CLASS 10

CBSE QUESTION & CONCEPT BANK

CHAPTER-WISE & TOPIC-WISE

SOCIAL SCIENCE

EDITION: Fourth

Published By: Physicswallah Limited

Physics Wallah Publication

ISBN: 978-93-7818-850-3

MRP: 699/-

Mobile App: Physics Wallah (Available on Play Store)

Website: www.pw.live

Youtube Channel: Physics Wallah - Alakh Pandey

Alakh Pandey - Class 10

Physics Wallah Foundation

NCERT Wallah

Email: publication@pw.live

SKU Code: BKP2603019477

Printed at: Fine Offset Printers(Tronica City)

About the Author

SIDDHARTH SHARMA, fondly known as Sid Sir, is a dedicated educator with over **12 years of teaching experience** (10 years offline & 2 years online). He holds a Bachelor of Science in Physics, Mathematics, and Geology, and is currently pursuing a Master of Arts in History.

He is a Teacher by profession and a mentor by passion, known for transforming students' perspective towards Social Science — from a subject they once disliked to one they genuinely love and enjoy.

With years of classroom experience, he deeply understands the real challenges students face. His offline teaching journey helped him connect personally with learners, identify their problems, and develop practical solutions — which are now reflected in this book.

Over the years, he has mentored lakhs of students, guiding them to achieve their dream scores in Board exams through conceptual clarity, smart strategies, and engaging teaching methods.

This book is a result of his love, dedication, and commitment to student success.

Students across platforms lovingly call him "**Sid Sir**" — a reflection of the trust, connection, and impact he has built in their academic journeys.

UJJVALA PUNJ is a passionate Social Science educator known for her engaging and student-friendly approach to teaching. With a strong academic foundation, holding both a Bachelor's and Master's degree in **Political Science from Delhi University**, she brings depth, clarity, and real-world relevance into every concept she teaches.

Driven by the belief that learning should be meaningful and relatable, Ujjvala simplifies complex topics by connecting them with everyday life. Her teaching style blends storytelling, practical examples, and interactive discussions, making Social Science not just easy to understand, but genuinely interesting for students.

Fondly appreciated for her fun and relatable vibe, Ujjvala creates a classroom environment where students feel comfortable, curious, and confident. She believes that education is not just about memorizing facts, but about understanding the world around us and developing a thoughtful perspective.

Her guiding philosophy, "**SST aapko jeena sikhati hai**," reflects her mission to help students see Social Science as a subject that goes beyond textbooks and shapes real-life thinking.

Through her dedication and unique teaching style, Ujjvala continues to inspire students to connect, question, and grow—both academically and personally.

PREFACE

In this era of cut-throat competition among Class 10th aspirants for great marks in Board Exams, only a few are prepared enough to achieve it. During the preparation, a student needs the most relevant study material to cover all topics, practice efficiently, and excel in Board exams and other 10th level competitive exams.

While there is an abundance of study materials available in the market, what we felt missing was a self-driven and well-planned study material. We have addressed this issue by introducing the CBSE Class 10th Question Concept Bank.

CBSE Class 10th Question & Concept Bank is a book that covers all the important concepts and theories, along with a rich amount of practice questions. This book is designed to provide you with the perfect guidance you need. The study material is consistent with the syllabus offered in NCERT Books and has been curated by the **Physics Wallah Editorial Team** under the careful observation of Physics Wallah Faculties.

Their invaluable contributions have enriched the very essence of our books.

This book consists of the following features:

The content is made in such a way that you can invest your time to make a strong fundamental that will get compounded and will pay you the interest in every upcoming year of your competitive exam's preparation and board exam preparation.

This will help you stay ahead of your competitors.

Our content will help you secure excellent marks in CBSE Class 10th Board Exam.

Following are the different sections that we have provided to develop your skills:

In Theory:

- Concept Maps
- NCERT Definitions
- Important Facts
- Important Concepts
- Classification
- Difference Between
- Real-life application-Based questions
- Myth Buster
- Mnemonics

In Questions (Competency Based):

- Multiple Choice Questions
- Assertion and Reason
- Subjective Questions (with VSA, SA, LA and Case Based Questions as per Latest Board Exam Pattern)
- Map-Based Questions (Wherever required)
- NCERT and NCERT Intext Questions
- Mistakes 101: What not to do!
- Nailing the Right Answer
- Answer key and Explanations with Marking Scheme as per the latest CBSE Board Pattern
- Topper's Explanations

Includes Questions & Explanations from:

Sample Question Paper issued by CBSE – **(CBSE SQP)**

Additional Practice Questions issued by CBSE – **(CBSE APQ)**

Competency Focused Practice Questions issued by CBSE – **(CFPQ)**

Previous Year Questions in CBSE Board Exams

A step to make our book even better for our students:

Provide your valuable feedback or Report the Error

View Errata (Error Correction from our end)

SYLLABUS ISSUED BY CBSE

SOCIAL SCIENCE

Code No. (087)

CLASS-X

(80 Marks)

<table>
<tr><th>Subject</th><th>Chapters Name</th><th>Marks</th></tr>
<tr><td>History</td><td>❒ The Rise of Nationalism in Europe.
❒ Nationalism in India:
❒ The Making of a Global World Sub topics 1 to 1.3
❒ Print Culture and the Modern World
❒ Map pointing</td><td>18+2</td></tr>
<tr><td>Political Science</td><td>❒ Power – sharing
❒ Federalism
❒ Gender, Religion and Caste
❒ Political Parties
❒ Outcomes of Democracy</td><td>20</td></tr>
<tr><td>Geography</td><td>❒ Resources and Development
❒ Forest and Wildlife Resources
❒ Water Resources
❒ Agriculture
❒ Minerals & Energy resources
❒ Manufacturing industries.
❒ Lifelines of National Economy (map pointing)
❒ Map pointing</td><td>17+3</td></tr>
<tr><td>Economics</td><td>❒ Development
❒ Sectors of the Indian Economy
❒ Money and Credit
❒ Globalization and The Indian Economy
❍ What is Globalization?
❍ Factors that have enabled Globalisation</td><td>20</td></tr>
<tr><td></td><td>Total</td><td>80</td></tr>
</table>

SUBJECT I: HISTORY

1. **THE RISE OF NATIONALISM IN EUROPE**

   The French Revolution and the Idea of Nation, The Making of Nationalism in Europe, The Age of Revolutions: 1830-1848, The Making of Germany and Italy, Visualising the Nation, Nationalism and Imperialism

2. **NATIONALISM IN INDIA**

   The First World War, Khilafat and Non-Cooperation, Differing Strands within the Movement, Towards Civil-Disobedience, The Sense of Collective Belonging

3. **MAKING OF A GLOBAL WORLD**

   The Pre-Modern World

4. **PRINT CULTURE AND THE MODERN WORLD**

   The First Printed Book and Print Comes to Europe, The Print Revolution and Its Impacts and The Reading Mania, The Nineteenth Century and India and the World of Print, Religious Reforms and Public Debates, New Forms of Publication and Print and Censorship

SUBJECT II: POLITICAL SCIENCE

1. **POWER-SHARING**

   Beligium and Sri Lanka, Majoritarianism in Sri Lanka, Accommodation in Belgium, Forms of Power-sharing

2. **FEDERALISM**

   What is Federalism?, What makes India a Federal Country?, How is Federalism Practiced?, Decentralisation in India

3. **GENDER, RELIGION AND CASTE**

Gender and Politics, Religion, Communalism and Politics, Caste and Politics

4. **POLITICAL PARTIES**

Political Parties Meaning, Function & Necessity, How many Parties Should We have?, National Parties and State Parties, Challenges to Political Parties & How can Parties be Reformed

5. **OUTCOMES OF DEMOCRACY**

How do We Assess Democracy's Outcomes? & Accountable, Responsive and Legitimate Government, Economic Growth and Development & Reduction of Inequality and Poverty, Accommodation of Social Diversity & Dignity and Freedom of the Citizens

SUBJECT III: GEOGRAPHY

1. **RESOURCES AND DEVELOPMENT**

Resources, Land Resources, Soil as a Resource

2. **FOREST AND WILDLIFE RESOURCES**

Flora and Fauna in India, Conservation of Forest and Wildlife in India

3. **WATER RESOURCES**

Water and Water Scarcity, Multipurpose River Projects, Rain Water Harvesting

4. **AGRICULTURE**

Farming, Crops

5. **MINERALS AND ENERGY RESOURCES**

Minerals, Energy Resources

6. **MANUFACTURING INDUSTRIES**

Manufacturing Industries and Industries, Industrial Pollution and Environmental Degradation

7. **LIFELINES OF NATIONAL ECONOMY**

Major Sea Ports, International Airports

SUBJECT IV: ECONOMICS

1. **DEVELOPMENT**

Income and Other Goals, National Development, Public Facilities, Sustainability of Development

2. **SECTORS OF THE INDIAN ECONOMY**

Sectors of Economic Activities, Comparing the Three Sectors, Primary, Secondary and Tertiary Sectors in India, Division of Sectors as Organised and Unorganised, Sectors in Terms of Ownership: Public and Private Sectors

3. **MONEY AND CREDIT**

Money as a Medium of Exchange & Modern Forms of Money, Loan Activities of Banks, Two Different Credit Situations & Terms of Credit, Formal Sector Credit in India, Self-Help Groups for the Poor

4. **GLOBALISATION AND THE INDIAN ECONOMY**

What is Globalisation?, Factors that have Enabled Globalisation

SOCIAL SCIENCE
QUESTION PAPER DESIGN
CLASS–X

Max. Time: 3 Hours **Max. Marks: 80**

S.No.	Typology of Questions	Total Marks	% Weightage
1.	**Remembering and Understanding:** Exhibiting memory of previously learned material by recalling facts, terms, basic concepts, and answers; Demonstrating understanding of facts and ideas by organizing, translating, interpreting, giving descriptions and stating main ideas.	24	30%
2.	**Applying:** Solving problems to new situations by applying acquired knowledge, facts, techniques and rules in a different way.	11	13.25%
3.	**Formulating, Analysing, Evaluating and Creating:** Examining and breaking information into parts by identifying motives or causes; Making inferences and finding evidence to support generalizations; Presenting and defending opinions by making judgments about information, validity of ideas, or quality of work based on a set of criteria; Compiling information together in a different way by combining elements in a new pattern or proposing alternative solutions.	40	50%
4.	Map Skill	5	6.25%
	Total	**80**	**100%**

Chapter-wise Weightage and Trend Analysis of
CBSE Past 5 Years' Papers

CHAPTERS	2022		2023		2024		2025		2026	
SOCIAL SCIENCE										
	DL	ODL	DL	ODL	DL	ODL	DL	ODL	DL	ODL
HISTORY										
The Rise of Nationalism in Europe	–	–	4	4	8	4	4	5	5	6
Nationalism in India	10	13	8	12	6	8	8	8	7	7
The Making of a Global World (*Some portion is Rationalised*)	–	–	3	–	2	3	3	1	3	3
The Age of Industrialisation (*Rationalised*)	–	–	1	–	–	–	–	–	–	–
Print Culture and the Modern World	–	–	4	3	4	5	5	6	5	4
GEOGRAPHY										
Resources and Development (*Some portion is Rationalised*)	–	–	1	1	1	2	3	2	2	2
Forest and Wildlife Resources (*Some portion is Rationalised*)	–	–	–	4	2	4	4	1	2	2
Water Resources	–	–	5	1	5	2	1	3	5	5
Agriculture (*Some portion is Rationalised*)	–	–	3	2	1	6	4	6	3	3
Minerals and Energy Resources	1	2	3	–	7	2	7	6	7	7
Manufacturing Industries (*Some portion is Rationalised*)	5	6	3	6	4	4	1	1	1	1
Lifelines of National Economy	5	3	5	2	1	1	1	2	1	1
POLITICAL SCIENCE										
Power-sharing	–	–	2	4	4	5	2	3	5	5
Federalism	–	–	5	1	5	4	6	6	3	4
Democracy and Diversity (*Rationalised*)	–	–	–	–	–	–	–	–	–	–
Gender, Religion and Caste (*Some portion is Rationalised*)	–	–	2	2	2	1	2	6	3	2
Popular Struggles and Movements (*Rationalised*)	4	5	–	–	–	–	–	–	–	–
Political Parties	5	12	4	4	4	4	4	2	4	6
Outcomes of Democracy	10	3	6	5	5	6	6	3	5	3
Challenges to Democracy (*Rationalised*)	–	–	–	–	–	–	–	–	–	–
ECONOMICS										
Development	–	–	5	5	6	5	5	2	6	6
Sectors of the Indian Economy	–	–	10	4	3	4	5	12	6	6
Money and Credit	5	5	5	4	5	5	5	3	4	4
Globalisation and the Indian Economy (*Some portion is Rationalised*)	5	5	3	6	6	6	5	3	4	4
Consumer Rights (*Rationalised*)	–	–	–	–	–	–	–	–	–	–

**The marks allotment mentioned above is chapter-wise and includes internal choice questions as well. Therefore, the total might not match the Maximum Marks of the respective Previous Year Paper. Here, DL is Delhi, ODL is Outside Delhi.*

Question Typology

YEAR	Objective Questions		Subjective Questions				
	MCQs	A/R	VSA	SA	LA	Case/Source Based type	Map-Based type
2026	18	2	4	5	4	3	2
2025	18	2	4	5	4	3	1
2024	19	1	4	5	4	3	1
2023	19	1	4	5	4	3	1
2022 (T-II)	-	-	5	3	2	2	1
2022 (T-I)	30	8	-	-	-	2	2

Evolving Trends in CBSE Exam Patterns

Social Science

2021

- Exam Not Conducted

2022

- Term-I (objective) and Term-II (subjective).
- 2 Marks VSA instead of 1 Mark
- 1 Section of Case based questions added.
- Questions with "OR" option reduced.

2023

- Matching Based Questions introduced.

2024

- Image Based Question introduced.
- Rationalised syllabus in Economics.
- Chapter "Lifelines of National Economy" to be used for map based questions only.

2025

- Weightage of Competency Based Questions increased.

2026

- Division of question paper into four sections- A, B, C and D representing 4 subjects (History, Geography, Political Science and Economics) not according to question typology like MCQs, VSA, LA etc. (as given in previous years).

HOW TO USE THIS BOOK

This book is structured to support your learning journey of preparing for your board exams through a variety of engaging and informative elements. Here's how to make the most of it:

CBSE Solved Paper of 2026 with Handwritten Style Answers: *Get yourself updated with the latest Board Question Papers. With handwritten answers, learn the practical application of concepts and effective answering techniques to achieve higher scores.*

CBSE Solved Paper

CBSE SOLVED PAPER 2026

Time allowed : 3 hours **Maximum Marks : 80**

GENERAL INSTRUCTIONS:

Read the following instructions very carefully and strictly follow them:

(i) *This question paper contains 38 questions. All questions are compulsory.*

(ii) *Question paper is divided into FOUR sections - Section A, B, C and D.*

Each Section carries 20 marks.

Section A : History

Section B : Geography

Section C : Political Science

Section D : Economics

SECTION-A (HISTORY) (20 M)

1. Arrange the following events in chronological order and choose the correct option: (*Re*) (1 M)

I. Salt Satyagraha

II. Kheda Satyagraha

III. Rowlatt Satyagraha

IV. Ahmedabad Mill Workers Satyagraha

Options:

(*a*) II, I, III, IV (*b*) II, IV, III, I (*c*) III, II, IV, I (*d*) II, I, IV, III

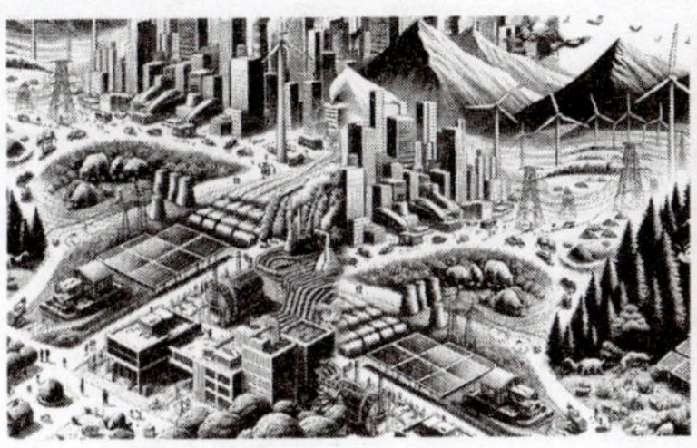

"Resources are materials or substances like water, minerals, and forest, used by us. Development involves using these resources wisely for our needs and future generations."

Preview

At the start of every chapter, you'll find a thoughtfully chosen image and a quote that captures the main idea and motivation of the topic. This approach aims to get your interest and give you a glimpse of the theme ahead.

Before diving into the details, we outline the syllabus and analyze the weightage given to each topic over the past five years. This helps you prioritize your study focus based on the significance of each section.

SYLLABUS & WEIGHTAGE

List of Concept Names	Years					
	2020	2021	2022	2023	2024	2025
Resources (Development of Resources, Resources planning in India, Conservation of Resources, Classification of resources)	1 Q (3 M)	Exam not Conducted	–	–	–	
Land Resources (Land utilisation and land use pattern in India, Land degradation and conservation measures)	–		–	–	1 Q (2 M)	
Soil as a Resource (Classification of soil, Soil erosion and soil conservation)	–		–	1 Q (1 M)	–	1 Q (3 M)

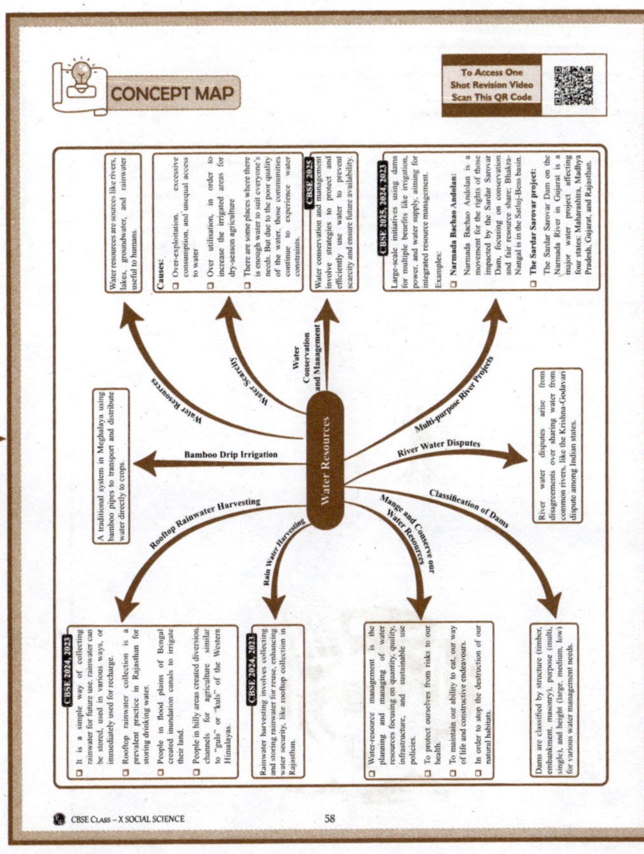

Concept Map

The concept map appears to be a comprehensive study aid that outlines key concepts in a structured format, featuring definitions, diagrams, and processes. For a student, it would serve as a visual summary, making complex ideas more accessible and aiding in revision and understanding of concept for their curriculum.

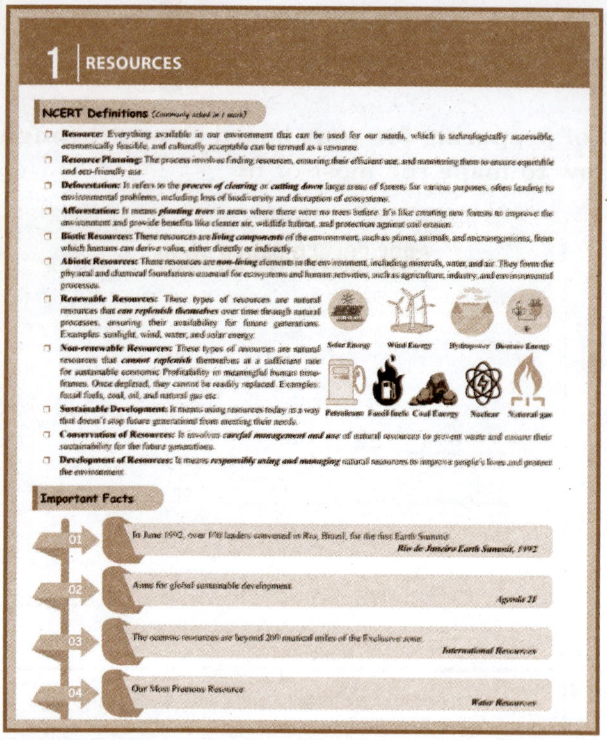

1 RESOURCES

NCERT Definitions

Important Facts

NCERT Definitions: *It simplifies complex topics into brief, easy-to-understand explanations.*

Important Facts: *Quick, bullet point facts that are crucial for exams.*

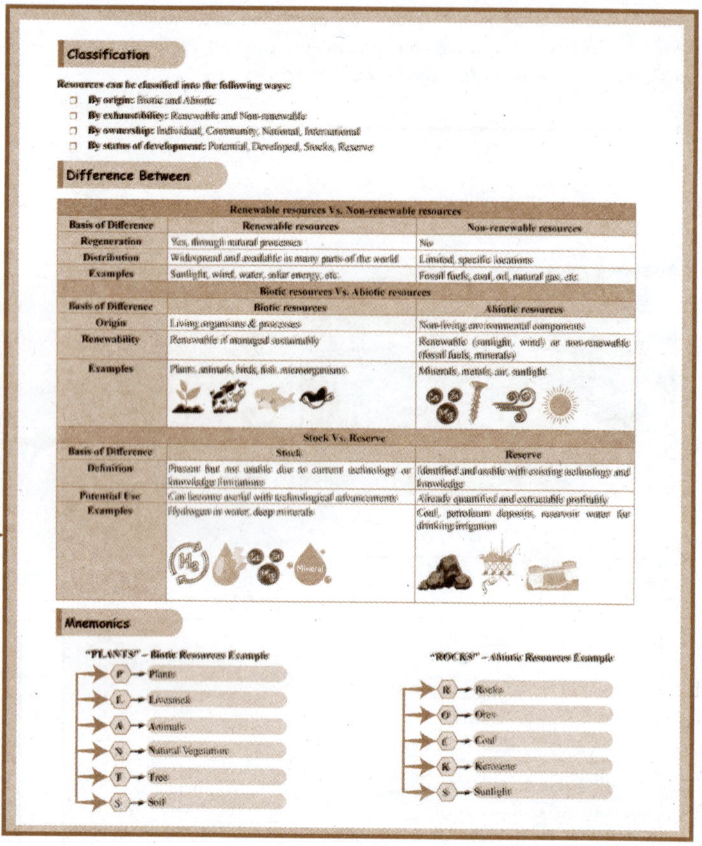

Classification

Difference Between

Mnemonics

Classification: *It organizes complex information into clear categories, making it easier for students to grasp differences, recognize patterns, and predict properties or behaviors in their learning.*

Difference Between: *Side-by-side comparisons to help distinguish similar concepts.*

Mnemonics: *Memory aids to help you retain and recall information.*

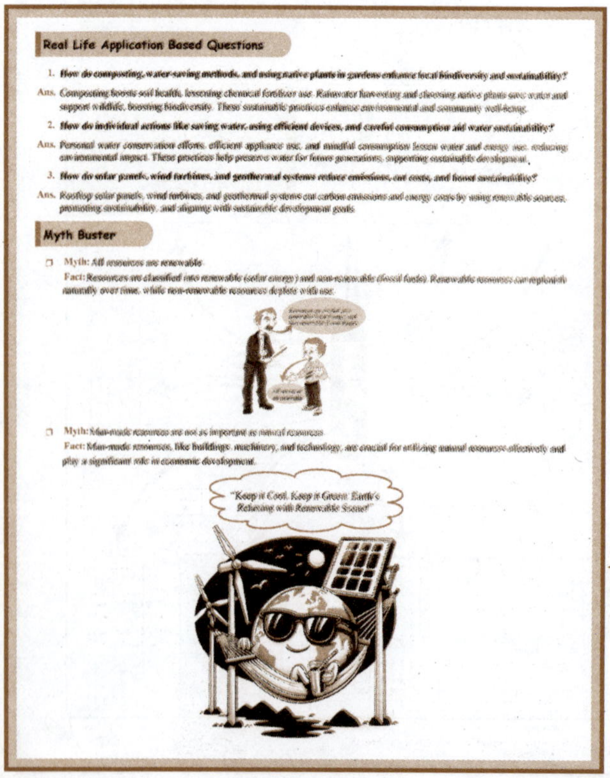

Real Life Application Based Questions

Myth Buster

Real-Life Application Based Questions: *Exercises that connect theory with practical scenarios. It will enhance your understanding and relevance of concepts.*

Myth Buster: *Clear up common misconceptions to ensure your understanding is accurate.*

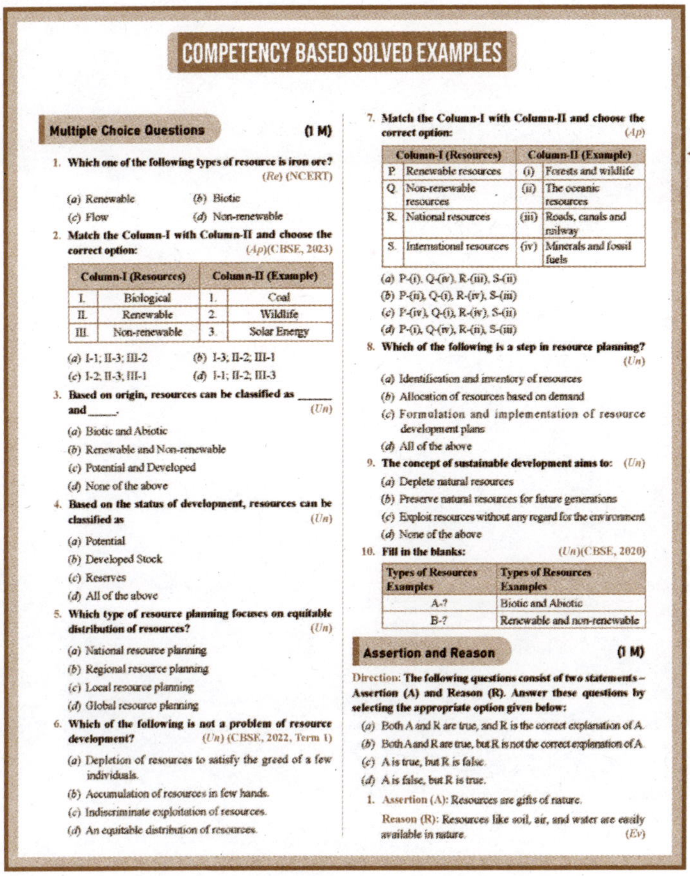

COMPETENCY BASED SOLVED EXAMPLES

Multiple Choice Questions **(1 M)**

1. **Which one of the following types of resource is iron ore?** *(Re)* (NCERT)
   (a) Renewable (b) Biotic
   (c) Flow (d) Non-renewable
2. **Match the Column-I with Column-II and choose the correct option:** *(Ap)*(CBSE, 2023)

	Column-I (Resources)		Column-II (Example)
I.	Biological	1.	Coal
II.	Renewable	2.	Wildlife
III.	Non-renewable	3.	Solar Energy

   (a) I-1; II-3; III-2 (b) I-3; II-2; III-1
   (c) I-2; II-3; III-1 (d) I-1; II-2; III-3
3. **Based on origin, resources can be classified as ______ and ______.** *(Un)*
   (a) Biotic and Abiotic
   (b) Renewable and Non-renewable
   (c) Potential and Developed
   (d) None of the above
4. **Based on the status of development, resources can be classified as** *(Un)*
   (a) Potential
   (b) Developed Stock
   (c) Reserves
   (d) All of the above
5. **Which type of resource planning focuses on equitable distribution of resources?** *(Un)*
   (a) National resource planning
   (b) Regional resource planning
   (c) Local resource planning
   (d) Global resource planning
6. **Which of the following is not a problem of resource development?** *(Un)* (CBSE, 2022, Term 1)
   (a) Depletion of resources to satisfy the greed of a few individuals.
   (b) Accumulation of resources in few hands.
   (c) Indiscriminate exploitation of resources.
   (d) An equitable distribution of resources.
7. **Match the Column-I with Column-II and choose the correct option:** *(Ap)*

	Column-I (Resources)		Column-II (Example)
P.	Renewable resources	(i)	Forests and wildlife
Q.	Non-renewable resources	(ii)	The oceanic resources
R.	National resources	(iii)	Roads, canals and railway
S.	International resources	(iv)	Minerals and fossil fuels

   (a) P-(i), Q-(iv), R-(iii), S-(ii)
   (b) P-(ii), Q-(i), R-(iv), S-(iii)
   (c) P-(iv), Q-(i), R-(iv), S-(ii)
   (d) P-(i), Q-(iv), R-(ii), S-(iii)
8. **Which of the following is a step in resource planning?** *(Un)*
   (a) Identification and inventory of resources
   (b) Allocation of resources based on demand
   (c) Formulation and implementation of resource development plans
   (d) All of the above
9. **The concept of sustainable development aims to:** *(Un)*
   (a) Deplete natural resources
   (b) Preserve natural resources for future generations
   (c) Exploit resources without any regard for the environment
   (d) None of the above
10. **Fill in the blanks:** *(Un)*(CBSE, 2020)

Types of Resources Examples	Types of Resources Examples
A-?	Biotic and Abiotic
B-?	Renewable and non-renewable

Assertion and Reason **(1 M)**

Direction: **The following questions consist of two statements – Assertion (A) and Reason (R). Answer these questions by selecting the appropriate option given below:**
(a) Both A and R are true, and R is the correct explanation of A.
(b) Both A and R are true, but R is not the correct explanation of A.
(c) A is true, but R is false.
(d) A is false, but R is true.

1. Assertion (A): Resources are gifts of nature.
   Reason (R): Resources like soil, air, and water are easily available in nature. *(Ev)*

Sovled Examples

For each topic, solved examples are provided including tagging of Competencies, PYQs, CBSE SQPs etc that exemplify how to approach and solve questions. This section is designed to reinforce your learning and improve problemsolving skills.

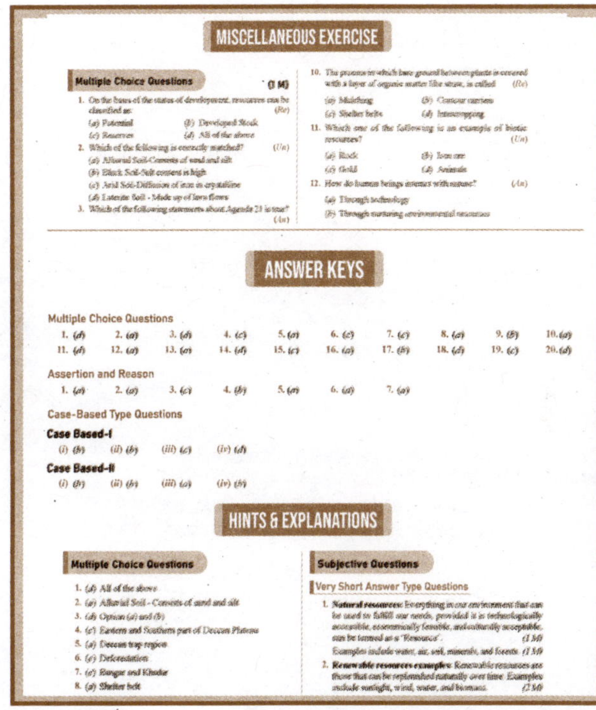

MISCELLANEOUS EXERCISE

Multiple Choice Questions **(1 M)**

ANSWER KEYS

Multiple Choice Questions

1. (d) 2. (a) 3. (d) 4. (c) 5. (a) 6. (c) 7. (c) 8. (a) 9. (b) 10. (a)
11. (d) 12. (a) 13. (a) 14. (d) 15. (c) 16. (a) 17. (b) 18. (d) 19. (c) 20. (d)

Assertion and Reason

1. (a) 2. (a) 3. (c) 4. (b) 5. (a) 6. (d) 7. (a)

Case-Based Type Questions

Case Based-I
(i) (b) (ii) (b) (iii) (c) (iv) (d)

Case Based-II
(i) (b) (ii) (b) (iii) (a) (iv) (b)

HINTS & EXPLANATIONS

Multiple Choice Questions

1. (d) All of the above
2. (a) Alluvial Soil - Consists of sand and silt
3. (d) Option (a) and (b)
4. (c) Eastern and Southern part of Deccan Plateau
5. (a) Deccan trap region
6. (c) Deforestation
7. (c) Bangar and Khadar
8. (a) Shelter belt

Subjective Questions

Very Short Answer Type Questions

Answer Key

At the end of each chapter, you'll find additional exercises intended to test your grasp of the material. These are great for revision and to prepare for exams.

Answer Key and Explanations including Topper's Explanations, Mistake 101 and Nailing the right answer to know how to write the ideal answer.

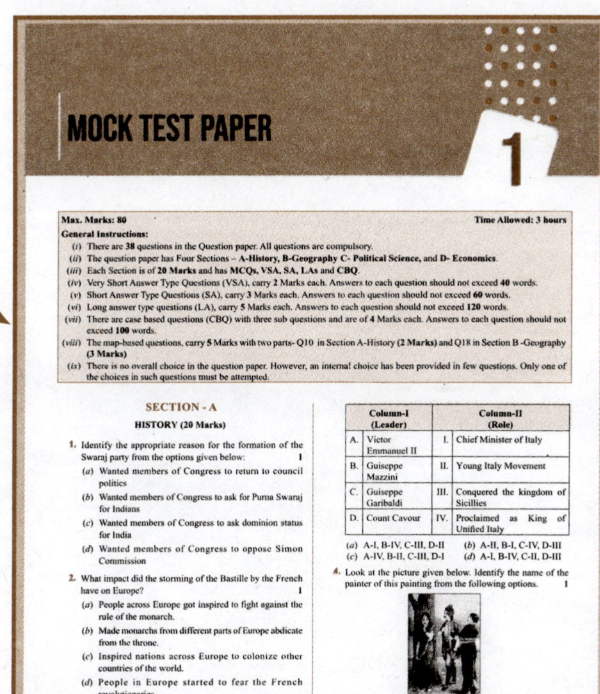

MOCK TEST PAPER 1

Max. Marks: 80 **Time Allowed: 3 hours**

General Instructions:
(i) There are **38** questions in the Question paper. All questions are compulsory.
(ii) The question paper has Four Sections – **A-History, B-Geography C- Political Science, and D- Economics.**
(iii) Each Section is of **20 Marks** and has **MCQs, VSA, SA, LAs** and **CBQ.**
(iv) Very Short Answer Type Questions (VSA), carry **2** Marks each. Answers to each question should not exceed **40** words.
(v) Short Answer Type Questions (SA), carry **3** Marks each. Answers to each question should not exceed **60** words.
(vi) Long answer type questions (LA), carry **5** Marks each. Answers to each question should not exceed **120** words.
(vii) There are case based questions (CBQ) with three sub questions and are of **4** Marks each. Answers to each question should not exceed **100** words.
(viii) The map-based questions, carry **5** Marks with two parts- Q10 in Section A-History **(2 Marks)** and Q18 in Section B -Geography **(3 Marks)**
(ix) There is no overall choice in the question paper. However, an internal choice has been provided in few questions. Only one of the choices in such questions must be attempted.

SECTION - A

HISTORY (20 Marks)

1. Identify the appropriate reason for the formation of the Swaraj party from the options given below: 1
   (a) Wanted members of Congress to return to council politics
   (b) Wanted members of Congress to ask for Purna Swaraj for Indians
   (c) Wanted members of Congress to ask dominion status for India
   (d) Wanted members of Congress to oppose Simon Commission
2. What impact did the storming of the Bastille by the French have on Europe? 1
   (a) People across Europe got inspired to fight against the rule of the monarch.
   (b) Made monarchs from different parts of Europe abdicate from the throne.
   (c) Inspired nations across Europe to colonize other countries of the world.
   (d) People in Europe started to fear the French revolutionaries.

	Column-I (Leader)		Column-II (Role)
A.	Victor Emmanuel II	I.	Chief Minister of Italy
B.	Guiseppe Mazzini	II.	Young Italy Movement
C.	Guiseppe Garibaldi	III.	Conquered the kingdom of Sicilies
D.	Count Cavour	IV.	Proclaimed as King of Unified Italy

(a) A-I, B-IV, C-III, D-II (b) A-II, B-I, C-IV, D-III
(c) A-IV, B-II, C-III, D-I (d) A-I, B-IV, C-II, D-III

4. Look at the picture given below. Identify the name of the painter of this painting from the following options. 1

Mock Test

Mock Test Papers: Test your preparedness with our Mock Test Papers designed to mirror the format and difficulty of real exams. Use the detailed explanations to identify areas of strength and opportunities for improvement.

CONTENTS

Upcoming CBSE SQPs/APQs can be accessed through this QR

Questions have been categorized according to the Bloom's Taxonomy (as per CBSE Board).

The following abbreviations have been used in the book:

(*Un*) - Understanding (*Re*) - Remembering (*Ap*) - Applying
(*An*) - Analysing (*Cr*) - Creating (*Ev*) - Evaluating

CBSE SOLVED PAPER 2026

Time allowed : 3 hours	Maximum Marks : 80

GENERAL INSTRUCTIONS:

Read the following instructions very carefully and strictly follow them:

(i) *This question paper contains 38 questions. All questions are compulsory.*

(ii) *Question paper is divided into **FOUR** sections - **Section A, B, C** and **D**.*
Each Section carries 20 marks.
Section A : History
Section B : Geography
Section C : Political Science
Section D : Economics

(iii) *This question paper has MCQs, VSAs, SAs, LAs and CBQs.*

(iv) *Multiple Choice Questions (MCQs) carry **1 mark** each.*

(v) *Very Short Answer Type Questions (VSAs) carry **2 marks** each. Answer to each question should not exceed **40 words**.*

(vi) *Short Answer Type Questions (SAs) carry **3 marks** each. Answer to each question should not exceed **60 words**.*

(vii) *Long Answer Type Questions (LAs) carry **5 marks** each. Answer to each question should not exceed **120 words**.*

(viii) *There are Cases Based Questions (CBQs) with three sub-questions and are of **4 marks** each. Answer to each question should not exceed **100 words**.*

(ix) *The map-based questions **(two questions)** carry **five** marks -*
Section A-(History) - 2 marks
Section B- (Geography) - 3 marks

(x) *Divide your answer sheet into four sections as per question paper*
Section A (History), Section B (Geography), Section C (Political Science),and Section D (Economics).
It is compulsory to answer each question in its respective section.
Do not mix answer of one section into the other section.

(xi) *Instructions are given with each section and question, wherever necessary.*

(xii) *There is no overall choice in the question paper. However, an internal choice has been provided in few questions. Only one of the choices in such questions has to be attempted.*

SECTION-A (HISTORY) (20 M)

1. Arrange the following events in chronological order and choose the correct option: **(*Re*) (1 M)**

I. Salt Satyagraha

II. Kheda Satyagraha

III. Rowlatt Satyagraha

IV. Ahmedabad Mill Workers Satyagraha

Options:

(*a*) II, I, III, IV (*b*) II, IV, III, I (*c*) III, II, IV, I (*d*) II, I, IV, III

Ans. *(b) Correct chronological order are:*

II. Kheda Satyagraha – 1917

IV. Ahmedabad Mill Workers Satyagraha – 1918

III. Rowlatt Satyagraha – 1919

I. Salt Satyagraha – 1930 *(1 Mark) [His, Ch.2, Pg.no. 31,39]*

2. Two statements are given below. They are Assertion (A) and Reason (R).Read both the statements carefully and choose the correct option: ***(Un)*** **(1 M)**

Assertion (A): The discovery of sea routes to Asia and America shrank the pre-modern world in the sixteenth century.

Reason (R): During this period European entry into Indian ocean expanded trade.

(*a*) Both (A) and (R) are true and (R) is the correct explanation of (A).

(*b*) Both (A) and (R) are true, but (R) is **not** the correct explanation of (A).

(*c*) (A) is true, but (R) is false.

(*d*) (A) is false, but (R) is true.

Ans. *(a) Both (A) and (R) are true and (R) is the correct explanation of (A).* *(1 Mark) [His, Ch.3, Pg.no. 51]*

3. Identify this image of the allegorical figure of a European nation during the nineteenth century from the following options: ***(Re)*** **(1 M)**

(*a*) Britannia (*b*) Marianna (*c*) Helvetia (*d*) Germania

Ans. *(d) This image shows Germania, the allegorical figure of the German nation in the 19th century.* *(1 Mark) [His, Ch.1, Pg.no. 23]*

4. Which one of the following pairs is correctly matched? ***(Re)*** **(1 M)**

Column-A (Writer)	Column-B (Contribution)
(*a*) Bal Gangadhar Tilak	Gulamgiri
(*b*) Jyotiba Phule	Amar Jiban
(*c*) Raja Rammohan Roy	Sambad Kaumudi
(*d*) Tarabai Shinde	Istri Dharam Vichar

Ans. *(c) Raja Rammohun Roy published the Sambad Kaumudi from 1821.* *(1 Mark) [His, Ch.5, Pg.no. 121]*

5. (A) Why did many Europeans migrate to America after sixteenth century ? Explain. ***(Un)*** **(2 M)**

OR

(B) How did trade and long distance travel contribute to the spread of diseases during ancient period? Explain. ***(Un)*** **(2 M)**

Ans. (A) Many Europeans migrate to America after sixteenth century because:

(i) Poverty, hunger, and deadly diseases were common in Europe. (1 Mark)

(ii) Religious conflicts and persecution of dissenters also forced thousands to leave Europe for a better life in America. (1 Mark)

[His, Ch.3, Pg.no. 55]

OR

(B) Trade and long-distance travel helped diseases spread in ancient times because people, goods, and animals moved from one place to another:

(i) Disease germs travelled with traders, travellers, and soldiers to new regions. (1 Mark)

(ii) Ships and trade routes carried infections like plague and smallpox, causing epidemics in distant lands. (1 Mark)

[His, Ch.3, Pg.no.55]

6. (A) "Print culture created the favourable conditions for the French Revolution." Explain the statement with examples. ***(An)* (3 M)**

OR

(B) "Throughout the nineteenth century, there were a series of innovations in printing technology." Explain the statement with examples. ***(Un)* (3 M)**

Ans. (A) Print culture created favourable conditions for the French Revolution in these ways:

(i) It spread the ideas of Enlightenment thinkers like Voltaire and Rousseau, who criticised tradition, Church authority and despotism. (1 Mark)

(ii) It encouraged debate and discussion, making people question old beliefs and social systems. (1 Mark)

(iii) Cheap pamphlets and cartoons mocked the monarchy, creating anger against the rulers. (1 Mark)

[His, Ch.5, Pg.no. 115]

OR

(B) The nineteenth century witnessed significant advancements in printing technology, which had a profound impact on society, culture, and communication:

(i) Richard M. Hoe's power-driven cylindrical press could print 8,000 sheets per hour and was useful for newspapers. (1 Mark)

(ii) In the late nineteenth century, the offset press was developed, which could print six colours at a time. (1 Mark)

(iii) Later, electrically operated presses, better paper-feeding methods and automatic paper reels improved printing further. (1 Mark)

[His, Ch.5,Pg.no. 118]

7. (A) Examine the nationalist tensions emerged in the Balkan region by the end of nineteenth century. ***(An)* (5 M)**

OR

(B) Examine the role of Giuseppe Mazzini in the unification of Italy during the nineteenth century. ***(An)* (5 M)**

Ans. (A) By the end of the 19th century, the Balkans became a region of intense nationalist tensions due to a mix of ethnic diversity, political instability, and the decline of the Ottoman Empire:

(i) The Balkans was a region of mixed ethnic groups such as Serbs, Greeks, Romanians and Bulgarians, which created rivalry. (1 Mark)

(ii) It was earlier controlled by the Ottoman Empire, but as the empire weakened, many nationalities demanded freedom. (1 Mark)

(iii) Each group began to develop strong nationalist feelings and wanted to form its own independent nation-state. (1 Mark)

(iv) The Balkan states were also jealous of each other and wanted to expand their territories. (1 Mark)

(v) Big powers like Russia, Austria-Hungary, Germany and Britain interfered in Balkan affairs for their own benefit, making the region highly unstable. (1 Mark)

[His, Ch.1, Pg.no.26]

OR

(B) Giuseppe Mazzini played an important role in the unification of Italy by spreading the idea of a united, independent and republican Italy:

(i) Mazzini was a revolutionary nationalist who believed that Italy should not remain divided into many small states. (1 Mark)

(ii) In 1831, he founded Young Italy, a secret society to unite Italian youth for the cause of nationalism. (1 Mark)

(iii) He also started Young Europe in Berne, which inspired people of other nations like Germany and Poland. (1 Mark)

(iv) Mazzini strongly supported a republic, not rule by kings, and spread ideas of liberty and nationhood. (1 Mark)

(v) Though his revolts failed, his ideas awakened national feelings and inspired leaders like Cavour and Garibaldi in the later unification of Italy. (1 Mark)

[His, Ch.1, Pg.no. 20,21]

8. Read the given source carefully and answer the questions that follow:

The sense of collective belonging

As the national movement developed, nationalist leaders became more and more aware of such icons and symbols in unifying people and inspiring in them a feeling of nationalism. Another means of creating a feeling of nationalism was through reinterpretation of history. By the end of the nineteenth century many Indians began feeling that to instill a sense of pride in the nation, Indian history had to be thought about differently. The British saw Indians as backward and primitive, incapable of governing themselves. In response, Indians began looking into the past to discover India's great achievements. They wrote about the glorious developments in ancient times when art and architecture, science and mathematics, religion and culture, law and philosophy, crafts and trade had flourished. This glorious time, in their view, was followed by a history of decline, when India was colonised. These nationalist histories urged the readers to take pride in India's great achievements in the past and struggle to change the miserable conditions of life under British rule.

(8.1) How did icons help to unite Indians during the freedom struggle ? **(*Un*) (1 M)**

(8.2) Why did nationalists feel the need to rewrite Indian history? **(*Un*) (1 M)**

(8.3) How did nationalist histories portray India's past and present? **(*Un*) (2 M)**

Ans. 8.1 Icons and symbols helped unite Indians by creating a shared national identity and inspiring a feeling of nationalism among people. (1 Mark)

8.2 Nationalists felt the need to rewrite Indian history because the British described Indians as backward and unfit to rule themselves. So, Indians wanted to present their glorious past and create pride in the nation. (1 Mark)

8.3 Nationalist histories showed India's past as glorious, when art, architecture, science, mathematics, religion, culture, law, philosophy, crafts, and trade had flourished. They showed India's present under British rule as a period of decline and miserable conditions. These histories encouraged people to feel proud of India's past and fight against colonial rule. (2 Mark)

[His, Ch.2, Pg.no.48]

9. Two places 'A' and 'B' have been marked on the given political outline map of India. Identify them with the help of the following informations and write their correct names on the lines drawn near them.

(A) The place where Gandhiji launched satyagraha, for the Indigo planters. **(*Re*) (1 M)**

(B) The place where the session of Indian National Congress was held. **(*Re*) (1 M)**

Ans. (A) Marked on map (1 Mark)

[His, Ch.2, Pg.no.32]

(B) Marked on map (1 Mark)

[His, Ch.2, Pg.no.33]

SECTION-B (GEOGRAPHY) (20 M)

10. Identify the soil with the help of the following informations given in the box and choose the correct option: ***(Un)*** **(1 M)**

- It is made up of extremely fine material.
- It is rich in soil nutrients.
- It is ideal for growing cotton.

(*a*) Alluvial Soil (*b*) Black Soil (*c*) Laterite Soil (*d*) Arid Soil

Ans. (b) Black Soil is made of extremely fine clay material and is rich in nutrients like lime and iron. Its excellent moisture-holding capacity makes it ideal and well-known for growing cotton. (1 Mark)

[Geo. Ch-1, Pg. no.7]

11. In which of the following States of India, has the largest area under permanent forests? ***(Re)*** **(1 M)**

(*a*) Uttar Pradesh (*b*) Madhya Pradesh (*c*) Gujarat (*d*) Maharashtra

Ans. (b) Madhya Pradesh has the largest area under permanent forests, constituting 75 per cent of its total forest area. Permanent forest areas are managed for both wood production and protective purposes, covering a large part of the state's land. (1 Mark)

[Geo. Ch-2, Pg. no.15]

12. Identify the correct option related to major crops grown in the 'Kharif' cropping season in India: ***(Re)*** **(1 M)**

(*a*) Paddy, Peas, Mustard (*b*) Paddy, Mustard, Gram

(*c*) Paddy, Jowar, Maize (*d*) Paddy, Maize, Gram

Ans. (c) Kharif crops are grown with the onset of the monsoon and are harvested in September–October. Kharif crops, also called the monsoon crops, These crops require warm, wet conditions.The important crops grown during this season include paddy, maize, jowar, bajra, tur (arhar), moong, urad, cotton, jute, groundnut and soyabean. (1 Mark)

[Geo. Ch-4, Pg. no.32]

13. Choose the appropriate option to fill in the blank: ***(Un)*** **(1 M)**

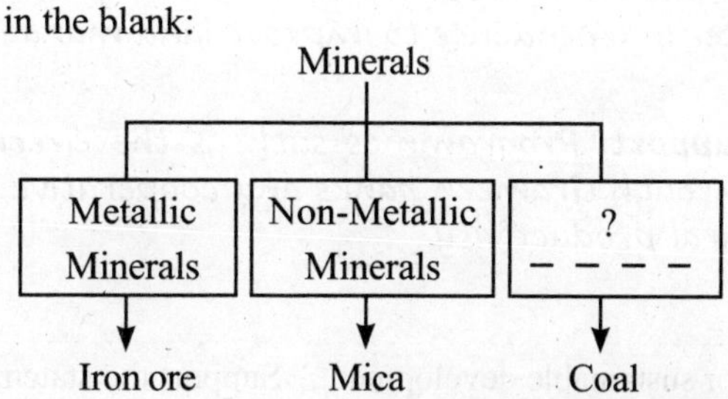

(*a*) Non-Ferrous minerals (*b*) Igneous minerals

(*c*) Energy minerals (*d*) Ferrous minerals

Ans. (c) Coal is used as a source of energy, mainly for producing electricity and running industries. Therefore, it is classified as an energy mineral. According to the classification of minerals, energy minerals include coal, petroleum, and natural gas, which are primarily used to generate energy. (1 Mark)

[Geo. Ch-5, Pg. no.43]

14. Which of the following is an example of 'current fallow land'? ***(Re)*** **(1 M)**

(*a*) Land left without cultivation for five agricultural years.

(*b*) Land left without cultivation for three agricultural years.

(*c*) Land left without cultivation for two agricultural years.

(*d*) Land left without cultivation for one agricultural year.

Ans. (d) Fallow lands are classified into two categories:

Current fallow: land left without cultivation for one or less than one agricultural year.

Other than current fallow: land left uncultivated for the past 1 to 5 agricultural years.

Since current fallow land refers to land that remains uncultivated for one agricultural year or less, the correct option is (d) Land left without cultivation for one agricultural year. (1 Mark)

[Geo. Ch-1, Pg. no.4]

15. Match Column-I with Column-II and choose the correct option: ***(An)*** **(1 M)**

Column-I (National Parks)	Column-II (States)
A. Sariska	i. Madhya Pradesh
B. Sunderban	ii. Uttarakhand
C. Corbett	iii. West Bengal
D. Bandhavgarh	iv. Rajasthan

	A	B	C	D
(*a*)	iii	ii	i	v
(*b*)	iv	ii	iii	i
(*c*)	iv	iii	ii	i
(*d*)	ii	iv	iii	i

Ans. (c)Match the National Parks with their respective States:

A. Sariska → iv. Rajasthan

B. Sunderban → iii. West Bengal

C. Corbett → ii. Uttarakhand

D. Bandhavgarh → i. Madhya Pradesh

(1 Mark)

[Geo. Ch-2, Pg. no.15]

16. Explain the measures made by government to improve Indian agriculture. ***(Un)*** **(2 M)**

Ans. The Indian government has introduced various institutional and technological reforms to improve agriculture:

(*i*) **Institutional Reforms:** Measures like abolition of the zamindari system, consolidation of land holdings, and cooperation were introduced after Independence to improve land management and agricultural development. (1 Mark)

(*ii*) **Technological and Financial Support:** Programmes such as the Green Revolution, crop insurance, Kisan Credit Card (KCC) and loans through Grameen banks and cooperative societies were introduced to support farmers and increase agricultural productivity. (1 Mark)

[Geo. Ch-4, Pg. no.38-39]

17. (A) "Conserving energy is essential for sustainable development." Support the statement with suitable arguments. ***(Ev)*** **(5 M)**

OR

(B) "Minerals are found in various forms and types, each having distinct properties." Support the statement with suitable arguments. ***(Ev)*** **(5 M)**

Ans. (A) "Conserving energy is essential for sustainable development" for the following reasons:

(*i*) **Energy is necessary for development:** Energy is required in every sector of the economy such as agriculture, industry, transport and households. Therefore, conserving energy ensures continuous economic development. (1 Mark)

(*ii*) **Rising energy consumption:** With development since Independence, the use of energy has increased rapidly. Conservation helps manage this rising demand and prevents wastage of resources. (1 Mark)

(*iii*) **Limited energy resources:** Many energy resources are limited in nature. Careful and judicious use of these resources is necessary so that they remain available for future generations. (1 Mark)

(*iv*) **Use of renewable energy:** Sustainable development encourages the use of renewable and non-conventional energy sources along with conservation of energy. (1 Mark)

(*v*) **Role of citizens:** People can help conserve energy by using public transport, switching off electricity when not in use and using energy-saving devices. Thus, "energy saved is energy produced." (1 Mark)

[Geo. Ch-5, Pg. no.55]

OR

Ans. (B) "Minerals are found in various forms and types, each having distinct properties" for the following reasons:

(i) **Variety in nature:** Minerals occur in many forms in nature, ranging from the hardest diamond to the softest talc, showing great variation in their physical properties. (1 Mark)

(ii) **Different compositions:** Minerals are formed from different combinations of elements under varying physical and chemical conditions, which leads to differences in their characteristics. (1 Mark)

(iii) **Different physical properties:** Because of different formation conditions, minerals show a wide range of colour, hardness, crystal form, lustre and density. (1 Mark)

(iv) **Occurrence in different rocks:** Minerals are found in igneous, metamorphic and sedimentary rocks, and sometimes occur in cracks, layers or beds. (1 Mark)

(v) **Different modes of occurrence:** Minerals may occur as veins and lodes, residual deposits, placer deposits in river sands, or in ocean water, showing their varied forms and types in nature. (1 Mark)

[Geo. Ch-5, Pg. no.42-43]

18. Read the given source carefully and answer the questions that follow:

Pradhan Mantri Krishi Sinchayee Yojana

Floods have not only devastated life and property but also caused extensive soil erosion. Sedimentation also meant that the flood plains were deprived of silt, a natural fertilizer, further adding on to the problem of land degradation. It was also observed that the multipurpose projects induced earthquakes, caused water-borne diseases and pests and pollution resulting from excessive use of water.

Irrigation has also changed the cropping pattern of many regions with farmers shifting to water intensive and commercial crops. This has great ecological consequences like salinisation of the soil.

Pradhan Mantri Krishi Sinchayee Yojana has been started which

ensures access to some means to protective irrigation for all agricultural farms in the country, thus bringing much desired rural prosperity. Some of the broad objectives of this programme are to enhance the physical access of water on the farm and expand cultivable area under assured irrigation (har khet ko pani), improve on farm water, use efficiency to reduce wastage and increase availability both in duration and extent, irrigation and other water saving technologies (per drop more crop) and

introduce sustainable water conservation practices, etc.

(18.1) Explain the role of floods in land degradation. **(*Un*) (1 M)**

(18.2) How has irrigation changed cropping pattern? **(*Un*) (1 M)**

(18.3) Explain any two objectives of the 'Pradhan Mantri Krishi Sinchayee Yojana'. **(*Un*) (2 M)**

Ans. 18.1 Floods devastate life and property, cause extensive soil erosion, and lead to sedimentation, depriving flood plains of fertile silt. (1 Mark)

18.2 Irrigation has encouraged farmers to shift towards water-intensive and commercial crops, leading to ecological problems such as salinisation of soil. (1 Mark)

18.3 Two objectives of the 'Pradhan Mantri Krishi Sinchayee Yojana'.

(i) To enhance physical access of water to farms and expand cultivable area under assured irrigation, ensuring "har khet ko pani." (1 Mark)

(ii) To improve water-use efficiency by reducing wastage and promoting water-saving technologies such as "per drop more crop." (1 Mark)

[Geo. Ch-3, Pg. no.23]

19. On the same outline map of **India** given for Q. No. 9. locate and label any **three** of the following with suitable symbols: **(*Ap*) (3 × 1 = 3 M)**

(*i*) The dam constructed on Satluj river

(*ii*) A nuclear power plant located in Gujarat

(*iii*) A software technology part located in Uttar Pradesh

(*iv*) An International Airport located in Maharashtra

Ans. (i) Marked on map [Geo.Ch-3,Pg.no.24]

(ii) Marked on map [Geo.Ch-5,Pg.no.53]

(iii) Marked on map [Geo.Ch-6,Pg.no.67]

(iv) Marked on map [Geo, Ch-7,Pg. no. 79]

(3 × 1 = 3 Marks)

SECTION-C (POLITICAL SCIENCE) (20 M)

20. Two statements are given below. They are Assertion (A) and Reason (R). Read both the statements carefully and choose the correct option: ***(Un)* (1 M)**

Assertion (A): Belgium's power sharing arrangements were designed to accommodate its linguistic and cultural divisions.

Reason (R): Belgian leaders recognised the existence of regional differences and cultural diversities.

(*a*) Both (A) and (R) are true and (R) is the correct explanation of (A)

(*b*) Both (A) and (R) are true, but (R) is not the correct explanation of (A).

(*c*) (A) is true, but (R) is false.

(*d*) (A) is false, but (R) is true.

Ans. (a) Both (A) and (R) are true and (R) is the correct explanation of (A) (1 Mark)

[Pol. Sci, Ch-1, Pg. no. 4]

21. Look at the given cartoon carefully and answer the question that follow: ***(An)* (1 M)**

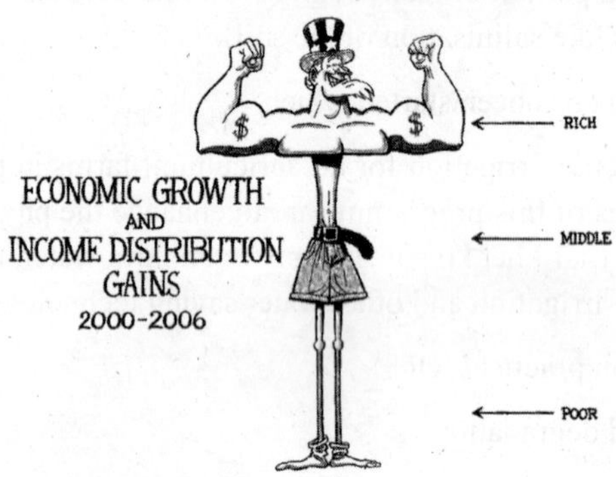

Which of the following concepts is best illustrated in the cartoon?

(*a*) Inclusive economic growth amongst nations

(*b*) Stagnation of economic development amongst nations

(*c*) Uneven distribution of wealth amongst nations

(*d*) Balanced economic growth amongst nations

Ans. (c) The cartoon shows a strong "rich" section while the "middle" and "poor" sections are weak and thin. This suggests that the benefits of economic growth are not shared equally. It highlights the uneven distribution of wealth. (1 Mark)

[Pol. Sci, Ch-5, Pg. no. 67]

22. Find the odd one out regarding the Political Parties of India: ***(An)* (1 M)**

(*a*) Bharatiya Janata Party & Aam Aadmi Party

(*b*) Indian National Lok Dal & Jananayak Janata Party

(*c*) National's People's Party & United Democratic Party

(*d*) Rashtriya Janata Dal & Loktantrik Samajwadi Party

Ans. (a) Bharatiya Janata Party & Aam Aadmi Party, these two are national political parties that operate across the country. The other options include regional parties that mainly work in specific states, so option (a) is the odd one out. (1 Mark)

[Pol. Sci, Ch-4, Pg. no. 54-56]

23. Read the given statements regarding urban local government and choose the correct option: **(*Un*) (1 M)**

I. Municipalities are setup in towns.

II. Big cities have Municipal Corporation.

III. Municipal chairperson is the head of Block Samiti.

IV. The officer in Municipal Corporation is called as Mayor.

(*a*) Only I, II and III are correct. (*b*) Only I, II and IV are correct.

(*c*) Only I, III and IV are correct. (*d*) Only II, III and IV are correct.

Ans. (b) Municipalities are set up in towns and Municipal Corporations exist in big cities. The head of a Municipal Corporation is called the Mayor. However, the Block Samiti is part of rural local government, so statement III is incorrect. (1 Mark)

[Pol. Sci, Ch-2, Pg. no. 25]

24. Suggest two ways to improve womens' participation in sports leadership roles. **(*Ap*) (2 M)**

Ans. In India, the participation of women in politics can be improved by: (Any two)

(i) **Reservation of Seats:** One way to solve this problem is to make it legally binding to have a fixed percentage of reserved seats for women in all the elected bodies. (1 Mark)

(ii) **Political Training:** Training women in leadership, election campaigning, and policy-making can equip them with the necessary skills to succeed in politics. (1 Mark)

(iii) **Awareness Campaigns:** Public campaigns to change societal attitudes, encourage women to vote, and highlight the importance of women's roles in decision- making can boost participation. (1 Mark)

[Pol. Sci, Ch-3, Pg. no. 35]

25. "Democracy is a better form of government compared with any other alternative." Examine the statement. **(*Ev*) (2 M)**

Ans. Democracy is a better form of government than any other form of government because it has the following features, which are often missing in other forms of government: (Any two)

(i) It promotes equality, dignity, and the active participation of citizens in governance. (1 Mark)

(ii) In a democracy, every citizen has the right to vote, ensuring that the government reflects the will of the people. (1 Mark)

(iii) This form of government also enhances individual dignity by acknowledging and protecting human rights, which are often suppressed in other forms of government. (1 Mark)

(iv) Democratic systems are designed to improve decision-making by incorporating diverse viewpoints and allowing for public debate, which leads to more informed and considered decisions. (1 Mark)

(v) Democracy provides mechanisms for resolving conflicts and correcting mistakes, which helps in maintaining social harmony and adapting to the changing needs and expectations of the public. (1 Mark)

[Pol. Sci, Ch-5, Pg. no. 64]

26. How does the 'system of three lists' function in Indian federalism? Explain with examples. **(*Un*, *Re*) (3 M)**

Ans. In Indian federalism, the 'system of three lists' functions in the following ways:

(i) Union List – It includes subjects of national importance on which only the Central Government makes laws, such as defence, foreign affairs, and currency. (1 Mark)

(ii) State List – It contains subjects like police, agriculture, and trade, where only State Governments can make laws. (1 Mark)

(iii) Concurrent List – Includes subjects of common interest to both the Union Government and the State Governments; both the Centre and State can legislate. If their laws conflict with each other, the law made by the Union Government will prevail. (1 Mark)

[Pol. Sci, Ch-2, Pg. no. 16-17]

27. (A) Explain the importance of political parties in Indian democracy. **(*Un*) (5 M)**

OR

(B) Explain the challenges faced by the political parties in India. **(*Un*) (5 M)**

Ans. (A) The importance of political parties in Indian democracy is:

(i) **Link between people and government** – Political parties connect citizens with the government. They convey public demands, opinions and problems to the rulers. (1 Mark)

(ii) **Contest elections** – Parties put forward candidates in elections. Without political parties, elections would become confusing and less organised. (1 Mark)

(iii) **Formation of government** – The party or alliance winning the majority forms the government and runs the administration. (1 Mark)

(iv) **Policy making** – Parties frame policies and programmes for the country. Different parties give people different choices and opinion in a democracy. (1 Mark)

(v) **Role of opposition** – Parties that do not form the government act as opposition. They question the government, check its actions, and help in maintaining accountability and democracy. (1 Mark)

[Pol. Sci, Ch-4, Pg. no. 48-50]

OR

(B) The challenges faced by the political parties in India are as follows:

(i) **Lack of internal democracy** – Power often remains in the hands of a few top leaders. Ordinary members do not get enough chances in decision-making. (1 Mark)

(ii) **Dynastic succession** – In many parties, leadership passes to family members. This reduces equal opportunity for capable and deserving people. (1 Mark)

(iii) **Money and muscle power** – Rich candidates and those using unfair influence often dominate party politics, affecting free and fair democracy. (1 Mark)

(iv) **No meaningful choice** – Sometimes parties appear very similar in policies, so voters may not get a strong alternative. (1 Mark)

(v) **Corruption** – Some parties are corrupt and focus more on winning elections for their own good rather than serving people, which weakens public trust in democracy. (1 Mark)

[Pol. Sci, Ch-4, Pg. no. 57-58]

28. Read the given source carefully and answer the questions that follow:

Forms of Power-sharing

The idea of power-sharing has emerged in opposition to the notions of undivided political power. For a long time, it was believed that all power of a government must reside in one person or group of persons located at one place. It was felt that if the power to decide is dispersed, it would not be possible to take quick decisions and to enforce them. But these notions have changed with the emergence of democracy. One basic principle of democracy is that people are the source of all political power. In a democracy, people rule themselves through institutions of self- government. In a good democratic government, due respect is given to diverse groups and views that exist in a society. Everyone has a voice in the shaping of public policies. Therefore, it follows that in a democracy, political power should be distributed among as many citizens as possible.

28.1 How does power sharing promote stability of political order? **(*Un*) (1 M)**

28.2 How are pressure groups part of the power sharing mechanism? **(*Un*) (1 M)**

28.3 How does power sharing contribute to the spirit of democracy? **(*An*) (2 M)**

Ans. 28.1 Power sharing promotes stability by reducing conflicts among social, religious, linguistic and regional groups. When all groups get a share in decision-making, they feel respected and included. This builds trust in the government and helps maintain peace, unity and political stability. (1 Mark)

28.2 Pressure groups are part of power sharing because they influence government decisions without forming the government. They represent the interests of different sections of society and make sure that diverse views are considered in public policies. (1 Mark)

28.3 Power sharing contributes to the spirit of democracy in the following ways:

- **Respect for all groups** – In a democracy, people are the real source of power. Power sharing gives respect to different social, religious and regional groups and makes them feel included in the system. (1 Mark)
- **People's participation in decision-making** – Power sharing allows more people to take part in making decisions and shaping public policies. This makes democracy more participatory, inclusive and responsive to the needs of all. (1 Mark)

[Pol. Sci, Ch-1, Pg. no. 8-9]

SECTION-D (ECONOMICS) (20 M)

29. Study the given data and answer the question that follow: ***(Ap)* (1 M)**

Comparative Data of few States			
	Infant Mortality Rate (2020)	**Literacy Rate (2017-18)**	**Net Attendance Rate (Class 1 to 5)**
State A	28	82	73
State B	6	94	94
State C	27	62	69

By how many of the following points does State B's literacy rate exceeds from State A in 2017-18?

(*a*) 12 (*b*) 10 (*c*) 16 (*d*) 14

Ans. (a) Number of points by which literacy rate of State-B exceeds from State-A in 2017-18

= 94 - 82

= 12 (1 Mark) [Eco, Ch-1, Pg. no. 10]

30. Identify the sector of economy with the help of information given in the box: ***(Un)* (1 M)**

- Ownership of assets and delivery of services in the hands of private individuals
- Activities are guided by the motive to earn profits

(*a*) Private Sector (*b*) Public Sector

(*c*) Joint Sector (*d*) Cooperative Sector

Ans. (a) In the Private Sector, businesses and industries are owned and managed by private individuals or companies, and their main objective is to earn profit. Examples: Tata Motors, Reliance Industries, Infosys. (1 Mark)

[Eco, Ch-2, Pg. no. 33]

31. Read the following case and choose the correct option:

Megha has taken a loan of 5 lakhs from bank to purchase a house. The annual rate on the loan is 12% and loan is to be repaid in 5 years in monthly instalments.

The 12% interest charged by the bank to Megha is related to which of the following? ***(Ap)* (1 M)**

(*a*) Collateral (*b*) Cost of Credit (*c*) Duration of Loan (*d*) Documentation

Ans. (b) The 12% interest charged by the bank is the extra amount that Megha has to pay for borrowing money from the bank. In economics, the interest paid on a loan is called the Cost of Credit because it is the price paid for using borrowed money. (1 Mark) [Eco, Ch-3, Pg. no. 44-45]

32. Which of the following is the main purpose of a trade barrier in global trade? Choose the correct option. ***(Un)* (1 M)**

(*a*) To promote the growth of foreign companies in a country

(*b*) To control the production of domestic industries

(*c*) To regulate foreign trade into the country

(*d*) To stop foreign trade between countries

Ans. (c) A trade barrier refers to restrictions such as taxes (tariffs), quotas, or rules imposed by the government on imports. The main purpose of trade barriers is to control or regulate the entry of foreign goods into a country so that domestic industries can be protected from too much foreign competition.

Therefore, trade barriers regulate foreign trade rather than completely stopping it. (1 Mark)

[Eco, Ch-4, Pg. no. 64]

33. Which of the following is an example of a renewable resource **(*Un*) (1 M)**

(*a*) Natural Gas (*b*) Crude Oil (*c*) Coal (*d*) Ground Water

Ans. (d) A renewable resource is a resource that can be replenished or renewed naturally in a short period of time. Groundwater is considered a renewable resource because it is recharged by rainfall and the water cycle.

On the other hand:

Natural gas, crude oil, and coal are non-renewable resources because they take millions of years to form and cannot be replaced quickly. (1 Mark)

[Eco, Ch-1, Pg. no. 14-15]

34. Choose the correct option to fill in the blank:

Infant Mortality Rate indicates the number of children that die before the age of ______ year(s) per 1000 live births in that particular year. **(*Re*) (1 M)**

(*a*) One (*b*) Two (*c*) Three (*d*) Four

Ans. (a) Infant Mortality Rate (IMR) refers to the number of children who die before completing one year of age per 1000 live births in a particular year. It is an important indicator used to measure the health condition and medical facilities of a country. (1 Mark)

[Eco, Ch-1, Pg. no. 10]

35. "Advancement in technology has stimulated the globalization process." Justify the statement with suitable arguments. **(*Un*) (3 M)**

Ans. "Advancement in technology has stimulated the globalisation process", this statement can be justified with the following points:

(i) **Communication Technology:** Innovations in communication technology, such as the internet, smartphones, and social media platforms, have revolutionized the way individuals and businesses interact globally. People can now communicate instantaneously across vast distances. (1 Mark)

(ii) **Transportation Technology:** Advances in transportation, like jet aircraft, large shipping containers, and improved logistics software, have dramatically reduced the time and cost of moving goods and people across the world. (1 Mark)

(iii) **E-Commerce:** Online shopping platforms and payment systems have transformed retail, allowing consumers to purchase goods from different countries easily. This not only provides consumers with more choices but also opens new markets for businesses. (1 Mark)

[Eco, Ch-4, Pg. no. 62-63]

36. Explain the role of Reserve Bank in Indian economy. **(*Un*) (3 M)**

Ans. The Reserve Bank of India plays a crucial role in India's economy:

(i) It acts as the country's central bank, regulating and overseeing the banking system. (1 Mark)

(ii) It formulates and implements monetary policies to control inflation and promote economic growth. (1 Mark)

(iii) It manages the country's foreign exchange reserves and plays a key role in maintaining the stability of the rupee. (1 Mark)

[Eco, Ch-3, Pg. no. 40-41]

37. "Different persons can have different developmental goals." Explain the statement with examples. **(*Un*) (3 M)**

Ans. Different people can have different developmental goals/ aspirations. Examples are given below:

(i) **Farmers who depend only on rain for growing crops:** Better seeds, artificial irrigation technologies, more water from canals, and higher prices of their crops are the developmental goals for farmers. (1 Mark)

(ii) **Landless rural labourers:** More days of work and better wages are the developmental goals for labour. (1 Mark)

(ii) **Urban unemployed youth:** The development goal of an urban unemployed youth would be to find a good job and to earn a decent wage with that work. (1 Mark) [Eco, Ch-1, Pg. no. 5-6]

38. (A) Describe the importance of tertiary sector in the economy. **(*Un*) (5 M)**

OR

(B) Describe the features of organised sector of the economy. **(*Un*) (5 M)**

Ans. (A) The importance of tertiary sector in India can be understood with the following points:

(i) **Support for Primary and Secondary Sectors:** The growth of agriculture and industry boosts services like transport and banking, increasing the importance of the tertiary sector. (1 Mark)

(ii) **Basic Services:** In any country, services like hospitals, education, and banking are essential. As India is developing, these basic services are becoming more important, making the tertiary sector vital. (1 Mark)

(iii) **Rising Income Levels:** As people's incomes rise, they demand more services like restaurants, tourism, and IT, which expands the tertiary sector. (1 Mark)

(iv) **Information Technology:** Recent years have seen a boom in information and communication technology services, making this sector more significant in India's economy. (1 Mark)

(v) **Employment Opportunities:** Despite many Indians being employed in the primary sector, the tertiary sector offers a growing number of jobs, especially in services like retail, IT, and transport. (1 Mark)

[Eco, Ch-2, Pg. no. 24-26]

OR

(B) The features of the organised sector are as follow:

(i) **Registered by the government:** The organised sector is properly registered with the government and follows official rules. (1 Mark)

(ii) **Follows government laws:** It works according to labour laws related to wages, working hours, and working conditions. (1 Mark)

(iii) **Fixed working hours:** Workers have fixed working hours and usually get extra payment for overtime worked. (1 Mark)

(iv) **Job security:** Employees in this sector have more secure jobs and are not removed easily without reason. (1 Mark)

(v) **Employee benefits are provided:** Workers in the organised sector get benefits like paid leave, provident fund, medical facilities, pension, and holidays etc. (1 Mark)

[Eco, Ch-2, Pg. no. 30-31]

Map for Q. no. 9 (Section A) & Q. no. 19 (Section B)

Map for Q. no. 9 (Section A) & Q. no. 19 (Section B)

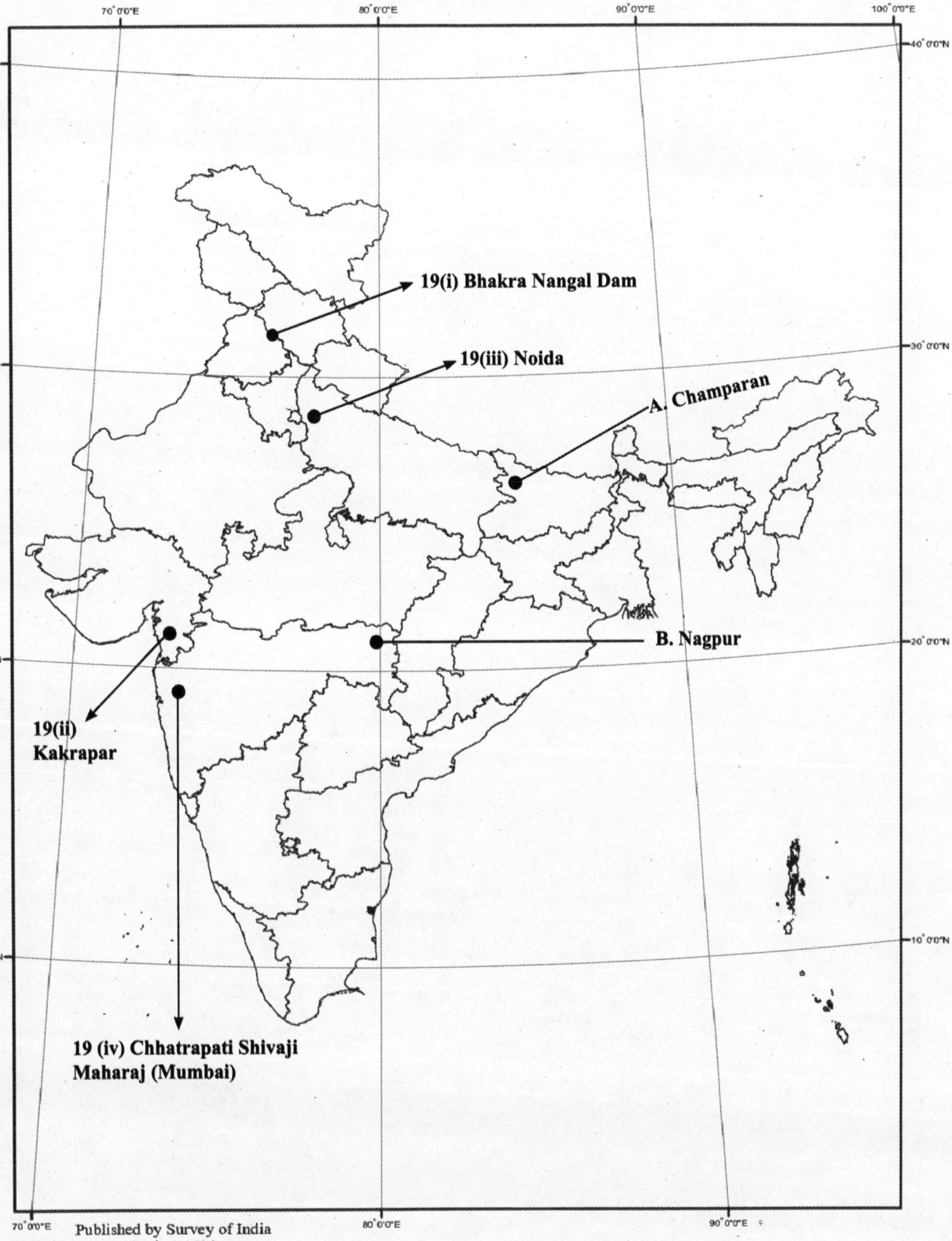

CBSE SOLVED PAPER 2025

Time allowed : 3 hours **Maximum Marks : 80**

GENERAL INSTRUCTIONS:

Read the following instructions very carefully and strictly follow them:

(*i*) This question paper contains **37** questions. **All** questions are **compulsory**.

(*ii*) Question paper is divided into **Six** Sections - Section **A**, **B**, **C**, **D**, **E** and **F**.

(*iii*) **Section A** - questions no. **1** to **20** are multiple choice type questions. Each questions carries **1** mark.

(*iv*) **Section B** - question number **21** to **24** are Very Short Answer type questions. Each question carries **2** marks. Answer to these questions should not exceed **40** words.

(*v*) **Section C** - question number **25** to **29** are Short Answer type questions. Each question carries **3** marks. Answer to these questions should not exceed **60** words.

(*vi*) **Section D** - question number **30** to **33** are Long Answer (LA) type questions. Each question carries **5** marks. Answer to these questions should not exceed **120** words.

(*vii*) **Section E** - question number **34** to **36** are **Case-based/Source-based questions** with three sub-questions. Each question carries **4** marks.

(*viii*) In **Section F** - question number **37** is Map skill based question with two parts -
37(*i*) History (**2** marks) and **37(*ii*)** Geography (**3** marks). This question carries total **5** marks.

(*ix*) In addition to this, NOTE that a separate question has been provided for Visually Impaired candidates in lieu of questions having visual inputs, Map etc. Such questions are to be attempted by Visually Impaired candidates only.

SECTION - A

1. Arrange the following historical events in chronological order and choose the correct option: ***(An) (1 Mark)***

I. Bardoli Satyagraha II. Rowlatt Satyagraha III. Champaran Satyagraha IV. Kheda Satyagraha

Options:

(*a*) I, II, III, IV (*b*) III, II, I, IV (*c*) II, I, IV, III (*d*) III, IV, II, I

1.(d) The correct chronological order is :
III. Champaran Satyagraha - 1917
IV. Kheda Satyagraha - 1918
II. Rowlatt Satyagraha - 1919
I. Bardoli Satyagraha - 1928

2. Which among the following newspapers is related to Bal Gangadhar Tilak? ***(Re) (1 Mark)***

(*a*) Hindustan (*b*) Bangla Patrika (*c*) Veer Bhoomi (*d*) Kesari

2.(d) When Punjab revolutionaries were deported in 1907, Balgangadhar Tilak wrote with great sympathy about them in his Kesari. This led to his imprisonment in 1908, provoking in turn widespread all over India.

3. In reference to the Germania allegory the "olive branch around the sword" symbolizes which one of the following? **(*Un*) (*1 Mark*)**

(*a*) Being freed (*b*) Heroism and strength (*c*) Willingness to make peace (*d*) Beginning of a new era

3. (c) In the Germania allegory, the "olive branch around the sword" symbolizes the willingness to make peace. The olive branch traditionally represents peace, and when it surrounds a sword, it indicates a readiness to maintain peace without compromising strength.

4. The germs of which disease paved the way for Europe's conquest of America in the later half of the sixteenth century? **(*Re*) (*1 Mark*)**

(*a*) Cholera (*b*) Smallpox (*c*) Jaundice (*d*) Malaria

4. (b) Smallbox was the most devasting disease brought by Europeans to the Americans. The indigenous population, having no immunity to this new disease, suffered massive fatalities.

5. Mrs. Monica, along with her family, clears a piece of land and grows grain and other food crops to feed her family. When the soil's fertility decreases, she prepares another piece of land for agriculture. Which of the following methods of agriculture does she use? **(*Un*) (*1 Mark*)**

(*a*) Plantation farming (*b*) Slash and burn farming

(*c*) Intensive subsistence farming (*d*) Commercial farming

5. (b) In slash and burn farming, farmers clear a piece of land, grow crops, and when the soil loss fertility, they move to another plot. This method is commonly practiced for subsistence farming.

6. Match Column-I with Column-II and choose the correct option: **(*Un*) (*1 Mark*)**

	Column-I		Column-II
A.	Sariska Wildlife Sanctuary	(*i*)	Uttarakhand
B.	Manas Tiger Reserve	(*ii*)	Rajasthan
C.	Periyar Tiger Reserve	(*iii*)	Assam
D.	Corbett National Park	(*iv*)	Kerala

(*a*) A-(*i*), B-(*ii*), C-(*iii*), D-(*iv*) (*b*) A-(*ii*), B-(*iii*), C-(*iv*), D-(*i*)

(*c*) A-(*iv*), B-(*i*), C-(*iii*), D-(*ii*) (*d*) A-(*ii*), B-(*i*), C-(*iv*), D-(*iiii*)

6. (b) A - (ii), B - (iii), C - (iv), D - (i)

7. Two statements are given below. They are Assertion (A) and Reason (R). Read both the statements and choose the correct option: **(*Un*) (*1 Mark*)**

Assertion (A): Most of the jute industry in India is located in a narrow belt along the banks of Hugli river.

Reason (R): India is the second largest exporter of jute.

(*a*) Both (A) and (R) are true and (R) is the correct explanation of (A).

(*b*) Both (A) and (R) are true, but (R) is not the correct explanation of (A).

(*c*) (A) is true, but (R) is false.

(*d*) (A) is false, but (R) is true.

7. (b) Both Statements are true. The Jute Industry in India is Concentrated along the Hugli River due to the availability of raw materials, transport facilities, and labor. However, India's position as the Second-largest Exporter of Jute is an independent fact and not the reason for the Industry's location.

8. Choose the correct option to fill in the blank: ***(Re)* (*1 Mark*)**

The process of removing barriers on foreign trade and investment by the government is known as ________.

(*a*) Import Tax (*b*) Export Tax (*c*) Liberalisation (*d*) Industrialisation

8. (c) Liberalisation refers to the removal of restrictions and trade barriers imposed by the government on foreign trade and investment. This policy aims to promote Economic integration by allowing free movement of goods, services, and capital across borders.

9. Identify the odd one out. ***(Re)* (*1 Mark*)**

(*a*) Hindustan Computers Limited (*b*) Bharti Airtel Limited

(*c*) Hindustan Unilever Limited (*d*) Bharat Heavy Electricals Limited

9. (d) Bharat Heavy Electricals Limited (BHEL) is a public Sector Company owned by the government of India, while the other three are private Sector Companies.

10. By which organization is the Human Development Report published? ***(Re)* (*1 Mark*)**

(*a*) World Trade Organisation (*b*) Amnesty International

(*c*) United Nations Development Programme (*d*) World Health Organisation

10. (c) The Human Development Report is published by the United Nations Development programme (UNDP). It Evalutes Countries based on health, Education, and per Capita income indicators to measuret overall human development.

11. Why is it not easy to get loans from the formal sector? Read the following reasons and choose the most appropriate option: ***(Un)* (*1 Mark*)**

I. Availability of Banks

II. Availability of Collateral

III. Long and Complicated Loan Process

IV. Awareness of Borrower

(*a*) Only I, II and III are correct. (*b*) Only II, III and IV are correct.

(*c*) Only I, II and IV are correct. (*d*) Only I, III and IV are correct.

11. (b) The main difficulties in getting loans from the formal sector are the requirements of collateral, complex loan procedures, and lack of borrower ~~awareness~~ awareness. Availability of bank is generally not an issue, but fulfilling the formal requirements is challenging.

12. Identify the sector on basis of the following characteristics and choose the correct option: ***(Re) (1 Mark)***

- The objective of this sector is to earn profit.
- This sector is owned by a person or company.
- Tata Iron and Steel is a example of this sector

(*a*) Cooperative Sector (*b*) Unorganised Sector (*c*) Public Sector (*d*) Private Sector

12. (d) The private sector is owned by individuals or companies with the primary objective of earning profit. Tata Iron and Steel is a prominent example of a private sector enterprise.

13. Data related to an imaginary country is given below. Study these data and answer the question that follows: ***(Un) (1 Mark)***

Age	Total Population	Net Attendance
7 and 8 years of age	1200	1000
14 and 15 years of age	1000	800
Total	2200	1800

The attendance percentage of this country of the age group of 14 and 15 years is ______.

(*a*) 90 percent (*b*) 80 percent (*c*) 70 percent (*d*) 60 percent

13. ~~(a)~~ (b) The attendance percentage for the age groups of 14 and 15 years is calculated as 80% using the given data.

Total population (14 and 15 years) : 1000
Net Attendance (14 and 15 years) : 800

$$\text{Attendance percentage} = \frac{\text{Net Attendance}}{\text{Total population}} \times 100$$

$$= \frac{800}{1000} \times 100 = 80\%$$

14. Two statements are given below. They are Assertion (A) and Reason (R). Read both the statements and choose the correct option: ***(An) (1 Mark)***

Assertion (A): Every party in India has to register with the Election Commission.

Reason (R): The Government provides election symbols to all political parties in India.

(*a*) Both (A) and (R) are true and (R) is the correct explanation of (A).

(*b*) Both (A) and (R) are true, but (R) is not the correct explanation of (A)

(*c*) (A) is true, but (R) is false

(*d*) (A) is false, but (R) is true.

14.(c) Every political party in India must register with the Election Commission. However, the government does not provides Election Symbols to all political parties.

15. Which of the following group is in majority in Sri Lanka? ***(Re) (1 Mark)***

(*a*) Tamil-speakers (*b*) Sinhala-speakers (*c*) Telugu-speakers (*d*) English-speakers

15.(b) Sinhala-Speaking people from the majority in Sri Lanka, making up approximately 74% of the population.

16. To reform the party system, which of the following tasks have been made compulsory for the political parties? Choose the most appropriate option. ***(Re) (1 Mark)***

I. It is now compulsory for all the political parties to file income tax returns.

II. It is now compulsory for all parties to have one-third women candidates.

III. It is now compulsory for all the political parties to hold their organisational election.

IV. It is now compulsory for all candidates to disclose information about pending criminal cases against them through affidavit.

(*a*) Only I, II and III are correct. (*b*) Only I, II and IV are correct.

(*c*) Only I, III and IV are correct. (*d*) Only II, III and IV are correct.

16.(c) It is compulsory for political parties to file income tax returns (I), holds organisational Elections (III), and for Candidates to disclose Criminal Cases through affidavits (IV). However, having one-third of women Candidates (II) is only a Suggestion, not a Compulsory rule.

17. Which of the following statements represent gender equality? ***(An) (1 Mark)***

(*a*) The value of women's vote is more than that of men

(*b*) Restricting women to household chores

(*c*) Providing more rights to men.

(*d*) Providing voting rights equally to men and women.

17.(d) Gender Equality means giving Equal rights and opportunities to both men and women. Providing Equal Voting rights ensures that both genders have the Same political power, which is a Key aspect of gender Equality. The other options either restrict women or favour Either men or women, which do not represent Equality.

18. Choose the correctly matched pair from the following: ***(Re) (1 Mark)***

(*a*) Concurrent List - Education (*b*) Concurrent List - Defence

(*c*) Concurrent List - Police (*d*) Concurrent List - Trade

18. (a) Education is included in the Concurrent list in the Indian Constitution. Both the Union and State Governments can legislate on matters related to Education.

19. In which one of the following organs of India are women taking advantage of reservation? **(*Re*) (*1 Mark*)**

(*a*) Municipality
(*b*) Legislative Council
(*c*) Rajya Sabha
(*d*) Judiciary

19. (a) Women taking advantage from reservation in local governance (municipalities and panchayats), where at least one-third of all seats are reserved for women.

20. Which one of the following languages is included in the Eighth Schedule of the Indian Constitution? **(*Re*) (*1 Mark*)**

(*a*) Bhojpuri
(*b*) Magadhi
(*c*) Rajasthani
(*d*) Tamil

20. (d) Tamil is one of the 22 languages recognized in the Eigth Schedule of the Indian Constitution.

SECTION - B

21. How is the distribution of power among different social groups beneficial for democracy? Explain. **(*An*) (*2 Marks*)**

21. Distribution of power among different social groups benefits democracy in the following ways: (Any two)

(i) Reduces Social Conflict: It reduces Conflicts between social groups, ensuring peace and unity by preventing one group from dominating others.

(ii) Enhances Inclusivity: It ensures minorities and disadvantages groups have a say in decision-making, promoting Equality and fairness.

(iii) Strengthens Democracy: Power sharing is the Core of a democratic Setup. It involves people in the governance process, making them feel included and responsible, which increases the legitimacy and stability of the government.

22. Explain any two benefits of globalisation. **(Un) (2 Marks)**

22. Two benefits of Globalisation :

(i) Increased Employment : Globalisation has led to the growth of multinational Companies, creating more job opportunities.

(ii) Access to New Markets : It allows producers to sell goods worldwide, Expanding markets and boosting Economic Growth.

23. Mention any two economic impacts of the First World War on India. **(Un) (2 Marks)**

23. Economic Impacts of the first world war on India were :

(i) Increased Taxation : The war led to higher defence Expenditure, financed by war loans and increased taxes, including Customs duties and newly introduced income tax.

(ii) Price Inflation : Prices doubled between 1913 and 1918, Causing ~~Serves~~ Server hardship for Common ~~peaste~~ people as the Cost of living rose significantly.

24. (A) Describe any two features of 'arid soils' **(Re) (2 Marks)**

24. (A) Arid Soils are characterized by unique properties due to Climatic Conditions and Soil Composition.

(i) Low fertility : Arid soils are Sandy, Saline, and lack organic matter, making them less fertile for agriculture.

(ii) High Evaporation : Due to high temperatures, moisture Quickly Evaporates, leaving the Soil dry and nutrient-deficient.

OR

(B) Describe any two features of 'forest soils'. **(Re) (2 Marks)**

(B) forest Soils are found in regions with dense Vegetation and exhibit unique Characteristics.

(i) Varied Texture : These soils are loamy and silty in Valleys, while Coarse-grained in upper slopes.

(ii) High fertility – forest soils in lower Valleys are rich in Organic matter and highly fertile for plant growth.

SECTION - C

25. Explain any three aims of Jal Jeevan Mission (JJM). (*Un*) (*3 Marks*)

25. The Jal Jeevan mission (JJM) aims to provide safe and adequate drinking water to every rural household.

(i) Piped water supply : It ensures potable piped water supply to rural households at 55 liters per capita per day.

(ii) Water Quality : It focuses on providing safe drinking water by addressing contamination issues and maintaining water quality.

(iii) Sustainability : JJM promotes water conservation through rainwater harvesting and groundwater recharge for long-term availability.

26. How does democracy establish an accountable, responsible and legitimate governance? Explain. (*Ap*) (*3 Marks*)

26. Democracy establishes an accountable, responsive and legitimate government in the following ways :

(i) Accountable Government : Through regular Elections and other mechanisms like the right to information, citizens can question, scrutinize, and replace their representatives, ensuring accountability.

(ii) Responsive Government : Democracy encourages the participation of citizens in decision-making process. Thus, the government must be responsive to their needs and aspirations to gain or maintain the support of the public.

(iii) Legitimacy : When people choose their leaders through voting, it makes the government more legitimate, strong and respected.

27. (A) Analyse the impacts of Gandhi-Irwin pact on the Indian freedom struggle. **(An) (3 Marks)**

27.(A) Impacts of Gandhi-Irwin Pact on the Indian freedom Struggle:

(i) Civil Disobedience Halted: Gandhi agreed to suspend the civil Disobedience Movement

(ii) Political Prisoners Released: The government agreed to release political prisoners except those involved in violence.

(iii) Round Table Conference: Gandhi Participated in the second Round table Conference in London.

OR

(B) Analyse the role of Alluri Sitaram Raju in the Indian National Movement. **(An) (3 Marks)**

(B) Role of Alluri Sitaram Raju in the Indian National Movement:

(i) led Gudem Rebellion: Raju led the tribal rebellion in Andhra Pradesh against colonial forest laws.

(ii) Inspired by Gandhi: He promoted Khadi and non-Cooperation but believed in armed struggle.

(iii) Folk Hero: After his capture and execution in 1924, he became a symbol of resistance.

28. Examine the importance of bank deposits. **(An) (3 Marks)**

28. The importance of bank deposits are:

(i) Safety and Interest: Bank deposits keep money safe while earning interest, ensuring the value of saving increase over time.

(ii) Easy Access: Depositors can withdraw money anytimes through deposits, enabling smooth cashless transactions.

(iii) Economic Growth: Banks use deposits to provide loans, supporting businesses and promoting overall economic development.

29. Explain the main features of the Indian federal system. **(Un) (3 Marks)**

29. The following are some of the main features of the Indian federal system:

(i) Division of Powers: The power is divided between the Central government and the Constituent units.

(ii) Rigid Constitution: The changes in the fundamental provisions of the Constitution require the consent of both levels of government to prevent abuse of power.

(iii) Independent Judiciary: A federal government has an independent Judiciary that severed as a check on the powers of both the Central government and the constituents units.

SECTION - D

30. (A) Analyse the contribution of Johann Gutenberg in the development of the printing press. **(An) (5 Marks)**

30.(A) Johan Gutenberg's Contribution to the development of the printing press:

(i) Invention of the printing press: Johan Gutenberg, a German goldsmith, developed the first-known printing press in the 1430s

(ii) Inspiration from olive press: He adapted the wine and olives press mechanism to create a printing press, enabling faster and more efficient printing.

(iii) Movable Metal Type: Gutenberg developed metal types for each letter of the alphabet, allowing reusable typefaces for different texts.

(iv) Printing of the Gutenberg bible: The first major book printed was the bible. Around 180 copies were printed, demonstrating the efficiency of the new technology.

(V) Impact on Print Culture: Gutenberg's invention made books cheaper, increased literacy, and spread knowledge across Europe, leading to the print revolution.

OR

(B) Analyse the development journey of print culture in India. **(*An*) (*5 Marks*)**

(B) The development journey of print culture in India:

(i) Introduction of printing press: The printing press first came to Goa with portuguese missionaries in the mid-16th Century. They printed religious texts in Konkani and tamil, with the first tamil book printed in 1579.

(ii) Expansion by Missionaries: Dutch protestant missionaries printed 32 tamil texts by 1710. Including translations of older works. Catholic priests printed the first Malayalam book in 1713.

(iii) Growth of English printing: James Augustus Hickey started the first printed English newspaper in India, the Bengal Gazette, in 1780, known for its independent stance.

(iv) Emergence of Indian-language press: Gangadhar Bhattacharya published the first Indian newspaper, the Bengal Gazette, in Bengali. Other regional newspaper, like the Bombay Samachar (Gujarati) and Jam-i-Jahan Nama (persian), soon followed.

(v) Role in Social and political Movements: Print culture helped spread reformist ideas, such as Rammohun Roy's Campaign against social evils through his newspaper Sambad Kaumudi.

31. (A) "Secularism is the very idea of Indian Constitution." Justify the statement. **(*Ev*) (*5 Marks*)**

31 (A) Secularism is the very idea of the Indian Constitution because:

(i) No official Religion: The Indian Constitution does not recognize any particular religion as the state religion ensuring that all religions are treated Equally.

(ii) Freedom of Religion : The Indian Constitution guarantees the freedom of religions to all citizens. Every citizens has the right to practice, profess, and and propagate any religion or choose not to follow any.

(iii) Prohibits discrimination : It specifically prohibits discrimination on the basis of religion, ensuring that no individual or group is treated unfairly because of their religious beliefs.

(iv) State Intervention : The Constitution allows the State to intervense in religious matters to ensure equality. For example, it bans untouchability and prevents discriminatory practices based on religion.

(v) Equality of all religions : No religion is considered superior or inferior to any other religion. All religions are treated equally under the law.

OR

(B) Suggest any five measures to establish the gender equality of labour. **(*Cr*) (*5 Marks*)**

(B) Five measures that may be taken to establish gender equality of labour are :

(i) Equal Remuneration for Equal work : The Equal remuneration Act, 1976 Mandates equal pay for men and women for the same work. However, women still face disparities, so it's important to enforce this law more strictly in all sectors.

(ii) Equal Education opportunities : Providing equal education for both boys and girls is crucial. When women gets the same education, they can access better jobs and earn a fair income, just like men.

(iii) Empowerment through Political Representation : More women in politics help address their needs better.

the women's Reservation Bill, which sets aside seats for women in the Lok Sabha and State Assemblies, is important for their empowerment.

(iv). Safe working Conditions: Implementing and Enforcing laws to ensure safe working conditions for women in all sectors can help reduce harassment and make women feel more secure at work

(v) Recognizing Household work: Household work should be equally shared between men and women. Recognizing the value of domestic work and promoting shared responsibilities can help achieve this balance.

32. (A) Distinguish between public and private sector of economy with examples. ***(Un)* (5 Marks)**

32(A) The distinction between the public and private sectors of the economy are:

features	Public Sector	Private Sector
Ownership	Owned and Controlled by the government.	Owned and Controlled by individuals or Companies.
Objective	Provide services and welfare to the public.	Earns profit through business activities.
Examples	Indian Railways, Post Office	Tata Iron and Steel, Reliance Industries.
Source of funds	funded by taxes and government revenue.	funded by private investments and profits.
Service priority	focuses on public welfare and development.	focuses on consumer satisfaction and profit.

OR

(B) Suppose you are the Sarpanch of your village. What suggestions will you give for creating additional employment in the village, so that the problem of unemployment of the residents of rural areas can be reduced? ***(Ap)* (5 Marks)**

(B) The Suggestions to Create additional employment and reduce unemployment in rural areas are:

(i) Promote Irrigation projects: Developing irrigation facilities through wells, Canals, or dams can enable farmers to grow multiple crops, & Creating more employment opportunities throughout the year.

(ii) Encourage Agro-Based Industries: Setting up agro-processing units like dal mills, Cold Storage, and fruit processing industries can generate jobs for villagers beyond agriculture.

(iii) Skill Development and Education: Providing vocational training in areas like Carpentry, tailoring and Computer Skills Can Equip villagers to find alternative Employment.

(iv) Improve Rural Infrastructure: Better roads, transportation, and Storage facilities will help farmers transport and Sell their produce Efficiently, boosting the rural Economy.

(V) Support Small-Scale Industries: Promoting Cottage industries like handicrafts, pottery, and handloom Can Create non-agricultural employment opportunities within villages.

33. (A) Describe the features of cropping patterns in India.

(Un) (5 Marks)

33.(A) India's Cropping patterns are shaped by geographical, Climatic, and Socio-economic factors, resulting in three major agricultural Seasons.

(i) Rabi crops: Sown in winter (October-December) and harvested in Summer (April-June); Examples include wheat, barley, gram, mustard, and peas.

(ii) Kharif crops: Grown during monsoon (June-September); Key crops include rice, maize, bajra, Cotton, Soybean, and pulses, requiring Significant rainfall.

(iii) Zaid crops: Short-Season Summer Crops grown between rabi and Kharif; Examples include watermelon, muskmelon, Cucumber, and fodder Crops.

(iv) Crop Rotation: farmers practice crop rotation to maintain soil fertility, reduce pests, and ensure balanced nutrient usage for sustainable farming.

(v) Regional Variations: Different crops grow based on regions - rice dominates eastern India, while wheat thrives in northwestern and central plains.

OR

(B) Describe the main characteristics of major millet crops grown in India. ***(Un) (5 Marks)***

(B) Major Millet crops in India, including Jowar, bajra, and ragi, are known for their resilience and nutritional value. The main characteristics of these crops are as follows:

(i) High Nutritional Value: Millets are rich in iron, calcium, fiber, and micronutrients, making them an essential part of a healthy diet.

(ii) Drought Resistance: These crops can withstand dry conditions and require minimal water, making them ideal for rain-fed areas.

(iii) Diverse Soil Adaptability: Millets grow well in sandy, loamy, red, black, and shallow soils, suitable for dry and semi-arid regions.

(iv) Major Growing Regions: Jowar is cultivated in Maharashtra and Karnataka, while Rajasthan and Uttar Pradesh lead in bajra production.

(v) Economic Importance: Millets are not only consumed domestically but also exported, boosting farmer's income and agricultural sustainability.

SECTION - E

34. Read the given source and answer the questions that follow:

IRON ORE

Iron ore is the basic mineral and the backbone of industrial development. India is endowed with fairly abundant resources of iron ore India is rich in good quality iron ores. Magnetite is the finest iron ore with a very high content of iron up to 70 per cent. It has excellent magnetic qualities, especially valuable in the electrical industry Hematite ore is the most important industrial iron ore in terms of the quantity used, but has a slightly lower iron content than magnetite (50-60 per cent). In 2018-19, almost the entire production of iron ore (97%) accrued from Odisha, Chhattisgarh, Karnataka and Jharkhand. The remaining production (3%) was from other states.

34.1 In which iron ore is the maximum iron content found? ***(Re) (1 Mark)***

34.1 Magnetite has the maximum iron content, with upto 70% iron, making it the finest quality iron ore.

34.2 Which is the most important industrial iron ore? **(Re) (1 Mark)**

34.2 The most important industrial iron ore is hematite due to the Quantity used, although it has a slightly lower iron Content (50-60 percent) Compared to magnetite.

34.3 "Iron ore is a basic mineral." Support the statement. **(Un) (2 Marks)**

34.3 Iron ore is a fundamental mineral for industrial and Economic development.

(i) Industrial Backbone: Iron ore is essential for steel production, which forms the foundation for industries like Construction, transportation, and manufacturing.

(ii) Economic Growth: It drives industrial growth, Creating Jobs and boosting Economic development by supporting infrastructure and technological advancements.

35. Read the given source and answer the questions that follow:

ORGANISED SECTOR

Kanta works in the organised sector. Organised sector covers those enterprises or places of work where the terms of employment are regular and therefore, people have assured work. They are registered by the government and have to follow its rules and regulations which are given in various laws such as the Factories Act, Minimum Wages Act, Payment of Gratuity Act, Shops and Establishments Act, etc. It is called Organised Sector because it has some formal processes and procedures. Some of these people may not be employed by anyone but may work on their own, but they too have to register themselves with the government and follow the rules and regulations.

35.1 Mention any one feature of the working conditions of organised sector. **(Re) (1 Mark)**

35.1 One feature of the working Conditions of the Organised Sector is Job Security, where employees have fixed working hours, regular wages, and benefits like paid leave and health insurance.

35.2 Explain any one benefit provided by the employers to the organised sector employees. **(Un) (1 Mark)**

35.2 One benefit provided by Employers in the Organised Sector is provident fund, which ensures financial Security for employees after retirements, along with paid leave and medical benefits.

35.3 Why is it necessary for all self-employed people to register with the government? **(Un) (2 Marks)**

35.3 The reasons for the necessity of self-employed people to register with the government are:

(i) Access to Benefits: Registration allows them to avail government schemes, loans, and subsidies that support business growth.

(ii) Legal Protection: It ensures their business operates under formal rules and regulations, protecting them from legal issues.

36. Read the given source and answer the questions that follow:

THE REVOLUTIONARIES

During the years following 1815, the fear of repression drove many liberal-nationalists underground. Secret societies sprang up in many European states to train revolutionaries and spread their ideas. To be revolutionary at this time meant a commitment to oppose monarchical forms that had been established after the Vienna Congress, and to fight for liberty and freedom. Most of these revolutionaries also saw the creation of nation-states as a necessary part of this struggle for freedom.

36.1 Mention any one political demand of the liberals. **(*Re*) (*1 Mark*)**

36·1 One major political demand of the liberals was the establishment of a constitutional government with national sovereignty and protection of individual rights and freedoms.

36.2 Mention the main cause for the rise of secret societies in European States. **(*Re*) (*1 Mark*)**

36·2 The main cause for the rise of secret societies in European States was the fear of repression by conservative forces after the Vienna Congress of 1815, which aimed to restore monarchical rule and suppress liberal and nationalist movements.

36.3 Analyse the reasons for many liberal-nationalists going underground after 1815. **(*An*) (*2 Marks*)**

36·3 Reasons for Many Liberal-Nationalists Going underground after 1815:

(i) Fear of Repression: The Congress of Vienna (1815) aimed to restore conservative monarchies, leading to strict surveillance and suppression of liberal-nationalist movements.

(ii) Opposition to Monarchical Rule: Liberal nationalists, who sought freedom and democratic reforms, were targeted by conservative regimes, forcing them to operate secretly to avoid persecution.

SECTION - F

37. (*i*) Two places **'A'** and **'B'** have been marked on the given political outline map of India (on page 23). Identify them with the help of the following information and write their correct names on the lines drawn near them: **(*2 Marks*)**

(*a*) The place where the session of Indian National Congress was held place in 1927. **(*Re*)**

(*b*) The place where Mahatma Gandhi broke the Salt Law. **(*Re*)**

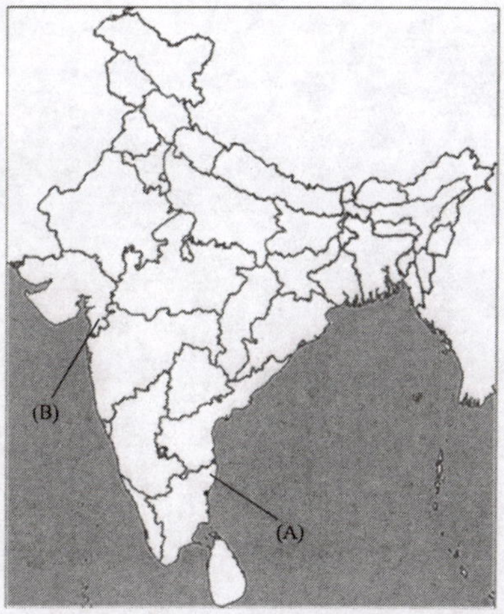

37 (i) (a) Madras
(b) Dandi

(*ii*) On the same political outline map of India, locate and label any **three** of the following with suitable symbols: **(*Un*) (*3 Marks*)**

(*a*) An international airport of West Bengal

(*b*) A software technology park of Karnataka

(*c*) A nuclear power plant located in Maharashtra

(*d*) A major sea port of Odisha

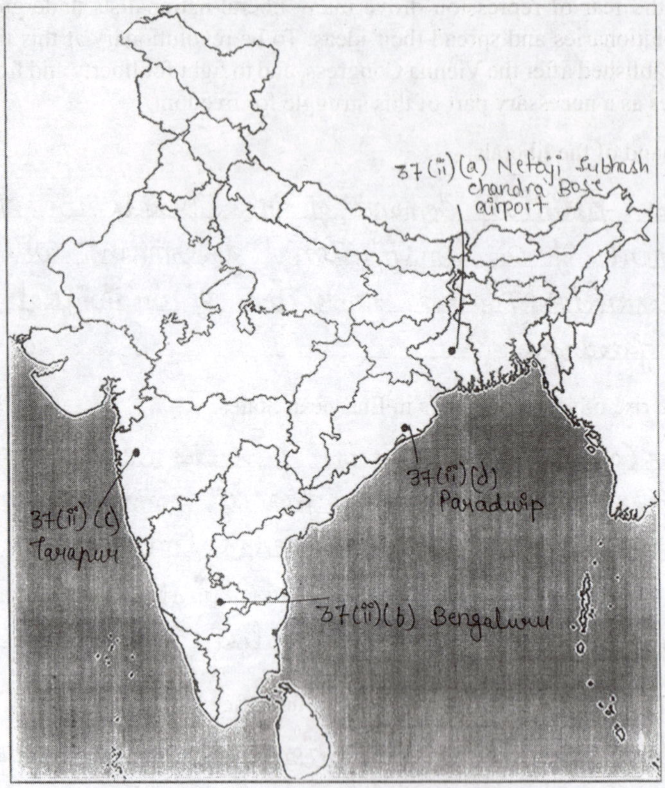

❑❑❑

RESOURCES AND DEVELOPMENT

1

"Resources are materials or substances like water, minerals, and forest, used by us. Development involves using these resources wisely for our needs and future generations."

SYLLABUS & WEIGHTAGE

List of Concept Names	Years					
	2020	2021	2022	2023	2024	2025
Resources (Development of Resources, Resources planning in India, Conservation of Resources, Classification of resources)	1 Q (3 M)	Exam not Conducted	–	–	–	
Land Resources (Land utilisation and land use pattern in India, Land degradation and conservation measures)	–		–	–	1 Q (2 M)	
Soil as a Resource (Classification of soil, Soil erosion and soil conservation)	–		–	1 Q (1 M)	–	1 Q (3 M)

CONCEPT MAP

To Access One Shot Revision Video Scan This QR Code

Resources and Development

Resources → CBSE 2020

Technologically accessible, economically feasible & culturally acceptable can be termed as a resources.

Development Resources

Essential for the future as resources are limited in supply. The Major Problems of indiscriminate are Ecological Problems, Depletion of resources, Scarcity of resources, and Unequal distributions

Classification of Resources

- **On the basis of origin:** biotic and abiotic
- **On the basis of exhaustibility:** renewable and non-renewable
- **On the basis of ownership:** individual, community, national and international
- **On the basis of status of development:** potential, developed stock and reserves.

Resource Planning in India → CBSE 2025

- Identification and inventory of resources across the regions of the country.
- Making of the planning structure with appropriate technology, skill, and institutions.
- Matching of resource development plans with overall national development plans.

Land Use Pattern in India

- Land use is shaped by topography, climate, soil, population, technology, and culture.
- The total geographical area of India is 3.28 million sq km.
- Net sown area ranges widely across states, exceeding 80% in Punjab and Haryana, but falls below 10% in Arunachal Pradesh, Mizoram, Manipur, and the Andaman Nicobar Islands.
- Forest area in the country is far lower than the desired 33% of geographical area, under the national forest policy (1952)
- Land degradation and conservation measures are about 130 Million of hectares of degraded in India.

Lnad Utilisation → CBSE 2024

- **Forests:** Land under forest, i.e. 22.78%
- **Land not available for cultivation:** Barren and wasteland, Land put to non-agricultural uses, e.g. buildings, roads, factories, etc.
- **Other uncultivated land:** Permanent pastures and grazing land, Land under miscellaneous tree crops groves, Culturable wasteland.
- **Fallow lands:** Left without cultivation for one or less than one agricultural year, left uncultivated for the past 1 to 5 agricultural years.
- **Net Sown Area:** Area sown more than once in an agricultural year plus net sown area is known as gross cropped area.

Lnad Under Important Relief Features

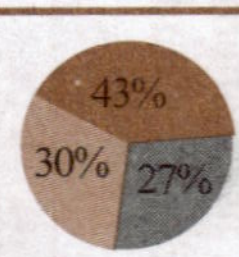

Plains & islands (43%)
Mountains (30%)
Plateaus (27%)

Soil Erosion & Soil Conservation

Soil Erosion: The removal of the topsoil by water, wind, or other natural forces, leading to reduced soil quality and land degradation.

Soil Conservation: Methods to protect soil from erosion and maintain its fertility, including planting trees, contour ploughing, and terrace farming.

Types of Soils → CBSE 2025, 2023

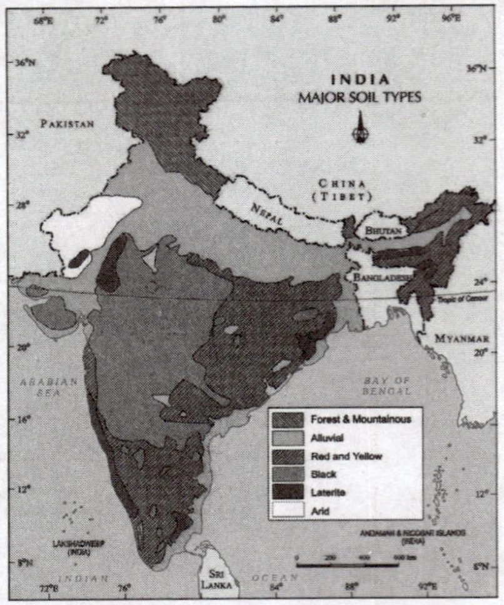

- **Alluvial Soil** (Region: eastern coastal plains and deltas of Mahanadi Godavari, etc.)
- **Black Soil** (Region: Deccan Trap Malwa, MP, Saurashtra)
- **Forest Soil** (Region: Jammu and Kashmir and other mountainous regions)
- **Red and Yellow Soils** (Region: Odisha, Chhattisgarh southern Deccan plateau)
- **Arid Soil** (Region: Rajasthan parts. of Gujarat)
- **Laterite Soil** (Region: Maharashtra, Bengal)

1 RESOURCES

NCERT Definitions *(Commonly asked in 1 mark)*

- **Resource:** Everything available in our environment that can be used for our needs, which is technologically accessible, economically feasible, and culturally acceptable can be termed as a resource.
- **Resource Planning:** The process involves finding resources, ensuring their efficient use, and monitoring them to ensure equitable and eco-friendly use.
- **Deforestation:** It refers to the ***process of clearing*** or ***cutting down*** large areas of forests for various purposes, often leading to environmental problems, including loss of biodiversity and disruption of ecosystems.
- **Afforestation:** It means ***planting trees*** in areas where there were no trees before. It's like creating new forests to improve the environment and provide benefits like cleaner air, wildlife habitat, and protection against soil erosion.
- **Biotic Resources:** These resources are ***living components*** of the environment, such as plants, animals, and microorganisms, from which humans can derive value, either directly or indirectly.
- **Abiotic Resources:** These resources are ***non-living*** elements in the environment, including minerals, water, and air. They form the physical and chemical foundations essential for ecosystems and human activities, such as agriculture, industry, and environmental processes.
- **Renewable Resources:** These types of resources are natural resources that ***can replenish themselves*** over time through natural processes, ensuring their availability for future generations. Examples: sunlight, wind, water, and solar energy.

Solar Energy Wind Energy Hydropower Biomass Energy

- **Non-renewable Resources:** These types of resources are natural resources that ***cannot replenish*** themselves at a sufficient rate for sustainable economic Profitability in meaningful human time-frames. Once depleted, they cannot be readily replaced. Examples: fossil fuels, coal, oil, and natural gas etc.

Petroleum Fossil fuels Coal Energy Nuclear Natural gas

- **Sustainable Development:** It means using resources today in a way that doesn't stop future generations from meeting their needs.
- **Conservation of Resources:** It involves ***careful management and use*** of natural resources to prevent waste and ensure their sustainability for the future generations.
- **Development of Resources:** It means ***responsibly using and managing*** natural resources to improve people's lives and protect the environment.

Important Facts

01 In June 1992, over 100 leaders convened in Rio, Brazil, for the first Earth Summit.
Rio de Janeiro Earth Summit, 1992

02 Aims for global sustainable development.
Agenda 21

03 The oceanic resources are beyond 200 nautical miles of the Exclusive zone.
International Resources

04 Our Most Precious Resource.
Water Resources

Classification

Resources can be classified into the following ways:

- **By origin:** Biotic and Abiotic
- **By exhaustibility:** Renewable and Non-renewable
- **By ownership:** Individual, Community, National, International
- **By status of development:** Potential, Developed, Stocks, Reserve

Difference Between

Renewable resources Vs. Non-renewable resources		
Basis of Difference	**Renewable resources**	**Non-renewable resources**
Regeneration	Yes, through natural processes	No
Distribution	Widespread and available in many parts of the world	Limited, specific locations
Examples	Sunlight, wind, water, solar energy, etc.	Fossil fuels, coal, oil, natural gas, etc.

Biotic resources Vs. Abiotic resources		
Basis of Difference	**Biotic resources**	**Abiotic resources**
Origin	Living organisms & processes	Non-living environmental components
Renewability	Renewable if managed sustainably	Renewable (sunlight, wind) or non-renewable (fossil fuels, minerals)
Examples	Plants, animals, birds, fish, microorganisms. 	Minerals, metals, air, sunlight 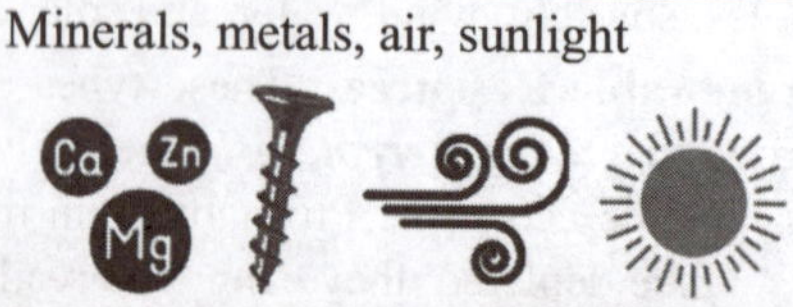

Stock Vs. Reserve		
Basis of Difference	**Stock**	**Reserve**
Definition	Present but not usable due to current technology or knowledge limitations	Identified and usable with existing technology and knowledge
Potential Use	Can become useful with technological advancements	Already quantified and extractable profitably
Examples	Hydrogen in water, deep minerals 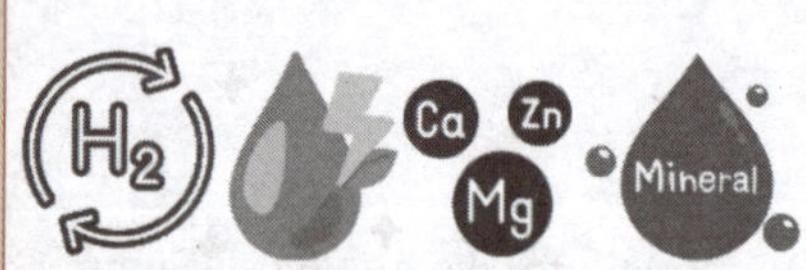	Coal, petroleum deposits, reservoir water for drinking/irrigation 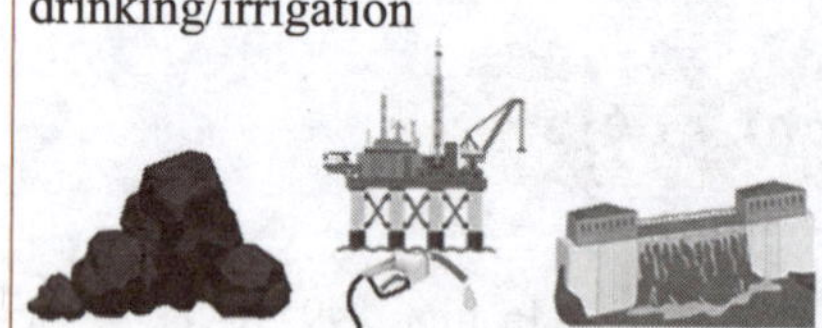

Mnemonics

"PLANTS" – Biotic Resources Example

- P → Plants
- L → Livestock
- A → Animals
- N → Natural Vegetation
- T → Tree
- S → Soil

"ROCKS" – Abiotic Resources Example

- R → Rocks
- O → Ores
- C → Coal
- K → Kerosene
- S → Sunlight

Real Life Application Based Questions

1. **How do composting, water-saving methods, and using native plants in gardens enhance local biodiversity and sustainability?**

Ans. Composting boosts soil health, lessening chemical fertilizer use. Rainwater harvesting and choosing native plants save water and support wildlife, boosting biodiversity. These sustainable practices enhance environmental and community well-being.

2. **How do individual actions like saving water, using efficient devices, and careful consumption aid water sustainability?**

Ans. Personal water conservation efforts, efficient appliance use, and mindful consumption lessen water and energy use, reducing environmental impact. These practices help preserve water for future generations, supporting sustainable development.

3. **How do solar panels, wind turbines, and geothermal systems reduce emissions, cut costs, and boost sustainability?**

Ans. Rooftop solar panels, wind turbines, and geothermal systems cut carbon emissions and energy costs by using renewable sources, promoting sustainability, and aligning with sustainable development goals.

Myth Buster

❒ **Myth:** All resources are renewable.

Fact: Resources are classified into renewable (solar energy) and non-renewable (fossil fuels). Renewable resources can replenish naturally over time, while non-renewable resources deplete with use.

❒ **Myth:** Man-made resources are not as important as natural resources.

Fact: Man-made resources, like buildings, machinery, and technology, are crucial for utilizing natural resources effectively and play a significant role in economic development.

COMPETENCY BASED SOLVED EXAMPLES

Scan Me for Detailed Explanations

Multiple Choice Questions (1 M)

1. Which one of the following types of resource is iron ore? ***(Re)* (NCERT)**

(*a*) Renewable (*b*) Biotic

(*c*) Flow (*d*) Non-renewable

2. Match the Column-I with Column-II and choose the correct option: ***(Ap)*(CBSE, 2023)**

Column-I (Resources)		Column-II (Example)	
I.	Biological	1.	Coal
II.	Renewable	2.	Wildlife
III.	Non-renewable	3.	Solar Energy

(*a*) I-1; II-3; III-2 (*b*) I-3; II-2; III-1

(*c*) I-2; II-3; III-1 (*d*) I-1; II-2; III-3

3. Mr. Sharma, a geography teacher, discusses with his class how Jharkhand, rich in mineral resources, faces environmental challenges.

What would be the most sustainable way to mitigate the environmental impact while continuing mining in Jharkhand? ***(Ev)***

(*a*) Increasing the area of open pit mines

(*b*) Implementing stricter environmental regulations

(*c*) Encouraging the export of raw minerals

(*d*) Reducing the overall extraction of minerals

4. Priya, a student from Jharkhand, noticed significant environmental changes due to mining activities around her hometown. Given this situation, which of the following is the most likely impact of mining on her region? ***(Ap)***

(*a*) Increase in agricultural productivity

(*b*) Enhancement of local biodiversity

(*c*) Increase in land degradation

(*d*) Improvement in air quality

5. At the World Resource Summit, various countries discussed strategies to combat resource depletion and ensure fair access. Countries like Agraria, known for its rich agricultural lands, and Mineria, known for its mineral wealth, debated the sharing of resources.

Agraria proposed a global resource-sharing agreement, suggesting that countries like Mineria should share their mineral resources with countries lacking them. What would be a critical factor to evaluate the feasibility of such an agreement? ***(Ev)***

(*a*) The historical trade relations between the countries involved

(*b*) The technological capabilities of the countries to utilize the resources

(*c*) The political stability and governance structures of the countries

(*d*) The equitable distribution of resources within each participating country

6. Which of the following is not a problem of resource development? ***(Un)*(CBSE, 2022, Term 1)**

(*a*) Depletion of resources to satisfy the greed of a few individuals.

(*b*) Accumulation of resources in few hands.

(*c*) Indiscriminate exploitation of resources.

(*d*) An equitable distribution of resources.

7. Match the Column-I with Column-II and choose the correct option: ***(Ap)***

Column-I (Resources)		Column-II (Example)	
P.	Renewable resources	(i)	Forests and wildlife
Q.	Non-renewable resources	(ii)	The oceanic resources
R.	National resources	(iii)	Roads, canals and railway
S.	International resources	(iv)	Minerals and fossil fuels

(*a*) P-(i), Q-(iv), R-(iii), S-(ii)

(*b*) P-(ii), Q-(i), R-(iv), S-(iii)

(*c*) P-(iv), Q-(i), R-(iv), S-(ii)

(*d*) P-(i), Q-(iv), R-(ii), S-(iii)

8. In the fictional country of Aridonia, resource management has become a critical issue due to the country's diverse geography and climatic conditions. The northern region, known for its rich mineral deposits, is facing challenges with mining practices causing environmental degradation. The southern region, abundant in water resources, is struggling with water wastage and pollution. The government, led by Prime Minister Elena, is implementing a comprehensive resource management plan to ensure sustainable development across the country.

Match the problems faced in different regions of Aridonia (Column-I) with the proposed solutions by Prime Minister Elena's administration (Column-II): ***(Ev)***

	Column-I		Column-II
(A)	Environmental degradation due to mining	(i)	Promotion of water-saving technologies
(B)	Water wastage and pollution	(ii)	Implementation of stricter pollution controls
(C)	Lack of sustainable agricultural practices	(iii)	Development of renewable energy sources
(D)	Over-reliance on non-renewable energy	(iv)	Introduction of sustainable farming techniques

(*a*) A-(ii), B-(i), C-(iv), D-(iii)

(*b*) A-(i), B-(ii), C-(iv), D-(iii)

(*c*) A-(iii), B-(ii), C-(i), D-(iii)

(*d*) A-(iv), B-(i), C-(ii), D-(iii)

9. **In the country of Ecotopia, resources are unevenly distributed. The northern region is rich in minerals and forests but has limited water resources. In contrast, the southern region has abundant water but lacks minerals and energy sources. The government, led by President Alex, is faced with the challenge of ensuring equitable resource distribution to avoid socio-economic disparities.**

President Alex is considering a policy to transport water from the southern to the northern region to support industrial growth. What factor should be most critically considered in this decision to ensure sustainable development? *(Ap)*

(*a*) The cost of infrastructure development

(*b*) The potential environmental impact on the southern region

(*c*) The availability of advanced technology for water transport

(*d*) The cultural acceptance of the policy by the northern population

Assertion and Reason (1 M)

Direction: The following questions consist of two statements – Assertion (A) and Reason (R). Answer these questions by selecting the appropriate option given below:

(*a*) Both A and R are true, and R is the correct explanation of A.

(*b*) Both A and R are true, but R is not the correct explanation of A.

(*c*) A is true, but R is false.

(*d*) A is false, but R is true.

1. **Assertion (A):** Resources are gifts of nature.

Reason (R): Resources like soil, air, and water are easily available in nature. *(Un)*

2. **Assertion (A):** Resource planning in India is guided by Five-Year Plans.

Reason (R): Five-Year plans outline the objectives, strategies, and allocation of resources for the economic and social development of the country. *(Ev)*

3. **Assertion (A):** Non-renewable resources are more sustainable than renewable resources.

Reason (R): Renewable resources can be replenished naturally or through human intervention, ensuring their continuous availability, while non-renewable resources are finite and get depleted over time. *(Ev)*

4. **Assertion (A):** Resource planning is an easy process in India.

Reason (R): Resource planning involves the identification and inventory of resources across the regions of the country. *(Un)*

5. **Assertion (A):** Renewable resources can be used indefinitely without depleting them.

Reason (R): Renewable resources are constantly replenished by natural processes. *(Un)*

Subjective Questions

Very Short Answer Type Questions (2 M)

1. **What are the benefits of technology in resource planning?** *(An)*

Ans. The benefits of technology in resource planning include:

***(i)* Improved Efficiency:** Technology automates repetitive tasks, reducing the time and effort required for planning and allocation of resources. *(1 M)*

***(ii)* Enhanced Accuracy:** Advanced software tools help in accurate forecasting and demand planning, reducing the risk of over or underutilization of resources. *(1 M)*

2. **In a small town, agricultural expert Mr. Amit Gupta and environmental planner Mrs. Sunita Rao are working together to draft a resource plan. They aim to enhance the town's development by optimizing the use of local resources such as rivers and fertile land, which have been underutilized due to a lack of technology and infrastructure.**

Explain how Mr. Gupta and Mrs. Rao can utilize resource planning to improve the agricultural output of the town. Consider the need for appropriate technology and institutional support in your response. *(Ap)*

Ans. Mr. Gupta and Mrs. Rao can enhance agricultural output through resource planning by:

***(i)* Technology Integration:** Implement modern agricultural technology like irrigation systems and high-yield seeds to maximize the use of rivers and fertile land. *(1 M)*

***(ii)* Institutional Support:** Establish local agricultural institutions to provide training and infrastructure, enhancing resource utilization and productivity. *(1 M)*

3. Provide two non-renewable resources. *(Re)*

Ans. Two non-renewable resources are:

Two non-renewable resources are **coal** and **petroleum**. Coal is used for electricity generation and as a fuel, while petroleum is used for transportation and manufacturing plastics. Both are extracted from the earth and cannot be replenished once used. *(2 M)*

4. Give two differences between renewable and non-renewable resources. *(Re)*

Ans. *(1+1 = 2 M)*

	Basis of Difference	Renewable resources	Non-Renewable resources
1.	Replenishment	Naturally replenished over short periods	Take millions of years to form; not replenished within a human time frame
2.	Availability	Often abundant and sustainable	Limited availability; can be exhausted

5. What are the challenges in resource planning in India? *(An)*

Ans. Resource planning in India faces difficulties due to:

Geographical Diversity: India's diverse geography, with mountains, plains, and coastlines, complicates resource allocation and management. *(1 M)*

Population Differences: Varying demographics and population densities challenge fair resource distribution. *(1 M)*

Short Answer Type Questions (3 M)

1. In a recent town hall meeting, the local government introduced a plan to develop a community park that integrates sustainable practices and utilizes natural resources efficiently. The park will feature areas for recreation, local flora, and structures built from recycled materials. Students from nearby schools, including yours, are invited to provide feedback on how to make the park a model of sustainability for other towns to follow.

How can the park demonstrate the effective use of renewable and non-renewable resources? *(Ev)*

Ans. To make the community park a model of sustainability and demonstrate the effective use of renewable and non-renewable resources, consider the following steps:

(Any Three)

(i) **Solar Panels:** Install solar panels for lighting and energy needs, harnessing renewable solar energy. *(1 M)*

(ii) **Rainwater Harvesting:** Implement systems to collect and utilize rainwater, conserving water resources. *(1 M)*

(iii) **Recycled Materials:** Use recycled materials for building structures and playgrounds, reducing waste and conserving non-renewable resources. *(1 M)*

(iv) **Local Flora:** Plant native species to preserve biodiversity and reduce the need for chemical fertilizers. *(1 M)*

2. Describe the importance of judicious use of resources. *(Un)***(CBSE, 2020)**

OR

Describe the different steps of 'resource planning'. *(Re)*

Ans. Key reasons for the judicious use of resources include:

(i) **Conservation of resources:** The judicious use of resources helps in the conservation of natural resources, which are finite and may become scarce if not used sustainably. *(1 M)*

(ii) **Sustainable development:** Sustainable development involves using resources wisely to meet current needs while ensuring future generations can meet theirs. *(1 M)*

(iii) **Economic benefits:** The judicious use of resources can lead to economic benefits, such as cost savings, increased efficiency, and reduced waste. *(1 M)*

OR

Ans. Resource planning involves the following steps:

(i) **Identification of resources:** The first step in resource planning is to identify the available resources, such as natural resources, human resources, and financial resources. *(1 M)*

(ii) **Inventory of Resources:** Assess the amount, quality, and accessibility of resources. *(1 M)*

(iii) **Resource Allocation:** Distribute resources according to priorities and goals. *(1 M)*

3. In a recent town meeting in Meerut, Uttar Pradesh, concerns were raised about the local river pollution worsening due to unchecked industrial waste dumping. The community is alarmed by the declining water quality and its effects on agriculture and health. As a response, the town council has decided to form a committee, including students from various schools, to propose sustainable solutions. You, as a student representative, need to prepare a proposal that addresses these concerns effectively.

Discuss how the concepts of sustainable development and resource planning can be applied to address river pollution in Meerut. *(Ev)*

Ans. To address river pollution in Meerut using the concepts of sustainable development and resource planning, consider these steps:

(i) **Implement Waste Treatment**: Enforce strict regulations on industrial waste, requiring industries to treat wastewater before release, reducing river pollution. *(1 M)*

(ii) **Educate and Engage**: Initiate community education programs to increase awareness about the effects of pollution and promote sustainable practices. *(1 M)*

(iii) **Regular Monitoring**: Establish a committee to monitor water quality regularly, ensuring compliance with environmental standards and taking action against violators. *(1 M)*

Long Answer Type Questions (5 M)

1. In Nagpur, Maharashtra, a recent government survey highlighted the city's potential for harnessing solar energy due to its high number of sunny days per year. However, the city faces challenges in managing its water resources, often experiencing water scarcity during the dry months. The local government has convened a panel including students, environmental experts, and urban planners to devise a strategic plan for resource management that utilizes the city's strengths while addressing its challenges.

As a student representative on the panel, analyze the situation in Nagpur by considering its resource strengths and deficits. Propose how integrated resource planning can help address these issues, focusing particularly on the potential for solar energy utilization and strategies for improving water resource management. *(An)*

Ans. To address Nagpur's strengths in solar energy and challenges in water scarcity, we propose:

(i) **High Solar Potential**: Nagpur's numerous sunny days make it ideal for solar energy projects. *(1 M)*

(ii) **Solar Panel Installation**: Encourage the installation of solar panels on rooftops to generate clean energy. *(1 M)*

(iii) **Rainwater Harvesting**: Implement rainwater harvesting systems to capture and store rainwater. *(1 M)*

(iv) **Efficient Water Use**: Promote the use of drip and sprinkler irrigation to conserve water in agriculture. *(1 M)*

(v) **Integrated Policy**: Develop policies that integrate solar energy utilization with effective water resource management. *(1 M)*

2. In the town of Shimla, Himachal Pradesh, which is known for its scenic landscapes and tourism, there has been a growing concern about the environmental impact of increased tourist activities, especially waste management and water usage. The local administration has been facing challenges in maintaining sustainability with fluctuating resources, particularly during peak tourist seasons. To address this, the administration has called for a collaborative approach involving local schools to educate and involve the community in sustainable practices.

Evaluate the current resource management practices in Shimla and suggest how these practices could be improved by integrating effective waste management and water conservation methods. Consider the town's reliance on tourism and the need for sustainable resource use to ensure long-term ecological and economic stability. *(Ev)*

Ans. To address Shimla's environmental concerns related to tourism, we suggest:

(i) **Current Practices**: Shimla struggles with waste management and water conservation during peak tourist seasons, leading to resource strain. *(1 M)*

(ii) **Waste Segregation**: Implement strict waste segregation and recycling programs in public areas and tourist spots. *(1 M)*

(iii) **Water Conservation**: Encourage rainwater harvesting in hotels and public buildings to reduce dependency on local water sources. *(1 M)*

(iv) **Education and Awareness**: Launch campaigns in local schools to educate the community and tourists on sustainable practices. *(1 M)*

(v) **Collaborative Efforts**: Involve local businesses, schools, and the administration in regular clean-up drives and sustainable resource use initiatives. *(1 M)*

3. Why is the issue of sustainability important for development? Explain *(Un)*

Ans. The issue of sustainability is crucial for development for several reasons:

- **Resource Preservation:** Sustainability ensures that resources are used judiciously so that future generations can also benefit from them, preventing resource depletion. *(1 M)*
- **Environmental Protection:** It emphasizes protecting the environment, reducing pollution, and combating climate change, which are essential for a healthy living planet. *(1 M)*
- **Economic Efficiency:** Sustainable practices promote economic efficiency by reducing waste and promoting renewable resources, which can be more cost-effective in the long run. *(1 M)*
- **Social Well-being:** It supports social equity and well-being, ensuring that development benefits are shared widely and do not compromise the needs of marginalized communities. *(1 M)*
- **Future Readiness:** Focusing on sustainability prepares societies to deal with future challenges, such as resource scarcity and environmental crises, ensuring long-term development success. *(1 M)*

Mistakes 101 : What not to do!

Confusion between Sustainability and Development

Tip: Development focuses on making life better and wealthier now, while sustainability is about using things carefully so the future can also thrive.

2 LAND RESOURCES

NCERT Definitions (Commonly asked in 1 mark)

- **Land:** A natural resource that supports natural vegetation, wildlife, human life, and economic activities.
- **Land Resources:** These resources include ***different kinds of land and soil*** on Earth used for farming, building homes, and supporting plants and animals. They represent the various ways we utilize the land.
- **Land relief features:** ***Different shapes*** and ***forms*** on the Earth's surface, like ***mountains*** and ***plains***.
- **Barren and wasteland:** Land that ***cannot be used for farming*** or ***construction*** due to ***poor soil*** or harsh conditions.
- **Fallow Lands:** Land not used for crops for a period to ***restore soil*** nutrients.
- **Land Degradation:** Damage to the land, making it ***less productive***, often due to ***overuse*** or ***poor practices***.

Important Facts

01 **India's land composition:** 43% plains, 30% mountains, and 27% plateaus provides diverse resources, that affect climate, agriculture, and lifestyle.

02 Grazing is one of the main reasons for land degradation in Gujarat, Rajasthan, Madhya Pradesh, and Maharashtra.

03 In the states of Punjab, Haryana, and western Uttar Pradesh irrigation is responsible for land degradation due to water logging leading to an increase in salinity and alkalinity in the soil.

04 Land degradation is caused by deforestation, overgrazing, mining, and poor agricultural practices. At present, there are about 130 million hectares of degraded land.

05 Current Degraded Land Area: Approximately 130 million hectares.

Classification

Based on Use		
S. No.	**Type of Land Use**	**Description**
1.	Agricultural Land	Used for farming, including cultivation of crops and orchards.
2.	Residential Land	Designated for housing and urban development.
3.	Recreational Land	Utilized for parks, gardens, playgrounds, and entertainment venues.

Based on Ownership		
S. No.	**Ownership Type**	**Description**
1.	Public Land	Land owned by the government including parks, government buildings, and roads.
2.	Private Land	Land owned by individuals or corporations for personal or commercial use.
3.	Community Land	Land owned collectively by a community or village, including common grazing grounds and water bodies.

Based on Location and Terrain		
S. No.	**Location and Terrain**	**Description**
1.	Urban Land	Located within city limits, characterized by high-density development.
2.	Rural Land	Found in countryside areas, primarily used for agriculture and residence.
3.	Mountainous Land	Situated in hilly or mountainous regions, utilized for tourism, forestry, and sometimes agriculture.

Based on Productivity		
S. No.	**Productivity Type**	**Description**
1.	Fertile Land	Highly productive, suitable for agriculture.
2.	Barren Land	Low or no productivity, unsuitable for cultivation.
3.	Marginal Land	Limited agricultural productivity, often used for grazing.

Difference Between

Criteria	Forest Land	Cultivated Land	Uncultivated Land
Area Coverage	Extensive; covers large areas in many countries	Smaller compared to forest land; varies by region.	Includes lands not suitable for farming; variable size.
Biodiversity	High biodiversity; home to various species.	Lower biodiversity; mainly crops and livestock	Varied biodiversity, depending on the land type.
Conservation Status	Often under protection for conservation.	Managed for agricultural productivity.	May be protected if ecologically valuable; otherwise not.
Land Utilisation	Mainly for ecological balance, wood, and habitat. (22.78% forested)	Used for growing food, feed, Fiber, and fuel.	May be used for grazing, left fallow, or not used due to poor soil/terrain.

Real Life Application Based Questions

1. **How does organic farming help connect people to their food sources?**

Ans. Organic farming connects people to their food sources in several ways:

- **Local produce:** Organic farming often involves local markets. This means people buy food grown close to where they live, connecting them to local farmers and the land.
- **Transparency:** Organic farming practices are more transparent. People can learn how their food is grown and what goes into it, which helps them feel more connected to their meals.
- **Community involvement:** Many organic farms encourage community participation, like farm visits or community-supported agriculture (CSA) programs, allowing people to be directly involved in the food production process.

2. How does land use planning meet the needs of urban and rural development?

Ans. Land use planning helps both cities and countryside areas by deciding how land should be used to meet people's needs and to protect the environment. In cities, it plans where houses, shops, and parks should be so people can live comfortably and travel easily. In the countryside, it helps decide where farms should be and protects natural areas to keep the environment healthy. This way, everyone gets to use the land in the best way possible, making sure there's space for both people and nature.

Myth Buster

- **Myth:** Land and soil are the same thing.

  Fact: Land encompasses various elements like water, forests, and cities, not just soil.

- **Myth:** Land management only involves taking care of soil.

  Fact: Soil is important, but land management should also consider other components.

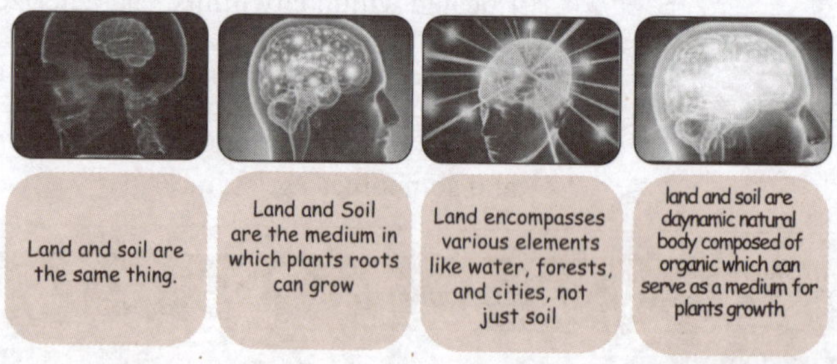

Scan Me for Detailed Explanations

COMPETENCY BASED SOLVED EXAMPLES

Multiple Choice Questions (1 M)

1. Deforestation due to mining has caused severe land degradation in which one of the following states? ***(Re)*(CBSE, 2022 Term 1)**

(*a*) Odisha (*b*) Tamil Nadu

(*c*) Kerala (*d*) Gujarat

2. Read the following data and choose the correct option:

(*i*) If a new environmental policy aims to increase forest cover to 30% by 2030, which land use category should be prioritized for reforestation based on the 2014-15 data? ***(An)***

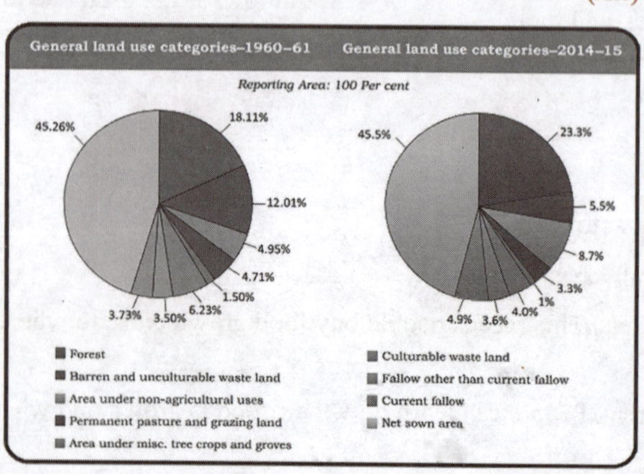

Source: Directorate of Economics and Statistics, Ministry of Agrivulture, 2017

(*a*) Barren and unculturable waste land

(*b*) Culturable waste land

(*c*) Permanent pasture and grazing land

(*d*) Fallow other than the current fallow

OR

(*ii*) Evaluate the effectiveness of land use changes from 1960-61 to 2014-15 in terms of sustainability. Which statement best reflects this evaluation? ***(Ev)***

(*a*) The changes have been largely sustainable as shown by increased forest and agricultural land.

(*b*) The increase in non-agricultural use reflects unsustainable urban expansion.

(*c*) Sustainability has not been achieved due to the reduction in permanent pastures.

(*d*) Land use has been optimized for both growth and sustainability.

3. Karan, a resident of Coimbatore, Tamil Nadu, is researching the impact of urbanization on local ecosystems. He notes that rapid city expansion has led to a decrease in the local bird populations. Which of the following measures would most effectively mitigate the impact of urbanization on bird habitats? ***(Ev)***

(*a*) Increasing commercial land use

(*b*) Developing more residential complexes

(*c*) Implementing green roofing systems

(*d*) Expanding paved areas

4. **In the fictional country of Greenlandia, excessive mining activities have led to severe land degradation. The government, with the help of environmental scientist Dr. Lila, is exploring ways to mitigate the negative impacts while continuing to meet economic needs.**

Dr. Lila suggests implementing stricter regulations on mining activities. Which of the following justifications best supports this policy from an environmental perspective? *(An)*

(*a*) It will increase government revenue through fines and penalties.

(*b*) It will protect biodiversity and prevent further loss of vegetation.

(*c*) It will encourage the use of alternative, sustainable resources.

(*d*) It will reduce the competition among mining companies.

5. **Interpret the following pie diagram and choose the correct option for the following question.** *(An)* **(CBSE SQP, 2025)**

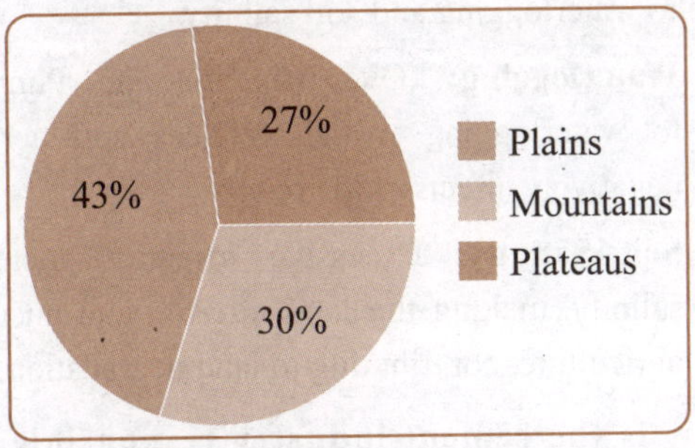

What is the significance of 43 percent land under plains?

(*a*) It provides facilities for agriculture and industry.

(*b*) It provides facilities for tourism.

(*c*) It ensures perennial flow of some river.

(*d*) It possesses rich reserves of minerals, fossil fuels and forests.

Note: The following question is for Visually Impaired Candidates only in lieu of Q. No. 5.

Transformation of things available in our environment involves an interactive relationship between .... Choose the correct option from below.

(*a*) Nature and technology

(*b*) Nature, technology, and institutions

(*c*) Nature and institutions

(*d*) Environment and human beings

6. **What is the main objective of land use planning?** *(Un)*

(*a*) To ensure optimal utilization of land resources

(*b*) To maximize agricultural production

(*c*) To promote industrialization

(*d*) To increase urbanization

7. **Uranium is found in Ladakh but has not been mined due to a lack of funding. What kind of resource is this?** *(Ap)***(CBSE CFPQ, 2023)**

(*a*) stock (*b*) reserves

(*c*) potential resources (*d*) developed resources

8. **Which of the following is NOT an important factor in the formation of soil?** *(Re)***(CBSE CFPQ, 2023)**

(*a*) running water (*b*) chemical reactions

(*c*) atmospheric pressure (*d*) change in temperature

9. **Most of the alluvial soil found in India is formed from the silt deposited by the Indo-Gangetic Brahmaputra rivers. Which of the following regions contains the parent rock that forms this silt?** *(Re)*

(*a*) Himalayas (*b*) Gangetic delta

(*c*) Northern plains (*d*) Eastern coastal plains

10. **Historically, colonising countries took advantage of India's rich resources to gain supremacy. Why was India not able to resist the exploitation of her resources?** *(Ev)***(CBSE CFPQ, 2023)**

(*a*) due to lack of use for products derived from natural resources

(*b*) due to the colonising countries' superior technology

(*c*) due to lack of awareness about India's resources

(*d*) due to over-utilisation of resources

Assertion and Reason (1 M)

Direction: The following questions consist of two statements – Assertion (A) and Reason (R). Answer these questions by selecting the appropriate option given below:

(*a*) Both A and R are true, and R is the correct explanation of A.

(*b*) Both A and R are true, but R is not the correct explanation of A.

(*c*) A is true, but R is false.

(*d*) A is false, but R is true.

1. **Assertion (A):** Land use planning is essential for sustainable development.

Reason (R): Land use planning helps to balance competing demands for land and minimize negative impacts on the environment and society. *(Ev)*

2. **An environmental scientist in Rajasthan is studying the effects of irrigation practices.**

Assertion (A): Overirrigation in arid regions like Rajasthan leads to soil salinity.

Reason (R): Over-irrigation in arid regions increases the groundwater level, leading to salinity. *(Ev)*

3. **Assertion (A):** Land degradation in India can be effectively controlled by implementing contour ploughing and strip cropping methods.

Reason (R): Contour ploughing and strip cropping are methods that only help in increasing crop yield but have no effect on soil erosion. *(Ap)*

4. **Assertion (A):** The forest area in India is significantly above the desired 33% as outlined in the National Forest Policy of 1952.

Reason (R): The availability of vast forest resources has led to the extensive development of the forest-based industry in India. ***(Ev)***

5. **Assertion (A):** Deforestation contributes to climate change.

Reason (R): Trees absorb carbon dioxide from the atmosphere through photosynthesis, so deforestation leads to an increase in atmospheric carbon dioxide levels, which contributes to climate change. ***(Ev)***

Subjective Questions

Very Short Answer Type Questions (2 M)

1. **What is the difference between land use and land cover?** ***(Un)***

Ans.

Aspect	Land Cover	Land Use	Marks
Definition	Refers to the natural surface of the earth	Describes how people utilize the land	*(1 M)*
Focus	Physical features like forests, water bodies, deserts. Examples: Forests, water bodies, grasslands	Human activities like farming, urban development, parks. Examples: Agriculture, residential areas, industrial zones	*(1 M)*

2. **In the rapidly developing city of Indore, Madhya Pradesh, urban planners are facing challenges with land management due to the city's diverse topography which includes both plain and plateau regions. The plateau areas are rich in minerals and ideal for industrial development, while the plains are primarily used for agriculture. To balance industrial growth with agricultural needs, the city council is in the process of revising its urban development plans.**

Evaluate the implications of Indore's land use policy focusing on its dual geography of plains and plateaus and discuss how the city can optimize its land use to enhance both industrial growth and agricultural productivity while ensuring sustainable environmental practices. ***(Ev)***

Ans. ***(i)*** **Implications of Indore's land use policy:** Indore's dual geography allows balanced development by utilizing plateaus for industry and plains for agriculture, ensuring optimal use and sustainable growth. *(1 M)*

(ii) **Optimizing land use for industrial and agricultural enhancement:** Indore can boost industry and agriculture by implementing sustainable practices like crop rotation and zoning, ensuring environmental protection and economic growth. *(1 M)*

3. **Which factor is mainly responsible for maximum land degradation in India?** ***(An)***

Ans. The main factor responsible for maximum land degradation in India is ***over irrigation***. Specifically, in states like Punjab, Haryana, and western Uttar Pradesh, over-irrigation has led to significant land degradation due to waterlogging, which subsequently increases salinity and alkalinity in the soil. *(2 M)*

4. **How is over-irrigation responsible for land degradation in Punjab?** ***(An)*** **(CBSE, 2019)**

Ans. Over-irrigation leads to land degradation in Punjab mainly due to waterlogging and soil salinity.

- **Waterlogging:** Over-irrigation in Punjab leads to waterlogging, which reduces soil aeration and negatively affects crop growth. *(1 M)*
- **Soil Salinity:** Excessive irrigation increases soil salinity, making the land infertile and unsuitable for agriculture, contributing to land degradation. *(1 M)*

5. **How is the cement industry responsible for land degradation?** ***(An)*** **(CBSE, 2019)**

Ans. The cement industry contributes to land degradation primarily through two processes:

- **Limestone Extraction:** The cement industry contributes to land degradation through the extensive extraction of limestone, depleting natural resources and altering landscapes. *(1 M)*
- **Pollution:** The industry also generates pollutants like dust and heavy metals, contaminating soil and water, further degrading land quality. *(1 M)*

Short Answer Type Questions (3 M)

1. **What are the different types of land use in India? Explain any three.** ***(Un)***

Ans. In India, land is utilized for various purposes. Three types of land use are:

(i) **Forests:** Used for ecological balance and providing resources like timber. *(1 M)*

(ii) **Net Sown Area:** Measures agricultural productivity, including all crop lands. *(1 M)*

(iii) **Fallow Lands:** Uncultivated to restore soil fertility, categorized as current or other based on duration left idle. *(1 M)*

Mistakes 101 : What not to do!

Lack of Elaboration: Students may need to provide more detailed explanations of each type of land use mentioned. Expanding on the significance, characteristics, and specific examples of forests, net sown area, and fallow lands could enhance the answer's depth and clarity.

2. **What is sustainable land use? How can it promote economic development while conserving natural resources?** ***(Un)***

Ans. Sustainable land use ensures long-term, eco-friendly land productivity and conservation. *(1 M)*

It promotes economic development by:

- **Enhancing Agricultural Productivity:** Implementing sustainable agricultural practices can improve soil health, increase crop yields, and ensure food security, contributing to economic growth. *(1 M)*
- **Conserving Resources:** It helps ensure they last longer, supports sustainable activities, and reduces restoration costs. *(1 M)*

3. **Give two examples of how human activities have impacted land resources negatively.** ***(Ap)***

Ans. Two examples of human activities have negatively impacted land resources are:

(i) **Deforestation:** The removal of trees for timber, agriculture, or urban expansion reduces forest cover, leading to soil erosion, and loss of habitat for species, and contributes to climate change by reducing carbon sequestration. *(1½ M)*

(ii) **Overuse of Chemical Fertilizers:** Excessive use of chemical fertilizers in farming contaminates soil and water bodies, harming soil fertility, aquatic life, and human health through polluted water and food. *(1½ M)*

Long Answer Type Questions (5 M)

1. **Evaluate the significance of land resources in supporting economic development and maintaining ecological balance in India. Discuss with examples.** ***(An)***

Ans. Land resources are signification for economic development and ecological balance in India.

(i) **Economic Support:** Fertile lands, particularly the alluvial soils of the Indo-Gangetic plains, drive agriculture, important for food security and economic stability. *(1 M)*

(ii) **Industrial Materials:** Regions like Jharkhand and Chhattisgarh, rich in minerals, to support India's manufacturing and economic growth. *(1 M)*

(iii) **Ecological Balance:** Forested areas, notably in the Western Ghats and Northeast, play a crucial role in climate regulation, water conservation, and biodiversity preservation. *(1 M)*

(iv) **Sustainable Development:** Adequate land use, including practices like terrace farming, aids in preventing soil erosion, promoting sustainable agriculture. *(1 M)*

(v) **Cultural Significance:** Land encompasses historical, cultural, and recreational areas, enriching India's heritage and social fabric. *(1 M)*

In essence, judicious management and sustainable practices of land resources are imperative for maintaining India's economic, environmental, and social health.

2. **Describe the role of land resources in sustaining rural and urban livelihoods. Discuss how land resource allocation impacts urban-rural dynamics in India.** ***(An)***

Ans. Role of Land Resources in Sustaining Rural and Urban Livelihoods:

- **Rural Livelihoods:** In rural areas, land is mainly used for agriculture, supporting crops, livestock, and forestry, crucial for food security and income. *(1 M)*
- **Urban Livelihoods:** Land in urban areas supports housing, industries, and infrastructure, crucial for jobs and city development. *(1 M)*

Impact of Land Resource Allocation on Urban-Rural Dynamics in India:

- **Migration:** Unequal land distribution and lack of employment in rural areas lead to migration towards cities, causing urban overcrowding and pressure on urban land resources. *(1 M)*
- **Agricultural Changes:** Land acquisition for urbanization reduces agricultural land, affecting food security and rural employment, and often leading to changes in rural lifestyles and economic activities. *(1 M)*
- **Infrastructure Development:** Urban land allocation boosts economy but may neglect rural infrastructure, increasing the urban-rural divide. *(1 M)*

3. **Explain how afforestation programs can help to prevent soil erosion and conserve natural resources in hilly areas.** ***(Cr)***

Ans. Afforestation programs can significantly prevent soil erosion and conserve natural resources in hilly areas:

(i) **Root Stabilization:** Trees' roots bind the soil, reducing soil displacement and preventing erosion. This helps maintain soil health and structure. *(1 M)*

(ii) **Water Absorption:** Tree roots absorb water, reducing surface runoff and lowering the risk of landslides and soil wash away, particularly in hilly terrains. *(1 M)*

(iii) **Increased Percolation:** Afforestation increases water infiltration into the soil, reducing soil erosion and contributing to groundwater recharge, which is vital for sustaining water resources. *(1 M)*

(iv) **Wind Barrier:** Trees act as windbreaks, reducing wind velocity and protecting the soil from being blown away, a process especially important in higher altitudes. *(1 M)*

(v) **Microclimate Improvement:** Trees from afforestation create a cooler, more humid environment, enhancing soil moisture and helping conserve resources. *(1 M)*

3 SOIL

NCERT Definitions *(Commonly asked in 1 mark)*

- **Soil:** The top layer of the earth's surface where ***plants grow***, composed of organic remains, clay, and rock particles.
- **Soil Erosion:** The ***removal of the topsoil*** by ***water, wind***, or other natural forces, leading to reduced soil quality and land degradation.
- **Soil Conservation:** ***Methods to protect soil*** from erosion and maintain its ***fertility***, including planting trees, contour ploughing, and terrace farming.
- **Contour ploughing:** Ploughing along the natural contours of land to prevent soil erosion.
- **Strip cropping:** Planting crops in strips to reduce soil erosion and protect the soil.
- **Soil Profile:** A ***vertical section*** of the soil from the ground surface downwards, showing different layers or ***horizons***.
- **Loamy Soil:** A type of soil that is ***well-balanced*** with ***sand, silt,*** and ***clay;*** it is fertile, well-drained, and easy to till, making it ideal for agriculture.
- **Alkaline Soil:** Soil with a ***pH level above 7***, which can affect the types of ***plants*** that can grow and may require management or treatment to improve fertility.
- **Leaching:** The process by which ***nutrients*** are ***washed out*** of the soil by rain or irrigation water, leading to reduced soil fertility.
- **Terracing:** It is an ***agricultural technique on sloped land*** where terraces are made to reduce soil erosion and runoff, making steep areas suitable for farming.

Important Facts

01 Soil forms over millions of years from the weathering of rocks and decay of organic matter.

02 Red and Yellow found ***in low rainfall areas***; supports crops like pulses and millets.

03 Laterite soil develops ***in wet and dry tropical areas***; suitable for tea and coffee.

04 Arid soil is sandy and dry, ***found in deserts***; becomes cultivable with irrigation.

05 Forest soil found ***in mountainous areas***, varies in texture; fertile in lower terrains.

Classification

S. No.	Type of Soil	Characteristics	Location/Distribution	Suitability for Crops
1.	**Alluvial Soil**	Rich in potash, phosphoric acid, and lime. Fine to coarse texture.	Plains of Punjab, Haryana, UP; Delta regions (eastern coastal plains).	Wheat, paddy, sugarcane, pulses
2.	**Black (Regur) Soil**	High in iron, magnesium, and calcium carbonate; poor in phosphoric contents. Retains moisture.	Deccan trap (Maharashtra, Saurashtra, Madhya Pradesh).	Cotton, soybean
3.	**Red and Yellow Soil**	Rich in iron oxides. Sandy to clay texture.	Eastern/southern Deccan Plateau (Odisha, Chhattisgarh, southern Ganga Plain).	Millets, pulses
4.	**Laterite Soil**	Rich in iron and aluminium oxides, porous, and low fertility.	Tropical regions (Western Ghats), hilly areas of Odisha and Assam.	Cashew nuts, tea, coffee, rubber
5.	**Arid and Desert Soil**	Sandy, low organic content, and poor water retention.	Arid regions of Rajasthan, Gujarat	Cactus, date palm

Difference Between

Soil Erosion Vs. Soil Conservation

S. No.	Criteria	Soil Erosion	Soil Conservation
1.	Definition	The removal of the top layer of soil by water or wind.	The set of practices used to prevent soil erosion.
2.	Causes	Deforestation, overgrazing, floods, and excessive farming.	Lack of sustainable land management practices.
3.	Impacts	Loss of fertile topsoil, reduced agricultural productivity.	Enhanced soil fertility, improved agricultural output.
4.	Preventive Measures	Avoid overgrazing, afforestation, proper drainage.	Contour ploughing, terracing, use of windbreaks.

Khadar Soil Vs. Bangar Soil

S. No.	Feature	Khadar Soil	Bangar Soil
1.	Regions	Lower reaches of river valleys.	Upper reaches of river valleys.
2.	Characteristics	New alluvial soil, fertile and dark in color.	Old alluvial soil, coarse and less fertile, lighter in color.
3.	Texture	Fine-grained, silty or clayey.	Coarse-grained, sandy, or loamy.
4.	Irrigation	Naturally irrigated by floods, suitable for wet crops like rice.	Requires artificial irrigation, suitable for dry crops like wheat and millet.
5.	Fertility	Khadar is highly fertile Soil containing clay and fine silt.	Bangar is less fertile Soil mixed with lime nodules

Real Life Application Based Questions

1. **What steps should be taken to implement an effective terracing project in hilly regions to combat soil erosion, and what types of vegetation are most effective in stabilizing these newly terraced areas?**

Ans. To start a terracing project in hilly areas to stop soil erosion, follow these steps:

- **Check the Area:** Find the slopes were soil washes away easily. Look at the type of soil and how steep the slopes are to figure out the best way to make terraces.
- **Plan the Terraces:** Draw a plan where each terrace follows the natural lines of the hill, making sure there's a way for water to run off without taking soil with it.
- **Build the Terraces:** Use materials found nearby to build the terraces. Make sure the walls are strong and there's a system to handle rainwater.
- **Choose Plants:** Pick plants with strong roots, like certain types of grass or bushes that are used to the local climate. These plants help keep the soil from moving.
- **Keep It Up:** Make sure to look after the terraces by checking the walls and plants and keeping everything in good shape.

Doing this helps stop soil from being washed away, keeps water where it's needed, and can make farming better on hilly land.

2. **How would you conduct a soil health assessment for your school garden, including tests for soil pH, nutrient levels, and water content? What steps will you take based on the results to ensure optimal plant growth and soil health?**

Ans. To conduct a soil health assessment for our school garden:

- **Collect Soil Samples:** Take small amounts of soil from different parts of the garden to get a good mix.
- **Test Soil pH:** Use a soil pH testing kit to find out if the soil is acidic, neutral, or alkaline. Plants grow best in different pH levels, so this will help decide what to plant.
- **Check Nutrients:** Get a soil nutrient testing kit to measure levels of important nutrients like nitrogen, phosphorus, and potassium.
- **Measure Water Content:** Check how moist the soil is to see if the area needs more or less watering.

Based on the results:

- If the soil is too acidic or alkaline, add lime or sulfur to balance the pH.
- If nutrients are low, use the right fertilizers to add what's missing.
- Adjust watering based on how dry or wet the soil is.

This helps our plants grow better and keeps the soil healthy for our school garden.

3. **What steps would you include in your watershed management plan to reduce soil erosion, improve water quality, and enhance sustainability in the area surrounding your school's nearby river?**

Ans. To create a watershed management plan for the area around our school's river:

- **Contour Plowing:** Suggest farming along the land's natural contours to reduce water runoff and soil erosion.
- **Check Dams:** Propose building small dams in the river to slow down water flow, reduce erosion, and help recharge groundwater.
- **Reforestation:** Plan to plant trees and shrubs around the riverbanks to stabilize soil and improve water absorption.
- **Trash Clean-Up:** Organize community clean-up days to remove litter from the river and surrounding areas to prevent pollution.
- **Awareness Campaigns:** Start campaigns in school and the community to educate about the importance of keeping the watershed area clean and conserving water.

By doing these steps, we can help reduce soil erosion, improve water quality, and make our local environment better and more sustainable.

Contour Plowing

Terracing

Crop rotation

Mnemonics

"GROUNDS" (Soil Erosion Causes)

- **G** → **Grazing:** Overgrazing by animals exposes soil.
- **R** → **Rainfall:** Heavy rainfall can cause soil erosion.
- **O** → **Over cultivation:** Excessive cultivation damages soil structure.
- **U** → **Urbanization:** Construction and urban development expose soil.
- **N** → **Nature:** Natural forces like wind and water contribute to erosion.
- **D** → **Deforestation:** Removal of trees increases soil erosion.
- **S** → **Slopes:** Steep slopes are prone to erosion.

"GUARD SOIL" (Soil Conservation Technique)

- **G** → **Ground Cover:** Implementing ground cover to protect soil.
- **U** → **Utilize Mulch:** Applying mulch to prevent erosion and retain moisture.
- **A** → **Afforestation:** Planting trees to stabilize soil and prevent erosion.
- **R** → **Retain Vegetation:** Preserving natural vegetation to prevent soil erosion.
- **D** → **Drainage Systems:** Installing proper drainage to manage water runoff.

COMPETENCY BASED SOLVED EXAMPLES

Scan Me for Detailed Explanations

Multiple Choice Questions (1 M)

1. **Which of the following is correctly matched?** *(Re)*(CBSE, 2023)
   (*a*) Alluvial Soil-Consists of sand and silt
   (*b*) Black Soil-Salt content is high
   (*c*) Arid Soil-Diffusion of iron in crystalline
   (*d*) Laterite Soil-Made up of Lava flows

2. **Which of the following pair is correctly matched?** *(Re)*(CBSE, 2023)
   (*a*) Alluvial Soil – Western Rajasthan
   (*b*) Black Soil – Northern Plain
   (*c*) Arid Soil – Deccan Plateau
   (*d*) Laterite Soil – Western Ghats

3. **Identify the soil that ranges from red to brown in colour and saline in nature:** *(Un)*(CBSE, 2022 Term-1)
   (*a*) Red soil (*b*) Laterite soil
   (*c*) Arid soil (*d*) Alluvial soil

4. **Which one of the following forces leads to maximum soil erosion in the plains?** *(Ap)*(CBSE, 2022 Term-1)
   (*a*) Wind (*b*) Glacier
   (*c*) Running water (*d*) Earthquake

5. **In Mumbai, Maharashtra, Sunita observes that despite industrial advancement, the local river systems are heavily polluted. What is the most probable cause of this pollution?** *(An)*
   (*a*) Agricultural runoff (*b*) Industrial waste
   (*c*) Natural soil leaching (*d*) Excessive rainfall

Assertion and Reason (1 M)

Direction: The following questions consist of two statements – Assertion (A) and Reason (R). Answer these questions by selecting the appropriate option given below:

(*a*) Both A and R are true, and R is the correct explanation of A.
(*b*) Both A and R are true, but R is not the correct explanation of A.
(*c*) A is true, but R is false.
(*d*) A is false, but R is true.

1. **Assertion (A):** Soil is a non-renewable natural resource.
   Reason (R): Soil formation takes thousands of years, and human activities can deplete soil faster than it can be regenerated. *(Ev)*

2. **Assertion (A):** The classification of soils is based on their texture.
   Reason (R): Different soil textures have different water-holding capacities and nutrient-retaining abilities, which influence their agricultural suitability. *(Ev)*

3. **Assertion (A):**Soil erosion cannot lead to the loss of topsoil and reduced agricultural productivity.
   Reason (R): Erosion removes the fertile top layer of soil, which contains essential nutrients and organic matter necessary for plant growth. *(Ev)*

4. **Assertion (A):** Contour plowing is an effective method to prevent soil erosion.
   Reason (R): By plowing parallel to the contour lines of a slope, contour plowing helps slow down water runoff, reducing soil erosion. *(Ev)*

5. **Assertion (A):** Terracing is a soil conservation practice used on steep slopes.
   Reason (R): Terracing involves creating flat platforms on steep slopes, which reduce the speed of water runoff and soil erosion. *(Ev)*

Subjective Questions

Very Short Answer Type Questions (2 M)

1. **What are the effects of soil erosion?** *(Uv)*

Ans. The effects of soil erosion include:

- **Loss of Fertile Topsoil:** Soil erosion removes the nutrient-rich upper layer of soil, reducing the land's ability to support plants and crops. *(1 M)*
- **Water Pollution:** When soil is eroded, it can carry pesticides and fertilizers into nearby water bodies, leading to water pollution and harming aquatic life. *(1 M)*

2. **What are the methods used for conserving soil?** *(Re)*

Ans. Methods for conserving soil include:

(*i*) Contour Plowing: Plowing along the contours of the land to reduce water runoff and prevent soil erosion. *(1 M)*

(*ii*) Afforestation: Planting trees to stabilize soil and increase water absorption. *(1 M)*

3. **Name two factors influencing soil formation.** *(Re)*

Ans. Factors Influencing Soil Formation:

(*i*) Climate: Temperature and rainfall affect the rate of weathering and organic matter decomposition, influencing soil characteristics. *(1 M)*

(*ii*) Parent Material: The type of rock from which the soil originates determines its texture, mineral content, and nutrient availability. *(1 M)*

4. **What is the importance of soil as a resource?** ***(Un)***

Ans. Importance of Soil as a Resource:

- **Supports Plant Life:** Soil supplies key nutrients, water, and support for plant growth, vital for food production and biodiversity. *(1 M)*
- **Sustains Ecosystems:** Soil is home to a vast array of organisms; it helps recycle nutrients, purifying water, and regulating the Earth's climate. *(1 M)*

Short Answer Type Questions (3 M)

1. **Describe any three main features of 'Alluvial soil' found in India.** ***(Un)*(CBSE, 2019)**

OR

Describe any three main features of 'Black soil' found in India. ***(Un)***

Ans. The three main features of Alluvial soil and Black soil are:

Alluvial Soil:

***(i)* Texture and Composition:** Alluvial soil is fine-grained and highly fertile, mainly composed of silt brought by river floods. It has a good mix of sand, silt, and clay. *(1 M)*

***(ii)* Distribution:** Found mainly in Indus, Ganges, and Brahmaputra River basins and floodplains, covering northern and eastern India. *(1 M)*

***(iii)* Agricultural Productivity:** Highly suitable for a wide range of crops like wheat, rice, sugarcane, and cotton due to its high fertility and moisture-retaining capacity. *(1 M)*

OR

Black Soil:

***(i)* Texture and Composition:** Black soil, or Regur, is deep, clayey, moisture-retaining, swelling when wet and shrinking, forming cracks when dry. *(1 M)*

***(ii)* Distribution:** Mainly found in the Deccan Plateau, covering states like Maharashtra, Madhya Pradesh, Gujarat, and Tamil Nadu. *(1 M)*

***(iii)* Suitability for Crops:** Especially favorable for growing cotton, hence also known as 'Cotton soil'. It is also good for crops like sorghum, millet, and oil seeds. *(1 M)*

2. **How does afforestation help in soil conservation?** ***(Ap)***

Ans. Afforestation helps in soil conservation through:

- **Root System Stabilization:** Tree roots bind soil to reduce erosion and prevent landslides. *(1 M)*
- **Water Retention:** Trees enhance soil's water absorption and retention, reducing runoff and maintaining groundwater. *(1 M)*
- **Organic Matter Addition:** Decomposed leaves and branches create humus, improving soil fertility and structure. *(1 M)*

3. **What is terrace farming and how does it help in soil conservation?** ***(Un)***

Ans. Terrace farming is the practice of cutting flat areas out of a hilly or mountainous landscape to grow crops.

Terrace Farming for Soil Conservation:

- **Reduces Runoff:** Shapes steep land into flat terraces, slowing water runoff and enhancing soil water absorption, minimizing erosion. *(1 M)*
- **Prevents Soil Erosion:** Terraces act as barriers, protecting topsoil from being washed away, vital for crop cultivation. *(1 M)*
- **Improves Water Usage:** Promotes efficient water retention and irrigation, conserving water and soil. *(1 M)*

Long Answer Type Questions (5 M)

1. **In the agricultural heartlands of India, particularly in the fertile plains of Punjab and the black soil regions of Maharashtra, farmers are encountering varying challenges related to soil management that affect their crop yields. The alluvial soils of Punjab, known for their richness and suitability for a variety of crops, contrast with the black soils of Maharashtra, which are ideal for cotton but require different management techniques due to their moisture retention properties and susceptibility to cracking in hot weather.**

Given the contrasting soil characteristics of alluvial and black soils, how should farmers in Punjab and Maharashtra adapt their farming practices to maximize agricultural productivity? Discuss specific cultivation techniques, irrigation methods, and crop rotation strategies appropriate for each soil type to enhance crop yield and soil health. ***(Ap)***

Ans. Given the contrasting soil characteristics of alluvial and black soils, how should farmers in Punjab and Maharashtra adapt their farming practices to maximize agricultural productivity:

***(i)* Deep Ploughing in Punjab:** Use deep ploughing to improve soil aeration and break up hard layers. This enhances root penetration and water absorption. *(1 M)*

***(ii)* Mulching in Maharashtra:** Apply mulching to retain soil moisture and prevent cracking in black soils, especially during hot weather. *(1 M)*

***(iii)* Drip Irrigation:** Use drip irrigation in both regions to conserve water, ensure efficient delivery to crops, and reduce water wastage. *(1 M)*

***(iv)* Crop Rotation in Punjab:** Rotate wheat, rice, and legumes to replenish soil nutrients, improve soil structure, and prevent pest buildup. *(1 M)*

***(v)* Crop Rotation in Maharashtra:** Rotate cotton with legumes like pigeon peas and soybeans to fix nitrogen, enhance soil fertility, and maintain crop productivity. *(1 M)*

2. **Analyse the measures adopted to prevent soil erosion** caused **due to natural forces.** ***(An)* (CBSE SQP, 2025)**

OR

"Mohan recently bought a farm and wants to grow crops such as sugarcane, cotton, and jowar. He is unfamiliar with the local soil types and climatic conditions." Help him identify the appropriate soil type and its properties for successful farming. ***(Ap)***

Ans. There are various measures which can be adopted to prevent soil erosion caused due to natural forces.

- Ploughing along the contour lines can decelerate the flow of water down the slopes. This is called contour ploughing. *(1 M)*
- Steps can be cut out on the slopes making terraces. Terrace cultivation restricts erosion. Western and central Himalayas have well developed terrace farming. *(1 M)*
- Large fields can be divided into strips. Strips of grass are left to grow between the crops. This breaks up the force of the wind. This method is known as strip cropping. *(1 M)*
- Planting lines of trees to create shelter also works in a similar way. Rows of such trees are called shelter belts. These shelter belts have contributed significantly to the stabilisation of sand dunes and in stabilising the desert in western India. *(1 M)*
- Natural forces like wind, glacier and water lead to soil erosion. *(1 M) (Any other relevant points)*

OR

Black soil is ideal for growing cotton, jowar and sugarcane.

- This type of soil is typical of the Deccan trap (Basalt) region spread over northwest Deccan plateau and is made up of lava flows. *(1 M)*
- They cover the plateaus of Maharashtra, Saurashtra, Malwa, Madhya Pradesh and Chhattisgarh and extend in the south east direction along the Godavari and the Krishna valleys. *(1 M)*
- The black soils are made up of extremely fine i.e. clayey material. They are well-known for their capacity to hold moisture. *(1 M)*
- In addition, they are rich in soil nutrients, such as calcium carbonate, magnesium, potash and lime. *(1 M)*
- These soils are generally poor in phosphoric contents.
- They develop deep cracks during hot weather, which helps in the proper aeration of the soil. *(1 M)*
- These soils are sticky when wet and difficult to work on unless tilled immediately after the first shower or during the pre-monsoon period. *(1 M)*

(Any five points or relevant point)

3. In the diverse landscapes of India, ranging from the arid regions of Rajasthan to the lush forests of the Western Ghats, soil conservation remains a crucial aspect of sustainable agriculture and environmental management. Each region presents unique challenges due to its specific soil type—whether it's the erosion-prone laterite soils of Karnataka or the fertile but fragile alluvial soils along the Ganges. Inspired by the successes and challenges of various regions, Dr. Ayesha Singh, a soil scientist, and Mr. Rohan Patel, an agricultural engineer, are tasked with developing a comprehensive soil conservation and management program tailored to these diverse conditions. *(Ap, Cr)*

Design a soil conservation program for addressing the challenges associated with laterite, arid, forest, and alluvial soils in India. Outline specific strategies for each soil type that include conservation techniques, agricultural practices to enhance soil health, and measures for community involvement in soil management.

Ans. Design a soil conservation program for addressing the challenges associated with laterite, arid, forest, and alluvial soils in India:

(*i*) Contour Ploughing for Laterite Soils: Implement contour ploughing and terracing in Karnataka to reduce soil erosion. *(1 M)*

(*ii*) Windbreaks for Arid Soils: Construct windbreaks and shelterbelts in Rajasthan to minimize wind erosion and use drought-resistant crops. *(1 M)*

(*iii*) Agroforestry for Forest Soils: Practice agroforestry in the Western Ghats to maintain forest cover and prevent soil erosion. *(1 M)*

(*iv*) Check Dams for Alluvial Soils: Build check dams and barriers along the Ganges to control flooding and prevent erosion. *(1 M)*

(*v*) Community Involvement: Engage local communities in all regions through education on sustainable practices, afforestation projects, and soil health awareness programs. *(1 M)*

MISCELLANEOUS EXERCISE

Multiple Choice Questions **(1 M)**

1. This is a cartoon on climate change.

Which of the following statements best describes the cartoon? *(An)*

(*a*) While the rich are benefitted from the depletion of resources, the poor are affected by its consequences.

(*b*) Resources are available to everyone equally, but the adverse effects are faced by the poor.

(*c*) Those who do not use natural resources sustainably are left to face its adverse effects.

(*d*) The rich try to reverse the effects of climate change by helping the poor.

2. Which of the following is correctly matched? *(Un)*

(*a*) Alluvial Soil-Consists of sand and silt

(*b*) Black Soil-Salt content is high

(*c*) Arid Soil-Diffusion of iron in crystalline

(*d*) Laterite Soil - Made up of lava flows

3. Which of the following statements about Agenda 21 is true? *(An)*

(*a*) It aims at achieving global sustainable development.

(*b*) It is an agenda to combat environmental damage, poverty and disease through global cooperation.

(*c*) One of the major objectives of Agenda 21 is that every local government should not draw its own local Agenda 21.

(*d*) Option (*a*) and (*b*).

4. Imagine you are a farmer in a region with a tropical climate experiencing alternate wet and dry seasons. You observe that the soil on your farm is reddish and has become less fertile due to heavy rainfall, leading to intense leaching of nutrients. Given this Image, which of the following soil types are you most likely dealing with, and what conservation techniques should you adopt to improve soil productivity?

(*i*) Which type of soil is described in the scenario? *(Un)*

(*a*) Black Soil (*b*) Laterite Soil

(*c*) Alluvial Soil (*d*) Arid Soil

OR

(*ii*) What conservation techniques should you consider to improve the soil productivity in this scenario? *(Ap)*

(*a*) Over-irrigation and use of chemical fertilizers

(*b*) Afforestation and proper management of grazing

(*c*) Extensive ploughing and use of synthetic pesticides

(*d*) Building concrete barriers to prevent soil erosion

5. Lakshmi, a farmer in the coastal region of Odisha, notices the soil in her fields retains moisture well, aiding in paddy cultivation. Which type of soil is most likely found in her fields? *(Un)*

(*a*) Black Soil (*b*) Laterite Soil

(*c*) Alluvial Soil (*d*) Arid Soil

6. Priyanka, a geography student in Arunachal Pradesh, notes that despite ample water resources, infrastructural deficiencies hinder development. What is most needed to improve this situation? *(Ap)*

(*a*) Reduction in water resources

(*b*) Enhanced agricultural techniques

(*c*) Better infrastructure

(*d*) More extensive land use

7. Which one of the following terms is used to identify the old and new alluvial respectively? *(Re)*

(*a*) Khadar and Tarai (*b*) Tarai and Bangar

(*c*) Bangar and Khadar (*d*) Tarai and Dvars

8. Which one of the following methods is used to break up the force of wind? *(Un)*

(*a*) Shelter belt (*b*) Strip Cropping

(*c*) Contour ploughing (*d*) Terrace farming

9. Which one of the following statements refers to the sustainable development? *(Un)*

(*a*) Overall development of various resources

(*b*) Development should take place without damaging the environment

(*c*) Economic development of people

(*d*) Development that meets the desires of the members of all communities

10. The process in which bare ground between plants is covered with a layer of organic matter like straw, is called ***(Re)***

(*a*) Mulching (*b*) Contour carriers

(*c*) Shelter belts (*d*) Inter cropping

11. In the country of Ecotopia, rapid industrialization has led to severe environmental issues, including deforestation, soil erosion, and water pollution. The government, led by President Samira, is working with environmental scientist Dr. Kumar to implement sustainable development practices. They are focusing on balancing economic growth with environmental conservation.

Consider the following statements about Ecotopia's environmental challenges and proposed solutions: ***(An, Ev)***

Statement-I: Dr. Kumar suggests implementing stricter regulations on industrial waste disposal to reduce water pollution.

Statement-II: President Samira plans to increase the country's reliance on renewable energy sources like wind and solar power.

Statement-III: The government encourages afforestation as a means to combat deforestation and improve biodiversity.

Statement-IV: Dr. Kumar proposes the use of traditional farming methods to improve soil health and prevent erosion.

Which statements are correct regarding the environmental policies proposed in Ecotopia?

(*a*) Statements-I and III

(*b*) Statements-II and IV

(*c*) Statements-I, II, and III

(*d*) All of the above

12. Match the Column-I with Column-II and choose the correct option: ***(Cr)***

A geography teacher is explaining the distribution of soil types and their agricultural uses in India to her class.

Column-I (Soil Type)		Column-II (Predominant Use)	
(A)	Black Soil	(i)	Tea and Coffee Plantation
(B)	Alluvial Soil	(ii)	Cotton Cultivation
(C)	Red Soil	(iii)	Rice and Wheat Cultivation
(D)	Laterite Soil	(iv)	Cashew Nut Cultivation

(*a*) A-(ii), B-(iii), C-(i), D-(iv)

(*b*) A-(ii), B-(iii), C-(iv), D-(i)

(*c*) A-(iii), B-(ii), C-(i), D-(iv)

(*d*) A-(ii), B-(i), C-(iii), D-(iv)

13. Under which of the following types of resource can solar energy be categorised? ***(Un)***

(*a*) Flow resource

(*b*) Human-made resource

(*c*) Non-recyclable resource

(*d*) Exhaustible resource

14. The alluvial soil consists of ***(Re)***

(*a*) Sand (*b*) Silt

(*c*) Clay (*d*) All of the above

15.

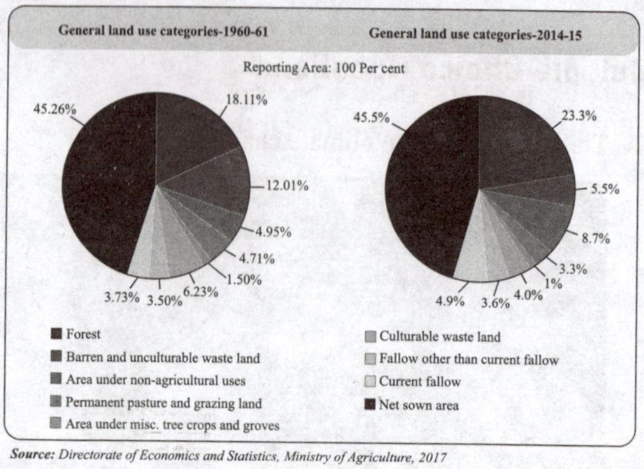

Source: *Directorate of Economics and Statistics, Ministry of Agriculture, 2017*

The percentage which of land-use categories is increased from 1960 to 2014? ***(Re)***

(*a*) Barren and unculturable waste land

(*b*) Culturable waste land

(*c*) Forest

(*d*) Permanent pasture and grazing land

16. Find the odd one out from the given options: ***(An)***

(*a*) Khadar soil (*b*) Red soil

(*c*) Black soil (*d*) Laterite soil

17. Laterite soil is very useful for growing: ***(Un)***

(*a*) Wheat (*b*) Tea & Coffee

(*c*) Jute (*d*) Cotton

18. Which one of the following type of resource is iron ore? ***(Re)(NCERT)***

(*a*) Renewable (*b*) Biotic

(*c*) Flow (*d*) Non-renewable

19. Which one of the following is the main cause of land degradation in Punjab? ***(Un)(NCERT)***

(*a*) Intensive cultivation (*b*) Deforestation

(*c*) Over irrigation (*d*) Overgrazing

20. Read the following statements and choose the correct option: ***(An)***

During a field study in Gujarat, Amit observed the effects of overgrazing on land quality.

Statement-I: Overgrazing can lead to soil compaction, reducing its fertility.

Statement-II: Soil compaction can increase water infiltration.

Choose the correct answer:

(*a*) Both statements are false.

(*b*) Statement-I is true, Statement-II is false.

(*c*) Statement-I is false, Statement-II is true.

(*d*) Both statements are true.

Assertion and Reason (1 M)

Direction: The following questions consist of two statements – Assertion (A) and Reason (R). Answer these questions by selecting the appropriate option given below:

(*a*) Both A and R are true, and R is the correct explanation of A.

(*b*) Both A and R are true, but R is not the correct explanation of A.

(*c*) A is true, but R is false.

(*d*) A is false, but R is true.

1. **Assertion (A):** The black soils are made up of extremely fine i.e., clayey material.

   Reason (R): They are well known for their capacity to hold moisture. *(An)*

2. **Assertion (A):** Alluvial soils are very fertile.

   Reason (R): Mostly these soils contain adequate proportion of potash., phosphoric acid, and lime. **(*An*)(KVS Hyderabad 2021-22)**

3. **Assertion (A):** Rajasthan and Gujarat have enormous potential for the development of wind and solar energy, but so far these have not been developed properly.

   Reason (R): Materials in the environment which have the potential to satisfy human needs but human beings do not have the appropriate technology to access these, are included among developed resources. *(An)*

4. **Assertion (A):** Biotic resources are obtained from biosphere and have life such as human beings, flora and fauna.

   Reason (R): Abiotic resources are those things which are composed of non living things, for example, rocks, air and metals. *(Un)*

5. **Assertion (A):** Forests are considered as renewable resources.

   Reason (R): Forests can be replanted and regrown after they are harvested. *(Un)*

6. **Assertion (A):** Renewable resources are more sustainable than non-renewable resources.

   Reason (R): Renewable resources can be naturally replenished, while non-renewable resources are finite and deplete over time. *(Un)*

7. **Assertion (A):** Overexploitation of natural resources leads to environmental degradation.

   Reason (R): Overexploitation disrupts ecological balance and can result in the loss of biodiversity. *(Un)*

Subjective Questions

Very Short Answer Type Questions (2 M)

1. What are natural resources? *(Un)*
2. Give examples of renewable resources. *(Re)*
3. Name some non-renewable resources. *(Re)*
4. What is sustainable development? *(Un)*
5. How does deforestation impact the environment? *(Un)*
6. What is the role of dams in water resource management? *(Un)*
7. How does overpopulation affect resources? *(An)*
8. What is the significance of recycling? *(Un)*

Short Answer Type Questions (3 M)

1. Imagine you are a farmer in the Chambal basin where soil erosion has significantly affected your land. Recently, you have noticed that deep gullies have formed, making parts of your land unfit for cultivation. Additionally, sheet erosion and wind erosion are contributing to the loss of topsoil, further reducing the fertility of your fields.

   Consider the effectiveness of contour ploughing and terrace cultivation in restoring the productivity of your land affected by soil erosion. Provide specific reasons for your evaluation based on the scenario described. *(Ev)*

2. Describe the importance of conservation of resources in the context of sustainable development. *(Un)*
3. Discuss the advantages and disadvantages of using renewable sources of energy. *(Ev)*
4. How does overpopulation affect the availability and management of resources? Explain with examples. *(An)*
5. Analyze the impact of deforestation on the environment and suggest measures to address it. *(An)*

Long Answer Type Questions (5 M)

1. In the rural regions of Haryana, where agriculture is the primary economic activity, a significant shift in land use patterns has been observed over recent decades. Influenced by population growth, modern farming techniques, and economic pressures leading to urbanization, there has been a notable decline in forested areas and permanent pastures. Concerns about environmental sustainability and the future of local agriculture have prompted the regional government to re-evaluate land management practices.

   Evaluate the effects of changing land use patterns on Haryana's rural environment and agriculture. In your answer, discuss the impact on local biodiversity, soil health, water resources, and agricultural economy, and suggest measures for sustainable land management. *(Ev, An)*

2. In states like Jharkhand, Chhattisgarh, Madhya Pradesh, and Odisha, extensive mining activities have significantly contributed to land degradation, impacting local communities that rely on the land for agriculture and natural resources. Concerned citizens, including environmental activist Sunita

Verma from Jharkhand and agricultural expert Anil Kumar from Odisha, are collaborating on a comprehensive initiative to address these issues. Their goal is to develop sustainable practices that can be implemented at the community level to mitigate the effects of land degradation and preserve the environment for future generations.

Consider the possible strategies that could be employed to manage the land degradation issues in Jharkhand, Chhattisgarh, Madhya Pradesh, and Odisha due to mining and deforestation. Consider the effectiveness of afforestation, management of grazing activities, and the regulation of mining operations in your analysis. **(Ev)**

3. Explain the classification of resources on the basis of exhaustibility. **(Un)**

4. How did Gandhiji voice his concern about resource conservation? Explain. **(Un)**

5. (*a*) Analyze the measures adopted to prevent soil erosion. Enumeratethe natural resources which lead to soil erosion. **(An)**

OR

(*b*) "There are many ways to solve the problems of land degradation."Substantiate the statement with illustrations. **(Ev) (CBSE APQ, 2023)**

Case Based Questions

Case Based-I

Read the following passage and answer the questions that follow:

Resources Planning

In the small town of Evergreen, rapid industrialization and agricultural expansion have led to significant environmental challenges. The town, once rich in natural resources, is now facing severe water scarcity, soil degradation, and loss of biodiversity. Mrs. Patel, the head of the town's environmental committee, is concerned about the unsustainable exploitation of resources. The local economy is heavily dependent on these activities, but the benefits are unequally distributed, with a small group of business owners profiting while the rest of the community struggles. Recognizing the urgent need for change, Mrs. Patel proposes a comprehensive resource planning initiative. This plan aims to implement sustainable practices, restore damaged ecosystems, and ensure that resource use benefits all residents. The committee is also exploring alternative livelihoods to reduce dependence on industries that harm the environment.

(*i*) What specific measures can Mrs. Patel's committee take to restore the degraded soil in Evergreen? *(1 M)* **(Ap)**

(*ii*) What are the potential long-term impacts on Evergreen if the town continues to rely heavily on unsustainable resource exploitation without implementing any conservation measures? *(1 M)* **(An)**

(*iii*) How can Evergreen's resource planning initiative promote sustainable economic development while addressing social inequalities and environmental challenges? *(2 M)* **(Cr)**

Case Based-II

Read the following passage and answer the questions that follow:

Soil Management and Conservation in India

India's diverse geography features various soil types, each presenting unique challenges for agriculture and conservation. Red and yellow soils, prevalent in parts of the Deccan plateau and the Piedmont zones of the Western Ghats, are characterized by their iron content which impacts their fertility. Laterite soils, common in tropical southern states, are highly acidic and subject to intense leaching, making them challenging for agriculture without proper management. Arid soils in the western regions, particularly Rajasthan, require innovative irrigation methods due to their high salinity and low moisture content. Forest soils, found in the mountainous and rainforest regions, are typically rich in organic matter but are prone to erosion if not properly managed. These conditions necessitate tailored agricultural practices and conservation efforts to maintain soil health and productivity across different landscapes.

(*i*) How can mulching be used to improve water retention and reduce soil erosion in red and yellow soils? *(1 M)* **(Ap)**

(*ii*) Analyze the impact of intensive agriculture on the nutrient depletion of laterite soils and propose a sustainable farming practice to mitigate this issue. *(1 M)* **(An)**

(*iii*) Design a soil conservation plan for arid soils in Rajasthan that integrates both traditional and modern irrigation techniques to enhance soil productivity. *(2 M)* **(Cr)**

Case Based-III

Read the information below and answer the questions that follow:

Resource planning is a complex process which involves : (i) identification and inventory of resources across the regions of the country. This involves surveying, mapping and qualitative and quantitative estimation and measurement of the resources. (ii) Evolving a planning structure endowed with appropriate technology, skill and institutional set up for implementing resource development plans. (iii) Matching the resource development plans with overall national development plans. India has made concerted efforts for achieving the goals of resource planning right from the First Five Year Plan launched after Independence. The availability of resources is a necessary condition for the development of any region, but mere availability of resources in the absence of corresponding changes in technology and institutions may hinder development. There are many regions in our country that are rich in resources but these are included in economically backward regions. On the contrary there are some regions which have a poor resource base but they are economically developed.

(*i*) What are the three main steps involved in resource planning? *(1 M)* **(Re)**

(*ii*) Why might the mere availability of resources not lead to the development of a region? *(1 M)* **(Un)**

(*iii*) Explain how the economic development of a region can be independent of its natural resource base, providing an example based on Indian regions. *(2 M)* **(An)**

Case Based-IV

Read the information below and answer the questions that follow:

The use of land is determined both by physical factors such as topography, climate, soil types as well as human factors such as population density, technological capability and culture and traditions etc. Total geographical area of India is 3.28 million sq km. Land use data, however, is available only for 93 per cent of the total geographical area because the land use reporting for most of the north-east states except Assam has not been done fully. Moreover, some areas of Jammu and Kashmir occupied by Pakistan and China have also not been surveyed.

(i) What factors determine the use of land? *(1 M)* **(Un)**

(ii) What percentage of India's total geographical area is covered by land use data? *(1 M)* **(Re)**

(iii) Explain why land use data is not available for certain areas of India. *(2 M)* **(An)**

Map Based Questions

1. Features are marked by numbers in the given outline map of India. Identify these features with the help of the following information and write their correct names on the lines marked in the map.

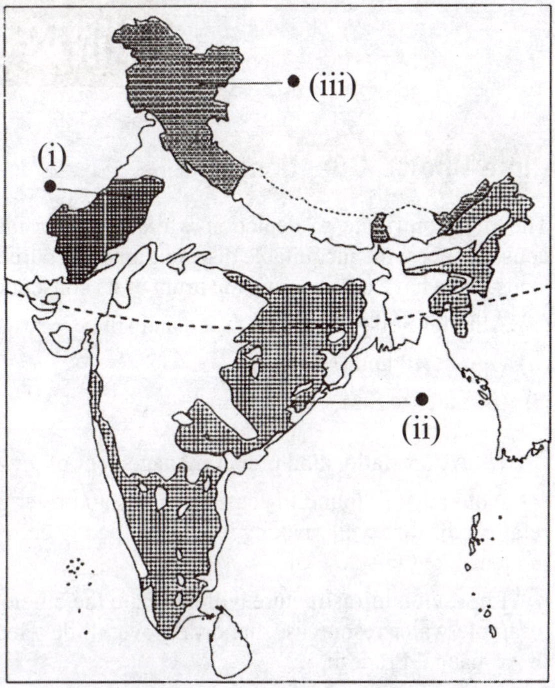

(i) A major soil type *(1 M)* **(Re)**

(ii) Soil type that is formed where the rainfall is low *(1 M)* **(Un)**

(iii) Soil type found mainly in hill slopes *(1 M)* **(Un)**

ANSWER KEYS

Multiple Choice Questions

1. (*d*) **2.** (*a*) **3.** (*d*) **4.** (*c*) **5.** (*c*) **6.** (*c*) **7.** (*c*) **8.** (*a*) **9.** (*b*) **10.** (*a*)
11. (*d*) **12.** (*a*) **13.** (*a*) **14.** (*d*) **15.** (*c*) **16.** (*a*) **17.** (*b*) **18.** (*d*) **19.** (*c*) **20.** (*b*)

Assertion and Reason

1. (*a*) **2.** (*a*) **3.** (*c*) **4.** (*b*) **5.** (*a*) **6.** (*a*) **7.** (*a*)

HINTS & EXPLANATIONS

Multiple Choice Questions

1. The rich contribute to depletion while the poor face the consequences; the inequitable distribution of resources also leads to the have nots bearing the brunt of its consequences.
2. (*a*) Alluvial Soil - Consists of sand and silt
3. (*d*) Option (*a*) and (*b*)
4. (*i*) (*b*) Laterite Soil

OR

(*ii*) (*b*) Afforestation and proper management of grazing
5. (*c*) Alluvial soil, found in coastal regions and river plains, retains moisture well, making it ideal for paddy cultivation in areas like Odisha.
6. (*c*) Improving infrastructure will facilitate the efficient use of ample water resources, supporting overall development in Arunachal Pradesh.
7. (*c*) Bangar and Khadar
8. (*a*) Shelter belt
9. (*b*) Development should take place without damaging the environment
10. (*a*) Mulching
11. (*d*) All proposed policies in the statements aim to address various environmental challenges in Ecotopia.
12. (*b*) A-(ii), B-(iii), C-(iv), D-(i)
13. (*a*) Flow resource
14. (*d*) All of the above
15. (*c*) Forest
16. (*a*) Khadar soil
17. (*b*) Tea & Coffee
18. (*d*) Non-renewable
19. (*c*) Over irrigation
20. (*b*) Overgrazing leads to soil compaction, reducing soil fertility. Compacted soil actually decreases water infiltration, not increases it, which negatively impacts soil health.

Assertion and Reason

1. (*a*) Both A and R are true, and R is the correct explanation of A.
2. (*a*) Both A and R are true, and R is the correct explanation of A.
3. (*c*) The assertion that Rajasthan and Gujarat have potential for solar and wind energy is true. However, the reason provided mischaracterizes undeveloped resources as "developed," which is inaccurate based on typical resource management terminology. Hence, A is true, but R is false.
4. (*b*) Both statements about biotic and abiotic resources are correct, but the reason does not explain why biotic r sources are derived from the biosphere; it merely defines what abiotic resources are. Hence, Both A and R are true, but R is not the correct explanation of A.
5. (*a*) Both A and R are true, and R is the correct explanation of A.
6. (*a*) Both A and R are true, and R is the correct explanation of A.
7. (*a*) Both A and R are true, and R is the correct explanation of A.

Subjective Questions

Very Short Answer Type Questions

1. **Natural resources:** Everything in our environment that can be used to fulfill our needs, provided it is technologically accessible, economically feasible, and culturally acceptable, can be termed as a 'Resource'. *(1 M)*

   Examples include water, air, soil, minerals, and forests. *(1 M)*
2. **Renewable resources examples:** Renewable resources are those that can be replenished naturally over time. Examples include sunlight, wind, water, and biomass. *(2 M)*
3. **Non-renewable resources:** These are resources that do not replenish or do so over extremely long geological periods. Examples include coal, petroleum, and natural gas. *(2 M)*
4. **Sustainable development:** It means development should take place without damaging the environment and should not compromise the needs of future generations. *(2 M)*
5. **Impact of deforestation:** Deforestation leads to loss of habitat for millions of species, increases greenhouse gases in the atmosphere, and disrupts water cycles, leading to environmental imbalances. *(2 M)*
6. **Role of dams:** Dams help in water resource management by storing water for irrigation, generating hydroelectric power, providing drinking water, and controlling floods. *(2 M)*
7. **Over population and resources:** Overpopulation increases demand for natural resources leading to their depletion, and causes environmental degradation due to the increased waste and pollution. *(2 M)*
8. **Significance of recycling:** Recycling helps in conserving natural resources, reducing waste and pollution, and saving energy. It leads to sustainable development by ensuring that resources are available for future generations. *(2 M)*

Short Answer Type Questions

1. The effectiveness of contour ploughing and terrace cultivation can be evaluated in the following ways:

   (*i*) Contour ploughing slows water runoff by ploughing along the contour lines, reducing soil erosion and preserving topsoil fertility. *(1 M)*

   (*ii*) Terrace cultivation creates flat areas on slopes, reducing surface runoff and preventing gully formation, making land suitable for cultivation again. *(1 M)*

(iii) Both methods improve water infiltration and reduce wind erosion, essential for restoring soil fertility and productivity in the Chambal basin. *(1 M)*

2. Conservation of resources in sustainable development:

- **Future generation needs:** Conserving resources ensures that future generations also have access to them, fulfilling the principle of sustainable development. *(1 M)*
- **Environmental protection:** Conservation helps in protecting ecosystems, reducing environmental degradation and pollution. *(1 M)*
- **Economic benefits:** Resource conservation leads to cost savings, efficient resource use, and long-term economic gains. *(1 M)*

3. Renewable energy advantages and disadvantages: *(1½ + 1½ = 3 M)*

Aspect	Advantages	Disadvantages	Overall Impact
Renewable Energy	Renewable energy sources like solar and wind are abundant and reduce reliance on fossil fuels.	Renewable energy can be inconsistent (e.g., solar energy depends on sunlight).	Despite disadvantages, renewable energies are crucial for sustainable development.
Environmental Impact	Leads to lower greenhouse gas emissions and cleaner air.	Initial setup costs can be high compared to traditional energy sources.	Reduces environmental impact and promotes a healthier planet.

4. Over population effects on resources:

- **Increased consumption:** Overpopulation leads to higher demand for natural resources such as water, land, and energy, leading to potential shortages. *(1 M)*
- **Waste management:** larger populations produce more waste, making management and disposal a significant challenge, contributing to pollution and health hazards. *(1 M)*
- **Resource depletion:** Overuse of resources due to large populations can lead to degradation of resources like forests, minerals, and biodiversity. *(1 M)*

5. Impact of deforestation and measures to address it:

- **Environmental impact:** Deforestation leads to loss of biodiversity, altered water cycles, and increased soil erosion, contributing to climate change. *(1½ M)*

Measures to address deforestation:

- **Afforestation:** Planting new trees to replace those cut down. *(½ M)*
- **Sustainable logging:** Implementing practices that allow forests to regenerate naturally. *(½ M)*
- **Legal actions:** Enforcing laws to prevent illegal logging and land clearing. *(½ M)*

Long Answer Type Questions

1. Evaluate the effects of changing land use patterns on Haryana's rural environment and agriculture:

***(i)* Biodiversity Loss:** A Decline in forested areas reduces wildlife habitats. *(1 M)*

***(ii)* Soil Degradation:** Loss of permanent pastures depletes organic matter, diminishing soil fertility. *(1 M)*

***(iii)* Water Scarcity:** Increased water consumption and overuse of groundwater lower water table levels. *(1 M)*

***(iv)* Reduced Arable Land:** Conversion of agricultural land for urban use impacts food production. *(1 M)*

***(v)* Sustainable Measures Needed:** Implementing afforestation, soil conservation, efficient water use, and sustainable farming practices can balance environmental sustainability with agricultural productivity. *(1 M)*

2. Consider the possible strategies that could be employed to manage the land degradation issues in Jharkhand, Chhattisgarh, Madhya Pradesh, and Odisha due to mining and deforestation:

***(i)* Afforestation:** Replanting trees to restore forest cover, stabilize soil, and enhance biodiversity, and engage local communities in tree-planting initiatives for better stewardship. *(1 M)*

***(ii)* Rotational Grazing:** Implementing controlled grazing patterns to prevent overgrazing and promote pasture recovery. *(1 M)*

***(iii)* Regulation of Mining Operations:** Enforcing stricter regulations and rehabilitating mined areas through soil restoration and reforestation. *(1 M)*

***(iv)* Contour Ploughing:** Ploughing along the contours to reduce soil erosion and retain soil moisture. *(1 M)*

***(v)* Sustainable Agricultural Practices:** Encouraging organic farming and crop rotation to maintain soil health and preserve soil nutrients. *(1 M)*

3. Classification of resources based on exhaustibility: *(2 + 2+ 1 = 5 M)*

Classification	Description	Examples	Implications for Use
Renewable Resources	Resources that can be replenished naturally and within a short time span.	Solar energy, Wind energy, Biomass	The sustainable use of renewable resources is crucial for long-term environmental balance.
Non-Renewable Resources	Resources that take millions of years to form and therefore are considered finite.	Fossil fuels like Coal, Petroleum, Natural minerals	Non-renewable resources should be used sparingly and with care to extend their lifespan and reduce environmental impact.

Implications for Use	Understanding the importance of resource management based on their rate of replenishment.	-	Encourages the sustainable use of resources to ensure availability for future generations and to maintain ecological balance.

4. Gandhiji's views on resource conservation:
   - **Philosophy:** Gandhiji emphasized 'Simple living and high thinking'. He believed that the Earth provides enough to satisfy everyone's needs, but not everyone's greed. *(2 M)*
   - **Economic and Environmental Ethics:** He advocated for sustainable living and the ethical use of resources, criticizing the mass production that leads to resource depletion and environmental degradation. *(1½ M)*
   - **Legacy and Relevance:** Gandhiji's principles promote a balanced approach to resource use, advocating for moderation and efficiency, which align with modern sustainable development goals. *(1½ M)*

5. (*a*) Measures to prevent soil erosion and natural causes:

   Measures:
   - **Terrace farming:** This reduces runoff and holds soil, making steep land more productive. *(1 M)*
   - **Afforestation:** Planting trees helps bind the soil and prevents erosion by wind and water. *(1 M)*
   - **Contour ploughing:** Ploughing along the contours of the land helps slow water runoff and captures soil. *(1 M)*
   - **Natural causes leading to soil erosion:** Water runoff, wind, glacier movements, and human activities like deforestation and overgrazing. *(2 M)*

   OR

   (*b*) Solutions for land degradation:
   - **Afforestation and reforestation:** Planting new trees and restoring forests can help replenish soil nutrients and prevent erosion. *(1 M)*
   - **Proper agricultural practices:** Techniques like contour ploughing, crop rotation, and use of organic fertilizers enhance soil health and prevent degradation. *(2 M)*
   - **Managing waste and industrial effluents:** Proper treatment and disposal of waste reduce soil and water contamination, thus preventing land degradation. *(2 M)*

Case Based Questions

Case Based-I

(*i*) Mrs. Patel's committee can use measures like reforestation, crop rotation, and the use of organic fertilizers to restore soil health in Evergreen. *(1 M)*

(*ii*) If Evergreen continues unsustainable practices, it may face severe resource depletion, loss of biodiversity, and long-term economic decline. *(1 M)*

(*iii*) Evergreen's resource planning initiative can promote sustainable development by encouraging renewable energy, supporting eco-friendly industries, and ensuring fair distribution of benefits, thus addressing environmental and social issues. *(2 M)*

Case Based-II

(*i*) Mulching helps to retain soil moisture, prevent the evaporation of water, and reduce surface runoff, thereby decreasing soil erosion and improving water retention in red and yellow soils. *(1 M)*

(*ii*) Intensive agriculture can rapidly deplete the nutrients in laterite soils, leading to decreased fertility. Crop rotation with legumes can help replenish nitrogen naturally and sustain soil health. *(1 M)*

(*iii*) The plan should include the use of drip irrigation systems to minimize water wastage and the introduction of saline-tolerant crop varieties. Additionally, incorporating organic amendments like compost could improve soil structure and fertility, enhancing productivity. *(2 M)*

Case Based-III

(*i*) The three main steps in resource planning are:

(*i*) identification and inventory of resources,

(*ii*) developing a planning structure with the right technology and skills, and

(*iii*) aligning resource development with national development plans. *(1 M)*

(*ii*) Mere availability of resources does not guarantee development due to potential lack of technology, skilled personnel, and proper institutional frameworks. *(1 M)*

(*iii*) Economic development can be independent of natural resources because regions with limited resources can excel economically through technology, services, and human resource development. For example, regions like Bangalore have limited natural resources but are economically developed due to IT and service sectors. *(2 M)*

Case Based-IV

(*i*) Land use is determined by physical factors like topography, climate, and soil types, as well as human factors like population density, technological capability, and culture and traditions. *(1 M)*

(*ii*) Land use data is available for 93% of India's total geographical area. *(1 M)*

(*iii*) Land use data is not available for certain areas due to incomplete reporting in most of the north-eastern states (except Assam) and unsurveyed areas of Jammu and Kashmir occupied by Pakistan and China. *(2 M)*

Map Based Questions

1. (*i*) Desert or Arid soil *(1 M)*

   (*ii*) Red and Yellow soil *(1 M)*

   (*iii*) Forest and Mountainous soil *(1 M)*

FOREST AND WILDLIFE RESOURCES

2

"Forests and wildlife are important, serving as the earth's lungs and biodiversity guardians. We must protect and cherish them for future generations"

SYLLABUS & WEIGHTAGE

List of Concept Names	Years					
	2020	2021	2022	2023	2024	2025
Flora and Fauna India (Causes of Depletion of the Flora and Fauna)	–	Exam not Conducted	–	–	–	
Conservation of forest and wildlife in India (Types and distribution of forests and wildlife resources, Community and Conservation)	–		–	–	1Q + 1Q + 1Q (4M)	1 Q (1 M)

CONCEPT MAP

To Access One Shot Revision Video Scan This QR Code

Forest and Wildlife Resources

Biodiversity or Biological Diversity

Biodiversity is the variety of all living forms and their ecosystems on Earth.

Flora

Flora represents all the plant life in a certain area, including various types of plants like trees and flowers.

Fauna

Fauna means all the animal life in a specific area, including different animals like tigers, birds, and insects.

Project Tiger-1973

- Tiger is one of the key wildlife species in the faunal web.
- The tiger population plummeted from 55,000 at the beginning of the 20th century to 1,827 by 1973.
- Threats to tigers include poaching, habitat loss, prey depletion, and human population growth.
- India and Nepal, home to two-thirds of the world's tigers, face significant challenges from poaching and illegal trade.

Sacred Groves (CBSE 2025)

Forest areas that are protected by local communities due to their religious significance.

Types and Distribution of Forest and Wildlife Resources

- In India, much of its forest and wildlife resources are either owned or managed by the government through the Forest Department or other government departments.
- **Classification of forests:**
  - **Reserved Forests:** Most valuable forests, cover half of the total forest land.
  - **Protected Forests:** Protected from any further depletion, one third of total forest area.
  - **Unclassed Forests:** Other forests and wastelands belong to both govt. and private individuals and communities.

Causes of Depletion of the Flora and Fauna

- **The various factors that cause depletion of the flora and fauna**
  - Large-scale development projects
  - Shifting cultivation
  - Mining
  - Grazing and fuel-wood collection
  - Over-population
- **Factors responsible for decline in India's biodiversity**
  - Habitat destruction
  - Hunting
  - Poaching
  - Over-exploitation
  - Environmental pollution
  - Poisoning
- Human beings transformed nature into a resource obtaining directly and indirectly from the forests and wildlife such as wood, barks, leaves, rubber, medicines, dyes, food, fuel, fodder, manure, etc. which depleted our forests and wildlife.

Conservation of Forest and Wildlife in India (CBSE 2024)

Conservation: Preserves the ecological diversity and our life support systems – water, air and soil.

- The Indian Wildlife (Protection) Act of 1972 was enacted to safeguard endangered species by prohibiting hunting, protecting habitats, and limiting wildlife trade.
- National parks and wildlife sanctuaries were established by central and state governments.
- The government launched protection projects for critically threatened animals, including tigers, one-horned rhinoceroses, Kashmir stags, three types of crocodiles, Asiatic lions, and more.
- By 1986, protections were extended to include hundreds of butterflies, moths, beetles, and a dragonfly.
- In 1991, plants were added to the protection list for the first time, starting with six species.

1 FLORA AND FAUNA IN INDIA

NCERT Definitions *(Commonly asked in 1 mark)*

- **Biodiversity (biological diversity):** This term refers to the ***variety*** of life on Earth, including different plants, animals, fungi, and microorganisms, as well as the diversity within and between species and ecosystems.
- **Ecosystem:** An ecosystem is a ***community of living organisms*** interacting with each other and their physical environment. This includes animals, plants, microorganisms, water, and soil.
- **Flora:** This term refers to the diverse ***plant life*** in a region, including trees, shrubs, grasslands, and both flowering and non-flowering plants, as seen in India's rich flora.
- **Fauna:** This term refers to the ***animal species*** in an area, such as India's diverse wildlife including tigers, rhinos, and elephants, encompassing mammals, birds, fish, and insects, each integral to the ecosystem.
- **Wildlife:** This term describes all ***undomesticated animals*** and other living creatures found in natural habitats. It includes a wide range of organisms from tiny insects to large animals like elephants and whales.
- **Biodiversity Hotspots:** Biodiversity hotspots are ***areas rich in biodiversity*** facing human threats, including India's Western Ghats, Himalayas, and Indo-Burma regions.
- **Protected Areas:** Protected Areas are regions ***designated to conserve*** wildlife and biodiversity.

Important Facts

01 India is rich in biodiversity, ranking among the world's top in flora and fauna.

02 In 1986, protection extended to include hundreds of butterflies, moths, beetles, and one dragonfly.

03 In 1991, plants were added to the protected list for the first time, starting with six species.

04 Numerous species face the risk of endangerment from human actions and shifts in the environment.

05 Home to a variety of unique animal species, contributing to its extensive biodiversity.

06 Unique and diverse plant life, crucial but under environmental stress.

07 Conservation efforts are underway to protect India's ecological wealth.

Important Concepts

Causes of Depletion of the Flora and Fauna:

- **Colonial Exploitation:** During colonial times, Indian forests were heavily exploited for railways, agriculture, commercial forestry, and mining to meet demands for wood, rubber, medicine, and fuel.
- **Agricultural Expansion:** After independence, India turned 26,200 sq. km of forests into farms between 1951 and 1980, worsening deforestation and harming tribal areas, mainly due to shifting cultivation in the northeast and central regions.
- **Multipurpose River Projects:** Multipurpose River projects in India have removed over 5,000 sq. km of forests since 1951, with projects like Narmada Sagar planning to clear an additional 40,000 hectares.

Difference Between

Flora Vs. Fauna		
Characteristic	**Flora**	**Fauna**
Definition	Refers to plant life specific to a region.	Refers to animal life specific to a region.
Diversity	Immensely rich in species, including unique regional plants like banyan trees, lichens, and various cultivated species.	Extremely diverse, includes unique regional animals like elephants, tigers, and blue whales.
Role in Ecosystem	Primary producers; crucial for the ecological system, providing oxygen, food, and supporting other species.	Consumers and decomposers; play vital roles in the ecosystem through various food chains and maintaining ecological balance.
Conservation Issues	Threatened by deforestation, environmental insensitivity, and climate change.	Endangered by habitat loss, poaching, pollution, and climate change.
Importance	Essential for air, food, medicine, and ecological services.	Crucial for biodiversity, ecological balance, and cultural significance.
Appearance	Lustrous (shiny)	Non-lustrous (except iodine)
Sonorous Density	Produce sound High density	Do not produce sound low density

Real Life Application Based Questions

1. **Explain how the introduction of non-native plant species can affect the local fauna in your area. Consider the real-life application of invasive species control measures.**

Ans. Impact of Non-native Plant Species:

- **Competition:** They out compete local plants for light and nutrients.
- **Fauna Impact:** Native animals lose food sources and habitats.
- **Biodiversity Loss:** Leads to reduced local wildlife variety.
- **Control Measures:** Remove invasive species, replant native plants.

2. **Describe how the planting of trees in urban areas can benefit local fauna and improve biodiversity.**

Ans. Benefits of Planting Trees in Urban Areas:

- **Habitats:** Trees offer homes for birds, insects, and small mammals.
- **Food Source:** Provide fruits, leaves, and seeds for urban fauna.
- **Air Quality:** Trees filter pollutants, improving air for all species.
- **Cooling Effect:** Lower temperatures help urban species thrive.
- **Biodiversity Increase:** More tree varieties attract diverse wildlife.

3. **How does reducing pesticide use in agricultural practices benefit the local flora and fauna?**

Ans. Benefits of Reducing Pesticide Use:

- **Healthier Soil:** Less chemical use leads to richer, natural soil.
- **Safer Plants:** Plants grow without absorbing harmful chemicals.
- **Protected Insects:** Beneficial insects like bees and butterflies thrive.
- **Food Chain:** Birds and mammals feeding on insects remain unpoisoned.
- **Water Quality:** Reduces chemical runoff into rivers and groundwater.
- **Biodiversity:** Supports a wider range of plant and animal life.

Myth Buster*

❒ **Myth:** Larger wildlife reserves always result in better conservation outcomes.

Fact: The effectiveness of wildlife reserves depends on proper management, local community involvement, and protection measures, not just on their size.

❒ **Myth:** All non-native plant species are harmful to local ecosystems.

Fact: While many non-native species can become invasive and harmful, not all non-native species are detrimental. Some can coexist without negatively impacting local ecosystems.

❒ **Myth:** Urban areas cannot support significant biodiversity.

Fact: Urban areas can support diverse flora and fauna through green spaces, urban forests, and gardens, contributing to biodiversity conservation.

❒ **Myth:** All regions in India have the same types of flora and fauna due to its vast biodiversity.

Fact: India's varied landscapes result in different ecosystems; hence, flora and fauna vary significantly across regions, like Rajasthan's deserts versus the Western Ghats' forests.

** Concepts beyond the board exam syllabus, offering deeper insight and critical thinking on NCERT topics.*

COMPETENCY BASED SOLVED EXAMPLES

Scan Me for Detailed Explanations

Multiple Choice Questions (1 M)

1. **What is the primary role of forests in the ecological system?** *(Un)*
   (*a*) To provide shelter for animals
   (*b*) To produce oxygen for humans
   (*c*) To act as a primary producer for all living beings
   (*d*) To regulate the earth's temperature

2. **Why are plants, animals, and micro-organisms important for humans?** *(Un)*
   (*a*) They create the quality of air and water
   (*b*) They are only used for food
   (*c*) They have no impact on humans
   (*d*) They are only part of natural beauty

3. **What is the reason for the great stress on India's flora and fauna?** *(Un)*
   (*a*) Climate change only
   (*b*) Pollution only
   (*c*) Insensitivity to the environment
   (*d*) Overpopulation only

4. **Why are diverse flora and fauna important for human lives?** *(Un)*
   (*a*) They provide food, water, and air quality regulation.
   (*b*) They provide entertainment for humans.
   (*c*) They are important for scientific research.
   (*d*) They have no direct impact on human lives.

5. **How have human activities affected the depletion of flora and fauna?** *(Ev)*
   (*a*) By over-harvesting resources such as timber and wildlife.
   (*b*) By polluting the environment with chemicals and waste.
   (*c*) By destroying natural habitats through deforestation and urbanization.
   (*d*) All of the above

Assertion and Reason (1 M)

Direction: The following questions consist of two statements – Assertion (A) and Reason (R). Answer these questions by selecting the appropriate option given below:

(*a*) Both A and R are true, and R is the correct explanation of A.
(*b*) Both A and R are true, but R is not the correct explanation of A.
(*c*) A is true, but R is false.
(*d*) A is false, but R is true.

1. **Assertion (A):** India is one of the world's richest countries in terms of its vast array of biological diversity.
   Reason (R): India has a diverse range of ecosystems, including forests, grasslands, wetlands, and coastal areas that support a wide variety of flora and fauna. *(Un)*

2. **Assertion (A):** Forests do not play a key role in the ecological system, as they are also the primary producers on which all other living beings depend.
   Reason (R): Forests provide shelter for animals and regulate the earth's temperature. *(Ev)*

3. **Assertion (A):** Human activities have led to the depletion of flora and fauna in India.
   Reason (R): Over-harvesting resources such as timber and wildlife has led to habitat destruction and loss of biodiversity. *(An)*

4. **Assertion (A):** Biodiversity is important for human survival.
   Reason (R): Plants, animals, and micro-organisms recreate the quality of the air we breathe, the water we drink, and the soil that produces our food. *(An)*

5. **Assertion (A):** Insensitivity to our environment has led to stress on India's flora and fauna.
   Reason (R): Human activities such as pollution and deforestation have led to habitat destruction and an increase in biodiversity. *(Ev)*

Subjective Questions

Very Short Answer Type Questions (2 M)

1. **What are some activities that contribute to the degradation of forests and wildlife?** *(Un)*

Ans. The activities leading to the degradation of forests and wildlife through:

- **Deforestation and overgrazing:** These activities remove the natural habitat of many species, leading to loss of biodiversity. *(1 M)*
- **Pollution and urban expansion:** These contribute to degradation by contaminating environments and reducing forest areas. *(1 M)*

2. **What are the primary causes of the depletion of flora and fauna in India?** *(Re)*

Ans. **Habitat destruction:** Activities like deforestation and urbanization lead to loss of natural habitats for flora and fauna. *(1 M)*

Poaching and pollution: Illegal hunting and environmental pollution further endanger various species and plant life. *(1 M)*

3. **What is the significance of biodiversity and ecosystems in India?** ***(Ap)***

Ans. The significance of biodiversity and ecosystems in India focusing on ecological and economic aspects are:

- **Ecological balance:** Biodiversity maintains ecological stability and supports vital processes like pollination and nutrient cycling. *(1 M)*
- **Supports livelihoods:** Ecosystems provide resources like food, medicine, and materials, crucial for human survival and economic activities. *(1 M)*

4. **What is meant by 'flora' and 'fauna'?** ***(An)***

Ans. Flora is the ***plant life*** found in a particular region or time, encompassing all varieties of plants, trees, and flowers. *(1 M)*

Fauna refers to all the ***animal life*** present in a specific area or period, including mammals, birds, insects, and other wildlife. *(1 M)*

5. **Name any four resources that are obtained from our biodiversity.** ***(Cr)***

Ans. From our biodiversity, we obtain crucial resources such as-

- **Medicinal plants:** Used for creating medicines and treatments. *(½ M)*
- **Timber:** Used in construction and furniture making. *(½ M)*
- **Food crops:** Provide nourishment and dietary diversity. *(½ M)*
- **Animal products:** Include milk, meat, and wool for various uses. *(½ M)*

Short Answer Type Questions (3 M)

1. **How many types of forest are classified in India? Explain it.** ***(Re)***

Ans. Forests are classified under the three categories: *(1 + 1 + 1 = 3 M)*

Type of Forest	Description	Percentage of Total Forests	Ownership
Reserved Forests	Strictly protected, mainly for conservation, no public entry.	More than half (50%+)	Government
Protected Forests	Protected but less strictly than reserved, some public access.	Almost one-third (~33%)	Government
Unclassed Forests	Managed by communities or private, minimal restrictions.	Remaining percentage	Government and private individuals and communities

2. **Explain the concept of biological diversity and its importance to the ecosystem services that support human life in India.** ***(Un)***

Ans. **Biological Diversity (Biodiversity):** The variety of all living organisms including plants, animals, and microorganisms, along with their ecosystems and genetic differences. *(1 M)*

Importance in Ecosystem Services:

- **Supports Ecosystem Functioning:** Biodiversity maintains ecosystem processes like soil formation, water cycling, and pollination, essential for human survival. *(1 M)*
- **Provides Resources:** Offers a range of materials for daily life, including food, medicinal resources, and raw materials, crucial for economic and health well-being in India. *(1 M)*

3. **Discuss the role of flora and fauna in sustaining ecosystems in India. Provide examples.** ***(An)***

Ans. **Flora and Fauna's Role:** They are crucial for maintaining natural balances, and supporting life cycles like pollination and seed dispersal, which are vital for ecosystem health. *(1 M)*

- **Examples:** The Bengal Tiger, by controlling herbivore populations, prevents overgrazing. The Banyan tree provides habitats for numerous species, aiding biodiversity. *(1 M)*
- **Ecosystem Support:** Together, they enrich the soil, purify the air, and regulate water cycles, supporting agriculture, forestry, and fisheries, essential for human survival in India. *(1 M)*

Mistakes 101 : What not to do!

Missing Interconnectedness: The answer could emphasize the interconnected nature of flora and fauna within ecosystems. Students might overlook discussing how disruptions in one species or habitat can have cascading effects on the entire ecosystem. Highlighting the delicate balance and interdependence among different species could enrich the answer.

4. **Explain the role of forests in maintaining the ecological balance.** ***(Un)***

Ans. **Oxygen Production/Carbon Absorption:** Forests contribute to climate regulation by producing oxygen and absorbing carbon dioxide, crucial for atmospheric balance. *(1 M)*

- **Habitat for Biodiversity:** They offer diverse habitats, supporting a wide range of species, crucial for maintaining ecological diversity and stability. *(1 M)*
- **Water Cycle and Soil Conservation:** Forests regulate the water cycle, control flooding, and prevent soil erosion, maintaining environmental health. *(1 M)*

5. **Why are flora and fauna considered integral to human existence? Provide examples from daily life.** *(Ap)*

Ans. Flora and fauna are important for human life:

- **Oxygen and Food:** Plants produce oxygen and are a primary food source. For example, trees like mango and banyan provide fruits and shelter. *(1 M)*
- **Ecological Balance:** Animals pollinate plants and control pest populations, keeping the environment balanced. Bees pollinate crops, supporting agriculture. *(1 M)*
- **Human Dependence:** Humans depend on flora and fauna for food, medicine, and clean air. Traditional medicines often use plant extracts, demonstrating our reliance on nature. *(1 M)*

Long Answer Type Questions (5 M)

1. **Explain how biodiversity contributes to the stability of an ecosystem. Illustrate your answer with examples of interdependencies among various species within Indian ecosystems.** *(An)*

Ans. Biodiversity significantly enhances ecosystem stability through interdependence and balance among species. In Indian ecosystems:

- **Biodiversity Importance:** Biodiversity, the variety of life, stabilizes ecosystems by allowing species to depend on each other for food, shelter, and the maintenance of the ecological balance. *(1 M)*
- **Pollination:** Bees and butterflies help pollinate plants and crops, which is essential for food production, showing how agriculture relies on these insects. *(1 M)*
- **Predator-Prey Balance:** Tigers in Indian forests control the population of herbivores like deer, preventing overgrazing and protecting vegetation diversity, which is vital for forest health. *(1 M)*
- **Nutrient Cycling:** Microorganisms break down dead matter, returning nutrients to the soil, and supporting plant growth and food chains. *(1 M)*
- **Human Dependence:** People rely on this biodiversity for food, medicine, and clean air, demonstrating our direct dependence on a balanced ecosystem. *(1 M)*

2. **Mr. Vikas, a young environmental activist is preparing a presentation on the importance of biodiversity conservation in India. he wants to highlight the challenges posed by habitat loss. Discuss the potential impact of habitat loss on India's rich biodiversity.** *(Ev)*

Ans. The potential impact of habitat loss on India's rich biodiversity is as follows:

(*i*) Species Extinction: Habitat destruction leads to the loss of flora and fauna, pushing many species towards extinction by eliminating their living and breeding environments. *(1 M)*

(*ii*) Disruption of Ecosystems: It disrupts natural processes like pollination, seed dispersal, and water purification, compromising ecosystem health and functionality. *(1 M)*

(*iii*) Genetic Diversity Loss: Shrinking habitats can lead to reduced genetic diversity as animal and plant populations are isolated, weakening their resilience to diseases and environmental changes. *(1 M)*

(*iv*) Impact on Livelihoods: Many communities depend on biodiversity for sustenance, medicine, and economic activities like ecotourism, which are jeopardized by habitat loss. *(1 M)*

(*v*) Climate Change Acceleration: The reduction in forest areas exacerbates climate change impacts by decreasing carbon sequestration capacities, leading to increased global warming. *(1 M)*

3. **Describe how communities have conserved and protected forests and wildlife in India?** *(Un)*

Ans. In India, communities have helped protect forests and animals in many ways:

- **Community Efforts:** In India, people living near forests have long protected their homes. They team up with the government to keep the forests safe, helping everyone live better. *(1 M)*
- **Standing Up:** For example, in Sariska, Rajasthan, locals stopped harmful mining by using laws meant to protect wildlife. This shows how people are actively protecting nature. *(1 M)*
- **Making Own Rules:** In Alwar, Rajasthan, villagers made their own rules to protect their forest, proving communities can look after their environment on their own. *(1 M)*
- **Chipko Movement:** This movement showed the world how standing together against cutting trees can save forests. It also taught the importance of planting native trees. *(1 M)*
- **Working With the Government:** In the Joint Forest Management program, communities and the government collaborate to care for forests. In exchange, locals get benefits like wood from these forests. *(1 M)*

2 CONSERVATION OF FOREST AND WILDLIFE IN INDIA

NCERT Definitions *(Commonly asked in 1 mark)*

- **Biosphere Reserves:** Areas where ***nature is protected*** while also allowing for sustainable human activities and learning about environmental balance.
- **National parks:** Protected areas ***for conserving wildlife and ecosystems***, restricting activities like hunting and logging to safeguard natural habitats and biodiversity.
- **Wildlife Sanctuaries:** Safe areas for ***animals*** where they can ***live without threat*** from humans.
- **Protected Forests:** Areas of forest that are ***protected by law*** to prevent further destruction and maintain biodiversity.
- **Reserve Forest:** Areas of forest that are preserved for their environmental importance and protected from any form of exploitation.
- **Unclassified Forests:** This types of forest are lands not specifically protected, **managed by local communities** or **private individuals,** often with varied natural environments.
- **Sacred Groves:** Forest areas that are ***protected by local*** communities due to their religious significance.
- **Endangered Species:** Types of animals or plants that are at risk of disappearing forever.
- **Wildlife conservation:** Safeguarding ***animal populations*** and their habitats to sustain biodiversity and ecological harmony.
- **Poaching:** The ***illegal hunting*** of animals around the world is called poaching.

Important Facts

01 The Indian Wildlife (Protection) Act was enacted in **1972** to safeguard wildlife.

02 India has established numerous wildlife sanctuaries and national parks.

03 The total forest and tree cover have expanded by **2, 261 sq. km** since **2019,** according to the **2021** State of Forest Report.

04 ***Project Tiger***, initiated in **1973,** aims to protect the dwindling tiger population.

05 India's rich biodiversity includes over ***two-thirds*** of the ***world's tiger population***.

Important Concepts

- **Community-based Conservation:** Community-based Conservation involves locals in managing natural resources sustainably.
- **Indian Wildlife (Protection)Act (1972):** This Act of 1972 promotes habitat preservation and was influenced by earlier conservation efforts and forest policies.

- **Chipko movement:** The Chipko movement demonstrated grass roots environmental activism by emphasizing the ımportance of trees for ecological balance.
- **Joint Forest Management:** JFM Since 1988 has engaged local communities in protecting forests for mutual benefits, including sharing forest products.

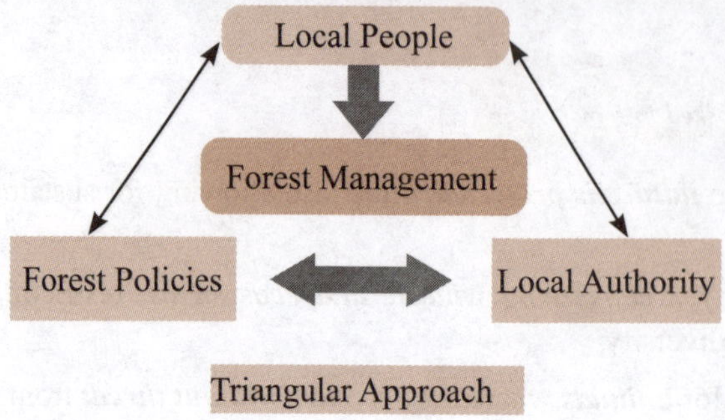

Fig: Joint Forest Management

India's Key Tiger Reserves

Tiger Reserves	States
Corbett National Park	Uttarakhand
Sundarbans National Park	West Bengal
Bandhavgarh National Park	Madhya Pradesh
Sariska Wildlife Sanctuary	Rajasthan
Manas Tiger Reserve	Assam
Periyar Tiger Reserve	Kerala

Important Dates

- **1952:** The species of Asiatic Cheetah was declared extinct in India.
- **1972:** The Indian Wildlife (Protection) Act was implemented.
- **1973:** "Project Tiger", a wildlife campaign around the world, was launched.
- **1988:** The Joint Forest Management Program was passed by the state of Odisha.

Classification

Classification of Forests

S.No.	Category	Reserved Forests	Protected Forests	Unclassed Forests
1.	Characteristics	Permanently reserved to produce forest products. More than 50% of the total forest land.	Almost one-third of forest area, is. protected from depletion. Protected from any further depletion. Almost 1/3 of the total forest area	Include inaccessible forests or wastelands. Consists of just 16% of the total forest area.
2.	Area	High conservation priority, largest areas in Madhya Pradesh, followed by Jammu and Kashmir, Andhra Pradesh, Uttarakhand, Kerala, Tamil Nadu, West Bengal, and Maharashtra. strict regulations.	Largest areas in Madhya Pradesh, followed by Jammu and Kashmir, Andhra Pradesh, Uttarakhand, Kerala, Tamil Nadu, West Bengal, and Maharashtra.	Mostly located in northeastern states and parts of Gujarat, managed by local communities.
3.	Management	No public entry or rights without permission.	Some rights and activities are allowed.	Generally open for community use and management.
4.	Location Examples	Madhya Pradesh, Uttarakhand, Maharashtra.	Bihar, Haryana, Punjab, Himachal Pradesh.	Northeastern states, parts of Gujarat.

Difference Between

Conservation of Forests Vs. Conservation of wildlife		
Aspect	**Conservation of Forests**	**Conservation of wildlife**
Objective	Preserve forest ecosystems for biodiversity, and ecological services.	Protect wild species and habitats for biodiversity.
Methods	Afforestation, reforestation, controlled logging.	Wildlife sanctuaries, national parks, anti-poaching laws.
Legal Framework	Forest Conservation Act, 1980; National Forest Policy.	Wildlife Protection Act, 1972; Project Tiger, Project Elephant.
Community Involvement	Joint Forest Management (JFM) for community participation.	Community reserves; involvement in movements like Chipko.
Challenges	Deforestation, fragmentation, climate change.	Habitat loss, poaching, illegal trade, conflicts.
Significance	Climate regulation, water cycle, livelihoods.	Ecosystem balance, gene pool preservation, ecological services.

National Park Vs. Wildlife Sanctuary		
Aspect	**National Park**	**Wildlife Sanctuary**
Objective	Conservation of ecosystems, landscapes, and biodiversity.	Protection of species, habitat conservation.
Human Activities	Cultivation, grazing, and forestry not allowed.	Cultivation, grazing, and forestry allowed under certain conditions.
Legal Protection	Private ownership is not permitted.	Private ownership permitted.
Area Coverage	Well-defined boundary.	Boundary not well defined.
Examples	Corbett National Park (Uttarakhand)	Bird Sanctuary Chilka (Odisha)
Tourism	Regulated tourism allowed minimal environmental disturbance.	Tourism is allowed with guidelines for wildlife protection.

Real Life Application Based Questions

1. If you found injured wildlife in your area, what steps would you take to help conserve it?

Ans. I would safely report the injured wildlife to local conservation authorities or wildlife rehabilitation centers, ensuring professional care and contributing to the conservation of local wildlife species.

2. How can avoiding products made from endangered species contribute to wildlife conservation?

Ans. Avoiding products made from endangered species reduces demand, helping to combat illegal wildlife trade and poaching, thus contributing to the conservation of these species and their natural habitats.

3. How does supporting eco-friendly products help in the conservation of forests?

Ans. Supporting eco-friendly products promotes sustainable resource use and reduces deforestation, thereby preserving forest ecosystems, biodiversity, and helping in the fight against climate change.

4. How does reducing, reusing, and recycling materials in your daily life contribute to forest conservation?

Ans. Reducing, reusing, and recycling lead to lower demand for forest products, decrease waste, and reduce pressure on forests, thereby aiding in their conservation and maintaining ecological balance.

Myth Buster

- **Myth:** National parks and wildlife sanctuaries are essentially the same, with no real difference in purpose or legal status.

  Fact: National parks strictly limit human activities to protect biodiversity, while wildlife sanctuaries permit controlled activities, focusing on species conservation.

- **Myth:** Only large forests need to be conserved.

  Fact: Even small forests and green spaces are important for maintaining biodiversity, local climate, and water cycles.

- **Myth:** Zoos and wildlife sanctuaries serve the same purpose.

  Fact: Zoos mainly focus on education and research, while wildlife sanctuaries prioritize the protection and natural living conditions of animals.

COMPETENCY BASED SOLVED EXAMPLES

Scan Me for Detailed Explanations

Multiple Choice Questions (1 M)

1. You are a part of a community living near a large forest region, which is home to a wide variety of plants and animals. Recently, a proposal for deforestation for the purpose of expanding urban areas has been put forward. As a young environmental activist, you are to present a case at the community meeting explaining why this forest, and its flora and fauna, are vital for the well-being of your community and the surrounding ecosystem. ***(Cr)***

(*a*) They provide aesthetic value only.

(*b*) They are indispensable for ecological balance but not directly linked to human survival.

(*c*) They are crucial for air quality, water, and soil, directly impacting human survival.

(*d*) Only flora is essential for oxygen supply, while fauna has limited ecological importance.

2. Match the following: ***(Re) (CBSE APQ, 2023)***

List-I		List-II	
A.	Reserved Forests	(*i*)	North Eastern States
B.	Protected Forests	(*ii*)	Andhra Pradesh
C.	Unclassed Forests	(*iii*)	Haryana

(*a*) A-(*i*), B-(*ii*), C-(*iii*) (*b*) A-(*iii*), B-(*ii*), C-(*i*)

(*c*) A-(*i*), B-(*iii*), C-(*ii*) (*d*) A-(*ii*), B-(*iii*), C-(*i*)

3. Which of the following options represent potential measures that can be taken to mitigate the threats posed on the tiger population and biodiversity? ***(Ev)***

(*i*) Banning hunting, giving legal protection to their habitats, and restricting trade in wildlife

(*ii*) Prohibiting the visit of public into forest area.

(*iii*) Establishing wildlife sanctuaries and National Parks

(*iv*) Converting forests into Reserved and Protected forests

Options:

(*a*) Statements (*i*) and (*ii*) are correct.

(*b*) Statements (*ii*), (*iii*) & (*iv*) are correct.

(*c*) Statement (*ii*) is correct.

(*d*) Statements (*i*), (*iii*) & (*iv*) are correct.

4. Conservation of forest is a key to the survival of human mankind. Some of the practices undertaken in India in this direction is Joint Forest Management. Identify the correct information related to Joint Forest Management. ***(Re)***

(*i*) It involves local communities in the management and restoration of degraded forests.

(*ii*) The programme has been in formal existence since 1980.

(*iii*) Jharkhand passed the first resolution for Joint Forest Management.

(*iv*) The members of local village communities are entitled to intermediary benefits like non timber forest producers.

Options:

(*a*) (*i*) and (*ii*) only (*b*) (*ii*) and (*iii*) only

(*c*) (*i*) and (*iv*) only (*d*) (*iii*) and (*iv*) only

Assertion and Reason (1 M)

Direction: The following questions consist of two statements – Assertion (A) and Reason (R). Answer these questions by selecting the appropriate option given below:

(*a*) Both A and R are true, and R is the correct explanation of A.

(*b*) Both A and R are true, but R is not the correct explanation of A.

(*c*) A is true, but R is false.

(*d*) A is false, but R is true.

1. Assertion (A): Conservation of forests and wildlife is not essential for maintaining ecological balance.

Reason (R): Forests and wildlife provide essential ecosystem services such as carbon sequestration, soil conservation, water regulation, and climate regulation. ***(An)***

2. **Assertion (A):** Community-based conservation strategies are more effective than top-down approaches in India.

   Reason (R): Local communities have a better understanding of their natural resources and are more likely to support conservation efforts if they are involved in decision-making and benefit-sharing. ***(Ap)***

3. **Assertion (A):** Habitat destruction is the smallest threat to wildlife in India.

   Reason (R): Habitat loss and fragmentation due to human activities such as deforestation, urbanization, and agriculture have led to a decline in wildlife populations. ***(An)***

4. **Assertion (A):** Protected areas are effective in conserving biodiversity in India.

   Reason (R): Protected areas such as national parks, wildlife sanctuaries, and biosphere reserves provide legal protection to important habitats and species. ***(Un)***

5. **Assertion (A):** Sustainable use of forest resources by local communities can contribute to conservation efforts in India.

   Reason (R): Encouraging sustainable use of forest resources can provide alternative livelihoods for local communities while reducing pressure on natural resources and promoting conservation. ***(Ap)***

Subjective Questions

Very Short Answer Type Questions (2 M)

1. **A small village "Vistrit" that depends heavily on a nearby forest for its resources and livelihoods. Recently, the forest area has been facing severe deforestation due to illegal logging activities. What role do forests play in the ecological system?** ***(An)***

Ans. The role of forests in the ecological system:

(*i*) Forests produce oxygen and maintain air quality. *(1 M)*

(*ii*) They support biodiversity and provide habitats for numerous species. *(1 M)*

2. **Aditi, a student, visits a small village in India where she notices a dense patch of forest untouched by human activity. Curious, she learns from the villagers that this area is known as a Sacred Grove, a place where they do not cut trees or hunt animals. The villagers explain that these groves are considered sacred and are protected due to religious and cultural beliefs. Aditi is fascinated to find out that such practices help in conserving biodiversity and preserving various plant species that might be rare or endangered. What is the significance of Sacred Groves in Indian culture?** ***(An)***

Ans. The significance of Sacred Groves in Indian culture:

(*i*) Sacred Groves are preserved for religious and cultural reasons, protecting biodiversity. *(1 M)*

(*ii*) They are considered sacred, and interference is prohibited, ensuring conservation. *(1 M)*

3. **A coastal city is planning a major development project that will involve clearing a significant portion of a nearby mangrove forest. The mangrove forest is known for its rich biodiversity. Based on the above information, explain why is biodiversity important for human survival.** ***(Un)***

Ans. The importance of biodiversity for human survival:

(*i*) Biodiversity provides essential resources like air, water, and food. *(1 M)*

(*ii*) It ensures ecosystem stability and resilience, supporting human life. *(1 M)*

4. **What is the main objective of Project Tiger, initiated in 1973?** ***(Re)***

Ans. Project Tiger's main objectives are:

- **Tiger Conservation:** Project Tiger aims to protect and increase the tiger population in India by creating safe habitats. *(1 M)*
- **Ecosystem Protection:** It also focuses on maintaining the health and diversity of ecosystems where tigers live. *(1 M)*

Short Answer Type Questions (3 M)

1. **Rakul, an environmental consultant tasked with advising a local government on the development of a new public park. The goal is to enhance the area's ecological health and biodiversity. As part of his report, Discuss the role of forests as primary producers and their importance in supporting diverse life forms.** ***(Un)***

Ans. Forests play a crucial role in maintaining ecological balance and supporting biodiversity, particularly through the following functions:

(*i*) Primary Producers: Forests act as primary producers in the ecological system, generating biomass from sunlight and soil nutrients, which form the base of food chains supporting diverse life forms. *(1 M)*

(*ii*) Biodiversity Support: They host a vast array of species, from the smallest microbes to large mammals and birds, enhancing the genetic diversity necessary for species adaptation and ecosystem resilience. *(1 M)*

(*iii*) Environmental Services: Beyond supporting biodiversity, forests contribute to the quality of air, water, and soil, crucial for the survival of all life forms, including humans. *(1 M)*

2. **Distinguish between reserve forest and protected forest.** ***(Re)* (CBSE, 2023)**

Ans. (Any three)

Criteria	Reserve Forests	Protected Forests	Marks
Definition	Strictly conserved areas with activity restrictions.	Conservation areas with less stringent rules.	*(1 M)*
Management	Aimed at biodiversity preservation and limited forestry.	Focuses on preventing depletion while allowing human activity.	*(1 M)*

Criteria	Reserve Forests	Protected Forests	Marks
Human Activity	Highly restricted to protect the ecosystem.	Allowed under controlled conditions for sustainable use.	*(1 M)*
Protection Level	High; activities closely monitored and regulated.	Moderate; aimed at balancing conservation with human needs.	*(1 M)*

Topper's Explanation

Reserved forests	Protected forests.
These forests are declared reserved by the forest department.	These are forests that are protected by the government.
These are the most valuable in terms of resources.	They are protected from further depletion, outside encroachments, etc.
These forests are found in Tamil Nadu, Kerala, Maharashtra and Andhra Pradesh.	These forests are found in Punjab, Haryana, Rajasthan, etc.
Around half of all forests are reserved forests.	Around one-third of forests are protected forests.

3. In a scenario, the Ministry of Environment and Forests drafts a proposal for a new national park in the Western Ghats, a region known for its rich biodiversity and endemic species. The region has seen a decline in several key species due to habitat loss and other human activities. How does the establishment of wildlife sanctuaries and national parks contribute to the conservation of endangered species and their habitats? *(An)*

Ans. The establishment of wildlife sanctuaries and national parks contributes to the conservation of endangered species and their habitats in the following ways:

***(i)* Protected Habitat:** National parks and sanctuaries offer a safe haven for endangered species by safeguarding their habitats from deforestation and encroachment. *(1 M)*

***(ii)* Biodiversity Preservation:** These areas conserve biological diversity by maintaining natural ecological processes and life support systems, crucial for species survival. *(1 M)*

***(iii)* Research and Monitoring:** They provide ideal sites for scientific research and regular monitoring of wildlife health and population dynamics. *(1 M)*

4. Your community is part of a region facing severe forest degradation and local authorities are proposing to implement the Joint Forest Management (JFM) program. You are a member of the village council tasked with evaluating this proposal. Explain how the Joint Forest Management (JFM) program involves local communities in forest conservation. *(Un)*

Ans. JFM programme was **initiated in Odisha in 1988** to involve communities in forest restoration.

***(i)* Community Participation:** JFM encourages local communities to partner with the forest department to manage and protect forest resources, fostering collective responsibility. *(1 M)*

***(ii)* Benefit Sharing:** Communities receive benefits such as a share of non-timber forest products and revenue from timber, incentivizing their active participation in conservation efforts. *(1 M)*

***(iii)* Decision-Making Involvement:** Villagers contribute to decision-making processes regarding forest management, enhancing sustainable practices and local engagement. *(1 M)*

5. Explain the significance of the Indian Wildlife (Protection) Act, 1972. *(Un)*

Ans. The Indian Wildlife (Protection) Act of 1972 is instrumental in several key areas:

- **Legal Framework:** The Act provides a legal structure for the protection of wildlife species by regulating hunting, trade, and management of habitats. *(1 M)*
- **Wildlife Protection:** It categorizes animals into schedules based on threat levels, giving special attention to endangered species. *(1 M)*
- **Conservation Areas**: Establishes protected areas like national parks, wildlife sanctuaries, and reserves to conserve biodiversity. *(1 M)*

Long Answer Type Questions (5 M)

1. You are a conservationist working with a tribal community in the Sariska Tiger Reserve. The community has noticed a significant decrease in the tiger population and an increase in illegal logging activities. As a conservationist, create a plan to protect the tiger population and to prevent further deforestation & illegal logging activities in the Sariska Tiger Reserve. *(Cr)*

Ans. A plan to protect the tiger population and deforestation can be understood by the following points:

***(i)* Strengthening Anti-Poaching Measures:** Implement rigorous anti-poaching patrols and surveillance using modern technology like drones and camera traps to monitor tiger movements and detect illegal activities. *(1 M)*

***(ii)* Community Engagement:** Involve the local tribal community in conservation efforts by providing them with training and employment as forest guards and eco-tourism guides, thereby giving them a stake in the preservation of their environment. *(1 M)*

***(iii)* Legal Enforcement:** Work with local law enforcement to ensure strict enforcement of wildlife protection laws, including harsher penalties for illegal logging and poaching. *(1 M)*

***(iv)* Habitat Restoration:** Initiate reforestation programs to restore degraded habitats, ensuring a stable prey base for tigers and improving the overall health of the forest ecosystem. *(1 M)*

***(v)* Awareness and Education:** Conduct awareness campaigns within the community and neighboring areas to educate people about the importance of tigers and forests, and the long-term benefits of conservation. *(1 M)*

2. Describe the impact of deforestation on biodiversity in India and discuss the significance of conservation programs like Project Tiger and Joint Forest Management (JFM) in addressing these impacts. *(An)*

Ans. Impact of Deforestation on Biodiversity: Deforestation in India significantly impacts biodiversity by destroying habitats, leading to species loss and disrupted ecosystems. It contributes to climate change, affecting water cycles and soil fertility. *(1 M)*

Significance of Conservation Programs:

- Initiated in 1973 to protect tiger habitats, successfully increasing tiger populations and demonstrating targeted conservation's effectiveness in preserving key species and ecosystems. *(1 M)*
- Introduced in the 1980s, JFM encourages community involvement in forest management. Combines local knowledge with conservation practices, restoring degraded forests and enhancing biodiversity. *(1 M)*
- **Successes of Conservation Programs:** These programs stress integrated conservation, combining government action and community involvement to counter deforestation's impact on India's biodiversity. *(1 M)*
- **Importance of Integrated Approaches in Conservation:** These programs emphasize integrating government and community efforts to combat deforestation's impact on India's biodiversity. *(1 M)*

3. How have National Parks and Wildlife Sanctuaries under this Act contributed to the protection of endangered species and habitats? Discuss with examples. *(An)*

Ans. National Parks and Wildlife Sanctuaries serve as crucial refuges for endangered species and ecosystems.

- **Legal Protection:** The Indian Wildlife (Protection) Act, 1972, established National Parks and Wildlife Sanctuaries, providing legal protection to habitats and species like the one-horned rhinoceros and the Bengal tiger. *(1 M)*
- **Habitat Conservation:** These areas preserve crucial habitats, reducing threats like habitat loss and fragmentation. Example: Kaziranga National Park is renowned for protecting the one-horned rhinoceros. *(1 M)*
- **Species Recovery:** Initiatives like Project Tiger have been launched to recover endangered species populations within these protected areas. *(1 M)*
- **Biodiversity Maintenance:** By preserving diverse ecosystems, they maintain ecological balance and support a variety of life forms. *(1 M)*
- **Research and Monitoring:** Enable scientific research and monitoring of wildlife, helping inform conservation strategies and actions. *(1 M)*

MISCELLANEOUS EXERCISE

Multiple Choice Questions **(1 M)**

1. A biodiversity conservation team was tasked with designing a wildlife sanctuary following the guidelines of the Indian Wildlife (Protection) Act. Select among the following how the protection of a wide range of animal species under this Act might contribute to the genetic diversity of the sanctuary's ecosystem. ***(Un)***

(*a*) It reduces genetic diversity by limiting the species under protection.

(*b*) It fails to affect genetic diversity due to ongoing species decline.

(*c*) It promotes genetic diversity through the protection of diverse species.

(*d*) It impacts only the genetic diversity of species introduced from other regions.

2. Mr. Prateek, an environmental officer whose task is to differentiate Protected Forests from Reserved Forests in terms of human activity and Conservation objectives. Choose the correct among the following for your differentiation: ***(Un)***

(*a*) Protected Forests allow limited sustainable tourism while Reserved Forests do not.

(*b*) Reserved Forests are open for agricultural use while Protected Forests are not.

(*c*) Protected Forests permit certain controlled human activities, unlike Reserved Forests.

(*d*) There is no significant difference; both categories allow for timber extraction.

3. Consider the scenario where the community of Sariska is facing a resurgence of illegal mining activities that threaten the local wildlife and disrupt the ecological balance. In tackling illegal mining issues in areas like Sariska Tiger Reserve, which of the following will be the reaction of local communities? ***(Ev)***

(*a*) They support mining activities for economic benefits.

(*b*) They collaborate with miners to regulate the activity.

(*c*) They protest against and report illegal mining activities.

(*d*) They invest in mining companies for community development.

4. In a village bordering a dense forest in India, the local community has taken an innovative approach to conservation by establishing a community-managed forest area similar to Bhairodev Dakav 'Sonchuri'. The area has been declared off-limits for hunting and industrial activity, managed solely by local rules set by the villagers. Analyzing the impact of such local conservation efforts, what is a key outcome of such initiatives? ***(An)***

(*a*) Increased forest degradation

(*b*) Enhanced community livelihoods

(*c*) Reduced biodiversity

(*d*) Expansion of industrial activities

5. Mr. Vishal, a wildlife conservation group member was tasked with setting up a new tiger reserve in a region known for its rich biodiversity. Given the following considerations, which would be the most crucial for ensuring the long-term sustainability of the tiger population in this new reserve? ***(Ap)***

(*a*) Proximity to urban areas for educational purposes.

(*b*) Adequate prey base, water sources, and minimal human interference.

(*c*) Focus on tourist attractions and infrastructure.

(*d*) Ease of access for forestry officials only.

6. The famous Chipko movement in the Himalayas has not only successfully resisted deforestation in several areas but has also shown that community afforestation with indigenous species can be enormously successful. How does the Chipko Movement exemplify community involvement in forest conservation? ***(Un)***

(*a*) By advocating commercial logging

(*b*) Through the establishment of wildlife sanctuaries

(*c*) By embracing tree-hugging to prevent deforestation

(*d*) By promoting industrial use of forest land

7. In the context of Project Tiger initiated in 1973, you are a wildlife conservationist tasked with presenting a report to a local community near a tiger reserve. Your goal is to educate them on the benefits of tiger conservation and how it can enhance their own livelihoods. Using the information about Project Tiger's impact on stabilizing and potentially increasing tiger populations, choose among the following how the conservation efforts can lead to economic and ecological benefits for the community. ***(Ev)***

(*a*) Conservation efforts have minimal impact on local communities and are primarily focused on the animals.

(*b*) Increased tiger populations scare away other wildlife, decreasing biodiversity.

(*c*) Conservation efforts, including eco-tourism, can boost local economies and promote biodiversity, benefiting both the tigers and the community.

(*d*) Tiger conservation takes up resources that would otherwise benefit local community development directly.

8. You are a botanist collaborating with the government on a project to preserve newly discovered medicinal plants. If a new species of plant with potential medicinal value is discovered, in which type of Indian forest is it most likely to be strictly conserved? **(*Re*)**

(*a*) Protected Forests (*b*) Reserved Forests

(*c*) Unclassed Forests (*d*) Community Forests

9. Rajat, a Geography student, is working on a project on biodiversity conservation in India. His task is to create a presentation that showcases the efforts in different Indian states to protect wildlife through the establishment of tiger reserves. He gathers information about various tiger reserves and the states where they are located. Rajat needs to accurately match the following tiger reserves with their respective states to complete his presentation. Help Rajat by choosing the correct state for each tiger reserve: **(*Re*)**

	Column-I (Tiger Reserves)		Column-II (States)
(A)	Corbett National Park	(i)	Rajasthan
(B)	Sunderbans National Park	(ii)	West Bengal
(C)	Bandhavgarh National Park	(iii)	Uttarakhand
(D)	Sariska Wildlife Sanctuary	(iv)	Madhya Pradesh

(*a*) A-(ii), B-(i), C-(iv), D-(iii)

(*b*) A-(i), B-(ii), C-(iv), D-(iii)

(*c*) A-(iii), B-(ii), C-(iv), D-(i)

(*d*) A-(iv), B-(iii), C-(i), D-(ii)

10. In a national quiz competition for students, you are presented with a challenge to match different types of forests in India to their unique characteristics based on their management and conservation importance. Use your understanding of the forest categorizations to align each forest type with the correct description. **(*Ap*)**

	Column-I		Column-II
(A)	Reserved Forests	(i)	Managed by local communities and includes forests and wastelands owned by government and private individuals.
(B)	Protected Forests	(ii)	Reserved and protected forests maintained for the purpose of producing timber and other forest produce, and for protective reasons.
(C)	Unclassed Forests	(iii)	Protected from any further depletion and significant in states like Bihar, Haryana, and Punjab.
(D)	Permanent Forests	(iv)	Considered most valuable for conservation, encompassing more than half of the forest land.

(*a*) A-(ii), B-(i), C-(iv), D-(iii)

(*b*) A-(i), B-(ii), C-(iv), D-(iii)

(*c*) A-(iii), B-(iv), C-(ii), D-(i)

(*d*) A-(iv), B-(iii), C-(i), D-(ii)

11. In a remote area of the Western Ghats, a community preserves a Sacred Grove, an untouched patch of forest revered for its cultural and ecological importance. This area is home to several endangered species and serves as a natural lab for ecological studies. Recently, a proposal has been made to develop part of the land adjacent to the Sacred Grove into a tourist resort, arguing it would boost local economy but potentially threatening the integrity of the grove. Based on the above scenario, which among the following measure could be implemented to ensure the Sacred Grove continues to protect biodiversity while potentially integrating sustainable tourism? **(*Cr*)**

(*a*) Establishing strict environmental guidelines for resort development

(*b*) Allowing limited tourist access to the grove under guided tours to raise awareness

(*c*) Creating a buffer zone around the Sacred Grove to minimize ecological disturbance

(*d*) Focusing solely on agricultural expansion to support the local economy instead of tourism

12. Which of the following states have a bulk of it under protected forests? **(*Re*)**

(*a*) Bihar, Haryana, Punjab, Himachal Pradesh, Odisha

(*b*) Sikkim, Manipur, Mizoram, Meghalaya, Nagaland

(*c*) Tamil Nadu, Maharashtra, Andhra Pradesh, Telangana

(*d*) Odisha, Jharkhand, Chhattisgarh, Madhya Pradesh

13. Which of the following is the correct statement? **(*Un*)**

(*a*) The famous Chipko movement in the Himalayas has not only successfully resisted deforestation in several areas.

(*b*) In India joint forest management (JFM) programme furnishes a good example for involving local communities in the management and restoration of degraded forests.

(c) The clear lesson from the dynamics of both environmental destruction and reconstruction in India is that local communities everywhere have to be involved in some kind of natural resource management.

(d) All of the above

14. Identify and Analyse the image given below and answer the following question:

The one-horned rhinoceros, shown in the image, is primarily found in which of the following national parks of India? **(Ap)**

(a) Jim Corbett National Park

(b) Kaziranga National Park

(c) Gir Forest National Park

(d) Sunderbans National Park

15. You are a policy advisor tasked with assessing the potential environmental impact of proposed changes to forest management policies in your region. The government is considering downgrading a significant area of Protected Forest to Unclassed Forest. Given the following outcomes, evaluate the most likely impact of this downgrade on wildlife populations: **(Ev)**

(a) Increased biodiversity due to diverse management practices.

(b) Possible decline in wildlife populations due to reduced legal protections.

(c) No impact, as all forest categories contribute equally to conservation.

(d) Enhanced wildlife populations due to community engagement.

Assertion and Reason (1 M)

Direction: The following questions consist of two statements – Assertion (A) and Reason (R). Answer these questions by selecting the appropriate option given below:

(a) Both A and R are true, and R is the correct explanation of A.

(b) Both A and R are true, but R is not the correct explanation of A.

(c) A is true, but R is false.

(d) A is false, but R is true.

1. In a village where a forested area, known as the "Sacred Grove," is preserved by the community. This area is significant for its religious rituals and is believed to bring blessings to the village. As a new member of the village council, you are tasked with explaining the importance of the Sacred Grove to visitors. You mention that these groves are protected by the community and are not subject to logging or other exploitative activities. Based on this scenario, answer the following:

Assertion (A): Sacred Groves are patches of forests preserved by local communities for religious and cultural reasons.

Reason (R): Sacred Groves are left untouched and protected from any form of exploitation by the local people. **(Un)**

2. A small village near a forest where the Joint Forest Management (JFM) program is being implemented. The villagers are actively involved in managing the forest resources to ensure sustainable use. However, there is some confusion among the villagers about the extent of their rights under this program. Some villagers believe they can sell timber and other forest products freely without government intervention. Based on this scenario, answer the following:

Assertion (A): The Joint Forest Management (JFM) program involves local communities in the management of forest resources.

Reason (R): JFM provides local communities with the right to sell timber and other forest products without government interference. **(Un)**

3. In the early 1970s, the Indian government observed a significant decline in the tiger population due to several factors. To address this issue, the government launched an initiative known as Project Tiger in 1973. At the same time, wildlife experts identified several key threats to tiger survival, including poaching, habitat loss, and a reduction in their prey.

Assertion (A): Project Tiger was launched in 1973 to conserve the tiger population in India.

Reason (R): The major threats to the tiger population include poaching, habitat loss, and depletion of prey species. **(Un)**

4. **Assertion (A):** Forests play a key role in the ecological system.

Reason (R): Forests are the primary producers on which all other living beings depend. **(Un)**

5. **Assertion (A):** Neglect of our environment has led to the destruction and extinction of many species of animals and plant life.

Reason (R): Decreasing Forest cover area is a major reason for the destruction of species. **(Ev)**

Subjective Questions

Very Short Answer Type Questions (2 M)

1. What is the significance of biodiversity and why is it crucial for human existence? *(Un)*
2. Suggest any two measures for the conservation of forest. *(Cr)* **(CBSE, 2024, DL)**

   OR

   Suggest any two measures for the conservation of wildlife. *(Cr)*
3. Identify two unique examples of community conservation efforts. *(Re)*
4. Describe the concept of Sacred Groves and their importance in biodiversity conservation. *(Un)*
5. What are the main threats to the tiger population in India? *(Re)*

Short Answer Type Questions (3 M)

1. "Forests play a key role in the ecological system." Highlight the value of forests in our life. *(Un)*
2. "The diverse flora and fauna of India is under threat". Justify by giving reasons. *(An)*
3. Mention any three factors which have led to the decline of India's biodiversity. *(An)*
4. With reference to the type and distribution of forests, answer the following questions:
   (*i*) How are they classified? *(Re)*
   (*ii*) Which type of forests are regarded most valuable as far as the conservation of forest and wildlife resources are concerned? *(Un)*
5. (*a*) Name any two states which have the largest area under permanent forests *(Re)*

   OR

   (*b*) Name any four states which have a large area under reserved forests. *(Re)*

Long Answer Type Questions (5 M)

1. "Conservation of rapid decline in wildlife population and forestry has become essential." Explain. *(Un)*

   OR

   Why do we need to conserve our forests and wildlife resources? Explain any two steps taken by the communities to protect our forest and wildlife resources. *(Ap)*
2. Why is conservation of forests and wildlife necessary? In what way have conservation projects changed in the recent years? *(An)*
3. As a researcher studying the impact of climate change on India's biodiversity, you observe that certain species are migrating to new areas while others are facing extinction. Present your findings on the impact of climate change on India's biodiversity and suggest measures to mitigate these effects. *(An, Ev)*

Case Based Questions

Case Based-I

Read the source given below and answer the following questions:

Project Tiger

Tiger is one of the key wildlife species in the faunal web. In 1973, the authorities realised that the tiger population had dwindled to 1,827 from an estimated 55,000 at the turn of the century. The major threats to tiger population are numerous, such as poaching for trade, shrinking habitat, depletion of prey base species, growing human population, etc. The trade of tiger skins and the use of their bones in traditional medicines, especially in the Asian countries left the tiger population on the verge of extinction. Since India and Nepal provide habitat to about two-thirds of the surviving tiger population in the world, these two nations became prime targets for poaching and illegal trading. "Project Tiger", one of the well publicised wildlife campaigns in the world, was launched in 1973. Tiger conservation has been viewed not only as an effort to save an endangered species, but with equal importance as a means of preserving biotypes of sizeable magnitude. Corbett National Park in Uttarakhand, Sunderbans National Park in West Bengal, Bandhavgarh National Park in Madhya Pradesh, Sariska Wildlife Sanctuary in Rajasthan, Manas Tiger Reserve in Assam and Periyar Tiger Reserve in Kerala are some of the tiger reserves of India.

(*i*) Considering the significant decrease in tiger populations due to various threats, propose a modern conservation strategy that could be implemented today. *(1 M) (Ap)*

(*ii*) Analyze the various threats to the tiger population. Which of these do you think has the most detrimental impact and why? *(1 M) (An)*

(*iii*) Discuss the effectiveness of establishing tiger reserves in combating the threats faced by tigers. Use examples to support your analysis. *(2 M) (An)*

Case Based-II

Read the source given below and answer the following question:

Sacred groves - a wealth of diverse and rare species

Nature worship is an age-old tribal belief based on the premise that all creations of nature have to be protected. Such beliefs have preserved several virgin forests in pristine form called Sacred Groves (the forests of God and Goddesses). These patches of forest or parts of large forests have been left untouched by the local people and any interference with them is banned. Certain societies revere a particular tree which they have preserved from time immemorial. The Mundas and the Santhal of Chota Nagpur region worship mahua (Bassia latifolia) and kadamba (Anthocaphalus cadamba) trees, and the tribals of Odisha and Bihar worship the tamarind (Tamarindus indica) and mango (Mangifera indica) trees during weddings. To many of us, peepal and banyan trees are considered sacred. Indian society comprises several cultures, each with its own set of traditional methods of conserving nature and its creations. Sacred qualities are often ascribed to springs, mountain peaks, plants and animals which are closely protected. You will find troops of macaques and langurs around many temples. They are fed daily and treated as a part of temple devotees. In and around Bishnoi villages in Rajasthan, herds of blackbuck, (chinkara), nilgai and peacocks can be seen as an integral part of the community and nobody harms them.

(i) Propose a community-based conservation project for your locality that incorporates elements from the concept of Sacred Groves. Highlight how you would involve different community members and integrate local cultural practices. *(1 M)* **(Cr)**

(ii) Describe how Sacred Groves are important for the preservation of species. Provide examples of how specific communities have used Sacred Groves to protect their local flora and fauna. *(1 M)* **(Un)**

(iii) Assess the impact of sacred groves on local wildlife populations, using examples of fauna, such as macaques, langurs, and blackbucks. *(2 M)* **(Ev)**

Case Based-III

Read the given source and answer the questions that follow. **(CBSE, 2023)**

Community and Conservation: Conservation strategies are not new in our country. We often ignore that in India, forests are also home to some of the traditional communities. In some areas of India, local communities are struggling to conserve these habitats along with government officials, recognizing that only this will secure their long-term livelihood. In Sariska Tiger Reserve, Rajasthan, villagers have fought against mining by citing the Wildlife Protection Act. In many areas, villagers themselves are protecting habitats and explicitly rejecting government involvement. The inhabitants of five villages in the Alwar district of Rajasthan have declared 1,200 hectares of forest as the Bhairodev Dakav 'Sanctuary', declaring their own set of rules and regulations which do not allow hunting, and protect wildlife against any outside encroachments.

(i) How are forests related to Communities? *(1 M)* **(Un)**

(ii) Explain the aim of the 'Wildlife Protection Act'. *(1 M)* **(Un)**

(iii) How are communities working for the conservation of Wildlife? Explain with an example. *(2 M)* **(An)**

Case Based-IV

Read the source given below and answer the following questions:

The Gharial is a river crocodile endemic to the Indian sub-continent. According to experts the drastic decline in the Gharial population can be attributed to a variety of causes including overhunting for skins and trophies, egg collection for consumption, killing for indigenous medicines, and killing by fishermen. The wild population of Gharials suffered a drastic decline of about 58% within a period of nine years from 1997 to 2006, due to an increase in the intensity of fishing and the use of gill nets. This occurs alongside the excessive and irreversible loss of riverine habitat due to developmental projects, sand mining, and agriculture. Despite a large restocking program for 30 years, resulting in over 5000 young Gharials being released into India's river system, only about 200 breeding adults still survive. "No matter how many Gharials are released in the wild, if their habitat continues to be destroyed, and they continued to be killed, this species will not be able to survive," explained an expert.

Source: The Times Of India, 31 January, 2013, 'The gharial's decline in UP.'

(i) Analyze the role of human activities in the decline of the Gharial population. What are the primary human-induced threats? *(1 M)* **(An)**

(ii) Describe the natural habitat of the Gharial and explain why this habitat is crucial for its survival. *(1 M)* **(Un)**

(iii) How might the decline of the Gharial population impact the ecosystem of India's river systems? Discuss two potential ecological consequences. *(2 M)* **(Ev)**

Map Based Questions

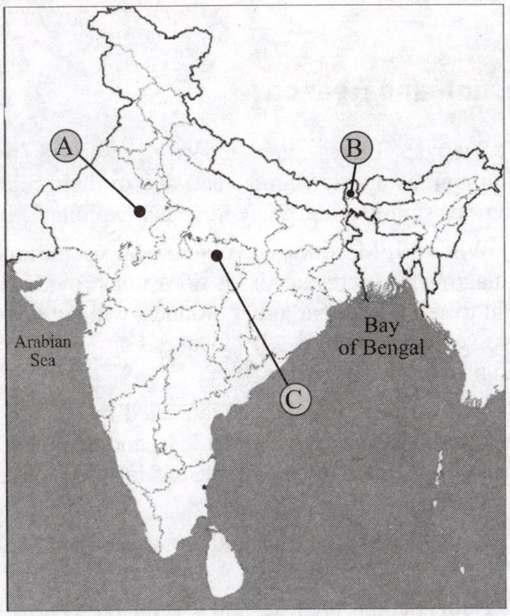

1. Point B is representing which of the following national park? ***(Re)***
   (*a*) Kanchenjunga National Park
   (*b*) Great Himalayas
   (*c*) Kaziranga National Park
   (*d*) Corbett National Park
2. Point A is representing which of the following national park? ***(Re)***
   (*a*) Ranthambore National Park
   (*b*) Great Himalayas
   (*c*) Dudhwa National Park
   (*d*) Corbett National Park
3. Point C is representing which of the following national park? ***(Re)***
   (*a*) Ranthambore National Park
   (*b*) Bandhavgarh National Park
   (*c*) Dudhwa National Park
   (*d*) Corbett National Park

ANSWER KEYS

Multiple Choice Questions

1. (*c*)	**2.** (*c*)	**3.** (*c*)	**4.** (*b*)	**5.** (*b*)	**6.** (*c*)	**7.** (*c*)	**8.** (*b*)	**9.** (*c*)	**10.** (*d*)
11. (*c*)	**12.** (*a*)	**13.** (*d*)	**14.** (*b*)	**15.** (*b*)					

Assertion and Reason

1. (*a*)	**2.** (*a*)	**3.** (*a*)	**4.** (*a*)	**5.** (*a*)

HINTS & EXPLANATIONS

Multiple Choice Questions

1. (*c*) By safeguarding a broad spectrum of animal species, the Act ensures the preservation and enhancement of genetic diversity within ecosystems, which is vital for the health and resilience of wildlife populations.
2. (*c*) Protected Forests in India allow for some degree of regulated human activity, including limited resource extraction and tribal habitation, ensuring a balanced approach to conservation and human needs.
3. (*c*) Local communities around Sariska have been instrumental in resisting illegal mining by leveraging legal frameworks and mobilizing collective action.
4. (*b*) Community-driven conservation areas like Bhairodev Dakav 'Sonchuri' aim to protect the environment while ensuring sustainable livelihoods for local inhabitants.
5. (*b*) For a tiger reserve to be effective and long-term sustainable, it must have a sufficient prey base, reliable water sources, and be located away from human settlements to minimize disturbances and ensure a conducive habitat for tigers.
6. (*c*) The Chipko Movement is a prime example of grassroots environmental activism, where community members physically embraced trees to halt their felling.
7. (*c*) By protecting tigers and their habitat, Project Tiger not only helps in stabilizing the animal's population but also promotes a richer biodiversity which can attract tourists. This, in turn, supports local businesses and reinforces the importance of sustainable environmental practices, providing a practical example of how conservation can enhance human well-being alongside wildlife preservation.
8. (*b*) When a new species of plant, especially one with potential medicinal value, is discovered, it is crucial to ensure its protection and conservation for further research and sustainable utilization. Reserved Forests provide the ideal environment for such conservation efforts because they are strictly regulated by the government, minimizing human interference and ensuring the preservation of biodiversity
9. (*c*) A-(iii), B-(ii), C-(iv), D-(i)
10. (*d*) A-(iv), B-(iii), C-(i), D-(ii)
11. (*c*) Creating a buffer zone would help mitigate the impact of nearby developments while preserving the core area of the Sacred Grove intact. This approach promotes a balance between economic development through sustainable tourism and the conservation of biodiversity.
12. (*a*) Bihar, Haryana, Punjab, Himachal Pradesh, Odisha
13. (*d*) All of the above
14. (*b*) Kaziranga National Park, Assam is renowned for its significant population of the one-horned rhinoceros. It was designated a UNESCO World Heritage site in 1985.
15. (*b*) Downgrading Protected Forests to Unclassed Forests might reduce the legal protections in place, potentially leading to habitat degradation or increased human-wildlife conflicts, thereby affecting wildlife populations adversely.

Assertion and Reason

1. (*a*) Sacred Groves are indeed preserved by local communities and left untouched due to their cultural and religious significance, preventing any exploitation.
2. (*a*) While JFM does involve local communities in managing forest resources, it does not provide them the right to sell timber and other products without government involvement. Instead, it focuses on protection and sustainable management.
3. (*a*) Project Tiger was indeed launched in 1973 to address the threats of poaching, habitat loss, and depletion of prey species, which are the major reasons for the declining tiger population.
4. (*a*) Both A and R are true, and R is the correct explanation of A.
5. (*a*) Both A and R are true, and R is the correct explanation of A.

Subjective Questions

Very Short Answer Type Questions

1. **Significance of Biodiversity:**
   - Biodiversity maintains ecological balance and supports essential life processes. *(1 M)*
   - It is indispensable for human existence as it ensures the provision of natural resources such as food, clean air, and fresh water, underpinning the sustainability of our environment. *(1 M)*
2. **Measures for the conservation of forests:**
   - **Implement afforestation programs:** Plant trees and restore degraded forests to increase forest cover and biodiversity. *(1 M)*
   - **Promote sustainable forest management:** Use resources judiciously, ensure the replanting of trees, and limit deforestation to maintain ecological balance. *(1 M)*

   OR

   Measures for wildlife conservation:
   - Establish protected areas like national parks, wildlife sanctuaries, and biosphere reserves to provide safe habitats for wildlife. *(1 M)*
   - Implement anti-poaching laws and strengthen enforcement to prevent illegal hunting and trade of wild animals and their products. *(1 M)*
3. **Community Conservation Examples:**
   - **Chipko Movement:** Initiated by Himalayan women, they embrace trees to thwart logging efforts, symbolizing non-violent resistance to save forests and preserve ecological balance. *(1 M)*
   - **Bishnoi Community:** In Rajasthan, protects wildlife, demonstrating environmental conservation. *(1 M)*

4. **Concept of Sacred Groves:**
   - Sacred Groves are undisturbed forest areas, safeguarded by local communities, embodying spiritual and cultural significance which aids in their protection. *(1 M)*
   - These groves are vital for biodiversity conservation, harboring rare flora and fauna, thus acting as natural reservoirs of rich biological heritage and ensuring ecosystem stability. *(1 M)*
5. **Threats to Tiger Population:**
   - Poaching for trade and shrinking habitats due to deforestation, significantly reducing their living space and survival chances. *(1 M)*
   - Depletion of prey base species and increasing human population encroachment into tiger habitats, leading to food scarcity and habitat loss. *(1 M)*

Short Answer Type Questions

1. **Value of Forests in Our Life:**
   - Forests act as crucial carbon sinks, reducing global warming by absorbing CO_2. They produce vital oxygen, supporting life on Earth. *(1 M)*
   - They are habitats for diverse species, maintaining biodiversity and ensuring ecosystem stability and resilience. *(1 M)*
   - Forests regulate water cycles and prevent soil erosion, supporting agriculture and safeguarding human communities. *(1 M)*
2. **Threats to India's Flora and Fauna:**
   - Habitat loss due to deforestation and urbanization reduces living spaces for wildlife, leading to biodiversity loss. *(1 M)*
   - Poaching and illegal trade threaten species survival, particularly for endangered animals like tigers and rhinos. *(1 M)*
   - Over-exploitation of resources and illegal wildlife trade lead to species depletion and biodiversity loss. *(1 M)*
3. **Factors Leading to Decline of India's Biodiversity:** **(Any three)**
   - **Deforestation:** Rapid urbanization and industrialization result in habitat destruction. *(1 M)*
   - **Pollution:** Water, air, and soil pollution adversely impact flora and fauna. *(1 M)*
   - **Poaching:** Illegal hunting for trade decimates wildlife populations *(1 M)*
   - **Climate Change:** Alters habitats, threatening species adaptation and survival. *(1 M)*
4. **Classification and Value of Forest Types:**
   (i) **Classification:** Indian forests are classified into Reserved, Protected, and Unclassed forests based on their conservation status and management practices. *(1 M)*
   (ii) **Most Valuable:** Reserved forests are considered the most valuable for the conservation of forest and wildlife resources due to their high level of protection and biodiversity. *(2 M)*
5. **Largest Permanent Forests by State:**
   - **Madhya Pradesh:** This state has the largest area under permanent forests, accounting for 75% of its total forest area, supporting biodiversity and conservation efforts. *(1½ M)*
   - **Jammu and Kashmir:** This state also has a significant percentage of its total forest area designated as reserved forests, contributing to the preservation of unique ecological systems. *(1½ M)*

   These areas are crucial for maintaining ecological balance and supporting diverse wildlife.

   OR

   States with Large Reserved Forests:
   - **Madhya Pradesh and Arunachal Pradesh** are renowned for their vast areas of reserved forests, playing a crucial role in conserving biodiversity and ecological systems. *(1 M)*
   - **Chhattisgarh:** Its large reserved forest areas contribute significantly to the conservation of wildlife and natural habitats. *(1 M)*
   - **Maharashtra:** With substantial reserved forests, it aids in maintaining ecological balance and supporting diverse species. *(1 M)*

Long Answer Type Questions

1. Essential Conservation Due to Wildlife and Forestry Decline:
   - **Rapid Decline:** The wildlife population and forests are diminishing at an alarming rate due to habitat loss, deforestation, and poaching, threatening biodiversity and ecosystem services. *(1 M)*
   - **Ecosystem Services:** Forests and wildlife play crucial roles in maintaining ecological balance, such as carbon sequestration, climate regulation, and supporting diverse life forms. The loss of these natural resources disrupts these vital functions. *(2 M)*
   - **Conservation Measures:** Implementing effective conservation strategies, such as protected areas, wildlife sanctuaries, and national parks, alongside community-based conservation efforts, is imperative to halt and reverse the decline, ensuring the sustainability of natural resources and the well-being of future generations. *(2 M)*

   OR

   Need for Conservation of Forests and Wildlife:
   (i) **Ecological Balance:** Conservation is crucial for sustaining biodiversity, ensuring the survival of various species and maintaining ecological processes, as highlighted in the provided materials. *(2 M)*
   (ii) **Survival and Well-being:** They provide essential services like clean air, water, and resources for survival, contributing to human well-being and economic development. *(1 M)*

   Community Steps for Protection:
   (i) **Sariska Tiger Reserve:** Local communities in Rajasthan have collaborated with authorities to combat mining and protect the habitat, aligning with conservation practices detailed in the text. *(1 M)*
   (ii) **Joint Forest Management (JFM):** Communities work alongside the government to manage and restore forest areas, enhancing both local livelihoods and forest conditions, as indicated in your document. *(1 M)*

2. Necessity of Conservation:

- **Ecological Balance:** Conservation is essential for sustaining ecological balance, supporting life processes, and ensuring biodiversity, which is crucial for the survival of various species including humans. *(1½ M)*
- **Resource Sustainability:** Ensures the availability of vital resources like food, medicinal plants, and clean water for future generations, highlighting the interdependence between humans and nature. *(1½ M)*

Changes in Conservation Projects:

- **Holistic Approach:** Recent years have seen a shift towards a more comprehensive approach in conservation projects, focusing not just on individual species but on entire ecosystems, aiming for overall biodiversity preservation. *(1 M)*
- **Community Involvement:** There is an increased emphasis on involving local communities in conservation efforts, recognizing their role and traditional knowledge in environmental stewardship. *(1 M)*

3. The impact of climate change on India's biodiversity and suggestive measures to mitigate the effects are as follows:

(*i*) **Findings on Migration and Extinction:** Climate change is causing shifts in species distribution, with some migrating to cooler areas and others unable to adapt, leading to increased risk of extinction for sensitive species. *(1 M)*

(*ii*) **Habitat Corridors:** Establish habitat corridors to connect fragmented ecosystems, allowing species to migrate safely in response to climate changes and maintain genetic diversity. *(1 M)*

(*iii*) **Climate-Resilient Species:** Promote the conservation and breeding of climate-resilient species to ensure the stability of ecosystems and prevent biodiversity loss. *(1 M)*

(*iv*) **Restoration Projects:** Implement large-scale ecosystem restoration projects to enhance habitat resilience and support species adaptation to changing climatic conditions. *(1 M)*

(*v*) **Policy Integration:** Integrate climate change adaptation strategies into national biodiversity conservation policies, ensuring that all conservation efforts consider the impacts of climate change and address them proactively. *(1 M)*

Case Based Questions

Case Based-I

(*i*) A modern strategy would include advanced technology like drone monitoring, genetic studies for breeding programs, and community-based conservation projects to ensure local involvement and sustainable practices. *(1 M)*

(*ii*) Poaching for trade is the most detrimental as it directly reduces tiger numbers rapidly and is driven by high-profit margins in illegal wildlife markets. *(1 M)*

(*iii*) Tiger reserves have been effective as they provide protected habitats, regulate poaching, and help maintain necessary ecological conditions for tigers to thrive, as evidenced by stabilized populations in areas like Corbett and Sunderbans. *(2 M)*

Case Based-II

(*i*) A community-based project might include creating small Sacred Groves in community parks, involving local schools to educate children about indigenous species, and organizing community planting days that celebrate local cultural traditions. *(1 M)*

(*ii*) Sacred Groves act as biodiversity hotspots, conserving rare species like the peepal tree and local fauna, which are revered and thus protected by local communities. *(1 M)*

(*iii*) Sacred groves provide refuge for diverse wildlife, ensuring survival by prohibiting hunting and habitat destruction. For example, macaques and langurs thrive around temple groves where they are fed and protected by devotees. *(2 M)*

Case Based-III

(*i*) Communities' direct needs for food, drink, medicine, culture, spirituality, and other things come from a variety of forest and wildlife components. *(1 M)*

(*ii*) The major goal of the Wildlife Protection Act is to safeguard the surviving individuals of endangered species by outlawing hunting, protecting their ecosystems through the law, and limiting trade in wildlife. *(1 M)*

(*iii*) (*a*) The Wildlife Protection Act has been used as a weapon by people in Rajasthan's Sariska Tiger Reserve to fight against mining. *(1 M)*

(*b*) In order to safeguard wildlife against outside encroachments, residents of five villages in Rajasthan's Alwar district have designated 1200 hectares of forest as the Bhairodev Dakav "Sonchuri." *(1 M)*

Case Based-IV

(*i*) The primary threats include overhunting for commercial purposes, habitat destruction due to developmental activities, and accidental killings by fishermen using gill nets. *(1 M)*

(*ii*) Gharials thrive in freshwater river systems with ample sandy banks for nesting. These areas provide food, nesting sites, and protection from predators. The loss of such habitats makes it difficult for Gharials to reproduce and sustain their population. *(1 M)*

(*iii*) The decline of the Gharial could lead to an imbalance in the aquatic ecosystem, potentially causing an overpopulation of certain fish species that Gharials prey on. This imbalance can disrupt the food chain and affect other species' populations. *(2 M)*

Map Based Questions

1. (*a*) Kanchenjunga National Park, Sikkim
2. (*a*) Ranthambore National Park, Rajasthan
3. (*b*) Bandhavgarh National Park, Madhya Paradesh

WATER RESOURCES

3

"Water is the driving force of all nature, the lifeblood of Earth's existence. In every drop, a world of possibility."

SYLLABUS & WEIGHTAGE

List of Concept Names	Years					
	2020	2021	2022	2023	2024	2025
Water and Water Scarcity (Water Scarcity and The Need for Water Conservation and Management)	–	Exam not Conducted	–	–	–	1Q (3 M)
Multipurpose River Projects (Multi-Purpose River Projects and Integrated Water Resources Management)	–		–	1Q(1 M) (MB)	1Q(1 M)	
Rain Water Harvesting (Rainwater Harvesting Techniques)	–		–	3Q(4M) (CB)	1Q(1 M)	

CONCEPT MAP

To Access One Shot Revision Video Scan This QR Code

Water Resources

Water Resources

Water resources are sources like rivers, lakes, groundwater, and rainwater useful to humans.

Water Scarcity

Causes:

- Over-exploitation, excessive consumption, and unequal access to water
- Over utilisation, in order to increase the irrigated areas for dry-season agriculture
- There are some places where there is enough water to suit everyone's needs. But due to the poor quality of the water, those communities continue to experience water constraints.

Water Conservation and Management

CBSE 2025

Water conservation and management involve strategies to protect and efficiently use water to prevent scarcity and ensure future availability.

Multi-purpose River Projects

CBSE 2025, 2024, 2023

Large-scale initiatives using dams for multiple benefits like irrigation, power, and water supply, aiming for integrated resource management.

Examples:

- **Narmada Bachao Andolan:**

  Narmada Bachao Andolan is a movement for the rights of those impacted by the Sardar Sarovar Dam, focusing on conservation and fair resource share; Bhakra-Nangal is in the Satluj-Beas basin.

- **The Sardar Sarovar project:**

  The Sardar Sarovar Dam on the Narmada River in Gujarat is a major water project affecting four states: Maharashtra, Madhya Pradesh, Gujarat, and Rajasthan.

River Water Disputes

River water disputes arise from disagreements over sharing water from common rivers, like the Krishna-Godavari dispute among Indian states.

Classification of Dams

Dams are classified by structure (timber, embankment, masonry), purpose (multi, single), and height (large, medium, low) for various water management needs.

Mange and Conserve our Water Resources

- Water-resource management is the planning and managing of water resources focusing on quantity, quality, infrastructure, and sustainable use policies.
- To protect ourselves from risks to our health.
- To maintain our ability to eat, our way of life and constructive endeavours.
- In order to stop the destruction of our natural habitats.

Rain Water Harvesting

CBSE 2024, 2023

Rainwater harvesting involves collecting and storing rainwater for reuse, enhancing water security, like rooftop collection in Rajasthan.

Rooftop Rainwater Harvesting

CBSE 2024, 2023

- It is a simple way of collecting rainwater for future use. rainwater can be stored, used in various ways, or immediately used for recharge.
- Rooftop rainwater collection is a prevalent practice in Rajasthan for storing drinking water.
- People in flood plains of Bengal created inundation canals to irrigate their land.
- People in hilly areas created diversion channels for agriculture similar to "guls" or "kuls" of the Western Himalayas.

Bamboo Drip Irrigation

A traditional system in Meghalaya using bamboo pipes to transport and distribute water directly to crops.

1 WATER AND WATER SCARCITY

NCERT Definitions (Commonly asked in 1 mark)

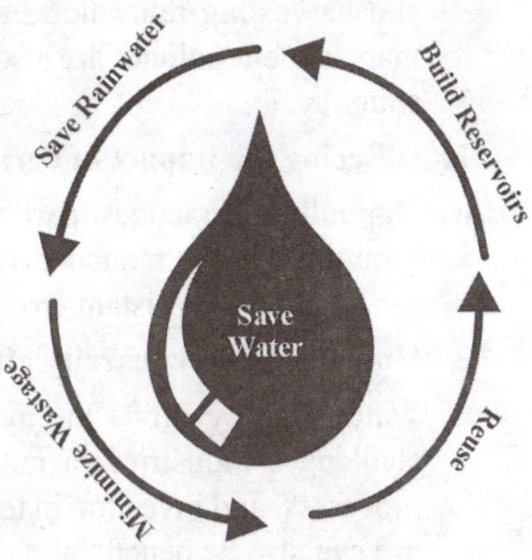

- **Water Resources:** Sources of water that are useful to humans, including rivers, lakes, groundwater, and rainwater.
- **Water Scarcity:** A situation where there is a ***shortage of water*** to meet the demand of a region, often due to overuse, pollution, and unequal access.
- **Reservoir:** A large **natural or artificial** lake used as a *storage for water supply*, created by damming rivers.
- **Water Cycle:** The continuous ***movement of water*** within the Earth's atmosphere, involving evaporation, condensation, precipitation, and runoff.
- **Drip Irrigation:** An ***efficient method*** of watering plants by delivering water directly to the roots through low-volume drips, reducing water waste.
- **Water Conservation and Management:** This involves actions and ***strategies to safeguard*** and use water resources wisely to prevent water scarcity and ensure availability for future needs.

Important Facts

01 ***Three-fourths*** of the Earth's surface is covered with water, but only a small part is usable freshwater.

02 By **2025**, it is predicted that nearly ***two billion people*** will face absolute water scarcity.

03 The Indian government has launched the ***Jal Jeevan Mission*** to improve water access and quality of life in rural areas.

04 The ***Jal Jeevan Mission*** by the Government of India aims to provide every rural household with **55 *litres*** of ***potable water*** per person per day.

05 Water scarcity is often caused by over-exploitation, excessive use, and unequal access to water.

Difference Between

Water Scarcity Vs. Water Resources		
Aspect	**Water Scarcity**	**Water Resources**
Definition	Lack of sufficient water for needs	Sources of water available
Causes	Over-exploitation, excessive use, unequal access, pollution, and large population demands.	Natural processes through hydrological cycle, including precipitation, surface runoff, and groundwater.
Effects	Droughts, health issues, conflicts.	Determines water availability.
Management	Conservation, efficient usage	Sustainable use, preservation
Examples	Cities facing groundwater depletion due to overuse and pollution.	Regions with abundant rainfall and well-managed reservoirs and dams.

Real Life Application Based Questions

1. **Explain how individuals can contribute to alleviating water scarcity in urban areas.**

Ans. Individuals can alleviate water scarcity by adopting water-efficient practices such as repairing leaks, using low-flow fixtures, and harvesting rainwater. Educating others about the importance of water conservation and advocating for sustainable water management policies are also crucial. These actions collectively reduce water demand and contribute to a more sustainable urban water cycle.

2. **Describe the impact of agricultural practices on water scarcity and a possible solution.**

Ans. Agricultural practices, particularly those relying on intensive irrigation, significantly contribute to water scarcity by depleting groundwater and reducing river flows. Adopting sustainable agricultural techniques, such as drip irrigation, crop rotation, and the use of drought-resistant crop varieties, can reduce water consumption and help mitigate water scarcity in farming regions.

3. **How does water scarcity affect industrial sectors, and what measures can industries take to mitigate this issue?**

Ans. Water scarcity limits the availability of water necessary for industrial processes, leading to increased costs and production challenges. Industries can mitigate this by implementing water recycling and reuse systems, improving water efficiency in industrial processes, and investing in technologies that require less water. Collaboration with local communities to ensure sustainable water use can also be beneficial.

4. **What is the significance of the Jal Jeevan Mission initiated by the Government of India?**

Ans. The Jal Jeevan Mission, initiated by the Government of India, aims to ensure that every rural household has access to safe and adequate drinking water through individual household tap connections. This mission is significant as it focuses on sustainable water supply management within communities, enhancing the quality of life and health standards. It addresses real-life challenges like water scarcity, ensuring long-term water availability and improving living conditions in rural areas.

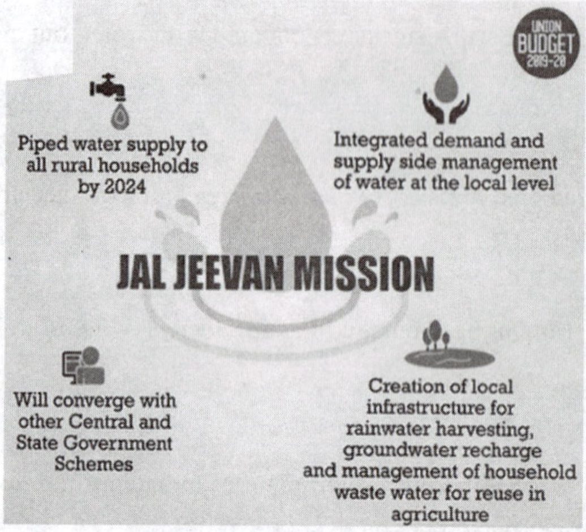

Myth Buster

- **Myth:** Water conservation is only necessary during droughts or in the summer.
  Fact: Water conservation is essential at all times to ensure sustainable usage and availability for the future, regardless of the season.
- **Myth:** Water management is solely a government responsibility (Lack of Public Engagement).
  Fact: Community awareness and participation are essential for sustainable water use.
- **Myth:** Water conservation is only necessary during droughts or in the summer.
  Fact: Water conservation is essential at all times to ensure sustainable usage and availability for the future, regardless of the season.
- **Myth:** Water management is solely a government responsibility (Lack of Public Engagement).
  Fact: Community awareness and participation are essential for sustainable water use.

COMPETENCY BASED SOLVED EXAMPLES

Scan Me for Detailed Explanations

Multiple Choice Questions (1 M)

1. Ankur, a resident from Rajasthan, decided to install a submersible water pump in his house, capable of extracting groundwater from depths of 250-300 m. This practice of installing similar pumps is becoming increasingly popular across the state. Which of the following will this growing practice MOST LIKELY lead to in the near future? *(An)* (CBSE APQ, 2023)

(*a*) decline in the groundwater quality

(*b*) reduced monsoon water resources

(*c*) increased number of waterborne diseases

(*d*) water scarcity resulting from excessive utilization

2. Imagine Darkland, a small town in India receives adequate rainfall throughout the year, yet the residents face significant challenges in accessing clean water. The local government has noted a growing concern among the populace regarding the frequent water shortages and the apparent abundance of water resources. Select the potential reason why this town might still experience water scarcity despite sufficient rainfall. *(An)*

(*a*) The town has excellent water conservation strategies.

(*b*) There is over-exploitation of the water resources and unequal distribution among the residents.

(*c*) The rainfall in the region is sporadic and unpredictable.

(*d*) The population density is too low to justify building adequate water infrastructure.

3. In rapidly growing cities, The Metro City is near a major river and has experienced significant population growth over the past decade. The city's infrastructure, however, has not been upgraded to meet the increasing water demand. A recent report highlights the risk of water scarcity affecting daily life, industrial activities, and sanitation services despite the proximity to abundant water resources. Given the situation in Metro City, which factor is primarily contributing to the impending water scarcity? *(Ev)*

(*a*) Insufficient annual rainfall

(*b*) Superior water quality that reduces perceived urgency for conservation

(*c*) Population density increasing faster than the available water supply can support

(*d*) Highly efficient water management systems already in place

4. In the fictional town of Greenfield, an emerging urban center that has recently attracted several large industrial plants and is also developing a hydroelectric power station on the nearby river. The local government is considering the introduction of a new water management plan in response to concerns about water scarcity affecting the community and ecological balance.

Identify which of the following statements are true regarding the impact of industrialization and urbanization on water resources: *(Un)*

Statement-I: Industrial units consume significant amounts of water, contributing to water scarcity.

Statement-II: All urban centers are self-sufficient in meeting their water needs.

Statement-III: Hydroelectric power, accounting for 22% of India's electricity, intensifies water demand.

Statement-IV: Jal Jeevan Mission aims to provide limited water access to urban households only.

(*a*) Statement-I & Statement-II are correct

(*b*) Statement-I & Statement-III are correct

(*c*) Statement-I & Statement-IV are correct

(*d*) Statement-I, II & III are correct

5. In the agricultural town of Harvestville, which frequently experiences dry seasons, local farmers face annual water shortages that threaten crop yields. To address these challenges, agricultural scientists propose a pilot project to introduce drought-resistant crops and promote dry farming techniques among the farming community. What potential impact could the adoption of drought-resistant crops and dry farming techniques have on Harvestville's persistent water scarcity issues? *(Ap)*

(*a*) They would increase dependence on limited groundwater supplies.

(*b*) They would not affect the overall water consumption in agriculture.

(*c*) They could reduce water scarcity by lowering agricultural water demands.

(*d*) They would exacerbate water scarcity due to increased water requirements.

Assertion and Reason (1 M)

Direction: The following questions consist of two statements – Assertion (A) and Reason (R). Answer these questions by selecting the appropriate option given below:

(*a*) Both A and R are true, and R is the correct explanation of A.
(*b*) Both A and R are true, but R is not the correct explanation of A.
(*c*) A is true, but R is false
(*d*) A is false, but R is true.

1. **Assertion (A):** Water scarcity is a significant issue in both arid and non-arid regions around the world.
   Reason (R): Unequal access to water and overuse in agriculture and industry contribute to water scarcity even in areas with sufficient rainfall. ***(Un)***
2. **Assertion (A):** The availability of water resources varies over space and time.
   Reason (R): Availability of water resources helps in storing water. ***(An)***
3. **Assertion (A):** Growing population is the main reason for water scarcity.
   Reason (R): Irrigation from tube wells and canals is responsible for water scarcity. ***(Un)***
4. **Assertion (A):** Climate change is a significant factor contributing to water scarcity.
   Reason (R): Climate change leads to changes in precipitation patterns and increased evaporation, reducing water availability. ***(Un)***
5. **Assertion (A):** Water scarcity is a result of the imbalance between water demand and supply.
   Reason (R): Rapid population growth and unsustainable water management practices contribute to water scarcity. ***(Un)***

Subjective Questions

Very Short Answer Type Questions (2M)

1. **Imagine you are a student living in a coastal area. After observing the weather patterns for a week, you notice that there is a regular cycle of evaporation and precipitation. Using your observations, What are the key processes involved in hydrological cycle?** ***(Un, Re)***

Ans. The hydrological cycle is the continuous movement of water on, above, and below the surface of the Earth. It includes processes like evaporation, condensation, precipitation, and runoff, making water a renewable resource. *(2 M)*

2. **You are a reporter for a local news channel in a region experiencing severe drought. You have been tasked with covering a story about the current water crisis. In your report, explain what water scarcity is and identify the primary factors contributing to this crisis in the region.** ***(Un)***

Ans. Water scarcity is the lack of sufficient available water resources to meet the demands within a region. Main causes include over-exploitation, excessive use, and unequal access among different social groups. *(2 M)*

3. **How can over-exploitation of groundwater lead to water scarcity?** ***(Un)***

Ans.
- **Depletion:** Over-exploitation involves extracting groundwater at a faster rate than it can be replenished, leading to a decline in groundwater levels. *(1 M)*
- **Reduced Availability:** As groundwater levels drop, wells and boreholes may dry up, reducing access to water for drinking, irrigation, and other uses, ultimately exacerbating water scarcity in the region. *(1 M)*

Short Answer Type Questions (3M)

1. **A national seminar on sustainable water management practices is being held, and participants are interested in understanding how water conservation practices have evolved in modern India. The discussion aims to explore both traditional methods and contemporary innovations in water conservation. How has the practice of water conservation evolved in modern India? Explain.** ***(Un)***

Ans. The practice of water conservation evolved in modern India:

(*i*) Modern India has adopted both traditional and advanced methods for water conservation, including rainwater harvesting and groundwater recharge systems. *(1 M)*

(*ii*) Policies like the Jal Jeevan Mission aim to provide piped water to rural households, ensuring sustainable water management. *(1 M)*

(*iii*) The use of water-efficient irrigation practices and awareness campaigns on water conservation have also contributed to the evolution of water conservation practices. *(1 M)*

2. **Describe the key components of the water cycle and their roles.** ***(Un)***

Ans. The key components of the water cycle are:
- **Evaporation:** Water from oceans, rivers, and lakes turns into vapor, contributing to cloud formation in the atmosphere. *(1 M)*
- **Condensation:** Water vapor cools and condenses to form clouds, leading to precipitation in the form of rain or snow. *(1 M)*
- **Precipitation and Collection:** Water falls back to earth as rain or snow, replenishing rivers, lakes, and groundwater, completing the cycle. *(1 M)*

3. **How does drip irrigation help conserve water in agriculture?** ***(Ap)***

Ans. Drip irrigation conserves water in agriculture by delivering it directly to the root zone of plants, reducing evaporation and runoff. *(1 M)*

- It provides water slowly, allowing it to be absorbed efficiently by the soil and roots, which leads to less water use and better crop health. *(1 M)*
- This method is particularly beneficial in arid regions, optimizing water use and improving agricultural productivity. *(1 M)*

4. Discuss the consequences of water scarcity on ecosystem health. *(An)*

Ans. Water scarcity leads to habitat loss for aquatic and terrestrial species, disrupting biodiversity and ecosystem balance. *(1 M)*

- It causes increased competition among species for limited water resources, stressing wildlife populations and plant life. *(1 M)*
- Reduced water availability can lead to the degradation of wetlands and forests, affecting ecosystem services and health. *(1 M)*

5. Why is sustainable management of water resources essential for human survival? *(Ap)*

Ans. Sustainable management ensures a steady supply of water for drinking, agriculture, and hygiene, critical for human survival. *(1 M)*

- It prevents conflicts over water by ensuring equitable distribution among communities and regions, promoting peace and security. *(1 M)*
- Protects ecosystems that provide vital services like clean air and water, supporting overall environmental health necessary for human life. *(1 M)*

Long Answer Type Questions (5 M)

1. Mr. Gautam, a city planner was tasked with addressing the water scarcity challenges in a rapidly urbanizing area that is also undergoing significant industrialization. The local government is considering expanding hydroelectric power facilities as part of the solution. Analyze the impact of industrialization and urbanization on water scarcity. Discuss the role of hydroelectric power in this context. *(An)*

Ans. The impact of industrialization and urbanization on water scarcity and the role of hydroelectric power can be understood by the following points:

(*i*) Urbanization increases water demand: Higher population densities in urban areas significantly boost domestic water needs, straining existing supplies and depleting groundwater levels. *(1 M)*

(*ii*) Industrial water consumption: Industries near urban centers consume vast water amounts and often pollute local water sources, worsening water scarcity. *(1 M)*

(*iii*) Water quality degradation: Urban and industrial waste contaminates water resources, reducing the availability of clean water for consumption and agriculture. *(1 M)*

(*iv*) Role of hydroelectric power: Hydroelectric projects manage water by storing it in reservoirs for power generation and supply during droughts, but disrupt natural water flows and ecosystems. *(1 M)*

(*v*) Environmental and social trade-offs: While providing renewable energy and aiding water management, hydroelectric facilities can cause environmental damage and community displacement. *(1 M)*

2. Describe the water cycle in detail, highlighting the significance of each stage. Explain how human activities impact the natural water cycle. *(Un)*

Ans. The water cycle, also known as the hydrological cycle, describes the continuous movement of water between the Earth's surface, atmosphere, and back again.

- **Evaporation:** Sun heats water bodies, turning water into vapor. This vapor rises into the atmosphere, playing a crucial role in cloud formation. *(1 M)*
- **Condensation:** Water vapor cools down in the atmosphere, forming clouds. This process is vital for precipitation, as it gathers water in the air. *(1 M)*
- **Precipitation:** Water returns to Earth as rain, snow, or sleet, replenishing rivers, lakes, and groundwater, essential for freshwater supplies. *(1 M)*
- **Collection:** Water collects in bodies like rivers, lakes, and oceans, and is absorbed into the ground, maintaining ecosystems and human water supplies. *(1 M)*
- **Human Impact:** Activities like deforestation, pollution, and overuse of water disrupt the natural cycle, leading to scarcity and quality issues, affecting ecosystems and human health. *(1 M)*

3. Explain the concept of drip irrigation and its advantages over conventional irrigation methods. Discuss the potential challenges and limitations of implementing drip irrigation systems. *(Cr)*

Ans. **Concept:** Drip irrigation involves delivering water directly to the plant roots through a network of pipes and drip emitters. This method is highly efficient as it reduces water wastage. *(1 M)*

- **Advantages:** Compared to conventional methods, drip irrigation conserves water, reduces evaporation, and minimizes weed growth. It ensures that water reaches directly to the roots, enhancing plant growth and yield. *(2 M)*
- **Challenges:** The initial setup cost of drip irrigation systems can be high, making it less affordable for small-scale farmers. Maintenance requires regular monitoring to prevent clogging of emitters and pipes. *(1 M)*
- **Limitations:** Drip irrigation may not be suitable for all types of crops and soil conditions. It also requires a reliable water source and technical knowledge for installation and operation. *(1 M)*

2 MULTIPURPOSE RIVER PROJECTS

NCERT Definitions *(Commonly asked in 1 mark)*

- **Hydraulic Structures:** Man-made constructions like ***dams and canals*** designed to control, manage, and utilize water for various purposes.
- **Dams:** Barriers constructed across waterways to store, manage, and regulate water for irrigation, power generation, and flood control.
- **Multi-purpose Projects:** Large-scale initiatives using dams for multiple benefits like irrigation, power, and water supply, ***aiming for integrated*** resource management.
- **Irrigated Agriculture:** The ***artificial application of water*** to land for crop production, which significantly increases water usage.
- **Environmental Movements:** Campaigns and actions by groups advocating ***for environmental protection*** and opposing harmful development projects. For example: Narmada Bachao Andolan and Tehri Dam Andolan etc.

Important Facts

01 In India, hydroelectric power contributes about **22% *to the total electricity*** production.

02 The Sardar Sarovar Dam on the Narmada River in Gujarat is one of ***India's largest water projects***, serving four states Maharashtra, Madhya Pradesh, Gujarat and Rajasthan and aiding drought-prone areas.

03 Sophisticated irrigation works have been found in historical sites across Kalinga (Odisha), Nagarjunakonda (Andhra Pradesh), Bennur (Karnataka), and Kolhapur (Maharashtra) etc.

04 In the 11th Century, Bhopal Lake was constructed, becoming one of the ***largest artificial lakes*** of that era.

05 In the 14th Century, ***Iltutmish*** built the ***Hauz Khas tank*** in Delhi to supply water to the Siri Fort area.

06 During ***Chandragupta Maurya's*** reign, ***extensive construction of dams***, lakes, and irrigation systems took place.

07 Jawaharlal Nehru referred to dams as the **'*temples of modern India*'**.

Important Concepts

- **Narmada Bachao Andolan:** A movement advocating for the rights and rehabilitation of people affected by the Sardar Sarovar Dam on the Narmada River. It emphasizes environmental conservation and equitable resource distribution. The Bhakra-Nangal Project has been constructed in the Satluj-Beas River basin.
- **Tehri Dam Andolan:** The "Tehri Dam Andolan" was part of environmental movements against large-scale displacement due to dam construction, focusing on local communities' sacrifices for national development without equitable benefits, highlighting conflicts over resource distribution and environmental concerns.
- **Hydrological cycle:** The hydrological cycle involves the continuous circulation of water through evaporation, condensation, precipitation, and runoff, connecting the Earth's oceans, land, and atmosphere.
- **River Water Disputed:** River water disputes occur when regions or states disagree over water distribution from shared rivers, often due to agricultural or industrial demands, like the Krishna-Godavari dispute among Indian states.

Classification

Classification of Dams			
S.No.	**Classification Basis**	**Type**	**Details**
1.	**Structure**	Timber Dams	Built from timber, used for temporary or small-scale water control.
		Embankment Dams	Made from earth and rocks, suitable for blocking streams and creating reservoirs.
		Masonry Dams	Constructed from concrete or stone, designed for durability and strength.
2.	**Intended Purpose**	Multi-purpose Dams	Used for water supply, hydroelectric power, irrigation, etc.
		Single-purpose Dams	Designed for one main function, such as flood control.
		Lustrous (shiny)	Non-lustrous (except iodine)
3.	**Height**	Large Dams	Higher than 15 meters, used for significant water storage.
		Medium Height Dams	Between 5 to 15 meters in height.
		Low Dams	Up to 5 meters in height, often used for minor storage or diversion.

Difference Between

Advantages Vs. Disadvantages of Multi-Purpose River projects			
S. No.	**Aspect**	**Advantages**	**Disadvantages**
1.	**Water Supply**	Provides water for irrigation, drinking, and industrial uses.	Large-scale displacements and loss of livelihood for local communities.
2.	**Electricity Generation**	Generates electricity to power industries and homes.	Can lead to environmental problems like deforestation and changes in land use.
3.	**Flood Control**	Helps in controlling floods by regulating water flow.	May cause poor sediment flow and excessive sedimentation, harming aquatic life.
4.	**Navigation**	Facilitates inland navigation and boosts local economies.	Fragmentation of rivers, affecting aquatic fauna and their migration.
5.	**Recreation**	Can be used for recreational purposes like water sports and tourism.	Leads to submergence of existing vegetation and soil, degrading ecosystems.

Water Conservation Vs. Water Management		
Aspect	**Water Conservation**	**Water Management**
Focus	Saving and reducing use	Planning and regulation
Methods	Rainwater harvesting, efficient fixtures	Dams, policies, resource allocation
Goal	Preserve water for future, reduce waste	Meet demands sustainably, ensure availability
Impact	Positive on ecosystems	Mixed, can disrupt ecosystems
Community Role	High, local actions	Requires higher-level coordination
Sustainability	High, enhances resource longevity	Depends on careful planning

Real Life Application Based Questions

1. What practical steps can schools take to educate students about Integrated Water Resources Management?

Ans. Schools can implement water-saving measures, organize educational programs on water conservation, engage students in projects related to water management, such as rain gardens or water recycling, and facilitate visits to water treatment plants or natural water bodies.

2. How does the construction of a multipurpose river project affect the daily life of nearby residents?

Ans. The construction of a multipurpose river project can lead to changes in water flow, affecting local fishing, agriculture, and water supply. Residents may benefit from improved infrastructure, electricity, and water availability but may also face relocation or environmental changes.

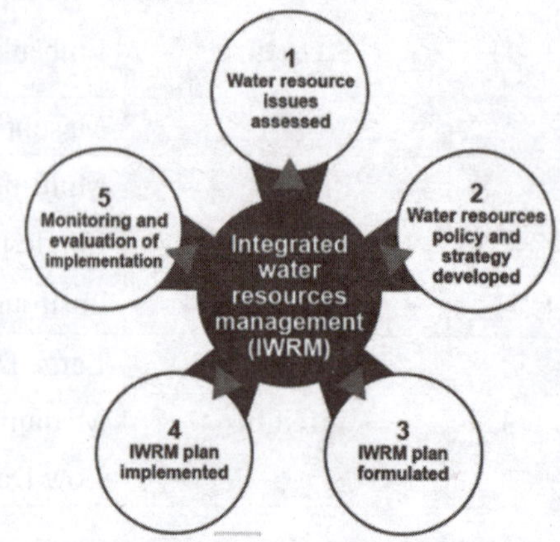

3. Describe the role of community participation in Integrated Water Resources Management.

Ans. Community participation ensures that water resource management is more inclusive and considers local needs and knowledge. This leads to more effective and sustainable water use and management practices, enhancing local ownership and stewardship of water resources.

Myth Buster

❒ **Myth:** Multipurpose River projects always lead to economic prosperity without any ecological cost.

Fact: While they contribute to economic development by providing water for irrigation, generating electricity, and preventing floods, they can also cause ecological damage, including habitat destruction and affecting local water tables.

❒ **Myth:** Environmental movements are against development and progress.

Fact: Environmental movements aim to ensure sustainable development. They advocate for balancing economic growth with ecological preservation and often push for the adoption of renewable energy and sustainable practices.

❒ **Myth:** Large dams are the only solution to water scarcity and energy needs.

Fact: While large dams provide significant water storage and hydroelectric power, alternatives like small-scale water harvesting and solar energy can also meet water and energy needs sustainably.

❒ **Myth:** The benefits of multipurpose river projects are shared equally by all.

Fact: Often, the benefits are disproportionately distributed, favoring urban over rural areas, and leading to conflicts over water rights and usage.

❒ **Myth:** Integrated Water Resources Management (IWRM) only applies to areas with water scarcity.

Fact: IWRM is applicable in all types of regions, whether water-scarce or water-abundant, to ensure sustainable and equitable use of water resource

COMPETENCY BASED SOLVED EXAMPLES

Scan Me for Detailed Explanations

Multiple Choice Questions (1 M)

1. Match the Column-I with Column-II and choose the correct option *(Re)*(CBSE, 2023)

Column-I (River)		Column-II (Dam)	
A.	Mahanadi	I.	Sardar Sarovar
B.	Narmada	II.	Hirakud
C.	Chambal	III.	Salal
D.	Chenab	IV.	Rana Pratap Sagar

(*a*) A-IV, B-III, C-II, D-I (*b*) A-III, B-IV, C-I, D-II
(*c*) A-II, B-I, C-IV, D-III (*d*) A-I, B-II, C-III, D-IV

2. In Bhakra – Nangal project water is being used for *(Un)*(CBSE APQ, 2023)

(*i*) Hydel power production
(*ii*) Irrigation
(*iii*) Transportation
(*iv*) Cleaning

(*a*) (*i*) and (*iv*) (*b*) (*ii*) and (*i*)
(*c*) Only (*iii*) (*d*) Only (*ii*)

3. Why are multipurpose projects often controversial? *(An)*

(*a*) High construction costs
(*b*) Opposition from local communities
(*c*) Lack of government support
(*d*) Limited ecological impact

4. Which factor is crucial in the planning and implementation of multipurpose projects? *(Ap)*

(*a*) Environmental impact assessment
(*b*) Political affiliation
(*c*) Economic competitiveness
(*d*) Technological advancement

5. What are multipurpose projects? *(Un)*

(*a*) Projects that serve multiple industries
(*b*) Projects that have multiple objectives and benefits
(*c*) Projects that involve multiple countries
(*d*) Projects that focus on multiple renewable energy sources

Assertion and Reason (1 M)

Direction: The following questions consist of two statements – Assertion (A) and Reason (R). Answer these questions by selecting the appropriate option given below:

(*a*) Both A and R are true, and R is the correct explanation of A.
(*b*) Both A and R are true, but R is not the correct explanation of A.
(*c*) A is true, but R is false
(*d*) A is false, but R is true.

1. You are part of a city council tasked with managing water resources in a growing urban area. The city has been facing severe water shortages, and many residents complain about irregular water supply. Upon investigation, you find that the city's water resources are rapidly depleting due to over-exploitation. Based on the above information, consider the following statements:

Assertion (A): Water resources are scarce in urban areas.

Reason (R): Over-exploitation of fragile water resources has caused their depletion. *(Un)*

2. The government is considering constructing a new dam on a river that flows through several villages and towns. There is a public debate about the potential benefits and drawbacks of this project. The proponents argue that the dam will bring several benefits, including electricity generation, improved irrigation, and a reliable water supply for domestic and industrial use. However, some local residents are concerned about the environmental and social impacts. Based on the above scneario, answer the following:

Assertion (A): Dams are built to impound rivers and rainwater, which can be used later for various purposes.

Reason (R): Dams help in generating electricity, irrigation, and providing water supply for domestic and industrial uses. *(An)*

3. You are working as a consultant for a coastal city that receives high annual rainfall. Despite this, the city faces severe water scarcity issues. During a community meeting, some residents believe that the scarcity is due to insufficient rainfall, while others think it might be due to other factors. Based on the above information, consider the following statements:

Assertion (A): Water scarcity is always caused by the lack of sufficient rainfall.

Reason (R): Water scarcity can occur even in regions with high rainfall if the available water is polluted or not properly managed. *(Ev)*

4. Assertion (A): Multipurpose projects must ensure water resource sustainability.

Reason (R): By integrating water management strategies, these projects can support both human and ecological needs effectively. *(Ap)*

Subjective Questions

Very Short Answer Type Questions (2 M)

1. **You are an environmental consultant tasked with advising a state government on the development of a new river project. The government is considering a multipurpose river project to address water management, energy production, and agriculture. What are multipurpose river projects?** ***(Un)***

Ans. Multipurpose river projects are infrastructure projects that provide multiple benefits such as irrigation, hydroelectric power, water supply, flood control, and recreation. *(2 M)*

2. **State any two sources from which freshwater can be obtained under the hydrological cycle.** ***(Re)***

Ans. (*i*) **Surface Runoff:** This is water from rain or snow that flows over the land's surface, collecting in rivers, lakes, and streams. *(1 M)*

(*ii*) **Groundwater:** This is water that seeps into the ground and is stored in underground aquifers, continually renewed and recharged through the hydrological cycle. *(1 M)*

3. **In whose kingdom in ancient India, dams and lakes were built?** ***(Re)***

Ans. **Chandragupta Maurya's Kingdom:** In ancient India, during his reign, extensive construction of dams, lakes, and irrigation systems was undertaken. *(1 M)*

Examples: Structures for water storage and management were significantly developed during this period. *(1 M)*

4. **What is a dam?** ***(Un)***

Ans. A dam is a barrier constructed across flowing water to control its flow or create a reservoir. *(1 M)*

It serves multiple purposes like irrigation, water supply, and hydroelectric power generation. *(1 M)*

5. **Make a list of inter-state water disputes.** ***(Cr)***

Ans. list of inter-state water disputes are:

- **Krishna-Godavari dispute:** This involves disagreements between Karnataka, Andhra Pradesh, and Maharashtra over water diversion at Koyna. *(1 M)*
- **Sabarmati-basin farmer's dispute:** Conflicts in Gujarat over water allocation between urban and agricultural uses, especially during droughts. *(1 M)*

Short Answer Type Questions (3 M)

1. **A panel discussion is being organized to debate the implementation of a new multipurpose river project in a region prone to both droughts and floods. The project aims to address water scarcity, provide irrigation, generate hydroelectric power, and control floods. However, there are concerns about the potential environmental and social impacts. Discuss the advantages and disadvantages of multipurpose river projects.** ***(Un, Re)***

Ans. The advantages and disadvantages are as follows:

(*i*) **Advantages:** Provide water for irrigation and drinking, generate hydroelectric power, and control floods and droughts. *(1 M)*

(*ii*) **Disadvantages:** Cause displacement of local communities, environmental degradation, such as altered river ecosystems, and reduced biodiversity. *(1 M)*

(*iii*) **Risks:** Sedimentation can reduce the effectiveness of these projects over time, leading to issues like decreased water storage capacity. *(1 M)*

2. **What is a multipurpose river valley project? Give any four objectives of the multi-purpose river valley projects.** ***(Un)***

Ans. A multipurpose river valley project involves constructing a dam on a large river to serve various needs like hydroelectric power, irrigation, and flood control. *(1 M)*

Objectives:

- **Electricity Generation:** To provide a source of hydroelectric power. *(½ M)*
- **Irrigation:** To supply water for agricultural fields. *(½ M)*
- **Water Supply:** For domestic and industrial uses. *(½ M)*
- **Flood Control:** To prevent the seasonal flooding of rivers. *(½ M)*.

3. **Describe the purpose and scale of the Sardar Sarovar Dam project on the Narmada River.** ***(Un)***

Ans. Purpose and Scale of the Sardar Sarovar Dam Project

- **Water Supply:** Aims to provide potable water to drought-prone areas, serving four states and supporting thousands of villages and towns. *(1 M)*
- **Irrigation and Agriculture:** Enhances irrigation facilities for vast agricultural lands, improving crop production and farmer livelihoods. *(1 M)*
- **Hydroelectric Power:** Generates significant hydroelectric power contributing to the regional and national energy grid. *(1 M)*

4. **List the historical sites in India known for their sophisticated irrigation works and describe one in detail.** ***(Ap)***

Ans.
- **List of Sites:** Kalinga (Odisha), Nagarjunakonda (Andhra Pradesh), Bennur (Karnataka), and Kolhapur (Maharashtra) are known for their ancient irrigation systems. *(1 M)*
- **Detail on Kalinga:** In Kalinga, sophisticated irrigation systems included canals and water storage facilities. These systems were used for diverting water from rivers to agricultural fields, ensuring water availability throughout the year. *(1 M)*
- **Impact:** The irrigation works supported agriculture, boosted local economies, and showcased advanced engineering skills of ancient India. *(1 M)*

5. **Discuss the importance of dams and lakes during Chandragupta Maurya's reign in the context of water management.** ***(An)***

Ans. Importance of Dams and Lakes During Chandragupta Maurya's Reign:

- **Construction and Use:** Chandragupta Maurya oversaw the construction of advanced hydraulic structures like dams and lakes for water management. *(1 M)*
- **Agricultural Impact:** These structures supported irrigation, boosting agriculture and supporting the empire's population. *(1 M)*
- **Historical Significance:** This era highlights the strategic use of water resources for the Mauryan empire's growth and stability. *(1 M)*

Long Answer Type Questions (5 M)

1. **In the fictional region of Aravalia, where the government plans to build a new multi-purpose river project called "Aravalia Renaissance Dam" on the River Narmali. The project aims to provide irrigation, hydroelectric power, and flood control, improving the local economy. However, environmental groups have raised concerns about potential negative impacts on the local ecosystem, including loss of biodiversity and displacement of communities. Analyze the dual role of multi-purpose river projects like "Aravalia Renaissance Dam" in promoting development and causing environmental degradation.** *(An)*

Ans. The dual role of multipurpose river projects in promoting development and causing environmental degradation can be understood by the following points:

(*i*) Development through infrastructure: Multi-purpose river projects facilitate infrastructure development by providing irrigation, hydroelectric power, and improved water supply, thereby supporting agricultural and industrial growth. fulfilling Nehru's vision of development. *(1 M)*

(*ii*) Economic benefits: These projects generate significant economic benefits by producing electricity, enhancing water availability for various uses, and sometimes enabling inland navigation which boosts trade and connectivity. *(1 M)*

(*iii*) Environmental impact: Dams alter natural river flows, disrupting sediment transport and aquatic ecosystems, which can lead to loss of biodiversity and changes in landscape. *(1 M)*

(*iv*) Displacement and social issues: Large-scale projects often result in the displacement of local communities, loss of livelihoods, and social strife due to relocation and inadequate compensation. *(1 M)*

(*v*) Water management challenges: While intended to control floods, dams have sometimes exacerbated flooding due to poor management and unexpected heavy rainfall. *(1 M)*

2. **What are the social consequences of multipurpose projects? Multipurpose projects have transformed the social landscapes Explain.** *(An)*

Ans. Social Consequences of Multipurpose Projects:

- **Displacement:** These projects result in large-scale displacement of local communities. People are often forced to leave their homes, land, and livelihoods, disrupting their traditional way of life. *(1 M)*
- **Social Inequality:** The transformation of social landscapes increases the gap between richer landowners, who benefit from new water resources, and the landless poor, who are often negatively affected without adequate compensation or rehabilitation. *(1 M)*
- **Cultural Disruption:** Local cultures, customs, and communal structures are significantly disrupted, leading to a loss of cultural heritage and traditional practices related to land and water use. *(1 M)*
- **Conflict and Agitation:** Projects can lead to social unrest and conflicts within communities, as seen with the agitation among Sabarmati-basin farmers in Gujarat over water allocation priorities during droughts. *(1 M)*
- **Economic and Food Security:** Changes in water distribution and land use can lead to alterations in the cropping pattern, affecting local economies and food security due to shifts towards water-intensive and commercial crops. *(1 M)*.

Mistakes 101 : What not to do!

Missing Counterarguments

Students might overlook addressing potential benefits of multipurpose projects, such as improved irrigation, electricity generation, or flood control. Including a balanced view with counterarguments could demonstrate a comprehensive understanding of the topic.

3 RAIN WATER HARVESTING

NCERT Definitions *(Commonly asked in 1 mark)*

- **Rain Water Harvesting:** The process of ***collecting and storing rainwater*** for reuse, mainly to supplement the main water supply and increase groundwater levels.
- **Rain Water Harvest Techniques:** Include rooftop harvesting, recharge pits, recharge trenches, recharge wells, and check dams, utilizing various structures to collect and store rainwater for future use.
- **Rooftop Rainwater Harvesting:** Collecting ***rainwater from rooftops*** to store for later use or recharge groundwater, reducing dependency on other water sources.
- **Bamboo Drip Irrigation System:** An age-old system used in Meghalaya, where ***bamboo pipes channel water*** to crops, reducing water wastage and enhancing water availability in hilly terrains.
- **Guls or Kuls:** Guls or Kuls are ***small channels*** that carry water from streams to fields in the mountains, helping to water crops.
- **Khadins and Johads:** In arid and semi-arid regions, agricultural fields were converted into rain-fed storage structures that allowed the water to stand and moisten the soil like the **'Khadins'** in Jaisalmer and **'Johads'** in other parts of Rajasthan.

Bamboo Drip Irrigation

Important Facts

01 In the first century B.C., Sringaverapura near Allahabad utilized a **sophisticated water harvesting** system to channel flood water from the river Ganga.

02 Traditional houses in arid regions like Bikaner, Phalodi, and Barmer had underground **'tankas'** for water storage.

03 Rooftop rainwater harvesting systems in Gendathur, Karnataka, help each household collect around 50,000 litres of water annually.

04 Rooftop rainwater harvesting is widespread in Shillong, Meghalaya, despite being near the **world's highest rainfall areas,** Cherapunjee and Mawsynram.

05 Rooftop water harvesting contributes to **15-25%** of a household's total water requirement in Shillong.

06 In Meghalaya, a 200-year-old method uses bamboo pipes to transport stream and spring water over long distances, culminating in a drip irrigation system.

07 Tamil Nadu is the first Indian state to **mandate rooftop rainwater harvesting** for all houses, with legal consequences for non-compliance.

Difference Between

Rooftop Rainwater Water Harvesting Vs. Surface Water Harvesting			
S. No.	**Aspect**	**Rooftop Rainwater Harvesting**	**Surface Water Harvesting**
1.	Definition	Collection and storage of rainwater directly from roof surfaces.	Collection and storage of runoff water from land surface.
2.	Area of Implementation	Mostly Urban and semi-urban areas, suitable for individual houses or buildings.	Rural and urban areas, applicable to agriculture fields, ponds, and reservoirs.
3.	Collection Source	Building roofs	Land surfaces
4.	Primary Use	Domestic purposes, groundwater recharge	Irrigation, aquaculture
5.	Cost and Maintenance	Low cost, easy maintenance	Higher cost, more maintenance
6.	Water Quality	High, with minimal treatment	Variable, may need treatment
7.	Regulation and Legal Framework	Mandated by law in some regions (e.g., Tamil Nadu).	Dependent on local water management policies and practices.

Real Life Application Based Questions

1. **How can homeowners in urban areas contribute to water conservation through rainwater harvesting?**

Ans. Urban households can use rooftop rainwater harvesting to collect and store rainwater for non-potable uses like gardening, flushing toilets, and washing cars, reducing their reliance on municipal water supply and lowering water bills.

2. **What is a simple way to start rainwater harvesting in a rural home?**

Ans. A rural household can start by collecting runoff from rooftops into a clean tank or underground pit. This stored water can then be used for irrigation or livestock, especially during dry seasons.

RAINWATER HARVESTING

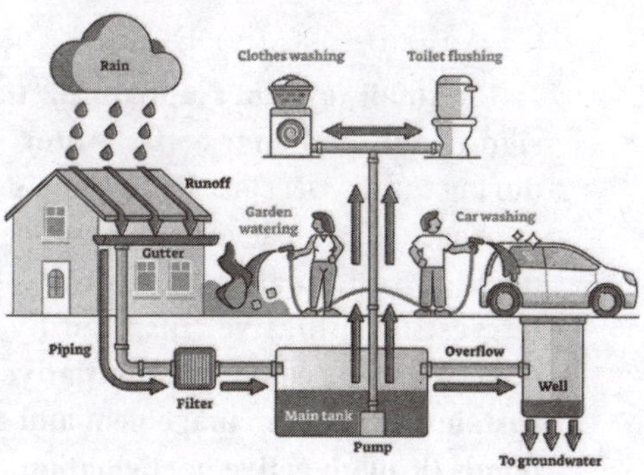

3. **How does rooftop rainwater harvesting help in areas facing water scarcity?**

Ans. Rooftop rainwater harvesting captures rain, reducing dependence on groundwater and surface water, thereby alleviating water scarcity and ensuring a sustainable water supply.

4. **How can schools contribute to promoting rainwater harvesting?**

Ans. Schools can install rainwater harvesting systems to collect and use rainwater for cleaning and gardening. They can also educate students about the importance of water conservation and rainwater harvesting through workshops and science projects.

Myth Buster

- **Myth:** Rainwater harvesting is only useful in rural areas.

  Fact: Both rural and urban areas can benefit from rainwater harvesting. Urban areas can reduce waterlogging, while rural areas can enhance water availability.

- **Myth:** Stored rainwater is unsafe for drinking.

  Fact: If collected and stored properly, rainwater is safe for drinking. Systems usually include filtration to ensure water quality.

- **Myth:** Bamboo drip irrigation is outdated and inefficient.

  Fact: Bamboo drip irrigation is a sustainable and efficient system suitable for hilly terrains, reducing water waste and aiding in precise water delivery to plants.

COMPETENCY BASED SOLVED EXAMPLES

Scan Me for Detailed Explanations

Multiple Choice Questions (1 M)

1. **A geography teacher, Mr. Kumar, decides to engage his class with a real-world application task during their study of traditional water conservation systems in different Indian regions. He assigns four groups in his class, each representing a historical community that implemented unique water conservation methods suitable to their geographical features and climate conditions.**
Each group is given a card describing one traditional water harvesting technique and a list of regions. The students need to match their assigned water harvesting technique to the correct region based on climatic conditions, geographical features, and historical usage. ***(Re)***

Column-I		Column-II	
(A)	'Guls' or 'Kuls'	(i)	Bikaner for drinking water storage
(B)	'Khadins'	(ii)	Western Himalayas for agriculture
(C)	'Tankas'	(iii)	Jaisalmer for rain-fed storage
(D)	'Inundation Channels'	(iv)	Bengal for field irrigation

(*a*) A-(ii), B-(iii), C-(i), D-(iv)
(*b*) A-(i), B-(ii), C-(iii), D-(iv)
(*c*) A-(ii), B-(i), C-(iii), D-(iv)
(*d*) A-(ii), B-(i), C-(iv), D-(iii)

2. **In the small town of Nandanvan, the community faces significant challenges with water scarcity, especially during the dry seasons. This year, as the monsoon season approached, a local environmental group, "AquaSave," decided to launch a community-driven Rainwater harvesting initiative. Inspired by successful models seen in other regions, the initiative aimed to promote sustainable water management and enhance community bonds through active participation.**

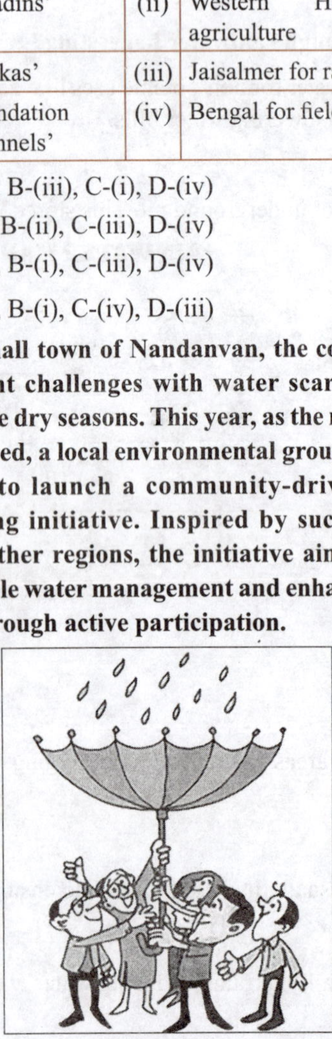

Which element in the image symbolizes community cooperation in sustainable practices? ***(Un)***
(*a*) The umbrella
(*b*) The raindrops
(*c*) The people holding the umbrella
(*d*) The colors used in the umbrella

3. **Which region in India commonly practices rooftop rainwater harvesting?** ***(Re)***
(*a*) Western Himalayas (*b*) Rajasthan
(*c*) Bengal (*d*) Jaisalmer

4. **What is the purpose of storing rainwater in rain-fed storage structures like 'khadins' and 'Johads'?** ***(Un)***
(*a*) To prevent soil erosion
(*b*) To create recreational water bodies
(*c*) To promote agriculture in arid regions
(*d*) To support industrial water needs

5. **In the context of a small rural community experiencing severe water scarcity, a revival of an abandoned dug well as a rainwater harvesting method has been implemented. This community, largely dependent on agriculture, has suffered due to insufficient rainfall and depleting groundwater levels, which has threatened both their crops and their daily water needs.**

Evaluate the sustainability of using abandoned dug wells for groundwater recharge compared to traditional water reservoirs. ***(Ev)***
(*a*) More sustainable as it prevents water loss through evaporation
(*b*) Less sustainable due to high maintenance costs
(*c*) Equally sustainable if managed properly
(*d*) Not sustainable as it contaminates groundwater

Assertion and Reason (1 M)

Direction: The following questions consist of two statements – Assertion (A) and Reason (R). Answer these questions by selecting the appropriate option given below:
(*a*) Both A and R are true, and R is the correct explanation of A.
(*b*) Both A and R are true, but R is not the correct explanation of A.
(*c*) A is true, but R is false
(*d*) A is false, but R is true.

1. **A town council is debating whether to invest in rainwater harvesting systems for public buildings and residential areas. Some members argue that with modern infrastructure and sufficient water resources, rainwater harvesting is outdated and unnecessary. Others believe it is still relevant and beneficial, especially in times of water stress or drought. Consider the following statements on the basis of above information:**

   Assertion (A): Rainwater harvesting is a traditional method that is still relevant today.

   Reason (R): Modern infrastructure and abundant water resources have eliminated the need for rainwater harvesting. ***(Un)***

2. **Assertion (A):** Rainwater harvesting is a sustainable solution for water scarcity.

   Reason (R): Rainwater harvesting helps in replenishing groundwater levels and reduces the strain on traditional water sources. ***(An)***

3. **Assertion (A):** Rainwater harvesting is a cost-effective method for water conservation.

   Reason (R): Rainwater harvesting systems require high initial investment and maintenance costs. ***(An)***

4. **Assertion (A):** . Assertion (A): Rooftop rainwater harvesting is mandated in Tamil Nadu for all houses.

   Reason (R): Rainwater harvesting effectively addresses urban water scarcity by augmenting the groundwater level. ***(Un)***

Subjective Questions

Very Short Answer Type Questions (2 M)

1. **State reasons for conservation of water resources.** ***(Un)***

Ans. The reasons for conservation of water resources are:

- Prevent health hazards from polluted water. *(½ M)*
- Ensure food security through consistent water supply. *(½ M)*
- Maintain livelihoods and productive activities. *(½ M)*
- Mitigate over-exploitation and mismanagement of water resources *(½ M)*

2. **In which state the farmers were upset over the higher priority given to the water supply in urban areas?** ***(Re)***

Ans. The farmers in the Sabarmati-basin in Gujarat were upset over the higher priority given to water supply in urban areas, especially during droughts. This situation led to near-riot conditions among the farmers. *(2 M)*

3. **Why is rooftop rainwater harvesting important?** ***(Ap)***

Ans. **Water Conservation:** Rooftop rainwater harvesting collects rainwater from roofs, reducing runoff and replenishing groundwater or storage tanks. *(1 M)*

This method provides a local and sustainable water source, reducing dependency on external water supplies and mitigating water scarcity, particularly in areas with unreliable water access. *(1 M)*

Short Answer Type Questions (3 M)

1. **A community in a semi-arid region like Rajasthan faces frequent water shortages, especially during dry seasons. The local government is considering implementing water harvesting techniques to address this issue. However, the community members are unfamiliar with the concept and its potential benefits. Explain the concept of water harvesting and its importance in semi-arid regions like Rajasthan.** ***(Un, An)***

Ans. The concept and importance of water harvesting can be understood by the following points:

(*i*) Water harvesting involves collecting and storing rainwater for future use, crucial in arid regions. *(1 M)*

(*ii*) Techniques like rooftop rainwater harvesting and underground tanks (tankas) are used to store water. *(1 M)*

(*iii*) It ensures a reliable water source during dry periods, helps recharge groundwater, and supports agriculture and daily needs. *(1 M)*

2. **What is palar pani? What is its significance in the arid regions of Rajasthan?** ***(Ap)***

Ans. Palar Pani is the purest form of natural water, collected as rainwater in underground tanks (tankas). *(1 M)*

Palar Pani is significant because:

- In arid regions of Rajasthan, it is a crucial source of drinking water during the dry seasons. *(1 M)*
- Helps in conserving groundwater and sustains life in extreme summer when other sources dry up. *(1 M)*

3. **Describe any three different rainwater harvesting systems practised in India.** ***(Ap)***

Ans. Three different rainwater harvesting systems practiced in India:

- **Rooftop Rainwater Harvesting:** Common in urban areas; water from roofs is channeled into storage tanks for later use. *(1 M)*
- **Bamboo Drip Irrigation:** Used in Meghalaya; bamboo pipes direct water from streams to agricultural fields. *(1 M)*
- **Johads:** Traditional earthen ponds used in Rajasthan to collect rainwater for agricultural and livestock needs. *(1 M)*

4. **Explain three traditional methods of rainwater harvesting in India. (Any three)** ***(An)***

Ans. (*i*) **Guls or Kuls:** In the Western Himalayas, people build diversion channels to direct water for agriculture. *(1 M)*

(*ii*) **Rooftop Rainwater Harvesting:** Common in Rajasthan, where rainwater from rooftops is stored in underground tanks (tankas) for later use. *(1 M)*

(*iii*) **Johads:** Earthen ponds used in Rajasthan to collect rainwater for agricultural and livestock needs. *(1 M)*

(*iv*) **Bamboo Drip Irrigation:** In Meghalaya, a network of bamboo tubes directs water from streams to fields. *(1 M)*

Long Answer Type Questions (5 M)

1. **Write how modern adaptations of traditional rainwater harvesting methods are being carried out to conserve and store water.** ***(An)***

Ans. Modern adaptations of traditional rainwater harvesting methods being carried out in India to conserve and store water include:

- **Rooftop Rainwater Harvesting:** Implemented widely, where rainwater from roofs is funneled through PVC pipes into filtration units before being stored in underground reservoirs or tankas, aiding in both direct use and groundwater recharge. *(1 M)*
- **Reviving and Upgrading Traditional Johads:** In Rajasthan, old johads are being renovated and integrated with modern engineering to enhance water storage capacity and recharge groundwater, supporting agriculture and local needs. *(1 M)*
- **Community-led Initiatives:** Example, Gendathur village in Karnataka, where residents collectively install rooftop harvesting systems, demonstrating a scalable model for water sustainability. *(1 M)*
- **Incorporating Technology in Irrigation:** Modern adaptations like drip irrigation from harvested water are being used to optimize water usage in agriculture. *(1 M)*
- **Public Awareness and Government Policies:** Promoting rainwater harvesting through educational programs and incentivizing its adoption via governmental schemes and regulations to ensure widespread implementation. *(1 M)*

Nailing the Right Answer

Lack of Clarity: Students may need to provide clearer explanations of how each modern adaptation works and its specific benefits. Adding more details on the mechanisms and outcomes of these methods could enhance the answer's clarity.

2. Explain how rooftop rainwater harvesting in semiarid regions of Rajasthan is carried out. ***(Re)***

OR

Write the features of the 'tankas built in the houses of Bikaner, Phalodi and Barmer ***(Re)***

Ans. Rooftop rainwater harvesting is carried out in semi-arid regions of Rajasthan through:

(i) **Collection System:** Homes in regions like Bikaner and Barmer collect rainwater from rooftops using PVC pipes, adapting traditional methods for modern needs. *(1 M)*

(ii) **Filtration Process:** The collected water is filtered through layers of sand and bricks, removing contaminants to ensure it is suitable for storage and use. *(1 M)*

(iii) **Storage in Tankas:** The filtered water is directed into underground tanks known as 'tankas'. These tankas are traditionally large, built within the main house or courtyard. *(1 M)*

(iv) **Non-collection of Initial Rainfall:** Initially, the first spell of rain is not collected to ensure roof and pipes are cleaned naturally. This maintains the purity of water collected subsequently. *(1 M)*

(v) **Utilization and Recharge:** The stored water is used during dry periods, and excess water helps in recharging the groundwater, making this a sustainable approach to water conservation in arid regions. *(1 M)*

OR

Ans. Five features of tankas built in the houses of Bikaner, Phalodi, and Barmer:

(i) **Large Capacity:** Tankas can be as large as a room, with some measuring up to 6.1 meters deep, 4.27 meters long, and 2.44 meters wide, suitable for storing significant amounts of rainwater. *(1 M)*

(ii) **Construction and Location:** They are traditionally constructed underground within the main house or the courtyard, integrating seamlessly with the house's structure. *(1 M)*

(iii) **Rooftop Connection:** These tankas are connected to the house's rooftops through pipes, allowing rainwater from the roofs to be directly channeled into them. *(1 M)*

(iv) **Initial Rain Rejection:** The first rain is not collected to clean debris and impurities from the collection surfaces. *(1 M)*

(v) **Usage:** The collected 'palar pani' is pure and mainly used for drinking during dry periods. *(1 M)*

3. Kushagra belongs to a rural family in arid Rajasthan. His community faces significant challenges in accessing clean water, primarily due to the region's dry climate and infrequent rainfall. The local government has introduced a rainwater harvesting project to help alleviate water scarcity. He and his family decided to implement this system in their home.

Explain how rainwater harvesting in Rajasthan adapts to its arid and semi-arid conditions and its impact on local households. ***(Ap)***

Ans. The adaptability of rainwater harvesting to arid and semi-arid conditions and its impact can be understood by the following points:

(i) **Customized Collection Systems:** In arid Rajasthan, families often construct rooftop rainwater harvesting systems where rainwater from roofs is channeled through pipes into underground tanks or **'tankas'** for storage. Other structures like **khadins** and **Johads** are also used in rain water harvesting. *(1 M)*

(ii) **Long-term Storage:** These underground 'tankas' are specifically designed to store water for long periods, ensuring a reliable supply during the prolonged dry seasons typical of the region. *(1 M)*

(iii) **Improving Water Quality:** Stored rainwater is generally cleaner and safer for consumption compared to the often saline or fluoride-contaminated groundwater in Rajasthan. *(1 M)*

(iv) **Reducing Dependence:** By harvesting rainwater, families reduce their dependence on distant water sources and erratic government supply, gaining autonomy over their water needs. *(1 M)*

(v) **Enhancing Livelihoods:** Access to consistent water supplies supports home gardening and small-scale agriculture, improving food security and family income. *(1 M)*

MISCELLANEOUS EXERCISE

Multiple Choice Questions (1 M)

1. Imagine a village in rural India where residents primarily rely on wells and local ponds for their daily water needs, often leading to waterborne diseases due to contamination. Recently, the government initiated the Jal Jeevan Mission in this village. Analyze and select how the implementation of the Jal Jeevan Mission could transform the lives of the villagers. *(Un)*

(a) It increases the villagers' reliance on traditional water sources.
(b) It provides each household with a reliable supply of clean drinking water.
(c) It encourages the purchase of expensive bottled water.
(d) It necessitates the reduction of water usage by villagers.

2. A small community in the valleys of the Himalayas, which is to be affected by the upcoming construction of a hydroelectric dam. This project is expected to provide significant benefits in terms of energy and water supply but will displace the local population and impact their traditional way of life. As a member of the local government's planning committee, you have been assigned to propose strategies to manage the social impacts of this dam construction effectively. Which approach would be the most ethical and sustainable to ensure that the community does not suffer due to these changes? *(Cr)*

(a) Increase the height of the dam to generate more electricity, disregarding the increase in the number of displaced families.
(b) Implement a comprehensive rehabilitation program that includes fair compensation, housing, and job training for displaced families to ensure they benefit from the dam.
(c) Build additional dams in the region to stimulate economic growth, hoping that the community will eventually benefit from increased job opportunities.
(d) Focus solely on the economic gains from the dam, ignoring the opposition from local communities and any social impacts.

3. Most farmers own wells and tube-wells in their farms for irrigation to increase their produce, what adverse effect can this have? *(Un)*

(a) Falling groundwater levels, adversely affecting water availability
(b) Imbalance in minerals for the soil
(c) Unequal distribution of water
(d) Could be technical defaults

4. Raj is a student who recently visited the Sutlej-Beas River basin for a school project. During his visit, he learned about the historical and modern purposes of dams. His group has been tasked to prepare a presentation that evaluates both the benefits and the environmental impact of dam construction. *(Un)*

Identify the correct statements based on the above scenario:

Statement-I: The primary purpose of building dams in ancient India was for irrigation only.

Statement-II: Modern dams serve multiple purposes including recreation and inland navigation.

Statement-III: Jawaharlal Nehru referred to dams as the economy boosters of modern India.

Statement-IV: Dams have no impact on the natural flow and sedimentation of rivers.

(a) Statement-I & Statement-II are correct
(b) Statement-I & Statement-III are correct
(c) Statement-I & Statement-IV are correct
(d) Statement-I, II & III are correct

5. What are the important things to do to prevent degradation of our natural ecosystems? *(Un)*

(a) Urbanization
(b) Industrialization
(c) Conserve and manage our water resources, to safeguard ourselves from health hazards
(d) Modem agriculture

6. You are an environmental researcher conducting a field study in western Rajasthan. You've observed that many villages now rely heavily on the Indira Gandhi Canal for their water needs, a shift from their traditional rainwater harvesting methods. As part of your research, you aim to evaluate the broader impacts of this shift on local water management strategies.

Based on your observations and interactions with the local community, which of the following conclusions best reflects the impact of the Indira Gandhi Canal on traditional water harvesting practices in the area? *(An)*

(a) The canal has enhanced the effectiveness and reliability of traditional water harvesting practices.
(b) The introduction of canal water has not altered the community's reliance on traditional rainwater harvesting.
(c) There has been a noticeable decline in the practice of traditional rainwater harvesting due to the availability of canal water.
(d) The community has transitioned entirely to using water from industrial sources, abandoning traditional methods.

7. In Shillong, a city known for its heavy rainfall, residents are surprisingly facing water shortages. As a geography consultant for the city council, you have been asked to propose a sustainable solution to address this paradox. Which of the following strategies would you recommend to ensure a steady supply of water throughout the year, especially during dry periods? **(Ap)**

(*a*) Implement flood control measures to prevent water runoff.

(*b*) Establish rooftop rainwater harvesting systems to collect and store rainwater.

(*c*) Introduce soil erosion control programs to preserve water quality.

(*d*) Develop groundwater recharge projects to increase water table levels.

8. Agricultural fields which are used as rainfed storage structures are called **(Re)**

(*a*) Cool (*b*) Khadins/Johads

(c) Recharge pits (*d*) None of the above

9. What is a barrier across flowing water that obstructs, directs or retards the flow, often creating a reservoir, lake or impoundment? **(Re)**

(*a*) Canal (*b*) Embankment

(c) Dam (*d*) Lake

10. Which of the following rivers is not having any multipurpose river project? **(Re)**

(*a*) Satluj-Beas (*b*) Mahanadi

(c) Narmada (*d*) Yamuna

11. In a scenario, the government plans to construct a new dam in the arid region of Kutch, which frequently experiences severe droughts and floods. The project, named "Kutch Harmony Dam" is designed to serve multiple purposes to address the region's unique challenges. As an environmental consultant tasked with assessing the project's alignment with Integrated Water Resources Management (IWRM) principles, which feature of the "Kutch Harmony Dam" project would best demonstrate these principles? **(Ev)**

(*a*) Prioritizing the dam primarily for urban domestic water supply without additional uses.

(*b*) Designing the dam to support hydroelectric power generation, irrigation for agriculture, and effective flood management controls.

(*c*) Limiting the dam's use to enhance agricultural output through irrigation alone.

(*d*) Building the dam without environmental impact assessments to expedite construction.

12. Which dam integrates conservation of water with flood control? **(Un)**

(*a*) Sutluj-Beas river basin (*b*) Bhakra-Nangal project

(c) Hirakud project (*d*) Tehri Dam

13. Why did Jawahar lal Nehru call dams the temples of India? **(Un)**

(*a*) They were multipurpose in nature

(*b*) Irrigation became better

(*c*) development of agriculture and the village economy with rapid industrialisation and growth of the urban economy

(*d*) Hydel power became ample

14. Which one of the following statements is not an argument in favour of multi-purpose river projects? **(Un)**

(*a*) Multi-purpose projects bring water to those areas which suffer from water scarcity.

(*b*) Multi-purpose projects by regulating water flow help to control floods.

(*c*) Multi-purpose projects lead to large-scale displacements and loss of livelihood.

(*d*) Multi-purpose projects generate electricity for our industries and our homes.

15. Find the odd one out from the given options? **(An)**

(*a*) Narmada (*b*) Ganga

(*c*) Mettur (*d*) Yamuna

16. Arrange the following projects from North to South? **(An)**

(*a*) Salal, Kota, Koyna, Mettur

(*b*) Kota, Koyna, Salal, Mettur

(*c*) Koyna, Mettur, Kota, Salal

(*d*) Mettur, Koyna, Kota, Salal

17. Which technique is shown in the image for conserving water? **(Re)**

(*a*) Watershed (*b*) Rainwater harvesting

(*c*) Rooftop saving (*d*) Saving water in umbrella

18. Consider the following statements **(Re)**

1. Rooftop rainwater harvesting is the most common practice in Shillong, Meghalaya

2. Rooftop harvesting was common across the towns and villages of the Thar.

3. Tamil Nadu is the first state in India which has made rooftop rainwater harvesting structure compulsory to all the houses across the state.

(*a*) 1 and 2 (*b*) 1 and 3

(*c*) 2 and 3 (*d*) 1, 2 and 3

Assertion and Reason (1 M)

Direction: The following questions consist of two statements – Assertion (A) and Reason (R). Answer these questions by selecting the appropriate option given below:

(*a*) Both A and R are true, and R is the correct explanation of A.

(*b*) Both A and R are true, but R is not the correct explanation of A.

(*c*) A is true, but R is false.

(*d*) A is false, but R is true.

1. **Assertion (A):** The availability of water resources varies over space and time.

   Reason (R): Availability of water resources help in storing water. ***(Un)***

2. **Assertion (A):** Dams are referred to as multipurpose projects.

   Reason (R): Dams are built for irrigation, electricity generation, flood control etc. ***(Re)***

3. **Assertion (A):** Groundwater is a highly overused resource.

   Reason (R): Groundwater is used for domestic and drinking purpose. ***(Un)***

4. **Assertion (A):** Water is a renewable resource.

   Reason (R): Freshwater is mainly obtained from surface run off and ground water that is continually being renewed. ***(Re)***

5. **Assertion (A):** Growing Population is the main reason for water scarcity.

   Reason (R): Irrigation from tube wells and canals is responsible for water scarcity. ***(An)***

6. **Assertion (R):** Water resources are essential for the survival and development of human beings.

   Reason (R): Water is required for various activities such as drinking, sanitation, agriculture, industry, and power generation. ***(Un)***

7. **Assertion (R):** Water scarcity is a major challenge faced by many regions in India.

   Reason (R): Uneven distribution of rainfall and overexploitation of water resources contribute to water scarcity in various parts of the country. ***(Un)***

8. **Assertion (R):** Sustainable management of water resources is crucial to ensure long-term availability and equitable distribution.

   Reason (R): Effective management practices like water conservation, rainwater harvesting, and efficient irrigation techniques help in optimizing water usage and reducing wastage. ***(Ap)***

9. **Assertion (A):** Pollution of water bodies poses a threat to both human health and ecosystem balance.

   Reason (R): Industrial effluents, untreated sewage, and agricultural runoff contribute to water pollution, affecting aquatic life and making water unfit for human consumption. ***(Un)***

10. **Assertion (A):** Integrated Water Resource Management (IWRM) aims to balance water usage for various sectors while preserving ecosystem integrity.

    Reason (R): IWRM considers the interconnectedness of water resources, promotes participatory decision-making, and emphasizes sustainable water management practices. ***(An)***

Subjective Questions

Very Short Answer Type Questions (2 M)

1. What is the importance of water resources? ***(Un)***
2. What are the main sources of freshwater? ***(Re)***
3. What is water scarcity? ***(Un)***
4. What is water conservation? ***(Un)***
5. What is water pollution? ***(Un)***
6. What is rainwater harvesting? ***(Un)***
7. What is groundwater depletion? ***(Un)***
8. What is the role of government in water resource management? ***(Un)***
9. How can wastewater treatment help in water conservation? ***(Ap)***
10. What are the challenges in implementing effective water resource management? ***(An)***
11. What is the role of rivers in water resource management? ***(Un)***
12. How does water availability impact ecosystems? ***(An)***

Short Answer Type Questions (3 M)

1. What are the consequences of water scarcity? ***(Un)***
2. How can governments address water scarcity? ***(Ap)***
3. What is the role of technology in addressing water scarcity? ***(An)***
4. How does climate change impact water scarcity? ***(An)***
5. What is the importance of public awareness in addressing water scarcity? ***(Un)***

Long Answer Type Questions (5 M)

1. Explain the concept of water scarcity and its causes. Discuss the impact of water scarcity on human life and suggest measures to overcome this problem. ***(An)***
2. Describe the various sources of water pollution. Discuss the harmful effects of water pollution on the environment and human health. Also, explain the methods to prevent water pollution. ***(An)***

3. Discuss the importance of water conservation. Explain different methods of water conservation that can be implemented at the individual and community levels. How can these methods help in sustainable water management? **(Ap)**

4. Explain the concept of rainwater harvesting. Discuss its significance in water conservation and sustainable development. Describe different techniques of rainwater harvesting and their benefits. **(Un)**

5. Describe the concept of watershed management. Explain the objectives and principles of watershed management. Discuss the role of community participation in successful watershed management. **(Un)**

6. Discuss the advantages and disadvantages of dams. Explain the various purposes served by dams and the potential negative impacts associated with their construction. Also, discuss alternative approaches to meet water demands without constructing large dams. **(An)**

Case Based Questions

Case Based-I

Read the source given below and answer the questions that follow: **(CBSE APQ, 2023)**

Given the abundance and renewability of water, it is difficult to imagine that we may suffer from water scarcity. The moment we speak of water shortages; we immediately associate it with regions having low rainfall or those that are drought prone. We instantaneously visualise the deserts of Rajasthan and women balancing many 'matkas' (earthen pots) used for collecting and storing water and travelling long distances to get water. True, the availability of water resources varies over space and time, mainly due to the variations in seasonal and annual precipitation, but water scarcity in most cases is caused by over-exploitation, excessive use and unequal access to water among different social groups.

(i) How do women collect water in Rajasthan? *(1 M)* **(Re)**

(ii) Why is water scarcity in most areas caused? *(1 M)* **(An)**

(iii) Do you think rainwater harvesting can help? Give reasons to justify your answer. *(2 M)* **(Ev)**

Case Based-II

Read the source given below and answer the following questions:

Hydraulic Structures in Ancient India

- In the first century B.C., Sringaverapura near Allahabad had a sophisticated water harvesting system channeling the flood water of the river Ganga.
- During the time of Chandragupta Maurya, dams, lakes and irrigation systems were extensively built.
- Evidences of sophisticated irrigation works have also been found in Kalinga, (Odisha), Nagarjunakonda (Andhra Pradesh), Bennur (Karnataka), Kolhapur (Maharashtra), etc.
- In the 11th Century, Bhopal Lake, one of the largest artificial lakes of its time was built.
- In the 14th Century, the tank in Hauz Khas, Delhi was constructed by Iltutmish for supplying water to Siri Fort area.

Source: Dying Wisdom, CSE, 1997.

(i) Analyze how the construction of dams and lakes during Chandragupta Maurya's time might have impacted the economic stability of local communities. *(1 M)* **(An)**

(ii) Considering the large-scale construction of dams and irrigation systems in ancient India, evaluate the potential environmental and social risks such projects might pose today. *(1 M)* **(Ev)**

(iii) Describe the economic significance of Bhopal Lake and the Hauz Khas tank in their respective eras. How did these structures contribute to the economic activities of the regions? *(2 M)* **(Un)**

Case Based-III

Read the given source and answer the questions that follow: **(CBSE, 2023)**

Rainwater Harvesting

Many thought that given the disadvantages and rising resistance against the multi purpose projects, water harvesting system was a viable alternative, both socioeconomically and environmentally. In ancient India, along with the sophisticated hydraulic structures, there existed an extraordinary tradition of water harvesting system. People had in-depth knowledge of rainfall regimes and soil types and developed wide ranging techniques to harvest rainwater, groundwater, river water and flood water in keeping with the local ecological conditions and their water needs. In hill and mountainous regions, people built diversion channels like the 'guls' or 'kuls' of the Western Himalayas for agriculture. 'Rooftop rainwater harvesting' was commonly practised to store drinking water, particularly in Rajasthan. In the flood plains of Bengal, people developed inundation channels to irrigate their fields. In arid and semi-arid regions, agricultural fields were converted into rain fed storage structures that allowed the water to stand and moisten the soil like the 'khadins' in Jaisalmer and 'Johads' in other parts of Rajasthan.

(i) Why is water harvesting system a viable alternative? *(1 M)* **(*Ev*)**

(ii) Describe the process of 'rooftop rainwater harvesting'. *(1 M)* **(*Un*)**

(iii) Mention any two methods adopted by ancient India for water conservation. *(2 M)* **(*Re*)**

Case Based-IV

Read the source given below and answer the following questions:

A dam is a barrier across flowing water that obstructs, directs or retards the flow, often creating a reservoir, lake or impoundment. "Dam" refers to the reservoir rather than the structure. Most dams have a section called a spillway or weir over which or through which it is intended that water will flow either intermittently or continuously. Dams are classified according to structure, intended purpose or height. Based on structure and the materials used, dams are classified as timber dams, embankment dams or masonry dams, with several subtypes. According to the height, dams can be categorised as large dams and major dams or alternatively as low dams, medium height dams and high dams.

(i) Considering the environmental, social, and economic factors, evaluate whether the construction of a new large dam in a densely populated river basin would be advisable. *(1 M)* **(*Ev*)**

(ii) What is meant by the term "spillway" in the context of dam construction, and why is it a critical feature? *(1 M)* **(*Un*)**

(iii) Analyze the benefits and drawbacks of multi-purpose projects like large dams, particularly focusing on their role in flood control and irrigation versus their social and environmental costs. *(2 M)* **(*An*)**

Map Based Questions

Features are marked by numbers in the given outline map of India. Identify these features with the help of the following information and write their correct on the lines marked in the map. **(*Re*)**

(i) A dam constructed across the Tungabhadra river. *(1 M)*

(ii) A dam constructed in Telangana. *(1 M)*

(iii) A dam constructed & across the Bhagirathi river. *(1 M)*

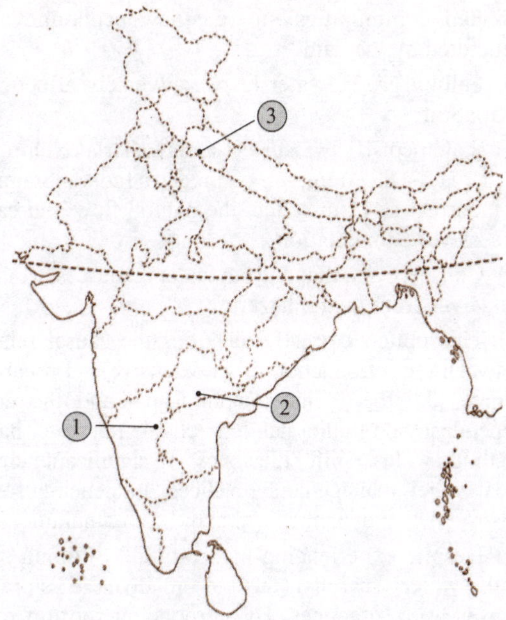

ANSWER KEYS

Multiple Choice Questions

1. (*b*)	**2.** (*b*)	**3.** (*a*)	**4.** (*a*)	**5.** (*c*)	**6.** (*a*)	**7.** (*b*)	**8.** (*b*)	**9.** (*c*)	**10.** (*d*)
11. (*b*)	**12.** (*c*)	**13.** (*c*)	**14.** (*c*)	**15.** (*c*)	**16.** (*a*)	**17.** (*b*)	**18.** (*d*)		

Assertion and Reason

1. (*d*)	**2.** (*a*)	**3.** (*a*)	**4.** (*a*)	**5.** (*b*)	**6.** (*c*)	**7.** (*a*)	**8.** (*a*)	**9.** (*a*)	**10.** (*b*)

HINTS & EXPLANATIONS

Multiple Choice Questions

1. (*b*) The Jal Jeevan Mission is designed to ensure that every rural household has a continuous supply of clean and potable piped water. This initiative aims to improve health standards by reducing the prevalence of waterborne diseases, thus enhancing the quality of life and promoting sustainable water usage practices in rural areas.
2. (*b*) This option not only addresses the immediate adverse effects of displacement caused by the dam construction but also provides a sustainable and ethical approach by ensuring the long-term welfare and integration of the affected communities into the new economic activities generated by the dam.
3. (*a*) Falling groundwater levels, adversely affecting water availability
4. (*a*) Statement-III is incorrect as Jawaharlal Nehru referred to dams as the 'temples of modern India'. Statement-IV is incorrect as Dams affect the natural flow and can cause excessive sedimentation.
5. (*c*) Conserve and manage our water resources, to safeguard ourselves from health hazards
6. (*c*) This option correctly identifies the causal relationship between the introduction of an extensive and reliable water source like the Indira Gandhi Canal and the decreased dependency on traditional, less reliable rainwater harvesting methods. This shift illustrates a significant change in local water management practices, influencing social and environmental dynamics within these communities.
7. (*b*) Despite experiencing high rainfall, Shillong struggles with water scarcity due to inadequate storage and conservation practices. By introducing rooftop rainwater harvesting, the city can capture excess rainfall during monsoons and store it for use during drier periods, thus ensuring a consistent water supply.
8. (*b*) Khadins/Johads
9. (*c*) Dam
10. (*d*) Yamuna
11. (*b*) Option (*b*) exemplifies the principles of Integrated Water Resources Management (IWRM) by ensuring that the dam serves various community needs—energy, agriculture, and disaster mitigation—thereby maximizing both economic and social welfare while aiming to sustain natural resources for future generations.
12. (*c*) Hirakud project
13. (*c*) Development of agriculture and the village economy with rapid industrialisation and growth of the urban economy
14. (*c*) Multi-purpose projects lead to large-scale displacements and loss of livelihood.
15. (*c*) Mettur
16. (*a*) Salal, Kota, Koyna, Mettur
17. (*b*) Rainwater harvesting
18. (*d*) 1, 2 and 3

Assertion and Reason

1. (*d*) A is true, but R is false
2. (*a*) Both A and R are true, and R is the correct explanation of A.
3. (*a*) Both A and R are true, and R is the correct explanation of A.
4. (*a*) Both A and R are true, and R is the correct explanation of A.
5. (*b*) A is true, but R is false
6. (*c*) This option correctly identifies the causal relationship between the introduction of an extensive and reliable water source like the Indira Gandhi Canal and the decreased dependency on traditional, less reliable rainwater harvesting methods. This shift illustrates a significant change in local water management practices, influencing social and environmental dynamics within these communities.
7. (*a*) Both A and R are true, and R is the correct explanation of A.
8. (*a*) Both A and R are true, and R is the correct explanation of A.
9. (*a*) Both A and R are true, and R is the correct explanation of A.
10. (*a*) Both A and R are true, and R is the correct explanation of A.

Subjective Questions

Very Short Answer Type Questions

1. The importance of water resources is two fold:
   (*i*) **Essential for life:** Water is crucial for drinking, cooking, and cleaning. It supports all forms of life. *(1 M)*
   (*ii*) **Supports agriculture and industry:** It is necessary for farming and industrial activities, impacting food and economic security. *(1 M)*
2. The main sources of freshwater are:
   - **Surface runoff:** This includes water from rivers and lakes, which collects as precipitation falls and flows over the land. *(1 M)*
   - **Groundwater:** Water that seeps down and accumulates underground in aquifers. It's continually renewed and recharged through the hydrological cycle. *(1 M).*
3. Water scarcity is caused by:
   - **Over-exploitation:** Using water faster than it can be replenished leads to shortages. *(1 M)*
   - **Unequal access:** Differences in availability among social groups, often caused by geographic and economic factors. *(1 M).*

4. Water conservation involves:
   - **Minimizing waste:** Using water efficiently and avoiding excess use. *(1 M)*
   - **Sustainable management:** Protecting water resources from pollution and overuse to ensure availability for future generations. *(1 M)*
5. Water pollution is caused by:
   - **Industrial waste:** Factories release pollutants into rivers, making the water hazardous for use. *(1 M)*
   - **Agricultural run-off:** Chemicals and fertilizers from fields seep into water bodies, contaminating them. *(1 M)*.
6. Rainwater harvesting is:
   - **Collection and storage:** Collecting rainwater from rooftops and other surfaces, storing it in tanks for later use. *(1 M)*
   - **Sustainable and economical:** Helps in reducing dependence on other water sources and conserves water. *(1 M)*.
7. Groundwater depletion is:
   - **Falling levels:** Excessive use of groundwater for irrigation and other needs causes water levels to fall. *(1 M)*
   - **Affects availability:** Leads to reduced water availability and food security for people. *(1 M)*.
8. The role of the government in water resource management involves:
   - **Ensuring supply:** Providing adequate and quality water to all citizens. *(1 M)*
   - **Regulating usage:** Managing water resources to prevent over-exploitation and ensure long-term availability. *(1 M)*.
9. Wastewater treatment helps in water conservation by:
   (i) **Recycling:** Cleaning used water so it can be reused, reducing the need for fresh water. *(1 M)*
   (ii) **Reducing pollution:** Prevents contaminated water from entering natural bodies, keeping them clean and usable. *(1 M)*
10. The challenges in implementing effective water resource management include:
    - **Over-exploitation and pollution:** Excessive use and contamination from industrial and agricultural activities. *(1 M)*
    - **Unequal access:** Disparities in water distribution among different social groups and regions. *(1 M)*
11. The role of rivers in water resource management includes:
    - **Supplying freshwater:** Rivers are a primary source of freshwater for domestic, agricultural, and industrial use. *(1 M)*
    - **Supporting ecosystems:** They help maintain natural landscapes and biodiversity. *(1 M)*
12. Water availability impacts ecosystems by:
    - **Supporting life:** Adequate water supports diverse plant and animal life, maintaining balance and biodiversity. *(1 M)*
    - **Influencing habitats:** Variability in water availability can create different habitats, affecting species distribution and ecosystem health. *(1 M)*

Short Answer Type Questions

1. The consequences of water scarcity are:
   - **Social impact:** Leads to unequal access to water, causing disparities among social groups. *(1 M)*
   - **Agricultural stress:** Over-exploitation for dry-season agriculture, leading to reduced water for food production. *(1 M)*
   - **Environmental degradation:** Depletion of water resources, affecting the balance and health of ecosystems. *(1 M)*
2. Governments can address water scarcity by:
   - **Regulating usage:** Implementing policies to manage water use and prevent over-exploitation. *(1 M)*
   - **Improving infrastructure:** Building dams, reservoirs, and treatment plants to enhance storage and supply. *(1 M)*
   - **Promoting conservation:** Encouraging water-saving practices and technologies among the public and industries. *(1 M)*
3. The role of technology in addressing water scarcity includes:
   - **Developing efficient irrigation methods:** Technologies like drip and sprinkler systems reduce water use in agriculture. *(1 M)*
   - **Water purification:** Advances in water treatment enable the use of recycled and desalinated water. *(1 M)*
   - **Monitoring and management:** Technology helps in better management of water resources through remote sensing and GIS. *(1 M)*
4. The climate change impacts water scarcity by:
   - **Altering precipitation patterns:** Leads to irregular rainfall, causing droughts in some areas and floods in others. *(1 M)*
   - **Increasing temperature:** Elevates evaporation rates, reducing water availability in lakes, rivers, and reservoirs. *(1 M)*
   - **Melting glaciers:** Initially increases water flow but eventually leads to a decrease in freshwater sources as glaciers retreat. *(1 M)*
5. The importance of public awareness in addressing water scarcity includes:
   - **Education:** Informing the public about the causes and effects of water scarcity leads to better water management. *(1 M)*
   - **Behavioral change:** Awareness encourages water-saving habits among individuals and communities. *(1 M)*
   - **Community involvement:** Active participation in local water conservation projects and initiatives. *(1 M)*

Long Answer Type Questions

1. Water scarcity is the lack of sufficient available water resources to meet the demands within a region. The main causes include overuse, pollution, and unequal distribution. This condition leads to several problems: *(1 M)*

The impact of water scarcity on human life is significant:

- **Health issues:** Limited access to clean water leads to hygiene problems and diseases. *(1 M)*
- **Agricultural problems:** Insufficient water for irrigation affects food production and can lead to hunger. *(1 M)*

Measures to overcome water scarcity:

- **Rainwater Harvesting:** Collect and store rainwater for use during dry periods. *(1 M)*
- **Water Conservation:** Educate the public on saving water and promote efficient usage. *(1 M)*

2. Water pollution originates from several sources:

- **Industrial waste:** Factories discharge pollutants directly into water bodies and Untreated sewage release introduces harmful pathogens. *(1 M)*
- **Agricultural runoff:** Excess fertilizers and pesticides wash into streams and rivers. *(1 M)*

Effects include:

- **Environmental damage:** Destroys aquatic habitats and decreases biodiversity. *(½ M)*
- **Human health risks:** Causes diseases like diarrhea and can contaminate drinking water. *(½ M)*

Prevention methods:

- **Waste treatment:** Industries should treat waste before discharge. *(1 M)*
- **Sustainable agriculture:** Use of less chemical fertilizers and more organic ones. *(½ M)*
- **Improved sewage systems:** Upgrade sewage treatment facilities to reduce contamination. *(½ M)*

Addressing these aspects can significantly reduce water pollution's impact on health and the environment.

3. Water conservation is crucial for sustaining life and preventing water scarcity. It involves various strategies:

- **At the individual level:** Use water-efficient appliances, fix leaks, and reduce unnecessary water use in daily activities. This reduces the personal consumption of water. *(½ M)*
- **At the community level:** Implement community rainwater harvesting systems, promote the reuse and recycling of water, and manage local water resources efficiently. Communities working together can significantly reduce overall water demand. *(1½ M)*

These conservation methods help in:

- **Ensuring sustainable water availability:** Guarantees water for future generations and maintains ecological balance. *(1 M)*
- **Preventing habitat destruction:** Reduces stress on natural water bodies and wildlife. *(½ M)*
- **Minimizing water-related conflicts:** Equitable distribution reduces disputes over water resources. *(½ M)*

Implementing these measures can lead to more sustainable water management and conservation efforts.

4. Rainwater harvesting involves collecting and storing rainwater for reuse, instead of allowing it to run off. *(1 M)*

It's significant for:

- **Water Conservation:** Reduces dependence on other water sources, conserving water. *(½ M)*
- **Reducing Soil Erosion:** By capturing runoff, it minimizes soil erosion and water pollution. *(½ M)*

Different techniques include:

- **Rooftop Harvesting:** Collecting rainwater from roofs. *(½ M)*
- **Surface Runoff Harvesting:** Capturing rainwater from surfaces like roads and fields. *(½ M)*

Benefits:

- **Prevents Flooding and Erosion:** Captures runoff, reducing flood risk and soil erosion. *(1 M)*
- **Enhances Water Availability:** Increases the local water supply, especially in water-scarce regions. *(1 M)*

5. It involves managing the precipitation and resources in a specific watershed area to prevent degradation and to utilize the water effectively. *(1 M)*

Objectives include:

- **Preventing soil erosion:** Protecting the land within the watershed from erosion. *(½ M)*
- **Enhancing water quality:** Ensuring that the water within the watershed is clean and safe. *(½ M)*

Principles involve:

- Community participation involves locals in management, ensuring their needs and knowledge shape strategies and Integrated management combines this with considering soil, water, and activities for holistic solutions. *(1½ M)*

Community participation is crucial as it ensures:

- Community participation in watershed management enhances sustainability and effectiveness, as locals contribute valuable insights and commitment. Combining this with integrated approaches that consider all environmental aspects ensures successful conservation and management efforts. *(1½ M)*

6. Dams serve multiple purposes but also have disadvantages:

Advantages of Dams:

- **Water Storage:** Dams store water for domestic, agricultural, and industrial use. *(½ M)*
- **Hydroelectric Power:** Generate renewable energy, providing electricity to many areas. *(½ M)*

Disadvantages of Dams:

- **Ecological Damage:** Alter natural habitats, affecting flora and fauna. *(½ M)*
- **Displacement:** Local populations may be relocated, losing homes and livelihoods. *(½ M)*

Purposes Served:

- **Irrigation:** Supports agriculture by providing consistent water supply. *(½ M)*
- **Flood Control:** Helps in managing flood risks by regulating river flow. *(½ M)*
- **Negative Impacts:** Dams cause sediment buildup affecting water capacity and disrupt ecosystems, and they can displace communities, especially indigenous ones, from their ancestral lands. *(1 M)*

Alternative Approaches:

(*i*) **Rainwater Harvesting:** Collecting rainfall to use during dry periods. (½ M)

(*ii*) **Water Recycling:** Treating and reusing wastewater for various needs. (½ M)

These alternatives offer sustainable ways to meet water needs, reducing the environmental and social issues linked to large dams.

Case Based Questions

Case Based-I

(*i*) Women collected and stored water by balancing many 'matkas' (earthen pots) and travelling long distances to get water. (1 M)

(*ii*) Water scarcity is caused due to the variations in seasonal and annual precipitation, but water scarcity in most cases is caused by over-exploitation, excessive use and unequal access to water among different social groups. (1 M)

(*iii*) Yes, rain water harvesting can help as agricultural fields were converted into rain fed storage structures that allowed the water to stand and moisten the soil like the 'khadins' in Jaisalmer and 'Johads' in other parts of Rajasthan. 'Rooftop rainwater harvesting' was commonly practised to store drinking water, particularly in Rajasthan. (2 M)

Case Based-II

(*i*) The construction of these hydraulic structures would have enabled more consistent and widespread irrigation, leading to improved agricultural yields and the cultivation of larger areas. This not only boosted food production but also supported local economies by increasing employment opportunities in the construction and maintenance of these structures, as well as in farming. (1 M)

(*ii*) The potential environmental and social risks associated with large-scale dam and irrigation projects today include displacement of communities, loss of biodiversity, and alteration of natural water courses which can lead to ecological imbalances. (1 M)

(*iii*) Bhopal Lake, constructed in the 11th century, was one of the largest artificial lakes of its time and significantly contributed to the irrigation and water supply in the region, which in turn supported agriculture and local livelihoods. (1 M)

Similarly, the tank in Hauz Khas, built in the 14th century, played a crucial role in supplying water to the Siri Fort area in Delhi. It not only provided the necessary water for domestic use and irrigation but also helped in maintaining ecological balance and supporting the local economy through increased agricultural outputs. (1 M)

Case Based-III

(*i*) The rainwater harvesting system is a viable alternative due to its socio-economic and environmental benefits. (1 M)

(*ii*) 'Rooftop Rainwater Harvesting' involves collecting rainwater from rooftops and storing it for various purposes. (1 M)

(*iii*) Two methods adopted by ancient India for water conservation include building diversion channels in hilly and mountainous regions and developing inundation channels in flood plains. (2 M)

Case Based-IV

(*i*) Constructing a new large dam in a densely populated river basin might not be advisable. Key criteria to consider include environmental impacts, such as habitat destruction and changes in the water table; social impact, particularly the displacement of communities; and economic impact, like the cost ofconstruction versus potential benefits from hydroelectric power and irrigation. (1 M)

(*ii*) A spillway is a structure built into a dam to provide a controlled path for excess water to pass through safely. It is critical because it helps prevent overtopping of the dam during high-flow periods, which can cause dam failure and downstream flooding. (1 M)

(*iii*) Multi-purpose projects like large dams offer several benefits, including flood control, irrigation, hydroelectric power, and water supply for domestic and industrial uses. (1 M)

However, they also carry substantial social and environmental costs. Dams often lead to the displacement of local communities and disrupt wildlife habitats. They can also cause sediment build-up, which affects river ecosystems downstream and leads to reduced water quality. The drawbacks sometimes outweigh the benefits, especially when alternative, less disruptive methods of water management and power generation are available. (1 M)

Map Based Questions

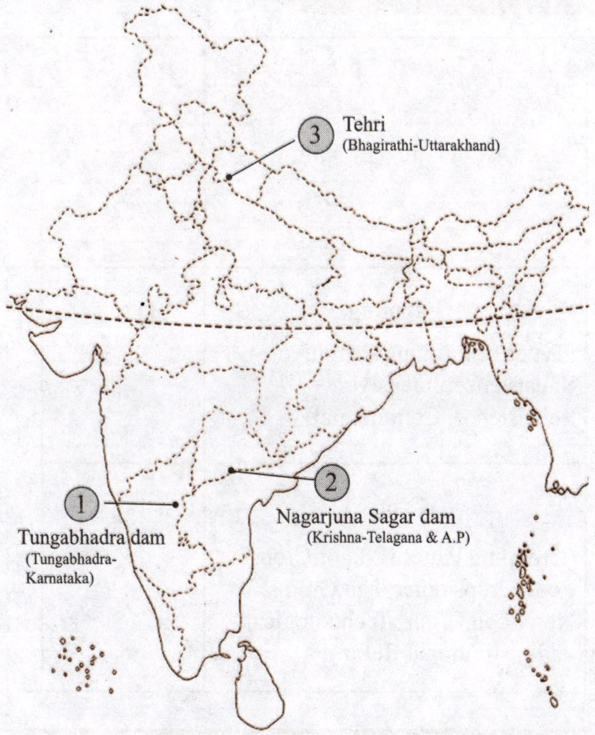

AGRICULTURE

4

"Agriculture is our wisest pursuit, because it will in the end contribute most to real wealth, good morals, and happiness."
—Thomas Jefferson

SYLLABUS & WEIGHTAGE

List of Concept Names	Years					
	2020	2021	2022	2023	2024	2025
Farming (Types of Farming-Primitive Subsistence, Intensive Subsistence, Commercial)	1 Q (5 M)	Exam not Conducted	–	1 Q (2 M)	1 Q (5 M)	1 Q (1 M)
Crops (Cropping Pattern-Major Crops, Food Crops other than Grains, Non Food Crops, Technological and Institutional Reforms)	–		–	–	1 Q (1 M)	1 Q (5 M)

CONCEPT MAP

To Access One Shot Revision Video Scan This QR Code

Agriculture

Subsistence Farming

Subsistence farming is a traditional method where families grow food for their own use with simple tools and local labour.

Types of Farming

CBSE 2024, 2023, 2020

- **Primitive Subsistence Farming:**
  Crops are grown for the farmer's family using basic tools and slash-and-burn techniques.
- **Intensive Subsistence Farming:**
  In densely populated areas, farmers maximize food production on small plots with irrigation and fertilizers.
- **Commercial Farming:**
  Modern technology is used to grow large quantities of crops for sale, like rice in Haryana and Punjab.

Jhumming Agriculture

Trees are cut and burned to clear land for crops, then after a few years, farmers move to new areas. This practice is common in Northeast India.

Jhumming farming is mostly done in some northeast parts of India.

Slash and Burn

CBSE 2025

- Jhumming-Assam, Meghalaya, Mizoram and Nagaland, Pamlou- Manipur, Dipa-Chhattishgarh
- 'Milpa' in Mexico and Central America, 'Conuco' in Venzuela, 'Roca' in Brazil, 'Masole' in Central Africa, 'Ray' in Vietnam

Cropping Pattern

CBSE 2025, 2024

The Cropping pattern in India involves three main seasons: Rabi, Kharif, and Zaid

Rabi Crops

CBSE 2024

Winter-grown crops like wheat and mustard, harvested in the summer.

Key Regions

Punjab, Haryana, Himachal Pradesh, Jammu and Kashmir, Uttarakhand, Uttar Pradesh.

Harvesting Period: April to June

Kharif Crops

CBSE 2024

Crops planted at the start of the rainy season, such as rice and maize, harvested in the fall.

Key Regions

Assam, West Bengal, Coastal Odisha, Andhra Pradesh, Telangana, Tamil Nadu, Kerala, Maharashtra, Uttar Pradesh, Bihar

Harvesting Period: September to October

Zaid Season

CBSE 2024

A brief farming period between Rabi and Kharif seasons for crops like watermelon and cucumber.

Key Regions

Various parts of India, mainly in northern and central regions.

Harvesting Period: Before Kharif season

Non-Food Crops

CBSE 2024

These are crops grown not for consumption but for other purposes such as manufacturing and industry.

Examples include cotton, jute, and oil seeds.

Harvesting Period: April to June

Food Grains

CBSE 2025, 2024

Staple crops such as rice, wheat, millets, and pulses, consumed as primary food sources.

1 FARMING

NCERT Definitions (Commonly asked in 1 mark)

- **Subsistence Farming:** Subsistence Farming is a ***traditional farming*** method where families grow food just for themselves, using simple tools and local labour.

Fig: Subsistance Farming.

- **Primitive Subsistence Farming:** A type of farming where crops are grown for the ***farmer's family needs***. It's done with simple tools and methods. Land is cleared by slashing and burning plants.
- **Intensive Subsistence Farming:** This farming happens where lots of people live. Farmers work hard to grow as much food as possible ***on small lands using*** man-made irrigation and fertilizers.

Fig: Intensive Subsistence Farming.

- **Commercial Farming:** This type of farming ***uses modern technology*** to grow large amounts of crops, which are then sold for money. Examples: Rice is commercial in Haryana and Punjab, but subsistence in Odisha.
- **Jhumming agriculture:** This is a way of farming where people ***cut down trees and burn*** them to clear land for growing crops. After using the land for a few years, they move to a new area. This kind of farming is mostly done in some northeast parts of India.

Fig: Jhumming agriculture.

- **Plantation Agriculture:** This is when big farms grow ***only one type of crop***, like tea or coffee, using lots of workers. The crops are usually sent away to be made into products.

Important Facts

01 Two-thirds of India's population engages in agriculture, producing most of the country's food and raw materials for industries.

02 India exports agricultural products such as tea, coffee, and spices.

03 '***Slash and burn***' agriculture, also known as Jhumming, involves moving to a new land when the current one loses fertility.

04 In India, 'slash and burn' agriculture is called different names in different states: Jhumming in the ***Northeast***, ***Bewar in Madhya Pradesh***, and ***Podu in Andhra Pradesh***.

05 Globally, similar practices Salsh and burn are called ***Milpa in Mexico***, ***Conuco in Venezuela***, ***Roca in Brazil***, and ***Ladang in Indonesia***.

Classification

Classification of farming systems in India		
Farming System	**Description**	**Names in India**
Primitive Subsistence Farming	Small scale, with primitive tools, depends on natural rainfall and soil fertility, involves family labour	Jhumming in Assam, Meghalaya; Bewar in Madhya Pradesh; Podu in Andhra Pradesh; Pamlou in Manipur
Intensive Subsistence Farming	Practiced in densely populated areas, involves high labour and inputs like fertilizers for more produce	Common in states with high population pressure like Uttar Pradesh, Punjab
Commercial Farming	Uses modern technology and inputs like HYV seeds, aimed at producing crops for sale	Rice in Haryana and Punjab; Plantation crops like tea in Assam and coffee in Karnataka
Plantation Farming	Single crop farming, large-scale, capital intensive, involves migrant labour	Tea in Assam and North Bengal; Rubber, coffee in Kerala and Karnataka

Difference Between

Subsistence Farming Vs. Commercial Farming		
Basis for Comparison	**Subsistence Farming**	**Commercial Farming**
Meaning	Farming practice in which crops are raised for personal consumption, it is known as subsistence farming	Farming practice, in which the farmer grows crops for the purpose of trade, it is called commercial farming
Land size	Small plot of land	Large plot of land
Labour type	Family members	Hired workers
Capital cost	Low capital input	High capital input
Types of fertilisers	Natural fertilisers	Chemical fertilisers
Tools/machines	Traditional tools/machines	High technology tools/machines
Output	For own use	For sale

Subsistence Farming

Commercial Farming

Primitive Subsistence Farming Vs. Intensive Subsistence Farming		
Feature	**Primitive Subsistence Farming**	**Intensive Subsistence Farming**
Tools	Primitive tools (hoe, dao)	Advanced tools, biochemical inputs
Land Size	Small patches	Small to moderate fields
Labour	Family/community	Family, very labour-intensive
Dependence on Nature	High (rely on monsoon)	Less (use of irrigation)
Soil Fertility	Shift cultivation	Use fertilizers
Productivity	Low	Higher
Objective	Food for family	Food for family, some surplus
Output	For own use	For sale

Real Life Application Based Questions

1. Why is rice grown as a commercial crop in Punjab different from its cultivation in Odisha?

Ans. In Punjab, rice cultivation is commercial due to extensive irrigation, mechanization, and the use of high-yielding varieties, aiming for profit and market supply.

In contrast, in Odisha, rice is primarily grown as a subsistence crop, relying on rainfall and traditional farming methods, primarily for local consumption and sustenance.

2. Why is primitive subsistence farming still practiced in some areas of India despite its lower productivity compared to modern agricultural techniques?

Ans. Primitive subsistence farming is still practiced in some areas of India for several reasons based on the provided document:

- **Traditional Approach:** It's deeply rooted in certain cultures and traditions.
- **Family Labour:** Utilizes family/community labour, making it cost-effective.
- **Low Investment:** Requires minimal investment in tools and technology.
- **Environmental Adaptation:** Relies on natural rainfall and soil fertility, suitable for specific environmental conditions.
- **Soil Fertility:** Allows soil fertility to replenish naturally over time through shifting cultivation methods like Jhumming.
- **Self-Sufficiency:** Aimed at meeting the needs of the farmer's family, not commercial profit.

3. How do farmers increase their yield in Intensive Subsistence Farming despite having small landholdings?

Ans. Farmers increase their yield in Intensive Subsistence Farming despite having small landholdings through:

- **High labour input:** Using more labour to intensively cultivate small plots.
- **Biochemical inputs:** Utilizing high doses of biochemical inputs and irrigation for higher production.
- **Improved farming techniques:** Implementing better farming methods and utilizing high-yielding variety seeds.
- **Improved seeds:** Utilizing high-yielding and disease-resistant crop varieties.

4. How does the high population density influence the practice of intensive subsistence farming in India?

Ans. High population density influences the practice of intensive subsistence farming in India through:

- **Small landholdings:** larger population leads to smaller land parcels for farming.
- **Greater labour utilization:** High population provides more labour, enabling intensive farming.
- **Increased demand:** Higher population density raises the demand for food, pushing for greater yields.
- **Resource strain:** More people lead to increased strain on water and soil, requiring efficient use.

Myth Buster

❒ **Myth: Primitive subsistence farming uses a lot of chemical fertilizers and pesticides.**

Fact: This type of farming relies on monsoon, natural fertility of the soil, and is practiced with primitive tools without modern inputs like fertilizers or pesticides.

❒ **Myth: Commercial farming is always sustainable and environmentally friendly.**

Fact: Commercial farming uses modern inputs for higher yields, but its focus on single-crop plantations can lead to soil degradation and biodiversity loss, making it not always sustainable.

❒ **Myth: All types of farming in India fully utilize modern agricultural technologies.**

Fact: Despite technological advances, many Indian regions still depend on traditional farming and monsoon rains, showing varied adoption of modern methods.

Scan Me for Detailed Explanations

COMPETENCY BASED SOLVED EXAMPLES

Multiple Choice Questions (1 M)

1. Rajesh, a farmer in the northeastern region of India, practices a traditional form of agriculture known as 'slash and burn'. He clears a new patch of forest every few years, cultivates it for a period, and then allows it to lie fallow to recover its fertility. How does Rajesh's method of farming impact the sustainability of his agricultural practices and the local ecosystem? *(Ev)*

(*a*) It enhances long-term soil fertility by continuous cultivation.

(*b*) It reduces the need for manual labor.

(*c*) It allows soil fertility to recover through natural processes when land is left fallow.

(*d*) It increases biodiversity through the introduction of new crops.

2. In a small village in central India where farmers practice primitive subsistence farming. This year, the monsoon rains arrived late, posing a significant challenge for the local farmers who depend solely on these rains for their crops. Analyze how the delay in monsoon affects the farming practices and livelihood of these farmers. *(An)*

(*a*) It encourages the adoption of advanced irrigation technologies.

(*b*) It leads to an increased use of drought-resistant crop varieties.

(*c*) It creates water shortages, impacting crop growth and threatening food security.

(*d*) Farmers use this time to take vacations due to the delayed farming season.

3. Identify the crop with the help of the following information and choose the correct option. *(Re)* **(CBSE, 2023)**

(*i*) This is the staple food crop.

(*ii*) This is a Kharif crop.

(*iii*) It requires high temperature and high humidity.

(*iv*) It requires above 100 cm of annual rainfall.

(*a*) Wheat (*b*) Maize

(*c*) Rice (*d*) Jowar

4. **In 2010-11, around ________ of the total workforce was employed by the farm sector, which makes more than half of the Indian population dependent on agriculture for sustenance.** *(Re)*

(*a*) 85 % (*b*) 40 %

(*c*) 52 % (*d*) 62 %

5. **In a scenario, three states of India- Haryana, Punjab, and Odisha are considered. There are different approaches to rice farming in Haryana, Punjab, and Odisha. why is rice considered a commercial crop in states like Haryana and Punjab, but not in Odisha?** *(Un)*

(*a*) Rice cultivation is banned in Odisha

(*b*) Rice does not require irrigation in Odisha

(*c*) Market-oriented production in Haryana and Punjab

(*d*) Rice is not consumed in Odisha

6. **Dr. Rao, an agricultural scientist, is tasked with evaluating the suitability of various Indian states for expanding bajra cultivation. Given the specific soil preferences of bajra, which state would Dr. Rao find most suitable for recommending large-scale bajra farming projects?** *(An)*

(*a*) Punjab, with its fertile alluvial plains.

(*b*) Rajasthan, known for its sandy soils and shallow black soil regions.

(*c*) Kerala, due to its humid tropical climate.

(*d*) West Bengal, given its predominantly clayey soil.

7. **A farmer named Rajesh is considering expanding his crop production to include maize on his farm near the Ganges River. He is aware that temperature and soil type are critical for the success of the crop. Given the typical conditions in this region during the growing season and the characteristics of soil, which of the following options should Rajesh choose for the best maize cultivation?** *(Ap)*

(*a*) 10°C to 15°C in sandy soil

(*b*) 21°C to 27°C in old alluvial soil

(*c*) 30°C to 35°C in clayey soil

(*d*) 18°C to 24°C in loamy soil

Assertion and Reason (1 M)

Direction: The following questions consist of two statements – Assertion (A) and Reason (R). Answer these questions by selecting the appropriate option given below:

(*a*) Both A and R are true, and R is the correct explanation of A.

(*b*) Both A and R are true, but R is not the correct explanation of A.

(*c*) A is true, but R is false

(*d*) A is false, but R is true.

1. **Ravi is a young student from a rural area who notices that his family's farm requires a lot of manual labor and frequent watering to produce enough crops for their needs. Despite working hard, they use simple tools and often face challenges like droughts and soil depletion. Ravi's friend, who lives in another region, mentions that they use modern techniques like HYV seeds and chemical fertilizers, requiring less labor but more technical knowledge and investment. Based on Ravi's observations and the description of his friend's farm, consider the following question and provide answer:**

Assertion (A): Intensive subsistence farming is highly labor-intensive.

Reason (R): This type of farming uses high doses of biochemical inputs and irrigation for higher production. *(Un)*

2. **Assertion (A):** Cooperatives play an important role in Indian agriculture.

Reason (R): Cooperatives provide farmers with access to credit, markets, and inputs such as seeds and fertilizers. *(Un)*

3. **Assertion (A):** Indian farmers should diversify their cropping patterns from cereals to high value crops.

Reason (R): This will increase income and reduce environmental degradation simultaneously. *(Un)* **(CBSE, 2022)**

4. **Assertion (A):** Small-scale farmers in India face several challenges such as lack of access to credit and markets.

Reason (R): Small-scale farmers have abundance resources and often rely on traditional farming methods that are less productive than modern techniques. *(An)*

5. **Assertion (A):** Agro-forestry is a sustainable farming method that benefits both farmers and the environment.

Reason (R): Agro-forestry involves growing trees along with crops or livestock, which helps to improve soil health, reduce erosion, and provide additional sources of income for farmers. *(Un)*

Subjective Questions

Very Short Answer Type Questions (1 or 2 M)

1. **By which name is specialized cultivation of fruits and vegetables known?** *(Un)*

Ans. Horticulture refers to the specialized cultivation of fruits, vegetables, and flowers. *(1 M)*

It aims at enhancing yield, quality, and nutritional value, significantly contributing to dietary needs and economic gains. *(1 M)*

2. **Describe "Jhum cultivation"?** *(Un)*

Ans. **Jhum cultivation** involves clearing forest land, burning the vegetation, and planting crops on the cleared land. *(1 M)*

Practiced mainly in **northeast India** (Assam, Meghalaya, Mizoram, Nagaland), it's a form of **slash and burn agriculture**. *(1 M)*

3. **What soil is perfect for the growth of cashew nuts?** *(Un)*

Ans. Cashew nuts thrive in **red laterite soil,** which is well-drained and rich in iron oxide. *(1 M)*

Tamil Nadu, Andhra Pradesh, and Kerala are ideal regions due to this soil type, supporting cashew cultivation. *(1 M)*

4. **"Agriculture and industry move hand in hand." Support the statement with examples.** *(Un)* **(CBSE, 2023)**

Ans. Agriculture and industry are closely linked, as seen through the following examples:

(i) **Raw Material Supply:** Agriculture provides raw materials for various industries; for instance, cotton farming supports the textile industry, and sugarcane cultivation is crucial for the sugar industry. *(1 M)*

(ii) **Plantation and Industry:** Plantation agriculture, like tea and coffee, integrates with industry as these crops are processed in factories before reaching the market, illustrating a direct link between farming and industrial activities. *(1 M)*

Short Answer Type Questions (3 M)

1. **Imagine you are an agricultural policymaker in India. You've observed that in regions where intensive subsistence farming is prevalent, the size of land holdings has significantly reduced due to the 'right of inheritance,' leading to fragmented agricultural plots. Discuss the impact of the 'right of inheritance' on land-holding size in the context of Intensive Subsistence Farming.** *(An)*

Ans. The impact of the 'right of inheritance' on land-holding size is as follows:

(i) The 'right of inheritance' refers to the **legal process** where **land** is **divided** among **heirs**. *(1 M)*

(ii) It results in **fragmentation of land**, leading to smaller, less economical land-holding sizes. *(1 M)*

(iii) This fragmentation forces farmers to **extract maximum yield** from limited land, **increasing pressure** on **agricultural resources**. *(1 M)*

2. **You are a farmer in a rural part of India practicing traditional subsistence farming. Describe the tools and labor used in this type of farming and explain why its land productivity is considered low.** *(Un)*

Ans. Tools and labor used in traditional subsistence farming and land productivity in the region are as follows:

(i) **Tools and Labor:** Basic tools like hoes and digging sticks are used, with labor provided by family or the local community, making it labor-intensive with minimal technology. *(1 M)*

(ii) **Dependency on Natural Factors:** Relies on monsoon rains and soil's natural fertility, without modern aids like fertilizers or irrigation. *(1 M)*

(iii) **Low Productivity:** Lack of modern inputs leads to lower soil fertility and productivity compared to modern methods. *(1 M)*

3. **Explain any three institutional reforms taken for the development of Indian agriculture.** *(Un)* **(CBSE, 2023)**

Ans. Three institutional reforms for Indian agriculture:

(i) **Land Reforms:** Implemented post-Independence strategies like consolidation of holdings and abolition of zamindari to improve land productivity. *(1 M)*

(ii) **Green and White Revolutions:** Launched to enhance crop yields and milk production respectively, focusing on technology and innovation. *(1 M)*

(iii) **Financial Support:** Introduced crop insurance, Grameen banks, Kissan Credit Card (KCC), and other schemes to provide financial aid and insurance to farmers. *(1 M)*

4. **Highlight the distinctions between primitive subsistence farming and commercial farming.** *(Un)* **(CBSE, 2019)**

Ans. *(1 + 1 + 1 = 3 M)*

Feature	Primitive Subsistence Farming	Commercial Farming
Tools and Techniques	Utilizes primitive tools like hoes, dao, and relies on manual labor.	Employs modern inputs like HYV seeds, chemical fertilizers, and mechanized equipment.
Purpose and Scale	Aimed at sustaining the farmer's family; practiced on small patches of land.	Geared towards market production; involves large-scale operations.
Dependence on Natural Factors	Relies heavily on natural rainfall and soil fertility.	Uses irrigation and other technologies to reduce dependency on natural factors.

Topper Explanation

The differences between primitive subsistence farming and commercial farming are

PRIMITIVE SUBSITENCE FARMING	COMMERCIAL FARMING
(i) This kind of farming is done to grow crops so as to sustain the family of the farmer	This kind of farming is done to produce crops for selling in the market to earn good profit.
(ii) This is done using primitive tools like dao, digging stick with the help of family or community labour.	This is done using capital intensive tools and waged labourers
(iii) The farmer depends on natural fertility and rain, hence production is low.	The farmers use high doses of modern inputs like HYV seeds, fertilisers, pesticides. The yield is high

Long Answer Type Questions (5 M)

1. Define plantation agriculture. Explain any four characteristics of plantation agriculture. *(Re, Un)*

Ans. Plantation Agriculture is a type of commercial farming where a single type of crop is grown on a large area. The plantation has an interface of agriculture and industry, utilizing capital-intensive inputs with the help of migrant labourers. *(1 M)*

Characteristics include:

- **Single Crop Focus:** A large area is dedicated to a single crop, such as tea, coffee, rubber, sugarcane, or banana, ensuring high volume production. *(1 M)*
- **Capital Intensive:** Requires significant investment in machinery, fertilizers, and other inputs to ensure high productivity. *(1 M)*
- **Labour Intensive:** Employs a large number of workers, often migrant labour, due to the intensive nature of the work. *(1 M)*
- **Market Oriented:** The production is primarily for the market, not for local consumption. This necessitates a well-developed network of transport and communication to link plantations with processing industries and markets. *(1 M)*

2. Explain any five features of primitive subsistence agriculture in India. *(Un)*

Ans. Primitive Subsistence Agriculture in India, also known as "slash and burn" agriculture.

Five features of primitive subsistence agriculture in India are:

(i) **Dependence on Natural Resources:** This farming method thrives on monsoon rains and soil's natural fertility, avoiding chemical inputs, which influences both the timing and location of cultivation. *(1 M)*

(ii) **Manual Labour and Primitive Tools:** Utilizing rudimentary tools such as hoes and digging sticks, it predominantly relies on manual labour from families or communities for cultivation. *(1 M)*

(iii) **Shifting Cultivation Method:** Farmers adopt the slash and burn approach, transitioning to new lands as soil fertility wanes, thereby giving time for the previously used land to naturally recover. *(1 M)*

(iv) **Subsistence Crop Diversity:** Emphasizing a variety of crops for family consumption over commercial sales, it supports dietary diversity. *(1 M)*

(v) **Cultural Integration:** Far beyond mere agricultural tactics, these practices are woven into the fabric of local cultures, symbolizing a deep connection between communities and their natural surroundings. *(1 M)*

3. Describe any four geographical conditions required for the growth of tea. Mention the two major tea producing states of South India. *(Re)*

Ans. Tea is the main beverage crop of India. Four geographical conditions requirements for its growth are:

(i) **Climate:** Tea plants grow well in tropical and subtropical climate. Tea thrives well in a hot and humid climate. *(1 M)*

(ii) **Soil:** The soil requirement is deep fertile well drained soil which is rich in humus and organic matter. *(1 M)*

(iii) **Temperature:** Ideal temperature for the growth is 20° C to 30° C. *(1 M)*

(iv) **Rainfall:** 150 to 300 cm annual rainfall is required. High humidity and frequent showers evenly distributed throughout the year are good for rapid development of tender leaves. *(1 M)*

The two major tea producing states of south India are: ***Tamil Nadu, Kerala***. *(1 M)*

4. Why is agriculture called the backbone of Indian economy? Explain. *(Cr) (CBSE, 2022)*

Ans. Agriculture is called the backbone of the Indian economy for several reasons. The following are some of the reasons why:

(i) **Employment:** Agriculture is the primary source of employment for a large percentage of the Indian population. Around 50% of the Indian workforce is employed in the agricultural sector, making it the largest employer in the country. *(1 M)*

(ii) **Contribution to GDP:** Agriculture contributes significantly to the Indian GDP. It accounts for around 17-18% of the country's GDP. *(1 M)*

(iii) **Food security:** Agriculture provides food security to the Indian population. The country's population depends on the agricultural sector for food, and any fluctuations in agricultural output can have a significant impact on the food security of the country. *(1 M)*

(*iv*) **Export earnings:** Indian agriculture generates significant export earnings for the country. India is one of the largest exporters of agricultural products in the world, and agricultural exports account for a significant portion of the country's total export earnings. *(1 M)*

(*v*) **Rural development:** Agriculture is closely linked to the development of rural areas in the country. The growth of the agricultural sector can lead to the development of rural infrastructure, such as roads, irrigation facilities, and power supply, which can help improve the standard of living of rural communities. *(1 M)*

5. **Analyses the challenges faced by the farming community in India.** *(An)*

Ans. Challenges Faced by India's Farming Community.

(*i*) **Reliance on Erratic Monsoon:** A substantial segment of Indian agriculture depends on monsoon rains. Inconsistent rainfall affects crop production, undermining food security and farmer livelihoods. *(1 M)*

(*ii*) **Fragmented Land Holdings:** Inheritance practices result in fragmented farms, limiting efficiency and modernization, which hampers productivity significantly. *(1 M)*

(*iii*) **Access to Modern Inputs:** Many farmers struggle to access high-yielding seeds, fertilizers, and technology. This gap reduces crop yields and agricultural efficiency. *(1 M)*

(*iv*) **Financial Challenges:** High input costs, low crop prices, and limited credit access lead to farmer indebtedness and exploitation by middlemen. *(1 M)*

(*v*) **Climate Change Effects:** Climate shifts threaten agriculture, demanding adaptation that many farmers are unprepared for, affecting crop timing and productivity. *(1 M)*

These challenges necessitate integrated policies for technological, financial, and knowledge-based support to sustain agriculture and improve farmer welfare in India.

Nailing the Right Answer

Oversimplification of Challenges

Students might oversimplify the challenges faced by the farming community by not elaborating on the complexities and interconnections of issues like erratic monsoon, fragmented land holdings, access to modern inputs, financial challenges, and climate change effects.

2 CROPS

NCERT Definitions (Commonly asked in 1 mark)

- **Cropping pattern:** The Cropping pattern in India involves three main seasons: Rabi, Kharif, and Zaid.
- **Rabi Crops:** These are crops ***grown in the winter*** and harvested in the summer, like wheat and mustard.
- **Kharif Crops:** Crops grown with the ***beginning of the rainy season,*** like rice and maize, and harvested in fall season.
- **Zaid Season:** This is a short farming season in ***between the Rabi and kharif seasons,*** during which crops like watermelon and cucumber are grown.
- **Green Revolution:** A time when agriculture in India changed a lot because of new methods and technology, leading to more food being grown.
- **White Revolution:** This was a big ***increase in milk production*** in India, also known as Operation Flood.
- **Bhoodan-Gramdan Movement:** A movement led ***by Vinoba Bhave*** where landowners gave parts of their land to the poor, making it a non-violent land reform effort.
- **Non-Food Crops:** These are crops grown not for consumption but for other purposes such as manufacturing and industry. Examples include cotton, jute, and oil seeds.
- **Food Grains:** These are ***staple crops*** consumed as the primary food source, including rice, wheat, millets, and pulses.

Important Facts

01 ***Kharif crops*** such as paddy and cotton grow with monsoon rains and are harvested in autumn or fall season. Rice, a kharif crop, needs ***temperatures above* 25°C** and over **100 cm *annual rainfall***.

02 The ***Zaid season*** fills the gap ***between Rabi and kharif*** with crops like watermelon and cucumber.

03 ***Wheat*** requires a cool growing season, **50-75 cm *of rainfall***, and is a staple in North-West India.

04 India, the ***largest pulse producer,*** cultivates crops like ***tur*** and ***moong*** which also enrich the soil.

05 ***Sugarcane*** prefers a hot, humid climate, significant rainfall, and is ***extensively grown*** in ***Uttar Pradesh*** and ***Maharashtra***.

06 ***Cotton*** needs ***high temperature, light rainfall,*** and is a important cash crop affecting the textile industry.

Classification

Classification of Cropping Season in India				
Season	**Sowing Period**	**Harvesting Period**	**Major Crops**	**Key Regions**
Rabi	October to December	April to June	Wheat, Barley, Peas, Gram, Mustard	Punjab, Haryana, Himachal Pradesh, Jammu and Kashmir, Uttarakhand, Uttar Pradesh
Kharif	June to July	September to October	Paddy, Maize, Jowar, Bajra, Tur, Moong, Urad, Cotton, Jute, Groundnut, Soybean	Assam, West Bengal, Coastal Odisha, Andhra Pradesh, Telangana, Tamil Nadu, Kerala, Maharashtra, Uttar Pradesh, Bihar
Zaid	End of Rabi season	Before Kharif season	Watermelon, Muskmelon, Cucumber, Vegetables	Various parts of India, mainly in northern and central regions

RABI CROPS

Wheat

Barley

Peas

Gram

KHARIF CROPS

Paddy

Maize

Bajra

Jowar

ZAID CROPS

Muskmelon

Cucumber

Watermelon

Vegetables

Difference Between

Food Crops Vs. Non-Food Crops		
Feature	**Food Crops**	**Non-Food Crops**
Types	Rice, wheat, millets, pulses	Cotton, jute, rubber
Purpose	For eating (humans/animals)	Industrial uses
Growing Season	Varied, e.g., rice is kharif, wheat is Rabi	Depends on the crop, e.g., cotton is a kharif crop
Temperature and Rainfall Requirements	Varies; rice requires high temperature and high humidity; wheat requires cool growing season	Varies; rubber requires moist and humid climate with high rainfall (rainfall more than 200 and temperature above 25°C.
Geographical Locations in India	Rice predominantly in eastern and southern states, wheat in northern and central states	Cotton in Maharashtra, Gujarat; Rubber in Kerala, Tamil Nadu
Usage Example	Rice and wheat as staple food, pulses for protein	Rubber for industrial raw materials, cotton for textile industry

Mnemonics

- Kharif crops examples

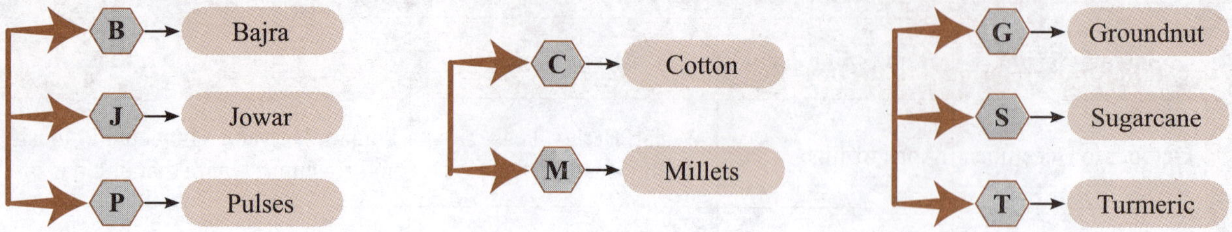

- Rabi crops examples

Real Life Application Based Questions

1. Why is it important for farmers in Punjab to understand the difference between Rabi and Kharif seasons?

Ans. It's important for farmers in Punjab to understand the difference between Rabi and Kharif seasons due to:

- **Crop Planning:** Deciding which crops to grow in each season to optimize yield and meet irrigation needs.
- **Resource Management:** Efficiently managing water, fertilizers, and other inputs based on seasonal requirements.
- **Market Demand:** Timing the harvest to meet market demand and ensure better prices.

2. How can the knowledge of major crops grown in India help in planning agricultural education in schools?

Ans. Understanding the major crops grown in India can aid in planning agricultural education in schools by:

- **Curriculum Relevance:** Tailoring the curriculum to include region-specific agricultural practices and crop details.
- **Skill Development:** Equipping students with practical knowledge and skills relevant to local agricultural needs and techniques.
- **Sustainability Education:** Teaching sustainable farming practices that align with regional crop cultivation.
- **Career Guidance:** Informing students about agricultural career opportunities in their region.

3. How can knowledge of the cropping pattern influence the market strategy of an agribusiness startup?

Ans. Knowledge of the cropping pattern can influence the market strategy of an agribusiness startup in several ways:

- **Product Demand:** Understanding what crops are grown allows the startup to tailor products or services to meet farmers' needs.
- **Seasonal Marketing:** Aligning marketing efforts with the cropping calendar to offer timely solutions.
- **Supply Chain Management:** Planning logistics and distribution according to harvest times to ensure fresh supply and reduce waste.
- **Market Expansion:** Identifying opportunities in different regions based on their specific cropping patterns.

4. Why should urban planners consider the cropping patterns of a region when designing urban expansion?

Ans. Urban planners should consider the cropping patterns of a region when designing urban expansion for several reasons:

- **Food Security:** Ensuring urban expansion does not encroach on fertile lands critical for local food production.
- **Sustainable Development:** Integrating green spaces and agricultural zones into urban planning for ecological balance.
- **Resource Management:** Aligning water and land use policies with agricultural needs to prevent resource depletion.
- **Cultural Preservation:** Respecting and maintaining the agricultural heritage and practices of the region.

Myth Buster

- **Myth: The same crops can be grown in any season regardless of the cropping pattern.**

  Fact: Different crops are suited to specific seasons; Rabi crops are winter crops, Kharif crops grow with the monsoon, and Zaid crops in summer.

- **Myth: Major crops refer only to the ones that are exported.**

  Fact: Major crops include staples and widely consumed crops within the country, such as rice, wheat, and millets, not just export crops.

- **Myth: Non-food crops are not important for the Indian economy.**

  Fact: Non-food crops like cotton and jute are crucial for the textile industry and significantly contribute to the economy.

Scan Me for Detailed Explanations

COMPETENCY BASED SOLVED EXAMPLES

Multiple Choice Questions (1 M)

1. As an agricultural consultant preparing materials for a workshop with farmers from different regions of India, you are tasked with demonstrating the different agricultural practices and inputs tailored to their specific needs. Use the given items in Column-I and match them with the appropriate concepts in Column-II based on their typical uses or characteristics in various regions of India. ***(Un)***

Column-I		Column-II	
(A)	Haryana and Punjab	(i)	Prevention from insects
(B)	Odisha	(ii)	Rice as a Commercial Crop
(C)	HYV Seeds	(iii)	Rice as a Subsistence Crop
(D)	Insecticide	(iv)	Modern Agricultural Input

(*a*) A–(i), B–(ii), C–(iii), D–(iv)
(*b*) A–(iii), B–(i), C–(iv), D–(ii)
(*c*) A–(ii), B–(iii), C–(iv), D–(i)
(*d*) A–(iv), B–(i), C–(ii), D–(iii)

2. Rohit, an agri-business entrepreneur, is considering the development of a new tea plantation in Assam. Given the scale of the operation and its implications, Rohit needs to carefully evaluate different aspects of plantation farming to ensure its success. As part of his business plan, he is evaluating the following statements. Determine which statements he should consider correct to effectively plan his tea plantation in Assam: ***(Ev)***

Statement-I: A single type of crop is grown on a large piece of land.

Statement-II: Migrant laborers are often employed in plantation farming.

Statement-III: Plantation farming does not rely on any transport and communication network for its development.

(*a*) Statement-I & Statement-II are correct
(*b*) Statement-I & Statement-III are correct
(*c*) Statement-II & Statement-III are correct
(*d*) Statement-I, Statement-II & Statement-III are correct

3. During a national-level debate competition, Nisha, representing her school, is presented with statements about India's cropping seasons. She needs to argue which statement is accurate, particularly focusing on the impact of Western temperate cyclones and the timing of crop harvesting. ***(Ev)***

Statement-I: Rabi crops are harvested during the monsoon season.

Statement-II: Western temperate cyclones facilitate rabi cropping in Northern India.

Statement-III: The green revolution had a negligible impact on rabi crops.

Statement-IV: Wheat and barley are important kharif crops.

(*a*) Only Statement-I is correct

(*b*) Only Statement-II is correct

(*c*) Statement-II & Statement-III are correct

(*d*) None of these

4. **You are a food export consultant preparing a report on the key fruit-producing regions in India. Analyze the following statements and identify which ones accurately reflect the prominent fruit production areas in the country:** *(Ev)*

Statement-I: Mangoes from Maharashtra are known globally.

Statement-II: Lichi is a major fruit produced in Maharashtra.

Statement-III: Himachal Pradesh is renowned for its production of apples, pears, and apricots.

(*a*) Statement-I & Statement-II are correct

(*b*) Statement-I & Statement-III are correct

(*c*) Statement-II & Statement-III are correct

(*d*) Statement-I, II & III are correct

5. **In a classroom activity designed to teach students about India's agricultural patterns, Mr. Kumar presents a matching exercise that requires understanding the timing of crop activities and regional crop specializations. The students must correctly align the sowing and harvesting periods with specific crops and match key crop-producing states to their respective crops.** *(Ap)*

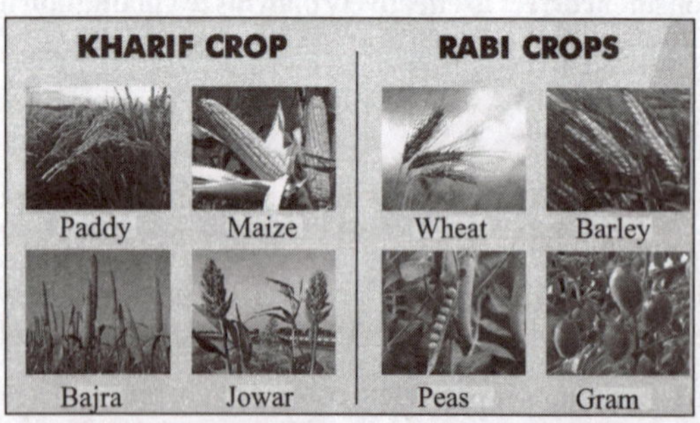

	Column-I		Column-II
(A)	Rabi crops sowing period	(i)	September-October
(B)	Kharif crops harvesting period	(ii)	Assam, West Bengal, Odisha
(C)	States known for wheat production	(iii)	October to December
(D)	Major rice-growing states	(iv)	Punjab, Haryana, and Uttar Pradesh

(*a*) A–(i), B–(ii), C–(iii), D–(iv)

(*b*) A–(iii), B–(i), C–(iv), D–(ii)

(*c*) A–(ii), B–(iii), C–(iv), D–(i)

(*d*) A–(iv), B–(i), C–(ii), D–(iii)

6. **Avinash, a progressive farmer in Telangana, is planning to utilize his newly acquired farmland to maximize his crop yield in alignment with the regional agricultural practices. Knowing that the monsoon season is crucial for the kharif crops, he seeks to choose the best crop that thrives in his region during this period.** *(Ap)*

(*a*) Wheat (*b*) Barley

(*c*) Paddy (*d*) Mustard

Assertion and Reason (1 M)

Direction: The following questions consist of two statements – Assertion (A) and Reason (R). Answer these questions by selecting the appropriate option given below:

(*a*) Both A and R are true, and R is the correct explanation of A.

(*b*) Both A and R are true, but R is not the correct explanation of A.

(*c*) A is true, but R is false

(*d*) A is false, but R is true.

1. **During a geography lesson, the teacher explained that farmers in India typically plant different crops according to the seasons. Rahul, a student, learned that Kharif crops are generally sown with the onset of the monsoon in June and harvested in September or October. However, he was puzzled when his friend mentioned that these crops often need a lot of water, mainly from rainfall, but not necessarily from irrigation systems. Considering the information Rahul received,answer the following:**

Assertion (A): Kharif crops are grown during the summer season in India.

Reason (R): Kharif crops depend on irrigation and do not require rainfall. *(Un)*

2. **Assertion (A):** Pulses are considered as a major source of protein in a vegetarian diet.

Reason (R): Being leguminous crops they help in restoring the soil fertility by fixing nitrogen from the air *(An)*

3. **Priya, a student, is researching the impact of the Green Revolution on India's agriculture for her school project. She discovers that regions like Punjab and Haryana saw significant increases in crop production, while other areas did not benefit as much. Her research also shows that the success of the Green Revolution relied heavily on the use of high-yielding variety (HYV) seeds, along with chemical fertilizers and pesticides, which were not equally accessible or affordable for all farmers across the country. Based on Priya's findings, analyse the following statements:**

Assertion (A): The 'Green Revolution' led to the concentration of agricultural development in selected regions.

Reason (R): The 'Green Revolution' was based on the use of high-yielding variety seeds, fertilizers, and pesticides. ***(Un)***

4. **Assertion (A):** Cotton cannot be grown in Assam.

Reason (R): The crop needs bright sunshine and 210 frost free days for its growth. ***(Ap)***

5. **Assertion (A):** Biochemical inputs and irrigation are used for obtaining higher production.

Reason (R): Doses of biochemical input are used to grow crops rapidly ***(Un)***

Subjective Questions

Very Short Answer Type Questions (2 M)

1. **Give one example of the main commercial crop cultivable in laterite soil.** ***(Re)***

Ans. ***Tea*** is the main commercial crop cultivated in laterite soil, thriving in a warm and moist climate. *(1 M)*

It is extensively grown in regions like ***Assam*** and ***North Bengal***, requiring well-drained fertile soil for growth. *(1 M)*

2. **Name one staple crop of India and the regions where it is produced.** ***(Re)***

Ans. Rice is a staple crop of India, essential for the majority's diet. *(1 M)*

Predominantly produced in the plains of north and northeastern India, coastal areas, and the deltaic regions like Punjab, Haryana, and Uttar Pradesh. *(1 M)*

3. **Which crop is the major crop of Rabi?** ***(Re)***

Ans. ***Wheat*** is the major Rabi crop in India. *(1 M)*

Primarily grown in ***Punjab***, ***Haryana***, ***Uttar Pradesh***, ***Bihar***, and ***Rajasthan*** during the winter season, harvested in the summer. *(1 M)*

4. **Which factors has helped Punjab and Haryana to grow more and more of rice?** ***(An)***

Ans. Irrigation facilities and ***high-yielding variety*** (HYV) seeds have significantly contributed to increased rice production in Punjab and Haryana. *(1 M)*

The ***Green Revolution*** also played a crucial role in enhancing the rice yield in these states. *(1 M)*

5. (a) **Explain any two efforts taken by the Government of India to modernise agriculture.** ***(Un)* (CBSE, 2023)**

OR

(b) **Explain any two features of Rabi cropping season.** ***(Re)***

Ans. (a) Two efforts taken by the Government of India to modernise agriculture are:

(i) **Green Revolution:** Introduced in the 1960s and 1970s, the Green Revolution promoted the use of high-yield variety seeds, fertilizers, and irrigation to boost crop production. *(1 M)*

(ii) **White Revolution (Operation Flood):** Launched to increase milk production in India, integrating rural milk producers with urban markets. *(1 M)*

OR

(b) Two features of Rabi cropping season are:

(i) **Sowing Time:** Rabi crops are sown in winter from October to December. *(1 M)*

(ii) **Harvest Time:** These crops are harvested in the summer from April to June, benefiting from winter precipitation influenced by western temperate cyclones. *(1 M)*

Topper Explanation

(b) The features of Rabi cropping season include:

(i) Rabi crops are sown in winter between October and December and are harvested in spring.

(ii) Rabi crops are dependent on winter rainfall and irrigation. Example of Rabi crops include wheat, barley, gram, peas and mustard.

Short Answer Type Questions (3 M)

1. **Raj, a smallholder farmer in Haryana, is considering switching from traditional farming methods to high-yielding variety seeds and chemical fertilizers, influenced by the success stories of nearby Punjab farmers during the Green Revolution. Analyze the potential changes Raj might experience in his farming operations, specifically during the rabi season. Discuss the broader implications such changes could have on the local cropping pattern and agricultural practices.** ***(Ev)***

Ans. The potential changes and implications of such changes are as follows:

(i) The **Green Revolution** introduced **high-yielding variety seeds, chemical fertilizers**, and advanced irrigation techniques. *(1 M)*

(ii) It significantly **increased** the **production of rabi crops** such as wheat in Punjab, Haryana, and other regions. *(1 M)*

(iii) The cropping pattern **shifted towards more intensive cultivation** of wheat and other rabi crops, supported by **modern agricultural practices**. *(1 M)*

2. **In which states three cops of paddy are grown? Which are they?** *(Re)*

Ans. **Assam, West Bengal, and Odisha** are states where three crops of paddy are grown annually due to favorable climatic conditions. *(1 M)*

The three crops are **Aus** (pre-monsoon crop), **Aman** (monsoon crop), and **Boro** (winter crop), each adapted to different growing seasons in these regions. *(2 M)*

3. **Rajat, a young farmer from Madhya Pradesh, has recently transitioned from traditional farming techniques to modern agricultural practices on his maize farm. Describe the changes Rajat might have implemented in his farming practices which could potentially increase the yield and quality of his maize production.** *(Ap)*

Ans. Rajat might have implemented the following farming practices on his maize farm:

(*i*) **Use of High-Yielding Varieties (HYVs) seeds:** The introduction of HYVs of maize has increased crop yields by providing plants that are genetically tailored to produce more grain per acre and resist certain pests and diseases. *(1 M)*

(*ii*) **Improved Irrigation Techniques:** Adoption of modern irrigation methods, such as drip and sprinkler systems, has improved water efficiency and availability to crops throughout the growing season, leading to better crop growth and higher yields. *(1 M)*

(*iii*) **Use of Fertilizers and Pesticides:** Modern agriculture employs scientifically formulated fertilizers and pesticides that boost crop growth and protect crops from pests and diseases, thereby enhancing productivity. *(1 M)*

4. **An international coffee company is looking to source high-quality Arabica coffee beans from India. They have asked their regional manager, Mr. Patel, to prepare a detailed report on the ideal geographical locations for Arabica coffee cultivation in India and the factors influencing its growth. Guide Mr. Patel in preparing his report by analyzing how the geographical locations in India influence the cultivation of the Arabica coffee variety.** *(Ev)*

Ans. The geographical locations in India Influence the cultivation of the Arabica coffee variety in the following ways:

(*i*) Arabica coffee is cultivated in high-altitude regions like **Baba Budan Hills** and **Nilgiri regions** in Karnataka, Kerala, and Tamil Nadu. *(1 M)*

(*ii*) These areas offer **ideal climatic conditions** like temperature (15-24°C) and rainfall ((150-250 cm), crucial for Arabica coffee growth. *(1 M)*

(*iii*) Rich, **well-drained**, and **slightly acidic soils** in these areas support optimal growth and quality of Arabica coffee beans. *(1 M)*

Long Answer Type Questions (5 M)

1. **Agriculture consultant Dr. Mehta is conducting a study to assess the potential impacts of climate change on wheat production in the Ganga-Satluj plains. Considering the climatic and soil requirements for wheat, analyze how a significant shift in rainfall pattern could impact wheat production in the Ganga-Satluj plains.** *(An)*

Ans. The impact of a shift in rainfall pattern on wheat production in the Ganga-Satluj plains is as follows:

(*i*) **Soil Moisture:** Wheat requires well-drained loamy soil with adequate moisture. A shift in rainfall patterns could lead to waterlogging or insufficient soil moisture, both detrimental to wheat growth. *(1 M)*

(*ii*) **Temperature:** Wheat thrives in cooler climates. Increased temperatures due to climate change can reduce grain quality and yield in the Ganga-Satluj plains. *(1 M)*

(*iii*) **Rainfall Timing:** Proper rainfall during the sowing and growing seasons is crucial. Unseasonal rains or droughts can disrupt the growth cycle, affecting wheat production. *(1 M)*

(*iv*) **Pest and Disease:** Changes in climate can increase the prevalence of pests and diseases, leading to lower wheat yields and higher production costs. *(1 M)*

(*v*) **Irrigation Dependency:** Farmers may become more reliant on irrigation, increasing water stress and impacting sustainable agricultural practices in the region. *(1 M)*

2. **Dr. Patel, a nutritionist at a community health center, is preparing a presentation to educate local farmers and families about the benefits of including millets in their diet, particularly focusing on ragi. She aims to highlight the nutritional benefits of ragi and advocate for its cultivation and consumption. What key points should Dr. Patel include to explain why ragi is considered a significant source of nutrients?** *(Un)*

Ans. Ragi is considered a significant source of nutrients because of the following reasons:

(*i*) Ragi, also known as finger millet, is rich in several essential nutrients that make it a valuable addition to a balanced diet. It is particularly high in calcium, iron, protein, fiber, and vitamins, especially vitamin D. *(1 M)*

(*ii*) The high calcium content in ragi makes it excellent for bone development and maintenance, which is crucial in both children and adults, potentially reducing the risk of osteoporosis. *(1 M)*

(*iii*) Its significant iron content helps combat anemia and boost overall energy levels and its protein content supports muscle repair and body growth. *(1 M)*

(*iv*) The presence of dietary fiber aids in digestion, helps in managing blood sugar levels, and contributes to heart health. *(1 M)* (*v*) Dr. Patel should emphasize that including ragi in the diet can lead to improved overall health outcomes for the community. Its nutritional benefits, coupled with its adaptability to grow in less fertile soil, and low water requirements, make it an excellent crop for local farmers to cultivate. *(1 M)*

3. As part of an agricultural development project, Mr. Verma is analyzing crop suitability for different regions in India to optimize crop yields and match them to local climates and soil types. His focus is on understanding the specific conditions under which Jowar and Bajra thrive and identifying the major states in India where these crops are traditionally cultivated. Based on this information discuss the agricultural conditions suitable for the growth of Jowar and Bajra and mention the major states where they are cultivated in India. ***(Un)***

Ans. The agricultural conditions suitable for Jowar and Bajra cultivation and their major states of production are as follows:

Jowar (Sorghum)

(*i*) It is predominantly a **rain-fed crop** grown in regions with an average **temperature** range of **26°C to 33°C**. *(1 M)*

(*ii*) It prefers **well-drained loamy to sandy-loam soils** and is quite drought-resistant but does require **moderate rainfall**, around **40-100 cm annually**. *(1 M)*

(*iii*) The major states in India where Jowar is extensively cultivated include **Maharashtra, Karnataka, Andhra Pradesh,** and **Madhya Pradesh**. *(1 M)*

Bajra (Pearl Millet)

(*iv*) It thrives in arid and semi-arid climates and prefers **sandy soils** and **shallow black soil**. It can grow in regions with **temperature** ranges from **25°C to 35°C** and requires **minimal rainfall**, about **40-75 cm annually**. *(1 M)*

(*v*) The leading producers of Bajra in India are Rajasthan, Uttar Pradesh, Maharashtra, Gujarat, and Haryana. *(1 M)*

4. A team of agricultural scientists is conducting a study on the diversity of horticulture crops across India. They aim to understand how regional climatic conditions affect the cultivation of these crops to develop region-specific agricultural guidelines for farmers. Help the team by discussing how the regional climatic conditions in different states of India influence the cultivation of various horticulture crops. ***(Ev)***

Ans. Geographical locations significantly influence the cultivation of horticulture crops in India as follows:

(*i*) **Climate Compatibility:** Mangoes thrive in the tropical climate of Maharashtra and Andhra Pradesh, while apples and apricots require the temperate climate of Jammu & Kashmir, and Himachal Pradesh. *(1 M)*

(*ii*) **Rainfall Patterns:** Oranges are predominantly grown in Nagpur and Meghalaya due to their moderate rainfall, essential for citrus growth. *(1 M)*

(*iii*) **Temperature Variations:** Bananas are cultivated in the warm, humid conditions of Kerala and Tamil Nadu, which are ideal for their growth. *(1 M)*

(*iv*) **Soil Type:** The alluvial soils of Uttar Pradesh and Bihar support litchi and guava cultivation, providing essential nutrients and drainage. *(1 M)*

(*v*) **Altitude:** Grapes flourish in the semi-arid climate and specific altitudes of Maharashtra and Telangana, ensuring optimal temperature and sunlight. *(1 M)*

MISCELLANEOUS EXERCISE

Multiple Choice Questions (1 M)

1. You are an agricultural economist analyzing the impact of the Minimum Support Price (MSP) policy on safeguarding farmers against exploitation by speculators and middlemen. How would you assess the effectiveness of the MSP in achieving this goal? *(Ev)*
   (*a*) Highly effective as it guarantees minimum profit
   (*b*) Moderately effective but dependent on proper implementation
   (*c*) Ineffective due to lack of awareness among farmers
   (*d*) Counterproductive as it leads to overproduction

2. Agriculture Officer Ms. Sharma is tasked with analyzing the potential for expanding rice cultivation in different states of India. Given the specific climatic needs of rice—high humidity and substantial rainfall—she must assess which state among the following is least suitable for expanding this crop. *(Ev)*
   (*a*) Punjab (*b*) West Bengal
   (*c*) Rajasthan (*d*) Assam

3. As a newly appointed agricultural officer in the Ganga-Satluj plains, Mr. Singh is tasked with developing strategies to maximize wheat production in the area. Considering the regional climate's suitability for wheat cultivation, why is this region critical for wheat production in India? Choose the best possible option among the following: *(Un)*
   (*a*) It provides the ideal hot and humid climate for wheat.
   (*b*) It offers the perfect cool growing season and adequate sunshine.
   (*c*) It is known for its heavy monsoonal rain beneficial for wheat.
   (*d*) It has black soil ideal for cotton, not wheat.

4. A farmer named Rajesh is considering expanding his crop production to include maize on his farm near the Ganges River. He is aware that temperature and soil type are critical for the success of the crop. Given the typical conditions in this region during the growing season and the characteristics of soil, which of the following options should Rajesh choose for the best maize cultivation? *(Ap)*
   (*a*) 10°C to 15°C in sandy soil
   (*b*) 21°C to 27°C in old alluvial soil
   (*c*) 30°C to 35°C in clayey soil
   (*d*) 18°C to 24°C in loamy soil

5. Agricultural officers are planning a workshop for farmers in a state known for its adaptable agricultural practices, where maize is cultivated in both the Kharif and Rabi seasons. This practice takes advantage of the state's unique climatic conditions, allowing for an extended growing period and increased crop output. which state is known to practice both cultivation cycles for maize? *(Un)*
   (*a*) Karnataka (*b*) Madhya Pradesh
   (*c*) Uttar Pradesh (*d*) Bihar

6. Keshav a farmer in India is planning to cultivate kharif pulses like tur (arhar) and moong. Given the dependency of these crops on monsoon rains, which states would be suitable for setting up his cultivation to ensure adequate water supply and optimal yield? *(An)*
   (*a*) Rajasthan (*b*) Maharashtra
   (*c*) Uttar Pradesh (*d*) All of the above

7. As a dietitian advising a vegetarian client on nutritional balance, you emphasize the importance of including certain foods in his diet. Considering the nutritional composition of various food groups, why would you particularly recommend incorporating pulses into their meals? *(Ev)*
   (*a*) They are high in fats.
   (*b*) They are a primary source of carbohydrates.
   (*c*) They are rich in proteins.
   (*d*) They provide essential amino acids only.

8. You are an agricultural consultant tasked with improving the sustainability of a sugarcane farm located in a region where the annual rainfall is less than 75 cm. Considering the high-water demand for sugarcane, which irrigation technique would you recommend to maximize water efficiency and ensure healthy crop growth? *(Ap)*
   (*a*) Flood irrigation (*b*) Drip irrigation
   (*c*) Sprinkler irrigation (*d*) No irrigation is required

9. Which of the following is true with reference to the climatic conditions required for the cultivation of sugarcane? *(Re)*
   A. It grows well in hot and humid climate.
   B. It needs temperature of 21°C-27°C
   C. It needs an annual rainfall between 75-100cm
   D. It can be grown on a variety of soils
   (*a*) Only (A) and (B) (*b*) Only (B) and (C)
   (*c*) Only (C) and (D) (*d*) All of the above

10. Which of the following climatic conditions is true with reference to the cultivation of cotton? *(Re)*
    A. It needs black soil
    B. It needs 210 frost free days and bright sunshine
    C. It needs 6 to 8 months to mature.
    D. It needs high temperature and light rainfall
    (*a*) Only A and B (*b*) Only B and C
    (*c*) Only C and D (*d*) None of these

11. You are managing a sugarcane plantation on land known for its less fertile soil. To improve soil fertility and meet the high nutrient demands of your sugarcane crop, which soil amendment practice would you implement to promote better growth and yield? ***(Ap)***

(*a*) Liming

(*b*) Applying high-nitrogen fertilizers

(*c*) Heavy irrigation

(*d*) No amendment is needed

12. As a consultant for a new tea production startup, you are analyzing the optimal locations for establishing tea plantations in India. Considering the climate and soil requirements of tea plants, where would you suggest setting up these plantations to ensure ideal growing conditions and high-quality tea production? ***(Ap)***

(*a*) It is uniformly distributed across all states.

(*b*) Limited to coastal regions only.

(*c*) Predominantly concentrated in tropical and sub-tropical regions.

(*d*) Exclusive to northern plains

13. Which country is the largest producer of pulses in the world? ***(Re)***

(*a*) China (*b*) Russia

(*c*) UK (*d*) India

14. As an agricultural analyst, you are preparing a report on global groundnut production trends for a major agribusiness firm. While analyzing the data from 2018, you need to identify which country led the world in groundnut production, surpassing India. ***(Re)***

(*a*) United States (*b*) Brazil

(*c*) China (*d*) Argentina

15. A coffee grower looking to expand Arabica coffee cultivation to new regions in India beyond Karnataka, Kerala, and Tamil Nadu. Considering the environmental needs of Arabica coffee, which other state would be most suitable for establishing new coffee plantations? ***(An)***

(*a*) Rajasthan due to its arid climate and sandy soil

(*b*) Punjab due to its fertile plains and extensive irrigation

(*c*) Meghalaya due to its high rainfall and hilly terrain

(*d*) Gujarat due to its industrial development

16. As an agricultural consultant presenting to a group of farmers, you are tasked with providing accurate information about cotton cultivation in India. Evaluate the following statements to determine which ones correctly reflect the characteristics and significance of cotton farming: ***(Ev)***

Statement-I: Cotton cultivation is predominant in the humid regions of India.

Statement-II: Maharashtra and Gujarat are among the top cotton-producing states in India.

Statement-III: Cotton is harvested within 3-4 months after planting.

Statement-IV: It is an essential raw material for the textile industry.

(*a*) Statement-I & Statement-II are correct

(*b*) Statement-I & Statement-III are correct

(*c*) Statement-II & Statement-III are correct

(*d*) Statement-II & Statement-IV are correct

17. The given picture shows a forest being cleared for agriculture. Many plants and animals have been killed or have moved away. What is being shown in the picture? ***(Re)***

(*a*) Hunting (*b*) Soil preparation

(*c*) Habitat destruction (*d*) Coal preparation process

18. Namit, an agronomist advises a tea plantation owner in Assam who is struggling with reduced yields due to unexpected frost events. To protect the tea crops and ensure their continued growth, what innovative approach would you recommend implementing on the plantation? ***(Cr)***

(*a*) Shift the plantation to a lower altitude with warmer conditions.

(*b*) Introduce genetically modified tea plants that can withstand frost.

(*c*) Utilize greenhouse technology to maintain optimal growth conditions.

(*d*) Increase the use of fertilizers and pesticides to enhance growth.

19. You are a consultant for an international coffee chain looking to source Arabica coffee from India due to its renowned quality. Your task is to identify the origin of Arabica coffee in India and determine the most suitable regions for its cultivation to ensure the best quality product for the chain. Which of the following statements accurately describes the historical introduction and current cultivation areas of Arabica coffee in India? ***(Un)***

(*a*) Arabica coffee was introduced from Brazil and is predominantly cultivated in Maharashtra, Gujarat, and Rajasthan.

(*b*) Arabica coffee was introduced from Ethiopia and is predominantly cultivated in Assam, West Bengal, and Odisha.

(*c*) Arabica coffee was introduced from Yemen and is predominantly cultivated in Karnataka, Kerala, and Tamil Nadu.

(*d*) Arabica coffee was introduced from Vietnam and is predominantly cultivated in Uttar Pradesh, Punjab, and Haryana.

Assertion and Reason (1 M)

Direction: The following questions consist of two statements – Assertion (A) and Reason (R). Answer these questions by selecting the appropriate option given below:

(*a*) Both A and R are true, and R is the correct explanation of A.

(*b*) Both A and R are true, but R is not the correct explanation of A.

(*c*) A is true, but R is false

(*d*) A is false, but R is true.

1. **Assertion (A):** Biochemical inputs and irrigation are used for obtaining higher production.

   Reason (R): Doses of biochemical input are used to grow crops rapidly. ***(An)***

2. **Assertion (A):** Tea cultivation, is a labour- intensive industry.

   Reason (R): Cultivation can be done throughout the year. Tea bushes require warm and moist frost- free climate.***(Un)***

3. **Assertion (A):** Plantation has an interface of agriculture and industry.

   Reason (R): Plantation is a type of commercial farming; a single crop is grown on a large area. ***(An)***

4. **Assertion (A):** Pulses are considered as a major source of protein in a vegetarian diet.

   Reason (R): Being leguminous crops they help in restoring the soil fertility by fixing nitrogen from the air. ***(Un)***

5. **Assertion (A):** In the 1980s and 1990s a comprehensive land development programme was initiated which included both institutional and technological reforms.

   Reason (R): Green revolution was based on the use of package Technology. ***(An)***

6. **Assertion (A):** Organic farming is much in vogue.

   Reason (R): In organic forming, crops are grown using high doses to increase production. ***(Ev)***

7. **Assertion (A):** Primitive Subsistence Farming is practised in areas of high population pressure on land.

   Reason (R): This type of farming depends on monsoon. ***(Un)***

Subjective Questions

Very Short Answer Type Questions (2 M)

1. Arjun, a factory manager, needs to decide on a material for manufacturing tires, hoses, and seals for various machines in his plant. He considers several options but eventually settles on rubber due to its unique properties and versatility. Explain why rubber is considered an important industrial raw material. ***(Un)***

2. What are some examples of horticultural crops? ***(Re)***
3. You are an agricultural consultant advising a group of new farmers in the coastal region of Odisha. These farmers are eager to diversify their crops and are considering rice due to its popularity and market demand. Discuss the specific climatic conditions required for rice cultivation. ***(Un)***
4. What is shifting agriculture also known as? ***(Re)***
5. What is a staple crop? ***(Un)***
6. What is the main characteristic of commercial farming? ***(Un)***
7. Agricultural officer, Ms. Sharma, is assigned to assist farmers in the semi-arid region of Marathwada, Maharashtra, where rainfall is scarce but sugarcane is a major crop. She is planning a workshop to educate local farmers about optimizing sugarcane cultivation under their specific climatic conditions. Describe those specific climatic conditions necessary for sugarcane production. ***(Ap)***
8. What are chemical fertilizers? ***(Un)***
9. "Agriculture and industry are not exclusive of each other. They move hand in hand". Justify your answer with examples. ***(An)* (CBSE SQP, 2025)**
10. What are the different types of farming systems practiced in India? ***(Re)***
11. What is subsistence farming? ***(Un)***

Short Answer Type Questions (3 M)

1. Define agricultural term used for cultivation of fruits and vegetables? Write its features with reference to India. ***(Re, Ap)* (CBSE SQP, 2025)**
2. Ramesh, a small-scale farmer, cultivates a variety of crops on his 2-acre farm in Rajasthan. This year, he plans to include pulses in his cropping pattern. Analyze the potential benefits Ramesh could observe in his soil's health and overall farm sustainability by integrating pulses into his crop rotation. ***(An)***
3. What is the difference between kharif and Rabi crops? ***(Un)***
4. A sustainable fashion brand is interested in developing eco-friendly products using jute. To ensure a reliable supply chain, they need to understand why jute production is concentrated in states like West Bengal, Bihar, Assam, Odisha, and Meghalaya in India. ***(An)***

5. Sunita, an entrepreneur from Gujarat, is considering venturing into the oilseed processing industry. She is particularly interested in understanding the agricultural and economic context of oilseed production in India, as it will influence her business strategy and operations. Assist Sunita by outlining the significance of oil seeds in India's agricultural sector. **(*Un*)**

6. What are plantation crops? **(*Re*)**
7. What is intensive agriculture? **(*Un*)**
8. What is modern agricultural practices, and how farming affects the environment. **(*Un*)**
9. Examine the crucial role played by agriculture in our economy and society. **(*Un*)**

Long Answer Type Questions (5 M)

1. What is contract farming and how does it benefit farmers? **(*Un*)**
2. What is primitive subsistence fariming? **(*Re*)**
3. What are the challenges faced by Indian farmers and how can we solve them. **(*An*)**
4. What is the impact of climate change on Indian agriculture? **(*An*)**
5. What are the different types of irrigation systems used in Indian agriculture? **(*Re*)**
6. Examines the difficulties that India's farming community faces. **(*Un*)**

Case Based Questions

Case Based-I

Read the source given below. Attempt any 5 questions out of 6 (Q. (*i*)-(*iv*)) questions.

Jhumming: The 'slash and burn' agriculture is known as 'Milpa' in Central America, 'Conuco' in Venzuela, 'Roca' in Brazil, 'Masola' in Central Africa, 'Ladang' in Indonesia, 'Ray' in Vietnam.

In India, this primitive form of cultivation is called 'Bewar' or 'Dahiya' in Madhya Pradesh, 'Podu' or 'Penda' in Andhra Pradesh, 'Pama Dabi' or 'Koman' or 'Bringa' in Odisha, 'Kumari' in Western Ghats, 'Valre' or 'Waltre' in South-eastern Rajasthan, 'Khil' in the Himalayan belt, 'Kuruwa' in Jharkhand, and 'Jhumming' in the North-eastern region. **(CBSE, 2022 Term 1)**

(*i*) How is Primitive Subsistence Agriculture related to Jhumming? **(*Un*)**

(*a*) It is based on shifting cultivation.
(*b*) It is intensive in nature.
(*c*) It is based on plantation cultivation.
(*d*) It depends on the cash crop.

(*ii*) The 'slash and burn' agriculture is known as 'Conuco' in which one of the following countries? **(*Re*)**

(*a*) Venezuela (*b*) Brazil
(*c*) Indonesia (*d*) Mexico

(*iii*) The 'slash and burn' agriculture is known as 'Roca' in which one of the following countries? **(*Re*)**

(*a*) Mexico (*b*) Indonesia
(*c*) Brazil (*d*) Venezuela

(*iv*) Identify the major problem of Jhumming cultivation. **(*Un*)**

(*a*) Single crop dominance (*b*) Modern inputs
(*c*) High cost (*d*) Low production

(*v*) In India 'slash and burn' agriculture is known as 'Bewar', in which one of the following states? **(*Re*)**

(*a*) Andhra Pradesh (*b*) Madhya Pradesh
(*c*) Rajasthan (*d*) Jharkhand

(*vi*) Match Column-I with Column-II and choose the correct options: **(*Re*)**

	Column-I		Column-II
A.	Andhra Pradesh	I.	Kuruwa
B.	Odisha	II.	Valre
C.	Rajasthan	III.	Penda
D.	Jharkhand	IV.	Pama Dabi

(*a*) A-III, B-IV, C-II, D-I (*b*) A-I, B-II, C-III, D-IV
(*c*) A-II, B-I, C-IV, D-III (*d*) A-IV, B-III, C-I, D-II

Case Based-II

Read the source given below and answer the following questions:

Bhoodan – Gramdan

Mahatma Gandhi declared Vinoba Bhave as his spiritual heir. He also participated in Satyagraha as one of the foremost satyagrahis. He was one of the votaries of Gandhi's concept of **gram swarajya.** After Gandhiji's martyrdom, Vinoba Bhave undertook **padayatra** to spread Gandhiji's message covered almost the entire country. Once, when he was delivering a lecture at Pochampalli in Andhra Pradesh, some poor landless villagers demanded some land for their economic well-being. Vinoba Bhave could not promise it to them immediately but assured them to talk to the Government of India regarding provision of land for them if they undertook cooperative farming. Suddenly, Shri Ram Chandra Reddy stood up and offered 80 acres of land to be distributed among 80 land-less villagers. This act was known as 'Bhoodan'. Later he travelled and introduced his ideas widely all over India. Some zamindars, owners of many villages offered to distribute some villages among the landless. It was known as **Gramdan.** However, many land-owners chose to provide some part of their land to the poor farmers due to the fear of land ceiling act. This Bhoodan-Gramdan movement initiated by Vinoba Bhave is also known as the **Blood-less Revolution**.

(*i*) Analyze the socio-economic impact of Vinoba Bhave's Bhoodan-Gramdan movement on rural communities in India during the 1950s and 1960s. *(1 M)* **(*An*)**

(*ii*) Explain the concept of Gram Swarajya as envisioned by Gandhi and how Vinoba Bhave's efforts contributed to this vision. *(1 M)* **(*Un*)**

(*iii*) Evaluate the effectiveness of the Bhoodan-Gramdan movement in achieving its goals compared to other land reform efforts in India. *(2 M)* **(*Ev*)**

Case Based-III

Read the source given below and answer the following questions:

Jhumming agriculture

The 'slash and burn' agriculture is known as 'Milpa' in Mexico and Central America, 'Conuco' in Venezuela, 'Roca' in Brazil, 'Masole' in Central Africa, 'Ladang' in Indonesia, 'Ray' in Vietnam. In India, this primitive form of cultivation is called 'Bewar' or 'Dahiya' in Madhya Pradesh, 'Podu' or 'Penda' in Andhra Pradesh, 'Pama Dabi' or 'Koman' or Bringa' in Odisha, 'Kumari' in Western Ghats, 'Valre' or 'Waltre' in South-eastern Rajasthan, 'Khil' in the Himalayan belt, 'Kuruwa' in Jharkhand, and 'Jhumming' in the North-eastern region. Rinjha lived with her family in a small village at the outskirts of Diphu in Assam. She enjoys watching her family members clearing, slashing and burning a patch of land for cultivation. She often helps them in irrigating the fields with water running through a bamboo canal from the nearby spring. She loves the surroundings and wants to stay here as long as she can, but this little girl has no idea about the declining fertility of the soil and her family's search for a fresh patch of land in the next season.

(*i*) Compare the names and regions of 'slash and burn' agriculture practices in India and the two other countries mentioned. *(1 M)* **(*Un*)**

(*ii*) Propose an alternative sustainable farming method that could be introduced to Rinjha's community to address the issue of declining soil fertility. *(1 M)* **(*Cr*)**

(*iii*) How can the practice of 'slash and burn' agriculture affect the long-term sustainability of the environment? Provide an example from the paragraph. *(2 M)* **(*Ap*)**

Map Based Questions

1. On the given political map of India, four leading wheat-growing states of India are marked by 1, 2, 3 and 4. Identify these and write their correct names on the line drawn against each in the given map. **(*Re*)**

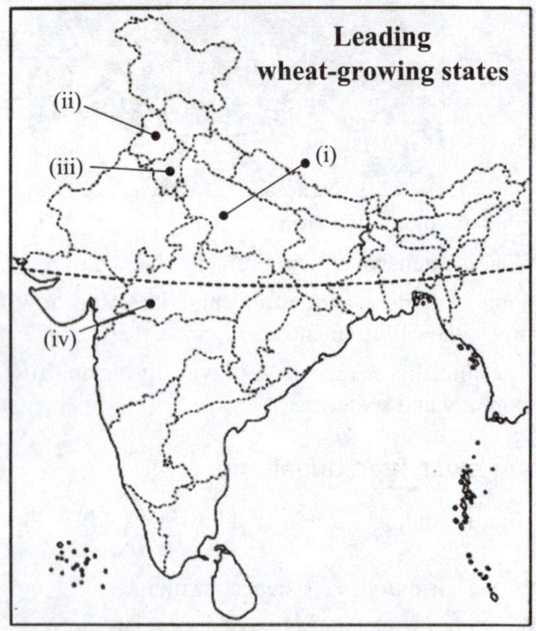

2. On the given political map of India, four leading rice-growing states of India are marked by 1, 2, 3 and 4. Identify these and write their correct names on the line drawn against each in the given map. **(*Re*)**

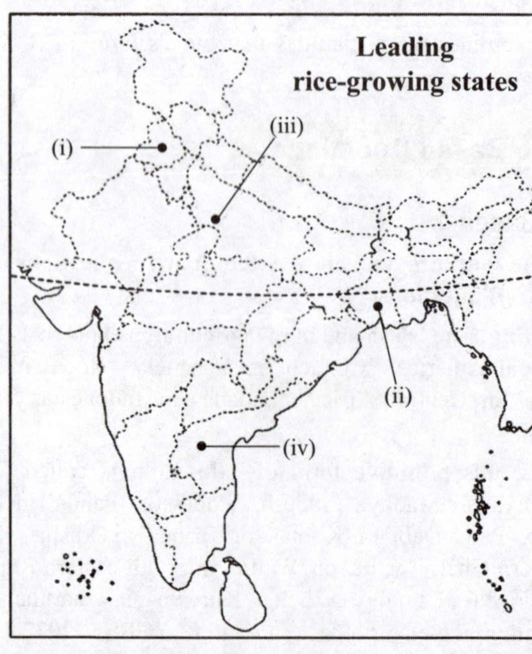

ANSWER KEYS

Multiple Choice Questions

1. (*b*)	**2.** (*c*)	**3.** (*b*)	**4.** (*b*)	**5.** (*d*)	**6.** (*d*)	**7.** (*c*)	**8.** (*b*)	**9.** (*d*)	**10.** (*b*)
11. (*b*)	**12.** (*c*)	**13.** (*d*)	**14.** (*c*)	**15.** (*c*)	**16.** (*d*)	**17.** (*c*)	**18.** (*c*)	**19.** (*c*)	

Assertion and Reason

1. (*a*) **2.** (*b*) **3.** (*a*) **4.** (*b*) **5.** (*b*) **6.** (*c*) **7.** (*b*)

Case Based Questions

Case Based-I

(*i*) (*a*) **(*ii*)** (*a*) **(*iii*)** (*c*) **(*iv*)** (*d*) **(*v*)** (*b*) **(*vi*)** (*a*)

HINTS & EXPLANATIONS

Multiple Choice Questions

1. (*b*) The MSP policy can protect farmers from exploitation by providing a guaranteed minimum price for their produce, thereby shielding them from market volatility. However, its effectiveness hinges on consistent and fair implementation, ensuring that farmers are adequately informed and can access the benefits of MSP.

2. (*c*) Rajasthan, known for its arid climate and low rainfall, would be less suitable for rice cultivation compared to the other options which have more conducive climatic conditions.

3. (*b*) The Ganga-Satluj plains provide an ideal cool growing season and sufficient bright sunshine necessary for wheat's optimal growth and ripening.

4. (*b*) Maize requires a temperature range of 21°C to 27°C for optimal growth, and it grows well in old alluvial soil, which offers adequate nutrients and water retention for the crop.

5. (*d*) In Bihar, maize is cultivated in both Kharif and Rabi seasons, leveraging the state's varying climatic conditions to optimize maize production.

6. (*d*) Each of these states have specific regions well-suited for the cultivation of kharif pulses, which rely heavily on the monsoon season to provide the necessary water for growth. This makes them ideal locations for farmers looking to cultivate these crops.

7. (*c*) Pulses are particularly valuable in vegetarian diets as they serve as a significant source of proteins, a crucial nutrient for muscle and tissue repair and growth, which might otherwise be lacking in a diet devoid of meat.

8. (*b*) Drip irrigation is recommended for areas with limited rainfall, as it conserves water by delivering it directly to the plant's root zone, minimizing evaporation and runoff, and ensuring that water use is as efficient as possible for the water-intensive sugarcane crop.

9. (*d*) All of the above

10. (*b*) Only (*b*) and (*c*)

11. (*b*) On less fertile lands, it is crucial to apply high-nitrogen fertilizers to enhance the soil's nutrient content. This practice supports the vigorous growth and high productivity of sugarcane, a crop that requires substantial nutrient inputs for optimal development.

12. (*c*) Tea cultivation requires a warm, moist, frost-free climate and fertile, well-drained soil, which confines its production primarily to the tropical and sub-tropical regions of India. Establishing plantations in these areas maximizes the chances of successful tea growth and quality harvests.

13. (*d*) India

14. (*c*) In 2018, China was the largest producer of groundnut surpassing India, indicating China's leading position in groundnut production.

15. (*c*) Meghalaya, with its high rainfall and hilly terrain, offers the necessary climatic conditions similar to those required by Arabica coffee. These environmental features make Meghalaya a suitable candidate for expanding coffee cultivation outside the traditional growing regions.

16. (*d*) Statements II and IV are accurate as Maharashtra and Gujarat are leading states in cotton production, and cotton is a vital raw material for the textile industry. In contrast, Statement-I is incorrect because cotton cultivation is prevalent in drier regions, not humid ones. Statement-III is also false, as cotton typically requires 6 to 8 months to mature.

17. (*c*) Habitat destruction

18. (*c*) Utilizing greenhouse technology offers a practical solution by creating a controlled environment that shields the tea plants from frost damage, thus maintaining optimal growth conditions and ensuring the stability of tea production despite climatic challenges.

19. (*c*) Arabica coffee, known globally for its superior quality, was first brought to India from Yemen. It thrives in the Nilgiri regions of Karnataka, Kerala, and Tamil Nadu, where the climatic conditions are ideal for cultivating this variety.

Assertion and Reason

1. (*a*) Both A and R are true, and R is the correct explanation of A.

2. (*b*) Tea cultivation is labour-intensive primarily because it requires abundant, cheap, and skilled labour for the maintenance and harvesting of tea bushes, not directly because it can be done throughout the year or because of its climate requirements. Hence, Both A and R are true, but R is not the correct explanation of A.

3. (*a*) Both A and R are true, and R is the correct explanation of A.

4. (*b*) Pulses are indeed a major source of protein, and while they do help in restoring soil fertility, this property does not explain their protein content. Hence,Both A and R are true, but R is not the correct explanation of A.

5. (*b*) The comprehensive land development program did include institutional and technological reforms, but these reforms were broader than the Green Revolution, which was just one part of the technological reforms. Hence, Both A and R are true, but R is not the correct explanation of A.

6. (*c*) Organic farming is indeed becoming more popular, but it is characterized by avoiding the use of synthetic chemicals and high doses of inputs, not using them. Hence, A is true, but R is false.

7. (*b*) Primitive Subsistence Farming is practiced under various environmental conditions, including those with high population pressure, but it is characterized more by its dependence on natural phenomena like the monsoon than by population pressure. Hence, Both A and R are true, but R is not the correct explanation of A.

Subjective Questions

Very Short Answer Type Questions

1. Rubber is a crucial industrial raw material and its significance and production in India can be outlined as follows:

   (*i*) **Versatile Applications:** Rubber is essential for manufacturing tires, footwear, industrial goods, and medical supplies, making it indispensable across various industries. *(1 M)*

   (*ii*) **Economic Contribution:** Rubber significantly contributes to the economy through exports and job creation in the processing and manufacturing sectors. *(1 M)*

2. Horticulture is the art of growing plants, like fruits, vegetables, and flowers.
   - **Fruits** such as mangoes, oranges, and bananas are examples of horticultural crops. *(1 M)*
   - **Vegetables** like peas, cauliflower, and tomatoes also fall under horticultural crops. *(1 M)*

3. To cultivate rice successfully in the coastal region of Odisha, the following climatic conditions are considered: **(Any two)**

   (*i*) **High Temperature:** Rice cultivation requires a warm climate with **temperatures** typically **above 25°C**. This is vital for germination and growth. *(1 M)*

   (*ii*) **Abundant Water:** Rice is a water-intensive crop. The coastal regions should utilize their proximity to water sources effectively, ensuring adequate flooding of rice paddies. *(1 M)*

   (*iii*) **High Humidity:** The area should have **high humidity levels**, ideally coupled with an **annual rainfall** of **over 100 cm.** In regions with less rainfall, irrigation methods may be necessary. *(1 M)*

4. **Shifting agriculture** is a traditional farming method where land is cultivated temporarily, then abandoned for its natural vegetation to regenerate. *(1 M)*

   It is also known as **"slash and burn"** agriculture, with regional names like **Jhumming** in India. *(1 M)*

5. A **staple crop** is a primary food source that forms the majority of a region's diet and sustains a large portion of its population. *(1 M)*

   Examples include **rice, wheat,** and **maize,** which are essential for daily consumption and nutritional needs.*(1 M)*

6. The main characteristic of **commercial farming** is the large-scale production of crops for sale, focusing on high yield and profit. *(1 M)*

   It involves the use of **modern technology, high-yielding varieties**, and inputs like chemical fertilizers and pesticides. *(1 M)*

7. Sugarcane cultivation thrives under specific climatic conditions: **(Any two)**

   (*i*) **Hot and humid climate:** Sugarcane requires a hot and humid climate, with temperatures ranging from **21-27°C** for optimal growth. *(1 M)*

   (*ii*) **Rainfall:** It needs substantial rainfall, between **75cm and 100cm annually**, evenly distributed throughout the growing period. *(1 M)*

   (*iii*) **Irrigation in Low Rainfall:** In regions with low rainfall, **irrigation** is **essential**, often requiring frequent and substantial watering to compensate for the lack of sufficient natural precipitation. *(1 M)*

8. **Chemical fertilizers** are man-made compounds applied to soil to provide essential nutrients that promote plant growth. *(1 M)*

They typically include key **nutrients like nitrogen, phosphorus, and potassium** to enhance crop yield and health. *(1 M)*

9. Agriculture and industry are not exclusive of each other. They move hand in hand. For instance, the agro-industries in India have given a major boost to agriculture by raising its productivity. They depend on the latter for raw materials and sell their products such as irrigation pumps, fertilisers, insecticides, pesticides, plastic and PVC pipes, machines and tools, etc. to the farmers. *(2 M)*

10. India practices various farming systems, including subsistence farming, intensive farming, commercial farming, and plantation farming. *(1 M)*

Other specific types include **shifting agriculture (slash and burn), mixed farming,** and **organic farming,** adapting to the diverse climatic conditions and cultural practices of the region. *(1 M)*

11. Subsistence farming is a self-sufficient farming system where crops and livestock are produced primarily for the consumption of the farmer's family, not for sale. *(1 M)*

It relies on traditional methods, with minimal use of chemical fertilizers and pesticides, often practiced in rural areas. *(1 M)*

Short Answer Type Questions

1. Horticulture is a term used for the cultivation of fruits and vegetables. Some features are—
   - India is one of the major producers of fruits and vegetables in the world. *(1 M)*
   - It is a producer of tropical and temperate fruits. *(1 M)*
   - India produces 13% of the world's vegetables. *(1 M)*

2. The cultivation of pulses benefits the soil and supports agricultural sustainability in India in the following ways:

   (*i*) **Nitrogen Fixation:** Pulses fix atmospheric nitrogen in the soil, reducing the need for chemical fertilizers and enhancing soil fertility. *(1 M)*

   (*ii*) **Soil Structure:** Their deep roots help in improving soil structure and increasing soil porosity, which aids in better water retention. *(1 M)*

   (*iii*) **Crop Rotation:** Including pulses in crop rotation breaks disease cycles and reduces pest populations, thereby sustaining crop health and reducing dependency on pesticides. *(1 M)*

3. *(1 + 1 + 1 = 3M)*

Aspect	Kharif Crops	Rabi Crops
Sowing Season and Harvesting Time	Sown with the onset of monsoon in June and harvested in September or October.	Sown at the end of monsoon or in winter (around October) and harvested in spring or early summer (around April).
Water Needs	High due to monsoon reliance.	Lower, relies more on irrigation.
Temperature Preferences	Thrive in warmer conditions.	Grow well in cooler conditions.

4. Jute production is mainly concentrated in states like West Bengal, Bihar, Assam, Odisha and Meghalaya due to the following reasons:

   (*i*) **Geographical and climatic conditions:** Jute grows well on well-drained fertile soils in the flood plains, where soils are renewed every year. *(1 M)*

   (*ii*) **Temperature:** Requires high temperature during the time of growth. *(1 M)*

   (*iii*) **Location-specific advantages:** States like West Bengal, Bihar, Assam, Odisha, and Meghalaya provide these ideal conditions. *(1 M)*

5. The significance of oil seeds in India's agricultural sector is as follows:

   (*i*) Oil seeds cover **approximately 12% of India's total cropped area,** indicating their significance. *(1 M)*

   (*ii*) India produces a **variety of oil seeds** such as **groundnut, mustard, and sesame,** reflecting biodiversity. *(1 M)*

   (*iii*) They have **multiple uses,** including as **edible oils** and **raw materials** for **industry products** like **soaps, cosmetics** and **ointments.** *(1 M)*

6. Plantation crops are those cultivated on large estates, focusing on a single cash crop intended for domestic or international markets. *(1 M)*
   - **Characteristics:** These crops require intensive labour and capital, often involving sophisticated farming techniques, irrigation, and processing facilities on or near the plantation. *(1 M)*
   - **Examples:** Common plantation crops in India include tea, coffee, rubber, sugarcane, and bananas, each requiring specific climatic conditions for optimal growth. *(1 M)*

7. Intensive agriculture is a farming system aimed at maximizing output from a limited area of land through the extensive use of labour, fertilizers, and other technological inputs. *(1 M)*
   - **Characteristics:** It features high crop density, frequent cropping, and the use of high-yielding variety seeds, often in areas with high population densities where land is at a premium. *(1 M)*
   - **Impact:** While it significantly increases food production, intensive agriculture can also lead to environmental issues like soil degradation, water pollution, and reduced biodiversity. *(1 M)*

8. Modern Agricultural Practices and Environmental Impact
   - **Modern Practices:** Utilizes advanced technology like HYV seeds, chemical fertilizers, and pesticides to increase farm output. Implements irrigation for consistent water supply. *(1 M)*

- **Benefits:** Enhances food production significantly, meeting the rising demand. Supports economic growth and makes efficient use of land. *(1 M)*
- **Environmental Effects:** Causes soil erosion, depletes water resources, and increases pollution. Affects biodiversity negatively and contributes to climate change. *(1 M)*

9. Role of Agriculture in Economy and Society
   - **Economic Backbone:** Agriculture contributes significantly to the GDP, providing raw materials for industries and exports like tea and spices. *(1 M)*
   - **Employment Source:** Employs two-thirds of India's population, mainly in rural areas, supporting families and communities. *(1 M)*
   - **Social Stability:** Ensures food security, maintaining societal stability and health. Cultivation practices reflect India's diverse cultures and traditions. *(1 M)*

Long Answer Type Questions

1. Contract farming is an agreement between farmers and a buyer (often a company) where farmers agree to produce a certain amount of a specific agricultural product. These agreements usually detail the quantity, quality, and timing of the production. *(2 M)*

   Benefits to Farmers:

   (i) **Assured Market:** Farmers have a guaranteed buyer for their produce, reducing the risk of fluctuating market demands. *(1 M)*

   (ii) **Stable Income:** Pre-agreed prices help in securing a stable income for farmers by protecting them from price volatility in the market. *(1 M)*

   (iii) **Access to Technology:** Companies often provide farmers with seeds, equipment, and expertise, leading to improved crop yields and practices. *(1 M)*

2. Primitive subsistence farming is an ancient form of agriculture where farmers use simple tools to grow crops on small patches of land for family consumption rather than for sale. *(1 M)*

   Characteristics:

   (i) **Manual Labour:** It relies heavily on human labour, using primitive tools like hoes and digging sticks. *(1 M)*

   (ii) **Slash-and-Burn Technique:** Farmers clear a piece of land by slashing the vegetation and burning it, to enrich the soil with ash, making it fertile for a short period. *(1 M)*

   (iii) **Shifting Cultivation:** Once the soil fertility decreases, farmers move to a new area, allowing the old plot to regenerate its fertility naturally over time. *(1 M)*

   (iv) **Dependence on Natural Conditions:** This type of farming depends on natural rainfall and soil fertility without the use of modern agricultural inputs like fertilizers and pesticides. *(1 M)*

3. The challenges faced by Indian farmers and improve their situation; the following steps can be implemented:

   (i) **Irrigation and Water Management:** Develop efficient water systems like drip irrigation and rainwater harvesting to counter unpredictable monsoons and water scarcity. *(1 M)*

   (ii) **Land Reforms:** Encourage land consolidation and cooperative farming to overcome the inefficiencies of small landholdings. *(1 M)*

   (iii) **Access to Affordable Credit:** Expand access to low-interest loans through rural banks and microfinance institutions to reduce dependence on high-interest loans from informal sectors. *(1 M)*

   (iv) **Subsidies for Inputs:** Provide subsidies for essential inputs like seeds, fertilizers, and modern equipment to lower farming costs. *(1 M)*

   (v) **Market Access:** Improve infrastructure for storage and transportation and implement minimum support price policies to ensure fair prices for crops, enhancing market access. *(1 M)*

4. Climate change significantly impacts Indian agriculture, affecting the livelihoods of millions:

   (i) **Unpredictable Rainfall:** Erratic monsoon patterns cause droughts or floods, damaging crops and reducing yields. Adaptation requires efficient water management and irrigation practices. *(1 M)*

   (ii) **Increased Temperatures:** Higher temperatures can stress crops, alter growing seasons, and reduce productivity, necessitating the development of heat-resistant crop varieties. *(1 M)*

   (iii) **Water Scarcity:** Rising temperatures lead to higher evaporation rates, exacerbating water scarcity. Implementing water-saving technologies like drip irrigation is essential. *(1 M)*

   (iv) **Pest and Disease Incidence:** Warmer conditions favor the spread of pests and diseases, impacting crop health. Integrated pest management strategies become crucial. *(1 M)*

   (v) **Soil Degradation:** Extreme weather events contribute to soil erosion and loss of fertility, calling for sustainable soil management practices. *(1 M)*

5. Indian agriculture utilizes a variety of irrigation systems to ensure water reaches farmlands efficiently.

   (i) **Canal Irrigation:** One of the most common systems, where water is diverted from rivers through a network of canals to agricultural fields. It's suitable for large-scale irrigation in plains. *(1 M)*

   (ii) **Tank Irrigation:** Store's rainwater in tanks for use during dry spells, common in peninsular India's uneven terrain. *(1 M)*

   (iii) **Tube Well Irrigation:** Uses deep wells and pumps to extract groundwater, effective in regions with abundant groundwater like the Gangetic plains. *(1 M)*

(*iv*) **Drip Irrigation:** Efficiently delivers water directly to plant roots via a system of pipes, saving water and ideal for dry areas and valuable crops. *(1 M)*

(*v*) **Sprinkler Irrigation:** Water is sprayed, or sprinkled, over the crops, mimicking rainfall. This method is suitable for uneven terrain and areas with water scarcity. *(1 M)*

6. Challenges Faced by India's Farming Community

(*i*) **Dependence on Monsoons:** Many farmers rely heavily on monsoon rains for irrigation. Inconsistent rainfall patterns, either too much or too little, severely impact crop yields. This uncertainty can lead to crop failure, affecting income and food security. *(2 M)*

(*ii*) **Small Land Holdings:** Due to inheritance laws, land holdings are fragmented, making farming inefficient. The small size of farms hinders the use of modern machinery and technology, limiting productivity and making farming less economically viable. *(1½ M)*

(*iii*) **Lack of Modern Inputs:** Limited access to high-quality seeds, fertilizers, and advanced farming techniques restricts the ability to increase crop yields. Many farmers lack the knowledge or financial resources to invest in modern agricultural practices. *(1½ M)*

Case Based Questions

Case Based-I

(*i*) (*a*) It is based on shifting cultivation

(*ii*) (*a*) Venezuela

(*iii*) (*c*) Brazil

(*iv*) (*d*) Low production

(*v*) (*b*) Madhya pradesh

(*vi*) (*a*) A-III, B-IV, C-II, D-I

Case Based-II

(*i*) The movement reduced landlessness and poverty, fostered community cooperation, and promoted Gram Swarajya. However, it faced resistance from landowners and uneven implementation, limiting its overall effectiveness compared to legislative land reforms. *(1 M)*

(*ii*) Gram Swarajya emphasizes self-sufficiency and local governance. Bhave's Bhoodan-Gramdan movement promoted equitable land ownership and cooperative farming, empowering rural communities and aligning with Gandhi's ideals of decentralized governance and self-reliance. *(1 M)*

(*iii*) The movement's voluntary, non-violent approach had localized success but faced limitations in participation and legal enforcement. *(1 M)*

Legislative land reforms had broader reach and enforcement, making the movement a complementary but less comprehensive approach. *(1 M)*

Case Based-III

(*i*) In India, 'slash and burn' is known as 'Jhumming' in the North-east and 'Podu' or 'Penda' in Andhra Pradesh. In Mexico and Central America, it is called 'Milpa', and in Brazil, it is known as 'Roca'. This shows cultural and geographical variations in similar practices. *(1 M)*

(*ii*) Agroforestry, integrating trees with crops and livestock, can improve soil fertility, reduce erosion, and provide additional income. This sustainable method can maintain soil health and offer a stable agricultural practice for Rinjha's community. *(1 M)*

(*iii*) 'Slash and burn' agriculture leads to deforestation and soil degradation, reducing long-term land productivity. As mentioned, Rinjha's family must find new land each season due to declining soil fertility, highlighting the unsustainable nature of this practice. *(2 M)*

Map Based Questions

1. (*i*) Uttar Pradesh *(1 M for each)*

(*ii*) Punjab

(*iii*) Haryana

(*iv*) Madhya Pradesh

2. (*i*) Punjab *(1 M for each)*

(*ii*) West Bengal

(*iii*) Uttar Pradesh

(*iv*) Andhra Pradesh

❑❑❑

MINERALS AND ENERGY RESOURCES

5

"From the depths of the Earth to the core of our daily lives, minerals and energy resources weave the fabric of our existence, powering our homes, fueling our travels, and shaping our world with their indispensable presence."

SYLLABUS & WEIGHTAGE

List of Concept Names	Years					
	2020	2021	2022	2023	2024	2025
Minerals (Mode of occurrence of Minerals, Types of Minerals, Conservation of Minerals)	–	Exam not Conducted	–	–	1Q (1 M)	(1Q + 1Q + 1Q) (4 M)
Energy Resources (Energy Resources, Conservation of Energy Resources)	1Q (1 M)		2 Q (2 M)	1Q (1 M)	1Q (1 M)	1Q (1 M)

CONCEPT MAP

To Access One Shot Revision Video Scan This QR Code

Minerals and Energy Resources

Minerals (CBSE 2025, 2024)

Meaning: Homogeneous naturally occurring substance with a definable internal structure.

Metallic

Ferrous (CBSE 2024)

Major Iron ores Belts:

- Odisha-Jharkhand belt,
- Durg-Bastar-Chandrapur belt lies in Chhattisgarh and Maharashtra
- Ballari-Chitradurga-Chikkamagaluru-Tumakuru belt in Karnataka
- Maharashtra-Goa belt includes the state of Goa & Maharashtra.

Manganese (CBSE 2025):

- Madhya Pradesh - 33%
- Odisha - 16%
- Andhra Pradesh - 10%
- Maharashtra - 27%
- Karnataka - 12%
- Other states - 2%

Non-Ferrous (CBSE 2025, 2024)

Copper: Used in electrical cables, electronics and chemical industries, The Balaghat mines in Madhya Pradesh, Khetri mines in Rajasthan and Singhbhum district of Jharkhand are leading producers of copper.

Bauxite: Deposits are found in the Amarkantak plateau, Maikal hills and the plateau region of Bilaspur-Katni

Precious

Gold, Silver & Platinum

Non-metallic (CBSE 2025)

Mica: Most indispensable minerals used in electronic industries, Mica deposits are found in the Chota Nagpur plateau, Koderma Gaya Hazaribagh belt of Jharkhand, Ajmer in Rajasthan and Nellore Mica belt in Andhra Pradesh.

Limestone: Found in sedimentary rocks. used raw material for the cement industry and essential for smelting iron ore in the blast furnace.

Energy Resources (CBSE 2025, 2024, 2023, 2022, 2020)

Conventional

Coal: Decaying plants in swamps produce peat, Lignite is a low grade brown coal, which is soft with high moisture content. Bituminous is the most popular coal in commercial use. Anthracite is the highest quality hard coal.

Petroleum: Major petroleum production states are Mumbai High, Gujarat and Assam.

Natural Gas: Discovered in the Krishna-Godavari basin, the Gulf of Cambay Andaman and Nicobar islands. Hazira-Vijaipur-Jagdishpur cross country gas pipeline Links Mumbai High and Basin with the fertilizer, power & industrial complexes in western and northern India.

Electricity

Thermal Electricity: Generated by using coal, petroleum and natural gas in thermal power plants.

Hydro Electricity: Generated by fast flowing water, and by multi-purpose projects like the Damodar Valley Corporation, the Kopili Hydel Project, etc. producing hydroelectric power.

Non-Conventional

Tidal Energy: Oceanic tides can be used to generate electricity. The Gulf of Khambat, the Gulf of Kuchchh in Gujarat on the western coast and Gangetic delta in Sunderban regions of West Bengal provide ideal conditions for utilising tidal energy.

Biogas: Shrubs, Farm waste, Animal and Human waste are used to produce biogas.

Wind Power: Located in Tamil Nadu, Andhra Pradesh, Karnataka, Rajasthan, Gujarat, Kerala, Maharashtra & Lakshdweep

Solar Energy: India has enormous possibilities of tapping solar energy. Photovoltaic technology converts sunlight directly into electricity

Nuclear or Atomic Energy (CBSE 2025): Uranium and thorium available in Jharkhand and in Rajasthan are used for generating atomic or nuclear power. The Monazite sands of Kerala is also rich in Thorium

Geo Thermal Energy: Refers to the heat and electricity produced by using the heat from the heat from the interior of the Earth. Parvati Valley in Himachal and Puga Valley in Ladakh are 2 experimental projects.

1 MINERALS

NCERT Definitions *(Commonly asked in 1 mark)*

- **Mineral:** A homogenous, naturally occurring substance with a definable internal structure.
- **Ore:** An accumulation of any mineral mixed with other elements.
- **Igneous Rocks:** Rocks formed through the cooling and solidification of magma or lava.
- **Metamorphic Rocks:** Rocks formed from the transformation of existing rock types, in the process called metamorphism, which means "change in form". These rocks can also contain minerals in veins and lodes.
- **Sedimentary Rocks:** Rocks formed by the deposition and solidification of mineral and organic particles on the Earth's surface and within bodies of water.

Important Facts

01 Our mineral intake represents only about **0.3 percent** of our **total intake of nutrients**, they are so potent and important that without them we would not be able to utilise the other 99.7 percent of foodstuffs.

02 **Although Over 2000 minerals** have been **identified**, only a few are abundantly found in most of the rocks.

03 **Fluoride** which is used to **reduce cavities**, comes from a **mineral fluorite**.

04 Most kinds of **toothpaste** are made **white** with **titanium oxide**, which comes from minerals called **rutile, ilmenite,** and **anatase**.

05 The **sparkle** in some kinds of **toothpaste** comes from **mica**.

06 The **toothbrush** and **tube** containing the paste are made of **plastics** from **petroleum**.

07 **Ferrous minerals** account for about **3/4th** of the total value of the production of metallic minerals.

08 Nearly **10 kg of manganese** is required to manufacture **one tonne** of **steel**.

09 **Odisha** was the **largest bauxite-producing state** in India in **2016-17**.

10 **Kudre** in Kannada means **horse**. The **highest peak** in the **western ghats** of Karnataka resembles the **face of a horse**. The **Bailadila** hills look like the **hump** of an **ox**, and hence its name.

Classification

Minerals are classified as follows:

- **Minerals**
  - **Metallic**
    - Ferrous (containing iron) e.g. iron ore, Manganese, nickel cobalt, etc.
    - Non-Ferrous e.g. copper, lead, tin, bauxite, etc.
    - Precious e.g. gold, silver, platinum, etc.
  - **Non-Metallic**
    - e.g. mica, salt, potash, sulphur, granite, limestone, marble, sandstone, etc.
  - **Energy Minerals**
    - Coal
    - Petroleum
    - Natural gas

Important Concepts

Mode of Occurrence of Minerals

- **In Igneous and Metamorphic rocks**, Minerals may be found in **cracks, crevices, faults, or joints**. The **smaller** occurrences are called **veins** and the **larger** are called **lodes**. Major metallic minerals like tin, copper, zinc and lead, etc. are obtained from veins and lodes.

  Formation: Minerals in Liquid/ molten and gaseous forms are forced upward through cavities towards the earth's surface. As they rise, they solidify and cool.
- **In sedimentary rocks**, Minerals are found in **beds or layers**. Examples of minerals in these rocks are coal, some forms of iron ores, gypsum, potash salt, sodium salt, etc.

  Formation: Deposition, accumulation, concentration, and evaporation.
- **Residual mass of weathered material** containing ores. An example of this form is Bauxite.

  Formation: The residual mass of weathered material is created by the decomposition of surface rocks and the removal of soluble elements.
- **Alluvial deposits** also known as **'placer deposits'**. Examples of minerals are Gold, Silver, Tin, Platinum, etc.

  Formation: These deposits are found in the Sands of valley floors and the base of hills. These deposits are not corroded by water.
- **Minerals found in ocean water.** Examples are common salt, magnesium, bromine and manganese

Rat-Hole Mining
In most of the tribal areas of north-east India, minerals are owned by individuals or communities. In Meghalaya, there are large deposits of coal, iron ore, limestone and dolomite etc. Coal mining in Jowai and Cherapunjee is done by family member in the form of a long narrow tunnel, known as 'Rat hole' mining. **Note:** The National Green Tribunal has declared such activities illegal.

Types/Classification of Minerals

Ferrous Minerals

- **Iron ore**
  - Iron ore is vital for the manufacturing sector, especially for producing steel, which is fundamental for various industries like construction, automotive, and machinery.

Types of Iron Ores:

- **Magnetite:** This is the highest quality of iron ore, containing up to **70%** iron. It is priced for its magnetic properties, making it especially valuable in the electrical industry.
- **Hematite:** The most important industrial iron ore in terms of usage. It contains a slightly lower iron content than magnetite, ranging from **50-60%**.

Production Concentration:

- The **major states** contributing to iron ore production include Odisha, Chhattisgarh, Karnataka, and Jharkhand. These states accounted for 97% of the total production in the 2018-19 period. The remaining 3% came from **other states**.

Major Iron ore belts in India:

- **Odisha-Jharkhand Belt:**
  This belt includes the Mayurbhanj and Kendujhar districts in Odisha and the Singbhum district in Jharkhand.
  Known for high-grade hematite iron ore found in the Badampahar mines in Odisha and in Gua and Noamundi in Jharkhand.
  The quality of ore in this belt is highly suitable for steel production.
- **Durg-Bastar-Chandrapur Belt:**
  It lies in Chhattisgarh and Maharashtra, Notable for the Bailadila range in the Bastar district of Chhattisgarh.
  This belt is famous for its 14 deposits of super high-grade hematite iron ore, which is among the best in the world for steel making.
  Iron ore from this belt is exported to countries like Japan and South Korea via the Vishakhapatnam port, highlighting its global importance.
- **Ballari-Chitradurga-Chikkamagaluru-Tumakuru Belt:**
  The unique aspect of the Kudremukh mine is its 100% export orientation, with the ore being transported as slurry through a pipeline to a port near Mangaluru for shipment.
- **Maharashtra-Goa Belt:**
  It Includes Goa and the Ratnagiri district of Maharashtra.
  Though the iron ore quality here may not match the high standards of the other belts, it is still efficiently exploited and exported.
  The main exporting port for this belt is Marmagao.

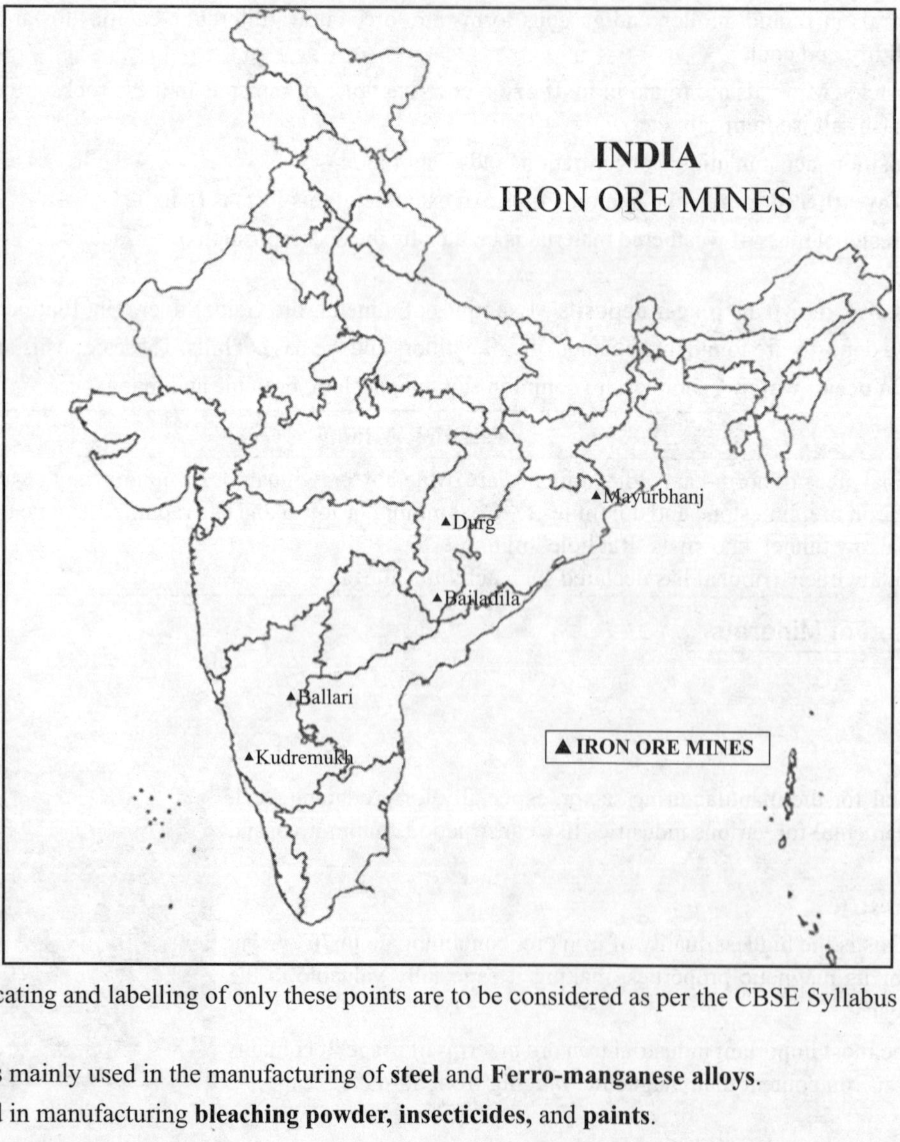

Note: Locating and labelling of only these points are to be considered as per the CBSE Syllabus 2024-25.

❑ Manganese

- Manganese is mainly used in the manufacturing of **steel** and **Ferro-manganese alloys**.
- It is also used in manufacturing **bleaching powder, insecticides,** and **paints**.

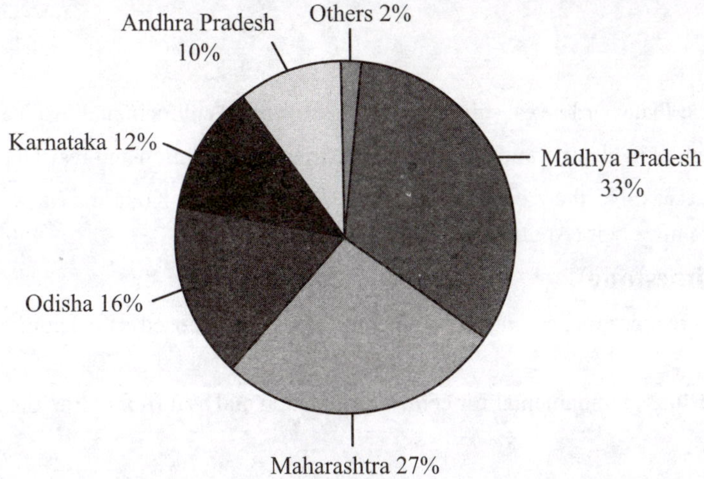

Production of Manganese showing state-wise share in per cent, 2018–19

Non-Ferrous Minerals

Non-ferrous minerals play a vital role in several metallurgical, engineering, and electrical industries.

❒ Copper

- **Importance:** Malleability, ductility, and excellent electrical conductivity.
- **Primary Applications:** Electrical cables, electronics, and the chemical industry.
- **Major Producing Areas:** Balaghat (Madhya Pradesh), Khetri (Rajasthan), Singhbhum (Jharkhand).
- **Challenge:** India faces a deficiency in copper reserves and production, leading to reliance on imports.

❒ Bauxite

- **Bauxite** is a **clay-like substance** from which aluminum is extracted.
- It forms through the **decomposition of rocks** containing **aluminum silicates**.
- **Importance of Aluminum:** Combines strength with lightness, good conductivity, and malleability.
- **Bauxite Deposits:** Found in Amarkantak plateau, Maikal hills, Bilaspur-Katni region.
- **Leading Producer:** Odisha, particularly the Panchpatmali deposits in the Koraput district.

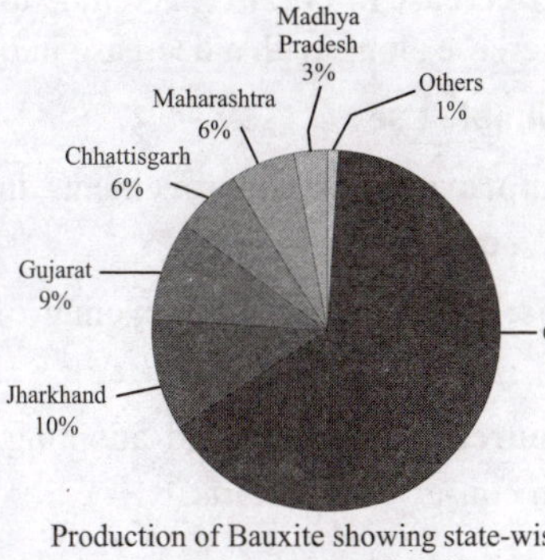

Production of Bauxite showing state-wise share in per cent, 2018–19

Non-Metallic Minerals

Mica

- **Physical Properties:** Plates or leaves, split into thin sheets, varied colors including clear, black, green, red, yellow, or brown.
- **Applications:** Essential in electric and electronic industries for insulation and resistance to high voltage.
- **Major Producing Areas:** Northern edge of the Chota Nagpur plateau, Koderma Gaya – Hazaribagh belt (Jharkhand), Ajmer (Rajasthan), Nellore mica belt (Andhra Pradesh).

Rock Minerals (Limestone)

- **Composition and Occurrence:** Found in sedimentary rocks, composed of calcium carbonates or a mix with magnesium carbonates.
- **Industrial Applications:** Fundamental for cement production and as a flux in iron ore smelting in blast furnaces.

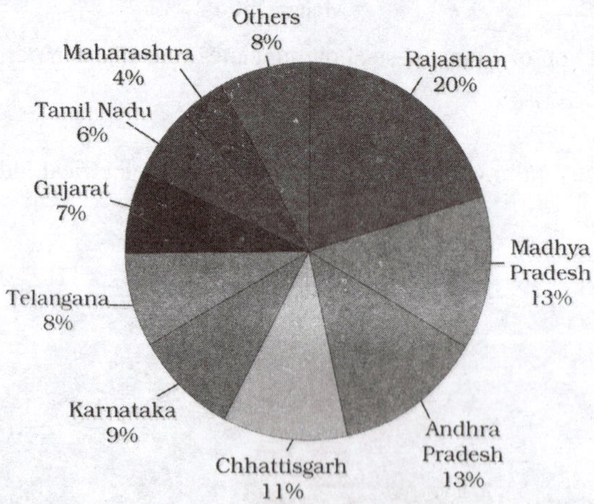

Production of Limestone showing state-wise share in per cent, 2018–19

Hazards of Mining
Health Risks to Miners: Exposure to dust and toxic fumes, leading to pulmonary diseases. Risks of collapsing mine roofs, inundation, and fires.
Environmental Impact: Contamination of water sources due to mining activities. Degradation of land and soil from waste dumping. Increased pollution in streams and rivers from slurry disposal.
Need for Regulations: Stricter safety regulations for miner protection. Implementation of environmental laws to reduce mining's impact.

Conservation of Minerals

- **Finite Resources:** Minerals, formed over **millions of years**, constitute **only 1%** of the **earth's crust**, highlighting their scarcity.
- **Non-renewable nature:** Once depleted, minerals **cannot be replenished** at a pace that matches their current consumption rate.
- **Extraction Costs & Decrease in Quality:** As minerals become scarcer, the financial and environmental costs of their extraction from deeper layers increase along with a decrease in quality.

  Strategies for Sustainable Use:

  - **Technological Improvements:** Improvements in technology are important for utilizing low-grade ores efficiently and reducing extraction costs.
  - **Recycling Efforts:** Emphasizing the recycling of metals and the use of scrap metals can significantly conserve mineral resources.
  - **Alternative Resources:** Exploring and adopting alternative resources can reduce the dependency on specific minerals, thereby helping in conservation efforts.

COMPETENCY BASED SOLVED EXAMPLES

Scan Me for Detailed Explanations

Multiple Choice Questions (1 M)

1. **Ananya finds an interesting crystal during a science project and brings it to her geologist aunt for examination. Her aunt explained that she could learn a lot about the crystal by studying its internal structure. Why might Ananya's geologist aunt be particularly interested in the crystal's internal structure?** ***(An)***

   (*a*) To determine its age
   (*b*) To classify it and understand its properties
   (*c*) To find its exact geographical location
   (*d*) To assess its economic value

2. **Health Nutri-Corp, a nutrition research organization, is hosting a seminar on the importance of minerals in human nutrition. During the seminar, two statements are presented regarding the role of minerals in the diet. Analyze the two statements given below about the role of minerals in human nutrition and which one is correct option.** ***(An)***

   Statement I: Minerals, though they constitute only 0.3% of total nutrient intake, are essential for various life processes in human nutrition.

   Statement II: Due to their minimal presence, minerals are not considered vital for the body's functioning.

   Choose the correct answer:
   (*a*) Both statements are false.
   (*b*) Statement I is true, Statement II is false.
   (*c*) Statement I is false, Statement II is true.
   (*d*) Both statements are true.

3. **The environmental science club at a school is creating an educational exhibit on different types of mineral deposits. As part of the exhibit, they want to include a section that explains various mineral formations and their characteristics. The students have researched and categorized the following formations: veins, lodes, placer deposits, and beds. They need to create a matching activity to help visitors understand where these mineral deposits are typically found.** ***(Un)***

	Column-I (Occurrences)		Column-II (Descriptions)
(A)	Veins	(i)	Large deposits found in faults or joints
(B)	Lodes	(ii)	Smaller deposits found in cracks and crevices
(C)	Placer deposits	(iii)	Minerals found in the sands of valley floors
(D)	Beds	(iv)	Layers of mineral deposits in sedimentary rocks

   Choose the correct options:
   (*a*) A-(ii), B-(i), C-(iii), D-(iv)
   (*b*) A-(i), B-(ii), C-(iv), D-(iii)
   (*c*) A-(iii), B-(iv), C-(ii), D-(i)
   (*d*) A-(iv), B-(iii), C-(i), D-(ii)

4. **During a school debate on natural resources, one team argues that India's mineral resources are unevenly distributed due to geological factors. The other team needs to provide specific examples of regions and their associated minerals to support this claim.** ***(Ev)***

   Statement I: Sedimentary rocks in Gujarat and Assam contain most of India's petroleum deposits.

   Statement II: The vast alluvial plains of North India are rich in economic minerals.

   Choose the correct answer:
   (*a*) Both statements are false.
   (*b*) Statement I is true, Statement II is false.
   (*c*) Statement I is false, Statement II is true.
   (*d*) Both statements are true.

5. **Which one of the following minerals is contained in the Monazite sand?** ***(Re)*(NCERT)**

   (*a*) Oil (*b*) Uranium
   (*c*) Thorium (*d*) Coal

6. **Which one of the following is an example of the Ferrous Metal?** ***(Re)*(CBSE, 2023)**

   (*a*) Copper (*b*) Tin
   (*c*) Bauxite (*d*) Nickel

Assertion and Reason (1 M)

Direction: The following questions consist of two statements – Assertion (A) and Reason (R). Answer these questions by selecting the appropriate option given below:

(*a*) Both A and R are true, and R is the correct explanation of A.
(*b*) Both A and R are true, but R is not the correct explanation of A.
(*c*) A is true, but R is false.
(*d*) A is false, but R is true.

1. **A government task force is evaluating the potential for increasing iron ore production in India to boost the country's industrial growth. They are reviewing geological reports to understand the distribution and quality of iron ores in various regions, aiming to recommend the most promising areas for new mining operations**

   Assertion (A): India is endowed with abundant resources of good quality iron ores.

   Reason (R): Magnetite has excellent magnetic qualities and contains up to 70% iron, making it highly valuable in the electrical industry. ***(Ev)***

2. **As a policy maker, you are drafting a policy to boost the production of certain minerals in India. You need to evaluate the importance of different metals and their sources to make informed decisions that will benefit the country's metallurgical and engineering industries.**

Assertion (A): Aluminium is an important metal because it combines the strength of metals like iron with extreme lightness.

Reason (R): Aluminium is mainly obtained from bauxite deposits found in the Amarkantak plateau, Maikal hills, and the Bilaspur-Katni plateau region. ***(Ev)***

3. **Assertion (A):** Coal is the most abundant fossil fuel in India.

Reason (R): India has large reserves of coal, which are mainly found in the Gondwana coalfields. ***(Un)***

4. **Assertion (A):** Non-metallic minerals like limestone and gypsum are essential for the cement industry.

Reason (R): Limestone and gypsum are used as raw materials in the production of cement, which is a primary building material. ***(Un)***

Subjective Questions

Very Short Answer Type Questions (1 or 2 M)

1. **What is a mineral?** ***(Un)*(NCERT)**

Ans. A mineral is defined as a homogenous, naturally occurring substance with a definable internal structure. Minerals are found in various forms in nature, ranging from the hardest diamond to the softest talc, showcasing a wide range of colors, hardness, crystal forms, lustre, and density. *(2 M)*

2. **You are an environmental scientist working with a team to assess the potential for mining in a newly discovered region. During your survey, a team member finds a rock containing a high concentration of a valuable mineral. define the term "ore" as used in the context of minerals.** ***(Re)***

Ans. An ore is a rock containing a high concentration of a valuable mineral. This significant concentration makes the extraction of the mineral economically feasible or commercially viable, enabling profitable mining operations. *(2 M)*

3. **The Ministry of Commerce and Industry is preparing a comprehensive report on the role of various minerals in driving India's economic growth. As part of this initiative, the Ministry is focusing on understanding the significance of ferrous minerals and their impact on different sectors of the economy.** ***(Un)***

Ans. Ferrous minerals, mainly iron ore, are vital for steel production, a backbone of industrial development and in economic impact, contributing 3/4th of the total value of metallic minerals. *(1 M)*

Sectors Benefited: They significantly support various sectors, including construction, automotive, and machinery, driving economic growth. *(1 M)*

4. **You are Rohit, a materials scientist working for a leading electronics manufacturing company, ElectronTech Innovations. The company is exploring alternative materials to enhance its product efficiency. The management has asked you to explain why mica is considered an important mineral for the electric and electronic industries?** ***(Un)***

Ans. Importance of Mica in Electric and Electronic Industries

(*i*) **Dielectric Strength:** Mica is essential due to its excellent di-electric strength, which allows it to withstand high voltages. *(½ M)*

(*ii*) Its low power loss factor ensures efficiency. *(½ M)*

(*iii*) Insulating properties make it ideal for use in electronic components. *(½ M)*

(*iv*) Resistance to high voltage prevents breakdown in electrical circuits. *(½ M)*

Short Answer Type Questions (3 M)

1. **"A concerted effort has to be made in order to use mineral resources in a planned and sustainable manner." Suggest and explain any three measures.** ***(Cr)***

Ans. **Recycling of Metals:** Recycling and reusing existing metals reduce the need for new mining, conserving resources and energy. *(1 M)*

- **Use of Low-Grade Ores:** Advancements in technology can make the extraction of minerals from low-grade ores more economically viable, reducing waste. *(1 M)*
- **Sustainable Mining Practices:** Implementing environmentally friendly mining techniques minimizes ecological damage and ensures that mineral resources are available for future generations. *(1 M)*

Nailing the Right Answer

- ❒ Clearly suggest measures like recycling of metals to conserve resources.
- ❒ Explain how the use of low-grade ores with advanced technology can reduce waste.
- ❒ Elaborate on the importance of sustainable mining practices to ensure resource availability for future generations.

2. **Geo-Explorers Ltd., a leading mining company, is conducting a training session for new employees to help them understand the diverse physical properties of minerals. during the session, a question arose about why minerals exhibit a wide range of physical properties such as colour and hardness.** ***(Un)***

Ans. Minerals exhibit a range of physical properties due to:

(*i*) **Chemical Composition:** Different elements and compounds create diverse colours. *(1 M)*

(*ii*) **Crystal Structure:** Variations in atomic arrangement affect hardness. *(1 M)* (*iii*) **Impurities:** Trace elements and inclusions change colour and hardness. for example, iron can give a red hue, while different carbon structures form diamond (hard) and graphite (soft). *(1 M)*

3. Distinguish between Ferrous and Non-Ferrous Minerals. *(3M)* ***(An)*(NCERT)**

Ans.

Aspect	Ferrous Minerals	Non-Ferrous Minerals
Composition	Contain iron	Do not contain iron
Examples	Iron ore, manganese	Copper, bauxite, lead, zinc
Uses	Used in steel and iron industries, manufacturing of machinery	Used in electrical, aerospace, and packaging industries

4. How are minerals formed in igneous and metamorphic rocks? *(3M)* ***(Re)*(NCERT)**

Ans. Cracks and Crevices Formation: In igneous and metamorphic rocks, minerals may occur in the cracks, crevices, faults, or joints, known as veins and lodes. *(1 M)*

- **Upward Movement:** Minerals in liquid/molten and gaseous forms are forced upward through cavities towards the Earth's surface. *(1 M)*
- **Cooling and Solidification:** As these mineral forms rise, they cool and solidify, resulting in the formation of metallic minerals like tin, copper, zinc, and lead. *(1 M)*

Mistakes 101 : What not to do!

- **Lack of Specific Examples:** Students might fail to provide specific examples of minerals formed in igneous and metamorphic rocks, which are essential for a comprehensive answer.
- **Incomplete Explanation:** The answer could be more detailed in explaining the process of mineral formation in igneous and metamorphic rocks, such as the role of pressure and temperature in metamorphic rock formation.
- **Missing Information:** The response could include information about the types of minerals commonly found in igneous and metamorphic rocks to enhance the answer's depth and accuracy.

5. Imagine you are an industrial engineer working for a company that manufactures steel. Your team is facing challenges in improving the quality and durability of the steel produced. After some research, you come across information about manganese as a potential solution.

Analyze the properties of manganese and explain how it can enhance the steel production process. ***(An)***

Ans. Manganese is a crucial metal in industry.

Properties of Manganese: Manganese is a **hard, brittle** metal with high tensile strength and it is highly **oxidizable**, forming manganese dioxide. *(1 M)*

Enhancement in Steel Production:

(*i*) **Deoxidizing Agent:** Manganese removes oxygen and sulfur impurities from steel, improving its ductility and toughness. *(1 M)*

(*ii*) **Wear Resistance:** Manganese increases the wear resistance of steel, making it more suitable for high-stress applications. *(1 M)*

6. The Steel Authority of India Limited (SAIL) is considering expanding its operations to include a new iron ore processing plant. As part of the feasibility study, the board needs to understand the differences between the two main types of iron ore, their properties, and their specific uses in the steelmaking process. As a consultant for SAIL, prepare a detailed report comparing the two main types of iron ore, highlighting their differences and uses. ***(An)***

Ans. Comparison of two main types of iron ore are Magnetite and Hematite: **(Any three)(1 M for each)**

Parameter	Magnetite	Hematite
Qualities	Excellent magnetic qualities and appears black or brownish-black in colour.	Most important industrial iron ore and has a reddish or reddish-brown colour.
Use	Valuable in the electrical industry	Widely used in various industries
Abundance and Iron Content.	Less abundant and up to 70% Iron Content.	More abundant and 50-60% Iron Content.
Comparison	Higher iron content, more valuable.	Lower iron content, more widely used.

Long Answer Type Questions (5 M)

1. Differentiate between metallic and non-metallic minerals with examples. ***(An)***

Ans. **(1 Mark for each points)**

Base	Metallic Minerals	Non-Metallic Minerals
Meaning	Minerals that contain metal in raw form and are generally hard substances.	Minerals that do not contain metals and encompass a vast range of minerals with diverse properties.
Conductivity	Good conductors of electricity and heat.	Poor conductors of electricity and heat.
Luster	Possess a shiny or metallic luster.	Do not exhibit a metallic luster; appearance can be dull, glassy, or pearly.

Examples	Iron ore (used in steel making), bauxite (used in aluminum production), copper (used in electrical wires).	Mica (used in electrical insulators), gypsum (used in plaster and drywall), limestone (used in cement production).
Economic Use	Mainly used in the manufacturing of machinery, vehicles, and construction materials.	Used in industries like construction, agriculture, pharmaceuticals, and cosmetics.

2. **Lokesh is a consultant for a mining company tasked with evaluating a potential mining site. To make an informed decision, he needs to analyze the various modes of occurrence of minerals found at the site. Discuss the different ways minerals can occur in nature and explain how each mode of occurrence influences the mining methods and the economic viability of extracting these minerals.** ***(An)***

Ans. Minerals occur in nature in several ways, affecting the mining methods and economic viability of extraction:

(*i*) **Igneous and Metamorphic Rocks:** Minerals in cracks, crevices, and faults (veins and lodes) require drilling and blasting, useful for minerals like tin and copper. Economically viable for high-concentration minerals like tin and copper. *(1 M)*

(*ii*) **Sedimentary Rocks:** Minerals like coal and gypsum in beds or layers are mined through surface mining, such as strip mining or open-pit mining, which are Cost-effective but can cause significant environmental impact. Common for coal and gypsum. *(1 M)*

(*iii*) **Residual Deposits:** Minerals like bauxite, from decomposed surface rocks, are extracted via open-cast mining, making it economically viable. *(1 M)*

(*iv*) **Alluvial Deposits:** Minerals like gold in valley floors and hill bases are extracted through placer mining, a cost-effective and less environmentally damaging method. *(1 M)*

(*v*) **Ocean Water:** Extracting minerals like salt and magnesium through evaporation is viable for minerals abundant in seawater. *(1 M)*

3. **What are the major iron ore belts in India?** ***(Re)***

Ans. ***(i)* Odisha-Jharkhand Belt:** This belt includes the Mayurbhanj and Kendujhar districts in Odisha and the Singbhum district in Jharkhand. It is known for high-grade hematite iron ore found in the Badampahar mines in Odisha and in Gua and Noamundi in Jharkhand. *(1¼ M)*

***(ii)* Durg-Bastar-Chandrapur Belt:** It lies in Chhattisgarh and Maharashtra, Notable for the Bailadila range in the Bastar district of Chhattisgarh. This belt is famous for its 14 deposits of super high-grade hematite iron ore, which is among the best in the world for steel making. *(1¼ M)*

***(iii)* Ballari-Chitradurga-Chikkamagaluru-Tumakuru Belt:** It lies in Karnataka and is rich in iron ore reserves, with the Kudremukh mines being a prominent feature. These mines are recognised for having one of the largest deposits in the world. *(1¼ M)*

***(iv)* Maharashtra-Goa Belt:** It Includes Goa and the Ratnagiri district of Maharashtra. Though the iron ore quality here may not match the high standards of the other belts, it is still efficiently exploited and exported. The main exporting port for this belt is Marmagao. *(1¼ M)*

4. **Ananya is a research analyst working for the National Mineral Development Corporation (NMDC). The NMDC has tasked you with preparing an insightful report on the impact of energy minerals on India's economy. In your report, you must:**

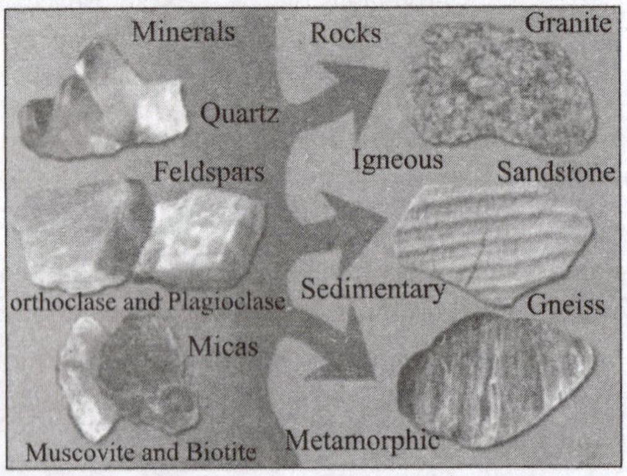

(*a*) Explain the classification of minerals. ***(Un)***

(*b*) Analyze the significance of energy minerals specifically in the context of India's economic growth. ***(An)***

Ans. (*a*) Minerals are classified based on their properties and uses. *(1 M for each)*

Metallic Minerals	Non-Metallic Minerals
(*i*) **Ferrous:** Containing iron, iron ore, manganese, nickel, cobalt	(*i*) **Example:** Mica, salt, potash, sulphur, granite, limestone, marble, sandstone.
(*ii*) **Non-ferrous:** copper, lead, tin, bauxite.	(*ii*) **Energy Minerals:** Coal, petroleum, natural gas.

(*b*) Role of Energy Minerals: *(Any two) (1 M for each)*

***(i)* Coal:** Essential for power generation, industrial fuel, and domestic energy needs.

***(ii)* Petroleum:** Provides fuel for heat and lighting, lubricants for machinery, and raw materials for various industries.

***(iii)* Natural Gas:** Used as a domestic and industrial fuel, for electricity generation, and as a raw material in chemical and fertilizer industries.

Economic Impact: Energy minerals are crucial for India's economic growth and development, ensuring energy security and supporting various sectors. *(1 M)*

2 ENERGY RESOURCES

NCERT Definitions *(Commonly asked in 1 mark)*

- **Conventional Sources of Energy:** Traditional energy sources including firewood, cattle dung cake, coal, petroleum, natural gas, and electricity (both hydel and thermal) that have been used for generations.
- **Non-Conventional Sources of Energy:** Modern energy sources that are considered alternative or renewable, including solar, wind, tidal, geothermal, biogas, and atomic energy.

Important Facts

01 According to one estimate **more than 70 percent of energy requirements** in **rural households** are met by **Firewood** and **cattle dung cake**.

02 **Assam** is the **oldest oil-producing state** in India.

03 From the initial **1,700 km, India's gas infrastructure** has expanded **more than tenfold** to approximately **18,500 km** of cross-country pipelines. It's expected to extend further to over **34,000 km**.

Classification

Sources of Energy are classified as follows

Basis	Conventional Sources of Energy	Non-Conventional Sources of Energy
Meaning	Traditional Energy sources	Modern Energy sources
Examples	Coal, petroleum, natural gas, and thermal electricity.	Solar energy, wind energy, bioenergy, geothermal energy, nuclear energy and tidal energy.
Availability	Limited and tend to get exhausted over time.	Virtually inexhaustible and replenish naturally.
Environmental Impact	Generally high, leading to pollution and contributing to climate change.	Much lower, considered environmentally friendly and sustainable.
Cost of Production	Lower initial costs but becomes expensive in the long term due to depletion and environmental damage.	Higher initial investment but lower operational costs and sustainable in the long term.
Renewability	Non-renewable; their formation takes millions of years.	Renewable; can be replenished naturally in a short period of time.

Important Concepts

Energy Resources

Conventional Sources of Energy:

❐ Coal

- Coal is a fossil fuel, formed from the remains of vegetation over millions of years through compression and heating.

Types of Coal:

- **Peat:** Initial stage, low carbon and high moisture content, low heating capacity.
- **Lignite:** Also known as brown coal with low grade, and high moisture content, primarily found in Neyveli, Tamil Nadu.
- **Bituminous:** Widely used for power generation and in industries, found in Jharia, Raniganj, and Bokaro.
- **Anthracite:** Highest quality coal with high carbon content.

  Gondwana Coalfields: Over 200 million years old, **found in the Damodar valley** (West Bengal-Jharkhand). Key sites include Jharia, Raniganj, and Bokaro.

  Tertiary Coalfields: About 55 million years old, **located in northeastern states** like Meghalaya, Assam, Arunachal Pradesh, and Nagaland.

❐ Petroleum

- **Petroleum**, also known as **mineral oil**, is a significant energy source in India, **second** only **to coal**.
- It serves various **purposes** including fuel for heat and lighting, lubricants for machinery, and raw materials for industries.
- Petroleum refineries act as a **"nodal industry"** for synthetic textile, fertiliser and numerous chemical industries.

Geological Features:

- Most petroleum in India is found associated with anticlines and fault traps in tertiary-age rock formations.
- It is commonly found in areas with folding, trapped in the crest of anticlines or domes, within porous limestone or sandstone layers.
- Non-porous layers above and below the oil-bearing layers prevent the oil from migrating.
- Petroleum is also found in fault traps, where porous rocks are adjacent to non-porous rocks, with gas typically found above oil due to its lighter nature.

Major Production Areas:

- **Mumbai High:** A crucial offshore oil field located off the western coast of India.
- **Gujarat:** Known for the **Ankeleshwar field**, it's a significant onshore petroleum production area.
- **Assam:** The oldest **oil-producing state in India**, with notable fields like Digboi, Naharkatiya, and Moran-Hugrijan.

❐ Natural Gas

- Natural gas, often found alongside petroleum deposits, is a **versatile fuel** used both domestically and industrially.

Uses of Natural Gas:

- **Power Generation:** Utilized in the power sector to generate electricity.
- **Industrial Heating:** Employed for heating purposes across various industries.
- **Raw Material:** Acts as a crucial input for chemical, petrochemical, and fertilizer industries.
- **Transport Fuel:** With infrastructure expansion, it's becoming a favored option for vehicles (as Compressed Natural Gas or CNG).
- **Domestic Fuel:** Increasingly used in homes for cooking (as Piped Natural Gas or PNG) due to the expansion of City Gas Distribution (CGD) networks.

Major Reserves and Production Areas:

- **Western Coast:** Mumbai High and allied fields, along with the Cambay basin, are significant sources of natural gas.
- **Eastern Coast:** The Krishna-Godavari basin has emerged as a new reservoir of natural gas.

- **Hazira-Vijaipur-Jagdishpur (HVJ) Pipeline:** A landmark **1,700 km** long cross-country gas pipeline **developed by GAIL** (India) that connects the Mumbai High and Bassein gas fields to fertilizer, power, and industrial complexes in western and northern India.

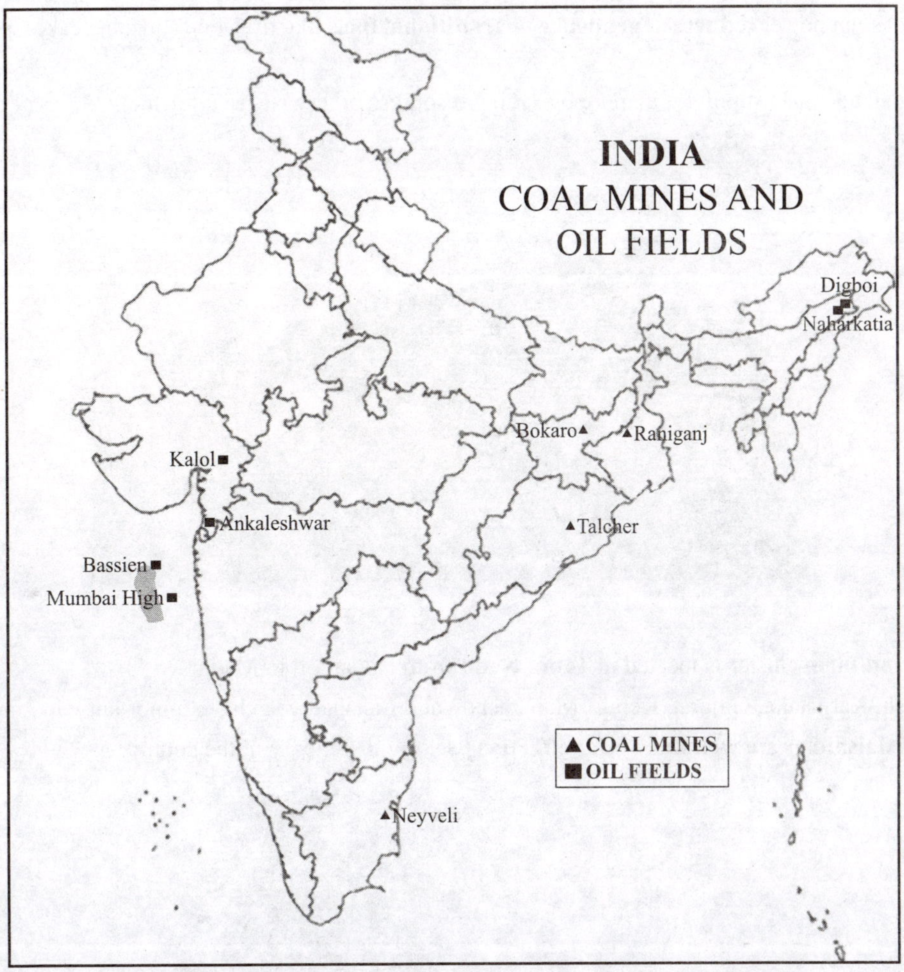

Note: Locating and labelling of only these points are to be considered as per the CBSE Syllabus 2024-25.

❒ Electricity

Methods of Generating Electricity:

- **Hydroelectricity:** It is a **renewable** form of energy produced by utilizing the kinetic energy of flowing water to drive hydro turbines. This method relies on renewable water resources. India boasts several multi-purpose projects like Bhakra Nangal, Damodar Valley Corporation, and the Kopili Hydel Project that contribute to hydroelectric power production.
- **Thermal Power:** It is a **non-renewable** form of energy generated by burning fossil fuels such as coal, petroleum, and natural gas. These fuels drive turbines to create electricity at thermal power stations. Unlike hydroelectricity, thermal power relies on non-renewable fossil fuels.

Non-Conventional Sources of Energy:

❒ Nuclear or Atomic Energy

- Nuclear or atomic energy is produced through alterations in the structure of atoms, a process that releases a significant amount of energy as heat.
- **Uranium** and **Thorium** are the **primary materials** used in generating **nuclear power**. India sources its Uranium from the mines in Jharkhand and the Aravalli ranges of Rajasthan.
- **The Monazite sands** of Kerala are notably **rich in Thorium**, a significant resource for India's nuclear energy sector.

❒ Solar Energy

- Given its geographical advantage, India has a vast **potential** for tapping into solar energy due to its **location** in the **tropical zone**.
- **Photovoltaic (PV) technology** plays a crucial role in converting sunlight directly into electricity, harnessing solar power efficiently.

Benefits for Rural and Remote Areas:

- Solar energy is becoming increasingly popular in India's rural and remote regions, offering a **reliable** and **sustainable energy source**.
- The adoption of solar power **reduces dependence on traditional fuels** like firewood and dung cakes, promoting environmental conservation.
- It also ensures an adequate supply of manure by saving resources otherwise used for fuel.

❒ Wind Power

- The **largest wind farm** cluster is located in **Tamil Nadu** from Nagarcoil to Madurai.
- Andhra Pradesh, Karnataka, Gujarat, Kerala, Maharashtra and Lakshadweep have important wind farms also.
- **Nagarcoil** and **Jaisalmer** are **well known** for **effective use** of wind energy in the country.

❒ Biogas

- Biogas is produced from organic materials such as shrubs, farm waste, and animal & human waste through the process of **decomposition**.
- The gas produced from the decomposition process has a **higher thermal efficiency** than conventional fuels like kerosene, dung cakes, and charcoal, making it a **preferable** choice for **domestic consumption**, especially in rural areas.
- Biogas plants can be established at various levels, including municipal, cooperative, and individual households.
- Biogas plants using **cattle dung** are known as **'Gobar gas plants'** in rural India.

Benefits:

- **Energy Production:** Offers a sustainable source of energy for cooking and lighting.
- **Improved Manure Quality:** The process enhances the quality of manure, providing a nutrient-rich fertilizer for agriculture.
- **Environmental Conservation:** Promotes the conservation of trees and manure by reducing the dependency on fuelwood and cow dung cakes for energy.

❒ Tidal Energy

Tidal energy involves harnessing the energy from oceanic tides to generate electricity, leveraging the natural ebb and flow of ocean tides.

Mechanism of Generating Tidal Energy:

- **Floodgate Dams:** Constructed across inlets, these structures capture water during high tide. The water is then retained and released through a turbine for power generation as the tide outside the floodgate recedes, driving the turbine to produce electricity.

Advantages of Tidal Energy:

- Tidal energy is a **renewable** and **clean source** of power that reduces dependency on fossil fuels and minimizes environmental impact.
- The **predictability** of tides **enhances** the **reliability** of tidal energy over other renewable sources like solar and wind.

Potential Sites in India:

- **Gulf of Khambhat and Gulf of Kuchchh:** Located on Gujarat's western coast, these gulfs are identified as promising sites for tidal energy due to their significant tidal range.
- **Gangetic Delta in the Sunderban Region:** The vast tidal flows in the Sunderban regions of West Bengal also offer ideal conditions for tapping into tidal energy.

❒ Geo-Thermal Energy

- Geothermal energy is the **heat** and **electricity generated** from the **Earth's interior heat**. This energy form is considered renewable and sustainable.

Mechanism of Geothermal Energy Production:

- The Earth's temperature increases with depth, leading to high temperatures at shallow depths in areas with a high geothermal gradient.
- Groundwater in such regions absorbs heat from surrounding rocks, becoming hot. When this heated water rises to the Earth's surface, it can transform into steam.
- This steam is then harnessed to drive turbines, which in turn generate electricity.
- There are **several hundred hot springs** in India, which could be used to generate electricity.

Experimental Projects in India:

- **Parvati Valley near Manikarn in Himachal Pradesh:** One of the first sites for geothermal energy exploration.
- **Puga Valley in Ladakh:** Another important site that demonstrates the potential for geothermal energy generation in India.

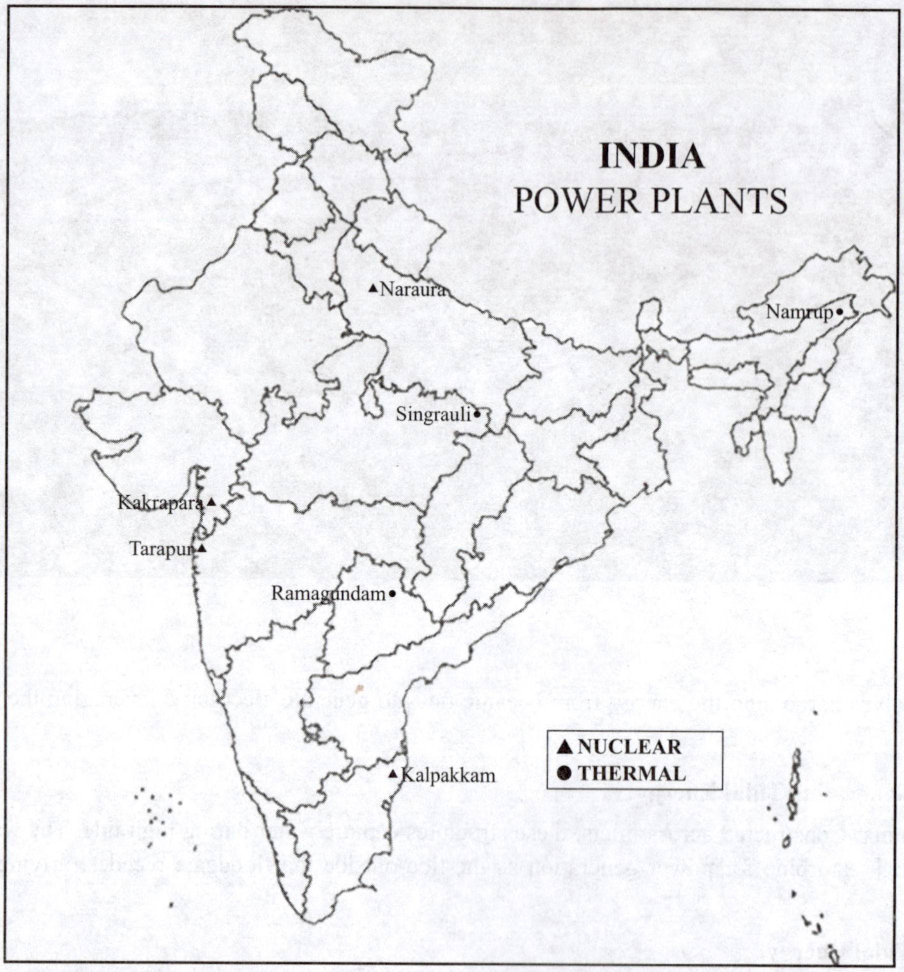

Note: Locating and labelling of only these points are to be considered as per the CBSE Syllabus 2024-25.

Conservation of Energy Resources

❐ **Need for Sustainable Energy Development:**

- Given the continuous rise in energy consumption, there is an urgent need to develop a sustainable path of energy development, focusing on energy conservation and the adoption of renewable energy sources.
- India ranks low in terms of energy efficiency on a global scale, indicating a considerable scope for improvement in how energy is used and conserved.

❐ **Strategies for Energy Conservation:**

- Promotion of energy conservation measures and an increased reliance on renewable energy sources are vital for achieving sustainable energy development.

❐ **Maxim "Energy Saved is Energy Produced":**

- The principle emphasizes the importance of energy conservation, suggesting that saving energy through efficient use and practices is similar to generating energy.

Mnemonics

❐ **Conventional sources of energy**

COMPETENCY BASED SOLVED EXAMPLES

Scan Me for Detailed Explanations

Multiple Choice Questions (1 M)

1. In which of the following States is Kalpakkam Nuclear Power Plant located? ***(Re)*(CBSE, 2020)**

(*a*) Gujarat (*b*) Odisha

(*c*) Kerala (*d*) Tamil Nadu

2. Observe the map given below showing the distribution of thermal and nuclear power plants across India.

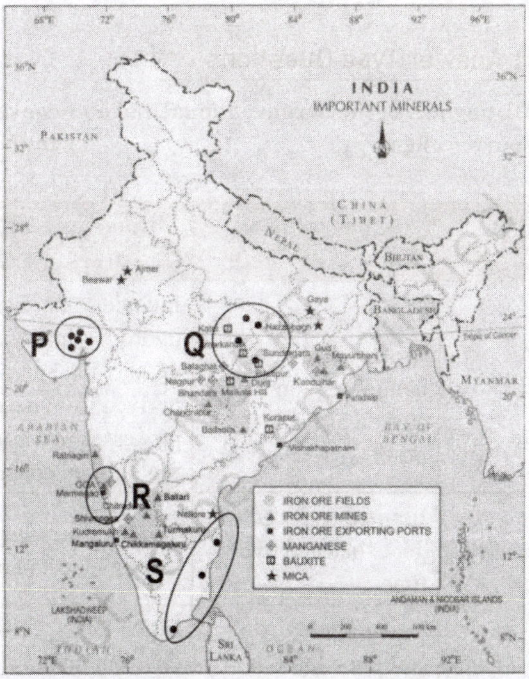

Air Quality Index (AQI) is used to measure real-time air pollution levels. A high AQI represents poor air quality. Accordingly, which of the following regions marked on the map is LIKELY to experience comparatively better AQI? ***(An)*(CBSE APQ, 2023)**

(*a*) P (*b*) Q

(*c*) R (*d*) S

3. Priya is an environmental activist who is organizing a community workshop on energy conservation practices in India. She wants to educate the attendees on various methods to save energy and promote sustainable development. Help Priya by identifying the correct statement regarding energy conservation in India from the following options. ***(Un)***

(*a*) Energy conservation is not necessary for economic development.

(*b*) Renewable energy sources do not contribute to sustainable energy development.

(*c*) Using public transport systems is one way to promote energy conservation.

(*d*) India is the most energy-efficient country in the world.

4. As the policy advisor, you are tasked with preparing a report that analyzes the potential long-term environmental and economic impacts if the country continues to use coal at the current rate. Based on your analysis, select the most likely outcome from the options below and provide your recommendations to the government to mitigate these impacts. ***(An, Ev)***

(*a*) Improvement in air quality and economic stability.

(*b*) Decrease in global temperatures and economic growth.

(*c*) Increase in air pollution and rising energy costs.

(*d*) Enhanced biodiversity and reduced mining costs.

5. Ravi is a young environmental scientist working on a project about India's oil and gas production regions. He is preparing a presentation for his community to highlight the significance of various oil-producing areas in India and their geological contexts. Help Ravi by matching the items in Column-I with the correct descriptions in Column-II. ***(Ap)***

	Column-I		Column-II
(A)	Ravi mentions an important offshore oil field that plays a crucial role in India's petroleum production.	(i)	oldest oil-producing state
(B)	Ravi talks about a state known for having a significant onshore oil field that contributes to the country's energy needs.	(ii)	Mumbai High
(C)	Ravi highlights the oldest oil-producing state in India, emphasizing its historical importance in the oil industry.	(iii)	Major onshore oil field
(D)	Ravi explains the geological age of most petroleum occurrences, indicating the period during which these resources were formed.	(iv)	Tertiary rock formations

(*a*) A-(iv), B-(iii), C-(i), D-(ii)

(*b*) A-(iii), B-(i), C-(iv), D-(ii)

(*c*) A-(i), B-(iv), C-(iii), D-(ii)

(*d*) A-(ii), B-(iii), C-(i), D-(iv)

Assertion and Reason (1 M)

Direction: The following questions consist of two statements – Assertion (A) and Reason (R). Answer these questions by selecting the appropriate option given below:

(*a*) Both A and R are true, and R is the correct explanation of A.

(*b*) Both A and R are true, but R is not the correct explanation of A.

(*c*) A is true, but R is false.

(*d*) A is false, but R is true.

1. **As a mining safety inspector, you are assessing the risks associated with mining operations in Jharia, where frequent mine fires and roof collapses occur. During your inspection, you notice a high level of dust and noxious fumes in the air, and many miners are complaining of respiratory issues. Additionally, you observe that safety measures and environmental laws are not strictly followed. evaluate the following statements.**

   Assertion (A): The dust and noxious fumes inhaled by miners make them vulnerable to pulmonary diseases

   Reason (R): Stricter safety regulations and implementation of environmental laws are essential to prevent mining from becoming a "killer industry." ***(Ev)***

2. **Assertion (A):** Wind energy is a renewable source of energy.

   Reason (R): Wind turbines convert kinetic energy from wind into electrical energy without producing any emissions or pollution. ***(An)***

3. **Assertion (A):** Non-Renewable energy sources like solar and wind power are considered environmentally friendly alternatives to fossil fuels.

   Reason (R): Non-Renewable energy sources do not produce harmful greenhouse gas emissions during power generation, unlike fossil fuels. ***(Un and En)***

4. **Assertion (A):** Hydroelectric power plants are not a sustainable source of energy.

   Reason (R): Hydroelectric power is generated by harnessing the energy of flowing water, which is a renewable resource. ***(Ev)***

Subjective Questions

Very Short Answer Type Questions (1 or 2 M)

1. **Sameer is an energy consultant at the Global Energy Research Institute (GERI). The government of India has tasked you with assessing the current state of atomic or nuclear power resources in the country. Identify the main resources for generating atomic or nuclear power in India.** ***(Re)***

Ans. The main resources for generating atomic or nuclear power in India are:

(i) **Uranium:** Sourced from mines in Jharkhand and the Aravalli ranges of Rajasthan. *(½ M)*

(ii) **Thorium:** Abundant in the Monazite sands of Kerala. *(½ M)*

Significance:

Uranium and Thorium are crucial for generating nuclear power, providing a stable and sustainable energy source, and reducing reliance on fossil fuels. *(1 M)*

2. **What are the common sources of energy in rural India?** ***(Re)***

Ans. Firewood and cattle dung cakes are the most common sources of energy in rural India. *(1 M)*

3. **How is solar energy trapped and used?** ***(Un)***

Ans. Solar Panels are used to trap the heat from the sun and are used to heat water in the glass panels. Solar technologies convert sunlight into electrical energy through photovoltaic (PV) panels. *(2 M)*

4. **How is Geo-thermal energy produced?** ***(Un)***

Ans. Geothermal energy refers to the heat and electricity produced by using the heat from the interior of the earth. Steam is generated when the underground water comes in contact with the points forming hot springs. *(2 M)*

5. **What are the full forms of CNG and LPG?** ***(Re)***

Ans. **CNG:** Compressed Natural Gas, used in vehicles. *(1 M)*

LPG: Liquified Petroleum Gas, used as a cooking medium. *(1 M)*

Short Answer Type Questions (3 M)

1. **Distinguish between conventional and non-conventional sources of energy.** ***(An)*(NCERT)**

Ans. *(1 M for each)*

Basis	Conventional Sources of Energy	Non-Conventional Sources of Energy
Origin	Mostly derived from fossil fuels like coal, natural gas, and oil, as well as nuclear power.	Include solar, wind, hydro, biomass, and geothermal energy, derived from natural processes that are replenished constantly.
Availability	Limited and tend to get exhausted over time.	Virtually inexhaustible and replenish naturally.
Environmental Impact	Generally high, leading to pollution and contributing to climate change.	Much lower, considered environmentally friendly and sustainable.

2. **Mohit is a student representative on the National Youth Council for Sustainable Development. The council is preparing a report on India's energy sector, focusing on the role of coal. Evaluate the economic and environmental impacts of coal usage in India.** ***(Ev)***

Ans. Coal is a crucial part of India's energy sector, some impacts of coal usage in India are:

(i) **Economic Impact:** Coal is essential for industrial and economic growth, powering major industries and generating electricity in India. *(1 M)*

(ii) **Environmental Impact:** However, coal mining and usage contribute significantly to air pollution and greenhouse gas emissions, impacting climate and health. *(1 M)*

(iii) **Resource Depletion:** Extensive coal usage depletes finite resources, necessitating sustainable energy alternatives to balance economic and environmental needs. *(1 M)*

3. The Indian Renewable Energy Agency (IREA) is exploring sustainable energy solutions for rural and remote areas of India. As part of their initiative, they are focusing on the benefits of solar energy. discuss the specific advantages of implementing solar energy in rural and remote regions of India. ***(Un)***

Ans. The specific advantages of Solar Energy in Rural India:

(i) **Abundant Resource:** India's tropical location ensures plentiful sunlight, making solar energy a reliable source. *(1 M)*

(ii) **Benefits for rural households:** Low maintenance costs and free electricity reduce economic burdens on rural households. *(1 M)*

(iii) **Environmental Impact:** Reduces reliance on firewood and kerosene, lowering deforestation and pollution. *(1 M)*

4. What are the two main ways of generating electricity? How are they different from each other?

Ans. Electricity is generated:

- By running water which drives hydro turbines to generate hydroelectricity. *(1 M)*
- By burning fuels such as coal, petroleum and natural gas to drive turbines to produce thermal power. *(1 M)*

They are different from each other in the sense that hydroelectricity is generated by water, which is a renewable source, whereas thermal electricity is generated using non-renewable fossil fuels. *(1 M)*

Long Answer Type Questions (5 M)

1. The Indian Ministry of Energy is developing a comprehensive energy strategy to address the growing demand for sustainable energy solutions. As part of this initiative, they are emphasizing the importance of non-conventional sources of energy. explain the significance of non-conventional sources of energy in India's energy strategy. discuss the different types of non-conventional energy sources along with their advantages. ***(Un)***

Ans. Significance in Energy Strategy: Non-conventional sources like solar, wind, tidal, and geothermal are vital for sustainable energy development, reducing dependency on finite fossil fuels. *(1 M)*

Types of Non-Conventional Energy Sources:

(Any four)(½ M for each)

(i) **Solar Energy:** Abundant in India, reduces reliance on traditional fuels, and provides clean energy.

(ii) **Wind Energy:** Effective in coastal regions, provides renewable and clean power.

(iii) **Biogas:** Converts organic waste into energy, improving waste management and providing a renewable source.

(iv) **Geothermal Energy:** Utilizes Earth's internal heat, providing a stable and sustainable energy source.

(v) **Tidal Energy:** Harnesses Ocean tides, offering a predictable and renewable energy source.

Advantages: They lower greenhouse gas emissions, create jobs, reduce energy costs, and support rural development. *(1 M)*

Significance: Non-conventional sources are essential for sustainable development, reducing dependency on finite fossil fuels, and ensuring energy security. *(1 M)*

2. Explain with examples the significance of the usage of non-conventional sources of energy for the country. ***(An and Ap)***

OR

"Non-conventional resources are the best option to conserve the natural resources" Substantiate this statement with Examples. (*Ap* and *An*) (CBSE SQP, 2023)

Ans. The significance of using non-conventional sources of energy for a country includes:

- **Renewable Energy:** Non-conventional sources like solar and wind are abundant and sustainable, reducing dependency on finite fossil fuels. *(1 M)*
- **Environmental Benefits:** They emit fewer pollutants, reducing greenhouse gas emissions and combating climate change. *(1 M)*
- **Economic Advantages:** Creates jobs in renewable energy sectors and lowers energy costs over time due to technological advancements. *(1 M)*
- **Energy Security:** Diversifies energy supply, reducing a country's vulnerability to energy price volatility and supply disruptions. *(1 M)*
- **Rural Development:** Solar and wind projects can provide power to remote areas, improving living conditions and reducing urban migration. *(1 M)*

3. Which is the most abundantly available fossil fuel in India? Assess the importance of its different forms. **(*Re* and *Ev*)(CBSE, 2015)**

Ans. Coal is the most abundantly available fossil fuel in India. *(1 M)* The different forms of coal hold varying importance:

- **Peat:** It has low carbon and high moisture content, with a low heating capacity. It is an early stage of coal formation and has limited commercial use. *(1 M)*
- **Lignite:** It is a low-grade brown coal with high moisture content. It is mainly used for electricity generation. *(1 M)*

- **Bituminous Coal:** This is the most popular coal in commercial use. Metallurgical coal is high grade bituminous coal which has a special value for smelting iron in blast furnaces. It plays a crucial role in the iron and steel industry. *(1 M)*
- **Anthracite:** It is the highest quality hard coal, known for its high carbon content and low moisture content. It is primarily used for heating purposes and has limited commercial significance. *(1 M)*

Each form of coal serves different purposes and contributes to meeting India's energy requirements in various sectors.

Topper's Explanation:

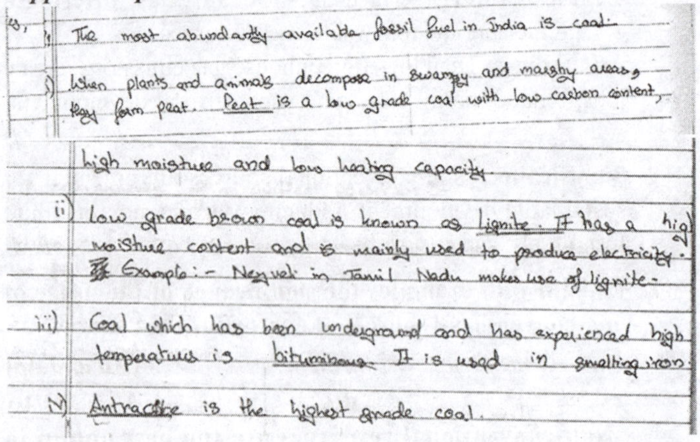
Ans, i) The most abundantly available fossil fuel in India is coal.

i) When plants and animals decompose in swampy and marshy areas, they form peat. Peat is a low grade coal with low carbon content, high moisture and low heating capacity.

ii) Low grade brown coal is known as lignite. It has a high moisture content and is mainly used to produce electricity. Example:- Neyveli in Tamil Nadu makes use of lignite.

iii) Coal which has been underground and has experienced high temperatures is bituminous. It is used in smelting iron.

iv) Antracite is the highest grade coal.

4. How is the per capita consumption of electricity considered as an index of development? Explain with examples. ***(Un)*(CBSE DL, 2024)**

OR

Explain with examples the significance of the usage of non-conventional sources of energy for the country.*(Un)*

Ans. The per capita consumption of electricity is a significant index of development for several reasons:

(i) **Indicator of Development:** Higher per capita electricity consumption signifies better living standards, advanced healthcare, and education, showcasing overall development. *(1 M)*

(ii) **Economic Growth:** Indicates industrialization and technological advancements contributing to a nation's economic strength. *(1 M)*

(iii) **Quality of Life:** Associated with better amenities and infrastructure, improving citizens' comfort and convenience. *(1 M)*

(iv) **Global Comparison:** Countries with higher consumption are often more developed, indicating their global economic position. *(1 M)*

(v) **Policy and Planning:** Guides governments in infrastructure and energy planning, targeting areas needing development. *(1 M)*

OR

The significance of using non-conventional sources of energy for a country includes:

(i) **Renewable Energy:** Non-conventional sources like solar and wind are abundant and sustainable, reducing dependency on finite fossil fuels. *(1 M)*

(ii) **Environmental Benefits:** They emit fewer pollutants, reducing greenhouse gas emissions and combating climate change. *(1 M)*

(iii) **Economic Advantages:** Creates jobs in renewable energy sectors and lowers energy costs over time due to technological advancements. *(1 M)*

(iv) **Energy Security:** Diversifies energy supply, reducing a country's vulnerability to energy price volatility and supply disruptions. *(1 M)*

(v) **Rural Development:** Solar and wind projects can provide power to remote areas, improving living conditions and reducing urban migration. *(1 M)*

5. Why is energy needed? How can we conserve energy resources? Explain. ***(Ap and Ev)***

Ans. Energy is essential for various activities such as cooking, transportation, and electricity generation. It plays a crucial role in economic development and improving the quality of life. Energy is required for industries, agriculture, and healthcare services. *(2 M)*

Conservation of Energy Resources:

- Use energy-efficient appliances and equipment and Opt for renewable energy sources like solar or wind power. *(1 M)*
- Practice energy-saving habits like turning off lights and appliances when not in use. *(1 M)*
- Promote public awareness and education about energy conservation. *(1 M)*

6. How are health and the environment affected by the process of mining? ***(An)***

OR

Analyze the impact of mining activities on the local environment and the health of the surrounding communities. ***(An)*(CBSE SQP, 2023)**

Ans. Mining activity is often called a "killer industry" due to the high risks involved. Here are the health and environmental impacts of it:

(i) **Air Pollution:** Mining activities release particulate matter and hazardous gases like Carbon monoxide and sulfur dioxide into the atmosphere, leading to respiratory problems among workers and nearby populations. *(1 M)*

(ii) **Water Contamination:** Chemicals used in mining operations can leach into water bodies, contaminating them with heavy metals and toxic substances, affecting both aquatic life and human health through water consumption. *(1 M)*

(iii) **Soil Degradation:** Mining disrupts the soil structure, leading to erosion, loss of fertile topsoil, and contamination with chemicals, affecting agricultural productivity and biodiversity. *(1 M)*

(iv) **Habitat Destruction:** Large-scale mining operations involve clearing vast areas of land, leading to the loss of habitats for many species, decreasing biodiversity, and altering ecosystems. *(1 M)*

(v) **Noise and Vibration:** Heavy machinery used in mining generates significant noise and ground vibrations, affecting the health of workers and causing distress to wildlife in the vicinity. *(1 M)*

MISCELLANEOUS EXERCISE

Multiple Choice Questions (1 M)

1. Which one of the following minerals is formed by the decomposition of rocks, leaving a residual mass of weathered material? ***(Un)*(NCERT)**

(*a*) coal (*b*) bauxite

(*c*) gold (*d*) zinc

2. Koderma, in Jharkhand, is the leading producer of which one of the following minerals? ***(Re)*(NCERT)**

(*a*) bauxite (*b*) mica

(*c*) iron ore (*d*) copper

3. Minerals are deposited and accumulated in the strata of which of the following rocks? ***(Re)*(NCERT)**

(*a*) sedimentary rocks (*b*) metamorphic rocks

(*c*) igneous rocks (*d*) none of the above

4. The Ministry of Mines is assessing the risk factors associated with the regional concentration of manganese production in India. They are reviewing data to develop strategies that could mitigate potential disruptions and ensure a stable supply chain. The provided pie chart displays the state-wise share of manganese production for the year 2018-19. analyze the following statements in the context of the provided data and determine their validity to help the Ministry in its assessment. ***(Ev)***

Statement I: Maharashtra and Madhya Pradesh together account for 60% of India's manganese production.

Statement II: This high concentration of production in two states suggests a need for diversification to mitigate risks associated with regional dependencies.

(*a*) Both statements are true.

(*b*) Both statements are false.

(*c*) Statement I is true; Statement II is false.

(*d*) Statement I is false; Statement II is true.

5. Choose the correct option from **Column-I** and **Column-II**. ***(Re)*(CBSE, 2020)**

	Column-I (Minerals)		Column-II (Examples)
(*a*)	Chandrapur thermal power plant	(*i*)	Odisha
(*b*)	Mayurbhanj iron ore mines	(*ii*)	Amarkantak
(*c*)	Kalol oil fields	(*iii*)	Gujarat
(*d*)	Bauxite mines	(*iv*)	Jharkhand

6. In a geography project, students are studying the mineral resources of north-east India. They discover that in this region, unlike the rest of the country, minerals are often owned by individuals or communities. This unique ownership has led to mining practices like 'Rat-hole' mining in Meghalaya. The students also learn about the legal actions taken by the National Green Tribunal against these practices due to environmental concerns. ***(Ap)***

Statement I: In north-east India, particularly in Meghalaya, minerals are owned by individuals or communities rather than being nationalized.

Statement II: The National Green Tribunal has declared 'Rat-hole' mining in Meghalaya illegal due to environmental concerns.

Choose the correct answer:

(*a*) Both statements are false.

(*b*) Statement I is true, Statement II is false.

(*c*) Statement I is false, Statement II is true.

(*d*) Both statements are true.

7. The National Metallurgical Institute is conducting a study on the distribution and quality of iron ores in India. They aim to determine the best sources for high-quality iron ores and their economic impact on industrial development and the Institute finds that the finest iron ore with a very high iron content and excellent magnetic qualities is valuable in the electrical industry. Which type of iron ore are they referring to? ***(Ap)***

(*a*) Hematite (*b*) Magnetite

(*c*) Siderite (*d*) Limonite

8. You are a logistics manager for a mining company that operates the Kudremukh mines in Karnataka. Your task is to optimize the transportation of iron ore to the port near Mangaluru. Which modern technique do you apply to ensure efficient and cost-effective transportation of iron ore from the Kudremukh mines to the port? ***(Ap)***

(*a*) The use of pipelines to transport ore as slurry.

(*b*) The construction of railroads for ore transport.

(*c*) The establishment of air transport routes for ore export.

(*d*) The development of advanced road networks.

9. India's reserves and production of non-ferrous minerals are not very satisfactory. As a student preparing for a geography quiz, you need to analyze the geographical distribution and economic importance of various non-ferrous minerals in India. Match the minerals with their corresponding leading production areas to understand the strategic locations of these resources. ***(An)***

Column-I (Mineral)		Column-II (Production Area)	
(A)	Copper	(i)	Amarkantak Plateau
(B)	Bauxite	(ii)	Khetri Mines
(C)	Mica	(iii)	Madhya Pradesh
(D)	Manganese	(iv)	Koderma

Choose the correct option:

(*a*) A-(ii), B-(i), C-(iv), D-(iii)

(*b*) A-(ii), B-(iii), C-(i), D-(iv)

(*c*) A-(iv), B-(i), C-(ii), D-(iii)

(*d*) A-(ii), B-(i), C-(iii), D-(iv)

10. Imagine you are a policy advisor named Ananya, working for the Ministry of Environment and Forests. You have been tasked with developing new regulations for the mining sector to ensure sustainable practices and prevent environmental degradation in this region. during your research, you come across the following information about mica. ***(Cr)***

Statement I: Mica deposits are found in the northern edge of the Chota Nagpur plateau.

Statement II: Mica is an essential mineral in the cement industry due to its excellent insulating properties. evaluate the accuracy of these statements and decide on the appropriate course of action to ensure sustainable mining practices in the Koderma-Gaya-Hazaribagh belt.

(*a*) Both statements are false.

(*b*) Statement I is true, Statement II is false.

(*c*) Statement I is false, Statement II is true.

(*d*) Both statements are true.

11. Imagine you are a resident in a mining town that has been experiencing continuous dust generation due to mining activities. Over the years, you have noticed changes in the environment and the health of the community. how would you propose addressing these issues to improve the quality of life in your town? ***(Cr)***

(*a*) Implementing measures to increase soil fertility and agricultural productivity.

(*b*) Taking steps to reduce contamination of air and water resources to prevent health issues.

(*c*) Encouraging activities that enhance local biodiversity and ecosystem stability.

(*d*) Focusing on reducing the overall mining output to minimize environmental impact.

12. You are the chief engineer at the plant, responsible for advising the management on the best type of coal to use. Analyze the following options and recommend the type of coal that should be chosen for the switch. Choose the appropriate options given below: ***(An)***

(*a*) Peat, because it has high moisture content

(*b*) Lignite, because it is soft and brown

(*c*) Bituminous, because it is popular in commercial use

(*d*) Anthracite, because it has the highest carbon content and heating capacity

13. Ananya is a high school student preparing for a science fair project on nuclear energy resources in India. She needs to present accurate information about the materials and locations associated with nuclear energy production in the country. Help Ananya by identifying the correct statements from her research notes. ***(Un)***

Statements:

(*i*) Ananya reads that Uranium and Thorium are essential materials used for generating atomic energy.

(*ii*) She finds a reference stating that the Monazite sands of Kerala are rich in Uranium.

(*iii*) She learns that altering atomic structures releases energy in the form of heat.

(*iv*) Ananya notes that nuclear power stations are located only in Jharkhand and Rajasthan.

(*a*) (*i*) and (*ii*) only (*b*) (*ii*) and (*iv*) only

(*c*) (*i*) and (*iii*) only (*d*) (*iii*) and (*iv*) only

Assertion and Reason (1 M)

Direction: The following questions consist of two statements – Assertion (A) and Reason (R). Answer these questions by selecting the appropriate option given below:

(*a*) Both A and R are true, and R is the correct explanation of A.

(*b*) Both A and R are true, but R is not the correct explanation of A.

(*c*) A is true, but R is false.

(*d*) A is false, but R is true.

1. Assertion (A): Mining activity is often called a "Killer Industry".

Reason (R): Mining helps in agriculture. ***(Ev)***

2. Assertion (A): Mica is a non-metallic mineral.

Reason (R): Mica mineral is the basic raw material for the cement industry. ***(Ev)***

3. Assertion (A): Minerals are an indispensable part of our lives.

Reason (R): Minerals have universal use, they are used to manufacture everything we use in our day-to-day lives. ***(An)***

4. Assertion (A): Natural gas is referred to as an environment-friendly fuel.

Reason (R): Natural gas contains low carbon dioxide emissions. ***(An)***

5. **Assertion (A):** Fossil fuels such as coal, oil, and gas are easily obtained from natural resources.
   Reason (R): Increased use of fossil fuels creates an unhealthy environment. ***(An)***
6. **Assertion (A):** Conservation of Energy Resources is essential.
   Reason (R): Energy is a basic requirement for economic development. ***(An)***

Subjective Questions

Very Short Answer Type Questions (1 or 2 M)

1. Why should the use of cattle cake as fuel be discouraged? ***(Ev)*(CBSE, 2016)**
2. How is iron ore transported from Kudremukh mines to a port near Mangaluru? ***(Re)***
3. How is hydroelectricity generated? ***(Un)***
4. What are the Khetri mines in Rajasthan famous for? ***(Re)***
5. Why is copper mainly used in electrical cables, electronics, and chemical industries? ***(Ap)***
6. How are bauxite deposits formed? ***(Un)***

Short Answer Type Questions (3 M)

1. Why is solar energy more developed in western Rajasthan? Give three points to support your answer. ***(An)***
2. The pie chart given below shows the production of manganese in different states. On the basis of diagram answer the following questions:

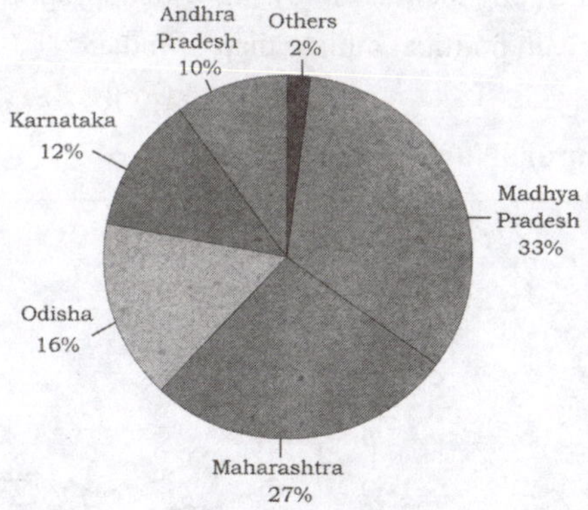

   (*a*) Which is the largest producer of Manganese? ***(Re)***
   (*b*) Mention any two uses of Manganese. ***(Re)***
3. What is Tidal energy? Name a region of India with proven ideal conditions for using tidal energy. ***(Un and Re)***

Long Answer Type Questions (5 M)

1. Describe the distribution of coal in India. ***(Un)*(NCERT)**
2. Why do you think that solar energy has a bright future in India? ***(Cr and Ev)*(NCERT)**
3. Why should we use renewable energy resources? Explain with arguments. ***(Ev)***

   OR

   Why is there a pressing need for using renewable energy sources in India? Explain any five reasons. ***(Ev)*(CBSE, 2014)**

Case Based Questions

Case Based-I

Read the source given below and answer the following questions:

Hazards of Mining

Ravi is a young environmental scientist working for the National Environmental Protection Agency (NEPA) in India. He has been assigned to study the impact of mining activities in the Jharia coal belt region. Ravi's task is to assess the environmental and health hazards associated with mining and propose sustainable solutions to mitigate these issues.

The mining activities in the Jharia coal belt have led to significant environmental and health hazards. The dust and noxious fumes inhaled by miners make them vulnerable to pulmonary diseases. The risk of collapsing mine roofs, inundation, and fires in coal mines are constant threats. Water sources in the region get contaminated due to mining, and the dumping of waste and slurry leads to land, soil, and river pollution. Recent reports indicate that over 50% of coal-belt mines are unsafe, and there are ongoing efforts to shift the population from these hazardous areas.

(*i*) Ravi needs to create a public awareness campaign highlighting the environmental azards of mining in Jharia. What key points should he include in his campaign to effectively communicate the risks to the local population? *(1 M)* ***(Un)***

(*ii*) Analyze the long-term environmental impacts of mining activities in Jharia. What patterns and issues can be identified from the given data and reports? *(1 M)* ***(An)***

(*iii*) Propose a sustainable plan that Ravi could recommend to the NEPA to mitigate the environmental and health hazards of mining in Jharia. Justify your recommendations with specific examples and strategies. *(2 M)* ***(Un)***

Case Based-II

Read the source given below and answer the following questions:

Conventional Sources of Energy: Coal

In India, coal is the most abundantly available fossil fuel. It provides a substantial part of the nation's energy needs. It is used for power generation, to supply energy to industry as well as for domestic needs. India is highly dependent on coal for meeting its commercial energy requirements as you are already aware coal is formed due to the compression of plant material over millions of years. Coal, therefore, is found in various forms depending on the degrees of compression and the depth and time of burial. Decaying plants in swamps produce peat, which has low carbon and high moisture content and low heating capacity. Lignite is a low-grade brown coal, which is soft with high moisture content. The principal lignite reserves are in Neyveli in Tamil Nadu and are used for the generation of electricity. Coal that has been buried deep and subjected to increased temperatures is bituminous coal. It is the most popular coal in commercial use. Metallurgical coal is high-grade bituminous coal which has a special value for smelting iron in blast furnaces. Anthracite is the highest quality hard coal. In India, coal occurs in rock series of two main geological ages, namely Gondwana, a little over 200 million years in age and in tertiary deposits which are only about 55 million years old. The major resources of Gondwana coal, which are metallurgical coal, are located in Damodar Valley (West Bengal- Jharkhand). Jharia, Raniganj, and Bokaro are important coalfields. The Godavari, Mahanadi, Son and Wardha valleys also contain coal deposits. Tertiary coals occur in the northeastern states of Meghalaya, Assam, Arunachal Pradesh and Nagaland. Remember coal is a bulky material, which loses weight on use as it is reduced to ash. Hence, heavy industries and thermal power stations are located on or near the coalfields.

(i) What policy measures can enhance the sustainability of coal-based energy? *(1 M)* **(Cr)**

(ii) Analyze the impact of geological factors on the types of coal found in India and how these affect the energy industry. *(1 M)* **(An)**

(iii) Ravi is a policy analyst evaluating India's dependency on coal for energy. Discuss the advantages and disadvantages of relying heavily on coal as a primary energy source for India. *(2 M)* **(Ev)**

Case Based-III

Read the source given below and answer the following questions:

Non-Conventional Sources of Energy

Non-Conventional Sources of Energy The growing consumption of energy has resulted in the country becoming increasingly dependent on fossil fuels such as coal, oil and gas. Rising prices of oil and gas and their potential shortages have raised uncertainties about the security of energy supply in future, which in turn has serious repercussions on the growth of the national economy. Moreover, the increasing use of fossil fuels also causes serious environmental problems. Hence, there is a pressing need to use renewable energy sources like solar energy, wind, tide, biomass and energy from waste material. These are called non-conventional energy sources. India is blessed with an abundance of sunlight, water, wind and biomass. It has the largest programmes for the development of these renewable energy resources. Nuclear or Atomic Energy is obtained by altering the structure of atoms. When such an alteration is made, much energy is released in the form of heat and this is used to generate electric power. Uranium and Thorium, which are available in Jharkhand and the Aravalli ranges of Rajasthan are used for generating atomic or nuclear power. The Monazite sands of Kerala is also rich in Thorium.

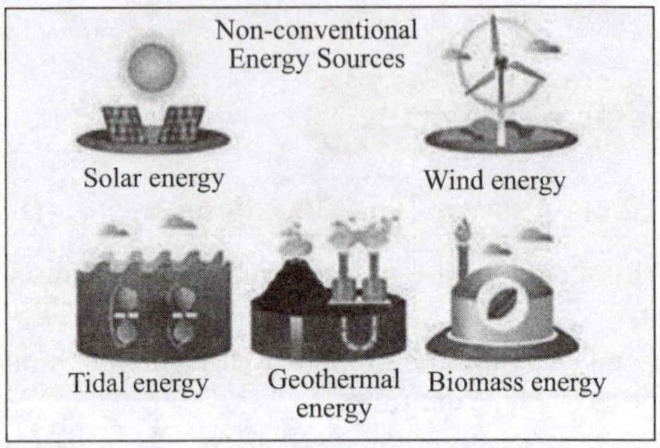

(i) Explain why there is a growing need for non-conventional energy sources in India. *(1 M)* **(Un)**

(ii) Analyze how India's geographical advantages contribute to its development of non-conventional energy sources. *(1 M)* **(An)**

(iii) Identify the six nuclear power stations in India and discuss the challenges these facilities face concerning location and resource management. *(2 M)* **(Re, Ev)**

Map Based Questions

1. Locate and label the following with appropriate symbol on the given political outline map of India: *(1 M)*
(Re)(CBSE, 2019, 2022)

Tarapur: Nuclear Power Plant

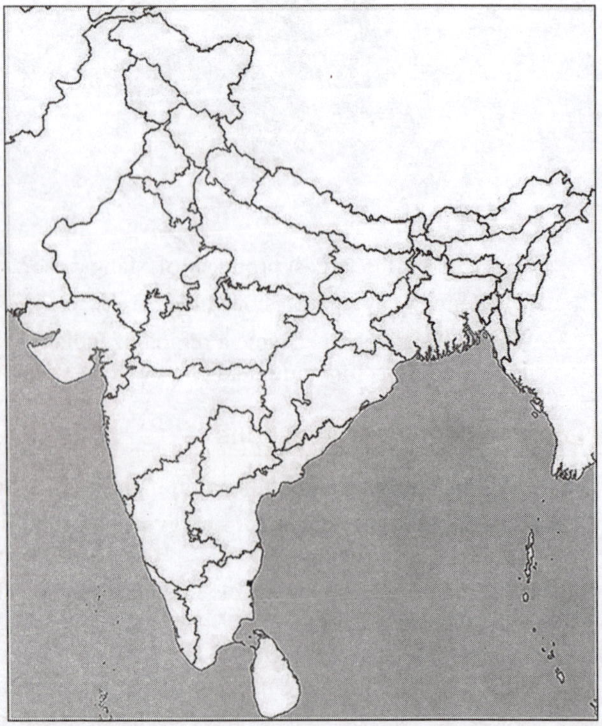

2. On the outline map of India, locate and label the following with appropriate symbol: *(1 M)* **(*Re*)(CBSE, 2020)**

Naraura: Nuclear Power Plant

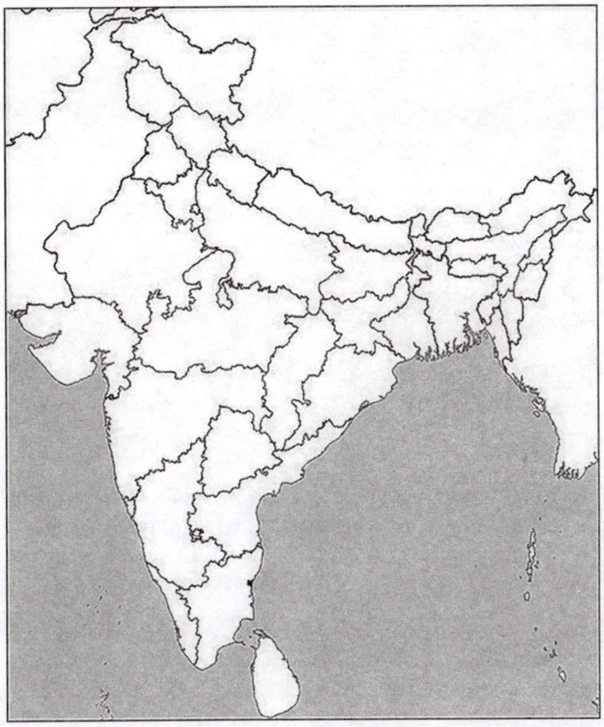

3. On the given map of India, locate and label the following with appropriate symbol. *(1 M)* **(*Re*)(CBSE, 2022)**

Kalpakkam: Nuclear Power Plant

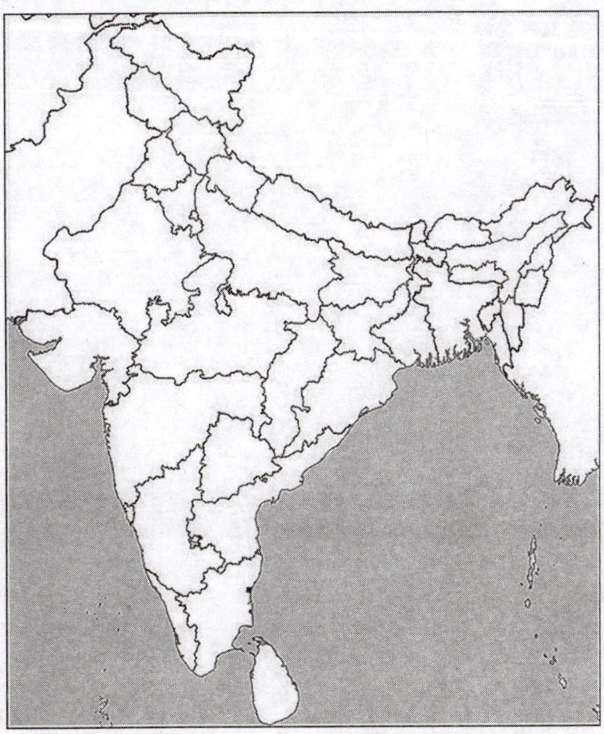

4. On the outline map of India locate and label the following with suitable symbol: *(1 M)* **(*Re*)(CBSE, 2023)**

Kakrapara: Atomic Power Station

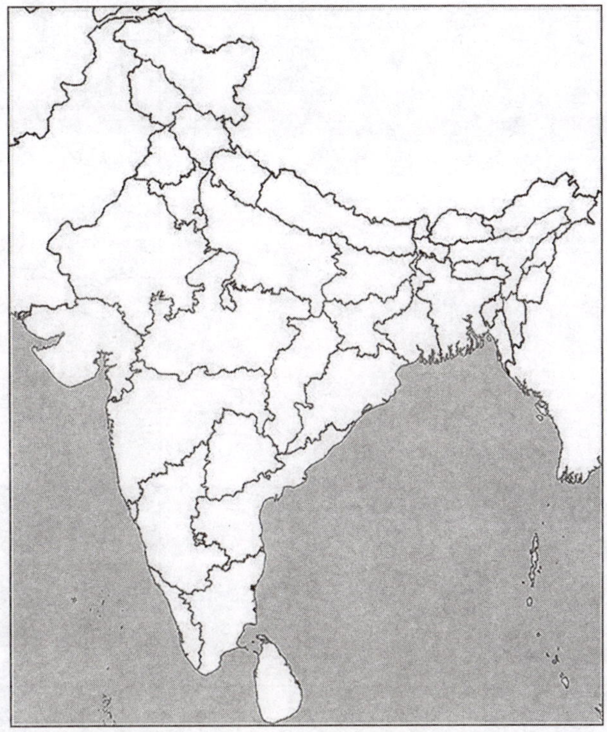

5. On the outline map of India locate and label the following with suitable symbol. *(1 M)* **(*Re*)(CBSE SQP, 2023)**

(*i*) A Coal mine in Tamil Nadu.

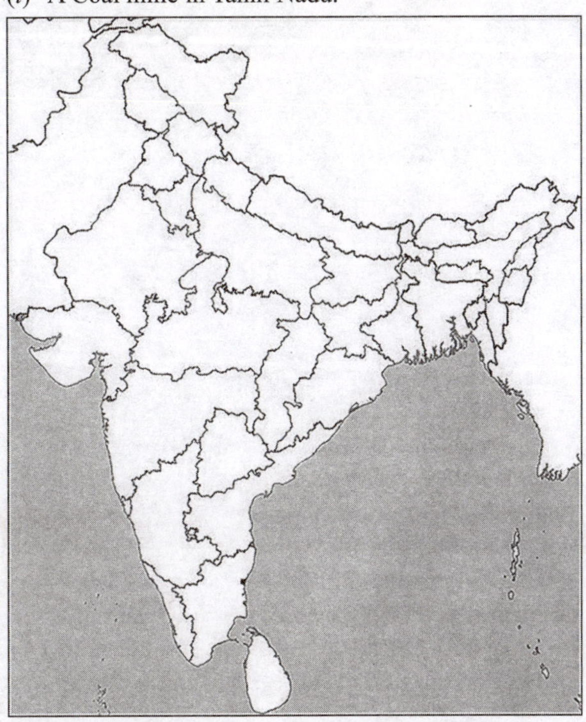

6. On the outline map of India, locate and label the following with suitable symbol: *(1 M)* **(*Re*) (CBSE APQ 2023)**

(*i*) a nuclear power plant in the state of Maharashtra .

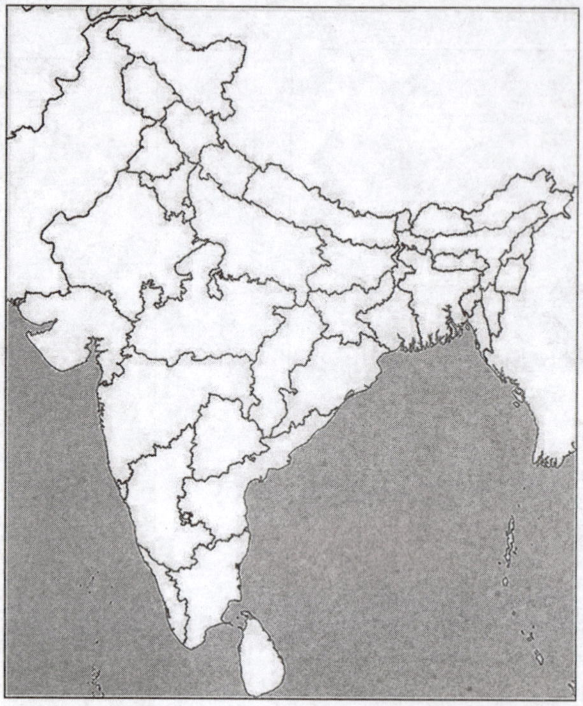

ANSWER KEYS

Multiple Choice Questions

1. (*b*) **2.** (*b*) **3.** (*a*) **4.** (*a*) **5.** (*c*) **6.** (*d*) **7.** (*b*) **8.** (*a*) **9.** (*a*) **10.** (*b*)
11. (*b*) **12.** (*d*) **13.** (*c*)

Assertion and Reason

1. (*c*) **2.** (*c*) **3.** (*a*) **4.** (*a*) **5.** (*d*) **6.** (*a*)

HINTS & EXPLANATIONS

Multiple Choice Questions

1. (*b*) bauxite
2. (*b*) mica
3. (*a*) sedimentary rocks
4. (*a*) Both statements are true as Maharashtra and Madhya Pradesh together account for 60% (33% + 27%), and high regional concentration suggests the need for production diversification.
5. (*c*) Kalol oil fields - (iii) Gujarat

Column-I	Column-II
(*a*) Chandrapur thermal power plant	(*iv*) Jharkhand
(*b*) Mayurbhanj iron ore mines	(*i*) Odisha
(*c*) Kalol oil fields	(*iii*) Gujarat
(*d*) Bauxite mines	(*ii*) Amarkantak

6. (*d*) (*i*) Statement I is true because in north-east India, particularly in Meghalaya, minerals are indeed owned by individuals or communities rather than being nationalized.

   (*ii*) Statement II is true because the National Green Tribunal has declared 'Rat-hole' mining in Meghalaya illegal due to environmental concerns.

   Which highlights the unique ownership of minerals in this region and the legal actions taken against environmentally harmful mining practices.
7. (*b*) Magnetite is the type of iron ore that the Institute is referring to. It is known for its very high iron content, which can be up to 70% and its excellent magnetic qualities. These properties make magnetite particularly valuable in the electrical industry, distinguishing it from other types of iron ores such as hematite, siderite, and limonite.
8. (*a*) Using pipelines to transport ore as slurry is an efficient and cost-effective method for transporting iron ore from the Kudremukh mines to the port near Mangaluru. This method reduces transportation costs and minimizes the environmental impact compared to other modes of transport like railroads, air transport, or road networks.
9. (*a*) (*i*) **Copper:** Leading production area is Khetri Mines in Rajasthan.

   (*ii*) **Bauxite:** Major deposits are found in the Amarkantak Plateau.

   (*iii*) **Mica:** Found in the Koderma region.

   (*iv*) **Manganese:** Major production area is Madhya Pradesh.
10. (*b*) Mica deposits are indeed found in the northern edge of the Chota Nagpur plateau, specifically in the Koderma-Gaya-Hazaribagh belt of Jharkhand, which is known to be the leading producer of mica in India so, Statement I as true.

    However, Statement II is incorrect. Mica is not used in the cement industry due to its insulating properties. Instead, mica is widely used in the electrical and electronics industries for its excellent insulating properties and ability to withstand high temperatures.
11. (*b*) Implementing measures to reduce air and water contamination directly addresses the core issues of dust generation and noxious fumes from mining, which significantly impact health and environmental quality in the community.
12. (*d*) Anthracite is the highest quality coal due to its high carbon content and superior heating capacity, making it the most efficient choice for power generation.
13. (*c*) (*i*) **Statement-I is correct:** Uranium and Thorium are used for generating atomic energy.

    (*ii*) **Statement-II is incorrect:** The Monazite sands of Kerala are rich in Thorium, not Uranium.

    (*iii*) **Statement-III is correct:** Alteration of atomic structures releases energy in the form of heat.

    (*iv*) **Statement-IV is incorrect:** nuclear power stations in India are located in various states, not just Jharkhand and Rajasthan.

Assertion and Reason

1. (*c*) Assertion is true but Reason is false. As mining does not help in agriculture.
2. (*c*) Assertion is true but Reason is false. Limestone is the basic raw material for the cement industry.
3. (*a*) Both Assertion and Reason are true and Reason is the correct explanation of Assertion.
4. (*a*) Both Assertion and Reason are true and Reason is the correct explanation of Assertion.
5. (*d*) Assertion is false as Fossil fuels such as coal, oil, and gas are formed from the remains of plants and animals that lived millions of years ago. The reason is true.
6. (*a*) Both Assertion and Reason are true and Reason is the correct explanation of assertion.

Subjective Questions

Very Short Answer Type Questions

1. (*a*) It creates pollution. *(1 M)*

   (*b*) By burning a manure resource is destroyed, which can improve soil fertility. *(1 M)*

Topper's Explanation:

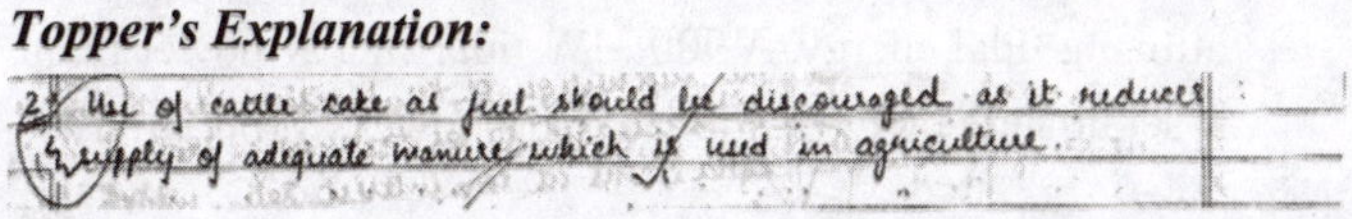
2) Use of cattle cake as fuel should be discouraged as it reduces supply of adequate manure which is used in agriculture.

2. Iron ore is transported as slurry through pipelines. The New Mangalore Port is one of the iron ore exporting ports of India. It caters to the Kudremukh mines in Karnataka. *(2 M)*

3. Hydroelectricity is produced by utilizing the gravitational force of falling water. To this end, the hydropower plant requires a dam. This dam is placed on a source of water, preferably a river. The dam is a massive wall that blocks the flow of the river, therefore, a lot of water collects behind the dam. *(2 M)*

4. Khetri is situated at the foothills of the Aravalli Range in Rajasthan famous for its Copper production. *(1 M)*

5. Copper is malleable, ductile and a good conductor of electricity. Therefore, it is mainly used in electrical cables, electronics and chemical industries. *(2 M)*

6. Bauxite deposits are formed by the decomposition of a wide variety of rocks rich in aluminium silicates. Bauxite deposits in India are found in the Amarkantak plateau, Maikal hills, and the plateau region of Bilaspur-Katni. *(2 M)*

Short Answer Type Questions

1. *(i)* Western Rajasthan is blessed with an abundance of sunlight. *(1 M)*

   (ii) It has less tree cover. *(1 M)*

   (iii) It has very little rainfall as it is located on the leeward side of the western ghats. *(1 M)*

2. *(a)* **Madhya Pradesh** is the largest producer of manganese in India approximately one-third of the country's total production. *(1 M)*

   (b) **Uses of Manganese:**

   - Manganese is mainly used in the manufacturing of steel and ferromanganese alloys. Nearly 10 kg of manganese is required to manufacture one tonne of steel. *(1 M)*
   - It is also used in manufacturing bleaching powder, insecticides, and paints. *(1 M)*

3. Oceanic tides can be used to generate electricity. Floodgate dams are built across inlets. During high tide, water flows into the inlet and gets trapped when the gate is closed. *(1 M)*

   After the tide falls outside the floodgate, the water retained by the floodgate flows back to the sea via a pipe that carries it through a power-generating turbine. *(1 M)*

   In India, the Gulf of Kuchchh provides ideal conditions for utilizing tidal energy. A 900 MW tidal energy power plant is set up here by the National Hydropower Corporation. *(1 M)*

Long Answer Type Questions

1. The distribution of coal in India is significant due to the country's extensive coal reserves, which play a crucial role in its energy sector and industrial production:

   (Any five points)

   (i) **Jharkhand:** Holds the largest reserves of coal and is known as the coal capital of India. Major coal fields include Jharia, Dhanbad, and Bokaro. *(1 M)*

   (ii) **Chhattisgarh:** The second-largest coal-producing state, featuring the Hasdeo-Arand coal fields and the Korba coalfield. *(1 M)*

   (iii) **Odisha:** Rich in coal reserves with significant coalfields like Talcher and Ib Valley. *(1 M)*

   (iv) **West Bengal:** Notable for the Raniganj coalfield, one of the oldest in the country. *(1 M)*

   (v) **Madhya Pradesh:** Contains major coalfields like Singrauli, the largest in the state, and Pench-Kanhan coalfield. *(1 M)*

   (iv) **Telangana:** Known for the Singareni coalfields, contributing significantly to the state's economy. *(1 M)*

2. Solar energy holds a bright future in India for several compelling reasons:

   (i) **Abundant Sunshine:** India enjoys a tropical climate, receiving an average of 300 sunny days a year, offering vast potential for harnessing solar energy. *(1 M)*

   (ii) **Government Support:** Initiatives like the National Solar Mission aim to promote solar energy through incentives, subsidies, and an ambitious target to significantly increase solar power capacity. *(1 M)*

   (iii) **Energy Security:** With rising fuel costs and the need to reduce dependence on imported fossil fuels, solar energy presents a sustainable and secure energy source. *(1 M)*

   (iv) **Rural Electrification:** Solar power can provide electricity to remote areas without access to the national grid, improving lives and reducing kerosene dependency. *(1 M)*

   (v) **Environmental Benefits:** Embracing solar energy aligns with India's commitment to reducing carbon emissions, combating climate change, and promoting sustainable development. *(1 M)*

3. Using renewable energy resources is crucial for several compelling reasons:

   (i) **Environmental Preservation:** Renewable sources like wind, solar, and hydro power produce minimal greenhouse gases and pollutants compared to fossil fuels, significantly reducing environmental degradation and combating climate change. *(1 M)*

   (ii) **Sustainable Supply:** Unlike finite fossil fuels, renewable resources are abundant and continuously replenished by nature, ensuring a long-term, sustainable energy supply. *(1 M)*

(*iii*) Economic Benefits: Investing in renewable energy technologies creates jobs in manufacturing, installation, and maintenance sectors, boosting local economies and reducing dependence on imported fuels. *(1 M)*

(*iv*) Energy Security: Diversifying energy sources with renewables reduces vulnerability to global fuel price fluctuations and supply disruptions, enhancing national energy security. *(1 M)*

(*v*) Health Benefits: By reducing air and water pollution, renewable energy improves public health, lowering healthcare costs associated with pollution-related diseases. *(1 M)*

Mistakes 101 : What not to do!

- Lack of Specific Examples
- Missing Counter arguments
- Not Addressing Cost-Effectiveness of Renewable Energy

Topper's Explanation:

26. There is a pressing need for using renewable energy sources in India.

(i) There is only limited supply of energy resources in India. Conventional sources are limited and it takes long time to renew back. So, renewable energy source should be use.
(ii) For a sustainable development, one should press on renewable energy resources because conventional sources should be left for future use.
(iii) Most of the conventional sources are pollutants it causes pollution when burnt in air. For eg:- coal, petroleum emits carbondioxide when burnt in air.
(iv) Renewable energy resources are eco-friendly. They can be retained back and also they do not cause pollution
eg:- Solar energy, wind energy.
(v) The cost of harnessing electricity (conventional source) is very expensive. But renewable source (electricity), initial cost is high but has a long run.

Case Based Questions

Case Based-I

(*i*) Ravi should include the following key points in his public awareness campaign: *(1 M)*

- Health risks from inhaling dust and fumes.
- Water contamination affects drinking water and agriculture.
- The environmental degradation caused by waste and slurry dumping.

(*ii*) Long-term environmental impacts of mining in Jharia include: *(1 M)*

- Air pollution causing respiratory problems.
- Water pollution affecting health and ecosystems.
- Soil degradation harming agriculture.

(*iii*) Ravi could recommend the following sustainable plan to the NEPA:

- Enforce air quality and dust control regulations, and develop a water management plan to prevent contamination. *(1 M)*
- Start mine reclamation projects and adopt cleaner mining technologies while promoting community engagement and education for sustainable practices. *(1 M)*

Case Based-II

(*i*) **Policy Measures:** Incentives for clean technology adoption and Penalties for non-compliance with environmental standards.Investments in education and training for renewable energy sectors. *(1 M)*

(*ii*) **Geological Factors:** Gondwana coal versus tertiary coal formations and different compression levels lead to various coal types (peat, lignite, bituminous, anthracite).

Impact on Energy Industry: Influence on the quality and grade of coal used for different purposes. Strategic placement of industries near coal deposits. *(1 M)*

(*iii*) **Advantages:** *(1 M)*

- Abundant availability in India.
- Key to power generation and industrial supply.
- Cost-effective for energy production.

Disadvantages: *(1 M)*

- Environmental pollution and carbon emissions.
- Health hazards due to mining activities.
- Dependency on a finite resource.

Case Based-III

(*i*) Rising fossil fuel costs, environmental issues, and energy security concerns drive India's shift towards abundant renewable sources like solar and wind for sustainable energy solutions. *(1 M)*

(*ii*) India's ample sunlight, wind, water, and biomass support large-scale renewable energy programs, reducing fossil fuel reliance and promoting sustainable development. *(1 M)*

(*iii*) Nuclear power stations in India include Tarapur (Maharashtra), Rawatbhata (Rajasthan), Kalpakkam (Tamil Nadu), Narora (Uttar Pradesh), Kakrapar (Gujarat), and Kudankulam (Tamil Nadu). Challenges include uranium shortages, safety concerns, and waste management. *(2 M)*

Map Based Questions

1.

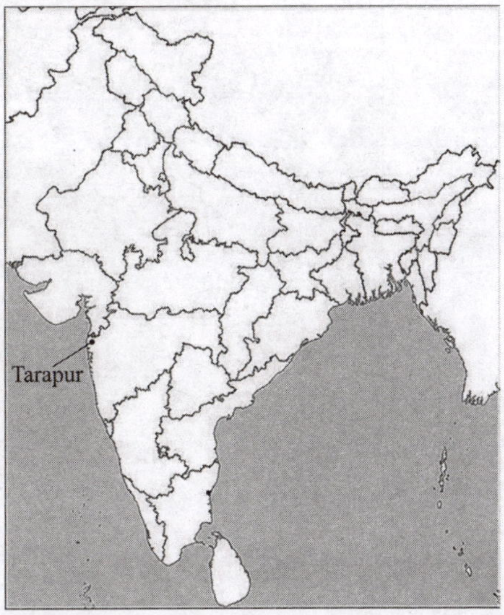

2.

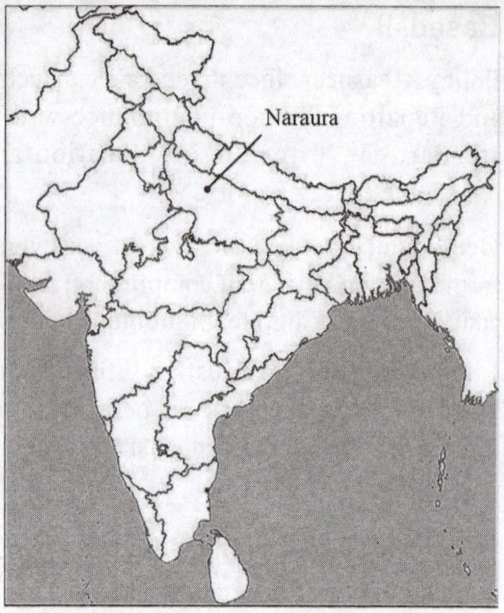

3.

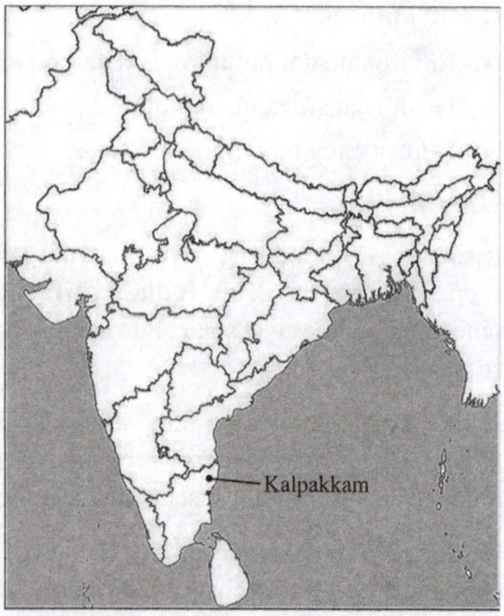

4.

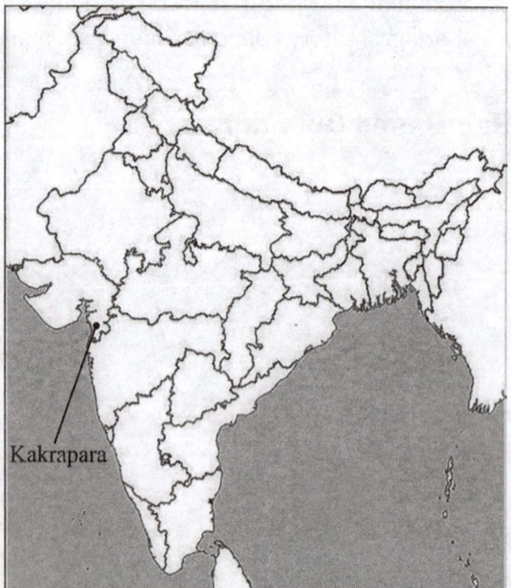

5.

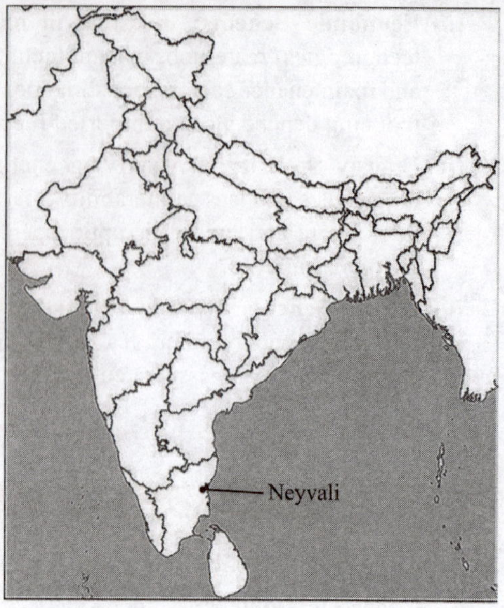

6.

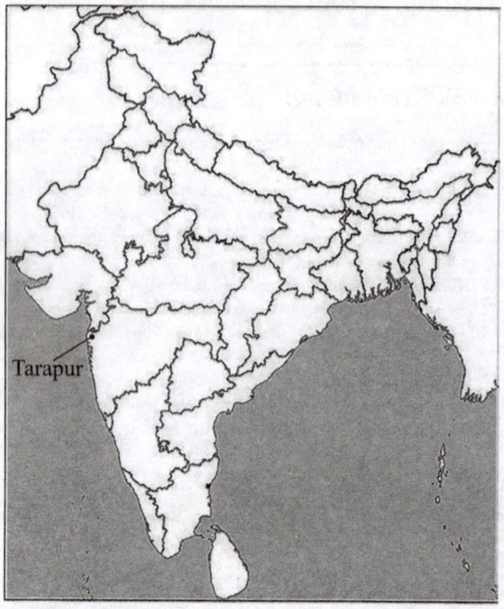

MANUFACTURING INDUSTRIES

6

Manufacturing industries play an important role in transforming raw resources into valuable goods, driving economic growth, and creating employment opportunities across various sectors.

SYLLABUS & WEIGHTAGE

List of Concept Names	Years					
	2020	2021	2022	2023	2024	2025
Manufactuing Industries and Industries (Importance of Manufacturing, Classification of Industries, Argo Based Industry and Mineral Based Industry)	4Q (1 M) 2Q (1 M) (MB)	Exam not Conducted	1Q (2 M)	1 Q (5 M) 1Q (1 M) (MB)	1 Q (3 M)	1 Q (1 M)
Industrial Pollution and Environmental Degradation (Control of Environmental Degradation) (Types of Pollution Air, Water, Thermal, Noise)	—		—	Q 1 (5 M)	—	1 Q (1 M)

CONCEPT MAP

To Access One Shot Revision Video Scan This QR Code

Manufacturing Industries

- **On the basis of ownership**
  - **Public Sector:** like BHEL, SAIL etc.
  - **Private Sector:** like TISCO, Bajaj Auto Ltd. etc.
  - **Joint sector industries:** like Maruti Udyog Ltd., Oil India Ltd. etc.
  - **Cooperative sector industries:** like AMUL, Indian Coffee House etc.
- **Based on the bulk and weight raw material and finished good**
  - **Heavy Industries:** like Iron and Steel Industries
  - **Light Industries:** like Automobile and Kitchen items etc.
- **On the basis of capital investment**
  - **Small Scale Industries:** Max. investment upto ₹ 1 crore
  - **Large Scale Industries:** Investment more than ₹ 1 crore.
- **On the basis of source of raw materials used** (CBSE 2024, 2023, 2022, 2020)
  - **Mineral based:** like Iron and Steel, Cement, Aluminium etc.
  - **Agro based:** like Cotton, Woolen, jute, silk etc. (CBSE 2025)
- **According to their main role** (CBSE 2024)
  - **Consumer industries:** like Sugar, toothpaste, paper etc.
  - **Basic or key industries:** like Copper smelting, Aluminium smelting etc.
- **Environmental Degradation** (CBSE 2023)
  - Minimising the use of water for processing by reusing and recycling, harvesting of rainwater, treating hot water and effluents before releasing, etc.
- **Industrial Pollution** (CBSE 2023)
  - **Air Pollution:** Caused by undesirable gases like SO_2 and CO_2.
  - **Noise Pollution:** Caused due to industrial and construction activities.
  - **Water Pollution:** Caused by organic and inorganic industrial wastes discharged into rivers.
  - **Thermal Pollution:** Occurs when hot water from factories and thermal plants drained into rivers and ponds.

1 MANUFACTURING INDUSTRIES AND INDUSTRIES

NCERT Definitions *(Commonly asked in 1 mark)*

- **Manufacturing:** The process of ***converting raw materials*** into finished products of higher value, often using machines in industries. For example, paper is made from wood, and sugar is made from sugarcane.
- **Basic industries:** Those industries that ***supply their products*** as raw materials to manufacture other goods. For example, Iron and Steel Industry.

Important Concepts

Importance of Manufacturing

Manufacturing sector is considered the ***backbone of development*** in general and economic development in particular mainly because–

- Manufacturing industries **boost agriculture** and **reduce dependence** on farming by offering jobs in other sectors.
- Industrial growth is important for **stopping unemployment** and **poverty**, aiming for equitable development across regions.
- Export of manufactured goods **expands trade** and **commerce**, and brings in much needed foreign exchange.
- Prosperous countries transform raw materials into diverse, **high-value products**. For India, expanding and **diversifying manufacturing** is key to prosperity.

Important Facts

01 The first successful textile mill was **established** in **Mumbai** in **1854**.

02 The **two world wars** were fought in Europe, India was a British colony. There was a demand for cloth in the U.K. hence, they gave a boost to the development of the **cotton textile industry**.

03 The **first jute mill** was set up near **Kolkata in 1855** at Rishra.

04 After Partition in 1947, the jute mills remained in India but **three-fourth** of the jute producing area went to **Bangladesh** (erstwhile East Pakistan).

05 **Iron and Steel Industry: Chota Nagpur** plateau region has the maximum concentration of iron and steel industries. **Iron ore**, **coking coal** and **limestone** are required in the ratio of approximately **4:2:1.**

Classification

Industries				
On the basis of raw material	**According to their main role**	**On the basis of capital investment**	**On the basis of ownership**	**Based on Bulk and weight of raw material and finished goods**
• Agro based industries • Mineral based industries	• Basic or key industries • Consumer industries	• Small scale industries • Large scale industries	• Public Sector Industries • Private Sector Industries • Joint Sector Industries • Cooperative Sector Industries	• Heavy industries • Light industries

Difference Between

1. On the basis of source of raw materials used Industries.			
Basics	**Agro-Based Industries**	**Mineral-Based Industries**	**Chemical Industries**
Meaning	Industries that use **plant and animal products to make goods**.	Industries that use **minerals** and **metals** as their main raw materials.	Comprising both **large and small scale** units growing rapidly in inorganic and organic sectors, producing a wide range of chemicals used in different industries.
Types	Textile Industry and Food Processing Industry	–	Fertilizer Industry, Cement Industry, Automobile Industry, & Information Technology and Electronics Industry
Examples	• **Textile industry** (using cotton, wool, jute, silk) • **Food processing industry** (using sugar, tea, coffee, edible oils).	• **Iron and steel industries** use iron ore, and • **Aluminium smelting** uses bauxite.	• **Organic sectors:** petrochemicals, which are used for manufacturing of synthetic fibers, synthetic rubber, plastics, dye-stuffs. • **Inorganic sectors:** sulphuric acid, nitric acid, alkalies, soda, etc. • **Fertilizer Industry:** Urea, phosphatic fertilizers • **Cement Industry:** Uses limestone, silica, gypsum • **Automobile Industry:** Uses steel, rubber, glass • **Information Technology and Electronics Industry:** Uses silicon, plastics, metals

2. According to their main role	
Basic or Key Industries	**Consumer Industries**
Those which supply their products as **raw materials to manufacture other goods.**	These industries produce goods **directly used by consumers.**
E.g. Iron and steel and copper smelting, aluminum smelting.	**E.g.** sugar, toothpaste, and fans.

3. On the basis of capital investment	
Small Scale Industry	**Large Scale Industry**
Investment allowed on the assets of a unit **up to ₹1 crore**	Investment allowed on the assets of a unit is **more than ₹1 crore**

4. On the basis of ownership			
Public Sector Industries	**Private Sector Industries**	**Joint Sector Industries**	**Cooperative Sector Industries**
Industries **owned and operated by government** agencies.	**Owned and operated by individuals** or **groups**.	Industries run **jointly** by the state and individuals or groups.	Industries owned and operated by the **producers or suppliers** of raw materials, workers, or both, pooling resources and sharing profits or losses proportionately.
E.g. BHEL (Bharat Heavy Electricals Limited) and SAIL (Steel Authority of India Limited), etc.	**E.g.** TISCO (Tata Iron and Steel Company) and Bajaj Auto Ltd. Dabur Industries, etc.	**E.g.** Oil India Ltd. (OIL) is jointly owned by public and private sector	**E.g.** Sugar industry in Maharashtra, the coir industry in Kerala.

5. Based on the bulk and weight of raw material and finished goods	
Heavy Industries	**Light Industries**
Industries like **iron and steel**, are characterized by heavy raw materials and finished goods, requiring significant transport and handling.	Industries that use light raw materials and produce **light goods**, such as **electrical appliances**, which are easier to transport and handle.

Note: Only these locating and labelling names are considered as per the CBSE Syllabus 2024-25.

Real Life Application Based Questions

Read the following source carefully and answer the questions that follow:

Shree Renuka Sugars is a global agribusiness and bio-energy corporation. The Company is one of the largest sugar producers in the world, the leading manufacturer of sugar in India, and one of the largest sugar refiners in the world. The company has its Corporate office in Mumbai (Maharashtra, India) and Head Office in Belgaum (Karnataka, India).

Production Process

Integrated **Sugar Mills**

Sugar Refineries

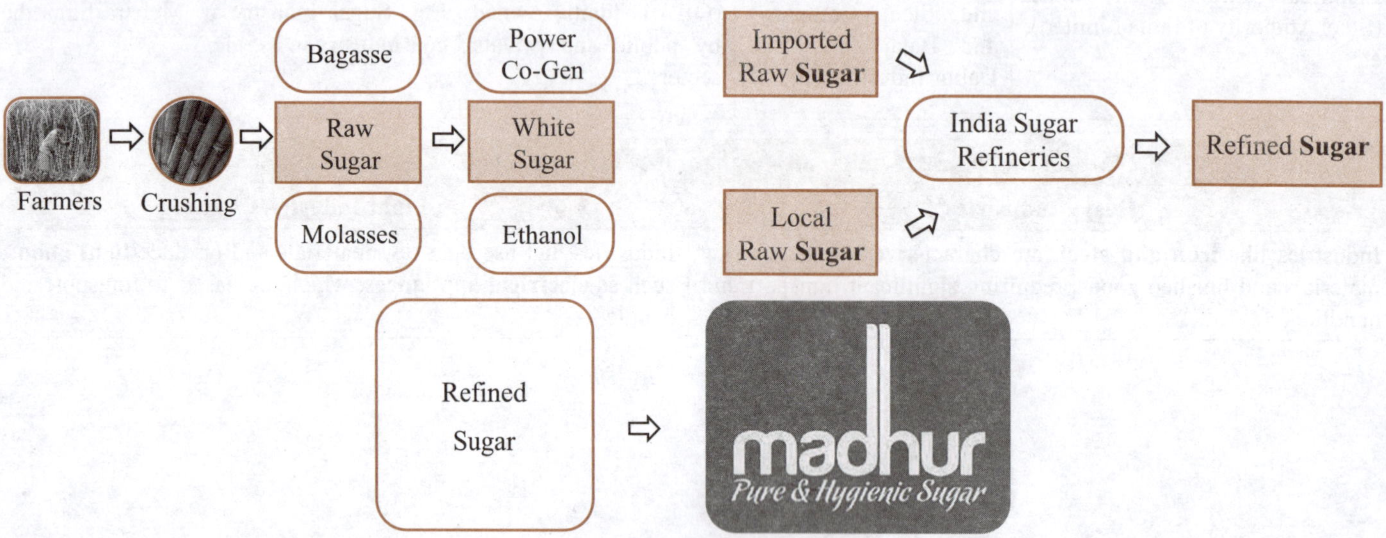

Turnkey EPC Plant Solutions for

- ❑ Fermentation
- ❑ Ethanol (Dehydration)
- ❑ Biogas
- ❑ Water Management Systems
- ❑ Distillation
- ❑ Evaporation
- ❑ Composting

1. **Identify one byproduct obtained during the sugar production process in integrated sugar mills.**

Ans. A byproduct obtained during the sugar production process is **molasses**.

2. **What is the main source of the raw material for India Sugar Refineries?**

Ans. The main source of raw material for India Sugar Refineries is **local raw sugar**.

3. **List two processes provided in Turnkey EPC Plant Solutions related to sugar production. Explain one in brief.**

Ans. Two processes provided in Turnkey EPC Plant Solutions related to sugar production are **Fermentation and Distillation.**

Fermentation is the process where sugar is **converted** into **alcohol under anaerobic** conditions.

Scan Me for Detailed Explanations

COMPETENCY BASED SOLVED EXAMPLES

Multiple Choice Questions

(1 M)

1. **Which one of the following industries uses bauxite as a raw material?** ***(Re)*(NCERT)**

(*a*) Aluminium Smelting (*b*) Cement
(*c*) Paper (*d*) Steel

2. **Which one of the following industries manufactures telephones, computer, etc.** ***(Re)*(NCERT)**

(*a*) Steel
(*b*) Electronic
(*c*) Aluminium Smelting
(*d*) Information Technology

3. **Suppose a developing country aims to boost its economy through various sectors. It prioritizes manufacturing because of its wide-reaching impacts on other sectors.**

Why might this country focus on enhancing its manufacturing sector as a strategic step towards economic development? ***(Ap)***

(*a*) To increase the import of raw materials and thus spend more foreign exchange.

(*b*) To directly increase agricultural production without technological inputs.

(*c*) To stimulate improvements in other sectors like agriculture through increased demand for agricultural products as raw materials.

(*d*) To solely focus on manufacturing, disregarding other sectors like services and agriculture.

4. **Consider a nation that has recently begun to diversify its economy through the development of manufacturing industries. Consider the Following statements:** ***(An)***

Statement I: The growth of manufacturing industries can lead to reduced unemployment by creating jobs in both secondary and tertiary sectors.

Statement II: The sole purpose of industrial development is to increase the country's exports.

Choose the correct answer:

(*a*) Both statements are false.

(*b*) Statement I is true; Statement II is false.

(*c*) Statement I is false; Statement II is true.

(*d*) Both statements are true.

5. **Match the Column-I with Column-II and choose the correct option:**

Review the different impacts of manufacturing on a country's economy. ***(An)***

	Column-I (Impact)		Column-II (Sector or Result)
(A)	Reduces dependence on agriculture	(i)	Export of manufactured goods
(B)	Increases foreign exchange	(ii)	Development of secondary and tertiary sectors
(C)	Eradicates unemployment	(iii)	Overall economic growth
(D)	Diversifies economy	(iv)	Modernization of agriculture

Choose the correct options given below:

(*a*) A–(i), B–(ii), C–(iii), D–(iv)

(*b*) A–(iii), B–(i), C–(iv), D–(ii)

(*c*) A–(ii), B–(iii), C–(iv), D–(i)

(*d*) A–(iv), B–(i), C–(ii), D–(iii)

6. **In a new economic policy, the government is considering incentives to promote specific types of industries based on their raw material source to boost sustainable economic growth.**

Which type of industry is likely to be prioritized for incentives if the government aims to support industries that reduce environmental impact and promote sustainable resource use? ***(An)***

(*a*) Agro-based industries, because they potentially use renewable resources.

(*b*) Mineral-based industries, due to their reliance on non-renewable resources.

(*c*) Consumer industries, as they directly fulfill consumer demands.

(*d*) Basic industries, because they provide essential raw materials to other industries.

7. **Considering an initiative to enhance self-reliance in manufacturing, a country is evaluating which industry sector to develop further. The government's focus is on balancing economic gain with strategic resource utilization.**

Which industry should be considered a key area for development to enhance the country's manufacturing self-reliance and why? ***(Ev)***

(*a*) Consumer industries, as they directly cater to the domestic market's daily needs.

(*b*) Basic or key industries, due to their role in supplying raw materials crucial for other industries.

(*c*) Light industries, for their less intensive use of raw materials and quicker turnover.

(*d*) Heavy industries, because of their potential to lead technological advancements and infrastructure development.

8. **Match the Column-I with Column-II and choose the correct option:**

A group of students is studying the impact of various types of industries based on ownership on the economy and workforce of a country. ***(Ap)***

	Column-I (Type of Industry Based on Ownership)		Column-II (Characteristic or Example)
(A)	Public sector	(i)	Operated by government agencies like SAIL
(B)	Private sector	(ii)	TISCO, Bajaj Auto Ltd.
(C)	Joint sector	(iii)	Oil India Ltd. (OIL), a collaboration between public and private stakeholders
(D)	Cooperative sector	(iv)	Sugar industry in Maharashtra, involves producers or suppliers pooling resources

Choose the correct options given below:

(*a*) A–(i), B–(ii), C–(iii), D–(iv)

(*b*) A–(iii), B–(i), C–(iv), D–(ii)

(*c*) A–(ii), B–(iii), C–(iv), D–(i)

(*d*) A–(iv), B–(i), C–(ii), D–(iii)

9. **Identify the industry with the help of following information:** ***(Ap)***

(*i*) India is the largest producer and stands at second place as an exporter after Bangladesh

(*ii*) Most of the mills are located in West Bengal

Choose the correct options given below:

(*a*) Jute textiles (*b*) Fertilizer Industry

(*c*) Chemical Industry (*d*) Iron & steel Industry

10. Arjun, an economic advisor, is tasked with suggesting improvements to the Indian textile industry to enhance global competitiveness.

Arjun is considering strategies to address the current situation where India excels in spinning but lags in weaving quality. Which policy initiative would best address this imbalance? *(Ap)*

(*a*) Subsidizing cotton production to increase raw material availability.

(*b*) Investing in technology upgrades for weaving to improve fabric quality.

(*c*) Increasing export duties on raw yarn to promote local fabric production.

(*d*) Expanding handloom weaving through subsidies and marketing support.

11. Priya, a consultant for sustainable industry practices, is evaluating the impact of the jute industry's location near the Hugli River on its operational efficiency and environmental sustainability.

What would be a critical factor for Priya to consider for the sustainability of the jute industry in this region? *(Ev)*

(*a*) The potential for water pollution and its management.

(*b*) The availability of cheap labor exclusively.

(*c*) Expansion of the road and railway network only.

(*d*) Relocation of industries away from urban centers like Kolkata.

Assertion and Reason (1 M)

Direction: The following questions consist of two statements – Assertion (A) and Reason (R). Answer these questions by selecting the appropriate option given below:

(*a*) Both A and R are true, and R is the correct explanation of A.

(*b*) Both A and R are true, but R is not the correct explanation of A.

(*c*) A is true, but R is false.

(*d*) A is false, but R is true.

1. A country invests heavily in manufacturing to not only modernize agriculture but also to balance regional economic disparities. *(Ev)*

Assertion (A): Investing in manufacturing industries is crucial for the eradication of unemployment and poverty in developing regions within a country.

Reason (R): Manufacturing provides jobs and stimulates local economies by producing goods that meet both local and international market demands.

2. Assertion (A): The non-cooking coal reserves are limited in India.

Reason (R): India is well endowed with nearly all the raw materials necessary for iron and steel industry. *(Un)*

3. Assertion (A): Agro-industries in India have given a major boost to agriculture by raising its productivity.

Reason (R): The primary function of agro-industries is to export raw materials. *(An)*

4. Assertion (A): India is the largest producer of raw jute and jute goods.

Reason (R): Most jute mills in India are located along the banks of the Hugli river. *(An)*

5. Assertion (A): The sugar industry is seasonal in nature.

Reason (R): The raw material for sugar, sugarcane, has a limited harvesting period. *(An)*

Subjective Questions

Very Short Answer Type Questions (2 M)

1. How is chemical industry in India diversified? Explain. ***(Ev)*(CBSE, 2022 Term 2)**

Ans. The chemical industry in India is diversified in the following ways: **(Any two)**

(*i*) Product range: The chemical industry in India produces a wide range of products such as dyes, fertilizers, pharmaceuticals, and plastics. *(1 M)*

(*ii*) Raw materials: The chemical industry in India uses a variety of raw materials such as minerals, oil and gas, and agricultural products. *(1 M)*

(*iii*) Market segments: The chemical industry in India caters to a variety of market segments such as agriculture, healthcare, and consumer goods. *(1 M)*

2. Classify industries on the basis of raw materials. ***(Re)*(CBSE, 2022 Term 2)**

Ans. Industries can be classified on the basis of raw materials in the following ways: **(Any two)**

- **Agro-based industries:** These industries use agricultural products such as cotton, jute, and sugarcane as raw materials. *(1 M)*
- **Mineral-based industries:** These industries use minerals such as iron ore, bauxite, and copper as raw materials. *(1 M)*
- **Forest-based industries:** These industries use forest products such as wood and pulp as raw materials. *(1 M)*

3. What is manufacturing? ***(Un)*(NCERT)**

Ans. The process of converting raw materials into finished products of higher value, often using machines in industries. For example, paper is made from wood, and sugar is made from sugarcane. *(2 M)*

4. What are basic industries? Give an example ***(Re)*(NCERT)**

Ans. Basic industries are those that supply their products as raw materials to manufacture other goods. *(1 M)*

Example: Iron and Steel Industry. *(1 M)*

5. **What are light industries?** ***(Un)***

Ans. Industries that use light raw materials and produce light goods are called light industries.

Example: Industries manufacturing sewing machine and electric fans. *(2 M)*

6. **Akola, Ram, and Shyam are in the village and are small-scale farmers who have recently transitioned into small-scale manufacturing business owners. They have started a cooperative that converts locally grown sugarcane into refined sugar and molasses. The cooperative not only aims to create more jobs but also seeks to enhance the economic conditions of their community, which has been heavily dependent on low-income agricultural practices.**

Ram and Shyam have noticed significant economic disparities between their village and the nearby urban areas. As a budding economist invited to advise them, analyze how their shift from agriculture to manufacturing might help reduce this disparity. Consider the broader impacts of such a transition on the village's economy and its residents. ***(An)***

Ans. The impact of transitioning to manufacturing includes the following:

(i) **Economic Diversification:** Transitioning from agriculture to manufacturing allows the village to diversify its economic activities. This reduces reliance on farming, which can be unstable due to factors like weather and market prices. *(1 M)*

(ii) **Job Creation and Skill Development:** Manufacturing can provide higher-income jobs and develop new skills among villagers, helping to bridge the economic gap with urban areas by boosting local income levels. *(1 M)*

7. **Assess the reasons for the concentration of the woollen textile industries in the sub-tropical region in India vs their absence in the southern part of India.** ***(An)*(CBSE APQ, 2023)**

Ans. The following reasons are: **(Any Two)**

- **Climatic conditions:** Southern India has a climate that is not favourable for wool production. *(1 M)*
- **Lack of raw material:** Sheep rearing is not widespread in southern India. *(1 M)*
- **Low demand:** The demand for woollen textiles is very low in southern India due to hot and humid temperatures. *(1 M)*

All these requirements are met in the sub-tropical region of India hence the woollen textile industry is concentrated in this region of India.

Short Answer Type Questions (3 M)

1. **Why did Mahatma Gandhi lay emphasis on spinning yarn and weaving khadi?** ***(Un)*(NCERT Intext)**

Ans. Mahatma Gandhi laid emphasis on **spinning yarn** and **weaving Khadi** to make India self-reliant and reduce dependence on imported clothes. To **provide scope** for incorporating traditional skills and designs of weaving in cotton, silk, zari, embroidery, etc. Handloom Khadi provided **large-scale employment** to weavers in their **homes** as a **cottage industry**. *(3 M)*

2. **Why is it important for our country to keep the mill sector loomage lower than power loom and handloom?** ***(Re)*(NCERT Intext)**

Ans. Our country needs to keep the mill sector looming lower than the power loom and handloom because:

- **Support Traditional Art:** Preserving the traditional and cultural heritage of handloom weaving. *(1 M)*
- **Employment:** Handlooms and power looms offer more employment opportunities compared to the mill sector. *(1 M)*
- **Diversity:** Promotes diversity in design and fabric, supporting local artisans and small businesses. *(1 M)*

3. **Describe the importance of manufacturing industries as a backbone of economic development of the country.** ***(Ev)*(CBSE, 2019)**

OR

Explain with examples the interdependence of agriculture and industries. ***(Ev)*(CBSE, 2017)**

OR

'Manufacturing sector is considered as the backbone of general and economic development.' Examine the statement in the context of India. ***(Ev)***

Ans. Manufacturing industries are crucial for our country's development because they do three important things:

- **Manufacturing Importance:** They not only modernize agriculture but also provide employment, thereby reducing dependency on agricultural income. *(1 M)*
- **Boost to Agriculture:** These industries boost agriculture by increasing its productivity. They supply machinery, fertilizers, and tools to the agriculture sector, enhancing the production process. *(1 M)*
- **Economic Growth:** They contribute to economic growth by increasing trade and foreign exchange earnings, making them essential for the country's wealth. *(1 M)*

Nailing the Right Answer

Highlight the role of manufacturing industries in modernizing agriculture and providing employment

4. **Community leaders Priya and Anil are exploring options to enhance local economic opportunities through new manufacturing initiatives, In the coastal city of Marina. Marina has abundant resources from both the sea and the hinterland, offering a unique advantage for both agro-based and mineral-based industries. The city is also known for its skilled but underemployed workforce. Priya believes that starting a consumer industry might better meet immediate local needs and ensure quick job creation, while Anil feels that a key industry could offer more sustainable growth and encourage further industrial development in the area.**

Analyze the potential impacts of establishing a consumer industry versus a key industry in Marina. Consider aspects such as the immediate economic benefits, long-term industrial growth, and the overall sustainability of each option. *(An)*

Ans. Analyzing the potential impacts of establishing a consumer industry versus a key industry in Marina:

(i) **Immediate Job Creation:** A consumer industry will provide quick employment opportunities for the skilled but underemployed workforce, addressing local needs swiftly. *(1 M)*

(ii) **Sustainable Growth:** Establishing a key industry promotes long-term economic stability by attracting further industrial development and diversifying the economic base. *(1 M)*

(iii) **Resource Utilization:** Both industries efficiently use abundant local resources, with consumer industries boosting local consumption and key industries enhancing industrial infrastructure for regional development. *(1 M)*

Long Answer Type Questions (4 or 5 M)

1. Explain the reasons for concentration of iron and steel industries in and around Chotanagpur region. *(An)*(CBSE, 2019)

OR

Explain any five factors that are responsible for the concentration of iron and steel industries mainly in Chhota Nagpur Plateau region. *(An)*(CBSE, 2019)

Ans. The Chhota Nagpur Plateau is ideal for iron and steel industries because:

- **Raw Materials Availability:** The Chhota Nagpur Plateau is rich in minerals like iron ore, coal, manganese, and limestone. This makes making steel cheaper. *(1 M)*
- **Low-Cost Labor:** Many people are willing to work for less money, which lowers the cost of making steel. *(1 M)*
- **Easy to Move Goods:** The Chhota Nagpur Plateau is well connected by road and rail networks. Good roads and trains make it easy to get materials in and sell products out. *(1 M)*
- **Water Supply:** The region has a good supply of water from rivers like the Damodar, which is crucial for the iron and steel manufacturing process. *(1 M)*
- **Support from Government:** The government helps by making it easier for steel factories to do well. *(1 M)*

Topper's Explanation (CBSE, 2019)

20 The reasons for the concentration of iron and steel industries in and around the Chotanagpur plateau are-

(i) Availibity of iron ore
The region is close to the iron mines, thus the raw material can be easily transported to the industries.

(ii) Proximity of other raw material
Limestone and coking coal is also readily and easily available for production

(iii) Good transport system.
The region is well connected through railways as well as roadways facilitating easy transportation of the raw material as well as the distribution of finished products.

(iv) Availibilty of labour
Cheap and skilled labour is easily available for the states of Uttar Pradesh, Bihar and Jharkhand.

(v) Port facilities
Kolkata port nearby facilitates the export of the finished goods

(vi) The industry has immense scope for development in the home market.

2. "The economic strength of a country is measured by the development of manufacturing industries". Explain with examples. *(Ev)*(CBSE, 2023)(CBSE, 2018)

OR

Why is the economic strength of a country measured by the development of manufacturing industries? Explain with examples. *(Ev)*(CBSE, 2018)

Ans. The economic strength of a country is significant determined by the development of its manufacturing industries. Here the reasons are: **(Any five)**

- **Job Creation:** Manufacturing industries offer various jobs, reducing agriculture dependence and unemployment, enhancing overall economic stability. *(1 M)*
- **Value Addition:** They add value to raw materials by transforming them into finished goods, for example, converting cotton into textiles or iron ore into steel. *(1 M)*
- **Self-Reliance:** Promote national self-reliance by reducing dependency on imports and producing goods domestically. *(1 M)*
- **Economic Growth:** Boost economic growth by increasing the country's GDP and improving living standards. *(1 M)*
- **Export Earnings:** Increase foreign exchange earnings through the export of manufactured goods, improving the country's trade balance. *(1 M)*
- **Regional Development:** Aid in balanced regional development by setting up plants in backward areas, reducing regional disparities. *(1 M)*
- **Innovation and Technology:** Encourage innovation and technological advancement, contributing to overall progress and competitiveness in the global market. *(1 M)*

Mistakes 101 : What not to do!

Students might forget to connect the development of manufacturing industries to key economic indicator like GDP growth, export earnings and job creation, which are crucial for assessing a country's economic strength.

3. **Explain the factors which are responsible for location of industries.** *(An)* **(CBSE, 2020)**

OR

Explain any five factors affecting the location of an industry. *(An)*

Ans. The location of industries is influenced by various factors, such as:

- Availability of raw materials, as industries tend to be located near the source of raw materials to reduce transportation costs. *(1 M)*
- Availability of labor and skilled workforce, as it is essential for the smooth functioning of industries. *(1 M)*
- Access to transportation and communication networks such as roads, railways, ports, and airports. *(1 M)*
- Availability of power and water supply, as industries require a lot of energy and water for their operations. *(1 M)*
- Government policies, such as incentives, subsidies, and tax breaks, can also influence the location of industries. *(1 M)*

4. **Why does the textile industry occupy an important position in the Indian economy?** *(Ev)***(CBSE, 2019)**

OR

Explain the contribution of the textile industry in the Indian Economy. *(Ev)***(CBSE, 2017)**

Ans. The textile industry is very important in the Indian economy for several reasons:

- **Major Role in Economy:** It contributes a lot to the country's industrial production and is a big part of our economy. *(1 M)*
- **Employment:** This industry creates lots of jobs for people, both directly and indirectly, helping many families. *(1 M)*
- **Foreign Exchange:** By exporting textiles to other countries, it earns valuable foreign exchange for India. *(1 M)*
- **Self-Reliant:** India's textile industry makes everything from raw materials to finished products, making us self-reliant. *(1 M)*
- **Support to Agriculture:** It supports agriculture by providing a market for cotton, jute, and other materials. *(1 M)*

5. **In the town of Neelkanth, there's a discussion about starting a new manufacturing project to boost local employment and economic growth. The town has access to a variety of raw materials, both agricultural and mineral. Local leaders, including Rohan and Amit, are debating whether to prioritize light industry or heavy industry for their new experience. They consider factors like local resources, capital investment, and the potential for export. The community is particularly interested in industries that could integrate well with the existing local agricultural base, yet could potentially transform into a key industry supplying materials to other sectors.**

Evaluate the potential benefits and challenges Neelkanth would face if it chose to develop a heavy industry based on local mineral resources versus a light industry utilizing local agricultural products. Analyze which type of industry might be more sustainable in the long term and support the overall economic development of Neelkanth. *(Ev)*

Ans. The impact of heavy versus light industry in Neelkanth involves considering several key factors:

(i) **Resource Utilization:** Heavy industry leverages local minerals, boosting the economy but requiring large investments. The light industry uses renewable agricultural resources, promoting sustainability. *(1 M)*

(ii) **Environmental Impact:** Heavy industry may increase pollution and energy use, necessitating robust environmental controls. Conversely, the light industry typically has a smaller environmental footprint. *(1 M)*

(iii) **Economic Stability:** Heavy industry might be vulnerable to global economic shifts, whereas light industry linked to daily consumer needs offers more stability. *(1 M)*

(iv) **Employment Opportunities:** Heavy industry creates specialized, high-paying jobs but may exclude unskilled locals. The light industry provides broader employment, suiting the existing workforce's skills. *(1 M)*

(v) **Sustainability and Growth:** Light industry, integrating with agriculture, enhances long-term sustainability, supporting local farmers and adapting to market and regulatory changes. *(1 M)*

6. **What is India's status in chemical production?** *(Un)*

Ans. India's status in chemical production is significant and diverse, covering both inorganic and organic chemical sectors through:

- **Rapid Growth:** India's chemical industry is rapidly growing and diversifying, making significant strides in both inorganic and organic chemicals. *(1 M)*
- **Wide Range:** The industry includes a wide range of products, from basic chemicals like sulphuric and nitric acids to more complex ones like fertilizers, synthetic fibers, and plastics. *(1 M)*
- **Major Producer:** India is a major producer of inorganic chemicals such as sulphuric acid, used in various manufacturing processes, including fertilizers and plastics. *(1 M)*
- **Petrochemicals:** The organic chemicals sector is notably strong in petrochemicals, which are crucial for manufacturing synthetic fibers, rubber, plastics, and dyes. *(1 M)*
- **Global Standing:** Thanks to its comprehensive and growing chemical industry, India stands as a key player in the global market, contributing significantly to the country's export earnings. *(1 M)*

2 INDUSTRIAL POLLUTION AND ENVIRONMENTAL DEGRADATION

NCERT Definitions *(Commonly asked in 1 mark)*

- **Environmental Degradation: Damage** to the natural environment caused by industrial activities, **including pollution** of land, water, and air, and the destruction of habitats.
- **Sustainable Development:** Economic development that is conducted **without depletion of natural resources**. It involves integrating **economic progress** with environmental conservation.

Important Concepts

Control of Environmental Degradation

(*i*) Minimising use of water for processing by reusing and recycling it .

(*ii*) Harvesting of rainwater to meet water requirements

(*iii*) Treating hot water and effluents before releasing them in rivers and ponds

(*iv*) Ground water resources also need to be regulated legally.

National Thermal Power Corporation (NTPC)

NTPC is a **major power** providing corporation in India. It has ISO certification for EMS (Environment Management System) 14001.

The corporation has a proactive approach for preserving the **natural environment** and **resources** like water, oil and gas and fuels in places where it is setting up power plants.

This has been possible through-

(*a*) Optimum utilisation of equipment **adopting latest techniques** and upgrading existing equipment.

(*b*) Minimising waste generation by maximising ash utilisation.

(*c*) Providing **green belts** for **nurturing ecological** balance and addressing the question of special purpose vehicles for afforestation.

(*d*) **Reducing environmental pollution** through ash pond management, ash water recycling system and liquid waste management.

(*e*) **Ecological monitoring**, reviews and online database management for all its power stations.

Sewage Treatment plant under Yammuna action plan at Faridabad

Ramagundan Plant

Classification

Industries are Responsible for four types of Pollution:

1. **Air pollution:** It is Caused by the presence of a high proportion of **undesirable gases**, such as sulphur dioxide and carbon monoxide.

2. **Water Pollution:** Caused by **organic and inorganic industrial** wastes and effluents discharged into rivers. It destroys aquatic life.

3. **Thermal Pollution:** Occurs when **hot water** from **factories** and thermal plants are **drained into rivers** and **ponds** before cooling.

4. **Noise Pollution:** Caused due to industrial and **construction activities**. This type of pollution results in increased **hearing impairment**, **heart rate** and **blood pressure**.

Real Life Application Based Questions

Read the following source carefully and Answer the Questions that follows:

It was originally a white monument, but because of pollution, the Taj Mahal is turning yellow - the sulphur dioxide getting in the atmosphere reacts with water molecules and becomes sulphuric acid, which slowly destroys the outer layer of the building.

1. **What color change is the Taj Mahal undergoing due to air pollution?**

Ans. The Taj Mahal is turning **yellow** due to air pollution.

2. **Which gas in the atmosphere is responsible for the discoloration of the Taj Mahal?**

Ans. The gas responsible for the discoloration of the Taj Mahal is **sulphur dioxide**.

3. **Explain how sulphur dioxide is contributing to the damage of the Taj Mahal's exterior.**

Ans. Sulphur dioxide in the air reacts with water to form **sulphuric acid**, which falls as acid rain. This acid rain slowly damages the outer layer of the Taj Mahal, causing it to lose its original white Colour.

Mnemonics

Types of Pollution: "LAWN"

- L → Land Pollution
- A → Air Pollution
- W → Water Pollution
- N → Noise Pollution

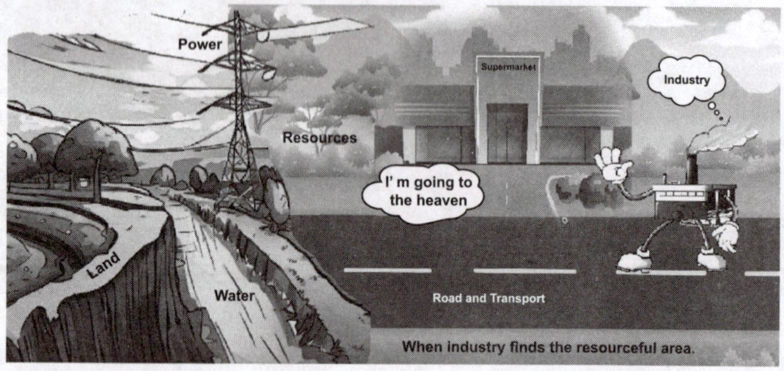

These are the four types of pollution caused by industries.

Scan Me for Detailed Explanations

COMPETENCY BASED SOLVED EXAMPLES

Multiple Choice Questions

(1 M)

1. **Rajiv, a local environmental officer, is assessing the impact of industrial emissions in his city, which is known for its chemical and paper factories.**

   What immediate action should Rajiv prioritize to reduce air pollution effectively in his city? *(Ap)*

   (*a*) Encourage factories to install air filters and scrubbers to reduce emissions.

   (*b*) Ban the use of all fossil fuels in industrial processes.

   (*c*) Implement strict noise control regulations in industrial areas.

   (*d*) Focus solely on improving waste disposal methods.

2. **Which pollution among of the following adversely affects human health, animals, plants, building and the atmosphere on the whole?** *(Un)*

   A. Noise pollution B. Thermal pollution

   C. Air pollution D. Water pollution

   Choose the correct options given below.

   (*a*) Both A and B (*b*) Both A and C

   (*c*) Only C (*d*) All of the above

3. **A recent study has shown an increase in water pollution in the Ganges River due to nearby industrial activities.**

   Which industries are most likely contributing to this increase in pollution and should be the focus of stricter regulations? *(An)*

   (*a*) Textile and dyeing industries that discharge dyes and heavy metals into the river.

   (*b*) Agricultural industries primarily contribute organic waste.

   (*c*) Information technology industries with minimal effluent discharge.

   (*d*) Food processing plants that largely emit organic wastes.

Assertion and Reason

(1 M)

Direction: The following questions consist of two statements – Assertion (A) and Reason (R). Answer these questions by selecting the appropriate option given below:

(*a*) Both A and R are true, and R is the correct explanation of A.

(*b*) Both A and R are true, but R is not the correct explanation of A.

(*c*) A is true, but R is false.

(*d*) A is false, but R is true.

1. **Assertion (A):** Industrial development cannot minimize environmental degradation.

   Reason (R): Environmental degradation depends on the raw material used. *(An)*

2. **Assertion (A):** Industrial pollution is the main cause of environmental degradation.

   Reason (R): Industries release harmful pollutants into the air, water, and soil, which can have negative impacts on human health and the environment. *(Un)*

3. **Assertion (A):** Harvesting of rainwater reduces industrial pollution of fresh water.

   Reason (R): Rainwater helps industry to meet water requirements. *(An)*

4. **Assertion (A):** Industrial pollution is the main cause of environmental degradation.

Reason (R): Industries release harmful pollutants into the air, water, and soil, which can have negative impacts on human health and the environment. *(An)*

Subjective Questions

Very Short Answer Type Questions (1 or 2 M)

1. **Name three major air pollutants.** *(Re)*

Ans. Air borne dust, smoke and undesirable gases are three major air pollutants. *(2 M)*

2. **Which machine helps in reducing noise pollution?** *(Un)*

Ans. Air duct Silencers, also known as sound alternators are designed to control noise pollution. *(1 M)*

3. **Name any two industries that are responsible for water pollution.** *(Re)*

Ans. Chemical, textile, dying and petroleum refineries are responsible for water Pollutions. *(2 M)*

4. **Business Process Outsourcing (BPO) is an example of ________ industry in India.** *(Un)(CBSE, 2020)*

Ans. Business Process Outsourcing (BPO) is an example of Information technology and Electronic industry in India. *(1 M)*

Short Answer Type Questions (3 M)

1. **How do industrial units cause air pollution?** *(Un)(CBSE, 2017)*

Ans. Air pollution is caused by the presence of high proportion of undesirable gases such as:

- **Smoke Emission:** Factories release smoke containing harmful gases like sulphur dioxide and carbon monoxide. *(1 M)*
- **Particulate Matter:** Industries emit dust, mist, and smoke, adding solid and liquid particles to the air. *(1 M)*
- **Burning Fossil Fuels:** The use of coal and oil in industries adds to air pollution by releasing more toxic gases. *(1 M)*

2. **Maya is the environmental engineer in EcoTech company leads efforts to reduce industrial pollution using advanced treatment and recycling technologies. Known for its extensive manufacturing sector that includes textile mills, chemical plants, and metal fabrication units, local environmental engineer Maya is leading a city-wide initiative to reduce industrial pollution. As part of this initiative, Maya is tasked with implementing advanced treatment and recycling technologies that align with the city's goal of becoming a model for sustainable industrial practices. The local government is supportive but concerned about the costs and the potential disruption to industrial operations.**

Based on the suggestions for controlling environmental degradation, analyze the specific strategies Maya could implement to manage water and air pollution in EcoTech's industrial sector. Discuss how these strategies could be integrated into existing industrial processes and the potential challenges and benefits they might bring to the local environment and the industry itself. *(Ev)*

Ans. Strategies Maya could implement to manage water and air pollution in EcoTech's industrial sector: *(Any Three)*

(*i*) **Advanced Filtration Systems:** Introduce high-efficiency particulate air (HEPA) filters in factories to capture airborne pollutants, reducing air pollution. *(1 M)*

(*ii*) **Wastewater Treatment Upgrades:** Upgrade existing wastewater treatment plants with modern technology like reverse osmosis systems to clean industrial effluents before discharge, improving water quality. *(1 M)*

(*iii*) **Recycling and Reuse Programs:** Implement systems for recycling water within industrial processes, decreasing water withdrawal and pollution. *(1 M)*

(*iv*) **Training and Awareness:** Conduct workshops to educate industry workers on the benefits and methods of pollution control, fostering a culture of environmental responsibility. *(1 M)*

3. **In the town of Riverwood, which is situated near a large river and relies heavily on tourism and fishing, local leaders are concerned about the impact of a nearby power station on the river's health and the local economy. The power station is under pressure to implement sustainable practices that can reduce its environmental footprint while continuing to meet the energy demands of the growing population.**

Examine how the power station in Riverwood could implement the strategy of creating green belts and managing ash ponds to minimize its impact on the river's ecosystem. What are the expected benefits of these actions for the local community and environment? *(Ap)*

Ans. The implementation of green belts and ash pond management at the Riverwood power station: **(Any Three)**

(*i*) **Green Belt Creation:** Plant trees and vegetation around the power station to act as a natural barrier, reducing soil erosion and water pollution. *(1 M)*

(*ii*) **Ash Pond Management:** Securely contain ash in lined ponds to prevent leaching into the river, safeguarding water quality. *(1 M)*

The expected benefits of these actions for the local community and environment are:

(*iii*) **Benefit - Ecosystem Health:** Green belts provide habitats for local wildlife, enhancing biodiversity around the river area. *(1 M)*

(*iv*) **Benefit - Community Impact:** Improved River health boosts tourism and fishing, crucial for the local economy. *(1 M)*

4. **What steps has NTPC taken to show the way in environmental management and conservation?** *(Un)*

Ans. The steps has NTPC taken to show the way in environmental management and conservation are:

- **Optimization of Resources:** Using equipment efficiently and adopting the latest technologies. *(1 M)*

- **Waste Minimization:** Maximizing the utilization of ash and minimizing waste generation. *(1 M)*
- **Environmental Protection:** Implementing ash pond management, water recycling, and ensuring ecological balance. *(1 M)*

Long Answer Type Questions (5 M)

1. How can the industrial pollution of fresh water be reduced? Explain with examples. ***(An)*(CBSE, 2023)**

OR

Explain the ways through which the industrial pollution of fresh water can be reduced. ***(Un)***

Ans. Industrial pollution of fresh water can be reduced in the following ways:

- **Treatment of effluents:** Industries can treat their effluents before releasing them into the water bodies. This can be done through physical, chemical, or biological methods. *(1 M)*
- **Recycling of water:** Industries can recycle the water used in their processes, which can reduce the amount of fresh water needed. *(1 M)*
- **Use of green technologies:** Industries can use green technologies that are less polluting and use less water. For example, industries can use renewable energy sources like solar or wind power. *(1 M)*
- **Pollution control norms:** Implementing strict pollution control norms and monitoring mechanisms to ensure industries comply with the regulations. *(1 M)*
- **Awareness campaign:** Raising awareness among industries and the public about the importance of environmental protection. *(1 M)*

2. 'The Challenge of sustainable development requires control over industries pollution'. Substantiate the statement with examples. ***(Ev)*(CBSE, 2019)**

Ans. Sustainable development means growing without harming the environment. Controlling industrial pollution is key to this:

- **Water Pollution:** Industries release harmful wastes into rivers. For example, chemical factories discharge dyes and detergents, polluting water and harming aquatic life. *(1 M)*
- **Air Pollution:** Factories emit gases like sulfur dioxide and carbon monoxide, causing air pollution. Smoke from burning fossil fuels adds to this problem, affecting health and climate. *(1 M)*
- **Soil Pollution:** Dumping industrial waste makes soil useless, affecting agriculture. Examples include the disposal of plastic and chemical wastes that degrade soil quality. *(1 M)*
- **Noise Pollution:** Machinery noise from industries can cause hearing loss and stress in humans. *(1 M)*
- Sustainable development needs industries to use clean technologies, treat wastes before disposal, and follow environmental guidelines to minimize pollution. *(1 M)*

3. In the small town of Riverview, which is nestled along a river and surrounded by fertile farmlands, community leader Anita is contemplating the introduction of a new industry that can utilize the local agricultural strengths. The town is known for its vibrant jute cultivation, but the jute is currently sold as raw material to industries far away, leading to minimal local economic benefit. Anita is considering establishing a jute processing plant right in Riverview to add value locally and create more jobs. However, she is also mindful of the challenges in setting up a new industry, including infrastructure needs and market access.

Given Riverview's agricultural backdrop and the presence of a skilled but underutilized workforce, assess the feasibility of establishing a jute processing plant in the town. Consider the potential economic benefits for the local community, the challenges of market and infrastructure development, and the environmental impact of such an industry. How could this industry align with sustainable development goals for Riverview? ***(An)***

Ans. The feasibility of a jute processing plant in Riverview:

(i) **Local Economic Boost:** Establishing the plant would create jobs and retain more economic value in Riverview, enhancing residents' incomes. *(1 M)*

(ii) **Infrastructure and Market Access:** Significant investment needed for infrastructure; remote location poses challenges for accessing broader markets. *(1 M)*

(iii) **Environmental Concerns:** Jute processing could impact the river and surrounding areas; adopting eco-friendly technologies and practices is vital. *(1 M)*

(iv) **Sustainable Development Alignment:** The plant can support sustainable economic growth and environmental stewardship (taking care of something) by integrating with local agricultural practices and implementing green technologies. *(1 M)*

(v) **Community Impact:** Besides economic benefits, the plant could strengthen community ties and preserve local agricultural traditions by involving jute farmers directly in the value chain. *(1 M)*

4. Discuss the steps to be taken to minimise environmental degradation by industry? **(NCERT)*(Cr)***

OR

Suggest any three steps to minimise the environmental degradation caused by the industrial development in India. ***(Cr)***

Ans. To minimize environmental degradation by industries, several steps need to be taken.

- Industries should adopt cleaner production techniques and ensure the treatment of emissions and effluents before release. *(1 M)*
- Implementing waste minimization practices and recycling can significantly reduce the amount of waste generated. *(1 M)*
- The use of renewable energy sources instead of fossil fuels can decrease air pollution. *(1 M)*
- Industries should also invest in green technologies and environmental control systems to monitor and manage their environmental impact. *(1 M)*
- Public awareness and community participation in environmental conservation efforts can further contribute to reducing industrial pollution and promoting sustainable industrial practices. *(1 M)*

MISCELLANEOUS EXERCISE

Multiple Choice Questions

(1 M)

1. Nikhil, a member of a planning committee focused on revitalizing the sugar industry in India, discusses strategies with the committee.

   Why might Nikhil and his committee consider promoting the cooperative model, particularly in states like Maharashtra and Karnataka for the sugar industry? ***(An)***

   (*a*) Because the high sucrose content of cane in these states ensures better profitability.

   (*b*) The cooler climate in these regions extends the crushing season, making operations more viable.

   (*c*) Cooperative models in these states have historically shown higher efficiency and success rates.

   (*d*) All of the above are reasons to promote the cooperative model in these states.

2. Meena, an environmental scientist, is designing a community workshop to educate the public about the effects of thermal pollution caused by local thermal power plants.

   What aspect of thermal pollution should Meena emphasize to illustrate its impact on aquatic life? ***(Ev)***

   (*a*) The role of thermal pollution in increasing river temperatures and decreasing oxygen levels in water.

   (*b*) The increase in noise pollution due to thermal power generation.

   (*c*) The direct effects of thermal pollution on soil fertility.

   (*d*) The contribution of thermal pollution to air quality degradation.

3. Which of the following is an example of a cooperative sector industry? ***(Un)***

   (*a*) BHEL

   (*b*) TISCO

   (*c*) Sugar industry in Maharashtra

   (*d*) Dabur Industries

4. What was a significant reason for the shift of the sugar industry to the southern and western states of India? ***(Un)***

   (*a*) Better soil quality

   (*b*) Higher sucrose content in cane

   (*c*) Lesser labor costs

   (*d*) Increase in local demand

5. What is the primary reason for the growth of the IT industry in Bengaluru? ***(Un)***

   (*a*) Educational facilities

   (*b*) Climate

   (*c*) Employment opportunities

   (*d*) Presence of entrepreneurs

6. Export of manufactured goods Expands ________, are brings in much needed foreign exchange. ***(Un)***

   (*a*) Trade and Commerce

   (*b*) People of a nation

   (*c*) Capacity of a nation

   (*d*) None of the above

7. This sewage treatment plant represents an initiative to mitigate pollution in the Yamuna River, aiming to improve water quality and support sustainable urban living.

   Sewage Treatment plant under Yamuna action plan at Faridabad

   (*i*) How can the process observed in the sewage treatment plant be applied to improve water management in drought-prone areas? ***(Ap)***

   (*a*) By using treated water for agriculture

   (*b*) By increasing water storage capacity

   (*c*) By enhancing rainwater harvesting

   (*d*) By redirecting river flow

   OR

   (*ii*) Propose a plan to use the output of this plant to support local agriculture. ***(Cr)***

   (*a*) Use treated water for irrigation

   (*b*) Extract nutrients from sludge as fertilizers

   (*c*) Develop hydroponic farms nearby

   (*d*) All of the above

8. The first textile mill was established in (Re)

(a) Mumbai (b) Delhi
(c) Patna (d) Kolkata

9. What is the rank of India in production of sugar? (Re)

(a) First (b) Second
(c) Third (d) Fourth

10. There are 60% of the mills in the state of (Re)

(a) Uttar Pradesh and Bihar
(b) Rajasthan and Haryana
(c) Kerala and Karnataka
(d) Jammu Kashmir and Ladakh

11. Which sector is the foundation sector of the economy? (Un)

(a) Sugar (b) Iron and steel
(c) Automobiles (d) Plastic

12. ______ has emerged as the electronic capital of India (Re)

(a) Bengaluru (b) Kota
(c) Lucknow (d) Patna

13. The second-largest metallurgical industry in India is (Re)

(a) Aluminium smelting
(b) Iron smelting
(c) Steel melting
(d) Cement melting

14. Which of the following is correct about Fertilizer Industry? (An)

1. The fertilizer industry is centered around the production of nitrogenous fertilizers.
2. After the Green Revolution the industry expanded to several other parts of the country. Gujarat, Tamil Nadu, Uttar Pradesh, Punjab and Kerala.

(a) Only 1 (b) Only 2
(c) Both 1 and 2 (d) Neither 1 nor 2

15. In which of the following year, the production of crude steel in India is below than 90? (An)

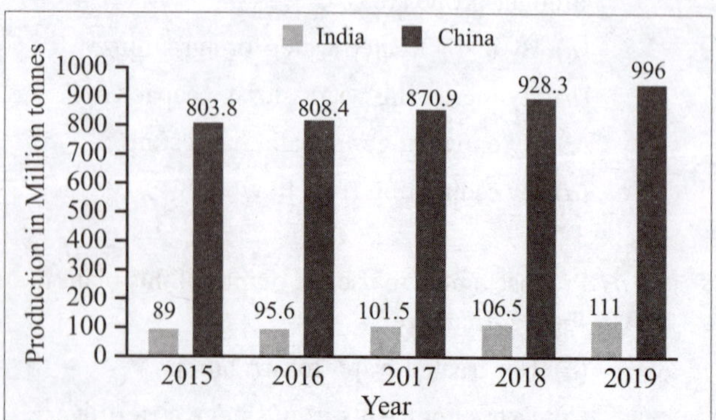

(a) 2016 (b) 2017
(c) 2019 (d) 2015

Assertion and Reason

(1 M)

Direction: The following questions consist of two statements – Assertion (A) and Reason (R). Answer these questions by selecting the appropriate option given below:

(a) Both A and R are true, and R is the correct explanation of A.
(b) Both A and R are true, but R is not the correct explanation of A.
(c) A is true, but R is false.
(d) A is false, but R is true.

1. **Assertion (A):** India is the largest producer of raw jute and jute goods.
Reason (R): Most jute mills in India are located along the banks of the Hugli river. (Ev)

2. **Assertion (A):** Aluminium smelting is an important metallurgical industry in India.
Reason (R): Aluminium is light, resistant to corrosion, and a good conductor of heat. (Ev)

3. **Assertion (A):** Industries gives boost to the agricultural sector.
Reason (R): Competitiveness of manufacturing industry has helped in increasing their production and also made production process efficient. (Un)

4. **Assertion (A):** Aluminium is a universally accepted metal for a large number of industries.
Reason (R): Aluminium is flexible and a good conductor of heat and electricity. (Un)

5. **Assertion (A):** Most of the Jute mills of India located in West Bengal.
Reason (R): Bus facility is available to export the manufactured goods. (An)

6. **Assertion (A):** Manufacturing industries are important for economic development.
Reason (R): Manufacturing industries help modernize agriculture and provide jobs in secondary and tertiary sectors. (An)

7. **Assertion (A):** Paper is manufactured from wood, while sugar is manufactured from sugarcane.
Reason (R): Primary materials are processed into finished goods in manufacturing industries. (An)

8. **Assertion (A):** Clothes can be manufactured from yarn, which is itself an industrial product.
Reason (R): Yarn is a primary material that can be processed into finished goods in manufacturing industries. (An)

9. **Assertion (A):** Wastes from nuclear power plants cause cancers, birth defects and miscarriages.
Reason (R): Rain water percolates to the soil carrying the pollutants to the ground and ground water also get contaminated. (An)

10. **Assertion (A):** In recent years, there is a tendency for the sugar mills to shift and concentrate in southern and western states
Reason (R): The cane produced in southern and western states has higher sucrose content. (An)

11. **Assertion (A):** Agriculture and industry are not exclusive of each other
Reason (R): The agro industries have given boost to agriculture by raising its productivity (An)

Subjective Questions

Very Short Answer Type Questions (2 M)

1. Arjun is the community leader In Technoville, his aim is to diversify the city's iron and steel-based industrial base by introducing chemical and fertilizer industries. This strategic shift considers global market dynamics, environmental impacts, and local skilled labor availability. Assess the decision's implications for employment, environmental sustainability, and industrial integration.

   Consider the impact of introducing chemical and fertilizer industries in Technoville on local employment, environmental sustainability, and integration with existing industries. *(An)*

2. Name some agro based industries. *(Re)*
3. What do you mean by joint sector industries? *(Un)*
4. Which inputs are required for iron and steel industry? *(Un)*
5. Which chemicals are categorized as "inorganic chemicals"? *(Un)*
6. How were cotton textiles produced in ancient India? *(Un)*
7. What is the position of India in the production of Gur and Khandearl in the world? *(Re)*

Short Answer Type Questions (3 M)

1. Entrepreneur Meena is considering establishing a new industry, In Agrihub the area is known for its cotton production and skilled labor in traditional textile techniques. Meena envisions revitalizing the local textile industry by combining traditional skills with modern technology to cater to domestic and international markets. Alternatively, she is exploring the jute industry due to its export potential and success in neighboring regions.

   What are the benefits and challenges Meena might face in developing a modernized cotton textile industry compared to starting a jute processing industry? *(An)*

2. Study the given table carefully and answer the following questions:

Sector	Share of Production	Loomage
Mills	6.00 percent	1.33 lakhs
Power Loom	51.17 percent	14 lakhs
Handloom	23.000 percent	NA

   (*i*) Name the sector which has the highest share in the production of fabric in India? *(Re)*

   (*ii*) Why is it important for our country to keep the mill sector loomage lower than power loom and handloom? *(An)*

3. In the developing region of SteelTown, local government and industry leaders, including Priya and Vijay, are evaluating the potential for setting up a new iron and steel manufacturing plant. This region has access to key raw materials like iron ore and coal, which are crucial for steel production. Additionally, SteelTown is strategically located near major transportation hubs, which could facilitate the distribution of finished steel products both domestically and internationally. Priya and Vijay are considering this venture not only to boost local employment but also to stimulate other sectors such as construction and automobile manufacturing through the supply of steel.

   Given the crucial role of the iron and steel industry as described, assess how the establishment of a new steel plant in SteelTown could impact the local economy and its adjacent industries. Consider the potential benefits such as job creation and industrial growth as well as the challenges including environmental impact and the need for substantial infrastructure development. *(Ev)*

4. "The industries have undergone significant changes due to advancement in technology and shifts in consumer preferences." Justify the statement. *(An)* **(CBSE, 2024 DL)**

Long Answer Type Questions (4 or 5 M)

1. Explain the ways through which the industrial pollution of fresh water can be reduced. *(Ap)***(CBSE, 2020)**
2. How do industries pollute the environment? *(Un)***(NCERT)**
3. Priya, the environmental officer, is tackling industrial pollution from the textile and chemical industries in Greenvale, which are crucial to the economy but harm air, water, and soil quality. Priya aims to implement modern technologies and regulations to reduce pollution and ensure sustainability without hindering industrial growth.

   Analyze potential strategies Priya could implement to reduce pollution in GreenVale's textile and chemical industries, considering the effects on both the environment and the local economy. How could these solutions balance industrial activity with environmental conservation? *(An)*

4. Why has the 'Chotanagpur Plateau region' the maximum concentration of Iron and Steel Industries? Analyze the reasons. *(An)*
5. How are integrated steel plants different from mini steel plants? What problems does the industry face? What recent developments have led to a rise in the production capacity? *(Un)*

Case Based Questions

Case Based-I

Read the given case and answer the questions that follow: (CBSE, 2022 Term 2)

Challenges faced by the Jute industry include stiff competition in the international market from synthetic substitutes and from other competitors like Bangladesh, Brazil, Philippines, Egypt and Thailand. However, the internal demand has been on the increase due to the Government policy of mandatory use of jute packaging. To stimulate demand, the products need to be diversified. In 2005, National Jute Policy was formulated with the objective of increasing productivity, improving quality, ensuring good prices to the jute farmers and enhancing the yield per hectare.

The main markets are U.S.A., Canada, Russia, United Arab Republic, U.K. and Australia. The growing global concern for environment friendly, biodegradable materials, has once again opened the opportunity for jute products.

(*i*) Mention any two challenges faced by 'jute industry' in India. (*1 M*) **(*Re*)**

(*ii*) What was the main objective of National Jute Policy formulated in 2005? (*1 M*) **(*Re*)**

(*iii*) How has jute industry once again opened the new opportunities for its products? (*2 M*) **(*Un*)**

Case Based-II

Read the following passage carefully and answer the questions that follow:

A cooperative sugar mill has been established in the small town of Dharapuram in Tamil Nadu, significantly influencing the local economy and the lives of the sugarcane farmers. This mill not only processes sugarcane from local farms but also actively participates in community development through various sustainability and educational programs. The mill has become a central part of the town's economic landscape, employing many locals and contributing to infrastructure improvements. The integration of modern technology in the mill has enhanced production efficiency, leading to better pricing and market access for the farmers' produce. Additionally, the mill's presence has encouraged younger generations to consider careers in agriculture and agro-based industries, shifting perceptions about employment in these sectors.

(*i*) How does the cooperative model of the sugar mill benefit the sugarcane farmers in Dharapuram? (*1 M*) **(*An*)**

(*ii*) What role does the sugar mill play in altering the employment landscape of Dharapuram? (*1 M*) **(*Ev*)**

(*iii*) Discuss the potential long-term impacts on agricultural practices in Dharapuram due to the mill's emphasis on sustainable farming techniques. (*2 M*) **(*Ev*)**

Case Based-III

Read the following passage carefully and answer the questions that follow:

Indore and Kanpur is the industrial city, known for its steel production, concerns over environmental degradation have grown significantly due to the emissions from various factories. In response, a local environmental NGO has initiated a collaborative project with the steel plants to implement green technologies and pollution control measures. The project aims to reduce air and water pollution by introducing advanced filtration systems, promoting the reuse of industrial waste, and developing community awareness programs about environmental sustainability. This initiative has started to show positive results, with noticeable improvements in local air and water quality. The community is also actively participating in various environmental conservation activities encouraged by the NGO.

(*i*) Evaluate how the introduction of green technologies in Indore's steel plants could potentially alter the local environmental quality. (*1 M*) **(*Ev*)**

(*ii*) Analyze the role of community involvement in enhancing the effectiveness of environmental sustainability programs in Indore. (*1 M*) **(*An*)**

(*iii*) Discuss the potential long-term economic benefits that Indore might experience from integrating environmental conservation practices in its industrial operations. (*2 M*) **(*Ev*)**

Map Based Questions

1. On the same given Map of India, locate and label the following: **(CBSE, 2022 Term 2) (*Re*)**

(*i*) Ramagundam Thermal Plant (*1 M*)

OR

(*ii*) Pune Software Technology Park (*1 M*)

2. Locate and label any **four** of the following with appropriate symbols on the same given political outline map of India. **(CBSE, 2020)(*Re*)**

Note: Only (*ii, iii, v*) in this chapter. (*4 M*)

Outine of India	
(*i*) Sardar Sarovar	Dam
(*ii*) Bhilai	Iron and Steel Plant
(*iii*) Pune	Software Technology Park
(*iv*) Kochi	Major Sea Port
(*v*) Indore	Cotton Textile Industry
(*vi*) Naraura	Nuclear Power Plant

3. Features are marked by numbers in the given political map of India. Identify these features with the help of the following information and write their correct names on the lines marked in the map. **(*Re*)**

(*i*) Cotton textile industry (*1 M*)

(*ii*) Woolen industry (*1 M*)

ANSWER KEYS

Answer Key

Multiple Choice Questions

1. (*d*) **2.** (*a*) **3.** (*c*) **4.** (*b*) **5.** (*a*) **6.** (*a*) **7.** (*a*) **or** (*d*) **8.** (*d*) **9.** (*b*) **10.** (*a*)
11. (*a*) **12.** (*a*) **13.** (*a*) **14.** (*c*) **15.** (*d*)

Assertion and Reason

1. (*a*) **2.** (*b*) **3.** (*a*) **4.** (*a*) **5.** (*b*) **6.** (*a*) **7.** (*a*) **8.** (*a*) **9.** (*b*) **10.** (*a*)
11. (*a*)

HINTS & EXPLANATIONS

Multiple Choice Questions

1. (*d*) All of the above are reasons to promote the cooperative model in these states.

2. (*a*) The role of thermal pollution in increasing river temperatures and decreasing oxygen levels in water.

3. (*c*) Cooperative sector industries are operated by the producers or the workers who share the resources and profits or losses proportionately, like the sugar industry in Maharashtra.

4. (*b*) Cane produced in the southern and western states has a higher sucrose content, leading to a longer crushing season.

5. (*a*) Bengaluru is known for its wide range of educational facilities which have been instrumental in the growth of the IT industry.

6. (*a*) Commerce of a nation

7. (*i*) (*a*) Using treated water for agriculture conserves fresh water resources and utilizes an otherwise waste product.

OR

(*ii*) (*d*) Utilizing treated water for irrigation, extracting nutrients for fertilization, and setting up hydroponic systems are all sustainable uses of resources from the plant.

8. (*d*) The first cotton textile mill in India was established at in Mumbai 1854.

9. (*b*) India stands second as a world producer of sugar but occupies the first place in the production of gur and Khandsari.

10. (*a*) Uttar Pradesh and Bihar

11. (*a*) Sugar

12. (*a*) Bengaluru

13. (*a*) Aluminium smelting

14. (*c*) Both 1 and 2

15. (*d*) 2015

Assertion and Reason

1. (*a*) India's position as the largest producer is aided by the conducive conditions along the Hugli river for jute mills.

2. (*b*) The properties of aluminium contribute to its importance but do not explain the industry's significance in metallurgy.

3. (*a*) Both A and R are true, but R is not the correct explanation of A.

4. (*a*) Both A and R are true, but R is not the correct explanation of A.

5. (*b*) The first jute mill was set up near Kolkata in 1855 at Rishra. After Partition in 1947, the jute mills remained in India but three-fourth of the jute producing area went to Bangladesh (erstwhile East Pakistan).

6. (*a*) Both A and R are true, but R is not the correct explanation of A.

7. (*a*) Both A and R are true, but R is not the correct explanation of A.

8. (*a*) Yarn, an industrial product, is a primary material used in textile manufacturing to make clothes, demonstrating its foundational role in transforming from raw form to finished apparel.

9. (*b*) Assertion and Reason both are true and Reason is the not correct explanation of assertion

10. (*a*) Assertion and Reason both are true and Reason is the correct explanation of assertion

11. (*a*) Assertion and Reason both are true and Reason is the correct explanation of assertion

Subjective Questions

Very Short Answer Type Questions

1. Introducing chemical and fertilizer industries in Technoville will create new jobs, improve sustainability by reducing reliance on heavy industries, and leverage existing infrastructure, but requires careful management of new environmental impacts. *(2 M)*
2. Cotton, woollen, jute, silk textile, rubber, sugar, tea, coffee and edible oil are some of the agro based industries. *(2 M)*
3. Joint sector industries are jointly run by the state and individuals or a group of individuals. Oil India Ltd. (OIL) is jointly owned by the public and private sectors. *(2 M)*
4. Iron ore, coking coal and limestone are required in the ratio of 4:2:1. Some quantities of manganese are also required to harden the steel. *(2 M)*
5. Inorganic chemicals include sulphuric acid (used to manufacture fertilizers, synthetic fibres, plastics, adhesives, paints, and dyes), nitric acid, alkalis, soda ash and caustic soda. *(2 M)*
6. In ancient India, cotton textiles were produced with hand spinning and handloom weaving techniques. *(2 M)*
7. India stands second as a world producer of sugar but has the first position in the production of Gur and Khandsari in the world. *(2 M)*

Short Answer Type Questions

1. Benefits and Challenges in Developing Cotton Textile Industry vs. Jute Processing Industry:

   (*i*) Cotton Textile Industry: *(1½ M)*
   - **Benefit:** Utilizes local skilled labor and traditional textile techniques.
   - **Challenge:** High initial investment for modernizing facilities.

   (*ii*) Jute Processing Industry: *(1½ M)*
   - **Benefit:** High export potential due to eco-friendly products.
   - **Challenge:** Requires expertise in jute processing which might be lacking locally.

2. (*i*) Power loom sector has the highest share in the production of fabric in India. *(1 M)*

   (*ii*) it important for our country to keep the mill sector looming lower than power loom and handloom because **(Any two)**

   (*a*) The power loom and the handloom can provide more employment to the rural people. *(1 M)*

   (*b*) Both of them promote decentralization and benefit a wider area of the country. *(1 M)*

   (*c*) Both of them require less investment as compared to mill sector loomage. *(1 M)*

3. The impact of establishing a new steel plant in Steel Town:

   (*i*) **Economic Growth:** The plant would create jobs and stimulate sectors like construction and automotive through steel supply, boosting the local economy. *(1 M)*

   (*ii*) **Infrastructure Demand:** Developing the plant requires significant infrastructure improvements, which can drive further investment in the region. *(1 M)*

   (*iii*) **Environmental Concerns:** Steel production has substantial environmental impacts, necessitating measures to manage pollution and resource use effectively. *(1 M)*

4. Industries have significantly evolved due to technology and consumer preferences.

   (*i*) Technological advancements have led to more efficient production methods, reducing costs and increasing output. *(1 M)*

   (*ii*) Changes in consumer preferences have pushed industries to innovate and diversify products to meet new demands. *(1 M)*

   (*iii*) Digitalization and the internet have transformed marketing strategies, allowing industries to reach a broader audience and customize products. These changes have collectively led to more dynamic, efficient, and consumer-responsive industries. *(1 M)*

   These points justify how industries have undergone significant changes due to advancements in technology and shifts in consumer preferences.

Long Answer Type Questions

1. Industrial pollution of fresh water can be reduced through various ways, such as:
   - Treating industrial wastewater before it is released into water bodies. *(1 M)*
   - Implementing strict regulations and standards to limit the amount of pollutants that industries can discharge. *(1 M)*
   - Promoting the use of eco-friendly technologies and practices, such as reducing water usage and recycling wastewater. *(1 M)*
   - Encouraging industries to shift towards cleaner sources of energy, such as solar and wind power. *(1 M)*
   - Creating awareness among industries and the public about the importance of water conservation and pollution prevention. *(1 M)*
2. Industries pollute the environment in several ways, leading to:
   - **Air Pollution:** They release harmful gases like sulfur dioxide and carbon monoxide into the air, causing air pollution. *(1 M)*
   - **Water Pollution:** This occurs when industries discharge untreated wastewater into rivers and lakes, contaminating water bodies with chemicals, heavy metals, and other pollutants. *(1 M)*

- **Land Pollution:** This is caused by the disposal of industrial waste, including toxic chemicals and non-biodegradable materials, which contaminate the soil. *(1 M)*
- **Noise Pollution:** This is generated from industrial operations, machinery, and construction activities, leading to hearing loss and stress in humans. *(1 M)*
- Industrial pollution adversely affects human health, wildlife, natural resources, and the climate. *(1 M)*

3. Strategies to Reduce Pollution in Greenvale's Textile and Chemical Industries:

(*i*) **Implement Modern Technologies:** Install **electrostatic precipitators**, fabric filters, and scrubbers to reduce air pollution. *(1 M)*

(*ii*) **Effluent Treatment Plants:** Establish **three-phase treatment plants** (mechanical, biological, chemical) for wastewater management. *(1 M)*

(*iii*) **Regulations and Monitoring:** Enforce strict **pollution control norms** and conduct regular **inspections**. *(1 M)*

(*iv*) **Green Practices:** Promote **recycling** and **reuse** of industrial waste, and use eco-friendly **raw materials**. *(1 M)*

(*v*) **Community Engagement:** Conduct **awareness programs** and involve the community in **monitoring and reporting** pollution incidents. *(1 M)*

4. The Reasons are:

- **Low Cost of Iron Ore:** The Chotanagpur Plateau region provides iron ore at low costs due to its rich deposits. *(1 M)*
- **High-grade Raw Materials:** Proximity to high-grade raw materials ensures efficient production processes. *(1 M)*
- **Cheap Labor:** The availability of cheap labor reduces production costs significantly. *(1 M)*
- **Vast Market Potential:** Its vast growth potential in the domestic market encourages industry localization. *(1 M)*
- **Transportation:** Well-connected transport infrastructure supports easy movement of raw materials and finished products. *(1 M)*

5. Integrated vs. Mini Steel Plants:

- **Integrated Steel Plants:** Handle the entire production process from extracting iron ore to manufacturing steel. They are large-scale operations. *(1 M)*
- **Mini Steel Plants:** Focus mainly on recycling scrap steel to produce new steel. They are smaller and have less extensive processes. *(1 M)*

Industry Challenges: **(Any-2)**

- **High Production Costs:** Both types of plants face high costs in energy, labor, and compliance with environmental standards. *(1 M)*
- **Environmental Regulations:** Meeting stringent environmental regulations adds to operational costs. *(1 M)*
- **Competition from Imports:** Cheap steel imports from other countries challenge domestic production. *(1 M)*

Recent Developments:

- Technological advancements, government support through policies, and an increase in demand have boosted production capacity. *(1 M)*

Case Based Questions

Case Based-I

(*i*) The two challenges of jute industry are:

(*a*) Stiff competition in the international market from synthetic substitutes. *(½ M)*

(*b*) Indian jute industry also faces competition from other jute supplier countries like Bangladesh, Brazil, Philippines, Egypt and Thailand. *(½ M)*

(*ii*) The main objective of National Jute Policy (2005) was to increase productivity, improve quality and to ensure good price to the jute farmers. *(1 M)*

(*iii*) The jute industry has reopened new opportunities for its products due to:

Environmental Concerns: The global shift towards environment-friendly and biodegradable materials has increased the demand for jute products. *(1 M)*

Government Policy: The mandatory use of jute packaging by the government has increased domestic demand, supporting the industry's growth. *(1 M)*

Case Based-II

(*i*) The cooperative model ensures farmers have direct stakes in the mill's profits, leading to fairer pricing for their sugarcane and shared decision-making in mill operations. *(1 M)*

(*ii*) The mill creates diverse job opportunities, from agricultural processing to administrative roles, reducing dependency on seasonal agricultural work. *(1 M)*

(*iii*) Long-term impacts may include increased adoption of sustainable farming, improved crop yields, and better soil health, contributing to environmental sustainability and economic resilience. *(2 M)*

Case Based-III

(*i*) Green technologies can significantly reduce harmful emissions and effluents, improving air and water quality, and thus enhancing public health and local biodiversity. *(1 M)*

(*ii*) Community involvement is crucial for the success of sustainability programs, as it increases awareness, encourages responsible environmental behavior, and ensures broader support for green initiatives. *(1 M)*

(*iii*) Long-term benefits could include reduced healthcare costs due to better air quality, increased attractiveness to eco-conscious investors, and sustainable industrial growth, preserving resources for future generations. *(2 M)*

Map Based Questions

1.

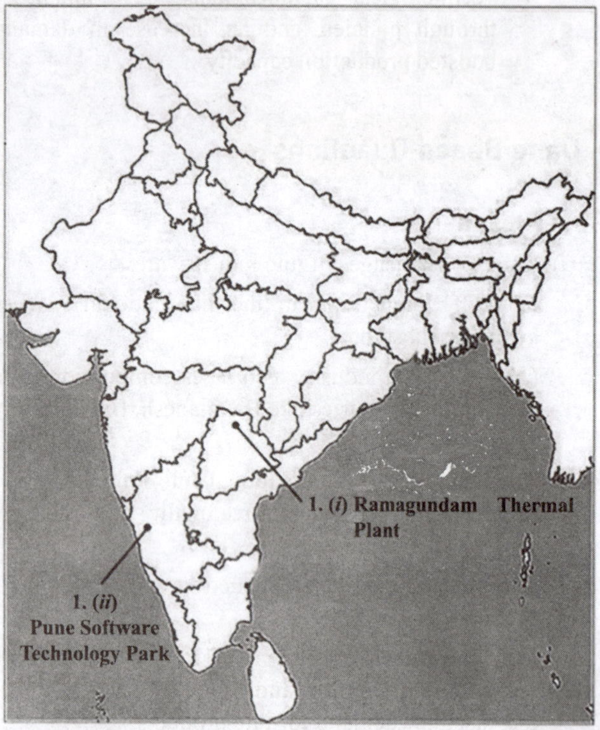

2.

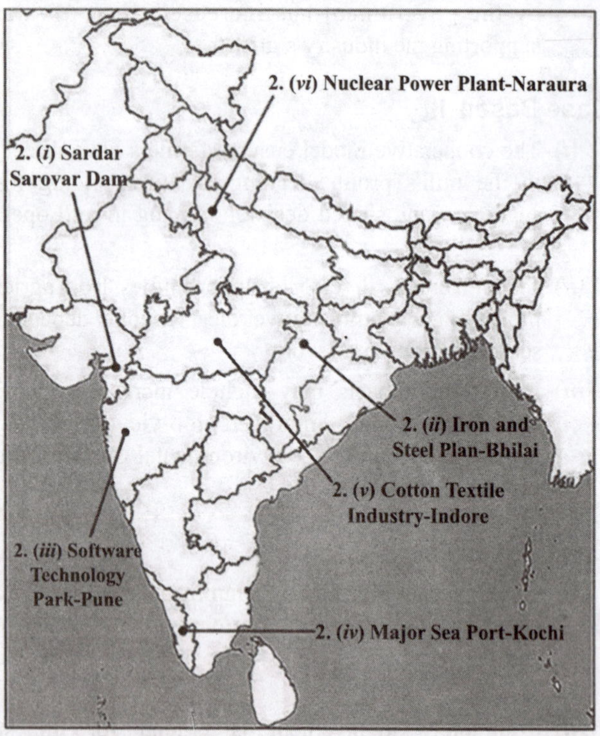

3.

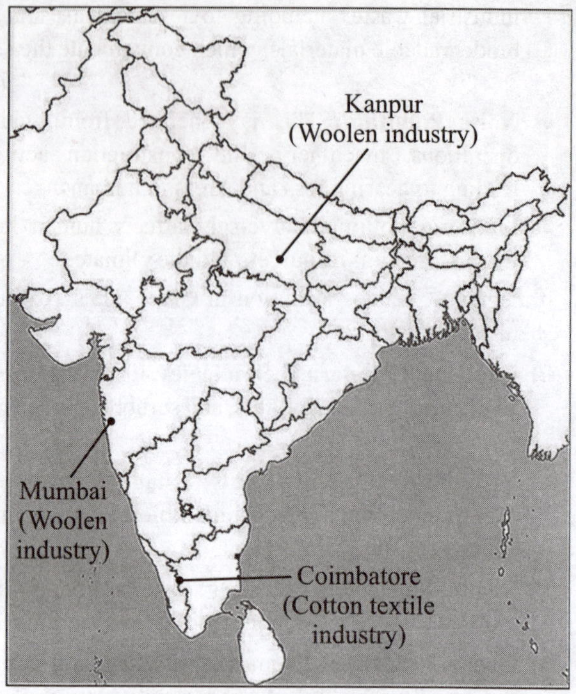

LIFELINES OF NATIONAL ECONOMY

7

"Transportation is crucial to a nation's economy, facilitating the delivery of finished products to consumers and supporting the production of goods and services. These activities are key determinants of a country's development pace. Consequently, efficient transportation systems are essential for rapid development."

SYLLABUS & WEIGHTAGE

List of Concept Names	Years					
	2020	2021	2022	2023	2024	2025
Major Sea Ports (Kandla, Mumbai, Mormugao, New Mangalore, Kochi, Tuticorin, Chennai, Vishakhapatnam, Paradip, Haldia)	1Q(1 M)	Exam not Conducted	—	1Q(1 M)	1Q(1 M)	1Q (1 M)
International Airports Amritsar (Raja Sansi - Sri Guru Ram Dass jee), Delhi (Indira Gandhi International), Mumbai (Chhatrapati Shivaji), Chennai (Meenam Bakkam), Kolkata (Netaji Subhash Chandra Bose), Hyderabad (Rajiv Gandhi)	1Q(1 M)		1Q(1 M)	1Q(1 M)	—	1Q (1 M)

CONCEPT MAP

To Access One Shot Revision Video Scan This QR Code

Lifelines of National Economy

Major Sea Ports

CBSE 2025, 2024, 2023, 2020

- ❑ Kandla (Gujarat)
- ❑ Mumbai (Maharashtra)
- ❑ Marmagao (Goa)
- ❑ New Mangalore (Karnataka)
- ❑ Kochi (Kerala)
- ❑ Tuticorin (Tamil Nadu)
- ❑ Chennai (Tamil Nadu)
- ❑ Vishakhapatnam (Andhra Pradesh)
- ❑ Paradip (Odisha)
- ❑ Haldia (West Bengal)

MAJOR PROTS OF INDIA

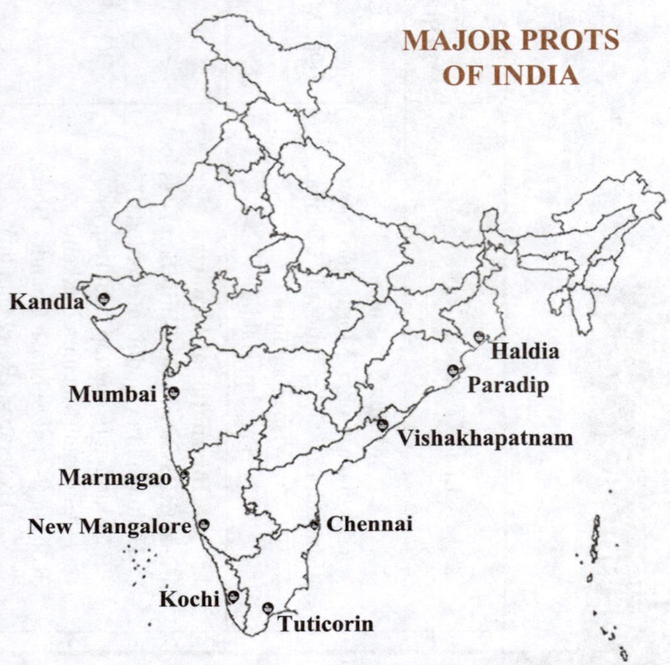

International Airports

CBSE 2025, 2023, 2022, 2020

- ❑ Amritsar (Raja Sansi - Sri Guru Ram Dass jee),
- ❑ New Delhi (Indira Gandhi International),
- ❑ Mumbai (Chhatrapati Shivaji),
- ❑ Chennai (Meenam Bakkam),
- ❑ Kolkata (Netaji Subhash Chandra Bose),
- ❑ Hyderabad (Rajiv Gandhi)

INTERNATIONAL AIRPORTS

MISCELLANEOUS EXERCISE

Map Based Questions

1. Locate and label the following with appropriate symbols on the same given political outline map of India.

(1 × 4 = 4 M)

(*i*) Kandla Sea Port

(*ii*) Chennai Sea Port

(*iii*) Haldia Sea Port

(*iv*) Kochi Sea Port

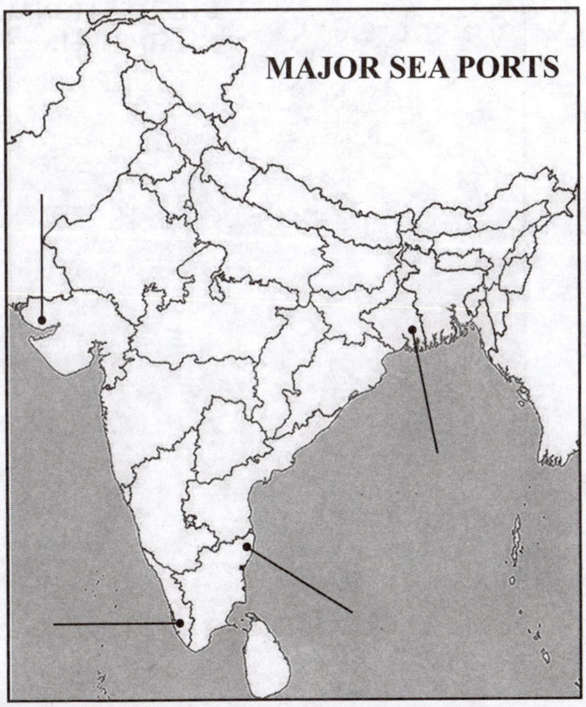

2. Locate and label the following with appropriate symbols on the same given political outline map of India.

(1 × 4 = 4 M)

(*i*) Mumbai Sea Port

(*ii*) Marmagao Sea Port

(*iii*) Tuticorin Sea Port

(*iv*) Vishakhapatnam Sea Port

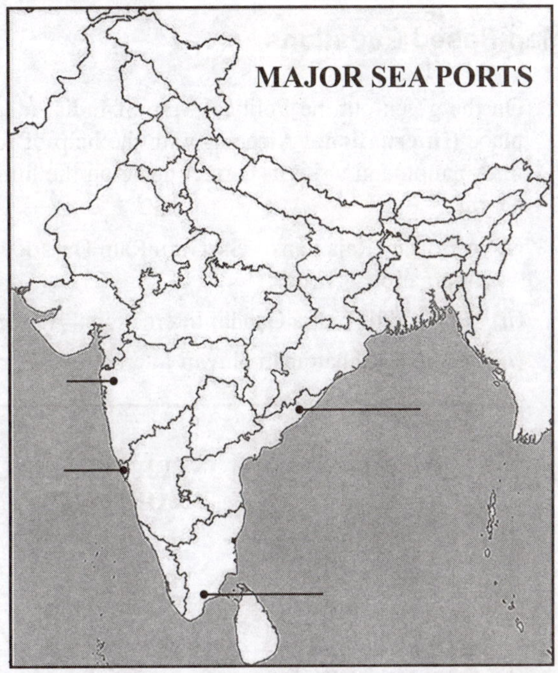

3. Locate and label the following with appropriate symbols on the same given political outline map of India.*(1 × 2 = 2 M)*

(*i*) Paradip Sea Port

(*ii*) New Managalore Sea Port

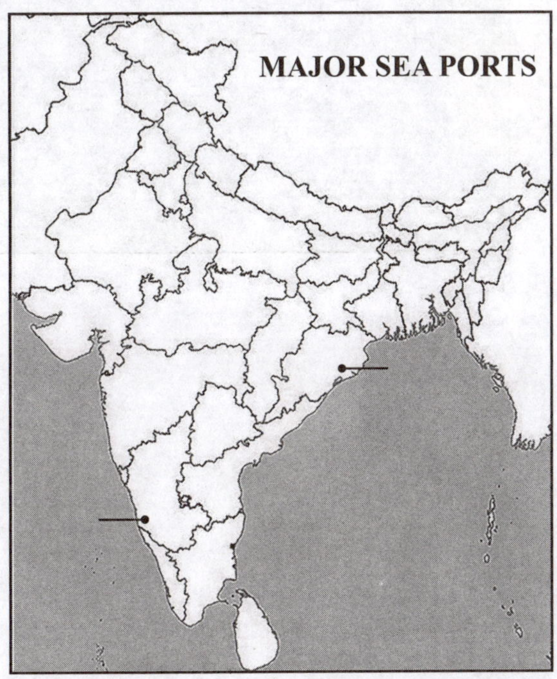

2 INTERNATIONAL AIRPORTS

MISCELLANEOUS EXERCISE

Map Based Questions

1. On the given outline Political Map of India, identify the place **(International Airport)** with the help of following information and write its correct name on the line marked near it: *(1 + 1 + 1 = 3 M)* ***(Re)***

(*i*) Amritsar (Raja Sansi - Sri Guru Ram Dass Jee International Airport)

(*ii*) New Delhi (Indira Gandhi International Airport)

(*iii*) Mumbai (Chhatrapati Shivaji International Airport)

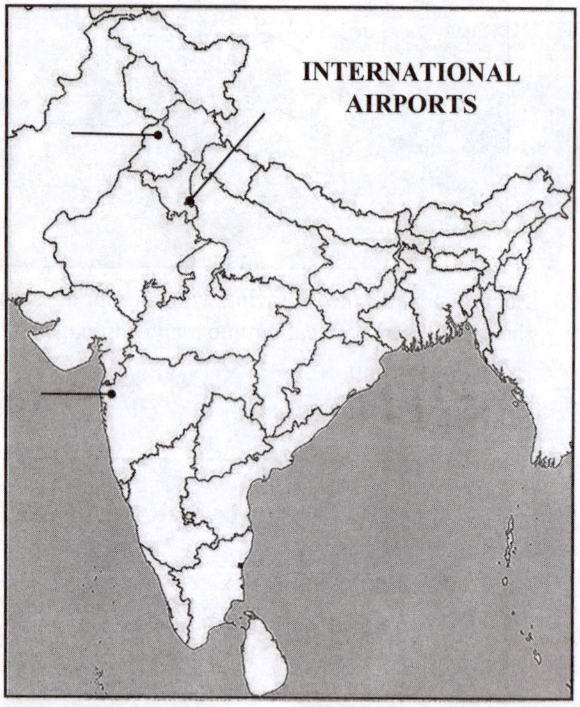

2. On the given outline Political Map of India, identify the place **(International Airport)** with the help of following information and write its correct name on the line marked near it: *(1 + 1 + 1 = 3 M)* ***(Re)***

(*i*) Chennai (Meenam Bakkam International Airport)

(*ii*) Kolkata (Netaji Subhash Chandra Bose International Airport)

(*iii*) Hyderabad (Rajiv Gandhi International Airport)

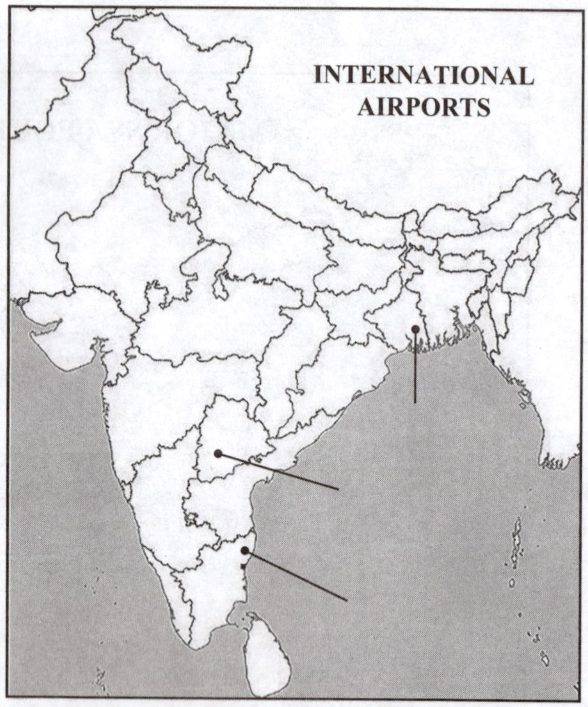

HINTS & EXPLANATIONS

1. Major Sea Ports

1.

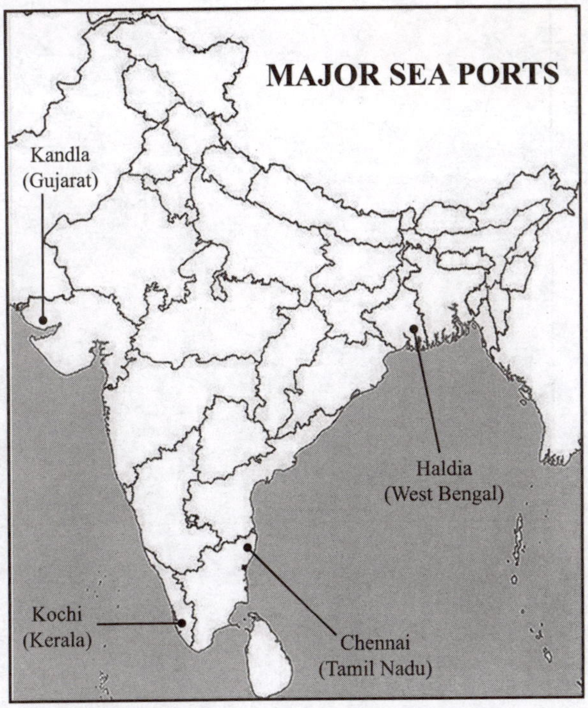

2.

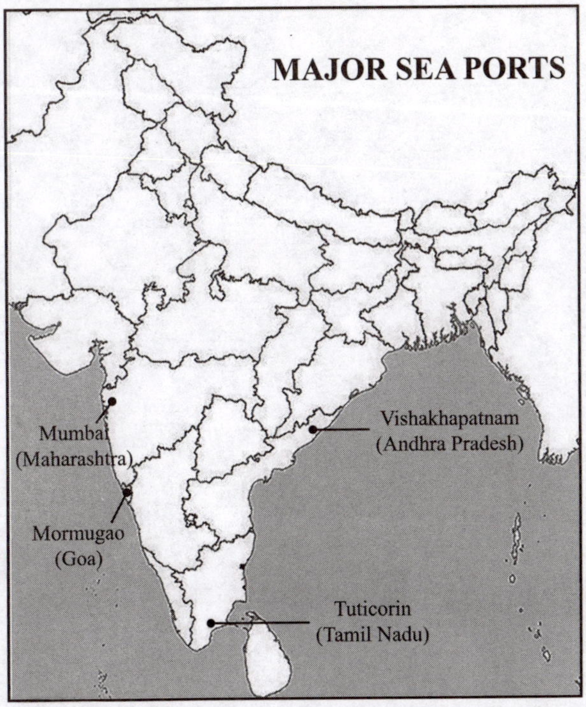

3.

2. International Airports

1.

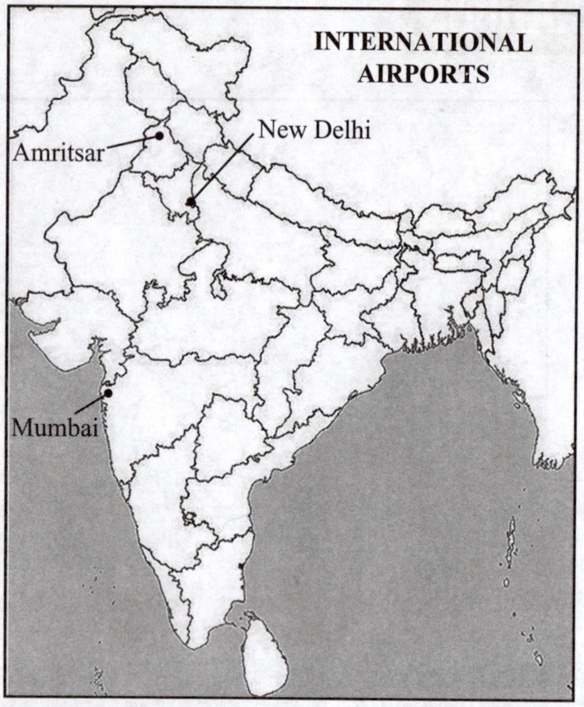

2.

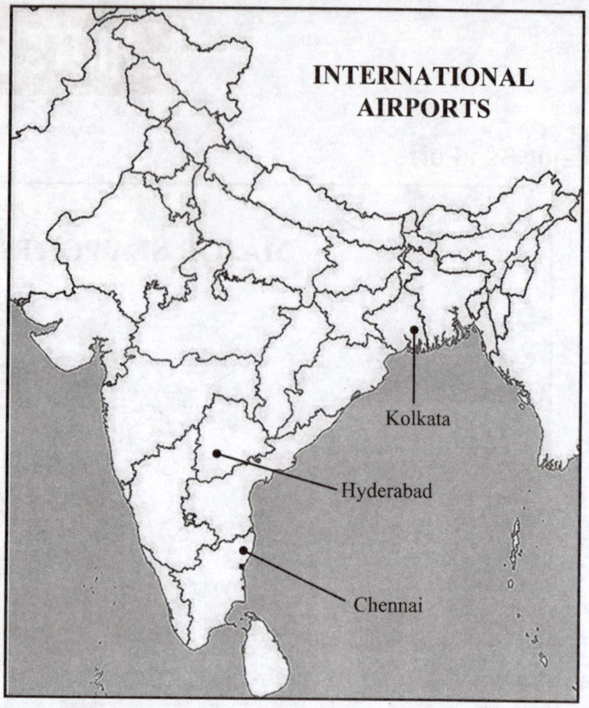

❑❑❑

ECONOMICS

DEVELOPMENT

1

"Development", explains how growth is not just about earning more money but also about making life better for everyone, considering what people need and dream of in different parts of the world.

SYLLABUS & WEIGHTAGE

List of Concept Names	Years					
	2020	2021	2022	2023	2024	2025
Income and other goals (What development different people, different goals)	—	Exam not Conducted	—	1Q (1M)		
National Development (How to compare different countries or states, income and other criteria)	1Q (1M)		—	1Q (1M)		1 Q (1 M)
Public Facilities (Human Development Report)	1Q (3M)		—	2Q (1M + 1M)	2Q (1M) 1Q (2M)	1 Q (1 M)
Sustainable Development	1Q (1M)		—	1Q (1M)		

CONCEPT MAP

To Access One Shot Revision Video Scan This QR Code

Development

Income and Other Goals

CBSE 2023

Income Goals, What people desire is regular work, Better wages and decent prices for their crops or other products that people produce.

National Development

CBSE 2025, 2024, 2023, 2022 Term-II, 2020

It means thinking about a fair and just path for all, like Social Economic & Political welfare of the people.

How to compare different Countries:

On the basis of Development & Per Capita Income.

How to compare different States:

On the basis of Income, Infant mortality rate, Literacy rate & Net attendance ratio.

Average Income: Average earnings per person in a specific area within a specific time frame. The average income is also called **Per Capita Income.**

Average Income or Per Capita Income is calculated:

$$\text{Per Capita Income} = \frac{\text{Total Income}}{\text{Total Population}}$$

Income and Other Criteria

Comparing states on the basis of (Haryana, Kerala, & Bihar)

Per Capita Income - Highest Harayana (₹2,36,147) & Lowest Bihar (₹40,982)

Infant mortality rate - Highest Bihar (32) & Lowest Kerala (7)

Literacy Rate % - Highest Kerala (94%) & Lowest Bihar (62%)

Net Attendance Ratio - Highest Kerala (83) & Lowest Bihar (43)

Development Goals and Mixed Goals

CBSE 2025, 2024, 2023

Characteristics of Development Goals

- ❒ More equitable distribution of resources.
- ❒ Different people have different aspirations for & nations of development.
- ❒ Each person seeks a different goals.
- ❒ Development goals can be conflicting.

Characteristics of Mixed Goals

- ❒ Thinking about Equality.
- ❒ Better lifestyle through better administration and principles.
- ❒ Freedom, Money, etc.

Meaning and Characteristics

Refers to the process by which an individual grows and changes throughout the life cycle.

Characteristics of Development

- ❒ Continuous process
- ❒ Income as an essential component
- ❒ Mixed goals
- ❒ Conflicting goals etc.

Sustainable Development

CBSE 2024, 2023, 2022 Term-II, 2020

Sustainable: Maintain for long term of time (for future generation) + **Development**: Economic Development (for current generation) = Sustainable development which meet needs of current generation without compromising ability of future generation to meet their needs.

Balance use of Natural Resources

Conservation & finding alternatives of non-renewable resources. Eg. Petrol.

Using renewable resources carefully. E.g. Ground water.

Features of Sustainable Development

- ❒ Efficient use of natural resources.
- ❒ No ↑ in the pollution.
- ❒ Improve Quality of human life.
- ❒ To fulfill the requirements of future generations.

Pillars of Sustainable Development

- ❒ Social Sustainability
- ❒ Economics Sustainability
- ❒ Environmental Sustainability

Human Development Report

CBSE 2025, 2020

Human development Report was introduced by UNDP [United Nations Development Programme] in 1990.

Components of Human Development Index

- ❒ Living Standard (Per Capita Income)
- ❒ Health Indicator (Life Expectancy at Birth)(BMI)
- ❒ Body Mass Index (BMI) = $\frac{\text{Weight in kilogram}}{(\text{Height in meter})^2}$
- ❒ Education Indicator (Literacy rate, Enrollment ratio)

Other Elements

- ❒ Consumption
- ❒ Environment
- ❒ Security, etc.
- ❒ Health
- ❒ Freedom

Public Facilities

CBSE 2023, 2020

Provided facilities by the government. E.g. Schools, Hospital, Community Halls, Transport, Electricity etc. These facilities are important as we cannot purchase every major facility.

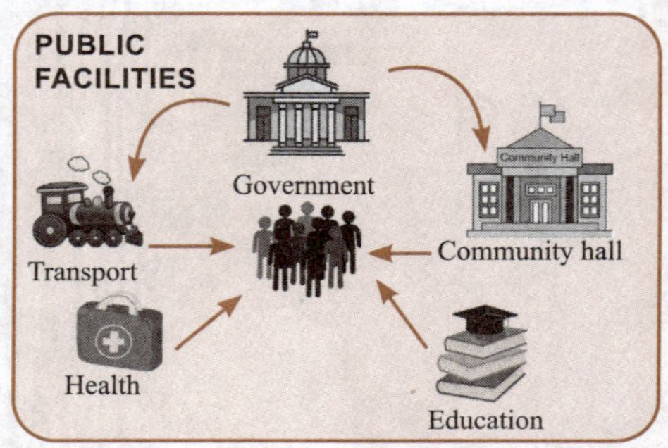

1 INCOME AND OTHER GOALS

NCERT Definitions *(Commonly asked in 1 mark)*

- **Development:** Refers to the process by which an individual **grows and changes** throughout the life cycle. It ensures a **good quality of life** for all people in terms of happiness, harmony, and satisfaction of essential needs.
- **Development Goals:** Objectives desired by individuals or groups for **improving life,** such as higher income, better education, and equality.
- **Income Goals:** It is a desire for **financial improvement** to enhance living standards.
- **Mixed Goal:** It means that development is a mix-up of all the goals like freedom, peace, harmony, a better lifestyle, money, respect towards others, and many more. For development people look at mix of goals which include **material things and non-material things**.

Important Concepts

What development promises: Different people different goals

- Different people can have different developmental goals/aspirations.

  Examples are given below:

Farmer

1. **Farmers who depend only on rain for growing crops:** For better seeds, artificial irrigation technologies, more water from canals, and higher prices of their crops are the developmental goals for farmers.

Labour

2. **Landless rural labourers:** More days of work and better wages are the developmental goals for labour.

Woman

3. **A rural woman from a land-owning family:** Opportunity to work, higher education, etc. are the developmental goals for rural women

Unemployed youth

4. **Urban unemployed youth:** Better employment opportunities are the developmental goal for urban unemployed youth.

Boy or Girl

5. **A Boy or Girl from a rich urban family:** Opportunities to study abroad and better jobs are the developmental goals for a Boy or Girl.

 ❑ **Conflicting Goals:** What may be development for one may not be development for others, it may be destructive.

Industry

For Example: Industries want big dams for their electricity and water supply. Water and Electricity are the main developmental goals for Industries, But this may submerge the land and disrupt the lives of people who are displaced – such as Tribal.

Note: It's Not Good for the Tribal Population. Because they have to leave their Place.

Tribal Population

Income and Other Goals

- **Material Things:** The things that one **can buy** with Money.

  Examples: Home, Car, Furniture, Clothes, etc.

House

Car

Furniture

Cloth

- **Non-Material Things:** The things that one **can not** buy with Money.

  Examples: Equality, Friendship, Security, Freedom, Respect, etc.

"Money is not enough for development, For proper development people look at mixed development goals which include material things and non-material things."

Mnemonics

Goals of development other than Income: **"FIRES"**

- F → Freedom
- I → Improvement in standard of living
- R → Respect
- E → Education
- S → Security

Scan Me for Detailed Explanations

COMPETENCY BASED SOLVED EXAMPLES

Multiple Choice Questions

(1 M)

1. **______ refers to the process by which an individual grows and changes throughout the life cycle.** *(Un)*

   (*a*) Economic
   (*b*) Development
   (*c*) Social
   (*d*) Environment

2. **Why are non-material goods like freedom and security crucial for development?** *(Ev)*

   (*a*) They can be easily traded
   (*b*) They add to material wealth
   (*c*) They contribute to overall well-being
   (*d*) They increase income

3. **What might be a developmental goal for a girl from a rich urban family?** *(Un)*

   (*a*) Equal political rights
   (*b*) Access to urban amenities
   (*c*) As much freedom as her brother
   (*d*) Higher per capita income

4. **Raj is a recent graduate from a university, struggling to find a job that matches his qualifications. On the other hand, Aman, a laborer, is working long hours but still earning barely enough to support her family.**

   Analyze the cartoon depicting their situations and discuss the socio-economic challenges they face. How can policy changes address their issues? *(An)*

Raj (Unemployed youth)

Aman (Labour)

(*a*) More days of work and better wages, Increasing technological jobs that they might not qualify for.

(*b*) Opportunities to study abroad, Reducing agricultural subsidies

(*c*) For better seeds, artificial irrigation technologies, Opportunity to work and higher education

(*d*) Better employment opportunities and More days of work and better wages

5. Development as Freedom is Amartya Sen's first book after receiving the Nobel and the most widely read of all of his works. Based on the author's World Bank Fellow Lectures in 1996, this descriptive, non-technical overview of welfare economics argues that 'development' should be viewed not in terms of economic measures (e.g. GDP growth, average annual income) but in terms of the real 'freedoms' that people can enjoy such as economic facilities and social opportunities. Sen describes human freedom as both the primary end objective and the principal means of development; economic measures are merely the means to this end. Sen frames development as the realisation of freedom and the abolishment of 'unfreedoms' such as poverty, famine, and lack of political rights.

Source: Terjesen, Siri. (2004). Amartya Sen'sDevelopment as Freedom.

In present-day Indian society, which of the following people would be the MOST 'unfree' as defined in this passage? (*Un*)

(*a*) Arvind, a shopkeeper who cannot afford to move from his 3 bedroom flat to a bigger house

(*b*) Afreen, a woman who is not allowed to pursue education

(*c*) Hiralal, a farmer has insurance against crop failure due to famine

(*d*) Anjana, a 15-year old, who does not have voting rights

6. Why may the notion of development differ among individuals? (*Un*)

(*a*) Different income levels

(*b*) Different social status

(*c*) Different personal aspirations

(*d*) Different educational backgrounds

7. If urban unemployed youth desire more days of work, what underlying issue does this reveal about the economy? (*Cr*)

(*a*) High levels of job satisfaction

(*b*) Efficient agricultural practices

(*c*) Insufficient employment opportunities

(*d*) Overpopulation in urban areas

8. Which of the following is the characteristics of development? (*Re*)

(*a*) Continuous process

(*b*) Income as an essential component

(*c*) Mixed goals

(*d*) All of the above

9. Development of a country is determined by (NCERT)

(*a*) Per Capita Income (*b*) Average Literacy Rafe

(*c*) Health Status (*d*) All of the above

10. What will be the top priority in the development goals of a jobless youth? (*Un*)

(*a*) More days of work and better wage

(*b*) Metal roads for transportation

(*c*) More Employment opportunities

(*d*) Establishment of a high school

11. Match the following List-I and List-II (*An*)

List-I Category of Person	List-II Developmental Goals / Aspirations
A. Landless rural labourers	(*i*) Education of her children in English medium schools earning more from the land by giving it on rent.
B. Prosperous farmers	(*ii*) More days of work and better wages
C. Urban unemployed youth	(*iii*) Low prices food grains, Cheap inputs like seeds, machinery, etc.
D. A rural woman from a landowning family	(*iv*) More opportunity for higher education

(*a*) A-(*iii*), B-(*ii*), C-(*iv*), D-(*i*)

(*b*) A-(*i*), B-(*iii*), C-(*iv*), D-(*ii*)

(*c*) A-(*ii*), B-(*iii*), C-(*iv*), D-(*i*)

(*d*) A-(*iv*), B-(*i*), C-(*ii*), D-(*iii*)

12. Development may mean different things for _______ (*Un*)

(*a*) Different people (*b*) Alien people

(*c*) Same people (*d*) All of the above

Assertion and Reason

(1 M)

Direction: The following questions consist of two statements – Assertion (A) and Reason (R). Answer these questions by selecting the appropriate option given below:

(*a*) Both A and R are true, and R is the correct explanation of A.

(*b*) Both A and R are true, but R is not the correct explanation of A.

(*c*) A is true, but R is false.

(*d*) A is false, but R is true.

1. **In India, individuals often believe that having more money can ensure a high quality of life. However, countries like Sweden demonstrate that collective provision of services, such as healthcare and education, can be more cost-effective and accessible for everyone.** ***(Ev)***

   Assertion (A): Money in your pocket can buy all the goods and services needed to live well.

   Reason (R): Collective provision of services is more cost-effective than individual provision.

2. **Assertion (A):** Non-material things such as friendship, freedom, and respect are equally important as material goods in life.

   Reason (R): The quality of life depends on non-material things such as friendship, freedom, and respect. In addition to material goods. ***(Ev)***

3. **Assertion (A):** Developmental goals of people are primarily focused on achieving a better income.

   Reason (R): Different people have same developmental goals, which may include equal treatment, freedom, security, and respect. ***(Un)***

4. **Assertion (A):** Job security is more important than high pay for people seeking employment.

   Reason (R): People consider factors such as facilities for their family, working atmosphere, and opportunities to learn before accepting a job. ***(Ev)***

Subjective Questions

Very Short Answer Type Questions

(1 or 2 M)

1. **"Different persons can have different developmental goals." Support the statement with an example.** ***(Un)*(CBSE, 2023)**

Ans. Different people can have different developmental goals/ aspirations.

Examples are given below:

- **Farmers who depend only on rain for growing crops:** Better seeds, artificial irrigation technologies, more water from canals, and higher Prices of their crops are the developmental goals for farmers. *(1 M)*
- **Landless rural labourers:** More days of work and better wages are the developmental goals for labour. *(1 M)*

2. **What may be the goal of a prosperous farmer in Punjab?** ***(Re)*(CBSE, 2019)**

Ans. The prosperous farmers of Punjab desire better irrigation facilities. As a developmental goal, they dream of sending their children to better schools and also acquiring better yielding crop varieties. *(2 M)*

3. **Imagine a village where Priya, a school teacher, dreams of having a well-equipped school to improve education quality, while Arjun, a local farmer, focuses on better irrigation facilities and higher crop prices. Both live in the same community but have different daily challenges and priorities.**

   Based on the scenario above, explain why Priya and Arjun might have different developmental goals. How do their individual circumstances influence their aspirations for development? ***(Ev)***

Ans. (*i*) **Priya's Perspective:**

- **Focus:** She aims to enhance educational quality with well-equipped facilities. *(½ M)*
- **Reason:** As a teacher, her priority is improving student learning outcomes. *(½ M)*

(*ii*) **Arjun's Perspective:**

- **Focus:** He seeks better irrigation and higher crop prices. *(½ M)*
- **Reason:** As a farmer, his main concern is agricultural productivity and income stability. *(½ M)*

4. **Can you imagine development goal of landless rural labour?** ***(Un)*(CBSE, 2019)**

Ans. The development goal of a landless rural labourer may include securing more days of work, better wages, quality education for their children and social equality. *(2 M)*

5. **What may be a development goal of farmers who depend only on rain for growing crops?** ***(Un)*(CBSE, 2019)**

Ans. The development goal for a farmer who is only dependent on rain for growing crops would be a good and sufficient monsoon season so that his crops get the needed irrigation and he can benefit from the good produce. *(2 M)*

6. **State any two goals of development other than income.** ***(Un)*(CBSE, 2018)**

Ans. The goals of development other than income are: **(Any 2)** *(1 M)*

(*i*) Equal Treatment

(*ii*) Job Security

(*iii*) Freedom

(*iv*) Respect

(*v*) Improvement in standard of living

Topper's Explanation

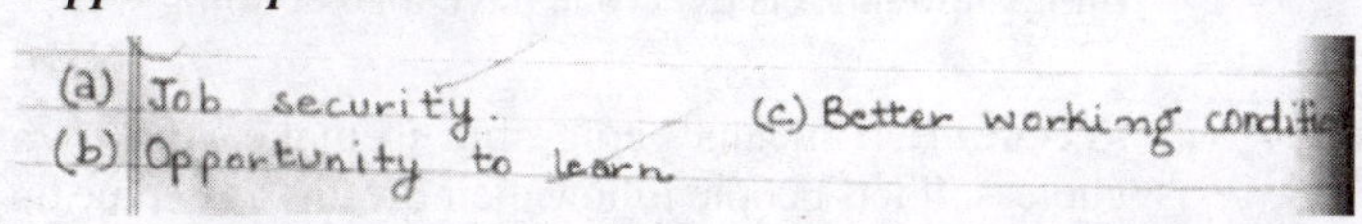
(a) Job security.
(b) Opportunity to learn
(c) Better working conditi[illegible]

7. **What may be a development goal of the urban unemployed youth?** ***(Ap)*(CBSE, 2019)**

Ans. The development goal of an urban unemployment youth would be to find a good job and earn a decent wage with that work. So, People will aspire to maintain a good standard of living. *(2 M)*

Short Answer Type Questions (3 M)

1. Write any three characteristics of development. ***(Re)***

Ans. The characteristics of development are: **(Any 3)**

(*i*) **Development is a Continuous process:** It is a continuous process that creates growth and brings in progress and positive change. *(1 M)*

(*ii*) **Income as an essential component:** It is the most important component of development, but along with income, people also seek equal treatment, good health, peace, literacy, job security, etc. *(1 M)*

(*iii*) **Mixed goals:** For development, people look at mixed goals such as freedom, money, equal opportunity, etc. *(1 M)*

(*iv*) **Conflicting goals:** Development for one may not be developed for another. It may be destructive for others. *(1 M)*

2. Why do different people have different goals for development? ***(Ev)(CBSE, 2019)***

Ans. Different people have different goals for development because:

Different people have different aspirations and desires. Some may like to have more income and better quality of education for their children, while others may require no social discrimination and high support prices for their crops. So according to the living conditions and the environment in which the person stays, he or she pursues the goals. People seek things that are most important for them i.e., that which can fulfill their aspirations or desires. *(3 M)*

Nailing the Right Answer

Connect the concept of individual goals to the broader idea of development and how it varies based on individual perspectives and priorities.

3. Apart from income which other things people look for growth and development. ***(Un)(CBSE, 2017)***

OR

Given some examples where factors other than income are important aspects of our lives ***(NCERT Intext)***

Ans. Apart from income, other things people look for growth and development are:

(*i*) **Equal Treatment:** This means everyone gets the same chance to succeed, no matter who they are. It makes things fair and lets everyone have a go at doing well. *(1 M)*

(*ii*) **Freedom:** It means being able to make your own choices. It lets people follow their dreams and come up with new ideas, making life better for themselves and others. *(1 M)*

(*iii*) **Security:** Feeling safe where you live and work is important. They also value job security, a good working environment, and the time to be with family, which all contribute significantly to their overall growth and development. *(1 M)*

4. Why do different persons have different notions of development? Which of the following explanations is more important and why? ***(Ev)(NCERT Intext)***

(*a*) Because people are different.

(*b*) Because life situations of persons are different.

Ans. (*b*) Different persons have different notions of development. This is because the life situations of people are different. *(1 M)*

- The development goals of a girl from a rich urban family will differ from a farmer in Rajasthan. It is because their conditions, lifestyle, and status are very different from each other. *(1 M)*
- People's goals depend on their present condition. Over a period of time if the conditions or situations change, then automatically the goals of a person will also change. *(1 M)*

5. Why is a safe and secure environment important for women to take up a variety of jobs or run a business? ***(Ev)***

Ans. The importance of a safe and secure environment for women to take up a variety of jobs or run a business as follows:

(*i*) Secure environment ensures women can work without fear, making it easier for them to pursue their professional goals. *(1 M)*

(*ii*) When women feel safe, they're more likely to take on different jobs or start their own businesses. This increases their chances to earn, learn new skills, and be independent. *(1 M)*

(*iii*) Feeling secure also encourages more women to step out into the world, make their own decisions, and contribute to the economy. *(1 M)*

Long Answer Type Questions (5 M)

1. What should India do or achieve to become a developed country? Explain. ***(Ev)***

Ans. India should focus on the following points to become a developed country:

(*i*) It should make provision for accommodating all its existing able people in jobs who are willing and able to do but unable to get a suitable job. *(1 M)*

(*ii*) It should reduce the gap between rich and poor people. *(1 M)*

(*iii*) Government should make provisions for making the country self-reliant by providing skill education to all. *(1 M)*

(*iv*) Primary health and education must be accessible to all evenly in the remote parts of the country. *(1 M)*

(*v*) Government should encourage small-scale industries and cottage industries by giving cheaper credit and training those who are willing to be an entrepreneur. *(1 M)*

2. **How does engaging in paid work increase the dignity of women in the household and society?** (*Ap* **or** *Un*)

Ans. When women engage in paid work, it enhances their dignity in the household and society in the following ways:

(*i*) It gives them a sense of independence, self-worth, and social recognition. (*1 M*)

(*ii*) Paid work enables women to contribute to the family income, which enhances their decision-making power in the household. (*1 M*)

(*iii*) Moreover, it helps them to break free from the traditional roles of a homemaker and helps them to assert themselves in society. (*1 M*)

(*iv*) A safe and secured environment may allow more women to take a variety of jobs or run a business. (*1 M*)

(*v*) As women engage in paid work they gain opportunities for professional development, social interaction and personal fulfilment. (*1 M*)

3. **In the role of a social researcher documenting regional aspirations, you are tasked with creating a report that contrasts the development goals of diverse economic groups in India. Your focus is on the prosperous farmers in Punjab, who have access to resources and technology, versus the landless laborers in Bihar, who strive for basic employment stability.**

Describe the distinct development goals for each group and analyze how their aspirations could potentially lead to conflicting interests. (*Cr*)

Ans. (*i*) **Prosperous Farmers in Punjab:**

(*a*) **Goals:** Prosperous farmers in Punjab aim for higher income through advanced farming techniques and support for high crop prices. (*1 M*)

(*b*) **Aspirations:** They desire modern infrastructure and technology to enhance productivity and market access. (*1 M*)

(*ii*) **Landless Laborers in Bihar:**

(*a*) **Goals:** These laborers seek basic employment opportunities and fair wages to sustain their livelihood. (*1 M*)

(*b*) **Aspirations:** Their primary concern is achieving job security and access to basic education and healthcare services. (*1 M*)

(*iii*) **Potential Conflicts:**

(*a*) **Conflicting Interests:** Policies favoring industrial agriculture can sideline small-scale farmers, intensifying rural inequalities. (*1 M*)

2 NATIONAL DEVELOPMENT

NCERT Definitions *(Commonly asked in 1 mark)*

- **National Development:** The process that involves improving the **well-being** of every individual in a country, like its economy growing, people being treated equally, taking care of the environment, and everyone living better lives or improving people's living standard.
- **Average Income:** The average income which is the **total income** of the country **divided** by its **total population**. Average income measures the average income **earned per person** in a given area (City, region, country, etc.) It is also called **Per Capita Income**.
- **Literacy Rate:** The percentage of people over the **age of 7** who are able to read and write, indicating the level of education in a region.
- **Infant Mortality Rate (IMR):** It indicates the number of children that **die before the age of one year** as a proportion of 1000 live children born in that particular year.
- **Net Attendance Ratio:** The proportion of children of official school age who are **enrolled in school**, indicating access to and the quality of education.
- **Purchasing power parity (PPP):** PPP is a **measure** of the **price of specific goods** in **different countries** and is used to compare the absolute purchasing power of the countries' currencies.

Important Facts

How to compare different countries

On the Basis of Development:

- **Developed** Countries for example U.S. and U.K.,
- **Developing** Countries for example India,
- **Underdeveloped** Countries for example Nepal and Bangladesh.

How to compare different States (Haryana, Kerala, Bihar)

On the basis of:

- **Income:** Highest Haryana (₹2,36,147) and Lowest Bihar (₹40,982)
- **Infant Mortality Rate:** Highest in Bihar (32) and Lowest in Kerala (7)
- **Literacy Rate:** Highest in Kerala (94%) and Lowest in Bihar (62%)
- **Net Attendance Ratio:** Highest Kerala (83) and Lowest Bihar (43).

State	Per Capita Income for 2018-2019 (in ₹)	Infant Mortality Rate per 1,000 live births (2018)	Literacy Rate % 2017-18	Net Attendance Ratio (per 100 persons) secondary stage (age 14 and 15 years) 2017-18
Haryana	2,36,147	30	82	61
Kerala	2,04,105	7	94	83
Bihar	40,982	32	62	43

Sources: Economic Survey 2020–21, P.A 157, National Sample Survey Organisation (Report No. 585), National Statistical Office, Government of India.

Classification

On the basis of Per Capita Income: In World Development Reports, brought out by the World Bank, It is an easy method to compare **developed and underdeveloped** countries.

This criterion is used in classifying countries into:

- **Higher Income or Rich Countries:** Those with Per capita Income of **US$ 49,300 per annum** and above in 2019.
- **Low-Middle Income Countries:** Those with per capita income of just **US$ 6700 per annum** in 2019. (India comes in the category of low-middle income).
- **Low-Income or Poor Countries:** Those with per capita income of **US$ 2500 or less**.

Note: Average Income or Per Capita Income is calculated as:

$$\text{Per Capita Income} = \frac{\text{Total Income}}{\text{Total Population}}$$

Difference Between

Literacy Rate	Attendance Ratio
The percentage of people over the age of seven who are able to read and write, indicating the level of education in a region.	Net Attendance Ratio is the total number of children of age group 14 and 15 years attending school as a percentage of total number of children in the same age group.
Indicates the result of past educational opportunities and initiatives.	Reflects current enrollment and participation in educational institutions.
It Can be high even if current school attendance is low due to past education efforts.	It Can be low even with a high literacy rate, indicating possible current issues in the education system.
Individual Goals	**National Goals**
Specific to the individual's aspirations and desires.	Collective aims for the country's progress.
It Can be diverse and even conflicting among different people.	Encloses a broader perspective, aiming for a balance of various aspirations.
May prioritize immediate and tangible outcomes.	Often focused on long-term and sustainable growth.
Examples: Better job, education, health.	**Examples:** Economic growth, infrastructure, public health.

Criteria	Economic Growth	Economic Development
Meaning	Refers to the raise in the value everything produced within the economy.	Process of rise in real national income due to structural changes for a long period.
Scope	Narrow	Broader
Indicators	This is indicated by an increase in GDP or GNP.	This is indicated by improvement in life expectancy, human development etc.
Country	It is generally used by developing countries like India.	It is generally used by developed countries like US and USA
Process	Rapid Process	Slow Process
Nature	Result of economic activities, often short- term	Long-term process involving improvements in quality of life.
Possible	Economic growth is possible without economic development	Economic development is not possible without economic growth.

Criteria	Developing Countries	Developed Countries
Economic	Achieve basic financial stability	Sustain high economic growth
Social	Improve basic health and education	Enhance quality of life and equality
Example	India	US., UK. etc.

Myth Buster*

❑ **Myth:** Misconception between Economic Growth and Economic Development

Fact: Students may think these terms are interchangeable when, in fact, economic growth refers to an increase in a country's income and can be quantified, while economic development is a broader concept that includes improvements in living standards, reduction in poverty, improved health and education, etc.

Mnemonics

National Development Aim: "SEED"

- **S** → Social and Equality
- **E** → Education
- **E** → Employment
- **D** → Development

Scan Me for Detailed Explanations

COMPETENCY BASED SOLVED EXAMPLES

Multiple Choice Questions

(1 M)

1. Which one of the following organisations prepares the 'World Development Report'? ***(Re)*(CBSE, 2023)**

(*a*) World Bank

(*b*) International Monetary Fund

(*c*) World Health Organisation

(*d*) International Labour Organisation

2. Consider the following data on education and health from two states, State X and State Y: ***(Ev)***

Indicator	State X	State Y
Per Capita Income (in ₹)	**1,50,000**	**1,20,000**
Literacy Rate (%)	70	90
Infant Mortality Rate (per 1000 live births)	60	30

Which state is likely more developed based on the Human Development Index (HDI) criteria?

(*a*) State X, because it has a higher per capita income.

(*b*) State Y, because it has better education and health outcomes.

(*c*) Both are equally developed.

(*d*) Cannot be determined from the given data.

3. The number of children that die before the age of one year in 1000 births is called ___________. ***(Un)***

(*a*) Infant Mortality Rate (*b*) Body Mass Index

(*c*) Net Attendance Ratio (*d*) Literacy Rate

4. Suppose there are four families in your locality, the average per capita income of whom is ₹10,000. If the income of three families is ₹6,000, ₹8,000, and ₹14,000 respectively, what would be the income of the fourth family? ***(Ap)*(CBSE, 2022 Term 2)**

(*a*) ₹15,000 (*b*) ₹12,000

(*c*) ₹14,000 (*d*) ₹10,000

** Concepts beyond the board exam syllabus, offering deeper insight and critical thinking on NCERT topics.*

5. **The literacy rate is highest in Kerala while the Infant mortality rate is highest in Bihar. In relation to this information which statement is true?** ***(An)***

(*a*) Most of the people in Kerala and Bihar are in good living conditions

(*b*) Both Bihar and Kerala lack basic necessities of life.

(*c*) The standard of living in Bihar is better than that of Kerala

(*d*) The standard of living in Kerala is better than that of Bihar

6. **Read the date given below and answer the questions.** ***(Un)*(CBSE SQP, 2023)**

Category	Male	Female
Literacy rate for rural population	76%	54%
Literacy rate for rural children in age group 10-14 years	90%	87%
Percentage of rural children aged 10-14 attending school	85%	82%

As per the date given above who has the least percentage of literacy rate in rural population?

(*a*) Male (*b*) Children

(*c*) Male & Female (*d*) Female

7. **Read the following data and answer the question that follow:** ***(An)*(CBSE, 2023)**

Some comparative Data on Haryana, Kerala and Bihar			
State	**Infant Mortality Rate (per thousand person)**	**Literacy Rate %**	**Net Attendance Ratio (per 100 person)**
Haryana	30	82	61
Kerala	7	94	83
Bihar	32	62	43

How much is the Net Absence Ratio of Haryana? Choose the appropriate option from the following:

(*a*) 39 (*b*) 27

(*c*) 38 (*d*) 18

8. **Assume there are four families in a locality. If the income of each family is ₹6,000, ₹4,000, ₹7,000 and ₹3,000 then find out the average income of the locality from the following options:** ***(An)* (CBSE, 2023)**

(*a*) ₹5,000 (*b*) ₹3,000

(*c*) ₹2,000 (*d*) ₹6,000

9. **In the successful state of Progresso, the government reported that due to successful policies and programs, the per capita income has risen from \$1,500 to \$1,800 in the span of one year. As an economics researcher at Progresso's Department of Economic Development, you're preparing a report on this change. Calculate the percentage increase in Progresso's per capita income over the year. In your report, choose the options given below that show the significance of this percentage change in terms of economic growth and the potential impacts on Progresso's residents' standard of living.** ***(Ap)***

(*a*) 15% (*b*) 20%

(*c*) 18% (*d*) 25%

10. **Which of the following is an example of an average used for comparing situations?** ***(Cr)***

COUNTRY WITH NO RICH AND NO POOR

COUNTRY WITH RICH AND POOR

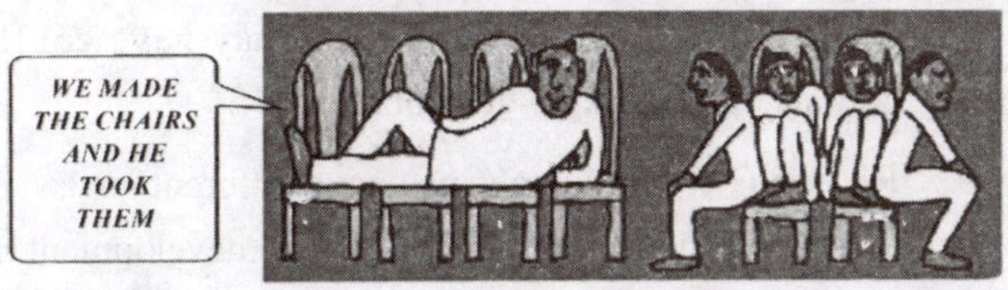

(*a*) When we compare the performance of cricket players, Income is used. The number of matches played excluding not outs by the total runs are divided.

(*b*) We find out the average daily income to compare the income of casual workers.

(*c*) We use averages to compute the performance of students in an examination wherein the sum of the profit.

(*d*) All of the above

11. **Read the data given below and answer the questions.** ***(An)*(CBSE APQ, 2023)**

State	Infant mortality rate per 1000 live births (2018)	Literacy rate% (2017-18)
Haryana	30	82
Kerala	7	94

As per the data given above, why has Kerala a low infant mortality rate?

(*a*) It has adequate provision of basic health and educational facilities.

(*b*) It has adequate provision of basic health and cultural facilities.

(*c*) It has adequate provision of basic social and educational facilities.

(*d*) It has adequate provision of basic health and technical facilities.

12. **Net Attendance ratio is the total number of children between the age group who attend school. (Secondary Stage)** ***(Un)***

(*a*) 4-5 years (*b*) 7-10 years

(*c*) 14 and 15 years (*d*) 15-20 years

Assertion and Reason

(1 M)

Direction: The following questions consist of two statements – Assertion (A) and Reason (R). Answer these questions by selecting the appropriate option given below:

(*a*) Both A and R are true, and R is the correct explanation of A.

(*b*) Both A and R are true, but R is not the correct explanation of A.

(*c*) A is true, but R is false.

(*d*) A is false, but R is true.

1. **Assertion (A):** The per capita income of a country is an important criterion for comparing the development of different countries.

   Reason (R): Higher income enables people to access more goods and services that they need. ***(An)***

2. **Assertion (A):** Different people may have conflicting notions of a country's development.

   Reason (R): Individuals may have different goals, and this may affect their idea of what national development means. ***(An)***

3. **Imagine comparing two countries, Bangladesh and Canada, based on their economic status. In 2019, Bangladesh had a per capita income of US$ 4,976, classifying it as a low-income country, whereas Canada, with a per capita income significantly higher, is considered a high-income country.**

   Assertion (A): Canada is classified as a high-income country according to the World Development Reports by the World Bank.

   Reason (R): The per capita income of Canada in 2019 was significantly above US$ 49,300 per annum. ***(Ev)***

4. **Assertion (A):** National development means thinking about questions related to fairness and justice.

   Reason (R): Conflicting notions of national development need to be resolved through a fair and just path that benefits a large number of people. ***(Ev)***

Subjective Questions

Very Short Answer Type Questions

(1 or 2 M)

1. **Define the term Literacy rate.** ***(Re)*(CBSE, 2020)**

Ans. Literacy rate refers to the percentage of the population with 7 years and above age who can read and write in a particular language. It is a measure of the education level of a population. *(1 M)*

2. **Study the table and answer the question given below.** ***(Ap)*(CBSE, 2020)**

Some comparative data on Haryana, Kerala and Bihar			
State	**Infant Morality Rate per 1,000 live births (2016)**	**Literacy Rate % 2011**	**Net Attendance Ratio (per 100 persons) secondary stage (age 14 and 15 years) 2013-14**
Haryana	33	82	61
Kerala	10	94	83
Bihar	38	62	43
Source: Economic Survey, 2017-18 Vol. 2, Government of India, National Sample Survey Organisation (Report No. 575)			

In comparison to Kerala which state has the highest infant mortality rate.

Ans. Based on the data provided in the table, it can be concluded that Bihar has the highest infant mortality rate in comparison to Kerala. *(1 M)*

3. **State the difference between literacy rate and attendance ratio.** ***(Un)***

Ans. *(2 M)*

Literacy Rate	Attendance Ratio
Literacy Rate measures the proportion of literate population in the 7-and-above age group.	Net Attendance Ratio is the total number of children of age group 14 and 15 years attending school as a percentage of total number of children in the same age group

4. **Study the statistics in the table and answer the questions that follows:** ***(Ap)***

₹	Member 1	Member 2	Member 3	Member 4
Income	15,000	6,000	8,000	9,000

Calculate the average income of the family:

Ans. ₹9,500

Average Income of the family:

= 15,000 + 6,000 + 8,000 + 9,000

Sum of Incomes = 38,000

$$\text{Average} = \frac{\text{Total Income}}{\text{No. of Members}} = \frac{38,000}{4} = ₹9,500$$ *(2 M)*

5. **Study the table and answer the question given below.** ***(Ap)***

Some Comparative Data on Haryana, Kerala And Bihar			
State	**Infant Mortality Rate per 1,000 live births (2018)**	**Literacy Rate % 2017-18**	**Net Attendance Ratio (per 100 persons) secondary stage (age 14 and 15 years) 2017-18**
Haryana	30	82	61
Kerala	7	94	83
Bihar	32	62	43
Sources: Economic Survey 2020-21, P.A 157, National Sample Survey Organisation (Report No. 585), National statistical office, Government of India.			

(*a*) In comparison to Kerala, which state has the highest Infant Mortality rate?

(*b*) Why does it have a low new attendance ratio?

Ans. (*a*) Comparing with Kerala, Bihar has the highest Infant Mortality Rate. *(1 M)*

(*b*) The low net attendance ratio may be due to factors like poverty, lack of schools, or cultural reasons where education is not prioritized. *(1 M)*

Short Answer Type Questions (3 M)

1. **Look at the picture given below. What should be the developmental goals for such an area?** ***(Ap & Cr)*(NCERT Intext)**

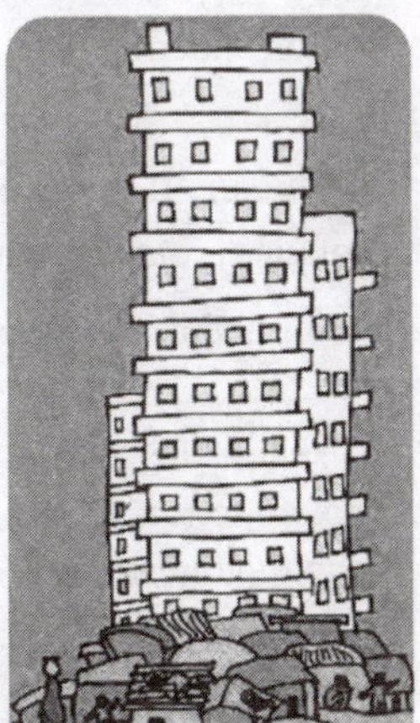

Ans. The developmental goals of this area must include **(Any 3)**:

(*i*) Availability of loans for constructing pucca houses with their own toilets. *(1 M)*

(*ii*) Ownership of land on which they live. *(1 M)*

(*iii*) Regular Employment. *(1 M)*

(*iv*) Availability of municipal services like water, electricity, and sanitation. *(1 M)*

(*v*) Medical facilities like dispensaries in the locality. *(1 M)*

2. **Define the term of Per Capita Income** ***(Un)*(CBSE, 2020)**

Ans. Per capita income refers to the average income earned per person in a particular area or county. Per Capita income is also known as average income. *(1 M)*

It reflects the people's standard of living and can be utilized to compare the economic conditions of various countries. *(1 M)*

Average income is calculated as:

$$\text{Per Capita Income} = \frac{\text{Total Income}}{\text{Total Population}}$$ *(1 M)*

3. **Although averages are useful for comparing countries, do they also hide disparities? Explain the meaning of this statement. Support the statement with suitable arguments.** ***(An)*(CBSE, 2019)**

Ans. Averages are useful for comparison but still hide disparities means that the average of everything gives us the mean value for comparison but,

(*i*) It does not indicate rising standard of living as average income only measures quantitive aspect. *(1 M)*

(*ii*) It does not tell us how equally or evenly income is distributed. *(1 M)*

(*iii*) It does not give information regarding the human development index such as infant mortality rate, literacy rate, etc. *(1 M)*

Topper's Explanation

Average income hide disparities. This can be proved by the following.

(i) Average income hide disparities in case there is no equitable distribution of income.

For example if a small population have a very high income, the total income as well as the average income rises thus hiding disparities about the actual situation

(ii) They average income do not indicate rising standards of living as development depends on non-materialistic factors like freedom, equality, respect, justice etc.

(iii) Average income do not tell us about the HDI as it depends on health and educational status also.

Long Answer Type Questions (4 or 5 M)

1. **What is the main criterion used by the World Bank in classifying different countries?** ***(Un)*(CBSE, 2017)**

Ans. Per Capita Income is the main criterion used by the World Bank in classifying different. *(1 M)*

In World Development Reports, brought out by the World Bank, It is an easy method to compare **developed and underdeveloped** countries. *(1 M)*

This criterion is used in classifying countries into:

- ***Higher Income or Rich Countries:*** Those with Per capita Income of **US$ 49,300 per annum** and above in 2019. *(1 M)*
- ***Low-Middle Income Countries:*** Those per capita income of **US$ 6700 per annum** in 2019 (India comes in the category of low-middle income). *(1 M)*
- **Low-Income or Poor Countries:** Those with per capita income of **US$ 2500 or less.** *(1 M)*

2. What is national development? What are the aspects covered under the national development? *(Un)*

Ans. The process that involves improving the well-being of every individual in a country, like its economy growing, people being treated equally, taking care of the environment, and everyone living better lives or improving people's living standard. *(1 M)*

The various aspects that come under national development are:

(*i*) To achieve national development, a country must use its resources efficiently and properly. *(1 M)*

(*ii*) The country should invest only in those schemes which help a large number of people. *(1 M)*

(*iii*) The Population increase must be managed efficiently and there must be an increase in the amount of food that is produced through agriculture. *(1 M)*

(*iv*) National development is achieved by focusing on improving social infrastructure that includes ensuring necessities like education and health care are available to all. *(1 M)*

3. Why do we use averages? Are there any limitations to their use? Illustrate with your own examples related to the development. *(Ev)*(NCERT)

Ans. Averages are used to compare differing quantities of the same category. *(1 M)*

For example: if we estimate the per capita income of two countries A and B with 5 people each, the salary of five people in country A is ₹28,000, ₹23,000, ₹23,500, ₹22,000, and ₹25,000 and the income of people living in country B are ₹50,000, ₹22,000, ₹1,50,000, ₹2500, and ₹4000.

The Average income of country A will be Total Income/ Total Population 1,21,500/5 = ₹24,300, and that of country B will be Total Income/Total Population 2,28,500/5 = ₹45,700.

This proves that the average of country B is higher than that of country A, and yet there is a disparity in the income distribution between country B, and the income is evenly distributed in country A. *(2 M)*

Limitations of their use

(*i*) It does not tell how income is distributed among the different sections of society. For example: - Per capita income does not show the actual distribution of income. *(1 M)*

(*ii*) It focuses only on the economic aspects ignoring the non-economic aspects of development. It hides disparities among people. *(1 M)*

4. The following table shows the proportion of undernourished adults in India. It is based on a survey of various states for the year 2001. Look at the table and answer the following questions. *(Ev)*(NCERT)

State	Male (%)	Female (%)
Kerala	22	19
Karnataka	36	38
Madhya Pradesh	43	42
All States	37	36

(*i*) Compare the nutritional level of the people in Kerala and Madhya Pradesh.

(*ii*) Can you guess why around 40 percent of people in the country are undernourished even though it is argued that there is enough food in the country? Describe in your own words.

Ans. (*i*) The nutritional level of the people of Kerala is quite higher than the people both males and females of Madhya Pradesh. Their ratio of undernourished is less than that of Madhya Pradesh. *(1 M)*

(*ii*) There is enough food in the country, even then 40% of the people in the country are undernourished because:

(*a*) A large number of people are so poor that they cannot afford nutritious food. *(1 M)*

(*b*) In most of the states, the Public Distribution System (PDS) does not function properly and poor people cannot get cheap food items. *(1 M)*

(*c*) There is a lack of educational and health facilities in many parts of the country. So many people remain backward and poor. As such, they are unable to get nutritious food. *(1 M)*

3 PUBLIC FACILITIES

NCERT Definitions *(Commonly asked in 1 mark)*

- **Public Facilities:** Those **basic facilities** are provided to all citizens **by the government** for their well-being and overall development like Health and education, water, sanitation, Schools, Hospital, Community Halls, Transport, Electricity, etc.
- **Public Distribution System (PDS):** PDS is like a **special store** set up by the government where people can get food and other important things for less money if they do not have a lot.
- **Life Expectancy:** Life Expectancy at **birth denotes,** as the name suggests, average expected length of life of a person at the time of birth.
- **Human Development Index (HDI):** A composite index measuring **average achievement** in key dimensions of human development like long and healthy life, being knowledgeable, and having a decent standard of living.
- **Gross National Income (GNI):** The total income from within a country plus income received from abroad.
- **Human Development Report:** A yearly report that **measures a country's development** not just by economic growth but also by social indicators like health and education, etc.
- **Gross Enrolment Ratio (GER) or Gross Enrolment Index (GEI):** It is a statistical measure used in the **education sector.** To determine the number of students enrolled in school at several different grade levels (*like primary or high school*), and use it to show the **ratio** of the number of students who live in that country to those who **qualify** for the particular grade level.

Important Concepts

Body Mass Index (BMI)

Body Mass Index is the criteria which is used to find out whether a person is nourished, undernourished or overweighted.

How to find body mass index?

$$\text{BMI} = \frac{\text{Weight in Kg}}{[\text{Height in meters}]^2}$$

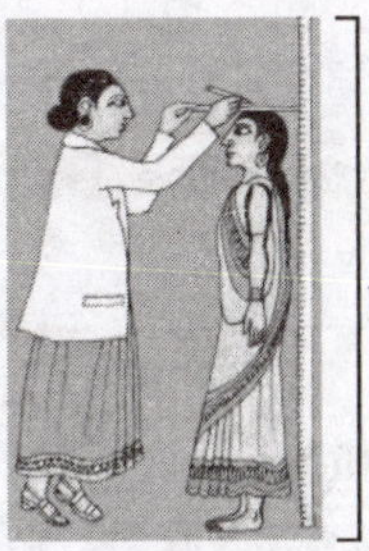

1.65 m

40 kg

For example: If a girl student is 14 years and 8 months old, weighs 40 kilogram and height 1.65 meters, her body mass index is 14.7 then she is undernourished.

$$\frac{40\text{kg}}{(1.65)^2} = 14.7$$

Body Mass Index = 14.7

Similarly, If the BMI of a boy aged 15 years and 6 months, weighs 70 kilogram and height 1.60 meters, his body mass index is 27.3 then he is overweight.

$$\frac{70\text{kg}}{(1.65)^2} = 27.3$$

Body Mass Index = 27.3

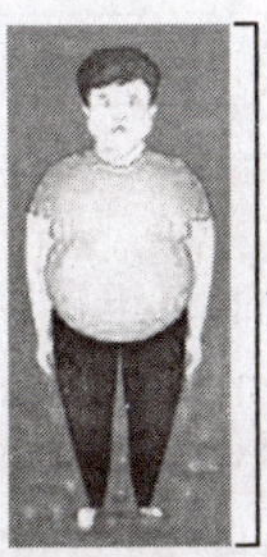

1.60 m

70 kg

BMI	Status
<18.4	Underweight
18.5-24.9	Normal
25.0-39.9	Overweight
>40.0	Obese

Classification

Human Development Report Published by

▼

United National Development Programme (UNDP)

For Comparing countries based on

Income, Education and Health

SOME DATA REGARDING INDIA AND ITS NEIGHBOURS FOR 2019				
Country	**Gross National Income (GNI) per capita (2011 PPP $)**	**Life Expectancy at birth**	**Mean Years of Schooling of People aged 25 and above**	**HDI Rank in the world (2018)**
Sri Lanka	12,707	77	10.6	73
India	**6,681**	**69.7**	**6.5**	**130**
Myanmar	4,961	67.1	5.0	148
Pakistan	5,005	67.3	5.2	154
Nepal	3,457	70.8	5.0	143
Bangladesh	4,976	72.6	6.2	134

Source: Human Development Report, 2020, United Nations Development Programme, New York.

Note:
1. HDI stands for Human Development Index. HDI ranks in the above table are out of 189 countries in all.
2. Per Capita Income is calculated in dollars for all countries so that it can be compared. It is also done in a way so that every dollar would buy the same amount of goods and services in any country.

(India Occupies 130 rank in the world on the basis of development)

Difference Between

Facilities	Urban Areas	Rural Areas
Healthcare	Generally better equipped	Often basic or limited
Education	More schools, higher education options	Fewer schools, limited higher education
Sanitation	Better sanitation facilities	Often lacks proper sanitation
Transportation	Better public transport, roads	Limited public transport, poorer road conditions

Private Security	Public Security
Protects individual or property. **Example:** Bodyguard, guard dog, parking security; security guard services, etc.	Protects entire communities **Examples:** Army, Police, Ambulance, Cybersecurity, food security, etc.
Operates for profit	Operates for public good
May not be accessible to all	Accessible to all citizens

Private Schooling	Public Schooling
May offer more resources.	Ensures basic education for all
Can be costly	Funded by the government
Choice of a few	The Rights of every child.

Myth Buster*

- **Myth:** Thinking that income in hand can guarantee access to all necessary services and a higher quality of life.

  Fact: Money can buy services, but public facilities like clean air, healthcare, and education often require collective action and state intervention to be accessible and effective for everyone. For example, wealthy individuals cannot purchase public security or ensure clean river water by themselves.

Mnemonics

Public Facilities provided by Govt: "CHHEST".

- C → Community
- H → Halls
- H → Hospitals
- E → Electricity
- S → Schools
- T → Transport

Component of Human Development Index "HELP".

- H → Health
- E → Education
- L → Life expectancy at birth
- P → Per Capita Income

Scan Me for Detailed Explanations

COMPETENCY BASED SOLVED EXAMPLES

Multiple Choice Questions

(1 M)

1. **Which of the following is the best example of a public good?** **(*Un*)(CFPQ, 2023)**

   (*a*) Medicines and Injections (*b*) Books and Stationary

   (*c*) Houses and Furniture (*d*) Law and Order

2. **"Given the data on Chandigarh and Bangalore, assess the implications of the number of hospitals, schools, and pollution levels on the quality of life in each city. Consider the balance between healthcare and education facilities and the environmental conditions represented by pollution levels:**

Facility	Chandigarh	Bangalore
Number of Hospitals	5	15
Number of Schools	10	25
Pollution Level	300	100

* *Concepts beyond the board exam syllabus, offering deeper insight and critical thinking on NCERT topics.*

Which option would you consider to be most accurate in evaluating the quality of life between these two cities based on the given data?" ***(Ap)***

(*a*) Chandigarh City, due to less congestion indicated by fewer hospitals and schools, which may suggest a smaller population and potentially a quieter, more relaxed living environment.

(*b*) Bangalore City, because of better public facilities, as indicated by a higher number of hospitals and schools, and lower pollution levels, suggesting a healthier and more resourceful living environment despite potential congestion.

(*c*) Both offer an equally good quality of life, as the number of facilities and pollution levels balance out differently for individual lifestyle preferences.

(*d*) The information provided is insufficient to determine which city offers a better quality of life since it lacks comprehensive details on factors like population size, quality of healthcare and education, employment opportunities, and others that affect living standards.

3. Read the following statements about Human Development and choose the correct option ***(An)*(CBSE, 2023)**

(*i*) It is the composite Index prepared by United Nations Development Programme (UNDP).

(*ii*) Parameters to measure it are Longevity, Literacy and Per Capital Income.

(*iii*) Countries are ranked according to Developed and Low Developing countries.

(*iv*) World Bank also prepares report of Human Development on the basis of Quality of Life.

(*a*) (*i*) and (*ii*) (*b*) (*ii*) and (*iii*)

(*c*) (*i*) and (*iii*) (*d*) (*ii*) and (*iv*)

4. What is not a fully adequate indicator of development? ***(An)***

(*a*) Per capita income

(*b*) Gross Domestic Product

(*c*) Human Development Index

(*d*) Public Distribution System

5. Which public facility is essential for a community to protect from diseases? ***(Un)***

(*a*) Education

(*b*) Public Distribution System

(*c*) Healthcare

(*d*) Roads

6. Study the data given below: ***(Ap)***

Country	Total GDP	GDP Per Capita
United States	$25,462,700,000,000	$75,269
China	$17,963,200,000,000	$12,598

Source: https://www.worldometers.info/gdp/gdp-by-country.

Despite having a higher total Income than the United States, China has a lower per capita Income. What is the reason for this?

(*a*) United States has a more equitable distribution of income

(*b*) China has more rich people than the poor people

(*c*) China has a smaller population than United States

(*d*) China has a bigger population than United States

7. What can money not buy? ***(Un)***

(*a*) Goods

(*b*) Services

(*c*) Pollution-free environment

(*d*) Education

8. How can the Public Distribution System (PDS) improve? ***(Un)***

(*a*) Wealth

(*b*) Health and nutritional status

(*c*) Per capita income

(*d*) Literacy rate

9. Read the following data: ***(Ap)***

Country	Means Years of Schooling of people aged and 25 above	HDI Rank (2018)
Sri Lanka	10.6	73
India	**6.5**	**130**
Pakistan	5.2	154
Myanmar	5.0	148

If an international education fund wants to invest in a country where increasing the mean years of schooling could substantially improve the HDI rank, where should they invest?

(*a*) Sri Lanka (*b*) India

(*c*) Pakistan (*d*) Myanmar

10. Which country is ranked higher than India in the HDI? ***(Un)***

(*a*) Nepal (*b*) Bangladesh

(*c*) Sri Lanka (*d*) Pakistan

11. HDI stands for ________. ***(Re)***

(*a*) Human Development Index

(*b*) Human Development Indicator

(*c*) Human Development Interaction

(*d*) Human Distribution Index

12. Which of the following countries has a better rank in the Human Development Index? ***(Re)*(CBSE, 2023)**

(*a*) Afghanistan (*b*) Myanmar

(*c*) India (*d*) Nepal

Assertion and Reason

(1 M)

Direction: The following questions consist of two statements – Assertion (A) and Reason (R). Answer these questions by selecting the appropriate option given below:

(*a*) Both A and R are true, and R is the correct explanation of A.

(*b*) Both A and R are true, but R is not the correct explanation of A.

(*c*) A is true, but R is false.

(*d*) A is false, but R is true.

1. **Assertion (A):** Public facilities are essential for the development of a country.

   Reason (R): Public facilities such as roads, hospitals, and schools provide essential services and infrastructure that contribute to the development of a country. ***(Un)***

2. **In Brazil, the Public Distribution System (PDS) provides subsidized food grains to ensure that all citizens have access to essential nutrients. Meanwhile, Mexico focuses its PDS on offering basic health amenities to improve the overall well-being of its population.**

   Assertion (A): The Public Distribution System (PDS) in Brazil ensures the nutritional well-being of its citizens.

   Reason (R): The PDS in Brazil provides subsidized food grains to its population. ***(Ev)***

3. **Assertion (A):** Money in your pocket can buy all the goods and services needed to live well.

   Reason (R): Collective provision of services is more cost-effective than individual provision. ***(An)***

4. **Assertion (A):** Kerala has a better Human Development Index than Haryana. ***(Re)***

   Reason (R): Kerala has adequate provision of health and educational facilities.

5. **Assertion (A):** Public Distribution System (PDS) ensures nutritional well-being.

   Reason (R): PDS provides basic health amenities. ***(Re)***

6. **Assertion (A):** Gross National Income alone can indicate a country's development level.

   Reason (R): Human Development Report uses more than income to rank countries. ***(Re)***

Subjective Questions

Very Short Answer Type Questions

(1 or 2 M)

1. **People only need a good income to have a good standard of living, as income can buy everything that one needs for a good life.**

   Is this statement correct? Give reason to support your answer. ***(An)(CFPQ, 2023)***

Ans. No *(½ M)*

People also depend on public services. *(½ M)*

2. **In Tamil Nadu, 90 percent of the people living in rural areas use a ration shop, whereas in West Bengal only 35 percent of rural people do so. Where would people be better off and why?** ***(Ap)(NCERT Intext)***

Ans. The health and nutritional status of people depend on the availability of cheap and reasonable quality food grains, sugar, and other items from the public distribution system (PDS). So, In Tamil Nadu, people would be better off due to better access to subsidized food, ensuring food security and affordability for a larger population provided facilities by the public distribution system. *(2 M)*

3. **A vessel dumped 500 tonnes of liquid toxic wastes into open-air dumps in a city and in the surrounding sea. This happened in a city called Abidjan in Ivory Coast, a country in Africa. The fumes from the highly toxic waste caused nausea, skin rashes, fainting, diarrhoea etc. After a month seven persons were dead, twenty in hospital, and twenty-six thousand treated for symptoms of poisoning. A multinational company dealing in petroleum and metals had contracted a local company of the Ivory Coast to dispose the toxic waste from its ship.**

   (*i*) **Who are the people who benefited and who did not?** ***(Un)***

   (*ii*) **What should be the developmental goal for this country?** ***(Ap)***

Ans. (*i*) Here are the reasons:

(*a*) **Benefited:** Multinational company and contracted local company. *(½ M)*

(*b*) **Not benefited:** Local people; they suffered from poisoning symptoms. *(½ M)*

(*ii*) Develop environmental regulations and waste management to protect health. *(1 M)*

4. **Human Development Index (HDI) level in India can be improved through ______________.** ***(Re)(CBSE, 2020)***

Ans. Human Development Index (HDI) level in India can be improved through better health and educational facilities. *(1 M)*

Topper's Explanation

(4) Investment in public facilities like healthcare and education.

Short Answer Type Questions

(3 or 4 M)

1. **Your friend is 1.50 cm tall and weighs 40 kg. Find out his BMI and comment on his report. What is BMI?** ***(Ap)***

Ans. Body mass index is the criteria which is used to find out whether a person is nourished, undernourished, and overweighted. *(1 M)*

Given, Weight = 40 kg

Height = 1.50 cm

The calculation is:

$$\text{BMI} = \frac{\text{Weight in kg}}{(\text{Height in meters})^2}$$

$$\text{BMI} = \frac{40}{(1.50)^2} = 17.8$$

Body Mass Index (BMI) is approximately 17.8. This BMI value indicates that a friend is underweight, suggesting a potential need to gain weight for optimal health. BMI is a measure that helps indicate whether a person has a healthy body weight for their height. *(2 M)*

2. Does availability of good health and educational facilities depend only on the amount of money spent by the government on these facilities? What other factors could be relevant? **(*Un*)(NCERT)**

Ans. No, it's not just about the money. Things like how well the facilities are run, the quality of teachers and doctors, and how easily people can access these services also really matter. *(1 M)*

The other factors that impact its success are:

- Effective implementation and monitoring of the policy instrument by government officials. *(1 M)*
- Creating a level of awareness about government policies and programmes through local bodies and village communities. *(1 M)*

3. A vessel dumped 500 tonnes of liquid toxic wastes into open-air dumps in a city and in the surrounding sea. This happened in a city called Abidjan in Ivory Coast, a country in Africa. The fumes from the highly toxic waste caused nausea, skin rashes, fainting, diarrhoea etc. After a month seven persons were dead, twenty in hospital, and twenty-six thousand treated for symptoms of poisoning. A multinational company dealing in petroleum and metals had contracted a local company of the Ivory Coast to dispose the toxic waste from its ship.

(*i*) Who are the people who benefited and who did not? **(*Un*)**

(*ii*) What should be the developmental goal for this country? **(*Ap*)**

Ans. (*i*) Here are the reasons:

(*a*) Benefited: Multinational company and contracted local company. *(½ M)*

(*b*) Not benefited: Local people; they suffered from poisoning symptoms. *(½ M)*

(*ii*) Develop environmental regulations and waste management to protect health. *(1 M)*

4. Explain the three components of the Human Development Index. **(CBSE, 2019)**

OR

Explain any four different indicators of economic development of different nations/states.

OR

What is Human Development? Explain its indicators. (Any 2) **(*Un*)(CBSE, 2020)**

Ans. Human development is the process of enlarging people's choices as well as raising the level of well-being so that they can lead a creative and purposeful life. *(1 M)*

<u>The UNDP considers four criteria as central indicators of human development are:</u>

(*a*) **Per Capita Income:** Estimates the economic prosperity and average income of individuals, reflecting the nation's wealth. It is the total income of a country divided by the total population. *(1 M)*

(*b*) **Education:** Education is an important indicator of human development as it helps individuals acquire knowledge and skills to participate in the economy and society. Education can be measured by literacy rates, enrollment rates, and the number of years of schooling. *(1 M)*

(*c*) **Health:** Health is another key indicator of human development. It is not only the absence of illness but also includes physical, mental, and social well-being. Health can be measured by life expectancy, infant mortality rates, and access to basic healthcare services. A healthy population is better able to participate in economic and social activities. *(1 M)*

(*d*) **Life Expectancy:** Life Expectancy at birth denotes, as the name suggests, average expected length of life of a person at the time of birth. *(1 M)*

5. Suggest any three ways to improve the public facilities in India. **(*Ap*)(CBSE, 2020)**

Ans. The ways to improve the public facilities in India are: **(Any-3)**

(*i*) By ensuring easy availability of dispensaries, doctors, and nurses in both urban and rural areas. *(1 M)*

(*ii*) Improving the Public Distribution System because it is another important facility that plays an important role in providing food security to the people. *(1 M)*

(*iii*) Improving infrastructure facilities like railways, airways, waterways, banking, etc. to become affordable for common people. *(1 M)*

(*iv*) Through increasing the number of hospitals, healthcare centers, and family welfare centers, especially in rural areas. *(1 M)*

(*v*) Organising free camps, polio awareness campaigns, and COVID-19 vaccination drives. *(1 M)*

6. Meena, a 25 Year old woman lives in a village. Her height is 1.45 m and weight is 36 km, while Teena of the same age and height weighs 48 kg. What can be said about their nutritional condition? **(*Ap*)**

Ans. Meena's BMI is approximately 17.1, which places her in the **"underweight"** category according to the BMI scale. This suggests that her nutritional intake might be insufficient for her height and age, indicating a potential need for a more nutritious diet to reach a healthier weight. *(1½ M)*

$$\text{BMI} = \frac{\text{Weight in kilogram}}{(\text{Height in meter})^2}$$

$$\text{Meena's BMI} = \frac{36}{1.45 \times 1.45} = 17.122$$

Teena's BMI is approximately 22.8, which falls within the **"normal"** weight range according to the BMI scale. This indicates that Teena has a healthier nutritional status compared to Meena, with her weight being appropriate for her height and age. *(1½ M)*

$$\text{BMI} = \frac{\text{Weight in kilogram}}{(\text{Height in meter})^2}$$

$$\text{Teena's BMI} = \frac{48}{1.45 \times 1.45} = 22.82$$

7. On what bases is the criterion used by the United Nations Development Programme (UNDP) for measuring development different from the one used by the World Bank? Explain. ***(Ev)*(CBSE, 2020)**

Ans. The basis for measuring development according to the World Bank and UNDP:

(*a*) According To UNDP **(Any 2)**

(***i***) **Literacy:** The percentage of the population of a given 7-and-above age group that can read and write. *(½ M)*

(***ii***) **Health facilities:** Medical services available to individuals or communities. *(½ M)*

(***iii***) **Living standard as criteria:** Refers to wealth, comfort, material goods, and necessities. *(½ M)*

(*b*) World Bank measures the same only on the basis of per capita income. Countries have been divided into three categories. Rich (High Income Group), Middle income group countries and Poor countries (Low Income Group) *(1 M)*

(*c*) World Bank only sees the average per capita income but UNDP sees the overall development. *(1 M)*

Long Answer Type Questions (4 or 5 M)

1. In what respect is the criterion used by the UNDP different from that of the World Bank? ***(Un)*(CBSE, 2017)**

Ans. World Bank's Criterion:

- The World Bank classifies countries based on **per capita** income. It considers higher income a sign of development, assuming it leads to better access to goods and services. *(2M)*

UNDP's Criterion:

- The UNDP uses a broader measure called the **Human Development Index (HDI)**. HDI considers **education levels, health status**, and **per capita income** to provide a more comprehensive view of human development. *(2M)*

Key Difference:

- While the **World Bank** focuses only on income, **UNDP** includes health and education, providing a multidimensional approach to assessing development. *(1M)*

2. The following table shows the proportion of adults (aged 15-49 years) whose BMI is below normal (BMI <18.5 kg/m^2) in India. It is based on a survey of various states for the year 2015-16. Look at the table and answer the following questions. ***(Ap)*(NCERT)**

State	Male (%)	Female (%)
Kerala	8.5	10
Karnataka	17	21
Madhya Pradesh	28	28
All States	20	23

Source: National Family Health Survey-4, 2015-16, http://rchiips.org

(***i***) **Compare the nutritional level of people in Kerala and Madhya Pradesh.**

(***ii***) **Can you guess why around one-fifth of people in the country are undernourished even though it is argued that there is enough food in the country? Describe in your own words.**

Ans. (*i*) In Kerala, 8.5% of males and 10% of females have a BMI below normal, indicating a lower proportion of undernourished individuals compared to Madhya Pradesh where 28% of both males and females have a BMI below normal. This suggests that the nutritional level of people in Kerala is better than that of Madhya Pradesh based on the BMI. *(1 M)*

(*ii*) Despite there being enough food in the country, around one-fifth of the population may still be undernourished due to various factors such as **(Any 4)**

(*a*) Unequal distribution of food resources,

(*b*) Lack of access to nutritious food,

(*c*) Poverty leading to food insecurity,

(*d*) Inadequate food distribution systems (In most of the states, the Public Distribution System (PDS), Does not function properly and poor people cannot get cheap food items.),

(*e*) Lack of awareness about balanced nutrition, and health issues impacting food absorption and utilization.

These factors can contribute to a significant portion of the population being undernourished even when there is enough food available in the country

3. Kerala, with lower per capita income has a better human development ranking than Haryana. Hence, per capita income is not a useful criterion at all and should not be used to compare states. Do you agree? ***(Ev)*(NCERT)**

Ans. I don't agree with the statement that per capita income is not at all a useful criterion to compare states. Here's why, *(1 M)*

(*i*) Per capita income measures the average money people earn; it's useful but doesn't tell the whole story. *(1 M)*

(*ii*) Kerala's better ranking in human development means it does well in health and education, despite lower per capita income. *(1 M)*

(*iii*) So, per capita income is a good start but we should also look at how healthy and educated people are to really understand development. *(1 M)* (*iv*) Development is about more than money; it's about quality of life too. Both income and human development factors are important to compare how well different states are doing. *(1 M)*

4. The map given below shows the Indian states with their categorisation on the basis of their Human Development Indices (HDI)

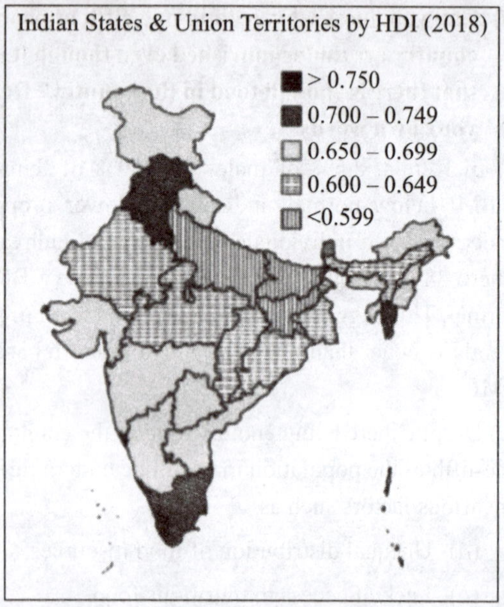

(*a*) Identify the top two states with the highest HDI. ***(Re)***

(*b*) Name any two states atthe bottom of the HDI ranking. ***(Re)***

(*c*) In 2020-21, Maharashtra is the richest state in India with a GDP of ₹26.61 lakh crore, but has a lower per capita income than Goa. What is the reason for this? ***(An)***

(*d*) Gujarat has a higher per capita income but lower HDI than Mizoram. What can be the reason for this? ***(An)***

(*e*) India's neighbouring country Sri Lanka has an HDI of 0.782 (2019), while India's HDI is 0.645 (2019). Name any one Indian state with an HDI similar to that of Sri Lanka, and one Indian state with the HDI closerto the national average. ***(Un)***

Ans. (*a*) Kerala, Goa *(Each Point Carries ½ M)*

(*b*) Uttar Pradesh, Bihar, Jharkhand

(Any Two Each Point Carries ½ M)

(*c*) Maharashtra's high population. *(1 M)*

(*d*) better health and education in Mizoram *(1 M)*

(*e*) • HDI closerto Sri Lanka-Goa/Kerala *(½ M)*

• HDI closerto the national average-Rajasthan/Madhya Pradesh/Chhattisgarh/Odisha/West Bengal/Assam. *(½ M)*

4 SUSTAINABILITY OF DEVELOPMENT

NCERT Definitions *(Commonly asked in 1 mark)*

- **Sustainable Development:** Development that **meets present needs** without compromising the ability of **future generations** to meet their own needs. Sustainable development requires balancing economic growth with environmental protection.
- **Groundwater Overuse:** The **excessive use** of groundwater at a rate faster than it can be replenished, leading to depletion.
- **Environmental Degradation:** The deterioration of the environment through depletion of resources, destruction of ecosystems, and extinction of wildlife.
- **Renewable Resources:** Those resources that **can be replenished** naturally over short periods of time, such as solar, wind, and water.
- **Non-renewable Resources:** Those resources which will **get exhausted** after a few years of use. We have a fixed stock on earth which **cannot be replenished** such as fossil fuels and minerals.

Difference Between

Renewable Resources	Non-renewable Resources
Those resources which are renewed or replenished naturally. **Examples:** Solar, wind, water.	Those resources which are non-renewed or non-replenished naturally. **Examples:** Coal, oil, Fossil fuels, etc
Sustainable usage possible	Lead to depletion and scarcity
Lower environmental impact	Often causes significant pollution

Pillar	Definition	Importance
Economic Sustainability	The capacity of an economy to support a high standard of living while preserving resources and integrity	Vital for long-term prosperity and responsible resource management
Social Sustainability	The ability to fulfill the basic needs of all members, including education, healthcare, and justice.	Ensures inclusive growth and societal well-being
Environmental Sustainability	The endurance of ecosystems to meet current and future needs without degradation.	Crucial for the health of the planet and its inhabitants

Mnemonics

Importance of Sustainable Development: "SAVE".

- S → Sustainability
- A → Awareness
- V → Values
- E → Environmental Conservation

COMPETENCY BASED SOLVED EXAMPLES

Scan Me for Detailed Explanations

Multiple Choice Questions

(1 M)

1. **"In the next 25 years, it is projected that 60 percent of the country will face severe resource depletion if current usage trends continue. This issue is particularly prevalent in agriculturally prosperous regions like Punjab and Western U.P., hard rock plateau areas in central and south India, some coastal areas, and rapidly growing urban settlements. Analyzing the situation and identifying the picture shows resources most likely to be overused according to the scenario.** ***(An)***

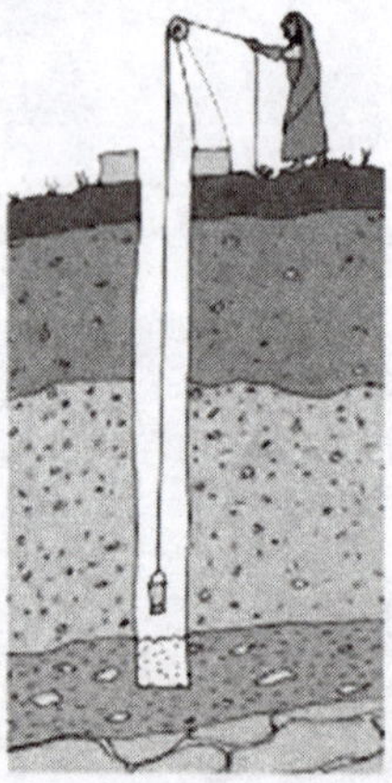

(*a*) Air (*b*) Women Power
(*c*) Groundwater (*d*) Soil"

2. **In the small town of Sundernagar, economic development varies widely. Some areas are flourishing with new technology companies and upscale shopping centers, while others still lack basic infrastructure like roads and schools. A recent government initiative plans to invest in sustainable projects to boost local economies but has sparked debate among residents. Some prioritize technological development and economic growth, while others advocate for sustainable practices that include improving local education and healthcare systems.** ***(Ap)***

Given the proposed government initiative in Sundernagar, which of the following best demonstrates a sustainable approach to improving the local economy?

(*a*) Increasing only the number of technology companies in the area.
(*b*) Building more roads to improve transportation without environmental assessments.
(*c*) Developing a mixed-use area that includes educational facilities, healthcare centers, and green parks.
(*d*) Privatizing water supply to increase efficiency.

3. **Which of the following is not a challenge to sustainable development?** ***(Un)***

(*a*) Climate change
(*b*) Population growth
(*c*) Technological advancement
(*d*) Resource depletion

4. **What is the main goal of sustainable development?** ***(Un)***

(*a*) Economic growth
(*b*) Environmental protection
(*c*) Social development
(*d*) Technological advancement

5. **What is the role of the government in promoting sustainable development?** ***(Un)***

(*a*) To regulate economic growth
(*b*) To protect the environment
(*c*) To promote social development
(*d*) All of the above

6. **In the town of Greenvale, the local council is facing a challenge. They need to balance the town's growth with the conservation of its natural surroundings for future residents. As a part of the Greenvale's Young Environmentalists Club, you've been invited to present your ideas on how the town can achieve this balance.**

As a young environmentalist, which principle would you advocate for that best describes the approach Greenvale should take towards sustainable development? ***(Ev)***

(*a*) Use of Greenvale's natural resources without considering the needs of the town's future inhabitants.
(*b*) Greenvale meets its current needs while ensuring that future generations can also fulfill their needs.
(*c*) Utilization of natural resources by past, present, and future residents of Greenvale without any specific strategy.
(*d*) Focus on the needs of Greenvale's future generation even if it means the current generation's needs are not fully met.

Assertion and Reason

(1 M)

Direction: The following questions consist of two statements – Assertion (A) and Reason (R). Answer these questions by selecting the appropriate option given below:

(*a*) Both A and R are true, and R is the correct explanation of A.
(*b*) Both A and R are true, but R is not the correct explanation of A.
(*c*) A is true, but R is false.
(*d*) A is false, but R is true.

1. **Assertion (A):** The present type and levels of development are not sustainable.
   Reason (R): Scientists have been warning about the unsustainability of present levels of development since the second half of the twentieth century. ***(Ev)***
2. **Assertion (A):** Groundwater is an example of a renewable resource.
   Reason (R): Renewable resources are replenished by nature, but even they may be overused. ***(Un)***
3. **Assertion (A):** Non-renewable resources will get exhausted after a few years of use.
   Reason (R): Non-renewable resources have a fixed stock on earth that cannot be replenished. ***(Un)***
4. **Assertion (A):** Development should be maintained at the present level for future generations.
   Reason (R): Maintaining the present level of development is desirable. ***(Ev)***
5. **Assertion (A):** Overuse of renewable resources may lead to their depletion.
   Reason (R): Renewable resources may be replenished by nature. ***(Ev)***

Subjective Questions

Very Short Answer Type Questions **(1 or 2 M)**

1. **Find out the present sources of energy that are used by the people in India. What could be the other possibilities fifty years from now?** ***(Ap)*(NCERT)**

Ans. The present sources of energy that are used by the people of India are electricity, coal, crude oil, cow dung, and solar energy. There are possibilities that fifty years from now, ethanol, bio-diesel, nuclear energy, and better utilization of wind energy, especially with the imminent danger of oil resources running out, be used by the people of India. *(2 M)*

2. **What is the sustainability of development?** ***(Un)***

Ans. Sustainability of development refers to the ability to meet the needs of the present generation without compromising the ability of future generations to meet their own needs. *(2 M)*

3. **Why is the sustainability of development important?** ***(Re)***

Ans. Sustainability of development is important because it ensures that natural resources are used in a way that they are available for future generations as well. *(1 M)*

4. **What are the three goals of sustainability?** ***(Re)***

Ans. The three pillars of sustainability are: *(1 M)*

(*i*) Economic sustainability
(*ii*) Social sustainability
(*iii*) Environmental sustainability.

5. **How can we achieve sustainable development?** ***(Ap)***

Ans. We can achieve sustainable development by using renewable resources, reducing waste and pollution, promoting education and awareness, and adopting environmentally friendly practices. *(2 M)*

6. **What are the consequences of unsustainable development?** ***(Ev)***

Ans. The consequences of unsustainable development include depletion of natural resources, loss of biodiversity, and environmental degradation, which ultimately affect the well-being of all living beings on the planet. *(2 M)*

Short Answer Type Questions **(3 M)**

1. **"The Earth has enough resources to meet the needs of all but not enough to satisfy the greed of even one person." How is this statement relevant to the discussion of development? Discuss.** ***(Ev)*(NCERT)**

Ans. "The Earth has enough resources to meet the needs of all but not enough to satisfy the greed of even one person." This statement is very relevant to the discussion of development.

(*i*) Development depends not just on the economic factors of the country but also on the resources that are available for the people of a country to use. *(1 M)*
(*ii*) Natural resources are non-renewable resources and it is people's responsibility to meet their needs and satisfy their greed. *(1 M)*
(*iii*) If there is not careful use of natural resources, future generations will not be able to use them which will result in the downfall of the development of a country. *(1 M)*

Nailing the Right Answer

Highlight the importance of both economic factors and available resources for development.
Emphasize the responsibility of individuals to use natural resources wisely.

2. **What are the three pillars of sustainable development?** ***(Re)***

Ans. The three pillars of sustainable development are:

(*i*) **Economic sustainability** means using resources in a way that promotes long-term economic growth. *(1 M)*
(*ii*) **Social sustainability** means ensuring that all members of society have access to basic necessities like healthcare and education. *(1 M)*
(*iii*) **Environmental sustainability** means using resources in a way that does not harm the environment and does not deplete resources. *(1 M)*

3. **What are the features of sustainable development? *(Un)***

Ans. The Features of Sustainable Development are: **(Any 3)**

(*i*) It Improves the quality of human life. *(1 M)*

(*ii*) It Minimizes the depletion of natural resources. *(1 M)*

(*iii*) It respects and cares for all kinds of life forms. *(1 M)*

(*iv*) It enables the communities to care for their own environment. *(1 M)*

(*v*) It ensures activities do not increase pollution beyond the ecosystem's capacity to absorb it. *(1 M)*

4. **What are some examples of sustainable development practices? *(Re)***

Ans. Some examples of sustainable development practices include using renewable energy sources like solar and wind power, reducing waste and pollution, protecting natural resources like forests and water sources, promoting sustainable agriculture practices, and promoting sustainable transportation methods like biking or public transportation. *(2 M)*

These practices help to ensure that resources are used in a way that does not harm the environment and promotes long-term economic growth. *(1 M)*

5. **Why is the issue of sustainability important for development? Explain with examples.** *(3 M)* **(CBSE, 2023, 2020 (5 M), NCERT)**

OR

Why has the issue of sustainability become essential for development in present times? Explain with example. *(3 M)* **(CBSE, 2024)**

Ans. The reasons why sustainability has become essential for development are:

(*i*) **Limited Resources:** Natural resources like coal, oil, and fresh water are getting used up fast. If we don't use them wisely, future generations will suffer. *(1 M)*

(*ii*) **Environmental Damage:** Overuse of resources causes pollution, deforestation, and climate change, which harm both nature and human life. *(1 M)*

(*iii*) **Groundwater Depletion:** Many parts of India, like Punjab and Western U.P., are overusing groundwater. If this continues, there will be a water crisis in the future. *(1 M)*

(*iv*) **Future Growth:** Development should not only focus on today's needs but also ensure that future generations have enough resources to grow. *(1 M)*

(*v*) **Sustainable Alternatives:** Using renewable energy like solar and wind power helps in reducing pollution and ensures long-term development. *(1 M)*

Topper's Explanation

29 Sustainable development refers to economic development without degrading the environment and ~~je~~ compromising with the needs of future generations.

1. Sustainable existence as a component of sustainable development is Important to ensure survival of life and maintain the quality of life. Human beings have indiscriminately exploited the resources of nature which has led to environmental degradation and disrupted the ecological balance. Global Warming, Climate Change, Depletion of renewable resources are global issues which don't respect national boundaries.

2. Excessive deforestation, burning of ~~fossil~~ fossil fuels have caused a lot of damage to our environment. Air pollution and land pollution have become very common these days.

3. Drying aquifiers, depleting water tables and contamination of water resources are very alarming. Over-utilisation of renewable resources which is degrading their quality and increasing their cost has posed a serious question on energy security in future. These resources like coal, petroleum are exhaustable in nature.

Conclusion - Therefore, It is Important to realise that nature has a lot to fulfil our needs but not our greeds. Use of sustainaible practices like using renewable resources and energy conservation are the need of the hour.

6. **Example 1: Grounds Water in India**

"Recent evidence suggests that the groundwater is under serious threat of overuse in many parts of the country. About 300 districts have reported a water level decline of over 4 metres during the past 20 years. Nearly one-third of the country is overusing their groundwater reserves. In another 25 years, 60 per cent of the country would be doing the same if the present way of using this resource continues. Groundwater overuse is particularly found in the agriculturally prosperous regions of Punjab and Western U.P., hard rock plateau areas of central and south India, some coastal areas and the rapidly growing urban settlements."

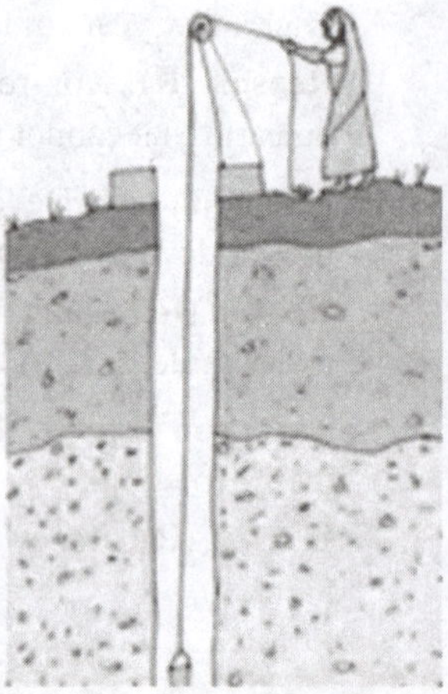

(*a*) **Why is groundwater overused? (NCERT Intext)**

(*b*) **Can there be development without overuse?**

Ans. (*a*) Groundwater is overused due to **high agricultural demands** in prosperous regions like Punjab and Western U.P., **urban expansion,** and lack of effective **water management** strategies. *(1½ M)*

(*b*) Yes, development can occur without overuse by implementing sustainable water management practices, promoting water conservation, and using alternative water sources like rainwater harvesting. *(1½ M)*

Long Answer Type Questions (5 M)

1. **List a few examples of environmental degradation that you may have observed around you. *(Re)*(NCERT)**

Ans. Some of the examples of environmental degradation in our surroundings include:

(*i*) Increase in air pollution due to smoke emissions from factories and vehicles. *(1 M)*

(*ii*) Increase in water pollution due to shops and small factories in residential areas. *(1 M)* (*iii*) Noise pollution due to the use of loudspeakers at night and blowing of horns unnecessarily on the roads by different vehicles. *(1 M)*

(*iv*) No proper disposal of waste and provision of dustbins in the streets or roadsides. *(1 M)*

(*v*) Some people urinate in the open on the roadside due to a lack of public conveniences. *(1 M)*

2. What are the challenges to achieving sustainable development? ***(Un)***

Ans. The challenges to achieving sustainable development include: **(Any-5)**

(*i*) **Overuse of Resources:** Like the depletion of groundwater in India due to over-extraction beyond natural replenishment rates. *(1 M)*

(*ii*) **Non-Renewable Resource Depletion:** The finite nature of resources like crude oil that cannot be replenished poses a significant challenge. *(1 M)*

(*iii*) **Environmental Degradation:** Cross-border environmental impacts that can lead to ecosystem damage and biodiversity loss. *(1 M)*

(*iv*) **Economic Pressures:** The demand for economic growth can conflict with the need to conserve natural resources. *(1 M)*

(*v*) **Poverty and Inequality:** Make it difficult for people to meet their basic needs, which can lead to the over-exploitation of natural resources. *(1 M)*

(*vi*) **Technological and Policy Limitations:** Lack of sustainable technologies and effective policies to manage resource use and environmental protection. *(1 M)*

3. Ram, Mohan, Rohan are a member of a city council in a developing country facing rapid industrial growth. The council is evaluating a proposal for a new industrial zone which promises significant economic benefits but poses risks to the local ecosystem, including a nearby river and forest area used by the community. Discuss the importance of sustainability in this scenario. What factors should the council consider to ensure that development is sustainable, and how can potential negative impacts on the environment and local community be mitigated? Use specific examples to justify your reasoning. ***(Ap)***

Ans. The importance of sustainability in developing an industrial zone in a developing country, the following factors should be considered, aiming for a balance between economic benefits and environmental protection:

(*i*) **Environmental Impact:** Assess the potential harm to the local ecosystem, including pollution of the nearby river and deforestation. Implement stringent environmental regulations to mitigate these risks. *(1 M)*

(*ii*) **Economic Benefits:** Recognize the potential for job creation and economic growth, but ensure these benefits do not come at the cost of environmental degradation. Engage in fair labor practices and ensure benefits are distributed equitably among the community. *(1 M)*

(*iii*) **Community Involvement:** Actively involve local communities in decision-making processes to ensure their needs and concerns are addressed. This fosters greater community support and sustainable outcomes. *(1 M)*

(*iv*) **Sustainable Practices:** Promote industries that practice sustainable methods, such as using renewable energy sources and recycling waste, to minimize environmental impact. *(1 M)*

(*v*) **Long-term Planning:** Implement regular environmental audits and update policies as necessary to adapt to changing environmental and economic conditions, ensuring long-term sustainability of the industrial zone. *(1 M)*

MISCELLANEOUS EXERCISE

Multiple Choice Questions

(1 M)

1. What is the primary purpose of earning an income? ***(Ev)***

(*a*) To achieve financial security

(*b*) To accumulate wealth

(*c*) To fulfill personal goals

(*d*) All of the above

2. "Analyze the pictures of Country-A and Country-B. Country-A depicts a uniform distribution of individuals with chairs, labeled 'COUNTRY WITH NO RICH AND NO POOR,' suggesting an even allocation of resources. In contrast, Country-B shows one individual with multiple chairs and others without any, labeled 'COUNTRY WITH RICH AND POOR,' reflecting a skewed distribution of resources. Based on these pictures, what can you infer about the economic structures of the two countries? ***(An)***

Country-A

Country-B

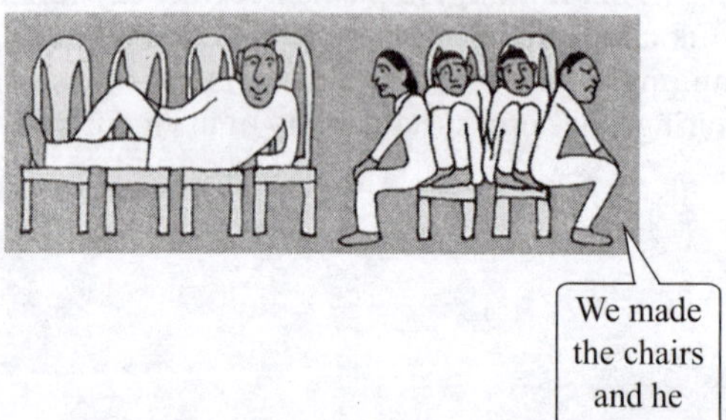

(*a*) Country-A practices equal wealth distribution, while Country-B shows wealth inequality.

(*b*) Country-A has a higher GDP than Country-B.

(*c*) Both countries prioritize wealth accumulation over public welfare.

(*d*) Country-B has achieved sustainable development, whereas Country-A has not.

3. Which of the following groups of people are likely to have the most conflicting developmental goals? ***(An)*(CFPQ, 2023)**

(*a*) Students and teachers

(*b*) Tribals and industrialists

(*c*) Small farmers and large farmers

(*d*) Municipal corporations and road-construction companies

4. Study the data given below: ***(An)*(CFPQ, 2023)**

Country	Total GDP	GDP Per Capita
Japan	$4,872,415,104,315	$38,214
Germany	$3,693,204,332,230	$44,680

Despite having a higher total income than Germany, Japan has a lower per capita income. What is the reason for this.

(*a*) Japan has a more equitable distribution of income

(*b*) Germany has more rich people than poor people

(*c*) Japan has a smaller population than Germany

(*d*) Japan has a bigger population than Germany

5. What is the relationship between respect for women and women's engagement in paid work? ***(An)***

(*a*) There is no relationship between the two

(*b*) Women's engagement in paid work increases respect for women

(*c*) Respect for women leads to more sharing of housework and greater acceptance of women working outside

(*d*) Women's engagement in paid work decreases respect for women

6. Suppose there are four families in your locality, the average per capita income of whom is ₹10,000. If the income of three families is ₹6,000, ₹8,000, and ₹14,000 respectively. ***(Ap)***

Person A	6000
Person B	8000
Person C	14000
Person D	Z
Average income	10000

Find Z the income of person D.

(*a*) ₹15,000 (*b*) ₹12,000

(*c*) ₹14,000 (*d*) ₹10,000

7. Read the data given below and answer the question.

State	Infant mortality rate per 1000 live births(2018)	Literacy rate% (2017-18)
A	30	82
B	7	94

As per the data given above, why state B has a low infant mortality rate?

(*a*) It has high per capita income.

(*b*) It has better infrastructure than state A.

(*c*) It has good teachers and schools.

(*d*) It has health care and education for all.

8. Which of the following statements defines sustainable development? ***(Un)*(CBSE, 2019)**

(*a*) Sustainable use of natural resources without considering the need of future generations

(*b*) Present generation fulfills its needs while considering the needs of the future generations as well.

(*c*) It means utilization of natural resources by the past, present and future generations

(*d*) To meet the needs of the future generation even if the needs of the present generation go unmet.

9. Which of the following is the most important factor for sustainable development? ***(Un)***

(*a*) Economic growth

(*b*) Environmental protection

(*c*) Social development

(*d*) Technological advancement

10. In the country of Sri Lanka, the government aims to improve its ranking in human development indices. The Prime Minister seeks your advice on which combination of factors to prioritize. Considering the overall well-being of the population, which combination of factors would you recommend focusing on simultaneously? ***(Ev)***

(*a*) Per capita income and defense spending.

(*b*) Literacy rates and healthcare facilities.

(*c*) Tourism and urbanization rates.

(*d*) Export rates and technology imports.

11. The literacy rate for all age groups, including young and old, was ______ for rural males and ______ for rural females. However, it is not just that these many adults could not attend school but that there are _____ who are currently not in school. ***(An)***

Category	Male	Female
Literacy rate for rural population	52%	19%
Literacy rate for children in age group 10-14 years	68%	39%
Percentage of rural children aged 10-14 attending school	64%	31%

(*a*) 68%, 39%, and 61.5%

(*b*) 52 %, 19 %, and 35.5%

(*c*) 76%, 54%, and 16.5%

(*d*) 64%, 39%, and 25.5%

12. UNDP stands for ____ ***(Re)***

(*a*) United Nations Diversity Playground

(*b*) United Nations Development Programme

(*c*) United Nations Democratic Programme

(*d*) None of these

13. Who publishes the "Human Development Report"? ***(Re)***

(*a*) UNICEF (*b*) WHO

(*c*) UNDP (*d*) United Nations

14. Match the following Column-I and Column-II Applying ***(Ap)***

	Column-I (Person in Harmony-Likely Developmental Aspiration)		Column-II (Goals)
(A)	**Arun (landless rural laborer):** Wants to provide a good education for his children.	(i)	Better employment opportunity Permanent Job, Having a self-owned home to live in.
(B)	**Balraj (prosperous farmer):** Seeks to reduce costs with cheaper farming inputs	(ii)	More days of work and better wages.
(C)	**Chetan (urban unemployed youth):** Aims to find stable and fair employment	(iii)	Low prices for food grains, cheap inputs like seeds, machinery, etc.
(D)	**Deepika (rural woman from a landowning family):** Aspires for higher education opportunities	(iv)	More opportunities for higher education.

Choose the correct match from the following options:

(*a*) A-Arun-(ii), B-Balraj-(iii), C-Chetan-(iv), D-Deepika-(i)

(*b*) A-Arun-(i), B-Balraj-(ii), C-Chetan-(iii), D-Deepika-(iv)

(*c*) A-Arun-(ii), B-Balraj-(iii), C-Chetan-(i), D-Deepika-(iv)

(*d*) A-Arun-(iv), B-Balraj-(i), C-Chetan-(ii), D-Deepika-(iii)

15. The facilities provided by the government that can be used collectively are called ________. ***(Re)***

(*a*) Public Distribution (*b*) Public Discussion

(*c*) Public Facilities (*d*) Public Formation

16. The Literacy rate of Kerala in 2011 was _______. ***(Re)***

(*a*) 62% (*b*) 94%

(*c*) 62% (*d*) 49%

17. Imagine that as part of an international economics class, students are participating in a simulation. They are assigned different countries to manage, each with unique economic profiles. The goal is to understand economic classification and the impact it has on global economics and funding opportunities. ***(Re, Ev)***

Statement-I: Countries with per capita income of US$ 49,300 per annum and above in 2019, are called high-income or rich countries.

Statement-II: Those with per capita income of US$ 2500 or less are called low-income countries.

(*a*) Both statements are true.

(*b*) Both statements are false.

(*c*) Statement-I is true, Statement-II is false.

(*d*) Statement-I is false, Statement-II is true.

18. The number of deaths of children less than one year of age per 100 live births is referred to as _____. **(Re)(CBSE, 2020)**

(a) Infant Mortality Rate (IMR)
(b) Human Development Index
(c) Body Mass Index
(d) Human Development Report

19. Assume there are four families in a country. The average per capita income of these families is ₹ 5000. If the income of three families is ₹ 4000, ₹ 7000, and ₹ 3000 respectively, what is the income of the fourth family? **(Ev)(NCERT)**

(a) ₹ 7500 (b) ₹ 3000
(c) ₹ 2000 (d) ₹ 6000

20. Which of the following neighbouring countries has better performance in terms of human development than India? **(An)(NCERT)**

(a) Bangladesh (b) Sri Lanka
(c) Nepal (d) Pakistan

21. Read the data given below and answer the question. Analyzing **(An)**

State	Per Capita Income (2018-19 in Rs)	Literacy Rate (%) 2017-18	Infant Mortality Rate per 1,000 live births (2018)	Net Attendance Ratio (age 14 and 15 years) 2017-18
Haryana	2,36,147	82	30	61
Kerala	2,04,105	94	7	83
Bihar	40,982	62	32	43

Which state has the highest per capita income, lowest literacy rate, the best performance in infant mortality rate, and highest net attendance ratio for the secondary stage?

(a) Haryana, Kerala, Kerala, Bihar
(b) Bihar, Kerala, Kerala, Haryana
(c) Haryana, Bihar, Kerala, Kerala
(d) Bihar, Haryana, Kerala, Kerala

22. Match the List-I with List-II. **(An)**

List-I	List-II
(a) Per Capita Income	(i) Renewable Resources
(b) Human Development Report	(ii) Average Income
(c) Body Mass Index	(iii) UNDP
(d) Sustainability of Development	(iv) Proper Nutrition

(a) A-(iii), B-(iv), C-(i), D-(ii)
(b) A-(ii), B-(iii), C-(iv), D-(i)
(c) A-(i), B-(iii), C-(ii), D-(iv)
(d) A-(iv), B-(ii), C-(i), D-(iii)

Assertion and Reason

(1 M)

Direction: The following questions consist of two statements – Assertion (A) and Reason (R). Answer these questions by selecting the appropriate option given below:

(a) Both A and R are true, and R is the correct explanation of A.
(b) Both A and R are true, but R is not the correct explanation of A.
(c) A is true, but R is false.
(d) A is false, but R is true.

1. **Assertion (A):** We compare the average income that is unevenly distributed income of the country divided by half of its population.
Reason (R): Average Income is also known as Per Capita income. **(Un)**

2. **Assertion (A):** Non-renewable resources are the resources that will get exhausted after years of use.
Reason (R): A fixed stock on earth that cannot be replenished such as fossil fuels and Minerals. **(Un)**

3. **Assertion (A):** Sustainable development is crucial for the economic growth of the countries.
Reason (R): Sustainable development guarantees that eco-friendly measures are adopted for carrying out the production processes. **(Ev)**

4. **Assertion (A):** Different people have different developmental goals.
Reason (R): The capitalist approach to development is harmful to the poor section of the society. **(Ev)**

5. **Assertion (A):** A high average income is not an indicator of the overall human development in a country.
Reason (R): Average income does not include indicators like level of literacy rate, health facilities in a country. **(An)**

6. **Assertion (A):** Suppose the literacy rate in a state is 78% and the net attendance ratio in secondary stage is 47%.
Reason (R): More than half of the students are going to other states for elementary level education. **(An)**

Subjective Questions

Very Short Answer Type Questions

(1 or 2 M)

1. Development as Freedom is Amartya Sen's first book after receiving the Nobel and the most widely read of all of his works. Based on the author's World Bank Fellow Lectures in 1996, this descriptive, non-technical overview of welfare economics argues that 'development' should be viewed not in terms of economic measures (e.g. GDP growth, average annual income) but in terms of the real 'freedoms' that people can enjoy such as economic facilities and social opportunities. Sen describes human freedom as both the primary end objective and the principal means of development; economic measures are merely the means to this end. Sen frames development as the realisation of freedom and the abolishment of 'unfreedoms' such as poverty, famine, and lack of political rights. **(An, Ev)**

Source: Terjesen, Siri. (2004). Amartya Sen'sDevelopment as Freedom.

Consider a situation where the government of a developing country has decided to undertake a large dam-building project. This project is touted to provide significant benefits such as hydroelectric power, improved irrigation, and flood control. However, this project alsoinvolves relocating several tribal communities that have lived in the project area for generations. These tribal groups are protesting the project, citing the loss of their ancestral lands and insufficient rehabilitation measures

2. Why Kerala has a low infant mortality rate? **(*Re*)**

3. Mention the formula to calculate the BMI (Body Mass Index) **(*Re*)(CBSE, 2019)**

OR

Riya, a 14-year-old student, has a BMI of 15.2, indicating that she is undernourished. Meanwhile, her friend Arjun, who is 15 years old, has a BMI of 28, showing that he is overweight. Both of them live in the same neighborhood and have different eating and exercise habits.

Evaluate how Riya and Arjun's lifestyle choices may contribute to their BMI differences. **(*Ev*)**

4. Define the term 'Per capita income'. **(*Re*)(CBSE, 2020)**

5. If there are 4 families in a country with a per capita income of ₹10,000. The income of 3 families is ₹8,000, ₹10,000, and ₹12000? What is the income of the 4th family? **(*Ev*)**

6. Choose the incorrect option from column A, and column B. **(*An*)(CBSE, 2020)**

Column-A Category of person	Column-B Development goals/ aspirations
1. Landless rural laborers	A. More days of work and better wages.
2. Prosperous farmers from Punjab	B. Availability of other sources of irrigation
3. Farmers who depend only on rain for growing crops	C. Assured higher support prices for their crops
4. A rural woman from a landowning family	D. Regular job and high wages to increase her income.

7. State any two goals of development other than income. What may be the goal of landless rural labourers regarding their income? **(*An*)(CBSE, 2018) and (CBSE, 2019)**

8. How can two people have different development goals? **(*An*)(CBSE, 2018)**

9. Define The term 'sustainable Development'. **(*Un*)(CBSE, 2022)**

Short Answer Type Questions (3 M)

1. Shyam is a 15-year-old student at Harmony High School. He loves playing cricket but has recently been experiencing low energy levels. The school nurse suggests that he should maintain a healthy Body Mass Index (BMI) to improve his energy and overall health. Shyam is also a member of the school's social science club, which is currently learning about different aspects of human development.

   (*i*) As a friend and fellow club member, advise Shyam on three lifestyle changes he can make to maintain a healthy BMI. Consider his daily routine and diet, and suggest practical steps he could take. **(*Ap*)**

   OR

   (*ii*) In your social science club, you are discussing the Human Development Index (HDI). Explain to the other members the three key components that make up the HDI and how they impact a country's development. **(*Ap*)**

2. Our development is the earth's destruction. Do you agree with the given statement? Give 2 reasons to support your answer. **(*Ev*)(CFPQ, 2023)**

3. On the basis of which three indicators of HDI 2004 Sri Lanka has a better rank than India? **(*An*)(CBSE, 2017)**

4. Describe any three public facilities needed for development. **(*Re*)**

5. "Imagine two states: 'State A' has a high average income but average public facilities and literacy rates. 'State B' (similar to Kerala) has a moderate average income but excellent public facilities and literacy rates. As a social analyst for 'State B,' you are tasked to prepare a report. Discuss how 'State B's' public facilities and literacy rates could contribute to its development in aspects other than income. Consider health, quality of life, and social equality in your analysis." **(*Ev*)**

6. In what respects is the criterion used by the UNDP for measuring development different from the one used by the World Bank? **(*An*)(NCERT)**

7. Ravi is a young software developer from a metropolitan city who aspires to work for a major tech company abroad, while Meena, a farmer in a rural area, wishes for better irrigation facilities and a stable market for her crops to secure her family's future.
   Analyze the aspirations of Ravi and Meena to illustrate how different individuals can have varying developmental goals based on their socio-economic backgrounds. Discuss how these differing goals impact their expectations from the government's development policies. **(*An*)**

8. How does the Human Development Report give a holistic view of development? **(*An & Un*)(CFPQ, 2023)**

Long Answer Type Questions (4 or 5 M)

1. List a few examples of environmental degradation that you may have observed around you. **(*Cr*)(NCERT)**

2. The table below shows the income of the citizens of two countries, A and B, assuming that they have only 4 citizens. **(*Ev*)(CFPQ, 2023)**

Country	Citizen I	Citizen II	Citizen III	Citizen IV
Country A	2,000	2,400	2,400	2,700
Country B	700	40,000	750	710

   (*a*) Calculate the per capita income of both the countries.

   (*b*) Which country has a higher per capita income?

   (*c*) Which country has a more equitable distribution of income?

   (*d*) Is the answer for (*b*) and (*c*) the same? Give reasons.

3. What is the main criterion used by the World Bank in classifying different countries? What are the limitations of this criterion, if any? ***(Un & An)*(NCERT)**

4. Three friends from different states—Rohan from Haryana, Maya from Kerala, and Aman from Bihar—are discussing the progress of their respective home states. They consider various factors like infant mortality rate, literacy rate, and net attendance ratio at the secondary stage. Each friend argues that their state is doing well in certain aspects while facing challenges in others.

Some comparative data on Haryana, Kerala and Bihar

State	Infant Mortablity Rate per 1,000 live births (2018)	Literacy Rate % 2017-18	Net Attendance Ration (per 100 persons) secondary stage (age 14 and 15 years) 2017-18
Haryana	30	82	61
Kerala	7	94	83
Bihar	32	62	43

Sources: Economic survey 2020-21, PA 157, National Sample Survey Organisation (Report No. 585). National statistical office, Government of India.

Imagine you are part of Rohan, Maya, and Aman's discussion. Based on the data provided in the table, how would you evaluate the development status of their states? Discuss how the indicators such as infant mortality rate, literacy rate, and net attendance ratio influence the overall development scenario of Haryana, Kerala, and Bihar. ***(Ev)***

OR

In the imagined nation of Greenwald, despite a high average income, the citizens face poor health services and low educational standards. Recent surveys have shown a decline in life expectancy and a high dropout rate from secondary schools. You are part of a team of policy analysts tasked with advising the government on development strategies. Analyze the situation in Greenwald and argue why focusing on improving health and education could be more significant indicators of development than average income. Provide suggestions on what kind of policies the government should implement to enhance these sectors. ***(An)***

Case Based Questions

(4 M)

Case Based-I

Average Income: While 'averages' are useful for comparison, they also hide disparities.

For example, let us consider two countries, A and B. For the sake of simplicity, we have assumed that they have only five citizens each. Based on data given in Table, calculate the average income for both the countries.

Comparison of Two Countries

Country	Monthly incomes of citizens (in Rupees)					
	I	II	III	IV	V	Average
Country A	9500	10500	9800	10000	10200	
Country B	500	500	500	48000		

Will you be equally happy to live in both these countries? Are both equally developed? Perhaps some of us may like to live in country B if we are assured of being its fifth citizen but if it is a lottery that decides our citizenship number then perhaps most of us will prefer to live in country A. Even though both the countries have identical average income, country A is preferred because it has more equitable distribution. In this country people are neither very rich nor extremely poor. On the other hand most citizens in country B are poor and one person is extremely rich. Hence, while average income is useful for comparison it does not tell us how this income is distributed among people.

COUNTRY WITH NO RICH AND NO POOR

COUNTRY WITH RICH AND POOR

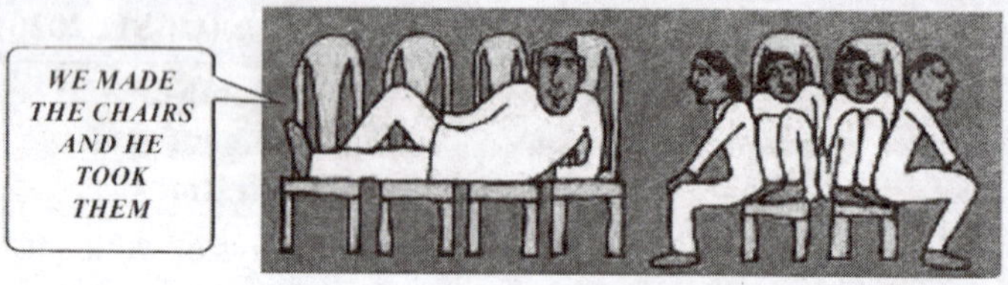

(Attempt Any Four)

(i) Give three examples where an average is used for comparing situations. ***(Re)***

(ii) Why do you think average income is an important criterion for development? Explain. ***(Un)***

(iii) Besides size of per capita income, what other property of income is important in comparing two or more societies? ***(Un)***

(iv) Suppose records show that the average income in a country has been increasing over a period of time. From this, can we conclude that all sections of the economy have become better? Illustrate your answer with an example. ***(An)***

(v) From the text, find out the per capita income level of about 10-15 low-income countries as per World Development Reports. ***(Un)***

Case Based-II

Read the information below and answer the questions that follow. ***(An)*(CBSE SQP, 2023)**

For comparing countries, their income is considered to be one of the most important attributes. Countries with higher income are more developed than others with less income. This is based on the understanding that more income means more of all things that human beings need. Whatever people like, and should have, they will be able to get with greater income. So, greater income itself is considered to be one important goal. Now, what is the income of a country? Intuitively, the income of the country is the income of all the residents of the country. This gives us the total income of the country. However, for comparison between countries, total income is not such an useful measure. Since, countries have different populations, comparing total income will not tell us what an average person is likely to earn. Are people in one country better off than others in a different country? Hence, we compare the average income which is the total income of the country divided by its total population. The average income is also called per capita income. In World Development Reports, brought out by the World Bank, this criterion is used in classifying countries. Countries with per capita income of US$ 49,300 per annum and above in 2019, are called high income or rich countries and those with per capita income of US$ 2500 or less are called low-income countries. The rich countries, excluding countries of. Middle East and certain other small countries are generally called developed countries.

(*i*) Explain the significance of per capita Income.

(*ii*) What are the classifications of countries based on per capita income, and which entity is responsible for determining these classifications?

Case Based-III

Read the Data and answer the following questions:

Some Data Regarding India and its Neighbours For 2019				
Country	**Gross National Income (GNI) per capita (2011 PPP $)**	**Life Expectancy at birth**	**Mean Years of Schooling of People aged 25 and above**	**HDI Rank in the world (2018)**
Sri Lanka	12,707	77	10.6	73
India	**6,681**	**69.7**	**6.5**	**130**
Myanmar	4,961	67.1	5.0	148
Pakistan	5,005	67.3	5.2	154
Nepal	3,457	70.8	5.0	143
Bangladesh	4,976	72.6	6.2	134

Source: Human Development Report, 2020, United Nations Development Programme, New York.

(*i*) Which country has the highest rank than India in the Human Development Report for 2018? ***(Un & Re)***

(*ii*) Which of the Asian countries has the least Human Development Index in the given table? ***(Un & Re)***

(*iii*) Which criterion is common in the inspection of development in the report of the United Nations Development Programme and World Bank? ***(Un)***

(*iv*) ____________ published by UNDP compares countries based on the educational levels of the people, their health status and per capita income. ***(Re)***

(*a*) Public Development Report

(*b*) Human Development Report

(*c*) Government Development Report

(*d*) Women Development Report

Case Based-IV

Read the information below and answer the questions that follow.

"Recent evidence suggests that the groundwater is under serious threat of overuse in many parts of the country. About 300 districts have reported a water level decline of over 4 metres during the past 20 years. Nearly one-third of the country is overusing their groundwater reserves. In another 25 years, 60 percent of the country would be doing the same if the present way of using this resource continues. Groundwater overuse is particularly found in the agriculturally prosperous regions of Punjab and Western U.P., hard rock plateau areas of central and south India, some coastal areas and the rapidly growing urban settlements."

Crude Oil Reserves		
Region/Country	**Reserves (2017) (Thousand Million Barrels)**	**Number of Years Reserves will last**
Middle East	808	70
United States of America	50	10.5
World	1697	50.2

Source: BP Statistical Review of World Energy, June 2018, P1.2

The table gives an estimate of reserves of crude oil (column 1). More importantly, it also tells us for how many years the stock of crude oil will last if people continue to extract it at the present rate. The reserves would last only 50 years more. This is for the world as a whole. However, different countries face different situations. Countries like India depend on importing oil from abroad because they do not have enough stocks of their own. If prices of oil increase this becomes a burden for everyone. There are countries like the USA which have low reserves and hence want to secure oil through military or economic power.

(*i*) Which of the following is not the reason for the overuse of groundwater? ***(An)***

(*a*) The ever-increasing population and the resultant higher demand for and unequal access to water.

(*b*) Water supplies are being over exploited to increase irrigated regions

(*c*) Dry season cultivation in order to promote increased demand for food

(*d*) Non-Renewable resources are those which will get unexhausted after a few years of use.

(*ii*) What do you mean by groundwater? ***(Un)***

(*a*) Groundwater is the water under the surface of the earth.

(*b*) Groundwater is the water over the surface of the earth.

(*c*) Groundwater is the water Upper the surface of the earth.

(*d*) Groundwater is the water behind the surface of the earth.

(iii) Which of the following is the importance of crude oil for the development process in the country? ***(Un & An)***

(*a*) Crude oil contributes 97% of the energy for transport such as cars, trains, and airplanes.

(*b*) Crude oil is necessary as without it no automobiles, industries, etc run.

(*c*) It is the most important raw material of the industrialized nations.

(*d*) All of the above

(iv) What percentage of India is currently overusing groundwater reserves? ***(An)***

(*a*) 10% (*b*) 25%

(*c*) 33% (*d*) 50%

Case Based-V

Read the following paragraph and answer the questions.

Human Development Report 2023-24

Drawing from the latest Human Development Report (2023-24) titled "Breaking the Gridlock: Reimagining Cooperation in a Polarized World," India's progress is evident with an improvement in its Human Development Index (HDI) value to 0.644 in 2022. This places the nation at rank 134 out of 193 countries. The report underscores the advancements across various HDI indicators for India, such as a rise in life expectancy from 67.2 to 67.7 years, an increase in expected years of schooling to 12.6, and a boost in Gross National Income (GNI) per capita from \$6,542 to \$6,951.

The 2023-2024 HDR builds on the 2021–2022 Human Development Report findings

Indicator	Value in 2021	Value in 2022	Change
Human Development Index (HDI)	–	0.644	Improvement
Rank among countries	–	134/193	–
Life Expectancy at Birth (years)	67.2	67.7	Increased by 0.5 years
Expected Years of Schooling	–	12.6	–
Mean Years of Schooling	–	6.57	–
Gross National Income (GNI) per capita (USD PPP)	\$6,542	\$6,951	Increased by \$409

Despite global HDI reaching record highs, disparities remain, with rich countries making robust recoveries, while half of the world's poorest have not yet regained their pre-crisis HDI levels. This illustrates a divided recovery, highlighting the urgency to address this through collective global action. The HDR emphasizes that India, like the Asia-Pacific region, has stood out for human development progress since 1990, yet it faces the challenge of significant gender gaps in labor force participation and other inequalities that need focused attention to achieve a more equitable future (UNDP) (HDR.)(UNDP).

Source: https://www.undp.org/

(i) What was India's Human Development Index (HDI) value in the 2023-24 report? ***(Un)***

(ii) How much did India's Gross National Income (GNI) per capita increase according to the 2023-24 report? ***(Ap)***

(iii) Discuss the significance of the progress in India's HDI value in relation to global disparities highlighted in the 2023-24 Human Development Report. Evaluating. ***(Ev)***

Case Based-VI

Read the source given below and answer the questions that follow: (CBSE SQP, 2024)

HUMAN DEVELOPMENT REPORT

Once it is realised that even though the level of income is important, yet it is an inadequate measure of the level of development, we begin to think of other criterion. There could be a long list of such criterion but then it would not be so useful. What we need is a small number of the most important things. Health and education indicators, such as the ones we used in comparison of Kerala and Punjab, are among them. Over the past decade or so, health and education indicators have come to be widely used along with income as a measure of development. For instance, Human Development Report published by UNDP compares countries based on the educational levels of the people, their health status and per capita income. It would be interesting to look at certain relevant data regarding India and its neighbours from Human Development Report 2006.

(i) On what basis the UNDP compares countries on Human Development? ***(An)***

(ii) Explain Human development briefly. ***(Un)***

(iii) Mention other aspects that should be considered in measuring human development. ***(Un)***

ANSWER KEYS

Multiple Choice Questions

1. (*d*)	**2.** (*a*)	**3.** (*b*)	**4.** (*d*)	**5.** (*c*)	**6.** (*b*)	**7.** (*d*)	**8.** (*b*)	**9.** (*b*)	**10.** (*b*)
11. (*b*)	**12.** (*b*)	**13.** (*c*)	**14.** (*c*)	**15.** (*c*)	**16.** (*b*)	**17.** (*a*)	**18.** (*a*)	**19.** (*d*)	**20.** (*b*)
21. (*c*)	**22.** (*b*)								

Assertion and Reason

1. (*d*)	**2.** (*a*)	**3.** (*a*)	**4.** (*b*)	**5.** (*a*)	**6.** (*c*)

Case Based Questions

Case Based-III

(iv) (*b*)

Case Based-IV

(i) (*d*) ***(ii)*** (*a*) ***(iii)*** (*d*) ***(iv)*** (*c*)

HINTS & EXPLANATIONS

Multiple Choice Questions

1. (*d*) Earning an income helps in achieving financial security, accumulating wealth, and fulfilling personal goals.

2. (*a*) The uniform height of the chairs in Country-A suggests an equal standing for all, symbolizing equal wealth distribution. In contrast, Country-B's varied chair heights suggest disparities in wealth, indicative of economic inequality.

3. (*b*) Tribals and Industrialists

4. (*d*) Japan has a bigger population than Germany

5. (*c*) Respect for women leads to more sharing of housework and greater acceptance of women working outside

6. (*b*) ₹12,000

Given,

Income of 3 Families = ₹6,000, ₹8,000, ₹14,000

The per capita income is 10,000

Per Capita Income = Total Income/Number of families.

Let 4 Families be W, X, Y, Z

10,000 = W + X + Y + Z / 4

Calculate the total income:

Total income = Average per capita income × Number of families

Total income = 10,000 × 4 = 40,000

10,000 = 6,000 + 8,000, 14,000 + Z

40,000 = 28,000 + Z

Z = ₹12,000

Therefore, the Income of the 4th Family is ₹12,000.

7. (*d*) It has health care and education for all.

8. (*b*) Present generation fulfills its needs while considering the needs of the future generations as well.

9. (*b*) Environmental protection is the most important factor for sustainable development because it ensures that resources are used in a way that does not harm the environment, which is essential for long-term economic and social development.

10. (*b*) Improving literacy rates and healthcare facilities directly enhances education and health, which are crucial components of human development and significantly impact overall well-being and quality of life.

11. (*b*) The illiteracy rate for all age groups, including young and old, was 52% for rural males and 19% for rural females. However, it is not just that these many adults could not attend school but that there are 35.5% who are currently not in school.

12. (*b*) United Nations Development Programme (UNDP) is a united nations agency that studies and looks after developing member countries by holding annual discussions and programmes.

13. (*c*) Human Development Report Published by UNDP compares countries based on the educational levels of the people, their health status and per capita income. It would be interesting to look at certain relevant data regarding India and its neighbours from Human Development Report 2020.

14. (*c*) A- Arun-(ii), B- Balraj-(iii), C- Chetan-(i), D- Deepika-(iv)

15. (*c*) The facilities provided by the government that can be used collectively are called public facilities. E.g. schools, colleges, healthcare, public transport, electricity, sanitation, safe drinking water, etc.

16. (*b*) Literacy Rate measures the proportion of literate population in the 7-and-above age group. The literacy rate of Kerala in 2011 was 94%.

17. (*a*) Both statements are true.

18. (*a*) Infant Mortality Rate (IMR)

19. (*d*) ₹ 6000

Average per capita income of four families = 5000

Total Income of three families = 4000 + 7000 + 3000 = 14000

$$\text{Per Capita Income} = \frac{\text{Total Income}}{\text{Total Population}}$$

$$5000 = 14000 + \frac{X}{4}$$

$$20{,}000 = 14000 - X$$

$$X = 20000 - 14000 = 6000$$

20. (*b*) Sri Lanka

Some Data Regarding India and its Neighbours For 2019				
Country	**Gross National Income (GNI) per capita (2011 PPP $)**	**Life Expectancy at birth**	**Mean Years of Schooling of People aged 25 and above**	**HDI Rank in the world (2018)**
Sri Lanka	12,707	77	10.6	73
India	**6,681**	**69.7**	**6.5**	**130**
Myanmar	4,961	67.1	5.0	148
Pakistan	5,005	67.3	5.2	154
Nepal	3,457	70.8	5.0	143
Bangladesh	4,976	72.6	6.2	134

Source: Human Development Report, 2020, United Nations Development Programme, New York.

21. (*c*) Haryana, Bihar, Kerala, Kerala.

22. (*b*) A-(*ii*), B-(*iii*), C-(*iv*), D-(*i*)

Assertion and Reason

1. (*d*) We compare the average income that is unevenly distributed income divided by its total population and not half of its population. However, Average income is also known as Per Capita income. Therefore, the reason is true.

2. (*a*) Both Assertion and Reason are true, and Reason is the correct explanation of Assertion.

3. (*a*) Both Assertion and Reason are true, and Reason is the correct explanation of Assertion.

4. (*b*) Different people may have different developmental goals because the idea of development is different for different groups of people and the capitalist approach to Development is harmful to poor sections of the society as it makes the rich richer and the poor poorer.

5. (*a*) Higher average income is not the only indicator of human development in a country. Other factors like level of literacy rate, health facilities and public facilities are also equally important.

6. (*c*) Net Attendance Ratio is the total number of children of age group 14 and 15 years attending school as a percentage of total number of children in the same age group. If the students were going to other states for higher education, the total students available in the state would go down and the net attendance ratio would not be so low. The low net attendance ratio is indicative of students dropping out of elementary school.

Subjective Questions

Very Short Answer Type Questions

1. "In this case of Amartya Sen's concept of 'Development as Freedom,' the large dam-building project raises critical issues:" **(Any Two)**

(*i*) Development for the government and for the people, destruction for the tribal minorities

(*ii*) Judiciary should intervene in matters of conflict between the government and the people.

(*iii*) Effects of dam-building projects on tribals

2. Kerala has a low Infant Mortality Rate because it has good conditions of basic health and educational facilities. *(1 M)*

3. It is a simple calculation using a person's height and weight.

$$\text{The formula is BMI} = \frac{\text{Weight (in kilogram)}}{(\text{Height in meter})^2}$$

Where kg is a person's weight in kilograms and m^2 is their height in metres squared. *(2 M)*

OR

Riya's low BMI may result from inadequate nutrition, possibly due to skipping meals or a diet low in essential nutrients. Arjun's high BMI could be due to excessive calorie intake, lack of physical activity, or unhealthy eating habits. *(2 M)*

4. The average income is the total income of the country divided by its total population. The average income is also called per capita income. *(2 M)*

5. $\text{Per Capita Income or Average Income} = \frac{\text{Total Income}}{\text{Total Population}}$. *(2 M)*

$$= \frac{[8{,}000 + 10{,}000 + 12{,}000 + A]}{4} = 10{,}000$$

$$= 10{,}000 \times 4 = [8{,}000 + 10{,}000 + 12{,}000 + A]$$

$$A = 40{,}000 - 30{,}000$$

$$A = ₹10{,}000$$

6.

4. A rural woman from a landowning family	D. Regular job and high wages to increase her income.

(1 M)

7. The goals of development other than income are: **(Any 2)** *(1 M)*

- Education
- Health
- Security
- Respect
- Equal treatment
- Freedom
- Improvement in standard of living

The development goals for landless rural labourers are:

More days of work and better wages, the best school to provide quality education to their children and no social discrimination and they too can become leaders in the village. *(1 M)*

8. Different people have different developmental goals because people come from different backgrounds and have different dreams and aspirations. *(2 M)*

9. Sustainable Development refers to the process of economic development which aims at maintaining the quality of life of both the present and future generations without harming natural resources and the environment. *(1½ M)*

Examples: Groundwater in India, Exhaustion of Natural Resources. *(½ M)*

Short Answer Type Questions

1. (*i*) Shyam, to enhance your energy for cricket, consider these three healthful habits:

(*a*) **Balanced Diet:** Shyam should include more fruits, vegetables, lean proteins, and whole grains in his meals. Reducing intake of sugary drinks and junk food can help manage weight and boost energy levels. *(1 M)*

(*b*) **Regular Exercise:** Incorporating at least 30 minutes of physical activity like brisk walking or cycling daily, apart from cricket practice, can enhance stamina and maintain BMI. *(1 M)*

(*c*) **Adequate Sleep:** Ensuring 7-9 hours of sleep nightly aids in recovery, metabolism regulation, and maintaining a healthy weight, vital for active teenagers. *(1 M)*

OR

(*ii*) In our club, let's explore the HDI's three pillars that shape a nation's progress:

(*a*) **Life Expectancy:** Reflects the overall health status of a population; longer life expectancy indicates better access to healthcare. *(1 M)*

(*b*) **Education Level:** Measured by the average years of schooling, it represents the intellectual wealth of a nation, influencing job prospects and economic growth. *(1 M)*

(*c*) **Standard of Living:** Assessed by GNI per capita, it evaluates economic stability and the average individual's capacity to access goods and services essential for a decent living. *(1 M)*

2. Yes, Development definitely leads to destructive when it comes to the wrong usage of resources

Agree **(Any-2)**

(*i*) Present type and levels of development being unsustainable.

(*ii*) Overexploitation of resources.

(*iii*) Destruction of habitat

(*iv*) Air, land and water pollution *(2 M)*

OR

Disagree **(Any-2)**

(*i*) Development can be earth-conscious

(*ii*) Sustainable development

(*iii*) Alternate energy sources

(*iv*) Reducing carbon footprint *(2 M)*

3. The three indicators of HDI 2004 on the basis of which Sri Lanka is better than India are:

(*i*) The Expected life of a person at birth, which is called life Expectancy at birth is higher in Sri Lanka than in India. *(1 M)*

(*ii*) The Per Capita Income of Sri Lanka is higher than India. *(1 M)*

(*iii*) The literacy ratio, that is Enrolment ratio in all levels of Schools in Sri Lanka is comparatively better than in India. Therefore, Sri Lanka is better than India in terms of HDI. *(1 M)*

4. Three public facilities necessary for development are:

(*i*) **Healthcare:** Access to hospitals and clinics improves survival rates and overall health, contributing to human wealth. *(1 M)*

(*ii*) **Education:** Schools help the population gain knowledge and skills for personal and economic growth. *(1 M)*

(*iii*) **Clean Water and Sanitation:** These are essential for preventing disease and maintaining a healthy workforce. *(1 M)*

5. To assess State B's development beyond income, consider the following:

(*i*) **Health Improvement:** Better public facilities such as healthcare improve the general health of the population, leading to longer lifespans and less disease burden. *(1 M)*

(*ii*) **Enhanced Quality of Life:** High literacy rates contribute to a more informed society, where people can make educated decisions about personal and community well-being. *(1 M)*

(*iii*) **Social Equality:** Excellent public services and education contribute to leveling the playing field, reducing disparities and promoting social mobility. *(1 M)*

6.
- UNDP (United Nations Development Programme) Focuses on life expectancy, education, and income to form the Human Development Index (HDI). *(1 M)*
- The World Bank uses primarily **per capita income to classify** countries into different income categories. *(1 M)*

In difference, UNDP's approach is broader, incorporating health and education alongside income, whereas the World Bank highlights economic output *(1 M)*

7. Ravi and Meena have different developmental goals based on their socioeconomic backgrounds. The following reasons are:

(*i*) **Ravi**, a young software developer, aspires to global opportunities, better income, and professional growth. *(1 M)*

(*ii*) **Meena**, a rural farmer, desires improved irrigation, stable markets, and better agricultural support. *(1 M)*

(*iii*) **These goals influence their expectations from government policies:** Ravi seeks tech advancement and global ties, while Meena prioritizes rural infrastructure and agricultural stability. *(1 M)*

8. The Human Development Report provides a comprehensive measure of development through key dimensions:

(*i*) **Per Capita Income:** Estimates the economic prosperity and average income of individuals, reflecting the nation's wealth. *(1 M)*

(*ii*) **Education Indicators:** Education is an important indicator of human development as it helps individuals acquire knowledge and skills to participate in the economy and society. Education can be measured by literacy rates, enrollment rates, and the number of years of schooling. *(1 M)*

(*iii*) **Health Indicators:** Health is another key indicator of human development. It is not only the absence of illness but also includes physical, mental, and social well-being. Health can be measured by life expectancy, infant mortality rates, and access to basic healthcare services. *(1 M)*

Long Answer Type Questions

1. Some of the examples of environmental degradation in our surroundings include: *(Each Point Carries 1 M)*

(*i*) Increase in air pollution due to smoke emissions from factories and vehicles.

(*ii*) Increase in water pollution due to shops and small factories in residential areas.

(*iii*) Noise pollution due to the use of loudspeakers at night and blowing of horns unnecessarily on the roads by different vehicles.

(*iv*) No proper disposal of waste and provision of dustbins in the streets or roadsides.

(*v*) Some people urinate in the open on the roadside due to a lack of public conveniences.

2. (*a*) Calculate the Per Capita Income

$$\text{Per Capita Income} = \frac{\text{Total Income}}{\text{Total Population}}$$

$$\text{Country - A} = \frac{2{,}000 + 2{,}400 + 2{,}400 + 2{,}700}{4} = 2{,}375$$

$$\text{Country - B} = \frac{700 + 40{,}000 + 750 + 710}{4} = 10{,}540$$

Therefore,

Country A = 2,375

Country B = 10,540 *(2 M)*

(*b*) Country B (10,540) has a higher Per Capita Income. *(1 M)*

(*c*) Country A has a more equitable distribution of Income. *(1 M)*

(*d*) No, because despite having a high per capita income, country B has a wide gap between the rich Citizen II and the rest of the citizens. *(1 M)*

3. **Per Capita Income** or **Average Income** is the main criterion used by the World Bank in classifying different countries. *(1 M)*

Limitations of this criterion:

(*i*) It does not tell us about how this average income is distributed among the people in the individual countries. *(1 M)*

(*ii*) Two countries with the same per capita income might be very different in income distribution. *(1 M)*

(*iii*) One might have equitable distribution of income while the other might have great disparities between the rich and the poor. *(1 M)*

4. In a discussion about the development status of Haryana, Kerala, and Bihar, considering factors like infant mortality rate, literacy rate, and net attendance ratio:

(*i*) **Infant Mortality Rate (IMR):** Kerala has the lowest IMR, indicating better health facilities. Lower IMR in Kerala reflects superior healthcare, while higher IMR in Haryana and Bihar suggests health services need improvement. *(1 M)*

(*ii*) **Literacy Rate:** Kerala's literacy rate is highest, suggesting better education policies. High literacy in Kerala aligns with strong education systems; lower rates in Haryana and Bihar point to areas for educational development. *(1 M)*

(*iii*) **Net Attendance Ratio:** Kerala also leads in secondary stage attendance, while Bihar lags. Kerala's higher attendance indicates successful education retention, determining Bihar's need for educational employment initiatives. *(1 M)*

(*iv*) **Overall Development:**

(*a*) **Conclusion:** Kerala excels in both health and education, Haryana has moderate success, and Bihar requires significant advancement in these sectors. *(1 M)*

(*b*) **Implications:** These indicators influence state policies on health and education, directing focus on infrastructure, accessibility, and quality of services. *(1 M)*

OR

In Greenwald, the high average income does not equate to development because:

(*i*) **Health Services:** Poor health services could lead to lower life expectancy and high disease rates, affecting productivity and well-being. *(1 M)*

(*ii*) **Education Standards:** Low educational standards can stunt personal and economic growth, limiting opportunities for innovation and skilled workforces. *(1 M)*

(*iii*) **Significance:** Improving health and education can lead to a more equitable, sustainable, and diverse economy, offering long-term benefits beyond income. *(1 M)* (*iv*) **Health Policy:** The government could prioritize healthcare funding, establish universal health coverage, and invest in preventive care and health education. *(1 M)*

(*v*) **Education Policy:** Policies should aim at enhancing educational infrastructure, increasing school enrollment, and improving the quality of education through teacher training and curriculum development. *(1 M)*

Case Based Questions

Case Based-I

(*i*) Three examples of using the average for comparing situations are as follows: *(1 M)*

(*a*) **Income of a country:** Average income (per capita income) is used to compare different countries.

(*b*) **Literacy rate:** Average literacy rate helps compare education levels in different states.

(*c*) **Infant mortality rate:** The average number of babies dying before age one helps compare healthcare facilities.

(*ii*) Average income (per capita income) is used to compare how well-off people are in different countries. Higher average income usually means better living standards. However, it does not show income distribution, meaning some people could be very rich while others are very poor. *(1 M)*

(*iii*) Income distribution is important. A country where a few people are rich and most are poor is not truly developed. For example, In Country A, income is fairly distributed, but in Country B, one person is very rich, and the rest are poor. *(1 M)*

(*iv*) No, because, Income may not be equally distributed. Some people may earn a lot while others remain poor. In Country B, the average income is high because one person earns ₹48,000, but the rest earn only ₹500. So, even if average income increases, some people may still struggle to get basic needs. *(1 M)*

(*v*) The per capita income level of middle-income countries as per the World Development Reports 2019 was between US $ 6700 per annum. Those with per capita income of US $ 2500 or less are called low-income countries. Typically low-income countries have an annual per capita income of around $1000 or less. *(1 M)*

Case Based-II

(*i*) The Per capita income enables comparisons between countries and provides insights into the relative economic performance and living standards across different nations. Per capita income also serves as an important indicator of the standard of living in a country. *(2 M)*

(*ii*) The courtiers are classified into **high income** or **rich countries** and **low income countries** based on their per capita Income. If it is **US $ 49,300** per annum they will be classified as a rich country and if the per capita income is **US $ 2500** per annum it will be called a **poor country**. The World Bank determines this classification. *(2 M)*

Case Based-III

(*i*) Sri Lanka is at the highest rank 73 while India is at rank 130. *(1 M)*

(*ii*) Bangladesh is at rank 134 according to the list of 2018. *(1 M)*

(*iii*) Per Capita Income *(1 M)*

(*iv*) (*b*) Human Development Report. *(1 M)*

Case Based-IV

(*i*) (*d*) Non-Renewable resources are those which will get exhausted after a few years of use. *(1 M)*

(*ii*) (*a*) Groundwater is the water under the surface of the earth. In the form of groundwater, almost 22% of the water is below the surface of the land. Groundwater is significant as it is used in rural and urban areas for the supply of water. *(1 M)*

(*iii*) (*d*) All of the above *(1 M)*

- Crude oil plays a crucial role in development because most of the petroleum and flammable gasses extracted from crude oil and petroleum products come under basic requirements.
- Crude oil is necessary as without it no automobiles, industries, etc run. It is the most important raw material of the industrialized nations. It can generate heat, drive machinery, and fuel vehicles and airplanes.
- Every year 18 million tonnes of crude oil are processed into synthetic materials.
- Oil within our materials:40% of all textiles contain oil; For functional clothing, this may be as much as 100%. The world consumes almost 14% billion liters of oil each day.

(*iv*) (*c*) It states that one-third (33%) of the country is already overusing groundwater reserves. If this continues, 60% of India will face groundwater depletion in the next 25 years. *(1 M)*

Case Based-V

(*i*) India's HDI value was 0.644 in 2022. *(1 M)*

(*ii*) India's GNI per capita increased from $6,542 to $6,951. *(1 M)*

(*iii*) India's HDI improvements reflect national progress, but global disparities continue as rich countries recover faster post-crisis, highlighting the need for action to address inequalities and support the lagging half of the world's poorest countries. *(2 M)*

Case Based-VI

(*i*) Human Development Report published by UNDP compares countries based on the educational levels of the people, their health status and per capita income. *(1 M)*

(*ii*) Human development is a process of enhancing the range of people's choices, increasing their opportunities for education, health care, income, and empowerment. It also covers the full range of human choices from a sound physical environment to economic, political, and social freedom. *(Any other relevant points)* *(2 M)*

(*iii*) Yes, there other aspects as well like- Life expectancy, access to public facilities such as water, sanitation, roads, electricity etc. *(1 M)*

❑❑❑

SECTORS OF INDIAN ECONOMY

2

"The Indian economy is diversified across three main sectors. The primary sector involves agriculture, the Secondary sector includes manufacturing, and the Tertiary sector covers services. Each sector plays a crucial role in economic development, employment, and GDP contribution."

SYLLABUS & WEIGHTAGE

List of Concept Names	Years					
	2020	2021	2022	2023	2024	2025
Sectors of Economic Activities	0	Exam not conducted	1 Q (2 M)	1 Q (1 M)	1 Q (1 M)	
Comparing the three Sectors (How do we count the various goods and services and know the total production in each sector?, Historical Change in Sectors)	2 Q (1 M + 3 M)		0	0	1 Q (1 M)	
Primary, Secondary and Tertiary Sectors in India (Rising Importance of the Tertiary Sector in Production, Where are most of the people employed?, How to Create More Employment?)	2 Q (1 M + 5 M)		0	3 Q (1 M + 2 M + 3 M)	1 Q (3 M)	1Q (5 M)
Division of Sectors as Organised and Unorganised (How to Protect Workers in the Unorganised Sector?)	0		0	1 Q (3 M)	0	1Q (4 M)
In Terms of ownership: Public and Private Sector	0		0	0	0	3Q (1 M+1M+5M)

CONCEPT MAP

To Access One Shot Revision Video Scan This QR Code

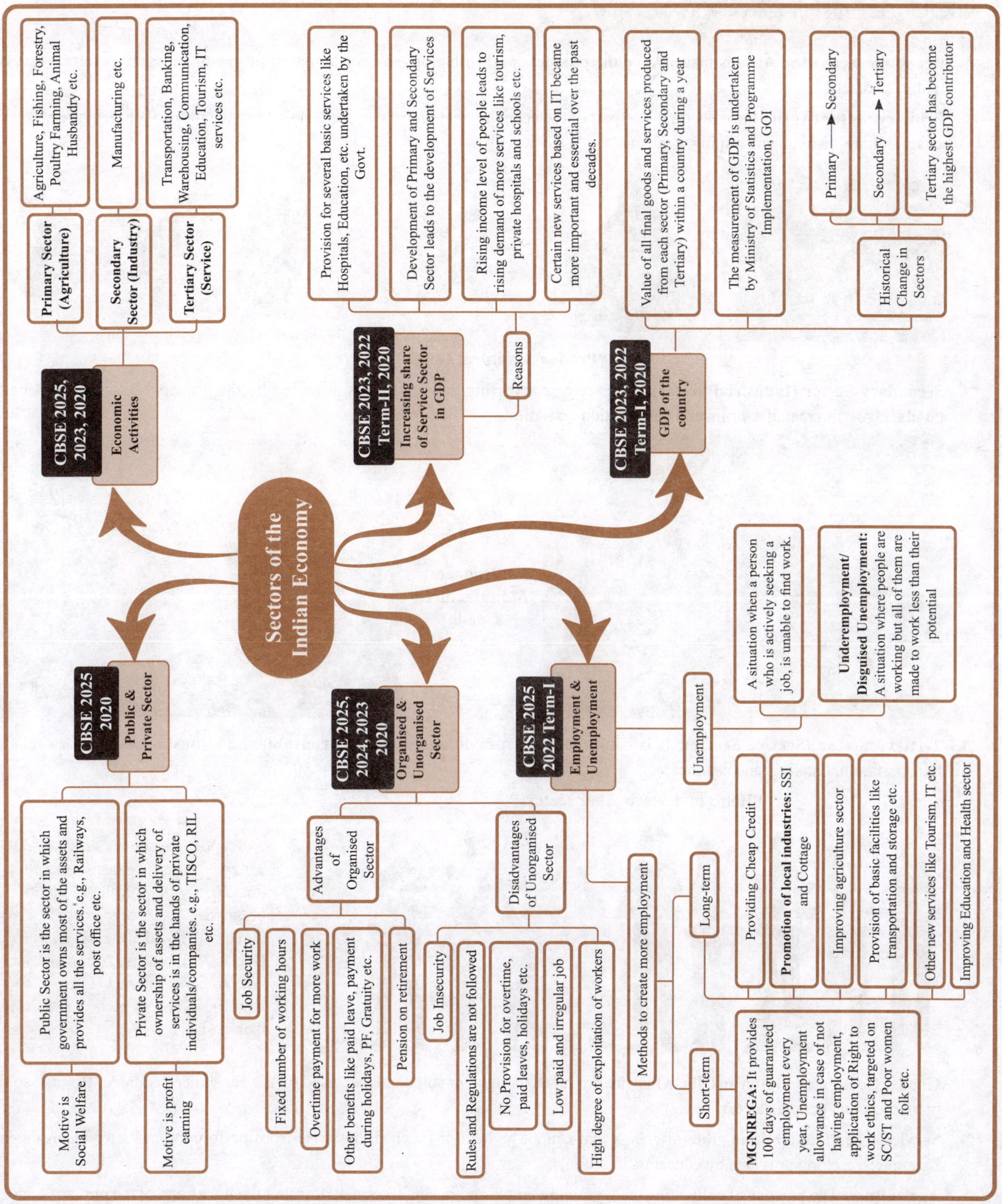

1 SECTORS OF ECONOMIC ACTIVITIES

NCERT Definitions *(Commonly asked in 1 mark)*

- **Economic Activities:** Actions that involve the production, distribution, and consumption of **goods and services** at all levels within a society.
- **Primary Sector (Agriculture Sector):** The part of the economy that draws **raw materials** from the **natural environment**, such as agriculture, fishing, and mining, coal, etc.

"Produces Natural Goods"

- **Secondary Sector (Industrial Sector):** This sector **converting raw materials** produced by the primary sector into **finished goods**, involving manufacturing and construction activities.

"Produces Manufactured Goods"

- **Tertiary Sector (Service Sector):** It is concerned with **providing services** to **consumers** and **businesses**, such as retail, transportation, banking, and healthcare.

"Helps to develop other sectors"

Note: Service sector also includes some essential services that may not directly help in the production of goods. For example: Teachers, Doctors, Washermen, Barbers, Cobblers, Lawyers, Administrator, Accountant, Internet Cafe, ATM Booths, Call Centers, Software Companies etc.

- **Goods:** Goods are **tangible products** that are produced, bought, or sold, and then used by the consumer. Example: Biscuits sold in markets that people can eat.
- **Services:** Services are **intangible offerings** that cannot be held or touched, but arise from performing tasks for a consumer. Example: Teaching provided by educators in schools.
- **Agriculture:** The practice of cultivating land, growing crops, and raising livestock, forming the **backbone** of the primary sector.

Classification

Economic Activity Classify into Three Sectors

On the basis of nature

- **Primary Sector (Agriculture Sector):** Natural Resources → Raw Materials (e.g., Cotton)
- **Secondary Sector (Industrial Sector):** Raw Materials → Manufactured Goods (e.g., Textiles)
- **Tertiary Sector (Service Sector):** Supports Production & Consumption (e.g., Banking Services), Provides Non-Goods-Based Services (e.g., IT Services)

Difference Between

Aspect	Primary (Agriculture) Sector	Secondary (Industrial) Sector	Tertiary (Service) Sector
Definition	Activities related to production of goods by exploiting natural resources	Activities in which natural products are changed into other forms through ways of manufacturing.	Activities that help in the development of the primary and secondary sectors.
Examples	Cultivating cotton, dairy farming, fishing, forestry.	Spinning yarn from cotton, making sugar from sugarcane, manufacturing bricks for construction.	Transporting goods, banking, communication, personal services like teaching and legal advice, IT services.
Products/Services	Natural products like cotton, milk, minerals, ores.	Manufactured goods like cloth, sugar, houses.	Services that help in development, like education, healthcare, and technology.

Real Life Application Based Questions

Read the following source carefully and answer the questions that follows:

- **Primary Sector:** In the Amul industry, the journey begins with cows producing milk, which is the essential **raw material** in this stage.

- **Secondary Sector:** The milk is then moved to factories, marking the beginning of the secondary sector. Here, it is processed and turned into various dairy products such as cheese, butter, and ice cream. This stage highlights the importance of the **manufacturing process**, as each product must meet high standards of quality and safety.

- **Tertiary Sector:** Finally, the tertiary sector involves marketing and distributing these products through a widespread network to **retailers** and **consumers**. This sector also includes **customer services**, ensuring consumer satisfaction. This stage completes the cycle from raw material to consumer product, showing the importance of each phase in **delivering** Amul's dairy products to the market.

1. **In which sector is cow milk classified in the Amul industry example?**

Ans. **Cow milk** is classified in the **Primary Sector** in the Amul industry example.

2. **What is the main activity in the tertiary sector according to the Amul example?**

Ans. The main activity in the tertiary sector, as per the Amul example, **is marketing** and **distributing dairy products**.

3. **Explain how the secondary sector contributes to the Amul industry, using the case study.**

Ans. In the Amul industry, the secondary sector takes **raw milk** and **processes** it **into various dairy products** like cheese, butter, and ice cream. This transformation underlines the sector's role in adding value and ensuring quality and safety standards.

Mnemonics

- "**TIP**" can also be used to remember three sectors of economic activities

T → **Tertiary sector (Service):** Trade, Transport, etc.

I → **Industrial sector (Secondary):** Manufacturing, Mining, Construction

P → **Primary sector (Agriculture):** Fishing, Forestry, etc.

Scan Me for Detailed Explanations

COMPETENCY BASED SOLVED EXAMPLES

Multiple Choice Questions

(1 M)

1. **Which one of the following pairs is correctly matched?** ***(Ev)*(CBSE, 2023)**

(*a*) Primary Sector - Flower Cultivator
(*b*) Secondary Sector - Milk Vendor
(*c*) Tertiary Sector - Fisherman
(*d*) Manufacturing Sector - Gardener

2. **Choose the incorrect pair from the following:** ***(Ev)*(CBSE, 2020)**

(*a*) Mailman - Tertiary sector
(*b*) Fisherman - Primary sector
(*c*) Carpenter - Primary sector
(*d*) Banker - Tertiary sector

3. **Which of the following profession belongs to the Tertiary Sector of economy?** ***(Re)*(CBSE, 2019)**

(*a*) Fisherman (*b*) Farmer
(*c*) Woodcutter (*d*) Teacher

4. **Which of the following shows an instance of dependence on the tertiary sector?** ***(Ap)*(CFPQ, 2024)**

(*a*) An ice cream producer buys milk from a dairy farmer.
(*b*) A farmer needs a savings account to deposit her money.
(*c*) An oil and gas company need big machines to drill the earth's surface.
(*d*) An educational organisation buys stationery from a local cottage industry directly.

5. **Which of the following is moving from primary to the tertiary sector?** ***(An)*(CFPQ, 2024)**

(*a*) A farmer is relocating to the city and joins a food delivery agency.
(*b*) A miner quits his job and starts working at an iron and steel factory.
(*c*) A taxi driver goes back to his village and opens his own grocery shop.
(*d*) A cattle farmer begins making milk products and selling them in the village

6. **A farmer wishes to expand his crop sales beyond his local village to a regional market. Analyze and select how the tertiary sector can play a crucial role in assisting this farmer in achieving his goals and thus enhance the overall agricultural output.** ***(Ap, An)***

(*a*) By providing educational services only
(*b*) By supplying raw materials used in manufacturing
(*c*) By offering support services like banking, transport, and communication
(*d*) By directly producing consumer goods

7. **Imagine you are the manager of a cotton fabric factory facing a major challenge. Due to a sudden transport strike, the delivery of essential raw materials to your factory has been halted. As a result, production is at risk of being significantly delayed or stopped. This scenario exemplifies a disruption in the link between which two sectors?** ***(Ap)***

(*a*) Primary and Secondary Sectors
(*b*) Secondary and Tertiary Sectors
(*c*) Tertiary and Quaternary Sectors
(*d*) Primary and Tertiary Sectors

8. Identify the sector shown in this picture? ***(Re)***

(*a*) Primary sector (*b*) Secondary sector
(*c*) Tertiary sector (*d*) None of these

9. Look at the given picture. The work being done in the picture comes under which one of the following economic sectors? ***(An)* (CBSE, 2024)**

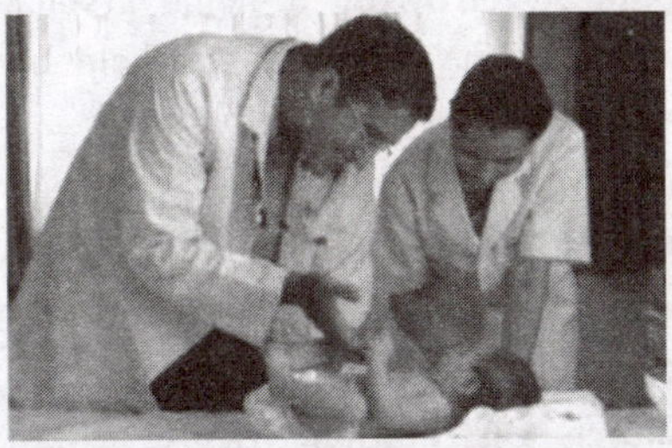

(*a*) Primary (*b*) Secondary
(*c*) Tertiary (*d*) Quaternary

10. If there is a disruption by transporters and lorries refuse to transport vegetables, milk, etc. from rural areas to urban areas, food will become scarce in urban areas, whereas farmers will be unable to sell their products. Which of the following sectors will be affected due to this situation stated above? ***(Ev)*(CBSE SQP, 2023)**

(*a*) Primary and Secondary
(*b*) Secondary and Tertiary
(*c*) Tertiary, Primary and Secondary
(*d*) Tertiary and Primary.

Assertion and Reason

(1 M)

Direction: The following questions consist of two statements – Assertion (A) and Reason (R). Answer these questions by selecting the appropriate option given below:

(*a*) Both A and R are true, and R is the correct explanation of A.
(*b*) Both A and R are true, but R is not the correct explanation of A.
(*c*) A is true, but R is false
(*d*) A is false, but R is true.

1. **Assertion (A):** An individual who produces flour from wheat is engaged in primary sector.
   Reason (R): When some process of production is used, the product becomes a part of secondary Sector. ***(Ev)***
2. **Assertion (A):** The service sector is the fastest-growing sector in the Indian economy.
   Reason (R): The demand for services such as healthcare, education, and IT has increased due to rising incomes and changing lifestyles. ***(Ev)***
3. **Assertion (A):** When we produce a good by exploiting natural resources, it is an activity of the primary sector
   Reason (R): It forms the base for all other products that we subsequently make. ***(Ev)***

Subjective Questions

Very Short Answer Type Questions (2 M)

1. Give one example each of primary and tertiary economic sectors. ***(Re)*(CBSE, 2019)**

Ans. **Example of Primary Sector:** Agriculture, fishing. *(1 M)*
Examples of Tertiary Sector: Banking, transportation. *(1 M)*

2. Find the odd one out and say why.
Teacher, doctor, vegetable vendor, lawyer ***(An)*(NCERT)**

Ans. Vegetable vendor is the odd one because he works in the primary sector, while teacher, doctor and lawyer provide services and come under tertiary sector. *(2 M)*

Short Answer Type Questions (3 M)

1. Explain the difference between primary, secondary and tertiary sectors using examples other than those mentioned in the text. ***(Un)* (NCERT Intext)**

Ans. *(3 M)*

Sector	Definition	Examples
Primary	Involves extraction and production of natural resources.	Agriculture (farming), fishing, forestry
Secondary	Involves transformation of raw materials into finished goods.	Manufacturing (textile production), construction
Tertiary	Provides services rather than goods. This sector provides services to both the primary and secondary sectors.	Banking, education, IT services

2. Classify the following list of occupations under primary, secondary and tertiary sectors: ***(Ap)*(NCERT Intext)**

- Tailor
- Basket weaver
- Flower cultivator
- Milk vendor
- Fishermen
- Priest
- Courier
- Workers in match factory
- Moneylender
- Gardener
- Potter
- Bee-keeper
- Astronaut
- Call centre employee

Ans.

Primary	Secondary	Tertiary
Flower cultivator	Basket weaver	Tailor
Fishermen	Workers in match factory	Milk vendor
Bee-keeper	Potter	Priest
Gardner		Courier
		Moneylender
		Astronaut
		Call centre employee

(3 M)

3. **Read the following source carefully and answer the questions that follow:** ***(Ap & Ev)*(NCERT Intext)**

Examples of Economic Activities	
Example	**What Does This Show?**
(*a*) Imagine what would happen if farmers refuse to sell sugarcane to a particular sugar mill. The mill will have to shut down.	This is an example of the secondary or industrial sector being dependent on the primary.
(*b*) Imagine what would happen to cotton cultivation if companies decide not to buy from the Indian market and import countries. Indian cotton cultivation will become less profitable and the farmers may even go bankrupt, if they cannot quickly switch to other crops. Cotton prices will fall.	
(*c*) Farmers buy many goods such as tractors, pumpsets, electricity, pesticides and fertilisers. Imagine what would happen if the price of fertilisers or pumpsets go up. Cost of cultivation of the farmers will rise and their profits will be reduced.	
(*d*) People working in industrial and service sectors need food. Imagine what would happen if there is a strike by transporters and lorries refuse to take vegetables, milk, etc. from rural areas. Food will become scarce in urban areas whereas farmers will be unable to sell their products.	

Ans. (*b*) This is an example of the primary sector being dependent upon the secondary sectors. *(1 M)*

(*c*) This is an example of the primary sector being dependent upon the tertiary sectors. *(1 M)*

(*d*) This is an example of the secondary and tertiary sectors being dependent on the primary sectors. *(1 M)*

Long Answer Type Questions (5 M)

1. **Do you think the classification of economic activities into primary, secondary and tertiary is useful? Explain how.** ***(An)* (NCERT)**

Ans. Yes, the classification of economic activities into primary, secondary, and tertiary sectors is useful: **(Any-5)**

- **Organized Growth:** It helps in understanding the structure of the economy and helps in its organized development. *(1 M)*
- **Policy Formulation:** Enables the government to formulate targeted policies for each sector. *(1 M)*
- **Specialization:** Encourages specialization of skills and labour in different sectors. *(1 M)*
- **Resource Distribution:** Helps in efficient resource distribution based on sectoral needs and priorities. *(1 M)*
- **Employment Strategies:** Guides strategies for employment generation and skill development. *(1 M)*
- **Economic Planning:** Facilitates better economic planning and forecasting by analyzing sector-specific data. *(1 M)*

2 COMPARING THE THREE SECTORS

NCERT Definitions *(Commonly asked in 1 mark)*

- **Gross Domestic Product (GDP):** The sum **total** of the **value of all final goods** and **services** produced within the country during a particular year. It is a broad measure of an economy's size.
- **Historical Change in Sectors:** Refers to the **modification** of **economic dominance** from primary, to secondary, and then to the tertiary sector.

Important Concepts

How do we count the various goods and services and know the total production in each sector? By using the method of value added at each stage.

Step 1: Start by determining the value of the product at each stage of production, from raw material to final sale

Step 2: Subtract the cost of raw materials and intermediate goods at each stage to calculate the value added at that stage.

Step 3: Add up the value added at all stages to get the total value of the good or service.

For Example,

To calculate the total value added, follow these steps:

1. **Raw Material Cost (Paper):** ₹10
2. **Value After Printing (Printing Cost Added):** ₹30 (Raw Material ₹10 + ₹20 for printing)
3. **Final Sale Price (Book Price):** ₹50

Calculation:

Stage 1: Value Added = ₹20 (Printing Cost)

Stage 2: Value Added = ₹20 (Selling Price - Value After Printing)

Total Value Added: ₹20 (Stage 1) + ₹20 (Stage 2) = ₹40

Important Facts

01 In India, the mammoth task of **measuring GDP** is undertaken by the central government Ministry of Statistics and Programme Implementation.

02 **GDP of the country** = Goods produced in Primary Sector + Goods produced in Secondary Sector + Goods produced in Tertiary Sector

Note: Only the value of **Final Goods and Services** is added in calculating the **GDP** of the country because the value of final goods already includes the value of all the intermediate goods that are used in making the final goods.

Classification

Goods are of Two Types

Intermediate goods	Final goods
↓	↓
Goods which are used for further production **Or** For Resale	A final good is a final product ready for sale that is used by the consumer to satisfy current wants or needs.

Example: Suppose a farmer grows sugarcane. A sugar factory uses this sugarcane to make sugar. A sweetshop uses this sugar to make sweets which are purchased by consumers

Sugarcane

→

Sugar

⇨

jalebi(Sweets)

Sugarcane and **sugar** are **intermediate goods** as they are used for further production

↓

Jalebi is **final goods** as it is used for consumption

Difference Between

Goods	Services
Tangible products that can be stored or stocked.	Intangible activities that cannot be stored.
Examples: Wheat, Biscuits.	**Examples:** Teaching, Haircutting.
Can be transferred from one person to another.	Cannot be transferred; they are experiential.
Value is added by changing the form or attributes.	Value is added through expertise or performance.
Production and consumption can be separated in time.	Production and consumption often occur simultaneously.

Past Trends	Current Trends
Majority of people are employed in agriculture.	More people are employed in services and industry.
Employment was more manual labor-oriented.	Employment is more diverse, including technology and services.
Less mobility between sectors.	Greater mobility and shifting between sectors.
Employment was dictated by tradition and necessity.	Employment is influenced by education, skill levels, and economic opportunities.
Agricultural sector was the main source of livelihood.	Service sector is becoming the main source of livelihood.

Real Life Application Based Questions

Read the following source carefully and answer the questions that follows:

COVID-19 pandemic has affected different sectors of the economy in different ways. For example, the service sector, which includes industries such as hospitality and tourism, has been hit hard due to travel restrictions and lockdowns.

On the other hand, the healthcare sector has seen a surge in demand for medical supplies and services. Understanding how different sectors are impacted by external factors like pandemics can help policymakers make informed decisions to support those sectors that are most affected.

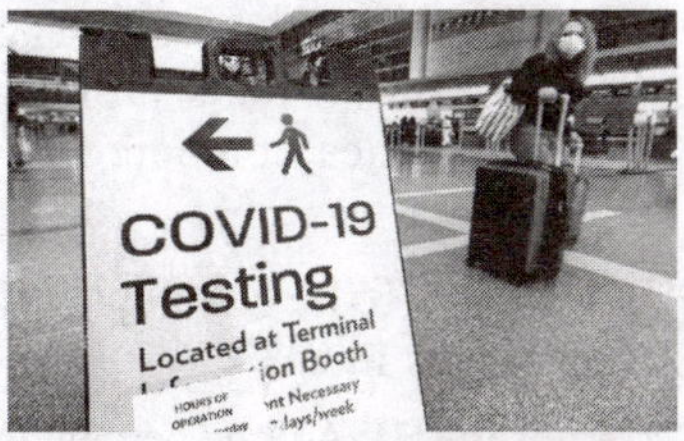

1. Which sector was negatively impacted by travel restrictions and lockdowns during the COVID-19 pandemic?

Ans. The service sector, including hospitality and tourism, was negatively impacted by travel restrictions and lockdowns.

2. Which sector experienced an increase in demand due to the COVID-19 pandemic?

Ans. The healthcare sector experienced an increase in demand for medical supplies and services during the COVID-19 pandemic.

Scan Me for Detailed Explanations

COMPETENCY BASED SOLVED EXAMPLES

Multiple Choice Questions

(1 M)

1. Activities that help in the development of the Primary and Secondary sectors come under which one of the following sectors? ***(Re)*(CBSE, 2022 Term 1)**

(*a*) Primary (*b*) Secondary
(*c*) Tertiary (*d*) Quaternary

2. At the initial stages of development, which one of the following sectors was the most important for economic activity? ***(Re)*(CBSE, 2022 Term 1)**

(*a*) Primary (*b*) Secondary
(*c*) Tertiary (*d*) Quaternary

3. Activities in which natural products are changed into other forms come under which one of the following sectors? ***(Re)*(CBSE, 2022 Term 1)**

(*a*) Primary (*b*) Secondary
(*c*) Tertiary (*d*) Quaternary

4. The products received by exploiting natural resources come under which one of the following section? ***(Re)*(CBSE, 2022 Term 1)**

(*a*) Quaternary
(*b*) Tertiary
(*c*) Secondary
(*d*) Primary

5. GDP is the total value of _________ produced during a particular year. ***(Re)*(NCERT)**

(*a*) all goods and services
(*b*) all final goods and services
(*c*) all intermediate goods and services
(*d*) all intermediate and final goods and services

6. In the village of Econville, a local farmer, Mr. Arjun, grows wheat and sells it to a bakery, Mr. Sweet's Bakery, at ₹20 per kg. The bakery uses this wheat to make delicious biscuits, which are then sold in the local market at ₹80 per packet. Assume that there are no other production costs involved. Select among the following how should this transaction be reflected in the GDP? ***(An)***

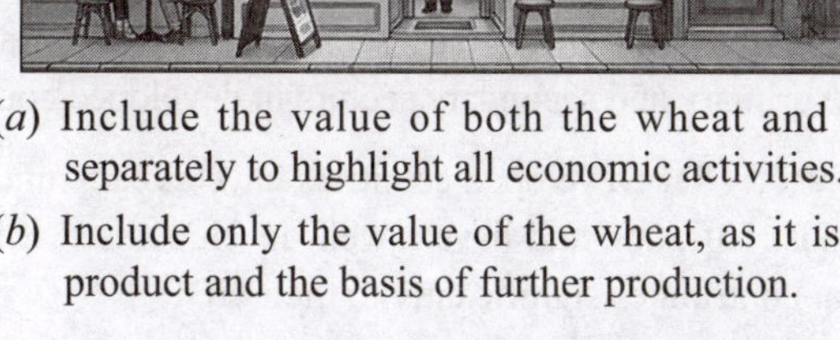

(*a*) Include the value of both the wheat and biscuits separately to highlight all economic activities.

(*b*) Include only the value of the wheat, as it is the raw product and the basis of further production.

(c) Include only the value of biscuits, as it represents the final consumption goods.

(d) Exclude both values, as they do not contribute directly to the village's retail market.

7. Nina is a baker. She uses eggs in her cakes. Will the value of these eggs be included in the calculation of the total domestic product? *(Ap)* **(CFPQ, 2024)**

(a) Yes, because eggs are a final product in themselves.

(b) Yes, because they are included in the primary sector.

(c) No, because they are included in the value of the cakes.

(d) No, because eggs have no value of their own without the cake.

8. Rajesh, who has been successfully managing a large agricultural farm (a primary sector business), decides to venture into the courier service industry (a tertiary sector business). Given his extensive experience in managing farm operations, he is considering which of his existing skills could be beneficial in his new venture. *(An)*

(a) They are not transferable due to sector differences

(b) Skills in resource management and logistics can be applied

(c) Only financial management skills are transferable

(d) Marketing skills are not applicable in the tertiary sector

9. Imagine a small economy where a miller buys grain worth ₹500 to produce flour, which is then sold to a bakery for ₹700. The bakery uses this flour to make bread that is sold to consumers for ₹1000. In calculating the Gross Domestic Product (GDP) of this economy, you observe that an assistant has included the value of grain, flour, and bread separately. what would be the consequence of this method of GDP calculation? *(Ap)*

(a) Overestimation of GDP

(b) Underestimation of GDP

(c) Accurate representation of GDP

(d) No impact on GDP

Assertion and Reason (1 M)

Direction: The following questions consist of two statements – Assertion (A) and Reason (R). Answer these questions by selecting the appropriate option given below:

(a) Both A and R are true, and R is the correct explanation of A.

(b) Both A and R are true, but R is not the correct explanation of A.

(c) A is true, but R is false

(d) A is false, but R is true.

1. **Assertion (A):** The tertiary sector is more important than the primary and secondary sectors in developed countries.

   Reason (R): Developed countries have already undergone industrialisation and have a well-developed service sector that contributes significantly to their GDP. *(An)*

2. **Assertion (A):** The primary sector is the most important sector in developing countries.

   Reason (R): Developing countries have a large population engaged in agriculture, mining, and other primary activities, which contribute significantly to their GDP. *(An)*

3. **Assertion (A):** The tertiary sector provides more employment opportunities than the primary and secondary sectors combined all over the world.

   Reason (R): The service sector is labour-intensive and requires a wide range of skills, leading to more employment opportunities compared to the primary and secondary sectors. *(An)*

4. **Assertion (A):** Agriculture is the primary sector of economic activity in India.

   Reason (R): A large percentage of the population is engaged in agriculture, and it contributes significantly to the country's GDP. *(An)*

5. **Assertion (A):** The Gross Domestic Product (GDP) of a country is the sum of the value of all final goods and services produced in the three sectors within a year.

   Reason (R): GDP is a key indicator of a country's economic health and includes the total production in the primary, secondary, and tertiary sectors. *(An)*

6. **Assertion (A):** To avoid double counting in GDP, only the final goods and services should be considered, not the intermediate goods.

   Reason (R): Counting only final goods and services ensures that the value of intermediate goods, which are used up in producing final goods, is not counted twice. *(An)*

7. **Assertion (A):** Not every good or service that is produced and sold needs to be counted to know the total production in each sector.

   Reason (R): The value of final goods already includes the value of all the intermediate goods. *(An)***(CBSE, 2019)**

Subjective Questions

Very Short Answer Type Questions (2 M)

1. Who is responsible for measuring GDP in India? *(Re)*

Ans. Ministry of Statistics and Programme Implementation, Government of India evaluates GDP in India. *(1 M)*

Short Answer Type Questions (3 M)

1. What does the history of developed countries indicate about the shifts that have taken place between sectors? *(Un)*

Ans. The history of developed countries indicates a significant shift between sectors, highlighting a common progression pattern:

- **Primary (Agriculture) to Secondary (Manufacturing):** Initially, economies are heavily reliant on agriculture. Over time, there's a shift towards manufacturing as countries develop. *(1½ M)*

- **Secondary (Manufacturing) to Tertiary (Services):** As manufacturing efficiency increases, there's a further shift towards service-based economies, where services become the largest sector. Most of the employed people in the developed countries are employed in this sector. *(1½ M)*

2. **"All the services of the 'service sector' are not growing equally well." Evaluate the statement.** ***(An)*****(CBSE, 2020)**

Ans. The statement "All the services of the 'service sector' are not growing equally well" can be evaluated as follows:

- **Growth Variation:** Some service sector areas, like IT, grow rapidly, while smaller services, like local shops, grow slowly. *(1 M)*
- **Skill Demand:** High-tech services expand quickly; basic services lag due to lower demand and support. *(1 M)*
- **Tech Impact:** Technology enhances sectors like finance but leaves traditional services behind. *(1 M)*

Long Answer Type Questions (5 M)

1. **For each of the sectors that we came across in this chapter why should one focus on employment and GDP? Could there be other issues which should be examined? Discuss.** ***(Ev)*** **(NCERT)**

Ans. Focus on:

- **Employment:** It shows how many jobs each sector creates, helping to understand where most people work and where more jobs might be needed. This is important for reducing unemployment and improving living standards. *(1 M)*
- **GDP Contribution:** It indicates how much value each sector adds to the economy. Sectors that contribute more to GDP are essential for economic growth and development. *(1 M)*

However, other issues are equally important to examine: **(Any-3)**

- **Income Inequality:** Even if a sector contributes significantly to GDP and employment, the distribution of income within that sector can be unequal. This needs attention to ensure fair economic growth. *(1 M)*
- **Environmental Impact:** Some sectors, especially manufacturing and agriculture, can have a substantial environmental impact. Sustainable practices are essential for long-term economic health. *(1 M)*
- **Sectoral Balance:** Depending too much on one sector can make an economy weak to sector-specific downturns. Balanced growth across sectors is healthier. *(1 M)*
- **Quality of Employment:** Beyond just creating jobs, the quality of those jobs (e.g., wages, working conditions) is crucial for worker well-being. *(1 M)*

3 PRIMARY, SECONDARY AND TERTIARY SECTORS IN INDIA

NCERT Definitions *(Commonly asked in 1 mark)*

- **Disguised Unemployment:** Disguised unemployment is a situation where **people are working** but all of them are **made to work less** than their **potential**.

  This kind of underemployment is **hidden in contrast** to someone who does not have a job and is clearly visible as unemployed is called disguised unemployment.
- **Underemployment:** Refers to a condition where people are **working less** than they are capable of or in positions that **do not utilize their skills**.
- **Casual Workers:** Those hired for **temporary** tasks without long-term contracts.
- **National Statistical Office (NSO):** The government agency responsible for **conducting statistical surveys** and **collecting data**.
- **Mahatma Gandhi National Rural Employment Guarantee Act (MGNREGA):** A social security measure that aims to guarantee the **'Right to Work'**.

Important Concepts

Methods to Create More Employment

1. **In a Short-term Method:** Mahatma Gandhi National Rural Employment Guarantee Act 2005 (MGNREGA 2005).

   (MGNREGA) The main **features** of the scheme are:
   - The scheme guarantees **100 days of wages employment** in a year to every household in 625 districts of the country.
   - The Gram Panchayat, after proper verification, will register households and **issue job cards** to them.
   - This act is also called **Right to Work** because if the government fails in its duty to provide employment, it will give unemployment allowances to the people.

> **Note: National Institute for Transforming India (NITI) Aayog**
> According to NITI Aayog, Estimates that nearly 20 lakh jobs can be created in the education sector alone.

2. **Long-Term Methods**
   - Providing Cheap Credit
   - Promotion of local industries like Small Scale Industries and Cottage
   - Improving agriculture sector
   - Provision of basic facilities like transportation and storage etc.
   - Other new services like Tourism, IT, etc.
   - Improving Education and Health Sector.

Rising Importance of the Tertiary Sector in Production

Tertiary Sectors have Replaced the Primary Sector as the Largest Producing Sector

Reasons for Tertiary Sector Growth:

- **Basic Services Requirement: Demand** for **basic services** like hospitals, educational institutions, postal services, police stations, banks, insurance companies, and defense.
- **Development-induced Services:** Greater development in the primary and secondary sectors has induced demand for service sector growth like **transport**, **trade**, **storage**, etc.
- **Rising Income Levels:** With the rise in income, certain services are demanded like tourism, which enhances the services sector.
- **New Services:** Due to globalisation, certain new services have entered the Indian market like **information technology** and **communication technology** which have become essential.

Important Facts

- **Graph-1** Shows the production of goods and services in the three sectors.

In 1973-74 Total GDP

- Largest Production in 1973-74 = Primary sector
- Least Production sector in 1973-74 = Secondary sector

In 2013-14 Total GDP

- Largest production sector in 2013-14 = Tertiary sector
- Least Production sector in 2013-14 = Primary sector

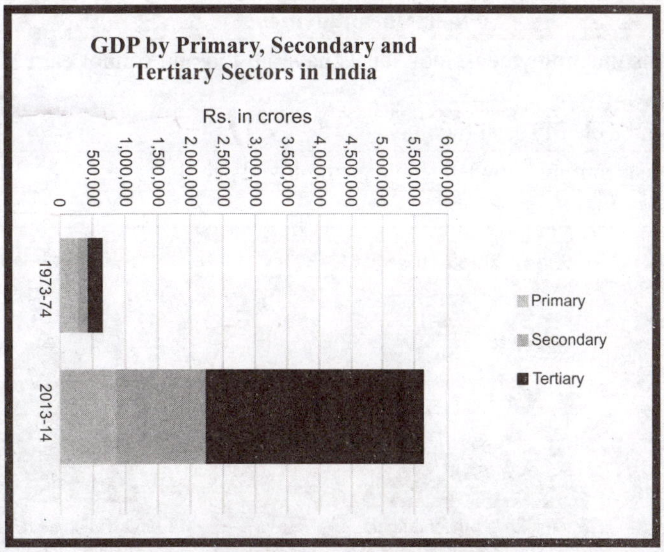

- **Graph-2** Presents the percentage share of the three sectors in GDP.

Sector	1973-74	2013-14
Primary	40%	11%
Secondary	11%	21%
Tertiary	49%	69%

Share of Sectors in GDP%

Note: Tertiary sector has grown the most **over forty years**

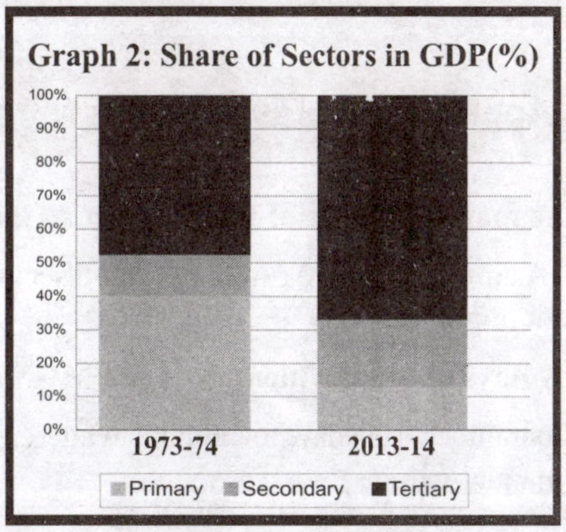

- **Graph-3** Shows the share of employment in the three sectors in 1977-78 and 2017-18. The primary sector continues to be the largest employer even now.

Sector	1977-78	2017-18
Primary	71%	44%
Secondary	11%	25%
Tertiary	18%	31%

Share of Sectors in Employment (%)

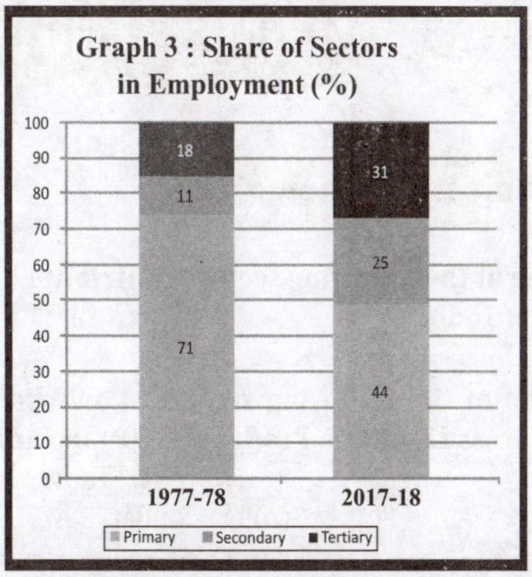

Classification

Types of Unemployment	
Type	**Characteristic**
Disguised Unemployment	People appear busy but output is less than potential
Casual Workers	Engaged in services like painting, plumbing without regular jobs
Underemployment	Full potential of workers is not utilized, leading to less income

Difference Between

Open Unemployment	Disguised Unemployment
In this unemployment, individuals have no job and cannot earn a living.	In this unemployment, Those who are unemployed work in places where no additional staff members are required.
It can be clearly seen by others.	This unemployment can't be clearly seen
It exists among knowledgeable unemployed people.	It is also most prevalent in the agricultural sector in remote areas

Under employment

I am a Ph.D but ending up flipping burgers

Unemployment

I have full time of scrolling through job listings

Working under MGNREGA

I think NREGA means 'No Real Effort Goes to Waste'

Real Life Application Based Questions

1. **What is the main objective of the Mahatma Gandhi National Rural Employment Guarantee Act, 2005?**

Ans. MGNREGA aims to improve rural livelihood security by offering 100 days of wage employment and enhancing infrastructure and employment opportunities.

2. **How many days of employment does the MGNREGA guarantee to rural households annually?**

Ans The Act guarantees 100 days of annual wage employment to every rural household willing to perform unskilled manual work.

Scan Me for Detailed Explanations

COMPETENCY BASED SOLVED EXAMPLES

Multiple Choice Questions

(1 M)

1. **Which one of the following sectors contribute highest in the GDP of India?** **(*Re*)(CBSE, 2023)**

OR

Which one of the following sectors shows the highest share of Gross Domestic Product (GDP) in India? **(*Re*)(CBSE, 2022 Term 2)**

(*a*) Primary (*b*) Secondary
(*c*) Tertiary (*d*) Quaternary

2. **Ramesh lives in a small village that suffers from water shortages and poor connectivity to nearby towns, especially during the monsoon season. The village council is discussing ways to improve the infrastructure and overall quality of life for its residents. During the meeting, one of the council members suggests utilizing MGNREGA (Mahatma Gandhi National Rural Employment Guarantee Act) funds. How can MGNREGA help Ramesh's village improve its infrastructure and address the issues of water shortage and connectivity?** **(*An*)**

(*a*) By constructing urban roads and highways
(*b*) By building schools and hospitals in cities
(*c*) By creating assets like wells, ponds, and roads in villages
(*d*) By providing free electricity to rural households

3. **Under MGNREGA 2005, all those who are able to, and are in need of, work in rural areas are guaranteed 100 days of employment in a year by the government. If the government fails in its duty to provide employment, it will give unemployment allowances to the people. Identify the right.** ***(Ap)*(CBSE APQ, 2023)**

(*a*) Right to work (*b*) Right to Freedom
(*c*) Right to livelihood (*d*) Right against Exploitation

4. **Choose the correct answer:**
Underemployment occurs when people ***(Re)*(NCERT Intext)**

(*a*) do not want to work
(*b*) are working in a lazy manner
(*c*) are working less than what they are capable of doing
(*d*) are not paid for their work

5. **Observe the graph given below and answer the following question based on it:**

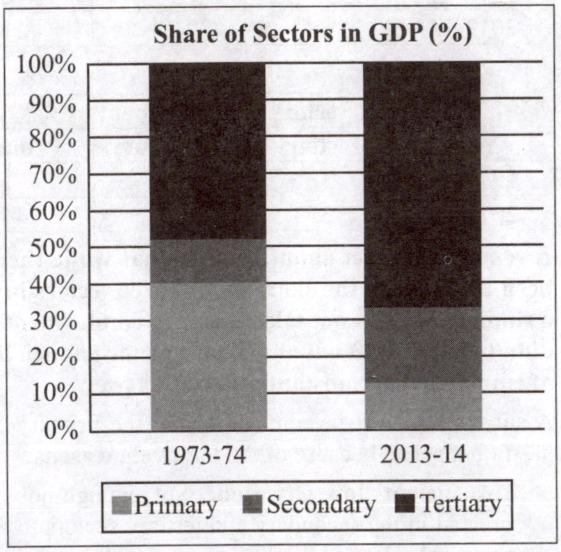

Evaluate the role of government policy in influencing the tertiary sector's growth as observed in the graph. Which of the following would be most effective? ***(Ev)***

(*a*) Subsidies for technology startups
(*b*) Investment in agricultural technologies
(*c*) Tariffs on imported goods
(*d*) Enhanced educational programs for service industries

6. **Imagine you are a policy analyst working for a state government facing a high level of disguised unemployment in its agricultural sector, primarily because many farmers are underutilized due to the limited scope of work available. The state is considering various strategies to tackle this issue effectively. Given the issue of disguised unemployment in the agricultural sector, which strategy could effectively reduce underemployment?** ***(An, Ev)***

(*a*) Increasing agricultural subsidies
(*b*) Encouraging industrialization to create new jobs
(*c*) Introducing more crops per year
(*d*) Expanding agricultural land

7. **Consider a city with a high rate of underemployment among service sector workers. Many workers are engaged in low-skill, low-wage jobs without the opportunity to utilize their full potential or improve their economic status. Evaluate the potential impacts of the following strategies on reducing disguised unemployment in the urban service sector and identify the most effective strategy.** ***(Ev)***

(*a*) Implementing advanced technological tools to enhance efficiency and job capabilities.
(*b*) Providing vocational training programs to enhance the skills of unskilled or under-skilled workers.
(*c*) Promoting entrepreneurship to create new business opportunities and jobs.
(*d*) Redistributing the existing workforce across different roles to better match skill sets and job requirements.

Assertion and Reason

(1 M)

Direction: The following questions consist of two statements – Assertion (A) and Reason (R). Answer these questions by selecting the appropriate option given below:

(*a*) Both A and R are true, and R is the correct explanation of A.
(*b*) Both A and R are true, but R is not the correct explanation of A.
(*c*) A is true, but R is false
(*d*) A is false, but R is true.

1. **Assertion (A):** Disguised unemployment is hidden in contrast to someone who does not have a job and is clearly visible as unemployed. Everyone is working, no one is fully employed.
Reason (R): In actual fact, labor efforts get divided. ***(An)***

2. **Assertion (A):** The tertiary sector has become the largest contributor to India's GDP in recent years.
Reason (R): The growth of the service sector has outpaced that of the primary and secondary sectors due to rising incomes, urbanisation, and changing lifestyles. ***(An)***

3. **Assertion (A):** The secondary sector has been losing its share in India's GDP over time.
Reason (R): Factors such as high input costs, lack of skilled labor, and inadequate infrastructure have made it difficult for manufacturers to compete globally ***(An)***

4. **Assertion (A):** The tertiary sector provides more opportunities for women than other sectors in India.
Reason (R): Service activities such as healthcare, education, and hospitality require a wide range of skills and are less physically demanding than other sectors. ***(An)***

5. **Assertion (A):** The tertiary sector contributes more to urbanisation than other sectors in India.
Reason (R): Service activities such as real estate, finance, and IT are concentrated in urban areas only and leading to more job opportunities and migration from rural areas. ***(An)***

6. **Assertion (A):** India's manufacturing sector has been declining in recent years.
Reason (R): Factors such as high input costs, lack of skilled labor, and inadequate infrastructure have made it difficult for manufacturers to compete globally. ***(Un)***

Subjective Questions

Very Short Answer Type Questions (2 M)

1. **Why should we be worried about underemployment?** ***(Un)*(NCERT Intext)**

Ans. We should worry about underemployment as due to it, the earning capacity of a person is decreased, resulting in a poor standard. Ultimately this can also lead to poverty. *(2 M)*

2. **Why do you think MGNREGA 2005 is referred to as 'Right to work'?** ***(Un)*(NCERT Intext)**

Ans. In MGNREGA, if the government fails to provide employment in rural areas, it will give unemployment allowances to the people. So, in effect, it is giving the person the right to work. *(2 M)*

3. **How to create more employment in rural areas? Explain with examples.** ***(Ap)*(CBSE, 2023)**

Ans. Creating more employment in rural areas can be done the the following ways: **(Any two)**

(i) **Developing infrastructure:** Developing infrastructure like roads, electricity, and water supply can help attract industries and businesses to rural areas, which can generate employment. *(1 M)*

(ii) **Skill development:** Providing training and skill development programs can help enhance the employability of rural youth. *(1 M)*

(iii) **Entrepreneurship:** Encouraging entrepreneurship and providing support for micro, small, and medium enterprises can create employment opportunities in rural areas. *(1 M)*

(iv) **Government schemes:** The government has launched several schemes like MGNREGA, which aim to create employment opportunities in rural areas. *(1 M)*

Short Answer Type Questions (3 M)

1. **Why is 'Tertiary Sector' becoming important in India? Explain.** ***(An)*(CBSE, 2023)**

Ans. There are many reasons why the service sector is becoming so important in India. Some of the reasons are being discussed here: **(Any three)**

(i) The service/tertiary sector is responsible for providing **public transportation, medical services, banking**, and **post office services** under the Government. *(1 M)*

(ii) The tertiary sector helps in the **development** of the **agricultural industry**. It also helps to flourish other industries like trade, transport, storage etc. *(1 M)*

(iii) The tertiary sector flourishes in tourism, retail, schools and private hospitals. *(1 M)*

(iv) The tertiary sector helps to **flourish services** related to communication and information technology. *(1 M)*

2. **Mr. Pawan, a village head, wanted to create more job opportunities to increase the income of the people of his village under MGNREGA act, suggesting three activities, so that Mr. Pawan could initiate in his village.** ***(Ap)*(CBSE SQP, 2023)**

Ans. For Mr. Pawan, the village head, to increase job opportunities under the MNREGA act, he could initiate the following activities in his village:

- **Water Conservation Projects:** The construction of check dams, ponds, and wells can help in water conservation and provide employment to villagers. *(1 M)*
- **Afforestation:** Planting trees around the village can improve the environment and provide work. *(1 M)*
- **Road Construction:** Building and repairing village roads can create jobs and improve transportation. *(1 M)*

3. **Compare Tables "A" & "B" and answer the question given below.** ***(An)*(CBSE SQP, 2023)**

Table- A

Share of Sectors in GDP in %			
Year	**Tertiary**	**Secondary**	**Primary**
1973-74	50	10	40
2013-14	68	21	11

Table- B

Share of Sectors in employment in %			
Year	**Tertiary**	**Secondary**	**Primary**
1977-78	18	11	71
2017-18	31	25	44

A remarkable fact about India is that while there has been a change in the share of the three sectors in GDP, a similar shift has not taken place in employment. Why didn't similar shift out of primary sector happen in case of employment? Substantiate your answer.

Ans. A substantial shift in employment in the primary Sector hasn't happened because of the following reasons:

- **Insufficient Job Creation:** Not enough jobs were created in the secondary and tertiary sectors to absorb the surplus labor from the primary sector. *(1 M)*
- **Underemployment in Agriculture:** Many workers in agriculture are underemployed, indicating they can leave without impacting production significantly. *(1 M)*
- **Imbalance in Sector Contribution:** Industrial and service sectors' output increased significantly, but job growth did not match. Many remain in the primary sector, despite its lower GDP contribution, while secondary and tertiary sectors are underemploy relative to their output. *(1 M)*

4. **Compare and contrast the changes in India with the pattern that was observed for developed countries. What kind of changes between sectors were desired but did not happen in India?** ***(An)*(NCERT Intext)**

Ans. *(i)* In developed countries, there was a shift from primary to secondary and then to tertiary sectors. *(1 M)*

(ii) In India, while the tertiary sector grew, the expected shift from primary to secondary did not happen significantly. *(1 M)*

(iii) The desired change was a larger move towards industrialization (secondary sector), which did not occur as expected. *(1 M)*

5. You are a consultant tasked with developing a proposal for a local government initiative aimed at boosting economic development in semi-rural areas. The proposal should focus on setting up a dal mill and cold storage facilities to stimulate local employment. Explain how setting up a dal mill and cold storage in semi-rural areas can create employment. ***(An)***

Ans. Employment Creation through Dal Mill and Cold Storage Facilities:

(*i*) **Direct Jobs:** Establishing a dal mill and cold storage will directly employ local labor for operations, management, and maintenance roles. *(1 M)*

(*ii*) **Agricultural Support:** Farmers gain better access to processing and storage, boosting agricultural productivity and creating more agricultural jobs. *(1 M)*

(*iii*) **Ancillary Services:** Supporting sectors like transportation, packaging, and retail benefit, generating additional employment opportunities in the community. *(1 M)*

6. How is the tertiary sector different from other sectors? Illustrate with a few examples. **(*Un*)(NCERT Intext)**

Ans. The tertiary sector is different from the primary and secondary sectors in several ways:

- The tertiary sector provides **services** rather than goods, unlike primary and secondary sectors. *(1 M)*
- Examples of the **tertiary sector** include banking, education, and healthcare services. *(1 M)*
- The tertiary sector **supports** the primary and secondary sectors by offering services such as transportation, storage, and banking which help in the development of these sectors. *(1 M)*

7. What do you understand by disguised unemployment? Explain with an example each from the urban and rural areas. **(*Un*)(NCERT)**

Ans. When more people are working in a job than actually needed. It looks like everyone is working but their full potential is not used. *(1 M)*

Rural Example	Urban Example
If a family farm needs 3 workers but employs 5, the extra 2 are disguisedly unemployed. They don't add to productivity. *(1 M)*	A family-run shop managed by 4 members could be run by just 2, the extra 2 are disguisedly unemployed. They are not increasing sales or service. *(1 M)*

8. Distinguish between open unemployment and disguised unemployment. **(*An*)(NCERT)**

Ans. *(3 M)*

Open Unemployment	Disguised Unemployment
Those unemployment, individuals have no job and cannot earn a living.	Those who are unemployed work in places where no additional staff members are required.
It can be clearly seen by others.	This unemployment can't be clearly seen.
It exists among knowledgeable unemployed people.	It is also most prevalent in the agricultural sector in remote areas.

9. Mr.Y from a city in India visits a rural area and finds five people working in a small agricultural farm. More than two people are not required to work in the farm and removing the other three will not affect production. How can one solve this problem of underemployment in rural areas? Explain. **(*Ap*) (CBSE SQP, 2024)**

Ans. If more men are working than required is called as disguised unemployment. In this case the other three who are not required should take up different jobs that would increase the total family income. **(Any 3 points)**

- Government can invest some money in transportation and storage of crops or make better rural roads so that mini-trucks reach everywhere. *(1 M)*
- Promotion of industries like setting up a dal mill, opening a cold storage could give an opportunity for farmers to store their products like potatoes and onions and sell them when the price is good. *(1 M)*
- In villages near forest areas, they can start honey collection centres where farmers can come and sell wild honey. It is also possible to set up industries that process vegetables and agricultural produce like potato, sweet potato, rice, wheat, tomato, fruits, which can be sold in outside markets and thus generate employment. *(1 M)*
- Government can plan to give loans at lower rates of interest to people in rural areas to start something new thereby solving problems of underemployment. *(1 M)*

10. Explain the objectives of implementing the NREGA 2005. **(*Un*)(NCERT)**

Ans. The objectives of implementing the NREGA 2005 were:

- NREGA 2005 was introduced with an aim to ensure **guaranteed 100 days** of **employment** in a year to all those who are in need of work. *(1 M)*
- It also states that in the case of employment is not provided under this act, **unemployment wages** will be given. *(1 M)*
- Additional **employment opportunities** need to be created for **people in villages** and **smaller towns**. *(1 M)*

Long Answer Type Questions (5 M)

1. Answer the following questions by looking at the graph-1 given below. ***(Re)*(NCERT Intext)**

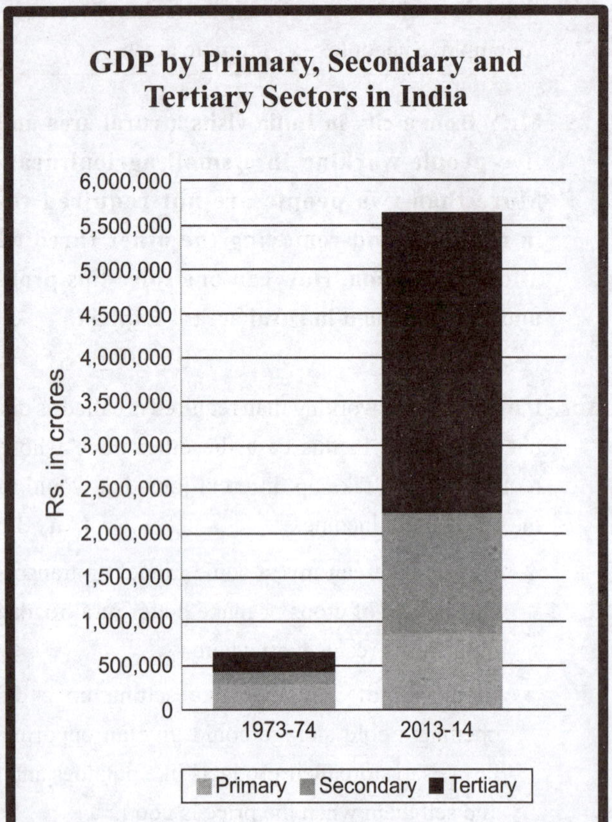

(i) Which was the largest producing sector in 1973-74?

(ii) Which is the largest producing sector in 2013-14?

(iii) Which is the least producing sector in 2013-14?

(iv) Can you say which sector has grown the most over forty years?

(v) What was the GDP of India in 2013-14?

Ans. (i) Primary sector. *(1 M)*

(ii) Tertiary sector. *(1 M)*

(iii) Primary Sector *(1 M)*

(iv) The GDP of India in 2013-14 was approx. 56,00,000 crore rupees as per the graph. *(1 M)*

(v) Tertiary sector has grown the most over forty years. *(1 M)*

2. You are a business analyst tasked with evaluating the role of technological advancements in the service sector of a developing economy. Over the past decade, there have been significant investments in information technology infrastructure, leading to the proliferation of internet services, IT companies, and digitally enhanced customer service facilities. Analyze the impact of technological advancements in the service sector. ***(An)***

Ans. The service sector provides support to primary and secondary sectors. The impact of technological advancements in the service sector of a developing economy is as follows:

(i) **Enhanced Efficiency and Productivity:** Technology, including automation and AI, streamlines processes, reducing manual labor and speeding up service delivery. *(1 M)*

(ii) **Improved Customer Experience:** Digital platforms like chatbots and mobile apps offer real-time support, personalized services, and 24/7 availability, boosting customer satisfaction. *(1 M)*

(iii) **Economic Growth and Job Creation:** IT infrastructure investments attract global companies and foster local startups, creating jobs in software development, cybersecurity, and data analytics. *(1 M)*

(iv) **Increased Access to Services:** Online banking, e-commerce, telemedicine, and e-learning reduce barriers to essential services, reaching remote and rural areas. *(1 M)*

(v) **Data-Driven Decision Making:** Big data and analytics provide insights into customer behavior and market trends, enabling informed decisions and better resource allocation. *(1 M)*

3. "Tertiary sector is not playing any significant role in the development of Indian economy." Do you agree? Give reasons in support of your answer. ***(Ev)*(NCERT)**

Ans. No, this statement is not true. The service sector is playing an important role in the development of the Indian Economy. In the year 2013-2014, the service sector replaced the primary sector as the most producing sector in the country. *(1 M)*

The Following reasons are:

- **Employment:** It provides key services like IT, transportation, and healthcare, creating numerous job opportunities, although not as much as the primary sector. *(1 M)*
- **Foreign Earnings:** Services like IT and call centers bring substantial foreign earnings to India. *(1 M)*
- **Support for Sectors:** Helps in the development of primary and secondary sectors through services like banking, communication, and transport. *(1 M)*
- **Social Services:** Education, healthcare, and public services improve the quality of life and productivity. *(1 M)*

4. The following table gives the GDP in Rupees (Crores) by the three sectors: ***(Ev)*(NCERT)**

Year	Primary	Secondary	Tertiary
2000	52,000	48,500	1,33,500
2013	8,00,500	10,74,000	38,68,000

(i) **Calculate the share of the three sectors in GDP for 2000 and 2013.**

(ii) **Show the data as a bar diagram similar to Graph 2 in the chapter.**

(iii) **What conclusions can we draw from the bar graph?**

Ans. (i)

In 2000	In 2013
Primary sector = 22.22%	Primary sector = 13.94%
Secondary sector = 20.73%	Secondary sector = 18.70%
Tertiary sector = 57.04%	Tertiary sector = 67.36%

(2 M)

Working Note:

In 2000

❒ Primary Sector = $\frac{52,000}{(52,000+48,500+1,33,500)}\times 100$

$=\frac{52,000}{2,34,000}\times 100 = 22.22\%$

❒ Secondary Sector = $\frac{48,500}{2,34,000}\times 100 = 20.73\%$

❒ Tertiary Sector = $\frac{1,33,500}{2,34,000}\times 100 = 57.04\%$

In 2013

❒ Primary Sector= $\frac{8,00,500}{(8,00,500+10,74,000+3,86,800)}\times 100$

$=\frac{8,00,500}{5742500}\times 100 = 13.94\%$ *(approx.)*

❒ Secondary Sector = $\frac{10,744,000}{57,42,500}\times 100 = 18.70\%$

❒ Tertiary Sector = $\frac{3,86,8000}{57,42,500}\times 100 = 67.36\%$

(ii)

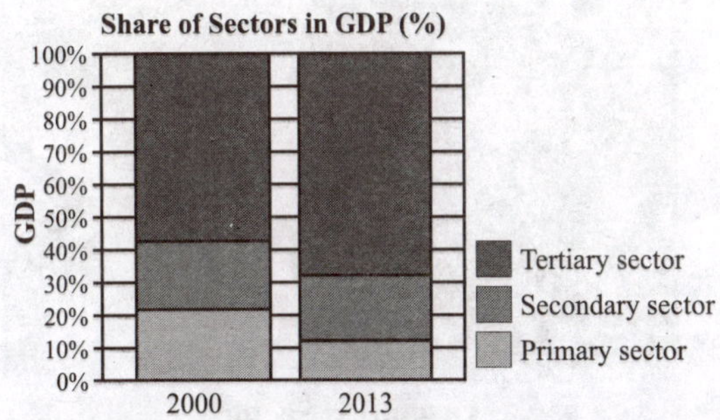

(2 M)

(iii) Conclusion is that the share of the tertiary sector in the GDP has increased by 10%, while that of the primary sector has halved approx. The secondary sector has grown by about 2%. *(1 M)*

4 | DIVISION OF SECTORS AS ORGANISED AND UNORGANISED

NCERT Definitions *(Commonly asked in 1 mark)*

- **Organised Sector:** Those sectors are places with **secured work**, regular terms, and benefits like leave, pension, etc. Follow government laws. Examples: Government jobs.

Organised Sector

Unorganised Sector

- **Unorganised Sector:** Those sectors which are jobs **without security**, rules not followed. Examples: Street vendors, and small traders.
- **Exploitation:** Refers to the **unfair treatment** or use, especially to benefit from someone else's work.
- **Seasonal Employment:** Jobs available **only at certain times** of the year.

Difference Between

Division of Sectors → **On the basis of employment condition**

Basis	Organised sector	Unorganised Sector
Term of employment	Regular.	Irregular.
Rules and Regulation of Govt.	It has to follow the rules and regulations of government.	It has rules but they don't follow the government's rules and regulations.
Job Security	Workers enjoy the security of employment.	Workers have no fixed employment.
Remuneration	Workers of this sector get paid during holidays, leave and overtime for more work etc.	Workers don't get paid for holidays or leave. And in case of less work they may be asked to leave their job.
Other benefits	Workers enjoy the other benefits like medical facilities etc.	Workers are not supposed to enjoy other benefits.

Organised sector

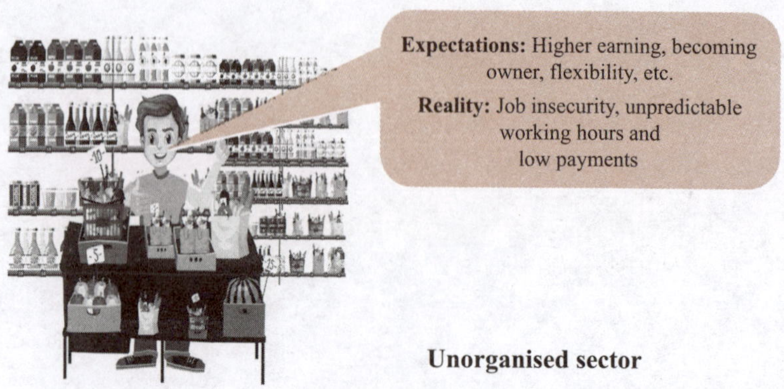

Unorganised sector

COMPETENCY BASED SOLVED EXAMPLES

Scan Me for Detailed Explanations

Multiple Choice Questions

(1 M)

1. **Which one of the following is an activity of the unorganised sector?** *(Ap)*(CBSE, 2023)
   (*a*) A teacher teaching in a school.
   (*b*) A worker going to work in a big factory.
   (*c*) A doctor treating patients in a hospital.
   (*d*) A daily wage labourer working under a contractor.
2. **________________ sector has some formal processes and Procedures.** *(Re)*
   (*a*) Unorganised sector (*b*) Organised sector
   (*c*) Both (*a*) and (*b*) (*d*) None of these
3. **Which one of the following is an example of organized sector activities?** *(Ap)* (CBSE, 2024)
   (*a*) A farmer irrigating his field.
   (*b*) A handloom weaver working in her house.
   (*c*) A headload worker carrying cement.
   (*d*) A teacher taking classes in a government school.
4. **Arjun Enterprises, a medium-sized garment manufacturing company, has recently set up several informal workshops across suburban areas. These workshops predominantly employ local laborers on a contract basis, paying them on a per-piece rate without providing formal employment benefits. Given this context, why do many organized sector enterprises like Arjun Enterprises choose to operate segments of their business in the unorganized sector?** *(An)*
   (*a*) To benefit from government subsidies
   (*b*) To evade taxes and avoid laws protecting laborers
   (*c*) Because of the higher skill level of unorganized sector workers
   (*d*) To access international markets
5. **A local government is considering programs to facilitate the movement of workers from the unorganized to the organized sector. This initiative aims to leverage the unique skills these workers have developed to enhance productivity and innovation within more structured environments. How might skills learned in the unorganized sector be beneficial if transferred to the organized sector?** *(Ap)*
   (*a*) No benefits as the sectors are unrelated
   (*b*) Better negotiation skills for wages
   (*c*) Adaptability and entrepreneurial skills
   (*d*) Specific technical skills only
6. **Rahul, a 30-year-old worker in a small garment manufacturing unit, faces job instability and lacks health benefits, common issues in the unorganized sector. Considering his need for a more secure job and healthcare benefits, evaluate his potential actions:** *(Ev)*
   (*a*) He could approach his current employer to formally request these benefits
   (*b*) He could lead an initiative to form a union with his co-workers to negotiate for better terms collectively
   (*c*) He might consider moving to a larger, well-established garment company in the organized sector known for providing job security and employee health benefits
   (*d*) To manage immediate financial needs, he could opt to work additional hours at the current job

Assertion and Reason

(1 M)

Direction: The following questions consist of two statements – Assertion (A) and Reason (R). Answer these questions by selecting the appropriate option given below:

(*a*) Both A and R are true, and R is the correct explanation of A.
(*b*) Both A and R are true, but R is not the correct explanation of A.
(*c*) A is true, but R is false
(*d*) A is false, but R is true.

1. **Assertion (A):** Mohan is a shopkeeper who pays his taxes on time. He has employed two workers Akash and Vivek in shop. He pays them well, however, none of the workers get any paid leaves in the year.

   Reason (R): Akash and Vivek are employed in unorganized sector. *(An)*
2. **Assertion (A):** The unorganised sector plays a crucial role in the Indian economy.

   Reason (R): It provides employment opportunities to a large number of people, especially in rural areas, and contributes significantly to the country's GDP. *(An)*
3. **Assertion (A):** The unorganised sector is the largest employer in India.

   Reason (R): A large percentage of the population is engaged in informal activities such as street vending, small-scale manufacturing, and domestic work, which are part of the unorganised sector. *(An)*
4. **Assertion (A):** The organised sector provides better working conditions than the unorganised sector in India.

   Reason (R): Organised sector activities such as formal employment, large-scale manufacturing, and corporate services offer better wages, job security, and social security benefits compared to informal activities. *(An)*

5. **Assertion (A):** The growth of the organised sector can lead to a reduction in poverty rates in India.

Reason (R): Formal employment opportunities can provide better wages and social security benefits leading to an increase in household income levels which can help reduce poverty rates over time. ***(An)***

Subjective Questions

Very Short Answer Type Questions (2 M)

1. **Differentiate between organized and unorganized sectors. (*Un*) (CBSE, 2024)**

Ans. Difference between Organised sector and unorganised sector is as follows:

Basis	Organised Sector	Unorganised Sector	
Term of Employment	The term of employment is regular.	The term of employment is irregular.	*(1 M)*
Job Security	Workers enjoy the security of employment.	Workers have no fixed employment.	*(1 M)*

2. **What is Organised Sector? Explain the main advantage of organised sector in respect of employment. (*Un*)(CBSE, 2020)**

Ans. Organised Sector is a sector where the employment terms are fixed and regular, and the employees get assured work. *(1 M)*

The main advantage of organised sector in respect of employment are:

(*i*) Job security *(½ M)*

(*ii*) Fixed working hours *(½ M)*

Short Answer Type Questions (3 M)

1. **Why is there a need to protect workers in the Unorganized Sector? Explain. (*Un*)(CBSE, 2023)**

Ans. Workers in the unorganised sector need protection because of the following reasons:

- **Wages:** The income of the workers is not fixed and they are hardly able to meet the needs to lead a decent livelihood. *(1 M)*
- **Job security:** There is no job security in this sector, anyone can be fired and removed from their work. *(1 M)*
- **Lack of Benefits:** Unlike organized sector workers, they often do not have benefits like health insurance, paid leave, or retirement pensions. *(1 M)*

2. **A worker in an urban area, who was working in a small factory, was not paid his wages properly, he was forced to work extra hours under poor working conditions, there was no job security, recently he lost his job and was found selling electrical items in a pushcart.**

Analyze the role of the government in protecting the workers working in an Unorganized sector. (*An*)(CBSE SQP, 2023)

Ans. The following are the ways in which the workers in the unorganized sector can be protected by the government.

- The small factories must be registered by the government and have to follow its rules and regulations which are given in various laws such as the Factories Act, Minimum Wages Act, Payment of Gratuity Act, Shops and Establishments Act, etc. *(1 M)*
- The government can provide loans to help unemployed educated youth start their own business. *(1 M)*
- The workers are supposed to get medical benefits and, under the laws, the factory manager has ensure facilities like drinking water and safe working. *(1 M)*

3. **Which sector, organised or unorganised, is preferable for employment? Explain. (*An*)(CBSE APQ, 2023)**

Ans. It is a preference that might depend on a variety of factors: People might prefer to work in the organised sector because of: *(1½ M)*

- Job security
- Social security benefits
- Regular income

People might prefer to work in the unorganised sector because of: *(1½ M)*

- Flexibility
- Escaping paperwork
- Quick employment opportunity

4. **Why is organized sector preferred by the employees? Explain. (*Un*)(CBSE, 2020)**

Ans. Employees prefer organized sector because of the following reasons:

- This sector gives many benefits to employees which are not present in unorganized sector like regular salary, leave benefits and social security benefits etc. *(1 M)*
- Workers in this sector enjoy the security of employment. *(1 M)*
- This sector follows the rules and regulations of government and many more reasons are there. *(1 M)*

5. **Sunil and Raman did their graduation from the same college. Sunil got employed in an unorganised sector and was not satisfied whereas Raman got employed in an organised sector and was happy and satisfied. Identify three reasons for Sunil's dissatisfaction as compared to Raman. (*Ap*) (CBSE SQP, 2024)**

Ans. Sunil's dissatisfaction in the unorganised sector as compared to Raman in the organised sector can be due to the following reasons:

(*i*) **Job Security and Stability:** Jobs in the unorganised sector are often temporary, and workers can be removed at any time without prior notice, whereas the organised sector provides job security with proper employment contracts. *(1 M)*

(*ii*) **Low Wages and Lack of Benefits:** In the unorganised sector, wages are generally low and irregular, with no additional benefits like provident fund, medical insurance, or paid leaves, unlike the organised sector where employees receive fixed salaries and additional perks. *(1 M)*

(*iii*) **Poor Working Conditions:** The unorganised sector often has poor working conditions, with long hours, lack of proper workplace facilities, and no legal protection, whereas the organised sector ensures a safe and comfortable working environment with regulated working hours. *(1 M)*

6. Over the forty years between 1973-74 and 2013-14, while production in all the three sectors has increased, it has increased the most in the tertiary sector. As a result, in the year 2013-14, the tertiary sector has emerged as the largest producing sector in India replacing the primary sector. Why do you think tertiary sector has become so popular in India? Support your answer giving any 3 reasons **(*An*)(CBSE SQP, 2024)**

Ans. **(Any 3 points)**

- In any country several services such as hospitals, educational institutions, post and telegraph services, police stations, courts, transport, banks, insurance companies, etc. are required, these can be considered as basic services. In a developing country the government must take responsibility for the provision of these services. *(1 M)*
- The development of agriculture and industry leads to the development of services such as transport, trade, storage and the like, as we have already seen. Greater the development of the primary and secondary sectors, more would be the demand for such services. *(1 M)*
- As income levels rise, certain sections of people start demanding many more services like eating out, tourism, shopping, private hospitals, private schools, professional training etc. *(1 M)*
- Over the past dècade or so, certain new services such as those based on information and communication technology have become important and essential. The production of these services has been rising rapidly. *(1 M)*

7. Workers are exploited in the unorganised sector. Do you agree with this view? Give reasons in support of your answer. **(*An*)(NCERT)**

Ans. Workers in the unorganized sector are often exploited. The following reasons are:

- **Lack of Job Security:** Workers in the unorganized sector do not have job security. They can be hired and fired at any time without any reason. *(1 M)*
- **Poor Working Conditions:** These workers often work in poor and unsafe conditions without access to basic amenities like clean drinking water or proper rest areas. *(1 M)*
- **No Regular Income:** There is no guarantee of regular income. This makes it difficult for workers to plan their expenses and save for the future. *(1 M)*

Long Answer Type Questions (5 M)

1. How would you distinguish between organised sector and unorganised sector? Explain in your words. **(*Un*)(NCERT Intext)(CBSE, 2020)**

OR

Distinguish the service condition of organised sector with that of unorganised sector. **(*An*)(CBSE, 2018)**

OR

Explain the differences between the organised and unorganised sector of economic activities. **(*Un*) (CBSE, 2024)**

Ans. **(5 M)**

Basis	Organised sector	Unorganised Sector
Term of employment	Regular.	Irregular.
Rules and Regulation of Govt.	It has to follow the rules and regulations of government.	It has rules but they don't follow the government's rules and regulations.
Job Security	Workers enjoy the security of employment.	Workers have no fixed employment.
Remuneration	Workers of this sector get paid during holidays, leave and overtime for more work etc.	Workers don't get paid for holidays or leave. And in case of less work they may be asked to leave their job.

Other benefits	Workers enjoy the other benefits like medical facilities etc.	Workers are not supposed to enjoy other benefits.

Topper's Explanation

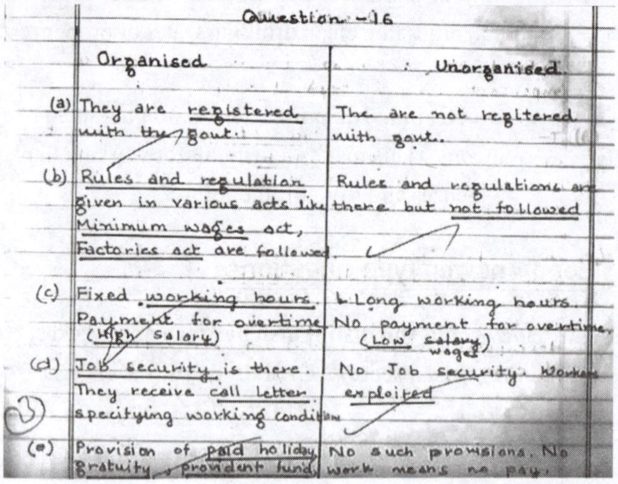
Question -16

	Organised	Unorganised
(a)	They are registered with the govt.	The are not regitered with govt.
(b)	Rules and regulation given in various acts like Minimum wages act, Factories act are followed.	Rules and regulations are there but not followed
(c)	Fixed working hours. Payment for overtime (High salary)	Long working hours. No payment for overtime. (Low salary wages)
(d)	Job security is there. They receive call letter specifying working condition	No Job security. Workers exploited
(e)	Provision of paid holiday, gratuity, provident fund.	No such provisions. No work means no pay.

2. The table below shows the estimated number of workers in India in the organised and unorganised sectors. Read the table carefully. Fill in the missing data and answer the questions that follow. ***(Ap)*(NCERT Intext)**

Workers In Different Sectors (In Millions)

Sector	Organised	Unorganised	Total
Primary	1		232
Secondary	41	74	115
Tertiary	440	88	128
Total	**82**		
Total in Percentage			**100%**

(*i*) What is the percentage of people in the unorganised sector in agriculture?

(*ii*) Do you agree that agriculture is an unorganised sector activity? Why?

(*iii*) If we look at the country as a whole, we find that ______% of the workers in India are in the unorganised sector. Organised sector employment is available to only about ______% of the workers in India.

Ans. (*i*) We can find out the number of people in an unorganised primary sector. But we can't find how many of these are engaged in agriculture. So it is not possible to answer this questions. *(1 M)*

(*ii*) Yes, I agree that agriculture in India is an activity of the unorganised sector, because of the following reasons: *(½ M)*

- Most of the workers working in agriculture do not get payment on regular basis *(½ M)*
- This sector faces the issue of underemployment *(½ M)*
- Most of the farmers are dependent on moneylenders and relatives for their debt requirements. Etc. *(½ M)*

(*iii*) 82.74%, 17.26%

Percentage of workers in unorganised sector

$$= \frac{(231 + 74 + 88)}{(232 + 115 + 128)} \times 100 = \frac{393}{475} \times 100 = 82.74\%$$

Percentage of workers in organized sector

$$= \frac{82}{475} \times 100 = 17.26\%$$ **(2 M)**

3. The workers in the unorganised sector need protection on the following issues: wages, safety and health. Explain with examples. ***(Ap)*(NCERT)**

Ans. The workers in the unorganised sector need protection on the following issues:

- **Wages:** Workers in the unorganised sector often receive less than minimum wage. Example: A street vendor earns irregular income, making it hard to meet basic needs. *(1 M)*
- **Safety:** These workers face unsafe working conditions. Example: A construction worker might work without safety gear, risking injuries. *(1 M)*
- **Health:** Lack of healthcare benefits can lead to untreated illnesses. Example: Domestic workers may not get sick leave or health insurance, affecting their health and work. *(1 M)*
- **Solution for Wages:** Implementing minimum wage laws and ensuring regular inspection can help. *(1 M)*
- **Solution for Safety and Health:** Providing safety gear and mandating health check-ups can improve conditions. *(1 M)*

4. Highlight any five benefits of the organised sector, with examples. ***(Re)*(CBSE, 2019)**

Ans. The benefits of the organised sector are as follows: **(Any 5)**

- Workers of the organised sector get regular and assured employment.
- Companies in the organised sector are registered/ enlisted under the government and have to follow its rules and regulations which are mentioned in various laws such as the Factories Act, Minimum Wages Act, and Payment of Gratuity Act.
- Workers in the organised sectors enjoy the privileges of job security and are expected to work only for a fixed number of hours.
- They also get several other benefits like paid leaves, provident fund, gratuity, etc.
- There is a provision for overtime payment, in case the workers do their duties after the fixed working hours.
- They also receive medical benefits, pensions, etc.

5 SECTORS IN TERMS OF OWNERSHIP: PUBLIC AND PRIVATE SECTORS

NCERT Definitions *(Commonly asked in 1 mark)*

- **Public Sector:** It is the sector in which the **government** owns most of the assets and provides all the services. E.g., Railways, post office, Defence, Airline, etc.

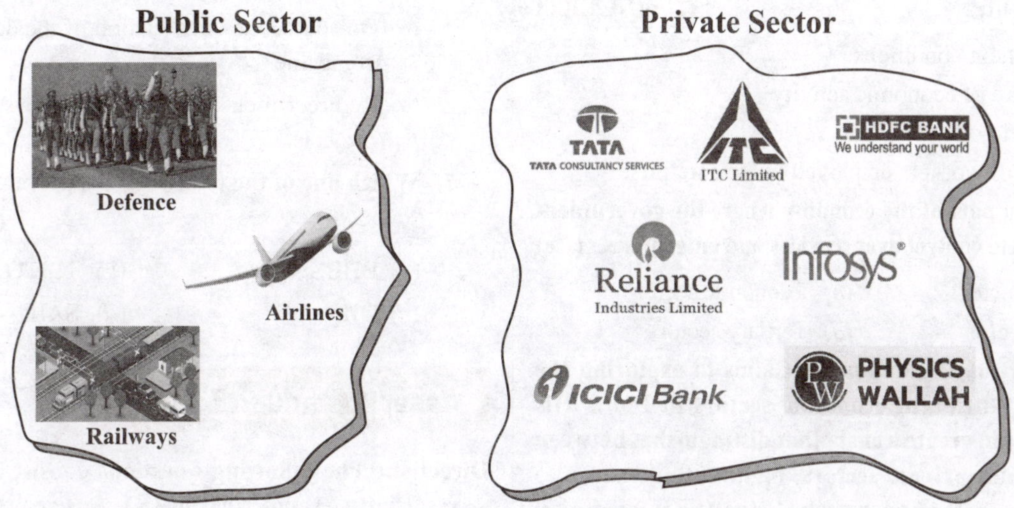

- **Private Sector:** It is the sector in which **ownership** of assets and **delivery of services** is in the hands of private individuals or companies. E.g., Tata Iron and Steel Company Limited (TISCO), and Reliance Industries Limited (RIL).

Important Concepts

Role of Public Sector

- Development of Infrastructure
- Development of backward areas
- Basic facilities like Education and Health
- Provide solutions to problems like malnutrition, high infant mortality rate etc.

Contrubution to Economic Developement

- Providing Essential Services at Reasonable Cost
- Benefits of public especially the poor like by giving wheat, kerosene oil etc. at lower price
- Setting up of Heavy Industries
- Social welfare not profit earning
- Educational and Health facilities free of cost

Difference Between

Economic Activity Classify into Two Sectors on the Basis of Ownership		
Basis	**Public Sector**	**Private Sector**
Meaning	Public sector organisations are owned, controlled and managed by the government or other state-run bodies.	Private sector organisations are owned, controlled and managed by individuals, groups or business entities.
Ownership	By Central, State or Local government bodies.	By Private individuals or entities.
Motive	Social welfare	Maximizing profit
Source of capital	Tax collections, excise and other duties, bonds etc.	Loans, issue of shares, issue of debentures etc.
Employment benefits	Job security, various allowances, retirement benefits etc.	Higher salary, better promotion chances, competitive environment, incentives etc.
Areas of operation	Police, military, mining, transportation banking, education etc.	Information technology, finance, FMCG goods, hospitality etc.

COMPETENCY BASED SOLVED EXAMPLES

Scan Me for Detailed Explanations

Multiple Choice Questions

(1 M)

1. **The sectors are classified into public and private sector on the basis of:** ***(Un)*(NCERT)**

   (*a*) Employment conditions

   (*b*) The nature of economic activity

   (*c*) Ownership of enterprises

   (*d*) Number of workers employed in the enterprise.

2. **________ is a part of the economy where the government holds complete control over services and enterprises.** ***(Re)***

   (*a*) Private sector (*b*) Economic sector

   (*c*) Public sector (*d*) Tertiary sector

3. **Rohit is part of a school project aims to exploring the functions of different economic sectors in India. His team decides to create a chart that distinguishes between the public and private sectors, highlighting examples and revenue methods for each. Using the information provided below, help Rohit and his team complete their chart by matching the appropriate descriptions and examples to the correct sector:** ***(Un)***

	Column-I		Column-II
(A)	Public Sector	(i)	Example of Private Sector
(B)	Private Sector	(ii)	Means of Government Earning
(C)	Tata Iron and Steel Company Limited (TISCO)	(iii)	Government provides services
(D)	Taxes and other ways	(iv)	Owned by Private Individuals or Companies

   (*a*) A-(iii), B-(iv), C-(i), D-(ii)

   (*b*) A-(iii), B-(iv), C-(ii), D-(i)

   (*c*) A-(ii), B-(iii), C-(i), D-(iv)

   (*d*) A-(iv), B-(i), C-(iii), D-(ii)

4. **In the fictional state of Aravalia, there is an urgent need for a new dam to support agricultural activities and provide stable water supply for the growing population. However, private companies are hesitant to invest in this large-scale infrastructure project due to the high costs and risks involved.**

   As an advisor to the Ministry of Infrastructure in Aravalia, evaluate the options below and recommend a strategy to the government for ensuring the dam project is undertaken. ***(Ev)***

   (*a*) Increase taxes on the private sector to fund the project directly.

   (*b*) Provide tax incentives and subsidies to encourage private sector investment in the dam.

   (*c*) Outsource the construction of the dam to international companies.

   (*d*) Redirect focus solely on smaller-scale infrastructure projects.

5. **Which one of the following is a private-sector industry?** ***(Re)*(CBSE, 2020)**

   (*a*) BHEL (*b*) TISCO

   (*c*) OIL (*d*) SAIL

Assertion and Reason

(1 M)

Direction: The following questions consist of two statements – Assertion (A) and Reason (R). Answer these questions by selecting the appropriate option given below:

(*a*) Both A and R are true, and R is the correct explanation of A.

(*b*) Both A and R are true, but R is not the correct explanation of A.

(*c*) A is true, but R is false

(*d*) A is false, but R is true.

1. **Assertion (A):** The public sector in India is responsible for providing essential services to all citizens.

   Reason (R): Public sector activities such as healthcare, education, and infrastructure development are aimed at providing basic services to all citizens irrespective of their income levels. ***(An)***

2. **Assertion (A):** The public sector is essential for providing basic services like roads, bridges, and railways.

   Reason (R): The government undertakes heavy spending to ensure that these facilities are available for everyone because the private sector might charge high rates for their use. ***(Un)***

3. **Assertion (A):** Private sector activities are guided by the motive to earn profits.

   Reason (R): Companies like Tata Iron and Steel Company Limited and Reliance Industries Limited are examples of private sector entities. ***(Un)***

4. **Assertion (A):** The government provides certain services at a reasonable cost to prevent private sector monopolies.

   Reason (R): The government needs to support activities like selling electricity at cost-friendly rates to ensure the survival of many industries, particularly small-scale units. ***(An)***

Subjective Questions

Very Short Answer Type Questions (2 M)

1. **How is Public sector different from Private sector?** ***(Un)*(CBSE, 2020)**

Ans. Public sector organisations are owned, controlled and managed by the government or other state-run bodies whereas Private sector organisations are owned, controlled and managed by individuals, groups or business entities. *(2 M)*

2. **Find the odd one out and say why** ***(Ap)*(NCERT)**

(*i*) Postman, cobbler, soldier, police constable

(*ii*) MTNL, Indian Railways, Air India, Jet Airways, All India Radio

Ans. (*i*) Cobbler is odd one because he works in the private sector while the postman, soldier and police constable work in the public sector or organized sector. *(1 M)*

(*ii*) Jet airways is the odd one because it is owned by a private co. while MTNL, Indian Railways, Air India and All India Radio are owned by the Government of India. *(1 M)*

Short Answer Type Questions (3 M)

1. **Mr. Y from a city in India visits a rural area and finds five people working in a small agricultural farm. More than two people are not required to work in the farm and removing the other three will not affect production. How can one solve this problem of underemployment in rural areas?** ***(Ap)*(CBSE APQ, 2023)**

Ans. In this situation solve this problem of underemployment in rural areas following the reasons: **(Any-3)**

- Government can invest some money in transportation and storage of crops, or **make better rural roads** so that mini-trucks reach everywhere. *(1 M)*
- The government can plan to give **loans** at **lower rates** of interest to people in rural areas to **start something new**. *(1 M)*
- People can start to **set up industries** that process vegetables and agricultural produce like potatoes, rice, wheat, tomato, fruits, etc. which can be sold in outside markets and thus generate employment. *(1 M)*
- In villages near forest areas, they can start honey collection centres where farmers can come and **sell wild honey**. *(1 M)*

2. **Sunil and Raman did their graduation from the same college. Sunil got employed in an unorganised sector and was unhappy whereas Raman got employed in an organised sector and was happy. Why do you think so?**

Write any 3 points of difference between the two sectors. ***(Ev or An)*(CBSE APQ, 2023)**

Ans. In this scenario, Here's how Sunil's and Raman's jobs are different:

- **Job Security:** Raman enjoys job security and benefits like paid leave and pension in the organized sector, unlike Sunil in the unorganized sector. *(1 M)*
- **Working Conditions:** Raman has fixed working hours and gets overtime pay, while Sunil faces uncertain working conditions without extra pay. *(1 M)*
- **Health and Safety:** Raman benefits from medical facilities and a safe workplace, which are often missing in Sunil's unorganized employment. *(1 M)*

3. **Over the forty years between 1973-74 and 2013-14, while production in all the three sectors has increased, it has increased the most in the tertiary sector. As a result, in the year 2013-14, the tertiary sector has emerged as the largest producing sector in India replacing the primary sector. Why do you think tertiary sector is becoming so popular in India? Substantiate your answer giving any 3 reasons.** ***(An)*(CBSE APQ, 2023)**

Ans. The reasons for the growing popularity of the tertiary sector in India are: **(Any-3)**

- **Basic Needs:** The growth of services like education, healthcare, and banking meets basic societal needs, moving demand in the tertiary sector. *(1 M)*
- **Support to Other Sectors:** Development in agriculture and industry increases demand for services like transport and trade, expanding the tertiary sector. *(1 M)*
- **Rising Incomes:** As people earn more, they spend more on services like dining out, tourism, and education, further boosting the tertiary sector. *(1 M)*
- **Technology and IT Services:** The rapid growth of information and communication technology services has significantly contributed to the expansion of the tertiary sector. *(1 M)*

4. **Give a few examples of public sector activities and explain why the government has taken them up.** ***(Un)*(NCERT)**

Ans. **Examples** of public sector activities are banking, transportation, electricity, water and many other basic things that are necessary for people. *(1 M)*

The government has taken up these public sector activities because it wants to provide proper **facilities** to the people of the country at **reasonable** price and providing these facilities to the citizens is the **responsibility** of the Government. *(2 M)*

5. **Explain how public sector contributes to the economic development of a nation.** ***(An)*(NCERT)**

Ans. The public sector contributes to the economic development of a nation in the following ways:

- **Infrastructure:** The public sector creates vital infrastructure like roads, bridges, and hospitals, supporting economic activities and improving living standards. *(1 M)*

- **Basic Services:** It provides essential services like education, healthcare, and water supply, essential for a country's development. *(1 M)*
- **Economic Equity:** Aims to provide services and goods ensuring equitable distribution of resources among all sections of society. *(1 M)*

Long Answer Type Questions (5 M)

1. Explain the differences between public and private sector of economic activities. ***(Un)*** **(CBSE, 2024)**

Ans. **(Any 5 points, each point carries 1 M)**

Basis	Public Sector	Private Sector
Meaning	Public sector organisations are owned, controlled and managed by the government or other state-run bodies.	Private sector organisations are owned, controlled and managed by individuals, groups or business entities.
Ownership	By Central, State or Local government bodies.	By Private individuals or entities.
Motive	Social welfare	Maximising profit
Source of capital	Tax collections, excise and other duties, bonds etc.	Loans, issue of shares, issue of debentures, etc.
Employment benefits	Job security, various allowances, retirement benefits etc.	Higher salary, better promotion chances, competitive environment, incentives, etc.
Areas of operation	Police, military, mining, transportation, banking, education, etc.	Information technology, finance, FMCG goods, hospitality, etc.

2. Explain the role of government in public sector. ***(An)***

Ans. The government plays a pivotal role in the public sector for several reasons:

- **Ownership and Services:** The government owns the majority of the help in the public sector, ensuring the provision of basic services like healthcare, education, and infrastructure to the public. *(1 M)*
- **Social Welfare:** The main Aim of social welfare over profit, the government undertakes projects that benefit society, including those that may not be profitable but are essential for public welfare. *(1 M)*
- **Economic Stability:** By investing in various sectors, the government promotes economic stability and growth, ensuring employment and development across the country. *(1M)*
- **Regulation and Control:** It regulates and controls critical sectors like banking, power, and water supply, ensuring their equitable and efficient distribution. *(1 M)*
- **Infrastructure Development:** Significant investments in infrastructure development such as roads, bridges, and railways facilitate overall economic growth and connectivity. *(1 M)*

MISCELLANEOUS EXERCISE

Multiple Choice Questions

(1 M)

1. Which one of the following pairs is correctly matched? ***(Ev)*(CBSE, 2023)**

(*a*) Primary Sector - Money Lender

(*b*) Secondary Sector - Priest

(*c*) Tertiary Sector - Bank

(*d*) Manufacturing Sector - Gardener

2. In Indian Economy, the three sectors (Primary, Secondary and Tertiary) are interdependent. However, the share of employment in the primary sector remains high. Most appropriate explanation for this could be: ***(Ap)* (CBSE SQP, 2024)**

(*i*) Government policies preferentially treat the primary sector

(*ii*) Indian economy is largely agrarian and majority of population is dependent on agriculture

(*iii*) Inadequate service sector jobs force people to continue working in primary sectors

(*iv*) Primary sector provides raw material for the secondary and tertiary sector.

Choose the correct option

(*a*) Only (*i*) and (*ii*) are true

(*b*) Only (*ii*) and (*iii*) are true

(*c*) Only (*iii*) and (*iv*) are true

(*d*) All are true

3. Agriculture sectors are related to ________ sector of the economy. ***(Re)***

(*a*) Primary sector

(*b*) Secondary sector

(*c*) Tertiary sector

(*d*) All of these

4. Rina's grandmother has been unwell for a few weeks. Rina's family decided to take her to a nearby hospital where she received comprehensive care from various medical professionals, including doctors, nurses, and lab technicians. The hospital also provided advanced diagnostic services and personalized treatment plans. Analyze the given scenario and determine which sector the healthcare industry primarily belongs to. ***(An)***

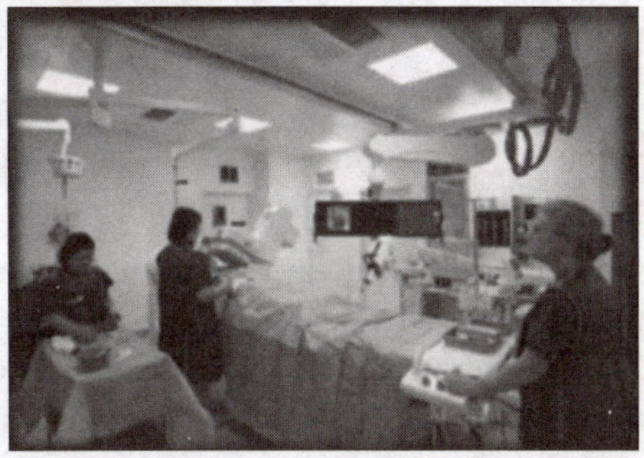

(*a*) Primary Sector (*b*) Secondary Sector

(*c*) Tertiary Sector (*d*) Quaternary Sector

5. Rahul is an economist analyzing the interconnectedness of various sectors of the economy. The image below shows a bustling construction site with workers and buildings under development. What primary sector activity is directly linked to the construction industry depicted in the image? ***(An)***

(*a*) Fishing (*b*) Mining

(*c*) Textile manufacturing (*d*) Retail trade

6. When a country progresses from underdeveloped to developing to developed, the sector that contributes the largest part to the national income, changes.

Which of the following shows this change? ***(Ap)* (CFPQ, 2024)**

(*a*) Primary → Tertiary → Secondary

(*b*) Primary → Secondary → Tertiary

(*c*) Tertiary → Primary → Secondary

(*d*) Tertiary → Secondary → Primary

Assertion and Reason

(1 M)

Direction: The following questions consist of two statements – Assertion (A) and Reason (R). Answer these questions by selecting the appropriate option given below:

(*a*) Both A and R are true, and R is the correct explanation of A.

(*b*) Both A and R are true, but R is not the correct explanation of A.

(*c*) A is true, but R is false

(*d*) A is false, but R is true.

1. **Assertion (A):** The private sector in India provides better quality services than the public sector.

   Reason (R): Private sector activities are driven by market competition leading to better quality services and products compared to public sector activities which may suffer from bureaucratic inefficiencies. ***(Ev)***

2. **Assertion (A):** The primary sector is more vulnerable to natural disasters than the secondary and tertiary sectors.

   Reason (R): Primary activities such as agriculture, forestry, and fishing are heavily dependent on natural resources and are therefore more vulnerable to natural disasters such as floods, droughts, and earthquakes. ***(An)***

3. **Assertion (A):** The secondary sector contributes more to exports than the primary and tertiary sectors combined globally

   Reason (R): Manufactured goods such as machinery, electronics, and automobiles are major exports for many countries, contributing significantly to their foreign exchange earnings. ***(Ev)***

4. **Assertion (A):** The organised sector has a higher productivity level than the unorganised sector in India.

   Reason (R): Organised activities involve higher levels of technology use and economies of scale leading to higher productivity levels compared to informal activities. ***(Ev)***

5. **Assertion (A):** Agriculture is an important sector in India's economy.

   Reason (R): Agriculture provides employment to a large number of people in rural areas and contributes significantly to India's GDP. ***(Un)***

6. **Assertion (A):** The service sector has contributed significantly to India's economic growth in recent years.

   Reason (R): The service sector is less vulnerable to external shocks such as changes in global commodity prices compared to other sectors. ***(Ev)***

7. **Assertion (A):** Public sector enterprises have played a key role in providing essential goods and service to citizens at affordable prices.

   Reason (R): Private sector enterprises are more efficient than public sector enterprises due to their profit oriented approach. ***(An)***

Subjective Questions

Very Short Answer Type Questions (1 or 2 M)

1. How is GDP calculated? ***(Un)*(CBSE, 2020)**
2. Suggest any one measure for the development of any activity of 'Secondary Sector'. ***(Ap)*(CBSE, 2020)**
3. Distinguish between 'primary' and 'secondary' sectors. ***(An)*(CBSE, 2019)**
4. When we produce goods by exploiting natural resources, in which category of economic sector such activities come? ***(Re)*(CBSE, 2018)**
5. Suman's family owns a small farm. She works there with her four siblings. They all put in two hours of work each morning and evening. There isn't any work to be done on the farm in between. Additionally, none of them have any other jobs. What type of unemployment is Suman and her family dealing with? Support the answer with a reason. ***(An)* (CFPQ, 2024)**
6. Raj and Sunita have recently started working. Raj has secured a position at a multinational corporation, while Sunita is working at a local grocery store owned by an individual. Both are concerned about their future in terms of job security and employee benefits. Analyze Raj and Sunita's employment situations to determine the differences in job security and benefits they might experience. ***(An)***
7. Study the given flowchart and answer the questions that follow:

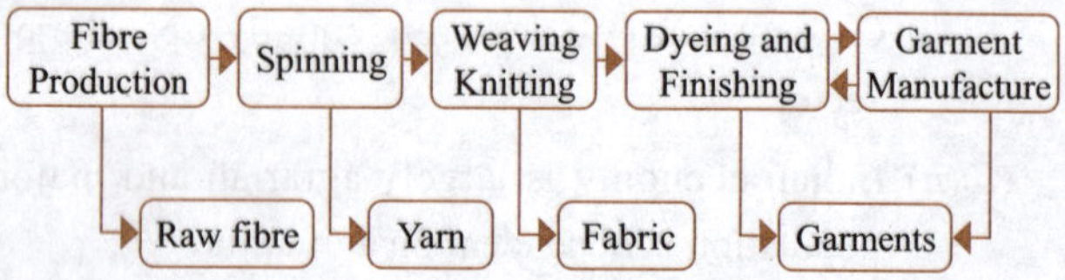

   (*i*) Which is the basic material required for garment manufacturing

   (*ii*) Give one example of value addition in the textile industry. ***(Un)*(CBSE, 2022)**

Short Answer Type Questions (3 M)

1. "All the services of the 'service sector' are not growing equally well." Evaluate the statement. ***(Ev)*(CBSE, 2020)**
2. "Tertiary sector activities help in the development of primary and secondary sectors." Evaluate the statement. ***(Ev)* (CBSE, 2020)**
3. 'Primary sector' was the most important sector of economic activity at initial stages of development". Evaluate the statement. ***(Ev)*(CBSE, 2020)**
4. Analyse the role of the manufacturing sector in the economic development of India. ***(An)*(CBSE, 2017)**
5. Imagine you are an economic advisor in the planning commission of a developing country facing significant employment challenges, especially in the secondary and tertiary sectors. Your task is to analyze and present a detailed report during the next committee meeting on the impacts of inadequate job creation in these sectors. Discuss the impact of not having enough job creation in the secondary and tertiary sectors on employment. ***(An, Ev)***

Long Answer Type Questions (5 M)

1. Why is agriculture called the backbone of Indian economy? Explain. ***(Un)*(CBSE, 2020)**
2. Highlight any five reasons for the importance of tertiary sector in India. ***(Re* or *Un)*(CBSE, 2019)**

Case Based Questions (4 M)

Case Based-I

A small clothing manufacturer, StitchWell Tailors, purchases raw cotton for Rs 100 per kg and dyes for Rs 200 per liter. They use these materials to produce designer shirts. Each shirt requires 2 kg of cotton and 0.5 liters of dye. The cost of labor to make each shirt is Rs 300. They sell each shirt for Rs 1000. StitchWell Tailors is known for its unique designs and quality, catering to local markets.

(i) What is the final product of this case? ***(Re)***

(ii) Is the labor cost considered separately in the GDP? ***(Un)***

(iii) Explain the concept of final goods using StitchWell Tailors in the GDP calculation. ***(Ap)***

Case Based-II

Fueled by economic reforms during the 1990s, India has experienced remarkable growth in the past 25 years, lifting 160 million people out of poverty. India is projected to be the fastest-growing major economy in 2017-2019 and will be the third largest economy in the world by 2030. Moreover, India will become the most populous country by 2022 according to the UN.

The current government has an ambitious reform agenda on many fronts to sustain this growth path and improve citizens' well-being. However, there is a fear that the economy is not creating enough "good jobs" to satisfy the appetites of aspiring youth.

The largest part of the labor force in India is informal, young, and underemployed, with low wages and unmet aspirations. In the book Dreamers: How Young Indians Are Changing Their World, Snigdha Poonan provides a fascinating portrayal of the main opportunities and challenges facing Indian millennials as they enter a more connected, entrepreneurial, and urbanized society. India's population is incredibly young: more than half of its citizens are under the age of 25 and it has the largest number of youth in the world (616.7 million in 2015).

Indian youth have big hopes and ambitions, yet many are not in education, employment, or training—oftentimes, they are unemployable. Many institutions in the country are already thinking about how to address the current challenges and disruptions in the labor market, namely informality, automation, digitalization, globalization, urbanization, and the youth bulge.

In the case of India, changing demographics and informality will probably be the most essential elements to address if continued economic growth, improvements in living conditions, and social cohesion are to be upheld. As many leaders have described in our interviews, the key issue that keeps them up at night is satisfying the enormous work needs for youth, to avoid an "Indian Spring."

(i) India is projected to be the fastest-growing major economy in 2017-2019 and will be the third largest economy in the world by ______. ***(Re)***

(*a*) 2030 (*b*) 2040
(*c*) 2050 (*d*) 2055

(ii) India will become the most ______ country by 2022 according to the UN. ***(Un)***

(*a*) Educated (*b*) Populous
(*c*) Youth (*d*) None of these

(iii) What are the issues with the largest part of the labor force in India? ***(Un)***

(*a*) Informal, young, and underemployed
(*b*) Low wages
(*c*) Unmet aspirations
(*d*) All of the above

(iv) In the case of India, what will probably be the most essential elements to address if continued economic growth, improvements in living conditions, and social cohesion are to be upheld? ***(Ap)***

(*a*) Changing demographics
(*b*) Informality
(*c*) Formality
(*d*) Both (*a*) and (*b*)

Case Based-III

Kanta

Kanta works in an office. She attends her office from 9.30 am. to 5.30 p.m. She gets her salary regularly at the end of every month. In addition to the salary. she also gets provident fund as per the rules laid down by the government. She also gets medical and other allowances. Kanta does not go to office on Sundays. This is a paid holiday. When she joined work. she was given an appointment letter stating all the terms and conditions of work.

Kamal

Kamal is Kanta's neighbour. He is a daily wage labourer in a nearby grocery shop. He goes to the shop at 7:30 in the morning and works till 8:00 p.m. in the evening. He gets no other allowances apart from his wages. He is not paid for the days he does not work. He has therefore no leave or paid holidays. Nor was he given any formal letter saying that he has been employed in the shop. He can be asked to leave anytime by his employer.

(i) What type of sector does Kanta work in? ***(Re)***

(ii) Does Kamal receive any medical and other allowances? ***(An)***

(iii) Do you see the differences in the conditions of work between Kanta and Kamal? ***(Un)***

Case Based-IV

Read the source given below. Attempt any 5 questions out of 6 questions. **(CBSE, 2022 Term 1)**

Take the case of Laxmi and her two-hectare plot of unirrigated land. The government can spend some money, or banks can provide a loan, to construct a well for her family to irrigate the land. Laxmi will then be able to irrigate her land and take a second crop, wheat, during the rabi season. Let us suppose that one hectare of wheat can provide employment to two people for 50 days (including sowing, watering, fertilizer application, and harvesting). So two more members of the family can be employed in her own field. Now suppose a new dam is constructed and canals are dug to irrigate many such farms. This could lead to a lot of employment generation within the agriculture sector itself, reducing the problem of underemployment.

(i) Which one of the following economic sectors is Laxmi related to? ***(Re)***

(*a*) Primary (*b*) Secondary

(*c*) Tertiary (*d*) Quaternary

(ii) In which one of the following sectors is underemployment seen at its maximum? ***(Un)***

(*a*) Industry (*b*) Agriculture

(*c*) Trade (*d*) Commerce

(iii) How does the construction of dams and canals create employment in large numbers in rural areas? ***(Ap)***

(*a*) A large number of engineers are needed.

(*b*) A large number of technicians are also required.

(*c*) Adjustment of large number of unskilled labourers.

(*d*) Executives and administrators can easily be adjusted.

(iv) Which one of the following means of irrigation generally falls under the Public Sector? ***(Re)***

(*a*) Well

(*b*) Tube well

(*c*) Tank

(*d*) Canal

ANSWER KEYS

Multiple Choice Questions

1. (*c*) 2. (*b*) 3. (*a*) 4. (*c*) 5. (*b*) 6. (*b*)

Assertion and Reason

1. (*d*) 2. (*a*) 3. (*d*) 4. (*a*) 5. (*a*) 6. (*b*) 7. (*b*)

Case Based Questions

Case Based-II

(*i*) (*a*) (*ii*) (*b*) (*iii*) (*d*) (*iv*) (*d*)

Case Based-IV

(*i*) (*a*) (*ii*) (*b*) (*iii*) (*c*) (*iv*) (*d*)

HINTS & EXPLANATIONS

Multiple Choice Questions

1. (*c*) Tertiary Sector - Bank
2. (*b*) Only (*ii*) and (*iii*) are true
3. (*a*) Agriculture and allied sectors are related to primary sector of the economy. Primary sector also includes activities like Fishing, poultry farming, Dairy etc.
4. (*c*) The healthcare industry primarily provides services, which places it in the tertiary sector of the economy.
5. (*b*) Mining provides raw materials such as metals and minerals, which are essential for construction.
6. (*b*) Primary $\rightarrow$ Secondary $\rightarrow$ Tertiary

Assertion and Reason

1. (*d*) While private sector activities can provide better quality services due to market competition; however, this may not be universally applicable across all industries or regions.
2. (*a*) Primary activities are heavily dependent on natural resources and are therefore more vulnerable to natural disasters than other sectors.
3. (*d*) Manufactured goods are major exports for many countries, but some developing countries also rely heavily on primary exports such as oil or minerals.
4. (*a*) Self Explanatory
5. (*a*) Both assertion and reason are true and reason is the correct explanation of assertion.
6. (*b*) The service sector has contributed significantly to India's economic growth due to its high productivity and value added services not bacause it is less vulnerable to external shocks.
7. (*b*) Public sector enterprises have played a key role in providing essential goods and services such as healthcare and education to citizens at affordable prices, while private sector enterprises may prioritize profit over social welfare.

Subjective Questions

Very Short Answer Type Questions

1. GDP is calculated by GDP of the country = Goods Produced in Primary Sector + Goods Produced in Secondary Sector + Goods Produced in tertiary Sector. *(2 M)*
2. For the development of the Secondary Sector, one measure can be:
   - **Improve Technology:** Upgrade technology in industries to increase productivity and improve the quality of products. *(1 M)*
   - **Skill Development:** Offer training programs to workers to enhance their skills for better performance in manufacturing. *(1 M)*
3. **Primary Sector** refers to the sector wherein the production of goods and services is done by the exploitation/extraction of natural resources. *(1 M)*

   Secondary Sector refers to the economic sector which transforms raw materials into finished goods through a manufacturing process. *(1 M)*

4. Activities that exploit natural resources fall into the category of Primary Sector. *(1 M)*

Topper's Explanation

"Primary Sector" also called "agriculture & related sector."

5. **Disguised unemployment/under-employment:** Labour is divided between Suman and her siblings and neither of them are using their labour to its full potential. *(2 M)*

6. Raj and Sunita's employment situations can be analyzed by the following points:

(*i*) In the organized sector (like MNC in this scenario), workers like Raj enjoy job security and are entitled to benefits like paid leave, provident fund, gratuity, medical benefits, and pensions. *(1 M)*

(*ii*) The unorganized sector (like the local grocery store, where Sunita works) lacks job security, with jobs being low-paid and often not regular, and lacking benefits like overtime pay or paid leave. *(1 M)*

7. (*i*) Fabric is the basic raw material for garment manufacturing. *(1 M)*

(*ii*) Fabric cutting. *(1 M)*

Short Answer Type Questions

1. All the services of the 'service sector' are not growing equally well because:
   - **Various Growth:** In the service sector, areas like IT and banking are growing fast. *(1 M)*
   - **Limited Growth:** However, small-scale services like street vending and repair services are growing slowly due to less investment and a lack of formal support. *(1 M)*
   - **Skill & Investment:** High-skilled services grow due to more investment and technology, unlike low-skilled ones. *(1 M)*

2. Tertiary sector activities help in the development of primary and secondary sectors due to:
   - **Support and Services:** The tertiary sector provides essential services like transportation, banking, and insurance which help in the growth of primary and secondary sectors. *(1 M)*
   - **Market Expansion:** It helps in marketing and selling the products of these sectors, increasing their reach and profit. *(1 M)*
   - Technological Assistance: Offers technological support and information, enhancing productivity and efficiency in primary and secondary sectors. *(1 M)*

3. The primary sector was the most important sector of economic activity at the initial stages of development because:
   - **Base of Economy:** Initially, the primary sector was the base as it included agriculture and natural resource extraction, essential for survival and growth. *(1 M)*
   - **Employment Source:** It employed the majority of the population, providing basic livelihood and nutrition. *(1 M)*
   - **Raw Material Supply:** Offers raw materials to the secondary sector for further processing and manufacturing, signifying its basic role. *(1 M)*

4. The manufacturing sector plays a essential role in India's economic development through:
   - **Industrial Growth:** Manufacturing boosts industrial sector growth, leading to advancements in technology and production methods. *(1 M)*
   - **Employment Generation:** Creates job opportunities for a large section of the population, reducing unemployment rates. *(1 M)*
   - **Export Enhancement:** Enhances the export potential of the country by producing goods for global markets, improving the trade balance. *(1 M)*

5. The impact of less job creation in secondary and tertiary sectors on employment can be understood by the following points:

(*i*) Despite significant growth in industrial output and services, employment growth in these sectors has not kept pace, leading to a skewed employment scenario. *(1 M)*

(*ii*) The tertiary sector's production rose by 14 times, but employment only rose five times, indicating a mismatch in job creation. *(1 M)*

(*iii*) This led to continued reliance on the primary sector for employment, despite its smaller contribution to GDP. *(1 M)*

Long Answer Type Questions

1. Agriculture is termed as the backbone of the Indian economy for several reasons:
   - **Majority Employment:** Agriculture employs the majority of India's population, supporting millions of families, particularly in rural areas. *(1 M)*
   - **Contribution to GDP:** Although its share has decreased, agriculture still contributes significantly to India's GDP, making it a key economic sector. *(1 M)*
   - **Raw Materials:** It provides essential raw materials to many industries such as cotton for the textile industry and sugarcane for the sugar industry. *(1 M)*
   - **Export Earnings:** Agricultural products form a substantial part of India's exports, earning valuable foreign exchange. *(1 M)*
   - **Food Security:** It ensures food security for the country, which is vital for socio-economic stability. *(1 M)*

2. Here are five reasons for the importance of the tertiary sector in India:
   - **Basic Services:** In any country, services like hospitals, education, and banking are essential. As India develops, these basic services become more important, making the tertiary sector vital. *(1 M)*

- **Support for Primary and Secondary Sectors:** The growth of agriculture and industry boosts services like transport and banking, increasing the importance of the tertiary sector. *(1 M)*
- **Rising Income Levels:** As people's incomes rise, they demand more services like restaurants, tourism, and IT, which expands the tertiary sector. *(1 M)*
- **Information Technology:** Recent years have seen a boom in information and communication technology services, making this sector more significant in India's economy. *(1 M)*
- **Employment Opportunities:** Despite many Indians being employed in the primary sector, the tertiary sector offers a growing number of jobs, especially in services like retail, IT, and transport. *(1 M)*

Topper's Explanation

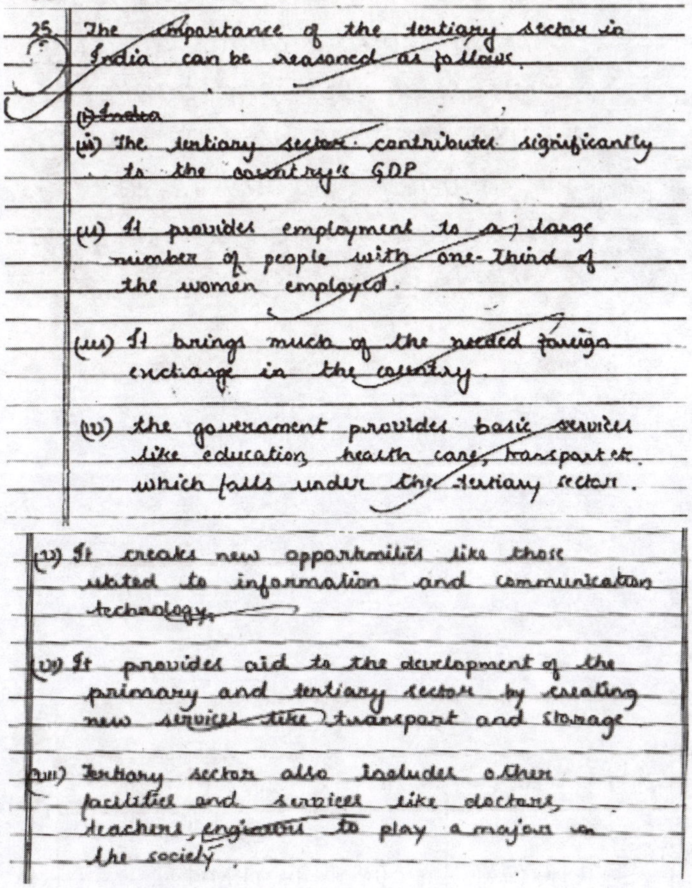

25. The importance of the tertiary sector in India can be reasoned as follows.

(i) ~~India~~

(ii) The tertiary sector contributes significantly to the country's GDP

(iii) It provides employment to a large number of people with one-third of the women employed.

(iv) It brings much of the needed foreign exchange in the country.

(v) the government provides basic services like education, health care, transport etc. which falls under the tertiary sector.

(vi) It creates new opportunities like those related to information and communication technology.

(vii) It provides aid to the development of the primary and tertiary sectors by creating new services like transport and storage

(viii) Tertiary sector also includes other facilities and services like doctors, teachers, engineers to play a major in the society.

Case Based Questions

Case Based-I

(i) The final product in this case study is the designer shirt. *(1 M)*

(ii) No, the labor cost is not considered separately; it's included in the price of the final product, the shirt. *(1 M)*

(iii) In StitchWell Tailors, the final goods are designer shirts, as they represent the end product sold to consumers. When calculating GDP, only the sale price of these shirts is considered to avoid double counting of raw materials and labor costs, thereby accurately reflecting the total economic value added. *(2 M)*

Case Based-II

(i) (*a*) India is projected to be the fastest-growing major economy in 2017-2019 and will be the third largest economy in the world by 2030. *(1 M)*

(ii) (*b*) India will become the most populous country by 2022 according to the UN. *(1 M)*

(iii) (*d*) The largest part of the labor force in India is informal, young and under employed with low wages and unmet aspirations. *(1 M)*

(iv) (*d*) In the case of India, changing demographics and informality will probably be the most essential elements to address if continued economic growth, improvements in living conditions, and social cohesion are to be upheld. *(1 M)*

Case Based-III

(i) Kanta works in the organised sector. This is indicated by her regular employment terms, provision of benefits, and a defined work schedule. *(1 M)*

(ii) No, Kamal does not receive any medical and other allowances. He only gets his wages with no additional benefits. *(1 M)*

(iii) Yes I see, The main differences in work conditions between Kanta and Kamal are: **(Any Two)**

- **Job Security:** Kanta has a secured job with a fixed schedule and salary, while Kamal works without job security or a fixed schedule. *(1 M)*
- **Benefits:** Kanta enjoys benefits like a provident fund and paid holidays; Kamal doesn't receive any benefits or paid leave. *(1 M)*
- **Work Agreement:** Kanta received a formal job letter; Kamal can be dismissed anytime without notice. *(1 M)*

Case Based-IV

(i) (*a*) Primary *(1 M)*

(ii) (*b*) Agriculture *(1 M)*

(iii) (*c*) Adjustment of a large number of unskilled labourers. *(1 M)*

(iv) (*d*) Canal *(1 M)*

MONEY AND CREDIT

3

"Money and Credit" talks about how money changed from trading goods directly to using cash and banks. It also explains how borrowing money (credit) is very important for people to grow their businesses or farms.

SYLLABUS & WEIGHTAGE

List of Concept Names	Years					
	2020	2021	2022	2023	2024	2025
Money as a medium of Exchange and Modern forms of Money (Currency, Deposits with Banks)	0	Exam not conducted	1 Q (2 M)	0	1 Q (1 M)	
Loan Activities of Bank, Two different credit situations and Terms of Credit (Positive Role of Credit, Negative Role of Credit)	1 Q (5 M)		0	0	0	1Q (3 M)
Formal Sectors Credit in India (Formal and Informal Credit who gets what?)	0		1 Q (3 M)	0	1 Q (1 M)	1Q (1 M)
Self Help Groups for the Poor	0		0	1 Q (5 M)	1 Q (3 M)	

CONCEPT MAP

To Access One Shot Revision Video Scan This QR Code

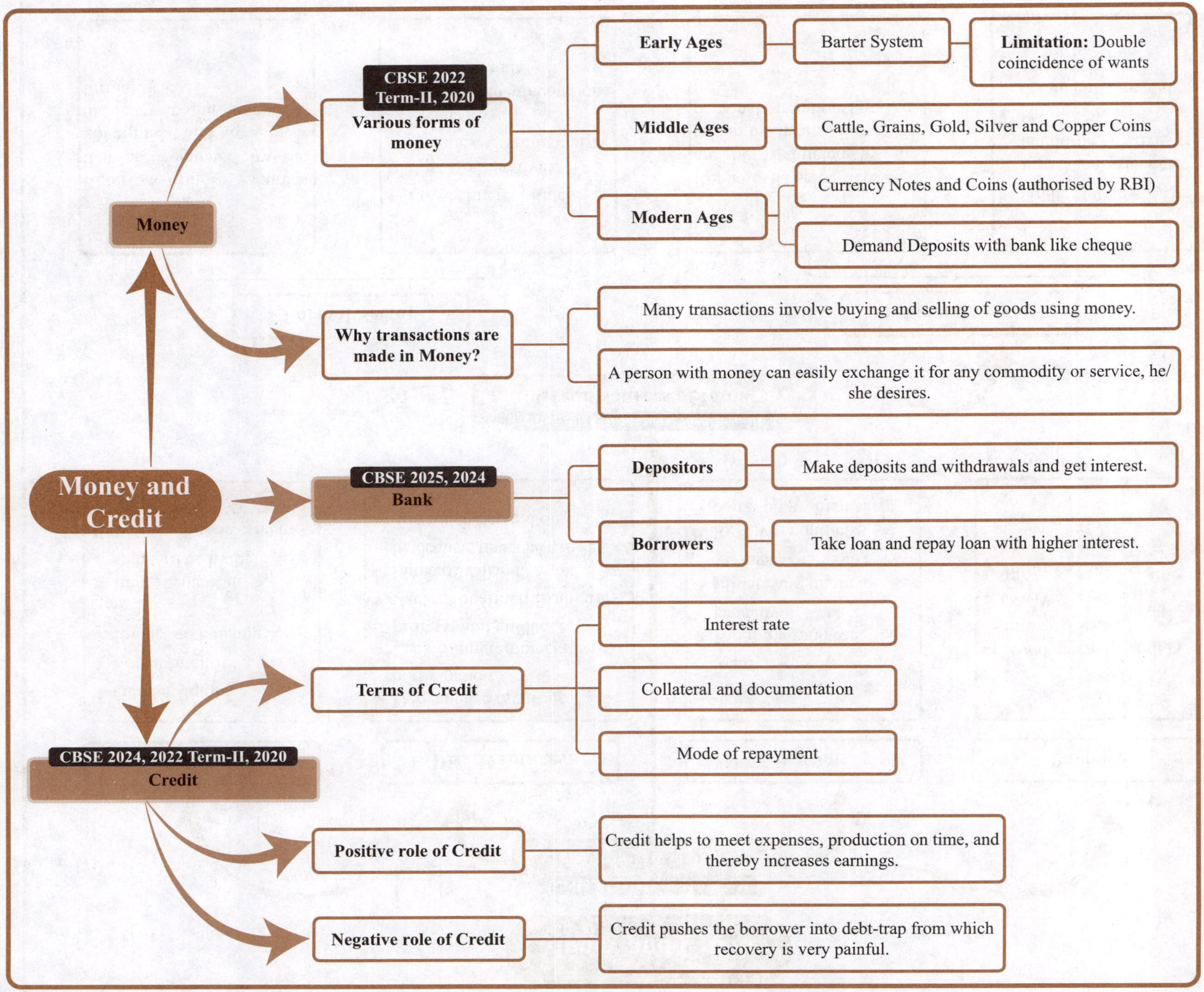

Money and Credit

Self Help Group

CBSE 2025, 2023, 2022 Term-II

Advantages

- Gender Equity
- Social Integrity
- Impact on housing & health
- Improvement in standard of living
- Women empowerment etc.

Disadvantages

- Dependence on group participation
- Lack of upgrading skills & professional guidance
- Lack of qualified facilitators
- Limited availability, Inadequate financial assistance
- Too much depend on Govt.
- NGOs etc.

Functions

- Offer collateral-free loans
- Build the functional capacity
- Initiate and maintain savings
- Resolves conflicts, common problems, etc.

Purpose

- Rural areas depend on informal sectors
- Poverty relief
- Improve social status etc.

Credit sources of India

CBSE 2025, 2024, 2023, 2022 Term-II

Formal Sector

Refer to those sources that are regulated by the government and are subject to legal requirements & formalities.

- Lower Interest Rates
- E.g., Cooperative societies, Commercial Banks, etc.
- Requires documentation and collateral.

Informal Sector

Refer to those sources that are not regulated by the government are based on personal relationships & trust.

- Higher Interest Rates
- E.g., Money lenders, landlords, relatives etc.
- Not requires documentation and collateral.

1 MONEY AS A MEDIUM OF EXCHANGE & MODERN FORMS OF MONEY

NCERT Definitions *(Commonly asked in 1 mark)*

- **Money:** An item used as a **medium of exchange** in daily transactions.
- **Barter System:** A system where **goods** and **services** are **exchanged** directly for other goods and services without using money.
- **Currency: Paper notes** and **coins** used as a medium of exchange.
- **Demand Deposits:** The deposits in the bank accounts can be **withdrawn on demand**, these deposits are called demand deposits.
- **Cheques:** A **written, dated**, and **signed instrument** that directs a bank to pay a specific sum of money to the bearer.

Important Concepts

Barter System Problems In Early Ages

- **Double Coincidence of Wants** should be Fulfilled (parties must agree to exchange goods and services.)

  For Example:

Note: Double Coincidence of Wants is an essential feature of the Barter System.

Money as a Medium of Exchange

- We see several transactions involving money in daily life

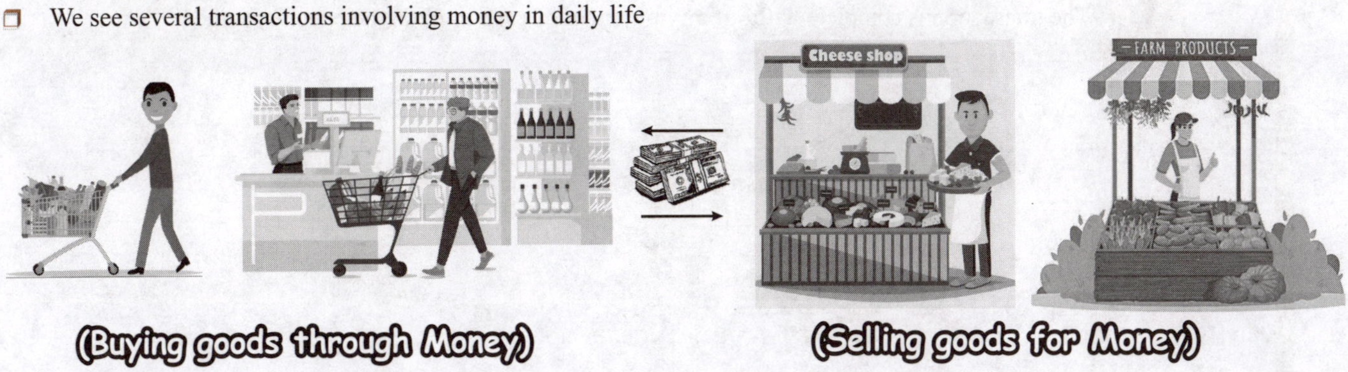

Everyone prefers to receive payment in money and then exchange the money for things that they want.

Currency

- In India, the **Reserve Bank of India issues** currency notes on behalf of the **central government**.
- As per Indian law, **no other individual or organisation** is allowed to issue currency.
- The law **legalises** the use of rupee as a medium of payment that **cannot be refused** in **settling** transactions in India.

Look at a 100 rupees note. What is written on top?

Deposits with Bank

- The other form in which people hold money is as deposits with banks.

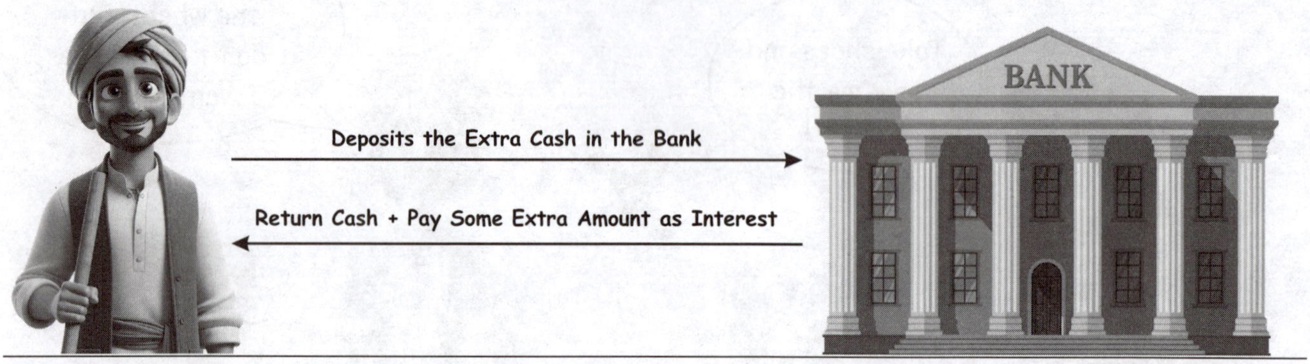

People also have the provision to withdraw the money as and when they require it.

Important Facts

01

Cheque Payments

The money is transferred from **one bank account** to **another bank account** in a couple of days. The transaction is complete **without any payment of cash** through the cheque payment.

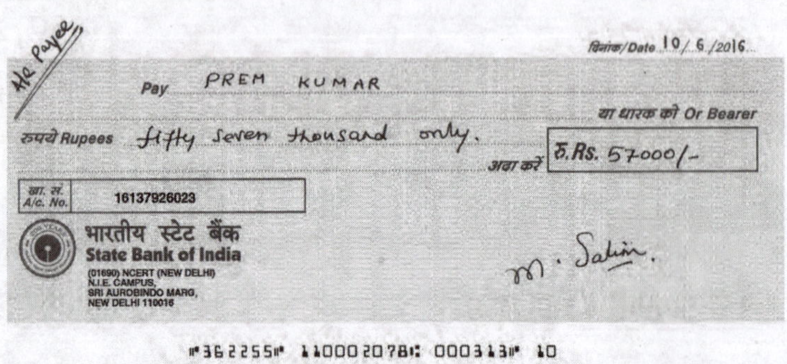

Classification

Medium of Exchange Transactions

- We have seen that money is something that can act as a 'medium of exchange'.
- "Today we have Money" But what about Thousands of Years Ago?

Early Ages

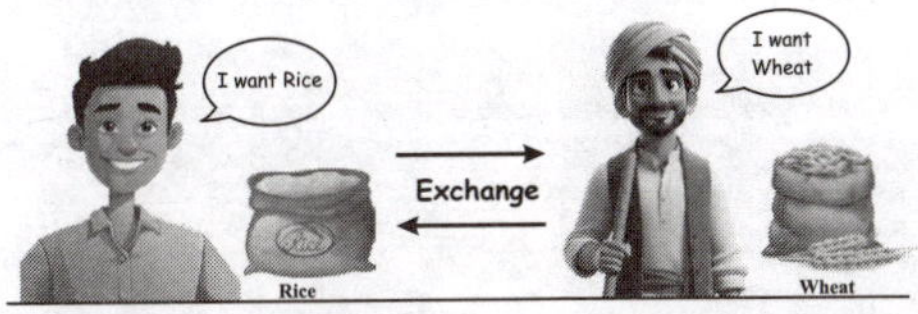

Goods or Services acts as an **intermediary** instrument in the exchange process.

Middle Ages

Metallics coins act as an intermediary instrument in the exchange process.

Modern Ages

Money acts as an intermediary instrument in the exchange process.

Difference Between

Evolution of Money from Early Ages to Modern Forms

Aspect	Early Ages (Barter System)	Middle Ages (Metallic Coins)	Modern Ages (Currency, Coins & Cheques)
Forms of Money	Direct exchange of goods and services without a universal medium.	Metallic coins made of precious metals used as a medium of exchange.	Paper notes and metal coins designated by the government as legal tender.
Example	Selling rice to purchase wheat.	Gold, silver, copper coins	Paper Notes like ₹100, ₹500 Coins like ₹1, ₹2, etc.
Convenience	Inconvenient, required double coincidence of wants	More convenient than barter, but still bulky	Highly convenient, easy to carry, universally accepted
Durability	Perishable goods, not durable	Durable but can degrade over time	Paper notes can wear out, but generally durable; coins are very durable
Value Basis	Subjective and based on mutual agreement.	Based on the metal content of the coins.	No intrinsic value; value is determined by government regulation and trust in the monetary system.

Mnemonics

Functions of Reserve Bank of India (RBI) **"BRIM"**.

B – **B**anker's Bank

R – **R**egulation of Banks

I – **I**ssuer of Currency

M – **M**aintain Cash Reserve

COMPETENCY BASED SOLVED EXAMPLES

Scan Me for Detailed Explanations

Multiple Choice Questions

(1 M)

1. **Which among the following issues currency notes on behalf of the Central Government? *(Re)*(CBSE, 2020)**
   (*a*) State Bank of India
   (*b*) Reserve Bank of India
   (*c*) Commercial Bank of India
   (*d*) Union Bank of India

2. **Mr. Arjun, a farmer needs a new pair of shoes for the upcoming farming season, and a shoemaker, Mr. Bose, requires wheat for his household. Analyze and select how money could simplify their exchange process in this situation. *(Ap, An)***

   (*a*) Both Mr. Arjun and Mr. Bose can engage in a direct swap of their goods without assessing their value.
   (*b*) Mr. Arjun and Mr. Bose can use the money to sell their goods independently and purchase what they need, avoiding the need for a direct swap.
   (*c*) Money enables Mr. Arjun and Mr. Bose to negotiate better terms in their barter arrangement.
   (*d*) Neither has to exchange anything if they both use money.

3. **What is the role of banks in creating and circulating modern forms of money? *(Un)***
   (*a*) Issuing loans that create new deposits in bank accounts which can be used for transactions with other parties.
   (*b*) Setting interest rates to control inflation.
   (*c*) Regulating the supply and demand for money in the economy.
   (*d*) Providing physical currency to customers.

4. **Rahul has a sack of cotton but he is in need of wheat and Anush has a sack of wheat and is in need of cotton, under this situation both will be able to exchange their goods. In case of absence of such coincidence of wants, they may not exchange their goods. Which one of the following would be the best option that describes the mutual exchange of goods and eliminates the exchange of goods? *(Ap)*(CBSE SQP, 2023)**
   (*a*) Double coincidence of want, Exchanging commodity for commodity
   (*b*) Double Coincidence of want, Credit on Commodity
   (*c*) Double coincidence of want, Loan on commodity
   (*d*) Double coincidence of want, Money

5. **Read the image of the cheque. Identify the cheque number from the given options: *(Re)***

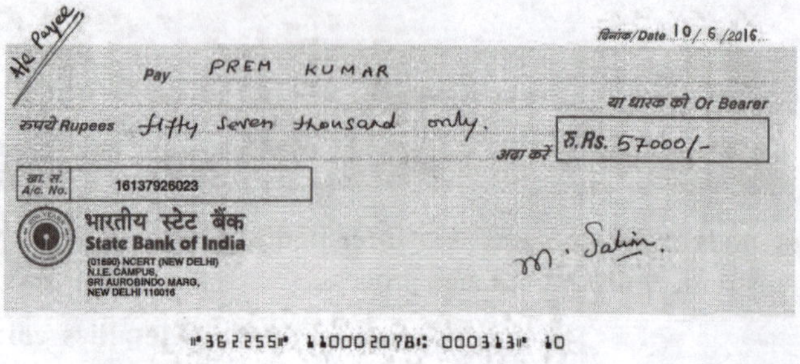

   (*a*) 362255 (*b*) 110002078
   (*c*) 000313 (*d*) 16137926023

OR

A shoe manufacturer, M. Salim has to make a payment to the leather supplier and writes a cheque for a specific amount. This means that the shoe manufacturer instructs his bank to pay this amount to the leather supplier. The leather supplier takes this cheque and deposits it in his own account in the bank. The money is transferred from one bank account to another bank account in a couple of days. The transaction is complete without any payment of cash.

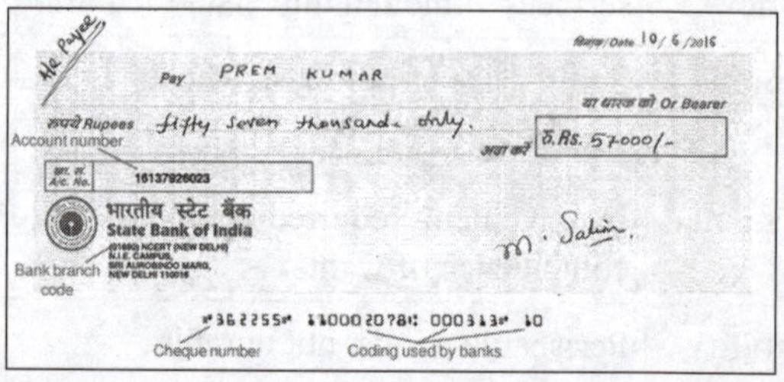

Analyze the cheque details and identify what the numerical code at the bottom of the cheque primarily represents: *(An)*
   (*a*) The amount of money to be transacted
   (*b*) A unique identifier for the cheque itself
   (*c*) The account number of the payer
   (*d*) Coding used by banks for processing

Assertion and Reason

(1 M)

Direction: **The following questions consist of two statements – Assertion (A) and Reason (R). Answer these questions by selecting the appropriate option given below:**
   (*a*) Both A and R are true, and R is the correct explanation of A.
   (*b*) Both A and R are true, but R is not the correct explanation of A.
   (*c*) A is true, but R is false.
   (*d*) A is false, but R is true.

1. **Assertion (A):** The use of money has made the barter system obsolete in modern times.

Reason (R): Barter system was based on the exchange of goods and services without using money as a medium of exchange. **(*Un* and *An*)**

2. **Assertion (A):** The value of money is determined by its purchasing power in the market.

Reason (R): Money can be exchanged for any commodity or service in the market, making its value dependent on the prices of goods and services. **(*Un* and *An*)**

Subjective Questions

Very Short Answer Type Questions (1 or 2 M)

1. **How do double coincidence of wants arise?** **(*Ap*)(CBSE, 2022 Term 2)**

Ans. (*i*) Double coincidence of wants arises when two parties are willing to exchange their goods or services but each party wants what the other party has to offer. (*1 M*)

(*ii*) For example, if a person wants to sell a book and buy a pen, he needs to find another person who wants to buy the book and sell the pen. If there is no match between the needs of the two parties, the exchange cannot take place. (*1 M*)

2. **What is barter system? What is the limitation of this system?** **(*Un*)**

Ans: Barter is a form of trading in which goods and services are exchanged directly for one another without the use of money as a medium of exchange. (*1 M*)

Limitation of barter system is "Double coincidence of wants". (*1 M*)

3. **How is money beneficial in transactions?** **(*Ap*)(CBSE, 2017)**

Ans. It allows a person to easily exchange it for any commodity or service required by him. (*1 M*)

It eliminates the need for a double coincidence of wants. It acts as a medium of exchange. (*1 M*)

4. **What is a 'cheque'? What is the advantage of using it for payment?** **(*Un* and *An*) (CBSE, 2017)**

Ans. A cheque is a piece of paper that instructs the bank to pay a specific amount from a person's account to the person named on the cheque. (*1 M*)

A Cheque is more convenient to carry than large amounts of cash. (*1 M*)

5. **Why one cannot refuse a payment made in rupees in India?** **(*Un*)**

Ans. The RBI issues currency notes on behalf of the Central Government. (*1 M*)

The law establishes the rupee as a legal currency that can be used to settle any transactions in India. (*1 M*)

Short Answer Type Questions (3 M)

1. **Give one example each of modern currency and older currency.** **(*Re*)(CBSE, 2019)**

Ans. An example of modern currency is the Euro, which is used by most European countries. An example of an older currency is the Roman denarius, which was used during the Roman Empire. (*1 M*)

2. **Describe the significance of the Reserve Bank of India.** **(*Un* and *An*)(CBSE, 2020)**

Ans. The Reserve Bank of India plays a crucial role in India's economy:

(*i*) It acts as the country's central bank, regulating and overseeing the banking system. (*1 M*)

(*ii*) It formulates and implements monetary policies to control inflation and promote economic growth. (*1 M*)

(*iii*) It manages the country's foreign exchange reserves and plays a key role in maintaining the stability of the rupee. (*1 M*)

Long Answer Type Questions (5 M)

1. **How has the use of money as a medium of exchange impacted the economy and society?** **(*An* and *Ev*)**

Ans. The use of money as a medium of exchange has had a significant impact on the economy and society. Here are some key ways in which this impact can be seen:

(*i*) Facilitates exchange: Money as a medium of exchange has made it easier for people to trade goods and services with one another. (*1 M*)

(*ii*) Increases efficiency: Money has made transactions more efficient by eliminating the need for bartering. With money, people can quickly and easily exchange value. (*1 M*)

(*iii*) Promotes economic growth: The use of money as a medium of exchange has helped to promote economic growth. It has allowed for the accumulation of capital, investment in businesses, and the creation of new jobs. (*1 M*)

(*iv*) Provides a measure of value: Money provides a common measure of value that allows people to compare the value of goods and services (*1 M*)

(*v*) Enables savings and investment: Money also enables people to save and invest, which can help them achieve long-term financial goals. This has led to the development of financial markets, where people can invest in stocks, bonds, and other financial instruments. (*1 M*)

2. **What role do banks play in the creation and circulation of modern forms of money, such as paper currency and digital currency?** **(*An*)**

Ans. Banks play a critical role in the creation and circulation of modern forms of money, including paper currency and digital currency. Here are some ways in which banks do so:

(*i*) **Creation of paper currency:** Bank, particularly the Central Bank (RBI), is responsible for the creation of paper currency. They have the authority to print and distribute physical cash. *(1 M)*

(*ii*) **Regulation of money supply:** Banks (particularly RBI) also regulate the money supply by using tools such as interest rates and reserve requirements to control the money supply and ensure price stability. *(1 M)*

(*iii*) **Creation of digital currency:** Banks are also involved in the creation of digital currency, which refers to electronic money that exists in digital form. Commercial banks create it through the process of deposit creation. *(1 M)*

(*iv*) **Credit Creation:** Through the provision of loans, credit cards etc., banks create credit. This credit increases the purchasing power of individuals and businesses, contributing to economic activity and growth. *(1 M)*

(*v*) **Security and fraud prevention:** Banks ensure the safety and security of digital currency by implementing measures like sophisticated encryption techniques and strict security protocols to prevent fraud and protect against hacking. *(1 M)*

3. **Consider a scenario where two small businesses operate in a bustling local market—one, a bakery specializing in artisan bread, and the other, a café offering gourmet coffee and sandwiches. They decide to collaborate to attract more customers. The bakery provides freshly baked bread to the cafe, which in turn, serves gourmet sandwiches made from this bread. How does the use of money, instead of bartering goods directly between the bakery and the café, enhance their business operations and economic activities within the market? Discuss the benefits of using money as a medium of exchange. (*Ap*)**

Ans. The role of money and its benefits of using as a medium of exchange can be understood by the following points:

(*i*) **Money, as a medium of exchange**, fundamentally changes how transactions are conducted, moving beyond the restrictive barter system. *(1 M)*

(*ii*) **It facilitates transactions** by providing a common value measure, making trade more straightforward and allowing for the specialization of labor. *(1 M)*

(*iii*) Economic activities are **enhanced** as money increases market **efficiency**, **expands trade opportunities**, and **encourages investment** and **savings**. *(1½ M)*

(*iv*) The case of the shoe manufacturer illustrates how money enables producers to easily convert their goods into a widely accepted medium, which can then be used to purchase diverse commodities. *(1½ M)*

2 LOAN ACTIVITIES OF BANKS, TWO DIFFERENT CREDIT SITUATIONS & TERMS OF CREDIT

NCERT Definitions *(Commonly asked in 1 mark)*

- **Banks: Financial institutions** that accept deposits from the public and create credit.
- **Loans:** Sums of money borrowed that are expected to be **paid back** with **interest**.
- **Depositors:** Individuals who place their **money** in a bank for **safekeeping**.
- **Credit (Loan):** Refers to an agreement in which the lender supplies the **borrower** with money, goods or services in **return** for the **promise** of **future payment**.
- **Debt-Trap:** A situation where a borrower is **unable to repay** their debt, leading to more borrowing and increasing debt.
- **Principal:** The **original sum** of money borrowed in a loan.
- **Interest:** The cost of borrowing money, typically a **percentage** of the **principal**.
- **Terms of Credit:** Interest rate, collateral and documentation requirement and the mode of repayment together comprise what is called the terms of credit.

Important Concepts

Loan Activities of Banks

The difference between what is charged from borrowers and what is paid to depositors is their main source of income.

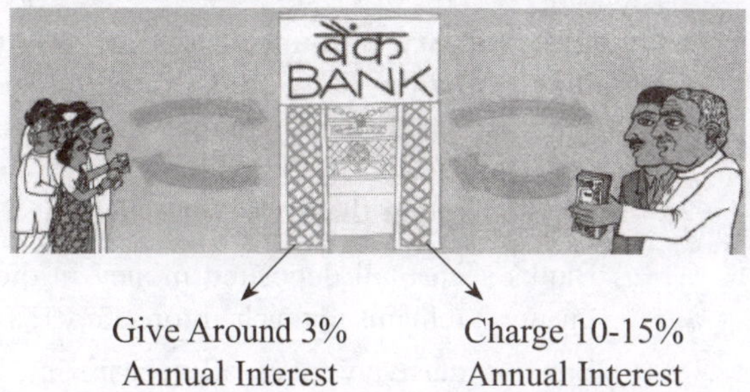

Terms of Credit

- **Interest Rate:** The proportion of a loan charged as interest to the borrower.
- **Collateral:** Collateral is an asset that the borrower owns (such as land, building, vehicle, live stocks, deposits with banks) and uses this as a guarantee to a lender until the loan is repaid.
- **Documentation Requirement:** Employment Record and Income earned by the borrower, other documents etc.
- **Mode of repayment**

  (*a*) Lump-sum (*b*) Installments (Monthly, Quarterly, Annually)

Difference Between

Two Different Credit Situation		
Basic Aspect	**Positive Impact**	**Negative Impact**
Economic Activity	Boosts business and income.	Can deepen poverty due to debt.
Financial Growth	Allows for expansion and profit.	High rates and failure can result in losses.
Employment	Creates job opportunities.	Reduces economic mobility and security.
Wealth Accumulation	Enables profit and reinvestment.	Leads to loss of assets and stress.
Credit Cycle	Positive reinforcement for growth.	Negative cycle leading to impoverishment.

Mnemonics

Terms of Credit **"CID"**

C → **C**ollateral

I → **I**nterest rate

D → **D**ocumentation

COMPETENCY BASED SOLVED EXAMPLES

Scan Me for Detailed Explanations

Multiple Choice Questions

(1 M)

1. **In one of the small villages, a farmer borrows money from the village moneylender at a high monthly interest rate but is not able to repay it back. Next, he borrows it from a bank at a lower interest rate. Gradually he earns and pays back the loan to the moneylender and the bank. Which of the following best describes the role of the bank in this credit situation?** ***(Un & Ap)* (CBSE, 2024)**
   (*a*) The bank acts as a cooperative lender.
   (*b*) The bank facilitates a debt-trap situation.
   (*c*) The bank ensures a fair exchange of goods.
   (*d*) The bank saves the farmer from debt-trap.
2. **Imagine you are a financial advisor at a community seminar explaining how banks function economically. One participant is curious about what banks do with the money people deposit. Based on your knowledge, how would you explain the use of these deposits?** ***(Un)***
   (*a*) Banks secure all deposited money in their vaults to ensure it remains untouched for safety reasons.
   (*b*) Banks exclusively invest all deposits into government securities to avoid any risks.
   (*c*) Banks utilize a significant portion of these deposits to extend loans to individuals and businesses, facilitating economic activity.
   (*d*) Banks are required to transfer all customer deposits directly to the central bank to safeguard national economic stability.
3. **A news report suggests that there's been a sudden rush of people withdrawing their savings from various banks due to a loss of public confidence in the banking system. As an economics student, analyze the potential issue that might arise from this situation.** ***(An)***

   (*a*) A surge in stock market activity as people invest their withdrawn funds.
   (*b*) A decline in interest rates for loans and savings due to surplus funds.
   (*c*) Banks might experience a liquidity crisis as they struggle to meet the increased demand for cash.
   (*d*) An increase in digital transactions as people move away from traditional banking.
4. **What do the banks do with the major deposits that they accept from the customers?** ***(Un)***
   (*a*) Banks use these deposits for their infrastructure.
   (*b*) Banks use a major portion of deposits to extend loans.
   (*c*) Banks use deposits to buy shares in the share market.
   (*d*) Banks use deposits to set up more branches in the country.
5. **Imagine you are a financial advisor analyzing the operations of a local bank. The bank is earning interest from the borrowers and also paying interest to the depositors. To calculate the bank's income, what would you consider as the primary source of the bank's profit?** ***(An)***

   (*a*) The difference between the amount deposited and borrowed by the bank to Reserve Bank of India.
   (*b*) The difference of amount of interest between what is charged from borrowers and what is paid to depositors.
   (*c*) The difference of interest rate between what is charged from borrowers and what is charged from depositor.
   (*d*) The difference between the amount deposited by the depositor and borrowed by the borrower.

Assertion and Reason

(1 M)

Direction: The following questions consist of two statements – Assertion (A) and Reason (R). Answer these questions by selecting the appropriate option given below:

(*a*) Both A and R are true, and R is the correct explanation of A.
(*b*) Both A and R are true, but R is not the correct explanation of A.
(*c*) A is true, but R is false.
(*d*) A is false, but R is true.

1. **Assertion (A):** The terms of credit vary substantially from one credit arrangement to another.
   Reason (R): They may vary depending on the nature of the lender and the borrower. ***(An)***
2. **Assertion (A):** Secured loans require collateral, while unsecured loans do not.
   Reason (R): Collateral provides security for lenders and reduces the risk of default by borrowers. ***(An)***

Subjective Questions

Very Short Answer Type Questions (1 or 2 M)

1. **What do you mean by the term 'collateral'?** ***(Un)***

Ans. Collateral is an asset owned by the borrower that is used as a guarantee to the lender until the loan is repaid. *(1 M)*

2. **Why do banks or lenders demand collateral against loans?** ***(Un)*(CBSE, 2019)**

OR

Why do lenders ask for collateral while lending? ***(Un)*(NCERT Intext)**

Ans. Collateral is used as a guarantee by the lender until the loan is repaid. If the borrower fails to repay the loan, the lender is free to sell the collateral and reimburse his amount. *(1 M)*

3. **Imagine you have just opened a savings account in a local bank and deposited a significant amount of money. Over time, you notice that the balance in your account has increased even though you haven't made any additional deposits. How do bank deposits become a source of income?** ***(Un)***

Ans. Bank deposits can earn money through the interest that banks pay. When we put our money in the bank, they use to give loans to others and share some of the profit with us as interest. *(2 M)*

4. **Given that a large number of people in our country are poor, does it in any way affect their capacity to borrow?** ***(An)*(NCERT Intext)**

Ans. Yes, it has an impact on borrowing capacity because Borrowing is determined by the amount of collateral available. People who are poor and have no security have very little or no borrowing capacity. *(2 M)*

Short Answer Type Questions (3 M)

1. **Explain the three important 'terms of Credit'.** ***(Un)*(CBSE, 2022 Term 2)**

Ans. Three important terms of Credits are:

***(i)* Interest Rate:** This refers to the amount that the borrower must pay in addition to the principal. *(1 M)*

***(ii)* Collateral:** It is the security that the borrower must give the lender as a deposit. The security can be real estate, a car, gold, or even livestock. *(1 M)*

***(iii)* Documents:** Salary slip, bank statements, and records of savings or fixed deposits are all acceptable forms of identification when applying for credit. The paperwork assures the lender. *(1 M)*

2. **Explain, why the banks do not lend credit to certain borrowers.** ***(Un)*(CBSE, 2022 Term 2)**

Ans. Banks do not lend credit to certain borrowers due to the following reasons:

***(i)* Low credit score:** Banks check the credit history of the borrower before approving a loan. If the borrower has a poor credit history or a low credit score, the bank may reject the loan application. *(1 M)*

***(ii)* Lack of collateral:** Banks require collateral to secure the loan. If the borrower does not have sufficient documents, the bank may reject the loan application. *(1 M)*

***(iii)* Unstable income:** Banks prefer borrowers with a stable income source. If the borrower's income is unstable or irregular, the bank may reject the loan application. *(1 M)*

3. **In high-risk situations, credit might create further problems for the borrower. Explain.** ***(An and Ev)*(NCERT)**

Ans. In high-risk situations, credit might worsen the borrower's problems. A borrower obtains credit from a lender for a specific amount of money at a high interest rate. If there is a failure and the borrower suffers a loss, he will fall further into the loan trap. This is referred to as a debt trap. *(1½ M)*

The borrower must repay the loans plus the lender's interest, and he falls further into the debt trap, worsening the borrower's problems. To repay the loan, the borrower must sell a portion of his or her Land. *(1½ M)*

4. **Illustrate with examples the role of 'loan' in 'businesses'.** ***(Ap)*(CBSE, 2017)**

OR

Analyse the role of credit for development. ***(An)*(NCERT)**

Ans.

- **Meeting Working Capital Needs:** Salim, a shoe manufacturer, obtains loans to meet the working capital needs for production, such as hiring more workers and buying raw materials. This credit enables him to complete production on time and increase his earnings. *(1 M)*
- **Facilitating Business Expansion:** By obtaining loans, businesses can expand their operations or take on larger orders they wouldn't have been able to fulfill otherwise. For example, Salim was able to accept and fulfill a large order for 3000 pairs of shoes due to the financial support from loans. *(1 M)*
- **Helping in Risk Management:** Credit allows businesses to manage risks better by ensuring they have the necessary funds to deal with unexpected challenges. E.g. a small farmer, took a loan to cover the costs of cultivation and could do so on time because of loan availability. It shows how businesses rely on loans to navigate uncertainties. *(1 M)*

Long Answer Type Questions (5 M)

1. **"Bank plays an important role in the economic development of the country." Support the statement with examples.** ***(Ap)*(CBSE, 2020)**

Ans. Banks play an essential role in the economic development of a country. Here are some examples that support this statement:

***(i)* Mobilizing savings:** Banks help mobilize savings from the public. They accept deposits from individuals and businesses and use these funds to lend to others. *(1 M)*

***(ii)* Providing credit:** Banks provide credit to individuals and businesses. This credit helps to finance investments in new businesses, expansions of existing businesses, and other productive activities. *(1 M)* (*iii*) **Facilitating trade:** Banks provide trade finance and other services that help facilitate international trade. This helps businesses to expand their operations and enter new markets, which can lead to increased economic activity and growth. *(1 M)*

(*iv*) **Promoting financial inclusion:** Banks help promote financial inclusion by providing access to financial services to people who may not have access to them otherwise. This helps to reduce poverty and promote economic development. *(1 M)*

(*v*) **Supporting government programs:** Banks support government programs by providing funding for infrastructure projects and other initiatives that promote economic development. *(1 M)*

2. "Credit sometimes pushes the borrower into a situation from which recovery is very painful." Support the statement with examples. **(*Ev*)(CBSE, 2020)**

Ans. Credit is an essential component of the financial system, but it can also lead to problems for borrowers. Here are some examples that support the given statement:

(*i*) **High Interest rates:** Borrowers who take out loans with high-interest rates may find it difficult to repay their loans. The high-interest rates can make it challenging for borrowers to keep up with their loan payments. *(1 M)*

(*ii*) **Over-indebtedness:** Borrowers who take out too many loans may become over-indebted. This can lead to financial stress and make it difficult for borrowers to meet their financial obligations. *(1 M)*

(*iii*) **Unforeseen circumstances:** Borrowers who take out loans may face unforeseen circumstances that make it difficult for them to repay their loans. For example, a borrower may lose their job or experience a medical emergency. *(1 M)*

(*iv*) **Predatory lending practices:** In some cases, lenders may engage in predatory lending practices that take advantage of vulnerable borrowers. These practices can lead to default to repay. *(1 M)*

(*v*) **Lack of financial literacy:** Borrowers who lack financial literacy may not fully understand the terms of the loans they are taking out. This can lead to default to repay the loan. *(1 M)*

3. A farmer has borrowed money from a money lender at a high rate of interest, as he could not pay the interest, he was forced to borrow from another landlord to settle the amount for the interest borrowed to the money lender. State the consequences he may face in this situation. **(*An*)(CBSE SQP, 2023)**

Ans. The Farmer has fallen into a "Debt trap", He is in a situation where he will not be able to repay the debt incurred because the Informal sector was the source of credit opted for by the farmer. *(1 M)*

He may face the following Consequences:

- The farmer may face ongoing harassment and physical harm from the men sent by the money lender. *(1 M)*
- He will not be able to make regular interest payments or repay the full amount borrowed. This could lead to significant stress and anxiety, as well as potential physical injuries. *(1 M)*
- Borrowing from another landlord to repay the original loan may create a cycle of debt for the farmer particularly if the interest rates on the second loan are also high. *(1 M)*

The farmer may experience personal consequences, such as mental stress, anxiety, and depression due to the constant pressure of repayments and harassment from the lenders. *(1 M)*

3 FORMAL SECTOR CREDIT IN INDIA

NCERT Definitions *(Commonly asked in 1 mark)*

- **Reserve Bank of India (RBI):** The central bank of India, which oversees the banking system.

Important Facts

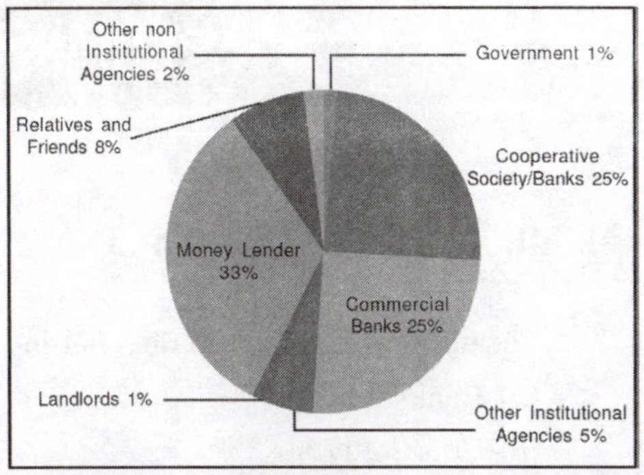

Sources of Credit per ₹ 1000 of Rural Households in India in 2012

- For these reasons, banks and cooperative societies need to lend more.
- This would allow many people could borrow cheaply for a variety of needs.
- They could grow crops, do business, set up small-scale Industries, etc.

Note: Cheap and affordable credit is crucial for the country's development.

Of all the loans taken by urban households, what percentage was formal and what percentage was informal?

Light Gray: Per cent of loans from the **INFORMAL** sector

Dark Gray: Per cent of loans from the **FORMAL** sector

Poor ⇒ Informal Sector

Rich ⇒ Formal Sector

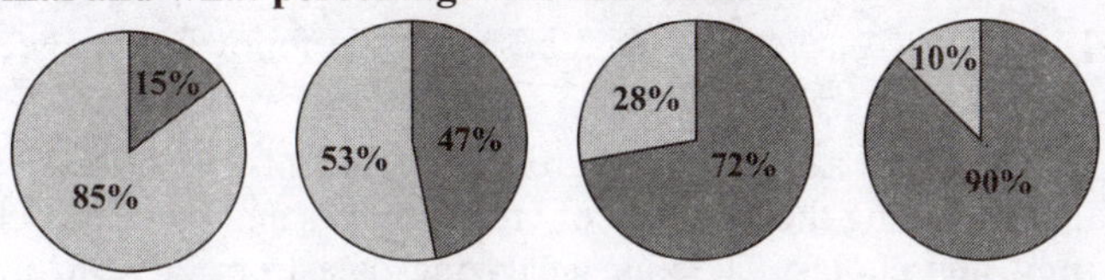

poor housholds | households with few assets | well-off households | rich households

- First, the formal sector still meets only about half of the total credit needs of the rural people.

  (Thus, it is necessary that banks and cooperatives increase their lending particularly in the rural areas, so that the dependence on informal sources of credit reduces.)
- Secondly, while formal sector loans need to expand, it is also necessary that everyone receives these loans.

Classification

The **various types of loans** can be conveniently grouped as

- Formal Source of Credit (Loans)
- Informal Source of Credit (Loans)

Difference Between

Basic Aspect	Formal Sector Credit (loans)	Informal Sector Credit (Loans)
Supervise	The Reserve Bank of India supervises its functioning.	There is no organisation which supervisor its functioning.
Interest Rates	Lower interest rates.	High interest rates.
Requirements	Requires documentation and collateral.	Not requiring documentation or collateral.
Impact	Contributes to development by providing affordable credit.	Can lead to a debt trap and hinder development.
Example	Loans from banks and cooperative 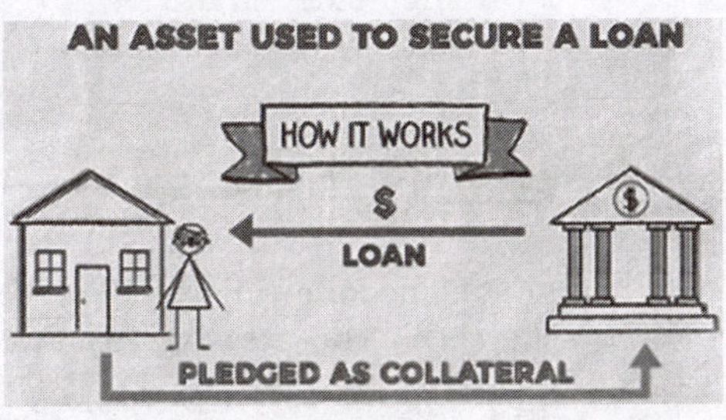	Moneylenders, Trader, Employees, Relative and Friends 

Myth Buster*

- **Myth:** Credit is always beneficial and leads to an improvement in income and welfare.

  Fact: While credit can be beneficial by enabling people to invest and increase their earnings, it can also lead to a debt trap al not used judiciously. For instance, crop failure can turn credit into a burdern, leading to a situation where the farmer is unable to repay and may lose their land or get caught in a cycle of debt.

COMPETENCY BASED SOLVED EXAMPLES

Scan Me for Detailed Explanations

Multiple Choice Questions

(1 M)

1. Formal sources of credit does not include ***(Re)*****(NCERT)**

(a) Banks

(b) Cooperatives

(c) Employers

Direction: Answer **Q-2 & 3** based on the following image and scenario:

In a village in India, a group of students is tasked with understanding the diversity of credit sources and their impact on rural households. They are analyzing data from 2012 to make recommendations for financial inclusion strategies:

Graph: Sources of Credit per ₹ 1000 of Rural Households in India in 2012

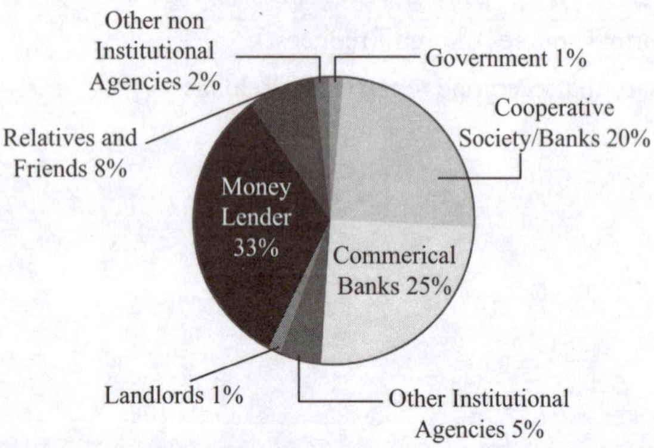

2. If the government plans to reduce the dependency on money lenders by rural households, which sector should it strengthen? ***(An)***

(a) Commercial Banks (b) Cooperative Society

(c) Either (a) or (b) (d) Relatives and Friends

3. Evaluate the role of cooperative societies/banks in rural credit systems. Based on the graph, how effective are they in comparison to commercial banks? ***(Ev)***

(a) Equally effective (b) Less effective

(c) More effective (d) Not at all effective

4. Which of the following is a formal sector credit institution in India? ***(Re)***

(a) Moneylenders (b) Friends and relatives

(c) Cooperatives (d) Relatives

5. Which of the following documents is required to get a loan from a formal sector credit institution in India? ***(Re)***

(a) Aadhaar card (b) Voter ID card

(c) PAN card (d) All of the above

6. Which of the following is a informal sector credit institution in India? ***(Re)***

(a) Commercial banks (b) Regional rural banks

(c) Moneylenders (d) Cooperative banks

7. In a simulation of a modern urban economy, students will explore how the financial status of households influences their access to formal and informal credit sources. Their task will be to analyze the implications of these credit sources on economic growth and personal financial health:

Graph: Of all the loans taken by urban households, what percentage was formal and what percentage was informal?

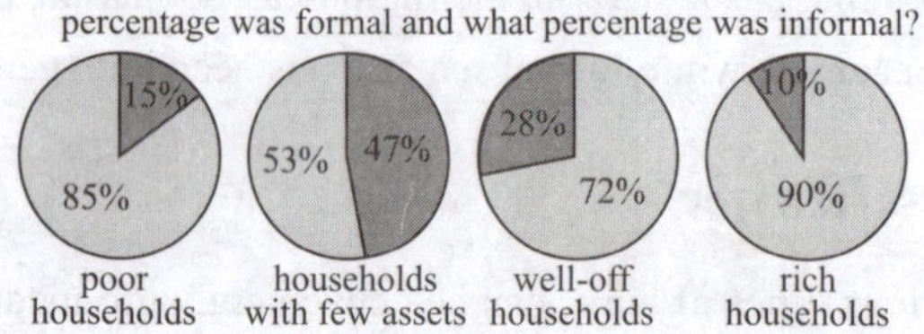

If they were to propose a financial scheme aimed at reducing poor households' dependence on informal credit, which feature would be most crucial? ***(An)***

(a) High-interest rates to ensure profitability

(b) Easy accessibility regardless of collateral

(c) Long-term repayment schedules

(d) Credit available only for entrepreneurial activities

8. Which of the following is not a feature of formal sector credit in India? ***(Re)***

(a) Regulated by the government

(b) Follows rules and regulations

(c) High-interest rates

(d) Provides loans to all sections of society

Assertion and Reason

(1 M)

Direction: The following questions consist of two statements – Assertion (A) and Reason (R). Answer these questions by

* *Concepts beyond the board exam syllabus, offering deeper insight and critical thinking on NCERT topics.*

selecting the appropriate option given below:

(*a*) Both A and R are true, and R is the correct explanation of A.

(*b*) Both A and R are true, but R is not the correct explanation of A.

(*c*) A is true, but R is false

(*d*) A is false, but R is true.

1. **Imagine a situation where a rural community decides to improve its irrigation systems to enhance agricultural productivity and ultimately economic development. They approach a local bank to secure a loan for this initiative. Discuss the role of the bank in facilitating economic growth through this loan and explain how the bank's use of public deposits to finance such loans supports the broader economy.**

   Assertion (A): The primary role of banks is to facilitate economic growth by providing loans.

   Reason (R): Banks use the majority of public deposits to meet the diverse loan requirements of the economy. ***(Un)***

2. **Consider a village in Rajasthan where farmers primarily rely on informal lending to finance their agricultural operations. This practice persists because the local banking services are not aligned with the specific needs of these farmers.**

   Assertion (A): In specific villages of Rajasthan, informal lending is the predominant method of borrowing.

   Reason (R): Banks in these areas do not tailor their loan products to the needs of the local population, unlike local lenders. ***(Un)***

3. **Assertion (A):** The Reserve Bank of India regulates the functioning of informal lenders in the country.

   Reason (R): Informal lenders are not regulated by any authority and operate freely. ***(An)***

Subjective Questions

Very Short Answer Type Questions (1 or 2 M)

1. **How do bank deposits become a source of income?** ***(Ev)***

Ans. Bank deposits can earn money through the interest that banks pay. When you put your money in the bank, they use it to give loans to others and share some of the profit with you as interest. *(2M)*

2. **Imagine a small village in rural India where the majority of the population is engaged in agriculture and small trades. The residents often face financial constraints, particularly during the off-harvest season. In such situations, instead of approaching banks, many villagers prefer to borrow money from local moneylenders, despite higher interest rates. Analyze the scenario above and discuss why poor households in the village might prefer to rely on informal sources of credit rather than bank loans.** ***(An)***

Ans. Poor households rely on informal sources of credit rather than on formal sources because of the following reasons:

(*i*) Poor households rely on **informal sources** due to the **absence of banks** in many rural areas and the difficulty in securing bank loans without proper documents and collateral. *(1 M)*

(*ii*) Informal lenders provide loans **without requiring collateral** and often **know the borrowers personally**, making access to credit easier for the poor. *(1 M)*

3. **State the role of Reserve Bank of India** ***(Un)***

Ans. The Reserve Bank of India (RBI) is the central bank of India and plays a crucial role in regulating the country's monetary policy. Its primary role is to maintain price stability and control inflation in the economy. *(2 M)*

4. **Read the following source and answer the questions that follow:** **(CSBE, 2022 Term 2)**

A House Loan

Megha has taken a loan of ₹5 lakhs from the bank to purchase a house. The annual interest rate on the loan is 12 per cent and the loan is to be repaid in 10 years in monthly installments. Megha had to submit to the bank, documents showing her employment records and salary before the bank agreed to give her the loan. The bank retained as collateral the papers of the new house, which will be returned to Megha only when she repays the entire loan with interest.

(*i*) From which source of credit Megha has taken loan? ***(Re)***

(*ii*) Explain the terms of credit given in the source. ***(Un)***

Ans. (*i*) Megha has taken a loan from the **formal sector** of credit (bank). *(1 M)*

(*ii*) **Terms of Credit:** The terms include **12% annual interest**, repayment in **10 years** with monthly installments, and her house documents as **collateral**. *(1 M)*

Nailing the Right Answer

The formal sector of credit refers to financial institutions such as banks and cooperative societies that are regulated by the government.

5. **Give any two examples of informal sector of credit.** ***(Re)*(CBSE, 2018)**

Ans. The examples of informal sector of credit are: **(Any 2)**

(*i*) Money Lenders *(½ M)*

(*ii*) Family Members *(½ M)*

(*iii*) Friends *(½ M)*

(*iv*) Relatives *(½ M)*

Topper's Explanation

(a) Credit from 'moneylenders.'

(b) Credit from 'family members.'

6. **Explain the reasons for necessity of supervision by the Reserve Bank of India of formal sources of loans.** ***(Ev)*(CBSE, 2019)**

Ans. The RBI monitors the banks to maintain the cash balance. The RBI sees the banks give loans not just to profit-making businesses and traders but also to small-scale industries, small cultivators, small borrowers, etc. *(1 M)*

Topper's Explanation

1 The supervision by the Reserve bank is necessary to ensure that
→ banks donot only give loans to profitable organisation and rich people
→ poor people can benefit from the formal sources of credit
→ bank maintains cash balance.

Short Answer Type Questions

(3 M)

1. Distinguish between formal and informal sources of credit. ***(An)*(CBSE, 2023)**

OR

Differentiate between formal and informal sources of Credit. ***(An)*(CBSE, 2022 Term 2)**

OR

What are the differences between formal and informal sources of credit? ***(An)*(NCERT Intext)**

Ans. **(Any 3)***(3M)*

Basic Aspect	Formal Sector Credit (loans)	Informal Sector Credit (Loans)
Supervise	The Reserve Bank of India supervises its functioning.	There is no organisation which supervisor its functioning.
Interest Rates	Lower interest rates	High interest rates.
Requirements	Requires documentation and collateral	Not requiring documentation or collateral
Example	Loans from banks and cooperative	Moneylanders, Trader, Employees, Relative and Friends

Topper's Explanation

Q1 (b)

		FORMAL SOURCES		INFORMAL SOURCES
SUPERVISION	1	supervised by RBI (Reserve Bank of India)	1	unsupervised
PREVALENCE	2	urban regions	2	rural regions
RATE OF INTEREST	3	low	3	high
RECORD-KEEPING	4	required	4	not necessary
SERVICE CONDITIONS	5	good	5	bad ; ~~workers~~ Borrowers are often harassed
COLLATERAL	6	required	6	usually not required
EXAMPLES	7	banks, cooperatives	7	moneylenders, relatives, traders

2. Dhananjay is a government employee and belongs to a rich household whereas Raju is a construction worker and comes from a poor rural household. Both are in need and wish to take loans. Create a list of arguments explaining who between the two would successfully be able to arrange money from a formal source. Why? ***(Ap* and *Cr)*(CBSE, 2016)**

Ans. Dhananjay might be more successful in arranging money from a formal source compared to Raju:

- **Formal sources favor collateral:** Dhananjay, being rich, likely has assets for loan security. Raju lacks this. *(1 M)*
- **Regular income:** As a government employee, Dhananjay's stable job ensures regular loan repayment. They prefer lending to individuals who can ensure regular repayment. *(1 M)*
- **Credit history:** If Dhananjay has taken and repaid loans before, he might have a good credit history, making formal institutions more likely to lend to him. *(1 M)*

Mistakes 101 : What not to do!

Thinking that just having a job is enough. It's not just about having a job but also about how stable and secure that job is for repaying loans.

3. In the wake of increasing financial irregularities reported in various small banks in India, a policy analyst at a leading think tank is tasked with assessing how the Indian government supervises the functioning of formal financial institutions to ensure their adherence to legal standards and protect the public interest. As a policy analyst, describe how the functioning of formal sources of loans, like banks and cooperatives, is supervised in India. Highlight the roles played by different regulatory bodies, such as the Reserve Bank of India (RBI), in maintaining oversight over these financial institutions. ***(Ev)***

Ans. The role of RBI can be understood by the following points:

(*i*) **Regulatory Body:** The Reserve Bank of India (RBI) primarily regulates banks and non-banking financial companies (NBFCs), ensuring adherence to financial standards and ethical lending practices. RBI ensures that banks maintain a minimum cash balance. *(1 M)*

(*ii*) **Auditing:** Regular audits are conducted to examine the financial health and integrity of lending institutions, ensuring transparency and accountability. *(1 M)*

(*iii*) **Consumer Protection:** The RBI monitors lenders to protect consumers from unfair practices, providing mechanisms to address complaints and disputes effectively. *(1 M)*

4. Why should credit at reasonable rates be available for all? ***(Ev)*(NCERT Intext)**

Ans. Access to credit at reasonable rates is crucial for economic development and social equity:

- **Promotes Growth:** Reasonable credit enables individuals to invest in businesses or education, fostering economic growth and job creation. *(1 M)*
- **Reduces Poverty:** Affordable loans help the poor improve their living standards, reducing poverty and inequality. *(1 M)*
- **Prevents Debt Traps:** Reasonable rates prevent debt traps caused by high-interest loans from informal lenders. *(1 M)*

5. Should there be a supervisor, such as the Reserve Bank of India, that looks into the loan activities of informal lenders? Why would its task be quite difficult? ***(Ev)*(NCERT Intext)**

Ans.

- Yes, there should be supervision to **prevent** exploitation through high-interest rates and unfair recovery practices. *(1 M)*
- However, supervising informal lenders is **challenging** because they are numerous, widely spread, and often operate without formal records. *(1 M)*
- Informal lenders have personal **connections** with borrowers, making it hard to regulate and oversee their activities. *(1 M)*

6. Why do you think that the share of formal sector credit is higher for the richer households compared to the poorer households? *(An)*(NCERT Intext)

Ans. The disparity in the share of formal sector credit between richer and poorer households can be attributed to several factors:

- Richer households have **more assets** to use as **collateral**, making it easier for them to secure loans from formal sources. *(1 M)*
- They have **better documentation** and credit histories, enhancing their trustworthiness in the eyes of formal institutions. *(1 M)*
- Poorer households lack collateral and proper documentation, leading them to depend on **informal sources**. *(1 M)*

7. Two families in a village—one wealthy and the other of modest means—both need to borrow money for agricultural activities. The wealthier family easily secures a loan from a formal banking institution, while the poorer family struggles to find a reliable lender and ends up borrowing from an informal source with higher interest rates. Analyze the reasons behind the disparity in access to formal sector credit between these two families. *(An)*

Ans. The disparity in the share of formal sector credit between wealthier and poorer households can be attributed to several factors:

(*i*) Richer households have more assets to use as collateral, making it easier for them to secure loans form formal sources. *(1 M)*

(*ii*) They have better documentation and credit histories, enhancing their trustworthiness in the eyes of formal institutions. *(1 M)*

(*iii*) Poorer households lack collateral and proper documentation, leading them to depend on informal sources. *(1 M)*

8. Explain any three functions of the Reserve Bank of India. *(Un)*(CBSE, 2019)

Ans. Three of the most important functions are:

- **Regulation of Banks:** The RBI supervises banks to ensure they follow safe banking practices and maintain adequate cash reserves. *(1 M)*
- **Monetary Authority:** It controls the supply of money in the economy to maintain price stability and ensure economic growth. *(1 M)*
- **Issuer of Currency:** The RBI is responsible for the issuance and management of the Indian currency. *(1 M)*

9. Describe the importance of formal sources of credit in economic development. *(Re)*(CBSE, 2019)

Ans. Importance of formal sources of credit in economic development:

(*i*) Formal sources provide cheap credit. *(1 M)*

(*ii*) Credit at an affordable rate is available through formal sources. *(1 M)*

(*iii*) Terms and conditions of credit through formal sources are regulated by the government. *(1 M)*

10. Describe the bad effects of informal sources of credit on borrowers. *(Ev)*(CBSE, 2019)

Ans. The following are the bad effects of informal sources of credit: **(Any-3)**

- **High Interest Rates:** Informal lenders often charge exorbitantly high-interest rates, making it difficult for borrowers to repay the loan, leading to a debt trap. *(1 M)*
- **Lack of Regulation:** Being unregulated, informal credit practices can lead to exploitation, including unfair terms and coercive collection practices. *(1 M)*
- **No Legal Protection:** Borrowers have no legal protection against malpractices, making them vulnerable to harassment and manipulation by lenders. *(1 M)*
- **Debt Trap:** The high costs of borrowing from informal sources can consume a major part of the borrower's income, leaving them in a perpetual cycle of debt. *(1 M)*

Long Answer Type Questions (5 M)

1. "Cheap and affordable credit is crucial for the country's development." Justify the statement. *(Ev)*(CBSE, 2023)

OR

Why is cheap and affordable credit important for economic development? Explain three reasons. *(Ev)*(CBSE, 2019)

OR

Why is cheap and affordable credit important for the country's development? Explain three reasons. *(Ev)*(CBSE, 2018)

Ans. Affordable and available credit is essential for development for several reasons:

- **Economic Growth:** Cheap credit allows people to invest in agriculture, start small businesses, or expand existing ones, fostering economic growth and job creation. *(1 M)*
- **Poverty Reduction:** Affordable loans enable the poor to improve their livelihoods, thereby helping to reduce poverty. *(1 M)*
- **Encourages Beginner:** Lower interest rates make loans attractive for beginners to invest in new ventures, driving innovation and development. *(1 M)*
- **Balances Inequality:** Providing affordable credit to lower-income groups helps reduce financial disparities within the country. *(1 M)*
- **Enhances Standard of Living:** Access to cheap credit improves people's ability to afford education, healthcare, and housing, thereby raising the overall standard of living. *(1 M)*

Topper's Explanation

Introduction : Cheap affordable credit is important for country's development :-

(a) It creates opportunities of self employment eg:- women in Bangladesh, through cheap affordable credit, set up various jobs like sewing for themselves.

(b) It helps the poor people to invest in new technology and resources like farmers to implement buy machines, fertilizers, etc and increase their earning and help in economic development also increasing per capita income of country.

(c) It helps to expand trade and commerce, development in industries, agriculture, and other sectors, thus leading to increase in GDP and foreign exchange earnings.

Conclusion - Hence, it is an index of country's development.

2. Why do we need to expand formal sources of credit in India? **(*An* or *Ev*)(NCERT)**

Ans. We need to expand formal sources of credit in India is essential due to the following reasons:

- **For Everyone:** Formal loans help everyone, especially farmers and small workers in villages, to get money when they need it. *(1 M)*
- **Reduced Exploitation:** By expanding formal credit, we reduce dependence on informal sources that often charge excessive interest rates, leading to debt traps for borrowers. *(1 M)*
- **Economic Development:** When people can borrow money easily, they can start new things like businesses or farming, which helps our country grow. *(1 M)*
- **Security and Trust:** When the loan process is clear and fair, people feel safer borrowing money and banks trust them more. *(1 M)*
- **Monitoring and Support:** Formal lending is monitored, offering support and advice to borrowers, ensuring that loans are used effectively for conscious purposes. *(1 M)*

3. In what ways does the Reserve Bank of India supervise the functioning of banks? Why is this necessary? **(*Ev*)(NCERT)**

OR

"The Reserve Bank of India supervises the functioning of formal sources of loans." Support the statement with examples. **(*Ev*)(CBSE, 2020)**

Ans. The Reserve Bank of India (RBI) supervises the functioning of banks through the following methods, which are essential for financial stability:

(*i*) Saving Money: The RBI makes sure banks keep some money saved so they can give it back when people need their deposits. *(1 M)*

(*ii*) Regular Inspections: RBI conducts inspections and checks to make sure banks are following rules and estimating their financial health. *(1 M)*

(*iii*) Regulating Interest Rates: The RBI helps decide how much interest banks can charge for loans or give on savings to help control how money moves in our country. *(1 M)*

(*iv*) Monitoring Loans: Ensuring that loans are distributed fairly across different sectors and economic groups. *(1 M)*

(*v*) Keeping Things Smooth: The RBI's job is to make sure banks are doing things right so that everyone's money is safe and the economy stays healthy. *(1 M)*

4. What are the three advantages and two disadvantages of unsecured loans? **(*An*)**

Ans. Unsecured loans offer several advantages and disadvantages as listed below:

Advantages:

- **No Collateral Required:** Borrowers do not need to provide assets as security, making it easier for those without collateral to get loans. *(1 M)*
- **Quick Processing:** These loans often have faster approval times since they require less paperwork and no property evaluation. *(1 M)*
- **Flexibility:** They can be used for various purposes, from emergency expenses to business investments. *(1 M)*

Disadvantages:

- **Higher Interest Rates:** Unsecured loans typically come with higher interest rates due to the increased risk for the lender. *(1 M)*
- **Credit Score Impact:** Failure to repay the loan can significantly damage the borrower's credit score, affecting their ability to secure future loans. *(1 M)*

5. Review any three merits and any two demerits of 'formal sector of credit' in India **(*Ev*)(CBSE, 2017)**

Ans. Here are three merits and two demerits of the formal sector of credit in India:

Merits:

- **Available of credit:** Formal credit institutions provide easy access to credit for various purposes, including agriculture, small-scale industries, and personal loans. *(1 M)*
- **Lower interest rates:** The formal sector of credit provides loans at lower interest rates than the informal sector, making it more affordable for borrowers. *(1 M)*
- **Safety and security:** Formal credit institutions are regulated by the government and follow strict guidelines, ensuring that the borrower's interests are protected. *(1 M)*

Demerits:

- **Lengthy loan approval process:** The formal sector of credit has a lengthy loan approval process, which can be a hindrance for borrowers in urgent need of funds. *(1 M)*
- **Stringent eligibility criteria:** The formal sector of credit has strict eligibility criteria that can exclude many borrowers, particularly those with poor credit histories *(1 M)*

4 SELF-HELP GROUPS FOR THE POOR

NCERT Definitions *(Commonly asked in 1 mark)*

- **Self-Help Groups (SHGs):** Groups formed by **community members** to support each other in saving and borrowing.

Important Concepts

Self Help Groups (SHGs)

- Self-help groups are small groups of **poor people** (about 10-15 members).
- They pool **(collect)** their savings (saving per member varies from **Rs 25 to Rs 100 or more**).
- Members can take **small loans** from the group itself to meet their needs.
- Group **charges interest** on these loans but this is still less than what the moneylender charges.
- Most of the important **decisions** regarding the savings and loan activities are taken by the **group members**.
- After a **year or two**, if the group is regular in savings, it becomes **eligible** for availing loan from the **bank**.
- Not only does it help women to become **financially self-reliant**, the regular meetings of the group provide a platform to discuss and act on a variety of **social issues** such as health, nutrition, domestic violence, etc.

Note: Poor people can easily get loans **without collateral** with the help of self-help groups.

Real Life Application Based Questions

Schemes for Women through Self Help Groups

Rs. 5.20 lakh crore bank credit accessed by SHGs under DAY-NRLM from FY 2013-14

Through Self-Help Groups (SHGs) under schemes like the Deendayal Antyodaya Yojana – National Rural Livelihoods Mission, women in rural areas receive financial support and training to start their own enterprises. This initiative helps in reducing poverty by offering women loans at lower interest rates and opportunities to engage in income-generating activities. Additionally, it encourages social empowerment by focusing on education, health, and nutrition, ensuring women's overall development and self-reliance.

Source: https://rural.gov.in/en/press-release/schemes-women-through-self-help-groups

Read the following source and answer the questions that follows:

1. **Name the government scheme that supports women through Self-Help Groups.**

Ans. The scheme is the Deendayal Antyodaya Yojana – National Rural Livelihoods Mission (DAY-NRLM).

2. **What is the main objective of the DAY-NRLM scheme?**

Ans. The DAY-NRLM scheme aims to support women in starting businesses and reduce poverty in rural areas.

3. **How does the DAY-NRLM scheme promote social empowerment among women?**

Ans. It focuses on education, health, and nutrition to empower women socially.

COMPETENCY BASED SOLVED EXAMPLES

Scan Me for Detailed Explanations

Multiple Choice Questions

(1 M)

1. **Who among the following takes the decision regarding saving and loan activities in the Self Help Groups (SHGs)?** ***(Re)*(CBSE, 2023)**

   (*a*) Manager of a Bank
   (*b*) Members of Non-Governmental Organisation (NGO)
   (*c*) Local Money Lenders
   (*d*) Members of Self-Help Group (SHG)

2. **In a SHG most of the decisions regarding savings and loan activities are taken by** ***(Re)*(NCERT)**

   (*a*) Bank
   (*b*) Members
   (*c*) Non-government organisation
   (*d*) None of the above

3. **In the rural village of Nandipur, the "Nandipur Weavers SHG" has faced a situation where one of their members, Mrs. Geeta, is unable to repay her loan due to a sudden family emergency. Analyze the mechanisms within the SHG that can help ensure the loan is recovered.** ***(An)***

   (*a*) The SHG takes immediate legal action against Mrs. Geeta for non-repayment.
   (*b*) Fellow members of the SHG intervene to collectively manage the repayment process.
   (*c*) The bank writes off the loan as a non-recoverable debt.
   (*d*) The SHG increases the interest rates for all members due to the default.

4. **Consider a rural village where a new SHG has been established. The group comprises some women from similar socio-economic backgrounds who are interested in starting small businesses but lack the capital. They gather weekly, contributing a small, fixed amount of money to a common fund.**

   Which of the following statements are true regarding Self Help Groups (SHGs)?

   Statement-I: SHGs consist of 5-10 members typically from different neighborhoods.

   Statement-II: Members meet occasionally to save money.

   Statement-III: SHGs enable members to access loans at lower interest rates than informal lenders.

   Statement-IV: Banks are more inclined to lend to SHGs due to the collective responsibility for loan repayment. ***(Un)***

   (*a*) Statement-I and II (*b*) Statement-III and IV
   (*c*) Statement-II and III (*b*) Statement-I and IV

5. **How do SHGs promote women's empowerment?** ***(Ev)***

   (*a*) By providing education to women
   (*b*) By providing job opportunities to women
   (*c*) By providing a platform for women to come together and take decisions
   (*d*) None of the above

6. **Which of the following is a benefit of an SHG for its members?** ***(Re)***

   (*a*) Access to formal sector credit
   (*b*) Higher interest rates on savings
   (*c*) No need to repay loans
   (*d*) All of the above

7. **In the village of Sunderpur, a group of women faced difficulties in securing individual loans due to their lack of collateral. These women formed a community group called "Sunderpur Sahayata Samiti" (SSS), a self-help group aiming to support each other financially. One day, they gathered to discuss how they could assist each other in accessing small loans for their farming needs without needing traditional collateral. They explored various options to manage and expand their collective savings. How do you think the "Sunderpur Sahayata Samiti" addresses the issue of lack of collateral among its members?** ***(Ap, An)***

   (*a*) By providing legal aid to negotiate with banks
   (*b*) By pooling savings and granting loans to members within the group
   (*c*) By guaranteeing bank loans with group assets
   (*d*) By offering financial literacy classes to improve creditworthiness

Assertion and Reason

(1 M)

Direction: The following questions consist of two statements – Assertion (A) and Reason (R). Answer these questions by selecting the appropriate option given below:

(*a*) Both A and R are true, and R is the correct explanation of A.
(*b*) Both A and R are true, but R is not the correct explanation of A.
(*c*) A is true, but R is false.
(*d*) A is false, but R is true.

1. **Assertion (A):** Self-help groups (SHGs) are formed by poor people to help themselves.

   Reason (R): SHGs are formed by NGOs and government agencies to help poor people. ***(Un)***

2. **Assertion (A):** SHGs encourage savings and thrift among poor people.

   Reason (R): SHGs discourage poor people from spending money on non-essential items. ***(An)***

3. **Assertion (A):** SHGs are only formed in urban areas.

Reason (R): Rural areas do not have the infrastructure to support the formation of SHGs. ***(An)***

4. **Assertion (A):** Self-help groups are instrumental in promoting economic democracy.

Reasoning (R): They contribute to a more equitable distribution of economic power and opportunities. ***(An)*(CBSE APQ, 2023)**

5. **Assertion (A):** SHGs help borrowers overcome the problem of lack of collateral.

Reason (R): SHGs can get timely loans for a variety of purposes and at a reasonable interest rate. ***(An)***

Subjective Questions

Very Short Answer Type Questions (2 M)

1. **What is the role of Self-Help Groups (SHGs) in promoting formal credit in rural areas?** ***(Un)***

Ans. Self-Help Groups (SHGs) play a crucial role in promoting formal credit in rural areas by providing collateral-free loans to their members and building their creditworthiness. *(2 M)*

2. **Give two reasons that prevent rural poor from getting a formal loan.** ***(Re)***

Ans. The two reason are:

(*i*) Lack of Collateral and documentation. *(1 M)*

(*ii*) Arrangements of informal sector loans are flexible in terms of timelines and interest rates etc. *(1 M)*

3. **What is the need for credit among farmers?** ***(Un)***

Ans. Farmers require credit to meet their various needs such as purchasing seeds, fertilizers, pesticides, machinery, etc. They also need credit to meet their household expenses and to repay their previous loans. *(2 M)*

4. **How can self-help groups be effective in reducing poverty among rural communities?** ***(An)***

Ans. Self-help groups can be effective in reducing poverty among rural communities by promoting savings, providing access to credit, and fostering community development. *(2 M)*

Short Answer Type Questions (3 M)

1. **Explain the functions of "Self Help Group".** ***(Un)*(CBSE, 2022 Term 2)**

Ans. The functions of Self Help Group (SHG) are: **(Any three)**

- **Mobilisation of savings:** SHGs mobilize the savings of their members, which are used for lending to the members. *(1 M)*
- **Providing Loans:** SHGs lend money to their members for various purposes such as starting a small business or meeting household expenses. *(1 M)*
- **Low-Interest Rates:** Interest on loans is lower compared to local moneylenders. *(1 M)*
- **Social empowerment:** SHGs promote social empowerment of their members by providing a platform for them to come together, discuss their problems and find solutions. *(1 M)*

2. **Why is it difficult for poor people to get loans from Banks?** ***(An)*(CBSE, 2017)**

Ans. Poor people find it difficult to get loans from banks because

- They lack collateral (like a house or land to secure the loan), lack proper documents, and have no regular income, making banks see them as high-risk borrowers. *(1½ M)*
- Poor people might not have a credit history, which banks use to judge if someone is likely to repay a loan. They also might live far from banks, making it hard to apply for a loan. *(1½ M)*

3. **Explain any three reasons for the banks and cooperative societies to increase their lending facilities in rural areas.** ***(Un)*(CBSE, 2019)**

Ans. Banks and cooperative societies should increase lending in rural areas to:

- **Boost Agriculture:** More loans help farmers buy seeds and equipment, leading to better crops and income. *(1 M)*
- **Support Small Businesses:** Loans can help start new businesses, creating jobs and improving the local economy. *(1 M)*
- **Reduce Poverty:** By providing affordable loans, banks can help lift people out of poverty, improving overall community well-being. *(1 M)*

Topper's Explanation

The banks and cooperative societies should increase their lending facilities in rural areas for the following reason⇒

(i) The poorer section of the society can get a greater share of formal credit and hence prosper.

(ii) The dependence on money lenders and traders, who charge extraorbitary high rates, decrease.

(iii) People can borrow cheaply for meeting the working capital requirement and thus develop their business and agriculture.

Long Answer Type Questions (4 or 5 M)

1. **Justify the role of 'Self Help Groups' in the rural economy.** ***(Ev)*(CBSE, 2023)**

Ans. Self Help Groups (SHGs) play a crucial role in the rural economy through the following:

- **Credit Access:** They help rural people, especially women, to save and borrow money, making it easier to manage their finances and start small businesses. *(1 M)*
- **Access to Loans:** They provide members with access to low-interest loans, enabling them to start small businesses or invest in agriculture, enhancing their income. *(1 M)*
- **Social Empowerment:** SHGs encourage women to work together, boosting their confidence and decision-making power in their households and communities. *(1 M)*

- **Economic Activities:** By providing loans, SHGs enable members to invest in agriculture or small businesses, enhancing their income and livelihoods. *(1 M)*
- **Skills Development:** They facilitate training and skill development, leading to better employment and entrepreneurship opportunities. *(1 M)*

2. Manav needs a loan to set up a small business. On what basis will Manav decide whether to borrow from the bank or the moneylender? Discuss.(*Ap* or *An*)(NCERT)

Ans. Manav will consider these points:

- **Interest Rate:** Banks usually have lower interest rates than moneylenders. So, he'll see which is cheaper. *(1 M)*
- **Loan Terms:** He'll look at how long it can take to pay back the loan and if the terms are fair and manageable. *(1 M)*
- **Paperwork and Collateral:** Banks need lots of documents and usually something big as collateral. Moneylenders are less strict but riskier. *(1 M)*
- **Reputation and Safety:** He'll think about how safe it is to borrow from either and if there's any risk like harassment. *(1 M)*
- **Future Support:** Getting a loan from a bank could help him in the long run, like making a credit history for future loans. *(1 M)*

3. What is the basic idea behind the SHGs for the poor? Explain in your own words. (*Un*)(NCERT)

Ans. The main idea behind Self Help Groups (SHGs) is:

- **Group Savings:** Poor people, especially women, come together to save money regularly. *(1 M)*
- **Self-Loans:** They use these savings to give loans to each other for their needs at lower interest rates than moneylenders. *(1 M)*
- **Support System:** Members support each other in business and personal matters, like a small community. *(1 M)*
- **Bank Trust:** When SHGs save regularly, banks are more willing to give them bigger loans. *(1 M)*
- **Empowerment:** Helps members become self-reliant, confident, and capable of making their own decisions. *(1 M)*

4. In India, about 80 per cent of farmers are small farmers, who need credit for cultivation. (*An*)(NCERT)

(*a*) Why might banks be unwilling to lend to small farmers?

(*b*) What are the other sources from which the small farmers can borrow?

(*c*) Explain with an example how the terms of credit can be unfavourable for the small farmer.

(*d*) Suggest some ways by which small farmers can get cheap credit

Ans. (*a*) Banks might hesitate because small farmers often lack collateral and proper documentation. *(1 M)*

(*b*) Small farmers can borrow from cooperatives, Self-Help Groups (SHGs), moneylenders, and government schemes. *(1 M)*

(*c*) A small farmer might borrow money from a moneylender at a high-interest rate and then lose crops to bad weather, making it hard to repay the loan. They fall into a debt trap, losing more money or even their land. *(1 M)*

(*d*) Small farmers can join SHGs, apply for government subsidies, use Kisan Credit Cards, and approach cooperative banks for lower interest rates. *(1 M)*

5. Why do most of the rural households still remain dependent on informal sources of credit? Explain. (*An*)(CBSE, 2021)

OR

'Poor households continue depending on informal sources of credit,' according to the report. What is the reason for this? Explain your reasoning. (*An*)

Ans. Rural households often remain dependent on informal sources of credit due to several key reasons:

- **Accessibility:** Informal lenders like moneylenders are readily available in rural areas, unlike banks which may be far away or not present. *(1 M)*
- **Collateral Requirement:** Banks usually require collateral for loans, which many rural households lack, making them turn to informal sources. *(1 M)*
- **Less Documentation:** Informal sources don't demand extensive paperwork, attracting those without formal documents. *(1 M)*
- **Quick Distribution:** Moneylenders provide loans quickly without procedural delays, required for urgent agricultural or personal needs. *(1 M)*
- **Flexibility and Relationship:** Rural borrowers prefer informal sources due to the flexible terms and personal relationship with the lender, despite higher interest rates. *(1 M)*

6. Self-help group borrowers overcome the problem of the lack of collateral. Examine the statement. (*An*)(CBSE, 2017)

OR

"The Self-Help Groups help borrowers to overcome the problem of lack of collateral security." Support the statement with examples. (*Ev*)(CBSE, 2020)

Ans. Self-help groups (SHGs) help borrowers overcome the collateral issues through the following ways:

- **Group Responsibility:** Members of an SHG collectively guarantee each other's loans. If one member can't pay, others chip in, removing the need for individual collateral. *(1 M)*
- **Regular Savings:** SHG members save money together regularly, building a fund that backs up the group's loans, acting as a form of collective collateral. *(1 M)*
- **Bank Trust:** Over time, SHGs develop a history of regular repayments and savings, gaining trust from banks, which then provide loans without individual collateral based on the group's credibility. *(1 M)*
- **Credit Accessibility:** SHGs make it easier for members, especially women and the economically weaker, to access credit for various purposes without the need for individual security. *(1 M)*
- **Empowerment:** This system empowers rural individuals who lack assets for collateral, enabling them to invest in businesses, agriculture, or education. *(1 M)*

7. **How can the formal sector loans be made beneficial for poor farmers and workers? Suggest any five measures.** **(Ap)**

Ans. To make formal sector loans more beneficial for poor farmers and workers, the following measures can be implemented:

- **Lower Interest Rates:** Providing loans at supported interest rates to make them affordable for poor farmers and workers. *(1 M)*
- **Collateral Flexibility:** The documentation process should not be complex. It should be an easy process, fast, and timely. *(1 M)*
- **Awareness and Education:** Educating them about formal loans and creating awareness among farmers about formal sector loans and their benefits. *(1 M)*
- **Micro-credit Schemes:** Introducing or expanding microcredit schemes and Self-Help Groups (SHGs) for easier access to credit. *(1 M)*
- **Easy Payback Plans:** Make payment plans that fit with when farmers sell crops or when people earn money to make it easier for them. *(1 M)*

8. **How are self-help groups the building blocks of the rural poor? Explain with examples.** **(*Cr*)(CBSE, 2022 Term 2)**

OR

"Self Help Groups (SHGs) are the building blocks of organisation of the rural poor." Support the statement with examples. **(*Ev*)(CBSE, 2020)**

Ans. Self-Help Groups (SHGs) serve as foundational elements for the rural poor in these ways:

- **Financial Inclusion:** SHGs include rural individuals who are typically excluded from formal banking, offering them a platform for saving and borrowing. *(1 M)*
- **Social Empowerment:** These groups often lead to increased social standing for members, particularly women, enabling them to make collective decisions and manage social issues. *(1 M)*
- **Economic Activities:** Members use loans for agricultural inputs, small-scale businesses, or emergency needs, improving their economic status. *(1 M)*
- **Education and Awareness:** Regular SHG meetings become venues for discussing various topics like health, nutrition, and rights, enhancing community knowledge. *(1 M)*
- **Linkages and Networks:** SHGs connect rural people to banks, government schemes, and markets, providing them with broader opportunities beyond their immediate locality. *(1 M)*

9. **"Self–help groups eliminate poverty and empower women". Substantiate with suitable answer.** **(*Ev*)(CBSE SQP, 2023)**

Ans. Self-Help Groups (SHGs) significantly contribute to poverty elimination and the empowerment of women through:

- **Access to Loans:** Women avail the facilities of loans from formal sources like banks at low rates of interest. *(1 M)*
- **Economic Empowerment:** SHGs provide women with a platform to save and access credit at affordable rates, which enables them to start and expand small businesses. *(1 M)*
- **Skill Development:** SHGs in India have also been successful in providing skill development and training opportunities to women. Through training programs, women are equipped with the necessary skills to start and run successful businesses. *(1 M)*
- **Social Empowerment:** Active participation in SHGs empowers women, boosts confidence, and elevates their social standing within the community. *(1 M)*
- **Other Factors:** Helps to improve other development factors such as literacy levels, improved healthcare, and better family planning. *(1 M)*

MISCELLANEOUS EXERCISE

Multiple Choice Questions

(1 M)

1. Select the formal sources of credit from the given sources and choose the correct option. ***(Un & Ap)* (CBSE, 2024)**

I. Bank II. Moneylender
III. Cooperatives IV. Businessman

Options :

(*a*) Only I and II (*b*) Only II and III
(*c*) Only I and III (*d*) Only I and IV

2. Which term refers to the difference between what banks charge from borrowers and what they pay to depositors? ***(Re)***

(*a*) Interest rate spread (*b*) Collateral requirement
(*c*) Mode of repayment (*d*) Documentation requirement

3. Mr.Y needs a loan to buy fertilisers to enhance crop production. He borrows loan from a bank as it is ***(Ap)*(CBSE APQ, 2023)**

(*i*) Cheap and affordable since rate of interest is lower
(*ii*) free from falling into a debt trap
(*iii*) going to ask him to sell his property
(*iv*) free of interest

(*a*) Only (*i*) (*b*) (*iii*) and (*iv*)
(*c*) (*i*) and (*ii*) (*d*) Only (*ii*)

4. At a community financial education workshop, you are discussing the role of banks in the economy. One attendee asks why banks offer interest on the money people deposit. Based on your knowledge, how would you explain the reason behind this practice? ***(An, Ev)***

(*a*) Banks have to give interest because the government says so.
(*b*) Banks pay interest as a fee for keeping and protecting people's money.
(*c*) Banks give interest to encourage people to deposit their money, which they then use to give out loans to others.
(*d*) Banks are like charities, and they give interest to help people out.

5. A local market operates under two systems: one where traders use money and another where a barter system is utilized. Traders include a vegetable vendor, a cloth merchant, a baker, and a furniture maker.
Select the correct statements regarding transactions involving money and barter system:

Statement-I: Money simplifies the buying and selling of goods.

Statement-II: A direct exchange of goods for goods is more efficient than using money.

Statement-III: Money acts as a promise for future payment in some transactions.

Statement-IV: The barter system requires a double coincidence of wants. ***(Un)***

(*a*) I and III (*b*) II and IV
(*c*) I, III, and IV (*d*) All of the above

6. Which of the following is a disadvantage of formal sector credit in India? ***(Un)***

(*a*) Low interest rates
(*b*) Timely availability of credit
(*c*) No collateral is required
(*d*) Limited access to credit in rural areas

7. Consider a small community, Greenfield, which decides to eliminate the use of money and revert to a barter system. As a local economist, analyze and select the most significant challenge Greenfield residents might face in their daily transactions under this new system. ***(An)***

(*a*) A noticeable increase in the value of their goods and services.
(*b*) Difficulty in finding exact matches for their wants and needs, known as double coincidence of wants.
(*c*) A reduction in the variety of goods and services available within the community.
(*d*) Simplification of transaction processes.

8. Mr. Singh, a farmer, is considering taking an agricultural loan by using his farmland as collateral. Given this scenario, analyze the possible reasons and implications of his decision. Discuss how this choice could reflect his financial planning or constraints. ***(An)***

(*a*) Mr. Singh is likely diversifying his agricultural practices and requires additional capital for investment.
(*b*) Mr. Singh might be facing financial difficulties, pushing him to risk his primary asset to secure necessary funds.
(*c*) Mr. Singh is planning to leverage his existing assets to expand into new agricultural markets.
(*d*) Mr. Singh anticipates a profitable return from his crops, enabling him to repay the loan ahead of schedule.

9. Mr. X has taken credit to make candles during the festive season. Choose the correct options that defines the importance of credit from the given options: **(CBSE SQP, 2024)**

(*i*) it plays a vital and positive role in meeting his target and accelerating his income
(*ii*) the credit helps him to meet the ongoing expenses of production
(*iii*) the credit helps him complete the production on time
(*iv*) it helps him in exercising restraint and get into the habit of taking more credit

(*a*) Only (*iv*) (*b*) (*iii*) and (*iv*)
(*c*) (*i*), (*ii*) and (*iii*) (*d*) Only (*ii*)

Assertion and Reason

(1 M)

Direction: The following questions consist of two statements – Assertion (A) and Reason (R). Answer these questions by selecting the appropriate option given below:

(*a*) Both A and R are true, and R is the correct explanation of A.
(*b*) Both A and R are true, but R is not the correct explanation of A.
(*c*) A is true, but R is false.
(*d*) A is false, but R is true.

1. **Assertion (A):** Rural poor families are still dependent on informal sources of credit.
   Reason (R): For obtaining loan from banks, collateral and special documents are required. ***(Un & An)* (CBSE, 2024)**
2. **Assertion (A):** The formal sector credit is accessible to only a small part of the Indian population.
   Reason (R): The informal sector provides credit to a much larger section of the population. ***(An)***
3. **Assertion (A):** SHGs provide a platform for women to come together and work towards their empowerment.
   Reason (R): Women are not interested in joining SHGs as they have other responsibilities to attend to. ***(An)***
4. **Assertion (A):** Collateral is a requirement for all types of loans.
   Reason (R): Collateral provides security for lenders and reduces the risk of default by borrowers.
5. **Assertion (A):** The mode of repayment refers to how frequently payments are made on a loan.
   Reason (R): Different modes of repayment can affect the total cost of borrowing by impacting interest rates or fees. ***(An)***
6. **Assertion (A):** Banks charge a higher interest rate on loans than what they offer on deposits.
   Reason (R): Banks need to earn a profit and cover their costs and risks associated with lending money. ***(An)***
7. **Assertion (A):** People take loans from banks to meet their financial needs.
   Reason (R): Banks use deposits made by people to lend money to others. ***(Un)***

Subjective Questions

Very Short Answer Type Questions

(1 or 2 M)

1. What are the four main activities of banks related to loans? What do banks use deposits for? ***(Un)***
2. What are the benefits of forming self-help groups for the poor? ***(Un)***
3. How can the government support the formation and development of self-help groups? ***(Un and An)***
4. What is a secured loan? How does it differ from an unsecured loan? ***(Un)***

Short Answer Type Questions

(3 M)

1. Examine any three situations in which credit pushes the borrower into a debt trap. ***(An)*(CBSE, 2019)**
2. Why is it necessary for the banks and cooperative societies to increase their lending facilities in rural areas? Explain. ***(An)*(CBSE, 2017)**
3. Teena wants to open a small Flowers shop near the temple for which she needs ₹45,000. Briefly explain which is the best credit source for her and why. ***(Ev)***
4. Why are formal sources of credit preferred over informal sources of credit? Give three reasons. ***(An)*(CBSE, 2018)**

   OR

   Why are service conditions of formal sector loans better than those of informal sector loans? Explain. ***(An)*(CBSE, 2019)**

Long Answer Type Questions

(5 M)

1. Describe circumstances that drive individuals to seek loans from informal sources of credit. ***(Un)*(CBSE APQ, 2023)**
2. State the potential negative economic implications that would arise in an economy in the absence of the concept of credit. ***(An)*(CBSE APQ, 2023)**
3. "The use of money spans a very large part of our everyday life." Support the statement with examples. ***(Ap)*(CBSE, 2020)**
4. A business owner decides to deposit the company's extra cash into a bank account at the beginning of the month. Explain how this action utilizes the concept of demand deposits and contributes to the business's financial management. ***(Ap)***
5. Miss X wants to start a savoury food store in her village. She wants to supplement her income to raise the standard of living of her family. How, do you think, self-help groups can help, support your answer with reasons?

   OR

   Money by providing the crucial intermediate step eliminates the need for double coincidence of wants. Justify the statement highlighting the significance of the modern form of money in India. **(CBSE SQP, 2024)**

Case Based Questions

Case Based-I

Read the given source and answer the questions that follow :

Loans from Cooperatives

Besides banks, the other major source of cheap credit in rural areas are the cooperative societies (or cooperatives). Members of a cooperative pool their resources for cooperation in certain areas. There are several types of cooperatives possible such as farmers cooperatives, weavers cooperatives, industrial workers cooperatives, etc. Krishak Cooperative functions in a village not very far away from Sonpur. It has 2300 farmers as members. It accepts deposits from its members. With these deposits as collateral, the Cooperative has obtained a large loan from the bank. These funds are used to provide loans to members. Once these loans are repaid, another round of lending can take place. Krishak Cooperative provides loans for the purchase of agricultural implements, loans for cultivation and agricultural trade, fishery loans, loans for construction of houses and for a variety of other expenses. **(CBSE, 2024)**

(i) How do 'Krishak Cooperatives' secure funds for providing loans to their members? ***(Re)***
(ii) What are the different types of loans that 'Krishak Cooperatives' offer to their members? ***(Re)***
(iii) Why are such cooperatives desirable in the rural areas? ***(Un & Ap)***

Case Based-II

Read the following paragraph and answer the questions.

Swapna's Problem

Swapna, a small farmer, grows groundnut on her three acres of land. She takes a loan from the moneylender to meet the expenses of cultivation, hoping that her harvest would help repay the loan. Midway through the season the crop is hit by pests and the crop fails. Though Swapna sprays her crops with expensive pesticides, it makes little difference. She is unable to repay the moneylender and the debt grows over the year into a large amount. Next year, Swapna takes a fresh loan for cultivation. It is a normal crop this year. But the earnings are not enough to cover the old loan. She is caught in debt. She has to sell a part of the land to pay off the debt.

(*i*) Considering Swapna's situation, What alternatives would you suggest for better financial security? (*Ev*)

(*ii*) Assess the impact of high interest rates on small farmers' ability to invest in innovative farming technologies. (*Ev*)

(*iii*) Imagine a scenario where Swapna had access to crop insurance and government subsidies. Propose a plan where these tools could help her manage the financial risks associated with farming. (*Cr*)

Case Based-III

Read the information below and answer the questions that follow:

Grameen Bank of Bangladesh

Grameen Bank of Bangladesh is one of the biggest success stories in reaching the poor to meet their credit needs at reasonable rates. Started in the 1970s as a small project, Grameen Bank 2018 had over 9 million members in about 81,600 villages spread across Bangladesh. Almost all of the borrowers are women and belong to the poorest sections of the society. These borrowers have proved that not only are poor women reliable borrowers, but that they can start and run a variety of small income-generating activities successfully.

"If credit can be made available to the poor people on terms and conditions that are appropriate and reasonable these millions of small people with their millions of small pursuits can add up to create the biggest development wonder."

(*i*) What is the Grameen Bank of Bangladesh? When did it start? (*Re*)

(*ii*) How many members did Grameen Bank of Bangladesh have? (*Re*)

(*iii*) What have the borrowers of Grameen Bank of Bangladesh proved? (*Un*)

Case Based-IV

Read the information below and answer the questions that follow:

Shyamal tells us that every season he needs loans for cultivation on his 1.5 acres of land. Till a few years back, he would borrow money from the village moneylender at an interest rate of five percent per month (60% per annum). For the last few years, Shyamal has been borrowing from an agricultural trader in the village at an interest rate of three percent per month. At the beginning of the cropping season, the trader supplies the farm inputs on credit, which is to be repaid when the crops are ready for harvest. Besides the interest charge on the loan, the trader also makes the farmers promise to sell the crop to him. This way the trader can ensure that the money is repaid promptly. Also, since the crop prices are low after the harvest, the trader is able to make a profit from buying the crop at a low price from the farmers and then selling it later when the price has risen.

(*i*) Explain the terms under which Shyamal borrows money from the agricultural trader. (*Un*)

(*ii*) Write one advantage and disadvantage Shyamal faces by borrowing from the agricultural trader instead of the village moneylender. (*An*)

(*iii*) How does the agricultural trader ensure his profit when lending money to farmers like Shyamal? (*Ap*)

Case Based-V

Read the following paragraph and answer the questions.

Festival Season

It is festival season two months from now and the shoe manufacturer, Salim, has received an order from a large trader in town for 3,000 pairs of shoes to be delivered in a month time. To complete production on time, Salim has to hire a few more workers for stitching and pasting work. He has to purchase the raw materials. To meet these expenses, Salim obtains loans from two sources. First, he asks the leather supplier to supply leather now and promises to pay him later. Second, he obtains loan in cash from the large trader as advance payment for 1000 pairs of shoes with a promise to deliver the whole order by the end of the month. At the end of the month, Salim is able to deliver the order, make a good profit, and repay the money that he had borrowed.

(*i*) Considering Salim's strategy to manage production and financial needs, discuss an alternative approach he could have used to secure resources without borrowing. (*Ap*)

(*ii*) Propose a marketing strategy that Salim could use to increase demand for his shoes during the off-peak season. (*Cr*)

(*iii*) Evaluate Salim's choice to borrow from the leather supplier and the trader. (*Ev*)

ANSWER KEYS

Multiple Choice Questions

1. (*c*) **2.** (*a*) **3.** (*c*) **4.** (*c*) **5.** (*c*) **6.** (*d*) **7.** (*b*) **8.** (*b*) **9.** (*c*)

Assertion and Reason

1. (*a*) **2.** (*b*) **3.** (*b*) **4.** (*d*) **5.** (*a*) **6.** (*a*) **7.** (*b*)

HINTS & EXPLANATIONS

Multiple Choice Questions

1. (*c*) Banks and Cooperatives are formal sources of credit as they follow government regulations and offer loans at reasonable interest rates. Moneylenders and businessmen are informal sources and not part of the formal credit system.

Topper's Explanation

C) Only I and III

2. (*a*) Interest rate spread

3. (*c*) i and ii

4. (*c*) Banks pay interest on deposits to attract and keep customers' money. This helps the bank because they can use this money to give loans to other people. When banks lend this money, they charge interest from the borrowers, which is usually higher than what they pay to the depositors. This difference in interest allows the banks to earn money and run their operations.

5. (*c*) Statements I, III, and IV correctly describe the functions and advantages of money in transactions. Statement II is incorrect because the text illustrates that money provides a more efficient means of exchange than a direct exchange of goods.

6. (*d*) Limited access to credit in rural areas

7. (*b*) In the barter system adopted by Greenfield, residents will face the significant challenge of the double coincidence of wants, where each participant in a trade must have what the other desires at the same time. This requirement complicates transactions because finding a person whose needs align perfectly with what one has to offer becomes a frequent and challenging obstacle, making trade less efficient compared to using money as a medium of exchange.

8. (*b*) Using farmland as collateral indicates that Mr. Singh might not have other assets or sufficient liquidity to secure a loan. This decision could stem from a need to manage immediate financial hardships or fund critical farming operations, reflecting a reliance on primary assets for financial support in challenging times.

9. (*c*) (*i*), (*ii*) and (*iii*)

Assertion and Reason

1. (*a*) Rural poor depend on informal credit sources because banks require collateral and official documents, which they often lack. This makes it difficult for them to access formal loans, leading to reliance on moneylenders despite high-interest rates.

Topper's Explanation

A) Both A and R are ~~tue~~ true + R is correct explanation

2. (*b*) Both A and R are true. But Reason is not the correct explanation of Assertion because primary reason the formal sector credit is accessible to only a small part of the Indian population is not just because the informal sector provides credit to a larger section. But it is also due to factors like the lack of banking services in certain areas, the stringent criteria for loan approval in the formal sector, and the lack of awareness or trust in formal banking systems among certain populations

3. (*b*) Both A and R are true. But Reason does not specify why SHGs provide a platform for women to come together.

4. (*d*) The assertion is false, but the reason is true. Collateral is not a requirement for all types of loans, but it does provide security for lenders and reduces the risk of default by borrowers.

5. (*a*) Both A and R are true and R is the correct explanation of A because the mode of repayment directly influences the total cost of borrowing through its impact on how interest accumulates and is paid over the duration of the loan.

6. (*a*) Self-Explanatory.

7. (*b*) Both A and R are true, but (R) is not the direct explanation of (A). People take loans to meet their financial needs, which could be for a variety of reasons such as buying a house, investing in business, or funding education.

Subjective Questions

Very Short Answer Type Questions

1. Deposits, withdrawals, loans, and loan repayments. *(1 M)*

   To meet the loan requirements of people. *(1 M)*

2. Self-help groups provide a platform for the poor to save, access credit, and engage in collective decision-making. *(1 M)*

   They also promote social capital and foster community development. *(1 M)*

3. The government can support the formation and development of self-help groups by providing financial assistance, technical support, and legal recognition. *(2 M)*

4. A secured loan is a type of loan that requires collateral to be provided by the borrower as security for the loan. *(1 M)*

   An unsecured loan does not require collateral. *(1 M)*

Short Answer Type Questions

1. Credit can push a borrower into a debt trap in the following situations:
   - **Multiple loans:** Taking multiple loans at the same time can lead to a debt trap, especially if the borrower is unable to repay the loans on time. *(1 M)*
   - **High-interest rates:** High-interest rates can make it difficult for the borrower to repay the loan, leading to a debt trap. *(1 M)*
   - **Lack of income:** Borrowers who do not have a steady source of income may find it difficult to repay the loan, leading to a debt trap. *(1 M)*

2. - It promotes financial inclusion, supports the growth of the agricultural sector, and stimulates economic development in these areas. *(1 M)*
   - The rural poor often face difficulty in accessing credit from formal sources, leading them to rely on informal sources, which charge high-interest rates and often trap them in debt cycles. *(1 M)*
   - By providing credit access to the rural poor, banks and cooperative societies can promote entrepreneurship and self-employment, leading to increased income levels and improved standards of living. *(1 M)*

3. - Teena, who wants to open a small flower shop near the temple, can consider getting a loan from a microfinance institution as the best credit source. *(1 M)*
   - Microfinance institutions provide small loans to entrepreneurs who do not have access to traditional banking services. *(1 M)*
   - These loans come with flexible repayment terms, low interest rates, and require minimal documentation. This makes them an ideal credit source for small businesses such as Teena's Flower Shop. *(1 M)*

4. Formal sources of credit are preferred over informal sources of credit for the following reasons:
   - **Lower interest rates:** Formal sources of credit charge lower interest rates as compare to informal sources of credit, which can charge excessive rates. *(1 M)*
   - **Transparency:** Formal sources of credit are more transparent than informal sources of credit. The terms and conditions (like interest rates, repayment schedules etc.) of formal sector loans are clearly laid out. *(1 M)*
   - **Legal protection:** Borrowers who take loans from formal sources are protected by law, which ensures that they are not exploited by the lenders. *(1 M)*

Long Answer Type Questions

1. - **Immediate financial requirement:** Informal sources of credit provide immediate access to funds whereas Formal financial institutions often involve lengthy procedures and paperwork. *(1 M)*
   - **Absence of collateral:** Formal sources require collateral against loans. Informal lenders, on the other hand, may not require collateral or may accept non-traditional assets as security, making it easier for these individuals to obtain loans. *(1 M)*
   - **Unavailability of documents:** Obtaining loans from formal sources often requires a substantial amount of documentation, including proof of identification, income, residence etc. In this case Informal sources are more accessible. *(1 M)*
   - **Informal economy and irregular income:** Informal lenders are more flexible and willing to extend credit based on personal relationships and community standing rather than based on regular income and various documents availability. *(1 M)*
   - **Limited/restricted access to formal sources of credit:** Geographic and socio-economic factors can restrict access to formal banking services. Rural areas, in particular, may lack banking infrastructure, making informal lenders the only available option. *(1 M)*

2. - **Limited access to funds for starting businesses or making investments:** Credit plays a crucial role in entrepreneurship and the expansion of existing businesses. Without it, potential entrepreneurs might struggle to gather the necessary capital to start a new businesses. *(1 M)*
   - **Limited capacity of savings:** Credit availability can indirectly encourage savings among individuals. In economies where credit is accessible, people may feel more secure in spending their savings on significant investments or expenses. *(1 M)*
   - **Limited ability to finance education and skill development:** Credit facilities, such as student loans, play a crucial role in higher education and skill development accessible. Without these, many individuals might be unable to afford the costs of tertiary education or vocational training. *(1 M)*

- **Limited ability to purchase high-worth items:** High-value assets like house and vehicles are typically purchased with the help of loans. In the absence of credit, the real estate and automotive industries would suffer significantly. *(1 M)*
- **Limited financial flexibility and convenience:** Without access to credit, both consumers and businesses would find it challenging to manage cash flow, handle emergencies, and make timely investments. *(1 M)*

3. - **Buying Essentials:** Money is fundamental for purchasing daily necessities such as food, clothing, and shelter, ensuring our basic needs are met. *(1 M)*
   - **Access to Services:** It allows us to access essential services like healthcare, education, and utilities (water, electricity), which are pivotal for maintaining a quality life. *(1 M)*
   - **Transportation and Mobility:** Money facilitates transportation, whether it's for daily commuting or occasional travel, enabling us to reach different places for work, leisure, or other purposes. *(1 M)*
   - **Investments and Savings:** It is instrumental in planning for the future through savings and investments, which help in securing financial stability and addressing unforeseen emergencies. *(1 M)*
   - **Leisure and Entertainment:** Money enables participation in leisure and entertainment activities, contributing to our overall well-being and happiness by allowing us to engage in hobbies, travel, and cultural experiences. *(1 M)*

4. Demand deposits are bank account deposits that can be withdrawn on demand. It is beneficial in several ways:
   - **Safety of Funds:** Depositing cash into a bank account safeguards the money against theft or loss, providing security and peace of mind for the business owner. *(1 M)*
   - **Accessibility:** Demand deposits allow for high liquidity, meaning funds can be withdrawn or transferred quickly and easily when needed, without significant processing delays. *(1 M)*
   - **Interest Earnings:** While typically lower than other investment forms, demand deposits often earn some interest, contributing to increased earnings for the business over time. *(1 M)*
   - **Cash Flow Management:** Managing cash flows effectively is critical for any business. Having funds in a bank account enables better tracking and management of cash flows. *(1 M)*
   - **Facilitating Transactions:** With cash deposited in a bank, a business can utilize various payment methods such as cheques, wire transfers, and online payments, facilitating smoother business transactions. *(1 M)*

5. Self Help Groups help the poor to become self-reliant in terms of savings and generating income. **(Any five)**
   - Can avail the facilities of loans from formal sources like banks at a low rate of interest. *(1 M)*
   - They do not demand collateral and so she can easily access. *(1 M)*
   - Self-help groups are exclusively meant for rural women like Miss X to make them economically independent through self-employment opportunities. *(1 M)*
   - This will help her to start and expand her business and thus improving the standard of living. *(1 M)*
   - Skill development: SHGs in India have also been successful in providing skill development and training opportunities to women. Through training programs, she can be equipped with the necessary skills to start and run a successful business. *(1 M)*
   - Social empowerment. By providing a platform for women to come together, share their experiences, and support each other, SHGs have empowered women to take charge of their lives and become active participants in their communities. *(1 M) (Any other relevant points)*

OR

- In a barter system where goods are directly exchanged without the use of money, double coincidence of wants is an essential feature. In contrast, in an economy where money is in use, money by providing the crucial intermediate step eliminates the need for double coincidence of wants. *(1 M)*
- People with the help of money can purchase whatever he needs. No goods or other items are needed for exchange anymore. Since money acts as an intermediate in the exchange process, it is called a medium of exchange. *(1 M)*
- Modern forms of money include currency — paper notes and coins. Unlike the things that were used as money earlier, modern currency is not made of precious metals such as gold, silver and copper. And unlike grain and cattle, they are neither of everyday use. The modern currency is without any use of its own. *(1 M)*
- It is accepted as a medium of exchange because the currency is authorised by the government of the country. In India, the Reserve Bank of India issues currency notes on behalf of the central government. As per Indian law, no other individual or organisation is allowed to issue currency. Moreover, the law legalises the use of rupee as a medium of payment that cannot be refused in settling transactions in India. No individual in India can legally refuse a payment made in rupees. Hence, the rupee is widely accepted as a medium of exchange. *(2 M) (Any other relevant points)*

Case Based Questions

Case Based-I

(i) Krishak Cooperatives accept deposits from their members and use them as collateral to obtain large loans from banks. These funds are then used to provide loans to their members. *(1 M)*

(ii) Krishak Cooperatives provide loans for agricultural implements, cultivation, agricultural trade, fishery, house construction, and other essential expenses needed by rural farmers. *(1 M)*

(iii) Cooperatives provide cheap and accessible credit to rural farmers, helping them buy seeds, fertilizers, and equipment. They also reduce dependence on moneylenders, offer financial stability, and promote self-sufficiency among small farmers and workers. This improves agricultural productivity and rural livelihoods. *(2 M)*

Topper's Explanation

36.1 This cooperative has 2300 farmers as members. It accepts deposits from each member which are used as collateral to obtain a large loan from the bank which are further used to provide loans to their members.

* Banks act as cooperative lenders here. Loans to buy raw materials, release their mortgaged land, for marketing their output etc are provided

36.2 Formal loans were extended by banks to the cooperatives which were further extended by them to their members. Cooperatives and Banks come in the formal source of credit

36.3 (1) Cooperative are useful because they reduce the heavy dependency of rural people on informal sources of credit which charge a very high interest rate and they help to avail loan facilities from banks by overcoming the lack of collateral issue

(2) They organise the rural poor and provide a platform for discussing social issues like health, education etc.

Case Based-II

(i) Alternatives such as microfinance institutions, government-backed loans, or cooperative society loans typically offer lower interest rates and are more forgiving during agricultural downturns. These sources also sometimes provide additional support services such as agricultural training and financial literacy programs. *(1 M)*

(ii) High-interest rates can significantly hinder small farmers' ability to invest in innovative technologies. The higher the interest, the more income is diverted toward repaying debts rather than investing in new technologies that could increase productivity and sustainability. This creates a cycle of low investment and limited growth potential. *(1 M)*

(iii) If Swapna had access to crop insurance, she could file a claim to receive compensation for the loss due to the pest attack, thus reducing her financial loss. Government subsidies could also lower the cost of inputs like seeds and pesticides, reducing her initial investment. Together, these tools would allow Swapna to absorb financial shocks better and continue farming without falling into debt. A proposed plan could include regular workshops by agricultural experts to assist farmers in choosing the right insurance and understanding the available subsidies. *(2 M)*

Case Based-III

(i) Grameen Bank of Bangladesh is a financial institution that provides credit to the poor, particularly women, in rural areas of Bangladesh. It started in 1970s. *(1 M)*

(ii) As of 2018, Grameen Bank of Bangladesh had over 9 million members in about 81,600 villages spread across Bangladesh. *(1 M)*

(iii) The borrowers of Grameen Bank of Bangladesh have proved that not only are poor women reliable borrowers, but that they can start and run a variety of small income-generating activities successfully. *(2 M)*

Case Based-IV

(i) Shyamal receives farm inputs on credit at the beginning of the cropping season, which he must repay after the harvest. Additionally, he must promise to sell the crop to the trader. *(1 M)*

(ii) Advantage for Shyamal includes a lower interest rate compared to the village moneylender, and the immediate provision of farm inputs needed for cultivation. *(1 M)*
Disadvantage includes a loss of freedom to sell his crops in the open market. *(1 M)*

(iii) The trader buys the crops at a low price immediately after harvest, when prices are typically lower, and sells them later at a higher price, ensuring a profit margin. *(1 M)*

Case Based-V

(i) An alternative approach Salim could have considered is forming a partnership with other small manufacturers to pool resources collectively or negotiating bulk purchase discounts for raw materials to reduce upfront costs. *(1 M)*

(ii) To boost demand during off-peak seasons, Salim could launch a marketing campaign focusing on versatility and durability, positioning his shoes as suitable for various occasions beyond festivals. *(1 M)*

(iii) Salim's choice to borrow from both the leather supplier and the trader is practical, providing him with necessary resources without immediate cash outflow. However, this could be seen as risky; it increases his debt and potentially compromises his business's financial stability if sales do not meet expectations. Ethically, relying on delayed payment to suppliers might strain relationships if not managed transparently. Nevertheless, if Salim maintains clear communication and fulfills his promises, these relationships can also strengthen, building trust and possibly leading to more favorable terms in the future. *(2 M)*

GLOBALISATION AND THE INDIAN ECONOMY

4

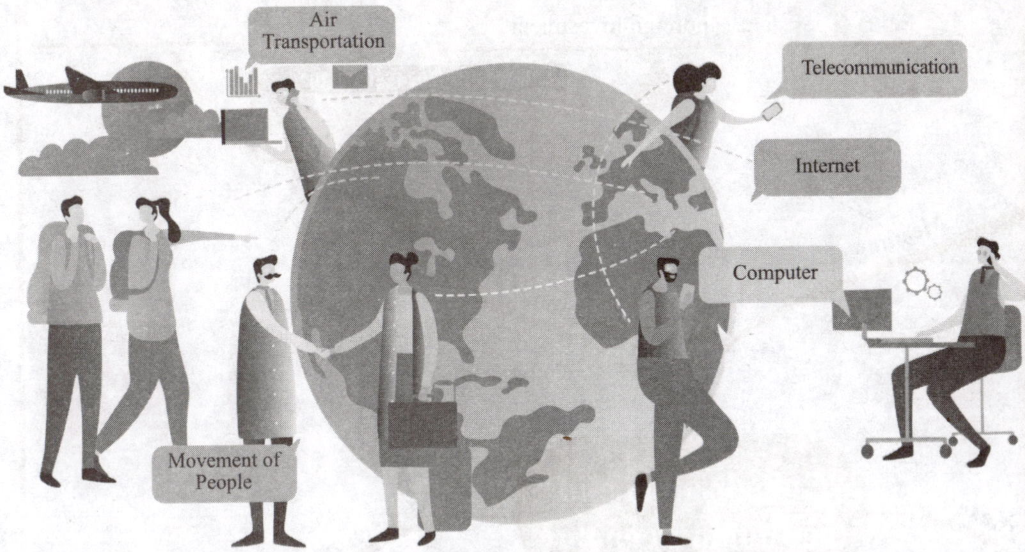

"Globalisation is growing fast because of new technology and easier trade rules. This has brought countries closer, making the world more connected."

SYLLABUS & WEIGHTAGE

List of Concept Names	Years					
	2020	2021	2022	2023	2024	2025
What is Globalisation?	0	Exam not Conducted	1 Q (5 M)	0	1 Q (1 M)	
Factors that have enabled globalisation (Technology, Liberalisation of foreign trade and foreign investment policy)	1 Q (1 M)		1 Q (5 M)	1 Q (5 M)	1 Q (5 M)	2 Q (1 M + 2 M)

CONCEPT MAP

To Access One Shot Revision Video Scan This QR Code

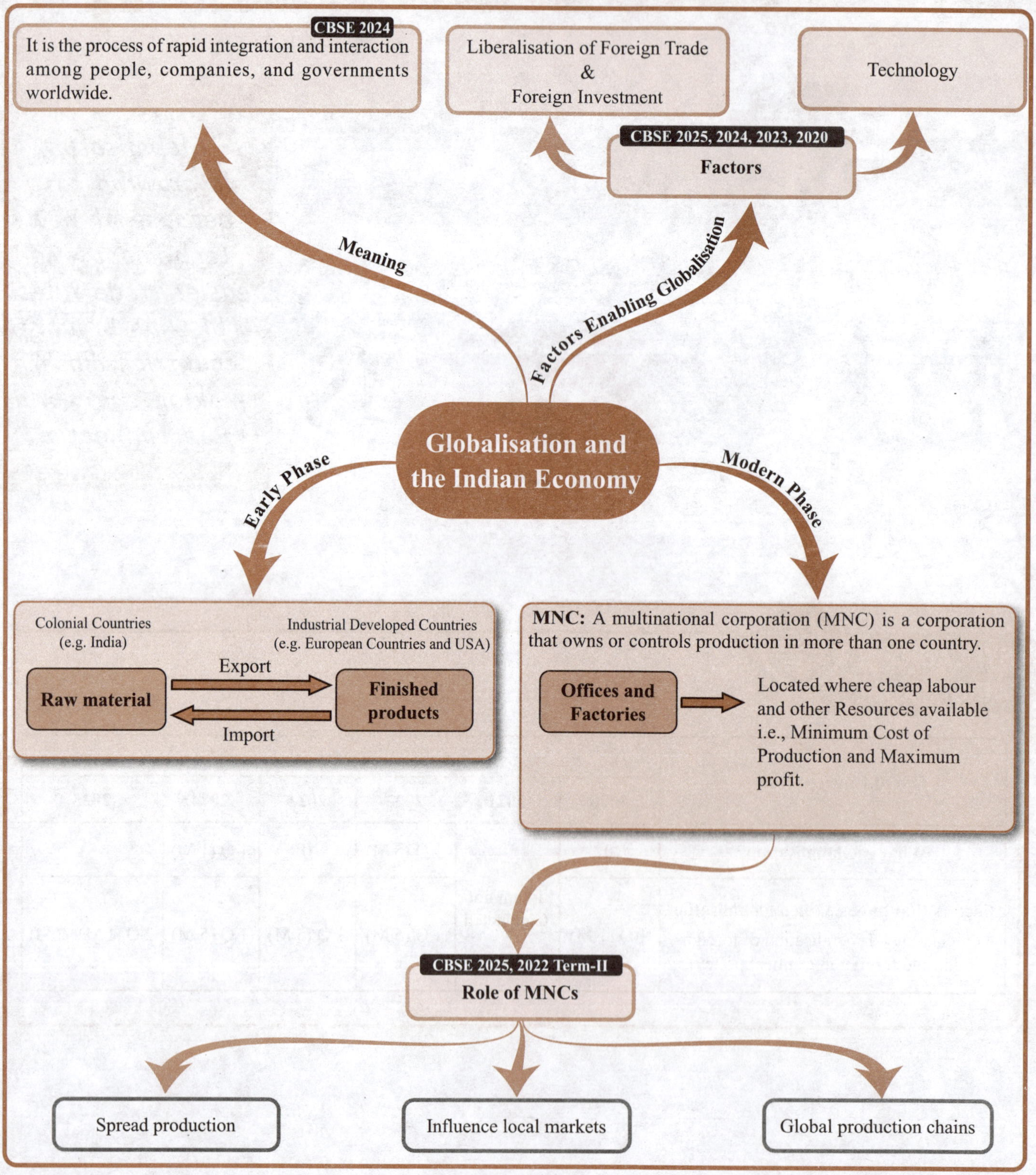

1 WHAT IS GLOBALISATION?

NCERT Definitions *(Commonly asked in 1 mark)*

- **Globalisation:** Globalisation is the process of rapid integration and interaction among people, companies; and governments worldwide. It involves the movement of goods, services, data, technology, and the economic resources of capital. It first appeared in the early 20th century.
- **MNC:** A multinational corporation (MNC) is a corporation/company that owns or controls production in more than one nation/country.

Important Concepts

Early Phase of Globalisation

- In the middle of the 20th century, colonial countries like India exported raw materials and foodstuffs to Industrial Developed countries like the USA and European countries & imported Finished products from these countries.

Modern Phase of Globalisation

- In the modern phase, MNCs emerged on the scene. These companies set up their offices and factories in areas where cheap labour and other resources were available so that the cost of production would be low and profit could be maximized.

Difference Between

Criteria	Multinational Corporations (MNCs)	Domestic Companies
Ownership & Control	Own and control production in more than 1 country.	Own and control production in its country of origin only.
Investment	Make Foreign Investments	Investments within the home country.
Role in Globalisation	Major role in Globalisation by integrating markets.	May benefit from Globalisation but have no major role.
Influence on local Economies	Significant impact on local markets and industries	Comparatively less impact on local markets.
Examples	Coca-Cola, Ford Motor, Deloitte, Unilever, Samsung etc.	BPCL, HPCL, Local law firm etc.

COMPETENCY BASED SOLVED EXAMPLES

Scan Me for Detailed Explanations

Multiple Choice Questions

(1 M)

1. The integration and interconnection among the economies of different countries is called: ***(Re)***

(*a*) Privatisation
(*b*) Liberalisation
(*c*) Globalisation
(*d*) Social Welfare

2. In the early phase of globalisation, India exported ____________ to European countries and imported ____________ from European countries. ***(Un)***

(*a*) Raw materials, Finished products
(*b*) Finished products, Raw materials
(*c*) Cloths, Raw material of cloths
(*d*) None of these

3. **A chocolate bar is made by an American company. Today, it is manufactured in India as well, at affordable prices. Which of the following is responsible for this?** ***(An)* (CFPQ, 2024)**

(*a*) Demand for export
(*b*) Complexity of production
(*c*) Removal of trade barriers
(*d*) Dispersal of production centres

4. **Offices and Factories of MNCs are located where ________________ is cheap.** ***(Un)***

(*a*) Machinery (*b*) Labour
(*c*) Land (*d*) None of these

5. **Look at the picture given below. Identify the type of the company from the following options.** ***(Un)***

(*a*) Multinational Company
(*b*) Domestic Company
(*c*) Multi-regional Company
(*d*) National Company

6. **Choose the correct option.**
Globalisation, by connecting countries, shall result in ***(Un)*(NCERT Intext)**

(*a*) lesser competition among producers
(*b*) greater competition among producers
(*c*) no change in competition among producers
(*d*) None of these

Assertion and Reason

(1 M)

Direction: The following questions consist of two statements – Assertion (A) and Reason (R). Answer these questions by selecting the appropriate option given below:

(*a*) Both A and R are true, and R is the correct explanation of A.
(*b*) Both A and R are true, but R is not the correct explanation of A.
(*c*) A is true, but R is false
(*d*) A is false, but R is true.

1. **Assertion (A):** In the middle of 20th century, colonial countries imported raw materials from industrial developed countries and exported finished product to these countries.

Reason (R): In the modern phase, multinational companies emerged on the ground. ***(Un)***

2. **Assertion (A):** Globalisation is related to only two or three countries.

Reason (R): MNCs play a major role in the globalisation process. ***(An)***

Subjective Questions

Very Short Answer Type Questions

(1 or 2 M)

1. **What is globalisation? Differentiate between multinational corporations and domestic companies.** ***(Un)*(CBSE, 2019)**

OR

What do you understand by globalisation? ***(Un)*(NCERT)**

Ans. Globalisation is the process of rapid integration and interaction among people, companies, and governments worldwide. *(1 M)*

The main difference between multinational corporations and domestic companies is that MNCs operate in two or more countries whereas domestic companies operate in only one country. *(1 M)*

2. **Why do MNCs set up their offices and factories in those regions where they get cheap labour and other resources?** ***(An)*(CBSE, 2016)**

Ans. MNCs set up offices and factories for production in regions where they get cheap labour and other resources. This is done so that the cost of production is low and the MNCs can earn greater profits. *(1 M)*

Topper's Explanation:

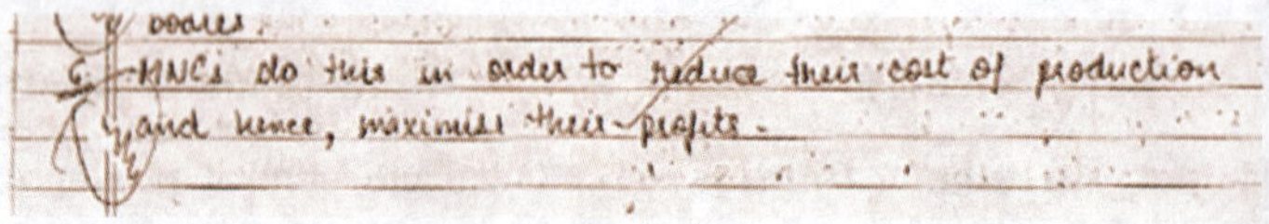

Short Answer Type Questions

(3 M)

1. **Assess any three advantages of globalisation.** ***(An)*(CBSE, 2019)**

Ans. The advantages of globalisation are as follows:

- **Access to New Markets:** Globalisation provides business units with the opportunity to expand into new markets, globally reach buyers, and increase revenue. *(1 M)*
- **Spread of knowledge and technology:** Globalisation spreads knowledge among buyers and sellers and it brings the latest technology globally. The MNCs use inputs with the latest technologies. *(1 M)*
- **Promotes economic growth:** Globalisation promotes economic growth by distributing resources more efficiently and also indirectly through complementary reforms in terms of capital and financial development. *(1 M)*

Long Answer Type Questions

(5 M)

1. **Why do multinational corporations set up their offices and factories in certain areas only? Explain any five reasons.** ***(Ap)*(CBSE, 2019)**

Ans. MNCs set up their offices and factories in certain areas only because of the following reasons:

- **Availability of Raw material:** MNCs will set up offices and factories in areas where raw material is available easily and at a low cost so that the cost of production would be minimal. *(1 M)*
- **Availability of labour at low costs:** these corporations set up their factories where labour and other resources are available at cheap rates. *(1 M)*
- **Availability of other factors of production:** Availability of other factors of production such as water, electricity and transport, as it eases the production and transportation of finished products. *(1 M)*
- **Smaller companies are available:** MNCs merge or acquire the business with smaller companies for production expansion and to earn more profit. Smaller companies at good market locations attract MNCs. *(1 M)*
- **Where government policies are favourable to investors:** Countries with favourable government policies towards investors attract MNCs so that more production and more profit can be earned. *(1 M)*

Nailing the Right Answer

Provide specific examples or case studies to support your points.
Use economic terminologies and concepts to showcase understanding.
Ensure clarity and coherence in your responses to maximize marks.

2. What are the various ways in which countries can be linked? **(*Un*)(NCERT Intext)**

Ans. Countries can be interconnected in various ways, including economically, culturally, politically, and socially

- **Trade:** Countries engage in importing and exporting goods and services, which connects their economies. This exchange enables access to a broader range of products, impacts pricing globally, and introduces competition across borders. *(1 M)*
- **Investments:** Multinational corporations (MNCs) play a significant role in global integration by investing in different countries. They establish factories, offices, or other operations abroad where they get cheap labour and other resources. *(1 M)*
- **Technology Transfer:** Countries are linked through the sharing and transfer of technology. MNCs often bring advanced technologies to the countries where they invest, which can encourage local innovation and development. *(1 M)*
- **Financial Markets:** Global financial markets link countries by allowing the flow of capital across borders. Investors in one country can invest in stock markets, bonds, or other financial instruments in another country, impacting economies worldwide. *(1 M)*
- **Labor Movements:** Although more restricted compared to goods, capital, and information, the movement of people for work also connects countries. Migrants can influence both their home and host countries economically through remittances, skills transfer, and cultural exchange. *(1 M)*

2 FACTORS THAT HAVE ENABLED GLOBALISATION

NCERT Definitions *(Commonly asked in 1 mark)*

- **Liberalisation:** The process of removing barriers or restrictions set by the government on foreign trade and investment is known as liberalisation. It's a part of economic reforms aimed at making economies more open and market-oriented.

Important Concepts

Technology:

Improvements in transportation technology:

- Improvements in transportation technology made faster delivery of goods at minimum cost.

  E.g. Goods are sent from one place to another through containers loaded onto ships, railways, planes, and trucks. It reduces port handling costs and the cost of air transport. It speeds up the export process, and ultimately, goods reach the market in a shorter time.

Developments in information and communication technology:

- The development of technology in the field of telecommunications (telegraph, fax, and telephone including mobile phones), has made it easy to access information quickly and to communicate from remote areas. It was made possible by satellite communication devices.
- Technological development in the field of the internet also made it possible to send and receive electronic mail (e-mail) and talk on voice mail worldwide at a minimum cost.

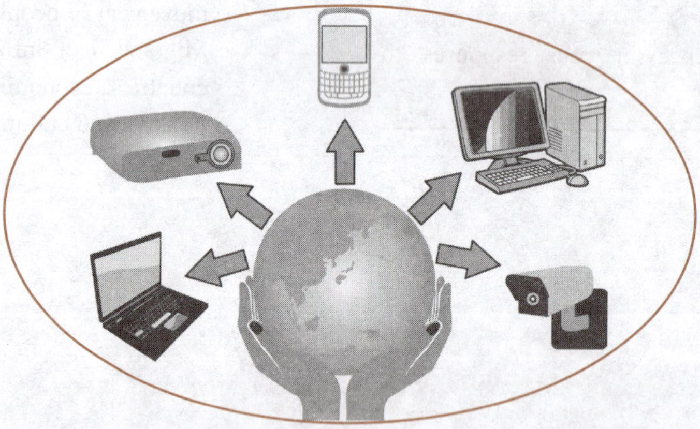

Liberalisation of foreign trade and foreign investment policy:

Foreign trade and Foreign investment after independence

- The Indian Government put barriers on foreign trade and foreign investment to protect domestic producers from foreign competition. In 1950s and 1960s Industries were starting to emerge, at that time competition from imports would not have been safe for their survival.

  E.g. tax imposed on imports of Chinese toys by the Indian government.
- The government permitted the import of only necessary items like fertilisers, machinery, petroleum etc.

Policy changes in Foreign trade and Foreign investment in 1991:

- In 1991, the government removed the barriers on foreign trade and foreign investment so that Indian producers could compete with foreign producers and the performance of producers within the country would improve by way of improved quality of products.
- The government adopted the policy of Liberalisation of foreign trade and foreign investment.

Mnemonics

Policy changes regarding Trade and Investment in India in 1991:

- **LG-** Liberalisation, Globalisation

Liberalisation **G**lobalisation

L G

COMPETENCY BASED SOLVED EXAMPLES

Scan Me for Detailed Explanations

Multiple Choice Questions

(1 M)

1. **Choose the correct option to fill the blank.**
Removing barriers or restrictions on business and trade set by the government is called as __________.
(*Re*) (CBSE, 2024)
(*a*) Disinvestment (*b*) Special Economic Zones
(*c*) Liberalisation (*d*) Foreign Direct Investment

2. **A multinational corporation (MNC) uses advanced data analytics and the internet to optimize its supply chain, ensuring that products from various parts of the world are available in markets where demand is highest.**
How do advancements in information technology contribute to the efficiency of MNC supply chains? (*Ap*)
(*a*) By predicting weather patterns only
(*b*) By facilitating faster physical transportation of goods
(*c*) By enabling real-time data analysis for demand forecasting and inventory management
(*d*) By decreasing the need for human labor in logistics

3. **Based on the image provided, which of the following statements best describes the impact of containerisation on global trade? (*Ap*)**

Containers for transport of goods

(*a*) Containers have increased the costs of goods globally due to higher transportation fees.
(*b*) Containerization has no significant impact on the speed or cost of transporting goods.
(*c*) Containers have decreased the need for manual labor in ports, increasing the efficiency of loading and unloading goods.
(*d*) The use of containers has slowed down the process of exporting goods to international markets.

Assertion and Reason

(1 M)

Direction: The following questions consist of two statements – Assertion (A) and Reason (R). Answer these questions by selecting the appropriate option given below:

(*a*) Both A and R are true, and R is the correct explanation of A.
(*b*) Both A and R are true, but R is not the correct explanation of A.
(*c*) A is true, but R is false
(*d*) A is false, but R is true.

1. **Assertion (A):** Tax on imports is an example of a trade barrier.
Reason (R): It is called a barrier because some restrictions have been set up. (*Ev*)

2. **Assertion (A):** Rapid improvement in technology has been one main factor that has stimulated the globalisation process.
Reason (R): Developing countries are to become at par with developed countries in terms of technological growth due to globalisation. (*An*)

Subjective Questions

Very Short Answer Type Questions

(1 or 2 M)

1. **Correct the following statement and rewrite it.**
(*Cr*)(CBSE, 2020)
Removing barriers or restrictions by the government is known as Globalisation.

Ans. Removing barriers or restrictions by the government is known as Liberalisation *(1 M)*

2. **What is meant by Trade barriers? State any one example of a trade barrier?** ***(Re & Un)*(CBSE, 2019)**

Ans. Trade barriers are restrictions imposed on the import and export of goods. *(1 M)*

Import duty is an example of trade barriers. *(1 M)*

3. **What do you understand by liberalisation of Foreign Trade?** ***(Un)*(NCERT Intext)**

Ans. Liberalisation of foreign trade refers to the removal or reduction of restrictions or barriers on the free exchange of goods between nations. This includes the elimination of tariffs, trade quotas, and other trade restrictions to encourage a more open and competitive international market. *(2 M)*

Short Answer Type Questions (3 M)

1. **Globalisation will continue in the future. Can you imagine what the world would be like twenty years from now? Give reasons for your answer.** ***(Ap)*(NCERT)**

Ans. Globalisation will continue in the future as well. After twenty years, we may see that:

- The efficiency of production will be increased.
- The market will become more competitive.
- The product quality will be improved.
- Trade and capital flows would increase
- There will be progress in every field. *(2 M)*

This will happen because the forces of globalisation will be strengthened much more in twenty years. The liberalization process will be accelerated, and trade restrictions will be removed even more. MNCs will merge with other businesses that make the same products. *(1 M)*

2. **In Araville, liberalization has allowed multinational corporations to enter the market, increasing product choices and sparking local economic growth. This policy shift introduces both competition for local businesses and a wealth of opportunities for consumers, enhancing overall market dynamism and community prosperity.**

Evaluate the effectiveness of foreign investment in improving the standard of living for Araville's residents. What measures can be taken to ensure that these benefits are distributed equitably? ***(Ev)***

Ans. The liberalization policy in Araville has opened up the market to multinational corporations, leading to an increase in product choices and economic growth. Here's how foreign investment can improve the standard of living and measures to ensure equitable benefits:

(i) **Enhanced Product Availability:** Foreign investment introduces a variety of products, improving consumer choice and satisfaction, thus potentially raising living standards. *(1 M)*

(ii) **Job Creation:** Multinationals often bring job opportunities in various sectors, boosting employment and income levels in Araville. *(1 M)*

(iii) **Community Development:** To distribute benefits equitably, the government could implement policies ensuring multinationals invest in local infrastructure and community programs. *(1 M)*

3. **"MNCs have been a major force in the globalisation process connecting distant regions of the world." Justify the statement.** ***(Ev)*(CBSE, 2022)**

OR

What is the role of MNCs in the globalisation process? ***(Un)*(NCERT Intext)**

OR

How do multinational corporations (MNCs) help in connecting distant countries? Explain with examples. ***(Ev)*(CBSE, 2017)**

Ans. In the process of globalisation, MNCs play an important role. Its role can be understood with the following points:

- **Economic Integration:** MNCs connect markets globally by investing across countries, and merging economies of the world. *(1 M)*
- **Technology Transfer:** They bring advanced technology to host countries, and encourage innovation and skills development. The globalisation process is sped up in this way. *(1 M)*
- **Job Creation:** MNCs establish operations worldwide in different countries and as a result create employment opportunities for the people residing in those countries. therefore, MNCs reduce the problem of unemployment. *(1 M)*

Mistakes 101 : What not to do!

Lack of Elaboration

❒ Students often provide points without elaborating on them, missing the opportunity to provide a deeper understanding of the concept.

Incomplete Explanation

❒ Some students might overlook the interconnectedness between economic integration, technology transfer, and job creation by not explaining how these aspects are interlinked in the globalization process.

Topper's Explanation:

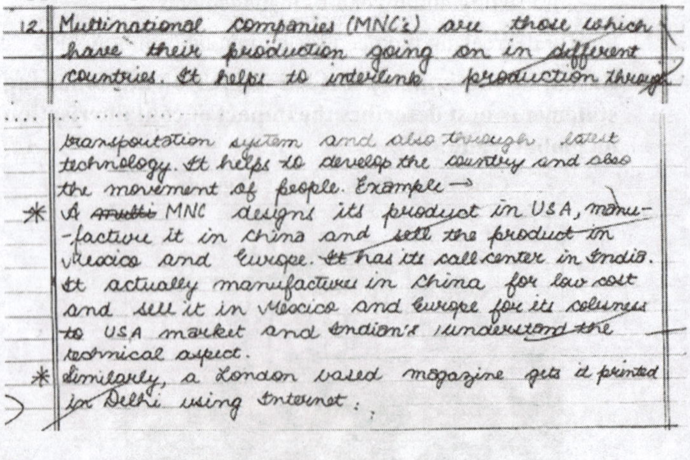
12. Multinational companies (MNC's) are those which have their production going on in different countries. It helps to interlink production through transportation system and also through latest technology. It helps to develop the country and also the movement of people. Example→

* A ~~multi~~ MNC designs its product in USA, manu-facture it in china and sell the product in Mexico and Europe. ~~It~~ It has its call center in India. It actually manufactures in China for low cost and sell it in Mexico and Europe for its colunies to USA market and Indian's understand the technical aspect.

* Similarly, a London based magazine gets it printed in Delhi using Internet.

Long Answer Type Questions (5 M)

1. **How do we feel the impact of globalisation on daily life? Explain with examples.** ***(Ap)*(CBSE, 2018)**

Ans. The impact of globalisation on daily life can be understood with the help of following points:

- Globalisation has improved transportation technologies, allowing for quicker and less expensive long-distance deliveries. *(1 M)*
- The invention of computers, the internet, mobile phones, and fax has made it much easier to communicate with people all over the world. *(1 M)*
- New jobs have been created in industries where multinational corporations have invested. *(1 M)*
- Prices for several goods have decreased due to competition among producers and manufacturers. *(1 M)*
- As a result of globalisation, some Indian corporations have become multinationals, creating more jobs. *(1 M)*

2. "Technology is the vital force in the modern form of globalisation." Explain the statement with suitable examples. **(*Un*)(CBSE, 2022)**

Ans. (i) Rapid improvement in technology has been one major factor that has stimulated the globalisation process. For instance, the past fifty years have seen several improvements in transportation technology. *(1 M)*

(ii) For Example, Goods are placed in containers that can be loaded intact onto railways, ships, planes, and trucks. Containers have led to a huge reduction in port handling costs and they increased the speed with which exports can reach markets. Besides, the cost of air transport has fallen. This has helped much greater volumes of goods to be transported by airlines. Therefore, This has made faster delivery of goods across long distances possible at lower costs. *(2 M)*

(iii) In recent periods, technology in the areas of telecommunications, the Internet, and computers has been changing rapidly. *(1 M)*

(iv) Telecommunication facilities (Eg. Telegraph, telephone including mobile phones, fax) are utilized to contact one another around the world, to access information instantly, and to communicate from remote areas. *(1 M)*

3. How have our markets transformed in recent years? Explain with examples. **(*An*)(CBSE, 2022 Term 2)**

Ans. Our markets have undergone significant transformations in recent years due to various factors such as globalisation, technology, and changing consumer preferences.

- Globalisation has led to an increase in trade and investment, resulting in the emergence of new markets and supply chains. *(1 M)*
- Technology has enabled the growth of e-commerce, online payments, and digital marketing, which has transformed the way businesses operate. *(1 M)*
- Changing consumer preferences have led to an increase in demand for sustainable and eco-friendly products, which has led to the growth of the green economy. *(1 M)*
- For example, the growth of e-commerce platforms like Amazon and Flipkart has transformed the retail industry. These platforms have made it easy for customers to shop online and get their products delivered to their doorstep. *(1 M)*
- Similarly, the rise of electric vehicles has transformed the automobile industry. Electric vehicles are more environmentally friendly than traditional gasoline-powered cars, and they offer better fuel efficiency and lower operating costs. *(1 M)*

4. "Liberalisation of foreign trade and foreign investment policy have shown far-reaching changes in India." Support the statement with suitable arguments. **(*Ev*)(CBSE, 2023)**

Ans. The statement "Liberalisation of foreign trade and foreign investment policy have shown far-reaching changes in India" can be supported with several arguments based on the impact of these economic policies:

- **Increase in Foreign Trade:** Liberalisation of foreign trade involves removing barriers on the import and export of goods and services. As a result, there was an increase in India's trade, with more diverse products entering the Indian market. *(1 M)*
- **Growth in Foreign Investment:** Liberalisation policies included relaxing norms and regulations for FDI. This attracted multinational companies to invest in India, bringing in capital, technology, and expertise. *(1 M)*
- **Technological Advancement:** With the entry of foreign companies and investments, India witnessed a significant transfer of technology. This helped in improving productivity and quality of products and boosting innovation and R&D activities in India. *(1 M)*
- **Expansion of Job Opportunities:** The entry of multinational corporations and the expansion of trade led to the creation of new job opportunities in various sectors. *(1 M)*
- **Impact on GDP and Economic Growth:** Liberalisation policies contributed to higher economic growth rates. The increased foreign trade and investment, led to an expansion in the industrial and service sectors, significantly contributing to India's GDP. *(1 M)*

MISCELLANEOUS EXERCISE

Multiple Choice Questions

(1 M)

1. Which of the following factors significantly contribute to the process of globalisation? Select the correct options.

1. Expansion of Multinational Corporations (MNCs).
2. Advancements in information and communication technology.
3. Nationalisation and trade barriers.
4. Cross-border movement of people for jobs and education.

Options: ***(An)* (CBSE SQP, 2024)**

(*a*) Statements 1 and 2 are appropriate.

(*b*) Statements 1, 2 and 3 are appropriate.

(*c*) Statements 2, 3 and 4 are appropriate.

(*d*) Only statement 3 is appropriate.

2. The process of integration between different countries is called as: ***(Re)*(CBSE SQP, 2023)**

(*a*) Privatisation (*b*) Globalisation

(*c*) Liberalisation (*d*) Competition

3. A high school in India collaborates with a school in Brazil for a student exchange program facilitated by advancements in technology and communications. They use various digital platforms for language learning and cultural exchange.

Which technological tool has been most effective in enhancing real-time global interactions between students from different countries? ***(Ap)***

(*a*) Printed newsletters (*b*) Email and voice-mail

(*c*) Social media platforms (*d*) Traditional mail services

4. Aman is an operational manager at a multinational company, tasked with optimizing the supply chain to enhance the efficiency of goods transportation across international borders using container ships like the one shown in the image.

Given the scenario, which term best describes the action of moving goods from one country to another as facilitated by the infrastructure shown in the image? ***(Un)***

(*a*) Import (*b*) Warehousing

(*c*) Export (*d*) Domestic distribution

5. The result of greater foreign investment and greater foreign trade has been ____________ across countries. Find the correct option from below. **(CBSE SQP, 2024)**

(*a*) greater bifurcation of production and markets

(*b*) greater segregation of production and markets

(*c*) greater differentiation of production and markets

(*d*) greater integration of production and markets

6. An educational NGO in India partners with several African countries to provide digital learning platforms. These platforms are used to deliver courses designed in India, supported by technology from Europe, and tailored for local African markets. This initiative has been facilitated by the NGO's ability to invest and operate across these diverse regions due to globalization.

What is a primary benefit of globalization in the context of this educational initiative? ***(Ap)***

(*a*) It allows for uniform educational content across different countries.

(*b*) It facilitates tailored educational services across diverse geographic regions.

(*c*) It restricts the type of educational materials that can be shared.

(*d*) It decreases the quality of education due to varying standards.

7. Imagine a scenario where the Indian government revises its policy to re-introduce tariffs on electronic goods to boost local manufacturing. As a result, international brands like Samsung and Apple face higher costs to sell their products in India, prompting them to consider setting up more manufacturing units within the country.

What is likely the most immediate impact of the Indian government reintroducing tariffs on imported electronic goods? ***(Ev)***

(*a*) Decrease in the variety of electronic goods available in Indian markets.

(*b*) Increase in the prices of imported electronic goods, making them less competitive.

(*c*) Increase in unemployment rates due to reduced imports.

(*d*) Decrease in the quality of electronic goods available.

8. Globalisation is the increasing interconnectedness of the world through the flow of goods, services, capital, ideas, and people. Which of the following examples represents globalisation? ***(Un)*(CBSE APQ, 2023)**

(*a*) an online advertising portal for goods sold by local vendors run by the Indian government

(*b*) an IKEA store in Bengaluru selling products manufactured in China

(*c*) a traditional Vietnamese market selling handicrafts in Hanoi

(*d*) a sunday market selling groceries produced locally

9. Evaluate the impacts of opening foreign trade on the global economy by identifying the appropriate statements among the following options: ***(Ev)*(CBSE SQP, 2023)**

(i) The choice of goods in the markets increases.

(ii) Producers from two countries closely compete against each other despite the distance between their locations.

(iii) Foreign trade thus results in connecting the markets or integration of markets in different countries.

(iv) The quality of the product is always good.

Options:

(*a*) Statements (i) and (ii) are appropriate.

(*b*) Statements (i), (ii) and (iii) are appropriate.

(*c*) All the statements are appropriate.

(*d*) Only statement (iv) is appropriate.

10. Identify the reason as to why MNC's would like to collaborate with India in producing goods. Choose from the appropriate statements among the following options: ***(An)*(CBSE APQ, 2023)**

(i) India has highly skilled engineers who can understand the technical aspects of production.

(ii) It also has educated English-speaking youth who can provide customer care services. This means 50-60 percent cost savings for the MNC.

(iii) It's the cheapest manufacturing location.

(iv) It's close to the markets in the US and Europe.

Options:

(*a*) Statements (i) and (ii) are appropriate.

(*b*) Statements (i), (ii) and (iii) are appropriate.

(*c*) All the statements are appropriate.

(*d*) Only statement (iv) is appropriate.

Assertion and Reason (1 M)

Direction: The following questions consist of two statements – Assertion (A) and Reason (R). Answer these questions by selecting the appropriate option given below:

(*a*) Both A and R are true, and R is the correct explanation of A.

(*b*) Both A and R are true, but R is not the correct explanation of A.

(*c*) A is true, but R is false

(*d*) A is false, but R is true.

1. **Assertion (A):** Globalisation leads to increased competition in international and domestic markets.

   Reason (R): Globalisation also makes the consumer better off as they have a wider variety of goods to choose from at higher prices. ***(Ev)***

2. A technology firm uses advanced computing to optimize logistics in distributing medical supplies worldwide, especially during health crises. ***(Ev)***

   Assertion (A): The rapid spread of medical information and resources across the globe is primarily facilitated by advancements in information technology.

   Reason (R): Modern information and communication technologies allow for quick adaptation and response in global health emergencies.

3. **Assertion (A):** Multinational Corporations can exert a strong influence on products at far locations.

   Reason (R): Multinational Corporations set up partnerships with local companies, use local companies for supplies, compete with local companies or acquire them. ***(An)***

4. **Assertion (A):** Rapid technological advancement has been a crucial driver in accelerating the globalisation process.

   Reason (R): Because of globalization, developing countries are expected to catch up to developed ones in terms of technological advancement. ***(Ev)***

Subjective Questions

Very Short Answer Type Questions (1 or 2 M)

1. Imagine a local smartphone manufacturing company in India, "TechBharat," which produces and sells smartphones within the Indian market only. On the other hand, consider Samsung, a multinational corporation that designs, manufactures, and sells smartphones globally.

   Discuss the role of globalisation in shaping the strategies of multinational corporations like Samsung compared to domestic companies like TechBharat. ***(An)***

2. AutoTech, a large multinational corporation, has chosen Marina, a small coastal town in India, as the site for its new car manufacturing plant. This decision is influenced by several strategic benefits, such as access to international markets in Southeast Asia and Africa, the introduction of advanced technology, and the creation of job opportunities for the local population.

   Evaluate how the influx of foreign investment from AutoTech could transform the local economy of Marina. ***(Ev, Re)***

Short Answer Type Questions (3 M)

1. What were the reasons for putting barriers to foreign trade and foreign investment by the Indian government? Why did it wish to remove these barriers? ***(Un and An)*(NCERT)**

2. How does foreign trade lead to the integration of markets across countries? Explain with an example other than those given here. ***(Ap)*(NCERT)**

Long Answer Type Questions (5 M)

1. Tax on imports is one type of trade barrier. The government could also place a limit on the number of goods that can be imported. This is known as quotas. Can you explain, using the example of Chinese toys, how quotas can be used as trade barriers? Do you think this should be used? Discuss. ***(An and Ev)*(NCERT Intext)**

2. "Globalisation is the process of rapid integration or interconnection between countries." Explain the statement with examples. ***(Un)* (CBSE, 2024)**

3. 'Improvement in technology has stimulated the globalisation process.' Explain the statement with examples. *(Un)* **(CBSE, 2024)**

4. How has Foreign trade been integrating markets of different countries? Explain with examples. *(An)***(CBSE, 2018)**

OR

"Foreign trade integrates the markets in different countries." Support the statement with arguments. *(An)***(CBSE, 2015)**

Case Based Questions

Case Based-I

Using IT in Globalisation

A news magazine published for London readers is to be designed and printed in Delhi. The text of the magazine is sent through the Internet to the Delhi office. The designers in the Delhi office get orders on how to design the magazine from the office in London using telecommunication facilities. The designing is done on a computer. After printing, the magazines are sent by air to London. Even the payment of money for designing and printing from a bank in London to a bank in Delhi is done instantly through the Internet (e-banking)!

Information and communication technology (or IT in short) has played a major role in spreading out production of services across countries. Let us see how.

(i) Explain the role of the internet in the design and printing process of the magazine described in the above case. *(Un)*

(ii) Write down IT tools speeding up the globalisation discussed in the above case. *(Re)*

(iii) Describe the significance of e-banking in the context of international transactions mentioned in the paragraph. *(Un)*

Case Based-II

Role of MNC in Globalisation

Ford Motors, an American company, is one of the world's largest automobile manufacturers with production spread over 26 countries of the world. Ford Motors came to India in 1995 and spent ₹ 1700 crore to set up a large plant near Chennai. This was done in collaboration with Mahindra and Mahindra, a major Indian manufacturer of jeeps and trucks. By the year 2017, Ford Motors was selling 88,000 cars in the Indian markets, while another 1,81,000 cars were exported from India to South Africa, Mexico, Brazil and United States of America. The company wants to develop Ford India as a component supplying base for its other plants across the globe.

(i) What kind of company is Ford Motor and why? *(Un)*

(ii) Why did Ford Motor develop India as its base for manufacturing car components for global operations? Give two reasons. *(An)*

(iii) What is Foreign Investment? How much did Ford Motor invest in India? *(Re)*

Case Based-III

Chinese manufacturers learn of an opportunity to export toys to India, where toys are sold at a high price. They start exporting plastic toys to India. Buyers in India now have the option of choosing between Indian and Chinese toys. Because of the cheaper prices and new designs, Chinese toys become more popular in the Indian markets. Within a year, 70 to 80 percent of the toy shops have replaced Indian toys with Chinese toys. Toys are now cheaper in the Indian markets than earlier. What is happening here? As a result of trade, Chinese toys come into the Indian markets. In the competition between Indian and Chinese toys, Chinese toys prove better. Indian buyers have a greater choice of toys at lower prices. For the Chinese toy makers, this provides an opportunity to expand their business. The opposite is true for Indian toy makers. They face losses, as their toys are selling much less.

(i) Why did Chinese toys become popular in the Indian market? *(An)*

(ii) How can Indian toy makers be protected from the loss? *(Cr)*

(iii) How has globalisation shown both positive and negative impacts in the above case? *(Ev)*

ANSWER KEYS

Multiple Choice Questions

1. (*b*) 2. (*b*) 3. (*c*) 4. (*c*) 5. (*d*) 6. (*b*) 7. (*b*) 8. (*b*) 9. (*b*) 10. (*a*)

Assertion and Reason

1. (*c*) 2. (*a*) 3. (*a*) 4. (*a*)

HINTS & EXPLANATIONS

Multiple Choice Questions

1. (*b*) Statements 1, 2 and 3 are appropriate.
2. (*b*) Globalisation
3. (*c*) Social media platforms have been the most effective technological tool in enhancing real-time global interactions among students, providing a dynamic and accessible way for continuous cultural and educational exchange.
4. (*c*) The image illustrates a port heavily equipped with containers ready to be loaded onto ships, a typical setup for exporting goods. This infrastructure is crucial for facilitating the movement of goods from one country to another, commonly referred to as exporting.
5. (*d*) greater integration of production and markets
6. (*b*) Globalization allows the NGO to tailor educational content specifically for diverse regions, utilizing technology and resources globally to address local educational needs effectively, enhancing learning outcomes.
7. (*b*) Reintroducing tariffs on imported electronics would make these goods more expensive compared to locally manufactured ones, potentially reducing their competitiveness in the Indian market and encouraging companies to consider local production to avoid tariffs.
8. (*b*) an IKEA store in Bengaluru selling products manufactured in China
9. (*b*) Statements i, ii and iii are appropriate.
10. (*a*) Statements i and ii are appropriate

Assertion and Reason

1. (*c*) Assertion is true but Reason is false.

   Globalisation also makes the consumer better off as they have a wider variety of goods to choose from at Lower prices.
2. (*a*) Advancements in information technology have indeed facilitated the rapid spread of medical information and resources globally, especially vital during health crises. Modern IT and communication technologies enable quick adaptations and immediate responses, which are essential in managing global health emergencies effectively.
3. (*a*) Both A and R are true and R is the correct explanation of A.
4. (*a*) Both A and R are true and R is the correct explanation of A.

Subjective Questions

Very Short Answer Type Questions

1. Globalisation impacts the business strategies of companies like Samsung and TechBharat in different ways:

   (*i*) **Wider Reach:** Samsung sells products globally, reaching more customers than TechBharat, which only sells in India. *(1 M)*

   (*ii*) **Innovation and Technology:** Exposure to global markets drives innovation, allowing Samsung to offer advanced technology products compared to TechBharat. *(1 M)*

   (*iii*) **Brand Recognition:** Samsung's international operations enhance its brand recognition and trust worldwide, attracting more consumers than a domestic-only brand like TechBharat. *(1 M)*
2. The transformative impact of AutoTech's foreign investment on Marina's economy through these key aspects: **(Any two)**

   (*i*) **Job Creation:** AutoTech's plant will provide numerous jobs, reducing unemployment and boosting local incomes. *(1 M)*

   (*ii*) **Skill Development:** Introducing advanced technologies and training programs will enhance the skills of local workers. *(1 M)*

   (*iii*) **Economic Growth:** Increased economic activity from manufacturing and exports will stimulate further development in Marina. *(1 M)*

Short Answer Type Questions

1. After independence, India was in a phase of building and nurturing its own industries. Allowing free foreign competition would have exposed these budding industries to international competition for which they were not prepared, possibly leading to their failure before they even had a chance to establish themselves. *(1½ M)*

However, over time, as the Indian economy matured and global perspectives changed, the need for these barriers to be reduced or removed became evident. By the early 1990s, the government recognized that integration into the global economy was essential for India's own economic growth. *(1½ M)*

Nailing the Right Answer

- Clearly outline the reasons for barriers to foreign trade and investment in a concise manner.
- Explain the impact of these barriers on India's industries and economy.
- Highlight the shift in perspective over time leading to the desire to remove these barriers.

2. Foreign trade leads to the integration of markets across countries by enabling the exchange of goods and services beyond domestic boundaries. *(1 M)*

   To illustrate this with an example not provided in the chapter, consider the global smartphone market. Smartphones designed in one country often incorporate components manufactured in multiple countries. For instance, a smartphone designed in the United States might use a microprocessor engineered in the U.S., a camera module developed in Japan, screen technology from South Korea, and assembly processes in China. Once assembled, these smartphones are then sold worldwide, from Europe to Asia to Africa, effectively integrating markets across these regions. *(2 M)*

Long Answer Type Questions

1. Introducing quotas can help mitigate the import of Chinese toys by capping the number of toys, thereby providing a buffer for Indian manufacturers to adapt, innovate, and become more competitive. This protection might allow them to sustain employment and contribute to the local economy. However, the downside is that it could lead to higher toy prices and less variety for Indian consumers compared to a scenario with unrestricted imports. *(2 M)*

   Whether quotas should be used is a matter of economic strategy and perspective. On one hand, they can protect and nurture domestic industries, contributing to economic sovereignty and job preservation. On the other hand, they can restrict consumer choice and potentially slow down market efficiency and the adaptation of domestic industries to global competition. The decision to use quotas should balance these considerations, taking into account the specific economic context, industry readiness, and the broader goals of national economic development. *(3 M)*

2. Globalisation refers to the process of rapid integration or interconnections between countries. Here are some examples to illustrate various aspects of globalisation:

   (i) **Economic Integration:** The rise of MNCs exemplifies economic globalisation. Companies like Apple, McDonald's, and Toyota have operations in multiple countries, sourcing raw materials, manufacturing products, and selling them in a global market. *(1 M)*

   (ii) **Cultural Exchange:** Globalization supports cultural exchange and influences as people, goods, and information cross borders. For instance, Hollywood movies are enjoyed worldwide. Food, fashion, and festivals from various cultures become globally accessible and celebrated. *(1 M)*

   (iii) **Technological Advancements:** The internet and mobile technology are important tools of globalisation, enabling instant communication and information exchange across the globe. Social media platforms like Facebook, Twitter, and Instagram connect people from different countries, fostering global dialogue and exchange of ideas. *(1 M)*

   (iv) **Political Cooperation:** International organizations and agreements such as the United Nations, World Trade Organisation, and the Paris Agreement on climate change illustrate political globalisation. These entities and pacts aim to address global issues that go beyond national borders. *(1 M)*

   (v) **Environmental Impact:** Globalisation has significant environmental implications, as increased trade and industrial activity contribute to resource depletion and pollution. *(1 M)*

3. "Improvement in technology has stimulated the globalization process" reflects the integral role technological advancements play in connecting the world. Here are various examples:

   (i) **Communication Technology:** Innovations in communication technology, such as the internet, smartphones, and social media platforms, have revolutionized the way individuals and businesses interact globally. People can now communicate instantaneously across vast distances. *(1 M)*

   (ii) **Transportation Technology:** Advances in transportation, like jet aircraft, large shipping containers, and improved logistics software, have dramatically reduced the time and cost of moving goods and people across the world. *(1 M)*

   (iii) **Information Technology:** The IT revolution has allowed for the efficient processing, storage, and distribution of vast amounts of data, facilitating global business operations and decision-making. *(1 M)*

   (iv) **E-Commerce:** Online shopping platforms and payment systems have transformed retail, allowing consumers to purchase goods from different countries easily. This not only provides consumers with more choices but also opens new markets for businesses. *(1 M)*

   (v) **Digital Media:** The rise of digital media platforms has democratized information flow, enabling news, entertainment, and cultural content to reach a global audience. Streaming services like Netflix and YouTube offer content from different countries and cultures and promote cultural exchange and global awareness. *(1 M)*

4. Foreign trade integrates markets of different countries through several ways:
   - **Expands Market Access:** It allows countries to reach beyond their domestic markets, offering goods globally, like Indian spices available worldwide. *(1 M)*
   - **Equalises Prices Globally:** Through trade, prices of similar goods in different countries tend to converge, as seen with crude oil prices. *(1 M)*
   - **Introduces Competitive Goods:** It brings foreign products into domestic markets, increasing choices, such as Chinese toys in India. *(1 M)*
   - **Promotes Specialization:** Countries specialize in producing goods they are most efficient at, like Japan's expertise in electronics. *(1 M)*
   - **Encourages Innovation:** Exposure to global markets compels companies to innovate, like the advancements in European automotive technology due to global competition. *(1 M)*

OR

Topper's Explanation:

18. "Foreign trade integrates the markets in different countries".

i) Foreign trade allows imports and exports of products in the market. When a product is imported, it provides competition to the local producers. This allows local producers to make their products better for competition with the first produc[t] thus integrating the producers and thereby the countries.

ii) Foreign trade helps in equalizing monetary ratios. Globalizatio[n] helps in this. By creating a monetary ratio in the market, the countries' markets get integrated.

iii) Foreign products brought in by trade provide choice to the buyers. Let us take the example of Chinese toys in the Indian market. Chinese toys are cheaper and are more modernized than Indian toys. This definitely would attract customers to purchase Chinese toys. Currently in India, over 70-[%] of the toys in the markets are Chinese toys. This means, Chinese toys have been in huge demand. As a result, more markets buy more Chinese toys thus creating more jobs for the producers and thus integrating the markets.

Case Based Questions

Case Based-I

(*i*) The internet plays a crucial role in enabling instantaneous communication and file transfer between the London office and the Delhi office. *(1 M)*

(*ii*) Telecommunication, Internet and Computer. *(1 M)*

(*iii*) E-banking enables secure and instant financial transactions across borders. In this scenario, it allows the London office to swiftly transfer funds to the Delhi office for the services rendered, eliminating the delays and complexities associated with traditional banking methods. *(2 M)*

Case Based-II

(*i*) Ford Motor is a multinational company (MNC) because it has production spread over 26 countries. *(1 M)*

(*ii*) Ford Motor developed India as its base for manufacturing car components because of the following reasons:

- **Cheaper cost of labour and other resources:** cost of labour and other resources like raw materials, power etc. are cheaper in India as compared to developed countries. *(1 M)*
- **Closeness to large number of buyers in India and China:** India and China provide easy access to a big market for multiple companies. These two countries comprise 30-35% of world population. *(1 M)*

(*iii*) The investment made from abroad is called Foreign investment. Ford Motor invested ₹ 1,700 crores. *(1 M)*

Case Based-III

(*i*) Because of the cheaper prices and new designs as compared to Indian toys, Chinese toys gained popularity in India. *(1 M)*

(*ii*) If the Indian government put trade barriers (like quota) on the import of chinese toys, It will protect Indian producers from the loss they suffer from the sale of toys. *(1 M)*

(*iii*) **Positive impacts of globalisation:**

- On entry of chinese toys in India, Indian buyers had a greater choice of toys at cheaper prices due to competition in the market. *(1 M)*

Negative impacts of globalisation:

- On the other hand, Indian buyers had to face losses as the sale of their toys were negatively affected due to competition with Chinese toys. *(1 M)*

History

THE RISE OF NATIONALISM IN EUROPE

1

Europe thus divided into nationalities freely formed and free internally, peace between States would have become easier: the United States of Europe would become a possibility.

SYLLABUS & WEIGHTAGE

List of Concept Names	Years					
	2020	2021	2022	2023	2024	2025
The French Revolution and the idea of Nation	1 Q (1 M)	Exam not Conducted	–	–	–	–
The Making of Nationalism in Europe (The Aristocracy and the New Middle class, what did liberal Nationalism stand for, A New Conservatism after 1815, The revolutionaries)	1 Q (5 M)		–	1 Q (3 M) 1 Q (1 M)	1 Q (5 M)	1 Q (4 M)
The Age of Revolution: 1830-1848 (The Romantic imagination and National feeling, Hunger, Hardsship and Popular revolt, 1848: The Revolution of the Liberals)	–		–	–	–	–
The Making of Germany and Italy (Germany: Can The Army be the Architect of a Nation, Italy Unified, The Strange Case of British)	–		–	–	1 Q (1 M) 1 Q (1 M)	–
Visualising the Nation	–		–	–	–	1 Q (1 M)
Nationalism and Imperialism	–		–	–	1 Q (1 M)	–

CONCEPT MAP

To Access One Shot Revision Video Scan This QR Code

The Rise of Nationalism in Europe

The French Revolution and the idea of Nation (CBSE 2025)

French Revolution-1789 (CBSE 2020)
- La patrie
- Le citoyen
- Tricolour French flag
- Equal Rights

Administrative Changes
- Emergence of Constitution of France
- Estates General renamed as the National Assembly
- Centralised Administration
- Uniform system of weights and measures
- French language made a common language

Napoleonic Code (CBSE 2020)
- Introduction of civil code (1804)
- Equality of all before law
- Privileges of high class abolished
- Feudal system ended
- Peasants freed from serfdom system
- Transport and communication improved

The age of Revolutions: 1830-1848 (CBSE 2022 Term-I)

Romantic Imagination & National Feeling

Romanticists criticised science and focussed instead on emotions, intuition and mystical feelings. Language and folklores were used to instil national spirit.

Hunger, Hardship & Popular Revolt

In 1830s, increased population, food shortages and widespread unemployment brought people out on the roads.

Liberal Revolts (CBSE 2022 Term-1)
- Upheaval in France in July 1830
- Uprising in Brussels
- Uprising in Greece 1821
- Treaty of Constantinople 1832

The Making of Nationalism in Europe (CBSE 2024)

Aristocracy and New Middle Class
- **Aristocrats:** numerically small dominant social and political class united by common way of life. Emergence of commercial classes-existence band on production for market.
- **New middle class:** working class, artisans, businessmen, professionals etc.

Liberal Nationalism (CBSE 2023, 2022 Term-I, 2020)
- **Political:** End of clerical privilege, autocracy, representative form of government through parliament, inviolability of private property, limited suffrage.
- **Economic:** Freedom of markets, abolition of state-imposed restrictions on movement of goods of capital.

Revolutionaries (CBSE 2023, 2022 Term-I)
- Secret societies sprang up in many parts of Europe to oppose monarchical forms and to fight for liberty and freedom.
- Giuseppe Mazzini, an Italian revolutionary founded 2 secret societies, Young Italy in Marseilles and Young Europe in Berne.

A New Conservatism after 1815 (CBSE 2022 Term-I)

Conservatists when they realised that modernisation could strengthen traditional institutions like the Monarchy introduced a modern army, an efficient bureaucracy, a dynamic economy, abolition of serfdom and feudalism. Treaty of Vienna (1815)

The Rise of Nationalism in Europe

The Making of Germany and Italy

Unification of Germany

CBSE 2024, 2022 Term-I

- Attempt to set up a constitutional monarchy at Frankfurt in 1848 was suppressed by the monarchy, Military and Junkers.
- Prussian Chief Minister Otto Von Bismarck takes the lead in German unification.
- He planned the unification with the help of the Prussian Army and Bureaucracy.
- Ensured unification after 3 wars with France, Austria and Denmark over 7 years.
- Process completed with the crowning of Kaiser William I as King of Germany.

Strange Case of Britain

English, Welsh, Scot or Irish (ethnicity) was the primary identities of inhabitants of Britain Isles. United Kingdom of Great Britain was formed as a result of the Act of Union (1707).

Unification of Italy

CBSE 2024, 2023, 2022 Term-I

- Idea of unification was first given by Guiseppe Mazzini through his secret society called young Italy.
- The lead was taken by the king of Sardinia, Victor Emmanuel II.
- Count Cavour, Chief Minister of Sardinia, led the unification process by alliance with France to defeat Austria and unify its Northern territories.
- Guiseppe Garibaldi led a movement in Western part by involving local peasant support to attack Spanish rule.
- Process completed with the crowning of Victor Emmanuel II as king of Italy in 1861.

Visualising the Nation

CBSE 2025

Allegory of the Nation

Female figure (allegory) chosen to personify the nation, to give the abstract idea of nation a concrete form. 'Germania' in Germany and 'Christened Marianne' in Italy was chosen.

Nationalism and Imperialism

CBSE 2025

Nationalism in the Balkans State

- Tensions of Europe after 1971 was the area called the Balkans.
- First world war (1914-1918)
- In 1914, Europe was disastrous because of Nationalism, aligned with imperialism.
- Anti-imperial movements were developed but they all struggled to form independent nation-states.

1 THE FRENCH REVOLUTION AND THE IDEA OF THE NATION

NCERT Definitions *(Commonly asked in 1 mark)*

- **Nationalism:** It is a feeling that combines all the people of the nation into a ***single unit***.
- **Sovereignty:** It means that a country or a government has the full and independent authority to make its own ***laws, decisions***, and ***control*** its own ***territory*** without interference from other nations.
- **La Patrie (The Fatherland):** This term is about more than just land; it's about ***feeling*** a strong love and bond with your country, a feeling that grew from the Revolution.
- **Le Citoyen (The Citizen):** This talks about how a person changes from being just a subject to becoming a citizen, realising their rights and responsibilities in their country. It means understanding one's place and role in a big group where everyone is treated the same.
- **Tricolour:** It's a symbol of ***liberty, equality, and fraternity***. The intertwining of blue, white, and red mirrors the unity and strength of the French people.
- **Utopian:** A ***vision of a society*** that is so ideal that it is unlikely to actually exist.
- **Plebiscite:** A ***direct vote by*** eligible voters to decide on an important public question.
- **Absolutist:** A government or system of government that does not limit the exercise of power. The term ***"monarchical"*** refers to a form of government that was centralised, militarised and oppressive.

Important Events

Event/Concept	Year	Significance
French Revolution	**1789**	Marked the first clear expression of nationalism, leading to the idea that sovereignty belongs to the people.
First French republic	**1792**	Establishment of the First French Republic.
Napolean Rise to Power	**1799**	Napoleon Bonaparte's rise to power, marking the end of the French Revolution.
Civil Code of 1804 (Napoleonic Code)	**1804**	Introduced equality before the law and secured property rights across the territories controlled by Napoleon.
Vienna Congress	**1815**	Aimed to restore Europe's pre-Napoleon borders and suppress revolutionary movements.
Frederic Sorrieu's Utopian Vision	**1848**	Visualised a utopian vision of democratic and social republics across the world.
Ernst Renan's Lecture	**1882**	Highlighted that a nation is defined by common glories in the past and a common will in the present.

Important Personalities

Frederic Sorrieu: He was a French artist famous for a series of four prints prepared in 1848 that visualized the dream of a world consisting of 'democratic and social Republics'.

Napoleon (1769-1821): A French military and political leader who gained prominence during the French Revolution. He ruled France from (1799 to 1815). He assumed absolute power in 1799 by becoming the first consul.

Difference Between

Nation-State Vs Modern State		
Aspect	**Nation State**	**Modern State**
Foundation	People have a shared identity based on ***language***, ***culture***, and ***customs***.	People of different identities coexist peacefully in a modern state.
Analogy	Like a family reunion where everyone shares common ancestors and stories.	Like a vibrant city where people from various backgrounds come together to live and work.
Key Features	Unity, cultural cohesion, and a deep sense of belonging and pride.	Diversity, legal-rational authority, and a focus on citizenship rights and responsibilities.
Governance	Often emphasises policies that reinforce a shared sense of identity and national unity.	Focuses on administrative efficiency, law, and order, catering to a diverse population.
Diversity	May struggle with diversity, aiming to maintain a sense of national homogeneity.	Embraces and manages diversity, often seeing it as a strength and enriching factor.
Adaptability	Can face challenges in adapting to global changes that dilute national homogeneity.	Highly adaptable, constantly evolving with demographic, technological, and economic shift

Myth Buster

- **Myth:** Napoleon's reforms uniformly liberated and benefited all conquered regions.

  Fact: The impact of Napoleon's reforms varied, with initial enthusiasm turning to hostility due to lack of political freedom, increased taxes, and forced conscription, highlighting the complex and often negative effects of French rule on local populations.

Mnemonics

The Civil Code of 1804: Usually known as the Napoleonic Code – are as follows:

'CABLE-TUG'

- **C** → Civil Code of 1804 (Napoleonic Code)
- **A** → Abolished (privileges based on birth, feudal system, serfdom, manorial dues, guild restrictions)
- **B** → Businessmen (benefitted from new freedoms and uniform laws)
- **L** → Law (equality before the law)
- **E** → Exported (Code exported to Dutch Republic, Switzerland, Italy, Germany)
- **T** → Transport (improved transport and communication systems)
- **U** → Uniform (laws, weights, measures, national currency)
- **G** → Goods (facilitated movement and exchange of goods and capital)

COMPETENCY BASED SOLVED EXAMPLES

Scan Me for Detailed Explanations

Multiple Choice Questions

(1 M)

1. Ravi is a student focused on art and symbolism, analyzing a painting depicting Christ, saints, and angels watching over a procession of nations. In the painting where Christ, saints, and angels oversee a procession of people from various nations, what do these celestial figures symbolize about the relationship between these nations? *(An)*

(*a*) Friendship among the nations
(*b*) Fraternity among the nations
(*c*) Love among the nations
(*d*) Freedom of the nations

2. Which of the following revolutions is called as the first expression of 'Nationalism'? **(*Re*)(CBSE, 2020)**

(*a*) French Revolution
(*b*) Russian Revolution
(*c*) Glorious Revolution
(*d*) The Revolution of the liberals

3. You are a member of a debating society in nineteenth-century Europe. You have been tasked with arguing the importance of liberalism during this period. Which concept of liberalism, primarily emphasizing individual freedom and equality before the law, influenced societal changes and political systems in your debate points? *(Cr)*

(*a*) The preservation of monarchy and traditional structures
(*b*) Universal suffrage and absolute democracy
(*c*) The end of autocracy and equality before the law
(*d*) Strong religious influences in politics

4. What impact did the storming of the Bastille by the French have on Europe? **(*An*)(CBSE CFPQ, 2023)**

(*a*) People across Europe got inspired to fight against the rule of the monarch.
(*b*) Made monarchs from different parts of Europe abdicate from the throne.
(*c*) Inspired nations across Europe to colonise other countries of the world.
(*d*) People in Europe started to fear the French revolutionaries.

5. Napoleon in the given picture is depicted as a postman. What do each letter falling from his bag represent? *(An)*

(*a*) Number of wars he fought
(*b*) Letters he posted to the monarchs
(*c*) Territories lost by him
(*d*) Areas conquered by him

Assertion and Reason

(1 M)

Direction: The following questions consist of two statements – Assertion (A) and Reason (R). Answer these questions by selecting the appropriate option given below:

(*a*) Both A and R are true, and R is the correct explanation of A.
(*b*) Both A and R are true, but R is not the correct explanation of A.
(*c*) A is true, but R is false
(*d*) A is false, but R is true.

1. **Assertion (A):** The French Revolution led to the transfer of sovereignty from the monarchy to a body of French citizens.
   Reason (R): The political and constitutional changes that came in the wake of the French Revolution proclaimed that it was the people who would henceforth constitute the nation and shape its destiny. *(Un)*
2. **Assertion (A):** The tricolour flag was chosen to replace the former royal standard during the French Revolution.
   Reason (R): The tricolour flag symbolized liberty, equality, and fraternity - values that were central to the revolution. *(Un)*
3. **Assertion (A):** Napoleon's French army brought democracy and accountability in governance across Europe by 1804.
   Reason (R): Napoleon simplified administrative divisions, abolished the feudal system, and freed peasants from serfdom and manorial dues. **(*Ev*)(CFPQ, 2023)**

Subjective Questions

Very Short Answer Type Questions

(1 or 2 M)

1. Name the Civil Code of 1804 which established equality before law and secured the right to property in France. **(*Re*)(CBSE, 2020)**

Ans. The Civil Code of 1804, which established equality before the law and secured the right to property in France, is known as the ***Napoleonic Code***. *(1 M)*

2. **Provide evidence to support the claim that the French Revolution was a turning point in European history.** ***(An)*(NCERT Intext)**

Ans. The French Revolution was a turning point in European history in below aspects;

(*i*) The French Revolution ended monarchy, heralding democracy in Europe, inspiring revolutionary movements across the continent. *(1 M)*

(*ii*) It induced profound social and political transformations, reshaping European society fundamentally. *(1 M)*

3. **Write one key feature of constitutional monarchy.** ***(Un)*(CFPQ, 2023)**

Ans. The key feature of constitutional monarchy is:

(*i*) The monarch exercises authority according to a written or unwritten constitution. *(1 M)*

4. **Why did Frederic Sorrieu present Utopian vision in his prints in 1848? Give one reason.** ***(Ap)*(CBSE, 2019)**

Ans. Frederic Sorrieu made his Utopian prints in 1848 to show his dream of a peaceful world where all countries are free and work together as friends.

He wanted to encourage people to believe in freedom and togetherness. *(1 M)*

Topper's Explanation

Frédéric Sorrieu presented the utopian vision in his prints in 1848 to inculcate a feeling of nationalism as well as fraternity among the people of the world.

Short Answer Type Questions (3 M)

1. **Summarise the attributes of a nation, as Renan understands them. Why, in his view, are nations important?** ***(Un)*(NCERT Intext)**

Ans. Ernst Renan was a French philosopher and attributes of a nation are according to him as follows:

(*i*) A nation is not formed by a common language, race, religion or territory. *(1 M)*

(*ii*) To form a nation, social capital, common glories and deeds of the past and common will are necessary. *(1 M)*

(*iii*) Inhabitants of a nation have the right to be consulted in reference of large scale solidarity. *(1 M)*

2. **Assess the influence of Napoleonic reforms on Europe beyond France.** ***(An)***

Ans. The influence of Napoleonic reforms on the rest of Europe was:

(*i*) Destroyed democracy: Through a return to monarchy, Napoleon destroyed democracy in France and the administrative field was made rational and efficient. *(1½ M)*

(*ii*) Napoleonic Reforms in European Territories: In the Dutch Republic, Switzerland, Italy, and Germany, Napoleon simplified the administrative divisions, abolished the feudal system, and freed the peasants from serfdom and manorial dues. *(1½ M)*

3. **"The fragmented states of our beloved Germany must come together as one nation. Only through unity can we ensure the rights and freedoms of our people. The old autocratic regimes suppress our liberties and hinder our progress. We, the liberals, must lead the charge towards a united and free Germany, where the ideals of liberalism can flourish."**

Analyze how Friedrich's views reflect the ideology of liberalism in the context of national unity. ***(An)***

Ans. Friedrich's views reflect the ideology of liberalism in this below context:

(*i*) Unity and Freedom: Friedrich's call for German unity reflects liberal nationalism's focus on collective identity and self-determination. *(1 M)*

(*ii*) Criticism of Autocracy: He opposes autocratic regimes, advocating for individual freedoms and democratic governance. *(1 M)*

(*iii*) Liberal Leadership: His call for liberals to lead the movement emphasizes the liberal belief in government by consent and democratic reforms. *(1 M)*

4. **What is the symbolism of Christ and Statue of Liberty in Frederic Sorrieu's painting?** ***(An)***

Ans. The symbolism of Christ and Statue of Liberty in Frederic Sorrieu's paintings follows:

(*i*) In Frederic Sorrieu's painting, Christ and the Statue of Liberty symbolise a utopian vision of universal brotherhood and democracy. *(1 M)*

(*ii*) Christ represents moral and spiritual guidance, advocating for peace and fraternity among nations. *(1 M)*

(*iii*) The Statue of Liberty embodies the ideals of freedom, enlightenment, and the rights of individuals, reflecting Sorrieu's hope for a world of democratic and social republics united in harmony. *(1 M)*

Long Answer Type Questions (5 M)

1. **How did the French Revolution contribute to the development of the idea of the nation?** ***(Un)***

Ans. The French Revolution played a significant role in developing the idea of the nation:

(*i*) The revolutionaries introduced various measures and practices that could create a sense of collective identity among the French people. *(1 M)*

(*ii*) They emphasized the notion of a united community enjoying equal rights under a constitution, with ideas such as la patrie (the fatherland) and le citoyen (the citizen). *(1 M)* (*iii*) The tricolour flag was chosen to replace the former royal standard, symbolizing liberty, equality, and fraternity - values that were central to the revolution. *(1 M)*

(*iv*) A centralised administrative system was put in place, and uniform laws were formulated for all citizens within its territory. *(1 M)*

(*v*) These measures helped create a sense of national unity and identity among the French people. *(1 M)*

2. How would you evaluate Napoleon as an administrator who created a more rational and efficient system? Elucidate with suitable examples. *(Ev)***(CBSE SQP, 2023)**

Ans. To evaluate Napoleon as an administrator who created a more rational and efficient system with suitable example as follows:

(*i*) **Napoleonic Code Implementation:** Established property rights, legal equality, and abolished birth-based privileges, becoming a model for regions under French influence. *(1 M)*

(*ii*) **Economic Liberation:** Businessmen, artisans, peasants, and workers experienced unprecedented freedom, fostering economic growth and productivity. *(1 M)*

(*iii*) **Feudal System Abolishment:** In territories like Italy, Germany, Switzerland, and the Dutch Republic, the Napoleonic reforms eradicated serfdom and manorial dues, modernizing the agrarian economy. *(1 M)*

(*iv*) **Removal of Guild Restrictions:** Enhanced urban economic activities by eliminating medieval guild restrictions, aiding artisans and townspeople. *(1 M)*

(*v*) **Infrastructure and Standardization:** Upgraded transport and communication systems, alongside the adoption of uniform laws, weights, and measures, facilitated cross-regional trade and commerce. *(1 M)*

3. Culture had played an important role in the development of nationalism in Europe during the 18th and 19th centuries. Support the statement with examples. *(An)*

Ans. Due to the following reasons, culture played an important role in the development of nationalism:

(*i*) Nationalist feelings in Europe were shaped by art, poetry, storytelling, and music. *(1 M)*

(*ii*) Romanticism was a cultural movement that influenced this situation. Romantic poet and artists were critical of reason and science. *(1 M)*

(*iii*) The development of a sense of shared collective heritage. *(1 M)*

(*iv*) Folk dancing, folk poetry, and folk melodies were seen as real expressions of the nation's spirit. *(1 M)*

(*v*) Another expression of nationalism was speaking in the vernacular language. *(1 M)*

4. Assess the impact of the French Revolution on the idea of nationhood. *(Ev)*

Ans. The French Revolution had a profound impact on the idea of nationhood:

(*i*) It promoted the concept of nationalism, emphasizing the idea of a nation as a community of people with shared identity, culture, and aspirations. *(1 M)*

(*ii*) The revolution fostered a sense of national unity among the French people, who rallied behind the ideals of liberty, equality, and fraternity. *(1 M)*

(*iii*) The Revolution also spread these ideas beyond France, inspiring nationalist movements across Europe and the world. *(1 M)*

(*iv*) It led to the emergence of nation-states and the formation of new political entities based on the principle of self-determination. *(1 M)*

(*v*) The French Revolution thus played a crucial role in shaping the modern concept of the nation and the aspirations of people for independence and self-governance. *(1 M)*

2 THE MAKING OF NATIONALISM IN EUROPE

NCERT Definitions *(Commonly asked in 1 mark)*

- **Conservatism:** A political philosophy that values ***tradition***, ***social stability***, and continuity over radical changes.
- **Zollverein:** A customs union among German states during the ***19th century*** to manage tariffs and economic policies.
- **Suffrage:** It refers to the ***right to vote*** in political elections, typically granted to citizens of a country or members of a particular community.
- **Elle:** It was used to measure ***cloth***, ***prevalent*** in the German state.

Important Facts

01 ***Mid-18th-century*** Europe lacked ***nation-states***, with regions like Germany, Italy, and Switzerland divided into smaller autonomous territories.

02 The ***Habsburg Empire*** was a mix of diverse peoples and languages, lacking a unified national identity.

03 The congress was hosted by the Austrian chancellor ***Duke Metternich*** and they drew up the Treaty of Vienna of ***1815***.

04 ***Liberal nationalism***, advocating freedom and equality before the law, gained popularity among the educated middle classes.

05 The ***Zollverein***, a customs union, helped stimulate economic unity and national sentiments in German states.

06 ***Post-Napoleon***, a conservative order sought to preserve traditional institutions, but faced challenges from liberal and nationalist movements

Important Personalities

Giuseppe Mazzini: A famous Italian revolutionary who was born in 1807 in Genoa. He was part of a ***secret society*** called carbonari and founded two underground societies called ***young Italy*** in Marseilles and ***young Europe*** in Berne.

Duke Metternich: An Austrian chancellor who hosted the Congress which was held at ***Vienna* in 1815** and was the chief architect of the treaty of Vienna.

Important Dates

- **1797:** Napoleon invades Italy; Napoleonic wars begin.
- **1814-1815:** Fall of Napoleon; the Vienna Peace Settlement.
- **1821:** Greek struggle for Independence began.

Difference Between

Conservatism Vs. Revolutionary		
Aspect	**Conservatism**	**Revolutionary**
Definition	Aimed to preserve existing social orders and traditions.	Wanted big changes and established new systems.
Key Supporters	Aristocracy, monarchy, The Church.	Middle-class professionals, intellectuals, workers.
Core Beliefs	Stability, hierarchy, gradual change.	Liberty, equality, fraternity; rapid and radical reforms.
Examples	Metternich of Austria, restoration of the Bourbon monarchy in France.	Mazzini in Italy, 1848 revolutions across Europe.

Aristocracy Vs New Middle Class		
Aspect	**Aristocracy**	**New Middle Class**
Social Origin	Traditionally inherited status, often linked to land ownership and titles.	Emerged from wealth acquired through industry, trade, and professions rather than inheritance.
Economic Basis	Wealth based on land ownership, agricultural rents, and hereditary privileges.	Wealth generated from industrial ventures, commerce, professions, and manufacturing.
Political Influence	Dominant in traditional monarchies; held significant power in government and society.	Sought political influence through merit, education, and economic contribution.
Lifestyle and Culture	Luxurious lifestyles, often maintaining multiple residences. Spoke French for diplomacy.	Wanted to move up, valued education and middle-class life.
Role in Society	Custodians of tradition and the existing social order. Served as the ruling class.	Agents of change, pushing for industrialization, modernization, and democratic reforms.

Myth Buster

- **Myth:** Conservatives wanted everything to go back to how it was before Napoleon.

  Fact: Conservatives liked some of Napoleon's changes because they made traditional institutions stronger, like having a modern army and getting rid of old feudal laws.

Mnemonics

Features of the Aristocratic class:

'ESTATES'

- **E** → **E**states and town-houses owned
- **S** → **S**peaking French for diplomacy
- **T** → **T**ies of marriage connect families
- **A** → **A**ristocratic
- **T** → **T**raditions uphold
- **E** → **E**lite society's norms
- **S** → **S**ocial standing secured

It helps recall the key actions taken during the Congress of Vienna:

'VIENNA'

- **V** → **V**ictory over Napoleon sealed
- **I** → **I**taly and Netherlands reshaped
- **E** → **E**urope's old monarchies restored
- **N** → **N**ew states buffer France
- **N** → **N**apoleonic changes reversed
- **A** → **A**lliance of Britain, Russia, Prusia.

COMPETENCY BASED SOLVED EXAMPLES

Scan Me for Detailed Explanations

Multiple Choice Questions

(1 M)

1. **Arrange the following in chronological order and choose the correct option:** ***(An)*(CBSE, 2023)**
   (i) Napoleonic wars
   (ii) The Treaty of Vienna
   (iii) Greek Struggle for Independence
   (iv) Slav Nationalism in Ottoman Empire
   (*a*) (iii), (ii), (i) and (iv) (*b*) (i), (ii), (iii) and (iv)
   (*c*) (iv), (iii), (ii) and (i) (*d*) (iv), (ii), (iii) and (i)
2. **Industrialisation began in which one of the following European countries in the second half of the eighteenth century?** ***(Re)*(CBSE, 2022 Term 1)**
   (*a*) Germany (*b*) France
   (*c*) Italy (*d*) England
3. **Which types of governments were mainly driven in Europe after the defeat of Napoleon in 1815?** ***(An)*(CBSE, 2022 Term 1)**
   (*a*) Conservative (*b*) Liberal
   (*c*) Federal (*d*) Feudal
4. **Which one of the following groups of countries collectively defeated Napoleon in 1815?** ***(Re)*(CBSE, 2022 Term 1)**
   (*a*) Britain, Russia, Prussia and Austria
   (*b*) Britain, Russia, Prussia and Australia
   (*c*) Britain, Russia, Netherlands and Germany
   (*d*) Britain, Luxembourg, Germany and Italy
5. **In which one of the following countries did the first liberalist-nationalist upheaval take place in July 1830?** ***(Re)*(CBSE, 2022 Term 1)**
   (*a*) France (*b*) Germany
   (*c*) England (*d*) Italy

Assertion and Reason

(1 M)

Direction: The following questions consist of two statements – Assertion (A) and Reason (R). Answer these questions by selecting the appropriate option given below:

(*a*) Both A and R are true, and R is the correct explanation of A.
(*b*) Both A and R are true, but R is not the correct explanation of A.
(*c*) A is true, but R is false
(*d*) A is false, but R is true.

1. **Assertion (A):** Conservatives advocated for the preservation of established institutions such as the monarchy, the Church, social hierarchies, property, and the family.
   Reason (R): Conservatives believed that these institutions were not essential for maintaining social order and stability. ***(An)***
2. **Assertion (A):** Liberalism advocated for the freedom of markets and the elimination of state-imposed restrictions on the movement of goods and capital in the economic sphere.
   Reason (R): Liberals believed that such economic freedom would lead to increased efficiency, prosperity, and individual liberty. ***(Un)***
3. **Assertion (A):** In Britain, the formation of the nation-state was not the result of a sudden upheaval.
   Reason (R): Ethnic groups in Britain extended its influence. ***(An)*(CBSE, 2022 Term 1)**

Subjective Questions

Very Short Answer Type Questions

(1 or 2 M)

1. **Explain the aim to form 'Zollverein', a Customs Union, in 1834 in Germany.** ***(Un)*(CBSE, 2019)**

Ans. The aim to form 'Zollverein', a Customs Union, in 1834 in Germany was to promote ***economic unity*** and ***remove trade barriers*** between the various German states. *(1 M)*

2. **How did the French Revolution contribute to the rise of nationalism in Europe?** ***(An)***

Ans. The French Revolution contributed to the rise of nationalism in Europe by ***promoting the idea*** that people should be loyal to their nation rather than their monarch or empire. It also inspired other nationalist movements throughout Europe. *(2 M)*

3. **Vinay is a resident of a newly conquered region under French control during Napoleon's rule. He has witnessed significant changes in the legal system and daily life due to the implementation of the Napoleonic Code. Describe how these changes have impacted his community, providing specific examples of both positive and negative effects.** ***(An)***

Ans. Positive Effects:

(*i*) **Legal Equality:** Abolished feudal privileges, establishing equality before the law for all citizens. *(½ M)*

(*ii*) **Property Rights:** Secured property rights, boosting investment and economic activity. *(½ M)*

Negative Effects:

(*i*) **Increased Taxation:** Higher taxes burdened many families, especially the poor. *(½ M)*

(*ii*) **Conscription:** Young men were conscripted into the army, reducing the local workforce and causing family hardships. *(½ M)*

4. **How did language contribute to the development of nationalism in Europe?** ***(Re)***

Ans. Languages played an important role in developing the nationalist sentiments:

(*i*) When Russia occupied Poland the Polish language was banned and it was replaced by the Russian language. *(1 M)*

(*ii*) Many members of the clergy in Poland began to use language as a weapon of national resistance. *(1 M)*

Short Answer Type Questions (3 M)

1. Sahil is researching the influence of the Napoleonic Code across various European regions once controlled by France. Explain how the implementation of this legal framework affected local legal systems, social hierarchies, and economic activities. ***(An)***

Ans. The implementation of the Napoleonic Code had significant impacts on the regions of Europe once controlled by France:

(*i*) **Local Legal Systems:** The Napoleonic Code established equality before the law and abolished feudal privileges, unifying legal systems in regions like the Dutch Republic and Italy. *(1 M)*

(*ii*) **Social Hierarchies:** It dismantled social hierarchies, promoting meritocracy and freeing peasants from serfdom, as seen in the Rhineland. *(1 M)*

(*iii*) **Economic Activities:** The Code facilitated freer trade by removing guild restrictions and standardizing weights and measures, boosting economic activities in regions like Germany. *(1 M)*

2. "Ideas of national unity in the early nineteenth century Europe were closely allied to the ideology of liberalism." Examine the statement. ***(An)*(CBSE, 2023)**

Ans. The ideas of national unity in early nineteenth century Europe were closely linked to the ideology of liberalism due to several key factors:

Statement:

(*i*) In early 19th-century Europe, ideas of national unity were intertwined with liberal ideologies, advocating freedoms, equal rights, and government by consent. *(1 M)*

(*ii*) Liberalism supported the end of autocratic privileges, promotion of constitutions, representative governments, and property rights, influencing nationalist movements. *(1 M)*

(*iii*) While emphasising legal and political equality, early liberals did not necessarily advocate for universal suffrage, reflecting limitations in their vision of equality. *(1 M)*

3. Examine any three effects of Print culture on the French Revolution. ***(An)*(CBSE, 2023)**

Ans. The print culture on the french revolution had several effects, including:

(*i*) **Spread of ideas:** Print culture disseminated Enlightenment and French Revolution ideas, mobilising people and fostering national identity through the wide reach of printed material. *(1 M)*

(*ii*) **Formation of public opinion:** It established a public sphere where individuals could share opinions and engage in debates, influencing public opinion and impacting political landscapes. *(1 M)*

(*iii*) **Rise of nationalism:** By promoting a common language and shared cultural narratives, print culture significantly contributed to the emergence and strengthening of nationalistic sentiments. *(1 M)*

4. How had Napoleonic code exported to the regions under French control? Explain with examples. ***(Ap)*(CBSE, 2019)**

Ans. The Napoleonic Code was exported to regions under French control through several significant reforms initiated by Napoleon here's a brief explanation with examples:

(*i*) **Legal Equality:** Implemented the principle of legal equality and the right to property across conquered regions. *(1 M)*

(*ii*) **Abolition of Feudalism:** Eliminate feudal privileges, freeing peasants from serfdom in areas like the Dutch Republic and Italy. *(1 M)*

(*iii*) **Economic Enhancement:** Improved transport and communication, facilitating trade and integration. *(1 M)*

Long Answer Type Questions (5 M)

1. 'The Treaty of Vienna depicted the spirit of conservatism.' Substantiate the statement with key features of the treaty. ***(Ev)***

Ans. The key features of the treaty are:

(*i*) **Restoration of Monarchies:** The main goal was to bring back the old monarchies that Napoleon had removed. For example, the Bourbon dynasty was restored in France. *(1 M)*

(*ii*) **Loss of French Territories:** France had to give up all the territories it had taken during Napoleon's rule. *(1 M)*

(*iii*) **Creation of Strong Boundaries:** To prevent France from expanding again, strong states were placed around it. The kingdom of the Netherlands (including Belgium) was created in the north, and Genoa was added to Piedmont in the south. *(1 M)*

(*iv*) **Territorial Adjustments:** Prussia got new lands on its western frontiers, while Austria was given control over northern Italy. *(1 M)*

(*v*) **Division of Poland and Saxony:** Russia took a part of Poland, and Prussia got a portion of Saxony. *(1 M)*

2. Aaron is a political strategist in 19th-century Europe tasked with preparing a presentation on the challenges and influences of Giuseppe Mazzini. His audience consists of young political activists interested in the history of European political movements. Describe the role of Giuseppe Mazzini in the nationalist movements of Europe and the opposition he faced How did his efforts impact the political landscape of the continent? ***(Un)***

Ans. Giuseppe Mazzini, a key figure in 19th-century European nationalism, played a pivotal role in inspiring and organising nationalist movements across the continent:

(*i*) Mazzini founded influential secret societies such as **Young Italy** and **Young Europe**, advocating for the unification and democratisation of nation-states. *(1½ M)* (*ii*) He faced significant opposition, notably from **Metternich**, who viewed him as a threat to the established conservative order. *(1½ M)*

(*iii*) Despite opposition, Mazzini's advocacy for **national unity** and **democratic republics** left a lasting impact on the political landscape of Europe, inspiring numerous nationalist movements. *(2 M)*

3. How did ideas of national unity in early nineteenth century Europe allied to the ideology of liberalism? Explain. **(*Un*) (CBSE, 2020)**

Ans. The ideas of national unity in early nineteenth century Europe were closely allied to the ideology of liberalism. The following are some ways in which these ideas were

Linked:

(*i*) **Common Values:** National unity and liberalism in early nineteenth-century Europe shared common values such as freedom, equality, and democracy, advocating for the power to be vested in the people rather than in monarchs. *(1 M)*

(*ii*) **Anti-monarchism:** Both ideologies opposed traditional monarchies of Europe, advocating for representative governments that would be accountable to the people. *(1 M)*

(*iii*) **Cultural Identity:** National unity and liberalism were grounded in a shared cultural identity, promoting the creation of nation-states that reflected the cultural identities of their people. *(1 M)*

(*iv*) **Emphasis on Individual Rights:** Both ideologies stressed the importance of individual rights, advocating for the freedom of individuals to live their lives without government interference. *(1 M)*

(*v*) **Emphasis on Education:** Education was seen as crucial for the development of a modern nation-state, with both national unity and liberalism stressing its importance. *(1 M)*

3 THE AGE OF REVOLUTIONS: 1830-1848

NCERT Definitions *(Commonly asked in 1 mark)*

- **Feminist:** A person who spreads awareness of ***women's rights*** and interests based on the belief of the social, economic and political equality of the genders.
- **Ideology:** System of ideas reflecting a particular ***social*** and ***political vision.***
- **Liberalism:** A belief in ***freedom*** and ***equal rights*** for everyone.
- **Romanticism:** It was a movement that valued ***emotions***, ***nature***, and ***individual expression*** over strict rules. It inspired art, literature, and thinking about freedom and creativity.

Important Facts

01 The first upheaval took place in France in ***July* 1830**. Liberal revolutionaries removed the Bourbon kings from power and established a constitutional monarchy with ***Louis Philippe*** as the leader.

02 The Greek War of Independence started in **1821**. The English poet ***Lord Byron*** joined the fight for Greece.

03 In **1832, the *Treaty of Constantinople*** officially acknowledged Greece as an independent country.

04 ***Culture*** played an important role in creating ***the idea of the nation***: art and poetry, stories and music helped express and shape nationalist feelings.

05 A German philosopher ***Johann Gottfried Herder* (1744-1803)** claimed that true German culture was to be discovered among the common people – ***das volk***. It was through folk songs, folk poetry and folk dances that the true spirit of the nation **(*volksgeist*)** was popularised.

06 The economic challenges of the **1830s**, compounded by food shortages and unemployment, sparked the revolutionary events of **1848** in ***Paris***, where protestors successfully pushed for the establishment of a Republic and voting rights for all adult males over **21**.

07 The **1848 *Revolutions*** across Europe were characterised by the liberal middle class advocating for democratic reforms, national unification, and constitutional governance, aiming to replace ***monarchical*** and ***aristocratic*** rule with systems based on equality and freedom.

08 The ***Frankfurt parliament*** was dominated by the middle classes who resisted the demands of workers and artisans and consequently lost their support.

09 The ***Habsburg rulers*** granted more autonomy to the Hungarians in **1867**.

Important Personalities

Louis Philippe: Head of France after the July Revolution 1830.

Friedrich Wilhelm IV: King of Prussia in 1848

Johann Gottfried Herder: German philosopher Johann Gottfried Herder (1744-1803) claimed that true German culture was to be discovered among the common people – das volk. It was through folk songs, folk poetry and folk dances that the true spirit of the nation (volksgeist) was popularised.

Louise Otto-peters: He (1819-95) was a political activist renowned for establishing a women's journal and later founding a feminist political association.

Important Dates

- **1831:** Giuseppe Mazzini established young Italy.
- **1832:** Greece gained independence, The Treaty of Constantinople.
- **1848:** Revolutions in Europe; artisans, industrial workers and peasants revolt against economic hardships; middle classes demand constitutions and representative governments; Italians, Germans, Magyars, Poles, etc. demand nation-states.

Difference Between

1830 Revolution Vs 1848 Revolution		
Criteria	**1830 Revolution**	**1848 Revolution**
Geographical Spread	Primarily France, with significant impacts in Belgium, Poland, and parts of Italy and Germany.	Spread all over Europe, like France, Germany, Italy, and Austria.
Main Causes	This was caused due to the presence of social and political inequalities in the society.	People faced economic problems due to Industrial Revolution inequalities.
Impact on Nationalism	Stirred nationalist feelings, leading to reforms and independence movements.	Markedly strengthened nationalist movements, aiming for nation-state unification and independence.
Role of the Middle Class	Played a significant role in initiating and supporting the revolutions.	Even more actively involved, pushing for democratic reforms and national unification.
Significance for Future	Set the stage for further liberal and nationalist movements.	Despite initial failures, laid the groundwork for future unification of Germany and Italy.

Myth Buster

- **Myth:** Revolutions were uniform across Europe.

  Fact: The revolutions of **(1830-1848)** were not uniform in their causes, objectives, or outcomes across different European regions. While they shared common themes of liberalism, nationalism, and a demand for constitutional government, local conditions and historical contexts played a crucial role in shaping each revolution.

Mnemonics

It helps to recall significant players in the Age of Revolution.

FB - Facebook; **PG** - Play Ground

- **F** → **France**
- **B** → **Belgium**
- **P** → **Poland**
- **G** → **Greece**

Scan Me for Detailed Explanations

COMPETENCY BASED SOLVED EXAMPLES

Multiple Choice Questions

(1 M)

1. **Which of the following term refers to the belief in and advocacy for the social, political and economic equality of women?** ***(Re)*(CBSE, 2024)**

   (*a*) Patriarchy (*b*) Matriarchy
   (*c*) Socialist (*d*) Feminists

2. **Who among the following reMed "When France sneezes, the rest of Europe catches cold"?** ***(Re)*(CBSE, 2022 Term 1)**

   (*a*) Lord Byron (*b*) Metternich
   (*c*) Johann Herder (*d*) Napoleon

3. **In 1824, Eugene Delacroix, a prominent French Romantic painter, completed a monumental painting titled "The Massacre at Chios." This painting captures the horrific event on the Greek island of Chios, where an estimated 20,000 Greeks were killed by Ottoman forces. The artwork emphasizes the anguish and suffering of the victims, especially women and children, using vivid colors and dramatic expressions to evoke strong emotions and sympathy for the Greek cause. Imagine you are an art historian studying Delacroix's painting, "The Massacre at Chios."**

   Based on your analysis, which of the following statements best describes the primary purpose of Delacroix's work? ***(An)***

   (*a*) To celebrate the victory of the Ottoman Empire over Greece.
   (*b*) To showcase the beauty and tranquility of Chios.
   (*c*) To evoke sympathy for the Greek victims and highlight their suffering.
   (*d*) To depict a peaceful co-existence between Greeks and Ottomans.

4. **Who among the following sought to put together a coherent program for a unitary Italian Republic during the 1830s?** ***(Re)*(CBSE, 2022 Term 1)**

   (*a*) Victor Emmanuel I (*b*) Victor Emmanuel II
   (*c*) Giuseppe Mazzini (*d*) Count Cavour

5. **Read the facts regarding the Revolution of the Liberals in Europe during 1848 and choose the correct option:** ***(Re)*(CBSE, 2022 Term 1)**

   (*i*) Abdication of the monarch
   (*ii*) Universal male suffrage had been proclaimed
   (*iii*) Political Rights to women were given
   (*iv*) Freedom of the press had been asked for

   Choose the correct answer from the given below:

   (*a*) Only (*i*) and (*ii*) are correct
   (*b*) Only (*i*), (*ii*) and (*iii*) are correct
   (*c*) Only (*i*) and (*iv*) are correct
   (*d*) Only (*i*), (*ii*) and (*iv*) are correct

Assertion and Reason

(1 M)

Direction: The following questions consist of two statements – Assertion (A) and Reason (R). Answer these questions by selecting the appropriate option given below:

(*a*) Both A and R are true, and R is the correct explanation of A.
(*b*) Both A and R are true, but R is not the correct explanation of A.
(*c*) A is true, but R is false
(*d*) A is false, but R is true.

1. **Assertion (A):** Culture played an important role in creating the idea of the nation.

   Reason (R): Weavers in Silesia had led a revolt against contractors who supplied raw materials and gave them orders for finished textiles but drastically reduced their payments. *(Ap)*

2. **Assertion (A):** The expression of nationalist sentiments through art and culture had a significant impact on the formation of nations.

   Reason (R): Artistic mediums such as painting, literature, and music served as powerful tools for expressing and shaping nationalist feelings, fostering a sense of shared identity and pride among the people. *(Ev)*

3. **Assertion(A):** After Russian occupation in Poland, the Russian language was imposed on its people.

   Reason(R): The use of Polish soon came to be a symbol of struggle against Russian dominance. *(An)*

4. **Assertion (A):** On 18 May 1848, 831 elected representatives marched in a festive procession to take their places in the Frankfurt parliament convened in the Church of St Paul.

   Reason (R): The Frankfurt parliament was a significant event in the history of Germany, representing a key moment in the push for political reforms and national unity. *(Ev)*

Subjective Questions

Very Short Answer Type Questions (1 or 2 M)

1. **What do you understand by the term Feminist?** *(Un)*

Ans. Feminist:

(*i*) Feminist is the person who supports or advocates for women's rights. *(1 M)*

(*ii*) He or she believes in equality in terms of rights either social or political for both men and women. *(1 M)*

2. **Who led the liberal-nationalist revolutions during this period?** *(Re)*

Ans. The 1848 revolution of the liberals refers to the various national movements pioneered by ***educated middle classes*** alongside the revolts of the ***poor, unemployed*** and ***starving peasants*** and workers in Europe. *(2 M)*

3. **Interpret the concept of 'liberalisation' in the field of economic sphere during the nineteenth century in Europe.** ***(Un)(CBSE, 2019)***

Ans. Liberalisation in the Economic Sphere (19th Century Europe):

(*i*) **Market Freedom:** Economic liberalization emphasized reducing state intervention in economic activities, advocating for free trade and the removal of customs barriers. *(½ M)*

(*ii*) **Capital Movement:** It supported the free movement of capital and goods across borders, promoting a unified economic territory for better trade efficiency. *(½ M)*

Short Answer Type Questions (3 M)

1. **Divya is a curator designing an exhibit on Romanticism's impact on European nationalism. The exhibit explains how Romanticism's emphasis on emotions, intuition, and mystical feelings fostered national unity. It showcases how Romantic poets, painters, and composers glorified the past and celebrated folk traditions, inspiring pride and a sense of cultural identity among European nations. As a visitor to Divya's exhibit, how did Romanticism's focus on emotions, intuition, and mystical feelings contribute to developing nationalist sentiments and national unity in 19th-century Europe?** *(Ev)*

Ans. Romanticism contributed to nationalism and unity in 19th-century Europe by:

(*i*) **Celebrating Folk Culture:** Romantic poets and artists highlighted local traditions, folklore, and languages, creating pride in cultural identity. *(1 M)*

(*ii*) **Emotional Bond with Homeland:** Emphasis on emotions and intuition strengthened people's connection to their nation. *(1 M)*

(*iii*) **Promoting Shared Heritage:** Romantic works glorified national history and struggles, inspiring unity and resistance against foreign domination. *(1 M)*

2. **How did the revolutions of 1830 and 1848 differ from each other?** *(An)*

Ans. The revolutions of 1830 and 1848 in France differed from each other in the following ways:

(Each point carries 1 Mark)

Aspect	Revolution of 1830	Revolution of 1848
Outcome for Monarchy	Led to a constitutional monarchy	Abolished the monarchy and declared a republic
Catalysts	Social and political inequalities	Economic hardships and industrial revolution impacts
Achievements	Achieved social equality	Achieved limited political equality

3. **Who were some of the prominent leaders of these revolutions?** *(Re)*

Ans. Some prominent leader as follows:

(*i*) **Giuseppe Mazzini:** Italian revolutionary who established Young Italy, advocating national unification and democracy, inspiring nationalists across Europe. *(1 M)*

(*ii*) **Count Camillo de Cavour:** Key architect of Italian unification, Cavour skillfully used diplomacy and strategic alliances, significantly advancing Italy's consolidation. *(1 M)*

(*iii*) **Giuseppe Garibaldi:** Celebrated for leading the Redshirts and uniting southern Italy, Garibaldi's military campaigns were crucial in the unification process, embodying the spirit of nationalism. *(1 M)*

4. **Why did these revolutions ultimately fail to achieve their goals?** ***(An)***

Ans. The key reasons why revolutions might fail:

(*i*) **Diverse Goals:** The revolutions lacked cohesive objectives across regions, with varying aspirations for independence, democracy, or social reform, leading to fragmented efforts. *(1 M)*

(*ii*) **Conservative Resistance:** Strong opposition from conservative forces, including monarchies and the aristocracy, effectively suppressed revolutionary movements, restoring old regimes. *(1 M)*

(*iii*) **Lack of Support:** Insufficient internal support and limited external assistance weakened revolutionary momentum, hindering sustained change and allowing for the quick re-establishment of conservative order. *(1 M)*

Long Answer Type Questions (5 M)

1. **Explain any five challenges which the Silesian weavers faced in 1845 when contractors reduced their payments?** ***(Un)*(CBSE CFPQ, 2023)**

Ans. The challenges found by the Silesian weavers in 1845:

(*i*) **Forced into Poverty:** The substantial reduction in payments by contractors forced many Silesian weavers into severe poverty. *(1 M)*

(*ii*) **Increased Unemployment Fear:** With the drop in wages, the fear of unemployment became more pronounced among the weavers, causing anxiety and uncertainty about their future and stability. *(1 M)*

(*iii*) **Food Shortages:** The limited income led to food shortages for the weavers and their families, making it challenging to secure adequate nutrition and maintain health, further affecting their ability to work efficiently. *(1 M)*

(*iv*) **Poor Health Conditions:** The lack of sufficient food resulted in deteriorating health conditions among the weavers and their families. *(1 M)*

(*v*) **Inaction of Silesian King:**The Silesian king's failure to act against the unjust practices of the contractors left the weavers defenseless and continued their exploitation. *(1 M)*

2. **Write a note on:** ***(Re)*(NCERT)**

(*a*) Guiseppe Mazzini
(*b*) Count Camillo de Cavour
(*c*) The Greek war of independence
(*d*) Frankfurt parliament
(*e*) The role of women in nationalist struggles.

Ans. (*a*) **Giuseppe Mazzini:** Italian nationalist, formed Young Italy and Young Europe, advocating for unified Italy; exiled for revolutionary activities, believed in nations as natural societal units. *(1 M)*

(*b*) **Count Camillo de Cavour:** Key in Italian unification, not a revolutionary; utilized diplomacy with France, leading Sardinia-Piedmont to overcome Austria, instrumental in unifying Italy. *(1 M)*

(*c*) **Greek War of Independence:** Started in 1821, Greeks fought Ottoman rule, influenced by European nationalism; received external support, culminating in independence acknowledged in 1832. *(1 M)*

(*d*) **Frankfurt Parliament:** Established in 1848 by German middle classes seeking unification; attempted to create a constitutional monarchy, dissolved due to lack of support and opposition. *(1 M)*

(*e*) **Role of Women in Nationalist Struggles:** Women actively engaged in liberal movements; faced challenges in gaining political rights, highlighting gender-based disparities within nationalist movements. *(1 M)*

3. **'Romanticism, a cultural movement sought to develop a particular form of nationalist sentiment.' Justify the statement with suitable arguments.** ***(Ev)***

Ans. Romanticism played a significant role in developing nationalist sentiment by emphasizing cultural identity and emotional connections. Here's how:

(*i*) **Glorification of Folk Traditions:** Romantic thinkers celebrated local folklore, songs, and traditions as symbols of national pride. For example, the Grimm Brothers collected German folktales to promote unity among Germans. *(1 M)*

(*ii*) **Emotional Connection to Homeland:** Romanticism emphasized emotions and intuition over reason. This created a deep emotional bond with one's homeland, strengthening nationalist feelings. *(1 M)*

(*iii*) **Celebration of Cultural Heritage:** Romantic artists and writers, like Johann Gottfried Herder, believed true national spirit (Volksgeist) was found in folk culture, promoting pride in one's heritage. *(1 M)*

(*iv*) **Role of Art and Literature:** Painters like Eugene Delacroix depicted nationalist struggles, while composers like Karol Kurpinski used folk music to inspire national unity, as seen in Poland's resistance to Russian dominance. *(1 M)*

(*v*) **Rejection of Foreign Domination:** Romantic nationalism encouraged people to oppose foreign rule by promoting their cultural uniqueness, leading to movements for national independence across Europe. *(1 M)*

4 THE MAKING OF GERMANY AND ITALY

NCERT Definitions (Commonly asked in 1 mark)

- **Ethnic:** Relates to a common *racial*, *tribal*, or *cultural* origin or background that a community identifies with or claims.
- **Junkers:** The German noble *landlords* and large *landowners* in Prussia who were a significant conservative political force and supported the monarchy and the military.
- **Young Italy:** A **secret society** founded by **Giuseppe Mazzini** aiming at the unification of Italy. It was part of a wider movement seeking to consolidate various Italian states and territories into a single nation.
- **Carbonari:** Members of a ***secret revolutionary society*** working to unify ***Italy*** in the early ***19th century***.

Important Facts

01 ***Nationalism in Europe*** shifted from its association with democracy and revolution to a tool for conservatives to promote state power after **1848**.

02 ***The liberal*** initiative by middle-class Germans in **1848** to unite the German confederation into a nation-state with an elected parliament was suppressed by monarchy, military, and Prussian landowners.

03 After that, Prussia led the effort to unite the nation. ***Otto von Bismarck***, who was the top leader of Prussia, planned how to make this happen.

04 The ***unification of Germany*** was achieved after Prussia won three wars against Austria, Denmark, and France over seven years, culminating in the establishment of the German Empire.

05 In ***January* 1871, *the Prussian king, William I***, was proclaimed German Emperor in a ceremony held at Versailles.

06 ***Italy*** was fragmented into several states in the ***mid*-19th *century***, with only Sardinia-Piedmont under Italian rule.

07 The rest were controlled by foreign powers like the Austrian Habsburgs, the Pope, and the Bourbon kings of Spain, leading to varied regional dialects of Italian.

08 ***Giuseppe Mazzini's*** efforts and ***Giuseppe Garibaldi's*** military campaigns were pivotal in unifying Italy, defeating Austrian and Spanish rule, leading to ***Victor Emmanuel II*** becoming the king of a united ***Italy in 1861***.

09 The formation of the ***United kingdom*** was shaped by England's increasing dominance over the diverse ***ethnic*** groups of the British Isles, Leveraging its growing wealth and power to unify English, Welsh, Scots, Irish cultures under a single national identity.

10 ***The English Parliament,*** empowered after **1688,** played a key role in forming a nation-state centered around England.

11 ***The Act of Union*** **(1707)** between England and Scotland that resulted in the formation of the 'United Kingdom of Great Britain' meant, in effect, that England was enable to impose its influence on Scotland.

Important Personalities

Otto Von Bismarck: He was the architect of a Prussian consolidation that was also a form of German unification. Once the empire was established, he actively and skilfully pursued pacific policies in foreign affairs, succeeding in preserving the peace in Europe for about two decades.

Count Camillo di Cavour: The Chief Minister of Piedmont, Count Camillo di Cavour, helped the kin in forming an alliance with France, and they defeated the Austrian forces in 1859. Camillo Paolo Filippo Giulio Benso, count of Cavour, Isolabella and Leri, generally known as Cavour, was an Italian statesman and a leading figure in the movement toward Italian unification.

Giuseppe Garibaldi: He was an Italian general, politician and nationalist who played a large role in the history of Italy. He has been hailed as one of the 'Fathers of the Fatherland' for his contribution to the Italian Risorgimento, which unified the fractured nation under one rule. He joined the war along with his armed volunteers called the 'Red shirts'. In 1860, Garibaldi and his troops marched into southern Italy and the kingdom of two sicilies.

Important Dates

- **1831:** Giuseppe Mazzini established young Italy.
- **1832:** Greece gained independence, The Treaty of Constantinople.
- **1848:** Revolutions in Europe; artisans, industrial workers and peasants revolt against economic hardships; middle classes demand constitutions and representative governments; Italians, Germans, Magyars, Poles, etc. demand nation-states.

Difference Between

Unification of Germany Vs. Unification of Italy		
Aspect	**Unification of Germany**	**Unification of Italy**
Main Leaders	Prussian monarchy, military, and Junkers (landowners)	Giuseppe Garibaldi, Count Cavour, Victor Emmanuel II
Dominant Power	Prussian state power dominated	Overthrow of foreign rulers (Austria, France, Spain)

Main Obstacles	Opposition from monarchy, military, and Junkers	Control by foreign powers (Austria, France, Spain)
Key Events	Repression of 1848 liberal initiative	Diplomatic efforts to overcome Austrian control by Cavour
Result	Dominance of Prussian power in unified Germany	Liberation of Italy from foreign rule and establishment of a united nation state

Myth Buster

- **Myth:** Nationalism was solely a peaceful and unifying force in the making of Germany and Italy.

  Fact: While nationalism did play a crucial role in unifying Germany and Italy, the process was not solely peaceful. It involved wars, strategic diplomatic maneuvers, and power politics.

  For example: the unification of Germany was significantly advanced by the Prussian victories in the Danish War (1864), the Austro-Prussian War (1866), and the Franco-Prussian War (1870-71). Similarly, the unification of Italy involved several military campaigns led by figures like Giuseppe Garibaldi, along with the strategic diplomacy of Count Camillo di Cavour.

Mnemonics

This phrase helps to remember Unification of Germany (1866-71):

"**P**russia Leads, **B**ismarck Builds, **K**aiser Crowned, **B**anking Begins, **P**russian Power"

- **P**russia Leads (Prussia's leadership).
- **B**ismarck Builds (Bismarck's nation-building role).
- **K**aiser Crowned (Kaiser William I's coronation).
- **B**anking Begins (The economic systems establishment).
- **P**russian Power (The outcome of Prussian dominance).

Scan Me for Detailed Explanations

COMPETENCY BASED SOLVED EXAMPLES

Multiple Choice Questions

(1 M)

1. Who among the following was the architect for the unification of Germany? ***(Re)*(CBSE, 2022 Term 1)**

(*a*) Otto Von Bismarck (*b*) William I

(*c*) Frederick III (*d*) William II

2. Who among the following was proclaimed King of United Italy in 1861? ***(Re)*(CBSE, 2022 Term 1)**

(*a*) Charles I

(*b*) Victor Emmanuel II

(*c*) Giuseppe Garibaldi

(*d*) Nero

3. Vimal analyzes various forms of political leadership through historical caricatures. One of the caricatures you are studying depicts Otto von Bismarck in the German Reichstag, taken from the Figaro, Vienna, dated 5 March 1870. In this caricature, Bismarck is shown wielding a whip, suggesting his methods of leadership and governance. Which of the following aspects of Bismarck is shown in this image? ***(An)***

(*a*) His democratic nature

(*b*) His violent and strict nature

(*c*) His sympathetic nature

(*d*) None of the above

4. Match the following and choose the correct option. ***(Ap)*(CBSE, 2023)**

	Leader		Role
A.	Victor Emmanuel II	I.	Chief Minister of Italy
B.	Guiseppe Mazzini	II.	Guiseppe Garibaldi
C.	Young Italy Movement	III.	Conquered the Kingdom of Sicillies
D.	Count Cavour	IV.	Proclaimed as King of Unified Italy

(*a*) A-I, B-IV, C-III, D-II
(*b*) A-II, B-I, C-IV, D-III
(*c*) A-IV, B-II, C-III, D-I
(*d*) A-I, B-IV, C-II, D-III

5. From which of the following countries Giuseppe Garibaldi belonged to? **(*Re*) (CBSE, 2024)**

(*a*) Austria (*b*) Italy
(*c*) Greece (*d*) Spain

Assertion and Reason

(1 M)

Direction: The following questions consist of two statements – Assertion (A) and Reason (R). Answer these questions by selecting the appropriate option given below:

(*a*) Both A and R are true, and R is the correct explanation of A.
(*b*) Both A and R are true, but R is not the correct explanation of A.
(*c*) A is true, but R is false
(*d*) A is false, but R is true.

1. Assertion (A): The dominance of foreign powers and the absence of a unified Italian monarchy hindered the process of Italian unification during the 19th century. **(*Un*)**

Reason (R): With only one Italian princely house ruling over Sardinia-Piedmont, the absence of a strong central Italian monarchy allowed foreign powers to exert influence over different regions, impeding the path towards Italian unification.

2. Assertion (A): Weavers in Silesia led a revolt against contractors in 1845.

Reason (R): Contractors had drastically reduced their payments. **(*Ap*)(CBSE, 2022 Term 1)**

Subjective Questions

Very Short Answer Type Questions

(1 or 2 M)

1. Explain the aim to form 'Zollverein', a Customs Union, in 1834 in Germany. **(*Un*)(CBSE, 2019)**

Ans. The aim to form 'Zollverein', a Customs Union, in 1834 in Germany was to promote economic unity and remove trade Barriers between the various German states. *(1 M)*

2. What measures did the new German state emphasise to modernise the country? **(*Re*)**

Ans. The new state placed a strong emphasis on modernising the currency, banking, legal and judicial systems in Germany. Prussian measures and practices often became a model for the rest of Germany. *(2 M)*

3. What was the result of the Act of Union (1707) between England and Scotland? **(*Un*)**

Ans. The result of the Act of Union (1707) between England and Scotland was;

(*i*) The Act of Union (1707) between England and Scotland resulted in the formation of the 'United Kingdom of Great Britain', where England was able to significantly influence Scotland. *(1 M)*

(*ii*) This union led to the suppression of Scotland's distinctive culture and political institutions, marking a significant shift towards a unified British identity under English dominance. *(1 M)*

4. How did the English nation extend its influence over other nations in the British Isles? **(*Un*)**

Ans. The English nation possessed the other three nations of the islands through a steady growth in property wealth and power. Besides this, the English language, British Flag and National Anthem were promoted as national symbols to identify the nationality of the nation. *(2 M)*

5. What instrument played a significant role in the formation of a nation-state with England at its center? **(*Re*)**

Ans. The English parliament, which had seized power from the monarchy in 1688 at the end of a protracted conflict, was the instrument through which a nation-state, with England at its centre, came to be forged. *(2 M)*

Short Answer Type Questions

(3 M)

1. Who gathered in the unheated Hall of Mirrors in the Palace of Versailles on 18 January 1871 to proclaim the new German Empire, and what does this event signify about the nation building process in Germany? **(*An*)**

Ans. Participants in the Proclamation: On the morning of 18 January 1871, German princes, army leaders, and key Prussian officials including Bismarck met in Versailles to announce Kaiser William I as the German Emperor. *(1½ M)*

Significance of the Event: This gathering highlighted Prussia's key role in uniting Germany, showing a move from people-driven to state-led nation building, and marked the start of a new, organized German nation under Prussian leadership. *(1½ M)*

2. Describe the role of Giuseppe Garibaldi in the unification of Italy and his famous expedition. **(*Un*)**

Ans. Giuseppe Garibaldi played a significant role in the unification of Italy.

(*i*) He was a prominent Italian freedom fighter and a member of the Young Italy movement. In 1860, Garibaldi led the famous Expedition of the Thousand to South Italy, also known as the Red Shirts. *(1 M)*

(*ii*) The expedition gathered a significant number of volunteers, around 30,000, who fought to unify Italy. In 1867, Garibaldi led an army to Rome to challenge the Papal States, but they were defeated by the combined French and Papal troops. *(1 M)*

(*iii*) Ultimately, in 1870, when France withdrew its troops during the war with Prussia, the Papal States were finally incorporated into Italy. *(1 M)*

3. Describe the political fragmentation of Italy during the mid nineteenth century and the diverse ruling powers in different regions. ***(Un)***

Ans. In the **mid-nineteenth century**, Italy was politically fragmented and divided among different rulers and foreign powers:

(*i*) **Northern Italy** was under the influence of Austria, directly controlling regions like Lombardy and Venetia, showcasing the dominance of foreign powers in Italian politics. *(1 M)*

(*ii*) **Central Italy** was ruled by the Papal States, indicating a significant religious influence over the political landscape, with the Pope governing these territories. *(1 M)*

(*iii*) **Southern Italy** and Sicily were under the Kingdom of the Two Sicilies, reflecting the regional division and local dynastic rule that characterized the Italian peninsula's fragmented nature. *(1 M)*

Long Answer Type Questions (5 M)

1. Explain the process of unification of Italy. ***(Ev)***

Ans. Unification of Italy:

(*i*) **Central Figures:** Giuseppe Garibaldi, Count Cavour, and Victor Emmanuel II were instrumental, leading diverse yet complementary efforts towards unification. *(1 M)*

(*ii*) **Pre-Unification Italy:** Initially fragmented into seven states, only Sardinia-Piedmont was under Italian rule, showcasing the divided Italian landscape. *(1 M)*

(*iii*) **External Domination:** The Austrian-Habsburgs controlled the north, the Papal States the center, and the Bourbons the south, indicating the extent of foreign influence. *(1 M)*

(*iv*) **Ideological Beginnings:** Mazzini's formation of secret societies like Young Italy ignited the nationalist movement, laying the ideological groundwork for unification. *(1 M)*

(*v*) **Military and Diplomatic Campaigns:** Count Cavour's diplomatic victory against Austria and Garibaldi's military conquest in the south were critical, culminating in Victor Emmanuel II's leadership unifying Italy under a single crown. *(1 M)*

2. Briefly trace the process of German unification. ***(Ev)(NCERT)***

Ans. The process of German unification:

(*i*) **Initial Movements:** Post-1848, nationalism in Germany evolved, focusing more on state power and less on democracy, particularly under Prussian influence. *(1 M)*

(*ii*) **Prussian Dominance:** Led by Otto von Bismarck, Prussia spearheaded the unification, utilizing its military and bureaucracy to consolidate the German territories. *(1 M)*

(*iii*) **Strategic Wars:** Bismarck engineered three crucial wars against Austria, Denmark, and France, strategically securing victories that were vital for unification. *(1 M)*

(*iv*) **Empire Proclamation:** In January 1871, the Prussian king, William I, was declared the German Emperor at Versailles, marking the official unification of Germany. *(1 M)*

(*v*) **Modernisation and Integration:** The new German Empire focused on modernizing its institutions, adopting Prussian systems as models, which fostered national integration and development. *(1 M)*

3. How was the history of nationalism in Britain unlike the rest of Europe? ***(An)(NCERT)***

Ans. The history of nationalism in Britain was unique compared to the rest of Europe due to several factors:

(*i*) **Early Unification:** Unlike other European nations, Britain achieved political unification much earlier, with England and Scotland forming the United Kingdom in 1707, which helped in early development of a British national identity. *(1 M)*

(*ii*) **Parliamentary Supremacy:** Unlike the autocratic regimes in much of Europe, Britain had a long-standing tradition of parliamentary democracy, shaping a distinct political culture. *(1 M)*

(*iii*) **Industrial Revolution:** Britain was the birthplace of the Industrial Revolution, advancing its technological and economic superiority, which bolstered national pride and identity. *(1 M)*

(*iv*) **Colonial Empire:** The vast British Empire, unlike European nationalist movements, provided a unique source of national pride, distinct from the continental struggles for independence or unification. *(1 M)*

(*v*) **Cultural Nationalism:** The promotion of English culture, language, and symbols like the Union Jack and national anthem played a crucial role in unifying the British identity, contrasting with the linguistic and cultural diversity in European nationalisms. *(1 M)*

5 VISUALISING THE NATION

NCERT Definitions *(Commonly asked in 1 mark)*

- **Allegory:** A symbolic representation where abstract ideas are portrayed through ***characters***, ***figures***, or ***events***. In the context of nationalism, countries were often personified by **female figures** to symbolize the nation itself.
- **Marianne:** An ***allegory*** of the ***French nation***, representing the Republic of France. Marianne embodies ***liberty***, ***republicanism***, and the French ***Revolution ideals***. She is characterised by symbols such as the Phrygian cap, representing freedom and the republic.
- **Germania:** The ***personification*** of the ***German nation***. Like Marianne, Germania symbolizes the unified German nation-state, embodying strength, courage, and the spirit of the German people. She is often depicted with the German eagle and a crown of oak leaves, denoting heroism.

Important Facts

01 The name ***Marianne***, commonly associated with Christianity, was adopted as an ***allegory*** for France. Statues of Marianne were erected in public squares to remind the public of the national symbol of unity and to persuade them to identify with it

02 **Marianne** images were marked on coins and stamps.

03 Similarly, **Germania** became the allegory of the German nation. In visual representations, Germania wears a crown of oak leaves, as the German oak stands for heroism.

04 **Meanings of the symbols:**

Attribute	Significance
Broken chains	Being freed
Breastplate with eagle	Symbol of the German empire-strength
Crown of oak leaves	Heroism
Sword	Readiness to fight
Olive branch around the sword	Willingness to make peace
Black, red and gold tricolour	Flag of the liberal-nationalists in 1848, banned by the Dukes of the German states
Rays of the rising sun	Beginning of a new era

Difference Between

Marianne Vs. Germania		
Aspect	**Marianne**	**Germania**
Symbolism	Personification of French Republic; Liberty, Equality, Fraternity	Symbol of German nation; Strength, Unity, Nationalism
Historical Context	Emerged during French Revolution; Late 18th century	Prominence during German unification; 19th century
Representation	Depicted in various art forms, official documents, currency	Featured in paintings, sculptures, literature
Cultural Impact	Enduring symbol of French Republic and democratic values	Played significant role in shaping German national identity

Myth Buster

- **Myth:** Only European countries utilized female allegories to personify their nations.

  Fact: While European countries popularized this practice, the use of personification and allegory to represent nations and their ideals is a global phenomenon, with various cultures adapting it to their own contexts and values.
- **Myth:** Allegorical figures like Marianne and Germania represent specific historical women.

  Fact: Marianne and Germania are allegorical figures representing the abstract idea of the nation, not any particular woman. They embody the collective identity and values of their respective nations, such as liberty, justice, and the republic for France, and heroism for Germany.

Scan Me for Detailed Explanations

COMPETENCY BASED SOLVED EXAMPLES

Multiple Choice Questions

(1 M)

1. How did artists in the eighteenth and nineteenth centuries represent a nation? ***(Un)***

(*a*) Through portraits of famous leaders

(*b*) By personifying the nation as a female figure

(*c*) Through landscape paintings

(*d*) All of the above

2. What does 'crown of oak leaves' symbolise? ***(Re)(CBSE SQP, 2023)***

(*a*) Freedom

(*b*) Readiness to fight

(*c*) Willingness to make peace

(*d*) Heroism

3. Following image is the personification of Germany commonly associated with the Romantic Era and the Revolutions of 1848. Identify its name from among the following options. ***(Re)***

(*a*) Germania (*b*) Marianne

(*c*) Philip Viet (*d*) La Italia

4. How were nations portrayed in visual art during the eighteenth and nineteenth centuries? ***(Un)***

(*a*) As male figures representing strength and power

(*b*) As landscapes representing natural beauty

(*c*) As female figures representing an allegory of the nation

(*d*) All of the above

5. **Which of the following aspects that signifies the image of 'Germania'?** *(Re)*
   (*a*) Fold and Cultural Tradition
   (*b*) Auterity and Asceticism
   (*c*) Revenge and Vengeance
   (*d*) Heroism and Justice

Assertion and Reason **(1 M)**

Direction: The following questions consist of two statements – Assertion (A) and Reason (R). Answer these questions by selecting the appropriate option given below:

(*a*) Both A and R are true, and R is the correct explanation of A.
(*b*) Both A and R are true, but R is not the correct explanation of A.
(*c*) A is true, but R is false
(*d*) A is false, but R is true.

1. **Assertion (A):** The personification of nations as female figures was a unique feature of European visual art during the eighteenth and nineteenth centuries.
   Reason (R): Other cultures did not use gendered allegories to represent their nations in visual art. *(Ev)*
2. **Assertion (A):** Artists in the eighteenth and nineteenth centuries personified nations as female figures.
   Reason (R): This was done to give the abstract idea of the nation a concrete form. *(Ev)*

Subjective Questions

Very Short Answer Type Questions **(1 or 2 M)**

1. **Who became the allegory of the German nation? Explain.** *(Un)*

Ans.
(*i*) Germania became the allegory of the German nation. She symbolizes the unity and identity of the German people. *(1 M)*
(*ii*) Germania is often depicted with ancient Roman features, reflecting Germany's historical and cultural roots. This figure is a personification of the nation's spirit and ideals. *(1 M)*

2. **French Revolution artists used the female allegory to portray ideas such as:** *(Un)*

Ans. During the French Revolution, artists used the female allegory:
(*i*) Marianne, to portray ideas such as liberty, equality, and fraternity. *(1 M)*
(*ii*) Marianne symbolizes the Republic's values and serves as a representation of the revolutionary ideals and the spirit of the French nation. *(1 M)*

3. **Artists in which century found a way out by personifying a nation?** *(Re)*

Ans. Artists in the 19th century found a way to express national identity by personifying nations through female allegories, such as Britannia for Britain, Germania for Germany, and Marianne for France, symbolising their ideals, culture, and unity. *(2 M)*

Short Answer Type Questions **(3 M)**

1. **You walk into a beautifully decorated room in the local museum where an interactive display about Marianne, the symbol of national unity in France, captures your attention. The display features a life-sized statue of Marianne, surrounded by historical artifacts and multimedia presentations. As you approach, a digital screen invites you to explore Marianne's significance. As you interact with the display, you notice a section that highlights various symbols of national unity from around the world. The screen poses an intriguing question: "Why do you think Marianne, depicted as a woman wearing a Phrygian cap, was chosen to symbolise the French Republic's values of liberty, equality, and fraternity?"** *(An)*

Ans. (*i*) **Symbol of Liberty:** Marianne, depicted with a Phrygian cap, symbolizes liberty. The Phrygian cap, also known as the liberty cap, was a powerful emblem of freedom during the French Revolution, representing the overthrow of tyranny. *(1 M)*
(*ii*) **Embodiment of Republican Values:** Marianne represents the core values of the French Republic—liberty, equality, and fraternity. Her image promotes these ideals, serving as a constant reminder of the principles that underpin the French nation. *(1 M)*
(*iii*) **Cultural and National Unity:** As a personification of the French nation, Marianne helps forge a collective identity and cultural unity. The choice of a common name like Marianne emphasizes the notion of a people's nation, accessible and relatable to all citizens. *(1 M)*

Long Answer Type Questions **(5 M)**

1. **Who were Marianne and Germania? What was the importance of the way in which they were portrayed?** *(Ev)(NCERT)*

Ans. Marianne: She was a personification of the French Republic, symbolizing liberty, reason, and the Republic. Her portrayal, often with a Phrygian cap, signified freedom and democracy. *(1 M)*
Germania: Represented the German nation, embodying strength, unity, and liberty. She was depicted with a crown, reflecting the unification of Germany under a single entity. *(1 M)*
Importance of Portrayal:
(*i*) These symbols were vital for rallying support for nationalist movements, helping to unify diverse groups by providing a common identity and purpose. *(1 M)*
(*ii*) Their representations in art and propaganda played a crucial role in inspiring and motivating the public, fostering a sense of national pride and belonging. *(1 M)*
(*iii*) The visual imagery associated with Marianne and Germania helped to communicate the ideals of the nation-state, freedom, and unity to a largely illiterate population, making complex political ideals more accessible. *(1 M)*

6 NATIONALISM AND IMPERIALISM

NCERT Definitions *(Commonly asked in 1 mark)*

- **Imperialism:** It is the ***state policy, practice***, or ***advocacy*** of extending power and dominion, especially by direct territorial acquisition or by gaining political and economic control of other territories and peoples.
- **The Balkans:** This refers to a region in ***Southeast Europe*** known for its diverse geography and various ethnic groups. It includes modern-day countries like Romania, Bulgaria, Albania, Greece, Macedonia, Croatia, Bosnia-Herzegovina, Slovenia, Serbia, and Montenegro.

Important Facts

01 ***The Balkan States*** were once part of the ***Ottoman Empire***. Influenced by romantic nationalism, they began to seek independence from Ottoman rule, claiming they were once independent before being controlled by foreign powers.

02 ***Each major power:*** Russia, Germany, England, and Austro-Hungary-wanted to reduce the influence of their rivals in the Balkans and expand their own control. This rivalry led to conflicts in the region, ultimately culminating in the First World War.

03 It was observed that nationalism along with imperialism led to the catastrophic events of the ***first world war* 1914** which did not affect Europe only but the whole world.

04 Although the source of ***nationalism*** originated in Europe and Later spread to the rest of the world, the colonial countries adopted the concepts of nationalism but were modified according to their purpose. Hence each nation had its own version of nationalism.

Important Dates

- **1905:** Slav nationalism gathers force in the Habsburg and Ottoman Empires.
- **1914:** First world war begins

Difference Between

Nationalism Vs. Imperialism

Aspect	Nationalism	Imperialism
Definition	Nationalism is a sense of pride, loyalty, and commitment to one's country, emphasizing unity, independence, and the celebration of national identity.	Imperialism is a policy of extending a country's power and influence through colonization, military force, or other means.
Goal	Promotes interests and rights of a specific nation or ethnic group, often seeking political independence and cultural identity.	Expands power, influence, and resources of the imperial nation, often through colonization and exploitation of resources and populations.

Examples	Movements for independence from colonial rule (e.g., India's struggle for freedom from British rule). Cultural movements celebrating national traditions, languages, and customs.	European colonisation of Africa, Asia, and the Americas during the 19th and early 20th centuries. Establishment of colonies for economic gain and strategic advantage (e.g., British colonisation of India).

Myth Buster

- **Myth:** Imperial powers only exploited their colonies without any benefit to the colonised regions.
  Fact: While imperialism often involved exploitation and subjugation, it also led to some economic development and modernization in the colonies. However, these changes primarily served the interests of the imperial powers and often disrupted local economies and societies.

Mnemonics

The Balkan States: "BAGS B SCRAM"

- B → Bosnia and Herzegovina
- A → Albania
- G → Greece
- S → Serbia
- B → Bulgaria
- S → Slovenia
- C → Croatia
- R → Romania
- A → North Macedonia (formerly known as the Former Yugoslav Republic of Macedonia)
- M → Montenegro

Scan Me for Detailed Explanations

COMPETENCY BASED SOLVED EXAMPLES

Multiple Choice Questions

(1 M)

1. **"Symbols in Nationalism" focusing on the artistic representation of nations during the 18th and 19th centuries, particularly on how the female form was used to personify nations: During the 18th and 19th centuries, the female form was commonly used to personify nations in artistic representations. Which of the following is a primary reason for this choice of symbolism?** *(An)*

   (*a*) The female form represented the nurturing aspect of the nation, akin to a mother figure.

   (*b*) Artistic styles of the period favored the depiction of women in all forms of art.

   (*c*) Male figures were considered inappropriate for national personification due to prevailing gender norms.

   (*d*) Nations wanted to highlight the role of women in their independence movements.

2. **Given below is the painting 'Imperial Federation - Map of the World showing the extent of the British Empire in 1886'.**

   Observe the painting and answer the question that follows.

   Which of the following elements depicted in the painting seem conflicting when presented together? *(An)***(CBSE APQ, 2023)**

   (*a*) The British soldiers and British colonies spread in both east and west

   (*b*) The variety of animals and costumed figures depicting countries and their people

   (*c*) Britannia, the personification of Britain, seated on top of the world and the words federation written at the top of the image

   (*d*) The words 'freedom' and 'fraternity' written at the top and Atlas, depicting human labour, holding the world upon his shoulders

3. **Which countries were part of the Balkan region during this period?** ***(Re)***

(*a*) Italy, France, and Spain

(*b*) Poland, Ukraine, and Belarus

(*c*) Romania, Bulgaria, and Albania

(*d*) Germany, Austria, and Hungary

4. **In a classroom activity designed to deepen understanding of symbolism in European historical artifacts, students are asked to match the following symbols with their respective meanings. This exercise aims to enhance their analytical skills by connecting symbols to the concepts they represent:** ***(Ap)***

Match the Following :

	Column-I (Symbol)		Column-II (Represents)
(A)	Imperial Crown	(i)	Military Honor
(B)	Iron Cross	(ii)	Royal Authority
(C)	Laurel Wreath	(iii)	Victory
(D)	Skeleton	(iv)	Human Costs

(*a*) A-(ii), B-(i), C-(iii), D-(iv)

(*b*) A-(i), B-(iii), C-(ii), D-(iv)

(*c*) A-(iii), B-(iv), C-(ii), D-(iv)

(*d*) A-(iv), B-(iii), C-(i), D-(ii)

5. **What impact did European ideas of nationalism have on anti-imperial movements in colonized countries?** ***(Un)***

(*a*) Rejection and resistance

(*b*) Adaptation and assimilation

(*c*) Collaboration and cooperation

(*d*) Acceptance and replication

Assertion and Reason **(1 M)**

Direction: The following questions consist of two statements – Assertion (A) and Reason (R). Answer these questions by selecting the appropriate option given below:

(*a*) Both A and R are true, and R is the correct explanation of A.

(*b*) Both A and R are true, but R is not the correct explanation of A.

(*c*) A is true, but R is false

(*d*) A is false, but R is true.

1. **Assertion (A):** The most serious source of nationalist tension in Europe after 1871 was Balkan.

Reason (R): A large part of the Balkan was under the control of Ottoman Empire. ***(An) (CBSE, 2024)***

Subjective Questions

Very Short Answer Type Questions (1 or 2 M)

1. **Which empire controlled a large part of the Balkans during this period?** ***(Re)***

Ans. The Ottoman Empire controlled a large part of the Balkans during this period. All through the nineteenth century the Ottoman Empire had sought to strengthen itself through modernisation and internal reforms but with very little success. *(2 M)*

2. **What type of movements emerged in response to imperial domination in colonised countries?** ***(Un)***

Ans. The anti-imperial movement was a political and social movement that emerged in response to the expansion of European empires and the colonisation of non-European countries. The movement was characterized by a strong opposition to imperialism. *(2 M)*

Short Answer Type Questions (3 M)

1. **Why did nationalist tensions emerge in the Balkans?** ***(An)(NCERT)***

Ans. Nationalist tensions emerge in the Balkans due to the following reasons:

(*i*) The Balkans was a region of geographical and ethnic variations. It included modern day Romania, Bulgaria, Albania, Greece, Macedonia, Croatia, Bosnia and Herzegovina, Slovenia, Serbia, and Montenegro. *(1 M)*

(*ii*) The widespread ideas of romantic nationalism as well as historical notions of independence combined with disintegration of the Ottoman Empire made this region very explosive. *(1 M)*

(*iii*) The Balkan states were envious of one another and every state wanted more territory, even at the expense of others. As a result, the region has become a scene of big power rivalry. *(1 M)*

2. **You are a university student participating in a history symposium that focuses on the impact of nationalism on European conflicts. Your presentation is on the concept of romantic nationalism and its specific role in escalating tensions in the Balkans during the late nineteenth century. In preparing your presentation, analyze how romantic nationalism contributed to the explosive situation in the Balkans.** ***(An)***

Ans. Romantic nationalism played a key role in escalating tensions in the Balkans in the late 19th century by:

(*i*) Romantic nationalism involves developing a national identity based on culture, language, and historical continuity. *(1 M)*

(*ii*) In the Balkans, this ideology inspired peoples under Ottoman rule to assert their distinct national identities. *(1 M)*

(*iii*) Nationalist movements sought to reclaim perceived historical sovereignty, contributing to regional tensions. *(1 M)*

Long Answer Type Questions (5 M)

1. Describe the explosive conditions prevailed in the Balkans after 1871 in Europe. *(Ev)*

Ans. Explosive Conditions in the Balkans After 1871:

(*i*) **Ethnic Diversity:** The Balkans comprised many ethnic groups like Serbs, Croats, Bulgarians, Greeks, and Romanians, creating frequent conflicts. *(1 M)*

(*ii*) **Decline of Ottoman Empire:** As the Ottoman Empire weakened, Balkan states began fighting for independence, increasing regional instability. *(1 M)*

(*iii*) **Rise of Nationalism:** The spread of romantic nationalism fueled the desire of Balkan communities to establish their independent nation-states. *(1 M)*

(*iv*) **Mutual Rivalries:** Balkan states were jealous of each other and often fought to expand their territories, causing further tension. *(1 M)*

(*v*) **Intervention by Major Powers:** European powers like Russia, Germany, Austria-Hungary, and Britain competed for influence in the region, turning the Balkans into a hotbed of conflicts. *(1 M)*

2. How did anti-imperial movements in colonised countries respond to European domination? *(An)*

Ans. Response of Anti-Imperial Movements to European Domination:

(*i*) **Rise of Nationalism:** Colonized people developed a strong sense of national identity, demanding self-rule and independence from European powers. *(1 M)*

(*ii*) **Mass Movements:** Leaders like Mahatma Gandhi in India, Ho Chi Minh in Vietnam, and Nelson Mandela in South Africa organized non-violent protests, armed struggles, and boycotts against colonial rule. *(1 M)*

(*iii*) **Use of Indigenous Culture:** Nationalists promoted local languages, traditions, and histories to revive their cultural identity and resist European influence. *(1 M)*

(*iv*) **International Support:** Many anti-imperial movements gained global sympathy and support from organizations like the United Nations and socialist countries. *(1 M)*

(*v*) **Formation of New Nations:** Through revolutions, negotiations, and wars, colonized regions gained independence, leading to the creation of new nation-states in Asia, Africa, and the Middle East. *(1 M)*

MISCELLANEOUS EXERCISE

Multiple Choice Questions

(1 M)

1. Sundar was a member of a cultural society in 19th-century Europe where Romanticism was flourishing. He's been tasked to organize an exhibition showcasing artworks, poems, and music that reflect the ideals of Romanticism. Which role did Romanticism play in the development of nationalism in Europe? ***(Un)***

(*a*) Promoted industrial advancement over cultural identity.

(*b*) Emphasised emotions and a shared heritage to foster national unity.

(*c*) Advocated for scientific rationalism as the basis for nationalism.

(*d*) Encouraged the separation of state and culture.

2. Why did nationalists in late-nineteenth-century India focus on recording and preserving folklore? ***(Un)***

(*a*) To create new forms of artistic expression that reflected modern India.

(*b*) To restore a sense of pride in traditional culture and national identity.

(*c*) To use folklore as a tool for economic development and modernization.

(*d*) To promote a uniform culture that could be adopted across all Indian regions.

3. Who was called the Árchitect of Germany's Unification? ***(Re)***

(*a*) Napoleon (*b*) Garibaldi

(*c*) Ottto Von Bismarck (*d*) Kaiser William II

4. After the Vienna Congress, a number of polish priests were sent to Siberia by the Russian authorities for ***(Re)***

(*a*) Not preaching in Russian language

(*b*) Bringing religious reform in Siberia

(*c*) Opposing constitutional reforms

(*d*) Holding secret meetings

5. Arrange the following events in chronological order and choose the correct option from the following: ***(Re)* (CBSE, 2024)**

I. Treaty of Constantinople

II. Defeat of Napoleon

III. Unification of Italy

IV. Unification of Germany

Options:

(*a*) I, II, IV and III (*b*) II, III, I and IV

(*c*) II, I, IV and III (*d*) IV, I, III and II

6. Marie Duval, a young Jacobin in Paris, believes in the French Revolution's ideals but is troubled by the new government's censorship and centralisation. She must decide whether to support the government or oppose these measures.Marie Duval is conflicted by the new government's censorship and centralization. What should she do to uphold the revolutionary ideals? ***(Cr)***

(*a*) Support the government's efforts for stability.

(*b*) Advocate for decentralisation and free speech.

(*c*) Encourage a return to monarchical rule.

(*d*) Focus on economic reforms first.

7. In mid-19th century Europe, Jean-Pierre, a French lawyer inspired by liberalism, joined movements demanding universal suffrage, facing dilemmas about balancing private property rights and social equity.Jean-Pierre must draft a constitution for a new democratic state. Which provision best resolves early liberalism's contradictions? ***(Cr)***

(*a*) Establishing universal suffrage for all adults.

(*b*) Limiting voting rights to property-owning men.

(*c*) Enforcing strict property rights while delaying political reforms.

(*d*) Granting temporary voting rights to non-property owners during emergencies.

8. Name the act that was passed by English and Scottish parliaments which resulted in the formation of the United kingdom of Great Britain. ***(Re)***

(*a*) The Act of Union, 1707

(*b*) Tax Reform Act, 1784

(*c*) Commutation Act, 1784

(*d*) None of the options

9. Maria, a young historian, is fascinated by the complex tapestry of cultures and languages within the Habsburg Empire in the 19th century. During a visit to Vienna, she stumbles upon a historical debate among scholars about the impact of such diversity on political unity. Maria wonders how the empire managed to maintain coherence despite its vast ethnic and linguistic differences. Which of the following factors played the most significant role in maintaining the political unity of the Habsburg Empire despite its ethnic and linguistic diversity? ***(Ap)***

(*a*) The implementation of a single official language across the empire.

(*b*) The establishment of a centralized administrative system under the emperor.

(*c*) The promotion of economic independence among different regions.

(*d*) The spread of a unifying religious ideology.

10. Which sentence best explains the Utopian Society? ***(Re)***

(*a*) A society where everyone is equal

(*b*) A society with a comprehensive constitution

(*c*) An idealist society which can never be achieved

(*d*) A democratic society

11. What happened at the Treaty of Constantinople of 1832? **(An)**

(*a*) Revolutionary nationalism in Europe sparked off

(*b*) Struggle for independence amongst the Greeks began

(*c*) Greece was recognised as an independent nation

(*d*) European civilisation and mobilised public opinion to support its struggle against a Muslim empire

12. What happened to Poland at the end of 18th century. Which of the following answers is correct? **(Re)**

(*a*) Poland achieved independence at the end of the 18th century.

(*b*) Poland came totally under the control of Russia and became part of Russia

(*c*) Poland became the part of East Germany.

(*d*) Poland was partitioned at the end of the 18th century by three Great Powers: Russia, Prussia and Austria

13. Who had sought to put together a coherent programme for a unitary Italian Republic in the 1830s ? **(Re)**

(*a*) Metternich (*b*) Otto von Bismarck

(*c*) Giuseppe Mazzini (*d*) Napoleon

14. Which English poet participated in the freedom struggle movement in Greece? **(Re)**

(*a*) Lord George Byron (*b*) Bourbon

(*c*) Metternich (*d*) Philippe

15. The first great revolution which gave the clear idea of nationalism with its core words: 'Liberty, Equality and Fraternity' was **(Re)**

(*a*) The Russian Revolution

(*b*) The French Revolution

(*c*) The American Revolution

(*d*) India's First War of Independence

16. Choose the correctly matched pair from the following: **(An)**

(*a*) Giuseppe Garibaldi – Britain

(*b*) Otto Von Bismarck – Italy

(*c*) Friedrich Wilhelm IV – Germany

(*d*) Giuseppe Mazzini – Italy

17. During a history quiz focusing on influential artists and their contributions to political ideas in the 19th century, students were asked: In 1848, which French artist created a series of four prints depicting his vision of a world composed of 'democratic and social Republics'? **(An)**

(*a*) Duke Metternich (*b*) Frédéric Sorrieu

(*c*) Kaiser Wilhelm (*d*) Louis XVI

18. Which language was spoken for purposes of diplomacy in the mid 18th century in Europe? **(Re)**

(*a*) German (*b*) English

(*c*) French (*d*) Spanish

19. Rakesh is an advisor to a modern-day leader of a European nation that seeks greater unity among its culturally diverse regions. Considering the historical role of Otto von Bismarck in the unification of Germany, which strategy would be most effective for achieving political unity in your diverse nation? **(Ap)**

(*a*) Promoting economic growth and technological advancement to connect different regions.

(*b*) Utilising diplomatic negotiation and political strategy to align regional interests.

(*c*) Implementing democratic reforms to engage various ethnic groups in the governance process.

(*d*) Prioritizing cultural programs to celebrate and integrate diverse heritages within the nation.

Assertion and Reason

(1 M)

Direction: The following questions consist of two statements – Assertion (A) and Reason (R). Answer these questions by selecting the appropriate option given below:

(*a*) Both A and R are true, and R is the correct explanation of A.

(*b*) Both A and R are true, but R is not the correct explanation of A.

(*c*) A is true, but R is false

(*d*) A is false, but R is true.

1. **Assertion (A):** Language, too, played an important role in developing nationalist sentiments.

Reason (R): After Russian occupation, the polish language was welcomed in schools and the Russian language was forced out. **(Ev)**

2. **Assertion (A):** A large part of the Balkans was under the control of the Ottoman Empire.

Reason (R): The spread of the ideas of romantic nationalism in the Balkans together with the disintegration of the Ottoman Empire made this region very explosive. **(Ev)**

3. **Assertion (A):** Italy was divided into seven states, of which only one was ruled by an Italian princely house.

Reason (R): The north was under the domination of the Bourbon kings of Spain. **(Ev)**

4. **Assertion (A):** From the very beginning, the French revolutionaries introduced various measures and practices like the idea of la patrie and le citoyen.

Reason (R): This was done to create a sense of collective identity amongst the French people. **(An)**

5. **Assertion (A):** Culture played an important role in creating the idea of the nation.

Reason (R): Weavers in Silesia had led a revolt against contractors who supplied raw material and gave them orders for finished textiles but drastically reduced their payments. **(Ev)**

6. **Assertion (A):** Giuseppe Mazzini worked with the conservatives for the monarchy.

Reason (R): Italy had to continue to be a patchwork of small states and kingdoms. **(Ev)**

Subjective Questions

Very Short Answer Type Questions (1 or 2 M)

1. Dr. Rohan Sharma was a professor of history, in the early 19th century. He has been invited to present a lecture on the impact of the French Revolution at a European history conference. Analyze how the principles of liberty, equality, and fraternity introduced during the French Revolution influenced the political and social changes in Europe. Provide two specific examples to support your analysis. *(An)*
2. Name the event that mobilised nationalist feelings among the educated elite across Europe in 1830-1848? *(Re)*
3. What was the major issue taken up by the liberal nationalists? *(Re)*
4. Name the Treaty of 1832 that recognised Greece as an independent nation. *(Re)*
5. What was the major change that occurred in the political and constitutional scenario due to the French Revolution in Europe? *(Un)*
6. Who was proclaimed German Emperor in a ceremony held at Versailles in January 1871? *(Re)*
7. What was the strong demand of the emerging middle classes in Europe during the nineteenth century? *(Un)*
8. Who was called as the architect of Germany's Unification? *(Re)*

Short Answer Type Questions (3 M)

1. Explain the conditions that were viewed as obstacles to the economic exchange and growth by the new commercial classes during the 19th century in Europe. *(Un)*
2. Describe the impact of the 'Revolution of Liberals' of 1848 in Europe. *(Un)*
3. How did Britain come into existence? *(Un)*

   OR

   Describe in brief the process by which the British nation came into existence. *(Un)*
4. In a vibrant classroom filled with students, you present images of Marianne of France and Germania of Germany as part of a cultural awareness campaign. You explain how these female allegories personify their nations and represent values like liberty, equality, and unity."How do Marianne and Germania as female allegories help shape national identity and promote unity in France and Germany?" *(Ap)*
5. What were Jacobin Clubs? How did their activities and campaigns help to spread the idea of nationalism abroad? Explain. *(An)*
6. Describe any three economic hardships faced by Europe in the 1830s. *(Re)*

   OR

   Describe the great economic hardship that prevailed in Europe during the 1830s. *(Re)*

Long Answer Type Questions (5 M)

1. What changes did Napoleon introduce to make the administrative system more efficient in the territories ruled by him? *(Re)*
2. How did the ideology of 'liberalism' affect the Europe in early nineteenth century? Explain. *(Un, An)* **(CBSE, 2024)**
3. Who hosted the 'Vienna Congress' in 1815 ? Analyse the main changes brought by the 'Vienna Treaty.' *(Ev)*
4. Explain the process of formation of United Kingdom of Great Britain. *(Un)* **(CBSE, 2024)**
5. The role of Romanticism in developing nationalist feelings among Europeans during the nineteenth century was? **(CBSE, 2019)**

Case Based Questions (4 M)

Case Based-I

Read the information below and answer the questions that follow:

Equality before the law did not necessarily stand for universal suffrage. You will recall that in revolutionary France, which marked the first political experiment in liberal democracy, the right to vote and to get elected was granted exclusively to property-owning men. Men without property and all women were excluded from political rights. In the economic sphere, liberalism stood for the freedom of markets and the abolition of state-imposed restrictions on the movement of goods and capital. During the nineteenth century this was a strong demand of the emerging middle classes. Napoleon's administrative measures had created out of countless small principalities a confederation of 39 states. Each of these possessed its own currency, and weights and measures. A merchant travelling in 1833 from Hamburg to Nuremberg to sell his goods would have had to pass through 11 customs barriers and pay a customs duty of about 5 per cent at each one of them. Duties were often levied according to the weight or measurement of the goods. As each region had its own system of weights and measures, this involved time-consuming calculation. The measure of cloth, for example, was the elle which in each region stood for a different length. Such conditions were viewed as obstacles to economic exchange and growth by the new commercial classes, who argued for the creation of a unified economic territory allowing the unhindered movement of goods, people and capital.

(i) What do you mean by the word suffrage? *(Re)*

(*a*) Gender equality (*b*) Right to vote
(*c*) Right to education (*d*) All of these

(ii) What were the hurdles is economic exchange during the 19th century? *(Un)*

(iii) What is the meaning of liberalism on the economic front? *(Un)*

Case Based-II

Read the information below and answer the questions that follow:

Ideas of national unity in early-nineteenth-century Europe were closely allied to the ideology of liberalism. The term 'liberalism' derives from the Latin root liber, meaning free. For the new middle classes liberalism stood for freedom for the individual and equality of all before the law. Politically, it emphasized the concept of government by consent. Since the French Revolution, liberalism had stood for the end of autocracy and clerical privileges, a constitution and representative government through parliament. Nineteenth Century liberals also stressed the inviolability of private property. The Rise of Nationalism in Europe 285 European governments were driven by a spirit of conservatism. Conservatives believed that established, traditional institutions of state and society – like the monarchy, the Church, social hierarchies, property and the family – should be preserved Most conservatives, however, did not propose a return to the society of pre revolutionary days. In the east, Russia was given part of Poland while Prussia was given a portion of Saxony. The main intention was to restore the monarchies that had been overthrown by Napoleon, and create a new conservative order in Europe. Conservative regimes set up in 1815 were autocratic. They did not tolerate criticism and dissent, and sought to curb activities that questioned the legitimacy of autocratic governments.

(i) Find the word which has the same meaning as "Free". ***(Ev)***

(ii) What was the meaning of liberalism at the time of the French Revolution? ***(Re)***

(*a*) Freedom of markets and abolition of state-imposed restrictions.

(*b*) End of autocracy and clerical privileges.

(*c*) It emphasised the concept of government by consent.

(*d*) All the above statements are correct.

(iii) What were the beliefs of conservatives? ***(Un)***

(iv) When was the conservative regime set up? ***(Re)***

(*a*) 1816 (*b*) 1815

(*c*) 1817 (*d*) 1818

ANSWER KEYS

Multiple Choice Questions

1. (*b*)	**2.** (*b*)	**3.** (*c*)	**4.** (*a*)	**5.** (*)	**6.** (*b*)	**7.** (*a*)	**8.** (*a*)	**9.** (*b*)	**10.** (*c*)
11. (*c*)	**12.** (*d*)	**13.** (*c*)	**14.** (*a*)	**15.** (*b*)	**16.** (*d*)	**17.** (*b*)	**18.** (*c*)	**19.** (*b*)	

Assertion and Reason

1. (*c*)	**2.** (*a*)	**3.** (*c*)	**4.** (*a*)	**5.** (*b*)	**6.** (*d*)

Case Based Questions

Case Based-I

(i) (*b*)

Case Based-II

(ii) (*b*) ***(iv)*** (*b*)

HINTS & EXPLANATIONS

Multiple Choice Questions

1. (*b*) Emphasised emotions and a shared heritage to foster national unity.

2. (*b*) To restore a sense of pride in traditional culture and national identity

3. (*c*) Ottto Von Bismarck

4. (*a*) Not preaching in Russian language

5. (*) *No option is correct as correct chronological order is II, I, III, IV

Treaty of Constantinople – 1832

Defeat of Napoleon – 1815

Unification Italy – (1859-1870)

Unification Germany – (1866-1871)

6. (*b*) Advocate for decentralisation and free speech.

7. (*a*) Establishing universal suffrage for all adults.

8. (*a*) The Act of Union, 1707
9. (*b*) The establishment of a centralized administrative system under the emperor.
10. (*c*) An idealist society which can never be achieved
11. (*c*) Greece was recognised as an independent nation
12. (*d*) Poland was partitioned at the end of the 18th century by three Great Powers: Russia, Prussia and Austria
13. (*c*) Giuseppe Mazzini
14. (*a*) Lord George Byron
15. (*b*) The French Revolution
16. (*d*) Giuseppe Mazzini – Italy
17. (*b*) Frédéric Sorrieu
18. (*c*) French
19. (*b*) Utilising diplomatic negotiation and political strategy to align regional

Assertion and Reason

1. (*c*) A is true but R is false.
2. (*a*) Both assertion and reason are true and reason is the correct explanation of assertion.
3. (*c*) Italy was divided into seven states of which only one, Sardinia-Piedmont was ruled by an Italian princely house. The north was under Austrian Habsburgs and the southern regions were under the domination of The Bourbon kings of Spain. Therefore assertion is true but reason is false
4. (*a*) Both assertion and reason are true and reason is the correct explanation of assertion. The French Revolution proclaimed that it was the people who would henceforth constitute the nation and shape its destiny. In the beginning, the French Revolutionaries introduced different measures and practices that would create a sense of collective identity amongst the French people. The centralized administrative system was one of the measures taken by them for making uniform laws for all citizens within its territory.
5. (*b*) Both assertion and reason are true but reason is not the correct explanation of assertion. Culture played an important role in creating the idea of the nation: art and poetry, stories and music helped express and shape nationalist feelings.
6. (*d*) Both assertion and reason are false.

Subjective Questions

Very Short Answer Type Questions

1. **Political Changes:**

(*i*) **Liberty:** Inspired democratic ideas and led to constitutional monarchies.

Example: July Revolution of 1830 in France established a constitutional monarchy under Louis-Philippe. (*1 M*)

Social Changes:

(*ii*) **Equality and Fraternity:** Abolished feudal privileges and promoted nationalism.

Example: Unification of Germany and Italy driven by movements for equality and shared cultural identity. (*1 M*)

2. The Greek War of Independence was the event that mobilised nationalist feelings among the educated elite across Europe in 1830-1848. (*1 M*)
3. The major issue taken up by the liberal nationalists;

(*i*) Liberal nationalists mainly fought for freedom of the press. (*1 M*)

(*ii*) They believed in the free expression of ideas, challenging the conservative order that imposed censorship to control information and suppress dissent. (*1 M*)

4. The Treaty of 1832 that recognised Greece as an independent nation;

(*i*) The Treaty of Constantinople of 1832 recognized Greece as an independent nation. (*1 M*)

(*ii*) This treaty marked the end of the Greek War of Independence against Ottoman rule. (*1 M*)

5. The major change that occurred in the political and constitutional scenario due to the French Revolution in Europe;

(*i*) The French Revolution led to the transfer of sovereignty from the monarchy to French citizens. (*1 M*)

(*ii*) It established the concept that the people constitute the nation and are the source of its political power. (*1 M*)

6. Kaiser William I [Prussian King] was proclaimed German Emperor in a ceremony held at Versailles in January 1871. (*1 M*)
7. The strong demand of the emerging middle classes in Europe during nineteenth century was market freedom and elimination of state-imposed restructure on the movement of goods and capital. (*2 M*)
8. Otto von Bismarck was called the architect of Germany's unification. His leadership and diplomatic strategies led to the unification of various German states into a single nation by 1871. (*1 M*)

Short Answer Type Questions

1. (*i*) The new commercial classes saw diverse currencies, weights, and measures as major obstacles to economic exchange and growth. (*1 M*)

(*ii*) Customs duties levied based on different regional standards made trade cumbersome and expensive, inhibiting the movement of goods. (*1 M*)

(*iii*) These conditions hindered efficient trade across regions, prompting demands for unified economic policies, standardization, and the creation of a single economic territory in Europe. (*1 M*)

2. The impact of the 'Revolution of Liberals' of 1848 in Europe was;

(*i*) The 1848 Revolution of Liberals led to widespread political upheaval across Europe, demanding democratic reforms and national unification. (*1 M*) (*ii*) It resulted in temporary concessions like constitutional monarchies, albeit with limited success in achieving long-term democratic change. *(1 M)*

(*iii*) The revolution sparked a wave of nationalism, influencing future movements for independence and democratic governance across various European nations. *(1 M)*

3. Britain came into existence as follows;

(*i*) Britain formation as a nation-state was a gradual process, not the result of a sudden upheaval. *(1 M)*

(*ii*) The Act of Union in 1707 between England and Scotland resulted in the formation of the **United Kingdom of Great Britain**, marking the beginning of a unified British state. *(1 M)*

(*iii*) This unification was further solidified through cultural and political dominance of England over Scotland, Wales, and Ireland. *(1 M)*

4. (*i*) **Personification of Nations:** Marianne and Germania, depicted as female allegories, personify their respective nations, making the abstract concept of the nation more relatable and emotionally resonant for the people. *(1 M)*

(*ii*) **Symbolism of Values:** Marianne symbolizes the French Republic's values of liberty, equality, and fraternity, while Germania embodies the strength and heroism of the German nation. These symbols promote national unity by embodying the ideals and virtues that citizens are encouraged to uphold. *(2 M)*

5. Jacobin clubs, formed by supporters of the French Revolution, played a pivotal role in spreading nationalism:

(*i*) Jacobin Clubs were political groups that supported revolutionary ideas and republican principles. *(1 M)*

(*ii*) They promoted democratic and republican ideals among the public, encouraging the overthrow of monarchies and establishment of republics across Europe. *(1 M)*

(*iii*) Their activities, including publications and public meetings, helped spread revolutionary ideas, influencing other nations to adopt similar nationalist movements. *(1 M)*

6. In the 1830s, Europe faced severe economic hardships due to:

(*i*) Widespread unemployment caused a significant rise in job seekers, leading to mass migrations from rural areas to overcrowded cities. *(1 M)*

(*ii*) Competition from industrialized England led to a crisis for small town producers, unable to compete with cheaper, machine-made imports. *(1 M)*

(*iii*) Peasant struggles under feudal burdens, exacerbated by rising food prices and bad harvests, caused widespread poverty in both towns and countryside. *(1 M)*

Long Answer Type Questions

1. Napoleon introduce to make the administrative system more efficient in the territories ruled by him as follows;

(*i*) Napoleon implemented the Napoleonic Code, abolishing feudal privileges and ensuring equality before the law, property rights, and a uniform legal framework. *(1 M)*

(*ii*) He restructured administrative divisions for more efficient governance, and abolished serfdom and manorial dues, freeing peasants. *(1 M)*

(*iii*) The feudal system was dismantled, and in cities, guild restrictions were removed to encourage economic activity. *(1 M)*

(*iv*) Improvements were made to transport and communication systems, enhancing mobility and facilitating the exchange of goods and capital. *(1 M)*

(*v*) These reforms modernized the administrative, legal, and economic systems across Napoleon's territories, promoting principles of rationalization and efficiency rooted in Enlightenment ideas. *(1 M)*

2. The ideology of 'liberalism' in early nineteenth-century Europe had profound impacts:

(*i*) **Political Change:** Liberalism advocated for constitutions, representative government, and individual freedoms, leading to political restructuring. *(1 M)*

(*ii*) **Economic Reform:** It supported free trade, opposed state restrictions, and encouraged the emergence of the bourgeoisie, which reshaped economic landscapes. *(1 M)*

(*iii*) **National Unification:** Liberal principles fueled movements for national unification in countries like Germany and Italy, promoting the idea of nation-states. *(1 M)*

(*iv*) **Social Impact:** It emphasized the rights and freedoms of individuals, influencing societal norms and values. *(1 M)*

(*v*) **Cultural Influence:** Liberalism encouraged the proliferation of new ideas in arts, science, and education, fostering a culture of inquiry and innovation. *(1 M)*

3. Vienna Congress Host and Main Changes Brought by the Vienna Treaty;

(*i*) The Vienna Congress in 1815 was hosted by the Austrian Chancellor, Duke Metternich. He played a pivotal role in guiding the deliberations of the congress, aiming to restore European stability post-Napoleonic wars. *(1 M)*

(*ii*) The main changes brought by the Vienna Treaty included the restoration of monarchies overthrown by Napoleon, establishing a balance of power to prevent future aggression. *(1 M)*

(*iii*) France was resized to its pre-Napoleonic borders, and a ring of strong states was created around it to prevent French expansion. *(1 M)*

(*iv*) The Kingdom of the Netherlands was established, and Genoa was added to Piedmont in Italy, aiming at strengthening states against France. *(1 M)*

(*v*) A German Confederation of 39 states was created under Austrian influence, replacing the Napoleonic reorganisation. *(1 M)*

4. The formation of the United Kingdom of Great Britain involved several significant steps:

(*i*) **Diverse Identities:** There was no British nation prior to the eighteenth century,the inhabitants of the British Isles primarily identified themselves as English, Welsh, Scots, or Irish, without a collective British nationality. *(1 M)* (*ii*) **Act of Union 1707:** This key event unified England and Scotland under one parliament, forming the 'United Kingdom of Great Britain'. The union was more of an English imposition over Scottish affairs, leading to significant cultural and political domination by England. *(1 M)*

(*iii*) **Incorporation of Ireland:** In 1801, following a failed revolt, Ireland was forcibly joined to the union, creating a more extensive British identity and further extending English influence. *(1 M)*

(*iv*) **Systematic Suppression:** Post-union, the British government systematically suppressed Scottish culture and political institutions, particularly targeting the Highlanders, prohibiting their language and national dress. *(1 M)*

(*v*) **Cultural Dominance:** The formation of the UK was not merely political but also cultural, promoting English language and symbols (Union Jack, national anthem) as unifying elements, subsuming the distinct identities of Scotland and Ireland. *(1 M)*

5. The role of Romanticism in developing nationalist feelings among Europeans during the nineteenth century was;

(*i*) **Emotional Appeal:** Romanticism was characterized by its emphasis on emotion and individualism, which resonated with growing nationalist sentiments. *(1 M)*

(*ii*) **Cultural Pride:** It celebrated folklore, local legends, and national histories, fostering a sense of unique cultural identity among different European peoples. *(1 M)*

(*iii*) **Heroic Figures:** Romantic artists and writers often depicted heroic figures and events from national pasts, which inspired pride and a sense of shared heritage. *(1 M)*

(*iv*) **Language Revival:** The movement also played a role in reviving and valuing vernacular languages, seen as a core element of national identity against dominant cultures. *(1 M)*

(*v*) **Natural Landscape:** Romanticism glorified the natural landscape of the homeland, strengthening the bond between people and their national territories. *(1 M)*

Topper's Explanations

15 (i) The feeling of nationalism didnot only come due to territorial expancion or war, culture played a major role in developing sense of nationalism.

(ii) Romanticism is a cultural movement that sought to develop a particular kind of nationalism.

(iii) Romantic poets didnot support the glorifying of science and reason, but rather focussed on mystic feelings, intitutions and emotion.

(iv) Folklores, folktales and folksong were collected as it was believed they gave the true manifestation of people's thoughts and lives.

(v) Historians argued true German culture was to be defined among the people (das volk).

Case Based Questions

Case Based-I

(*i*) (*b*) Right to vote.

(*ii*) The Napoleon administration oversaw a confederation of 39 states, each with its own currency, weights, and measurements. Merchants faced customs duties of about 5% and navigated through 11 barriers, and the measurement of goods like cloth varied by region, complicating economic transactions in the 19th century.

(*iii*) On the economic front liberalism stood for freedom of markets and the abolition of the restrictions imposed by states on the translocation of goods and capital.

Case Based-II

(*i*) 'Liber' is the word which means the same as free.

(*ii*) (*b*) End of autocracy and clerical privileges.

(*iii*) The beliefs of conservatives were to preserve the established, traditional institutions of the state and society such as monarchy, church, social hierarchies, property and the families.

(*iv*) (*b*) The conservative regime was established in the year 1815.

NATIONALISM IN INDIA

2

"Under the wide skies of our country, we all walked together, creating unity from our many differences. Guided by Gandhi's determination, we followed a path of peaceful resistance, reflecting our country's united desire for freedom and fairness."

SYLLABUS & WEIGHTAGE

List of Concept Names	Years					
	2020	2021	2022	2023	2024	2025
The First World War, Khilafat and Non-cooperation (The idea of Satyagraha, The Rowlatt Act, Why Non-Cooperation)	1 Q (1 M)	Exam not Conducted	2 Q (1 M) 1 Q (2 M)	2 Q (1 M)	1 Q (1 M)	1 Q (1 M), 1 Q (2 M)
Differing Strands within Movement (The Movement in the Towns, Rebellion in the Countryside, Swaraj in the Plantations)	1 Q (3 M) 2 Q (1 M)		1 Q (3 M)	—	1 Q (1 M)	1 Q (3 M)
Towards Civil Disobedience (The salt march and the civil Disobedience Movement, How Participants saw the movement, The limits of civil Disobedience)	1 Q (5 M)		1 Q (2 M)	1 Q (5 M)	—	1 Q (3 M), 2 Q (1 M),
The Sense of Collective Belonging	1 Q (1 M)		—	—	—	

CONCEPT MAP

To Access One Shot Revision Video Scan This QR Code

Nationalism in India

The First World war, Khilafat & Non-Cooperation
CBSE 2025, 2020

The way of Changes Nationalism
CBSE 2024

Satyagraha — CBSE 2022 Term-II

- Satyagraha is Mahatma Gandhi's concept of peaceful protest (fighting with peace).
  - Champaran Satyagraha 1916.
  - Mill worker's movement in Ahmedabad 1918.
  - Kheda Satyagraha 1918.

Rowlatt Act

- Rowlatt Act (1919) was passed in a hurry by the Imperial Legislative Assembly despite the opposition from the Indian members of the council.
- Local leaders were asserted in Amritsar and Gandhiji was barred from entering Delhi, martial law was ?imposed in Amritsar
- A number of people gathered in Jallianwala Bagh to celebrate Baisakhi unaware of the martial law.
- celebrate Baisakhi unaware of the martial law. General Dyer ordered open fire on them killing hundreds of people.
- People in India opposed the killings by attacking government offices, police stations etc.

Non-Cooperation Movement — CBSE 2022 Term-II , 2020

- Surrender of Govt. Titles.
- Boycott of civil services, army, police, courts and legislative councils. Schools and foreign goods.

Rise of Nationalism after First World War

Reason — CBSE 2022 Term-II

- Increase in custom duties and introduction of income tax due to war loans.
- Extreme hardships due to increase in price of essential goods.
- Forced recruitment in the army.
- Shortage of food due to crop failure, famines and epidemics.

Differing strands within Movement
CBSE 2020

The Movcment in the Towns

- Students left government schools, officers resigned, lawyers gave up their practices, and traders and merchants boycotted foreign goods.
- The movement experienced a slowdown due to the high price of Khadi cloth and the absence of adequate alternative Indian institutions to replace British-established systems.

Movement in the Countryside

- In Awadh Peasants were led by Ram Chandra - a Sanyasi, who had earlier been to Fiji as an indentured labourer.
- Peasants had to do begar and work at the landlord's farms without any payment. Peasants movement demanded abolition of begar and reduction of revenues.
- The movement in the countryside was against talukdars and landlords who demanded high rents and other cesses.

Swaraj in the Plantations — CBSE 2023, 2020

- Under the Inland Emigration Act of 1859, workers were not allowed to leave the plantations without permission, which was seldom granted.
- Workers defied the authorities, left the plantations.

Nationalism in India

Towards Civil Disobedience
CBSE 2025, 2024

Aspects of the Movement

Re-launch of the Movement

- Mahatma Gandhi relaunched the Civil Disobedience Movement.
- For over a year, the movement continued, but by 1934 it lost its momentum.

Gandhi-Irwin Pact

- The pact was signed on March 5, 1931, wherein Mahatma Gandhi agreed to attend the Round Table Conference.
- The British government consented to release political prisoners as part of the pact's conditions.
- Held in London in 1931, this conference concluded without achieving any substantive results.

Salt March

CBSE 2025, 2022 Term-II

- The Salt Satyagraha was a large-scale civil disobedience movement started by Mahatma Gandhi in response to the imposition of a salt tax in India by the British administration.
- Mahatma Gandhi initiated the Salt March from Sabarmati to Dandi with 78 followers, embarking on a profound act of civil disobedience.
- Arriving at Dandi on April 6, 1930, Gandhi defied British law by producing salt from sea water, symbolically challenging British authority.

Simon Commission

- The Simon Commission was established by Britain's Tory government
- Sir John Simon, to review nationalist demands and recommend changes to India's constitutional framework.
- The commission was met with widespread protest and the slogan "Go back Simon" in India due to its all-English membership.
- The Simon Commission proposed 'dominion status' as a topic for future discussions on India's Constitution.

Withdrawal of Non-Cooperation Movement

- Gandhiji ended the movement due to escalating violence.
- There was significant debate within the Congress about participating in council elections.

Formation of Swaraj Party

- C. R. Das and Motilal Nehru established the Swaraj Party within the Congress to advocate for council entry.
- Jawaharlal Nehru and Subhash Chandra Bose pressed for mass agitation and for full independence.

Effect of Civil Disobedience Movement

CBSE 2020

- The movement spread to the entire nation.
- Colonial laws were violated, salt manufactured in numerous places.
- Foreign clothes were burnt and picketing liquor shops.
- Peasants refused to pay revenue and chaukidari tax.

Different Perspective of The Movement

CBSE 2024

Business Class

- They wanted protection against imports of foreign goods.
- The Indian Industrial and Commercial Congress was established in 1920 and FICCI in 1927 by leading Indian industrialists.
- These groups opposed colonial economic policies and supported the initial launch of the Civil Disobedience Movement.

Poor Peasants

CBSE 2020

- The poor peasants were interested in the reduction of the revenue demand.
- Congress was unwilling to support 'no rent' campaigns in most of the places.

Rich Peasants

CBSE 2023

- The wealthy Patidars of Gujarat and the Jats of Uttar Pradesh were involved in the movement in the countryside.
- For them the fight for Swaraj was struggle against high revenues.

Industrial Worker

- The Industrial Working Classes did not participate in the Civil disobedience Movement in large numbers except in the Nagpur region.
- There were strikes by railway workers in 1930 and dock workers in 1932.

Participation of Women

- They participated in protest marches, manufactured salt and picketed foreign cloth and liquor shops.
- In Urban areas these women were from high-caste families; in rural areas they came from rich peasant households.

Nationalism in India

Towards Civil Disobedience

Feeling of Collective Belonging CBSE 2020

- People began to see themselves as members of a unified nation, recognizing a common bond among diverse communities.
- To foster nationalism, communities developed folklore, and created national figures, symbols, and icons that encapsulated shared values and aspirations.

Positive and Negative aspects of Nationalism

- The Indian national struggle united various groups and classes in a collective effort for independence.
- Conflicts among different groups occasionally emerged, sometimes leading to the movement's failure.

Quit India Movement

- Launched in 1942 after the failure of the Cripps Mission.
- Led by Mahatma Gandhi with the slogan "Do or Die."
- Involved diverse sections of society including students, workers, and women.
- Marked by severe crackdowns, mass arrests, and violence.
- Weakened British control and paved the way for India's independence in 1947.

1 THE FIRST WORLD WAR, KHILAFAT AND NON-COOPERATION

NCERT Definitions *(Commonly asked in 1 mark)*

- **Forced Recruitment:** The compulsory enlistment of individuals into the ***military service*** without their consent.
- **Satyagraha:** A form of ***nonviolent*** resistance or ***civil resistance*** initiated by Mahatma Gandhi to fight against injustice and achieve political objectives.
- **Rowlatt Act:** Enacted in **1919**, it allowed the British government to imprison any person suspected of terrorism living in British India without trial.
- **Boycott:** An act of protest and civil disobedience involving the refusal to buy, use, or participate in something as a form of protest.
- **Colonialism:** ***The policy*** or ***practice*** of gaining full or partial political control of another country, occupying it, and exploiting it economically.
- **Hartal:** A ***demonstration*** against a political situation or a government action.

Important Facts

01 During the First World War **(1914-1918)**, the British government raised taxes and prices in India, causing economic difficulties and food shortages due to crop failures.

02 Many Indian men were forcibly ***recruited*** into the British army, leading to widespread anger and resentment.

03 The ***Rowlatt Act of*** **1919** allowed imprisonment without trial, which infuriated Indians and led to nationwide protests.

04 The ***Jallianwala Bagh*** massacre in **1919**, where British troops killed peaceful protesters in Amritsar, united Indians in their opposition to British rule.

05 The ***Khilafat Movement*** emerged to protect the Ottoman Caliphate, aligning Indian Muslims with the Indian National Congress and Gandhi, showing Hindu-Muslim unity.

06 ***Gandhi*** led the ***Non-Cooperation Movement***, urging Indians to boycott British goods, services, and institutions, gaining widespread support from various social groups.

07 The movement ended after the violent ***Chauri-Chaura*** incident in **1922**, as Gandhi wanted to maintain a commitment to ***non-violence***.

08 Despite its end, the ***Non-Cooperation Movement*** fostered a strong sense of Indian nationalism and laid the groundwork for future independence efforts.

Important Personalities

Mahatma Gandhi: Mahatma Gandhi by name of Mohandas Karmachand Gandhi, (born October 2, 1869 Porbandar, India died January 30, 1948 Delhi, India), Indian Lawyer, politician, social activist and writer who became the leader of the nationalist movement against the British rule in India.

Jawaharlal Nehru: On November 14, 1889, Pandit Jawaharlal Nehru was born. From the 1930s onwards, Nehru rose to become one of India's most powerful political figures, thanks to Gandhi's acknowledgment. After significant discussion, Nehru accepted the partition proposal for India in 1947 and was sworn in as India's first Prime Minister after independence.

Muhammad Ali and Shaukat Ali: Mohammad Ali and his brother, Maulana Shaukat Ali, along with other Muslim leaders, formed the All India Khilafat Committee with the goal of establishing political unity among Muslims and defending the caliphate via their influence. They urged the British in 1920 to protect the caliphate.

Important Dates

- **1913:** Mahatma Gandhi launched satyagraha in South Africa against the racist regime.
- **1914-18:** First World War took place.
- **1918-19:** UP peasants organised by Baba Ramchandra.
- **1915:** Mahatma Gandhi returned from South Africa.
- **1916:** Champaran Movement was launched.
- **1917:** Kheda Movement was started in Gujarat to support the peasants who could not pay the revenue due to crop failure and plague epidemic.
- **April 1919:** Gandhian hartal against Rowlatt Act: Jallianwala Bagh Massacre.

Difference Between

Khilafat Vs Non-Cooperation Movement

Aspect	Khilafat Movement	Non-Cooperation Movement
Core Issue	Aimed to protect the Ottoman Caliphate and Islamic symbols of power.	Sought Swaraj and protested against unjust British laws.
Leadership	Predominantly led by Muslim leaders like the Ali brothers.	Spearheaded by Mahatma Gandhi with a broader leadership base.
Nature of Participation	Focused engagement from the Muslim community.	Encompassed a wide array of Indian society including various religions and classes.
Relation to British Rule	Was a specific grievance relating to an international Islamic issue.	Direct challenge to British authority and laws in India.
Outcome and Legacy	Contributed to Hindu-Muslim unity temporarily but did not achieve its primary goals.	Marked a significant step in the Indian independence movement, despite its suspension in 1922.

Myth Buster

- **Myth:** The Non-Cooperation Movement was solely a reaction to the Rowlatt Act and Jallianwala Bagh Massacre.

  Fact: While the Rowlatt Act and the Jallianwala Bagh Massacre were pivotal events that catalyzed the Non-Cooperation Movement, the movement itself was a culmination of widespread dissatisfaction and anger against colonial rule. The movement grew out of a variety of grievances against the colonial government, including economic distress caused by World War I, the imposition of oppressive laws, and the disregard for Indian sentiments (like those expressed through the Rowlatt Act). It also drew from earlier movements and the collective desire for Swaraj or self-rule, aiming to unify various sections of Indian society against the British regime.

- **Myth:** Nationalism in India was a uniform movement with a singular objective and method, spearheaded exclusively by the Indian National Congress under Mahatma Gandhi's leadership.

  Fact: Nationalism in India was a complex phenomenon that encompassed a diverse range of social groups, each with its own set of aspirations, objectives, and methods of struggle. While the Indian National Congress, particularly under Mahatma Gandhi, played a pivotal role in the national movement, there were various other streams and leaders contributing to the struggle. These included movements led by figures like Subhas Chandra Bose, Bhagat Singh, and organizations like the Muslim League

Mnemonics

The effects of World War I in India.

"DIFFER"

- **D** – **D**efence Expenditure Increased
- **I** – **I**nflation
- **F** – **F**orced Recruitments
- **F** – **F**amine
- **E** – **E**pidemic
- **R**

Gandhi's early Satyagrahas in India.

"NACK"

- **N** – **N**on-cooperation Movement (1920)
- **A** – **A**hmedabad Mill Workers' Movement (1918)
- **C** – **C**hamparan Satyagraha (1916)
- **K** – **K**heda Satyagraha (1918)

COMPETENCY BASED SOLVED EXAMPLES

Scan Me for Detailed Explanations

Multiple Choice Questions

(1 M)

1. **The following image is of a march by Indian workers in South Africa. Mahatma Gandhi led the workers when he was arrested. This march was from NewCastle to Transvaal. Identify the year in which this march took place among the following options.** *(An)*

(*a*) November, 1913 (*b*) December, 1913

(*c*) November, 1914 (*d*) December, 1914

2. **How was the Rowlatt Act of 1919 perceived in terms of fundamental rights and civil liberties by Indians?** *(Un)*(CBSE APQ, 2023)

(*a*) It was viewed as a regressive legislation in favour of the majority Indians.

(*b*) It was considered as severely curtailing the right to personal liberty.

(*c*) It was seen as a necessary measure to prevent communal tensions.

(*d*) It was regarded as a safeguard for protecting British soldiers.

3. **What was the significance of Mahatma Gandhi's satyagraha movements in Champaran and Kheda?** *(Re)*

(*a*) They aimed to promote non-violence and truth

(*b*) They focused on educational reforms

(*c*) They aimed to abolish the caste system

(*d*) They fought for farmers' rights and relief from oppressive systems

4. **Arrange the following statements in sequential order based on the events that shaped the Non-cooperation movement.** *(An)*(CBSE SQP, 2023)

(*i*) General Dyer opened fire at the large crowd gathered in the enclosed ground of Jallianwala Bagh.

(*ii*) "Forced recruitment" carried out by the British government and the economic hardships faced by the people during the first world war.

(*iii*) The defeat of the Ottoman Emperor of Turkey led to the formation of the Khilafat movement.

(*iv*) Gandhiji launched a nationwide satyagraha against the Rowlatt act.

Options:

(*a*) (*iv*), (*iii*), (*ii*), (*i*) (*b*) (*ii*), (*i*), (*iv*), (*iii*)

(*c*) (*i*), (*iv*), (*iii*), (*ii*) (*d*) (*i*), (*ii*), (*iii*), (*iv*)

5. **As a young journalist in 1917 Champaran, you are observing Gandhi's application of satyagraha among the local farmers. Based on your observations, which of the following best represents the principle of satyagraha Gandhi is using?** *(An)*

(*a*) By leading an armed revolt against British planters

(*b*) By initiating a non-violent protest to support peasants against oppressive plantation systems

(*c*) By negotiating trade agreements with the British

(*d*) By encouraging peasants to pay higher taxes

Assertion and Reason

(1 M)

Direction: The following questions consist of two statements – Assertion (A) and Reason (R). Answer these questions by selecting the appropriate option given below:

(*a*) Both A and R are true, and R is the correct explanation of A.

(*b*) Both A and R are true, but R is not the correct explanation of A.

(*c*) A is true, but R is false

(*d*) A is false, but R is true.

1. **Assertion (A):** The growth of modern nationalism in India was intimately connected to the anti-colonial movement.

Reason (R): The sense of being oppressed under colonialism provided a shared bond that tied many different groups together. *(Un)*

2. **Assertion (A):** Jawaharlal Nehru played a crucial role in the growth of modern nationalism in India.

Reason (R): He advocated for non-violent civil disobedience and mobilized different social groups for the national movement. *(Un)*

3. **Assertion (A):** The Rowlatt Act triggered widespread opposition and led to the launch of non-violent civil disobedience movements in India.

Reason (R): The Rowlatt Act granted the government extensive powers to repress political activities and detain individuals without trial. *(An)*

Subjective Questions

Very Short Answer Type Questions (1 or 2 M)

1. Why did Mahatma Gandhi travel to Champaran in Bihar in 1917? Explain. ***(Un)*(CBSE, 2022 Term 2)**

Ans. Mahatma Gandhi traveled to Champaran in Bihar in 1917:

(*i*) Mahatma Gandhi traveled to Champaran in Bihar in 1917 to investigate the plight of indigo farmers who were being forced to grow indigo by the British planters. *(1 M)*

(*ii*) Gandhi's visit to Champaran led to the formation of the Champaran Satyagraha, which was one of the first non-violent protests against British rule in India. *(1 M)*

2. The First World War had ended with the defeat of Ottoman Turkey. And there were rumours that a harsh peace treaty was going to be imposed on the Ottoman emperor—the spiritual head of the Islamic world (the Khalifa). To defend the Khalifa's temporal powers, a Khilafat Committee was formed in Bombay in March 1919.

How did this event bring Muslims under the umbrella of a unified national movement? ***(Un)***

Ans. The Khilafat Movement played a crucial role in bringing Muslims under the umbrella of a unified national movement in these ways:

(*i*) A young generation of Muslim leaders like the brothers Muhammad Ali and Shaukat Ali began discussing with Mahatma Gandhi the possibility of united mass action on the issue. *(1 M)*

(*ii*) At the Calcutta session of the Congress in September 1920, he convinced other leaders of the need to start a non-cooperation movement in support of Khilafat as well as for swaraj. *(1 M)*

3. Imagine you are a social historian studying the impact of the Non-Cooperation Movement on various worker groups in India. You are particularly interested in the experiences of plantation workers in Assam during this period. You want to investigate how their understanding of swaraj affected their behavior in a case study that you write. ***(Cr)***

Ans. To investigate the impact of the Non-cooperation movement on the plantation workers in Assam. We could approach the study by focusing on the following key aspects:

(*i*) **Interpretation of swaraj:** For plantation workers in Assam, swaraj meant the freedom to move freely in and out of the plantations and maintain a connection with their home villages. *(1 M)*

(*ii*) **Actions taken:** Thousands of workers defied the authorities, left the plantations, and attempted to return home, believing that Gandhi Raj would grant them land and freedom. *(1 M)*

Short Answer Type Questions (3 M)

1. "The effects of Non-Cooperation Movement on the economic front were more dramatic." Support the statement with examples. ***(Ev)*(CBSE, 2022 Term 2)**

Ans. The Non-Cooperation Movement had a significant impact on the economic front due to the:

(*i*) The Non-Cooperation Movement led to a significant boycott of foreign goods, especially foreign cloth, which dramatically affected British economic interests in India. *(1 M)*

(*ii*) Indian weavers and local industries received a substantial boost due to the emphasis on swadeshi goods, fostering economic self-reliance and striking at the heart of the colonial economic structure. *(1 M)*

(*iii*) Economic hardships and resentment against colonial tax impositions galvanized many Indians, including those in rural areas, to actively participate in the movement, demonstrating its widespread economic impact. *(1 M)*

2. Why did Mahatma Gandhi decide to withdraw the Non-Cooperation Movement in February 1922? Explain. ***(Un)*(CBSE, 2022 Term 2)**

Ans. Primarily due to the violent incident at Chauri Chaura:

(*i*) Mahatma Gandhi decided to withdraw the Non Cooperation Movement in February 1922 due to the Chauri Chaura incident. *(1 M)*

(*ii*) The incident involved the burning of a police station by a group of protestors, which resulted in the death of 22 policemen. *(1 M)*

(*iii*) Gandhi felt that the movement had taken a violent turn, which went against the principles of nonviolence, and he called for its withdrawal to prevent further violence. *(1 M)*

Long Answer Type Questions (5 M)

1. Mahatma Gandhi's concept of satyagraha was central to the Indian independence movement. Imagine you are a journalist in the early 20th century who has the opportunity to interview Mahatma Gandhi. During the interview, Gandhi explains that satyagraha is not merely passive resistance but involves active, non-violent resistance to injustice. Based on this explanation, how would you, as the journalist, describe the principles of satyagraha to your readers? ***(Cr)***

Ans. Principles of Satyagraha as Explained by Mahatma Gandhi:

(*i*) **Active Resistance:** Satyagraha is not passive but involves active, non-violent resistance to injustice. It requires courage and strength, not submission. *(1 M)*

(*ii*) **Truth (Satya):** The power of satyagraha lies in the adherence to truth. Gandhi emphasized the need to search for and uphold truth in every action. *(1 M)* (*iii*) **Non-Violence (Ahimsa):** Satyagraha is based on non-violence. It seeks to win over the oppressor through love and patience, appealing to their conscience. *(1 M)*

(*iv*) **Self-Sacrifice:** A satyagrahi must be willing to endure suffering without retaliation. The goal is to transform the oppressor's heart, not to defeat them through force. *(1 M)*

(*v*) **Moral High Ground:** Satyagraha aims to create moral pressure on the oppressor by demonstrating the justice of the cause and the dignity of the resisters. *(1 M)*

2. What is meant by the idea of satyagraha? (*Un*)(NCERT)

Ans. The idea of Satyagraha, formulated by Mahatma Gandhi, is a profound concept that played a crucial role in India's struggle for independence, embodying the following principles;

(*i*) **Principle of Truth and Non-violence:** Advocates for resolving conflicts through the moral power of truth, emphasizing non-violence. *(1 M)*

(*ii*) **Self-suffering:** Involves the satyagrahi enduring suffering instead of inflicting harm, to appeal to the oppressor's conscience. *(1 M)*

(*iii*) **Active Resistance:** Contrary to passive resistance, it entails actively opposing injustice through non-violent means, showcasing moral courage. *(1 M)*

(*iv*) **Moral Victory:** Aims not to defeat but to convert the oppressor, fostering an environment of respect and mutual understanding. *(1 M)*

(*v*) **Social Unity and Change:** Seeks to unite individuals across diverse societal divisions to collectively address and rectify social injustices, such as untouchability, and to champion communal harmony. *(1 M)*

2 DIFFERING STRANDS WITHIN THE MOVEMENT

NCERT Definitions *(Commonly asked in 1 mark)*

- **Picket:** A form of demonstration or protest by which people block the entrance to a ***shop***, ***factory*** or ***office***.
- **Begar:** Labour that villagers were ***forced to contribute*** without ***any payment***.
- **Nai-Dhobi Bandh:** In **1919**, the panchayats of Awadh organised a ***nai-dhobi bandh*** in ***Pratapgarh*** district to deny landlords the services of barbers and washer-men.
- **Plantation:** A group of particular ***plants*** that are being ***cultivated***, an ***agricultural*** estate that is usually worked by labourers.

Important Facts

01 The ***Non-Cooperation-Khilafat Movement*** saw diverse social group participation, each with different aspirations. The term 'Swaraj' meant different things to different people within this movement.

02 In towns, the movement witnessed ***middle-class*** participation with students leaving schools, headmasters and teachers resigning, and lawyers abandoning their practices. The economic front saw a ***boycott*** of ***foreign goods***, leading to a significant drop in the import of foreign cloth.

03 In the ***countryside***, the movement expanded to include ***peasant*** and ***tribal*** struggles against landlords and ***British authorities***. Notable was the struggle in Awadh led by ***Baba Ramchandra*** and the peasant movement in Gujarat led by Vallabhbhai Patel.

04 The ***Civil Disobedience Movement***, initiated by Mahatma Gandhi with the Salt March, aimed at directly breaking colonial laws, including the manufacturing of salt, boycotting foreign goods, and refusing to pay taxes.

05 The participation of various social groups, including ***rich peasant communities***, ***poorer peasants***, ***business classes***, ***industrial working classes***, and ***women***, highlighted the movement's diverse appeal and objectives.

06 The movement faced limitations, particularly from groups like the 'untouchables', led by ***Dr. B.R. Ambedkar***, who sought political solutions for social disabilities, and sections of the Muslim community that felt alienated due to rising Hindu-Muslim communal tensions.

Important Personalities

Alluri Sitaram Raju: Alluri Sitaram Raju is famous for his involvement in the national struggle for the Independence of India. In Andhra Pradesh he led the protest against the Begar.

Baba Ramchandra: During Non Cooperation Movement, peasants movements were led by Baba Ramchandra In Awadh, who had earlier been to Fiji as an indentured labourer.

C.R. Das: Chittaranjan Das, also known as Deshbandhu (Friend of the Nation), was a Bengali nationalist and Indian freedom fighter who founded the Swaraj Party. He was born on November 5, 1870, and died on June 16, 1925.

Sardar Vallabh Bhai Patel: On October 31, 1875, Vallabhbhai Patel was born. He was a senior member of the Indian National Congress and one of India's most powerful leaders, he led the peasant movement in Bardoli, Gujarat, against enhancement of land revenue in 1928, this Satyagrah is known as Bardoli Satyagraha. anti-British peasant movements based on Gandhi's nonviolent beliefs.

Important Dates

- **1921:** Khilafat and Non – Cooperation Movement started by Mahatma Gandhi and Ali brothers.
- **1922, February:** Non Cooperation Movement was called off & Chauri-Chaura incident.
- **1924, May:** Alluri Sitaraman Raju arrested ending a two year armed tribal struggle.
- **1927:** Formation of Federation of the Indian Chamber of Commerce and Industries (FICCI).
- **1928:** Nehru Report (The Indian Constitution was drafted by Motilal Nehru)
- **1929, December:** Lahore Session of Congress and demand of Complete Independence "Purna Swaraj".

Difference Between

Rowlatt Act Vs. Jallianwala Bagh Massacre

	Rowlatt Act	Jallianwala Bagh Massacre
Time line	A legislative act passed by the British government in 1919.	A tragic event occurred on 13 April 1919 in Amritsar, Punjab.
Action by British	Allowed the government to detain individuals without trial.	British troops opened fire on a peaceful gathering, killing hundreds.
Symbol of	Represented the repressive nature of British colonial rule.	Symbolized the brutal extremes of British repression in India.
Effect of INM	Led to widespread anger and protests across India.	Acted as a catalyst for a stronger unified national movement.
Impact of Civilians	Was part of legislative repression; indirect impact on the populace.	Had a direct, devastating impact on Indian civilians, creating immediate outrage.

Myth Buster

- **Myth:** Non-Cooperation Movement was Entirely Non-violent

  Fact: Though Mahatma Gandhi advocated for non-violence, instances of violence occurred, like the Chauri Chaura incident, leading Gandhi to halt the movement. This shows the challenge of maintaining non-violence in mass movements.

- **Myth:** All Indians Supported the Idea of Swaraj in the Same Way

  Fact: Swaraj meant different things to different groups. While some viewed it as complete independence, others had specific expectations, such as trade benefits or social reforms. The movement's appeal varied among different communities, highlighting diverse motivations and expectations within the independence movement.

Mnemonics

Economic Impact of Non-Cooperation Movement

"Be Proud, Buy Indian, Halve imports."

Be	**P**roud	**B**uy	**I**ndian,	**H**alve	Imports
↓	↓	↓	↓	↓	
Boycott	Picketing	Bonfire	Increase	Halving	

Scan Me for Detailed Explanations

SOLVED EXAMPLES

Multiple Choice Questions

(1 M)

1. **Certain events are given below. Choose the appropriate chronological order:** ***(An)*(CBSE,2020)**

   (i) Coming of Simon Commission to India.

   (ii) Demand of Purna Swaraj in Lahore Session of INC.

   (iii) Government of India Act, 1919.

   (iv) Champaran Satyagraha.

   Choose the correct option:

   (*a*) (iii)-(ii)-(iv)-(i) (*b*) (i)-(ii)-(iv)-(iii)

   (*c*) (ii)-(iii)-(i)-(iv) (*d*) (iv)-(iii)-(i)-(ii)

2. **Rina is a young woman living in a small town in India during the 1920s. She regularly attends community meetings where leaders discuss the ongoing Non-Cooperation Movement. One day, Rina hears a passionate speech by a local leader who emphasises the importance of "Swaraj." The leader explains that "Swaraj" is not just about political freedom but also about self-reliance and self-governance in every aspect of life. Inspired, Rina decides to start a community garden to reduce dependency on British imports and promote local produce.**

   Based on this scenario, what does the term "Swaraj" most closely mean in the context of the Non-Cooperation Movement? ***(Ev)***

   (*a*) Complete independence from British rule.

   (*b*) Improvement of social services.

   (*c*) Adoption of Western customs and practices.

   (*d*) Establishment of a communist state.

3. **Jawaharlal Nehru visited various villages in Awadh, listening to the peasants' complaints about high rents and arbitrary evictions imposed by the landlords. He encourages them to organise non-violent protests and assures them of the Indian National Congress's support. How did Jawaharlal Nehru contribute to the peasant movement in Awadh in 1920?** ***(An)***

   (*a*) By providing financial assistance to the peasants to pay off their debts.

   (*b*) By writing letters to the British government demanding immediate reforms.

   (*c*) By personally visiting villages, understanding the peasants' grievances, and mobilizing them for non-violent protests.

   (*d*) By suggesting the peasants migrate to other regions to escape the landlords' oppression.

4. **What happened to the plantation workers who left the tea gardens to return to their villages during the Non-Cooperation Movement?** ***(Re)***

   (*a*) They successfully reached their destinations

   (*b*) They were caught by the police and beaten up

   (*c*) They joined the peasant movement in Awadh

   (*d*) They started a peaceful protest in Assam

5. **The following image is a very famous event of India's National Movement that took place in Chauri Chaura in 1922, where a peaceful demonstration turned into a violent clash with the police. Hearing of the incident Mahatma Gandhi called a halt to the Non-Cooperation Movement. Identify the district where this event took place among the following options.** ***(Re)***

(*a*) Hoshiarpur (*b*) Gorakhpur
(*c*) Meerut (*d*) Delhi

Assertion and Reason

(1 M)

Direction: The following questions consist of two statements – Assertion (A) and Reason (R). Answer these questions by selecting the appropriate option given below:

(*a*) Both A and R are true, and R is the correct explanation of A.
(*b*) Both A and R are true, but R is not the correct explanation of A.
(*c*) A is true, but R is false
(*d*) A is false, but R is true.

1. **Assertion (A):** The Non-Cooperation Movement led to a significant decline in the import of foreign cloth in India.

   Reason (R): The movement encouraged the boycott of foreign goods, including cloth, leading to a decrease in their import. ***(Ev)***

2. **Assertion (A):** The peasant movement in Awadh during the Non-Cooperation Movement adopted violent methods to protest against oppressive landlords.

   Reason (R): The peasant movement demanded reduction of revenue, abolition of begar, and social boycott of oppressive landlords. ***(Ev)***

3. **Assertion (A):** The plantation workers in Assam defied the authorities and left the tea gardens during the Non-Cooperation Movement.

   Reason (R): The plantation workers believed that Mahatma Gandhi's movement would bring them freedom and land in their own villages. ***(Ev)***

4. **Ravi is a historian studying the lives of workers in colonial Assam. He comes across the story of Ramesh, a tea plantation worker in Assam in the late 19th century. Ramesh and his fellow workers faced severe restrictions on their movement due to specific legislation passed by the British colonial government. This law was designed to ensure that workers could not leave the tea plantations without permission, thus tying them to their place of employment.**

   Assertion (A): The Inland Emigration Act of 1859 restricted the movement of factory workers in Assam.

   Reason (R): The Act was designed to prevent workers from leaving the industrial areas without permission. ***(An)***

Subjective Questions

Very Short Answer Type Questions

(1 or 2 M)

1. **What were the main aspirations of the various social groups participating in the Non-Cooperation Movement?** ***(Un)***

Ans: The main aspirations of various social groups participating in the non-cooperation movement were as follows:

(*i*) The Non-Cooperation Movement 1921 united Indians against the British atrocities in India. People belonging to all social groups joined Gandhi in his movement. *(1 M)*

(*ii*) The Members of the Congress including Gandhi announced the Non-Cooperation Movement. *(1 M)*

2. **What was the impact of the boycott movement on the import of foreign cloth?** ***(Un)***

Ans: The impact of the boycott movement on the import of foreign cloth is;

(*i*) In many places merchants and traders refused to trade in foreign goods or finance foreign trade. *(1 M)*

(*ii*) As the boycott movement spread, and people began discarding imported clothes and wearing only Indian ones, production of Indian textile mills and handlooms went up. *(1 M)*

3. **Who led the peasant movement in Awadh?** ***(Un)***

And. The peasant movement in Awadh was led by Baba Ramchandra, a Sanyasi with a past as an indentured labourer in Fiji. Their demands were focused on reducing rents, abolishing Begar, and boycotting landlords. *(2 M)*

4. **What happened to the plantation workers who left the tea gardens during the Non-Cooperation Movement?** ***(Un)***

Ans: During the Non-Cooperation Movement, plantation workers left the tea gardens to head to their homes, believing they would receive land. However, they were stopped due to a railway and steamer strike, arrested by the police, and brutally beaten. *(2 M)*

5. **How did Non-Cooperation movement start with participation of middle-class people in the cities? Explain its impact on the economic front.** ***(Un)(CBSE, 2018)***

Ans: The Non-Cooperation movement started with middleclass participation in the cities.

(i) Thousands of students left government controlled schools and colleges, headmasters and teachers resigned, and lawyers gave up their legal practices. *(1 M)*

(ii) The council elections were boycotted in most provinces except Madras, where the Justice Party, the party of the non-Brahmans, felt that entering the council was one way of gaining some power; something that usually only Brahmans had access to. *(1 M)*

Topper's Explanations

Introduction : The Non cooperation movement started in Jan 1921. Each group took it in its way. In the cities middle class group participated :-

(a) Students left govt schools, headmasters & teachers resigned, lawyers gave up their practice.

(b) Everyone joined the movement by boycotting European goods, using Swadeshi products, Dealers refused to trade in European products.

Short Answer Type Questions (3 M)

1. You are a young journalist in the early 20th century, covering the diverse reactions to Mahatma Gandhi's call for Swaraj (self-rule). While traveling through various regions, you interact with different groups, including tribal peasants and plantation workers. These interactions reveal that their interpretations of Swaraj are not uniform but shaped by their unique experiences and needs. As you prepare your article, explain how tribal peasants and plantation workers might have interpreted Mahatma Gandhi's idea of Swaraj differently. *(An)*

Ans: Tribal peasants and plantation Workers' Interpretation of Swaraj:

(i) **Tribal peasants:** Saw swaraj as freedom from restrictions on forest use and an end to forced labor (begar). *(1 M)*

(ii) **Plantation workers:** Viewed swaraj as freedom to move freely and maintain connections with their native villages. *(1 M)*

(iii) **Difference:** Tribal peasants' focus was on livelihood and traditional rights, while plantation workers focused on freedom of movement and escaping the constraints of the plantations. *(1 M)*

Proposed strategy to unite Rich and Poor Peasards:

2. What were the challenges faced by the Awadh peasant movement during the Non-Cooperation Movement? *(An)*

Ans: The Awadh peasant movement encountered several challenges during the Non-Cooperation Movement;

(i) The Awadh peasant movement faced challenges during the Non-Cooperation Movement, particularly in aligning with Congress's non-violent stance. *(1 M)*

(ii) While peasants demanded land reforms and reduced revenue, their violent actions, like attacking houses and looting, conflicted with Congress's methods. *(1 M)*

(iii) This misalignment caused tensions and led to disapproval from the mainstream Congress leadership, affecting the movement's unity. *(1 M)*

3. How did the Non-Cooperation Movement impact the Indian textile industry? *(An)*

Ans. The Non-Cooperation Movement had a significant impact on the Indian textile industry;

(i) The boycott of foreign cloth led to a decrease in its import, resulting in a surge in the production of Indian textile mills and handlooms. *(1½ M)*

(ii) This shift towards indigenous textiles aligned with the movement's emphasis on promoting Swadeshi (indigenous) goods and reducing dependence on foreign products, contributing to the growth and revitalization of the Indian textile sector. (1½ M)

Long Answer Type Questions (5 M)

1. 'Workers of Assam had their own understanding of Mahatma Gandhi and the notion of Swaraj'. Explain with examples. *(An)***(CBSE, 2023)**

Ans: (i) The workers of Assam had their own understanding of Mahatma Gandhi and the notion of Swaraj, which was shaped by their experience of exploitation and oppression. *(1¼ M)*

(ii) They saw Mahatma Gandhi as a leader who could unite the different communities and fight against British imperialism, but they also had their own demands and concerns. *(1¼ M)*

(iii) The tea garden workers in Assam saw Gandhi's Swaraj as a means to attain social justice and economic freedom. They saw it as an opportunity to achieve better wages, working conditions, and living standards. *(1¼ M)*

(iv) The workers also organized themselves into unions and went on strike to demand their rights. They saw Gandhi's non-violent methods as a way to achieve their goal peacefully. *(1¼ M)*

2. How did the Non-Cooperation Movement impact the Indian economy? *(An)*

Ans: The Non-Cooperation Movement had a significant impact on the Indian economy in these ways:

(i) **Economic Disruption:** The boycott of British institutions and foreign goods disrupted the existing economic system. *(1 M)*

(ii) **Reduction in Foreign Imports:** There was a notable decrease in foreign goods' importation, particularly foreign cloth, which halved between 1921 and 1922. *(1 M)*

(iii) **Support for Local Goods:** Indian merchants and traders' refusal to deal in foreign goods led to a rise in production from Indian textile mills and handlooms. *(1 M)* (*iv*) **Economic Challenges:** The movement faced challenges as Khadi, promoted as an alternative to foreign cloth, was more expensive, hindering poor people from sustaining the boycott. *(1 M)*

(*v*) **Institutional Challenges:** The effort to establish alternative Indian institutions faced difficulties, leading to a gradual reversion to the government-controlled system. *(1 M)*

3. "The most striking evidence of continued popular militancy came from the ever- restive semi-tribal Rampa region in the north of the Godavari, scene of a veritable guerrilla war between August 1922 and May 1924. [The leader of the revolt] won the grudging admiration of the British As a formidable guerrilla tactician. That the Government had to spend over Rs 40 lakhs in those days to defeat the rebellion speaks volumes about the success of the Rampa rebellion."

Source: The Hindu

State the causes of the rebellion that the passage talks about. ***(Re)***

Ans: Causes of the Rampa Rebellion:

(*i*) The rebellion happened in the Gudem Hills of Andhra Pradesh. *(1 M)*

(*ii*) The colonial government had closed large forest areas and prevented people from entering the forests to graze their cattle, or to collect fuelwood and fruits. *(1 M)*

(*iii*) It enraged the hill people. *(1 M)*

(*iv*) Not only were their livelihoods affected but they felt that their traditional rights were being denied. *(1 M)*

(*v*) When the government began forcing them to contribute begar for road building,the hill people revolted. *(1 M)*

3 TOWARDS CIVIL DISOBEDIENCE

NCERT Definitions (Commonly asked in 1 mark)

- **Civil Disobedience Movement:** Initiated by Gandhi to resist ***British laws non-violently***. Marked by the Salt March, it called for the violation of the salt laws, among other forms of resistance.
- **Simon Commission:** A British committee formed to report on the ***political situation*** in India. The commission faced opposition for not including Indian members.
- **Purna Swaraj:** The goal of the Indian National Congress declared in **1930**, demanding complete independence from British rule.
- **Poona Pact:** An agreement between Mahatma Gandhi and Dr. B.R. Ambedkar in 1932, resolving the conflict over separate electorates for ***"Depressed Classes"*** by providing reserved seats in the general electorate.

Important Facts

01 The ***Civil Disobedience Movement*** was triggered by the ***Salt March***, marking a key turning point in the Indian struggle for independence by directly challenging British authority.

02 The movement involved widespread ***non-violent resistance*** and ***civil disobedience*** across India, including the refusal to pay taxes, boycotting of foreign goods, and the non-payment of revenue to the British government.

03 Despite initial successes, the movement faced severe repression from the British government, leading to the arrest of thousands of activists including Gandhi , and causing Gandhi to suspend the movement temporarily in **1931** following the ***Gandhi-Irwin Pact***.

04 The ***second Round Table Conference,*** attended by ***Gandhi*** in ***London***, ended in failure, leading to the resurgence of the Civil Disobedience Movement until it gradually lost momentum by **1934**.

Important Personalities

Motilal Nehru: A very famous leader of India who drafted the constitution of India in 1928 which was known as Nehru Report. He also played an important role in the formation of Swaraj Party in 1922.

Lala Lajpat Rai: He was an eminent freedom fighter. He protested against the Simon Commission.

Viceroy Irwin: Lord Irwin is also known as Edward Frederick Lindley Wood. The Gandhi–Irwin Pact was a political agreement signed by Mahatma Gandhi and Lord Irwin, the then Viceroy of India, on March 5, 1931, in London, before the Second Round Table Conference.

Sir John Simon: He was the head of the Simon Commission which was an all white committee.

Dr. Bhimrao Ambedkar: The founder of Distressed Class Association, a prominent lawyer who later on drafted Indian Constitution

Important Dates

- **1930:** Distressed Class Association was formed by Dr. B R Ambedkar.
- **1930:** Salt Law was broken through Dandi March **(12 *March* 1930 *to* 6 *April* 1930)**
- **1930, March:** Civil Disobedience Movement was launched.
- **1930:** First Round Table Conference took place. Congress didn't participate.
- **1931:** Gandhi ji ends Civil Disobedience Movement.
- **1931:** Gandhi Irwin Pact was signed. Key Dates and Personalities
- **1931, December:** Second Round Table Conference took place. M K Gandhi and B R Ambedkar participated.
- **1932:** Poona pact between M K Gandhi and Dr. B R Ambedkar.
- **1932:** Civil Disobedience Movement was relaunched.
- **1942:** Quit India Movement was launched.

Difference Between

Civil Disobedience Movement vs. Salt March

Aspect	Civil Disobedience Movement	Salt March
Scope	A broader movement involving the violation of laws set by the British government.	A specific act within the Civil Disobedience Movement focusing on the salt laws.
Nature of Protest	Encompassed various forms of non-violent protests and non-cooperation.	Started with Gandhi's march from Sabarmati Ashram to Dandi to make salt illegally.
Objective	Aimed at challenging the legitimacy of British laws and rule.	Highlighted the exploitative nature of the British salt tax.
Participation	Participants included people from various strata of society.	Acted as a catalyst, inspiring widespread participation in the Civil Disobedience Movement.

Myth Buster

- **Myth:** Civil Disobedience was solely about protesting and breaking the salt tax law.

  Fact: While the salt tax was a significant aspect of Civil Disobedience, the movement encompassed a broader spectrum of actions and demands. It aimed at challenging various laws and policies of the British government, and the salt march was just one part of the multifaceted struggle for freedom. The movement included a boycott of foreign goods, refusal to pay taxes, and mass protests against British institutions and laws.

Mnemonics

Effect of Civil Disobedience Movement (1930-1934):

"Flabrs"

F – **Forest laws violated** (Violation of Forest Laws)

L – **Laws violated** (Violation of Laws)

A

B – **Boycott actions** (Boycott Actions)

R – **Revenue non-payment** (Refusal to pay revenue)

S – **Spread of the movement** (Nationwide Spread)

Scan Me for Detailed Explanations

COMPETENCY BASED SOLVED EXAMPLES

Multiple Choice Questions

(1 M)

1. **The Indian masses willingly participated in the Civil Disobedience Movement, despite the challenges faced during the Non-Cooperation Movement. Accordingly, which of the following quotes BEST reflects the outlook of the masses?** *(Ev)*(CBSE APQ, 2023)

   (*a*) 'The greatest glory in living lies not in never falling, but in rising every time we fall'

   (*b*) 'An eye for an eye only ends up making the whole world blind'

   (*c*) 'Injustice anywhere is a threat to justice everywhere'

   (*d*) 'Obedience is the key to a peaceful society'

2. **Identify the correct option that describes the movement given below.** *(Re)*(CBSE SQP, 2023)

   The movement broke colonial laws and also refused cooperation with the British

   (*a*) Rowlatt Satyagraha Movement

   (*b*) Civil Disobedience movement

   (*c*) Non Cooperation Movement

   (*d*) Quit India Movement

3. **The Indian masses willingly participated in the Civil Disobedience Movement despite the challenges faced during the Non-Cooperation Movement. Which of the following quotes BEST reflects the outlook of the masses?** *(An)*

   (*a*) 'The greatest glory in living lies not in never falling, but in rising every time we fall'

   (*b*) 'An eye for an eye only ends up making the whole world blind'

   (*c*) 'Injustice anywhere is a threat to justice everywhere'

   (*d*) 'Obedience is the key to a peaceful society'

4. **Arrange the following events in the correct chronological order leading up to the Civil Disobedience Movement:**

   1. **Boycott of the Simon Commission**
   2. **Poorna Swaraj resolution passed**
   3. **Letter with 11 demands sent to Viceroy Irwin**
   4. **Salt March** *(Un)*

   Options:

   (*a*) 4, 3, 2, 1 (*b*) 2, 1, 3, 4

   (*c*) 1, 4, 3, 2 (*d*) 1, 2, 3, 4

5. **Observe the image given below**

INDIA'S PEACE ASSURED BY COMPROMISE

Viceroy and Gandhi Reach Agreement on Major Points in Dispute

CIVIL DISOBEDIENCE TO CEASE AT ONCE

Congress Cancels Demand for Police Inquiry—Salt Making Permitted on Coast

   What was the agreement between Gandhi and the Viceroy? *(Un)*

   (*a*) The British government will lift the ban on meetings, demonstrations, and boycotts.

   (*b*) The British government will reserve seats for depressed classes in the councils.

   (*c*) Gandhi will participate in the Round Table Conference.

   (*d*) Gandhi will accept dominion status for India.

6. **What led to the temporary suspension of the Civil Disobedience Movement in 1931?** *(Re)*

   (*a*) The release of political prisoners

   (*b*) The signing of the Gandhi-Irwin Pact

   (*c*) The success of the Round Table Conference

   (*d*) The British government's repression of protesters

Assertion and Reason

(1 M)

Direction: The following questions consist of two statements – Assertion (A) and Reason (R). Answer these questions by selecting the appropriate option given below:

(a) Both A and R are true, and R is the correct explanation of A.
(b) Both A and R are true, but R is not the correct explanation of A.
(c) A is true, but R is false
(d) A is false, but R is true.

1. **Assertion (A):** The Non-Cooperation Movement gained widespread support from various sections of Indian society.
   Reason (R): It was based on nonviolent principles and aimed to mobilize the masses against British rule. ***(Ev)***
2. **Assertion (A):** The Poona Pact made the depressed classes a formidable political force for the first time in history.
   Reason (R): Dr. B.R Ambedkar and Gandhi agreed to make separate electorates for the depressed classes in the Poona Pact. ***(An)***
3. **Assertion (A):** The Simon Commission was met with widespread protests in India.
   Reason (R): Indians demanded greater representation and participation in the Commission. ***(Ev)***
4. **Assertion (A):** The Poona Pact of 1932 aimed to improve the political representation of dalits in India.
   Reason (R): It was a compromise between the Congress and British government to address dalit concerns. ***(An)***
5. **Assertion (A):** The Civil Disobedience Movement marked a shift towards more radical forms of protest in the Indian freedom struggle.
   Reason (R): Indians were frustrated with the slow progress of the Non-Cooperation Movement. ***(Ev)***

Subjective Questions

Very Short Answer Type Questions (1 or 2 M)

1. **Mention any two causes that led to the Civil Disobedience Movement. *(Un)*(CBSE, 2022 Term 2)**

Ans: Two causes that led to the Civil Disobedience Movement were:

***(i)* Salt Tax:** British imposition of salt tax severely impacted India's poor who depended on salt for daily needs. *(1 M)*

***(ii)* Simon Commission:** Exclusion of Indian members from the Simon Commission reviewing India's constitution was viewed as a slight to self-rule aspirations. *(1 M)*

2. **You are a historian tasked with creating an educational documentary on Mahatma Gandhi's Civil Disobedience Movement. One segment focuses on Gandhi's letter to Viceroy Irwin, dated January 31, 1930. Explain how Gandhi's demands in this letter addressed the interests of various classes in Indian society, such as peasants, industrialists, and workers. *(Ap)***

Ans: In his letter to Viceroy Irwin, Gandhi made demands that addressed the needs of differnet groups: **(Any two)**

(*i*) **Peasants:** He called for a reduction in land taxes to ease their financial burden. *(1 M)*

(*ii*) **Industrialists:** He demanded the end of the salt tax and British monopoly on salt, which hurt local industries. *(1 M)*

(*iii*) **Workers:** Gandhi pushed for better working conditions and fair treatment for workers. *(1 M)*

3. **What was the main demand of the Lahore Congress in December 1929? *(Re)***

Ans: The main demand of the Lahore Congress in December 1929 was;

(*i*) The Lahore Congress, under Jawaharlal Nehru's presidency, formalized the demand for 'Purna Swaraj' or complete independence for India, rejecting any form of British dominion. *(1 M)*

(*ii*) It was decided that January 26, 1930, would be celebrated as Independence Day, marking the commitment to a struggle for full sovereignty. *(1 M)*

4. **What was the significance of women's participation in the Civil Disobedience Movement? *(Un)***

Ans: The significance of women's participation in the Civil Disobedience Movement:

(*i*) Women's active roles in protests and boycotts during the Civil Disobedience Movement challenged traditional gender norms and increased their public visibility. *(1 M)*

(*ii*) Their participation demonstrated widespread societal support for the movement, symbolizing unity and empowerment across gender lines. *(1 M)*

5. **When did Mahatma Gandhi call off the Civil Disobedience Movement and enter into a pact with Irwin? *(Re)***

Ans: Mahatma Gandhi called off the Civil Disobedience Movement and entered into a pact with Lord Irwin on 5 March 1931, leading to the Gandhi-Irwin Pact which allowed Gandhi to participate in the Second Round Table Conference in London. *(2 M)*

Short Answer Type Questions (3 M)

1. **Describe the implications of the First World War on the economic and political situation of India. *(An)*(CBSE, 2020)**

Ans: The First World War had significant implications on the economic and political situation of India;

(*i*) **Economic**

(a) India became a prominent exporter of raw materials and food grains, leading to inflation and widespread poverty. *(1 M)*

(b) The war led to a significant increase in India's debt, which had to be repaid with interest. *(1 M)*

(*ii*) **Political:** India's contribution to the war was not recognized, fueling the demand for self-governance. *(1 M)*

2. **Describe the role of poor peasantry in the 'Civil Disobedience Movement'. *(Un)*(CBSE, 2020)**

Ans: The poor peasantry played a crucial role in the 'Civil Disobedience Movement.'

(*i*) **Mass Support:** The poor peasantry formed the backbone of the Civil Disobedience Movement, ensuring its status as a mass movement. *(1 M)*

(*ii*) **Affected by British Policies:** Suffering greatly under British rule, their participation was driven by a direct impact on their livelihoods. *(1 M)* (*iii*) **Inclusivity of the Movement:** Their involvement highlighted that the freedom struggle included all societal layers, not just the educated or affluent. *(1 M)*

3. Given the economic hardships faced by the rich and poor peasants, imagine you are a leader of a peasant community during the Civil Disobedience Movement. Propose a strategy to unite these groups for a common cause despite their differing priorities. *(Cr)*

Ans: Proposed strategy to unite Rich and Poor Peasants:

(*i*) **Common Economic Hardships:** Both groups faced severe economic difficulties due to falling incomes and high revenue demands. *(1 M)*

(*ii*) **Unification Strategy:** Form a unified front focusing on overall financial relief, including both revenue reduction and rent remission. Organise joint protests and campaigns emphasizing mutual benefits. *(1 M)*

(*iii*) **Conflict Resolution:** Create committees comprising representatives from both groups to address specific grievances and ensure equitable focus on both rent and revenue issues, thereby maintaining solidarity. *(1 M)*

Long Answer Type Questions (5 M)

1. Examine the progress of the Civil Disobedience Movement in the countryside. *(An)***(CBSE, 2023)**

Ans: The progress of the Civil Disobedience Movement in the countryside as follow:

(*i*) In the countryside, the Civil Disobedience Movement saw peasants protesting against oppressive practices and policies, demonstrating the expansion of the freedom struggle beyond urban centers. *(1 M)*

(*ii*) Different regions experienced the movement uniquely, with localized issues and leadership shaping the nature of rural protests and demands. *(1 M)*

(*iii*) Participation varied, with some areas showing intense engagement while others were less active, reflecting regional economic conditions, leadership effectiveness, and the impact of repressive measures. *(1 M)*

(*iv*) The movement influenced subsequent rural mobilizations and contributed to a growing consciousness and politicization among rural populations. *(1 M)*

(*v*) Overall, the Civil Disobedience Movement in the countryside marked a significant phase in India's struggle for independence, illustrating the depth and diversity of anti-colonial sentiment across the nation. *(1 M)*

2. Who had organized the dalits into the 'Depressed Classes Association' in 1930? Describe his achievements. *(Un)***(CBSE, 2019)**

Ans: Dr. B.R. Ambedkar had organised the dalits into the Depressed Classes Association in 1930. The Depressed Classes Association was in favour of a separate electorate for dalits. *(1 M)*

Achievements:

- It uplifted the dalits against the dominance of upper caste hindus. *(1 M)*
- It gave the depressed classes, reserved seats in Provincial and Central Legislative Councils in proportion to their population. *(1 M)*
- The Depressed Classes Association. enhanced the dignity of marginalised sections of society such as SC, ST, OBC. *(1 M)*
- Ambedkar accepted Gandhi's position and as a result, the Poona Pact was signed. *(1 M)*

3. Explain the reasons behind Mahatma Gandhi's decision to withdraw the Non-Cooperation Movement in February 1922 and the formation of the Swaraj Party within the Congress. How did the younger leaders like Jawaharlal Nehru and Subhas Chandra Bose differ in their approach from the more moderate leaders? *(An)*

Ans: **Withdrawal of Non-Cooperation Movement:** Gandhi called off the movement in February 1922 due to the violent incident at Chauri Chaura, where protestors clashed with police, leading to the death of 22 policemen. This violence went against his principle of non-violence. *(2 M)*

- **Formation of the Swaraj Party:** Frustrated by the suspension of the movement and motivated to continue the struggle within the legislative councils, leaders like Motilal Nehru and C.R. Das formed the Swaraj Party in January 1923 to argue for reforms from within the government structures. *(1½ M)*
- **Difference in Approaches:** Younger leaders like Jawaharlal Nehru and Subhas Chandra Bose were critical of the moderate methods and pushed for radical measures and immediate complete independence, rather than the gradual and conciliatory approach of moderate leaders. *(1½ M)*

4. You are an advisor to Mahatma Gandhi during the Civil Disobedience Movement. Gandhi has asked you to prepare a comprehensive report evaluating the challenges faced by the Congress in maintaining unity among various social and religious groups. Analyze the differing objectives and aspirations of these groups, the strategies employed by the Congress to address these challenges, and the impact of these efforts on the overall success of the movement. *(Ev)*

Ans: Report on challenges faced by the congress in maint aining unity during the civil Disobedience Movement.

(*i*) The Civil Disobedience Movement aimed for India's independence through non-violent means, led by the Indian National Congress. *(1 M)*

(*ii*) The Dalits were initially ignored by the Congress to avoid offending conservative sanatanis. Gandhi's efforts to include them through the satyagraha and renaming them harijan faced limited success due to demands for reserved seats and a separate electorate, leading to the Poona Pact. *(1 M)*

(*iii*) Muslim participation was tepid post the Non-Cooperation-Khilafat Movement. The Congress's association with Hindu nationalist groups like the Hindu Mahasabha deepened communal divides. *(1 M)*

(*iv*) Efforts to forge unity, such as negotiations between the Congress and the Muslim League, failed over representation issues. Jinnah's willingness to forego separate electorates in exchange for reserved seats was thwarted by opposition from the Hindu Mahasabha. *(1 M)*

(*v*) These challenges led to an atmosphere of suspicion and distrust among communities, limiting the movement's inclusiveness and overall impact. *(1 M)*

4 THE SENSE OF COLLECTIVE BELONGING

NCERT Definitions *(Commonly asked in 1 mark)*

- **Bharat Mata:** A ***personification*** of India as a mother goddess, which emerged as a symbol of Indian nationalism, inspiring devotion and national pride among Indians.
- **Folklore Revival:** The process of collecting and preserving ***folk tales, songs,*** and legends to foster a sense of national identity and pride in India's cultural heritage.
- **Swadeshi Movement:** A part of the Indian independence movement that emphasized the importance of ***self-reliance*** through the ***boycott of British goods*** and the promotion of Indian-made products.
- **Swaraj Flag:** Introduced by Gandhi, symbolising the goal of ***self-rule*** and ***independence*** for India, with the spinning wheel representing self-reliance and non-violent resistance.

Important Facts

01 The concept of ***nationalism in India*** was significantly shaped by cultural processes, including the spread of folklore, songs, and the arts, fostering a sense of ***unity*** and ***national identity***.

02 The concept of ***collective belonging*** in India was significantly shaped by the shared experiences of colonial exploitation and the struggle for independence, leading to the emergence of a unified national identity among diverse social, cultural, and religious groups.

03 The portrayal of ***Bharat Mata*** as a mother figure symbolizing India played a crucial role in evoking emotional bonds of patriotism among Indians, transcending regional and communal divides.

04 The ***Swadeshi Movement's*** emphasis on the boycott of British goods and the promotion of Indian-made products served not only as an economic strategy but also as a means of asserting Indian autonomy and national pride.

05 The revival of ***folklore***, through the collection and celebration of folk tales and songs, was part of a broader cultural movement to rediscover and valorize India's indigenous heritage and history, fostering a sense of pride and unity among the Indian populace.

06 The adoption of the ***tricolour flag*** as a symbol of the ***national movement*** encapsulated the collective aspirations and diverse cultural identities of India, contributing to the development of a shared sense of national belonging.

07 Nationalist leaders like ***Rabindranath Tagore*** and ***Mahatma Gandhi*** played pivotal roles in the cultural and ideological formation of collective belonging, using literature, art, and political action to articulate visions of an independent and united India.

Important Personalities

Rabindranath Tagore: He wrote the national anthem of India (Jan – Gan – Man) and collected the folklores, myths and ballads of India to revive Indian Culture.

Abanindranath Tagore: One of the greatest painters of India who painted Bharat Mata for the first time.

Bankim Chandra Chatterji: The author of Anandmath who wrote Vande Matram and used the word Bharat Mata for the first time.

Difference Between

	Salt March Vs Quit India Movement	
Aspect	**Salt March**	**Quit India Movement**
Part of Movement	A pivotal part of the Civil Disobedience Movement initiated in 1930.	Launched in 1942, demanding an end to British rule in India.
Initiation	Gandhi led a march from Sabarmati Ashram to Dandi to make salt, defying British laws.	Was a leaderless movement, with Gandhi giving the call to "Do or Die".
Specificity	Targeted a specific law (salt tax) symbolizing British exploitation.	A more aggressive and broad-based movement with no specific target other than British exit.

Mnemonics

Cultural Elements in the Indian National Movement;
"SPICE"

- **S** → Songs (Patriotic songs)
- **P** → Pride (Depiction of Bharat Mata invoking national pride)
- **I** → Identity (Collection and popularization of folklore for national identity)
- **C** → Chronicle (Reinterpretation of history)
- **E** → Emblems (Icons and symbols)

Myth Buster

- **Myth:** All Indian communities embraced national symbols like Bharat Mata.

  Fact: National symbols tended to reflect Hindu iconography, which didn't resonate with all, highlighting the challenge in creating a unified national identity.

- **Myth:** The folk revival was seen as an unequivocal return to a glorious past.

  Fact: While aimed at fostering national pride, the focus on Hindu history sometimes excluded non-Hindu narratives, necessitating a more inclusive approach to history.

COMPETENCY BASED SOLVED EXAMPLES

Scan Me for Detailed Explanations

Multiple Choice Questions

(1 M)

1. **Who among the following wrote the Vande Mataram?** ***(Re)*(CBSE, 2020)**

   (*a*) Rabindranath Tagore

   (*b*) Bankim Chandra Chattopadhyay

   (*c*) Abanindranath Tagore

   (*d*) Dwarkanath Tagore

2. **During a history lesson about Bal Gangadhar Tilak, students are asked to identify the key aspects of his image that contributed to his reputation as a significant figure in the Indian freedom struggle.Which of the following aspects best signify the image of Bal Gangadhar Tilak?** ***(Un)***

   (*a*) Symbol of Ashoka's Pillar

   (*b*) Shri Krishna Rath in Mahabharat

   (*c*) The rising sun

   (*d*) Symbol of unity

3. **What did the nationalists believe was the true picture of traditional culture?** ***(Un)***

   (*a*) Folklore and songs

   (*b*) Historical documents

   (*c*) Scientific advancements

   (*d*) Foreign influences

4. **What did the tricolour flag represent during the Swadeshi movement in Bengal?** ***(Re)***

   (*a*) Unity among Hindus and Muslims

   (*b*) Eight provinces of British India

   (*c*) Gandhian ideal of self-help

   (*d*) Defiance against British rule

5. **Who created the image of Bharat Mata, which became associated with the identity of India?** ***(Re)***

   (*a*) Rabindranath Tagore

   (*b*) Bankim Chandra Chattopadhyay

   (*c*) Abanindranath Tagore

   (*d*) Natesa Sastri

Assertion and Reason

(1 M)

Direction: The following questions consist of two statements – Assertion (A) and Reason (R). Answer these questions by selecting the appropriate option given below:

(*a*) Both A and R are true, and R is the correct explanation of A.

(*b*) Both A and R are true, but R is not the correct explanation of A.

(*c*) A is true, but R is false

(*d*) A is false, but R is true.

1. **Assertion (A):** As the national movement developed, nationalist leaders became more and more aware of such icons and symbols in unifying people and inspiring in them a feeling of nationalism.

   Reason (R): During the Swadeshi movement in Bengal, the tricolour flag (red, green and yellow) was designed. ***(Ev)***

2. **Assertion (A):** Many Indians felt that rethinking Indian history was necessary to cultivate a sense of national pride by the end of the nineteenth century.

   Reason (R): Existing historical narratives were influenced by colonial perspectives and failed to accurately represent the depth and contributions of Indian civilization. ***(Ev)***

Subjective Questions

Very Short Answer Type Questions

(1 or 2 M)

1. **In which novel was the hymn 'Vande Mataram' included?** ***(Re)***

Ans: The hymn ***'Vande Mataram'*** was included in the novel ***"Anandamath"*** written by Bankim Chandra Chattopadhyay. This novel, set in the background of the Sannyasi Rebellion in the late 18th century, effectively used the hymn to inspire Indian nationalism. *(2 M)*

2. **What did the tricolour flag designed during the Swadeshi movement in Bengal represent?** ***(Re)***

Ans: The tricolour flag designed during the Swadeshi movement in Bengal represent:

   (*i*) The tricolour flag designed during the Swadeshi movement featured red, green, and yellow colors. It included eight lotuses, representing the eight provinces of British India, symbolizing unity among the diverse regions. *(1 M)*

(*ii*) It represented the eight provinces of British India, with eight lotuses, and Hindus and Muslims with a crescent moon. *(1 M)*

3. Who designed the Swaraj flag? ***(Re)***

Ans: By 1921, Mahatma Gandhi designed the Swaraj flag. This was a tricolour flag and had a spinning wheel in the centre of a red, green and white banner. The red stripe was for Hindus, and the green was for Muslims. The white band represented peace and the rest of the communities living in India. *(2 M)*

Short Answer Type Questions (3 M)

1. Nationalism spreads when people begin to believe that they are all part of the same nation when they discover some unity that binds them together.

How did nationalists such as Rabindranath Tagore and Natesa Sastri use folk art and music to bring this about? ***(Un)***

Ans: Nationalists like Rabindranath Tagore and Natesa Sastri used folk art and music to promote nationalism by:

(*i*) Rabindranath Tagore collected ballads, nursery rhymes, and myths. *(1 M)*

(*ii*) Some nationalists felt it was essential to preserve such folk traditions to discover one's national identity and restore a sense of pride. *(1 M)*

(*iii*) Natesa Sastri published a massive four-volume collection of Tamil folk tales - ***The Folklore of Southern India.*** *(1 M)*

2. How did symbols, such as flags, contribute to the growth of nationalism? ***(Un)***

Ans: Symbols like flags played a significant role in the growth of nationalism;

(*i*) They served as visual representations of the nation, inspiring a sense of unity and pride. *(1 M)*

(*ii*) The tricolour flag used during the Swadeshi movement in India symbolised unity among Hindus and Muslims and represented resistance against British rule. *(1 M)*

(*iii*) Such symbols became rallying points for people, fostering a collective identity and a shared sense of purpose in the struggle for independence. *(1 M)*

Long Answer Type Questions (5 M)

1. What were the challenges faced in achieving inclusivity within the nationalist movement? ***(An)***

Ans: The challenges faced in achieving inclusivity within the nationalist movement:

(*i*) Glorification of certain cultural symbols, often rooted in Hindu iconography, created a sense of exclusion for people from other communities. *(1¼ M)*

(*ii*) This led to feelings of marginalization and hindered the unity of the movement. *(1¼ M)*

(*iii*) Diverse groups and classes participated in the nationalist struggle with varied aspirations and expectations, which sometimes led to disunity and conflicts within the movement. *(1¼ M)*

(*iv*) Efforts were made by the Indian National Congress to resolve differences and ensure that one group's demands did not alienate others, but maintaining unity remained a challenge. *(1¼ M)*

2. Discuss the role of visual symbols and representations in shaping nationalist sentiments during the Indian independence movement. ***(An)***

Ans: Visual symbols and representations played a crucial role in shaping nationalist sentiments during the Indian independence movement:

(*i*) They served as powerful tools for fostering a sense of identity, unity, and resistance against British rule. *(1 M)*

(*ii*) The image of Bharat Mata, created by Bankim Chandra Chattopadhyay, became synonymous with the identity of India and inspired devotion to the motherland. *(1 M)*

(*iii*) The tricolour flags used during the Swadeshi movement, with their symbolism of Hindu-Muslim unity, became potent symbols of defiance and solidarity. *(1 M)*

(*iv*) Mahatma Gandhi's Swaraj flag, with its spinning wheel, represented self-help and self-sufficiency, resonating with the ideals of the independence struggle. *(1 M)*

(*v*) These visual symbols provided tangible representations of the movement, enabling people to identify and rally around a shared cause. *(1 M)*

MISCELLANEOUS EXERCISE

Multiple Choice Questions

(1 M)

1. Identify the appropriate reason for the formation of the Swaraj party from the options given below: ***(An)***
   (*a*) Wanted members of Congress to return to council politics
   (*b*) Wanted members of Congress to ask for Purna Swaraj for Indians
   (*c*) Wanted members of Congress to ask dominion status for India
   (*d*) Wanted members of congress to oppose simon commission
2. In a small Indian village, Ramesh, a young lawyer, speaks to villagers about an oppressive law passed by the British government. This law has allowed authorities to detain protesters without trial, causing fear among the people. ***(Cr)***
   Identify the act Ramesh is referring to, which includes the following provisions:
   (*i*) Passed by the Imperial Legislative Council.
   (*ii*) Gave power to repress political activities.
   (*iii*) Allowed detention of political prisoners without trial for two years.
   Option:
   (*a*) Rowlatt Act
   (*b*) Vernacular Press Act
   (*c*) Government of India Act
   (*d*) Inland Emigration Act
3. Imagine you are an economic analyst in the late 1920s, tasked with evaluating the impact of the worldwide economic depression on various sectors in India. Your focus is on the agricultural sector and the lives of Indian peasants during this period. What was the primary cause of these difficulties for Indian peasants during the late 1920s? ***(Ap)***
   (*a*) Increased agricultural prices and exports.
   (*b*) Led to the establishment of the Swaraj Party.
   (*c*) Caused agricultural prices to fall and exports to decline.
   (*d*) Improved the economic condition of the countryside.
4. The Simon Commission was boycotted because; ***(Re)***
   (*a*) There was no Indian in the commission
   (*b*) It supported the Muslim League
   (*c*) Congress felt that the people deserved swaraj
   (*d*) There were differences among the members.
5. You are a member of a planning committee for a protest against unjust laws in your town, inspired by historical movements. After studying the strategies used by Mahatma Gandhi in the 1920s during India's struggle against colonial rule, decide which approach would best suit your current objectives. ***(Un)***
   (*a*) Employing violent protests to demand immediate action against unfair laws.
   (*b*) Organising inclusive, nonviolent mass movements to unify different community groups.
   (*c*) Engaging in negotiations to secure incremental economic reforms from local authorities.
   (*d*) Severing ties with key stakeholders to pressure the local government into compliance.
6. Which one of the following pairs regarding Indian nationalism is correctly matched? ***(Re)*(CBSE, 2024)**

	Leaders		Contribution
(*a*)	Sardar Patel	:	Hindustan Socialist Republican Army
(*b*)	Bhagat Singh	:	Swaraj Party
(*c*)	C.R. Das	:	Bardoli Satyagraha
(*d*)	Jawahar Lal Nehru	:	Oudh Kisan Sabha

7. Hind Swaraj was written by Gandhiji in which year? ***(Re)***
   (*a*) 1905 (*b*) 1906
   (*c*) 1909 (*d*) 1908
8. ______ Act passed by British government in India in 1919? ***(Re)***
   (*a*) Govt. of India (*b*) Martial
   (*c*) Rowlatt (*d*) None of these
9. Arrange the following in the correct sequence. ***(An)***
   A. Non-cooperation and khilafat movement
   B. Second round table conference
   C. Chauri chaura
   D. Ambedkar establishes depressed classes, associations
   (*a*) A-C-D-B (*b*) C-B-D-A
   (*c*) B-A-D-C (*d*) D-A-C-B
10. Who presided over the December 1929 session of the congress at Lahore and what was its demand? ***(Re)***
    (*a*) Jawaharlal Nehru, the demand was for Poorna swaraj or full independence
    (*b*) Subhas Chandra Bose and "Poorna Swaraj" was its demand
    (*c*) Mahatma Gandhi. He asked for peaceful transfer of power by the British
    (*d*) Jawaharlal Nehru, the demand was for more representation of Indians in the councils
11. Name the industrial organization established by Indian merchants and industrialists to protect their business interests. ***(Re)***
    (*a*) The confederation of Indian industry (CII)
    (*b*) The Indian industrial and commercial congress (1920)
    (*c*) The federation of the Indian chambers of commerce and industry (FICCI) in 1927
    (*d*) Both (*a*) and (*c*)
12. People belonging to different communities, regions or language groups developed a sense of collective belonging through ***(Un)***
    (*a*) Experiences of linked struggles
    (*b*) A variety of cultural processes through which nationalism captured peoples imagination

(c) History and fiction, folklore and songs popular prints and symbols all developed nationalism.

(d) All the above

13. What exactly do you mean when you say 'Begar'? **(Re)**

(a) A law prohibiting plantation workers from leaving the tea gardens without authorization.

(b) During World War I, soldiers were obliged to be recruited in rural regions.

(c) Forced labour that villagers were forced to perform without being compensated.

(d) As a kind of protest, refusing to deal with people and associate with them, or participating in activities.

14. What were the impacts of civil disobedience movement? **(An)**

(a) Increased the strength of the National Movement

(b) Instilled political consciousness and a strong sense of patriotism in the people's thoughts.

(c) Liberate women from their homes and make them equal players in the struggle for freedom

(d) All the above

15. Who painted the portrait of Bharat Mata imparting knowledge, food, and clothing in 1905? **(Re)**

(a) Abnindranath Tagore

(b) Rabindranath Tagore

(c) Bankim Chandra Chattopadhyay

(d) None of these are true

16. In his book 'Hind Swaraj,' Gandhiji wrote: **(Re)**

(a) The British must withdraw from India.

(b) Indians must refuse to cooperate with the British.

(c) The government must renounce its right to produce salt.

(d) Indians must be involved in the country's government.

17. Awadh Kisan Sabha was led by which of the following leaders? **(Re)**

(a) Jawaharlal Nehru (b) Mahatma Gandhi

(c) Motilal Nehru (d) Subhash Chandra Bose

18. Muslim league was formed in **(Re)**

(a) 1908 (b) 1907

(c) 1906 (d) 1905

Assertion and Reason **(1 M)**

Direction: The following questions consist of two statements – Assertion (A) and Reason (R). Answer these questions by selecting the appropriate option given below:

(a) Both A and R are true, and R is the correct explanation of A.

(b) Both A and R are true, but R is not the correct explanation of A.

(c) A is true, but R is false

(d) A is false, but R is true.

1. **Assertion (A):** In 1917, Gandhiji organised a satyagraha to support the peasants of the Kheda district of Gujarat.

Reason (R): The peasants were affected by the Forced Recruitment of the villagers in the World War 1. **(Ev)**

2. **Assertion (A):** The council elections were boycotted in most provinces except Madras.

Reason (R): Justice Party came to power In Madras- where only Brahmans had access to take part in Council Elections. **(Ev)**

3. **Assertion (A):** Dyer entered the area, blocked the exit points, and opened fire on the crowd, killing hundreds.

Reason (R): His object, as he declared later, was to 'produce a moral effect', to create in the minds of satyagrahis a feeling of terror and we. **(An)**

4. **Assertion (A):** Foreign goods were boycotted, liquor shops picketed, and foreign cloth burnt in huge bonfires.

Reason (R): Students and teachers began trickling back to government schools and lawyers joined back work in government courts. **(An)**

5. **Assertion (A):** Bankim Chandra Chattopadhyay wrote 'Vande Mataram' as a hymn to the motherland and it was later included in his novel Anandamath and widely sung during the Swadeshi movement.

Reason (R): Rabindranath Tagore painted his famous image of Bharat Mata, which is portrayed as an ascetic figure, who is calm, composed, divine and spiritual. **(Ev)**

6. **Assertion (A):** The Muslim political organizations in India were very responsive to the civil disobedience movement

Reason (R): After the decline of the Non-Cooperation-Philately movement, a large section of Muslims felt alienated from the Congress. **(Ev)**

7. **Assertion (A):** Dr B.R. Ambedkar, who organized the dalits into the depressed classes, Association in 1930, clashed with mahatma Gandhi at the second round table conference by demanding separate electorates for dalits.

Reason (R): In the countryside rich peasant communities-like the patidars of Gujarat and the jats of Utter Pradesh- were active in the movement. Being producers of commercial crops, they were very hard hit by the trade depression and falling prices. **(Ev)**

Subjective Questions

Very Short Answer Type Questions **(1 or 2 M)**

1. Name the two main leaders of Khilafat committee' formed in the year 1919. **(Re)(CBSE, 2020)**
2. Name the writer of the book ''Hind Swaraj". **(Re)**
3. Trace the reason because of which Gandhiji started Satyagraha in 1919. **(Un)**
4. What did British do to repress the Rowlatt Satyagrahis? **(Re)**
5. The resolution of Poorna Swaraj was adopted at which session of the congress? **(Re)**
6. Why was the Simon Commission boycotted in India? **(Un)**
7. Why was the Inland Emigration Act of 1859 trouble some for plantation workers? **(Un)(CBSE, 2020)**
8. Mention any two Impacts of the first world war on the Indian economy. **(An)(CBSE, 2022)**

Short Answer Type Questions (3 M)

1. Why did Gandhiji decide to launch a nationwide Satyagraha against the proposed Rowlatt Act 1919? Explain any three reason. *(Un)*
2. What is meant by the idea of Satyagraha? *(Re)*

   OR

   Explain the idea of Satyagraha according to Gandhiji. *(Un)*
3. Ramesh, a 21-year-old living in a small Indian town in 1919. After World War I,His family struggled with rising costs and economic hardships. At a town hall meeting, local leaders discuss these issues.

   He stand up and ask:

   "World War I has ended, but our struggles have intensified. The cost of living is unbearable. How will you address these economic challenges and ensure fair prices for our produce and goods?" *(Ev)*
4. How had the first World War created a new economic situation in India? Explain with three examples. *(Un)*
5. What were the three proposals regarding Non-Cooperation movement, as suggested by Mahatma Gandhi? *(Un)*
6. Write about the Rowlatt act, 1919. *(An)*
7. How did Mahatma Gandhi successfully organize Satyagraha movement in various places just after arriving India? explain by giving three examples. *(Un)*
8. Discuss the various stage of the Non-Cooperation movement launched by Mahatma Gandhi. *(Re)*
9. Why did the different social groups join the Civil Disobedience Movement? Explain. *(Re)*

   OR

   How did women participate in the Civil Disobedience Movement? Explain. *(Un)*
10. Describe any three causes that led to the Non-Cooperation Movement. *(An)***(CBSE, 2024)**

    OR

    Describe any three causes of 'Civil Disobedience Movement'. *(An)***(CBSE, 2024)**
11. Mahatma Gandhi launched a more broad based movement in India by joining Khilafat Movement. Explain the statement with any three arguments in the context of Non-cooperation movement. *(An)***(CBSE, 2022)**

Long Answer Type Questions (5 M)

1. Explain the implications of the First World War' on the economic and political situation of India. **(An)**

   OR

   How did the first World War create a new economic situation in India. *(Un)* **(CBSE, 2022)**
2. In 1920, Ramesh, a merchant from Bombay, joined the Non-Cooperation Movement. He stops importing British goods, closes his shop selling foreign clothes, and relies on local weavers and craftsmen. Over the next year, he sees significant changes in his business and the local market. Explain how Ramesh's participation in the Non-Cooperation Movement reflects the broader impact of the movement on the Indian economy. *(An)*
3. Describe the development which led to the launching of Non-cooperation movement. *(Un)*
4. Explain Gandhiji view on Satyagraha. Which quality of Mahatma Gandhi turned the freedom struggle in to a mass movement? *(Un)*
5. Why did Mahatma Gandhi relaunch the civil disobedience movement with treat apprehension? Explain. *(An)*
6. Why was congress reluctant to allow women to hold any position of authority within the organization? How did women participate in Civil disobedience movement? Explain. *(An)*

Case Based Questions (4 M)

Case Based-I

Read the information below and answer the questions that follow:

The movement in the towns The movement started with middle class participation in the cities. Thousands of students left government-controlled schools and colleges, headmasters and teachers and resigned. lawyers gave up their legal notices. The council elections were practices. boycotted in most except Madras, provinces except where the Justice Party, the party of the non

Brahmans, felt that entering the council was one way of gaining some power-something that usually only Brahmans had access to The effects of non-cooperation on the economic front were more dramatic. Foreign goods were boycotted, liquor shops picketed, and foreign cloth burnt in huge bonfires The import of foreign cloth halved between 1921 and 1922, its value dropping from 102 crore to 57 crore. In many places merchants and traders refused to trade in foreign goods or finance foreign trade. As the boycott movement spread and people began discarding imported clothes and wearing only Indian ones, production of Indian textile mills and handlooms went up.

(i) Explain the role of Justice Party in council elections. *(Un)*

(ii) How was the effects of 'non-cooperation on the economic front' dramatic? *(An)*

(iii) Explain the effect of Boycott movement on foreign textile trade. *(Un)***(CBSE, 2020)**

Case Based-II

Read the information below and answer the questions that follow.

Not all social groups were moved by the abstract concept of swaraj. One such group was the nation's 'untouchables', who from around the 1930s had begun to call themselves dalit or oppressed. For long the Congress had ignored the dalits, for fear of offending the sanatanis, the conservative high-caste Hindus. But Mahatma Gandhi declared that Swaraj would not come for a hundred years if untouchability was not eliminated. He called the 'untouchables' harijan, or the children of God, organized Satyagrahs to secure them entry into temples, and access to public wells, tanks, roads and schools. He himself cleaned toilets to dignify the work of the the sweepers, and persuaded upper castes to change their heart and give up 'the sin of untouchability'. But many dalit leaders were keen on a different political solution to the problems of the community. They began organising themselves, demanding reserved seats in educational institutions, and a separate electorate that would choose dalit members for legislative councils. Political empowerment, they believed, would resolve the problems of their social disabilities. Dalit participation in the Civil Disobedience Movement was therefore limited, particularly in the Maharashtra and Nagpur region where their organisation was quite strong.

(*i*) Why weren't the 'untouchables' moved by the abstract concept of Swaraj? ***(An)***

(*ii*) What were the demands of Dalit leaders? ***(Re)***

(*iii*) How did Gandhiji persuade Upper castes to open their hearts for Untouchables? ***(Un)***

Case Based-III

Read the information below and answer the questions that follow.

Tribal peasants interpreted the message of Mahatma Gandhi and the idea of swaraj in yet another way. In the Gudem Hills of Andhra Pradesh, for instance, a militant guerrilla movement spread in the early 1920s – not a form of struggle that the Congress could approve. Here, as in other forest regions, the colonial government had closed large forest areas, preventing people from entering the forests to graze their cattle, or to collect fuelwood and fruits. This enraged the hill people. Not only were their livelihoods affected but they felt that their traditional rights were being denied. When the government began forcing them to contribute begar for road building, the hill people revolted. The person who came to lead them was an interesting figure. Alluri Sitaram Raju claimed that he had a variety of special powers: he could make correct astrological predictions and heal people, and he could survive even bullet shots. Captivated by Raju, the rebels proclaimed that he was an incarnation of God. Raju talked of the greatness of Mahatma Gandhi, said he was inspired by the Non-Cooperation Movement, and persuaded people to wear khadi and give up drinking. But at the same time he asserted that India could be liberated only by the use of force, not non-violence. The Gudem rebels attacked police stations, attempted to kill British officials and carried on guerrilla warfare for achieving swaraj. Raju was captured and executed in 1924, and over time became a folk hero.

(*i*) How did Tribal peasants interpret the message of Mahatma Gandhi? ***(An)***

(*ii*) Why were the Tribal peasants enraged by the British Government? ***(Un)***

(*iii*) Write a short note on Alluri Sitaram Raju. ***(Re)***

Case Based-IV

Read the source given below and answer the questions that follow:

Emboldened with this success, Gandhi ji in 1919 decided to launch a nationwide Satyagraha against the proposed Rowlatt Act (1919). This Act had been hurriedly passed through the Imperial Legislative Council despite the united opposition of the Indian members. It gave the government enormous powers to repress political activities, and allowed detention of political prisoners without trial for two years. Mahatma Gandhi wanted non-violent civil disobedience against such unjust laws, which would start with a hartal on 6 April.

(*i*) Why did the British introduce the Rowlatt Act? ***(Un)***

(*ii*) Examine the effect of this Act on Indians. ***(An)***

(*iii*) How did Mahatma Gandhi respond to the Rowlatt Act? Provide one reason for his reaction. ***(Un)***

Map Based Questions

Find the answers of the following statements and Locate them on the map.

(*i*) The centre/place of calling off/withdrawing of the Non-Cooperation Movement. ***(Re)***

(*ii*) The place is known for the movement of Indigo peasants during the British Period. ***(Re)***

(*iii*) The place where Gandhiji started the Satyagraha in favor of cotton mill workers. ***(Re)***

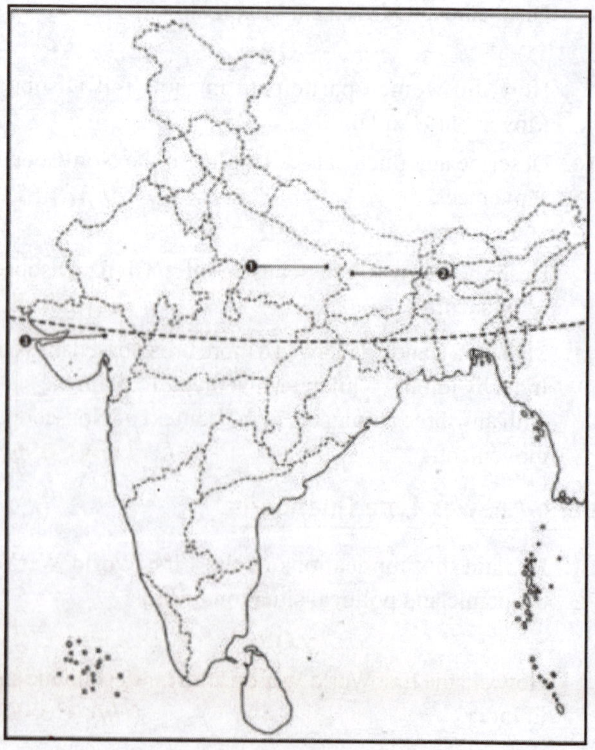

ANSWER KEYS

Multiple Choice Questions

1. (*a*)	**2.** (*a*)	**3.** (*c*)	**4.** (*a*)	**5.** (*b*)	**6.** (*d*)	**7.** (*c*)	**8.** (*c*)	**9.** (*a*)	**10.** (*d*)
11. (*d*)	**12.** (*d*)	**13.** (*c*)	**14.** (*d*)	**15.** (*a*)	**16.** (*b*)	**17.** (*a*)	**18.** (*c*)		

Assertion and Reason

1. (*c*)	**2.** (*a*)	**3.** (*a*)	**4.** (*c*)	**5.** (*d*)	**6.** (*d*)	**7.** (*b*)

HINTS & EXPLANATIONS

Multiple Choice Questions

1. (*a*) Swaraj Party was formed because the members of congress party wanted to return to council politics. It was a political party founded in India in January 1923 by Chittaranjan Das.

2. (*a*) Rowlatt Act

3. (*c*) Caused agricultural prices to fall and exports to decline.

4. (*a*) There was no Indian in the commission, The Simon Body was a legal commission assigned to look into India's constitutional structure and making recommendations for reforms. It was a all-white commission with no Indian representation

5. (*b*) Organising inclusive, nonviolent mass movements to unify different community groups.

6. (*d*) Jawahar Lal Nehru : Oudh Kisan Sabha

7. (*c*) Hind Swaraj was written by Mahatma Gandhi in 1909.

8. (*c*) Rowlatt act (1919) was passed in a hurry by the Imperial Legislative Assembly despite the opposition from the Indian members of the council. It gave boundless powers to the government to crush Indian political activities.

9. (*a*) A, C, D, B

10. (*d*) The Indian Industrial and commercial congress formed in 1920 & the Federation of the Indian chamber of commerce and industries (FICCI) was set up in 1927 led by several Indian industrialists and Indian Merchants.

11. (*d*) People felt to began united by the experience of the linked struggle, a variety of cultural processes through which nationalism captured people's imagination and history, fiction folklore, songs and popular prints and symbols.

12. (*d*) All of the above

13. (*c*) Begar means forced labor that villagers were forced to perform without being compensated.

14. (*d*) It carried on the Non-Cooperation Movement's unresolved issues. It (i) Increased the strength of the National Movement. (ii) Instilled political consciousness and a strong sense of patriotism in the people's thoughts. (iii) Liberate women from their homes and make them equal players in the struggle for freedom.

15. (*a*) Abnindranath Tagore painted the portrait of Bharat Mata imparting knowledge, food, and clothing in 1905.

16. (*b*) Mahatma Gandhi argued in his book Hind Swaraj that British authority was formed in India with the assistance of Indians, and that it had only sustained because of this assistance.

17. (*a*) Awadh Kisan Sabha was led by Jawaharlal Nehru. It was set up in the year 1920.

18. (*c*) The Muslim League was set up on 30th December 1906 by Mohammad Ali Jinnah.

Assertion and Reason

1. (*c*) Assertion is true but reason is false because Kheda Movement was started in Gujarat to support the peasant who could not pay the revenue due to crop failure and plague epidemic.

2. (*a*) Both assertion and reason are true and reason is the correct explanation of assertion. The council elections were boycotted in most provinces except Madras. Justice Party came to power In Madras which was a non Brahmans Party.

3. (*a*) Both assertion and reason are true and reason is the correct explanation of assertion. Because General Dyer wanted to terrorize the revolutionaries.

4. (*c*) assertion is true but reason is false All the protest took place in support after Non Cooperation Movement.

5. (*d*) Only assertion is true but reason is false as All the songs and hymns were composed to create a sense of nationalism among the citizens.

6. (*d*) Assertion is false but reason is true. Because 1920s the Congress came to be more visibly associated with openly Hindu religious nationalist groups like the Hindu Mahasabha. As relations between Hindus and Muslims worsened

7. (*b*) Both assertion and reason are true but reason is not the correct explanation of assertion. Because Gandhi ji believed that separate electorates for dalits would slow down the process of their integration into society.

Subjective Questions

Very Short Answer Type Questions

1. The two main leaders of the Khilafat Committee formed in the year 1919 were Muhammad Ali and Shaukat Ali. *(1 M)*

2. The writer of the book 'Hind Swaraj' is Mahatma Gandhi. This seminal work, published in 1909, outlines his views on Indian self-rule and nonviolent resistance. *(1 M)*

3. The reason because of which Gandhiji started Satyagraha in 1919:
   (*i*) Gandhiji initiated Satyagraha in 1919 to oppose the Rowlatt Act, which allowed detention without trial. *(1 M)*
   (*ii*) The movement marked a shift to non-violent resistance, featuring a nationwide hartal on April 6. *(1 M)*

4. Mahatma Gandhi initiated the Satyagraha movement in 1919 primarily to protest against the Rowlatt Act. This legislation empowered the government to detain people suspected of sedition without trial, significantly curtailing civil liberties and justice. *(2 M)*

5. The resolution of Poorna Swaraj was adopted at the Lahore Congress session in December 1929. *(1 M)*

6. The Simon Commission boycotted in India in these reasons:
   (*i*) The Simon Commission was boycotted due to its all-British composition, excluding Indian representation. *(1 M)*
   (*ii*) This exclusion led to widespread protests from all political parties in India. *(1 M)*

7. The Inland Emigration Act of 1859 trouble some for plantation workers, was;
   (*i*) The Inland Emigration Act of 1859 restricted plantation workers' movement, binding them to tea gardens without permission to leave. *(1 M)*
   (*ii*) This act severely limited their freedom, preventing returns to their villages and maintaining oppressive conditions. *(1 M)*

8. Impacts of the first world war on the Indian economy:
   (*i*) **Increased Defense Expenditures:** Higher taxes and customs duties were introduced to finance war expenses. *(1 M)*
   (*ii*) **Economic Hardship:** Prices of essential goods nearly doubled, severely affecting the living standards of common people. *(1 M)*

Topper's Explanations:

(Q1) The First World War created a new economic and political situation in India.
1. EXPENDITURE: There was a huge increase in the defense expenditure which was financed by war loans and increasing taxes: custom duties were raised and income tax was introduced.
2. PRICES: Prices of goods increased, almost doubling between 1921 and 1928. This caused extreme hardship for the common people.

Short Answer Type Questions

1. Gandhiji decided to launch a nationwide Satyagraha against the proposed Rowlatt Act(1919) because of the following reasons:-
   (*i*) Rowlatt act (1919) was passed in a hurry by the Imperial Legislative Assembly despite the opposition from the Indian members of the council. *(1 M)*
   (*ii*) It gave boundless powers to the government to crush Indian political activities. *(1 M)*
   (*iii*) It allowed detention of political prisoners without any trial for two years on the basis of suspicion. *(1 M)*

2. The idea of satyagraha according to Gandhiji are: **(Any three)**
   (*i*) The concept of satyagraha emphasised the importance of truth and the necessity to seek it out. *(1 M)*
   (*ii*) Satyagraha was a novel method of mass agitation, which stressed the principle of truth, tolerance, non-violence and peaceful protests. *(1 M)*
   (*iii*) Physical force is not required to battle the oppressor for a true cause and strive against injustice. *(1 M)*
   (*iv*) Gandhi believed that the Satyagraha battle will be won and this battle also unite the Indians by this dharma of truth and non-violence. *(1 M)*
   (*v*) Satyagraha was a unique tool to fight injustice. *(1 M)*

3. (*i*) The Khilafat movement (1919–1924), led by Muhammad Ali and Shaukat Ali, was a popular movement against the loss of the Caliph's political powers after Ottoman Turkey's defeat in World War I. *(1 M)*
   (*ii*) Gandhiji backed it because he viewed it as an opportunity to unite Muslims under a unified National Movement. *(1 M)*
   (*iii*) In 1919, the Khilafat Committee was founded to defend Khalifa's political powers, as he was regarded as the spiritual leader of Islam. *(1 M)*

4. New political and economic situation occurred in India after the First World War.
   (*i*) It resulted in a huge rise in defence expenditures, as well as increased customs duties and the introduction of an income tax to fund the war. *(1 M)*
   (*ii*) Forced recruitment in rural areas caused widespread anger. *(1 M)*
   (*iii*) Between 1913 and 1918, the price of necessary commodities doubled leading to extreme hardship for the common people. *(1 M)*

5. Gandhiji proposed that the movement would follow some stages:

(i) Surrender of titles that the government had awarded. *(1 M)*

(ii) Boycott of civil services, army, police, courts and legislative, councils, schools, and foreign goods. *(1 M)*

(iii) In case the government continues to use repressive measures, a full civil disobedience campaign would be launched. *(1 M)*

6. The Rowlatt Act included following provisions:

(i) It gave immense powers to the government to repress political activities. *(1 M)*

(ii) It allowed detention of political prisoners without trial. *(1 M)*

(iii) It was passed by Imperial Legislative Assembly despite the strong opposition of the Indian members. *(1 M)*

7. After reaching India, Mahatma Gandhi successfully launched Satyagraha Movement in various places:

(i) In 1915, he traveled to Champaran in Bihar to inspire the peasants to struggle against the repressive plantation of indigo. *(1 M)*

(ii) In1917, he organized a Satyagraha to support the peasants of the Kheda district of Gujarat who were affected by crop failure and plague epidemic and could not pay the revenue. *(1 M)*

(iii) Mahatma Gandhi visited Ahmedabad in 1918 to organize the Satyagraha Movement among cotton mill laborers. *(1 M)*

8. The three main stages of Non-Cooperation are:

(i) **First Stage:** In protest, Indians who had gained British titles and honours rejected them. *(1 M)*

(ii) **Second Stage:** Large-scale protests, including hartals, were held. All government institutions were boycotted, including schools, colleges, offices, and legislatures. A number of important leaders have been detained and imprisoned. *(1 M)*

(iii) **Third Stage:** Non-payment of taxes was the third and most critical stage of the campaign. People were told not to pay taxes to the government until their demands were realised at a congress session held in Ahmedabad in 1921. *(1 M)*

9. Civil Disobedience Movement saw the participation of Different social groups:

(i) **Poor Peasants:** They wanted unpaid rent to be remitted, joined radical movement led by the socialist and communist. *(1 M)*

(ii) **Rich Peasants:** The Patidar and Jats demanded reduction in tax and participated in the boycott program. *(1 M)*

(iii) **Industrialists and Business Class:** Prominent industrialist like Purshottamdas, G D Birla formed FICCI and Indian Industrial and commercial congress in1920. *(1 M)*

10. The three causes that led to the 'Non-Cooperation Movement' include:

(i) **Opposition to the Rowlatt Act:** Introduced in 1919, this act allowed the government to imprison individuals without trial, which led to widespread anger and protests. *(1 M)*

(ii) **Jallianwala Bagh Massacre:** The brutal killing of unarmed civilians in Amritsar in 1919 fueled outrage against British rule and garnered support for the Non-Cooperation Movement. *(1 M)*

(iii) **Economic Hardships:** Post-World War I, Indians faced severe economic distress due to high taxes and inflation, pushing them to support the movement seeking relief and autonomy. *(1 M)*

OR

The three causes that led to the Civil Disobedience Movement include:

(i) **Salt Tax:** Gandhi's identification of the salt tax as a symbol of British oppression led to the Salt March, demonstrating the movement's capacity to mobilize a wide range of the Indian population against British rule. *(1 M)*

(ii) **Simon Commission:** The appointment of the all-British Simon Commission in 1928 to recommend India's future constitution, without any Indian members, sparked widespread protests and a sense of betrayal among Indians. *(1 M)*

(iii) **Resistance to British Laws and Goods:** The movement expanded to widespread non-compliance with colonial laws, boycotts of foreign goods, refusal to pay taxes, and resignations from government posts, symbolizing a mass defiance against British authority. *(1 M)*

11. Mahatma Gandhi's strategy of launching a broad-based movement by joining the Khilafat Movement in the context of the Non-Cooperation Movement, here are three arguments;

(i) **Unity Across Communities:** Gandhi united Hindus and Muslims by supporting the Khilafat Movement, strengthening the Non-Cooperation Movement. *(1 M)*

(ii) **Shared Grievances:** Both movements opposed British injustices, amplifying their impact. *(1 M)*

(iii) **Increased Participation:** Integrating the Khilafat cause brought significant Muslim support, diversifying the movement's base. *(1 M)*

Topper's Explanations

1. LIMITS: Mahatma Gandhi's Satyagrahas in Champaran, Kheda and Ahmedabad were limited to a particular social group. The Rowlatt Act Satyagraha was also limited to cities and towns. Mahatma Gandhi now felt the need to launch a more broad-based movement in India. But he ~~believe~~ thought that no such movement could be started without the united cooperation of Hindus and Muslims.

KHILAFAT ISSUE: The First World War ended with the defeat of Ottoman Turkey. There were rumours that a harsh peace treaty was going to be imposed on the Ottoman emperor – the spiritual head of the Islamic World – the Khalifa. This enraged the Muslims in India and a Khilafat Committee was formed in Bombay in March 1919 to defend the Khalifa's temporal powers.

UMBRELLA MOVEMENT: A young generation of Muslim leaders like Muhammad Ali and Shaukat Ali, began discussing with Mahatma Gandhi, the possibility of a combined struggle for Khilafat as well as swaraj. Mahatma Gandhi saw this as an opportunity to bring the Muslims under a united umbrella movement.

Long Answer Type Questions

1. The First World War led to a new political and economic situation in India:
   (*i*) Villagers were called upon to supply soldiers, forced recruitment in rural areas caused widespread resentment *(1 M)*
   (*ii*) Prices of essential commodities doubled between 1913 and 1918 leading to extreme hardship to the common people *(1 M)*
   (*iii*) It led to huge increase in defense expenditure, Custom duties were raised, income tax was introduced to finance the war *(1 M)*
   (*iv*) In 1918-19, 1920-21 crops failed in many parts of India resulting in acute food shortage. *(1 M)*
   (*v*) Influenza epidemic spread. According to the census in 1921, 12-13 million people perished due to famines and epidemics. *(1 M)*
2. Impact of Ramesh's Participation in the Non-Cooperation Movement on the Indian Economy;
   (*i*) **Reduction in British Imports:** Ramesh stopped importing British goods, contributing to the broader boycott, which decreased foreign cloth imports significantly from ₹102 crore to ₹57 crore between 1921-1922. *(1 M)*
   (*ii*) **Boost to Local Industry:** By closing his shop selling foreign clothes and relying on local weavers and craftsmen, Ramesh supported the rise in production of Indian textile mills and handlooms. *(1 M)*
   (*iii*) **Economic Self-Reliance:** This shift reduced dependence on British imports, fostering economic self-reliance and increasing demand for indigenous products. *(1 M)*
   (*iv*) **Middle-Class Involvement:** Ramesh's actions reflected the broader involvement of the middle class in the Non-Cooperation Movement, which actively promoted Indian goods. *(1 M)*
   (*v*) **Long-Term Economic Adjustments:** The movement faced challenges, such as the higher cost of khadi, indicating necessary economic adjustments for sustainable change. *(1 M)*
3. Mahatma Gandhi successfully organized Satyagraha movements in various places
   (*i*) In 1916, he travelled to Champaran in Bihar to inspire the peasants to struggle against the oppressive plantation system. *(1 M)*
   (*ii*) Then in 1917, he organized a Satyagraha to support the peasants of the Kheda district of Gujarat. *(1 M)*
   (*iii*) In 1918, he went to Ahmedabad to organize a Satyagraha movement amongst cotton mill workers. *(1 M)*
   (*iv*) In 1919, he decided to launch a nationwide Satyagraha against the proposed Rowlatt Act. *(1 M)*
   (*v*) At the Calcutta session of the Congress in September 1920, he convinced other leaders of the need to start a non-cooperation movement in support of Khilafat as well as for Swaraj. *(1 M)*
4. Satyagraha highlighted the importance of truth and the need to search it out:
   (*i*) It meant that if the cause was just, if the struggle was against injustice, then fighting the oppressor did not require physical force. *(1 M)*
   (*ii*) A satyagrahi could win the conflict via nonviolence without seeking revenge or being violent. *(1 M)*
   (*iii*) This could be achieved by appealing to the oppressor's conscience. *(1 M)*
   (*iv*) Rather than being forced to accept truth via violence, people, especially oppressors, had to be encouraged to see the truth. *(1 M)*
   (*v*) He believed that the nonviolence dharma could bring all Indians together. *(1 M)*
5. Relaunch of Civil Disobedience Movement:
   (*i*) When the Civil Disobedience Movement became violent in locations like Peshawar and Sholapur, Mahatma Gandhi decided to call it off. Gandhiji's call was partly inspired by the British government's harsh response. *(1 M)*
   (*ii*) As Gandhiji returned to India, he discovered a new kind of repression. The new policies of the British government were a main force that made him relaunch the movement. *(1 M)*
   (*iii*) The failure of negotiations at the Round Table Conference in London further aggravated the situation as Gandhiji came back disappointed. *(1 M)*
   (*iv*) Jawaharlal Nehru and Ghaffar Khan were put in jail. *(1 M)*
   (*v*) The government's policies also declared the congress illegal and placed limitations on gatherings, demonstrations, and boycotts. The national crisis eventually pushed Gandhiji to resume the movement, although he did so with caution. *(1 M)*
6. Congress reluctant in the participation of women:
   (*i*) Congress was keen only on the symbolic presence of women within the organization. *(1 M)*

(*ii*) Gandhiji was convinced that it was the duty of women to look after home and hearth, be good mothers and good wives. *(1 M)*

Participation of women in Civil disobedience movement:

(*i*) During Gandhiji salt march, thousands of women came out of their homes to participate in protest marches. *(1 M)*

(*ii*) Women were from high caste families and from rich peasant households participated. *(1 M)*

(*iii*) Moved by Gandhiji's call, they began to see service to nation as a sacred duty of women. *(1 M)*

Case Based Questions

Case Based-I

(*i*) The council elections were not boycotted in Madras where the Justice party was leading .Non Brahmans did not join the non cooperation group, nor it boycotted the elections, which was in favor of the Justice party because earlier only Brahmins had access to the council elections. *(1 M)*

(*ii*) The effects of non-cooperation on the economic front were more dramatic. Foreign goods were boycotted, liquor shops picketed, and foreign cloth burnt in huge bonfires The import of foreign cloth halved between 1921 and 1922, its value dropping from 102 crore to 57 crore. In many places merchants and traders boycotted the foreign goods. *(1 M)*

(*iii*) In many places merchants and traders refused to deal in the foreign goods(clothes).The boycott movement spread and people refused to buy imported clothes and wearing only Indian ones, production of Indian textile mills and handlooms increased. *(2 M)*

Case Based-II

(*i*) For long the Congress had ignored the dalits, for fear of offending the conservative high-caste Hindus therefore 'untouchables' were not moved by the abstract concept of swaraj. *(1 M)*

(*ii*) Dalit leaders started demanding reserved seats in educational institutions and a separate electorate that would choose dalit members for legislative councils. , they believed that political empowerment would resolve the problems of their social disabilities. *(1 M)*

(*iii*) Gandhi ji persuaded Upper castes to open their hearts for Untouchables by calling the 'untouchables' harijan, or the children of God, by organizing Satyagrahs to secure their entry into temples, and by providing them access to public wells, tanks, roads and schools etc. He himself cleaned toilets to dignify the work of the sweepers. *(2 M)*

Case Based-III

(*i*) Tribal peasants of Andhra Pradesh interpreted the message of Mahatma Gandhi in their own way. 'Swaraj' meant the freedom to use forests and forest produce to them. Alluri Sitaram Raju provided the leadership to the tribal movement. *(1 M)*

(*ii*) The Tribal peasants were enraged by the British Government because colonial government had closed large forest areas, prevented people from entering the forests to graze their cattle, or to collect fuelwood and fruits. Their livelihoods were affected. They felt that they are being deprived of their traditional rights. The government began forcing them to contribute 'begar' for road building. This enraged the hill people. *(1 M)*

(*iii*) Alluri Sitaram Raju lead the tribal movements in Andhra Pradesh claimed that he had a variety of special powers, he could make correct astrological predictions and heal people, and he could survive even bullet shots, he was inspired by the Non-Cooperation Movement, and persuaded people to wear khadi and give up drinking. But at the same time he asserted that India could be liberated only by the use of force, not non-violence. *(2 M)*

Case Based-IV

(*i*) One of the primary reasons for the Rowlatt Act was to suppress the growing nationalist movements and unrest in India. The Rowlatt Act gave the colonial authorities all powers to arrest and detain individuals without trial, making it easier to suppress political opposition and prevent further nationalist agitation. *(1 M)*

(*ii*) The Act gave the authorities the power to prohibit public gatherings and censor the press:

This curbed the freedom of speech and assembly, as Indians were no longer free to express their political views, hold public meetings, or publish materials critical of British rule without risking arrest and prosecution. *(1 M)*

(*iii*) Mahatma Gandhi wanted non-violent civil disobedience against such unjust laws, which would start with a hartal on 6 April. Gandhiji in 1919 decided to launch a nationwide satyagraha against the proposed Rowlatt Act (1919). *(2 M)*

Map Based Questions

(*i*) Chauri-Chaura *(1 M)*

(*ii*) Champaran *(1 M)*

(*iii*) Kheda *(1 M)*

❑❑❑

THE MAKING OF A GLOBAL WORLD

3

"Global interconnectedness, fueled by trade, migration, labor, and capital movements, traces back through history. Comprehending these phases is essential for understanding the complexities of today's global interactions and interdependencies."

SYLLABUS & WEIGHTAGE

List of Concept Names	Years					
	2020	2021	2022	2023	2024	2025
The Pre-modern world (Silk Routes Link the World, Food Travels: Spaghetti and Potato, Conquest, Disease and Trade)	1 Q (1 M)	Exam not Conducted	–	–	1 Q (2 M) 1 Q (1 M)	1 Q (1 M)

CONCEPT MAP

To Access One Shot Revision Video Scan This QR Code

The Making of a Global World

Features of Pre-modern World
CBSE 2024, 2020

- Human societies have become steady more interlinked.
- Travellers, Traders, Priest and Pilgrims travelled vast distance.
- Indus Valley civilisation was linked with west Asia.
- Cowries were used as a form of currency.

Important aspect
CBSE 2025, 2024

Conquest, Disease and Trade
CBSE 2025, 2023

- In 16th century, Europe sailors found a sea route to Asia and America.
- The Portugese and Spanish conquest and colonisation of America was under way.
- The most powerful weapon of Spanish conquers, was small pox which they carried to America.

Food Travells

- Traders and Travellers introduced new crops of the land they travelled.
- Potatoes, Soya, Maize, Ground nuts, Tomatoes, Chillies introduced in Europe and Asia after America wad discovered.
- Noodles travelled west from China to become Spaghetti.

Silk Routes
CBSE 2025

- Interconnected modern trade and cultural link between distant parts of the world.
- Most well known silk route connected China to Europe.

1 THE PRE-MODERN WORLD

NCERT Definitions *(Commonly asked in 1 mark)*

- **Globalisation:** It is generally associated with economy as the free movement of capital, ***goods***, ***technology***, ***ideas and people*** across the globe.
- **Silk Routes:** The route taken by traders to carry silk cargoes from ***China*** to the ***West***, which affected cultures of China, Central Asia and the West.
- **Cowries:** ***Seashells*** used as currency, highlighting early forms of economic exchange connecting regions like the Maldives, China, and East Africa.
- **Cultural Exchange:** The movement of religious beliefs, ideas, and cultural practices alongside goods and commodities across trade routes.
- **Christopher Columbus:** His voyages led to the introduction of American food crops like ***potatoes*** and ***tomatoes*** to Europe and Asia, significantly impacting global diets.
- **Irish Potato Famine:** An example of how a reliance on a single crop can lead to disaster, reflecting the importance of agricultural diversity.
- **Conquest and Disease:** How European expansion was facilitated not just by military might but also by the ***spread of diseases*** to which indigenous populations had no immunity.
- **Colonisation of America:** The processes and consequences of European conquests in the ***Americas***, significantly shaping ***global history***.
- **Dissenter:** One who refuses to accept established ***beliefs*** and ***practices***.

Important Facts

01 Since ancient times, human societies have progressively become more interlinked, with ***travelers, traders, and pilgrims*** connecting distant lands.

02 The ***Silk Routes*** connected Asia to Europe and northern Africa, serving not only as trade paths but also as channels of **cultural interaction** from before the Christian era up to the fifteenth century.

03 Coastal trade linking the ***Indus Valley Civilisation*** with present-day West Asia was active around 3000 BCE, suggesting early global economic exchanges.

04 ***Cowries*** from the ***Maldives*** were used as currency and reached as far as ***China*** and ***East Africa***, showing ancient international trade practices.

05 The ***sixteenth century*** saw European sea voyages successfully reaching Asia and crossing to America, significantly shrinking the pre-modern world.

06 ***Smallpox***, brought by Europeans, decimated indigenous American populations, easing the way for conquest due to their lack of immunity.

07 ***Agricultural producers***, especially ***wheat*** and ***cotton growers***, responded to the global market demands, profoundly impacting their societies.

Difference Between

Silk Routes vs Food Travels:		
Aspect	**Silk Routes**	**Food Travels**
Connectivity	Network of trade routes connecting Asia with Europe and Africa.	The exchange of food cultures and crops across continents.
Main Commodities	Primarily used for trading silk, spices, and metals.	Led to the introduction of new foods like potatoes and maize in Europe and Asia.
Cultural Exchange	Facilitated cultural and religious exchanges, spreading Buddhism.	Influenced by explorations like those of Christopher Columbus.
Historical Period	Active from before the Christian era till the 15th century.	Highlighted global cultural contacts even in the pre-modern world.
Economic Empact	Represented the interconnectedness of ancient economies.	Showed how new crops could transform diets and economies.

Myth Buster

- **Myth:** The pre-modern world saw limited intercontinental trade and cultural exchange.

  Fact: As early as 3000 BCE, active coastal trade linked civilizations across continents. The Silk Routes, for example, connected various regions of Asia with Europe and northern Africa, facilitating not only trade but also the exchange of ideas, culture, and inventions long before the modern era.

- **Myth:** Globalization is a modern phenomenon, only emerging in the last 50 years.

  Fact: The roots of globalization extend far back in history. The pre-modern world was already interconnected through trade, migration, and the spread of ideas and diseases. For instance, as early as 3000 BCE, there was active coastal trade linking the Indus Valley civilizations with present-day West Asia.

Mnemonics

Global interconnectedness:

'STRIP'

- S → Silk Routes
- T → Trade
- R → Religious and cultural exchanges
- I → Indus Valley Civilization
- P → Potato and other American food crops

Goods Traded

'SPICE'

- S → Silk
- P → Porcelain
- I → Ivory
- C → Cotton
- E → Exotic spice

COMPETENCY BASED SOLVED EXAMPLES

Scan Me for Detailed Explanations

Multiple Choice Questions

(1 M)

1. **Consider the scenario of a merchant traveling along the Silk Routes during the pre-modern era. This merchant engages with various cultures along the way, trading goods like silk and pottery. How these interactions might contribute to the spread of religious ideas and cultural practices, specifically focusing on Buddhism and Christianity.** ***(Ev)***
   (*a*) The Silk Routes limited cultural interactions to the exchange of goods such as silk and pottery.
   (*b*) The Silk Routes facilitated extensive cultural exchanges, including the spread of religions such as Buddhism and Christianity.
   (*c*) Cultural interactions along the Silk Routes were strictly regulated by the governments of the regions involved.
   (*d*) The Silk Routes were primarily used for political negotiations between empires, with little cultural exchange.

2. **Consider the statements given below and choose the correct answer:** ***(An)*(CBSE APQ, 2023)**
   Statement I: In Globalisation besides the movements of goods, services, investments and technology, there is one more way in which the countries can be connected.
   Statement II: Countries can be connected through the movement of people. between countries.
   (*a*) Statement I and II are correct.
   (*b*) Statement I is correct and II is incorrect.
   (*c*) Statement I is incorrect and II is correct.
   (*d*) Both are incorrect.

3. **The process of integration between different countries is called as _______.** ***(Re)*(CBSE SQP, 2023)**
   (*a*) Privatization (*b*) Globalisation
   (*c*) Liberalization (*d*) Competition

4. **Manaku was a trader from the Indus Valley civilization tasked with establishing a new trade route to East Africa. During his journey, He encounters various traders and learns about different forms of currency used in other civilizations.**
   Which of the following items, carried by you for trade, would be recognised and accepted as a form of currency in the markets of East Africa, based on historical trade practices? ***(Re)***

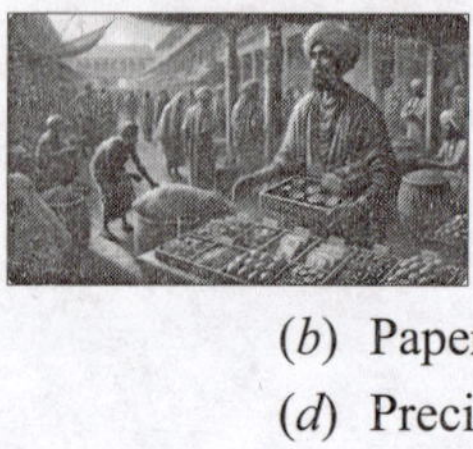

   (*a*) Coins (*b*) Paper money
   (*c*) Cowries (*d*) Precious metals

Assertion and Reason

(1 M)

Direction: The following questions consist of two statements – Assertion (A) and Reason (R). Answer these questions by selecting the appropriate option given below:

(*a*) Both A and R are true, and R is the correct explanation of A.
(*b*) Both A and R are true, but R is not the correct explanation of A.
(*c*) A is true, but R is false.
(*d*) A is false, but R is true.

1. **Assertion (A):** Until the nineteenth century, poverty and hunger were common in Europe.
   Reason (R): Cities were crowded and deadly diseases were widespread. ***(An)***

2. **Assertion (A):** Until well into the eighteenth century, China and India were among the world's richest countries.
   Reason (R): However, from the fifteenth century, China is said to have restricted overseas contacts and retreated into isolation. ***(An)***

3. **Assertion (A):** Spaghetti and potatoes are examples of foods that have traveled across the world.
   Reason (R): Traders and travelers introduced new crops to the lands they traveled, leading to the spread of food items like spaghetti and potatoes. ***(Un)***

Subjective Questions

Very Short Answer Type Questions

(2 M)

1. **How did the 'small pox' prove as the most powerful weapon of the Spanish conquerors in the mid sixteenth century? Explain** ***(Un)*(CBSE, 2023)**

Ans. The most powerful weapon of the Spanish conquerors were diseases like smallpox that they carried with them. Because of their long isolation, America's original inhabitants had no immunity against these diseases that came from Europe. Smallpox proved to be a deadly killer of the native inhabitants. *(2 M)*

2. **The silk routes are a good example of vibrant pre -modern trade and cultural links between distant parts of the world. Substantiate the statement with illustrations.** ***(Un)* (CBSE APQ, 2023)**

OR

"The Silk route was a good example of vibrant pre-modern trade and cultural links between distant parts of the world." Explain the statement with any two examples. ***(Un)* (CBSE, 2024)**

Ans. The name 'silk routes' points to the importance of West-bound Chinese silk cargoes along this route.

Chinese pottery, textiles and spices from India and Southeast Asia also travelled the same route. In return, precious metals – gold and silver – flowed from Europe to Asia. *(2 M)*

3. 'All through history, human societies have become steadily more interlinked.' Justify this statement with illustrations. ***(Un)*(CBSE APQ, 2023)**

Ans. Travellers, traders, priests and pilgrims travelled vast distances for knowledge, opportunity and spiritual fulfilment, or to escape persecution.

They carried with them goods, money, values, skills, ideas, inventions, and even germs and diseases. *(2 M)*

4. "The most powerful weapon of the Spanish conqueror was not a conventional military weapon at all". Justify the above statement by giving two reasons. ***(Ev)*(CBSE SQP, 2023)**

Ans. The Spanish conqueror's most powerful weapon was not a conventional military weapon because;

(*i*) They used germs like smallpox which spread deep into the continent before any European could reach there. *(1 M)*

(*ii*) America's original inhabitants had no immunity against these diseases that came from Europe. *(1 M)*

Short Answer Type Questions (3 M)

1. How had Indian trade been beneficial for the British during the seventeenth century? Explain. ***(Un)*(CBSE, 2020)**

Ans. Indian trade was beneficial for the British during the seventeenth century due to the following reasons:

(*i*) India was a source of raw materials, such as cotton, silk, and spices, which were in high demand in Europe. *(1 M)*

(*ii*) The British established various trading posts and monopolies, such as the East India Company, which helped them control and dominate trade in the region. *(1 M)*

(*iii*) The profits generated from Indian trade helped fuel the Industrial Revolution in Britain. *(1 M)*

2. You are an advisor to a medieval trade guild exploring new buisness opportunities along the Silk Routes. Prepare a detailed proposal highlighting how engaging in trade along these routes can benefit the guild economically and culturally. ***(Ap)***

Ans. Proposal for Engaging in Trade Along the Silk Routes:

(*i*) **Economic Benefits:**

- **Diverse Market Access:** Trading along the Silk Routes will provide access to a wide range of markets from East Asia to Europe, increasing demand for our guild's products. *(1½ M)*

(*ii*) **Cultural Benefits:**

- **Knowledge Exchange:** Interaction with traders from various regions will facilitate the exchange of knowledge, including new technologies, production techniques, and agricultural practices. *(1½ M)*

Long Answer Type Questions (5 M)

1. You are participating in a debate competition representing your school, and the topic is "Factors Influencing the Portuguese and Spanish Conquest of America Beyond Military Superiority." Your task is to present a compelling argument on this topic.Prepare a detailed argument that explain the various factors that influenced the Portuguese and Spanish conquest of America aside from their military firepower. ***(Ev)***

Ans. The various factors that influenced the Portuguese and Spanish conquest of America aside from their military firepower:

(*i*) The Portuguese and Spanish conquest of America was not solely due to superior firepower. *(1 M)*

(*ii*) The most powerful weapon was the germs like smallpox carried by Europeans. *(1 M)*

(*iii*) America's original inhabitants had no immunity to these diseases. *(1 M)*

(*iv*) Smallpox spread rapidly, decimating communities before Europeans arrived. *(1 M)*

(*v*) This massive population decline facilitated easier conquest and colonization by Europeans. *(1 M)*

MISCELLANEOUS EXERCISE

Multiple Choice Questions

(1 M)

1. Tracing the origins of common foods reveals the interconnection of different cultures. Which of the following examples best illustrates how global exploration and cultural exchange influenced culinary traditions? ***(Un)***

   (*a*) Potatoes and tomatoes, originally from the Americas, became staples in European diets after the 16th century.

   (*b*) Wheat, native to the Middle East, became a primary food source in North America by the 20th century.

   (*c*) Rice, a staple in Asia, was introduced to Europe in the Middle Ages and replaced traditional grains.

   (*d*) Corn, originally from Europe, was brought to Africa in the 19th century and became a major part of their diet.

2. Ravi is a young merchant living in the city of Samarkand during the 1st century CE. He has been trading silk and spices with various regions using the Silk Road. One day, he decides to embark on a journey to expand his business further west. As he prepares for his trip, he studies a map detailing the main routes of the Silk Road and the regions it connects. Ravi notices that the Silk Routes were important trade routes in the pre-modern world, connecting different regions. Based on the map he studied, which regions did the Silk Routes primarily connect? ***(Un)***

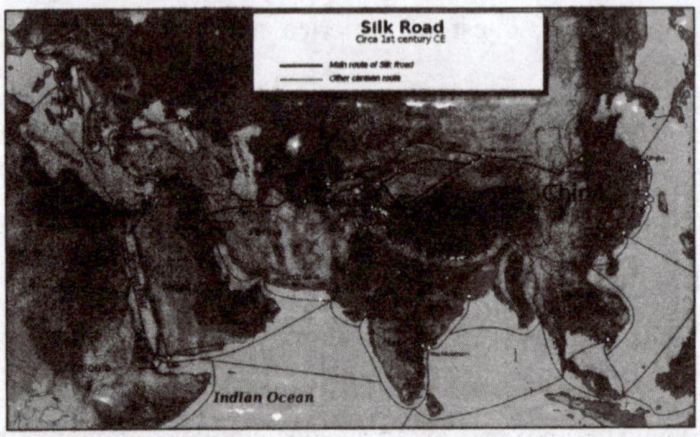

   (*a*) Asia and Europe

   (*b*) Africa and South America

   (*c*) North America and Australia

   (*d*) Antarctica and Asia

3. How did the global transfer of disease in the pre-modern world help in the colonization of the Americas? ***(Un)***

   (*a*) It weakened the immune systems of Native Americans, making them more susceptible to European diseases

   (*b*) It strengthened the immune systems of Native Americans, making them resistant to European diseases

   (*c*) It had no impact on the colonization of the Americas

   (*d*) None of the above

4. Which country introduced 'Corn Laws' to restrict the import of corn? ***(Re)***

   (*a*) France (*b*) Britain

   (*c*) Germany (*d*) Spain

Assertion and Reason

(1 M)

Direction: The following questions consist of two statements – Assertion (A) and Reason (R). Answer these questions by selecting the appropriate option given below:

(*a*) Both A and R are true, and R is the correct explanation of A.

(*b*) Both A and R are true, but R is not the correct explanation of A.

(*c*) A is true, but R is false

(*d*) A is false, but R is true.

1. **Assertion (A):** We consider globalisation as rapid growth of global trade in the last 50 years.

   Reason (R): But globalisation has a long history which emerged with centuries of trade, migration and voyages. ***(Ev)***

2. **Assertion (A):** Indus valley had no active foreign trade.

   Reason (R): For more than a millennium cowries, the currency has been found in China and East Africa. ***(An)***

3. **Assertion (A):** Pre-modern trade and cultural exchange existed between distant regions.

   Reason (R): Chinese silk was transported through silk routes to western world. ***(Un)***

4. **Assertion (A):** The silk routes were regarded as the most important route linking the distant parts of the world.

   Reason (R): Routes existed even before the Christian Era and flourished till the 15th century ***(Re)***

Subjective Questions

Very Short Answer Type Questions

(2 M)

1. "Traders and traveller introduced new crops to lands they travelled." Substantiate this statement with illustrations. ***(Un)* (CBSE SQP, 2023)**

2. "New crops can significantly impact survival and well-being." Provide evidence to support this statement. ***(An)* (CBSE SQP, 2024)**

3. You are part of a cultural delegation visiting cities along the ancient Silk Routes. Prepare a presentation detailing how historical globalisation through these routes influenced the spread of religions such as Christianity, Islam, and Buddhism. ***(Cr)***

4. You are an explorer in the early 16th century who has just arrived in the Americas. How might the arrival of European explorers like yourself impact the native populations? *(An)*

5. Why was the Indian subcontinent central to the flows of the trading network before the sixteenth century ? Explain. *(Un)* (CBSE, 2024)

Short Answer Type Questions (3 M)

1. "The decade of 1830 had brought great economic hardship in Europe". Support the statement with arguments. *(Un)*

2. How were the silk routes a good example of vibrant premodern trade and cultural links? Explain. *(Un)*

3. Explain how the global transfer of disease in the pre-modern world helped in the colonisation of the Americas. *(An)*

Long Answer Type Questions (5 M)

1. "The new crops could make the difference between life and death". Explain the above statement in context of the Irish Potato Famine. *(An)*

2. Ananya, an Indian student in Italy, discovers the connection between Italian pasta and Chinese noodles. Inspired by a discussion with Giuseppe, a local eatery owner, she researches the historical spread of foods like tomatoes, spices, and potatoes, realising how food has facilitated long-distance cultural exchanges. Discuss with examples how food has served as a medium for long-distance cultural exchange and enriched global cultures. *(Un)*

ANSWER KEYS

Multiple Choice Questions

1. *(a)* 2. *(a)* 3. *(a)* 4. *(b)*

Assertion and Reason

1. *(b)* 2. *(d)* 3. *(a)* 4. *(b)*

HINTS & EXPLANATIONS

Multiple Choice Questions

1. *(a)* Potatoes and tomatoes, originally from the Americas, became staples in European diets after the 16th century.
2. *(a)* Asia and Europe
3. *(a)* It weakened the immune systems of Native Americans, making them more susceptible to European diseases.
4. *(b)* Britain

Assertion and Reason

1. *(b)* Both A and R are true, but R is not the correct explanation of A.
2. *(d)* A is false, but R is true.
3. *(a)* Both A and R are true, and R is the correct explanation of A.
4. *(b)* Both A and R are true, but R is not the correct explanation of A.

Subjective Questions

Very Short Answer Type Questions

1. "Traders and traveller introduced new crops to lands they travelled"
   (i) It is believed that noodles travelled West from China to become Spaghetti. Perhaps Arab Traders took Pasta to the fifth century Cecily and Island now in Italy. *(1 M)*
   (ii) Similar food was known in India and Japan, so that the truth about their origins may never be known. *(1 M)*

2. *(i)* Europe's poor began to eat better and live longer with the introduction of the humble potato. *(1 M)*
   (ii) Ireland's poorest peasants became so dependent on potatoes that when disease destroyed the potato crop in the mid-1840s, hundreds of thousands died of starvation. Thus new crops can significantly impact survival and well-being. *(1 M)*

3. Presentation on historical globalisation and the spread of Religions through the silk routes:
   (i) Early Christian missionaries and Muslim preachers traveled along the silk routes to Asia, spreading their religions. *(1 M)*
   (ii) Buddhism from eastern India also spread through the silk routes to several directions, influencing various cultures along the way. *(1 M)*

4. The arrival of European explorers, including myself, brings diseases like smallpox to the Americas, which devastates native populations who lack immunity. This leads to a significant decline in their numbers, making it easier for Europeans to conquer and colonize their lands. *(2 M)*

5. Indian subcontinent was central to the flows of the trading network before the sixteenth century Key reasons include:
   (i) **Geographical Position:** India was situated at the crossroads of major trade routes connecting the East

and the West, facilitating the exchange of goods like spices, textiles, and precious stones. *(1 M)*

(*ii*) **Silk Routes:** India was also connected to the Silk Routes, which were overland trade routes linking Asia to Europe. Goods such as textiles, spices, and other luxury items from India moved across these routes, enriching the global trade network. *(1 M)*

Topper's Explanation

21.(1) Before the european sailors discovered Asia and America, Indian Ocean used to bustle with trade of goods, services, knowledge, customs, traditions etc till the 15th century which made the Indian subcontinent central to the flows of the trading network as it placed a crucial role at the point of intersection

(2) Till the 15th century, India and China were the richest countries which largely dominated the global trade and were pre-eminent in Asian trade of spices, textiles etc. However, The dynamics of global trade changed as the center shifted towards west as China restricted over-seas trade and retracted in isolation.

Short Answer Type Questions

1. The decade of 1830 brought great economic hardship in Europe due to several reasons:

(*i*) **Agricultural Decline:** The 1830s saw reduced agricultural productivity in Europe due to adverse weather and disease outbreaks, leading to food shortages. *(1 M)*

(*ii*) **Manufacturing Slump:** Economic recession globally reduced demand for European manufactured goods, affecting industries and workers. *(1 M)*

(*iii*) **Rising Unemployment:** Rural workers moving to cities due to agricultural issues caused urban unemployment and poverty to spike. *(1 M)*

2. The Silk Routes were a significant example of vibrant premodern trade and cultural links for the following reasons:

(*i*) **Varied Trade Goods:** The Silk Routes facilitated the exchange of diverse products like Chinese silk, Indian textiles, and Southeast Asian spices, connecting multiple civilizations across continents. *(1 M)*

(*ii*) **Cultural Interactions:** Alongside trade, these routes enabled significant cultural exchanges, spreading religions, art, and knowledge across Asia, Africa, and Europe. *(1 M)*

(*iii*) **Economic Integration:** The thriving trade on Silk Routes exemplified early economic globalization, showcasing interdependence and wealth generation across regions. *(1 M)*

3. The global transfer of disease in the pre-modern world played a significant role in the colonization of the Americas in the following ways:

(*i*) Europeans brought diseases like smallpox to the Americas, to which the indigenous populations had no immunity, leading to massive fatalities. *(1 M)*

(*ii*) The significant reduction in the native population due to diseases facilitated easier European colonization, as weakened societies could offer less resistance. *(1 M)*

(*iii*) The depopulation of native communities opened up lands for European settlers, accelerating colonization and resource exploitation. *(1 M)*

Long Answer Type Questions

1. (*i*) **Potatoes Became Important:** Potatoes from America turned into the main food in Ireland, helping everyone eat better. *(1 M)*

(*ii*) **Dependence:** People in Ireland mostly ate potatoes because they were easy to grow and filled them up. *(1 M)*

(*iii*) **Disease Hit:** In the 1840s, a bad disease killed off the potatoes, leaving people without enough food. *(1 M)*

(*iv*) **Consequences:** Because of no potatoes, around a million people died, and another million left Ireland to find a better place to live. *(1 M)*

(*v*) **Impact:** This disaster deeply affected Ireland's population, economy, and fueled anti-British sentiment, influencing Ireland's history and independence movement. *(1 M)*

2. Food has always been a significant medium for long-distance cultural exchange, enriching global cultures in diverse ways:

(*i*) **Spaghetti and Noodles:** It is believed that noodles traveled from China to the West and evolved into spaghetti, highlighting the cultural exchange between Asia and Europe. *(1 M)*

(*ii*) **Tomatoes, Potatoes, and Chillies:** These crops, originally from the Americas, were introduced to Europe and Asia after the discovery of the Americas by Columbus, revolutionizing cuisines worldwide. *(1 M)*

(*iii*) **Spices:** Indian and Southeast Asian spices were traded along the Silk Routes, enhancing European cuisine and leading to further culinary integration and experimentation. *(1 M)*

(*iv*) **Tea and Coffee:** Tea from China and India became staples in British culture, while coffee from Africa and the Middle East spread globally, becoming central to various social rituals. *(1 M)*

(*v*) **Sugar and Chocolate:** Sugarcane, cultivated in the Caribbean and South America, along with cocoa from the Americas, became integral to European confectionery traditions. *(1 M)*

❑❑❑

PRINT CULTURE AND THE MODERN WORLD

4

"In the dance of ink and paper, where each press of the Gutenberg machine whispers revolution, we find the birth of a new world—a world where knowledge spreads faster than ever, bridging minds and crafting the future of societies."

SYLLABUS & WEIGHTAGE

List of Concept Names	Years					
	2020	2021	2022	2023	2024	2025
The first Printed Books and Print Comes to Europe (Print in Japan, Gutenberg and the printing press)	–	Exam not Conducted	–	–	–	1 Q (5 M)
The Print revolution and its impact and the Reading Mania (A New Reading Public, Religious Debates and the fear of Print, Print and Dissent, 'Tremble, therefore, tyrants of the world', Print culture and French Revolution)	–		–	1 Q (3 M)	–	
The Nineteenth Century and India and the World of Print (Children, Women and workers, further innovations, Manuscripts Before the age of print , Print comes to India)	1 Q (1 M) 1 Q (3 M)		–	–	–	1 Q (5 M)
Religious Reform and Public Debates, New Forms of Publication (Women and Print, Print and the poor people)	1 Q (1 M)		–	–	3 Q (1 M) 1 Q (2 M)	1 Q (1 M)

CONCEPT MAP

To Access One Shot Revision Video Scan This QR Code

Print Culture and the Modern World

The First Printed Books and Print Comes to Europe (CBSE 2020)

The First Printed Book

The First Printed Book
- China, Japan and Korea invented the very first type of print technology, which was a hand printing system.

Contribution

China
- Shanghai emerged as the center of the new print culture.
- Merchants utilized printed materials extensively.
- Affluent women started to read and publish their poetry and plays.

Japan
- Buddhist missionaries introduced print technology.
- The "Diamond Sutra" is considered the oldest known book in Japan.
- The printing of visual materials fostered unique publishing practices.

Print Culture in Europe

Origins
- Introduction of Chinese paper to Europe in the 11th century.
- Marco Polo's introduction of woodblock printing from his travels in Asia.
- Italians began producing books with woodblocks, and soon the technology spread to other parts of Europe.

Manuscript Culture
- The production of handwritten manuscripts could not satisfy the ever-increasing demand-for books because:
  - Copying was an expensive, laborious and time-consuming business.
  - Manuscripts were fragile, awkward to handle.

First Printing Press
- Johann Gutenberg developed the printing press for the first time in the 1430's Strasbourg.
- For the printing press, he used an olive press model and molds for the letters of the alphabet.
- The first book he printed with this technology was the Bible.

The Print Revolution & Its Impact and The Reading Mania

The Reading Mania

Increased Literacy Rates
- Literacy rates surged in Europe through the 17th and 18th centuries.
- Churches set up schools in villages, bringing education to a broader audience.

Emergence of New Readers
- The market was flooded with books catering to new demographics, including peasants, artisans, and women.
- Pedlars sold books, reaching audiences beyond the cities and towns.

Tremble, therefore, Tyrants of the World
- People believed books as a means of spreading progress and enlightenment.
- Printing Press believed to be a means of ending despotism.

The Print Revolution and its Impact

A New Reading Public
- Printers began publishing popular ballads and folk tales and such books would be profusely illustrated.
- Printed material was orally transmitted.

Religious Debate
- In 1517, the religious reformer Martin Luther wrote Ninety-Five Theses criticizing many of the practices and rituals of the Roman Catholic Church.
- This led to a division within the Church and the Beginning of the Protestant Reformation.

Fear of Print
- People believed this can lead to the fear of the spread of rebellious and irreligious thoughts.

Print Culture and the Modern World

The Nineteenth Century and India and the World of Print

CBSE 2025

Print in India

CBSE 2020

Manuscripts before the age of Print

- In India, manuscripts were copied on palm leaves or on handmade paper.

Print comes to India

- In the mid-sixteenth century, the printing press first came to Goa with Portuguese missionaries.
- By 1710, Dutch Protestant Missionaries had Printed 32 Tamil texts.
- James Augustus Hicky began to edit ***'Bengal Gazette'*** in 1780.

Important Aspect

Children, Women and Workers

- Children's Press was set up in France in 1857.
- Women became important as readers as well as writers.
- Penny Magazines were especially meant for women, manuals teaching proper behaviors and housekeeping.

Further Innovations

- By mid 19th Century, ***Richard M. Hoe*** perfected the power driven cylindrical press.
- In the late 19th century, an offset press was developed that can print up to six colours at a time.
- By the 20th century, electrically operated presses accelerated printing operations.

Religious Reform and Public Debates, New Forms of Publication and Print and Censorship

CBSE 2025

Religious Reforms and Public Debates

CBSE 2025, 2024, 2020

- Raja Ram Mohan Roy released a publication called ***"Sambad Kaumudi"*** in the year 1821.
- In response, Hindu traditionalists started publishing a paper titled ***"Samachar Chandrika"*** also beginning in 1821.
- Muslim communities produced translations of sacred texts in Persian and Urdu.
- A variety of religious texts began to be widely printed in local languages starting in the 1880s.

New Forms of Publication

CBSE 2023

Rise of the Novel

- The novel as a literary form found its unique place in India, reflecting the diverse experiences and emotions of its people.
- New Literary Forms- lyrics, short stories, essays.

Women & Print

- The prevalence of reading among women rose in middle-class households.
- Rashsundari Devi authored 'Amar Jiban,' recognized as the first extensive autobiography by a woman.
- Tarabai Shinde and Pandita Ramabai penned works that examined women's lives.
- In the early 20th century, journals composed by women began to gain popularity

Print & the Poor People

- In the 19th century, very cheap and small books were brought to markets.
- From the late nineteenth century, issues of caste discrimination began to be written about in many printed tracts and essays.
- A Kanpur mill worker published 'Sacchi Kavitayen' under the name of 'Sudarshan Chakra'.

Print and Censorship

CBSE 2020

Facts

- By the **1820s,** the Calcutta Supreme Court passed certain regulations to control press freedom.
- In **1835,** Thomas Macaulay formulated new rules that restored the earlier freedoms.
- In **1878,** the Vernacular Press Act was passed, modelled on the Irish Press Laws.

1 THE FIRST PRINTED BOOKS AND PRINT COMES TO EUROPE

NCERT Definitions (Commonly asked in 1 mark)

- **Hand Printing:** It developed in ***East Asia,*** involving the creation of books by manually ***rubbing paper*** against inked ***woodblocks***.
- **Accordion Book:** ***A traditional Chinese book*** format resulting from hand printing, characterized by folded and stitched pages due to the inability to print on both sides of the paper.
- **Calligraphy:** The art of beautiful and stylized writing, especially significant before the ***advent of printing***, where texts were ***manually written*** and illustrated with ***high precision***.
- **Vellum:** A high-quality ***parchment*** made from ***animal skin***, used for luxury manuscripts before the widespread use of paper and print.
- **Platen:** In letterpress printing, platen is a board which is pressed onto the back of the paper to get the impression from the type. At one time it used to be a ***wooden board***; later it was made of ***steel***.
- **Compositor:** The person who composes the ***text for printing***.
- **Galley:** ***Metal frame*** in which types are laid and the text composed.

Important Facts

01 The earliest print technology originated in ***China***, ***Japan***, and ***Korea***, featuring a system of hand printing from ***AD 594***.

02 The ***seventeenth century***, print in ***China*** expanded beyond official use to leisure reading.

03 The late ***nineteenth century*** introduced Western mechanical printing, transforming ***Shanghai*** into a print culture hub.

04 Buddhist missionaries from ***China*** introduced ***hand-printing*** technology to ***Japan*** around **(AD 768-770)**.

05 ***Marco Polo*** introduced ***woodblock printing*** technology to Italy from China in **1295**, facilitating the spread of book production across Europe.

06 The demand for books led to the widespread use of ***woodblock printing*** for texts and illustrations, surpassing the capabilities of handwritten manuscript production by the early ***fifteenth century***.

07 ***Gutenberg*** used his skills as a goldsmith and his knowledge of presses to create the first printing press by **1448**, and he printed the first ***Bible*** with it.

08 After ***Gutenberg's*** invention, lots of printing presses started up all over Europe between **1450** and **1550**, making many more books.

09 This technological advancement resulted in a print revolution, with **20 *million*** copies of printed books in the late ***fifteenth century*** and about **200 *million*** by the ***sixteenth century***.

Important Personalities

Marco Polo: An explorer who returned to Italy after years of exploration in China and brought back with him the knowledge of woodblock printing.

Johann Gutenberg: Gutenberg was the son of a merchant and grew up on a large agricultural estate. Developed the first-known printing press in the 1430s in Strasbourg, Germany, and printed the Bible, marking the start of the print revolution in Europe.

Important Dates

- **AD 594:** Books in China were printed by rubbing paper against the inked surface of woodblocks.
- **AD 768-770:** Buddhist missionaries from China introduced hand-printing technology into Japan.
- **11th century:** Chinese paper reached Europe via the Silk Route.
- **1295:** Marco Polo returned to Italy from China, bringing with him the knowledge of woodblock printing, which began to spread across Europe.
- **1430s:** Johann Gutenberg developed the first-known printing press in Strasbourg, Germany.

Difference Between

Hand Printing Vs. Mechanical Printing

Aspect	Hand Printing (Before 15th Century)	Mechanical Printing (After 15th Century)
Origin	Developed in China, Japan, and Korea.	Invented by Johann Gutenberg in Germany.
Technique	Involved rubbing paper against inked woodblocks.	Utilized movable metal types and printing presses.
Production Speed	Slow, labor-intensive process.	Much faster, enabling mass production.
Cost	Expensive and accessible to a few.	Reduced cost, making books more accessible.
Readership	Limited to elites and scholars.	Expanded to include a wider public, fostering literacy.

Myth Buster

- **Myth:** The printing press was a European invention that originated without any foreign influence.

  Fact: The earliest kind of print technology was developed in China, Japan, and Korea, well before it appeared in Europe. Marco Polo, upon returning to Italy from China, brought knowledge of woodblock printing to Europe, indicating the influence of Asian printing technology on Europe.

Mnemonics

The manual technique of printing used in ancient times:

"HAND"

- **H** – Hand Printing
- **A** – Accordion
- **N** – New Technology from East Asia
- **D** – Development in China, Japan, Korea

To remember the sequence and significance of how Chinese paper reached Europe in the 11th century.

"PAPER"

- **P** – Paper reaches Europe
- **A** – Arrives in the 11th Century
- **P** – Polo brings woodblock
- **E** – Europe learns printing
- **R** – Rises in book production

COMPETENCY BASED SOLVED EXAMPLES

Scan Me for Detailed Explanations

Multiple Choice Questions

(1 M)

1. **Given that Western printing techniques and mechanical presses were introduced to China in the late nineteenth century, what would be a possible solution to improve the efficiency of book production?** *(Ap)*

   (*a*) Continue using hand printing
   (*b*) Use cheaper quality paper
   (*c*) Adopt Western printing techniques and mechanical presses
   (*d*) Reduce the number of books printed

2. **How were books printed in China from AD 594 onwards?** *(Re)*

   (*a*) By using metal type for printing
   (*b*) By hand-printing using woodblocks
   (*c*) By using mechanical presses
   (*d*) By using digital printing technology

3. **During the seventeenth century, China experienced significant cultural and social transformations. As urban centers flourished, there was a remarkable diversification in the use of print technology. This period**

saw a shift from the traditional usage of print for official and scholarly purposes to a more widespread adoption across various aspects of daily life.What led to the diversification of print use in China in the seventeenth century? *(An)*

(*a*) Urban culture blooming
(*b*) Western printing techniques
(*c*) Increase in trade information
(*d*) Introduction of civil service examinations

4. **In the late 19th century, Western printing techniques and mechanical presses were imported into China as Western powers established their outposts. This period saw the transformation of cities like Shanghai into hubs of the new print culture, catering to the needs of Western-style schools and institutions.**

Consider the following statements:

Statement I: Western printing techniques and mechanical presses were imported in the late 19th century as Western powers established their outposts in China.

Statement II: Beijing became the hub of the new print culture, catering to Western-style schools.

Which of the following options is correct? *(Ev)*

(*a*) Statement I is correct and II is incorrect.
(*b*) Statement I is incorrect and II is correct.
(*c*) Both I and II are incorrect.
(*d*) Both I and II are correct.

5. **What led to the diversification of print use in China in the seventeenth century?** *(An)*

(*a*) Urban culture blooming
(*b*) Western printing techniques
(*c*) Increase in trade information
(*d*) Introduction of civil service examinations

Assertion and Reason

(1 M)

Direction: The following questions consist of two statements – Assertion (A) and Reason (R). Answer these questions by selecting the appropriate option given below:

(*a*) Both A and R are true, and R is the correct explanation of A.
(*b*) Both A and R are true, but R is not the correct explanation of A.
(*c*) A is true, but R is false
(*d*) A is false, but R is true.

1. **Assertion (A):** By the 17th century, the use of print diversified in China because of a blooming urban culture.

Reason (R): The imperial state in China was the major producers of printed materials. *(An)*

2. **Johann Gutenberg invented the printing press in the mid-15th century. This invention drastically changed the landscape of book production. Before the printing press, books were painstakingly copied by hand, a process that was time-consuming and expensive. The printing press allowed for the mass production of books, making them more accessible and affordable to the general public. This led to an increase in literacy rates and the spread of new ideas.**

Assertion (A): Gutenberg's printing press revolutionized book production in Europe.

Reason (R): The printing press allowed for faster and more efficient production compared to handwritten manuscripts. *(Un)*

3. **Assertion (A):** The printing press had a greater impact on the dissemination of knowledge than hand printing.

Reason (R): The printing press not allowed for the mass production of books, making them more accessible to a larger audience. *(Ev)*

Subjective Questions

Very Short Answer Type Questions

(1 or 2 M)

1. **You are an exchange student in Japan attending a seminar on cultural history. The speaker discusses the introduction of hand-printing technology by Buddhist missionaries in the 8th century. They invite participants to share their thoughts on how this technology might have influenced Japanese society.** *(Cr)*

Ans. The introduction of hand-printing technology by Buddhist missionaries in the 8th century significantly influenced Japanese society by:

(*i*) **Cultural and Educational Spread:** Facilitating the dissemination of religious texts and educational materials, thus enhancing literacy and cultural development. *(1 M)*

(*ii*) **Artistic Development:** Promoting the creation and distribution of illustrated manuscripts and prints, which enriched Japanese art and literature. *(1 M)*

2. **Who is credited with inventing the printing press?** *(Re)*

Ans. Inventor of the Printing Press: Johann Gutenberg, a German craftsman and inventor, is credited with the invention of the printing press in the 1430s. *(1 M)*

Development Location: The printing press was developed in Strasbourg, Germany. *(1 M)*

3. **What impact did mechanical printing have on book production in Europe?** *(Un)*

Ans. The impact of mechanical printing on book production in Europe:

(*i*) Mechanical printing, starting with Gutenberg's press in the 1430s, significantly increased book production compared to hand-copied texts. *(1 M)*

(*ii*) The cost and time of book production dropped, and accessibility increased, leading to a flood of books and the growth of a new reading public. *(1 M)*

4. **How had hand printing technology been introduced in Japan?** ***(Re)*(CBSE, 2019)**

Ans. Around 768–770 AD, Chinese Buddhist missionaries introduced hand printing to Japan. *(1 M)*

5. **Why was printing of textbooks sponsored by the Imperial State in China?** ***(Un)*(CBSE, 2019)**

Ans. The printing of textbooks was sponsored by the Imperial State in China to promote education and literacy among the population, as well as to spread the ideas of Confucianism and loyalty to the emperor. *(1 M)*

Short Answer Type Questions (3 M)

1. **How had the Imperial State in China been the major producer of printed material for a long time? Explain with examples.** ***(Un)* (CBSE, 2019)**

Ans. The Imperial State in China as a major producer of printed material with example as follows;

(*i*) Starting AD 594, China's major print production involved paper rubbed on inked woodblocks, driven by bureaucratic needs. *(1 M)*

(*ii*) The Imperial State sponsored vast textbook printing for civil service exams, expanding with the 16th-century candidate surge. *(1 M)*

(*iii*) By the 17th century, China's urban cultural growth led to print's diversification, making reading a widespread leisure pursuit. *(1 M)*

2. **'By the seventeenth century, as urban culture bloomed in China, the uses of print diversified'. Explain the statement by giving suitable examples.** ***(An)*(CBSE SQP, 2024)**

Ans. (*i*) Print was no longer used just by scholar officials. Merchants used print in their everyday life, as they collected trade information. *(1 M)*

(*ii*) Reading increasingly became a leisure activity. The new readership preferred fictional narratives, poetry, autobiographies, anthologies of literary masterpieces, and romantic plays. *(1 M)*

(*iii*) Rich women began to read, and many women began publishing their poetry and plays. Wives of scholar-officials published their works and courtesans wrote about their lives. *(1 M)*

3. **As a student in pre-colonial India, you learn from beautifully illustrated and meticulously written manuscripts on palm leaves and handmade paper. However, you notice they are fragile, expensive, and accessible only to the wealthy. Based on your experiences as a student in pre-colonial India, explain the characteristics and limitations of handwritten manuscripts before the introduction of printing.** ***(Un)***

Ans. Characteristics:

(*i*) **Material and Craftsmanship:** Made from palm leaves and handmade paper, featuring intricate calligraphy and illustrations. *(1 M)*

(*ii*) **Languages:** Written in Sanskrit, Arabic, and Persian, covering religious texts, poetry, and scientific treatises. *(1 M)*

(*iii*) **Limitations:** Fragile, expensive, and accessible mainly to the wealthy; few villagers could read them, relying on teachers to read aloud. *(1 M)*

Long Answer Type Questions (5 M)

1. **Discuss the impact of print technology on society and culture in China during the seventeenth century.** ***(An)***

Ans. During the seventeenth century in China, print technology had a significant impact on society and culture:

(*i*) The uses of print diversified beyond scholar-officials to encompass a broader readership. Merchants started using print to collect trade information, and reading became a popular leisure activity. *(1 M)*

(*ii*) The new readership preferred fictional narratives, poetry, autobiographies, anthologies of literary masterpieces, and romantic plays. *(1 M)*

(*iii*) Women, including rich women, wives of scholar officials, and courtesans, began reading and publishing their works. *(1 M)*

(*iv*) This new reading culture was accompanied by a shift from hand printing to mechanical printing, with Western printing techniques and mechanical presses being imported from the West. *(1 M)*

(*v*) This led to the establishment of Shanghai as the hub of the new print culture, catering to Western-style schools. *(1 M)*

2. **Compare the early forms of print technology in China, Japan, and Europe.** ***(An)***

Ans. Comparison the early forms of print technology in China, Japan, and Europe:

Region	China	Japan	Europe	Mark
Start of Print Technology	AD 594	Around AD 768-770	11th century (paper arrival); 1430s (movable type)	*(1 M)*
Primary Technology	Woodblock printing	Woodblock printing	Gutenberg Press with movable type	*(1 M)*
Key Development	Accordion books	Buddhist scriptures	Mass production of texts	*(1 M)*
Notable Publications	Buddhist texts, government documents	Diamond Sutra (AD 868)	Gutenberg Bible	*(1 M)*
Cultural Impact	Used for bureau-cratic and educational purposes	Enhanced religious and cultural dissemination	Revolutionised access to printed materials, boosting literacy and learning	*(1 M)*

2 THE PRINT REVOLUTION AND ITS IMPACT AND THE READING MANIA

NCERT Definitions *(Commonly asked in 1 mark)*

- **Ballad:** A historical account or ***folk tale*** in verse, usually ***sung*** or ***recited***.
- **Taverns:** Places where people gathered to ***drink alcohol***, to be ***served food***, and to meet friends and exchange news.
- **Protestant Reformation:** A ***sixteenth-century*** movement to reform the ***Catholic Church*** dominated by Rome. Martin Luther was one of the main Protestant reformers. Several traditions of anti-Catholic Christianity developed out of the movement.
- **Inquisition:** A former ***Roman Catholic court*** for identifying and punishing ***heretics***.
- **Heretical:** Beliefs which do not follow the accepted teachings of the ***Church***. In medieval times, heresy was seen as a threat to the right of the Church to decide on what should be believed and what should not. Heretical beliefs were severely punished.
- **Satiety:** The state of being fulfilled much beyond the point of satisfaction.
- **Seditious:** ***Action, speech or writing*** that is seen as opposing the government
- **Denominations:** Sub groups within a ***religion***.
- **Almanac:** An annual publication giving ***astronomical data***, information about the movements of the sun and moon, timing of full tides and eclipses, and much else that was of importance in the everyday life of people.
- **Chapbook:** A term used to describe ***pocket sized books*** that are sold by travelling pedlars called ***chapmen***. These became popular from the time of the sixteenth-century print revolution.
- **Despotism:** A system of governance in which absolute power is exercised by an individual, unregulated by ***legal*** and ***constitutional checks***.

Important Facts

01 The printing press made books ***cheaper*** and easier to make, so more people could buy and read them, creating a big group of new readers.

02 ***Printers*** published stories and songs that people already liked, adding pictures to them, so even those who couldn't read could still enjoy the stories, mixing the old way of sharing stories by talking with the new way of reading from books.

03 Print made it ***easy*** for people, including those who challenged the status quo, to share their ideas widely and start debates.

04 ***Martin Luther's*** printed writings in 1517 criticized the Catholic Church and started a big change in the church known as the Protestant Reformation.

05 The ***Catholic Church*** started to strictly control books and created a list of banned books in **1558** because they were worried about how people's personal interpretations could challenge their teachings.

06 By the late **18th *century***, literacy rates in some parts of Europe were between **60% and 80%.**

07 Affordable books, like ***penny chapbooks*** in England and ***"Bibliothèque Bleue"*** in France, were sold, so even poor people could buy them.

08 ***Newspapers*** and ***journals*** were important for spreading information about wars, trade, and events in other regions.

Important Dates

- **1517:** Martin Luther wrote Ninety Five Theses.

Difference Between

Impact on Religion Vs. Impact on Politics

Aspect	Impact on Religion	Impact on Politics
Spread of Texts	Facilitated the spread of religious texts and reform ideas.	Enabled the dissemination of political thoughts and ideologies.
Influence on Debates	Contributed to the Protestant Reformation and other religious debates.	Supported the growth of nationalism and democratic ideas.
Personal Interpretation	Allowed for personal interpretation of religious texts.	Promoted public participation in political discourse.
Encouraging Literacy	Encouraged literacy with religious motivations.	Literacy driven by political awareness and the desire for participation.
Propagation of Views	Diverse religious views were more easily propagated.	Unified political movements across regions through shared texts.

Myth Buster

- **Myth:** Print Culture Only Benefited the Elite.

  Fact: While initially print culture was more accessible to the elite due to literacy rates, it rapidly expanded to include broader segments of society. The print revolution made books cheaper, allowing a wider public to access reading material. This democratized knowledge and fostered a more literate society.
- **Myth:** Print Culture Only Fostered Serious Literature and Religious Texts

  Fact: While religious texts and serious literature benefited from print, the print revolution also gave rise to diverse forms of popular literature. This included almanacs, folk tales, and later, newspapers and journals that blended information with entertainment, significantly enriching the cultural landscape.

Mnemonics

The effects of World War I in India:
"BROAD"

B – **B**ooks reach wider sections
R – **R**ebellious fears arise
O – **O**rally transmitted tales
A – **A**rt illustrated books
D – **D**istribution widens

For remembering the key elements of how books were sold:
"PIPED"

P – **P**edlars employed
I – **I**deas widely published
P – **P**hilosophers' and scientists' works
E – **E**mployed by booksellers
D – **D**issemination through peddlers

Scan Me for Detailed Explanations

COMPETENCY BASED SOLVED EXAMPLES

Multiple Choice Questions

(1 M)

1. **Sarah, a young scholar in 16th-century Europe, has just come across a pamphlet criticizing the Church's practices. Inspired, she prints her own thoughts and distributes them, leading to widespread debate in her town. Her actions catch the attention of the local authorities, who are divided on whether to suppress this new form of expression or embrace it. Which of the following best evaluates the impact of Sarah's actions on her society?** ***(Ev)***

   (*a*) Authorities suppressed all printed materials.

   (*b*) It fostered debate and critical thinking.

   (*c*) It had little impact due to illiteracy.

   (*d*) It led to unrestricted printing and freedom.

2. **You are a member of the clergy in early modern Europe, witnessing the rapid spread of printed books. While some view this as a positive development, you and others in your community have concerns about the potential impacts of this new technology. Why are you and some others apprehensive about the widespread circulation of printed books in early modern Europe?** ***(An)***

   (*a*) They feared books would become too expensive.

   (*b*) They worried it would lead to a loss of traditional hand-copied manuscripts.

   (*c*) They feared it could spread rebellious and irreligious thoughts.

   (*d*) They believed it would reduce the demand for religious texts

3. **How did publishers persuade the common people to welcome printed books?** ***(Re)***

   (*a*) By reducing the cost of books

   (*b*) By distributing books for free

   (*c*) By organizing reading competitions

   (*d*) By publishing popular ballads and folk tales

4. **What was one of the fears associated with the wide circulation of printed books?** ***(An)***

   (*a*) Loss of religious authority

   (*b*) Increased literacy rates

   (*c*) Decline in trade and commerce

   (*d*) Rise of agricultural innovations

5. **Who wrote the Ninety Five Theses, which challenged the Roman Catholic Church and led to the Protestant Reformation?** *(An)*

(*a*) Isaac Newton (*b*) Thomas Paine
(*c*) Martin Luther (*d*) Voltaire

6. **What was the impact of print culture on literacy rates in Europe?** *(Re)*

(*a*) Literacy rates declined significantly
(*b*) Literacy rates remained unchanged
(*c*) Literacy rates increased in most parts of Europe
(*d*) Literacy rates fluctuated unpredictably

7. **You are an advisor to a European monarch in the late 18th century. With the rise of printed literature spreading revolutionary ideas, there is growing concern about maintaining social order and the authority of the state. The monarch seeks your advice on measures to control the influence of printed literature. What measures could authorities take to control the influence of printed literature?** *(Cr)*

(*a*) Promote more printing of revolutionary literature.
(*b*) Ban all printed materials.
(*c*) Maintain an index of prohibited books and impose controls on publishers.
(*d*) Encourage public debates on printed materials.

8. **Who said, "The printing press is the most powerful engine of progress and public opinion is the force that will sweep despotism away"?** *(Re)*

(*a*) Johann Gutenberg
(*b*) Martin Luther
(*c*) Louis-Sebastien Mercier
(*d*) Voltaire

Assertion and Reason

(1 M)

Direction: The following questions consist of two statements – Assertion (A) and Reason (R). Answer these questions by selecting the appropriate option given below:

(*a*) Both A and R are true, and R is the correct explanation of A.
(*b*) Both A and R are true, but R is not the correct explanation of A.
(*c*) A is true, but R is false
(*d*) A is false, but R is true.

1. **Assertion (A):** Access to books created a new culture of reading.

   Reason (R): Books were not only expensive but also not produced in sufficient numbers before the age of print. *(An)*

2. **Assertion (A):** Earlier, reading was restricted to the elites.

   Reason (R): Common people relied on an oral culture and did not have access to books. *(Ev)*

3. **Assertion (A):** Knowledge was transferred orally in the pre-print era.

   Reason (R): People heard sacred texts read out, ballads recited, and folk tales narrated collectively. *(An)*

Subjective Questions

Very Short Answer Type Questions

(2 M)

1. **How did the print revolution change the accessibility of books?** *(Un)*

Ans. The print revolution changed the accessibility of books as these aspect:

(*i*) **Reduction in Costs:** The print revolution significantly reduced the cost of producing books, making them financially accessible to a broader segment of society. *(1 M)*

(*ii*) **Increase in Production:** With the introduction of mechanical printing, notably the Gutenberg press, the volume of books produced increased exponentially. *(1 M)*

2. **What impact did the print revolution have on literacy rates?** *(Un)*

Ans. The impact of the print revolution on literacy rates:

(*i*) **Increased Book Availability:** The print revolution significantly increased the availability of books due to the rise in production volumes, making educational materials more accessible to the public. *(1 M)*

(*ii*) **Lowered Costs:** As the cost of books decreased, more individuals could afford to purchase them, facilitating self-education and learning at home. *(1 M)*

3. **Why were religious authorities and monarchs apprehensive about print?** *(Un)*

Ans. Religious authorities and monarchs;

(*i*) **Religious authorities:** Religious leaders and monarchs worried that print could easily spread rebellious and irreligious ideas, undermining their authority. *(1 M)*

(*ii*) **Historical Examples:** Events like the Protestant Reformation, fueled by widespread printed criticisms, showcased print's potential to challenge established powers. *(1 M)*

Short Answer Type Questions

(3 M)

1. **How had the printing press created a new culture of reading in Europe? Explain with examples.** *(Un)(CBSE, 2019)*

Ans. The printing press created a new culture of reading in Europe by:

(*i*) Making books more affordable, leading to the growth of literacy. *(1 M)*

(*ii*) Encouraging the spread of new ideas and the growth of knowledge. *(1 M)*

(*iii*) Facilitating the dissemination of information, leading to the growth of journalism. *(1 M)*

2. Thomas visits a city to observe Gutenberg's mechanical printing press. He notes the differences in the book production process, the cost, and the accessibility of books compared to traditional hand-copying methods. Based on Thomas's observations,Discuss the potential changes in the cost and accessibility of books due to the printing press. *(Ev)*

Ans. The potential changes in the cost and accessibility of books due to the printing press as follows:

(i) **Reduced Cost of Production:** The Gutenberg press significantly reduced the time and labor needed to produce books, lowering the cost per book compared to traditional hand-copying methods. *(1 M)*

(ii) **Increased Book Production:** The efficiency of the printing press allowed for the mass production of books. For instance, by the second half of the 15th century, 20 million copies of printed books were available, drastically increasing the supply. *(1 M)*

(iii) **Wider Accessibility:** Books became more affordable and widely available, enabling more people, including commoners and students, to access and own books. *(1 M)*

3. How did the print revolution influence the development of public opinion? How did the print revolution impact scientific progress? *(An)*

Ans. Influence on Public Opinion:

- The print revolution provided a platform for diverse voices, enabling the dissemination of different perspectives and ideas, essential for shaping public opinion. *(1½ M)*

Impact on Scientific Progress:

- Print allowed for the wider distribution of scientific knowledge, making it accessible to a larger audience beyond the elite. *(1½ M)*

Long Answer Type Questions (5 M)

1. Discuss the fears and criticisms surrounding the print revolution, particularly from religious authorities and monarchs. *(An)*

Ans. Fears and criticisms surrounding the print revolution, particularly from religious authorities and monarchs as follows:

(i) **Martin Luther's Actions:** Luther's posting of the Ninety-Five Theses criticized church practices, marking a significant moment in religious reforms. *(1 M)*

(ii) **Widespread Impact:** The printing press enabled Luther's ideas to spread quickly, leading to major divisions within the Church and sparking the Protestant Reformation. *(1 M)*

(iii) **Leaders' Concerns:** Religious authorities and monarchs were worried that printing could spread challenging ideas that threatened their control. *(1 M)*

(iv) **Response to Threat:** Their fear led to stringent measures to control the printing of materials considered dangerous or rebellious. *(1 M)*

(v) **Censorship Implemented:** This resulted in strict regulations over what could be published, including the creation of an Index of Prohibited Books to suppress dissenting views. *(1 M)*

2. How did the print revolution shape the intellectual and cultural climate of the 18th century, particularly in relation to the French Revolution? Also Examine the impact of the print revolution on literacy rates and the proliferation of reading material in early modern Europe. *(An)*

Ans. The impact of the print revolution on the 18th-century cultural climate and literacy:

(i) **Enlightenment Spread:** The print revolution spread Enlightenment ideas that encouraged questioning traditional norms and authorities, setting the stage for the French Revolution. *(1 M)*

(ii) **Revolutionary Influence:** Printed materials, like pamphlets and satires, criticized the monarchy and fueled public desire for change during the French Revolution. *(1 M)*

(iii) **Boost in Literacy:** Cheaper and more accessible books from the print revolution significantly raised literacy rates across Europe. *(1 M)*

(iv) **Diverse Materials:** A wider range of reading materials became available, including almanacs and newspapers, meeting the interests of an increasingly literate population. *(1 M)*

(v) **Educational Growth:** More schools used printed books to educate the masses, further enhancing literacy and enabling broader discussions and engagement with new ideas. *(1 M)*

3 THE NINETEENTH CENTURY AND INDIA AND THE WORLD OF PRINT

NCERT Definitions (Commonly asked in 1 mark)

- **Mass Literacy:** The significant increase in the ***ability to read*** and write across various segments of ***society*** during the **19th *century***, driven by educational reforms and the increased availability of printed materials.
- **Manuscripts: *Handwritten texts*** prevalent in India before the introduction of printing technology, copied on palm leaves or paper, often beautifully illustrated.
- **Bengal Gazette:** Also known as ***Hicky's Gazette***, the first newspaper printed in India by James Augustus Hickey in **1780**, marking the beginning of print journalism in India.
- **Vernacular Press Act (1878):** A legislation enacted by the British colonial government to curtail the freedom of the Indian press, especially those ***vernacular papers*** that were critical of ***colonial rule***.

Important Facts

01 Compulsory education laws in the late **19th *century*** made children a significant group of readers, increasing the demand for school textbooks and children's literature.

02 A specialized children's press was established in ***France*** in **1857**, indicating the start of targeted literature for young readers, including the publication of fairy tales and folk tales.

03 **"*Penny Magazines*"** targeted women and included manuals for proper behavior and housekeeping.

04 Lending libraries in **19th-*century*** England became educational platforms for white-collar workers, artisans, and lower-middle-class individuals.

05 In the ***mid*-19th *century*, *Richard M. Hoe*** perfected the power-driven cylindrical press.

06 The late **19th *century*** saw the development of the offset press capable of printing up to ***six colors*** simultaneously.

07 Electrically operated presses in the **20th *century*** accelerated printing processes.

08 Prior to the advent of printing, Indian manuscripts were transcribed onto ***palm leaves*** or crafted from ***handmade paper***.

09 In the **1500s**, ***Portuguese missionaries*** introduced the printing press to ***Goa***, marking the beginning of print in India.

10 By the year **1674**, approximately fifty books had been published in the ***Konkani*** and ***Kannada*** languages.

11 The year **1579** saw Catholic priests in Cochin produce the inaugural Tamil book.

12 In **1713**, Catholic priests were responsible for printing the earliest Malayalam book.

13 Protestant missionaries from the Netherlands had translated and printed thirty-two Tamil texts by the year **1710**.

14 The ***Bengal Gazette***, a weekly publication, was launched by ***James Augustus Hickey*** in **1780**.

Difference Between

Impact on Women Vs. Impact on Workers

Aspect	Impact on Women	Impact on Workers
Access to Education	Enabled access to education and literacy, empowering women.	Provided political and social awareness, uniting workers against exploitation.
Platform for Expression	Women authors and poets found a platform for their writings.	Workers used print to share their experiences and organize movements.
Thematic Publications	Journals and magazines targeted at women discussed issues like education and reform.	Cheap books and pamphlets made education and self-improvement accessible to workers.
Challenging Traditional Roles	Challenged traditional roles and advocated for women's rights.	Highlighted the plight of workers and the need for labor rights.
Growth of Readership	Contributed to the growth of a female reading public.	Fostered a culture of reading and discussion among the working class.

Myth Buster

- **Myth:** Print Culture Was Uniform Across India.
  Fact: The impact and development of print culture varied significantly across different regions of India. Factors such as language, colonial policies, socio-economic conditions, and the efforts of missionaries and reformers influenced how print culture evolved in different areas.
- **Myth:** Print Culture Automatically Led to Increased Literacy Rates Across India.
  Fact: The spread of print culture created opportunities for increased literacy, but actual literacy rates varied widely. Factors such as gender, caste, economic status, and regional disparities influenced who had access to education and printed materials.

Mnemonics

To remember the progression of the printing press in India:

"GANGA"

Goa receives the first printing press

Arrival with Portuguese missionaries

New technology for India

Gazette, the Bengal Gazette starts

Augustus Hicky begins editing

Scan Me for Detailed Explanations

COMPETENCY BASED SOLVED EXAMPLES

Multiple Choice Questions

(1 M)

1. **Consider the statements given below and choose the correct answer.** ***(Ev)*(CBSE SQP, 2023)**

   Statement-I: From 1780, James Augustus Hickey began to edit the Bengal Gazette, a weekly magazine that described itself as 'a commercial paper open to all, but influenced by none.'

   Statement-II: Hickey also published a lot of gossip about the Company's senior officials in India.

   (*a*) Statement-I is correct and II is incorrect.
   (*b*) Statement-I is incorrect and II is correct
   (*c*) Both I & II are incorrect
   (*d*) Both I & II are correct

2. **Why was reading manuscripts not easy in India? Choose the appropriate reason from the following options:** ***(Un)*(CBSE, 2020)**

   (*a*) Manuscripts were highly cheap.
   (*b*) Manuscripts were widely spread out.
   (*c*) Manuscripts were written in English and Hindi.
   (*d*) Manuscripts were fragile.

3. **In which country was a children's press, dedicated solely to literature for children, established in 1857?** ***(Re)***

   (*a*) France (*b*) Germany
   (*c*) England (*d*) United States

4. **Who were some of the well-known women novelists of the nineteenth century?** ***(Re)***

   (*a*) Grimm Brothers
   (*b*) Jane Austen, the Bronte sisters, George Eliot
   (*c*) Richard M. Hoe
   (*d*) Penny magazines

5. **Which category of readers became important with the introduction of compulsory primary education in the late nineteenth century?** ***(Un)***

   (*a*) Elite class (*b*) Peasants
   (*c*) Children (*d*) White-collar workers

6. **While exploring an art museum, Arjun came across a section dedicated to ancient Indian manuscripts. He was particularly drawn to an exhibit labeled "Pages from the Gita Govinda of Jayadeva, eighteenth century." The manuscript was displayed with its delicate palm-leaf pages arranged in an accordion format. The detailed illustrations and the unique way the pages were bound intrigued him, reminding him of the rich cultural heritage of India. What unique feature of the Gita Govinda manuscript display the museum intrigued Arjun?** ***(Un)***

   (*a*) It is a printed manuscript in book format.
   (*b*) It is a handwritten manuscript in scroll format.
   (*c*) It is a palm-leaf handwritten manuscript in accordion format.
   (*d*) It is a printed manuscript in digital format.

7. **When did the printing press first arrive in Goa, India?** ***(Re)***

   (*a*) 16th century (*b*) 17th century
   (*c*) 18th century (*d*) 19th century

8. **In 1780, James Augustus Hickey began publishing the Bengal Gazette, which criticised senior officials of the East India Company. In response, Governor-General Warren Hastings persecuted Hickey and supported officially sanctioned newspapers to counter the negative information. What does the conflict between Hickey and Hastings suggest about the press in colonial India?** *(An)*

(*a*) It was a tool for the British to promote their policies.
(*b*) It provided a platform for dissent against the colonial government.
(*c*) It had no significant influence on public opinion.
(*d*) It was used mainly for commercial advertisements.

Assertion and Reason (1 M)

Direction: The following questions consist of two statements – Assertion (A) and Reason (R). Answer these questions by selecting the appropriate option given below:

(*a*) Both A and R are true, and R is the correct explanation of A.
(*b*) Both A and R are true, but R is not the correct explanation of A.
(*c*) A is true, but R is false
(*d*) A is false, but R is true.

1. **Assertion (A):** The distribution, application, and preservation of knowledge were fundamentally altered with the invention of printing.

   Reason (R): Printing enabled intellectuals to produce, comment on, and evaluate texts which spread as ideas across Europe. ***(Ev)* (CBSE APQ, 2023)**

2. **Assertion (A):** The establishment of a children's press in France in 1857 was a response to the growing demand for literature aimed specifically at children.

   Reason (R): As primary education became compulsory, children became an important category of readers, necessitating the production of school textbooks and dedicated literature for children. *(Ev)*

3. **Assertion (A):** The printing press was first brought to Goa by Britishers missionaries in the mid-sixteenth century.

   Reason (R): Portuguese missionaries in Goa utilized the printing press to print tracts and books in languages like Konkani and Kanara. *(An)*

4. **Assertion (A):** Dutch Protestant missionaries played a significant role in printing Tamil texts during the early 18th century.

   Reason (R): By 1810, Dutch Protestant missionaries had printed 32 Tamil texts, including translations of older works. *(Ev)*

Subjective Questions

Very Short Answer Type Questions (1 or 2 M)

1. **In the late nineteenth century, the introduction of compulsory primary education created a new group of readers in Europe. As literacy rates increased, especially among children, the demand for school textbooks and children's literature surged, reshaping the publishing industry and making children significant consumers of printed material. What category of readers became important with the introduction of compulsory primary education in the late nineteenth century?** *(Un)*

Ans. (*i*) The children became an important category of readers with the introduction of compulsory primary education. *(1 M)*

(*ii*) This led to a surge in the demand for school textbooks and children's literature, reshaping the publishing industry. *(1 M)*

2. **Who were some well-known women novelists of the nineteenth century?** *(Re)*

Ans. Some well-known women novelists of the nineteenth century were Jane Austen, the Bronte sisters, and George Eliot. *(1 M)*

3. **What category of readers became important with the introduction of compulsory primary education in the late nineteenth century?** *(Un)*

Ans. Introduction of compulsory primary education in the late nineteenth century:

(*i*) **Primary Focus on Children:** Compulsory education laws made children a central focus for educational publications. *(1 M)*

(*ii*) **Educational Materials:** The demand for school textbooks and educational materials surged as more children attended school. *(1 M)*

4. **When did the printing press first come to Goa?** *(Re)*

Ans. The printing press first arrived in Goa with Portuguese missionaries in the mid-16th century. Here are the key points:

(*i*) **Introduction Timeline:** The printing press was introduced to Goa in the mid-16th century. *(1 M)*

(*ii*) **Missionary Influence:** It was brought by Portuguese missionaries who were significant in spreading the technology in the region. *(1 M)*

5. **Who printed the first Tamil book in India?** *(Re)*

Ans. The first Tamil book in India was printed by Catholic priests in 1579 at Cochin. These priests were part of the Portuguese missionaries, including Jesuits, who brought the printing press to India in the mid-16th century. *(2 M)*

Short Answer Type Questions (3 M)

1. **What were some technological innovations in printing during the nineteenth century?** *(Re)*

Ans. Some technological innovations in printing during the nineteenth century was:

(*i*) **Power-driven Cylindrical Press:** Developed by Richard M. Hoe of New York, which could print 8,000 sheets per hour, greatly increasing the speed of printing operations. *(1 M)*

(*ii*) **Offset Press:** Introduced in the late nineteenth century, this press could print up to six colors simultaneously, enhancing the quality and variety of printed materials. *(1 M)* (*iii*) **Automatic Paper Reels and Photoelectric Controls:** These innovations improved the feeding of paper and the accuracy of color registration, further optimizing the printing process. *(1 M)*

2. How did the nineteenth century contribute to the expansion of readership among children, women, and workers? ***(Un)***

Ans. The nineteenth century contributed to the expansion of readership among children, women, and workers:

(*i*) **Children:** Compulsory education laws increased literacy and demand for educational books. *(1 M)*

(*ii*) **Women:** Rising literacy due to educational reforms and targeted publications like novels and magazines increased women's readership. *(1 M)*

(*iii*) **Workers:** Improved access to political tracts and newspapers broadened worker engagement and literacy. *(1 M)*

3. What kind of books were available in India before the introduction of print culture? ***(Un)***

Ans. Books available in India before print culture:

(*i*) **Manuscript Form:** Books were handmade manuscripts, often written on palm leaves or handmade paper. *(1 M)*

(*ii*) **Rich Content:** Included diverse subjects like religious scriptures, epic poetry, and scientific texts, available in multiple languages. *(1 M)*

(*iii*) **Exclusive Access:** Artistic and detailed, these manuscripts were costly and primarily accessible to the affluent and scholars. *(1 M)*

Long Answer Type Questions (5 M)

1. Discuss the major factors that contributed to the spread of mass literacy in Europe during the nineteenth century. ***(An)***

Ans. The major factors that contributed to the spread of mass literacy in Europe during the nineteenth century:

(*i*) **Compulsory Education:** Many European countries introduced compulsory primary education, ensuring a broader base of children received formal schooling. *(1 M)*

(*ii*) **Children's Presses and Textbooks:** The establishment of dedicated children's presses and widespread publication of school textbooks made educational materials more accessible to young learners. *(1 M)*

(*iii*) **Influential Literary Efforts:** Writers and collectors like the Grimm Brothers compiled and popularized folk tales and fairy tales, enriching children's literature. *(1 M)*

(*iv*) **Lending Libraries:** The emergence of lending libraries provided access to books for those who could not afford to purchase them, further promoting literacy across different social classes. *(1 M)*

(*v*) **Cultural and Social Support:** There was a growing recognition of the importance of literacy, leading to increased investment in education and literacy programs by governments and philanthropists. *(1 M)*

2. How did print publications foster pan-Indian identities and connect communities in colonial India? ***(Re)***

Ans. Print publications significantly fostered pan-Indian identities and connected communities in colonial India in several key ways:

(*i*) Newspapers and printed materials conveyed news and information across different regions. *(1 M)*

(*ii*) Print publications facilitated the exchange of ideas and knowledge between diverse communities. *(1 M)*

(*iii*) The availability of printed materials in various languages promoted a shared cultural and intellectual heritage. *(1 M)*

(*iv*) Print created a sense of interconnectedness among communities across India. *(1 M)*

(*v*) Newspapers and printed materials contributed to the formation of pan-Indian identities by providing a common source of information and discussion. *(1 M)*

3. What were the characteristics and limitations of handwritten manuscripts in India before the introduction of printing? ***(An)***

Ans. The characteristics and limitations of handwritten manuscripts in India before the introduction of printing:

(*i*) Handwritten manuscripts in India were created on palm leaves or handmade paper, often with beautifully illustrated pages. *(1 M)*

(*ii*) They were expensive and fragile, requiring careful handling and preservation. *(1 M)*

(*iii*) The script was written in different styles, making them challenging to read easily. *(1 M)*

(*iv*) Manuscripts were not widely used in everyday life due to their cost, fragility, and difficulty in reading. *(1 M)*

(*v*) Despite the development of an extensive network of village primary schools in pre-colonial Bengal, students often only learned to write and did not read texts, as teachers dictated portions from memory. *(1 M)*

4. Explain how print culture assisted the growth of nationalism in India? ***(Un)(NCERT)***

Ans. Print culture assisted the growth of nationalism in India in following ways:

(*i*) Indians began publishing newspapers such as the Bengal Gazette brought out by Gangadhar Bhattacharya, who was close to Rammohun Roy. A number of newspapers and journals were published by the end of the eighteenth century. *(1 M)*

(*ii*) Following the 1857 rebellion, vernacular newspapers became more assertively nationalist. Angry Englishmen demanded that the 'native' press should shut down. *(1 M)*

(*iii*) The Vernacular Press Act, which was passed in 1878,gave the government full authority to censor reporting and opinions in the Vernacular press. *(1 M)*

(*iv*) Despite repressive actions, the number of nationalist newspapers rose, reporting on colonial misrule and encouraging nationalist activity. *(1 M)*

(*v*) Punjab revolutionaries were deported in 1907, Bal Gangadhar Tilak wrote about them in his Kesari with great sympathy. This resulted in his arrest in 1908,which caused massive protests across India. *(1 M)*

4 RELIGIOUS REFORM AND PUBLIC DEBATES, NEW FORMS OF PUBLICATION AND PRINT AND CENSORSHIP

NCERT Definitions *(Commonly asked in 1 mark)*

- **Ulama:** Legal scholars of Islam and the sharia (a body of Islamic law).
- **Fatwa:** A legal pronouncement on Islamic law usually given by a mufti (legal scholar) to clarify issues on which the law is uncertain.
- **Religious Reform:** Efforts aimed at modifying religious beliefs and practices by challenging existing orthodoxies and introducing new doctrines, often facilitated by the print medium in the 19th and early 20th centuries.
- **Censorship:** The suppression or prohibition of any parts of books, films, news, etc. that are considered obscene, politically unacceptable, or a threat to security. Governments often use censorship to control the flow of information and suppress dissent.

Important Facts

01 In the **early 19th century**, vigorous debates emerged concerning religious matters.

02 **Diverse groups** presented fresh interpretations of various religious beliefs.

03 **Rammohun Roy** released the **Sambad Kaumudi** in **1821**.

04 The publication of **Persian** newspapers **'Jam-i-Jahan Nama'** and **'Shamsul Akhbar'**, along with the Gujarati **'Bombay Samachar'** in **1822**, signified the spread of debate across linguistic lines.

05 In **1810**, the first printed edition of **Tulsidas' Ramcharitmanas**, a 16th-century text, was published in **Calcutta**.

06 **The novel** in India evolved to reflect local styles and themes, and affordable books on social issues like caste discrimination became widespread in the **19th century**.

07 **Raja Ravi Varma's** artwork reached a mass audience, and there was a cultural shift as more women began to receive education at home, despite some societal apprehensions.

08 **Ram Chaddha** published the fast-selling **Istri Dharm Vichar** to teach women how to be obedient wives.

09 The establishment of public libraries in the early **20th century** made books more accessible to the public, especially in urban and affluent rural areas.

10 Literature addressing caste discrimination, such as **Jyotiba Phule's "Gulamgiri"**, emerged in the **late 19th century**.

11 Prominent activists like **B.R. Ambedkar** and **Periyar** wrote influential works on **caste issues**, widely read across India.

12 Worker-authored literature, such as **"Chhote Aur Bade Ka Sawal"** by **Kashibaba**, highlighted the interconnectedness of caste and class exploitation.

Difference Between

Religious Reform Vs. Public Debates

Aspect	Religious Reform	Public Debates
Purpose	Aimed at addressing and reforming religious practices and beliefs.	Focused on discussing social, political, and economic issues openly.
Leadership	Often spearheaded by individual leaders or reform movements.	Engaged the wider public, including intellectuals, activists, and the common people.
Media Utilization	Used print media to spread reformist ideas and criticize orthodox practices.	Utilized a variety of print formats (newspapers, pamphlets, journals) to present diverse viewpoints.
Organizational Impact	Led to the founding of new religious and social organizations.	Encouraged the formation of public opinion and collective actions.
Focus	Focused more on moral and spiritual enlightenment.	Broader in scope, addressing a range of contemporary concerns beyond religion.

Myth Buster

- **Myth:** Print Led to Immediate Widespread Public Debates.

  Fact: The initiation of public debates through print was gradual and faced various obstacles, including literacy rates, societal norms, and censorship. Print created the potential for wider public engagement, but actual participation in debates and the impact of these debates varied widely across different segments of society.
- **Myth:** Print Culture Erased Oral Traditions.

  Fact: While print culture transformed the dissemination of religious, social, and political ideas, it did not erase oral traditions. In many communities, oral storytelling, religious preaching, and public debates continued to coexist with printed materials, each influencing and enriching the other.

Mnemonics

To remember the publication of ideas against social evils,

"SCRIPT"

- **S** → Social evils challenged in print
- **C** → Common languages for the masses
- **R** → Raja Ram Mohan Roy's Sambad Kaumudi
- **I** → Influence of Samachar Chandrika
- **P** → Persian and Urdu scriptures
- **T** → Texts widely in vernacular by the 1880s

COMPETENCY BASED SOLVED EXAMPLES

Scan Me for Detailed Explanations

Multiple Choice Questions

(1 M)

1. **Which one of the following aspects was common among the writings of Kailashbashini Debi, Tarabai Shinde and Pandita Ramabai?** *(Re)*(CBSE, 2023)
   (*a*) Demanded economic equality for the masses.
   (*b*) Highlighted the experiences of women.
   (*c*) Raised awareness about cultural heritage.
   (*d*) Motivated Indians for their national freedom.
2. **Amir, a young scholar from North India, witnessed the increasing influence of various Muslim sects that used Urdu print to disseminate their religious views. His family, traditional followers of a local Sufi order, were concerned about the divisive potential of these publications. Aamir, curious about the impact of these printed materials, decided to investigate how they shaped public opinion and inter-sect relations. What critical role did Urdu print play in shaping the religious and social dynamics of North India in the late 19th century?** *(An)*
   (*a*) Spread official propaganda.
   (*b*) Increased sectarian awareness and rivalry.
   (*c*) Unified Muslim sects under one interpretation.
   (*d*) Discouraged public religious discussions.
3. **What role did newspapers play in creating pan-Indian identities?** *(Un)*
   (*a*) They encouraged debates and controversies.
   (*b*) They connected communities and people across different regions.
   (*c*) They disseminated religious texts.
   (*d*) They facilitated the import and sale of slaves.
4. **What is the main theme depicted in the woodcut "Ghor Kali (The End of the World)"?** *(Un)*

   (*a*) The harmony of family relations
   (*b*) The dominance of traditional gender roles
   (*c*) The destruction of proper family relations
   (*d*) The celebration of cultural heritage
5. **In the late 19th century, a new visual culture emerged due to the establishment of printing presses. What kind of images were reproduced in multiple copies?** *(Re)*
   (*a*) Paintings by famous artists
   (*b*) Caricatures and cartoons
   (*c*) Religious scriptures
   (*d*) Woodblock prints
6. **What was the consequence of Balgangadhar Tilak writing sympathetically about the deported Punjab revolutionaries in his newspaper?** *(Re)*
   (*a*) The government appreciated his support
   (*b*) The newspaper faced censorship
   (*c*) He was awarded a prestigious literary prize
   (*d*) There were widespread protests in India
7. **Which act provided the colonial government extensive rights to censor reports and editorials in the vernacular press?** *(Re)*
   (*a*) The English Press Act
   (*b*) The Indian Censorship Act
   (*c*) The Vernacular Press Act
   (*d*) The Colonial Printing Control Act

Assertion and Reason

(1 M)

Direction: The following questions consist of two statements – Assertion (A) and Reason (R). Answer these questions by selecting the appropriate option given below:

(*a*) Both A and R are true, and R is the correct explanation of A.
(*b*) Both A and R are true, but R is not the correct explanation of A.
(*c*) A is true, but R is false
(*d*) A is false, but R is true.

1. **Assertion (A):** After the mid 19th century women's schools were set up in the cities and towns.

   Reason(R): Many journals begans carry the writings of women and explained why women should be educate. *(An)*
2. **Assertion (A):** Visual images produced by painters like Raja Ravi Varma played a significant role in shaping popular ideas about modernity, tradition, religion, politics, society, and culture during the late nineteenth century.

   Reason (R): With the establishment of printing presses and the availability of multiple copies, these visual images could be reproduced and circulated widely, thus influencing public perception and discourse on various aspects of life. *(Ev)*

Subjective Questions

Very Short Answer Type Questions (1 or 2 M)

1. Why was the Vernacular Press Act passed in 1878? *(Un)*(CBSE, 2020)

Ans. The Vernacular Press Act was passed in 1878 by the British colonial government in India. The act was aimed at controlling the Indian-language press, which was becoming increasingly critical of British policies. *(1 M)*

2. Why was 'Gulamgiri' book written by Jyotiba Phule in 1871? *(Un)*(CBSE, 2020)

Ans. To critique the caste system prevalent in India at that time. The book was aimed at empowering the Dalits and Other Backward Classes (OBCs), who were oppressed by the upper castes, and advocating for their social and political upliftment. *(1 M)*

3. Lives and feelings of women in India began to be written in particularly vivid and intense ways in the late 19th century. Justify this statement with two examples. *(An)*

Ans. Justification of the statement with example:

(*i*) From the 1860s, a few Bengali women like Kailashbashini Debi wrote books highlighting the experiences of women about how women were imprisoned at home, kept in ignorance, forced to do hard domestic labour and treated unjustly by the very people they served. *(1 M)*

(*ii*) In the 1880s, in present-day Maharashtra, Tarabai Shinde and Pandita Ramabai wrote with passionate anger about the miserable lives of upper-caste Hindu women, especially widows. *(1 M)*

4. Why had Englishmen demanded a clamp down on the 'Vernacular Press' in the 19th century? *(Un)*(CBSE, 2019)

Ans. Englishmen demanded a clamp down on the 'Vernacular Press' in the 19th century:

(*i*) **Rising Nationalism:** The vernacular press played a significant role in promoting Indian nationalism which threatened British colonial rule. *(1 M)*

(*ii*) **Spread of Critical Ideas:** Newspapers in local languages often criticized colonial policies and spread dissenting ideas among the masses, which the British viewed as a threat to their control. *(1 M)*

Topper's Explanations

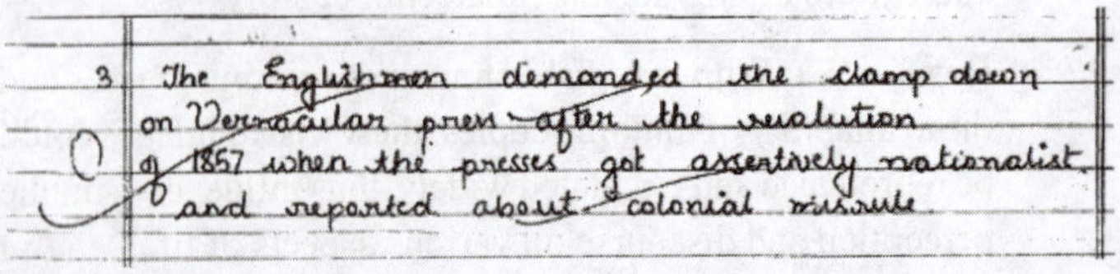

3 The Englishmen demanded the clamp down on Vernacular press after the revolution of 1857 when the presses got assertively nationalist and reported about colonial misrule.

Short Answer Type Questions (3 M)

1. Provide evidence to support the claim that print culture helped in the growth of nationalism in India? *(An)*(CBSE SQP, 2023)

Ans. Print culture played a significant role in the growth of nationalism in India by spreading nationalist ideas and creating awareness among people. The following points provide evidence:

(*i*) **Spread of Nationalist Ideas:** Newspapers and books in local languages helped people understand British policies. Papers like Kesari and Bengalee inspired many. *(1 M)*

(*ii*) **Bringing People Together:** Print media connected people from different regions and backgrounds, creating a shared sense of identity. *(1 M)*

(*iii*) **Inspiration from Leaders:** Writings of Mahatma Gandhi, Bankim Chandra Chattopadhyay's Anandamath, and Bhagat Singh motivated people to fight for freedom. *(1 M)*

2. How did the availability of printed materials and changing social attitudes impact women's literacy and writings? *(Un)*

Ans. Impacts of printed materials and changing social attitudes on women's literacy and writings;

(*i*) **Educational Access:** Increased availability of printed educational materials improved literacy among women. *(1 M)*

(*ii*) **Female Writers:** More literate women began to write, adding diverse voices to literature. *(1 M)*

(*iii*) **Changing Attitudes:** Societal support for women's education grew, enhancing their participation in literary and intellectual pursuits. *(1 M)*

3. You are a student in 1920s India, eagerly reading nationalist newspapers and magazines like *Young India* and *Kesari*, which discuss the independence movement and stories of freedom fighters. Your grandfather often shares how similar pamphlets and books inspired his generation. Based on the scenario, explain how the availability and spread of printed materials helped in fostering a sense of nationalism among the Indian population in the early 20th century. *(Un)*

Ans. The availability and spread of printed materials in the early 20th century significantly fostered a sense of nationalism among the Indian population by:

(*i*) **Dissemination of Nationalist Ideas:** Newspapers and magazines like *Young India* and *Kesari* published articles on the independence movement and freedom fighters, spreading nationalist ideas widely. *(1 M)*

(*ii*) **Inspiration and Unity:** Printed materials inspired readers by sharing stories of bravery and sacrifice, fostering a sense of unity and purpose among the Indian population. *(1 M)* (*iii*) **Public Engagement:** The availability of these publications allowed the common people to engage with the independence movement, increasing awareness and participation in the struggle for freedom. *(1 M)*

4. How did visual culture change with the rise of printing presses? ***(Un)***

Ans. Visual culture change with the rise of printing presses are:

(*i*) Visual images could be easily reproduced in multiple copies, leading to the production of mass-circulated prints and calendars. *(1 M)*

(*ii*) Artists like Raja Ravi Varma created images for mass circulation, shaping popular ideas about modernity, tradition, religion, politics, society, and culture. *(1 M)*

(*iii*) Caricatures and cartoons began to be published, offering commentary on social and political issues, including imperial rule and nationalist sentiments. *(1 M)*

Long Answer Type Questions (5 M)

1. What were the effects of print on the accessibility of religious texts in vernacular languages? ***(An)***

Ans. The effects of print on the accessibility of religious texts in vernacular languages:

(*i*) Print made religious texts more widely available and accessible to the general public. *(1 M)*

(*ii*) It encouraged the reading and study of religious texts in vernacular languages. *(1 M)*

(*iii*) Printed texts enabled the faithful to engage with religious scriptures and teachings in their native languages. *(1M)*

(*iv*) The portability of printed texts allowed individuals to carry and study them at their convenience. *(1 M)*

(*v*) Print publications facilitated the reading and dissemination of religious texts among larger groups of people. *(1 M)*

2. How did caste discrimination become a prominent theme in printed tracts and essays during this period? Provide Four examples. ***(An)***

Ans. Caste discrimination became a prominent theme in printed tracts and essays during this period through the efforts of various social reformers and movements: *(1 M)*

(*i*) **Jyotiba Phule's Influence:** Jyotiba Phule wrote "Gulamgiri" in 1871, which critiqued the caste system and called for its eradication, highlighting the injustices faced by lower castes. *(1 M)*

(*ii*) **B.R. Ambedkar's Writings:** B.R. Ambedkar, through his writings like "Annihilation of Caste," challenged the hierarchical social order and advocated for the rights and empowerment of marginalized communities. *(1 M)*

(*iii*) **E.V. Ramaswamy Naicker's Efforts:** E.V. Ramaswamy Naicker, known as Periyar, also contributed significantly by writing against caste discrimination and pushing for social reforms to achieve equality. *(1 M)*

(*iv*) **Local Protests and Sects:** Various local protest movements and new religious sects published tracts and essays that criticized ancient scriptures and proposed visions of a more equitable future without caste discrimination. *(1 M)*

3. How did the revolt of 1857 impact the attitude towards freedom of the press in colonial India? ***(Re)***

Ans. The Revolt of 1857 significantly influenced the colonial authorities' attitude towards freedom of the press in India:

(*i*) The revolt of 1857 had a significant impact on the attitude towards freedom of the press in colonial India. *(1 M)*

(*ii*) Enraged Englishmen demanded a clampdown on the 'native' press, fearing its potential role in inciting rebellion and anti-colonial sentiments. *(1 M)*

(*iii*) There was a shift in the colonial government's attitude towards press freedom. They began debating and implementing measures of stringent control to curtail press freedom and increase censorship. *(1 M)*

(*iv*) The revolt of 1857 heightened concerns about the press being a powerful tool for nationalist movements, leading to a more restrictive approach towards the dissemination of information and expression of dissent *(1 M)*

(*v*) In 1878, the Vernacular Press Act was passed, modeled on the Irish Press Laws. *(1 M)*

MISCELLANEOUS EXERCISE

Multiple Choice Questions (1 M)

1. Ravi, a young journalist in 19th-century India, is intrigued by the new offset printing press and its potential to promote literacy and social awareness in rural areas. What is the most significant impact of the new offset printing press according to Ravi's analysis? ***(Ev)***
   (*a*) More colorful newspapers.
   (*b*) Increased literacy rates.
   (*c*) Unemployment for scribes.
   (*d*) Benefits only urban areas.
2. In which countries the earliest type of print Culture was developed. ***(Re)***
   (*a*) Japan (*b*) China
   (*c*) Korea (*d*) All of these.
3. At which of the following city of India, first printing press was established. ***(Re)***
   (*a*) Calcutta (*b*) Ahmedabad
   (*c*) Goa (*d*) Bombay
4. Arrange the following in sequence. ***(Ap)***
   1. Martin Luther Ninety Five theses.
   2. The first Tamil Book printed.
   3. The first Malayalam book was printed.
   4. Vernacular press. Put passed.

   (*a*) 4, 3, 2, 1 (*b*) 1, 4, 3, 2
   (*c*) 3, 2, 4, 1 (*d*) 1, 2, 3, 4
5. Who among the following was against caste system. ***(Re)***
   (*a*) Dr. BR Ambedkar (*b*) E.V Ramaswamy
   (*c*) Jyotiba Phule (*d*) All of these
6. Which of the following related to women novelists? ***(Un)***
   (*a*) Kailashbashini Devi (*b*) Tarabaishinde
   (*c*) Jane Austen (*d*) All of these
7. Jane Austen, and Boonie sisters are the Native of. ***(Un)***
   (*a*) China (Asia) (*b*) Africa
   (*c*) Europe (*d*) Australia
8. What did Gandhi ji say necessary of Nationalism? ***(Re)***
   (*a*) Liberty of speech
   (*b*) liberty of press
   (*c*) Freedom association
   (*d*) All of the above
9. According to Gandhi ji what do mean of Swaraj. ***(Re)***
   (*a*) Achieve education
   (*b*) Achieve nationalism
   (*c*) Achieve freedom of press
   (*d*) None of these.
10. Who was Menocchio? ***(Re)***
    (*a*) A calligrapher (*b*) Religious reformer
    (*c*) Italian miller (*d*) Lalin schooler
11. Which of the following is incorrect. ***(Ev)***
    (*a*) Primary Dutch Education Compulsory bite nineteenth. Century.
    (*b*) Book Jacket-Twentieth Century.
    (*c*) Periodical press-early eighteenth Century.
    (*d*) Ramcharitmanas Seventeen Century.
12. Raja Ravi Verma was famous for: ***(Re)***
    (*a*) Writer (*b*) Poet
    (*c*) Painter (*d*) Calligrapher
13. What were the objectives of established in 1980s by the libraries workers. ***(Re)***
    (*a*) Reduce drinking (*b*) Promote literally
    (*c*) Promote nationalism (*d*) All of these
14. Which of the following incorrect. ***(Ev)***
    (*a*) The first tamil book printed in Madras.
    (*b*) Martin Luther wrote ninety five theses.
    (*c*) In 1870, Hindi printing began seriously
    (*d*) Fairy Tales printed by the Grimm Brothers.
15. Arrange in the sequence. ***(Ap)***
    A. James Augustus Hickey edit the Bengal Gazette.
    B. First Malayalam book was printed.
    C. Hindi printing began officially
    D. Punjab revolutionaries depo.

    (*a*) A, B, C, D (*b*) C, B, A, D
    (*c*) C, A, B, D (*d*) B, A, C, D

Assertion and Reason (1 M)

Direction: The following questions consist of two statements– Assertion (A) and Reason (R). Answer these questions by selecting the appropriate option given below:

(*a*) Both A and R are true, and R is the correct explanation of A.
(*b*) Both A and R are true, but R is not the correct explanation of A.
(*c*) A is true, but R is false.
(*d*) A is false, but R is true.

1. **Assertion (A):** The Ulama were very anxious about the collapse of muslim dynasties. *(Ev)*

   Reason (R): They published persian and Urdu translate holy scriptures and printed religion Newspaper.

2. **Assertion (A):** The first printing press came to Goa with French missionaries.

   Reason (R): French protestant missionaries had printed 32 Tamil book. *(An)*

3. **Assertion (A):** India had a very rich and ancient tradition of hand written Manuscripts·

   Reason (R): Mostly Indian manuscripts were written in Hindi, Urdu and Sanskrit. *(Un)*

4. **Assertion (A):** The spread of print culture in India assisted the decline of nationalism.

   Reason (R): Print culture allowed for the dissemination of nationalist ideas and facilitated communication among different regions. *(Ev)*

5. **Assertion (A):** The Vernacular Press Act was passed in response to nationalist newspapers becoming more assertive.

   Reason (R): The Vernacular Press Act gave the colonial government extensive rights to censor reports and editorials in vernacular newspapers. *(Re)*

6. **Assertion (A):** Print technology had a positive impact on poor people in 19th century India.

   Reason (R): Print technology allowed for greater access to education and literature among poor people. *(Ev)*

7. **Assertion (A):** The spread of print culture in Europe led to the growth of literacy rates.

   Reason (R): Print technology made it easier and cheaper to produce books, which increased access to education. *(Ev)*

8. **Assertion (A):** The introduction of woodblock printing in Europe was a significant development.

   Reason (R): Woodblock printing allowed for the mass production of images and text. *(An)*

9. **Assertion (A):** The Vernacular Press Act had a negative impact on freedom of speech in India.

   Reason (R): The act gave the colonial government extensive powers to censor reports and editorials in vernacular newspapers. *(Ev)*

10. **Assertion (A):** Print technology does not played a role in shaping national identity in India.

    Reason (R): Print technology allowed for nationalist ideas to be disseminated more widely. *(Ev)*

Subjective Questions

Very Short Answer Type Questions (1 or 2 M)

1. Name the countries where the earliest kind of Print technology was developed. *(Re)*
2. Define to the Ballads. *(Re)*
3. What is Chapbook? *(Re)*
4. In which languages are Jesuit priests' printed books? *(Un)*
5. Write the names of two Persian Newspapers. *(Re)*
6. Write the names of two Persian Newspapers. *(Re)*
7. Who Invented the Printing press? *(Re)***(CBSE, 2020)**

Short Answer Type Questions (3 M)

1. How hand printing technology was introduced in Japan? *(Un)***(CBSE, 2019)**
2. Maria, a university student, is preparing a presentation on the role of religious institutions in the development of education for her history class. She focuses on the seventeenth and eighteenth centuries in Europe, a period when churches played a pivotal role in increasing literacy rates. Her research highlights the various methods employed by religious institutions to promote education and literacy among the population. How did religious institutions contribute to the increase in literacy rates in Europe during the seventeenth and eighteenth centuries, and what methods did they use? *(An)*
3. Emma, a historian, is examining the diary of a commoner from eighteenth-century Europe for her research on the spread of scientific and philosophical ideas among the general population. The diary provides vivid accounts of how reading periodicals influenced the diarist's daily life, shaping public opinion and making complex ideas accessible. Emma prepares to analyze the diary entries to understand the broader impact of the periodical press on society. How did reading periodicals shape public opinion and make scientific and philosophical ideas accessible to common people in eighteenth-century Europe, as evidenced by the diary entries of a commoner? *(An)*
4. Write any three characteristics features of the printed books in the late 17th century. *(Re)*
5. Explain the three features of the first printed Bible. *(Un)*
6. "Issues of caste discrimination began to be written about in many printed tracts and essays in India in the late nineteenth century." Support the statement with two suitable examples. *(Re)***(CBSE, 2019)**

Long Answer Type Questions (5 M)

1. Mei, a young merchant in China, witnesses the growing influence of print technology in urban centers. She observes how print materials are used not only for official examinations but also for leisure reading, commercial purposes, and spreading new ideas. Mei interacts with various social groups, including scholars, traders, and artists, to understand the societal and cultural changes brought by print technology.Explain how the availability of printed materials for official examinations influences the education and career opportunities of scholars. *(Un)*
2. Describe the new forms of publications that came out at the end of the 19th century and in the beginning of the 20th century *(An)*
3. Explain how print culture affected. Women in the 19th century in India. *(An)*

Case Based Questions

(4 M)

Case Based-I

Read the information below and answer the questions that follow. **(CBSE, 2020)**

Source-1:

Religious Reform and Public Debates There were intense controversies between social and religious reformers and the Hindu orthodoxy over matters like widow immolation, monotheism, Brahmanical priesthood, and idolatry. in Bengal, as the debate developed, tracts and newspapers proliferated, circulating a variety of argument.

Source-2:

New Forms of Publication New literary forms also entered the world of reading lyrics, short stories, essays about social and political matters. In different ways, they reinforced the new emphasis on human lives and intimate feelings, about the political and social rules that shaped such things.

Source-3:

Since social reforms and novels had already created a great interest in women's lives and emotions, there was also an interest in what women would have to say about their own lives.

(*i*) Evaluate how the print shaped the nature of the debate in the early nineteenth century in India. (*Ev*)

(*ii*) To what extent do you agree that print opened up new worlds of experience and gave a vivid sense of the diversity of human lives? (*Ev*)

(*iii*) To what extent did the print culture reflect a great interest in women's lives and emotions? Explain. (*An*)

Case Based-II

Read the information below and answer the questions that follow.

Why Newspapers?

'Krishnaji Trimbuck Ranade inhabitant of Poona intends to publish a Newspaper in the Marathi Language with a view of affording useful information on every topic of local interest. It will be open for free discussion on subjects of general utility, scientific investigation and the speculations connected with the antiquities, statistics, curiosities, history and geography of the country and of the Deccan especially...the patronage and support of all interested in the diffusion of knowledge and Welfare of the People is earnestly solicited.' Bombay Telegraph and Courier, 6 January, 1849 'The task of the native newspapers and political associations is identical to the role of the Opposition in the House of Commons in Parliament in England. That is of critically examining government policy to suggest improvements, by removing those parts that will not be to the benefit of the people, and also by ensuring speedy implementation. These associations ought to carefully study the particular issues, gather diverse relevant information on the nation as well as on what are the possible and desirable improvements, and this will surely earn it considerable influence.

F' Native Opinion, 3 April, 1870.

(*i*) Explain the main reason for publishing newspaper by Krishnaji? (*An*)

(*ii*) How was the task of native newspaper and political association seen identical to the role of opposition? (*Un*)

(*iii*) Analyze the reasons of popularity of newspapers during 19th century. (*An*)

Case Based-III

Read the following source carefully and answer the questions that follow:

Printed Words

This is how Mercier describes the impact of the printed word, and the power of reading in one of his books:

'Anyone who had seen me reading would have compared me to a man dying of thirst who was gulping down some fresh pure water... Lighting my lamp with extraordinary caution, I threw myself hungrily into the reading. An easy eloquence, effortless and animated, carried me from one page to the next without my noticing it. A clock struck off the hours in the silence of the shadows, and I heard nothing. My lamp began to run out of oil and produced only a pale light, but still I read on. I could not even take out time to raise the wick for fear of interrupting my pleasure. How those new ideas rushed into my brain! How my intelligence adopted them!'

(*i*) How does the passage reflect the immersive nature of reading of Mercier? (*An*)

(*ii*) Why did Mercier describe himself as a virtual writer? (*Un*)

(*iii*) How did reading influence Mercier's intellectual capacity and his engagement with new concepts? Explain in any two points. (*Ev*)

ANSWER KEYS

Multiple Choice Questions

1. (*b*) **2.** (*d*) **3.** (*c*) **4.** (*d*) **5.** (*d*) **6.** (*d*) **7.** (*c*) **8.** (*d*) **9.** (*c*) **10.** (*c*)
11. (*d*) **12.** (*c*) **13.** (*d*) **14.** (*d*) **15.** (*d*)

Assertion and Reason

1. (*a*) **2.** (*d*) **3.** (*c*) **4.** (*d*) **5.** (*a*) **6.** (*a*) **7.** (*a*) **8.** (*a*) **9.** (*a*) **10.** (*d*)

HINTS & EXPLANATIONS

Multiple Choice Questions

1. (*b*) Increased literacy rates.
2. (*d*) All of these.
3. (*c*) Goa
4. (*d*) 1, 2, 3, 4
5. (*d*) All of these
6. (*d*) All of these
7. (*c*) Jane Austen
8. (*d*) All of the above
9. (*c*) Achieve freedom of press
10. (*c*) Italian miller
11. (*d*) Ramcharitmanas Seventeen Century.
12. (*c*) Painter
13. (*d*) All of these
14. (*d*) Fairy Tales printed by the Grimm Brothers
15. (*d*) B, A, C, D

Assertion and Reason

1. (*a*) Both A and R are true, and R is the correct explanation of A.
2. (*d*) A is false, but R is true
3. (*c*) A is true, but R is false
4. (*d*) A is false, R is true.
5. (*a*) Both the assertion and reason are true, and the reason explains why the assertion is true.
6. (*a*) Both the assertion and reason are true, and the reason explains why the assertion is true.
7. (*a*) Both the assertion and reason are true, and the reason explains why the assertion is true. The spread of print culture in Europe led to the growth of literacy rates by making it easier and cheaper to produce books. This increased access to education, which helped more people learn how to read and write.
8. (*a*) Both the assertion and reason are true, and the reason explains why the assertion is true.
9. (*a*) The Vernacular Press Act had a negative impact on freedom of speech in India because it gave the colonial government extensive powers to censor reports and editorials in vernacular newspapers. This limited people's ability to express their opinions freely.
10. (*d*) A is false, R is true.

Subjective Questions

Very Short Answer Type Questions

1. The earliest kind of print technology was developed in the following countries:

   (*i*) **China:** The development of woodblock printing technology occurred around AD 600. *(1 M)*

   (*ii*) **Korea:** Innovations continued in Korea where metal movable type printing was developed in the 13th century before spreading to other regions. *(1 M)*

2. A ballad refers to a song or a poem that usually tells a story. These are mostly passed orally. *(1 M)*
3. **Chapbook:** It is a term used to describe pocket-size books that are sold by travelling peddlers called chapmen. These became popular from the time of the sixteenth-century print revolution. *(2 M)*
4. Jesuit priests learnt Konkani and printed several tracts. By 1674, about 50 books had been printed in the Konkani and Kannada languages. *(1 M)*
5. The names of two Persian newspapers are- Jam-i-Jahan Nama and Shamsul Akhbar. *(1 M)*
6. Johann Gutenberg invented the printing press in the 1430s in Strasbourg, Germany. *(1 M)*

Topper's Explanations

7) The Printing Press was invented by Johann Gutenberg.

Short Answer Type Questions

1. (*i*) Hand Printing was introduced in Japan by Buddhist missionaries around (768 AD to 770AD.). *(1 M)*

   (*ii*) The Diamond Sutra was the first printed book of Japan. It contained six sheets of text and wood cut illustrations. Urban society was shown in printed artwork in the late eighteenth century. *(1 M)*

   (*iii*) Libraries were flooded by books which were hand printed on cooking, women musical instrument, flower arrangement habits. *(1 M)*

2. During the seventeenth and eighteenth centuries, religious institutions significantly contributed to increasing literacy rates in Europe by employing various methods:

   (*i*) **Establishment of Schools**: Churches established numerous schools in both rural and urban areas, making basic literacy education accessible to a broader population. *(1 M)*

   (*ii*) **Printing Religious Texts**: Religious institutions printed and distributed Bibles, catechisms, and other religious texts, encouraging reading and literacy among believers. *(1 M)*

   (*iii*) **Encouraging Reading**: Clergy promoted the reading of religious texts as part of spiritual development, fostering a culture of reading within communities. *(1 M)*

3. Reading periodicals shape public opinion and make scientific and philosophical ideas:

   (*i*) **Dissemination of Ideas:** Periodicals simplified and spread scientific and philosophical ideas, making them accessible to the common people. *(1 M)*

   (*ii*) **Shaping Public Opinion:** They informed readers about ongoing debates, influencing their views and fostering public discourse. *(1 M)*

   (*iii*) **Daily Life Impact:** Periodicals became part of daily routines, encouraging critical thinking and intellectual engagement. *(1 M)*

4. Three characteristic features of printed books in the late 17th century:

   (*i*) **Introduction of Printing in Paris:** Paris became a pivotal center for the development of print culture soon after Johannes Gutenberg's printing innovations spread across Europe. *(1 M)*

   (*ii*) **Academic and Cultural Hub:** With its vibrant intellectual scene, including universities and scholarly activities, Paris fostered the growth and innovation of print technology. *(1 M)*

   (*iii*) **Literary and Scholarly Publications:** It became known for a wide range of publications, from scholarly texts to literature, contributing significantly to the dissemination of new ideas across Europe. *(1 M)*

5. The Bible was printed by Gutenberg, three features of the Bible are:

   (*i*) Above 180 copies of the Bible printed by Gutenberg of which no more than 50 have survived. *(1 M)*

   (*ii*) The book was printed in the new Gutenberg press with metal type, but the borders were illuminated by hand. *(1 M)*

   (*iii*) No two copies of the Bible were the same. Every page of each copy was different. *(1 M)*

6. The statement about caste discrimination issues discussed in printed tracts and essays in late 19th century India:

   (*i*) **Jyotiba Phule's Writings:** Jyotiba Phule, a pioneer of the low caste protest movements, openly critiqued the caste injustices in his book Gulamgiri (1871),which extensively discussed the plight and discrimination faced by lower castes in society. *(1½ M)*

   (*ii*) **Periyar and Ambedkar's Contributions:** In the 20th century, prominent leaders like B.R. Ambedkar and E.V. Ramaswamy Naicker, known as Periyar, also wrote extensively on caste issues. *(1½ M)*

Topper's Explanations

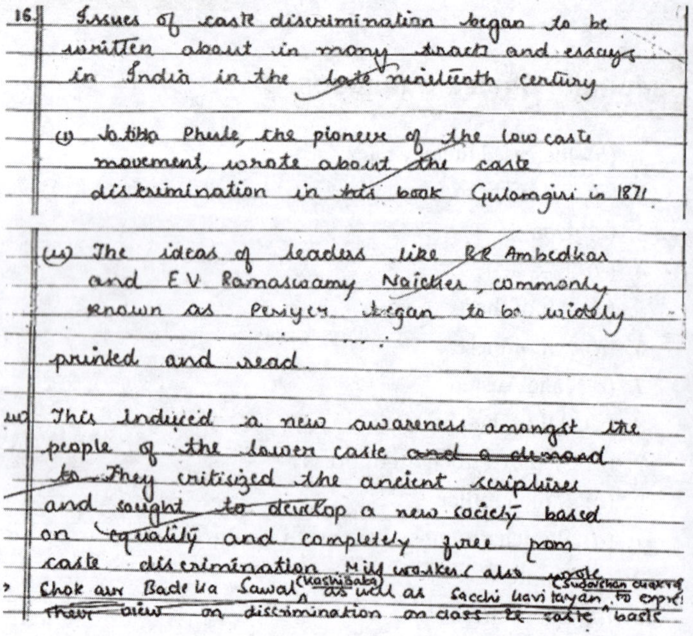
16. Issues of caste discrimination began to be written about in many tracts and essays in India in the late nineteenth century

(i) Jotiba Phule, the pioneer of the low caste movement, wrote about the caste discrimination in his book Gulamgiri in 1871.

(ii) The ideas of leaders like BR Ambedkar and E V Ramaswamy Naicker, commonly known as Periyar began to be widely printed and read.

(iii) This induced a new awareness amongst the people of the lower caste ~~and a demand to~~. They criticized the ancient scriptures and sought to develop a new society based on equality and completely free from caste discrimination. Mill workers also wrote Chok aur Bade ka Sawal (Kashibaba) as well as Sacchi Kavitayan (Sudarshan Chakra) to express their view on discrimination on class & caste basis.

Long Answer Type Questions

1. The availability of printed materials and influences the education and career opportunities of scholars:

   (*i*) **Wider Distribution:** Imperial sponsorship of printed textbooks increased study material availability, aiding effective preparation for exams. *(1 M)*

   (*ii*) **Standardisation:** Printed materials standardized knowledge, ensuring equal access to information for all scholars. *(1 M)*

   (*iii*) **Higher Literacy Rates:** Availability of printed texts encouraged literacy, boosting reading and writing skills among potential scholars. *(1 M)*

   (*iv*) **Efficient Learning:** Printed materials made studying more efficient, allowing scholars to cover more content in less time. *(1 M)*

   (*v*) **Career Opportunities:** Success in civil service exams, facilitated by accessible printed materials, opened prestigious bureaucratic career paths, enhancing social mobility and intellectual growth. *(1 M)*

2. At the turn of the 20th century, new publication forms emerged, reflecting societal changes and technological advancements:

(i) **Novels:** Became popular, exploring personal experiences and relationships, offering insights into human emotions and societal norms. *(1¼ M)*

(ii) **Short Stories and Essays:** Gained traction, discussing social, political, and intimate issues, influencing public perspectives. *(1¼ M)*

(iii) **Visual Culture:** Enhanced by printing innovations, including widely circulated paintings by artists like Raja Ravi Varma, and the spread of cheap prints and calendars that affected views on modernity and tradition. *(1¼ M)*

(iv) **Caricatures and Cartoons:** Appeared in journals and newspapers, providing commentary on social and political issues, using humor and satire to influence public opinion. *(1¼ M)*

3. Print culture had a transformative impact on women in 19th-century India, promoting education and social change. Here are the effects explained concisely:

(i) **Education Opportunities:** Increased access to print led to more educational opportunities for women, fostering literacy and allowing participation in cultural and intellectual discussions. *(1 M)*

(ii) **Emergence of Women Writers:** More literate women like Rashsundari Debi started writing, offering perspectives on women's issues and experiences. *(1 M)*

(iii) **Social Reform Advocacy:** Printed works empowered women to challenge oppressive norms and practices, such as child marriage and Sati. *(1 M)*

(iv) **Expressive Platform:** Print provided a new platform for women to express and publish their creative works, broadening their cultural impact. *(1 M)*

(v) **Empowerment through Resistance:** Despite societal resistance, print enabled women to advocate for their rights and promote empowerment through literacy. *(1 M)*

Case Based Questions

Case Based-I

(i) Print media spread new ideas quickly, enabling inclusive debates and challenging traditional norms, which fostered public discussions and social reforms in early 19th-century India. *(1 M)*

(ii) Print culture expanded debates by making diverse ideas accessible, fostering widespread public engagement across social boundaries. *(1 M)*

(iii) The print culture reflected a great interest in women's lives and emotions by providing a platform for women to express their opinions and ideas. *(1 M)*

- Social reforms and novels had already created a great interest in women's lives and emotions, and the print culture helped to reinforce this interest by enabling women to express their opinions through various literary forms. *(1 M)*

Case Based-II

(i) The primary aim was to disseminate knowledge and promote the welfare of the people. *(1 M)*

(ii) 'The task of the native newspapers and political associations is identical to the role of the Opposition in the House of Commons in Parliament in England. *(1 M)*

(iii) The popularity of newspapers in the 19th century can be attributed to increased literacy rates and education, which created a larger readership base. *(1 M)*

- People's ability to read led to a growing demand for news and information. Newspapers also served as platforms for expressing opinions and discussing public issues, fostering participation and involvement in societal discussions. *(1 M)*

Case Based-III

(i) The thirst, hunger, and focus of Mercier reflect the immersive nature of reading. *(1 M)*

(ii) Mercier describes himself as a "virtual writer" because It focuses on his deep engagement and immersive experience with reading, not writing. *(1 M)*

(iii) **Intellectual Nourishment:** Mercier compares his reading experience to a man dying of thirst drinking fresh water, illustrating how reading served as essential nourishment for his intellect, expanding his mind with new ideas and perspectives just as water revitalizes the body. *(1 M)*

Engagement with New Concepts: The passage highlights how absorbed Mercier was in his reading, to the extent that he lost track of time and his surroundings. This deep engagement allowed new ideas to "rush into his brain," suggesting that reading significantly enhanced his understanding and adoption of new concepts. *(1 M)*

❑❑❑

POLITICAL SCIENCE

1 POWER-SHARING

"I bring peace, harmony, fraternity, and unity.
I prevent discrimination, disintegration, conflicts, and abuse of power.
I ensure equality, justice, political stability, and fair representation.
Overall, I strengthen democracy."
— Power-sharing

SYLLABUS & WEIGHTAGE

Concept Names	Years					
	2020	2021	2022	2023	2024	2025
Belgium and Sri Lanka	1 Q (1 M)	Exam not Conducted	—	—	—	1 Q (1 M)
Majoritarianism in Sri Lanka	—		—	1 Q (1 M)	—	—
Accommodation in Belgium	1 Q (1 M)		—	1 Q (1 M)	1 Q (1 M) 1 Q (4 M)	—
Forms of power sharing	2 Q (1 M + 1 M)		—	1 Q (2 M)	—	1 Q (2 M)

CONCEPT MAP

To Access One Shot Revision Video Scan This QR Code

Power Sharing

Case Study: Sri Lanka (CBSE 2020)

Location & Population (CBSE 2025, 2020)

- An island nation, few kilometres off the southern coast of Tamil Nadu.
- The population of about two crore, the same as in Haryana
- **Majority-**
  - 74% Sinhalese speakers
- **Minority-**
  - 18% Tamil speakers (Hindus or Muslims)
    - → 13% Sri-Lankan Tamils
    - → 5% Indian Tamils
  - 7% Christians(Tamils and Sinhala speaker)

Reason of Conflict

Sinhala leaders adopted majoritarian measures to establish Sinhala supremacy after independence in 1948.

Response to Conflict → MAJORITARIANISM

- Paid no attention to minorities need and wishes.
- Sinhala was recognised as the only official language by an act in 1956.
- Preference to Sinhalese in government jobs and universities.
- Protected and fostered Buddhism.

Outcomes

- Feeling of alienation among Sri-Lankan Tamils
- **Tamils Started demanding-**
  - Recognition of Tamil as an official language
  - Regional autonomy
  - Equality of opportunity in jobs and education
  - Independent Tamil Ealam (State) in northern and eastern part of Sri Lanka
  - **Civil War-**
    - → Thousands of people were killed from both communities.
    - → Families were forced to leave the country as refugees.
    - → Many people lost their livelihood.

Case Study: Belgium

Location & Population (CBSE 2025)

- A small country in Europe(Smaller than Haryana).
- Share border with the Netherlands, France, Luxembourg, and Germany.
- Population- little over one crore(about the half of the Haryana's population)
- **Majority-**
  - Country- Dutch(59%, Flemish)
  - Capital city(Brussels)- French(80%)
- **Minority-**
  - Country- French(40%, Wallonia)
  - Capital city(Brussels)- Dutch(20%)

Reason of Conflict (CBSE 2025)

- The french speaking community was relatively rich and powerful.
- Dutch-speaking (majority) community got the benefit of economic development and education much later then the minority French-speaking community

Outcomes

- No civic strife between the two major communities
- Prevented the possible division of the country on linguistic lines.

Response to Conflict → ACCOMMODATION (CBSE 2024, 2020)

- Recognised the existence of regional differences and cultural diversities
- Amended constitution four times between 1970-1993 to ensure peaceful co-existence
- **Elements of Belgium model-**
  - Equal no. of Dutch and French speaking ministers in central government.
  - Support of majority of members from each linguistic group to prevent dominance of any one group.
  - Devolution of power to state government.
  - State government not subordinate to central government.
  - Separate government for brussel in which both communities have equal representation.
  - Community government- Elected by people belonging to one language community.

Power Sharing

Why power sharing is desirable?

Prudential Reasons

It can lead to better outcomes like less conflict, and more stability and keep the country running smoothly.

Moral Reasons

It is the right thing to do in a democracy because it respects everyone's rights and opinions.

Forms of Power Sharing

CBSE 2023

(i) Horizontal Division of Power CBSE 2025, 2024, 2020

- Between the different organs of the government - Legislature, Executive and Judiciary.

(ii) Vertical Division of Power

- Between the different levels of government - Central, State & Local self government.

(iii) Power Sharing among different social groups CBSE 2025

- Between various social groups such as linguistic and religious groups.
- E.g.: Belgium's Community Government

(iv) Power Sharing among Influential groups

- Political Parties, Business men, Industrialists, Farmers Industrial workers.
- E.g.: Coalition Government.

Advantages of Power sharing

CBSE 2023

- Bring peace, harmony and unity.
- Prevent discrimination, disintegration, conflicts and abuse of power.
- Ensure fair representation and political stability.

1 BELGIUM AND SRI LANKA

NCERT Definitions *(Commonly asked in 1 mark)*

- **Power Sharing:** It refers to the division of power among different branches of government or between different levels of government, communities, or political groups. For example: Belgium's model of power sharing, where power is shared among centers, states, and linguistic groups.
- **Ethnic:** It refers to a group of people who share a common culture, language, or ancestry. In Belgium the Dutch speakers (Flemish region) and French speakers (Walloon region) are the example of this.
- **Minority:** A minority is a smaller group within a larger population that might have different language, religion, or cultural practices than the majority. For example Tamil-speakers in Sri Lanka.
- **Majority:** This term is often used to describe the group that has more people compared to other groups within the population of a country or society. For example, Sinhala speakers in Sri Lanka.

Important Facts

Belgium

- Ethnic composition(based on language):
  - 59% speak Dutch (Flemish region)
  - 40% speak French (Wallonia region)
  - 1% speak German
- Capital city(Brussel):
  - 80% speak French
  - 20% speak Dutch

The Dutch-speaking people constituted a majority in the country, but a minority in the capital city Brussel.

Sri Lanka

- Ethnic composition (based on language):
  - 74% Sinhalese speaking people
  - 18% Tamil speaking people
    - 13% Sri-Lankan Tamils
    - 5% Indian Tamils
- Religion
  - Most of the Sinhalese people are Buddhists.
  - Most of the Tamils are Hindus or Muslims.
  - There are about 7 percent Christians, who are both Tamil and Sinhala.

Difference Between

Belgium Vs. Sri Lanka		
Aspect	**Belgium**	**Sri Lanka**
Location	• Small country of Europe. • Share borders with France, the Netherlands, Germany, and the Luxembourg.	• Island nation of South Asia. • Few kilometres off the southern coast of Tamil Nadu.
Population	• Little over one crore (about half of Haryana's population).	• About two crore (similar to Haryana's population)
Major Language Distribution	• Dutch in the Flemish region. • French in Walloon region.	• Sinhala in the majority. • Tamil in the north and east.

Mnemonics

- Ethnic Communities of Sri Lanka:
  "MISS"
  - **M** → **Muslim**
  - **I** → **Indian Tamils**
  - **S** → **Sri Lankan Tamils**
  - **S** → **Sinhalese**

- Countries sharing border with Belgium:
  "Not For Low Goals"
  - **N** → **Netherland**
  - **F** → **France**
  - **L** → **Luxembourg**
  - **G** → **Germany**

COMPETENCY BASED SOLVED EXAMPLES

Scan Me for Detailed Explanations

Multiple Choice Questions

(1 M)

1. Which one of the following is a major caste group of Sri Lanka. ***(Re)*(CBSE DL, 2020)**

(*a*) Christian and Tamil (*b*) Buddhist and Hindu

(*c*) Sinhali and Tamil (*d*) Sinhali and Christian

2. Consider the following two statements on power sharing and select the answer using the codes given below: **(*Un* and *An*) (NCERT Exercise)**

A. Power sharing is good for democracy.

B. It helps to reduce the possibility of conflict between social groups.

Which of these statements are true and false?

(*a*) A is true but B is false (*b*) Both A and B are true

(*c*) Both A and B are false (*d*) A is false but B is true

3. Study the map thoroughly and choose the correct option: **(*An*)**

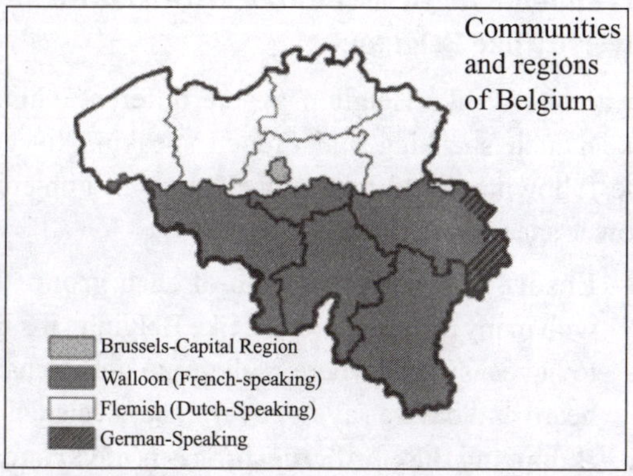

Which of the following language are dominantly present in belgium:

(*a*) German (*b*) Dutch

(*c*) French (*d*) Sinhala

4. Most of the Sinhala-speaking people are **(*Re*)**

(*a*) Buddhists (*b*) Hindus

(*c*) Muslims (*d*) Christians

5. Which one of the following countries does not share its boundary with Belgium? **(*Re*)**

(*a*) France (*b*) The Netherlands

(*c*) Sweden (*d*) Luxembourg

6. Consider the following statements on Power sharing and choose the correct option. **(*An*)(CBSE, 2023)**

(*i*) Imposing the will of majority community over others.

(*ii*) It helps in reducing the possibility of conflict between the social groups.

(*iii*) Power sharing is a good way to ensure the stability of political order.

(*iv*) It brings socio-political opposition among parties.

(*a*) (*i*) and (*iii*) (*b*) (*ii*) and (*iii*)

(*c*) (*i*) and (*iv*) (*d*) (*i*) and (*ii*)

7. Which of the following is the capital city of Belgium? **(*Re*)**

(*a*) Netherland (*b*) Brussels

(*c*) Europe (*d*) France

8. Consider the following statements on Power Sharing and choose the correct option: **(*Ev*)(CBSE, 2023)**

(*i*) Majoritarianism is the real spirit of democracy.

(*ii*) It creates balance and harmony in different groups.

(*iii*) It reduces the possibility of conflict among social groups.

(*iv*) Power sharing is the essence of democracy.

(*a*) (*i*), (*ii*) and (*iii*) (*b*) (*ii*), (*iii*) and (*iv*)

(*c*) (*i*), (*iii*) and (*iv*) (*d*) (*i*), (*ii*) and (*iv*)

Assertion and Reason

(1 M)

Direction: The following questions consist of two statements – Assertion (A) and Reason (R). Answer these questions by selecting the appropriate option given below:

(*a*) Both A and R are true, and R is the correct explanation of A.

(*b*) Both A and R are true, but R is not the correct explanation of A.

(*c*) A is true, but R is false.

(*d*) A is false, but R is true.

1. **Assertion (A):** Belgium is a small country in United States, smaller in area than the state of Haryana.
   Reason (R): It has borders with France, the Netherlands, Germany and Luxembourg. **(*Re*)**
2. **Assertion (A):** The minority french speaking community was resented by Dutch speaking community.
   Reason (R): French speaking community was relatively rich and powerful and dutch speaking community got the benefit of economic development and education much later. **(*Ev*)**
3. **Assertion (A):** Power sharing can help to prevent conflict in society.
   Reason (R): Power sharing ensures that different social groups are included in decision-making processes, reducing marginalisation and fostering inclusivity. **(*Ev* and *An*)(CBSE APQ, 2023)**
4. **Assertion (A):** The Sri Lankan government recognised sinhala as the only official language of Sri Lanka.
   Reason (R): The Sri Lankan government wanted to establish Tamil supremacy. **(*Ev* and *An*)(CBSE APQ, 2023)**

Subjective Questions

Very Short Answer Type Questions

(2 M)

1. **Study the map thoroughly and mention the languages that are dominantly present in Belgium.** **(*Re*)(CBSE SQP, 2023)**

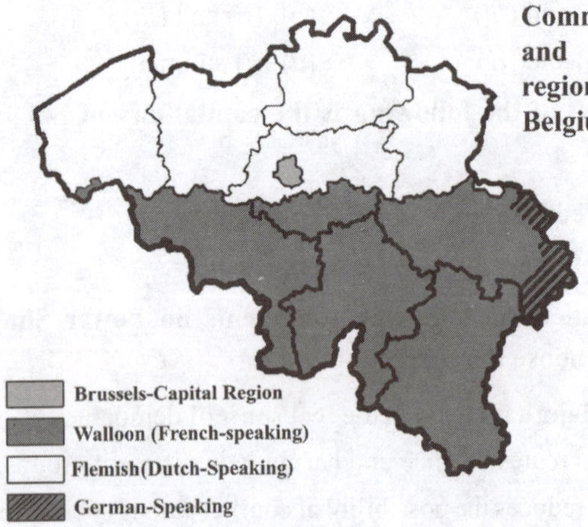

Ans. As per the map, in Belgium-

- The dominant languages are the **Dutch** and the **French**. *(1 M)*
- Dutch is spoken by the majority in the **Flemish region**. Whereas French is spoken by a large population in the **Wallonia region**. *(1 M)*

2. **Name two major ethnic groups in Sri Lanka and their primary religions.** **(*Re*)**

Ans. The two major ethnic groups in Sri Lanka are:

- **Sinhala speakers:** Sinhala speakers make up about 74% of the country's population, and their primary religion is Buddhism. *(1 M)*
- **Tamil speakers:** Tamil speakers make up about 18% of the country's population, and they are primarily Hindus or Muslims. *(1 M)*

Short Answer Type Questions

(3 M)

1. **Why is Brussels unique in the context of language distribution in Belgium?** **(*An*)**

Ans. Brussels is unique in the context of language distribution in Belgium because: **(Any two)**

- **Presence of Both Communities:** In the rest of the country, regions are divided where either Dutch or French-speaking people live. For example, in the Walloon region, a French-speaking community lives and in the Flemish region Dutch-speaking people live but in the region of the capital city Brussels, we can see the presence of both linguistic communities. *(1½ M)*
- **Majority French-Speaking Population Despite Flemish Region:** Brussel is the capital city of Belgium and is located in the Dutch-speaking Flemish region. But despite being in the Dutch-speaking Flemish region, it has a majority of French speakers. *(1½ M)*
- **Dutch-Speaking Minority in Brussels:** It presents a special situation where the Dutch-speaking majority in the country becomes a minority in their capital city Brussels. *(1½ M)*

2. **Analyze the challenges in implementing power-sharing arrangements in a country with significant ethnic diversity like Belgium.** **(*An*)**

Ans. In a country like Belgium, where different ethnic groups like Dutch speaking and French speaking live together, the following could be the challenges in implementing a power-sharing arrangement:

- **Ensure fair representation of each group:** In places with many different groups, like Belgium, it's important to have a system where each group gets a chance to be heard and have a say in government decisions. *(1½ M)*
- **Balancing the conflicting interests of various groups:** This means finding a fair solution that considers the different wants and needs of various groups. The government tries to listen to everyone and find a balance that works for all so that no one group's needs overpower the others. *(1½ M)*

Long Answer Type Questions

(5 M)

1. Compare the situation of Belgium and Sri Lanka considering their location, size, and cultural aspects. *(An)* **(CBSE, 2019)**

Ans. *(1 + 1 + 3 = 5M)*

Aspects	Belgium	Sri Lanka
Location	• Belgium is a small country in Europe. Share borders with the Netherlands, France, Germany, and Luxembourg	• Sri Lanka is an island nation in South Asia located in the Indian Ocean, a few kilometers away from the southern coast of Tamil Nadu (India).
Size	• Belgium is a small country with an area smaller than the Indian state of Haryana, and it has a population of little over one crore which is about half of Haryana's population.	• Sri Lanka is a small country about the same size as Haryana in India. It has a population of about 2 crores, approximately the same as Haryana.
Cultural Aspects	• In Belgium, there are two major communities: the Dutch and the French. • The majority of people speak Dutch (59%), followed by French (40%), and German (1%). • Belgium shares power well with equal representation for French and Dutch speakers in central government, a federal structure for regions, and community governments for cultural autonomy.	• In Sri Lanka, there are two major social groups: the Sinhalese and the Tamils. • Sinhala speakers are in the majority (74%), and Tamil speakers (18%) are in the minority. • Sri Lanka didn't share power well. The government favoured Sinhala speakers, leaving Tamil speakers feeling left out. This led to the Civil War.

Nailing the Right Answer

- Use two columns, one for Belgium and the other for Sri Lanka.
- Include all the headings(Location, Size, cultural aspect) seperately for comparison criteria.
- Explain each heading as per the marks allotted.

2 MAJORITARIANISM IN SRI LANKA

NCERT Definitions *(Commonly asked in 1 mark)*

- **Majoritarianism:** It is a belief or practice where the majority group in a society has the power to make decisions that affect everyone. E.g.: Government's policies that favoured the Sinhala-speaking majority over Tamil-Speaking in Sri Lanka.

- **Civil War:** A violent conflict between opposing groups within a country that becomes so intense that it appears like a war. For example, war between the Sinhala-speaking majority and Tamil-speaking minority in Sri Lanka.

Difference Between

Sri Lanka Before Vs. After the Civil War	
Sri Lanka Before Civil War	**Sri Lanka After Civil War**
Sri Lanka was noted for its excellent economic development, education, and health record.	Significant setback to the country's social, cultural, and economic life, highlighting how unresolved ethnic and political conflicts badly affect a country's progress.

Myth Buster

- **Myth:** When one group makes the country's decisions, without considering what the other group wants is known as Majoritarianism.

  Fact: The concept of majoritarianism is only applicable when the majority population of the country makes all the decisions without considering and consulting the minority population. When decisions are made by a minority of the population, disregarding the preferences of the majority group, it is not termed majoritarianism but rather represents a concept of minority rule.

  Example: The 1971 war between East Pakistan (now Bangladesh) and West Pakistan (Pakistan) illustrate minority rule where despite a larger population, East Pakistan was marginalized politically, economically, and linguistically by West Pakistan's government.

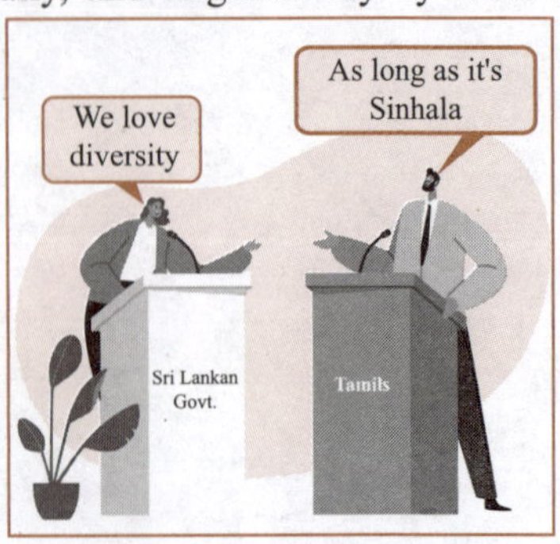

Important Dates

- **1948:** Sri Lanka gained independence.
- **1956:** An act made Sinhala the only official language of Sri Lanka.

COMPETENCY BASED SOLVED EXAMPLES

Scan Me for Detailed Explanations

Multiple Choice Questions

(1 M)

1. **In 1956, the Sri Lankan government passed an Act that recognized ________ as the only official language.** ***(Re)***

   (*a*) Tamil (*b*) Sinhala
   (*c*) English (*d*) Buddhist

2. **Which of the following statements accurately distinguishes between Majoritarianism and Power sharing?** ***(Un)*(CBSE SQP, 2023)**

   (*a*) Majoritarianism emphasises the dominance of the majority community, while Power sharing emphasises the sharing of power among different groups.
   (*b*) Majoritarianism emphasises the need for consensus building, while Power sharing emphasises the exclusion of minority groups.
   (*c*) Majoritarianism emphasises the importance of accommodating minority interests, while Power sharing emphasises the need for majority rule.
   (*d*) Majoritarianism emphasises the need for peaceful resolution of conflicts, while Power sharing emphasises the use of force to impose the majority's will.

3. **The preferential policies implemented by the Sri Lankan government favored ________ for university positions and government jobs.** ***(Re)***

   (*a*) Tamil applicants
   (*b*) English-speaking applicants
   (*c*) Sinhala applicants
   (*d*) Buddhist applicants

4. **A war-like conflict between two opposite groups within a country is called ________.** ***(Re)***

   (*a*) Cold war (*b*) Civil war
   (*c*) Ethnic war (*d*) None of these

5. **Find the incorrect option.** ***(An)***

   A. Sri Lanka emerged as an independent country in 1958.
   B. Majoritarianism measures adopted by Belgium ultimately led to the civil war.
   C. Power sharing is a good way to ensure the stability of political order.
   D. In 1956, an Act was passed to recognise Sinhala as the only official language, thus disregarding Tamil.

   (*a*) C and D (*b*) B and C
   (*c*) A and B (*d*) A, B and D

6. **Which demand of the Sri-Lankan Tamils was repeatedly denied?** ***(Re)* (CBSE APQ, 2023)**

   (*a*) Their demand of separate electorate
   (*b*) Their demand for freedom of expression.
   (*c*) Their demand for the right to vote.
   (*d*) Their demand for more autonomy to provinces populated by the Tamils.

7. **Analyze the map of Sri Lanka's ethnic communities and consider the historical and social factors that have shaped the current distribution of ethnic groups. Which approach would be most innovative and sustainable to address the ethnic conflict in Sri Lanka?** ***(An)***

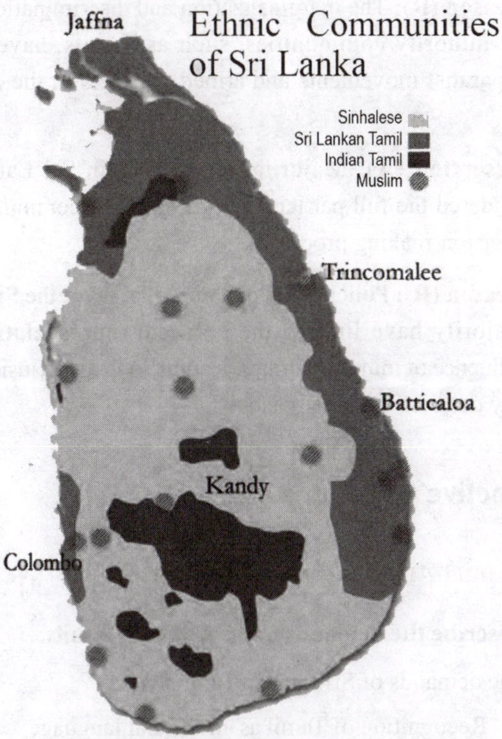

   (*a*) Establishing a bilingual education system across the country.
   (*b*) Offering autonomy to regions based on ethnic majority.
   (*c*) Conducting yearly cultural exchange programs between ethnic groups.
   (*d*) All of the above.

Assertion and Reason

(1 M)

Direction: **The following questions consist of two statements – Assertion (A) and Reason (R). Answer these questions by selecting the appropriate option given below:**

(*a*) Both A and R are true, and R is the correct explanation of A.

(*b*) Both A and R are true, but R is not the correct explanation of A.

(*c*) A is true, but R is false

(*d*) A is false, but R is true.

1. **Assertion (A):** The Sinhala community sought to establish dominance over government by virtue of their majority.

   Reason (R): The democratically elected government adopted a series of majoritarian measures to establish Sinhala supremacy. *(An and Un)*

2. **Assertion (A):** Tamils felt none of the major political parties led by the buddhist Sinhala leaders were sensitive to their language and culture.

   Reason (R): Tamils was treated equals as Sinhala. *(Ev)*

3. **Assertion (A):** Majoritarianism has played a role in the escalation of violence and civil war in Sri Lanka.

   Reason (R): The marginalization and discrimination faced by minority communities, such as Tamils, have fueled separatist movements and armed conflicts in the country. *(An)*

4. **Assertion (A):** Majoritarian politics in Sri Lanka has hindered the full participation of minority communities in decision-making processes.

   Reason (R): Policies and practices that favor the Sinhalese majority have limited the political representation and influence of minority groups, leading to their exclusion from key decision-making positions. *(Ev)*

Subjective Questions

Very Short Answer Type Questions (1 or 2 M)

1. **Describe the demands of Sri Lankan Tamils.** *(Re)*

Ans. The demands of Sri Lankan Tamils were:

- Recognition of Tamil as an official language *(½ M)*
- Provision of regional autonomy *(½ M)*
- Equality of opportunity in securing education and jobs *(½ M)*
- An independent Tamil Eelam (state) in northern and eastern parts of Sri Lanka *(½ M)*

2. **How did the feeling of alienation develop among the Sri Lankan Tamils?** *(Un)*(CBSE, 2019)

Ans. The feeling of alienation developed among the Sri Lankan Tamils because the government favoured the Sinhala majority, making Sinhala the only official language and prioritizing Sinhalas in jobs and education, ignoring Tamil rights and interests. *(1 M)*

Short Answer Type Questions (3 M)

1. **What were the reasons for the civil war in Sri Lanka?** *(An)*

Ans. The reasons for the Civil War in Sri Lanka were:

- **Majoritarian Measures in Sri Lanka:** The democratically elected government in Sri Lanka adopted a series of majoritarian measures to establish Sinhala supremacy in Sri Lanka *(1 M)*
- **Preferential Policies for Sinhalese:** The government followed preferential policies that favored Sinhalese in respect of jobs, education, religion and many more. *(1 M)*
- **Alienation of Sri Lankan Tamils:** All the measures taken by the government gradually increased the feeling of alienation among the Sri Lankan Tamils. They felt themselves deprived which ultimately led to the civil war. *(1 M)*

2. **Apart from Sri Lanka, another example of majoritarianism is the situation in Nazi Germany under Adolf Hitler's leadership.**

   The Nazi government believed that one group, the Aryan race, was better than others. They thought this group had the right to control everything in politics, society, and the economy. Unfortunately, they didn't care about the rights, dignity, and lives of other groups, especially the Jews.

   This way of favoring the majority led to a very sad and terrible event called the Holocaust. During this time, around six million Jewish people, along with other minority groups, were persecuted and killed by the government.

   (*a*) What can we learn from the Holocaust about majoritarianism? *(2 M) (Ev)*

   (*b*) Suggest ways to prevent such cruelty and suppression of rights in the future. *(1 M) (Cr)*

Ans. (*a*) The Holocaust teaches us that when the majority is allowed to control everything without considering the rights of minorities, terrible things can happen. It can lead to Cruelty against humanity and the suppression of fundamental human rights. *(2 M)*

(*b*) To prevent such cruelty in the future, we must ensure that everyone's rights are respected, regardless of their race, religion, or background. We need to promote equality and tolerance to build a better and safer world for everyone. *(1 M)*

3. **What were the Majoritarian measures taken in Sri Lanka to establish Sinhala supremacy?** *(Re)*

Ans. Majoritarian measures taken in Sri Lanka to establish Sinhala supremacy were:

- In 1956, an Act was passed which recognised Sinhala as the only official language, thus disregarding Tamil language. *(1 M)*

- Preferences were given to Sinhala applicants for university positions and government jobs, etc. *(1 M)*
- A new Constitution declares that the state will protect and promote Buddhism. Sri Lankan Tamil felt that none of the major political parties led by Buddhist Sinhala leaders were sensitive to their language and culture. *(1 M)*

4. Using Sri Lanka's example, where majoritarian measures were adopted by the democratically elected government, analyze:

(*i*) How the recognition of Sinhala as the only official language in 1956 impacted the Tamil community. ***(An)***

(*ii*) What was the impact of the majoritarian measures adopted by the Sri Lankan government? ***(An)***

Ans. (*i*) In 1956, a law was passed making Sinhala the only official language and ignoring Tamil. This decision made Tamil speakers feel left out and unfairly treated based on their language. *(1 M)*

(*ii*) The majoritarian measures adopted by the government led to the feeling of alienation among Sri Lankan Tamils where Tamils started demanding for separate Tamil Ealam state, recognition of Tamil as an official language, and equality of opportunity in securing education and jobs. But their demand were repeatedly denied which ultimately led to the civil war. *(2 M)*

Long Answer Type Questions (5 M)

1. Imagine a classroom where the teacher asks the students to vote on what movie they want to watch during a fun day. There are 30 students in the class. 18 students prefer action movies, while 12 students prefer animated movies. The teacher chooses the majority's choice and selects an action movie for the class to watch.

(*a*) What does the above example show? *(1 M)* ***(Un)***

(*b*) If this decision-making pattern is routinely followed, what could be the long-term effects on minority students' participation and interest in class activities? *(2 M)* ***(An)***

(*c*) Discuss the importance of inclusive decision-making in diverse groups, and how it can be beneficial to both minority and majority in the long run. *(2 M)* ***(Ev and Cr)***

Ans. (*a*) The example demonstrates majoritarianism, where the majority's choice (action movie) is favored, disregarding the preferences of the minority (animated movie fans). *(1 M)*

(*b*) If this decision-making pattern is routinely followed, then it may lead to minority students feeling ignored and disengaged from class activities. Over time, they might become less interested in participating, which could affect their overall growth, and engagement in the classroom. *(2 M)*

(*c*) Inclusive decision-making ensures that all voices are heard and considered. This fosters a sense of belonging and respect among all students, leading to better cooperation and understanding between the minority and the majority. Ultimately, inclusive decision-making benefits the entire class by creating a more cohesive and supportive learning environment. *(2 M)*

3 ACCOMODATION IN BELGIUM

NCERT Definitions (Commonly asked in 1 mark)

- **Community Government:** This is a special kind of government which is elected by people belonging to one language community – Dutch, French and German-speaking – no matter where they live. This government has the power regarding cultural, educational and language-related issues.
- **Democratic Rule:** This is the rule where people have the power to govern themselves, either directly or through the representatives elected by them, and influence decisions.
- **Tyranny of the Majority:** "Tyranny of the majority" refers to a situation where the larger group or majority in a society uses its power to oppress, mistreat, or disregard the rights of the smaller group or minority.

Classification

Reasons for power sharing:

A. Prudential reason

B. Moral reason

Difference Between

Moral reasons Vs. Prudential reasons of Power-Sharing		
Aspect	**Prudential reasons**	**Moral reasons**
Definition	These are practical reasons for making decisions. In the context of power-sharing, it means supporting power-sharing because it can lead to better outcomes like less conflict, and more stability and keep the country running smoothly.	These are the moral reasons based on what is right and just. Regarding power sharing, it's about the belief that sharing power is the right thing to do in a democracy because it respects everyone's rights and opinions.
Focus	On Reducing conflicts and ensuring political stability.	All people have a voice in governance
Aim	Achieving a stable and harmonious society where conflicts are minimized.	Respecting and valuing every citizen's participation in the democratic process.

Belgium Vs. Sri Lanka's approach to Ethnic Diversity		
Aspect	**Belgium**	**Sri Lanka**
Approaches to Ethnic Diversity	Belgium opted for a complex but effective power-sharing model to respect and include its diverse communities, preventing linguistic or cultural conflict.	Sri Lanka, in contrast, adopted majoritarian measures, where the dominance of a majority community led to national disunity and conflict.

Important Dates

- **1970-1993:** Belgium changed its constitution four times to find a way for everyone to live peacefully in the same country.

COMPETENCY BASED SOLVED EXAMPLES

Scan Me for Detailed Explanations

Multiple Choice Questions

(1 M)

1. What was the purpose of the amendments to the Belgian constitution between 1970 and 1993? ***(Un)***

(*a*) To establish separate state governments

(*b*) To promote regional differences

(*c*) To divide the country on linguistic lines

(*d*) To enable peaceful coexistence within the same country

2. Which of the following was the primary objective of Belgium to form the separate government in Brussels? ***(Un)*(CBSE, 2024)**

(*a*) Promoting cultural events.

(*b*) Managing international relations.

(*c*) Enforcing local laws.

(*d*) Ensuring linguistic accommodation.

3. What lesson can be learned from the examples of Belgium and Sri Lanka? ***(Un)***

(*a*) Power sharing is not necessary in democracies.

(*b*) Unity in a country can be achieved by ignoring the interests of different communities.

(*c*) Power sharing and respecting the interests of different communities can help maintain the unity of a country.

(*d*) The European Union chose Brussels as its headquarters because of Belgium's complicated arrangements.

4. In a class discussion on the Belgian model of power-sharing, you are tasked with critically evaluating each component listed below. Determine which of these elements does not align with the principles of the Belgian power-sharing model ***(Ev)***

(*a*) Some laws can only be passed with a majority from each linguistic group.

(*b*) The central government has an equal number of Dutch and French ministers.

(*c*) State governments of the two linguistic regions enjoy some powers of the central government.

(*d*) Territories based on language were abolished and people were encouraged to live amongst each other.

5. When many countries of Europe came together to form the European Union, ______ was chosen as its headquarters. ***(Re)*(CBSE SQP, 2023)**

(*a*) Brussels (*b*) Paris

(*c*) London (*d*) Zurich

6. Which of the following statements accurately describes a "community government"? ***(Re)*(CBSE AQP, 2023)**

(*i*) 'community government' is elected by people belonging to one language community – Dutch, French and German-speaking – no matter where they live.

(*ii*) This government has the power regarding cultural, educational and language-related issues.

(*iii*) This government has the power regarding economical, educational and language-related issues.

(*iv*) 'community government' is elected by people belonging to one language community – Dutch, Spanish and German-speaking – no matter where they live.

(*a*) Only (*i*) (*b*) Only (*iii*)

(*c*) Only (*iv*) (*d*) Both (*i*) and (*ii*)

Assertion and Reason

(1 M)

Direction: The following questions consist of two statements – Assertion (A) and Reason (R). Answer these questions by selecting the appropriate option given below:

(*a*) Both A and R are true, and R is the correct explanation of A.

(*b*) Both A and R are true, but R is not the correct explanation of A.

(*c*) A is true, but R is false.

(*d*) A is false, but R is true.

1. **Assertion (A):** The accommodation of linguistic diversity in Belgium has been a challenging process.

   Reason (R): Belgium is a country with two main linguistic communities, French-speaking (Wallonia) and Dutch-speaking (Flemish), which have different cultural and political identities. ***(An)***

2. **Assertion (A):** In Belgium, there is a mutually acceptable arrangement for sharing power

   Reason (R): The leaders realised that the unity of the country is possible only by respecting the feelings and interests of different communities and regions. ***(Ev)***

3. **Assertion (A):** Regional autonomy has played a significant role in the accommodation policies of Belgium.

   Reason (R): Sri Lanka has devolved certain powers and decision-making authority to its regional governments to accommodate regional differences and aspirations. ***(An)***

Subjective Questions

Very Short Answer Type Questions

(1 or 2 M)

1. State any one step taken in Belgium to rule out the problem of regional differences and cultural diversities. ***(Un)*(CBSE, 2020)**

Ans. Adoption of a federal system of government. Under this system, power is divided between the central government and the regional governments, allowing each region to have some degree of autonomy and control over its affairs. *(1 M)*

2. *"In Belgium, a unique power-sharing model was established to accommodate the diverse linguistic and regional communities, promoting stability and unity within the country."* ***(Un)***

What does the above statement illustrate about the relationship between power-sharing and national unity?

Ans. (*i*) The statement illustrates that power-sharing can strengthen national unity by acknowledging and respecting the diversity within a country. *(1 M)*

(*ii*) Involving various groups in governance reduces conflicts and fosters cooperation because no single group can dominate others, and all people feel respected and valued. *(1 M)*

3. What is the purpose of equal representation in Brussels? *(Un)*

Ans. The purpose is to maintain balance and avoid potential conflicts between the linguistic communities. By ensuring equal representation in Brussels, both communities have equal a say in the governance and decision-making process and thus, no single community can make decisions unilaterally. *(2 M)*

Short Answer Type Questions (3 M)

1. Reflecting on the power-sharing arrangements in Belgium, a historian commented, *"The intricate system of government in Belgium, including community governments for different linguistic groups, not only preserves peace but also respects the unique cultural identities of these groups."*

Discuss how this arrangement has contributed to political stability and cultural integrity in Belgium. *(Ev)*

Ans. (*i*) **Political Stability:** It allows each linguistic group to govern themselves in matters related to their cultural, educational, and language-related issues. This autonomy ensures that each community's specific needs and preferences are addressed, leading to greater satisfaction among the groups and reducing the likelihood of conflict. *(1 ½ M)*

(*ii*) **Cultural Integrity:** By allowing each community to manage its educational and cultural policies, Belgium has successfully preserved the unique identities of its diverse linguistic groups. This respect for cultural integrity also helps in maintaining peace among the communities. *(1 ½ M)*

2. State one prudential reason and one moral reason for power sharing with an example from the Indian context. *(An)***(NCERT)**

Ans. **Prudential Reason:** Power-sharing promotes stability and prevents conflicts. In India, diverse communities like Hindus, Muslims, Sikhs, and others coexist. Sharing power ensures representation for all, reducing the chances of tensions and unrest. *(1½ M)*

Moral Reason: It's the essence of democracy. It reflects fairness and equality. For instance, India's reservation system ensures political participation for historically marginalized communities, morally upholding the principles of justice and inclusivity. *(1½ M)*

3. Describe the elements of the Belgian model for accommodating diversities *(Re)***(CBSE, 2020)**

Ans. Some elements of Belgian model are: **(Any Three)**

- The constitution prescribes equal representation of Dutch and French-speaking ministers in the central government. *(1 M)*
- Special laws require the support of the majority of members from each linguistic group, preventing unilateral decision-making by any single community. *(1 M)*
- Many powers of the central government have been delegated to state governments of the two regions. *(1 M)*
- Brussels has a separate government with equal representation for both linguistic communities. *(1 M)*
- There is a community government elected by people belonging to each language community, with powers regarding cultural, educational, and language-related issues. *(1 M)*

Topper's Explanation

• The central government prescribes that the number of Dutch and French speaking ministers shall be equal in the central government. Some laws require support of majority of members in both groups, thus no one group can take decisions unilaterally.

• Many powers of the central government have been given to the State governments in both the regions which are not subordinate to the central government.

• Brussels has a separate government in which both the communities have equal representation. French agreed to equal representation in Brussels because Dutch agreed to equal representation in the central government.

• The Community government is elected by members of one language group no matter where they live. Dutch, German or French. It has power related to the educational, language and cultural issues.

Long Answer Type Questions (5 M)

1. Why is the Belgian model considered innovative and What has the Belgian model helped to prevent? *(An)*

Ans. The Belgian model is considered innovative because:

- It recognizes and addresses regional differences and cultural diversities within the country. *(1 M)*
- It establishes mechanisms for power-sharing and decision-making that involve both linguistic communities, ensuring a balanced representation in the government. *(1 M)*
- The inclusion of community and regional government allows for more localized governance and decision-making on specific issues. *(1 M)*
- The Belgian model has helped to avoid civic strife between the two major linguistic communities in Belgium and a possible division of the country along linguistic lines. *(1 M)*
- By implementing power-sharing mechanisms, equal representation, and decentralized governance, the model has fostered cooperation and prevented conflicts that could have led to the fragmentation of the country. *(1 M)*

2. Explain how the bilingual street signs in Belgium, such as the ones shown in the image, contribute to the nation's policy of power-sharing among linguistic communities. What could be the potential benefits of this approach in maintaining social harmony and unity? *(Ap)*

Ans. The bilingual street in Belgium contribute to the nation's policy of power-sharing among linguistic communitiec in the following ways:

(*i*) The bilingual street signs in Belgium, in both french and dutch language, shows the country's commitment to accommodate its linguistic diversity. *(1 M)*

(*ii*) This practice is part of Belgium's power-sharing policy, where equal importance is given to both major language groups, French and Dutch, to ensure that neither feels marginalized or less represented. *(1 M)*

Potential benefit of this approach in maintaining social harmony and unity:

(*i*) It helps prevent linguistic or cultural conflicts by promoting an environment of inclusivity and respect. *(1 M)*

(*ii*) Each linguistic community sees its language reflected in everyday aspects like navigation and public information, enhancing mutual respect and unity among diverse groups. *(1 M)*

(*iii*) This policy is crucial in a country where language has historically been a source of tension, as it helps to bridge divides and foster a sense of belonging and identity among all citizens. *(1 M)*

4 FORMS OF POWER-SHARING

NCERT Definitions (Commonly asked in 1 mark)

- **Federal Government:** A system of government where the power is divided between a central authority and various constituent units of the country. For example, the division of power between central and state government in India.
- **Checks and Balances:** A system where different branches of government can check each other to prevent any one branch from becoming too powerful. For Example: The judiciary can check the powers of the legislature and executive by declaring certain laws and actions unconstitutional.

Classification

Forms of power-sharing

- **Horizontal Distribution of Power:** Power is shared among different organs of the government at the same level (executive, legislative, judiciary).
- **Vertical Division of Power:** Power is shared between different levels of government, from the central to local government.
- **Power Sharing Among Social Groups:** Ensuring representation for different religious, linguistic, and social groups.
- **Power Sharing in Political Parties and Movements:** Power is shared through competition and coalition among various political parties and influenced by pressure groups and movements.

Difference Between

Different Forms of Power-Sharing

Aspect	Horizontal Distribution of Power	Vertical Division of Power	Sharing Among Different Social Groups	Sharing Among Political Parties, Pressure Groups and Movements
Definitions	Power is shared among government branches (executive, legislative, judiciary).	Power is shared between different levels of government, from the central to regional government.	Power is shared by including diverse social groups in governance.	Power is shared through political competition and influence.
Purpose	Prevents any one branch from becoming too powerful.	Allowing regions autonomy while maintaining national unity.	Ensures representation for all social groups.	Making governance more inclusive and prevents monopolies of power.
Example	Legislature (Parliament), Executive (Government), and Judiciary (Courts).	Federal system of India.	Belgium's community governments.	Coalition governments

Mnemonics

Forms of power-sharing

Have Very Strong Principles

- **Horizontal:** Among government organs
- **Vertical:** Among government levels
- **Social Groups:** Among different social groups
- **Political Parties:** Among parties and movements

COMPETENCY BASED SOLVED EXAMPLES

Scan Me for Detailed Explanations

Multiple Choice Questions

(1 M)

1. **Why do you think power is shared among different organs of government i.e. executive, legislature and judiciary called horizontal distribution of power? What does it result in?** *(Un)*(CBSE APQ, 2023)
   (*a*) because it allows different organs of government placed at the same level to exercise different powers. This results in a balance of power among various institutions.
   (*b*) because it allows different organs of government placed at the same level to exercise different powers. This results in an imbalance of power among various institutions.
   (*c*) because it allows different organs of government placed at the same level to exercise the same powers. This results in a balance of power among various institutions.
   (*d*) because it does not allow different organs of government placed at the same level to exercise different powers. This results in a balance of power among various institutions.
2. **What role do 'checks and balances' play in a democratic country?** *(Ap)*(CBSE, 2024)
   Choose the most suitable option from the following.
   (*a*) To establish a direct form of government without representatives.
   (*b*) To create a separation of powers to prevent from authoritarianism.
   (*c*) To prevent any change to the Constitution.
   (*d*) To ensure absolute power for one branch of government.
3. **"Multiple political parties have come together to form the government despite having diverse political ideologies".**
   What form of power-sharing does the above statement demonstrate? *(Ap)*
   (*a*) Federal Government (*b*) Community Government
   (*c*) Separation of Powers (*d*) Coalition Government

Assertion and Reason

(1 M)

Direction: The following questions consist of two statements – Assertion (A) and Reason (R). Answer these questions by selecting the appropriate option given below:

(*a*) Both A and R are true, and R is the correct explanation of A.
(*b*) Both A and R are true, but R is not the correct explanation of A.
(*c*) A is true, but R is false
(*d*) A is false, but R is true.

1. **Assertion (A):** Vertical power sharing allows for the representation of diverse regional interests in government and promotes local autonomy.
   Reason (R): Vertical power sharing is a form of power-sharing in which power is divided between the central government and regional governments. *(Un)*
2. **Assertion (A):** Coalition governments are a form of power-sharing in which single political party governs.
   Reason (R): Coalition governments can help to ensure that diverse political views are represented in government and promote compromise and cooperation among different parties. *(Un)*

Subjective Questions

Very Short Answer Type Questions

(2 M)

1. **India often sees coalition governments, especially at the national level, where multiple political parties cooperate to form a government. This situation necessitates power-sharing among various political, regional, and ideological groups. What might be the challenges and benefits of such power-sharing arrangements among different political, regional, and ideological groups?** *(An)*

Ans. The challenges and benefits of such power- sharing among different political, regional, and ideological groups are:
   (i) **Benefit:** It provide more representative governance, and represent a wide range of people and their different views. *(1 M)*
   (ii) **Challenge:** Different parties often have conflicting interests and policies. This can cause instability in governance and make it difficult to make decisions and implement policies effectively. *(1 M)*

2. **What is the purpose of power sharing in democracy?** *(Un)*

Ans. The purpose of power sharing is to:
- Prevent the concentration of power in a few hands by involving different groups in decision-making *(1 M)*
- Ensure the representation and participation of diverse groups in decision-making. *(1 M)*

Short Answer Type Questions

(3 M)

1. **"In modern democracies, power-sharing arrangements can take many forms." Explain the statement.** *(Un)* (CBSE, 2023)

Ans. In modern democracies, power-sharing arrangements can take many forms, like: **(Any three)**

- **Horizontal Sharing:** Power is shared between different branches like the executive, legislature, and judiciary. *(1 M)*
- **Vertical Sharing:** Power is spread out between central, state, and local governments to manage things at different levels. *(1 M)*
- **Social Groups:** Power is also shared among different religious and ethnic groups to ensure everyone's voice is heard. *(1 M)*
- **Political Parties:** Different political parties may join together in coalitions to govern, sharing power among them. *(1 M)*

2. Describe the horizontal power sharing arrangements. ***(Un)*(CBSE, 2020)**

Ans. Horizontal power-sharing in a democracy involves:

- Sharing power among different organs of the government like the legislature, executive, and judiciary. This ensures no single organ has unlimited power. *(1 M)*
- Each organ checks the others, maintaining a balance of power. *(1 M)*
- This setup is known as a system of checks and balances because it prevents the misuse of power and ensures accountability within the government. *(1 M)*

Long Answer Type Questions (5 M)

1. What are the two advantages of power-sharing arrangements in a democracy? *(Ev, An)*

Ans. Power-sharing arrangements in a democracy offer several advantages that contribute to a more inclusive and stable governance system. For example:

- Power-sharing ensures that decision-making is not concentrated in the hands of a single individual or group, but rather distributed among different institutions, such as the legislature, executive, and judiciary. This helps to prevent the abuse of power and ensures a system of checks and balances. *(2½ M)*
- Power-sharing allows for the representation and participation of diverse groups in the decision-making process. This ensures that the interests of different segments of society are taken into account and reduces the chances of marginalization or exclusion. *(2½ M)*

MISCELLANEOUS EXERCISE

Multiple Choice Questions

(1 M)

1. In an Indian state, communities X and Y have been engaged in a long-standing conflict over issues of co-existence and resource sharing. The tensions have intensified, leading to a demand from both communities for self-administration. What is the BEST resolution to this conflict? ***(Ap)*(CBSE APQ, 2023)**

(*a*) collapsing the present government due to its inefficiency in governing the state

(*b*) delaying the demands of self-administration and maintaining the current power structure

(*c*) imposing strict regulations to control the movements and interactions of both communities

(*d*) establishing a power-sharing arrangement where both communities have a role in decision-making

2. A belief that the majority community should be able to rule a country in whichever way it wants, by disregarding the wishes and needs of the minority is ***(Re)***

(*a*) Power Sharing

(*b*) Central Government

(*c*) Majoritarianism

(*d*) Community Government

3. *"Everything would come to an end if the legislative, executive, and judicial powers of government were to be exercised by the same person or authority."*

~Montesquieu, French jurist

Which of the following is the BEST explanation of this quote? ***(Ev)***

(*a*) All work in a country will stop in the absence of power-sharing.

(*b*) Separation of powers is needed to strengthen democracy.

(*c*) Governments can only function if powers are distributed.

(*d*) People cannot exist in a nation if powers are not divided.

4. Division of powers between higher and lower levels of government is called ***(Re)***

(*a*) Horizontal distribution (*b*) Parallel distribution

(*c*) Vertical division (*d*) Diagonal division

5. Match list-I with list-II and select the correct answer using the codes below in the lists: ***(Re)*(CBSE SQP 2024)**

	List-I		List-II
1.	Ethnic	A.	Either only one or two level government
2.	Majoritrianism	B.	a violent conflict opposing groups within a country
3.	Civil war	C.	Belief that the majority community should be able to rule a country
4.	Unitary system	D.	a social division based on culture

	1	2	3	4
(*a*)	D	A	C	B
(*b*)	B	D	A	C
(*c*)	C	A	B	D
(*d*)	D	C	B	A

6. Proportionality is an important practice in power-sharing which includes proportional allocation of jobs, representation, and participation by ethnic group leaders, etc. Which of the following is an example of proportionality? ***(Ap)*(CFPQ)**

(*a*) Many political organisations demanded an independent Tamil state in Sri Lanka.

(*b*) Roles and responsibilities are allotted to both the Central and the State governments in India.

(*c*) Around 24% of total seats in Lok Sabha are reserved for members belonging to SC-ST categories.

(*d*) The minority French-speaking community (around 45%) is more rich and powerful than the majority Dutch-speaking community in Belgium.

7. Read the following headline in a newspaper.

A government in a conflict-ridden country offered a power-sharing agreement to a militant group as part of a negotiation to cease hostilities.

Which type of reasoning for power-sharing is demonstrated here? ***(Un)***

(*a*) Moral reason (*b*) Prudential reason

(*c*) Both (*a*) and (*b*) (*d*) Any other

8. Consider the following statements about power-sharing arrangements in Belgium and Sri Lanka. ***(An)***

(A) In Belgium, the Dutch-speaking majority of people tried to impose their domination on the minority French-speaking community.

(B) In Sri Lanka, the policies of the government sought to ensure the dominance of the Sinhala-speaking majority.

(C) The Tamils in Sri Lanka demanded a federal arrangement of power sharing to protect their culture, language and equality of opportunity in education and jobs.

(D) The transformation of Belgium from a unitary government to a federal one prevented a possible division of the country on linguistic lines.

Which of the statements given above are correct?

(*a*) A, B, C and D (*b*) A, B and D

(*c*) C and D (*d*) B, C and D

9. Identify the correct option based on the horizontal power sharing arrangement. ***(Re)***

(*a*) Central government, state government, local bodies.

(*b*) Legislature, executive, judiciary.

(*c*) Among different social groups.

(*d*) Among different pressure groups.

10. Match List-I (forms of power sharing) with List-II (forms of government) and select the correct answer using the codes given below in the lists: ***(Un)(NCERT)***

	List-I		List-II
1.	Power shared among different organs of government.	**A.**	Community government
2.	Power shared among governments at different levels	**B.**	Separation of powers
3.	Power shared by different social groups	**C.**	Coalition government
4.	Power shared by two or more political parties	**D.**	Federal government

	1	2	3	4
(*a*)	D	A	B	C
(*b*)	B	C	D	A
(*c*)	B	D	A	C
(*d*)	C	D	A	B

11. Different arguments are usually put forth in favour of and against power sharing. Identify those which are in favour of power sharing and select the answer using the codes given below? Power sharing: ***(An and Un)(NCERT)***

A. reduces conflict among different communities

B. decreases the possibility of arbitrariness

C. delays decision making process

D. accommodates diversities

E. increases instability and divisiveness

F. promotes people's participation in government

G. undermines the unity of a country

(*a*) A B D F (*b*) A C E F

(*c*) A B D G (*d*) B C D G

Assertion and Reason

(1 M)

Direction: The following questions consist of two statements – Assertion (A) and Reason (R). Answer these questions by selecting the appropriate option given below:

(*a*) Both A and R are true, and R is the correct explanation of A.

(*b*) Both A and R are true, but R is not the correct explanation of A.

(*c*) A is true, but R is false.

(*d*) A is false, but R is true.

1. Assertion (A): Power sharing is good for democracy.

Reason (R): It helps in reducing the possibility of conflict among social groups. ***(Un)(NCERT)***

2. Assertion (A): Power-sharing can only emerge in a democratic setup.

Reason (R): In an ideal democracy, political power is distributed among as many people as possible. ***(An)(CFPQ)***

3. Assertion (A): French speaking community in Belgium was rich and powerful.

Reason (R): Belgian Government favoured French speaking community. ***(Re)***

4. Assertion (A): In a democracy, everyone has voice in the shaping of public policies.

Reason (R): India has federal system. ***(Un and Re)***

5. Assertion (A): Belgium and Sri Lanka both faced ethical tension among different communities.

Reason (R): Both the countries resolved the conflict by power sharing arrangement which gave equal representation to all the communities. ***(Re and Ev)***

6. Assertion (A): There was a feeling of alienation among Sri Lankan Tamils.

Reason (R): The Sri Lankan government denied them equal political rights and discriminated against them in getting jobs and other opportunities. ***(Un)***

7. Assertion (A): Sinhala was recognized as only official language of Sri Lanka.

Reason (R): The government of Sri Lanka wanted to establish the supremacy of Sinhala community. ***(Un)***

Subjective Questions

Very Short Answer Type Questions

(1 or 2 M)

1. Why is horizontal distribution of power sharing important? Explain. ***(Un)(CBSE, 2024)***

2. Read the following passage and pick out any one of the prudential reasons for power sharing offered in this ***(An)(NCERT)***

"We need to give more power to the panchayats to realise the dream of Mahatma Gandhi and the hopes of the makers of our Constitution. Panchayati Raj establishes true democracy. It restores power to the only place where power belongs in a democracy – in the hands of the people. Giving power to Panchayats is also a way to reduce corruption and increase administrative efficiency. When people participate in the planning and implementation of developmental schemes, they would naturally exercise greater control over these schemes. This would eliminate the corrupt middlemen. Thus, Panchayati Raj will strengthen the foundations of our democracy."

3. My friend's grandfather had gone to Belgium during the 1950's and 1960's and worked in a chocolate factory. He expressed that 'he witnessed tensions between the Dutch speaking and French-speaking communities during this time in Belgium'. Justify his statement with two reasons. ***(An)***

4. Read the following lines from an article written by a group of authors. ***(Un)*(CFPQ)**

"The rise of majoritarianism in recent years may weaken power-sharing in Indian democracy. There is a need for constitutional provisions to protect minority rights."

Which type of reasoning for power-sharing is visible here?

5. (*a*) State whether the following statement is true or false. ***(An)***

"Power sharing is effective only for small countries like Belgium."

(*b*) Given an example to support your answer. ***(Ap)* (CFPQ)**

Short Answer Type Questions (3 M)

1. After reading this chapter, three students drew different conclusions. Which of these do you agree with and why? Give your reasons in about 50 words. ***(Ev)*(NCERT)**

Thomman - Power sharing is necessary only in societies which have religious, linguistic or ethnic divisions.

Mathayi – Power sharing is suitable only for big countries that have regional divisions.

Ouseph – Every society needs some form of power sharing even if it is small or does not have social divisions

2. Attempts at forced integration often sow the seeds of disintegration". Support the statement with suitable arguments. ***(Ev)***

3. Both Belgium and Sri Lanka are democracies, but they follow different systems of power sharing". Support the statement by giving two points of difference. ***(An)***

4. One of the remedies that are suggested for societies struggling with civil conflict are power-sharing arrangements that accommodate the various parties involved in the civil conflict. Power-sharing guarantees each of the critical players, a significant payoff from cooperation and peaceful behavior:

This peaceful behaviour can be maintained in the power-sharing arrangements in two ways:

(1) by providing minimum benefit to each party from cooperation in collective decisions, and

(2) through provisions that protect group autonomy in sensitive policy areas.

(*i*) In Lebanon, The Prime Minister must be a Sunni Muslim and the Deputy Prime: Minister must be an Orthodox Christian. Which of the two ways of maintaining peaceful behaviour given above is this an example of? ***(Un)***

(*ii*) Give one example each for the two ways of maintaining peaceful behaviour in the context of power sharing arrangement in Belgium. ***(Ap)***

Source: Power sharing, Agency and Civil Conflicts, Scott Gates, 2007.

5. Evaluate the power sharing system in India. ***(Ev)*(CBSE, 2019)**

Long Answer Type Questions (5 M)

1. In a classroom of 35 students, the teacher proposes a movie day and asks for a vote on which genre to watch. After counting the votes, it's revealed that 20 students prefer comedy movies, while 15 students lean towards horror movies. Seeing that the majority prefers comedy, the teacher announces that they'll be watching a comedy movie for the fun day activity. This leads to feelings of exclusion or dissatisfaction among the minority group. Teacher after being aware of this situation continued with the decision for a comedy movie.

(*a*) What does the above example show? ***(Un)***

(*b*) What could be the right thing to do in such a scenario? ***(Cr)***

(*c*) What could be inclusive decision-making in the above case? ***(Cr)***

2. How is the idea of power sharing emerged? Explain different forms that have common arrangements of power sharing. ***(Re* and *Un)*(CBSE, 2019)**

3. Here are some examples of power sharing. Which of the four types of power sharing do these represent? Who is sharing power with whom? ***(An)*(NCERT)**

(*a*) The Bombay High Court ordered the Maharashtra state government to immediately take action and improve living conditions for the 2,000-odd children at seven children's homes in Mumbai.

(*b*) The government of Ontario state in Canada has agreed to a land claim settlement with the Aboriginal community. The Minister responsible for Native Affairs announced that the government will work with aboriginal people in a spirit of mutual respect and cooperation.

(*c*) Russia's two influential political parties, the Union of Right Forces and the Liberal Yabloko Movement, agreed to unite their organisations into a strong right-wing coalition. They propose to have a common list of candidates in the next parliamentary elections.

(*d*) The finance ministers of various states in Nigeria got together and demanded that the federal government declare its sources of income. They also wanted to know the formula by which the revenue is distributed to various state governments.

4. Sharing of powers makes a country more powerful and united'. Justify the statement. ***(Ev)***

5. Discuss the importance of power sharing in a democracy with reference to the case studies of Belgium and Sri Lanka. ***(Cr* and *An)***

Case Based Questions (4 M)

Case Based-I

Read the information below and answer the questions that follow.

Power sharing arrangements can also be seen in the way political parties, pressure groups and movements control or influence those in power. In a democracy, the citizens must have freedom to choose among various contenders for power. In contemporary democracies, this takes the form of competition among different parties. Such competition ensures that power does not remain in one hand. In the long run, power is shared among different political parties that represent different ideologies and social groups. Sometimes this kind of sharing can be direct, when two or more parties form an alliance to contest elections. If their alliance is elected, they form a coalition government and thus share power. In a democracy, we find interest groups such as those of traders, businessmen, industrialists, farmers and industrial workers. They also will have share in governmental power, either through participation in governmental committees or bringing influence on the decision-making process.

(*i*) Power sharing is an essential component of democracy. Give a single case to support the claim. **(*Ap*)**

(*ii*) How do political parties, pressure groups, and movements help restrict or influence those in positions of authority? **(*An*)**

(*iii*) How does forming alliances show power sharing? **(*An*)**

Case Based-II

Read the passage given below and answer the questions based on it. **(CFPQ)**

Between 1992-95, a conflict broke out between three ethnic groups in the Bosnian territory. These three ethnic groups are the Bosnian Serbs, the Bosnians Croats and the Bosnian Muslims.

These ethnic groups had religious differences as the Serbs were Orthodox, the Croats were Catholics and the Muslims followed Islam.

As a compromise, Dayton agreement was designed. It proposed power-sharing as a solution to reduce the conflict. Dayton consisted of both territorial and political power-sharing.

A system was chosen where the national ethnicities were separated by territory. There is Significant autonomy granted to the separate entities, since they each have their own presidents, parliaments and other governing bodies, which are responsible for policy making on the entity level.

So instead of having one president, the entire population of Bosnia is represented by a three-presidency which consist of a Bosniak, a Croat and a Serb. The 42 seats of the House of Representatives are chosen by proportional representation which results in a corresponding reflection of the population. The seats in the other house, House of Peoples, are equally divided amongst the ethnicities. There is clear political and territorial power sharing found within the case of Bosnia-Herzegovina.

Although the Dayton Agreement did stop the violence and stabilised the conflict, it seems to have made the ethnic differences more rigid.

Source(edited): The Experience of power sharing through Bosnia- Herzegovina, Wageningen University, 2014.

(*i*) What was the reason for the conflict in the Bosnian teritory? **(*Re*)**

(*ii*) Mention the two forms of power-sharing that were proposed as a solution to the conflict. **(*Un*)**

(*iii*) Mention one example each for the two forms of power sharing that was adopted in the Bosnian territory. **(*Ap*)**

(*iv*) Mention one positive effect that power sharing had on the conflict in the Bosnian territory. **(*Un*)**

ANSWER KEYS

Multiple Choice Questions

1. (*d*) **2.** (*c*) **3.** (*b*) **4.** (*c*) **5.** (*d*) **6.** (*c*) **7.** (*b*) **8.** (*d*) **9.** (*b*) **10.** (*c*) **11.** (*a*)

Assertion and Reason

1. (*a*) **2.** (*b*) **3.** (*c*) **4.** (*b*) **5.** (*c*) **6.** (*a*) **7.** (*a*)

HINTS & EXPLANATIONS

Multiple Choice Questions

1. (*d*) The best way to resolve long-standing conflicts between communities is by establishing a power-sharing arrangement where both communities have an active role in decision-making.
2. (*c*) Majoritarianism refers to a system where the majority community imposes its will on the minority without considering their needs or interests.This often leads to.the marginalization of the minority groups.
3. (*b*) Montesquieu's quote emphasizes the importance of separating the legislative, executive, and judicial powers to prevent the concentration of authority in one entity, which is crucial for maintaining a democratic system and preventing tyranny.
4. (*c*) The division of power between different levels of government, such as central, state, and local governments, is called vertical division of power.
5. (*d*) 1-D, 2-C, 3-B, 4-A
6. (*c*) Proportionality in power-sharing ensures that different groups receive representation in proportion to their population. Reservations in the Lok Sabha for SC-ST communities is an example of proportionality, ensuring that these groups have a voice in the decision-making process..
7. (*b*) The reasoning demonstrated here is prudential because it focuses on the practical benefits of power-sharing to achieve peace and stability.
8. (*d*) B, C, and D
9. (*b*) Horizontal power-sharing refers to the division of power among the three organs of government: the legislature, executive, and judiciary. This system ensures that no branch becomes too powerful, and each can check the others, maintaining a balance of power.
10. (*c*) 1-B, 2-D, 3-A, 4-C
11. (*a*) A B D F

Assertion and Reason

1. (*a*) Self-explanatory
2. (*b*) Both A and R are true, but R is not the correct explanation of A.
3. (*c*) The leaders of belgium adopted power sharing arrangement that promoted equal representation of the communities and recognised cultural differences and regional diversities by accommodating both groups. The Belgian government didn't favour either of the community.
4. (*b*) Both A and R are true, but R is not the correct explanation of A.
5. (*c*) Both the countries (Belgium & Sri Lanka) did not resolve the ethnic conflict by power sharing arrangement. Sri Lankan government adoped the majoritarian measures.
6. (*a*) Self-explanatory
7. (*a*) Both A and R are true, and R is the correct explanation of A.

Subjective Questions

Very Short Answer Type Questions

1. The horizontal distribution of power sharing is important because:
   (*i*) It establishes a system of checks and balances among various branches of government, such as the legislature, executive, and judiciary. *(1 M)*
   (*ii*) It stops one branch from having all the power, so no single branch can dominate or misuse power, reducing the risk of authoritarian rule and defends democracy. *(1 M)*
2. A prudential reason for power sharing mentioned in the passage is that giving more power to panchayats because it will reduce corruption and increase administrative efficiency by allowing people to have greater control over developmental schemes. *(2 M)*
3. During the 1950's and 1960's the minority French-speaking community was relatively rich and powerful in Belgium. This was resented by the Dutch-speaking community who got the benefit of economic development and education much later. *(2 M)*
4. The statement reflects moral reasoning for power-sharing. This reasoning emphasizes the fundamental value of ensuring minority rights and representation in a democracy, advocating for fairness and protection against the tyranny of the majority. *(1 M)*
5. The statement "Power sharing is effective only for small countries like Belgium" is false. Power sharing is a broad concept applicable and effective in large and diverse countries as well, ensuring representation and stability across different social and political groups. *(1 M)*

Short Answer Type Questions

1. I agree with Ouseph's conclusion that every society needs some form of power-sharing, even if it's small or does not have social divisions. Power-sharing promotes inclusivity, prevents abuse of power, and fosters cooperation, which are essential for any society to function democratically and fairly, regardless of its size or internal divisions. *(3 M)*
2. (*a*) The above statement is true. If the rulers are willing to share power and accommodate the reasonable demands of the minority community, social divisions become less threatening for the country, as we can see in the case of Belgium. *(1½ M)*
   (*b*) However, suppressing such a demand in the name of national unity often has the opposite effect. As a result, such attempts at forced integration frequently sowed the seeds of disintegration. An example of this can be seen in the case of Sri Lanka. *(1½ M)*
3. Belgium and Sri Lanka dealt with the issue of power sharing differently. **(Any two)**
   - The Belgian government has no preferential policies in terms of jobs and education, whereas the Sri Lankan government has preferential policies that favoured, Sinhala applicants for university positions and government jobs. *(1½ M)*

- In Belgium, there is a special government called 'community government' which has the power regarding cultural, educational and language based issues. However, in Sri Lanka, there were no such provisions and no major political parties were sensitive to 'Tamil' language and culture as well. *(1½ M)*
- In Belgium, there is no discrimination between religions however, in Sri Lanka, a new constitution declares that the state will protect and promote Buddhism. *(1½ M)*

4. (*i*) The arrangement in Lebanon is an example of the second way of maintaining peaceful behavior through provisions that protect group autonomy in sensitive policy areas. This ensures each group has a stake and say in the government, promoting peace. *(1 M)*

(*ii*) Belgium Examples:

a. **Minimum benefit from cooperation:** Ensures equal representation of Dutch and French-speaking ministers, preventing any one community from dominating. This ensures cooperation across language groups and fosters cooperation and peace. *(1 M)*

b. **Protecting group autonomy:** "Community government" that allows different language communities (Dutch, French, German-speaking) to have autonomous control over cultural, educational, and language-related issues. *(1 M)*

5.

- India's power-sharing system distributes power among the legislature, executive, and judiciary to prevent any one branch from becoming too powerful. *(1 M)*
- It allocates power between central and state governments, ensuring local governance and regional interests are addressed. *(1 M)*
- Power-sharing extends to various social groups, providing representation to religious and linguistic minorities, thus maintaining national unity by respecting diversity. *(1 M)*

Topper's Explanation

Power sharing in India is done in different ways, each with its own benefits

HORIZONTAL DISTRIBUTION OF POWER AND ITS BENEFITS

Power is shared among different organs of the government, namely the legislature, the judiciary and the executive, placed at the same level. Different organs exercise different powers as well as checks the other organ.

VERTICAL DIVISION OF POWER AND ITS BENEFITS

India is a federal country that divides its power amongst the national government and the government at local and state level. This allows the issues and problems to be settled easily and effectively and the state can function as autonomous body. They are not subordinate of the central government.

POWER SHARING AMONGST DIFFERENT COMMUNITIES AND BENEFITS

Power is shared among different religious, linguistic and regional groups.

There are legal provisions made whereby the weaker section of the society and women are represented in the assemblies and legislature.

POWER SHARING AMONGST DIFFERENT PARTIES AND BENEFITS

Due to the system of elections power is shared among different parties who represent different groups and communities. This allows different ideas and views to enjoy representation, although it leads to political unstability.

Due to the above reasons, the power sharing in India has actual made India more powerful and promoted unity amongst citizens. It has allowed people to participate in the decision making that affects them.

Long Answer Type Questions

1. (*a*) The scenario demonstrates the application of majority rule, where the choice favored by the majority (comedy movies) is chosen over the minority preference (horror movies). *(1 M)*

(*b*) The right thing to do in such a scenario is to looking for a more inclusive decision-making approach, which involve considering both groups' preference and can balance between the majority preferenec and minority interest to ensure everyone feels included and valued. *(1 M)*

(*c*) Inclusive decision making could involve:

(*i*) **Combine Genres:** Opt for a movie that blends elements of comedy and horror, satisfying both groups. *(1 M)*

(*ii*) **Host Two Movie Sessions:** Plan for two movie days instead of one, showing a comedy on one day and a horror movie on the other. *(1 M)*

(*iii*) **Split Screening Time:** If time allows, watch a short comedy first, followed by a horror movie, ensuring both preferences are respected. *(1 M)*

2. **Emergence of Power Sharing:** The idea of power-sharing has emerged in opposition to the notions of undivided political power where it was believed that all power must reside in one person/group located at one place for quick decision-making and enforcement. *(1 M)*

Forms of Power Sharing:

- **Horizontal Distribution:** Power is shared among different organs of the government, like the legislature, executive, and judiciary, ensuring a system of checks and balances. *(1 M)*
- **Vertical Distribution:** Power is shared among different levels of government (federal, state, and local), known as federalism, to accommodate regional interests and promote governance at a closer level to the people. *(1 M)*
- **Social Groups:** Power sharing among different social groups (like linguistic, religious, or ethnic groups) to ensure representation and prevent marginalization. *(1 M)*

- **Political Parties and Pressure Groups:** Power sharing through competition and coalition formation among political parties and influence by pressure groups and movements to ensure that no single party or group dominates. *(1 M)*

3. (*a*) **Horizontal Power Sharing:** The Bombay High Court's directive represents a case of horizontal power sharing, where the judiciary checks the state government's actions, ensuring accountability and safeguarding citizens' rights. *(1¼ M)*

   (*b*) **Power sharing between the government social groups:** The Ontario government's settlement with the Aboriginal community exemplifies power sharing between the government and different social groups, acknowledging and respecting the rights and autonomy of indigenous communities. *(1¼ M)*

   (*c*) **Political Party Coalition:** The coalition between Russia's political parties is an example of power sharing among political parties, where they agree to unite for greater political influence, sharing power to govern more effectively. *(1¼ M)*

   (*d*) **Vertical Power sharing:** The finance ministers' demand in Nigeria shows power sharing among different levels of government (vertical distribution), where states seek transparency and fairness in the distribution of federal revenue. *(1¼ M)*

4. Sharing power makes a country more powerful and united because:
   - **Prevents Conflict:** Sharing power reduces the chances of conflict between different communities, as seen in Belgium, leading to a more peaceful and stable nation. *(1 M)*
   - **Promotes Stability:** It ensures political stability by including diverse groups in the decision-making or governance process, making policies more acceptable. *(1 M)*
   - **Promotes Unity:** By recognizing the existence of diverse groups and ensuring their representation in governance, countries foster a sense of belonging and unity among all. *(1 M)*
   - **Enhances Cooperation:** The Belgian model demonstrates how equal representation and cooperation between communities can lead to innovative governance solutions, making the country more cohesive. *(1 M)*
   - **Avoids Dominance:** Unlike Sri Lanka, where majoritarian policies led to civil unrest, sharing power prevents any one community from dominating others, ensuring fairness and equality. *(1 M)*

5.
   - **Introduction to Power Sharing:** Power sharing is a vital component of democracy, ensuring that power isn't concentrated in the hands of a few but is distributed among various organs of the government and society. *(1 M)*
   - **Case Study of Belgium:** Belgium showcases a positive example of power-sharing, where the innovative constitutional arrangements ensure equal representation and autonomy for both Dutch and French-speaking communities. *(1 M)*
   - **Case Study of Sri Lanka:** Sri Lanka's approach to power-sharing was hindered by the dominance of the Sinhala-speaking majority, neglecting the rights and demands of the Tamil-speaking minority, leading to a prolonged civil conflict. *(1 M)*
   - **Lessons Learned:** The comparison between Belgium and Sri Lanka illustrates that inclusive power-sharing can prevent conflict and maintain unity, whereas neglecting it can lead to division and unrest. *(1 M)*
   - **Conclusion on the Importance of Power Sharing:** Power sharing in democracies is not just a matter of political necessity but a Moral necessity as well, ensuring stability, reducing conflicts, and fostering a sense of belonging among diverse groups. *(1 M)*

Case Based Questions

Case Based-I

(*i*) The case of Belgium supports power sharing in democracy. Belgium resolved its internal ethnic conflict by amending its constitution four times to equally distribute power among its diverse linguistic groups, thus avoiding potential conflict and ensuring political stability. *(1 M)*

(*ii*) Political parties, pressure groups, and movements make sure that the people in power listen to everyone. They help by talking about what different people need and making sure no one person or group has all the control. *(1 M)*

(*iii*) (*a*) When political parties form alliances to contest elections, it demonstrates power sharing as these parties agree to work together and share governance responsibilities if they win. *(1 M)*

(*b*) Due to the formation of alliance, a single political party cannot exercise supreme powers/authority thus it automatically leads to power sharing. *(1 M)*

Case Based-II

(*i*) The reason for the conflict in the Bosnian territory was the ethnic and religious differences among the Bosnian Serbs, Croats, and Muslims. *(1 M)*

(*ii*) The two forms of power-sharing that were proposed as a solution to the conflict were territorial and political power sharing. *(1 M)*

(*iii*) An example of territorial power-sharing is the division of Bosnia into separate entities with significant autonomy. Political power-sharing is exemplified by the three-presidency system, representing each ethnic group. *(1 M)*

(*iv*) One positive effect of power-sharing on the conflict in Bosnia was the end of violence and the stabilization of the region, despite making ethnic differences more rigid. *(1 M)*

❑❑❑

FEDERALISM

2

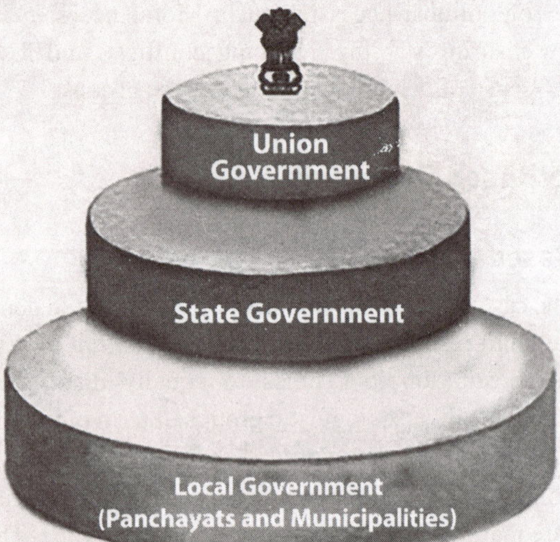

Federalism isn't about States' rights. It's about dividing power to better protect individual liberty.

SYLLABUS & WEIGHTAGE

List of Concept Names	Years					
	2020	2021	2022	2023	2024	2025
What is Federalism?	1 Q (3 M)	Exam not Conducted	—	—	1 Q (1 M)	1 Q (3 M)
What makes India a federal country?	—		—	1 Q (1 M)	1 Q (1 M)	1 Q (1 M)
How is federalism practiced? (Linguistic State, Language policy, Centre-state relations)	—		—	1 Q (4 M)	—	1 Q (1 M)
Decentralisation in India	—		—	1 Q (1 M)	1 Q (4 M)	1 Q (1 M)

CONCEPT MAP

To Access One Shot Revision Video Scan This QR Code

Federalism

Meaning
- A system of government in which the power is divided between central authority and various constituent units.

Features (CBSE 2020)
- Multiple levels (tiers) of Government.
- Each tier is accountable to the people.
- Each level has its own jurisdiction, specified in the constitution, guaranteeing their authority.
- Changes to fundamental provisions require the consent of both levels of Government.
- Courts interpret the Constitution & resolve disputes between levels of Government.
- Revenue sources for each level are specified to ensure financial autonomy

Type of federations
- **Coming Together Federation:** Independent states voluntarily coming together (example -USA, Switzerland, Australia)
- **Holding Together Federation:** Large country divides power between constituent states and the national government (example - India Spain, Belgium).

What Makes India A Federal Country? (CBSE 2025)

Constitution
- Establishes a two-tier system of government namely union government (represent the country) and state government (represent a particular state). In 1992, the third tier was added with panchayats and municipalities.

Independent Judiciary
- Judiciary interpret and oversee the implementation of constitutional provisions & in case of a dispute regarding the division of powers, the court makes the decision.

Amendment Process
- Requires two-third majority in both the houses of the parliament and ratification by the legislature of at least half of the total states.

Power sharing arrangements (CBSE 2025, 2023)
- Power sharing arrangements between union and state government.

State Government Legislate over

State list - Contains subject of state and local importance. Such as police, trade, agriculture etc.

Concurrent list - Both union and state government can make laws but in case of Conflict, the union government's law prevail

Special power (under article 371) - Granted to states like Assam, Nagaland, Arunachal Pradesh and Mizoram. Aim is to protect Culture, land rights and ensure preferential employment for indigenous people.

Union Government Legislate over (CBSE 2024, 2023)

Union list - Subjects of national importance such as defence, banking, foreign affair etc.

Concurrent list - Includes subjects of common interests to both union and state government such as education forest, trade union. In case of conflicts, union government's law prevail.

Union territories - Small areas that neither become independent state nor merge with existing States. E.g.- Chandigarh, Delhi etc.

Residuary power - Subjects that do not fall in any of the three lists or all subjects that came up after the constitution was made.

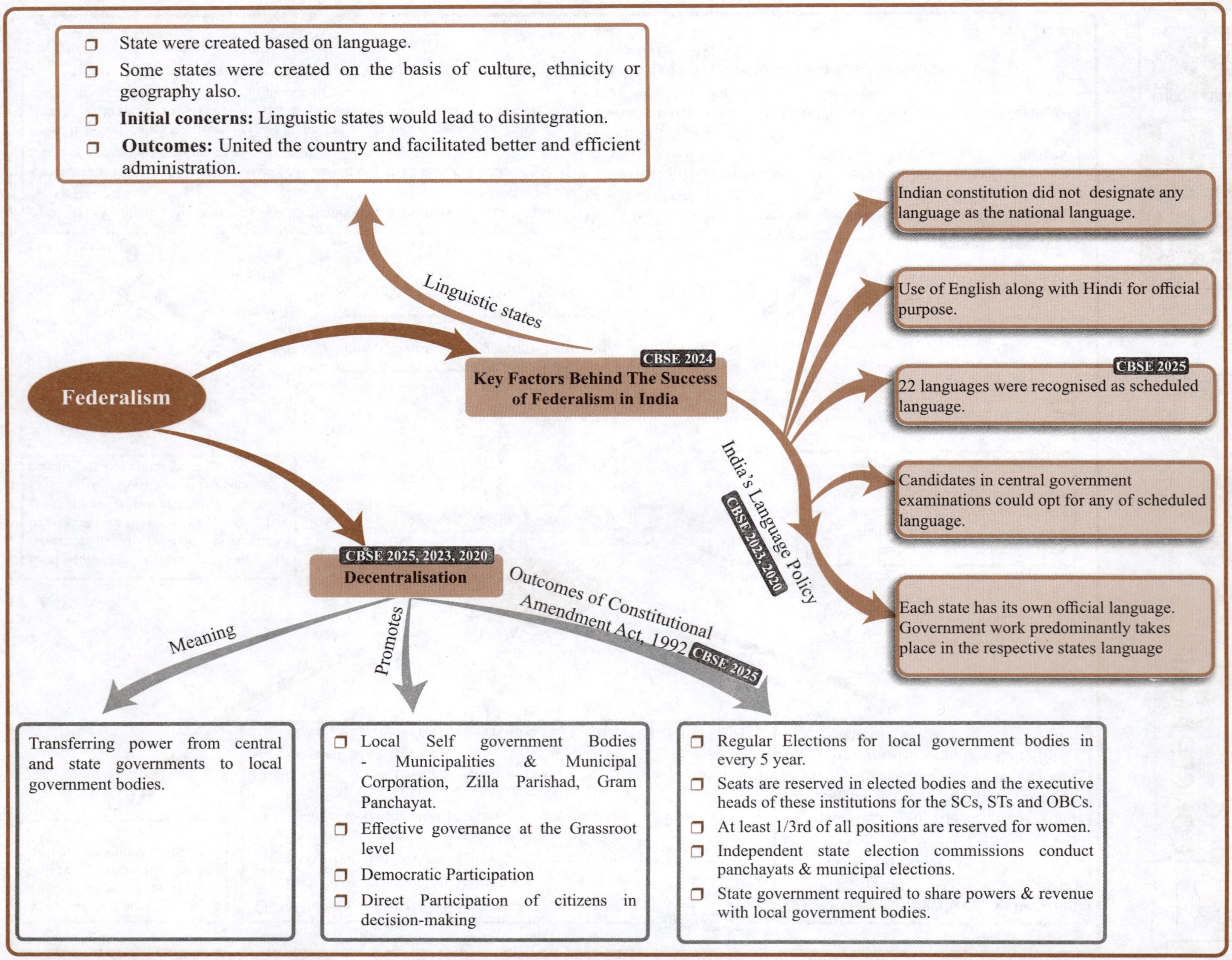
Federalism
Key Factors Behind The Success of Federalism in India
CBSE 2024
Linguistic states
State were created based on language.
Some states were created on the basis of culture, ethnicity or geography also.
Initial concerns: Linguistic states would lead to disintegration.
Outcomes: United the country and facilitated better and efficient administration.
India's Language Policy
CBSE 2023, 2020
Indian constitution did not designate any language as the national language.
Use of English along with Hindi for official purpose.
22 languages were recognised as scheduled language.
CBSE 2025
Candidates in central government examinations could opt for any of scheduled language.
Each state has its own official language. Government work predominantly takes place in the respective states language
Decentralisation
CBSE 2025, 2023, 2020
Meaning
Transferring power from central and state governments to local government bodies.
Promotes
Local Self government Bodies - Municipalities & Municipal Corporation, Zilla Parishad, Gram Panchayat.
Effective governance at the Grassroot level
Democratic Participation
Direct Participation of citizens in decision-making
Outcomes of Constitutional Amendment Act, 1992
CBSE 2025
Regular Elections for local government bodies in every 5 year.
Seats are reserved in elected bodies and the executive heads of these institutions for the SCs, STs and OBCs.
At least 1/3rd of all positions are reserved for women.
Independent state election commissions conduct panchayats & municipal elections.
State government required to share powers & revenue with local government bodies.

1 WHAT IS FEDERALISM?

NCERT Definitions *(Commonly asked in 1 mark)*

- **Federalism** is a system of government in which the power is divided between a central authority and various constituent units of the country. Each level of government has its own set of powers and responsibilities.
- **Unitary system:** It is a system where there's only one level of government that holds all the power. In this system, the central government has the authority to make decisions for the entire country, and any lower levels of government, like provinces or local governments, are subordinate to it. For example, Sri Lanka where the national government has all the power.
- **Central government:** The highest level of government in a country, responsible for governing the entire nation and typically handling matters of common national interest.
- **Regional government:** Governments at the level of provinces, states, or regions, which have their own set of powers and responsibilities distinct from those of the central government. Regional governments look after much of the day-to-day administering of their state

Important Facts

01
- The *USA*, *Switzerland* and *Australia* follows the route of *coming together Federation*.

02
- *India*, *Spain* and *Belgium* follows the route of *holding together Federations*.

Classification

1. **Routes of Federation Formation:**
- **Coming Together Federations:** Independent States coming together on their own to form a bigger unit.
- **Holding Together Federations:** A large country decides to divide its power between the constituent States and the national government.

2. **Forms of government:**
- **Federal form of government:** Power divided between central and regional governments
- **Unitary form of government:** All power is centralized in a single national government.

Difference Between

Federalism vs Unitary system		
Aspect	**Federalism**	**Unitary System**
Power Distribution	Divided between central and regional governments	The central government holds all the power.
Number of Government Tiers	Two or more	One
Jurisdiction	Each tier has specific legislative, tax, and administrative powers.	Central government dictates to sub-units

Constitutional Changes	Requires consent of both tiers.	Central government's authority.
Financial Autonomy	Revenue sources specified for each tier.	States have no financial autonomy. The central government controls the finances.
State/Provincial Autonomy	Significant autonomy	Limited or no autonomy
Example	India, USA	France, Sri Lanka

Coming Together Federation v/s Holding Together Federation		
Feature	**Coming Together Federation**	**Holding Together Federation**
Formation	Independent states unite	A large nation divides power between the constituent states and the national government
Power Distribution	Usually equal among states	Central government tends to be stronger
State Autonomy	High autonomy for states	Varies, can be less for some states
Examples	USA, Switzerland, Australia	India, Spain, Belgium

Myth Buster

- **Myth:** All federal systems are identical and have equal power distribution between central and state governments.
  Fact: In different countries, the balance of power between the central government and state governments can be different. This happens because of historical reasons.
  Example: In some countries like the USA and Switzerland, the states have similar powers. But in others like India and Belgium, the central government has more power despite having a federal system.

Mnemonics

- Countries with coming together federations

  USA

  U → United States of America(USA)

  S → Switzerland

  A → Australia

- Countries with holding together federations

  SBI

  S → Spain

  B → Belgium

  I → India

Important Dates

- **1993:** Belgium shifted from a unitary to a federal form of government.

COMPETENCY BASED SOLVED EXAMPLES

Scan Me for Detailed Explanations

Multiple Choice Questions

(1 M)

1. **A third party were to step in and directly intervene to resolve the conflict between the centre and the state government, what body of the government would that be?** ***(Re)***

   (*a*) The media

   (*b*) The judiciary

   (*c*) The Executive

   (*d*) The legislature

2. **Study the map given below and answer the question.** ***(An)***

   Which continent shown on the map has the most countries with federal political systems?

(*a*) Europe	(*b*) Africa
(*c*) Asia	(*d*) North America

3. **What is the role of the highest court in a federal system?** ***(Re)***

   (*a*) To only interpret the constitution.

   (*b*) To resolve disputes between different government levels.

   (*c*) To legislate new laws.

   (*d*) Both (*b*) and (*c*)

4. **When Santosh was asked to pick the from odd one out from from USA, Spain, Switzerland, Australia he picked Spain, which is the correct answer.** ***(An)***
   What could be the reason for this?

   (*a*) It is a "holding together" federation.

   (*b*) It is the only country that has a federal government.

   (*c*) It is the only country that does not account for regional diversity.

   (*d*) All the states in Spain have equal power and can rule above the central Government.

5. **Read the statement given below and identify the trend followed from the options given below:** ***(Ev)***

   Statement: One of the key changes made in the Constitution of Belgium was to reduce the power of the Central Government and to give these powers to the regional governments.

   (*a*) Federal system where the national government has all the powers.

   (*b*) Unitary system where the national government has all the powers.

   (*c*) Shift from a federal to a unitary form of government.

   (*d*) Shift from a unitary to a federal form of government

Assertion and Reason

(1 M)

Direction: The following questions consist of two statements – Assertion (A) and Reason (R). Answer these questions by selecting the appropriate option given below:

(*a*) Both A and R are true, and R is the correct explanation of A.

(*b*) Both A and R are true, but R is not the correct explanation of A.

(*c*) A is true, but R is false

(*d*) A is false, but R is true.

1. **Assertion (A):** Federalism promotes diversity and unity within a country.

   Reason (R): By allowing for regional autonomy, federalism allows for the preservation of local cultures and traditions while still maintaining national unity under a common framework. ***(Un)***

2. **Assertion (A):** The United States is an example of a federal system of government.

   Reason (R): In the United States, power is not divided between the federal government and individual states. ***(Re)***

3. **Assertion (A):** Federalism can help prevent the concentration of power.

   Reason (R): By dividing power between multiple levels of government, federalism ensures that no one has too much control over decision-making or resources. ***(An)***

4. **Assertion (A):** The exact balance of power between the central and the state government is same across different countries.

   Reason (R): The balance of power between the central government and the state government depends mainly on the historical context in which the federation was formed. ***(An)***

Subjective Questions

Very Short Answer Type Questions (2 M)

1. **What is federalism? How many levels of government are there in a federation? *(Un)***

Ans. (*i*) Federalism is a system of government where power is divided between a central authority and various constituent units of a country. *(1 M)*

(*ii*) Typically, there are two levels of government in a federation. One is the government for the entire country and others are governments at the level of states or provinces. *(1 M)*

2. **What is holding together federation? Also provide some example of holding together federation. *(Un)***

Ans. (*i*) When a large country decides to divide its power between the constituent states and the national government it is known as holding together federation. *(1 M)*

(*ii*) In this federation central government tends to be more powerful. India, spain and Belgium are the example of holding together federation. *(1 M)*

Short Answer Type Questions (3 M)

1. **Point out one feature in the practice of federalism in India that is similar to and one feature that is different from that of Belgium. *(Un)*(NCERT)**

Ans. (*i*) One feature in the practice of federalism in India that is similar to that of Belgium is that the central government has to share its power with the state/provincial governments. *(1½ M)*

(*ii*) One feature in the practice of federalism in India that is different to that of Belgium is that Unlike India, it has a third form of government called the community government in addition to central and state governments, which is elected by people belonging to one language community. *(1½ M)*

2. **What is the main difference between a federal form of government and a unitary one? Explain with examples. *(Un)*(NCERT)**

Ans.

Criteria	Federal System	Unitary System
Power Distribution	Powers are divided between the central government and state/ provincial governments.	All powers are centralised in the national government.
Relationship Between Levels	Central and state/ provincial governments operate independently.	Sub-national units (if any) are subordinate to the central government.
Constitutional Structure	The Constitution allocates powers to both levels of government.	The Constitution may not provide for power sharing; central authority holds ultimate power.

(1 + 1 + 1 = 3M)

> **Nailing the Right Answer**
>
> (*i*) Use two columns, one for the Federal System and the other for the Unitary System.
>
> (*ii*) Include headings for comparison criteria.

3. **Name the two ways through which the federation can be formed, and by considering all the clues identify the type of federation and give reasons to support your answer *(An)***

Clue-I: Very often different constituent units of the federation have unequal powers.

Clue-II: Some units are granted special powers

Clue-III: The Central Government tends to be more powerful vis-a-vis the States.

Ans. (*i*) There are mainly two ways to form a federation-Coming together federations and Holding togethon federations. The above clues refer to the Holding together federations. *(1½ M)*

(*ii*) In holding together federations, Central government tends to be more powerful and constituent units often have unequal powers, and some may have special powers as well to protect their cultural heritage. *(1½ M)*

4. **Study the map given below and answer the following questions.**

(*i*) **Based on the map, name three large countries that have a federal political system. *(Re)***

Ans. Russia, Canada, and the United States of America are the three large countries highlighted on the map that have a federal political system. *(1 M)*

(ii) Can you identify an exception to the rule that most of the large countries of the world are federations, as seen on this map? ***(Un)***

Ans. Yes, China is a large country highlighted on the map in white, indicating it does not have a federal system. This makes it an exception to the general trend where most large countries are federations. *(1 M)*

(iii) Which is the largest federal country in the world? ***(Re)***

Ans. Russia is the largest country in the world by land area and is shown on the map as having a federal political system, making it the largest federal country globally *(1 M)*

5. Highlight three major distinctions between the federation of the 'Coming together' type and the 'holding together' type. ***(Ev)***

Ans. The three major distinctions between the federations of 'coming together' and 'holding together' are:

(1 + 1 +1 = 3 M)

Coming together Federation	Holding Toghether Federation
In this type independent states come together on their own to form bigger unit.	In this type, a large country decide to divide power between the Constituent States and the National government.
In this category, all the constituent States usually have equal power and states are not sub-ordinate to the centre.	In this, the Central Goverment tends to be more powerful vis-a-vis the states.
Examples are USA, Switzerland and Australia	Examples are India, Spain and Belgium.

6. "The exact balance of power between the central and the state government varies from one federation to another." Substantiate the statement with suitable examples. ***(An)*(CBSE APQ, 2023)**

Ans. (*i*) Countries have different ways of sharing power between the central and regional governments. This balance of power in federations depends on the historical context in which the federations are formed. *(1 M)*

(*ii*) For example, in "coming together" federations constituent states join voluntarily and often have significant power. In contrast, "holding together" federations often see a more powerful central government. *(1 M)*

(*iii*) This shows that federal systems can be different, based on unique historical contexts, highlighting the responsiveness of federalism to accommodate regional diversity while maintaining unity. *(1 M)*

Long Answer Type Questions **(5 M)**

1. What are the key features of federalism? ***(Re)***

Ans. The key features of federalism are:

(*i*) **Dual Governance:** Federalism establishes two levels of government, each with its own powers and functions. The national government deals with nationwide issues, while regional governments handle local matters. *(1 M)*

(*ii*) **Constitutional Framework:** The powers and functions of different levels of government are clearly outlined in the constitution, ensuring a division of powers that is legally recognized and enforceable. *(1 M)*

(*iii*) **Supremacy of the Constitution:** The Constitution is the highest law of the land, and all individuals, institutions, and government actions must comply to it. *(1 M)*

(*iv*) **Independent Judiciary:** The highest court acts as an umpire if disputes arise between different levels of government in the exercise of their respective powers. The Courts also have the power to interpret the powers of different levels of government. *(1 M)*

(*v*) **Revenue Sharing:** Both levels of government have their revenue sources defined by the constitution. Financial autonomy ensures that both central and regional governments can undertake their responsibilities effectively. *(1 M)*

2 WHAT MAKES INDIA A FEDERAL COUNTRY

NCERT Definitions *(Commonly asked in 1 mark)*

- **Union List:** It is the list which includes the subjects of national interest that only the central government can make laws on.
- **State List:** It is the list which includes the subjects important to states, where only state governments can legislate.
- **Concurrent List:** It is the list which includes the subjects on which both central and state governments can make laws, with central laws prevailing in case of conflict.

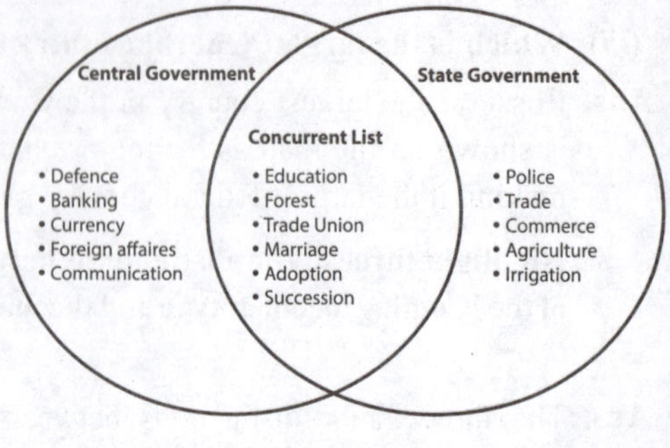

- **Residuary Powers:** Subjects that do not fall in any of the three lists or subjects that came up after the constitution was made are the residuary subjects and union government has the power the legislate on these subjects. E.g. Computer software.
- **Union Territories:** Areas which are too small to become an independent state but which could not be merged with any of the existing states. These regions don't have the same powers as states and are directly governed by the central government.

Important Facts

01 The Indian constitution did not use the word ***federation*** but the Indian union is based on the principle of federalism.

02 Assam, Arunachal Pradesh, and Nagaland have special status under ***Article 371*** of the Constitution due to their unique social and historical contexts.

03 **Union Territories** in India, such as Chandigarh and Delhi, do not possess the same powers as states.

04 In India, the Constitution originally provided for a ***two-tier system*** of government, the Union Government and the State governments. Later, ***a third tier*** of federalism was added in the form of ***Panchayats*** and ***Municipalities***.

Difference Between

Union List, State List and Concurrent List

Category	Union List	State List	Concurrent List
Legislation	Only Union Government can make laws	Only State Governments can make laws	Both can make laws, Union law prevails in conflict
Scope	National importance	State and local importance	Common interest to both Union and State
Examples	Defence, foreign affairs, banking, currency	Police, trade, agriculture, irrigation	Education, forests, trade unions, marriages

Real Life Application Based Questions

1. **Suppose the Government of Rajasthan was opposed to the Central Government's nuclear policy. Could it prevent the Government of India from conducting nuclear tests in Pokhran, Rajasthan?**

Ans. No, the state government cannot prevent the central government from conducting nuclear tests, as defense and nuclear policy are under the Union List, over which only the central government has authority.

Myth Buster

- **Myth:** All Indian states have the same powers.

  Fact: Some Indian states have ***special rights under article 371*** due to their unique social and historical circumstances.

Mnemonics

Lists which divides legislative powers between the Union Government and the State Governments.

U Should **C**ome

- U → Union list
- S → State list
- C → Concurrent list

States that enjoy a special status and powers under article-371

MAAN

- M → Mizoram
- A → Arunachal Pradesh
- A → Assam
- N → Nagaland

Scan Me for Detailed Explanations

COMPETENCY BASED SOLVED EXAMPLES

Multiple Choice Questions

(1 M)

1. **Which list in the Indian Constitution includes subjects of national importance?** ***(Re)***

   (*a*) State List

   (*b*) Concurrent List

   (*c*) Union List

   (*d*) Residuary List

2. **Match the Column-I with Column-II and choose the correct option:** ***(Re)*(CBSE, 2023)**

	Column-I (Subjects)		Column-II (List)
A.	E-Programming	(*i*)	Concurrent List
B.	Police	(*ii*)	Union List
C.	Education	(*iii*)	State List
D.	Defence	(*iv*)	Residuary List

   (*a*) A-(*iv*), B-(*iii*), C-(*i*), D-(*ii*)

   (*b*) A-(*iii*), B-(*iv*), C-(*i*), D-(*ii*)

   (*c*) A-(*iv*), B-(*i*), C-(*iii*), D-(*ii*)

   (*d*) A-(*iv*), B-(*ii*), C-(*i*), D-(*iii*)

3. **What happens if there is a conflict between the laws made by the Union Government and the State Government on the subject of concurrent list.** ***(Ap)***

   (*a*) The State laws will prevail.

   (*b*) The Union laws prevail.

   (*c*) The laws will be nullified.

   (*d*) The judiciary will decide the outcome.

4. **Which areas in the Indian Union have limited powers and are directly governed by the Central Government?** ***(Re)***

   (*a*) Union Territories (*b*) State Governments

   (*c*) Princely States (*d*) Municipalities

5. **How can the power-sharing arrangement between the Union Government and the State Governments be changed?** ***(An)***

(*a*) By a simple majority in the Parliament

(*b*) By approval from the President

(*c*) By approval from the Supreme Court

(*d*) By two-thirds majority in the Parliament and ratification by state legislatures

6. You are participating in a quiz competition focused on the Indian Constitution and its governance structure. Your task is to evaluate the accuracy of the following statements about the Indian Constitution and its federal setup: ***(Ev)***

(*i*) The Indian Constitution explicitly uses the term 'federation' to describe the country's structure.

(*ii*) The Constitution provided for a two-tier system of government which was later expanded.

(*iii*) The addition of Panchayats and Municipalities represents the third tier of federalism in India.

(*iv*) Different tiers in the Indian federal system operate independently within their jurisdiction.

(*a*) Only (*i*) and (*iii*) are correct.

(*b*) Only (*i*), (*ii*), and (*iv*) are correct.

(*c*) Only (*ii*), (*iii*), and (*iv*) are correct.

(*d*) All statements are correct.

7. If the Indian government consider a constitutional amendment to alter the power-sharing dynamics between the Union and State governments. Evaluate which steps are required for such an amendment to take place. ***(Ev)***

(*i*) The amendment requires approval from both Houses of Parliament.

(*ii*) A simple majority in Parliament.

(*iii*) The amendment must be ratified by the legislatures of at least half of the States.

(*iv*) The Supreme Court has to approve the amendment."

(*a*) (*i*) and (*iii*) (*b*) (*ii*) and (*iv*)

(*c*) (*i*), (*ii*) and (*iii*) (*d*) All of the above

8. Consider the following statements regarding language policy of the Indian Federation. ***(Re)*****(CBSE, 2020)**

(*i*) Hindi was identified as the official language.

(*ii*) Besides Hindi, there are 21 other languages recognised as scheduled languages.

(*iii*) English can be used along with Hindi for official purposes.

Choose the right option from the following:

(*a*) (*i*) and (*iii*) (*b*) (*i*) and (*ii*)

(*c*) Only (*i*) (*d*) (*i*), (*ii*) and (*iii*)

9. In the context of Indian federalism, certain states have been granted special status under Article 371 due to unique historical and social contexts. How do these special provisions primarily aim to benefit these states? ***(An)***

(*a*) By granting complete autonomy from the central government

(*b*) By providing exclusive economic benefits and subsidies

(*c*) By protecting the land rights of Indigenous peoples and their cultural heritage

(*d*) By allowing these states to form their foreign policies.

10. Read the statement given below and choose the code. ***(Ev)***

Statement I: In case of any dispute about the division of powers, the Supreme Court makes a decision.

Statement II: In the Indian Union, all States have equal powers.

(*a*) Statement I is correct and II is incorrect.

(*b*) Statement I is incorrect and II is correct

(*c*) Both I & II are incorrect

(*d*) Both I & II are correct

Assertion and Reason **(1 M)**

Direction: The following questions consist of two statements – Assertion (A) and Reason (R). Answer these questions by selecting the appropriate option given below:

(*a*) Both A and R are true, and R is the correct explanation of A.

(*b*) Both A and R are true, but R is not the correct explanation of A.

(*c*) A is true, but R is false

(*d*) A is false, but R is true.

1. **Assertion (A):** The rigidity of the amendment procedure for changing the power-sharing arrangement between the Union and State Governments protects the federal structure of India.

   Reason (R): Such amendments require a simple Parliament process as they are essential for the dynamic federal governance of India. ***(Ev)***

2. **Assertion (A):** Federalism in India allows for greater representation of diverse regional interests within a unified national framework.

   Reason (R): In India, power is equally divided between the central government and states governments. ***(Ev)***

3. **Assertion (A):** The adoption of federalism in India was influenced by the country's diverse linguistic, religious, and regional identities.

Reason (R): The Indian Constitution was created after Independence when several princely states became part of the country. To manage diversity effectively, the Constitution declared India as a Union of States with power-sharing arrangements between the central government and individual states. ***(Un)***

4. **Assertion (A):** The presence of state governments in India signifies the federal character of the country.

   Reason (R): State governments in India have their own legislative and executive powers, indicating the distribution of authority between the central government and states. ***(An)***

Subjective Questions

Very Short Answer Type Questions (2 M)

1. **What are the three lists mentioned in the Indian Constitution?** ***(Re)***

Ans. The three lists mentioned in the Indian constitution are the union list (which includes subjects of national importance), the state list (which includes subjects of state and local importance), and the concurrent list (includes subjects of common interest to both the union government and the state governments). *(2 M)*

2. **Who has the power to legislate on "residuary" subjects in India?** ***(Re)***

Ans. Subjects that do not fall into any of the three lists or subjects that come up after the constitution was made are known as residuary subjects, and according to the constitution, the Union government has the power to legislate on these residuary subjects. *(2 M)*

Short Answer Type Questions (3 M)

1. **What are the special provisions enjoyed by certain states in India?** ***(Un)***

Ans. (*i*) States like Assam, Nagaland, Arunachal Pradesh, and Mizoram enjoy special powers under Article 371 of the Indian Constitution due to their peculiar social and historical circumstances. *(1½ M)*

(*ii*) These special powers are specially enjoyed in relation to the protection of land rights of indigenous peoples, their culture, and preferential employment in government services. *(1½ M)*

2. **Explain the areas where the state government can make laws.** ***(Un)***

Ans. The areas where state government can make laws are:

(*i*) **State list:** Contains subject of state and local importance, such as police, trade, agriculture, etc. *(1 M)*

(*ii*) **Concurrent list:** Both union and state governments can make law but in case of Conflict, the union government's law prevails. *(1 M)*

(*iii*) **Special power (under article 371):** Granted to states like Assam, Nagaland, Arunachal Pradesh and Mizoram. The aim is to protect Culture, land rights and ensure preferential employment for indigenous people. *(1 M)*

Long Answer Type Questions (5 M)

1. **Explain the area where the Union government can make laws.** ***(Un)***

Ans. The union government can make laws on:

(*i*) **Union list:** This list includes subjects of national importance, such as defense, foreign affairs, banking, communications, and currency. The central government has the power to legislate on this list because we need a uniform policy on these matters throughout the country. *(1¼ M)*

(*ii*) **Union territories:** The union territories do not have the powers of a State. The Central Government has special powers in running these areas. *(1¼ M)*

(*iii*) **Residuary power:** These are the subjects that do not fall into any of the three lists or that came up after the Constitution was made. According to our constitution, the Union Government has the power to legislate on these 'residuary' subjects. *(1¼ M)*

(*iv*) **Concurrent list:** Both the Union as well as the State Governments can make laws on the subjects mentioned in this list but if their laws conflict with each other, the law made by the Union Government will prevail. *(1¼ M)*

2. **What makes India a federal country?** ***(Un)***

Ans.
- **Written constitution:** The country having a federal system necessarily has a written constitution for the clear demarcation of power. As India has a written constitution it supports the case of India being a federal country. *(1 M)*
- **Three-tier Government:** The Constitution establishes a two-tier system of government namely union government and state government. In 1992, a third tier was added with panchayats and municipalities *(1 M)*
- **Division of Powers:** The Constitution of India clearly divides the powers of the Central and State governments, and both have their separate areas of jurisdiction. *(1 M)*
- **Independent Judiciary:** India has an independent judiciary with the power of judicial review. The Supreme Court of India is the highest judicial authority in the country and has the power to interpret the Constitution and resolve disputes between the Central and State governments. *(1 M)*
- **Amendment Process:** Constitutional Amendment requires a two-thirds majority in both the houses of parliament and ratification by the legislature of at least half of the total states. *(1 M)*

3 HOW IS FEDERALISM PRACTICED?

NCERT Definitions *(Commonly asked in 1 mark)*

- **Linguistic States:** These are states formed based on the languages spoken by the majority of people in an area. This helps people in the state communicate better and feel more connected.
- **Official Language:** The languages that a country or region officially uses for its government and public works. It's used in laws, government offices, and official documents.
- **Scheduled Language:** These are specific languages that the Indian Constitution recognizes and supports under the ***eighth schedule*** of the Indian Constitution. There are 22 scheduled languages.
- **Coalition Government:** A government formed by multiple political parties coming together. When no single party wins enough seats to rule alone, they join with other parties to form the government.

Important Facts

01 Our Constitution did not give the status of national language to any one language

02 **Hindi** is the **official language** and not the national language.

03 The Indian constitution under the ***8th schedule*** recognizes **22 official languages**, including Hindi and English, as well as many regional languages such as Bengali, Tamil, Telugu, etc. to protect linguistic diversity.

04 The state boundaries of many states were changed on the basis of language, culture, ethnicity or geography in 1947.

05 The formation of linguistic States did not lead to disintegration as many leaders were afraid of but has made the country more united. It has also made administration easier.

Classification

Basis of reorganization of state in India in 1947:

1. **Based on language:** This was done to ensure that people who spoke the same language live in the same state.
2. **Based on culture, ethnicity, or geography:** Some States were created not on the basis of language but to recognise differences based on culture, ethnicity or geography.

Difference Between

Centre-State Relations in India Before and after 1990		
Aspect	**Pre-1990**	**Post-1990**
Political Scenario	Dominated by a single party at both Central and State levels.	Rise of regional parties and coalition governments at the Centre.
Centre-State Relations	The Central government could weaken State powers, often dismissing State governments led by rival parties.	Stronger autonomy for State governments, less arbitrary dismissal due to a Supreme Court judgment.
Power Sharing	Centralised power, less respect for State autonomy.	Enhanced power-sharing, and respect for State autonomy in governance.
Impact of Judiciary	Limited role in preventing arbitrary dismissal of State governments.	Significant role in safeguarding state autonomy against arbitrary dismissal.

Mnemonics

States created based on culture, ethnicity, or geography (not on linguistic basis): **JNU**

- J → Jharkhand
- N → Nagaland
- U → Uttarakhand

Important Dates

1990s – Beginning of the era of coalition governments at the Centre.

– The Supreme Court made it difficult for the Central Government to dismiss state governments arbitrarily through a major judgment.

Scan Me for Detailed Explanations

COMPETENCY BASED SOLVED EXAMPLES

Multiple Choice Questions

(1 M)

1. When Sunil looked at this cartoon, he said that this could not happen in the USA. Why did he say this? ***(An)***

(*a*) There are more individual states in the USA than in India.

(*b*) The central government holds absolute authority over the entire country.

(*c*) The individual states in the USA cannot make their own laws, unlike in India.

(*d*) The central government in the USA does not hold more power than the individual states.

2. How many languages are recognized as Scheduled Languages by the Indian Constitution? ***(Re)***

(*a*) 22 (*b*) 15

(*c*) 21 (*d*) 25

3. What led to a new culture of power sharing and respect for state autonomy in India? ***(Un)***

(*i*) Emergence of coalition governments

(*ii*) Centralization of power at the Centre

(*iii*) Dismissal of state governments by the Central Government
(*iv*) Supreme Court's judgment.
(*a*) Only (*i*) (*b*) (*i*) and (*iv*)
(*c*) Only (*iv*) (*d*) (*ii*) and (*iv*)

4. Analyze how the policy of allowing the use of English along with Hindi for official purposes has impacted India's unity and governance. ***(An)***
(*a*) It has led to linguistic divisions and weakened unity
(*b*) It has accommodated diversity and strengthened federalism
(*c*) It has marginalized non-English speakers
(*d*) It has undermined the importance of Hindi

5. Propose an initiative that could further strengthen linguistic harmony and federalism in India, drawing from the success of existing policies. ***(An)***
(*a*) Implementing a single national language policy
(*b*) Encouraging inter-state language learning programs
(*c*) Banning regional languages in official communication
(*d*) Promoting only English for inter-state communication

Assertion and Reason (1 M)

Direction: The following questions consist of two statements – Assertion (A) and Reason (R). Answer these questions by selecting the appropriate option given below:
(*a*) Both A and R are true, and R is the correct explanation of A.
(*b*) Both A and R are true, but R is not the correct explanation of A.
(*c*) A is true, but R is false
(*d*) A is false, but R is true.

1. **Assertion (A):** The Central Government's willingness to continue the use of English alongside Hindi was primarily to cater to non-Hindi speaking regions.
Reason (R): This decision was taken to prevent the kind of linguistic conflicts experienced in Tamil Nadu across the country. ***(Un)***
2. **Assertion (A):** Hindi was adopted as the official language of India to foster national unity.
Reason (R): Hindi is the mother tongue of half of the Indians, facilitating better communication and integration. ***(Ap)***
3. **Assertion (A):** The main difference between a federal form of government and a unitary one is the distribution of power between different levels of government.
Reason (R): In a unitary system, power is divided between central and regional governments, while in a federal system, power is concentrated at the national level with little or no autonomy given to regional governments. ***(Ev)***

Subjective Questions

Very Short Answer Type Questions (2 M)

1. What was the response of the Indian leaders when the demand for linguistic states was raised? ***(Re)***
Ans. When the demand for linguistic states was raised, initially the government was worried that creating states based on language would break the country apart, and they resisted linguistic states for some time. But later, they agreed to the idea, and it turned out that having linguistic states made people more united and administration simpler. *(2 M)*

2. What were some factors that contributed to the success of federalism in India? ***(An)***
Ans. Factors that contributed to the success of federalism in India were:
(*i*) The creation of linguistic States, language policy, and the restructuring of Centre-State relations. *(1 M)*
(*ii*) These factors played a significant role in strengthening federalism in India and made the country more united and has also made administration much more easier. *(1 M)*

Short Answer Type Questions (3 M)

1. What changes occurred in Centre-State relations after 1990? What role did the Supreme Court play in this? ***(An)***
Ans. (*i*) After 1990, the rise of regional parties and coalition governments at the Centre significantly improved Centre-State relations. States gained more autonomy, and a culture of power-sharing emerged. *(1½ M)*
(*ii*) The Supreme Court played a crucial role by passing a judgment that made it difficult for the central government to dismiss state governments arbitrarily, thus strengthening federal power sharing and respect for state autonomy. *(1½ M)*

Long Answer Type Questions (5 M)

1. Explain the language policy of India. ***(Un)***
Ans. (*i*) **No National Language:** The Indian Constitution doesn't designate any language as the national language of India. *(1 M)*
(*ii*) **Official Language:** Hindi is identified as the official language. It is the mother tongue of around 40% of Indians. *(1 M)*
(*iii*) **Safeguards for Other Languages:** To protect linguistic diversity, the Constitution recognizes 22 languages as Scheduled Languages, giving people the option to use them in exams for Central Government positions. *(1 M)*
(*iv*) **State Official Languages:** States have their own official languages, and much of the government work in each state is conducted in its official language. *(1 M)*
(*v*) **Continuation of English:** Originally, English was supposed to cease being used for official purposes in 1965. However, due to demand, especially from non-Hindi speaking states like Tamil Nadu, English continued alongside Hindi. *(1 M)*

4 DECENTRALISATION IN INDIA

NCERT Definitions *(Commonly asked in 1 mark)*

- **Decentralisation:** The transfer of power from central and state governments to local government.
- **Local Government:** These are government offices that operate at a local level, closer to the people, such as in villages (Panchayats) or towns (Municipalities). They handle day-to-day issues and decisions that affect local communities directly.
- **Panchayati Raj:** A system where villages have their councils called Panchayats. It's like having a small government for the village itself, where villagers can have a say in their governance and development.
- **Gram Panchayat:** A council at the village level which includes ward members (Panch) and a president (Sarpanch). They are chosen by the village's adult population and make decisions for the village's welfare.
- **Panchayat Samiti/Block/Mandal:** A group of several Gram Panchayats form a Panchayat samiti, with its members elected by Panchayat members within that area. It represents a middle tier between the Gram Panchayat and Zilla Parishad.
- **Zilla Parishad:** It is the top level of the Panchayati Raj system. All the panchayat samitis or mandals in a district together constitute the zilla (district) parishad. It includes elected members, MPs, and MLAs, and focuses on larger district-level development plans.
- **Municipality:** Local government for towns and smaller cities handling urban issues like water supply and waste management. Elected bodies consisting of peoples's representatives run it with a chairperson at the head.
- **Municipal Corporation:** Similar to a municipality but for larger cities. It has more power and resources to manage the complex issues of big cities. It is also under the control of elected representative run it with a mayor at the head.

Important Facts

01 India has a ***three-tier system*** of government: central, state, and local government.

02 In ***1992***, Amendments to the Constitution were made to strengthen local governments by making elections mandatory, reserving seats for marginalized groups, and ensuring financial autonomy and powers.

03 Urban local governments include municipalities for towns and municipal corporations for larger cities.

04 Now it is constitutionally ***mandatory*** to hold ***regular elections*** for local government bodies.

05 An independent institution called the State Election Commission has been created in each State to conduct panchayat and municipal elections.

06 The State governments are required to share some powers and revenue with local government bodies and the nature of sharing varies from State to State.

07 In local government bodies, ***at least 1/3rd*** of all the positions are reserved for ***women***.

08 Seats in the elected bodies and the executive heads of these institutions are reserved for the Scheduled Castes, Scheduled Tribes and Other Backward Classes.

Classification

Types of Local Governments:

- **Rural Local Governments**

  Panchayati Raj:
  - Gram Panchayat (village level)
  - Panchayat Samiti (block level)
  - Zilla Parishad (district level)
- ***Urban Local Governments***
  - Municipalities (towns)
  - Municipal Corporations (larger cities)

Difference Between

Local Government before vs after Constitutional Amendment in 1992.

Feature	Before the 1992 Amendment	After the 1992 Amendment
Elections	Elections to local governments were not held regularly.	It became constitutionally mandatory to hold regular elections for local government bodies.
Reservation of Seats	No specific provisions for the reservation of seats for SCs, STs, OBCs, and women.	Seats are reserved in elected bodies for SCs, STs, OBCs, and at least one-third of the seats are reserved for women.
Financial Autonomy	Local governments did not have any powers or resources of their own and were directly under the control of state governments.	State governments are required to share some powers and revenue with local government bodies, although the extent of this varies from state to state.
Election Commission	No independent body for conducting elections to local governments.	An independent institution called the State Election Commission was created in each State to conduct panchayat and municipal elections.
Women's Participation	Very limited participation of women in local governance.	Significant increase in women's representation and participation in local governance due to mandatory reservation.
Decentralisation	Very little decentralization in effective terms. Local issues and decisions were largely managed by state governments.	Enhanced decentralization with more powers given to local bodies, aiming for better governance at the village and town levels.

Myth Buster

- **Myth:** The establishment of local governments in India has fully achieved its goal of self-governance, effectively decentralizing power to the grassroots level.

  Fact: Gram sabhas are not held regularly. Most state governments have not transferred significant powers to the local governments. Nor have they been given adequate resources. We are thus still a long way from realizing the ideal of self-government.

Important Dates

1992- The constitution was amended to make the third-tier of democracy more powerful and effective.

COMPETENCY BASED SOLVED EXAMPLES

Scan Me for Detailed Explanations

Multiple Choice Questions

(1 M)

1. **In the context of Indian federalism, the decentralization of power introduced a third tier of governance to address local issues effectively. This tier, aimed at fostering direct democratic participation and more efficient local management, includes various local government structures.**

   Based on the description, which of the following best captures the essence of decentralized governance in India? ***(Un)***

   (*a*) Decentralization primarily enhances the financial independence of local bodies without altering their administrative roles.

   (*b*) The decentralization process, initiated in 1992, aimed to empower local governments by mandating regular elections and resource sharing, thus deepening democracy.

   (*c*) The third tier of governance mainly serves as an advisory body to the central and state governments, with no significant decision-making authority.

   (*d*) Decentralization was introduced to increase the central government's control over rural and urban areas by establishing local surveillance units.

2. **What was the major step taken towards decentralization in 1992 in India?** ***(Re)***

   (*a*) Abolishing local government bodies

   (*b*) Increasing the power of state governments

   (*c*) Amending the Constitution to empower local government

   (*d*) Introducing direct rule by the central government

3. **What is the role of the State Election Commission in local government elections?** ***(Re)***

   (*a*) Appointing the President of the local government bodies

   (*b*) Conducting panchayat and municipal elections

   (*c*) Allocating resources to union government.

   (*d*) Overseeing the functioning of state governments

4. **A few gram panchayats are grouped together to form** ***(Re)***

   (*a*) Gram Panchayat

   (*b*) Zilla Parishad

   (*c*) Municipal Corporation

   (*d*) panchayat samiti or block or mandal

5. **In an interactive game designed to test your understanding of local governance and local government functions. You need to match the terms in Column-I with the appropriate descriptions in Column-II based on your knowledge:** ***(Re)***

Column-I (Local Governance Structures)		Column-II (Functions)	
(A)	Gram Panchayat	(*i*)	Handles urban planning and infrastructure for large cities
(B)	Zilla Parishad	(*ii*)	Manages local welfare schemes and development at the village level
(C)	Municipal Corporation	(*iii*)	Coordinates development activities across multiple villages within a district
(D)	Panchayat Samiti	(*iv*)	Governs an entire district's rural development projects

   (*a*) A-(*ii*), B-(*iv*), C-(*i*), D-(*iii*)

   (*b*) A-(*iii*), B-(*i*), C-(*iv*), D-(*ii*)

   (*c*) A-(*iv*), B-(*ii*), C-(*i*), D-(*iii*)

   (*d*) A-(*ii*), B-(*iii*), C-(*i*), D-(*iv*)

Assertion and Reason

(1 M)

Direction: The following questions consist of two statements – Assertion (A) and Reason (R). Answer these questions by selecting the appropriate option given below:

(*a*) Both A and R are true, and R is the correct explanation of A.

(*b*) Both A and R are true, but R is not the correct explanation of A.

(*c*) A is true, but R is false

(*d*) A is false, but R is true.

1. **Assertion (A):** A major step towards decentralization was taken in 2000.

   Reason (R): The constitution was amended to make the third tier of democracy more powerful and effective. ***(Ap)***

2. **Assertion (A):** Zilla Parishad Chairperson is the political head of the zilla parishad.

   Reason (R): Mayor is the head of municipal corporation. ***(Re)***

3. **Assertion (A):** When power is taken away from central and state governments and given to local governments it is called decentralisation.

   Reason (R): At least one fourth of all positions are reserved for women in local government bodies. ***(An)***

Subjective Questions

Very Short Answer Type Questions

(2 M)

1. **Assess the need for local government.** ***(Ev)***

Ans. The local government is essential because there are a large number of issues which can better addressed when local people are involved. People have better knowledge of their problems. They also have better ideas to spend money and how to manage things more efficiently. *(2 M)*

2. **State any two differences between the local government before and after the Constitutional amendment in 1992.** **(*An*)(NCERT)**

Ans. **(Any Two)**

Local government before 1992	Local government after 1992
Elections to the local bodies were conducted by state bodies	An independent institution called the State Election Commission has been created in each State to conduct panchayat and municipal elections.
Not mandatory to hold regular elections for local bodies.	Mandatory to hold regular elections for local government bodies.
Local governments did not have any powers or resources of their own.	The State governments are required to share some powers and revenue with local government bodies.
There was no specific provision for the reservation of seats for SC/STs or women.	Provisions for reservation of seats for Scheduled Castes, Scheduled Tribes, and women (at least one-third of positions).

(1 + 1 = 2 M)

3. **Why is it important for a village to conduct regular gram sabha meetings?** **(*Ap*)**

Ans. Gram sabha meetings are important because they allow all adult villagers to discuss and decide on the village's budget and review the performance of the gram panchayat. This promotes democratic participation and effective decision-making and ensures that decisions reflect the community's needs. *(2 M)*

Short Answer Type Questions (3 M)

1. **Do you take decentralisation as means to minimise the conflicts? Give your view point.** **(*Ev*)**

Ans. Yes, Decentralisation can be used as a means to reduce conflicts because:

(*i*) **Promotes Local Governance:** Decentralisation supports local governance, which allows communities to address their issues directly. This enhances community participation and decision-making at the local level, leading to more relevant and accepted solutions. *(1½ M)*

(*ii*) **Efficient Problem-Solving:** Local governments have a better understanding of their problems, which leads to more effective and relevant solutions to local issues. This targeted problem-solving can prevent conflicts that arise due to inefficiencies and misaligned policies of centralized governance. *(1½ M)*

2. **How does decentralisation through local government contribute to the overall development of India?** **(*Ap*)**

Ans. Decentralization through local government contributes significantly to the overall development of India in the following ways.

(*i*) **Inclusive Growth:** It promotes inclusive growth by empowering marginalized communities and ensuring their representation in decision-making processes. *(1 M)*

(*ii*) **Economic Development:** Decentralization promotes region-specific development strategies. This approach leads to balanced economic growth across various parts of the country, reducing regional disparities and boosting national development. *(1 M)*

(*iii*) **Boosts Development:** Focused attention on local infrastructure, education, and health services directly impacts the overall development of the area and, subsequently, the nation. *(1 M)*

3. **Describe any three provisions of amendment made in 'Indian Constitution' in 1992 for making 'Three-Tier' government more effective and powerful.** **(*Cr*)(CBSE, 2018)**

Ans. Amendments in Indian Constitution in 1992, For making the 'Three-Tier' government most effective and powerful were:

(*i*) It is constitutionally mandatory to hold regular elections to local government bodies. *(1 M)*

(*ii*) Seats reserved for women, Scheduled Caste, Scheduled Tribes and Other Backward Classes. *(1 M)*

(*iii*) The state governments are required to share some powers and revenue with local government bodies. *(1 M)*

4. **Read the statements given below regarding Federalism in India.**

Statement I: India's constitution originally provided for a two-tier system of government.

Statement II: Later, a third tier of federalism was added.

Explain what trend these statements - S1 and S2 - reflect in the governance system of India. **(*An*)**

Ans. (*i*) These statements reflect a trend towards increased decentralization and democratization of governance in India. *(1 M)*

(*ii*) Initially, the Indian Constitution established a two-tier government structure. Later, to enhance governance closer to the grassroots level, a third tier was introduced through the addition of Panchayats and Municipalities. *(1 M)*

(*iii*) This evolution draws attention to India's commitment to federalism and the principle of local governance, where decisions are made at the most immediate (or local) level possible. *(1 M)*

5. **"Local Government is an effective way to uphold the democratic principle of decentralization, and strengthens democracy." Justify this statement with valid points.** **(*Ev*)**

Ans. The statement "Local Government is an effective way to uphold the democratic principle of decentralization" can be justified in the following ways:

- **Decentralization of Power:** Local government ensures the decentralization of power by giving authority to local bodies, allowing decisions to be made at the grassroots level, which helps in solving local problems more effectively. *(1½ M)*
- **Strengthens democracy:** It strengthens democracy by encouraging active participation from the people in local governance, making them more involved in decision-making and increasing accountability at the local level. *(1½ M)*

Long Answer Type Questions (5 M)

1. How has decentralization in India evolved over time, and what measures have been taken to strengthen local government? *(An)*

Ans. (*i*) Decentralization in India has evolved gradually and it aimed to enhance local self-government and promote democratic participation. *(1 M)*

(*ii*) Initially, local government bodies such as gram panchayats and municipalities were set up, but they lacked powers and resources. *(1 M)*

(*iii*) In 1992, a major step was taken to strengthen local government by amending the Constitution. *(1 M)*

(*iv*) This ensured regular elections, reservations for marginalized groups, and sharing of powers and revenue with local government bodies. *(1 M)*

(*v*) The creation of independent State Election Commissions and the mandatory reservation of one-third of positions for women further empowered local government. *(1 M)*

2. What is the rationale for decentralisation of power? Explain the structure of Rural local government in India. *(Un)*

Ans. The main rationale for decentralization in India is to bring power sharing within the states and promote grass-roots democracy by empowering local government. This is to address diverse needs more efficiently and empower people at the grassroot level. It helps in promoting direct participation, which is the foundation of democracy. *(2 M)*

Structure of Rural Local Government:

(*i*) **Gram Panchayat:** A council consisting of several ward members often called Panch, and a president or sarpanch. It is the decision making body for the entire village. *(1 M)*

(*ii*) **Panchayat Samiti or Mandal or Block:** A few Gram Panchayats are grouped together to form this government body. The members of this body are elected by the entire panchayat members in that area. *(1 M)*

(*iii*) **Zilla (district) Parishad:** All the mandals in a district together constitute the Zila Parishad. Most of the members are elected. *(1 M)*

MISCELLANEOUS EXERCISE

Multiple Choice Questions

(1 M)

1. Which of the following are examples of 'Coming together federations'? ***(Re)***

(*a*) Germany, Spain, and Belgium
(*b*) India, USA, and Britain
(*c*) USA, Switzerland, and Australia
(*d*) Belgium, China and Sri Lanka

2. Match the Column-I with Column-II and choose the correct option: ***(Re)*(CBSE, 2023)**

Column-I (Subject)		Column-II (List)	
A.	Banks	(*i*)	Concurrent List
B.	Agriculture	(*ii*)	Union List
C.	Education	(*iii*)	State List
D.	Computer	(*iv*)	Residuary Subjects

(*a*) A-(*iv*), B-(*iii*), C-(*i*), D-(*ii*)
(*b*) A-(*iii*), B-(*iv*), C-(*i*), D-(*ii*)
(*c*) A-(*ii*), B-(*iii*), C-(*i*), D-(*iv*)
(*d*) A-(*iv*), B-(*ii*), C-(*i*), D-(*iii*)

3. Which of the following statements about Federalism in the Indian Constitution are correct? ***(Re)* (CBSE SQP, 2024)**

1. India is declared as a Union of States.
2. Power-sharing between the Union and State governments is a basic feature.
3. The power-sharing arrangement is easy to change.
4. Changes in power-sharing require a 1/3rd majority in both houses of Parliament.

Options

(*a*) 1 and 2 (*b*) 2 and 3
(*c*) 1 and 3 (*d*) 2 and 4

4. Evaluate the statement and choose the correct option: ***(Ev)***
"*Decentralization has completely shifted power dynamics from state to local governments.*"

(*a*) True, as local governments are now fully autonomous.
(*b*) False, state governments still play a significant role in overseeing local functions.
(*c*) True, as local governments control all public services.
(*d*) False, as local governments don't have any power of their own.

5. After the 1992 amendment to the Indian Constitution, local governments received constitutional status, enhancing the democratic at the grassroots level. Despite these improvements, certain challenges persist in fully actualizing the potential of local self-governance.

Which of the following options best describes a significant issue that local governments face despite constitutional empowerment? ***(An)***

(*a*) Local governments now hold more power than state governments, leading to conflicts.
(*b*) Despite holding elections, local governments often lack sufficient autonomy and resources to function effectively.
(*c*) The reservation of seats for marginalized communities has led to a decrease in the quality of governance.
(*d*) The establishment of State Election Commissions has led to increased central interference in local governance.

6. Read the passage below.

Australia became a nation on 1 January 1901, when the British Parliament passed legislation enabling the six Australian colonies to collectively govern in their own right as the Commonwealth of Australia. It was a remarkable political accomplishment that had taken many years and several referenda to achieve. ***(Ap)***

Source: Official website of the National Museum of Australia

From this, we can infer that Australia is an example of a __________.

(*a*) united democracy
(*b*) unitary government
(*c*) 'coming together' federation
(*d*) 'holding together' federation

7. The head of urban local self-government is __________. ***(Re)***

(*a*) Sarpanch (*b*) Ward commissioner
(*c*) Mukhiya (*d*) Mayor

8. The Constitution mandated that _______ number of seats be reserved for women in the panchayats and municipalities ***(Re)***

(*a*) One-fourth (*b*) One-third
(*c*) Three-fourth (*d*) One-sixth

9. The distinguishing feature of a federal government is: ***(Un)*(NCERT)**

(*a*) National government gives some powers to the provincial governments.
(*b*) Power is distributed among the legislature, executive and judiciary.
(*c*) Elected officials exercise supreme power in the government.
(*d*) Power is divided between different levels of government.

10. The principle of subsidiarity emphasises that decisions should be made by the people who are most affected by them, promoting decentralisation, efficiency, and citizen participation in governance, with higher levels of authority intervening only when lower level authorities are unable to address certain issues effectively. ***(An)*(CBSE APQ, 2023)**

Which of the following constitutional principles/legislations is in close alignment with the principle stated above?

(*a*) separation of power between the executive, legislature, and judiciary

(*b*) division of power between the central, state, and local government

(*c*) right of individuals to form and join political parties of their choice

(*d*) reservation for women in the highest law-making bodies

11. Which of the following statements is correct regarding revenue sources in a federal setup? ***(Un)***

(*a*) States either have no financial powers or have independent sources of revenue.

(*b*) States are dependent on the central government's revenue/funds.

(*c*) Sources of revenue for each level of government are specified to ensure its financial autonomy.

(*d*) States have no financial autonomy.

12. Which of the following languages is recognized as the national language by the Constitution of India? ***(Re)***

(*a*) Hindi (*b*) English

(*c*) Tamil (*d*) None of these

13. The people of Belgium have successfully dealt with their country's power sharing problem and is leading a happy and peaceful life. Which route to federation have they opted for? ***(Un)* (CBSE SQP, 2024)**

(*a*) Coming together (*b*) Cooperative Federation

(*c*) Holding Together (*d*) Competitive Federation

14. Identify the administrative level of Indian Government with the help of the information given below and choose the correct option: ***(Un)*(CBSE, 2023)**

(*i*) Power shared between Central to Local Government.
(*ii*) The State Governments are required to share some powers and revenue with them
(*iii*) It is called a three tier government.

(*a*) Dictatorial System

(*b*) Unitary Federal System

(*c*) Decentralised System

(*d*) Imperialistic System

15. Which of the following statements are correct regarding 'Holding together federation': ***(An)***

A. A large country divides its power between constituent states and the national government.

B. The Central government tends to be more powerful vis-a-vis the States.

C. Constituent states have equal powers.

D. Constituent states have unequal powers.

(*a*) Only A (*b*) A and D

(*c*) B and D (*d*) A, B, and D

16. Below given are statements on the practice of federalism in India. ***(Ap and An)***

A. Local governments did not have any power or resources of their own.

B. It became constitutionally mandatory to hold regular elections to local government bodies.

C. The state governments are required to share some powers and revenue with local government bodies.

D. No seats are reserved in the elected bodies for SCs, STs, and other backward classes.

Which of these hold true in the context of decentralization after 1992?

(*a*) B and C (*b*) A and C

(*c*) A and D (*d*) B and D

17. Match the **Column-I** with **Column-II** and choose the correct option: ***(Re)* (CBSE 2024)**

Column-I (List)		Column-II (Jurisdiction Sphere)	
I.	Union list subjects	A.	State Government alone make laws on it
II.	State list subjects	B.	For uniformity Central Government Legislates on it
III.	Concurrent subjects	C.	Subjects under Jurisdiction of Centre and State Governments.
IV.	Residuary subjects	D.	Central Government legislates on new subjects

	I	II	III	IV
(*a*)	A	B	C	D
(*b*)	C	D	A	B
(*c*)	D	C	B	A
(*d*)	B	A	C	D

18. In a representative democracy, which of the following best describes the role of elected representatives? ***(Un)*(CBSE APQ, 2023)**

(*a*) They have absolute power and authority to make decisions without consulting the public.

(*b*) They are accountable to the public and make decisions on behalf of their constituents.

(*c*) They act as mere figureheads with no real power or influence in the government.

(*d*) They serve lifetime appointments and cannot be removed from office.

19. Match the Column-I with Column-II and select the correct answer using the codes given below the column: **(*Re*)(NCERT)**

	Column-I		Column-II
A.	Union of India	(*i*)	Prime Minister
B.	State	(*ii*)	Sarpanch
C.	Municipal Corporation	(*iii*)	Governor
D.	Gram Panchayat	(*iv*)	Mayor

(*a*) A-(*iv*), B-(*i*), C-(*ii*), D-(*iii*)

(*b*) A-(*ii*), B-(*iii*), C-(iv), D-(*i*)

(*c*) A-(*i*), B-(*iii*), C-(*iv*), D-(*ii*)

(*d*) A-(*iii*), B-(*iv*), C-(*i*), D-(*ii*)

20. Consider the following two statements.

A. In a federation, the powers of the federal and provincial governments are clearly demarcated.

B. India is a federation because the powers of the Union and State Governments are specified in the Constitution and they have exclusive jurisdiction on their respective subjects.

C. Sri Lanka is a federation because the country is divided into provinces.

D. India is no longer a federation because some powers of the States have been devolved to the local government bodies. **(*An*)(NCERT)**

Which of the statements given above are correct?

(*a*) A, B, and C (*b*) A, C, and D

(*c*) A and B only (*d*) B and C only

Assertion and Reason

(1 M)

Direction: The following questions consist of two statements – Assertion (A) and Reason (R). Answer these questions by selecting the appropriate option given below:

(*a*) Both A and R are true, and R is the correct explanation of A.

(*b*) Both A and R are true, but R is not the correct explanation of A.

(*c*) A is true, but R is false

(*d*) A is false, but R is true.

1. Assertion (A): The Constitution originally provided for a three-tier system of the government.
Reason (R): These different tiers enjoy separate jurisdiction. **(*An*)**

2. Assertion (A): India has a federal system.
Reason (R): Under a unitary system either there is only one level of government or the sub-units are subordinate to the central government. **(*Ev*)**

3. Assertion (A): It is very difficult to make changes in the fundamental provisions of the Indian constitution.
Reason (R): Fundamental provisions of the constitution cannot be unilaterally changed by one level of government. **(*Ev*)**

4. Assertion (A): Switzerland and Australia are 'coming together' federations.
Reason (R): These States come together on their own to form a bigger unit, so that by pooling sovereignty and retaining identity, they can increase their security. **(*Ev*) (NCERT)**

5. Assertion (A): When power is taken away from Central and State governments and given to local governments, it is called decentralization.
Reason (R): Rural local government is known as municipalities. **(*An*)**

6. Assertion (A): All States in the Indian Union have identical powers.
Reason (R): Most federations that are formed by 'holding together' do not give equal power to its constituent units. **(*Ev*)**

7. Assertion (A): The areas, like Chandigarh, or Lakshadweep or the capital city of Delhi, are called Union Territories.
Reason (R): The state government has special powers in running these areas. **(*An*)**

Subjective Questions

Very Short Answer Type Questions (2 M)

1. Distinguish between unitary and federal systems of government. **(*An*)(CBSE APQ, 2023)**

2. In the fictitious democratic state of Lokapur, the election for the local Panchayat has brought several events into the limelight. One such issue is the auctioning of Panchayat positions to the highest bidder, as reported by the local news. This controversial practice has sparked a debate on the integrity of democratic processes at the grassroots level. Furthermore, the state has seen a remarkable election where over 1 million women have been elected to Panchayats, signaling a shift towards gender inclusivity in local governance.

On the following developments in Lokapur, discuss their implications for the democratic process and local governance. **(*An*)**

3. Mention any two reasons to state that India is a federal country. **(*Re*)(CBSE SQP, 2023)**

4. What is the system of Panchayati Raj? **(*Un*)**

5. An analysis by Vidushi Joshi in the International Journal of Advanced Legal Research (IJALR) provides a comparative look at federalism in India and the USA, discussing how each country's historical and constitutional frameworks shape their current federal structures. The article notes how both nations handle the distribution of power between central and state governments, albeit in different manners reflecting their unique political and social contexts.

Based on Vidushi Joshi's analysis in the International Journal of Advanced Legal Research (IJALR), how do the federal structures of India and the United States differ in terms of power distribution between central and state governments? ***(An)***

Short Answer Type Questions (3 M)

1. Describe the nature of the Panchayati Raj system in India. ***(Un)*(CBSE, 2020)**
2. Describe any three features of 'federal government. ***(Un)*(CBSE, 2020)**

OR

Describe any three characteristics of the Indian federal system. ***(Un)*(CBSE, 2024)**

3. Describe any three features of 'unitary government. ***(Un)*(CBSE, 2020)**
4. Discuss the MOST LIKELY impact if India operated without a federal system. Build the answer around these points: ***(An)*(CBSE APQ, 2023)**
   - regional autonomy
   - effectiveness in governance
   - decision-making process
5. The Indian constitution provides 3 lists to distribute the legislative power. State any two subjects that are included in the union list. In which list the subject "Education" is included and why? ***(Re)*(CBSE SQP, 2023)**
6. Name any two subjects that are included in Concurrent List. How are laws made on these subjects? Explain. ***(Re)*(CBSE, 2019)**

Long Answer Type Questions (5 M)

1. What is the significance of federalism in a country like India? ***(Un)***
2. During a national debate on governance systems, a panelist argues that India does not truly operate under a federal system due to its centralized legislative tendencies. To counter this claim, another panelist, who is a constitutional expert, presents evidence to support India's federal structure. Provide your response based on your understanding of India's governance framework. ***(Cr)***
3. A policy debate is being held at a national conference on language policy. The discussion focuses on the constitutional approach to language management in India, a country with significant linguistic diversity. The panelists are asked to explain the framework of India's language policy. Provide a comprehensive response to this scenario, outlining the constitutional provisions and their implications for managing linguistic diversity in India. ***(Cr)***
4. What role does decentralization play in Indian federalism? ***(Un)***
5. How federalism practised in india? ***(Ap)***

Case Based Questions (4 M)

Case Based-I: Read the information below and answer the questions that follow. (CBSE, 2023)

Language Diversity of India

How many languages do we have in India? The answer depends on how one counts it. The latest information that we have is from the Census of India held in 2011. This census recorded more than 1300 distinct languages which people mentioned as their mother tongues. These languages were grouped together under some major languages. For example languages like Bhojpuri, Magadhi, Bundelkhandi, Chhattisgarhi, Rajasthani and many others were grouped together under 'Hindi'. Even after this grouping, the Census found 121 major languages. Of these 22 languages are now included in the Eighth Schedule of the Indian Constitution and are therefore called 'Scheduled Languages'. Others are called 'Non-Scheduled Languages'. In terms of languages, India is perhaps the most diverse country in the world.

(i) Explain the importance of language diversity in India. ***(Un)***

(ii) Differentiate between Scheduled and Non-Scheduled Languages. ***(An)***

(iii) 'The fusion of languages has united the country into one cultural entity.' Explain the statement with an example. ***(Ap)***

Case Based-II: Read the information below and answer the questions that follow. (CBSE, 2023)

Decentralisation in India

This new system of local government is the largest experiment in democracy conducted anywhere in the world. There are now about 36 lakh elected representatives in the panchayats and municipalities etc., all over the country. This number is bigger than the population of many countries in the world. Constitutional status for local government has helped to deepen democracy in our country. It has also increased women's representation and voice in our democracy. At the same time, there are many difficulties. While elections are held regularly of Panchayats and people participate enthusiastically in it but meeting of gram sabhas are not held regularly.

(i) Why is Indian decentralisation considered as the largest experiment in democracy? ***(Un)***

(ii) Analyse how constitutional status for local government has helped to deepen democracy in India? ***(An)***

(iii) Explain any two steps taken by the Indian Government for decentralization. ***(Re)***

Case Based-III: Read the information below and answer the questions that follow.

Centre State Relations

Restructuring the Centre-State relations is one more way in which federalism has been strengthened in practice. How the constitutional arrangements for sharing power work in reality depends to a large extent on how the ruling parties and leaders follow these arrangements. For a long time, the same party ruled both at the Centre and in most of the States. This meant that the State governments did not exercise their rights as autonomous federal units. When the ruling party at the State level was different, the parties that ruled at the Centre tried to undermine the power of the States. In those days, the Central Government would often misuse the Constitution to dismiss the State governments that were controlled by rival parties. This undermined the spirit of federalism. All this changed significantly after 1990. This period saw the rise of regional political parties in many States of the country. This was also the beginning of the era of COALITION GOVERNMENTS at the Centre. Since no single party got a clear majority in the Lok Sabha, the major national parties had to enter into an alliance with many parties including several regional parties to form a government at the Centre. This led to a new culture of power sharing and respect for the autonomy of State Governments. This trend was supported by a major judgement of the Supreme Court that made it difficult for the Central Government to dismiss state governments in an arbitrary manner. Thus, federal power sharing is more effective today than it was in the early years after the Constitution came into force.

(i) What are Coalition Governments? Explain its significance. ***(Un)***

(ii) How did coalition governments at the Centre impact federalism in India? ***(Ap)***

(iii) "Federal power-sharing is more effective today than it was in the early years after the Constitution came into force." Elaborate. ***(Ev)***

ANSWER KEYS

Multiple Choice Questions

1. (*c*)	**2.** (*c*)	**3.** (*a*)	**4.** (*b*)	**5.** (*b*)	**6.** (*c*)	**7.** (*d*)	**8.** (*b*)	**9.** (*d*)	**10.** (*b*)
11. (*c*)	**12.** (*d*)	**13.** (*c*)	**14.** (*c*)	**15.** (*d*)	**16.** (*a*)	**17.** (*d*)	**18.** (*b*)	**19.** (*c*)	**20.** (*c*)

Assertion and Reason

1. (*d*)	**2.** (*b*)	**3.** (*a*)	**4.** (*a*)	**5.** (*c*)	**6.** (*d*)	**7.** (*c*)

HINTS & EXPLANATIONS

Multiple Choice Questions

1. (*c*) USA, Switzerland, and Australia are examples of 'Coming together federations'.

2. (*c*) A-(ii), B-(iii), C-(i), D-(iv)

3. (*a*) Statements 1 and 2 are correct. Statement 3 and 4 are incorrect because the power-sharing arrangement is rigid and cannot be changed easily. Also, changes in power-sharing need approval by a $2/3^{rd}$ majority in both houses, not $1/3^{rd}$.

4. (*b*) While decentralization has increased local governance powers, state governments still oversee and regulate significant aspects of local administration.

5. (*b*) Even after the constitutional amendments, many local governments struggle with inadequate financial resources and limited autonomy, hindering their ability to address local issues effectively. *(1 M)*

6. (*c*) Australia is an example of a 'coming together' federation where independent states (colonies) voluntarily unite to form a federation, sharing sovereignty while retaining individual autonomy.

7. (*d*) The head of urban local self-government is Mayor.

8. (*b*) The Constitution mandated that one-third number of seats be reserved for women in the panchayats and municipalities.

9. (*d*) In a federal government, power is shared between two or more levels, like central and state governments, ensuring autonomy in their areas. When power is distributed among the legislature, executive, and judiciary, it refers to the separation of powers, not federalism.

10. (*b*) division of power between the central, state, and local government

11. (*c*) Sources of revenue for each level of government are specified to ensure its financial autonomy.

12. (*d*) Constitution of India does not recognise any language as the national language of India.

13. (*c*) Belgium followed the holding together model of federation, where power was decentralized to accommodate different linguistic groups while maintaining the unity of the country.

14. (*c*) Decentralised system

15. (*d*) A, B, and D

16. (*a*) In the context of decentralization in India after 1992, only b and C are correct. The other option shows the case before 1992.

17. (*d*) I-B, II-A, III-C, IV-D

18. (*b*) They are accountable to the public and make decisions on behalf of their constituents.

19. (*c*) A-(i), B-(iii), C-(iv), D-(ii)

20. (*c*) A and B only

Assertion and Reason

1. (*d*) The constitution originally provided for a two-tier system of government. Later, a third tier was added in the form of panchayats and municipalities.

2. (*b*) Both A and R are true, but R is not the correct explanation of A.

3. (*a*) Self-explanatory.

4. (*a*) Self-explanatory.

5. (*c*) The rural local government is known as Panchayati raj.

6. (*d*) All states in the Indian Union do not have identical powers; some states like Assam, Mizoram, Arunachal Pradesh, and Nagaland enjoy some special power due to their peculiar social and historical circumstances.

7. (*c*) The central government has special powers in running these areas.

Subjective Questions

Very Short Answer Type Questions

1.
- Under the unitary system, either there is only one level of government or the sub-units are subordinate to the central government. The central government can pass on orders to the provincial or the local government. *(1 M)*
- However, in a federal system, the central government cannot order the state government to do something. State government has powers of its own for which it is not answerable to the central government. Both these governments are separately answerable to the people. *(1 M)*

2. The implication of the events are as follows:

(*i*) **The auctioning of panchayat positions:** It undermines the essence of democracy which is based on fair and free elections. It could lead to governance by those with financial power rather than by those with the welfare of the people in mind. *(1 M)*

(*ii*) **One million elected women in panchayats:** It is a positive development, fostering gender balance and potentially bringing new perspectives to local governance that can address women's issues more effectively. *(1 M)*

3. The following are the reasons to state that India is a federal Country:

- **Division of Powers:** The Constitution of India clearly demarcates the powers of the Central and State governments, and both have their separate areas of jurisdiction. *(1 M)*

- **Independent Judiciary:** India has an independent judiciary with the power of judicial review. The Supreme Court of India has the power to interpret the Constitution and resolve disputes between the Central and State governments. *(1 M)*

4. The system of Panchayati Raj in India is a three-tier structure of local governance, consisting of village (Gram Panchayat), block (Panchayat Samiti), and district (Zilla Parishad) levels. It aims to bring administration closer to the people, encouraging direct participation in decision-making at the local level. *(2 M)*

5. India and the United States both have a federal structure. Yet it is very different from each other as India has a centralized federal structure where the central government holds more powers. In contrast, the U.S. has a decentralized structure where states have significant autonomy over their internal affairs, and the central government has limited interference in state policies. *(2 M)*

Short Answer Type Questions

1. Nature of the Panchayati Raj System in India.

(i) **Three-tier structure:** Comprises Gram Panchayats (village level), Panchayat Samitis (block level), and Zilla Parishads (district level). *(1 M)*

(ii) **Decentralisation:** Empowers local governance by transferring administrative and financial responsibilities to the grassroots level. *(1 M)*

(iii) **Democratic participation:** Facilitates direct involvement of the people in decision-making through regular elections and Gram Sabha meetings. *(1 M)*

Topper's Explanations **(CBSE, 2020)**

- Every village or group of villages has a gram panchayat which consists of several ward members [panch] and a president [sarpanch]. It is elected by all the adult ward members living in that ward.
- It is under the supervision of the gram sabha which consists of the adult members of that population who meet a few times a year to discuss the performance of the gram sabha and the annual budget.
- A few Gram Sabhas form a Panchayat Samiti or Block or Mandal elected by all the Panchayat members in that area.
- A few Panchayat Samitis constitute the Zilla Parishad which consists of MLAs, members of legislative assemblies, and other ministers.
- Zilla Parishad chairperson is the political head of Zilla Parishad.

2. The three characteristics of the Indian federal system are:

(i) **Division of powers:** The power is divided between the central government and the constituent units. Both levels of government have their own areas of jurisdiction and are independent of each other. *(1 M)*

(ii) **Rigid Constitution:** The fundamental provisions of the constitution cannot be solely changed by one level of government. Such changes require the consent of both the level of government. *(1 M)*

(iii) **Independent judiciary:** A federal government has an independent judiciary that serves as a check on the powers of both the central government and the constituent units. The judiciary is responsible for interpreting the constitution and ensuring that both levels of government remain within their constitutional limits. *(1 M)*

Topper's Explanation **(CBSE, 2024)**

2B. Three characteristics of the Indian federal system are -

1. It is an example of holding together federation wherein the centre tends to be more powerful vis-à-vi the states. The Constitution declares India to be a Union of states with a three tier system (3 levels) - Central, State and local governments which comprise of municipalities and panchayats.

2. The jurisdictions of each tier of government is clearly specified in the constitution which ensures that the presence and authority of each level is constitutionally guaranteed. Constitution provides a three fold distribution comprising of union, state and concurrent lists. Each level has its own jurisdiction in legislative, adminstrative and affairs related to taxation.

3. Judiciary acts as an umpire incase a dispute arises between the levels of the government and has the power to interpret the constitution and the powers of each and every tier of the government. Federal structure helps us to strengthen the unity of the country and accomodate its regional diversity.

3. The following are some of the features of unitary government.

(i) Concentration **of power:** In unitary government power is concentrated in the hands of the central government. *(1 M)*

(ii) **No division of powers:** Unlike the federal government, there is no division of powers between the central government and the constituent units. *(1 M)*

(iii) **No written constitution:** Unitary government does not necessarily have a written constitution that outlines the powers of the central government and the constituent units. *(1 M)*

4. ***(i)*** **Regional autonomy:** Regional governments would have little or no decision-making power. Regional autonomy and aspirations might get suppressed. *(1 M)*

(ii) **Effectiveness in Governance:** Local issues might not receive due attention, leading to a disconnect between grass root reality and governance leading to less effectiveness in governance. *(1 M)*

(iii) **Decision-making process:** The decision-making process might become undemocratic and less inclusive. It is likely to neglect regional aspirations. *(1 M)*

5. *(i)* The subjects that are included in the Union List are those that are under the exclusive jurisdiction of the Union Government. Some of the subjects that are included in the Union List are:

- Defense of the country
- Foreign affairs and relations *(1 M)*

(ii) *(a)* The subject "Education" comes under the Concurrent List, which means that both the Union Government and the State Governments have the power to make laws on this subject. *(1 M)*

(b) The Concurrent List contains subjects that are of common interest to both the Union and the State Governments. Education is included in this list because it is of the common interest to both the union and state government. *(1 M)*

6. • The two subjects that are included in the concurrent list are Education and Forests. *(1 M)*

• Both the Union and State Governments can make laws on these subjects as this list contains the subjects which are of common interest to both the Union and state governments. *(1 M)*

• If there is a conflict between the central and state laws, the law made by the Union Government prevails. *(1 M)*

Long Answer Type Questions

1. The significance of federalism in a country like India are:

(i) **Diversity Management:** Federalism allows India, a diverse country with many languages, cultures, and traditions, to respect and manage this diversity effectively by giving regional governments power. *(1 M)*

(ii) **Local Governance:** It empowers local areas through their state or regional governments, making decision-making more relevant and efficient for local needs and aspirations. *(1 M)*

(iii) **Unity and Integrity:** By distributing power, federalism helps maintain India's unity, preventing conflicts between different regions and promoting national harmony. *(1 M)*

(iv) **Economic Efficiency:** Different states can focus on their strengths and develop policies that suit their unique economic conditions, boosting overall national growth. *(1 M)*

(v) **Political Stability:** Federalism offers a platform for various political voices and regional parties to contribute to the country's governance, enhancing democratic participation and stability. *(1 M)*

2. In my opinion, India is a federal country. India has so many features that a federal country has, supported the claim of India being federal. For example:

(i) **Written constitution:** The country having a federal system necessarily has a written constitution for the clear demarcation of power. As India has a written constitution it supports the case of India being a federal country. *(1 M)*

(ii) **Three-tier Government:** The Constitution establishes a two-tier system of government namely union government and state government. In 1992, a third tier was added with panchayats and municipalities *(1 M)*

(iii) **Division of Powers:** The Constitution of India clearly demarcates the powers of the Central and State governments, and both have their separate areas of jurisdiction. *(1 M)*

(iv) **Independent Judiciary:** The Supreme Court of India is the highest judicial authority in the country and has the power to interpret the Constitution and resolve disputes between the Central and State governments. *(1 M)*

(v) **Rigid Amendment Process:** Constitutional Amendment requires a two-thirds majority in both the houses of parliament and ratification by the legislature of at least half of the total states. *(1 M)*

3. The framewark and rationale behind the India's language policy:

(i) **No National Language:** India's constitution does not designate any language as the national language. This approach fosters inclusivity among India's diverse linguistic groups. *(1 M)*

(ii) **Hindi as the Official Language:** Hindi is recognized as the official language of India, used primarily for governmental purposes, which is the mother tongue for about 40% of the population. *(1 M)*

(iii) **Recognition of Scheduled Languages:** The constitution recognizes 22 languages as Scheduled Languages. This ensures that people can use these languages for official purposes, including in examinations and for central government examinations. *(1 M)*

(iv) **State Official Languages:** Individual states in India have the autonomy to designate their own official languages, which are used in state administration and local governance. *(1 M)*

(v) **Continued Use of English:** Originally set to be phased out in 1965, English continues to be used officially alongside Hindi due to demand from non-Hindi-speaking regions, promoting accessibility and inclusivity in governance. *(1 M)*

4. Decentralisation plays a significant role in enhancing the federal structure of India, and its key contributions can be summarized through the following aspects:

(i) Decentralization in Indian federalism empowers local governments by transferring authority, resources, and responsibilities from central and state levels to enhance governance at grassroots. *(1 M)*

(ii) It Brings governance closer to the people, ensuring their direct involvement in decision-making processes, which leads to more responsive and people-focused governance. *(1 M)*

(iii) Local governments are empowered to make decisions based on their specific regional contexts, improving the efficiency and effectiveness of governance. *(1 M)*

(iv) Strengthening democracy by encouraging public participation, making the democratic process more inclusive and representative. *(1 M)*

(v) Decentralization balances power among central, state, and local governments, strengthens the federal structure of India, and accommodates its diverse societal needs. *(1 M)*

5. Here's how federalism operates in India: **(Any five)**

(*i*) **Clear Division of Powers:** The Indian Constitution specifies the powers of each level of government through three lists - the Union List, State List, and Concurrent List. This ensures a clear demarcation of responsibilities between the central and the state government. *(1 M)*

(*ii*) **Changes Require Consensus:** Any amendment to the Constitution requires the approval of both the Central and State Governments. *(1 M)*

(*iii*) **Judicial Oversight:** The judiciary, especially the Supreme Court, plays a crucial role in resolving disputes between different levels of government, further ensuring that the division of power is respected and maintained. *(1 M)*

(*iv*) **Financial Autonomy:** Each level of government has its own sources of revenue as defined by the Constitution, ensuring financial autonomy and enabling them to function effectively. *(1 M)*

(*v*) **Decentralisation to Local Governments:** The introduction of Panchayati Raj institutions and urban local bodies has further decentralized power, bringing governance closer to the people and enhancing democratic participation at the grassroots level. *(1 M)*

(*vi*) **Special Status and Provisions:** Some states and regions in India have been granted special status under the Constitution, acknowledging their unique needs and circumstances. *(1 M)*

Case Based Questions

Case Based-I

(*i*) India's language diversity makes its culture rich and diverse. It helps people from different backgrounds respect each other's culture, encourage culture exchange and respect for all communities. *(1 M)*

(*ii*) Scheduled Languages are those which are included in the Eighth Schedule of the Indian Constitution, comprising 22 major languages. Non-Scheduled Languages, on the other hand, refer to languages not included in the Eighth Schedule. *(1 M)*

(*iii*) The fusion of languages in India promotes cultural unity. For example-using languages likes Hindi and English across India help in brining people together, even though they may speak different local languages. This shows how languages can help unite a country. *(2 M)*

Case Based-II

(*i*) Indian decentralisation is considered the largest experiment in democracy because it involves about 36 lakh elected representatives, more than the population of many countries, reflecting massive democratic engagement. *(1 M)*

(*ii*) Granting constitutional status to local governments in India has significantly deepened democracy by ensuring regular elections, expanding women's participation, and enabling direct local decision-making, thus enhancing democratic engagement at the grassroots level. *(1 M)*

(*iii*) The Indian Government has implemented several measures to encourage decentralization:

- **Amendment of the Constitution in 1992:** This amendment made it mandatory to hold regular elections for local government bodies like panchayats and municipalities. It also ensured the reservation of seats for Scheduled Castes, Scheduled Tribes, and women to ensure their representation. *(1 M)*
- **Power and Revenue Sharing:** The state governments must share some powers and revenue with local bodies. This change aims to empower local bodies to manage and resolve local issues more effectively. *(1 M)*

Case Based-III

(*i*) A Coalition government is a type of government which is formed when there is no clear majority. The parties enter into an alliance to form the government. *(1 M)*

(*ii*) Coalition governments at the Centre encouraged power-sharing and respect for state autonomy, reducing arbitrary dismissals of the state government and strengthening federalism through alliances with regional parties and Supreme Court rulings. *(1 M)*

(*iii*) (*a*) This statement holds true especially after 1990s with the beginning of era of Coalition Governments which led to a new culture of power-sharing and respect for the autonomy of State Governments. *(1 M)*

(*b*) Supreme Court too passed a major judgement that made it difficult for the Central Government to dismiss state governments in an arbitrary manner making federal power sharing more effective today than it was in the early years. *(1 M)*

GENDER, RELIGION AND CASTE

3

"The State shall not discriminate against any citizen on grounds only of religion, race, case, sex, place of birth or any of them."

– Article 15(1)
(The Indian Constitution)

SYLLABUS & WEIGHTAGE

List of Concept Names	Years					
	2020	2021	2022	2023	2024	2025
Gender and Politics (Public/private division, women's political representation)	—	Exam not Conducted	—	1 Q (2 M)	Q 1 (1 M) Q 1 (2 M)	1 Q (1 M) 1 Q (5 M)
Religion, Communalism and Politics (Communalism, Secular Sate)	1 Q (1 M)		—	—	—	1 Q (5 M)
Caste and Politics (Caste Inequalities, Cast in Politics, Politics in Caste)	1 Q (3 M)		—	—	—	—

CONCEPT MAP

To Access One Shot Revision Video Scan This QR Code

Gender, Religion and Caste

Basis of Social Differences → Gender, Religion, Caste

Gender (CBSE 2025, 2023, 2020)

Meaning

Biological difference between males and females.

Gender division of labour

- **Meaning:** Social division under which unequal roles are assigned.
  - ▲ **Males:**

    Roles Assigned: Earning and all the work outside home.

    Result: Men becoming more powerful enjoying greater freedom and social respect.
  - ▲ **Females:**

    Roles Assigned: Household work, cooking, taking care of kids etc.

    Result:

    Minimum role in public life, women confined to home, no freedom

    Womens started demanding for voting rights, enhancement in political and legal status,improvement in educational and career opportunities, equality in personal and family life. It led to Improvement in women's role in public life.

Women in India

- **Status in Society** Indian women have low respect in society due to patriarchal society.
- **Literacy Rate:** only 54% compared with 76% among men
- **Unpaid Work:** Women works one hour more than men but do not get paid for household work.
- **Wage Difference:** Despite of Equal Renumeration Act 1976, women workers get less pay than men for equal work.
- **Child Sex Ratio:** Girl child is aborted due to preference of male which led to a decline in child sex ratio (914 girls per 100 boys).
- **Violence against Women:** Exploitation, harassment and violence against women have increased in urban areas.
- **Political Representation:** Proportion of women in legislature is low.
- **Reservation of Seats:** In 1992, 1/3rd seats in local government bodies is reserved for women (the same proposal for reserved seats in Lok Sabha and state legislature is pending in parliament). Now, there are more than 10 lakh elected women representatives in rural and urban local bodies.

Caste

Religion

Religious Division

Meaning:

- Division of society on the basis of religion
- Leads to discrimination and opperession of minorities
- Also leads to Communalism.

Communalism (CBSE 2020)

Meaning

- When one community tries to promote itself on the cost of the other.
- **Communal Politics:** Using religion in politics to gain dominance
- **Forms of communalism:**
  - ▲ Religious beliefs in the superiority of one's religion
  - ▲ Use of sacred symbols, religious leaders, emotional appeal in politics
  - ▲ Communal violence, riots, massacre between different communities

Gender, Religion and Caste

Basis of Social Differences

- Gender
- Religion
- Caste

Caste

Brief

- Caste inequalities create social division
- In India, untouchability is an extreme form of casteism
- Government prohibited untouchability.
- Urbanisation and occupational mobility reduced caste hierarchy.

Caste in Politics

CBSE 2020

Meaning:

- Using caste in politics to gain dominance

Negative Aspect

- ▲ Parties choose candidate according to caste composition of the electorate and not on qualification basis.
- ▲ Parties favour a particular caste to gain support

Positive Aspect

- ▲ Lower caste got the better representation in the government.
- ▲ Everyone gets a fair chance to contest in the elections

India as a Secular State

CBSE 2025, 2020

- No official religion, of the country
- People have freedom to practice, follow and propagate their religion
- No discrimination on the basis of religion.

Politics is Caste

Influence of politics in caste:

- Each caste tries to gather more subcaste to increase its number
- One caste may make alliance with other castes to gain political support
- New kind of caste group such as 'backward' and 'forward' caste has emerged.

1 GENDER AND POLITICS

NCERT Definitions *(Commonly asked in 1 mark)*

- **Sexual division of labour:** A system where all home-based work is done by women or managed by them through domestic helpers and men do all the work outside the home. This is not because men can't do it, but because of old ideas that home tasks are for women.
- **Feminist:** A person (man or woman) who supports equal rights and opportunities for women and men. Feminists work to make sure women can do the same things as men and are treated fairly and fight for equality for women in all areas of life.
- **Patriarchy:** A type of society where men have more power and women are less valued. This system gives men more control over many parts of life, including politics and family.

Important Facts

01 ***Literacy Rate*** among women is 54% compared to men's 76%.

02 Sex-selective abortion caused the child sex ratio in the country to drop significantly to just 914 girls per thousand boys.

03 This ratio declined below 850 or 800 for every 1000 boys in certain areas. For example- in some areas of Delhi

04 Despite the Equal Remuneration Act of 1976, which states that people should be paid equally for the same work, women consistently earn less than men across various fields like sports, cinema, factories, and agriculture, even when they perform the same tasks.

05 In local government bodies like panchayats and municipalities, one third of all the seats are reserved for women.

Important Dates

- **1976:** The Equal Remuneration Act was enforced.

Difference Between

Gender Equaulity vs Patriarchy	
Gender Equality	**Patriarchy**
Both men and women have the same rights and chances in life	Men are often seen as the main decision-makers.

Both women and men can do any job, like being a doctor, engineer, or leader.	Often sees women as mainly responsible for housework and taking care of children.
Aimed at equality in personal and family life as well	A system where men have more power in families and society.
Equal pay for both in the workplace.	Men's work is often valued more and Women may earn less than men.

Real Life Application Based Questions

1. **Rina works as a human resource manager at a multinational corporation. She noticed that women are less represented in senior management roles within the company despite equal qualifications. What measures can she propose to improve gender equality in senior management positions in her company?**

Ans. To improve gender equality, she can propose to implement policies such as flexible work hours and remote working options to accommodate women who might have domestic responsibilities. Additionally, establishing mentorship programs that specifically target the development of women in the workforce and creating awareness programs to challenge existing stereotypes could be effective.

Myth Buster

- **Myth:** The low participation of women in politics is due to a lack of interest or capability on their part.

  Fact: Women's lower participation in politics is due to historical discrimination and societal barriers, not because of any lack of interest or capability. There have been active movements demanding equal rights and representation for women in politics.

- **Myth:** To empower women and promote their participation in decision-making, the one-third seats are reserved for women in all the legislative bodies.

  Fact: 1/3rd of seats for women are only reserved in local government bodies – in panchayats and municipalities and not in all the legislative bodies. A bill with this similar proposal of reservation of at least one-third of seats in the Lok Sabha and State Assemblies for women has been pending before the Parliament for more than a decade.

Scan Me for Detailed Explanations

COMPETENCY BASED SOLVED EXAMPLES

Multiple Choice Questions

(1 M)

1. **Given below is a cartoon created by Neelabh Banerjee, the renowned Indian cartoonist, illustrator, and comics artist.** ***(An)*(CBSE APQ, 2023)**

Source: asiapacific.unwomen.org

What is the cartoon trying to depict?

(*a*) the sexual division of labour in India

(*b*) natural and unchangeable gender divisions

(*c*) income generating activities done by women in rural India

(*d*) the ability of men to contribute equally to domestic work as women

2. **Based on the 'time use survey' conducted in six states of our country, which of the following statements is/are correct?** ***(An)***

Daily time use (hours: minutes)		
Activities	**Men**	**Women**
Income generating work	6:00	2:40
Household and related work	0:30	5:00
Talking, Gossip	1:25	1:20
No work/Leisure	3:40	3:50
Sleep, self-care, reading etc.	12:25	11:10

Source: Government of India, Time Use Survey, 1998-99.

(i) **Men spend more time on household and related work compared to women.**

(ii) **Women spend more time on income-generating work compared to men.**

(iii) **Men have less leisure time compared to women.**

(iv) **Women spend less time on sleep, self-care, and reading compared to men.**

(a) (i) and (iv) only (b) (iii) and (iv)

(c) (ii), (iii) and (iv) only (d) (i), (ii), (iii) and (iv)

3. **Which one of the following countries has the highest representation of women in their National Parliament?** ***(Re)*(CBSE, 2023)**

(a) Russia (b) Australia

(c) Sweden (d) India

4. **Which one of the following statements is true based on the graph?** ***(Ev)***

Women in national parliaments in different regions of the world (in %)

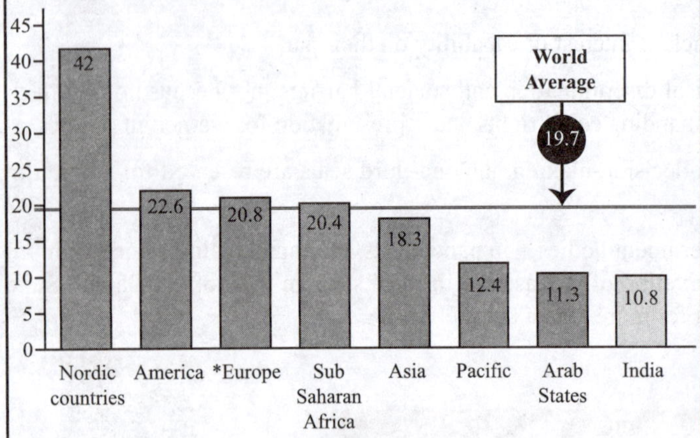

Region

* Europe– OSCE (Organisation for Security and Cooperation in Europe) member countries excluding Nordic countries.

Note: Figures are for the percent of women in the directly elected chambers of parliament as on 31st December 2011.

(a) The Pacific States have the highest representation of women in national parliaments.

(b) India surpasses the world average for women's representation in national parliaments.

(c) The Nordic countries are below the world average for women's representation in national parliaments.

(d) The America have a higher percentage of women in national parliaments compared to the Asia region.

5. **Which of the following statement is true regarding Feminist Movements?** ***(An)***

(a) A group which favors giving more power to working women at the rural and urban levels.

(b) A movement that believes in giving exclusive rights to females in urban areas.

(c) Radical women's movements aimed at equality in personal and family life as well.

(d) It is the practice of placing a feminine and masculine point of view in decision-making.

6. **In light of the gender inequalities in employment, consider the following statements about the role of gender in the workplace and select the correct option.**

(i) **Gender divisions in employment often result in unequal pay for equal work between men and women.**

(ii) **Men are commonly underrepresented in professions such as nursing and primary education due to societal stereotypes.**

(iii) **The public/private division of labor assigns men primarily to domestic tasks and women to external income-generating roles.**

(iv) **Legal measures like the Equal Remuneration Act, of 1976, are aimed at eliminating wage disparity based on gender.**

Which of the statements is/are correct? ***(An)***

(a) (i) and (iv) only

(b) (ii) and (iii) only

(c) (i), (ii) and (iv) only

(d) All of the above

7. **What does the reservation of seats for women in local government bodies signify in the politics?** ***(An)***

(a) It signifies the end of caste-based discrimination in politics.

(b) It ensures that only women from upper castes can be elected to local government bodies.

(c) It represents an effort to improve political representation of women.

(d) It has no impact on caste politics.

Assertion and Reason

(1 M)

Direction: The following questions consist of two statements – Assertion (A) and Reason (R). Answer these questions by selecting the appropriate option given below:

(a) Both A and R are true, and R is the correct explanation of A.

(b) Both A and R are true, but R is not the correct explanation of A.

(c) A is true, but R is false

(d) A is false, but R is true.

1. **Assertion (A):** Women's political participation is crucial for achieving gender equality in society.

Reason (R): Women's perspectives and experiences are often different from men's, and their inclusion in decision-making processes can lead to more equitable policies. ***(Un)***

2. **Assertion (A):** In many parts of India, women are paid less than men for the same work.

Reason (R): The Equal Remuneration Act 1976 mandates equal pay for equal work irrespective of the gender. ***(Ev)***

3. **Assertion (A):** The literacy rate among women in India is lower compared to men.

Reason (R): Societal norms and values have historically prioritized men's education over women's. *(An)*

4. **Assertion (A):** Women's representation in India's legislative bodies is significantly low.

Reason (R): The only reason is the lack of adequate legal provisions mandating women's representation in politics. *(Ev)*

5. **Assertion (A):** Women in India face discrimination and disadvantage in various aspects of life.

Reason (R): Patriarchal norms and cultural practices have perpetuated gender inequality in Indian society. *(An)*

6. **Assertion (A):** Education is key to empowering women in India.

Reason (R): Education can help women gain economic independence, challenge gender stereotypes, and increase their participation in politics and society. *(An)*

Subjective Questions

Very Short Answer Type Questions (1 or 2 M)

1. **Suggest any one way to protect women from domestic oppression.** *(Ap)*(CBSE, 2020)

Ans. One way to protect women from domestic oppression is to raise awareness about women's rights against domestic violence through education, campaign and community outreach programs. *(1 M)*

2. **Shruti performed a web search for 'Teacher' and found that 80% of the images had women, while a search for 'Pilot' mainly showed men. Discuss how these web search results reflect societal perceptions and the sexual division of labour. Explain with an example.** *(An)*(CBSE APQ, 2023)

Ans.
- The over-representation of women as teachers and men as pilots supports traditional notions of job roles. The role of teaching is considered a caregiving job suitable for women while the role of pilot is regarded as a physically and mentally demanding job ideal for men. *(1 M)*
- Another example which shows the societal perception and sexual division of labour is a job of a nurse which is associated more with women and job of an engineer which is generally associated with men. *(1 M)*

Mistakes 101 : What not to do!

Some students may overlook the historical context that has shaped these societal perceptions, failing to connect the present-day gender biases to their roots in the past.

3. **"Women face discrimination in various ways in our society." Explain any two ways.** *(Un)*(CBSE, 2023)

OR

Mention different aspects of life in which women are discriminated or disadvantaged in India. *(Un)*(NCERT)

Ans. In India, women are discriminated against and disadvantaged in the following ways: **(Any two)**
- They are not provided with adequate education. Thus, the literacy rate among women is only 54 percent compared with 76 percent among men. *(1 M)*
- In almost all areas of work, from sports and cinema to factories and fields, women are paid less than men, even when both do exactly the same work. *(1 M)*
- In many parts of India parents prefer to have sons and due to the preference for the boy child, female child is aborted in many parts of the country. *(1 M)*
- On average an Indian woman works one hour more than an average man every day. Yet much of her work is not paid and therefore often not valued. *(1 M)*

4. **Rina works all day at home, managing household chores and taking care of her children. Her husband, on the other hand, works a paid job outside. Discuss how the sexual division of labor affects the value of Rina's work in society.** *(An)*

Ans. The sexual division of labor affects the value of Rina's work in the following ways:
- **Undervalued Household Work:** Rina's household work is not valued as much as her husband's paid job. *(1 M)*
- **Lack of Recognition:** Rina's contributions at home are essential but remain undervalued and unrecognized by society. *(1 M)*

Short Answer Type Questions (3 M)

1. **How does the underrepresentation of women in politics impact the policymaking process and the interests of women?** *(Ev)*

Ans. The underrepresentation of women in politics has significant implications for policymaking and the interests of women because:
- When women's perspectives and experiences are not adequately represented, policies and decisions may overlook or neglect issues that specifically affect women. *(1½ M)*
- This can lead to a lack of gender-sensitive policies addressing matters such as reproductive rights, childcare, domestic violence, and gender-based discrimination. *(1½ M)*

2. **"Women still lag much behind men in India despite some improvements since independence." Analyze the statement.** *(An)*(CBSE, 2019)

Ans. The statement stands true. In our country, women still lag much behind men despite some improvements since Independence. This can be understood with the help of the following examples:

- **Educational Barriers:** The literacy rate among women is only 54 percent as compared with 76 percent among men, because parents prefer to spend their resources on their boys' education. *(1 M)*
- **Political Presence:** Despite some progress, women's representation in politics remains low, highlighting the ongoing struggle of gender equality. *(1 M)*
- **Economic Disparity:** The proportion of women in the highest-paid and most valued jobs is still very small. On average, an Indian woman works one hour more than an average man every day. Yet, much of their work is often not valued *(1 M)*

Long Answer Type Questions (5 M)

1. Discuss how the participation of women in politics has evolved over time and its impact on society. Consider the challenges they have faced and the progress made towards gender equality in the political arena. *(Ev)*

Ans. ***(i)*** **Historical Exclusion:** Traditionally, women were excluded from political roles as they were seen mainly as caregivers. This limited their public and political participation. *(1 M)*

(ii) **Feminist Movements:** Over time, feminist movements globally fought for women's rights, including the right to vote and hold public office, leading to gradual inclusion in politics. *(1 M)*

(iii) **Legal and Social Progress:** Laws and policies, like reservation of seats in local bodies in India, have encouraged women's participation. *(1 M)*

(iv) **Challenges Persist:** Despite progress, women's representation in legislative bodies remains low compared to men. Women in politics face underrepresentation in higher strata of power. *(1 M)*

(v) **Impact on Society:** Increased female political participation has led to more attention to women's issues and gender equality, highlighting the need for diverse perspectives in governance for balanced and inclusive development. *(1 M)*

2 RELIGION, COMMUNALISM AND POLITICS

NCERT Definitions *(Commonly asked in 1 mark)*

- **Family laws:** Those laws that deal with family related matters such as marriage, divorce, adoption, inheritance, etc. In our country, different family laws apply to followers of different religions.
- **Communalism:** When people think that one's religion is the main part of their identity and interests, leading to conflicts and issues in society. It often divides people and can cause violence.
- **Secular State:** A country that does not favor any particular religion. In a secular state, everyone has the freedom to follow any religion or not to follow religion at all.
- **Secularism:** The belief that religion should not be involved in government and law. A secular country doesn't support one religion over others and allows everyone to follow their own beliefs.

Important Facts

01 The Indian Constitution does not recognise any religion as the ***official religion*** of the state.

02 The ***constitution prohibits*** discrimination on the grounds of religion.

03 The constitution provide to all individuals and communities freedom to profess, practice and propagate any religion,or not to follow any.

Difference Between

Communalism Vs. Secularism	
Communalism	**Secularism**
Favors one religion over others, which can lead to unfair treatment and fights.	Keeps religion separate from government to ensure everyone is treated equally regardless of their religion.
Can cause violence and arguments between different religious groups.	Encourages respect and fairness among all religions, preventing favoritism, conflict or violence.
Uses religion to divide people and gain political support.	Makes sure government decisions and laws are fair and don't favor any religion.
Creates division and weakens the unity of a country by focusing on religious differences.	Prevent division and make the country more united.
Is seen as harmful to society because it promotes separation and conflict based on religion.	Viewed as beneficial for democracy and cultural diversity, supporting peace and cooperation.

Real Life Application Based Questions

1. **Imagine you are the mayor of a diverse city with significant populations of multiple religious communities. Recent events have led to heightened tensions between these communities. What initiatives would you introduce to foster peaceful coexistence and mutual respect among different religious groups in your city?**

Ans. I would initiate dialogue to promote understanding and respect among different communities. It will address complaints and misunderstandings which may resolve the issue and foster peaceful coexistence and mutual respect among different religious groups in the city.

Scan Me for Detailed Explanations

COMPETENCY BASED SOLVED EXAMPLES

Multiple Choice Questions

(1 M)

1. **Consider the following statements on the meaning of communal politics. Communal politics is based on the belief that:** *(Ev)*(NCERT)

   A. One religion is superior to that of others.

   B. People belonging to different religions can live together happily as equal citizens.

   C. Followers of a particular religion constitute one community.

   D. State power cannot be used to establish the domination of one religious group over others.

   Which of the statements is/are correct?

   (*a*) A, B, C, and D (*b*) A, B, and D

   (*c*) A and C (*d*) B and D

2. **Read the given statements:** *(Re)*(CBSE, 2024)

• India has no official religion.
• All the communities have freedom to profess and practice any religion in India.

   Which one of the following constitutional term is used for the above statements?

   (*a*) Republic (*b*) Secular

   (*c*) Sovereign (*d*) Socialist

3. **During a visit to your school, a guest speaker explained the measures taken by the Indian Constitution to ensure a secular state. The speaker highlighted that one of these provisions is crucial in maintaining India's secularism. Which constitutional provision did the speaker most likely highlight to emphasize India's secular nature?** *(Re)*

   (*a*) Equal wages for equal work.

   (*b*) No official religion for the state.

   (*c*) Prohibition of untouchability.

   (*d*) Reservations for women in local government bodies

4. **Which among the following statements about India's Constitution is wrong? It** *(Ev)*(NCERT)

   (*a*) prohibits discrimination on grounds of religion.

   (*b*) gives official status to one religion.

   (*c*) provides to all individuals freedom to profess any religion.

   (*d*) ensures equality of citizens within religious communities.

Assertion and Reason

(1 M)

Direction: The following questions consist of two statements – Assertion (A) and Reason (R). Answer these questions by selecting the appropriate option given below:

(*a*) Both A and R are true, and R is the correct explanation of A.

(*b*) Both A and R are true, but R is not the correct explanation of A.

(*c*) A is true, but R is false

(*d*) A is false, but R is true.

1. **Assertion (A):** The Constitution provides to all individuals and communities freedom to profess, practice and propagate any religion, or not to follow any.

   Reason (R): The Constitution prohibits discrimination on the grounds of religion. *(Ev)*

2. **Assertion (A):** Communal politics can lead to the belief that followers of different religions can live as equal citizens.

   Reason (R): Communalism involves seeing religion as the principal basis of social community. *(Ev)*

3. **Assertion (A):** India does not have an official religion.

   Reason (R): The Indian Constitution provides for a secular state ensuring equality of all religions before the law. *(Ev)*

Subjective Questions

Very Short Answer Type Questions

(2 M)

1. **Suggest any one way to create communal harmony among various communities of India.** *(Cr)*(CBSE 2020)

Ans. Promoting cultural exchange programs can help build communal harmony among various communities in India. By understanding and appreciating the diverse cultures, traditions, and practices, mutual respect and unity can be fostered. *(2 M)*

2. **What is the significance of a secular state?** *(Un)*

Ans. (*i*) A secular state does not consider anyone's religion as an official religion of the state. A secular state also treats all its citizens equally, regardless of religion. *(1 M)*

(*ii*) It allows freedom of religion, prevents discrimination based on religion, and maintains equality within religious communities, ensuring a harmonious coexistence and safeguarding minority rights. *(1 M)*

3. **What is communalism politics?** *(Re)*

Ans. (*i*) Communalism politics involves using religion as a way to gain power. It prioritizes one religion over others and can result in discrimination and violence. *(1 M)*

(*ii*) It involves highlighting differences between various religious communities which often leads to division, discrimination, and conflict within society. *(1 M)*

4. **What is the main argument of the women's movement regarding family laws?** *(Un)*

Ans. Women's movement has argued that family laws of all religions discriminate against women. So they have demanded that government should change these laws to make them more equitable laws, advocating for equal rights in marriage, divorce, inheritance, and aiming for gender equality in personal and family life. *(2 M)*

Short Answer Type Questions (3 M)

1. **Mention any three features of 'secularism' described in the Indian Constitution.** **(CBSE, 2020)**

OR

Mention any two constitutional provisions that make India a secular state. *(Re)***(NCERT)**

Ans. The following are some of the features of secularism as described in the Indian Constitution:

- **No state religion**: The Indian Constitution does not recognize any particular religion as the state religion. The government is not allowed to promote any particular religion or discriminate against any particular community on the basis of religion. *(1 M)*
- **Freedom of religion:** The Indian Constitution guarantees the freedom of religion to all citizens. Every citizen has the right to practice, profess, and propagate any religion of their choice. *(1 M)*
- **Equality of all religions:** The Indian Constitution ensures equality of all religions. No religion is considered superior or inferior to any other religion. All religions are treated equally under the law. *(1 M)*

Topper's Explanations **(CBSE, 2020)**

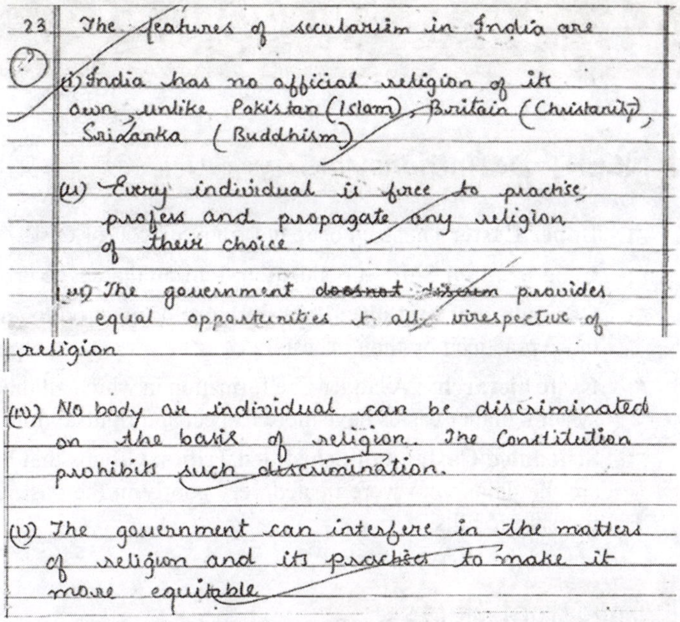

23 The features of secularism in India are

(i) India has no official religion of its own, unlike Pakistan (Islam), Britain (Christianity), Srilanka (Buddhism)

(ii) Every individual is free to practise, profess and propagate any religion of their choice.

(iii) The government doesnot ~~discrim~~ provides equal opportunities to all irrespective of religion

(iv) No body or individual can be discriminated on the basis of religion. The Constitution prohibits such discrimination.

(v) The government can interfere in the matters of religion and its practices to make it more equitable

Long Answer Type Questions (5 M)

1. **Examine how religion, communalism, and politics are interlinked in the context of Indian democracy. Discuss the role of secularism in maintaining democratic values.** *(Ev)*

Ans. Religion, communalism and politics are interlinked in Indian democracy in the following ways:

- **Religion and Politics:** In India, religion deeply influences politics. Leaders often use religious sentiments to attract votes, leading to communalism where politics is driven through religion rather than public welfare. *(1 M)*
- **Communalism's Effect:** Communalism divides people based on religion, leading to conflicts and riots. It goes against the idea of democracy, which is about unity and equal rights for all, regardless of religion. *(1 M)*
- **Secularism for Democracy:** India's constitution promotes secularism, meaning the state has no religion. It ensures freedom to practice any religion, aiming to maintain harmony and equal treatment of all religions. *(1 M)*
- **Role of Secularism:** Secularism fights communalism by keeping religion separate from state affairs. It helps in focusing on common issues like development and social justice, ensuring that religion doesn't influence political decisions. *(1 M)*
- **Conclusion:** For a healthy democracy, secularism is crucial. It allows diverse religions to coexist peacefully, ensuring that political decisions are made for the common good, not based on religious biases. *(1 M)*

3 CASTE AND POLITICS

NCERT Definitions *(Commonly asked in 1 mark)*

- **Upper Caste:** Those who are not from SC, ST, or OBC.
- **Urbanization:** Shift of population from rural areas to urban areas.
- **Occupational Mobility:** Shift from one occupation to another, usually when a new generation takes up occupations other than those practiced by their ancestors.
- **Caste hierarchy:** A ladder-like formation in which all the caste groups are placed from the 'highest' to the 'lowest' castes. In this system, higher castes have more respect and rights, while lower castes have less.
- **Scheduled Castes and Scheduled Tribes:** Groups that have been historically discriminated against in India. Scheduled Castes are the dalits who were treated very poorly in the past, and Scheduled Tribes are the adivasis who lived apart from others in forests and hills.

Important Facts

01 The proportion of people living below the poverty line is highest among the Scheduled Tribes and lowest among the 'upper' castes.

02 Urbanization and occupational mobility have led to the weakening of traditional caste hierarchies, but caste identities still influence politics.

Classification

Discrimination in Indian Society is based on:

- **Gender** (Man or Woman)
- **Religion** (Hindu, Muslim, etc.)
- **Caste** (Upper caste or lower caste)

Myth Buster

- **Myth:** Politics based on caste or communal identities is always harmful to society and democracy.

  Fact: While politics based on these caste or communal identities can have negative effects, it can also be a way for disadvantaged groups to bring attention to their issues and ensure their representation in the democratic process, thus enhancing social equality and inclusiveness. However, these identities must not overshadow other pressing issues like development and corruption.

- **Myth:** The caste system is no longer relevant in urban areas.

  Fact: Despite changes and urbanization, caste continues to influence people's lives in India, including urban areas. Even now most of the people marry within their own caste or tribes, untouchability has also not ended completely.

COMPETENCY BASED SOLVED EXAMPLES

Scan Me for Detailed Explanations

Multiple Choice Questions

(1 M)

1. **What are the factors that have contributed to changes in the caste system in modern India?** *(Re)*

   A. Urbanization
   B. Occupational mobility
   C. Growth of literacy and education
   D. Weakening of position of land lords in the villages

   (*a*) Only A and B (*b*) A, B and C
   (*c*) Only D (*d*) A, B, C and D

2. **What role does caste politics play in empowering disadvantaged communities?** *(Un)*

   (*a*) It helps them demand their share of power
   (*b*) It leads to discrimination against particular castes
   (*c*) It promotes social exclusion
   (*d*) It hinders access to land and resources

3. **Which statement best describes the dual role of caste in Indian politics?** *(An)*

   (*a*) Caste only serves to divide society and has no place in politics.
   (*b*) Caste politics can both help marginalized communities gain power and divert attention from broader issues like economic development.
   (*c*) Engaging in caste politics is illegal under Indian law.
   (*d*) Caste is irrelevant in modern Indian politics.

4. **How does the caste system influence political representation in India?** *(An)*

   (*a*) By ensuring that only upper-caste individuals can become political leaders.
   (*b*) By political parties considering the caste composition of constituencies when choosing candidates.
   (*c*) By legally prohibiting members of certain castes from holding public office.
   (*d*) By restricting voting rights to certain castes.

Assertion and Reason

(1 M)

Direction: The following questions consist of two statements – Assertion (A) and Reason (R). Answer these questions by selecting the appropriate option given below:

(*a*) Both A and R are true, and R is the correct explanation of A.
(*b*) Both A and R are true, but R is not the correct explanation of A.
(*c*) A is true, but R is false
(*d*) A is false, but R is true.

1. **Assertion (A):** The reservation system in India is not effective in promoting social mobility for historically marginalized castes.
   Reason (R): By reserving seats in educational institutions and government jobs for members of historically marginalized castes, the reservation system has helped to promote social mobility and reduce caste-based discrimination. *(Ev)*

2. **Assertion (A):** Political parties in India often consider the caste composition of electorates during elections.
   Reason (R): Every parliamentary constituency in India has a clear majority of one single caste. *(Ev)*

3. **Assertion (A):** The Scheduled Castes and Scheduled Tribes in India continue to face economic disadvantages.
   Reason (R): Historic inequalities and restrictions on access to resources have had long-lasting impacts. *(Ev)*

4. **Assertion (A):** Caste-based politics can divert attention from crucial issues.
   Reason (R): Focusing on caste alone in politics can overshadow broader and more pressing societal needs like economic development and corruption. *(Ev)*

Subjective Questions

Very Short Answer Type Questions

(2 M)

1. **"The practice of caste-based politics in India has often been criticized for perpetuating division, yet it plays a significant role in representing marginalized communities." Evaluate the statement.** *(Ev)*

Ans. The statement stands true and can be justified with the help of following examples: ***(Any Two)***

(*i*) **Representation for Marginalized Communities:** Caste-based politics help marginalized communities gain political representation. Political representation ensures that their issues and concerns are addressed at both local and national levels. *(1 M)*

(*ii*) **Political Awareness:** It has brought awareness and a sense of identity to the lower castes, empowering them to fight for their rights and demand equal treatment and opportunities. *(1 M)*

(*iii*) **Policy Focus on Social Justice:** Caste-based politics often leads to policies aimed at social justice, such as reservations in education and employment, which help reduce disparities caused by historical injustices. *(1 M)*

2. **Why is caste-based politics considered unhealthy for a democracy?** *(An)*

Ans. (*i*) Caste-based politics is considered unhealthy for a democracy because it can divert attention from critical issues like development, poverty, and corruption. *(1 M)*

(*ii*) It may lead to division, conflict, and even violence, undermining social harmony and focusing on narrow interests for political gain rather than the common good. *(1 M)*

3. **State two reasons to say that caste alone cannot determine election results in India.** *(Ap)***(NCERT)**

Ans. Caste cannot solely determine election results in India because: **(Any two)**

- No parliamentary constituency in the country has a clear majority of one single caste. So, the party needs to win the confidence of more than one caste and community to win elections. *(1 M)*
- Urbanization, education, and economic status influence voter behavior more significantly in many areas, reducing the impact of caste alone. *(1 M)*
- Voters are becoming more issue-oriented rather than caste-oriented, prioritizing performance, leadership, governance, corruption, and development issues over caste identity. *(1 M)*

Short Answer Type Questions (3 M)

1. "Caste inequalities are still prevalent in India." Examine the statement. ***(An)*(CBSE, 2019)**

OR

State how caste inequalities are still continuing in India ***(Ap)*(NCERT)**

Ans. The Statement "Caste ineuqalities are still prevalent in India" stands true and can be justified by the following points:

- Caste inequalities in India are weakening with the rise of economic development, large-scale urbanization, occupational mobility, and growth of literacy, and education. But it is not gone completely and is still prevalent in India. *(1 M)*
- Even today, most people marry within their own caste or tribe. Discrimination based on caste, including untouchability has not ended completely, despite constitutional prohibition. *(1 M)*
- On the economic front as well, the proportion of people living below the poverty line is highest among the Scheduled Tribes and lowest among the 'upper' castes. *(1 M)*

Topper's Explanation:

Caste inequalities are still prevalent in India. This statement can be justified by the following →

(i) Although the constitution has prohibited caste discrimination; it is still practiced in parts of the country.

(ii) People still now marry within the same caste.

(iii) The decades of advantages and disadvantages are ~~followed~~ felt even today.

(iv) People who earlier had access to education have done very well in accessing modern education. But people who didnot have access to education or were prohibited, have lagged behind.

(v) The economic status still now follow the caste hierarchies - the upper class the best off the lower caste the worst and the OBCs in between

2. Mention the problem of 'Casteism' in Indian politics. ***(Re)*(CBSE 2020)**

Ans. Casteism is a significant problem in Indian politics. The following are some of the ways in which casteism manifests itself in Indian politics:

- **Vote-bank politics:** Political parties often use caste as a means to form vote banks. They appeal to specific castes to secure their votes, which can lead to a divided society. *(1 M)*
- **Compromising quality:** The candidate is selected based on caste rather than qualification or capabilities to gain support from the major caste group of that constituency, affecting governance quality. *(1 M)*
- **Promotes Division:** Focusing on caste can divert attention from crucial national issues like development, income inequality, and poverty. It also fosters division rather than unity. *(1 M)*

3. Why are caste barriers breaking down in India? Explain with three reasons. ***(An)***

Ans. Caste barriers in India are breaking down due to several factor like:

- **Urbanization:** It has led to more people moving to cities where caste identities are less valued. People from different castes live and work together, diluting caste boundaries. *(1 M)*
- **Educational advancements:** It have made it possible for individuals from historically marginalized castes to access better job opportunities, reducing economic disparities based on caste. *(1 M)*
- **Legislative reforms and policies:** Reservations in education and employment, have helped lower-caste groups improve their social and economic status, challenging traditional caste hierarchies. *(1 M)*

Long Answer Type Questions (5 M)

1. Examine how the caste system influences politics in India. Discuss both its positive and negative impacts on Indian democracy. ***(An)***

Ans. ***(i)* Caste and Political Identity:** The caste system in India has a significant influence on politics. Political parties often nominate candidates based on the caste composition of constituencies to attract votes from specific caste groups. *(1¼ M)*

***(ii)* Vote Banks:** Caste acts as a vote bank where political parties make promises to gain support from certain caste groups. This sometimes results in caste-based policies and promises during election campaigns rather than common good. *(1¼ M)*

***(iii)* Positive Impact:** Caste politics has helped bring attention to the needs and rights of underrepresented and marginalized communities, ensuring their better representation in politics and policy-making. *(1¼ M)*

***(iv)* Negative Impact:** Excessive focus on caste can lead to neglect of other important issues such as economic development, education, and health. It can also foster division and conflict between different caste groups, risking social harmony and national integration. *(1¼ M)*

MISCELLANEOUS EXERCISE

Multiple Choice Questions

(1 M)

1. When we speak of gender divisions, we usually refer to: **(Re)(NCERT)**

   (*a*) Biological difference between men and women

   (*b*) Unequal roles assigned by the society to men and women

   (*c*) Unequal child sex ratio

   (*d*) Absence of voting rights for women in democracies

2. In India seats are reserved for women in **(Re)(NCERT)**

   (*a*) Lok Sabha (*b*) State legislative assemblies

   (*c*) Cabinets (*d*) Panchayati Raj bodies

3. In rural India, reserving seats for women in local government bodies like Panchayats has become increasingly prevalent. Which of the following outcomes is MOST LIKELY to occur as a direct result of this practice shortly? **(An)**

   (*a*) Increased participation of women in local governance

   (*b*) Decrease in overall efficiency of local governance

   (*c*) Reduced influence of caste in local elections

   (*d*) Increased communal tensions in rural areas

4. __________ provides that equal wages should be paid to equal work. **(Re)**

   (*a*) Equal Wages Act, 1977

   (*b*) Equal Remuneration Act, 1976

   (*c*) Wages act 1980

   (*d*) Equal Income Act. 1978

5. Which of these countries has an official religion? **(Re)**

   (*a*) Pakistan (*b*) England

   (*c*) Sri Lanka (*d*) All of these

6. Caste continues to be very strongly linked to economic status in many important ways. The effects of centuries of accumulated advantages and disadvantages continue to be felt. Moreover, new kinds of inequalities have also developed.

   The passage states that_________. **(An)**

   (*a*) In terms of proportions, lower castes are still financially worse off than upper castes.

   (*b*) Lower castes today are economically better off than upper castes due to government policies.

   (*c*) Differences in economic status today have more to do with choices of individual castes rather than caste hierarchy.

   (*d*) Caste hierarchy has changed in the last thirty years and upper castes have become lower castes and vice versa.

7. In a recent school debate, students discussed the role of gender in politics. Several viewpoints were presented: **(An)**

   A. First student argued that gender division is a form of hierarchical social division.

   B. The second student claimed that the role of women in public life remains minimal in many societies.

   C. Third student claimed that women have always had equal political rights as men.

   D. The fourth student mentioned that feminist movements have significantly contributed to achieving equality in both personal and family life.

   Based on the debate, which student(s) provided accurate statements about gender and politics?

   (*a*) The first student only

   (*b*) The first, second, and fourth student.

   (*c*) The second and third student

   (*d*) All four students

8. In the town of Harmonyville, several events took place during the recent election campaign:

   (*i*) **Event A:** A political party invited a prominent religious leader to endorse their candidate in a large public rally.

   (*ii*) **Event B:** Flyers were distributed in the town, claiming that one religion is superior to others and urging people to vote based on this belief.

   (*iii*) **Event C:** Political party organized a series of events to unite people from different religious backgrounds and promote peaceful coexistence.

   (*iv*) **Event D:** Reports emerged of political groups mobilizing support exclusively from their religious communities.

   Which of the following events are examples of communal politics? **(An)**

   (*a*) Event A and Event B

   (*b*) Event A, Event B, and Event D

   (*c*) Event C and Event D

   (*d*) All of the above

9. Match List-I with List-II and select the correct answer using the codes given below the lists: **(Re)(NCERT)**

	List-I		List-II
A.	A person who believes in equal rights ande opportunities for women and men	(*i*)	Communalist
B.	A person who says that religion is the principal basis of community	(*ii*)	Feminist

C.	A person who thinks that caste is the principal basis of community	(*iii*)	Secularist
D.	A person who does not discriminate other on the basis of religious beliefs	(*iv*)	Castiest

	A	B	C	D
(*a*)	(*ii*)	(*iii*)	(*i*)	(*iv*)
(*b*)	(*ii*)	(*i*)	(*iv*)	(*iii*)
(*c*)	(*iv*)	(*iii*)	(*i*)	(*ii*)
(*d*)	(*iii*)	(*i*)	(*ii*)	(*iv*)

10. Identify the reasons that shows that only caste cannot determine elections in India. **(*An*)**

(*i*) No party wins the votes of all the voters of a caste or community.

(*ii*) No parliamentary constituency in the country has a clear majority of one single caste.

(*iii*) Some political parties are known to favour some castes and are seen as their representatives

(*iv*) Mobilising and securing political support has brought new consciousness among the lower castes.

(*a*) (*i*) and (*ii*) (*b*) (*i*) and (*iv*)

(*c*) (*ii*) and (*iii*) (*d*) (*ii*) and (*iv*)

11. Consider the following statements: **(*Re*)**

(*i*) Gandhiji believed that religion can never be seperated from politics.

(*ii*) Gandhiji believed that politics must be guided by ethics drawn from religion.

Which of the statements given above is/are correct?

(*a*) (*i*) only (*b*) (*ii*) only

(*c*) Both (*i*) and (*ii*) (*d*) Neither (*i*) nor (*ii*)

12. Which of the following is the true meaning of 'Equal treatment of women' as a necessary ingredient of a democratic society? **(*Ev*) (CBSE SQP, 2024)**

(*a*) Women are always treated with respect and dignity.

(*b*) It is now easier for women to legally wage struggle for their rights.

(*c*) Most societies across the world are now women dominated.

(*d*) Women are now treated as equals in the political arena.

Assertion and Reason **(1 M)**

Direction: The following questions consist of two statements – Assertion (A) and Reason (R). Answer these questions by selecting the appropriate option given below:

(*a*) Both A and R are true, and R is the correct explanation of A.

(*b*) Both A and R are true, but R is not the correct explanation of A.

(*c*) A is true, but R is false

(*d*) A is false, but R is true.

1. Assertion (A): When parties chose candidates in elections, they keep in mind the caste composition of the electorate

Reason (R): To ensure necessary support to win elections **(*Un*)**

2. Assertion (A): Sex-selective abortion led to decline of sex ratio in India.

Reason (R): Desire of a male child make Indian families abort girls. **(*An*)**

3. Assertion (A): Women paid less than men, even, when both do exactly the same work.

Reason (R): Women are less productive and creative than men. **(*An*)**

4. Assertion (A): The literacy rate among women is only 76 per cent compared with 54 per cent among men. **(*An*)**

Reason (R): Parents prefer to spend their money and resources for their boy's education rather than spending on girls. **(*An*)**

5. Assertion (A): Women's movement have demanded that government should change family laws.

Reason (R): Women's movement argued that family law of all religion discriminate against women. **(*An*)**

Subjective Questions

Very Short Answer Type Questions **(2 M)**

1. Describe the positive impact of casteism with regard to political expression. **(*An*)**

2. What are some perceptions of an ideal woman in society? **(*An*)**

3. What is the sexual division of labour? **(*Re*)**

4. What is the significance of the Panchayati Raj system in enhancing women's political participation? **(*An*)**

5. Explain the role of feminist movements in political mobilization based on gender. **(*An*)**

Short Answer Type Questions **(3 M)**

1. In India, women continue to face several systemic challenges. Given the increasing awareness and initiatives, women's representation in politics has seen some improvement, yet remains low. Provide three measures to enhance the participation of women in politics. **(*Ap*)**

2. "The promotion of gender equality in educational opportunities leads to increased political participation by women."

(*i*) What does the statement imply about the relationship between education and political participation among women? **(*An*)**

(*ii*) How does the promotion of gender equality in education represent a shift in societal norms? **(*An*)**

3. How can communalism pose a great threat to Indian democracy? **(*An*)**

4. What is the status of women's representation in India's legislative bodies? **(*Re*)(NCERT)**

5. Read the statements regarding the political representation of women in India:

   Statement-1 (S1): Historically, the representation of women in Indian legislatures has been significantly low.

   Statement-2 (S2): Recent years have seen efforts to increase women's representation through various legislative and policy measures.

   Explain the trend these statements - S1 and S2 reflect in the context of gender equality in Indian politics. *(An)*

Long Answer Type Questions (5 M)

1. Explain the challenges and progress in gender equality in India since independence. *(An)*
2. In the Panchayati Raj System, one-third of the seats have been reserved for women. Do you feel that the same should be done for the State Legislature and the Parliament? Support your answer with arguments. *(An)*
3. Write a short note about communalism. *(Un)*
4. As a social scientist, you have been invited to present at an international conference on gender equality. Your focus is on the feminist movement in India and its impact on gender equality over the years. Prepare a detailed analysis of how the feminist movement has influenced gender equality in India. *(An)*
5. You are working for a think tank that focuses on the intersection of religion, communalism, and politics in Indian democracy. You are tasked with preparing a report that will be presented to policymakers to help them understand these interlinkages and the importance of secularism in maintaining democratic values. Write a comprehensive report examining the influence of religion on politics, the impact of communalism, the role and significance of secularism and how secularism helps in maintaining democratic values. *(Cr)*

Case Based Questions

Case Based-I

No wonder the proportion of women among the highly paid and valued jobs is still very small. On an average an Indian woman works one hour more than an average man every day. Yet much of her work is not paid and therefore often not valued. The Equal Remuneration Act 1976 provides that equal wages should be paid to equal work. However, in almost all areas of work, from sports and cinema, to factories and fields, women are paid less than men, even when both do exactly the same work.

(i) Why do women not get equal pay as males? *(An)*

(ii) Which act has been formulated by government of India to ensure equal wages for equal work? *(Re)*

(iii) In what fields of work women still do not get equal wages? *(An)*

Case Based-II

Communalism was and continues to be one of the major challenges to democracy in our country. The makers of our Constitution were aware of this challenge. That is why they chose the model of a secular state. This choice was reflected in several constitutional provisions. There is no official religion for the Indian state. Unlike the status of Buddhism in Sri Lanka, that of Islam in Pakistan and that of Christianity in England, our Constitution does not give a special status to any religion. The Constitution provides to all individuals and communities freedom to profess, practice and propagate any religion, or not to follow any religion.

(i) What is a secular state? *(Un)*

(ii) What has constitution done to ensure secularism in our country? *(An)*

(iii) How has India taken a different path than other nations like Sri Lanka, Pakistan, and England in the context of religion? *(An)*

Case Based-III

The gender division tends to be understood as natural and unchangeable. It is not based on biology but on social expectations and stereotypes. The result of this division is that though women constitute half of humanity, their role in public life, especially politics, is minimal in most societies. Issues related to women are not given adequate attention. This has led many feminists and women's movements to the conclusion that unless women control power, their problems will not get adequate attention. In India, the percentage of elected women members in Lok Sabha touched 10 percent of its total strength for the first time in 2009. Their share in the state assemblies is less than 5 per cent. One way to solve women's problems is to have a fair proportion of women in the elected bodies. In Panchayats and Municipalities, one-third of seats in local government bodies are reserved for women. Now there are more than 10 lakh elected women representatives in rural and urban local bodies. Gender division is an example that some form of social division needs to be expressed in politics. This also shows that disadvantaged groups do benefit when social divisions become a political issue.

(i) What is the main reason for the minimal representation of women in politics according to the passage? *(An)*

(ii) Why do feminists and women's movements believe that women need to control power in order to address their problems adequately? *(An)*

(iii) How has India attempted to address the underrepresentation of women in politics? *(An)*

ANSWER KEYS

Multiple Choice Questions

1. (b) 2. (d) 3. (a) 4. (b) 5. (d) 6. (a) 7. (b) 8. (b) 9. (b) 10. (a)
11. (c) 12. (b)

Assertion and Reason

1. (a) 2. (a) 3. (c) 4. (d) 5. (a)

HINTS & EXPLANATIONS

Multiple Choice Questions

1. (b) Unequal roles assigned by the society to men and women
2. (d) Panchayati Raj bodies
3. (a) Reserving seats for women in Panchayats aims to enhance their participation in local governance, providing them with more decision-making power and representation.
4. (b) The Equal Remuneration Act, 1976
5. (d) All of these
6. (a) Despite changes over the years, the economic status of lower castes remains worse off compared to upper castes. The old hierarchy still influences economic conditions, and lower castes have higher proportions of people living in poverty.
7. (b) The first student correctly described gender division as hierarchical. The second student accurately noted that women's public role remains minimal. However, the third student's claim that women have always had equal rights is incorrect, and feminist movements have indeed aimed at equality (fourth student). Therefore, the viewpoint of only first, second and fourth student are accurate.
8. (b) Communal politics involves using religion to gain political support, often pitting one religious group against another. Events A, B, and D fit this description, as they use religious endorsement, superiority claims, and mobilization based on religion.
9. (b) A-(*ii*), B-(*i*), C-(*iv*), D-(*iii*)
10. (a) (*i*) and (*ii*)
11. (c) Gandhiji emphasized that politics should be guided by moral values derived from religion, rather than being secular or detached from religious ethics.
12. (b) It is now easier for women to legally wage struggle for their rights.

Assertion and Reason

1. (a) Self-explanatory.
2. (a) Self-explanatory.
3. (c) It is due to gender discrimination, gender division of labor, and societal norms and not because women are less productive and less creative than men.
4. (d) The literacy rate of women is 54% and men is 76%.
5. (a) Self-explanatory.

Subjective Questions

Very Short Answer Type Questions

1. Caste-based Political expression has positively impacted Indian society by giving caste groups who were dicriminated in the past a political voice, addressing historical injustice through reservations, and raising awareness about caste discrimination and unequal resource access, leading to the formulation of policies for a fairer and more inclusive society. *(2 M)*
2. Perceptions of ideal women vary in society, but some prevalent notions include the belief that women's main responsibility is housework and child -care. This Stereotype assigns women the role of house makers and less value on their paid work. *(2 M)*
3. The term "sexual division of labor" refers to traditional roles where men handle jobs outside the home, and women are primarily responsible for domestic chores and child care. This division isn't biological but arises from societal norms. *(2 M)*
4. The Panchayati Raj system played a very significant role in enhancing the women's involvement in politics because:
   - The Panchayati Raj system reserves one-third of seats for women, promoting their political involvement and decision-making at local level. *(1 M)*
   - This has led to over one million elected women representatives in local bodies, demonstrating significant progress in gender equality in politics. *(1 M)*

5. Feminist movements play a significant role in political mobilization based on gender by:
- Advocating for equal rights and opportunities for women in all spheres, including politics, which has increased women's participation in political processes. *(1 M)*
- Challenging gender stereotypes and societal norms that limit women's roles, thereby empowering more women to take on leadership and decision-making roles in politics. *(1 M)*

Short Answer Type Questions

1. In India, the participation of women in politics can be enhance by:
   - **Reservation of Seats:** One way to solve this problem is to make it legally binding to have a fixed percentage of reserved seats for women in all the elected bodies. *(1 M)*
   - **Political Training:** Training women in leadership, election campaigning, and policy-making can equip them with the necessary skills to succeed in politics. *(1 M)*
   - **Awareness Campaigns:** Public campaigns to change societal attitudes, encourage women to vote, and highlight the importance of women's roles in decision-making can boost participation. *(1 M)*
2. (*i*) (*a*) The statement implies that there is a direct relationship between increased educational opportunities for women and their enhanced participation in political processes. *(1 M)*

   (*b*) As education levels increase among women, they gain more knowledge, skills, and confidence, which empowers them to engage more actively in politics either as voters, candidates, or in any other political roles. *(1 M)*

   (*ii*) Promoting gender equality in education suggests a societal move towards valuing and utilizing the potential of women equally in public spheres, including politics, which historically have been male-dominated domains. *(1 M)*
3. **Threats of communalism to Indian democracy:**
   - Communalism creates division along religious lines, which can lead to conflict and violence, risking national unity. *(1 M)*
   - It leads to a political environment where parties and policies are crafted around religion to gain power, which may ignore minority groups and disrupt secular governance. *(1 M)*
   - Communal tensions can divert government and societal focus from developmental goals to managing conflicts, thus delaying economic and social progress. *(1 M)*
4. (*i*) **Low Representation:** Despite progress, women's representation in India's legislative bodies remains low. Women made up just over 10% in the Lok Sabha and even less in State Assemblies. *(1 M)*

   (*ii*) **Efforts for Improvement:** Measures like reserving seats in local government bodies (Panchayats and Municipalities) for women have been introduced to improve their representation. *(1 M)*

   (*iii*) **Pending Legislation:** A bill proposing at least one-third reservation for women in the Lok Sabha and State Assemblies has been pending, for more than a decade, indicating ongoing efforts to enhance women's political participation. *(1 M)*
5. (*i*) Statement I points out the longstanding issue of women's underrepresentation in politics, reflecting traditional gender roles and societal norms. *(1 M)*

   (*ii*) Statement II indicates proactive efforts, including policies like the Women's Reservation Bill, to enhance women's participation in political decision-making. *(1 M)*

   (*iii*) These reflect a shift towards greater gender equality in governance, promoting a more inclusive and representative political landscape. *(1 M)*

Long Answer Type Questions

1. (*i*) Since independence, India has made progress toward gender equality, yet challenges persist. Legislative and societal efforts have improved women's educational, professional, and political participation. *(1 M)*

   (*ii*) Laws against discrimination and for equal pay have been enacted, alongside other action like reservation in local governance. *(1 M)*

   (*iii*) Despite these efforts, women face societal stereotypes, under representation in higher political offices, and economic disparities. The sexual division of labor and low political representation highlight ongoing biases. *(1 M)*

   (*iv*) However, feminist movements have forced changes, pushing for more equitable laws and societal norms. *(1 M)*

   (*v*) The journey toward gender equality is ongoing, requiring continuous effort to break down deep-rooted discrimination and ensure equal rights and opportunities. *(1 M)*
2. Yes, in my opinion it is reasonable to consider extending the reservation system for women to the State Legislature and the parliament for several compelling reasons, like:
   - **Increased representation:** Reservation of seats for women ensures that women are represented in decision-making bodies. This helps to ensure that women's perspectives and experiences are taken into account when policies are being formulated. *(1¼ M)*
   - **Empowerment of women:** Reservation of seats for women empowers women, giving them a voice in the political process. This can help to increase women's confidence and self-esteem, and can also help to challenge gender-based stereotypes and discrimination *(1¼ M)*
   - **Improved governance:** women's participation in politics has been shown to lead more inclusive and equitable policies. This is because women tend to prioritise issues as health, education, and social welfare for woman as well, which are often neglected in male-dominated political Systems. *(1¼ M)*

- **Address the gender imbalance:** The reservation system has been successful in increasing women's participation in local government bodies and extending it to higher levels of government could help to address the gender imbalance in politics and in society more effeciently. *(1¼ M)*

3. (*i*) **Definition:** Communalism in politics involves prioritizing one religious identity over other identities. *(1 M)*

   (*ii*) **Communal Violence:** An extreme form of communalism results in communal violence, riots, and massacres, as witnessed during the Partition of India and Pakistan. *(1 M)*

   (*iii*) **Secular State Provisions:** The Indian Constitution do not promote communalism. The Indian Constitution establishes India as a secular state, prohibiting discrimination based on religion and ensuring equality before the law for all religious communities. *(1 M)*

   (*iv*) **Political Mobilization:** Communal politics often involves the use of religious symbols and leaders to mobilize voters. *(1 M)*

   (*v*) **Conclusion:** Communalism represents a significant challenge to Indian democracy, threatening the secular fabric of the nation. Fighting communalism requires both constitutional safeguards and active efforts to promote communal harmony. *(1 M)*

4. The feminist movements greatly impacted gender equality in India. This can be understood with the help of the following points:

   (*i*) **Raising Awareness:** The feminist movement has played a crucial role in highlighting the issues of gender inequality and discrimination against women in various areas of life. *(1 M)*

   (*ii*) **Legislative Reforms:** It has led to significant legislative changes aimed at improving the status of women, including laws related to dowry, domestic violence, and equal pay for equal work. *(1 M)*

   (*iii*) **Education and Employment:** Feminist movement has contributed to increased access to education and employment opportunities for women, challenging traditional roles and stereotypes. *(1 M)*

   (*iv*) **Political Representation:** The movement has pushed for greater political representation for women, leading to policy changes like reserving seats for women in local government bodies. *(1 M)*

   (*v*) **Conclusion:** The feminist movement has had a significant impact on gender equality in India, influencing society's attitudes, laws, and policy decisions towards a more equitable treatment of women. *(1 M)*

5. (*i*) **Influence of Religion on Politics:** In India, religion deeply influences politics. Leaders often use religious sentiments to attract votes, leading to communalism where politics is driven through religion rather than public welfare. *(1 M)*

   (*ii*) **Impact of Communalism:** Communalism divides people based on religion, leading to conflicts and riots. It goes against the idea of democracy, which is about unity and equal rights for all, regardless of religion. *(1 M)*

   Role and Significance of Secularism:

   (*i*) **Secularism for Democracy:** India's constitution promotes secularism, meaning the state has no religion. It ensures freedom to practice any religion, aiming to maintain harmony and equal treatment of all religions. *(1 M)*

   (*ii*) **Role of Secularism:** Secularism fights communalism by keeping religion separate from state affairs. It helps in focusing on common issues like development and social justice, ensuring that religion doesn't influence political decisions. *(1 M)*

   (*iii*) **Significance of Secularism:** For a healthy democracy, secularism is crucial. It allows diverse religions to coexist peacefully, ensuring that political decisions are made for the common good, not based on religious biases *(1 M)*

Case Based Questions

Case Based-I

(*i*) Women do not get equal pay as men due to social stereotypes and undervaluation of their work, both in households and workplaces. *(1 M)*

(*ii*) The Equal Remuneration Act, of 1976 ensures equal wages for men and women for equal work. *(1 M)*

(*iii*) Women continue to face wage disparities. Despite equal capability and work hours, their remuneration remains less compared to their male counterparts in almost all fields like sports, cinema, manufacturing, and agriculture. *(2 M)*

Case Based-II

(*i*) A secular state is one where no religion is given official status or preference over another, ensuring equal treatment to all under the law. *(1 M)*

(*ii*) To ensure secularism, the Indian Constitution prohibits any official state religion and guarantees every individual the freedom to practice, profess, and propagate their religion or any religion or choose not to follow any religion. *(1 M)*

(*iii*) India chose to be a secular state, ensuring no official religion of the state and allowing freedom to practice, profess, or not follow any religion, unlike Sri Lanka, Pakistan, and England where Buddhism, Islam, and Christianity were recognized as their states' official religions. *(2 M)*

Case Based-III

(*i*) The minimal representation of women in politics is primarily due to societal norms and stereotypes that underestimate women's roles and capabilities. *(1 M)*

(*ii*) Feminists argue that without political power, women cannot effectively influence or enact policies that directly address and improve their societal and legal status. *(1 M)*

(*iii*) India has introduced measures such as reserving one-third of the seats in Panchayati Raj institutions for women, significantly increasing their representation and involvement in governance, which has been crucial for supporting gender-specific issues and rights. *(2 M)*

POLITICAL PARTIES

4

"Political parties bridge citizens and governance, balancing representation and efficiency, facing challenges with reforms for transparency and inclusivity for a strong democracy."

SYLLABUS & WEIGHTAGE

List of Concept Names	Years					
	2020	2021	2022	2023	2024	2025
Why do we need political parties? (Meaning, functions, and necessity)	1 Q (3 M)	Exam not conducted	—	1 Q (3 M)	1 Q (1 M)	—
How many parties should we have? (One-party system, Two-party system, and Multi-party system)	1 Q (2 M)		1 Q (2 M)	1 Q (1 M)	—	—
National parties and State parties	1 Q (3 M)		—	—	—	1 Q (1 M)
Challenges to political parties and How can parties be reformed?	—		—	—	1 Q (3 M)	1 Q (1 M)

CONCEPT MAP

To Access One Shot Revision Video Scan This QR Code

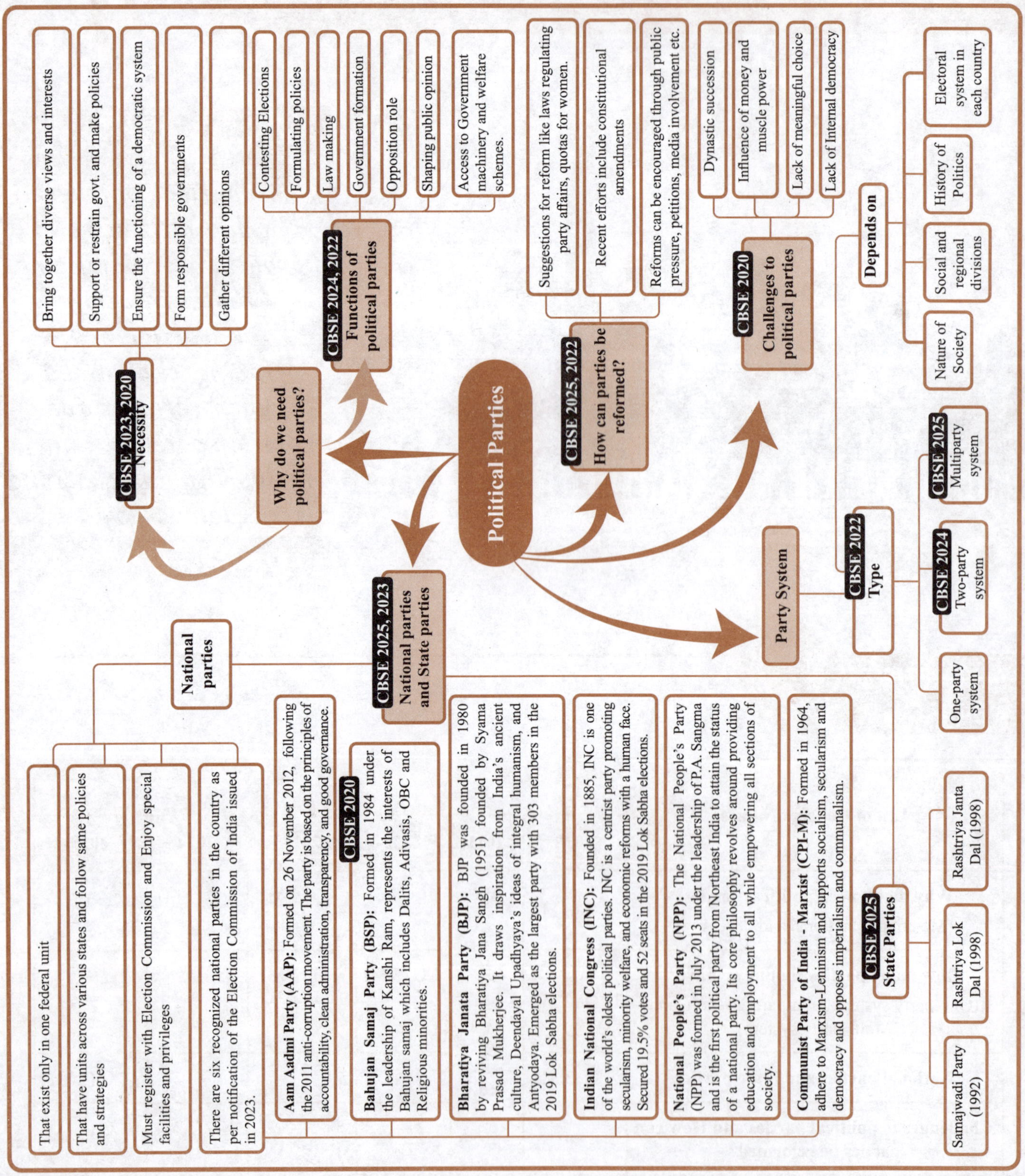

1 WHY DO WE NEED POLITICAL PARTIES?

NCERT Definitions *(Commonly asked in 1 mark)*

- **Political Party:** A political party is a group of people who come together to contest elections and hold power in the government. They agree on some policies and programs for society with a view to promote the collective good.
- **Partisans:** Partisanship means always taking one side and inability to take a balanced view on an issue. A partisan strongly supports a particular party, group, or side.
- **Ruling Party:** The ruling party is the political party that runs the government. It is the party that has won the majority of seats in the legislature and is responsible for making and implementing policies.

Important Facts

01 Election Commission has officially banned wall writing by parties during election times.

02 In India, top party leaders choose candidates for contesting elections.

Important Concepts

Functions of Political Parties

- **Contest Elections:** Parties select candidates to contest elections. In India, top leaders usually choose candidates.
- **Form Policies and Programs:** They propose different policies and programs for the public to choose from during elections.
- **Make Laws:** Political parties play a major role in the law-making process in the legislature.
- **Form and Run Governments:** The ruling party makes important policy decisions and runs the government.
- **Act as Opposition:** The losing parties play the role of opposition by criticizing the government's policies and actions.
- **Shape Public Opinion:** Parties shape public opinion. They raise and highlight issues.
- **Provide Access to Government:** They help citizens connect with government schemes and services through their local leaders.

Difference Between

Ruling Party Vs. Opposition Party

Aspect	Ruling Party	Opposition Party
Role	Governs the country or state.	Challenges and scrutinizes the government's policies and actions.
Responsibility	Implements policies and laws.	Provides alternative policies and holds the government accountable.
Position	Holds a majority in the legislature.	Usually has fewer seats than the ruling party.

Myth Buster

- **Myth:** Only National Parties Play a Crucial Role in Democracy.

  Fact: Both national and regional parties are essential in democracy, ensuring broad representation, influencing coalitions, and enriching the democratic process.

- **Myth:** Political parties are corrupt.

  Fact: While corruption exists in many parties, not all political parties engage in corrupt practices.

Scan Me for Detailed Explanations

COMPETENCY BASED SOLVED EXAMPLES

Multiple Choice Questions

(1 M)

1. **'Opposition slams minister's remark; condemns rising fuel prices.' The above statement shows the important function of opposition parties in a democracy**

   Which of the following options does NOT fall under the functions of an opposition party? ***(Re)***

   (*a*) Auditing the government's spending and budget

   (*b*) Criticising the government for its shortcomings and mistakes

   (*c*) Asking questions from the government to ensure accountability

   (*d*) Mobilising the support of other parties to oppose the decisions of the government

2. **What role do these images illustrate about political parties during election times?** ***(Un)***

   (*a*) Artistic expression in public spaces

   (*b*) Informational campaigns to educate voters

   (*c*) Use of public space for advertising by political parties

   (*d*) Vandalism and public disturbance

3. **Which component is not a part of a political party?** ***(An)*(CBSE APQ, 2023)**

   (*a*) The leaders (*b*) The active members

   (*c*) The voters (*d*) The followers

4. **How do political parties typically select their candidates for elections?** ***(Re)***

   (*a*) Through appointment by the judiciary

   (*b*) By lottery system

   (*c*) Based on personal recommendations

   (*d*) Through internal party processes

5. **What role do opposition parties play in a democracy?** ***(Un)***

   (*a*) They implement government policies

   (*b*) They criticize the ruling party and offer alternative views

   (*c*) They decide on the allocation of public funds

   (*d*) They control the military forces

Assertion and Reason

(1 M)

Direction: The following questions consist of two statements – Assertion (A) and Reason (R). Answer these questions by selecting the appropriate option given below:

(*a*) Both A and R are true, and R is the correct explanation of A.

(*b*) Both A and R are true, but R is not the correct explanation of A.

(*c*) A is true, but R is false

(*d*) A is false, but R is true.

1. **Assertion (A):** Political parties are necessary for the functioning of a democracy.

   Reason (R): Political parties provide people access to government machinery and welfare schemes implemented by governments. ***(Un)***

2. **Assertion (A):** Political parties should not be responsive to people's needs and demands.

   Reason (R): If political parties fail to meet people's expectations, they risk being rejected in the next elections. ***(An)***

3. **Assertion (A):** Political parties perform various functions such as mobilizing voters, formulating policies, and holding elected officials accountable.

   Reason (R): These functions are necessary for ensuring that democracies function effectively. ***(Un)***

4. **Assertion (A):** It is often said that political parties are facing a crisis.

   Reason (R): They are very unpopular and the citizens are indifferent to political parties. ***(Un)*(CBSE APQ, 2023)**

5. **Assertion (A):** Political parties are important in the functioning of democracy.

Reason (R): The media plays an important role in the making of Political parties. ***(Un)*(CBSE, 2023)**

Subjective Questions

Very Short Answer Type Questions (1 or 2 M)

1. **What is a political party?** ***(Re)***

Ans. A political party is a group of people who organize to contest elections and hold power in the government, aiming to implement policies for the society's benefit. It plays a crucial role in a democracy by representing different views and interests. *(2M)*

2. **What are the components of a political party?** ***(Re)***

Ans. A political party typically consists of two main components:

- **Leaders:** The individuals who guide the party's decisions and strategies. *(1 M)*
- **Active Members:** The dedicated party workers who support daily operations and campaign activities. *(1 M)*

3. **Suggest any one way to promote the public participation in the Political Parties for enhancing the quality of democracy.** ***(Cr)* (CBSE, 2020)**

Ans. One way to promote public participation in political parties is by encouraging youth and marginalized groups to join political parties. Political parties should provide opportunities for these groups to participate in decision-making processes and leadership positions. *(1 M)*

4. **Differentiate between ruling and opposition parties.** ***(Un)*(CBSE, 2022 Term 2)**

Ans. Difference between ruling and opposition party: *(2 M)*

Ruling Party	Opposition parties
Ruling parties are the ones who hold the majority in the government and are responsible for governing.	Opposition parties are those who do not hold the majority and are responsible for holding the government accountable.
The ruling party has the power to implement its policies and agenda.	Opposition parties can only propose policies and offer criticism.

Short Answer Type Questions (3 M)

1. **How do political parties function within a democratic system? Explain.** ***(Re)* (CBSE, 2024)**

Ans. Within a democratic system, political parties function in such ways: **(Any three)**

- **Present Policies and Leaders:** They present different policies and leaders, offering voters choices in elections on who should govern. *(1 M)*
- **Raise Public Concerns:** By raising public concerns in legislative bodies, parties bring people's issues to the government, ensuring that the government considers various perspectives. *(1 M)*
- **Ensure accountable government:** Through debates and votes, they shape legislation and oversee government actions. *(1 M)*
- **Enhance Political Understanding:** Parties help people understand politics better. They teach and inform people about complicated things and help citizens to make informed choices. *(1 M)*

2. **Analyze the need of Political Parties in the Democracy.** ***(An)*(CBSE, 2023)**

Ans. The political parties are very important in democracy. They perform the following functions:

- **Present Policies and Leaders:** Political parties give people choices in elections. They present different policies and leaders, offering voters options on who should govern. *(1 M)*
- **Raise Public Concerns:** They bring people's issues to the government. By raising public concerns in legislative bodies, parties ensure that the government considers various perspectives. *(1 M)*
- **Ensure accountable government:** Help make laws and check on the government. Through debates and votes, they shape legislation and oversee government actions. *(1 M)*

Long Answer Type Questions (5 M)

1. **A research institute has been tasked with designing a framework to evaluate the performance of political parties in a democratic country. Discuss the key indicators that the institute should consider while designing this framework.** ***(Cr)***

Ans. The key indicator that the institute must consider while designing the framework are: **(Any Five)**

- **Electoral Success:** This indicator measures how successfully a political party wins elections. High electoral performance indicates strong public support and legitimacy. *(1 M)*
- **Policy Implementation:** Evaluating how well a party translates its manifesto promises into actual policies and actions once in power. This shows the party's capability to govern and fulfill its commitments. *(1 M)*
- **Internal Democracy:** Assessing the degree of internal democracy within the party, such as how candidates are selected and how decisions are made. *(1 M)*
- **Transparency and Accountability:** The extent to which a party is transparent in its operations and accountable to its members and the public. *(1 M)*
- **Inclusiveness:** Measuring the extent to which a party includes and represents various social groups, including minorities and marginalized communities. *(1 M)*
- **Responsiveness:** Assessing how responsive a party is to the needs and demands of the public. This includes the party's ability to address public concerns and adapt to changing circumstances. *(1 M)*

2 HOW MANY PARTIES SHOULD WE HAVE?

NCERT Definitions *(Commonly asked in 1 mark)*

- **One-Party System:** A system where only one political party is allowed to control and run the government. Example: China.
- **Two-Party System:** A system where two major political parties dominate the elections and power, while other parties have a minor role. Example: USA, UK.
- **Multi-Party System:** A system where more than two political parties compete for power, often forming alliances to govern. Example: India.
- **Coalition:** A group of political parties that come together to contest elections and form a government. Example: UPA, NDA, and Left Front in India.

Important Facts

01 India has more than 750 registered political parties with the Election Commission.

02 In a democracy, any group of citizens can form a political party.

03 A political party system (one-party system, two-party system, multi-party system) is based on the nature of society, its social and regional divisions, the history of politics, and the system of elections.

Classification

Type of Party System
- One-Party System → Only one party controls the government.
- Two-Party System → Two major parties dominate elections.
- Multi-Party System → Many parties compete, often forming alliances.

Difference Between

Feature	One-Party System	Two-Party System	Multi-Party System
Number of Main Parties	Only one party	Two major parties	Many competing parties
Competition in Elections	No competition	Limited competition	Very competitive
Choices for voters	None	Limited	Multiple
Example Countries	China	USA, UK	India
Democratic Nature	Not democratic	Democratic	Democratic

Myth Buster

- **Myth:** A two-party system is always better than a multi-party system.
  Truth: There's no "best" system. It depends on the country's diversity, history, and political structure.
- **Myth:** One-party systems are more efficient in decision-making because there is no opposition or debate.
  Truth: While one-party systems may seem efficient, they often lack checks and balances. Decisions are made quickly, but they may not reflect the diverse needs and opinions of the people, which is essential for a truly democratic and fair society.

Scan Me for Detailed Explanations

COMPETENCY BASED SOLVED EXAMPLES

Multiple Choice Questions

(1 M)

1. Which one of the following country has two party system? ***(Re)* (CBSE, 2023)**

(*a*) China (*b*) Russia
(*c*) America (*d*) India

2. Which one of the following countries have One Party System? ***(Re)* (CBSE, 2023)**

(*a*) China (*b*) India
(*c*) Pakistan (*d*) America

3. According to the infographic about party membership, which statement is correct about India's party membership trend from 1996 to 2004? ***(Ap)***

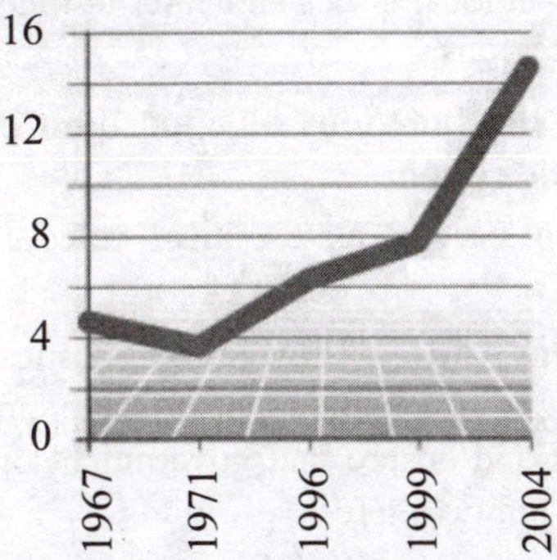

Fig: Those who say they are member of a political party

(*a*) Party membership in India steadily declined.
(*b*) Party membership in India was constant throughout the years.
(*c*) Party membership in India increased.
(*d*) There is no available data for India's party membership between 1996 and 2004.

4. "Over 750 parties registered by the Election Commission of India". What might be a potential outcome for the democratic process? ***(Ev)***

(*a*) Enhanced policy implementation efficiency
(*b*) Increased representation of diverse opinions
(*c*) Simplified electoral choices for voters
(*d*) Reduced political fragmentation

5. Which of the following is the PRIMARY factor which contributed to the emergence of multiple political parties at the same level in India? ***(Un)* (CBSE APQ, 2024)**

(*a*) a federal political system
(*b*) varied economic conditions
(*c*) linguistic and regional diversity
(*d*) low levels of literacy and political awareness

Assertion and Reason

(1 M)

Direction: **The following questions consist of two statements – Assertion (A) and Reason (R). Answer these questions by selecting the appropriate option given below:**

(*a*) Both A and R are true, and R is the correct explanation of A.
(*b*) Both A and R are true, but R is not the correct explanation of A.
(*c*) A is true, but R is false
(*d*) A is false, but R is true.

1. **Assertion (A):** More than 750 parties are registered with the Election Commission of India.
   Reason (R): Only one party is sufficient to control and run the government. ***(Re)***
2. **Assertion (A):** In some countries, only one party is allowed to control and run the government in democracy.
   Reason (R): These are called two-party system. ***(Un)***
3. **Assertion (A):** A multi-party system is better for democracy.
   Reason (R): A multi-party system allows for a greater diversity of voices and perspectives to be represented in government. ***(An)***

Subjective Questions

Very Short Answer Type Questions

(2 M)

1. Can the ideal number of major parties be determined for all democracies? ***(An)***

Ans. No, the ideal number of political parties cannot be determined for all democracies. It depends on the country's social, regional, and political diversity. Each country develops its party system based on its unique historical, geographical, and cultural conditions. *(2 M)*

2. **In a country, though people are allowed to form parties, only one party controls and forms the government. What type of party system can we say operates in this country? Why?** *(Ap)*

Ans. In a country where only one party controls and forms the government, the system can be described as a "one-party system." Since only one party controls and forms the government, it would seem that the electoral system does not permit free competition for power, leading to the dominance of a single party in the political system. *(2 M)*

3. **In a hypothetical democratic nation with a population that is religiously homogenous, should there still be multiple political parties?** *(Ap, Cr)*

Ans. Yes, even if the population shares the same religion, people will have different views on economic policies, social reforms, education, healthcare, and governance. Multiple parties ensure these different opinions are represented in the political process. *(2 M)*

Short Answer Type Questions (3 M)

1. **Examine the reason for accepting a multi-party system in India.** *(An)*

Ans. In India, the multi-party system was adopted due to the following reasons: **(Any three)**

- **Social and Regional Diversity:** India has vast social, cultural, and regional diversity. India's vast social and geographical diversity cannot be represented by just two or three parties. *(1 M)*
- **Better Representation:** A multi-party system allows representation of different communities, languages, and interests, ensuring everyone's voice is heard in the democratic process. *(1 M)*
- **Coalition Governments:** Since no single party often wins a clear majority, the multi-party system encourages alliances to govern. This promotes power sharing and checks dominance by one party. *(1 M)*
- **Inclusive Democracy:** The multi-party system reflects India's diverse society. It encouraging healthy competition among parties and making the government respond better to the needs of the people. *(1 M)*

2. **A country facing slow decision-making is considering adopting a one-party system to make governance more efficient. Would this approach strengthen or weaken democracy?** *(Ev)*

Ans. This approach would weaken the democracy because:

- **Loss of Democratic Competition:** A one-party system may speed up decision-making, but it eliminates competition, which is essential for a fair and healthy democracy. *(1 M)*
- **Restricted People's Choice:** In a democracy, citizens must have the right to choose between different political alternatives. A one-party system denies this freedom. *(1 M)*
- **Risk of Power Misuse:** Without opposition, there is no check on the ruling party's power, and the ruling party can misuse power, increasing the chances of authoritarian rule, as seen in countries like China. *(1 M)*

Long Answer Type Questions (5 M)

1. ***"The multiparty system in India often seems chaotic and leads to political instability. However, it also allows for a wide range of interests and opinions to be represented in the political process."*** **Justify the statement with relevant points, referring to India.** *(An)*

Ans. The statement can be justify with the help of the following arguments:

- **Political Instability:** Because there are so many parties, it's common to have coalition governments. These coalitions can be unstable and sometimes lead to frequent changes in leadership, which can make the India's political system seems chaotic and can lead to political instability. *(1 M)*
- **Representation of Diverse Interests:** India has many different cultures, languages, and religions. The multiparty system allows these different groups to have their voices heard in politics, making sure everyone is represented. *(1 M)*
- **Federal Structure:** India's government structure supports regional parties that represent local interests. This system allows regional parties to participate in national politics and address local issues effectively. *(1 M)*
- **Democratic Evolution:** The multi-party system evolved in India because it ensures that various interests and regional issues are represented in the governance, which is very important to keep this country united. *(1 M)*
- **Examples:** Regional parties like the Trinamool Congress in West Bengal and the DMK in Tamil Nadu show how the multiparty system works. These parties focus on local issues and cater to the specific needs of their regions. *(1 M)*

2. **Examine the functions of opposition parties within a democratic system.** *(An)*

Ans. Opposition parties play critical roles in a democratic system:

- **Prevent Abuse of Power:** By questioning government decisions, opposition parties help prevent abuses of power and ensure that government operations remain in the public interest. *(1 M)*
- **Alternative Policies:** Opposition parties propose alternative policies and programs. This contributes to a more informed public debate and helps voters see different solutions to national issues. *(1 M)*
- **Public Representation:** They represent the interests and voices of those not in government, ensuring diverse viewpoints are considered in national discussions. *(1 M)*
- **Check and Balance:** They serve as a check on the ruling party, scrutinize its policy decisions, and ensure that the majority does not override the minority's rights. *(1 M)*
- **Electoral Choice:** By providing alternatives, they give voters choices in elections, which is fundamental for the healthy democracy, encouraging participation and engagement in the political process. *(1 M)*

3 NATIONAL PARTIES AND STATE PARTIES

NCERT Definitions (Commonly asked in 1 mark)

- **National Party:** These are political parties that are present in several or all states of a country. They are recognized by the Election Commission of India if they meet certain electoral criteria (6% of votes in 4 states and at least 4 Lok Sabha seats).
- **State Party:** These are political parties that primarily operate in one state or a few states. They may not have a nationwide presence but are recognized by the Election Commission based on specific electoral criteria (6% of votes and 2 seats in legislative assemblies)
- **Recognised Political Parties:** Recognised Political Parties are political parties that meet certain criteria set by the Election Commission of India. These parties are given special privileges, such as a unique election symbol that only their official candidates can use.

Important Facts

01 The Election Commission recognizes 6 national parties as per 2023 data, namely the Aam Aadmi Party (AAP), Bahujan Samaj Party (BSP), Bharatiya Janata Party (BJP), Communist Party of India-Marxist (CPI-M), Indian National Congress (INC), and National People's Party (NPP).

02 The Indian National Congress, founded in 1885, is one of the oldest party in the world.

Classification

Types of parties	
National parties	**State parties**
(*i*) Aam Aadmi Party (AAP)	(*i*) Samajwadi Party
(*ii*) Bahujan Samaj Party (BSP)	(*ii*) Rashtriya Janata Dal
(*iii*) Bharatiya Janata Party (BJP)	(*iii*) Biju Janata Dal
(*iv*) Communist Party of India - Marxist (CPI-M)	(*iv*) Telangana Rashtra Samithi
(*v*) Indian National Congress (INC)	(*v*) Mizo National Front
(*vi*) National People's Party (NPP)	(*vi*) Sikkim Democratic Front, etc.

Comparison

Aspects	National Parties	State Parties
Scope	Operate in **multiple** states across the country.	Operate **mainly in** one or **a few states.**
Election Criteria	Recognized by Election Commission if they secure **6% votes in four states** and win **four seats in Lok Sabha.**	recognized if they secure **6% votes in a state** and win at least **two seats** in State elections.
Influence	Have a **countrywide presence** and influence.	Have a **limited presence** in one or a few states.
Example	Bharatiya Janata Party (BJP), Indian National Congress (INC), Communist Party of India (Marxist) (CPI-M)	Samajwadi Party (SP), All India Trinamool Congress (AITC), Rashtriya Janata Dal (RJD)

Myth Buster

- **Myth:** A party must be a National Party or must have a nationwide presence to get a unique election symbol.
  Fact: The Election Commission provides unique election symbols to recognized parties, whether national or state-level.
- **Myth:** Regional parties are always focused on local issues and cannot address national concerns.
  Fact: While regional parties may prioritize local concerns, they also engage with national issues by entering into alliances with national parties and have been part of coalition governments, influencing policies on a national scale as well

Scan Me for Detailed Explanations

COMPETENCY BASED SOLVED EXAMPLES

Multiple Choice Questions

(1 M)

1. A political party formed in 2013 has its main base in the North East of India. The party believes in diversity and regional development, and it emphasizes education and employment for all. This party was recognized as a national party in 2019. Which party is this? ***(Re)***

(*a*) National People's Party (NPP)

(*b*) Bharatiya Janata Party (BJP)

(*c*) Communist Party of India (CPI)

(*d*) Indian National Congress (INC)

2. Subhash lobbies with various government offices to work specifically for the interests of the Scheduled Tribes.

Which of the following parties is he MOST LIKELY to be associated with? ***(Ap)***

(*a*) All-India Trinamool Congress

(*b*) Indian National Congress

(*c*) Communist Party of India

(*d*) Bahujan Samaj Party

3. Which party played a dominant role in Indian politics at the national and state level for several decades after India's Independence? ***(Re)***

(*a*) Bahujan Samaj Party (BSP)

(*b*) Communist Party of India (CPI)

(*c*) Indian National Congress (INC)

(*d*) Nationalist Congress Party (NCP)

4. Match Column-I with Column-II: ***(Re)***

Column-I		Column-II	
(A)	Formed in 1925. Opposed to the forces of secessionism and communalism.	(i)	 Bahujan Samaj Party (BSP)
(B)	Formed in 1980. Wants a uniform civil code for all people living in the country irrespective of religion.	(ii)	 Communist Party of India (CPI)
(C)	Formed in 1984 under the leadership of Kanshi Ram.	(iii)	 Bhartiya Janta Party (BJP)
(D)	Formed in 1885. Supports new economic reforms but with a human face.	(iv)	 Indian National Congress (INC)

(*a*) A-(iv), B-(i), C-(iii), D-(ii)

(*b*) A-(ii), B-(iii), C-(i), D-(iv)

(*c*) A-(iv), B-(iii), C-(ii), D-(i)

(*d*) A-(iii), B-(i), C-(iv), D-(ii)

Assertion and Reason

(1 M)

Direction: **The following questions consist of two statements – Assertion (A) and Reason (R). Answer these questions by selecting the appropriate option given below:**

(*a*) Both A and R are true, and R is the correct explanation of A.

(*b*) Both A and R are true, but R is not the correct explanation of A.

(*c*) A is true, but R is false

(*d*) A is false, but R is true.

1. **Assertion (A):** National parties have a wider presence and appeal than state parties in India.
   Reason (R): National parties have a broader ideological base and are able to attract voters from across the country, while state parties are limited to a particular region or state. ***(An)***

2. **Assertion (A):** State parties play an important role in regional politics in India.
Reason (R): State parties are better equipped to understand and address local issues than national parties. *(An)*

3. **Assertion(A):** Only those recognized as national parties can contest elections at the Union level.
Reason(R): Recognition of a political party as a national party is accorded by the Election Commission. *(An)*

Subjective Questions

Very Short Answer Type Questions (2 M)

1. **A party has won the following percentage of seats in the 4 states where it has contested in the state legislative assembly election.**

State	% of Votes Won	No of Seats Won
State A	19	10
State B	16	4
State C	35	42
State D	7	1

The party has not won any Lok Sabha seats.

(i) What type of political party will it be classified as? Why? *(Ap)*

(ii) Can it be classified as a national party? Justify your answer. *(Ap)*

Ans. (i) It will be recognised as a state party in States A, B, and C. This is because it has won at least 6% of votes and at least 2 seats in the state legislative assembly elections in those states. *(1 M)*

(ii) The party cannot be classified as a national party even though it has won more than 6% of votes in four state assembly elections, as the party has not won any Lok Sabha Seat. *(1 M)*

2. **The Aam Aadmi Party (AAP) has formed governments in Delhi and Punjab. It has recently expanded its reach in Gujarat but has limited influence in southern and eastern states.**

What is the current status of AAP according to the Election Commission? Why? *(Re)*

Ans. • **Current Status:** The Aam Aadmi Party (AAP) is recognized as a national party by the Election Commission of India. *(1 M)*

• **Reason :** Despite its limited presence in some regions, AAP has met the criteria of becoming a national party. *(1 M)*

3. **Explain the role of Election Commission regarding recognition of Political Parties in India.** *(Un)*(CBSE,2023)

Ans. The Election Commission of India plays a crucial role in the recognition of political parties:

• It maintains the register of political parties and grants them recognition as national or state parties based on their performance in elections. *(1 M)*

• Monitors the financial and organizational aspects of political parties and ensures Political parties adhere to the guidelines and regulations set by the Election Commission. *(1 M)*

Short Answer Type Questions (3 M)

1. **Read the statements given below regarding political parties in India.**

Statement 1 (S1): National political parties have a significant influence over the country's policies and governance.

Statement 2 (S2): Regional political parties are gaining prominence and are essential for representing local issues.

Explain what trend these statements - S1 and S2 - reflect in the political landscape of India? *(An)*

Ans. The statements reflect the trend of:

• **Balance of Power:** The statements show a balance of power where national parties deals with the national level issues and policies, while regional parties focus on local issues. *(1 M)*

• **Increased Representation:** Regional parties gaining prominence means more localized representation in governance. It allows people from different regions to have their unique concerns and interests heard and acted upon *(1 M)*

• **Strengthening Democracy:** The presence of both strong national and regional parties ensure wider range of voices and opinions are included in the political process. This helps in making the government more responsive and accountable to the people. *(1 M)*

2. **What privileges are given to recognized political parties by the Election Commission of India? How are political parties recognized as state and national parties in India?** *(An)*

Ans. **Privileges to Recognised Party:** The Election Commission of India gives special privileges, like a unique election symbol to a recognized political parties, which only their candidates can use. *(1 M)*

Recognition criteria for national parties and state parties are as follows:

• **National Party Criteria:** A party is recognized as a national party if it secures at least 6% of the total votes in four states or wins four seats in the Lok Sabha elections. Example: Bharatiya Janata Party (BJP). *(1 M)*

• **State Party Criteria:** A party becomes a state party by securing at least 6% of votes in a state election and winning at least two seats. Example: Bahujan Samaj Party (BSP). *(1 M)*

3. **Explain the role and significance of the Bahujan Samaj Party (BSP) in Indian politics.** *(Un)*

Ans. Role and Significance of Bahujan Samaj Party(BSP):

- **Formation and Leadership:** The Bahujan Samaj Party (BSP) was founded in 1984 by Kanshi Ram with the aim of representing the Bahujan Samaj, which includes Dalits, adivasis, OBCs, and religious minorities. *(1 M)*
- **Welfare of Oppressed Sections:** The party advocates for the upliftment and welfare of the oppressed sections of society, particularly focusing on securing their political and social rights. *(1 M)*
- **Philosophy and Inspiration:** BSP's ideology is deeply influenced by the teachings of prominent leaders like Sahu Maharaj, Mahatma Phule, Periyar Ramaswami Naicker, and Babasaheb Ambedkar. *(1 M)*

Long Answer Type Questions (5 M)

1. **How do state parties have influenced the political system in India? What role do they play in shaping national politics and federalism?** *(An)*

Ans. State parties have had a significant impact on India's political system. Here's how they influence the system:

- **Growth of Regional Parties:** State parties have become stronger over the years, focusing on local issues. Parties like the Samajwadi Party in Uttar Pradesh and the Biju Janata Dal in Odisha represent the interests of their states. *(1 M)*
- **Impact on National Politics:** Many state parties have a big role in national politics. They form alliances with national parties to help create governments. *(1 M)*
- **Strengthening Federalism:** State parties help strengthen India's federal system. They make sure that the different states are heard and have a say in how the country is run. *(1 M)*
- **Coalition Governments:** Since no single national party can get a majority by itself, national parties often form alliances with state parties to form a government. This allows more groups to be represented in the Parliament. *(1 M)*
- **Diversity in Politics:** Although coalitions can be complicated, state parties bring in different opinions and ideas, making the political system more diverse and fairer. *(1 M)*

2. **How do national parties and state parties differ in terms of their influence and role in Indian politics? Provide examples to support your answer.** *(An)*

Ans. National parties and state parties are different in the following ways:

- **Geographical Reach:** National parties have a presence across multiple states, while state parties are confined to specific regions. *(1 M)*
- **Policy Focus:** National parties focus on broader national issues, whereas state parties prioritize state-specific concerns like regional identity and development. *(1 M)*
- **Electoral Performance:** National parties often dominate Lok Sabha elections, while state parties perform better in State Legislative Assembly elections. *(1 M)*
- **Role in Coalition Governments:** National parties usually lead coalition governments, while state parties are crucial partners in forming these coalitions. *(1 M)*
- **Example:** BJP is a national party with a strong presence in states like Uttar Pradesh and Gujarat, while the Trinamool Congress is a state party dominant in West Bengal. *(1 M)*

4 CHALLENGES TO POLITICAL PARTIES AND HOW CAN PARTIES BE REFORMED?

NCERT Definitions *(Commonly asked in 1 mark)*

- **Defection:** It refers to the act of a political leader or elected representative leaving the political party they originally belonged to and joining another party, often for personal gain such as a higher position, power, or financial rewards.
- **Affidavit:** A signed document submitted to an officer by a candidate who contests elections, where a person makes a sworn statement regarding her personal information, like giving details of his property and criminal cases pending against him.
- **Dynastic Succession:** The process where leadership positions in a political party are passed down within a family, often without open competition or transparent elections.
- **Internal Democracy:** The system within a political party where the members are allowed to participate in decision-making, have the right to hold elections, and access party information. It ensures the party's functioning is transparent and inclusive.

Important Facts

01 It is mandatory for every candidate who contests elections to file an affidavit giving details of his property and criminal cases pending against him.

02 The Election Commission passed an order making it necessary for political parties to hold their organizational elections and file their income tax returns.

03 The Constitution was amended to prevent elected MLAs and MPs from changing parties. If any MLA or MP changes parties; he or she will lose the seat in the legislature.

Difference Between

Internal Democracy vs Dynastic Succession

Internal Democracy	Dynastic Succession
In internal democracy, all decisions including leadership, are made based on group discussions, voting, and fair representation of members.	In dynastic succession, leadership is passed down within one family, with limited or no opportunity for others to rise.
Encourages participation from all members.	Limits participation.
The leadership is chosen based on merit.	Only family members are given top positions, regardless of their experience or popularity.
Diverse leadership.	Same family controlling the party for a long time.

Important Concepts

Challenges Faced by Political Parties:

- **Lack of Internal Democracy:** Political parties often concentrate power in the hands of a few leaders, making it difficult for other members to influence decisions or rise to top positions.
- **Dynastic Politics:** Many parties are controlled by families, leading to unfair advantage for family members, regardless of their qualifications or popularity.
- **Money and muscle power:** Rich individuals or criminal candidates influence elections, undermining fairness and democracy.
- **Lack of Meaningful Choice:** Parties often offer similar policies, reducing the range of options for voters.

Efforts to reform political parties:

- **Constitutional Amendment:** Constitution was amended to prevent elected representatives from changing parties to gain personal benefits. If they do, they lose their seat.
- **Supreme Court Order:** Candidates must file affidavits disclosing their assets and criminal records, making information public, and reducing criminal influence.
- **Election Commission Order:** Political parties are required to hold internal elections and file income tax returns to promote transparency.

Suggestion to reform political parties:

- A law to regulate the internal affairs of political parties.
- Political parties should maintain a register of their members, follow their own constitution, and act as a judge in case of party disputes.
- Hold open elections to the highest posts.
- Mandatory to give about one-third tickets to women candidates.
- The government should give parties money to support their election expenses. This support could be given in cash and kind: petrol, paper, telephone, etc.

COMPETENCY BASED SOLVED EXAMPLES

Scan Me for Detailed Explanations

Multiple Choice Questions

(1 M)

1. During an election campaign, it is required to submit various documents to ensure transparency and legality. One crucial document is the affidavit, which plays an important role in the electoral process. Which statement best reflects the true nature of affidavits in the election process? *(Re)*

A. A signed document was submitted to an officer.

B. Contain details of his property are criminal cases pending against him.

C. There is a system of checking if the information given by the candidate is correct.

D. It is not mandatory for every candidate who contests election to file an affidavit.

(*a*) Only (A) (*b*) Both (B) and (C)

(*c*) Only (C) (*d*) Both (A) and (B)

2. What is the growing concern regarding the role of money and muscle power in parties? *(Un)*

(*a*) Inefficient campaign strategies

(*b*) Lack of public support

(*c*) Increased influence during elections

(*d*) Declining party memberships

3. In the recent national election, several political entities and individuals have engaged in various efforts to influence public policy. Which of the following scenario most accurately demonstrates how political parties influence and shape public policy? *(An)*

(*a*) A local neighborhood association mobilizes volunteers to clean up parks and streets, operating independently of any political affiliations or agendas.

(*b*) A major political party, aiming to address climate change, develops a comprehensive platform advocating for increased investment in renewable energy sources and actively campaigns on this issue across the country.

(c) An independent candidate with a strong personal following enters the race, focusing primarily on their charisma and leaving their policy positions vague and undefined.

(d) Various non-governmental organizations conduct extensive efforts to alter federal regulations on environmental protection, working independently of any political party influence.

4. What measure was taken to prevent elected representatives from changing parties? *(Re)*

(a) Mandating disclosure of property and criminal cases

(b) Amending the Constitution

(c) Enforcing internal party elections

(d) Implementing state funding of elections

5. Parties often face criticism for issues like lack of transparency, corruption, and internal conflicts. These challenges undermine public trust and the effectiveness of democratic governance.
Should measures be taken to improve the functioning and transparency of political parties? *(Ev)*

(a) Yes, but only for major national parties.

(b) No, because current practices are sufficient.

(c) Yes, to ensure better governance and public trust.

(d) No, as it could disrupt party operations.

Assertion and Reason

(1 M)

Direction: The following questions consist of two statements – Assertion (A) and Reason (R). Answer these questions by selecting the appropriate option given below:

(a) Both A and R are true, and R is the correct explanation of A.

(b) Both A and R are true, but R is not the correct explanation of A.

(c) A is true, but R is false

(d) A is false, but R is true.

1. Assertion (A): There is a lack of meaningful choices available to voters.

Reason (R): There is a decline in ideological differences among political parties. *(An)*

2. Assertion (A): Political parties can be reformed by increasing transparency in their funding and expenditure.

Reason (R): Many political parties in India receive funding from unknown sources and do not disclose their expenditure, leading to corruption and lack of accountability. *(An)*

3. Assertion (A): Political parties need to adopt a more inclusive approach towards women, youth, and marginalized communities.

Reason (R): These groups are often underrepresented or excluded from the decision-making process within political parties. *(An)*

Subjective Questions

Very Short Answer Type Questions (2 M)

1. What measures were taken to prevent elected representatives (MLAs and MPs) from changing parties for personal gain? *(Re)*

Ans. Measures taken to prevent elected representatives (MLAs and MPs) from changing parties for personal gain are:

- The Constitution was amended to stop elected representatives (MLAs and MPs) from changing parties. *(1 M)*
- The new law says that if an MLA or MP changes their party, they will lose their seat in the legislature. This has helped reduce the practice of defection (changing parties for benefits). *(1 M)*

2. 'In Goa, 7 powerful families are contesting 35% of the assembly seats' states a headline in a recent newspaper article.
Which challenge of political parties does it MOST LIKELY illustrate? *(An)*

Ans.
- The headline about seven powerful families contesting a significant portion of the Goa assembly seats illustrates the challenge of dynastic succession in political parties. *(1 M)*
- This shows a scenario where politics is dominated by certain families, which can stop other people from having a fair chance to participate and represent in government. *(1 M)*

Short Answer Type Questions (3 M)

1. Analyse any three challenges faced by political parties in India. *(An) (CBSE, 2024)*

Ans. The Main challenge faced by political parties are:

- **Lack of internal democracy:** Power is concentrated in the hands of a few leaders, and ordinary members have little say in decision-making. *(1 M)*
- **Dynastic succession:** Family members often control top positions, which can be unfair to other party members. *(1 M)*
- **Limited choice for voters:** Political parties often offer very similar policies, reducing meaningful options for the public. *(1 M)*

Topper's Explanation **(CBSE, 2024)**

27. hallenges faced by political parties are as follow's –

1 Lack of Internal Democracy : There is concentration and accumulation of power in the hands of party leaders at the top and the ordinary members of the party often ~~lack~~ lack the means and influence to voice their opinion. Membership registers are not maintained, regular organisational meetings are not conducted. Devotion and commitment to the party leaders are valued more than the devotion towards the party principles and constitution.

2. Dynastic Succession – Leaders at the top often misuse their power to support their families and relatives. Free, fair and open elections are not conducted for the top positions. As a result, People who lack support, potential and skills come to power

because of favourism. In various political parties, leaders often belong to the same family generation after generation. Consequently, Deserving candidates are unable to get free and fair opportunities.

3. Increasing role of power and might along with lack of meaningful choice – Growing role of power, money and might is an alarming concern for most of the democracies all across the globe. Criminals are often nominated as party candidates as they have various links and contacts. Rich people who can gather funds in order to win the elections are favoured. Various industrialists and businessmen who finance the parties influence its policies and decisions. Decreasing ideological differences on the economic front are also a concern for democrats. Political leaders often change parties for gaining power which leaves no meaningful choice for the citizens.

2. What role does money and muscle power play in political parties? *(An)*

Ans. Money and muscle power influence the political parties in the following ways:

- **Influence of Wealth:** Political parties often choose candidates who can spend large amounts of money on election campaigns. This gives rich people and companies more control over party decisions and policies. *(1 M)*
- **Use of Muscle Power:** Some parties support candidates with strong local influence, sometimes even with criminal backgrounds, if they are able to win elections, which harms fair political competition and democracy. *(1 M)*
- **Unfair Competition:** Money and muscle power in politics creates an uneven playing field, making it harder for honest and less wealthy candidates to win elections. *(1 M)*

3. The anti-defection law was enacted to ensure stability in the government by preventing elected members from frequently switching parties. However, this has led to some unintended consequences during the legislative debates. During a crucial session on environmental policy, several lawmakers found themselves unable to vote according to their conscience or the specific needs of their constituencies because of party whip directives. Given this scenario, what are two possible ill effects of the anti-defection law? Discuss how these effects could impact democratic principles and governance. *(An)*

Ans. Two ill effects of the anti-defection law are:

- **Restriction on Lawmakers' Independence:** It can stop lawmakers from voting based on what they truly think is correct and the unique needs of the people they represent. This can go against the democratic principle of reflecting different views of the people. *(1½ M)*
- **Lack of Internal Party Debate:** By enforcing strict adherence to party lines, the law can hinder healthy debate within parties. This might lead to a political environment where significant issues are not thoroughly debated, potentially leading to less effective governance. *(1½ M)*

Long Answer Type Questions (5 M)

1. Political parties need to face certain challenges in order to remain effective instruments of democracy" Explain the statement with example. *(An)(CBSE, 2020)*

Ans. In order to remain effective instrument of democracy, political parties need to overcome the following challenges:

- **Lack of Internal Democracy:** Power often remains concentrated in the hands of top leaders. Regular internal elections, transparent functioning, and member participation are usually missing. *(1 M)*
- **Dynastic Succession:** Leadership positions in many parties are passed down to family members rather than capable individuals. This prevents capable leaders from rising and makes the system unfair. *(1 M)*
- **Money and Muscle Power:** Parties often give tickets to wealthy candidates or those with strong influence. This limits the chances of honest and deserving people to contest elections. *(1 M)*
- **Lack of Meaningful Choice:** Many parties now follow similar policies, making it hard for voters to choose based on clear ideological differences, leaving voters with limited options for genuine change. *(1 M)*
- **Accountability Issues:** Leaders often prioritize personal loyalty over accountability to the people and party principles. As a result, they focus more on staying in power rather than addressing public issues *(1 M)*

2. There are various reforms taken to strengthen parties in India so that they perform their function well." Explain the statement with examples. *(Cr) (CBSE, 2022 Term 2)*

Ans. To address challenges, several reforms have been introduced to strengthen political parties in India:

- **Anti-Defection Law:** The Constitution was amended to prevent MPs and MLAs from changing parties after elections, ensuring stability in the government. *(1 M)*
- **Candidate Affidavit:** It is mandatory for candidates to disclose their criminal records, assets, and liabilities, promoting transparency during elections. *(1 M)*
- **Organizational Elections:** The Election Commission has mandated political parties to conduct regular internal elections and file income tax returns to promote accountability. *(1 M)*
- **State Funding of Elections:** There is a proposal for state funding of elections to reduce the influence of money power and provide a level playing field. *(1 M)*
- **Women's Representation:** Suggestions include reserving one-third of party tickets for women to enhance their participation in politics and decision-making bodies. *(1 M)*

Topper's Explanation **(CBSE, 2022 Term 2)**

Q3) (b) Some reforms taken to strengthen parties in India so that they can perform their function well, are:-

1. ANTI-DEFLECTION LAW: Deflection refers to changing party alliance from the party on which one got elected to another party.
   (i) The law was changed in order to prevent MPs and MLAs from changing party alliance to become ministers or for cash rewards.
   (ii) Any MP or MLA who changes party alliance loses his/her seat in the legislative.
   (iii) While this has strengthened democracy it has also made dissent more difficult.

2. AFFIDAVIT: (i) Affidavit is a signed document submitted to an officer in which the person makes a sworn statement regarding his/her personal information.
   (ii) The Supreme Court passed an order making it compulsary for the elected representatives to file an

3. INCOME TAX: An order was passed to make it compulsary for parties to hold their organisational elections and file their income tax returns.

4. INTERNAL AFFAIR REGULATION: Political parties must:
   (i) maintain a register of their members
   (ii) have their own formal constitution
   (iii) act as a judge in case of internal disputes
   (iv) have an independent format authority
   (v) hold open and transparent elections to the highest posts.

5. RESERVATION: About one-third seats should be reserved for women candidates.

6. GOVERNMENT SUPPORT: The governments should provide support to parties for election campaign in cash or kind.

PEOPLE'S PARTICIPATION: People can help strengthen political parties by:
   (i) protests and rallies
   (ii) joining parties themselves

MISCELLANEOUS EXERCISE

Multiple Choice Questions

(1 M)

1. Choose the country having the multi party system from the following options *(Re)*

(*a*) United Kingdom (*b*) USA
(*c*) India (*d*) China

2. Choose the right option to fill in the blank.

The emergence of ____________ is directly connected to the rise of political parties. *(Re)* **(CBSE SQP 2024)**

(*a*) Monitory democracies
(*b*) Direct democracies
(*c*) Representative democracies
(*d*) Constitutional democracies

3. Which of the following statements Is correct keeping the requirement of formation of government? *(An)* **(CBSE SQP 2024)**

Statement I: It is possible for independent candidates to form a government.

Statement II: Government formation is exclusively reserved for political parties.

Statement III: The formation of government is limited to only elected political parties.

Statement IV: Government can only be formed by political parties that are elected and hold a majority.

Options:

(*a*) Statement (i) and (ii) are right.
(*b*) Statement (i), (ii) and (iii) are right.
(*c*) Statement (iii) is right.
(*d*) Statement (iv) is right.

4. Indian National Congress is a ________. *(Re)*

(*a*) National Party (*b*) Regional Party
(*c*) Local Party (*d*) International Party

5. Which one of the following countries has two-party system? *(Re)* **(CBSE, 2024)**

(*a*) China (*b*) United Kingdom
(*c*) India (*d*) Pakistan

6. The party wants to build a strong India by drawing inspiration from India's ancient culture and values ________. *(Re)*

(*a*) INC (*b*) BJP
(*c*) BSP (*d*) Akali Dal

7. In a country, a constitutional reform has been proposed to transition from a multi-party system to a one-party system. Proponents argue that this will create unity and streamline governance, while critics argue that it undermines the fundamental democratic principle of choice and competition in policy-making. Read the statement given by proponents and critique and choose the correct options while keeping India's diversity in mind: *(Ev)*

Statements-I: A one-party system is a good democratic option.

Statements-II: Political parties in a democracy put forth different programs and policies for voters to choose from.

(*a*) Statements-I and Statements-II are Correct
(*b*) Statements-I and Statements-II are Incorrect
(*c*) Statements-I is Correct but Statements-II is Incorrect.
(*d*) Statements-I is Incorrect but Statements-II is Correct.

8. A person who is strongly committed to a party, group or faction. *(Un)*

(*a*) Partisan (*b*) Leader
(*c*) Partite (*d*) None of these

9. During an election period, a political party decides to utilize digital platforms extensively for campaigning rather than traditional methods due to a ban on wall writing by the election commission. Considering their strategy, evaluate the following statements: *(Ev)*

(*i*) The use of digital platforms allows for targeted messaging and analytics-driven campaigning.
(*ii*) Traditional campaigning methods are more effective and reach a wider audience than digital campaigns.
(*iii*) Digital campaigning could potentially exclude voters in regions with limited internet access.

Which of the statements are correct?

(*a*) (*i*) and (*ii*) only (*b*) only (*ii*)
(*c*) (*i*) and (*iii*) only (*d*) (*i*), (*ii*), and (*iii*)

10. Vikram, a citizen from Uttar Pradesh, decided to support a new regional political party that promises to focus on local issues and governance. The rise of such regional parties has been observed in many states. *(Ev)*
What could be the possible implication of such situation?

(*a*) Diminished influence of national parties, affecting their ability to implement nationwide policies.
(*b*) Increased political fragmentation, making it challenging to form stable governments.
(*c*) Enhanced focus on regional issues, potentially leading to effective local governance.
(*d*) Improved representation of regional interests, potentially leading to more equitable national policies.

11. In India, political parties play a crucial role in shaping the democratic process. However, the dominance of a few major political parties often leads to criticisms. Which of the following is a likely reason for such criticism? *(An)*

(*a*) Enhanced democratic representation
(*b*) Increased policy diversity
(*c*) Reduced effective opposition
(*d*) Improved governmental transparency

12. Changing party allegiance from the party on which a person got elected (to a legislative body) to a different party is called. **(Re)**

(a) Defection (b) Diversion
(c) Separation (d) Cancellation

13. Who among the following is the founder of the Bahujan Samaj Party? **(Re)**

(a) Kanshi Ram (b) Sahu Maharaj
(c) B.R. Ambedkar (d) Jyotiba Phule

Assertion and Reason **(1 M)**

Direction: The following questions consist of two statements – Assertion (A) and Reason (R). Answer these questions by selecting the appropriate option given below:

(a) Both A and R are true, and R is the correct explanation of A.
(b) Both A and R are true, but R is not the correct explanation of A.
(c) A is true, but R is false
(d) A is false, but R is true.

1. **Assertion (A):** National parties are compelled to form alliances with state parties when they do not secure a majority in Lok Sabha.
Reason (R): This does not contribute to the strengthening of federalism and democracy in our country. **(Un)**

2. **Assertion (A):** Political parties are essential for representing diverse opinions and interests in a democracy.
Reason (R): The effectiveness of a democracy is often undermined by factionalism and partisanship within political parties. **(Ev)**

3. **Assertion (A):** Democrats are worried about the increasing role of rich people and big companies in democratic politics.
Reason (R): Rich people and companies that give funds to the parties tend to have influence on the policies and decisions of the party. **(An)**

4. **Assertion (A):** Many elected representatives were indulging in Defection.
Reason (R): Defection brings political stability. **(An)**

5. **Assertion (A):** The challenges parties face is lack of internal democracy within parties.
Reason (R): Very often parties do not seem to offer a meaningful choice to the voters **(An)**

Subjective Questions

Very Short Answer Type Questions **(1 or 2 M)**

1. Why one-party system is not considered a good democratic system? **(An)**
2. Correct the following statement and rewrite it: Bahujan Samaj Party(BSP) was formed under the leadership of Mayawati. **(Ap)(CBSE, 2020)**
3. Ms. Gupta observes that in her village, political parties are deeply involved in creating social divisions, often influencing elections through caste-based politics. How can Ms. Gupta and her fellow villagers work towards reducing this influence and promoting unity? **(Cr)**
4. Examine the possible consequences on the basic rights of party members within political organisations that lack internal democracy. **(An) (CBSE SQP 2024)**
5. How is one-party system different from two-party system? Explain with examples. **(Re)(CBSE, 2022 Term 2)**
6. Suggest any one way to make political parties more responsive to the people's need and demand. **(Cr)(CBSE, 2020)**

Short Answer Type Questions **(3 M)**

1. Describe any three main features of Multi-Party system **(Un)**
2. How are political parties recognized as regional and national parties in India? Explain with examples. **(Ap)(CBSE, 2019)**
3. Imagine you are a member of a committee tasked with evaluating recent efforts to reform political parties in India. In your report, describe the main reform measures introduced to improve political parties in India. How have these reforms bring the transparency, accountability, and effectiveness in political parties? **(Cr)**
4. How does the dynastic succession affect political parties? **(Un)**
5. How do state or regional political parties contribute in strengthening federalism and democracy in India? Explain with examples **(Ap)**
6. Explain, how the rise of political parties is directly linked to the emergence of representative democracies. **(Ap)(CBSE, 2022 Term 2)**
7. Why are political parties considered essential in modern representative democracies? **(Ap)**

Long Answer Type Questions **(5 M)**

1. "Examine any five major challenges faced by the political parties in India. **(An) (CBSE, 2022 Term 2)**
2. "Political parties play an important role in democratic countries." Justify the statement. **(Ev) (CBSE, 2022 Term 2)**
3. Analyse the role of a multi-party system in a democratic country like India. **(An) (CBSE SQP 2024)**
4. Evaluate the significant distinction between the national and regional parties and assess the requirements for a regional party to become a national party. **(Ev) (CBSE SQP 2024)**

5. Describe the necessity of political parties in democratic countries. *(Un)* **(CBSE, 2020)**

6. A recent study has highlighted significant discontent among the lower and mid-level members of the major political parties. These members express frustration over their limited influence in decision-making processes, which are predominantly controlled by a small group of top leaders. This situation has sparked debates on the effectiveness and democratic nature of these parties.

   Given the situation, why is the lack of internal democracy within political parties considered a challenge to India's democracy? If it persists what could be its implication? *(An)*

7. Describe any five functions of political party. *(Re)* **(CBSE, 2020)**

Case Based Questions

Case Based-I

Read the Following Source and answer the questions that follow:

Political parties are easily one of the most visible institutions in a democracy. For most ordinary citizens, democracy is equal to political parties. If you travel to remote parts of our country and speak to the less educated citizens, you could come across people who may not know anything about our Constitution or about the nature of our government. But chances are that they would know something about our political parties. At the same time, this visibility does not mean popularity. Most people tend to be very critical of political parties. They tend to blame parties for all that is wrong with our democracy and our political life. Parties have become identified with social and political divisions.

(i) Why have political parties become the most visible institutions in a democracy? *(Un)*

(ii) How do political parties contribute to both the functioning and the criticism of democratic systems? *(An)*

(iii) What is the general perception of political parties among ordinary citizens, and why? *(Un)*

Case Based-II

Read the Following Source and answer the questions that follow:

A political party is a group of people who come together to contest elections and hold power in the government. They agree on some policies and programs for society to promote the collective good. Since there can be different views on what is good for all, parties try to persuade people why their policies are better than others. They seek to implement these policies by winning popular support through elections.

(i) What is the main purpose of a political party? *(Un)*

(ii) Why do political parties try to persuade people about their policies? *(Ap)*

(iii) How do political parties seek to implement their policies? *(Ap)*

Case Based-III

Read the Following Source and answer the questions that follow:

Recent Efforts to Reform Political Parties

The Constitution was amended to prevent elected MLAs and MPs from changing parties. This was done because many elected representatives were indulging in DEFECTION in order to become ministers or for cash rewards. Now the law says that if any MLA or MP changes parties, he or she will lose the seat in the legislature. This new law 'has helped bring defection down. At the same time, this has made any dissent even more difficult. MPs and MLAs have to 'accept whatever the party leaders decide. The Supreme Court passed an order to reduce the influence of money and criminals. Now, it is mandatory for every candidate who contests elections to file an affidavit giving details of his property and criminal cases pending against him. The new system has made a lot of information available to the public. But there is no system of checking if the information given by the candidates is true.

(i) Why was the anti-defection law implemented? *(Un)*

(ii) Discuss the dual impact of the anti-defection law in terms of reducing political defections and its impact on democratic dissent within parties. *(An)*

(iii) What was the Supreme Court's order regarding candidates contesting elections, and what has been the effect of this order? *(Un)*

ANSWER KEYS

Multiple Choice Questions

1 (*c*)	2. (*c*)	3. (*d*)	4. (*a*)	5. (*b*)	6. (*b*)	7. (*d*)	8. (*a*)	9. (*c*)	10. (*c*)
11. (*c*)	12. (*a*)	13. (*a*)							

Assertion and Reason

1 (*c*)	2. (*b*)	3. (*a*)	4. (*c*)	5. (*b*)

HINTS & EXPLANATIONS

Multiple Choice Questions

1. (*c*) India has the multi party system.
2. (*c*) The emergence of representative democracies is directly connected to the rise of political parties.
3. (*d*) Statement (iv) is right.
4. (*a*) The Indian National Congress (INC) is a national party.
5. (*b*) United Kingdom
6. (*b*) BJP wants to build a strong India by drawing inspiration from India's ancient culture and values.
7. (*d*) Keeping India in mind, Statement I is incorrect because it limits diverse representation, which is very crucial for maintaining peace, harmony, stability, and unity in the country.
8. (*a*) Partisan is the person committed strongly to a party group or a faction.
9. (*c*) It is not necessarily true that traditional methods reach a wider audience when compared to digital campaigns. Additionally, It depends on various factors including the audience demographics and how much access they have to technology.
10. (*c*) The rise of regional political parties in India will lead to a stronger focus on local issues, as these parties aim to address the specific needs and concerns of their regions to gain popular support in elections, leading to effective local governance.
11. (*c*) The dominance of a few major political parties leads to reduced effective opposition, limiting diverse perspectives and scrutiny. This concentration of power weakens the ability to hold the government accountable.
12. (*a*) Defection means switching political parties from the one in which a person was elected to a new one.
13. (*a*) Bahujan Samaj Party was formed in 1984 under the leadership of Kanshi Ram.

Assertion and Reason

1. (*c*) National parties do form alliances when needed, but these alliances often help strengthen democracy and federalism by including diverse interests.
2. (*b*) Both A and R are true, but R does not explain A.
3. (*a*) Self-explanatory
4. (*c*) Defection is often criticized for undermining political stability rather than enhancing it. It can lead to unstable governments, frequent no-confidence motions can erode public trust in the political system. The Anti-Defection Law in India was enacted to prevent such instability by discouraging defection.
5. (*b*) Both A and R are true, but R is not the correct explanation of A as lack of internal democracy is a different issue from the lack of meaningful choices for voters.

Subjective Questions

Very Short Answer Type Questions

1. A one-party system is not good for democracy because: **(Any One)**
   - **Lack of Choice:** In a one-party system, people do not have the option to choose between different political parties. Only one party controls the government, which is against the democratic principle of free competition. *(2 M)*
   - **Risk of Dictatorship:** Since there is no opposition, the ruling party can misuse power, make unfair laws, and suppress different opinions. This can lead to authoritarian rule, as seen in China. *(2 M)*
2. The Bahujan Samaj Party (BSP) was established by Kanshi Ram, not Mayawati. It was founded in 1984, with the aims to represent and empower the Dalits, Adivasis, OBCs, and religious minorities, advocating for their rights and welfare. *(2 M)*

3. Ms. Gupta and her fellow villagers can take these steps to reduce the bad influence and promote unity: **(Any two)**

- **Promote Awareness:** Educate villagers about the importance of voting based on issues rather than caste, helping them make informed decisions. *(1 M)*
- **Encourage Dialogue:** Organize community meetings to discuss and address social divisions, fostering unity and mutual understanding. *(1 M)*
- **Support Development-Focused Candidates:** In elections, support the candidates who focus on development and inclusivity rather than divisive politics. *(1 M)*

4. In political organisations that lack internal democracy, the basic rights of party members are often compromised. The possible consequences include: **(Any two)**

- **Lack of Participation:** Power remains concentrated in the hands of a few leaders, making it difficult for members to voice concerns or challenge leadership decisions. *(1 M)*
- **Lack of Transparency:** Ordinary members do not have access to information or influence in decision-making. *(1 M)*
- **Right to Equality of Opportunity:** Due to the absence of fair internal elections, not everyone would get an equal chance to rise within the party as leadership positions often remain within certain families or groups, preventing talented and deserving members from rising. *(1 M)*

5. Differences between one-party and two-party system follows: **(Any two)**

One-party system	Two-party system
A one-party system is a political system in which only one political party is allowed to hold power.	In contrast, a two-party system is a political system in which two major parties compete for power.
There is no competition or choice for the voters, and the ruling party has unchecked power.	In a two-party system, the parties offer different political ideologies and policies, and the voters have a choice between them.
Examples of countries with one-party systems include China and North Korea.	Examples of countries with two-party systems include the United States and the United Kingdom.

(1 + 1 = 2 M)

6. One way to make political parties more responsive is by enforcing internal democracy. If parties hold regular elections and listen to their members, it will bring diverse viewpoint in governance, leading to better governance and decision-making. *(2 M)*

Short Answer Type Questions

1. The following are the features of a multi-party system:

- **Multiple Parties Compete for Power:** In a multiparty system, several political parties compete for power. This allows voters to choose from a variety of parties that represent different interests and views. *(1 M)*
- **Coalition Governments:** Since no single party usually gets a clear majority in a multiparty system, coalitions are formed. This means different parties join together to run the government. *(1 M)*
- **Diverse Representation:** This system allows for the representation of diverse social, cultural, and regional groups, ensuring that more people have a voice in the government. *(1 M)*

2. Political parties in India are recognized as regional or national based on criteria set by the Election Commission of India. The recognition process is:

- **National Party:** A party is recognized as a national party if it secures at least 6% of the total votes in Lok Sabha elections or Assembly elections in four or more states and wins at least four Lok Sabha seats. Example: Bharatiya Janata Party (BJP). *(1½ M)*
- **State Party (Regional Party):** A party is recognized as a state party if it secures at least 6% of the total votes in Legislative Assembly elections of a state and wins at least two seats. Example: Samajwadi Party (SP) in Uttar Pradesh. *(1½ M)*

3. Some efforts to reform the political parties in India are:

- **Anti-Defection Law:** An amendment to the Constitution was made to prevent elected MLAs and MPs from switching parties, reducing defection for personal gain and enhancing effectiveness in governance by maintaining political stability. *(1 M)*
- **Supreme Court Mandate:** The Supreme Court passed an order that says Candidates must disclose their assets and criminal cases against them, increasing transparency. *(1 M)*
- **Election Commission Order:** Political parties must conduct organizational elections and file income tax returns, promoting internal democracy and financial accountability. *(1 M)*

4. Dynastic succession affect political parties in the following ways:

- **Limited Leadership Choice:** When political power is passed down within a family, it limits opportunities for others with fresh ideas or experience to lead. *(1 M)*
- **Weakening Democracy:** It can reduce the democratic nature of a party, as decisions may focus on maintaining power within the family rather than serving the people's interests. *(1 M)*

- **Unfair Advantage:** Family members often get top positions regardless of their ability or popularity, leading to policies that may favor personal interests over public needs. *(1 M)*

5. State and regional political parties play a crucial role in strengthening federalism and democracy in India. Their contribution can be understood through the following points:
   - **Promoting Regional Interests:** State parties focus on local issues and ensure that regional voices are heard at the national level. *(1 M)*
   - **Strengthening Federalism:** Coalition governments often rely on regional parties, strengthening federalism and leading to more balanced decision-making. *(1 M)*
   - **Encouraging Political Diversity:** With multiple regional parties, elections become more competitive, giving voters wider choices. This enhances democracy by ensuring better representation. *(1 M)*

6. The rise of political parties is directly linked to the emergence of representative democracies because: **(Any three)**
   - **Need for Representation:** As societies grew larger and more complex, direct democracy became impractical, and it became necessary to have representatives who could voice diverse opinions and interests. *(1 M)*
   - **Formation of Responsible Government:** Political parties help in forming structured governments by grouping representatives with common policies and ideologies, ensuring stability and accountability in governance. *(1 M)*
   - **Link between People and Government:** Political parties connect citizens with the government, providing a platform to express demands, participate in decision-making, and access welfare schemes. *(1 M)*
   - **Formation of Government:** Political parties help in forming and running governments by recruiting leaders, contesting elections, and implementing policies. Without political parties, governance would lack stability and organization. *(1 M)*
   - **Policy Formation and Decision-Making:** Parties group similar views and interests together, simplifying complex public opinions into clear policy directions, making governance efficient. *(1 M)*

7. Political parties are considered essential in modern representative democracies for several reasons:
   - **Representation:** They organize diverse societal interests, providing a platform for various groups to be represented in the political process. *(1 M)*
   - **Governance:** Parties form governments, shape policies, and make crucial decisions that guide national direction. *(1 M)*
   - **Accountability:** They hold the government accountable, offering alternatives and facilitating public engagement and scrutiny. *(1 M)*

Long Answer Type Questions

1. The challenges faced by political parties are as under:
   - **Lack of internal democracy:** In political parties, a small number of people hold the majority of the power. In such situations, a party's other members are given no consideration. Few members who have grown excessively powerful take charge of all decisions. *(1 M)*
   - **Dynastic succession:** Families of political party members typically receive very easy entry. In these situations, the unqualified family members attend the party while the deserving are excluded. *(1 M)*
   - **Factionalism:** Factionalism within the party, which can lead to a lack of unity and unstable political system, leading to frequent change in the government. *(1 M)*
   - **Money and muscle power:** The influence of money and muscle power in elections, which leads to corruption and unfair practices. *(1 M)*
   - **Lack of Meaningful Choice:** Political parties often offers very similar polices, reducing meaningful options for the voters. *(1 M)*

2. Political parties play an essential role in democratic countries. Here are some justifications for the statement: **(Any five)**
   - **Ensures people's participation in decision making:** Political parties provide a platform for citizens to express their opinions and participate in the decision-making process. *(1 M)*
   - **Ensures efficient government:** Opposition parties criticise the government for its wrong policies and failures which helps to create a competitive political environment, which promotes accountable and effecient government. *(1 M)*
   - **Ensures representation:** Political parties ensures the representation of every section of the society. Political parties helps to represent diverse interests and view points. *(1 M)*
   - **Accountability:** Political parties make sure that leaders in charge are responsible for their actions. *(1 M)*
   - **Political education:** Political parties play an important role in political education as they help to educate citizens about the political process and the importance of participation. *(1 M)*
   - **Political stability:** Political parties help to promote political stability. They help to avoid situations of political instability and conflict that can arise in the absence of organised political parties. *(1 M)*

3. India follows a multi-party system, which plays a crucial role in its democratic framework:
   - **Representation of Diversity:** India is a diverse country with multiple languages, religions, and cultures. A multi-party system ensures that different social and regional interests are represented in governance. *(1 M)*

- **Encourages Political Competition:** It provides multiple choices to voters, leading to better governance as parties compete to gain public support. *(1 M)*
- **Prevents Dominance of a Single Party:** Unlike a one-party system, it prevents any single party from holding absolute power, ensuring checks and balances in governance. *(1 M)*
- **Coalition Governments:** When no party wins a majority, multiple parties join together to form a government through negotiation and discussion. *(1 M)*
- **Strengthens Federalism:** Regional parties play a key role in state politics, making governance more inclusive and effective at both national and state levels. *(1 M)*

4. Political parties in India are classified into national and regional parties based on their influence and reach.

- **National vs. Regional Reach:** National parties operate across multiple states and follow uniform policies, whereas regional parties focus on specific states and local issues. *(1 M)*
- **Representation in Elections:** National parties contest Lok Sabha elections nationwide, while regional parties primarily contest state elections. *(1 M)*
- **Recognition by Election Commission:** A national party must secure 6% of votes in at least four states and win four Lok Sabha seats, whereas a regional party needs 6% of votes and two seats in one state. *(1 M)*
- **Participation in Governance:** National parties contest both Lok Sabha and Assembly elections, while regional parties mainly focus on state elections but may support coalition governments at the center. *(1 M)*
- **Criteria for Becoming a National Party:** A regional party must secure at least 6% of the total votes in four or more states and win at least four Lok Sabha seats to gain national party status. *(1 M)*

5. Political parties are necessary for a democracy because they perform important functions that help in the smooth functioning of the government. Here are five key reasons why political parties are needed: **(Any five)**

- **Contest Elections:** Political parties select candidates and contest elections. For example, in India, parties like the BJP and Congress put forward candidates to run elections. *(1 M)*
- **Policy Making:** Parties propose different policies and programs. Voters choose from these during elections. *(1 M)*
- **Forming and Running Governments:** The party that wins the majority forms the government and makes policy decisions. *(1 M)*
- **Opposition Role:** Parties that do not win form the opposition, critiquing and providing alternatives to the government's policies. *(1 M)*
- **Access to Government:** Political parties often act as intermediaries between the government and the people, making it easier for citizens to get their issues addressed. *(1 M)*
- **Representation:** Political parties represent the interests and views of the people. They provide a platform for citizens to express their political opinions and preferences. *(1 M)*
- **Accountability:** Political parties hold the government accountable for its actions. They provide a check on the power of the government and ensure that the government acts in the best interests of the people. *(1 M)*
- **Political education:** Political parties educate people about the political issues and the policies of different parties. They help people make informed decisions about who to vote for and what policies to support. *(1 M)*

Topper's explanation **(CBSE, 2020)**

31) A political party is a group of people that come together to contest elections and hold power in the government. They agree on some policies and programmes for the society to promote the collective good.

Necessity of political parties:

-> The need for political parties can be seen in a situation where no political parties exist. Then, every candidate will be independent and will not be able to make a promise for any policies. They will be responsible for their own constituency but no one will be responsible for how the country is run.

-> For example, though no political parties exist officially in Panchayat elections, it can be seen that villages split up into some factions and each puts up its panel of candidates. This is what a political party does.

-> The emergence of political parties can be linked to representative democracy, as societies become large and complex.

-> People need some ways to elect representatives, bring people together to form a responsible government, form policies, support, reject them, and make laws for the country.

Hence there is a need for political parties in India.

6. (*b*) The lack of internal democracy within the political party is considered a challenge to India's democracy because:

- **Loss of Public Trust:** People might lose faith in democracy if they see that parties aren't fair internally. This can reduce participation and trust in the democratic process. *(1 M)*
- **Concentration of Power:** it centralizes power in the hands of a few leaders. This undermines democratic principles, as decisions are made without proper consultation and participation from the party members. *(1 M)*

Its Implications:

- **Risk of Political instability:** A persistent lack of internal democracy can lead to factionalism, where dissatisfied members may break away to form their own parties. *(1 M)*

- **Risk of Authoritarian Rule:** When power is concentrated in the hands of a few, it can lead to authoritarian behavior where leaders might ignore democratic norms and rule as they want. *(1 M)*
- **Ineffective Decision-Making:** Decisions made by a small group of top leaders may not reflect the needs and desires of the larger membership or electorate, leading to ineffective policies and a potential loss of voter support. *(1 M)*

7. Political parties perform several functions within a democratic system. The following are some of the functions of political parties:
   - **Contesting elections:** Political parties contest elections at all levels of government, from local to national. They choose candidates who represent their party and its views. *(1 M)*
   - **Forming government:** Political parties form government when they win elections. They take responsibility for governing and implementing policies and programs that benefit the people. *(1 M)*
   - **Representation:** Political parties represent the interests and views of the people. They provide a platform for citizens to express their political opinions and preferences. *(1 M)*
   - **Articulating policies:** Political parties articulate policies that reflect the views and interests of their members and supporters. They provide a vision for the country and set out a plan for achieving that vision. *(1 M)*
   - **Accountability:** Political parties hold the government accountable for its actions. They provide a check on the power of the government and ensure that the government acts in the best interests of the people. *(1 M)*

Case Based Questions

Case Based-I

(i) The political parties have become the most visible institution in democracy because they actively engage citizens in the political process, contest elections, and represent various interests, making them well-known even in remote areas. *(1 M)*

(ii) Political parties organize elections, represent diverse interests, and form governments, facilitating democratic system. However, they face criticism for fostering divisions, prioritizing their interests, and being involved in corruption and inefficiency. *(1 M)*

(iii)
- The general perception of political parties among ordinary citizens is often critical. People tend to blame political parties for the problems in democracy, associating them with social and political divisions. *(1 M)*
- This critical view arises because parties are seen as self-interested groups that prioritize their power and interests over the collective good of society. *(1 M)*

Case Based-II

(i) The main purpose of a political party is to contest elections, hold power in the government, and agree on policies and programs for society to promote the collective good. *(1 M)*

(ii) Political parties try to persuade people about their policies because they aim to show why their policies are better than other and seek to gain popular support and form government through elections. *(1 M)*

(iii) Political parties seek to implement their policies by winning popular support through elections. By gaining the trust and votes of the people, they can achieve the power needed to put their policies into action. *(2 M)*

Case Based-III

(i) The anti-defection law was implemented to curb elected representatives from switching parties for personal gain, such as becoming ministers or receiving cash rewards. *(1 M)*

(ii) The law against defection has made it harder for MLAs and MPs to switch parties, reducing political instability and corruption. However, it also makes it difficult for them to disagree with their party leaders, limiting their freedom to express different opinions or stand up against party decisions. *(1 M)*

(iii)
- The Supreme Court mandated that every candidate must file an affidavit disclosing their property and pending criminal cases against him. *(1 M)*
- This has increased transparency by providing the public with detailed information about candidates. However, a limitation is that there is no system in place to verify the accuracy of the information provided. *(1 M)*

❑❑❑

OUTCOMES OF DEMOCRACY

5

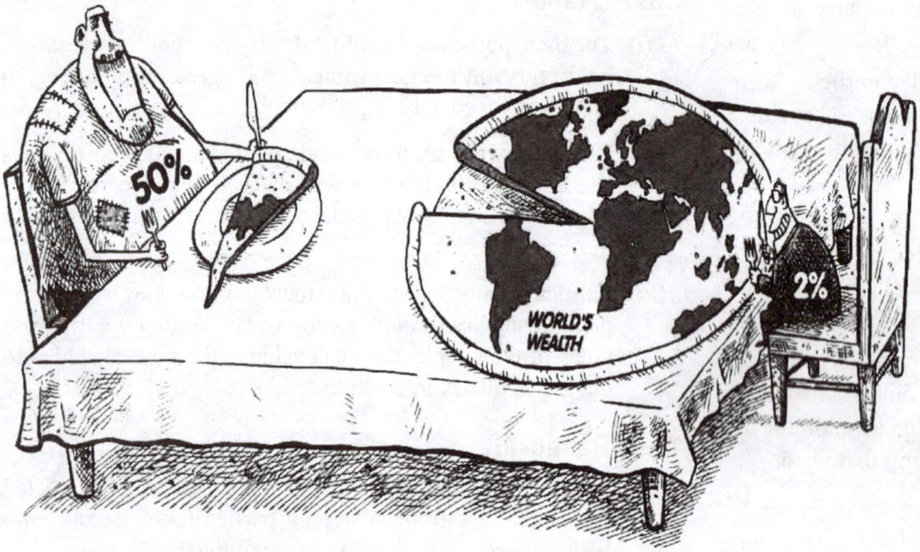

> "A nation will not survive morally or economically when so few have so much, while so many have so little."
> –Bernie Sanders

SYLLABUS & WEIGHTAGE

Concept Names	Years					
	2020	2021	2022	2023	2024	2025
Accountable, responsive and legitimate government	—	Exam not Conducted	—	1 Q (1 M)	1 Q (1 M) 1Q (5 M)	1 Q (3 M)
Economic growth and development & Reduction of inequality and poverty	—		1 Q (3 M)	—	1 Q (5 M)	—
Accommodation of social diversity & Dignity and freedom of citizens	1 Q (5 M)		—	1 Q (5 M)	—	—

CONCEPT MAP

To Access One Shot Revision Video Scan This QR Code

Democracy

Meaning: A form of government where citizen have the power to choose their leader and have a say in decisions affecting them.

Democracy Or Dictatorship — CBSE 2023, 2020

Democracy is better because dictatorships is often lack in:

- ❑ Promoting equality among
- ❑ Facilitating better decision-making
- ❑ Providing peaceful way to resolve conflicts
- ❑ Provision of correcting mistakes
- ❑ Improving dignity and freedom of people.

Outcomes of Democracy (CBSE 2024)

Political Outcomes (CBSE 2025, 2024)

Expectations (CBSE 2023)

- ❑ **Accountable government:** Answerable to the citizen for the actions taken.
- ❑ **Responsive government:** Consider the needs and expectations of the people in decision-making.
- ❑ **Transparency:** Citizens can examine all the actions/decisions taken by the government.
- ❑ **Elections:** Regular, free and fair elections.
- ❑ **Public Debates:** Open public debates on major policies and legislation
- ❑ **Political Equality:** All individual have equal weight in electing representatives
- ❑ **Corruption Free:** Democracy is supposed to be free from corruption.

Outcomes

- ❑ Successful in setting up regular and free elections, but falls short in providing fair chance to everyone in elections.
- ❑ Successful in setting up condition for open public debates, but falls short in subjective every decision to public debates.
- ❑ Do not show good record when it comes to sharing information with citizens.
- ❑ Democracy is not free from corruption.
- ❑ Successful in providing political equality

Economic Outcomes (CBSE 2022)

Expectations

- ❑ Democracy is expected to bring economic growth and development.
- ❑ Government keenly take up the problem of poverty.
- ❑ Democracy is expected to decrease the income disparity between the people.

Outcomes

- ❑ Democracy did not appear to be very successful in ensuring economic growth and development.
- ❑ Democratically elected governments do not appear to be as keen to address the question of poverty as one may expect.
- ❑ Many democracies have failed in reducing economic disparities.

Social Outcomes (CBSE 2025, 2023, 2022)

Expectations (CBSE 2022)

- ❑ Accommodation of Social Diversity- Proper handling of social difference, divisions and conflicts
- ❑ Dignity and Freedom of People- Respect and freedom of every individual living in the country.
- ❑ Equal treatment of women- Equal treatment of women in society and treating them with respect.
- ❑ Equal status of all castes- Respect and equal position in society to the backward classes.

Outcomes

- ❑ Democracy stands much superior to any to any other form of government in promoting dignity and freedom of the individual.
- ❑ Democracy accommodates social diversity.

1 HOW DO WE ASSESS DEMOCRACY'S OUTCOMES? & ACCOUNTABLE, RESPONSIVE, AND LEGITIMATE GOVERNMENT

NCERT Definitions *(Commonly asked in 1 mark)*

- **Democracy:** A form of government where people have the power to choose their leaders and have a say in decisions affecting them. It aims to treat everyone equally and fairly, enhancing individual dignity and improving decision-making quality.
- **Accountable Government:** An accountable government is one where government officials are responsible to citizens, ensuring their actions and decisions meet the needs and rights of the community, and are open to scrutiny.
- **Responsive Government:** A responsive government is one that listens to its citizens, considering their needs and expectations in decision-making. This ensures policies and actions reflect the public's interests and demands.
- **Legitimate Government:** A legitimate government is one that is accepted by its people as lawful and right, established through democratic elections. It has the authority to govern because it follows established laws and has the consent of the people.
- **Transparency:** This means the government's actions are open to the public. In a democracy, citizens have the right to know what decisions are being made and how those decisions are made.

Important Facts

01 The process of decision-making in democracies, is slower due to deliberation and negotiation, but considered more acceptable and effective.

02 Democracies are not guaranteed to be free from corruption, but they are expected to develop better mechanisms for accountability than non-democracies.

Difference Between

Accountable, Responsive and Legitimate Government			
Feature	**Accountable Government**	**Responsive Government**	**Legitimate Government**
Definition	Government officials are answerable for their actions and decisions to the people.	Government meets the needs and expectations of its citizens.	Government is recognized as rightful and just by its citizens.
How it Works	Through mechanisms like elections, and public forums where officials must explain and defend their actions.	By actively listening to citizen's needs and promptly addressing them through policies and services.	Through fair elections. Where citizens feel their government is their own choice.
Importance	Ensures transparency and ensures officials don't misuse their power.	Makes sure the government's actions align with the people's needs and welfare.	Builds trust and support among the people for the government's authority and decisions.
Example	Citizens using Right to Information laws to check on government activities.	Government adjusting policies based on public feedback or crisis response.	High voter turnout in elections showing people's support and belief in their government's system.

Democratic Vs. Non-Democratic Regime (In respect of accountable, responsive and legitimate government)		
Aspect	**Democratic Regimes**	**Non-Democratic Regimes**
Decision-Making Speed	**Slower** due to deliberation and negotiation.	**Faster** as it doesn't involve deliberation in assemblies or concern for public opinion.
Efficiency and Effectiveness	May take more time but decisions are more acceptable to people and can be more effective.	Quick decisions but may not be accepted by the people, leading to problems.
Transparency	**High transparency**; citizens can examine decision-making processes.	Often **lacks transparency**; decision-making processes are not open to scrutiny.
Accountability and Participation	Government is accountable; mechanisms exist for citizen participation.	Lack of accountability and limited to no mechanisms for citizen participation.
Elections and Public Debate	Regular, free elections and open public debate are common.	Lacks free elections and open public debate.
Fairness in Elections	Strives for fair elections but often falls short in providing a fair chance to everyone.	Does not prioritize fair elections or equal opportunities.
Legitimacy	Seen as **legitimate** because it is the people's own government.	**Lacks legitimacy**; not seen as the people's own government.
Support and Suitability	**High support globally**; seen as suitable for their country by its citizens.	**Lacks support**; people prefer democracy for their countries.

Real Life Application Based Questions

1. **How can a citizen in a democracy verify that a decision was made through the correct procedures?**

Ans. Democracies ensure decisions are transparent. By utilising the laws like the Right to Information Act a citizen can inquire about the progress and procedures involved in decision-making.

2. **How can democracies better involve citizens in the decision-making process on major policies?**

Ans. (*i*) Holding regular public consultations and hearings on major policy proposals allows citizens to voice their opinions directly.

(*ii*) Using digital platforms to collect feedback, conduct polls, and enable discussions on policy matters can make participation more accessible to all citizens.

Myth Buster

- **Myth:** Democracy can address all socio-economic and political problems.

  Fact: Democracy is just a form of government. It can only create conditions for achieving something. The citizens have to take advantage of those conditions to overcome problems or achieve some goals.

- **Myth:** Non-Democratic system are better as democracies are inherently inefficient and slow in decision-making.

  Fact: Democratic processes involve deliberation and negotiation leading to some delays, but this approach ensures that decisions are more acceptable to people. In democracies, leaders have to answer to the people which often lead to more sustainable and inclusive outcomes than in non-democratic systems.

Scan Me for Detailed Explanations

COMPETENCY BASED SOLVED EXAMPLES

Multiple Choice Questions (1 M)

1. **Based on the cartoon "Governmental Secrecy", which outcome of democracy is most critically highlighted by the cartoon, and what does it suggest about the relationship between the government and its citizens?** *(An)*

Governmental Secrecy

(*a*) The cartoon suggests that democracies are completely transparent, with no secrecy between the government and its citizens, ensuring full accountability.

(*b*) The cartoon indicates that democracies are highly efficient in sharing all information with citizens, thus eliminating any form of secrecy.

(*c*) The cartoon highlights that despite the principles of democracy, there is often a significant gap in transparency, with the government knowing much more about its citizens than the citizens know about governmental activities.

(*d*) The cartoon shows that in democracies, citizens have more information about the government than the government has about them, ensuring complete transparency.

2. _________ is the democracy in which the citizens elect their representatives. ***(Re)***

(*a*) Direct democracy (*b*) Indirect democracy

(*c*) Dictatorship (*d*) None of these

3. Imagine you are a journalist in a country transitioning to a democratic system. You have been invited to write an article assessing the success of this new democracy. While preparing for your article, you come across various aspects of the new government's functioning. Which aspect would you highlight as a potential threat to the democratic process? ***(An)***

(*a*) The government holds regular, free, and fair elections.

(*b*) Citizens actively participate in public debates on major policies.

(*c*) The government exercises centralized control over media.

(*d*) Citizens have the right to access information about government functioning.

4. Which of the following would be the most effective measure to assess whether democracy is functioning effectively in terms of being accountable, responsive, and legitimate? ***(Ev)***

(*a*) Monitoring the luxury lifestyles of elected officials to ensure they are not engaging in corrupt practices.

(*b*) Ensuring that all governmental decisions are made swiftly, without public debate or consultation.

(*c*) Establishing mechanisms such as regular, free, and fair elections, and the citizens' right to information about governmental functioning.

(*d*) Comparing the economic growth rates of democratic governments with those of non-democratic governments.

5. Which of the following is NOT a reason why democratic governments are considered legitimate? ***(Re)***

(*a*) They are elected by the people.

(*b*) They are faster in decision-making than autocracies.

(*c*) They are more likely to adhere to procedural norms.

(*d*) They are considered people's government.

6. "A government must ensure that the majority group does not make all the decisions and becomes a superior social group." ***(Ap)***

Which of the following questions BEST aligns with the suggestion given above?

(*a*) "How can a government increase the political participation of its citizens?"

(*b*) "What can be done to ensure the economic development of the country?"

(*c*) "What can the leaders do to ensure that citizens' diversity is respected?"

(*d*) "How can you make sure free and fair elections are conducted?"

Assertion and Reason

(1 M)

Direction: The following questions consist of two statements – Assertion (A) and Reason (R). Answer these questions by selecting the appropriate option given below:

(*a*) Both A and R are true, and R is the correct explanation of A.

(*b*) Both A and R are true, but R is not the correct explanation of A.

(*c*) A is true, but R is false

(*d*) A is false, but R is true.

1. Assertion (A): Democracy is a legitimate government.

Reason (R): Regular, free and fair elections are the spirit of democracy. ***(Ap)*(CBSE, 2020)**

2. Assertion (A): Responsiveness is an important characteristic of a democratic government.

Reason (R): A responsive government listens to the needs and concerns of its citizens, and takes appropriate action to address them. ***(Un)***

3. Assertion (A): Legitimacy is essential for a government to function effectively.

Reason (R): A legitimate government has the support and trust of its citizens, which allows it to make decisions and implement policies with greater ease. ***(Ap)***

4. Assertion (A): Democracies are based on political inequality.

Reason (R): All individuals have equal say in electing representatives. ***(Un)***

5. Assertion (A): Democracies are preferred because they provide a framework where the government is accountable and responsive to its citizens.

Reason (R): In democracies, the public has mechanisms to participate in decision-making and hold the government accountable through regular and free elections. ***(Ev)***

Subjective Questions

Very Short Answer Type Questions

(2 M)

1. Analyze the public perception of democracy versus dictatorship in South Asia by analyzing the picture. What conclusions can be drawn about the overall support for democracy in this region? ***(An)***

	Bangla-desh	India	Nepal	Pakistan	Sri Lanka
■ Democracy is preferable	69	70	62	37	71

Sometimes dictatorship is better	6	9	10	14	11
Doesn't matter to me	25	21	29	49	18

Source: *SDSA Team, State of Democracy in South Asia, Delhi Oxford University Press, 2007*

Ans. The data shows that:

(*i*) Democracy is overwhelmingly preferred in South Asia, considering it suitable for their countries. *(1 M)*

(*ii*) The preference for democracy is highest in Sri Lanka (71%) and Bangladesh (69%) and lowest in the pakistan where only 37% prefer democracy. *(1 M)*

2. Why do some people believe that democracy is less effecient? ***(An)***

Ans. Democracy is sometimes seen as less effective because it requires a lot of discussion and agreement among many people, which can take a lot of time. Though democracy is slow when compared to other form of government but people consider it good as the decisions made are more sustainable and inclusive. *(2 M)*

3. What is the key advantage of democratic government over alternatives? ***(Un)***

Ans. The main advantage of a democratic government over alternatives is its legitimacy. It's chosen by the people, making it truly "the people's government." This ensures rulers are accountable and responsive to the citizens, promoting a sense of ownership and participation among the citizens. *(2 M)*

Short Answer Type Questions (3 M)

1. Read the sources given below and answer the questions that follow: **(CBSE, 2020)**

Over a hundred countries of the world today claim and practice some kind of democratic politics: they have formal constitutions, they hold elections, they have parties and they guarantee rights of citizens. While these features are common to most of them, these democracies are very much different from each other in terms of their social situations, their economic achievements and their cultures. Clearly, what may be achieved or not achieved under each of these democracies will be very different.

(*i*) Explain the fascination for democracy amongst various countries. ***(Un)***

(*ii*) Explain democracy on the basis of expected and actual outcome. ***(An)***

Ans. (*i*) People are fascinated by democracy because it gives them the power to choose their leaders and have a say in important decisions. This idea of having a voice in how your country is run attracts the countries worldwide, regardless of their differences. *(1 M)*

(*ii*) **Expected vs. Actual Outcomes of Democracy:**

- **Expected Outcomes:** In a democracy, people expect fair and free elections, protection of rights, and governments that listen to them. They hope for equality, better living conditions, and freedom. *(1 M)*
- **Actual Outcomes:** In reality, while democracies do hold elections and have laws to protect people's rights, not all are equally successful. Some countries do better in making sure everyone is heard and taken care of, but others might struggle with issues like inequality or not being able to respond quickly to people's needs. *(1 M)*

2. A social scientist conducted a study on the global acceptance of different political systems. He gathered survey data from various countries, showing a strong preference for democracy over other forms of government. Analyze why democracy is overwhelmingly supported worldwide. Consider the various factors that contribute to its global acceptance. ***(An)***

Ans. Democracy is widely favored globally because:

(*i*) It promotes equality, ensures citizen participation in governance, and upholds individual dignity. *(1 M)*

(*ii*) It also allows people to choose their leaders and influence decisions. *(1 M)*

(*iii*) The fundamental principles of democracy, such as freedom and equality, gain strong support worldwide, making it a preferred form of government over alternatives like dictatorship or authoritarian regimes. *(1 M)*

Long Answer Type Questions (5 M)

1. "Democracy's ability to generate its own support is also its outcome and it cannot be ignored." Explain the statement. ***(Un)*****(CBSE, 2022 Term 2)**

Ans. (*i*) Democracy's ability to generate its own support as an outcome signifies that people naturally value democratic principles and choose democracy over other forms of government. *(1 M)*

(*ii*) This preference is evident globally. People in various countries, regardless of whether they live in democratic or non-democratic regimes, tend to support the idea of democracy. *(1 M)*

(*iii*) People believe in having a government elected by them and feel that democracy suits their country. It reflects people's belief in democracy as a fair and just method of governance. *(1 M)*

(*iv*) Even when individuals criticize their democratic systems or express dissatisfaction with certain aspects, their engagement and demands for improvement further validate democracy's significance. *(1 M)*

(*v*) This continuous cycle of support, critique, and evolution underlines democracy's capacity to sustain and enhance itself. *(1 M)*

2. "Democracy produces an accountable, responsive and legitimate government." Support the statement with arguments. ***(Ev)*****(CBSE, 2023)**

OR

How does democracy produce an accountable, responsive and legitimate government? ***(Ev)*****(NCERT)**

Ans. Democracy produces an accountable, responsive, and legitimate government. It can be understood by the following arguments:

- **Accountable Government:** Democracy ensures that government officials are accountable to the people. Through regular elections and other mechanisms like the right to information, citizens can question, scrutinize, and replace their representatives, ensuring accountability. *(1¼ M)*

- **Responsive Government:** Democratic governments must be responsive to their citizens' needs and desires, ensuring that policies reflect public preferences and contribute to the common good. *(1¼ M)*
- **Legitimacy:** When people choose their leaders through voting, it makes the government more legitimate, strong, and respected. *(1¼ M)*
- **Public Participation:** Democracy encourages the participation of citizens in decision-making processes, ensuring that the government is responsive to their needs and aspirations to gain or maintain the support of the public. *(1¼ M)*

3. Why is Democratic Government considered as Legitimate Government? Explain. ***(Un)*(CBSE, 2023)**

or

How is democracy a legitimate government ? Explain with examples. ***(Un, An)* (CBSE, 2024)**

Ans. A democratic government is considered legitimate because,

- **Representation Through Election:** It is formed through the process of regular, free, and fair elections. This system ensures that the government is created by the choice of its people, making it their representative. *(1 M)*
- **Public Participation:** In a democracy, every citizen has the right to vote and influence the government's formation, giving it a strong basis of support and consent from the public. *(1 M)*
- **Accountability and Responsiveness:** Additionally, a democratic government is accountable and responsive to its citizens. It must listen to them, address their needs, and allow for participation in decision-making. *(1 M)*
- **Consent and Support:** This openness and inclusiveness increase people's trust and confidence in the government, further establishing its legitimacy. *(1 M)*
- **Openness and Inclusiveness:** Therefore, democracy is seen as a "government of the people, by the people, and for the people," which is why it gathers widespread approval and is considered legitimate. *(1 M)*

Topper's explanation **(CBSE, 2024)**

1. Democracy is a legitimate government because it comprises of a government which is freely and fairly elected by the citizens of the country. It gives prime importance to the people of the country who have a right to choose their leaders and participate in the decision making process whenever necessary.

2. It produces a fair, accountable government which is responsive to the needs of the citizens. All democratic governments are expected to follow fair rules and regulations and maintain transparency at all times. Free and fair elections are regularly conducted where people have a right to rectify their mistakes and are placed on an equal political footing.

3. Democracy enhances the dignity of an individual by following an accomodative policy with mutual respect for social differences. It is based on the idea of deliberation and negotiation to ensure that different views are heard and considered during policy formations.

4. Democracies might produce a slow, ineffecient government but at the end of the day, It is people's own government which raises the people from the status of object to citizens as they are able to rationalize and think for themselves. Power and rule of law, reason and justice are given supreme Importance

5. Democratic governments are concerned about the well being of the poorest of the poor and aim at reducing income disparities. They are able to generate immense support for themselves which is an open testimony to their legitimacy and credibility. They organise public debates and are accountable to the parliament for their actions.

2 ECONOMIC GROWTH AND DEVELOPMENT & REDUCTION OF INEQUALITY AND POVERTY

NCERT Definitions *(Commonly asked in 1 mark)*

- **Economic Growth:** Economic growth is when a country's production of goods and services increases over time.
- **Economic Development:** Economic development is about improving the well-being and quality of life of people in a country. It's not just about having more money or products; it's about making sure people have better health care, education, and jobs etc.
- **Economic Inequality:** Economic inequality refers to a situation when wealth or income is distributed unevenly among people in a society. Some people have a lot of money and resources, while others have very little.

Important Facts

01 Between 1950 and 2000, dictatorships have a slightly higher rate of economic growth.

02 Democracies are expected to reduce economic disparities. However, they have not been very successful in this area.

Evidence : Growing economic inequalities in many democratic regime

: In Bangladesh, more than half of its population lives in poverty.

Difference Between

Democracy Vs. Disctatorship

Aspect	Democracy	Dictatorship
Promotion of Equality	Democracies aim to promote equality among citizens	Dictatorships do not necessarily prioritize citizen equality.
Enhancing Dignity	Democracies enhance individual dignity by allowing freedoms and rights	Individual dignity may be compromised under dictatorship.
Decision-making Quality	Democratic decisions tend to involve more deliberation, which can improve quality but may take more time.	Dictatorships might make quicker but not always popular or well-considered decisions.
Conflict Resolution	Democracies provide mechanisms for resolving conflicts peacefully	Might suppress conflicts rather than resolving them, leading to long-term unrest.
Correction of Mistakes	Allows for correction through democratic processes like elections and judicial review.	Limited scope for correction, as disagreement is often not tolerated.

Myth Buster

- **Myth:** Democracies cannot achieve economic growth as effectively as dictatorships.

  Fact: The relationship between regime type and economic growth is not direct. Democracies provide a framework for stability, rights, and freedoms that can foster economic growth but the actual economic growth is mainly depends on the factors such as investment climate, policies adopted by the government of the country, global economic conditions, country's population size, cooperation from other countries, etc.

- **Myth:** High economic growth in democracies benefits all citizens equally.

  Fact: Economic growth in a democracy does not necessarily mean that the wealth is evenly distributed. Often, economic benefits are unevenly distributed which favor the wealthy, leaving others with minimal to no improvements in their living conditions.

- **Myth:** Democracy's success is only measured by economic performance.

  Fact: While economic performance is important, democracy's outcomes are also assessed through the quality of governance, the level of social equality, the extent of freedom and dignity provided to citizens, and the ability to accommodate social diversity.

- **Myth:** The evidence shows that a country should choose dictatorship regime over democracy for economic growth.

  Fact: The evidence does not conclusively favour dictatorships over democracies in terms of economic performance because the difference is negligible. Also, the type of regime is not solely responsible for economic growth.

COMPETENCY BASED SOLVED EXAMPLES

Scan Me for Detailed Explanations

Multiple Choice Questions

(1 M)

1. **Which of the following is NOT yet achieved from democracy?** *(An)*
   (*a*) Uniform benefit of economic growth across the country.
   (*b*) Enhances the dignity of the individual.
   (*c*) Provides a method to resolve conflicts.
   (*d*) Improves the quality of decision-making.

2. **Based on economic outcomes observed from 1950 to 2000, which statement accurately reflects the comparison between democracies and dictatorships regarding economic growth?** *(Re)*
   (*a*) Dictatorships consistently show lower rates of economic growth compared to democracies.
   (*b*) Democracies have a slightly higher rate of economic growth than dictatorships.
   (*c*) There is negligible difference in the rates of economic growth between poor countries under dictatorships and democracies.
   (*d*) Economic growth in democracies is directly correlated with the level of democratic participation.

3. **Based on the cartoon "The Rich Get Buff", what critical issue regarding economic growth and income distribution is highlighted?** *(An)*

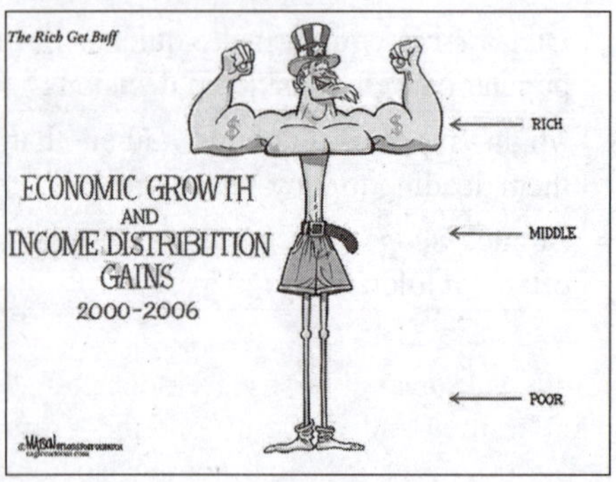

   (*a*) The cartoon suggests that economic growth is evenly distributed across all social classes.
   (*b*) The cartoon highlights the problem of income inequality, with the wealthy benefitting disproportionately from economic growth.
   (*c*) The cartoon indicates that the middle class benefits the most from economic growth.
   (*d*) The cartoon shows that economic growth primarily benefits the poor.

4. **"Democracies often struggle with economic inequalities, with a significant portion of wealth concentrated among a small segment of the population, despite being based on political equality."** *(An)*

   Which statement best captures the dilemma faced by democracies regarding economic inequality?
   (*a*) Democracies are successful in eliminating economic inequalities among their citizens.
   (*b*) In democracies, economic growth automatically leads to the equitable distribution of wealth among all citizens.
   (*c*) Despite political equality, democracies face challenges in reducing economic disparities and ensuring equitable wealth distribution.
   (*d*) Economic disparities do not exist in democracies due to their inherent principle of equality among citizens.

Assertion and Reason

(1 M)

Direction: The following questions consist of two statements – Assertion (A) and Reason (R). Answer these questions by selecting the appropriate option given below:

(*a*) Both A and R are true, and R is the correct explanation of A.
(*b*) Both A and R are true, but R is not the correct explanation of A.
(*c*) A is true, but R is false.
(*d*) A is false, but R is true.

1. **Assertion (A):** Democracies are based on political equality.

   Reason (R): All individuals have equal weight in electing representative. *(Ev)*

2. **Assertion (A):** In democracies, economic growth does not always lead to the reduction of poverty.

   Reason (R): While democracies promote political equality and provide mechanisms for accountability, they do not guarantee the equitable distribution of economic gains, which is necessary for substantial poverty reduction. *(Ev)*

3. **Assertion (A):** In poor countries, the rate of economic growth under dictatorships and democracies is drastic.

Reason (R): The form of governance does not directly determine a country's economic growth rate, which is influenced by external and internal factors. *(Un)*

4. **Assertion (A):** Democracies have not always succeeded in reducing economic inequalities among their citizens.

   Reason (R): Despite economic growth, wealth distribution in democracies often remains uneven, with a significant portion of wealth concentrated among a small segment of the population. *(Ev)*

5. **Assertion (A):** Economic growth and development is a desirable outcome of democracy.

   Reason (R): Democracy provides a conducive environment for economic progress and prosperity. *(An)*

Subjective Questions

Very Short Answer Type Questions (2 M)

1. **Can democracy reduce economic inequality? Give reasons for your answer.** *(Ev and Cr)*

Ans. Yes, democracy can reduce economic inequality because it provide a condusive environment for growth by ensuring stability, economic freedom etc. Democracies also ensures free and fair election where people can choose a leader who take the issue of economic inequality very seriously and work towards reducing it through policies and other neccessary steps. *(2 M)*

2. **Why is economic development not guaranteed in all democracies?** *(Un)*

Ans. Economic development is not guranteed in all democracies because:

- Economic development in democracies is influenced by various factors beyond the political system, such as, population size, global economic conditions, and the policies adopted by the country. *(1 M)*
- While democracy provides a conducive environment for growth, it does not automatically ensure economic development without effective policies and governance. *(1 M)*

Short Answer Type Questions (3 M)

1. **Analyse the outcomes of democracies in terms of economic growth and development.** *(An)*(CBSE, 2022 Term 2)

Ans. The outcomes of democracies in terms of economic growth and development are:

- Democracy does not guarantee superior economic growth. Democracies' impact on economic growth and development is not uniform. *(1 M)*
- Economic development in democracies depends on various factors, such as political stability, rule of law, investment climate, and national policies. *(1 M)*
- While democracy doesn't guarantee superior economic growth, it fosters a framework for sustainable and inclusive development. *(1 M)*

2. **Read the statements given below regarding the outcomes of democracies.**

   Statement 1 (S1): Democratic countries often experience economic inequalities, with a significant wealth gap between the rich and the poor.

   Statement 2 (S2): Democracies provide political equality, where every citizen has an equal vote in electing representatives.

   Explain what these statements - S1 and S2 - reflect in the context of economic and political outcomes in democracies. *(An)*

Ans. (*i*) These statements reflect that while democracies promote political equality, they often struggle with economic inequality. *(1 M)*

(*ii*) In democratic nations, every citizen has an equal vote, ensuring political equality (S2). However, economic disparities persist, with a significant gap between the rich and the poor (S1). *(1 M)*

(*iii*) For example, in India, despite equal voting rights, the top 20% of the population controls a disproportionate share of wealth, while the bottom 20% struggles to meet basic needs. *(1 M)*

Long Answer Type Questions (5 M)

1. **Analyse the political outcomes associated with democracy.** *(An)* (CBSE, 2024)

Ans. The Political outcomes associated with democracy are: **(Any five)**

(*i*) **Accountable government:** Democratic leaders must answer to the public and justify their actions, promoting transparency and reducing corruption. *(1 M)*

(*ii*) **Responsive governance:** Democracies are compelled to address the concerns and needs of their citizens, ensuring that policies reflect public preferences and contribute to the common good. *(1 M)*

(*iii*) **Legitimate authority:** Even if democracies are perceived as slow or less efficient, they are considered legitimate and represent people's own government. When people choose their leaders through voting, it makes the government more legitimate, strong, and respected. This helps everyone to respect the rules, the rulers and how the country is run. *(1 M)*

(*iv*) **Policy transparency:** Open debates, free media, and public scrutiny in democracies encourage transparency in policymaking, allowing citizens to be informed and engaged. *(1 M)*

(*v*) **Handling of social diversity:** Democracies accommodate social diversities and prevent conflicts from becoming explosive, fostering a more harmonious society. *(1 M)*

(*vi*) **Promotion of dignity and freedom:** Democracies are really good at respecting and protecting the rights and freedom of people. They have rules that make sure everyone is treated fairly and equally. *(1 M)*

3 ACCOMMODATION OF SOCIAL DIVERSITY & DIGNITY AND FREEDOM OF THE CITIZENS

NCERT Definitions *(Commonly asked in 1 mark)*

- **Social Diversity:** Mix of different cultures, races, genders, religions, and other characteristics in a society.
- **Corruption:** Corruption involves dishonest or unethical conduct by people in power, typically for personal gain. It undermines fairness and justice, leading to a misuse of resources and eroding public trust in institutions and leaders.

Important Facts

01 Democracy is superior to other forms of government in promoting dignity and freedom of the individual including marginalized groups, through legal and moral principles. as it acknowledges all individuals as equal.

02 Non-democratic regimes often turn a blind eye or suppress internal social differences.

03 The principle of democratic governance involves majority rule with respect for minority rights, ensuring that no group is excluded from participating in the democratic process.

Difference Between

Expectation Vs. Actual Outcomes of Democracy

Aspect	Expectations from Democracy	Actual Outcomes
Government Accountability	Democracy should produce a government that is accountable to the citizens and responsive to their needs and expectations.	Generally better in setting up free elections and public debates but often fall short in transparency and in being fully responsive and accountable to all citizens.
Economic Growth	Democracies are expected to ensure economic growth.	The economic growth rate in democracies is not significant.
Reduction of Inequality and Poverty	Democracies are expected to reduce economic disparities and poverty.	Not very successful in reducing economic inequalities or poverty. The distribution of wealth remains unequal in many democratic countries.
Accommodation of Social Diversity	Democracies lead to a harmonious and peaceful society by accommodating social diversities.	Handle social differences and conflicts through negotiation and legal frameworks. However, the effectiveness varies among different democracies.
Freedom and Dignity of Citizens	Democracy is expected to promote the dignity and freedom of individuals.	Generally uphold individual freedom and dignity, though challenges remain in fully achieving these ideals for all citizens.

COMPETENCY BASED SOLVED EXAMPLES

Scan Me for Detailed Explanations

Multiple Choice Questions

(1 M)

1. **We felt that democracy was better because it:** *(Un)*
   (*i*) Promotes equality among citizens;
   (*ii*) Enhances the dignity of the individual
   Which of the above statements given above is/are correct?
   (*a*) (*i*) only
   (*b*) (*ii*) only
   (*c*) Both (*i*) and (*ii*)
   (*d*) Neither (*i*) nor (*ii*)
2. **In a democracy, minority groups have legal protections and are given platforms to voice their concerns. However, these groups still face social discrimination and exclusion. What does this scenario reveal about the complexities of social equality in democracies?** *(Ev)*
   (*a*) Legal protections are sufficient to ensure social equality.
   (*b*) Social discrimination is unrelated to the political system.
   (*c*) Achieving social equality requires both legal protections and broader social change.
   (*d*) Minority groups do not need additional platforms in democracies.
3. **In a democracy, an individual has the right and means to examine the procedure of decision-making. This is known as** *(Re)*
   (*a*) Transparency (*b*) Dictatorship
   (*c*) Equality (*d*) Legitimacy
4. **What is the significance of public dissatisfaction with democracy?** *(Ev)*
   (*a*) It indicates the failure of democracy as a system of governance
   (*b*) It highlights the success of democracy in empowering citizens to voice their concerns
   (*c*) It suggests that citizens have no awareness of their democratic rights
   (*d*) It signifies the need for a transition to an autocratic regime
5. **Based on the outcomes of democracy, which statement accurately reflects the comparison between democracies and dictatorships regarding social harmony?** *(Un)*
   (*a*) Democracies always resolve social conflicts completely.
   (*b*) Dictatorships handle social differences better than democracies.
   (*c*) Democracies can handle social differences and conflicts better than non-democratic regimes.
   (*d*) Social harmony is not affected by the type of government.

Assertion and Reason

(1 M)

Direction: The following questions consist of two statements – Assertion (A) and Reason (R). Answer these questions by selecting the appropriate option given below:

(*a*) Both A and R are true, and R is the correct explanation of A.
(*b*) Both A and R are true, but R is not the correct explanation of A.
(*c*) A is true, but R is false
(*d*) A is false, but R is true.

1. **Assertion (A):** Accommodation of social diversity is essential for a smooth functioning of democracy.
   Reason (R): A diverse society does not requires representation and inclusion of all groups in decision-making processes to ensure that policies and laws are fair and equitable for all citizens. *(Ev)*
2. **Assertion (A):** Democracy is best suited to address and manage conflicts among different groups, even if complete resolution may not be achievable.
   Reason (R): Democracy provides a framework that promotes respect for differences and facilitates the development of mechanisms for negotiation, enabling societies to effectively manage conflicts among different groups. *(An)*
3. **Assertion (A):** Democracy promotes dignity and freedom of the individual.
   Reason (R): Every individual wants to receive respect from fellow beings, and democracy recognizes this by ensuring that all individuals are equal. *(Un)*
4. **Assertion (A):** Public expression of dissatisfaction with democracy shows the failure of the democracy.
   Reason (R): When people express dissatisfaction with democracy, it shows that they have developed awareness and critical thinking skills to expect accountability from power holders, transforming them from subjects into citizens. *(Ap)*

Subjective Questions

Very Short Answer Type Questions

(2 M)

1. **Why is it important to accommodate social diversity?** *(Un)*

Ans. It's essential to accommodate social diversity because it fosters unity and strengthens the nation. If not managed well it may lead to conflict, violence, and unrest in the society. By valuing differences, democracy can tackle discrimination, promote inclusiveness and create a more equitable environment for everyone. *(2 M)*

2. **How can a democracy safeguard the dignity and freedom of its citizens?** *(Ap)*

Ans. A democracy can safeguard the dignity and freedom of its citizens by:

- Enacting laws that protect human rights, ensuring equal opportunities for all, and promoting social justice. *(1 M)*
- Fostering a culture of respect, tolerance, and inclusivity where individuals feel valued and can exercise their freedoms without fear of discrimination or oppression. *(1 M)*

Short Answer Type Questions (3 M)

1. **What is the best-suited system to handle social differences, division, and conflicts in between democracy and dictatorship?** *(Ev)*

Ans. Democracy is better suited to handle social differences, divisions, and conflicts than dictatorship because:

- Democracy promotes equality and dignity, allowing for peaceful negotiation of differences and conflicts. In contrast, dictatorships often suppress diversity and disagreement, leading to unrest and unstability. *(1½ M)*
- Democracy's inclusive and participative nature fosters a harmonious society, despite being slower in decision-making. On the other hand, dictatorship might make quick decisions but not always responsive or well considered decisions which may not be accepted by people, leading to conflict. *(1½ M)*

2. **In a democracy, citizens often voice their dissatisfaction with government policies and decisions and it is not considered a failure of democracy as a system of governance rather public dissatisfaction with democracy is considered a testimony to its success. Discuss how this dissatisfaction reflects the strengths of a democratic system.** *(An)*

Ans. Public dissatisfaction with democracy is seen as a testimony to its success because:

(*i*) It indicates that citizens have the freedom to express their views and demand accountability from the government. *(1 M)*

(*ii*) Continuous dissatisfaction and critical evaluation of democracy by its citizens are essential for its growth and improvement. *(1 M)*

(*iii*) It drives the system towards addressing its shortcomings and evolving to meet the changing needs of its society. *(1 M)*

Long Answer Type Questions (5 M)

1. **How has democracy strengthened the claims of disadvantaged and discriminated castes in India?** *(An)*

Ans. In India, democracy has played a significant role in supporting the rights of disadvantaged and discriminated castes in the following ways:

- It gives everyone, no matter their caste, an equal chance to vote, share their opinions, and choose their leaders. *(1 M)*
- This helps make sure that even those from lower castes can have a say in how the country is run and what laws are made. *(1 M)*
- Democracy also pushes for treating everyone with respect and gives a platform for fighting against unfair treatment based on caste. *(1 M)*
- While there are still issues and inequalities that exist, democracy offers a way to challenge and slowly change these problems. *(1 M)*
- It's about giving everyone a fair chance and making sure that all voices, especially those that have been ignored in the past, are heard and valued. *(1 M)*

2. **"Democracy stands much superior to any other forms of governments in promoting dignity and freedom of the individual." Support the statement with arguments.** *(Cr)***(CBSE, 2023)**

Ans. Democracy stands much superior to any other form of government in promoting the dignity and freedom of the individual, because:

- **Equality and Respect:** Democracy ensures that every individual is treated with equality and respect, unlike authoritarian systems where individuals' freedoms can be suppressed. *(1 M)*
- **Legal and Moral Recognition:** Democratic societies legally and morally recognize the dignity and freedom of every individual, providing a framework for protecting these rights. *(1 M)*
- **Self-expression and Participation:** Democracies allow individuals to express themselves freely and participate in the governance process, promoting freedom and dignity. *(1 M)*
- **Non-discrimination:** Democratic systems aim to eliminate discrimination and promote equality, ensuring that all individuals, regardless of their background, have the opportunity to live with dignity. *(1 M)*
- **Responsive Governance:** Democracies provide mechanisms for individuals to hold the government accountable, ensuring that their dignity and freedoms are respected and upheld. *(1 M)*

3. **"Democracies accommodate social diversities and provide dignity and freedom to the citizens." Justify the statement.** *(An)***(CBSE, 2022)**

Ans. Democracies accommodate social diversities and provide dignity and freedom to the citizens because of the following reasons: **(Any five)**

- **Protection of Minority Rights:** Democracies aim to protect the rights of minorities and ensure their representation in decision-making processes. *(1 M)*
- **Equality Before the Law:** In democratic societies, all citizens are treated equally under the law. Discrimination based on race, religion, gender, or ethnicity is prohibited, promoting a sense of dignity and respect for every individual. *(1 M)*
- **Constitutional Provisions:** In a democratic country like India, the Constitution guarantees fundamental rights to all citizens, irrespective of their backgrounds. These rights, such as the right to equality, and the right to practice any religion, ensure that citizens have the dignity and freedom to live according to their beliefs and choices. *(1 M)*
- **Freedom of Speech and Expression:** Democracies foster an environment where individuals can freely express their thoughts and opinions without any fear. *(1 M)*
- **Social and Cultural Pluralism:** Democracies embrace diversity and recognize the coexistence of various cultures, religions, languages, and traditions. *(1 M)*
- **Representative Government:** Democratic systems ensure that citizens from different backgrounds and regions are represented in the government. *(1 M)*

MISCELLANEOUS EXERCISE

Multiple Choice Questions

(1 M)

1. Read the following statements regarding democracy and choose the correct option. ***(Un)***
   I. Promotes equality among citizens
   II. Government by few individuals
   III. Protection of human rights
   IV. Ensures checks and balance system
   (*a*) I, II and III (*b*) II, III and IV
   (*c*) I, III and IV (*d*) I, II and IV
2. Which type of government is likely to be more acceptable to the people in the world? ***(Re)*(CBSE, 2023)**
   (*a*) Democratic (*b*) Military
   (*c*) Dictatorship (*d*) Theocratic
3. Match the term(column-I) with its definition (Column-II): ***(Re)***

Column-I (Term)		Column-II (Definition)	
(A)	Social Diversity	(i)	Ensures fair distribution of wealth and opportunities among all citizens
(B)	Economic Growth	(ii)	A situation where citizens lack basic needs like food and shelter.
(C)	Equality	(iii)	The nation experiences increased productivity and higher standards of living.
(D)	Poverty	(iv)	A variety of cultural, ethnic, and social differences within society.

   (*a*) A-(iv), B-(iii), C-(i), D-(ii)
   (*b*) A-(iii), B-(ii), C-(i), D-(ii)
   (*c*) A-(i), B-(ii), C-(iii), D-(iv)
   (*d*) A-(iv), B-(ii), C-(i), D-(iii)
4. Analyse the data and answer the question that follows: ***(An)***

Name of the Countries	% share of national income	
	Top 20%	Bottom 20%
South Africa	64.8	2.9
Brazil	63.0	2.6
Russia	53.7	4.4
USA	50.0	4.0
United Kingdom	45.0	6.0
Denmark	34.5	9.6
Hungary	34.4	10.0

***Fig:** Inequality of income in selected countries*

   Which democratic country has a relatively more equitable income distribution?
   (*a*) South Africa (*b*) Russia
   (*c*) United States (*d*) Denmark
5. What is the primary purpose of democratic elections? ***(Ap)***
   (*a*) To determine the ruler's eligibility
   (*b*) To give citizens the right to choose their rulers
   (*c*) To establish a hierarchy of power within the government
   (*d*) To ensure efficient decision-making processes
6. A democratic government in a multicultural society has successfully managed to maintain peace and harmony among different ethnic groups through inclusive policies.
   What key democratic principle is being demonstrated here? ***(Un)***
   (*a*) Economic development.
   (*b*) Military control.
   (*c*) Social diversity accommodation.
   (*d*) Political instability.
7. Match the following elements of democratic governance (Column-I) with their corresponding descriptions (Column-II): ***(Re)***

Column-I (Element)		Column-II (Description)	
(A)	Transparency	(i)	The process of openly discussing and debating policies and decisions.
(B)	Deliberation	(ii)	The state of being answerable to the people for decisions and actions.
(C)	Legitimacy	(iii)	The right of citizens to access information about government actions.
(D)	Accountability	(iv)	The quality of being accepted and recognized by the people.

   (*a*) A-(iv), B-(i), C-(iii), D-(ii)
   (*b*) A-(iii), B-(i), C-(iv), D-(ii)
   (*c*) A-(iii), B-(i), C-(ii), D-(iv)
   (*d*) A-(iii), B-(ii), C-(iv), D-(i)
8. Which of the following statements is not true about Democracy? ***(An)*(CBSE APQ, 2023)**
   (*a*) People wish to be ruled by representatives elected by them.
   (*b*) It is free of corruption.
   (*c*) It is expected to produce good governments.
   (*d*) Guarantees rights of citizens.

9. Which of the following is a DEFINITE indicator of the successful implementation of democratic governance? **(*An*)(CBSE APQ, 2023)**
   (*a*) free economy dictated by market forces
   (*b*) provision of basic amenities to the citizens
   (*c*) establishment of central financial institutions
   (*d*) establishment of institutions to protect people's rights

10. In a representative democracy, which of the following best describes the role of elected representatives? **(*An*)(CBSE APQ, 2023)**
   (*a*) They have absolute power and authority to make decisions without consulting the public.
   (*b*) They are accountable to the public and make decisions on behalf of their constituents.
   (*c*) They act as mere figureheads with no real power or influence in the government.
   (*d*) They serve lifetime appointments and cannot be removed from office.

11. Given the expectation that democracies should reduce economic disparities, what has been the actual outcome regarding economic inequalities in democracies? **(*An*)**
   (*a*) Democracies have been very successful in reducing economic inequalities.
   (*b*) Economic growth in democracies is always accompanied by an increase in inequalities.
   (*c*) In actual life, democracies do not appear to be very successful in reducing economic inequalities.
   (*d*) Democracies always ensure a just distribution of goods and opportunities among their citizens.

12. In the context of democracies, which of the following ideas is correct – democracies have successfully eliminated: **(*An*)(NCERT)**
   (*a*) conflicts among people
   (*b*) economic inequalities among people
   (*c*) differences of opinion about how marginalised sections are to be treated
   (*d*) the idea of political inequality

13. In the context of assessing democracy which among the following is odd one out. Democracies need to ensure: **(*Ev*)(NCERT)**
   (*a*) free and fair elections
   (*b*) dignity of the individual
   (*c*) majority rule
   (*d*) equal treatment before law

14. Studies on political and social inequalities in democracy show that **(*An*)(NCERT)**
   (*a*) democracy and development go together.
   (*b*) inequalities exist in democracies.
   (*c*) inequalities do not exist under dictatorship.
   (*d*) dictatorship is better than democracy.

15. A country with a democratic government has a high poverty rate. The richest 20% control a significant portion of the wealth, while the bottom 20% remain poor despite being a democracy. **(*Un*)**
   Which of the following best explains this scenario?
   (*a*) The government is not accountable
   (*b*) The democratic system is not functioning
   (*c*) Economic growth is not evenly distributed
   (*d*) There is no economic freedom

Assertion and Reason

(1 M)

Direction: The following questions consist of two statements – Assertion (A) and Reason (R). Answer these questions by selecting the appropriate option given below:

(*a*) Both A and R are true, and R is the correct explanation of A.
(*b*) Both A and R are true, but R is not the correct explanation of A.
(*c*) A is true, but R is false
(*d*) A is false, but R is true.

1. **Assertion (A):** Democracies are expected to produce governments that are accountable to the citizens and responsive to their needs.
   Reason (R): In a democracy, citizens have the power to elect their rulers, which in turn makes the rulers accountable and responsive to the electorate's needs and expectations. **(*Un*)**

2. **Assertion (A):** Democracies are better than non-democracies in ensuring that decisions are made following procedures and are more acceptable to the people.
   Reason (R): Democratic processes inherently require deliberation, negotiation, and adherence to established procedures making the outcomes more legitimate to the people. **(*An*)**

3. **Assertion (A):** Democracies are expected to be more efficient in decision-making and implementation than non-democracies.
   Reason (R): Democratic decision-making involves deliberation and negotiation, which can lead to delays. **(*Ev*)**

4. **Assertion (A):** Democracy is an accountable, responsive and legitimate government.
   Reason (R): Democracies have regular, free, and fair elections. Elections and decision-making are based on norms and procedures. **(*Un*)**

5. **Assertion (A):** There is an overwhelming support for the idea of democracy all over the world.
   Reason (R): Democracy has successfully reduced economic inequalities. **(*An*)**

6. **Assertion (A):** Democracy allows for peaceful resolution of conflicts.
   Reason (R): Democratic systems provide a method for resolving conflicts through peaceful means, such as negotiation and dialogue. **(*Re*)**

7. **Assertion (A):** A public expression of dissatisfaction with democracy shows the success of the democratic project.
   Reason (R): It transform people from the status of subject into that of a citizen. **(*Ev*)**

8. **Assertion (A):** Democracies do not appear to be very successful in reducing economic inequalities.
   Reason (R): Democracies are based on political equality. **(*An*)**

Subjective Questions

Very Short Answer Type Questions (2 M)

1. Rani researched the development indicators of various countries and noticed that democratic countries like India and South Africa have high economic inequality, while countries like Denmark and Hungary have lower inequality. Discuss the reasons for such disparity. **(*An*)**

2. Rajesh, a resident of a small town, discovered that the local municipality was not addressing the issues of poor road conditions. He filed an RTI application to inquire about the budget allocation and expenditures for road repairs.
   (*i*) Which democratic principle was being violated in the delay of addressing the road conditions? **(*An*)**
   (*ii*) Which democratic principle was invoked through Rajesh's RTI application? **(*An*)**

3. Which form of government is better democratic or non-democratic? Support your answer with reasonable arguments. **(*Ev*)**

4. Discuss the most likely impact on accountability of the government and corruption level if democracy does not ensure transparency. **(*Ev*)**

5. What are the two key aspects that democracy must provide? **(*Re*)**

6. In the course of researching for a project on political systems, Pranav stumbled upon the concept that democracy involves extensive discussions and deliberations, which often results in decision-making processes being perceived as slow. Curious about this, he asked his professor why democracies prioritize such lengthy discussions. His professor explained that this process, while seemingly slow, actually serves a vital purpose. Explain why the professor might value these prolonged discussions in a democratic setting. **(*Un*)**

7. Explain any two limitations that has been observed in democracies. **(*Un*)**

Short Answer Type Questions (3 M)

1. Discuss the role of newspapers in shaping public opinion and the democratization of information during the modern period. **(*An*)(CBSE APQ, 2023)**

2. Read the following excerpt about the Right to Information Act (RTI) in India and answer the question that follows.
   "The Right to Information Act (RTI) of 2005 empowers citizens to request information from any public authority, promoting transparency and accountability in governance. The Act mandates timely response to citizen requests, enhancing the accessibility of information and enabling people to make informed decisions about public matters."
   Source: *NCERT*
   Examine how the implementation of the Right to Information Act has impacted transparency and accountability in governance, using examples. **(*An*)**

3. Identify the challenges to democracy in the following descriptions. Also suggest policy/institutional mechanism to deepen democracy in the given situations: **(NCERT)**
   (*i*) Following a High Court directive a temple in Orissa that had separate entry doors for dalits and non-dalits allowed entry for all from the same door. **(*Ap*)**
   (*ii*) A large number of farmers are committing suicide in different states of India. **(*Ap*)**
   (*iii*) Following allegation of killing of three civilians in Gandwara in a fake encounter by Jammu and Kashmir police, an enquiry has been ordered. **(*Ap*)**

4. What other positive outcomes make democracy preferable despite differences in economic growth rates? **(*Ev*)**

5. Democracy has proven to be very successful in reducing economic inequality and poverty." Do you agree? Give arguments in support of your answer. **(*Ev*)**

Long Answer Type Questions (5 M)

1. How is democracy a better from of government in comparision to dictatorship? Explain. **(*Un*)(CBSE, 2023)**

2. 'Democratic system is better than any other form of governments.' Support the statement with examples. **(*Ev*)(CBSE, 2020)**

   OR

   "Democracy is a better form of government than any other form of government." Justify the statement. **(*Ev*)(CBSE, 2019)**

3. Analyse the positive outcomes of the democracy. **(*An*) (CBSE, 2024)**

4. "Democracies do not appear to be very successful in reducing economic inequalities." Justify the statement. **(*Ev*)(CBSE, 2019)**

5. A think tank has been given the task to design an outline to measure how successful has democracy been in any country. Discuss the key indicators that the think tank should consider while designing this outline and explain why these factors are crucial in assessing the outcomes of democracy. **(*Cr*)(CBSE APQ, 2023)**

6. Free and fair media is one of the most important outcomes of democracy. Comment. **(*Ev*)(CBSE APQ, 2023)**

Case Based Questions

Case Based-I

Nannu is a daily wage earner. He lives in Welcome Mazdoor Colony, a slum habitation in East Delhi. He lost his ration card and applied for a duplicate one in January 2004. He made several rounds to the local Food & Civil Supplies office for the next three months. But the clerks and officials would not even look at him, leave alone do his job or bother to tell him the status of his application. Ultimately, he filed an application under the Right to Information Act asking for the daily progress made on his application, names of the officials, who were supposed to act on his application and what action would be taken against these officials for their inaction. Within a week of filing application under the Right to Information Act, he was visited by an inspector from the Food Department, who informed him that the card had been made and he could collect it from the office. When Nannu went to collect his card next day, he was given a very warm treatment by the Food & Supply Officer (FSO), who is the head of a Circle. The FSO offered him tea and requested him to withdraw his application under the Right to Information, since his work had already been done.

(*i*) What does Nannu's example show? (*An*)

(*ii*) What impact did Nannu's action have on officials? (*Un*)

(*iii*) How does Nannu's experience illustrate the importance and effectiveness of the Right to Information Act for citizens? (*An*)

Case Based-II

If you consider all democracies and all dictatorships for the fifty years between 1950 and 2000, dictatorships have slightly higher rate of economic growth. The inability of democracy to achieve higher economic development worries us. But this alone cannot be reason to reject democracy. As you have already studied in economics, economic development depends on several factors: country's population The Rich Get Buff size, global situation, cooperation from other countries, economic priorities adopted by the country, etc. However, the difference in the rates of economic development between less developed countries with dictatorships and democracies is negligible. Overall, we cannot say that democracy is a guarantee of economic development. But we can expect democracy not to lag behind dictatorships in this respect.

(*i*) What factors influence economic development in a country? (*Re*)

(*ii*) Can we conclude that democracy is not effective for economic development? (*An*)

(*iii*) A country should opt. for dictatorships rather than democracy to ensure economic growth. Do you agree with this statement? (*Ev*)

ANSWER KEYS

Multiple Choice Questions

1. (*c*)	**2.** (*a*)	**3.** (*a*)	**4.** (*d*)	**5.** (*b*)	**6.** (*c*)	**7.** (*b*)	**8.** (*b*)	**9.** (*d*)	**10.** (*b*)
11. (*c*)	**12.** (*d*)	**13.** (*c*)	**14.** (*b*)	**15.** (*c*)					

Assertion and Reason

1. (*a*)	**2.** (*a*)	**3.** (*d*)	**4.** (*a*)	**5.** (*c*)	**6.** (*a*)	**7.** (*a*)	**8.** (*b*)

HINTS & EXPLANATIONS

Multiple Choice Questions

1. (*c*) I, III and IV

2. (*a*) Democratic government is likely to be more acceptable to the people in the world.

3. (*a*) A-(iv), B-(iii), C-(i), D-(ii)

4. (*d*) Denmark has a more equitable income distribution, with the top 20% earning 34.5% and the bottom 20% earning 9.6% of the national income, indicating a relatively fairer income distribution than other countries.

5. (*b*) To give citizens the right to choose their rulers

6. (*c*) This demonstrates the principle of social diversity accommodation, where the democratic government ensures peace and harmony by including and respecting various ethnic groups. This approach helps in managing social differences and conflicts.

7. (*b*) A-(iii), B-(i), C-(iv), D-(ii)

8. (*b*) It is free of corruption.

9. (*d*) Democratic governance is successful when people's rights are protected, and there are institutions in place to ensure justice, equality, and freedom. These institutions, like the judiciary, human rights commissions, safeguard the rights of citizens and ensure that the government acts fairly and transparently.

10. (*b*) They are accountable to the public and make decisions on behalf of their constituents.

11. (*c*) In actual life, democracies do not appear to be very successful in reducing economic inequalities.

12. (*d*) Democracy ensures equal political rights for all, like the right to vote and participate in governance, removing political inequality. However, issues like conflicts, economic inequalities, and differences of opinion (options a, b, and c) can still exist. Democracies provide a platform to address these issues, but they are not completely eliminated.

13. (*c*) Democracy ensures free and fair elections, dignity of individuals, and equal treatment before the law. However, majority rule (option c) can sometimes override minority rights, which contradicts the democratic principle of inclusivity. Hence, it is the odd one out.
14. (*b*) Studies on political and social inequalities in democracy show that inequalities exist in democracies.
15. (*c*) Even in democracies, economic growth may not benefit all segments of the population equally, leading to persistent poverty.

Assertion and Reason

1. (*a*) Self-explanatory
2. (*a*) Self-explanatory
3. (*d*) Democracy involves procedures and deliberation, ensuring acceptability but doesn't guarantee efficiency.
4. (*a*) Self-explanatory
5. (*c*) Democracies do not appear to be very successful in reducing economic inequalities.
6. (*a*) Self-explanatory
7. (*a*) Self-explanatory
8. (*b*) Both Assertion and Reason are true but Reason is not the correct explanation of Assertion.

Subjective Questions

Very Short Answer Type Questions

1. The economic outcomes are not the same in both the country despite having the same political system because:
   (*i*) Economic development in democracies is influenced by various factors beyond the political system, such as population size, global economic conditions, and the policies adopted by the country. *(1 M)*
   (*ii*) While democracy provides a conducive environment for growth, it does not automatically ensure economic development without effective policies and governance. *(1 M)*
2. (*i*) The delay in addressing the road conditions violated the principle of an accountable and responsive government, as the officials were not taking prompt action to resolve the issue. *(1 M)*
   (*ii*) By filing an RTI application, Rajesh invoked the principle of transparency and the right to information. *(1 M)*
3. Democratic government are better than non-democratic government because:
   - Democracies ensure accountable governments, as leaders are elected by citizens and must satisfy their needs. On the other hand, non-democracies ignore people's demands, leading to dissatisfaction and unrest. *(1 M)*
   - Democracies promote equality and protect individual dignity, whereas non-democracies may compromise these values. Hence, democratic governance is preferable for representing the will and welfare of the people. *(1 M)*
4. If transparency is not ensured it may impact the accountability and corruption in the following ways:
   (*i*) **Accountability:** Accountability of the government would diminish, as citizens would not have the means to scrutinize government actions and decisions, which may also lead to unresponsive governance. *(1 M)*
   (*ii*) **Corruption levels:** Corruption would likely increase, as non-transparent systems provide opportunities for misuse of power without fear of detection or punishment. *(1 M)*
5. The two key aspects that democracy must provide are:
   - A government that is accountable and responsive to its citizens' needs and expectations. *(1 M)*
   - Guarantee that citizens have the right to participate in decision-making that impacts them, ensuring control over their rulers. *(1 M)*
6. The professor might value these prolonged discussions in a democratic setting because:
   (*i*) In a democracy, lengthy discussions and deliberations in decision-making ensure that all opinions are considered, leading to more inclusive and well-considered decisions. *(1 M)*
   (*ii*) Furthermore, while this might slow down the decision-making process, it tends to make decisions that are more effective and acceptable to a broader section of society, reducing conflicts and increasing acceptance and adherence with the law. *(1 M)*
7. Two limitations that have been observed in democracies are:
   - Democracies often fail to reduce economic disparities, the rich often get richer while the poor struggle to meet basic needs. *(1 M)*
   - The poor constitute a large proportion of voters, despite being ruled by the majority democracies may not always focus on poverty reduction as much as expected, neglecting the needs of the majority who are poor. *(1 M)*

Short Answer Type Questions

1. (*i*) Newspapers play a critical role in shaping public opinion by providing a platform for debate and discussion. *(1 M)*
   (*ii*) They contribute to the democratization of information by ensuring that different viewpoints are accessible to the public, which is important for a healthy democratic society. *(1 M)*
   (*iii*) It led to increased awareness about social, Political, and economic issues and helped individuals make informed decisions and participate actively in the democratic process. *(1 M)*
2. The Right to Information Act has significantly improved transparency and accountability in the following ways:
   (*i*) By enabling citizens to request information, the act ensures that public authorities are answerable to the people. *(1 M)*

(*ii*) This empowerment of citizens to seek information helps in making informed decisions and holds government officials accountable for their actions, thereby fostering a more responsive governance system. *(1 M)*

(*iii*) For example, RTI applications have been instrumental in exposing irregularities in public projects, such as uncovering corruption in the allocation of funds for infrastructure projects. *(1 M)*

3. (*i*) **Temple Entry Issue in Orissa:** The challenge here was social discrimination. A policy to deepen democracy could include educational programs to promote social equality and legal enforcement against discrimination. *(1 M)*

(*ii*) **Farmers' Suicides:** The challenge is economic distress among farmers. Policy measures could include better support for farmers through subsidies, access to credit, and agricultural counseling services. *(1 M)*

(*iii*) **Fake Encounter Allegations in Jammu and Kashmir:** The challenge is the misuse of power. Strengthening judicial oversight and establishing independent bodies to investigate such allegations can help deepen democracy. *(1 M)*

4. Despite differences in economic growth rates, democracy is preferred because:
   - It promotes equality among citizens, enhances individual dignity, allows for effective decision-making, and provides mechanisms for correcting mistakes. *(1 M)*
   - It also creates a government that is accountable and responsive to its citizens' needs. *(1 M)*
   - These outcomes underline democracy's value beyond just economic criteria, making it a desirable form of governance. *(1 M)*

5. No, I don't agree. In fact, democracy has failed to reduce economic inequality and poverty. This is evident from the following points:
   - While democracy ideally supports fairness and participation, there is evidence suggesting that democracies have not necessarily performed better than dictatorships in terms of economic growth. *(1 M)*
   - Democracies like South Africa and Brazil show high degrees of inequality, where the top 20% of the population controls the majority of national income, leaving minimal resources for the bottom 20%. *(1 M)*
   - The growth in democracies has often been accompanied by increasing economic disparities between rich and poor rather than reducing them. *(1 M)*

   These pattern highlights the inability of democracies to effectively reduce economic disparities and poverty.

Long Answer Type Questions

1. Democracy is a better form of government in comparison to dictatorship because it has the following features, which are often missing in dictatorships:
   - It promotes equality, dignity, and the active participation of citizens in governance. *(1 M)*
   - In a democracy, every citizen has the right to vote, ensuring that the government reflects the will of the people. *(1 M)*
   - This form of government also enhances individual dignity by acknowledging and protecting human rights, which are often suppressed in dictatorships. *(1 M)*
   - Democratic systems are designed to improve decision-making by incorporating diverse viewpoints and allowing for public debate, which leads to more informed and considered decisions. *(1 M)*
   - Democracy provides mechanisms for resolving conflicts and correcting mistakes, which helps in maintaining social harmony and adapting to the changing needs and expectations of the public. *(1 M)*

2. The statement 'Democracy is a better form of government than any other form of government' stands true because:
   - Democracy allows for the participation of all citizens in the decision-making process to ensure that policies are more representative of the people's interests. *(1 M)*
   - Democracy provides for the protection of individual rights and freedoms because democratic governments are accountable to the people and must respect their rights. *(1 M)*
   - Democracy allows for peaceful and non-violent transfer of power as there is a set procedure for transferring power from one government to another. *(1 M)*
   - Democracy promotes transparency and accountability in governance. Democratic governments are subject to scrutiny by the media and the public, and must answer to them. *(1 M)*
   - However, while democracy is generally considered to be a better form of government, it is not without its flaws. For example, it can be slow and inefficient, and often leads to the formation of unstable coalition governments. *(1 M)*

3. There are so many positive outcomes of democracy: **(Any five)**
   - **Promotes equality:** Democracies ensure that all citizens have equal rights and opportunities, fostering a society where people are treated fairly regardless of their background. *(1 M)*
   - **Enhances dignity:** By allowing individuals to have a voice and participate in decision-making, democracies uphold the dignity and freedom of every person, enabling them to contribute to societal progress. *(1 M)*
   - **Improves decision-making:** With diverse view points and participation, democratic systems can produce more thoughtful, inclusive, and effective policies that reflect the will and needs of the people. *(1 M)*
   - **Resolves conflicts:** Democracy offers peaceful means of resolving disagreements through debate, discussion, and legal frameworks, which helps maintain harmony in society. *(1 M)*

- **Facilitates learing and correction:** The ability to change leaders and policies through elections and peaceful resolution allows democracies to learn from and correct past mistakes. *(1 M)*
- **Handling of social diversity:** Democracies accommodate social diversities and prevent conflicts from becoming explosive, fostering a more harmonious society. *(1 M)*

4. (*i*) While democracies promote political equality, ensuring that everyone has an equal say in electing their leaders, they haven't been very successful in reducing economic disparities. *(1¼ M)*

(*ii*) For example, in countries like South Africa and Brazil, a small percentage of the population, the top 20%, controls a massive portion of the national income, while the poorest 20% have very little. *(1¼ M)*

(*iii*) The poor constitute a large proportion of our voters and no party will like to lose their votes. Yet democratically elected governments do not appear to be as keen to address the question of poverty as you would expect them to. *(1¼ M)*

(*iv*) In many democracies, the number of poor people is very high, and they don't see the benefits of their country's wealth. So, while in theory, democracy should help everyone equally, in real life, a lot of people still don't have enough money to meet basic needs like food and a home. *(1¼ M)*

5. When designing an outline to measure the success of democracy in a country, a think tank should consider the following key indicators:

- **Electoral Process:** Regular, free, and fair elections are essential as they ensure leaders are elected democratically and are accountable. *(1¼ M)*
- **Accountability and Responsiveness:** Governments must be accountable to the citizens, responding effectively to their needs and expectations. This is crucial as it measures the government's connection and responsiveness to the people. *(1¼ M)*
- **Civil Liberties:** A successful democracy must uphold civil liberties and human rights, ensuring freedom of speech, religion, and assembly. The protection of citizens' freedom of speech ensures that individuals can live without fear of persecution or restriction by the state. *(1¼ M)*
- **Government Transparency:** The ability of citizens to access information regarding governmental activities and policies, promoting accountability. *(1¼ M)*

6. Free and fair media is indeed one of the most important outcomes of democracy. It is not just a result of democracy but a pillar that sustains it. This is because:

- **Voice and Accountability:** Media serves as a watchdog, ensuring that government actions are transparent and leaders are held accountable. *(1 M)*
- **Public Opinion:** It shapes and expresses public opinion, allowing citizens to be informed and make educated decisions while electing a candidate. *(1 M)*
- **Checks and Balances:** Independent media acts as a check on government power, preventing abuses and corruption. *(1 M)*
- **Representation:** Media provides a platform for diverse voices and opinions, fostering a more inclusive society. *(1 M)*
- **Education:** Through reporting, analysis, and debate, media educates the public on important issues, encouraging people's participation. *(1 M)*

Case Based Questions

Case Based-I

(*i*) Nannu's example shows the power and effectiveness of the Right to Information Act in holding government officials accountable and ensuring transparency in their actions. *(1 M)*

(*ii*) Nannu's action prompted the officials to quickly process his application and treat him with respect, showing the effectiveness of citizen's empowerment tools in a democracy. *(1 M)*

(*iii*) Nannu's experience demonstrates the power of the Right to Information Act as a tool for accountability and transparency. By filing an application under this act, he compelled government officials to speed up the processing of his ration card, showing how citizens can use the law to demand fair treatment and prompt action from government agencies. *(2 M)*

Case Based-II

(*i*) Economic development in a country is influenced by factors such as the country's population size, the global situation, cooperation from other countries, and the economic priorities adopted by the country. *(1 M)*

(*ii*) While the data shows dictatorships had slightly higher growth rates, still we cannot conclude that democracy is not effective for economic development because economic development depends upon various sectors besides government type like population size, government policies etc. *(1 M)*

(*iii*) No, I don't agree because the difference in the rates of economic development between dictatorships and democracies is negligible. When we find such significant difference in the rates of economic growth between the countries under dictatorship and democracy, it is better to prefer democracy as it has several other positive outcomes which are not present under dictatorships. *(2 M)*

MOCK TEST PAPER

Scan Me
for Detailed
Mock Test
Explanations

MOCK TEST PAPER 1

Max. Marks: 80 **Time Allowed: 3 hours**

General Instructions:

(*i*) There are **38** questions in the Question paper. All questions are compulsory.
(*ii*) The question paper has Four Sections – **A-History, B-Geography C- Political Science,** and **D- Economics**.
(*iii*) Each Section is of **20 Marks** and has **MCQs, VSA, SA, LAs** and **CBQ.**
(*iv*) Very Short Answer Type Questions (VSA), carry **2** Marks each. Answers to each question should not exceed **40** words.
(*v*) Short Answer Type Questions (SA), carry **3** Marks each. Answers to each question should not exceed **60** words.
(*vi*) Long answer type questions (LA), carry **5** Marks each. Answers to each question should not exceed **120** words.
(*vii*) There are case based questions (CBQ) with three sub questions and are of **4** Marks each. Answers to each question should not exceed **100** words.
(*viii*) The map-based questions, carry **5** Marks with two parts- Q10 in Section A-History **(2 Marks)** and Q18 in Section B -Geography **(3 Marks)**
(*ix*) There is no overall choice in the question paper. However, an internal choice has been provided in few questions. Only one of the choices in such questions must be attempted.

SECTION - A

HISTORY (20 Marks)

1. Identify the appropriate reason for the formation of the Swaraj party from the options given below: **1**

(*a*) Wanted members of Congress to return to council politics
(*b*) Wanted members of Congress to ask for Purna Swaraj for Indians
(*c*) Wanted members of Congress to ask dominion status for India
(*d*) Wanted members of Congress to oppose Simon Commission

2. What impact did the storming of the Bastille by the French have on Europe? **1**

(*a*) People across Europe got inspired to fight against the rule of the monarch.
(*b*) Made monarchs from different parts of Europe abdicate from the throne.
(*c*) Inspired nations across Europe to colonize other countries of the world.
(*d*) People in Europe started to fear the French revolutionaries.

3. Match the **Column-I** with **Column-II** and choose the correct option from the following: **1**

	Column-I (Leader)		Column-II (Role)
A.	Victor Emmanuel II	I.	Chief Minister of Italy
B.	Guiseppe Mazzini	II.	Young Italy Movement
C.	Guiseppe Garibaldi	III.	Conquered the kingdom of Sicillies
D.	Count Cavour	IV.	Proclaimed as King of Unified Italy

(*a*) A-I, B-IV, C-III, D-II (*b*) A-II, B-I, C-IV, D-III
(*c*) A-IV, B-II, C-III, D-I (*d*) A-I, B-IV, C-II, D-III

4. Look at the picture given below. Identify the name of the painter of this painting from the following options. **1**

(*a*) Raja Ravi Verma (*b*) Rabindra Nath Tagore
(*c*) Abanindranath Tagore (*d*) Samant Das Gupta

5A. Mention any two ways in which trade and cultural exchange took place across continents in the pre-modern world? **2**

OR

5B. "How did the introduction of new crops like potato impact people's lives in Europe during the pre-modern world? Give any two points." **2**

6A. "How did the spread of print culture in India contribute to the rise of nationalism? Explain with any three suitable examples." **3**

OR

6B. "The spread of print culture in India became an effective tool of resistance against colonial rule." Justify the statement with three suitable arguments or examples. **3**

7A. "Culture had played an important role in the development of nationalism in Europe during the 18th and 19th centuries". Support the statement with examples. **5**

OR

7B. Describe any three the steps taken by the French revolutionaries to create a sense of collective identity amongst the French people. **5**

8. Read the given text and answer the following questions: (1 + 1 + 2 = 4) **4**

Gutenberg was the son of a merchant and grew up on a large agricultural estate. From his childhood, he had seen wine and olive presses. Subsequently, he learnt the art of polishing stones, became a master goldsmith, and also acquired the expertise to create lead moulds used for making trinkets. Drawing on this knowledge, Gutenberg adapted existing technology to design his innovation. The olive press provided the model for the printing press, and moulds were used for casting the metal types for the letters of the alphabet. By 1448, Gutenberg perfected the system. The first book he printed was the Bible. About 180 copies were printed and it took three years to produce them. By the standards of the time, this was fast production. The new technology did not entirely displace the existing art of producing books by hand. In fact, printed books at first closely resembled the written manuscripts in appearance and layout. The metal letters imitated the ornamental handwritten styles. Borders were illuminated by hand with foliage and other patterns, and illustrations were painted. In the books printed for the rich, space for decoration was kept blank on the printed page. Each purchaser could choose the design and decide on the painting school that would do the illustrations.

8.1 What was the major drawback of new technology?

8.2 Which previous knowledge did Gutenberg draw on to design his innovation in the form of a printing press?

8.3 Write two features of the first book printed by Gutenberg.

MAP SKILL BASED QUESTIONS (2 Marks)

9. Two places **A** and **B** have been marked on the given outline map of India. Identify them and write their correct names on the lines drawn near them. **(1 + 1 = 2)**

A. The place where Indian National Congress session was held in December, 1920.

B. The place associated with calling off the Non-Cooperation Movement.

SECTION - B

GEOGRAPHY (20 Marks)

10. Considering the multi-purpose Sardar Sarovar Dam, which river's basin has been developed for irrigation, drinking water supply, and hydroelectric power generation under this project? **1**

(*a*) Ganga (*b*) Godavari
(*c*) Mahanadi (*d*) Narmada

11. The image shows an indigenous irrigation technique that uses bamboo channels to transport water from hill springs to farms. In which Indian region is this eco-friendly method widely practised? **1**

(*a*) Western Ghats (*b*) Eastern Himalayas
(*c*) Western Rajasthan (*d*) Meghalaya

12. Read the following features of a soil and name the related soil: **1**

(*i*) It soil is ideal for growing cotton
(*ii*) Also called regur soil
(*iii*) Well known for its capacity to hold moisture.

(*a*) Black soil (*b*) Alluvial soil
(*c*) Laterite soil (*d*) Red soil

13. The image shows a one-horned rhinoceros, an endangered species protected in its natural habitat. In which of the following Indian national parks is this animal primarily found? **1**

(*a*) Jim Corbett National Park
(*b*) Kaziranga National Park
(*c*) Gir Forest National Park
(*d*) Sunderbans National Park

14. Ankur, a resident from Rajasthan, decided to install a submerisble water pump in his house, capable of extracting groundwater from depths of 250-300 m. This practice of installign similar pumps is becoming increasingly popular across the state. Which of teh following will this growing practice MOST LIKELY lead to in the near future? **1**

(*a*) Decline in the groundwater quality

(*b*) Reduced monsoon water resources

(*c*) Increased number of waterborne diseases

(*d*) Water scarcity resulting from excessive utilization

15. In Bhakra – Nangal project water is being used for: **1**

(*i*) Hydel power production

(*ii*) Irrigation

(*iii*) Transportation

(*iv*) Cleaning

(*a*) (*i*) and (*iv*) (*b*) (*ii*) and (*i*)

(*c*) Only (*iii*) (*d*) Only (*ii*)

16. In what ways does excessive irrigation contribute to land degradation in Punjab? Explain any two factors. **2**

17A. Priya is preparing a presentation on India's economic strengths for her school's annual fest. While researching, she finds that manufacturing industries are called the "backbone of the economy."

Justify this statement by highlighting any five ways manufacturing supports India's economic development. **5**

OR

17B. Tanmay is preparing a research project on India's manufacturing strengths. While studying, he comes across data highlighting the vast scale of India's chemical industry.

Can you help Tanmay understand the present status of the chemical industry in India and its key features? **5**

18. Read the text carefully and answer the following questions: (1 + 2 + 1 = 4) **4**

In the 1960s and 1970s, conservationists demanded a national wildlife protection programme. The Indian Wildlife (Protection) Act was implemented in 1972, with various provisions for protecting habitats. An All-India list of protected species was also published. The thrust of the programme was towards protecting the remaining population of certain endangered species by banning hunting, giving legal protection to their habitats, and restricting trade in wildlife. Subsequently, central and many state governments established national parks and wildlife sanctuaries about which you have already studied. The central government also announced several projects for protecting specific animals, which were gravely threatened, including the tiger, the one-horned rhinoceros, the Kashmir stag or hangul, three types of crocodiles freshwater crocodile, saltwater crocodile and the Gharial, the Asiatic lion, and others. Most recently the Indian elephant, black buck (chinkara), the great Indian bustard (godawan) and the snow leopard, etc, have been given full or partial legal pro-tection against hunting and trade throughout India

18.1 What is the purpose of the Indian Wildlife (Protection) Act of 1972?

18.2 Name two specific animals that have been given full or partial legal protection under this Act.

18.3 How have central and state governments contributed to wildlife conservation since the implementation of the Wildlife Protection Act? Explain with an example.

MAP SKILL BASED QUESTIONS (3 Marks)

19. On the same outline map of India locate and label the following with suitable symbols: **1**

I. (*p*) The nuclear power plant located in Gujarat, near the Tapi River, known for producing atomic energy.

OR

(*q*) The western coastal major port in Karnataka that handles exports of iron ore and petroleum products.

II. Any two of the following: **(1 × 2 = 2)**

(*i*) Bailadila Iron Ore Mines

(*ii*) An International Airport in New Delhi

(*iii*) Kandla Sea Port

SECTION - C

POLITICAL SCIENCE (20 Marks)

20. Which of the following languages is recognized as the national language by the Constitution of India? **1**

(*a*) Hindi (*b*) English

(*c*) Tamil (*d*) None of these

21. _________ reasons stress that power sharing will bring out better outcomes **1**

(*a*) Prudential (*b*) Moral

(*c*) Economic (*d*) Social

22. '*In Goa, 7 powerful families are contesting 35% of the assembly seats*' states a headline in a recent newspaper article. **1**

Which challenge of political parties does it MOST LIKELY illustrate?

(*a*) Lack of internal democracy

(*b*) Influence of money and muscle power

(*c*) Dynastic succession

(*d*) Lack of Meaningful Choices

23. Which of the following statements accurately reflects the data on the percentage of women in national parliaments from the chart? **1**

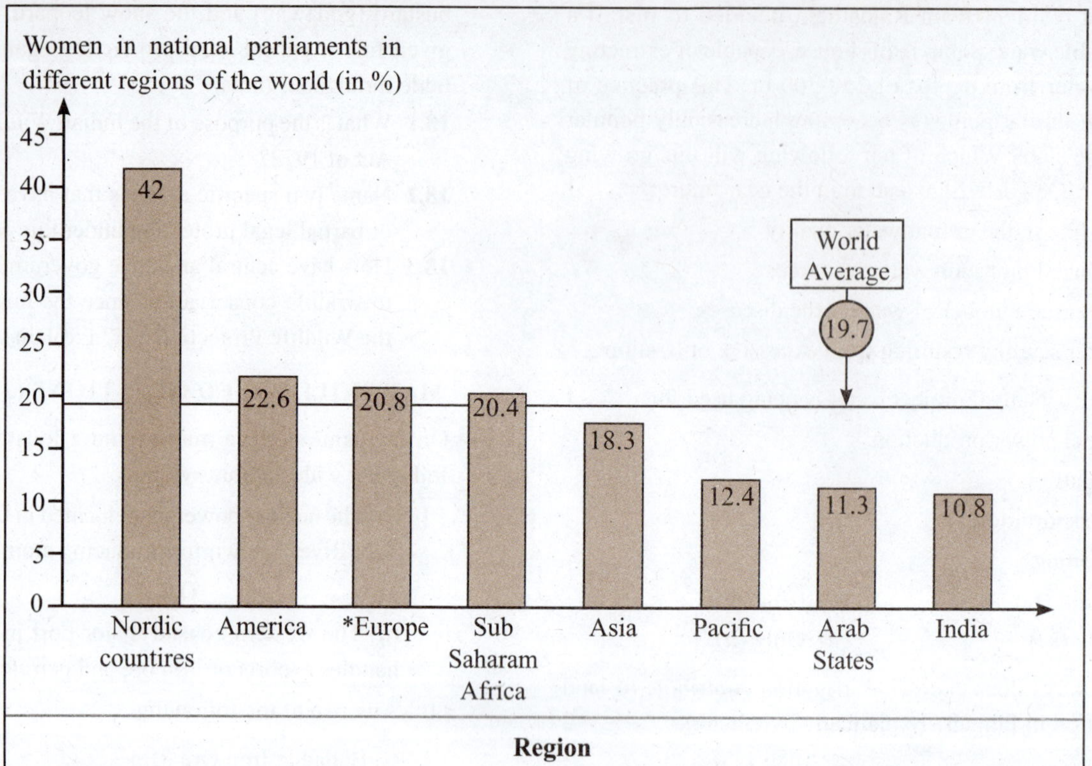

***Europe:** OSCE (Organisation for Security and Cooperation in Europe) member countries excluding Nordic countries.

Note: *Figures are for the percent of women in the directly elected chambers of parliament as on 31st December 2011.*

(*i*) Europe (excluding Nordic countries) has a higher percentage of women in national parliaments compared to the Pacific region.

(*ii*) The world average percentage of women in national parliaments is above 20%.

(*iii*) Sub-Saharan Africa has a higher percentage of women in national parliaments than Asia.

(*iv*) The percentage of women in national parliaments in the Pacific region is the lowest among all regions listed.

(*a*) (*i*), (*ii*) and (*iii*)

(*b*) (*ii*) and (*iii*) only

(*c*) (*i*) and (*iii*) only

(*d*) (*i*), (*ii*), (*iii*) and (*iv*)

24. How do most democracies perform when it comes to providing fair elections? **2**

25. There are mainly two ways to form a federation. By considering all the clues identify the type of federation and give reasons to support your answer. **2**

Clue I: Very often, different constituent units of the federation have unequal powers.

Clue II: Some units are granted special powers

Clue III: The Central Government tends to be more powerful vis-à-vis the States.

26. Describe the nature of the Panchayati raj system in India. **3**

27A. Analyse how the participation of women in politics has evolved and its impact on society. **5**

OR

27B. Analyse the impact of the feminist movement on gender equality in India. **5**

28. Read the given text and answer the following questions: (1 + 1 + 2 = 4) **4**

If you consider all democracies and all dictatorships for the fifty years between 1950 and 2000, dictatorships have slightly higher rate of economic growth. The inability of democracy to achieve higher economic development worries us. But this alone cannot be reason to reject democracy. As economic development depends on several factors: country's population size, global situation, cooperation from other countries, economic priorities adopted by the country, etc. However, the difference in the rates of economic development between less developed countries with dictatorships and democracies is negligible. Overall, we cannot say that democracy is a guarantee of economic development. But we can expect democracy not to lag behind dictatorships in this respect.

28.1 What factors influence economic development in a country?

28.2 Can we conclude that democracy is not effective for economic development?

28.3 A country should opt. for dictatorships rather than democracy to ensure economic growth. Do you agree with this statement?

SECTION - D

ECONOMICS (20 Marks)

29. Study the statistics in the table and answer the questions that follows: 1

₹	Member 1	Member 2	Member 3	Member 4
Income	15,000	6,000	8,000	9,000

Calculate the average income of the family:

(*a*) ₹950 (*b*) ₹9500

(*c*) ₹2500 (*d*) ₹3000

30. Megha has taken a loan of ₹ 5 Lakhs from the banks to purchase a house. The annual interest rate on the loan is 12 percent and the loan is to be repaid in 10 years in monthly installments. Megha had to submit to the bank, documents showing her employment records and salary before the bank agreed to give her the loan. The bank retained as collateral the papers of the new house, which will be returned to Megha only when she repays the entire loan with interest. 1

From which sources of credit Megha has taken loan?

(*a*) Informal source (*b*) Formal source

(*c*) Individual source (*d*) None of the above

31. What is the primary factor that has stimulated the process of Globalisation? 1

(I) Increase in foreign investment.

(II) Rise of trade barriers between countries.

(III) Rapid improvement in technology, especially in communication and transportation.

(IV) Decrease in multinational corporations' activities.

(*a*) Statements I and II are appropriate.

(*b*) Statements I, II and III are appropriate.

(*c*) All the statements are appropriate.

(*d*) Statement III is appropriate.

32. Ramesh, a small-scale farmer, needs a loan to buy seeds and fertilizers for the upcoming planting season. He decides to take a loan from a local money lender who offers the loan without any formal paperwork or collateral.

What potential risk does Ramesh face by taking a loan from the local moneylender? 1

(*a*) The loan interest rate might be higher, leading to a larger debt burden if he fails to repay on time.

(*b*) The loan might come with government subsidies and lower interest rates.

(*c*) The loan repayment terms might be more flexible compared to bank loans.

(*d*) The moneylender might offer additional financial advice and support.

33. In a rural village, the majority of the population is engaged in agriculture. The villagers grow crops and raise livestock for their livelihood. There are a few small shops and a local craftsman who makes pottery. The village does not have any large industries or factories. 1

Which sector of the economy is most dominant in this village?

(*a*) Primary Sector (*b*) Secondary Sector

(*c*) Tertiary Sector (*d*) Quaternary Sector

34. Which of the following is a significant impact of globalisation on the indian economy? 1

(*a*) Decrease in competition among local producers.

(*b*) Improved access to international market for indian companies.

(*c*) Reduced foreign investment in india.

(*d*) Isolation of indian market from global trends.

35A. Apart from income which other things people look for growth and development. 3

OR

35B. Write down some characteristics of development. 3

36. Assess any three advantages of globalisation. 3

37. Aman is a farmer who grows wheat. He wants to exchange his wheat for a pair of shoes. He meets Ravi, a shoemaker, but Ravi needs clothes, not wheat.

Based on this situation, answer the following:

(*i*) What kind of system is being used by Aman and Ravi? 1

(*ii*) Mention any two limitations of this system. 2

38A. What is organised and unorganised sector? The workers in the unorganised sector need protection on the following issues: wages, safety, and health. Explain with examples. 5

OR

38B. Highlight five reasons for the importance of the tertiary sector in India. 5

Map for Q. no. 9 (Section A) & Q. no. 19 (Section B)

MOCK TEST PAPER 2

Max. Marks: 80 **Time Allowed: 3 hours**

General Instructions:

(*i*) There are **38** questions in the Question paper. All questions are compulsory.

(*ii*) The question paper has Four Sections – **A-History, B-Geography C- Political Science, and D- Economics.**

(*iii*) Each Section is of **20 Marks** and has **MCQs, VSA, SA, LAs** and **CBQ**.

(*iv*) Very Short Answer Type Questions (VSA), carry **2** Marks each. Answers to each question should not exceed **40** words.

(*v*) Short Answer Type Questions (SA), carry **3** Marks each. Answers to each question should not exceed **60** words.

(*vi*) Long answer type questions (LA), carry **5** Marks each. Answers to each question should not exceed **120** words.

(*vii*) There are case based questions (CBQ) with three sub questions and are of **4** Marks each. Answers to each question should not exceed **100** words.

(*viii*) The map-based questions, carry **5** Marks with two parts- Q10 in Section A-History **(2 Marks)** and Q18 in Section B -Geography **(3 Marks)**

(*ix*) There is no overall choice in the question paper. However, an internal choice has been provided in few questions. Only one of the choices in such questions must be attempted.

SECTION - A

HISTORY (20 Marks)

1. Imagine you are an economic analyst in the late 1920s, tasked with evaluating the impact of the worldwide economic depression on various sectors in India. Your focus is on the agricultural sector and the lives of Indian peasants during this period. What was the primary cause of these difficulties for Indian peasants during the late 1920s? **1**

(*a*) Increased agricultural prices and exports.

(*b*) Led to the establishment of the Swaraj Party.

(*c*) Caused agricultural prices to fall and exports to decline.

(*d*) Improved the economic condition of the countryside.

2. Which of the following option best signifies this caricature? **1**

(*a*) Otto Von Bismarck in the German Reichstag (Parliament)

(*b*) Victor Emmanuel II in the Italian Parliament

(*c*) Kaiser William II in the Prussian Parliament

(*d*) Napoleon Bonaparte in the French Parliament

3. Arrange the following statements in sequential order based on the events occurs **1**

A. Quit India movement was launched

B. Poona Pact was signed

C. Gandhi Irwin pact was signed.

D. Civil disobedience movement was launched

Options:

(*a*) (A),(B),(C) and (D) (*b*) (D),(C),(B) and (A)

(*c*) (B),(A),(D) and(C) (*d*) (A),(D), (C)and (B)

4. Given below is the painting 'Imperial Federation - Map of the World showing the extent of the British Empire in 1886'. Observe the painting and answer the question that follows: **1**

Which of the following elements depicted in the painting seem conflicting when presented together?

(*a*) The British soldiers and British colonies spread in both east and west

(*b*) The variety of animals and costumed figures depicting countries and their people

(c) Britannia, the personification of Britain, seated on top of the world and the words federation written at the top of the image

(d) The words 'freedom' and 'fraternity' written at the top and Atlas, depicting human labour, holding the world upon his shoulders

5A. Provide evidence to support the claim that the French Revolution was a turning point in European history. **2**

OR

5B. Analyze the impact of industrialisation on the development of nationalism in Europe? **2**

6. Thomas visits a city to observe Gutenberg's mechanical printing press. He notes the differences in the book production process, the cost, and the accessibility of books compared to traditional hand-copying methods. Based on Thomas's observations, Discuss the potential changes in the cost and accessibility of books due to the printing press. **3**

7A. Mention four main proposals with reference to the Non-Cooperation Movement as suggested by Mahatma Gandhi. **5**

OR

7B. Discuss the role of visual symbols and representations in shaping nationalist sentiments during the Indian independence movement. **5**

8. Read the given text and answer the following questions: (1 + 1 + 2 = 4) **4**

Source-1: Religious Reform and Public Debates

There were intense controversies between social and religious reformers and the Hindu orthodoxy over matters like widow immolation, monotheism, Brahmanical priesthood, and idolatry. in Bengal, as the debate developed, tracts and newspapers proliferated, circulating a variety of arguments.

Source-2: New Forms of Publication

New literary forms also entered the world of reading lyrics, short stories, essays about social and political matters. In different ways, they reinforced the new emphasis on human lives and intimate feelings, about the political and social rules that shaped such things.

Source-3: Women and Print

Since social reforms and novels had already created a great interest in women's lives and emotions, there was also an interest in what women would have to say about their own lives.

8.1 Evaluate how the print shaped the nature of the debate in the early nineteenth century in India.

8.2 To what extent do you agree that print opened up new worlds of experience and gave a vivid sense of the diversity of human lives?

8.3 To what extent did the print culture reflect a great interest in women's lives and emotions? Explain.

MAP SKILL-BASED QUESTION (2 Marks)

9. Two places **A** and **B** have been marked on the given outline map of India. Identify them and write their correct names on the lines drawn near them. **(1 + 1 = 2)**

A. The place where Indian National Congress session was held in 1927

B. The place where Gandhi ji started first Satyagraha.

SECTION - B

GEOGRAPHY (20 Marks)

10. In the fictional country of Greenlandia, excessive mining activities have led to severe land degradation. The government, with the help of environmental scientist Dr. Lila, is exploring ways to mitigate the negative impacts while continuing to meet economic needs. Dr. Lila suggests implementing stricter regulations on mining activities. Which of the following justifications best supports this policy from an environmental perspective? **1**

(a) It will increase government revenue through fines and penalties.

(b) It will protect biodiversity and prevent further loss of vegetation.

(c) It will encourage the use of alternative, sustainable resources.

(d) It will reduce the competition among mining companies.

11. Raj is a student who recently visited the Sutlej- Beas River basin for a school project. During his visit, he learned about the historical and modern purposes of dams. His group has been tasked to prepare a presentation that evaluates both the benefits and the environmental impact of dam construction. Identify the correct statements based on the above scenario: **1**

Statement-I: The primary purpose of building dams in ancient India was for irrigation only.

Statement-II: Modern dams serve multiple purposes including recreation and inland navigation.

Statement-III: Jawaharlal Nehru referred to dams as the economic boosters of modern India.

Statement-IV: Dams have no impact on the natural flow and sedimentation of rivers.

(a) Statement-I & Statement-II are correct

(b) Statement-I & Statement-III are correct

(c) Statement-I & Statement-IV are correct

(d) Statement-I, II & III are correct

12. Read the following features of a soil and name the related soil: **1**

(i) This soil develop in areas of high temperature and heavy rainfall.

(*ii*) Humus content is low

(*iii*) Good for tea, coffee,cashew nut etc.

(*a*) Laterite soil (*b*) Black soil

(*c*) Alluvial soil (*d*) Red and yellow soil

13. You are an agricultural consultant advising a group of new farmers in the coastal region of Odisha. These farmers are eager to diversify their crops and are considering rice due to its popularity and market demand. Discuss the specific climatic conditions required for rice cultivation. **2**

14. Ananya, a research analyst at National Mineral Development Corporation (NMDC), is preparing a report on the impact of energy minerals on India's economy. Her research highlights the use of coal, uranium, and natural gas in various sectors such as power generation, manufacturing, and transportation. She observes that energy security is essential for industrial growth, employment generation, and GDP contribution.

Based on the above case, analyze how energy minerals contribute to India's economic development. Mention any three specific sectors where their role is crucial. **3**

15A. The Indian Ministry of Energy is developing a comprehensive energy strategy to address the growing demand for sustainable energy solutions. As part of this initiative, they are emphasizing the importance of non-conventional sources of energy. explain the significance of non-conventional sources of energy in India's energy strategy. discuss the different types of non-conventional energy sources along with their advantages. **5**

OR

15B. Lokesh is a consultant for a mining company tasked with evaluating a potential mining site. To make an informed decision, he needs to analyze the various modes of occurrence of minerals found at the site. Discuss the different ways minerals can occur in nature and explain how each mode of occurrence influences the mining methods and the economic viability of extracting these minerals. **5**

16. Read the given text and answer the following questions: (1 + 1 + 2 = 4) **4**

Manufacturing Industries

Manufacturing Industries not only help in modernizing agriculture, which forms the backbone of our economy, they also reduce the heavy dependence of people on agricultural income by providing them jobs in secondary and tertiary sectors. Industrial development is a pre-condition for eradication of unemployment and poverty from our country. This was the main philosophy behind public sector industries and joint sector ventures in India. It was also aimed at bringing down regional disparities by establishing industries in tribal and backward areas. Export of manufactured goods expands trade and commerce, and brings in much needed foreign exchange. Countries that transform their raw materials into a wide variety of finished goods of higher value are prosperous. India's prosperity lies in increasing and diversifying its manufacturing industries as quickly as possible. Agriculture and industry are not exclusive of each other. They move hand in hand. For instance, the agro-industries in India have given a major boost to agriculture by raising its productivity.

16.1 How do manufacturing industries help in modernizing agriculture in India?

16.2 Why is industrial development crucial for eradicating unemployment and poverty in India?

16.3 Explain how the relationship between agriculture and industry benefits both sectors in India.

MAP SKILL-BASED QUESTION (3 Marks)

17. On the same outline map of India, locate and label the following with suitable symbols: **1**

I. (*p*) The eastern state known as the largest producer of jute in India.

OR

(*q*) A neighboring state of West Bengal also produces jute.

II. Any two of the following: **(1 × 2 = 2)**

(*i*) The highest gravity dam in India located on the Sutlej River in Himachal Pradesh.

(*ii*) The dam built on the Chambal River in Rajasthan, important for irrigation and electricity.

(*iii*) A major multipurpose dam built on the Narmada River in Gujarat.

SECTION - C

POLITICAL SCIENCE (20 Marks)

18. A belief that the majority community should be able to rule a country in whichever way it wants, by disregarding the wishes and needs of the minority is called ________. **1**

(*a*) Power Sharing (*b*) Central Government

(*c*) Majoritarianism (*d*) Community Government

19. *"Everything would come to an end if the legislative, executive, and judicial powers of government were to be exercised by the same person or authority." ~Montesquieu, French jurist*

Which of the following is the BEST explanation of this quote? **1**

(*a*) All work in a country will stop in the absence of power-sharing.

(*b*) Separation of powers is needed to strengthen democracy.

(*c*) Governments can only function if powers are distributed.

(*d*) People cannot exist in a nation if powers are not divided.

20. There are two statements marked as Assertion (A) and Reason (R). Mark your answer as per the codes provided below: **1**

Assertion (A): Public expression of dissatisfaction with democracy shows the failure of the democracy.

Reason (R): When people express dissatisfaction with democracy, it shows that they have developed awareness and critical thinking skills to expect accountability from power holders, transforming them from subjects into citizens

(*a*) Both Assertion (A) and Reason (R) are the true and Reason (R) is a correct explanation of Assertion (A).

(*b*) Both Assertion (A) and Reason (R) are the true but Reason (R) is not a correct explanation of Assertion (A).

(*c*) Assertion (A) is true and Reason (R) is false.

(*d*) Assertion (A) is false and Reason (R) is true.

21. Match Column-I with Column-II and select the correct answer by using the codes given below: **1**

	Column-I		Column-II
A.	Power shared among different organs of government	(*i*)	Community government
B.	Power shared among governments at different levels	(*ii*)	Separation of powers
C.	Power shared by different social groups	(*iii*)	Coalition government
D.	Power shared by two or more political parties	(*iv*)	Federal government

(*a*) A-(*i*), B-(*iv*), C-(*ii*), D-(*iii*)

(*b*) A-(*iii*), B-(*i*), C-(*ii*), D-(*iv*)

(*c*) A-(*ii*), B-(*iv*), C-(*i*), D-(*iii*)

(*d*) A-(*iii*), B-(*ii*), C-(*i*), D-(*iv*)

22. Read the passage below.

Australia became a nation on 1 January 1901, when the British Parliament passed legislation enabling the six Australian colonies to collectively govern in their own right as the Commonwealth of Australia. It was a remarkable political accomplishment that had taken many years and several referenda to achieve. **1**

Source: Official website of the National Museum of Australia

From this, we can infer that Australia is an example of a ________.

(*a*) United democracy

(*b*) Unitary government

(*c*) 'Coming together' federation

(*d*) 'Holding together' federation

23. Analyze the data and answer the question that follows: **1**

Inequality of Income in Selected Countries		
Name of the Countries	**% Share of national income**	
	Top 20%	**Bottom 20%**
South Africa	64.8	2.9
Brazil	63.0	2.6
Russia	53.7	4.4
USA	50.0	4.0
United Kingdom	45.0	6.0
Denmark	34.5	9.6
Hungary	34.4	10.0

Fig: Inequality of income in selected countries

Which democratic country has a relatively more equitable income distribution?

(*a*) South Africa (*b*) Russia

(*c*) United States (*d*) Denmark

24. Based on the cartoon "The Rich Get Buff", what critical issue regarding economic growth and income distribution is highlighted? **1**

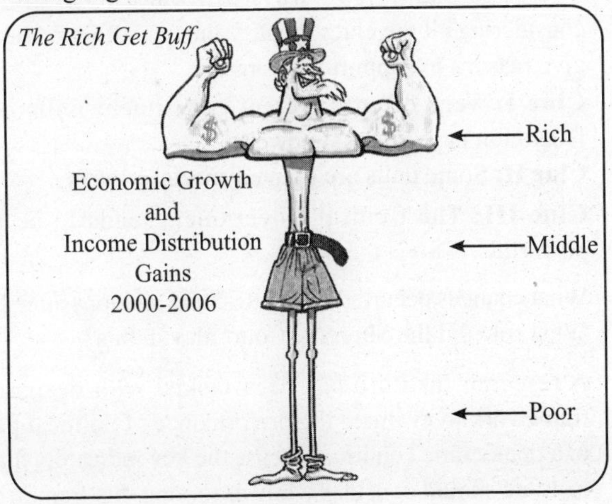

(*a*) The cartoon suggests that economic growth is evenly distributed across all social classes.

(*b*) The cartoon highlights the problem of income inequality, with the wealthy benefitting disproportionately from economic growth.

(*c*) The cartoon indicates that the middle class benefits the most from economic growth.

(*d*) The cartoon shows that economic growth primarily benefits the poor.

25. *"Democracies often struggle with economic inequalities, with a significant portion of wealth concentrated among a small segment of the population."* 1

Which statement best captures the dilemma faced by democracies regarding economic inequality?

(*a*) Democracies are successful in eliminating economic inequalities among their citizens.

(*b*) In democracies, economic growth automatically leads to the equitable distribution of wealth among all citizens.

(*c*) Democracies face challenges in reducing economic disparities and ensuring equitable wealth distribution.

(*d*) Economic disparities do not exist in democracies due to their inherent principle of equality among citizens

26. Analyze the map and answer the question that follows:

(*a*) Identify an exception to the rule that most of the world's large countries are federations from the map. 1

(*b*) Which is the largest federal country in the world? 1

27. There are mainly two ways to form a federation. By considering all the clues identify the type of federation and give reasons to support your answer.

Clue I: Very often different constituent units of the federation have unequal powers.

Clue II: Some units are granted special powers

Clue III: The Central Government tends to be more powerful vis-a-vis the States. 2

28. What changes occurred in Centre-State relations after 1990? What role did the Supreme Court play in this? 3

29A. A research institute has been tasked with designing a framework to evaluate the performance of political parties in a democratic country. Discuss the key indicators that the institute should consider while designing this framework. 5

OR

29B. Why is the lack of internal democracy within political parties considered a challenge to India's democracy? 5

SECTION - D

ECONOMICS (20 Marks)

30. The following table shows the proportion of adults (aged 15-49 years) whose BMI is below normal (BMI <18.5 kg/m^2) in India. It is based on a survey of various states for the year 2015-16. Look at the table and answer the following questions. 1

State	Male (%)	Female (%)
Kerala	8.5	10
Karnataka	17	21
Madhya Pradesh	28	28
All States	**20**	**23**

Which of the following states has the least female adults below normal BMI?

(*a*) Karnataka

(*b*) Kerala

(*c*) Madhya Pradesh

(*d*) All of the above

31. Besides banks, the other major source of cheap credit in rural areas are the cooperative societies (or cooperatives). Members of a cooperative pool their resources for cooperation in certain areas. There are several types of cooperatives possible such as farmers cooperatives, weavers cooperatives, industrial workers cooperatives, etc. Krishak Cooperative functions in a village not very far away from Sonpur. It has 2300 farmers as members. It accepts deposits from its members. With these deposits as collateral, the Cooperative has obtained a large loan from the bank. These funds are used to provide loans to members. Once these loans are repaid, another round of lending can take place. 1

Krishak Cooperative provides loans for the purchase of agricultural implements, loans for cultivation and agricultural trade, fishery loans, loans for construction of houses and for a variety of other expenses.

Why is Arun one of the few people in Sonpur to take a bank loan?

(*a*) Other people in the village prefer to borrow from moneylenders.

(*b*) Banks demand collateral which everyone cannot provide.

(*c*) Interest rates on bank loans are the same as the interest rates charged by traders.

(*d*) Bank loan have strict documentation requirements.

32. In the village of Econville, a local farmer, Mr.Arjun, grows wheat and sells it to a bakery, Mr.Sweet's Bakery, at ₹20 per kg. The bakery uses this wheat to make delicious biscuits, which are then sold in the local market at ₹80 per packet. Assume that there are no other production costs involved. Select among the following how should this transaction be reflected in the GDP? **1**

(*a*) Include the value of both the wheat and biscuits separately to highlight all economic activities.

(*b*) Include only the value of the wheat, as it is the raw product and the basis of further production.

(*c*) Include only the value of biscuits, as it represents the final consumption goods.

(*d*) Exclude both values, as they do not contribute directly to the village's retail market.

33. A non-profit organization uses internet technology to launch a global campaign for environmental awareness. They use live streaming tools to conduct webinars and interactive sessions with participants from over 30 countries. How does internet technology specifically support global environmental campaigns? **1**

(*a*) By allowing real-time monitoring of environmental changes only.

(*b*) By enabling high-definition video streaming of local issues globally.

(*c*) By facilitating interactive and educative sessions across different time zones.

(*d*) By limiting participation to environmental experts.

34. Priya, a college student, wanted to purchase a laptop for her studies. She applied for a loan at a nearby bank. The bank asked her for documents like her ID proof, address proof, and college admission letter. After verification, the bank approved her loan at a reasonable interest rate. **1**

What does this case highlight?

(*a*) Banks provide loans to college students.

(*b*) Documentation is not necessary for obtaining loans.

(*c*) Formal sources of credit have certain eligibility criteria.

(*d*) College students should not buy laptops.

35A. Imagine you are an economic advisor in the planning commission of a developing country facing significant employment challenges, especially in the secondary and tertiary sectors. Your task is to analyze and present a detailed report during the next committee meeting on the impacts of inadequate job creation in these sectors. Discuss the impact of not having enough job creation in the secondary and tertiary sectors on employment. **3**

OR

35B. You are part of a policy analysis team in the Ministry of Finance. The team is tasked with evaluating the government's role in infrastructure development. Analyze why the government engages in activities such as constructing roads, and bridges, and providing irrigation systems, especially considering that these projects require substantial resources and coordination. **3**

36. Although averages are useful for comparing countries, do they also hide disparities? Explain the meaning of this statement. Support the statement with suitable arguments. **3**

37A. Consider a scenario where two small businesses operate in a bustling local market—one, a bakery specializing in artisan bread, and the other, a café offering gourmet coffee and sandwiches. They decide to collaborate to attract more customers. The bakery provides freshly baked bread to the cafe, which in turn, serves gourmet sandwiches made from this bread. How does the use of money, instead of bartering goods directly between the bakery and the café, enhance their business operations and economic activities within the market? Discuss the benefits of using money as a medium of exchange. **5**

OR

37B. A business owner decides to deposit the company's extra cash into a bank account at the beginning of the month. Explain how this action utilizes the concept of demand deposits and contributes to the business's financial management. **5**

38. Read the text carefully and answer the following questions: (1 + 1 + 2 = 4) **4**

Using IT in Globalisation

A news magazine published for London readers is to be designed and printed in Delhi. The text of the magazine is sent through the Internet to the Delhi office. The designers in the Delhi office get orders on how to design the magazine from the office in London using telecommunication facilities. The design is done on a computer. After printing, the magazines are sent by air to London. Even the payment of money for designing and printing from a bank in London to a bank in Delhi is done instantly through the Internet (e-banking)!

38.1 Explain the role of the internet in the design and printing process of the magazine described in the above case.

38.2 Write down IT tools speeding up the globalisation discussed in the above case.

38.3 Describe the significance of e-banking in the context of international transactions mentioned in the paragraph.

Notes

Notes